A FLEXIBLE ORGA... FOR INSTRUCTORS

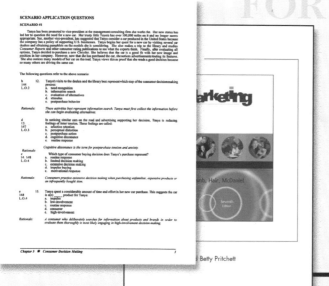

Text Learning Objectives

form the framework for organizing your lectures, selecting support materials, and customizing tests for your students.

Test Bank Questions

are grouped by learning objective, so that you can thoroughly test all objectives—or emphasize the ones you feel are most important. Relevant, well stated questions make it easy to prepare tests that cover the objectives at the level of difficulty appropriate for your students.

ExamView®

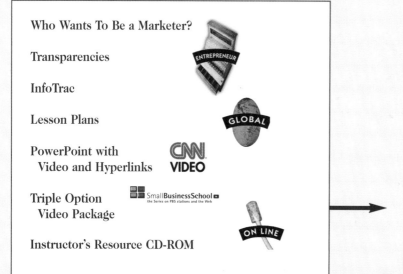

Who Wants To Be a Marketer?

Transparencies

InfoTrac

Lesson Plans

PowerPoint with
Video and Hyperlinks

Triple Option
Video Package

Instructor's Resource CD-ROM

All Lecture Support Materials

come together under their appropriate objectives in the Instructor's Handbook Lecture Outlines, for thorough coverage of all objectives. Annotations tell you the appropriate times to integrate text special features, transparencies, additional examples, supplemental articles and activities, and end-of-chapter pedagogy into your lectures.

Marketing ⁷ᵉ

Charles W. Lamb, Jr.

M.J. Neeley Professor of Marketing
M.J. Neeley School of Business
Texas Christian University

Joseph F. Hair, Jr.

Alvin C. Copeland Endowed Chair
of Franchising and Director,
Entrepreneurship Institute
Louisiana State University

Carl McDaniel

Chair, Department of Marketing
College of Business Administration
University of Texas at Arlington

THOMSON
---™
SOUTH-WESTERN

Australia · Canada · Mexico · Singapore · Spain · United Kingdom · United States

THOMSON
SOUTH-WESTERN

Marketing, 7e
Charles W. Lamb, Joseph H. Hair, and Carl McDaniel

Editor-in-Chief:
Jack Calhoun

Team Leader:
Melissa Acuña

Acquisitions Editor:
Steve Hazelwood

Developmental Editor:
Jamie Gleich-Bryant

Marketing Manager:
Nicole Moore

Production Editor:
Amy McGuire

Manufacturing Coordinator:
Diane Lohman

Compositor:
Pre-Press Company, Inc.

Printer:
Transcontinental Printing, Inc.
Beauceville, QC

Design Project Manager:
Carrie Hochstrasser

Internal Designer:
Christy Carr

Cover Designer:
Anne Marie Rekow

Photography Manager:
Deanna Ettinger

Photo Researcher:
Charlotte Goldman

Library of Congress Cataloging-in-Publication Data
Lamb, Charles W.
Marketing / Charles W. Lamb, Jr., Joseph F. Hair, Jr., Carl McDaniel.
—7th ed.
p. cm.
Includes bibliographical references and index.
ISBN 0-324-14798-8
1. Marketing. 2. Marketing—Management. I. Hair, Joseph F. II McDaniel, Carl D. III. Title.
HF5415 .L2624 2002b
658.8—dc21

Package ISBN: 0-324-14798-8
Text ISBN: 0-324-18818-8
Xtra! CD ISBN: 0-324-18817-X
Infotrac ISBN: 0-534-55853-4
Non-Infotrac Package ISBN:
0-324-19131-6

To my grandsons, Cameron
and Chandler Stock.

—*Charles W. Lamb, Jr.*

To my loving and supportive wife Dale,
and my son Joe, III, and his wife
Kerrie.

—*Joseph F. Hair, Jr.*

To Ann and Billy Boswell—
The finest sister and brother-in-law
a person could have.

—*Carl McDaniel*

Brief Contents

Your Guide to Features

Your Guide to Features

Contents

PART 4

ABOUT THIS EDITION

You are holding a textbook that has experienced a dramatic increase with each edition in the number of colleges and university student-users. We are very grateful to the hundreds of professors that have selected our text to give college students their first exposure to the dynamic world of marketing. We are honored that a vast majority of professors stay with our text edition after edition. Our research gives us an indication why this is true. *Students find* Marketing, *by Lamb, Hair, and McDaniel, the most exciting, readable, and enjoyable text of their college career.*

OUTLINE

SO WHAT'S NEW...

If you are already familiar with *Marketing*, you may be asking, "So what's new?" The answer is quite a bit. In addition to the dozens of new examples in each chapter, we have added new content and revised and updated existing material throughout the book.

BRAND NEW CONTENT

PART 1 We have streamlined Chapter 2 (Marketing Strategy) to make the discussion of strategy more relevant for today's marketing environment. Chapter 3 (Marketing Environment and Marketing Ethics) has a new section on American values and new content on demographics, including material and an exhibit on women as principal economic decision makers. We have revised the section on older consumers and included a completely new section on multicultural marketing. Chapter 4 (Developing a Global Vision) has been greatly revised to reflect constant changes in the global marketplace. We have updated the section on the impact of globalization on trade and added new content on the U.S. Commercial Service which includes a new exhibit on how the service helps companies that want to go global. There is updated information on direct foreign investment, new sections on the Free Trade Agreement of the Americas (FTAA), the Association of South East Asian Nations (ASEAN), and the Asia-Pacific Economic Cooperation (APEC), plus a map that depicts the member countries of the trade agreements discussed in the chapter.

PART 2 Chapter 5 (Consumer Decision Making) has new material on trends in gender marketing, and Chapter 6 (Business Marketing) has a completely revised section on business marketing on the Internet. Chapter 7 (Segmenting and Targeting Markets) now includes updated information based on the 2000 census, plus a thoroughly revised section on bases for segmenting business markets.

PART 3 Part 3 begins with Chapter 9 (Product Concepts), which has a new section on global brands. Chapter 10 (Developing and Managing Products) follows with new exhibits on the history of new product introductions and the diffusion process, plus a completely new section on on-line test marketing. We have revised the discussion on how services differ from goods in Chapter 11 (Services and Nonprofit Organization Marketing). Distribution concepts can be difficult, so we have revised Chapter 12 (Supply Chain Management) to give students an introduction to supply chain management that sticks to the basics. We have condensed the chapter in several areas to make it more readable.

PART 5 Chapter 15 (Advertising and Public Relations) has a new section on Internet advertising, plus we describe new and innovative ways of advertising, and Chapter 16 (Sales Promotion and Personal Selling) has an expanded discussion of point-of-purchase programs.

PART 6 Chapter 17 (Pricing Concepts) opens Part 6 with more examples of elastic and inelastic demand, a thoroughly revised and expanded section on the impact of Internet and extranets on pricing, and a revised section on Internet auctions. Chapter 18 (Setting the Right Price) follows with expanded discussions of choosing a pricing strategy, predatory pricing, and bundling and services. The chapter also has a new section on the implications of zero-percent financing and a revised section on value pricing, with a new section on dangers of pricing products too low.

PART 7 Much is revised in Part 7. Chapter 19 (Internet Marketing) is completely revised for every edition of *Marketing* to reflect the constantly evolving world of Internet marketing and e-commerce. Chapter 20 (Customer Relationship Management) is a new chapter that introduces the company-wide business strategy (CRM) designed to optimize profitability, revenue, and customer satisfaction by focusing on highly defined and precise customer groups. And Chapter 21 (One-to-One Marketing) simplifies the introduction to database marketing and abridges the discussion of data mining, now covered in depth in Chapter 20.

So What's New...

OPENING VIGNETTES

7

Hair care in the United States is a $45 billion industry. Hair care for kids under age twelve makes up approximately $5 billion of that market. Therefore, servicing only kids excludes nearly 90 percent of the market, and thus does not appear to represent a viable market segment. Furthermore, stylists have traditionally avoided this market because the customers tend to wiggle and wail and may even bite the hand that shears them.

However, the kids' haircutting industry is growing. Since 1995, at least four new children's haircutting chains have opened around the country. They join established kids' salons such as Cartoon Cuts, a $4.5 billion, sixteen-unit outfit whose first facility opened in Fairfax, Virginia, in 1991, and $2 million-plus Kids' Hair, Inc., which launched the first of ten stores in 1992 in Edina, Minnesota. The growth spurt is similar to that of children's specialty retail stores like GapKids and Gymboree, which emerged in the

sophisticated mapping that superimposes spending habits on demographic and economic data such as median home values, household income, and number and ages of children, allow the company to pinpoint the most lucrative spots for new sites.

While the chains have similarities—all claim to have superior customer service and consistent offerings—each one has its own variation on the kids theme. Cool Cuts, for example, divides its waiting area into two sides. For kids age six and under, a gated-in play space is stocked with Legos and videos such as *Barney* and *Sesame Street*. For older children there is an area stocked with Nintendo 64 stations. Kid Snips sells toys and splashes whimsical jungle creatures on its walls. Stylists at Cartoon Cuts wash as well as cut their customers' hair, dousing the suds with hoses that project from the trunks of green fiberglass elephants. For the most part,

Each chapter begins with a new, current, real-world story about a marketing decision or situation facing a company. These vignettes have been carefully prepared to stimulate student interest in the topics to come in the chapter and can be used to begin class discussion. A special section before the chapter summary called **Connect It** answers the teaser questions posed in the opening vignette and helps illustrate how the chapter material relates to the real world of marketing. In the Seventh Edition, you'll read about companies like Coach, Coleman, *Maxim*, Red Bull, the Dallas Mavericks, and Universal Studios.

GLOBAL PERSPECTIVE BOXES

GLOBAL PERSPECTIVES

Powering into Europe

Coca-Cola Company sees the fragmented and fast-growing European sports-drink market as an important opportunity, which is why the company is investing $40 million to $50 million to launch Powerade in Europe. It is Coke's biggest marketing push in Europe in six years. "There is an open field in Europe. It's not like the United States," says Keith Pardy, director of strategic marketing for Coca-Cola West Europe.

Sports drinks command an even higher premium in Europe than in the United States, where the market is well established. A 500-milliliter bottle of a sports drink costs between 90 pence and £1 ($1.31–$1.45) in Britain, for example, compared with about 75 pence for the same size bottle of Coke or Pepsi.

Moreover, Coke believes Europeans aged 13 to 29, the target market for Powerade, increasingly are making sports a bigger part of their lives. Coke says its new Powerade drink increases endurance

during exercise by combining the benefits of a sports drink with the energy boost of drinks such as Red Bull, made by a closely held Austrian company. The formula in Europe is the same as in the new vitamin-B–enhanced U.S. Powerade, but the taste is slightly different because of certain European regulations on ingredients, Mr. Pardy says. The look is the same as in the United States, with a futuristic letter "P" logo.

As in the United States, Coke is marketing Powerade to the likes of surfers and skateboarders. Posters to be placed in gyms across Europe as part of the advertising campaign for Powerade will allude to "extreme sports" challenges, for example. But the company hopes the drink will eventually transcend its original use, and that European youths will begin drinking sports beverages more generally, as youths do in the United States.

"We want to grow the market in Europe to the point where you'll use it whenever you need en-

durance, beyond sports occasions," Mr. Pardy says.

Powerade will be launched in Britain, Ireland, France, Germany, Spain, Sweden, Turkey, Italy, Poland, Hungary, and Greece. The drink, which will be sold in citrus, orange, and vivid-blueberry flavor, will be distributed first through vending machines in gyms, sports centers, and soccer stadiums before moving to convenience stores and supermarkets.

Advertising for the drink will span billboards, television commercials, sponsorships with sports figures, the Internet, and direct mail. Most of the advertising will be directed at a male audience, as the sports-drink market is generally skewed more toward men in Europe.[28]

Describe Coke's target market strategy for Powerade in Europe. Explain the marketing mix that the company plans to employ.

Today most businesses compete not only locally and nationally, but globally as well. Companies that have never given a thought to exporting now face competition from abroad. Thinking globally should be a part of every manager's tactical and strategic planning. Accordingly, we address this topic in detail early in Chapter 4. We have also integrated numerous global examples within the body of the text and identified them with the icon shown in the margin.

Global marketing is fully integrated throughout the book, cases, and videos, as well. Our **Global Perspectives** boxes, which appear in most chapters, provide expanded global examples of the marketing issues facing companies in countries from Asia to Africa to Europe. Each box concludes with thought-provoking questions carefully prepared to stimulate class discussion. You'll read about the Chinese supply chain, marketing beverages in developing nations, exporting marketing savvy, and the impact of the euro on pricing in Europe, among others.

ETHICS IN MARKETING

In this edition we continue our emphasis on ethics. The **Ethics in Marketing** boxes, complete with questions focusing on ethical decision making, have been revised in each chapter. This feature offers provocative examples of how ethics comes into play in many marketing decisions. Is it ethical to target teens at school? What about using sex as an advertising appeal? Or conducting racial profiling at retail stores? Students will consider these and many other hotly debated ethical questions.

ETHICS IN MARKETING

All for the Cause

Modern-day "cause marketing" goes back to 1974 and the inception of the Ronald McDonald House Charities. Since then, the trend has been building steadily. The 1980s saw Pizza Hut, Lens-Crafters, and Home Depot launch nationwide drives to benefit charities. In the 1990s, many major retail, automotive, and cosmetic companies embraced a variety of causes, from child and family issues to breast cancer.

The trend isn't simply a case of corporate consciousness-raising; consumers are increasingly demanding that corporations "give back." According to a joint study by branding and communications firm Cone and research firm Roper Starch Worldwide, nearly two-business practice. Roughly the same fraction agree that, all else being equal, they would be likely to switch brands or retailers to those associated with a good cause.

Dan Cunningham, chief chokolada (yes, that's his official title) of Dan's Chocolates, needed to convince the nation that fresh chocolate, shipped within seven days of manufacture from his Madison, Wisconsin, factory, is better than chocolate found lingering on retail shelves. So he devised "The Great Chocolate Challenge," the first nationwide chocolate tasting party.

For ten days in April, he offered the first ten thousand visitors to his site a six-piece chocolate sampler for a $1 donation to char-and ship the chocolate, and another $2 million on radio ads in seven cities. The company also placed banners on the Blue Mountain Arts Web site.

The result? The campaign quadrupled orders and site traffic, and almost ten percent of "Challengers" became return customers. "We did more business in the month of May than we did the entire first quarter," says Ted Richardson, Dan's chief marketing officer. Though it's hard to separate the impact of Mother's Day from the promotion, no one's arguing with the $50,000 that Dan's donated to charity at the end of the Challenge.[25]

Is it ethical to use donations to charity to increase sales?

REVIEW IT

In order to make our **Integrated Learning System** even more effective, we have distributed the end-of-chapter discussion and writing questions within the chapter summary in a **Review It** section. Questions are numbered according to the learning objective to which they correspond. For example, the summary point for learning objective 5 in Chapter 15 has four related questions. They are numbered 5.1, 5.2, 5.3, and 5.4. This reorganization helps students identify questions pertinent to the learning objective they are studying, allowing each chapter to function as a series of modules that can be read over multiple study sessions.

REVIEW IT

(5) **Discuss the role of public relations in the promotional mix.** Public relations is a vital part of a firm's promotional mix. A company fosters good publicity to enhance its image and promote its products. Popular public relations tools include new-product publicity, product placement, consumer education, event sponsorship, issue sponsorship, and Internet Web sites. An equally important aspect of public relations is managing unfavorable publicity in a way that is least damaging to a firm's image.

5.1 How can advertising and publicity work together? Give an example.

5.2 *WRITING* As the new public relations director for a sportswear company, you have been asked to set public relations objectives for a new line of athletic shoes to be introduced to the teen market. Draft a memo outlining the objectives you propose for the shoe's introduction and your reasons for them.

5.3 *WRITING* Reports have just surfaced that your company, a fast-food chain, sold contaminated food products that have made several people seriously ill. As your company's public relations manager, devise a plan to handle the crisis.

5.4 *WRITING* *INFOTRAC COLLEGE EDITION* The Ford/Firestone tire recall of 2000 was one of the biggest public relations nightmares of recent memory. How well did the companies handle the situation? Use InfoTrac (**http://www.infotrac-college.com**) to run a keyword search on "Ford public relations." Read a selection of the articles, and then write an analysis of CEO Jacques Nasser's performance in the face of this crisis. What did he do well? What could he have done better? Evaluate his solution to the problem. Has Ford recovered from the recall? What about Firestone?

THINK ABOUT IT

In today's business environment, ethics are extremely important. In recent years, there have been numerous scandals and trials that stem from a lack of ethical judgment. In 2002, over 150 companies revised their earnings forecasts, signaling that perhaps their accounting methods were questionable. And who can forget the scandals linked to Adelphia, Tyco, ImClone, WorldCom, and of course Enron and Arthur Andersen?

Although, some might say that these

THINK ABOUT IT

Ethics Exercise

People feel better when they think that they are getting a great bargain when they shop. Knowing this, some retailers mark up items above the traditional retail price and then offer a 60 percent discount. If they had simply discounted the normal retail price by 20 percent the resulting "sale price" would have been the same. One retailer says that he is just making shoppers happy that they got a great deal when he inflates the retail price before discounting.

Questions

1. What do you think?

2. Does the AMA Code of Ethics address this issue? Go to **http://www.marketingpower.com** and review the code. Then, write a brief paragraph summarizing what the AMA Code of Ethics contains that relates to retail pricing.

occurances are the work of a few bad apples spoiling the bunch, it is clear that ethical decision making plays a very important role in a company's success and prosperity. **Think About It** is a new ethics exercise appearing in every chapter. A brief scenario presents students with a situation in which the right thing to do may or may not be crystal clear. To help students make appropriate ethical decisions, we always refer students back to the AMA's Code of Ethics, found on-line at **http://www.marketingpower.com**. This gives students a resource for the exercise and also helps reinforce the ethical standards that marketers should uphold.

So What's New...

TRY IT: ENTREPRENEURSHIP CASE

Entrepreneurship, whether in the newest dot com or in America's largest corporations, is what fueled the greatest period of expansion in American history. Thirteen chapters have new entrepreneurship cases highlighting the challenges facing entrepreneurs in the 21st century. **Try It** cases focus on a wide variety of companies, like Look-Look (a marketing research company specializing in cool spotting), Identix (maker of optical identification systems based on a person's biological features, such as eye patterns or fingerprints), Global Lightwave (an Israeli optics company), IslanderISP (an Internet service provider started by high-school students on Seattle's exclusive Mercer Island suburb), Noodé (a skin care company and product line for Generations X and Y), and mytoybox.com.

But we also recognize that entrepreneurial activities take place across the Fortune 500, so we profile industry giants like W. W. Grainger, which offers over 600,000 maintenance, repair, and operating items, and Valvoline. Both have used a highly entrepreneurial approach in various parts of their business. Your students will find these cases an exciting and challenging aspect of each chapter. But our coverage of small business issues doesn't stop there.

Many students will either work for a small business or strike out on their own to form an organization. For this reason, we continue to include **Apply It: Application for Entrepreneurs** at the end of each chapter. **Try It** cases apply general marketing concepts to the world of start-ups and small business. The **Apply It** exercises are mini-cases designed to illustrate how small business can create strategies and tactics using the material in the chapter. In addition, small business examples throughout each chapter are identified by the icon in the margin.

WATCH IT

Video is a valuable teaching tool, so this edition has a completely new video package that combines short, medium, and long segments. **Watch It** gives students a brief description of segments relating to that chapter. For instance, in Chapter 9 (Product Concepts), the short segments are ads for Kenmore, Chrysler, Radio Shack, and AOL with WebMD; the medium segment is about organic labeling; and the long segment is about Fluker Cricket Farms in Baton Rouge, Louisiana. Students are prepared for video viewing in or out of class by reading the **Watch It** at the end of the chapter.

FLIP IT, CLICK IT, AND SPIN IT

Because we offer a comprehensive set of learning resources, students may not know what is available to help them study. The Seventh Edition adds three brief new sections at the end of each chapter to help students identify the study aids that are right for them. **Flip It** describes learning opportunities in the Grademaker Study Guide and Workbook, **Click It** reminds students of the many resources at their disposal at **http://lamb.swlearning.com**, and **Spin It** lists the materials for review on their Xtra! CD-ROM.

FLIP IT

Flip to Chapter 10 in your *Grademaker Study Guide* for more review opportunities, including the pretest, vocabulary review, study test questions, and a marketing application based on product concepts. Can you describe the product life cycle? Do you know which marketing mix strategies work best at each point in the product life cycle? What about the diffusion of innovation? If you're unsure, then pick up your *Grademaker* and review.

CLICK IT

The *Marketing* Web site links you to all the Internet-based activities in this chapter, like the "Use It," "Review It" questions 2.4, 2.5, 4.1, and 6.1, and the On-Line exercises in the chapter margins. As a review, do the Chapter 10 quiz and crossword puzzle. And don't forget the Career Exersite that gives you resources for exploring product-development career opportunities. Review the main concepts in the PowerPoint presentation for Chapter 10, too. Go to **http://lamb.swlearning.com**, read the material, and follow the links right from the site.

SPIN IT

Spin your Xtra! CD-ROM to test your understanding of the new-product development concepts in the chapter by completing the worksheets for Exhibits 10.2, 10.3, 10.5, 10.6, 10.8, and 10.9. If your instructor has assigned a marketing plan project, worksheets on Xtra! can help you organize your work. In addition to the quiz on the Web site, there's another quiz on the Xtra! CD-ROM, plus video of the authors answering frequently asked questions about new products and product diffusion, such as "Why do so many new products fail?" and "Why is such a small proportion of the new products introduced each year 'new-to-the-world' products?"

MARKETING MISCUES

Mistakes can have tough consequences, but they also offer a great lesson. This is especially true in marketing. At the end of each part you will find new cases that describe good and bad ideas that couldn't make it in the rough and tumble marketplace. Often amusing and always interesting, these cases about Kmart, Metricom, Moxi, Jeremy's Microbatch Ice Cream, Duracell, Apple, and Eli Lilly will help your students avoid the same mistakes made by these well-known companies.

MARKETING MISCUES

Kmart's Blue Lights Are in the Red, and There's Nothing Special about It

Is there anything special about Kmart anymore? Do consumers know what Kmart and its brands stand for? Does Kmart have an image in the retail marketplace? Answers to these questions were crucial to Kmart's long-term survival as the company entered into Chapter 11 bankruptcy proceedings in early 2002. Kmart's case was the largest retail bankruptcy filing in U.S. history, as well as the sixth-largest bankruptcy case in U.S. history.

More than a hundred years ago, Sebastian Kresge opened his first five-and-dime store in Michigan. This store was the first of what would come to be known as the S. S. Kresge Company. The company's business philosophy was to offer products that consumers needed at prices they could afford. In doing so, management expected that customers would keep returning. The company thought it had found the key to customer loyalty.

Unfortunately for Kresge, another retailing guru would soon enter the picture. In 1962, when Kresge launched the Kmart concept, Sam Walton was setting in motion the debut of Wal-Mart. Kmart never expected that the retailing showdown with Wal-Mart would ultimately result in Kmart's appearance in bankruptcy court. For forty years, it battled Wal-Mart, and in the end, Kmart had lost. What went wrong?

According to market analysts, Kmart made a series of strategic and tactical blunders. Strategically, Kmart failed to differentiate itself as a retailer. In-

concerns such as poor customer service, long checkout lines, inconsistent price marking, dingy stores, empty shelves, and old merchandise as issues that led to Kmart's downfall.

Some would say that this downfall should not have come as a surprise to Kmart management, employees, and customers. Kmart appeared to have focused solely on its competition and what they were doing rather than focusing on its customers and what they wanted. In the end, Kmart could not differentiate itself from Wal-Mart because it could not price below it. Nor could Kmart sway Target customers because it appeared unable to provide the in-store experience that made customers feel chic as they purchased discounted clothing.

At the time of its bankruptcy filing, Kmart was the third largest retailer in the United States, with 2,100 stores across the United States and Puerto Rico. While Kmart was filing Chapter 11, Wal-Mart boasted sales of $200 billion, with growth rates of 15 to 20 percent, and Target's 1,055 stores posted record sales revenue of $37 billion. With competition like this, there was doubt as to whether Kmart could rectify its past strategic missteps and differentiate itself in the retail marketplace. Could Kmart devise a unique and compelling strategy that would leave the company's fractured image behind? Or, should Kmart's blue lights be turned off forever?

Questions

1. Is this an example of poor strategy formulation or poor strategy implementation?

CRITICAL THINKING CASES

Making smart decisions is at the heart of successful marketing. **Critical Thinking Cases** at the end of each part put your students in the role of decision maker. They will evaluate the marketing plans of well known organizations like Hewlett-Packard, Square Two Golf, Segway, Philip Morris, Morpheus, Nokia, and Peapod.

CRITICAL THINKING CASE

Nokia's $20,000 Cellular Phone

Nokia's luxury-edition cellphone has it all— platinum or 18-karat gold housing, crystal screen, soft leather casings, upgradable internal components— all for only $21,240 (24,000 euros)! Why, such a high-priced cellphone? Will anyone buy it?

The Mobile Phone Industry

The mobile phone industry has burgeoned in the past few years. By 2003, cellular penetration is expected to be as high as 80 percent in many European countries and slightly greater than 30 percent in the United States. Product innovation and pricing appear to be the drivers for this level of market penetration. Price-sensitive consumers are expected to purchase the low-end cellphones, while price-insensitive consumers will demand the latest and greatest in cellular technology.

By 2000, the mobile phone industry was thought to be the world's largest consumer electronics industry in terms of unit sales. Although overall market penetration has been phenomenal, such growth levels are not expected to continue. Rather, experts predict only modest growth in the mid- and late 2000s. Since first-time users accounted for over half of mobile phone purchases at the start of 2000, replacement sales are expected to comprise around 75 percent of sales in later years.

The mobile phone industry is dominated by major competitors including Ericsson (Sony), Motorola, Nokia, Qualcomm, Samsung, and Sanyo. Each of these companies offers cellular phones with nu-

Attempting to differentiate its product offerings while building on its branding efforts, Nokia has founded the world's first luxury mobile phone company. This new, independent subsidiary, Vertu, Ltd., started operations in early 2002 and will cater to very wealthy consumers. A senior vice president in Nokia's Asia-Pacific division, Nigel Litchfield, will serve as president of London-based Vertu, Ltd.

Historically, Nokia has been known for marketing well-designed, user-friendly phones that are popular with the everyday phone user. The new Vertu phones, however, focus on the phone as a status symbol of the very wealthy and take Nokia into a niche market. Selling under the Vertu brand, the company's most expensive product carries a hefty price tag of $21,240. For this premium price, the rich and discerning customer gets a cellular phone that makes a fashion statement. In addition to its platinum handset and crystal display screen, this limited-edition luxury phone features evolutionary technology that will allow the phone's internal mechanisms to be upgraded while keeping the outside casing intact. The lower end of this elite product will feature similar internal technology inside a stainless steel casing. The low-end price is expected to be around $5,300. These luxury phones will be available by private showing only in the most distinguished shopping areas of Paris, London, Los Angeles, New York, and Hong Kong.

Nokia is not the only company offering limited-edition, high-end cellular phones. For many years, Ericsson has made gold-plated phones, and Motorola has an 18-karat gold, diamond-studded phone. Priced

WHAT MAKES *MARKETING 7E* SO POPULAR WITH STUDENTS?

WE GRAB THEIR ATTENTION

We have done extensive research to provide a comprehensive, up-to-the-minute introduction to the field of marketing. Because we weave hundreds of real-world examples into our discussions, our text is called lively and interesting. You should know that this never means superficial or shallow. The latest concepts are covered in detail in a lucid manner with numerous illustrations. For example, in Chapter 3 on the marketing environment, you'll read this passage.

> In recent years there has been explosive population increases among African Americans, Hispanics, and Asians, with those groups now accounting for 79 million out of 281 million Americans. Collectively, they represent an estimated $1 trillion in annual spending power. Hispanics are the fastest growing segment of the population. The diversity of the U.S. population is projected to stabilize around 2023, as the birthrate of minorities levels off.

Is this straightforward information that students need to know? Absolutely. Does that mean that students find this and the other concepts and research-based facts presented in their book very compelling, let alone interesting? Maybe, maybe not. But what we do is combine this information with examples of how real companies are using that information to their benefit (or not using them, to their detriment). The passage below is also in Chapter 3, and it shows how Procter & Gamble, one of the largest global consumer products companies, is using demographic statistics (like those above) in its Multicultural Market Development Organization.

> Procter & Gamble has created a new "Multicultural Market Development Organization" to reach minority markets. Now, every six months, the firm sends out 4.5 million copies of its promotional magazine "Avanzando con tu Familia," or "Getting Ahead with your family." That's one copy for every two Hispanic households. Marketers have reworked the Spanish slogan for Cover Girl makeup, and product developers are creating new Secret deodorant scent names that they hope will appeal to Hispanic consumers. In addition, P&G's new line of Pampers diapers with a "cloth-like backside" come in boxes written in both English and Spanish.

This is just one example of how we have illustrated the principles and concepts in this book with literally hundreds of fresh, new examples.

IT'S EASY TO LEARN

Since the First Edition, one of the hallmarks of *Marketing* has been its **Integrated Learning System.** Many of today's students are not only students–many work, commute and some even have families of their own. This can make it hard to read a chapter in a single sitting. In fact, it can take anywhere from two to five sittings to completely read through a chapter once. With all the starting and stopping of studying, it can be hard to retain the chapter concepts.

Our unique **Integrated Learning System** breaks each chapter into modules organized around the learning objectives, which are placed in the margin throughout the chapter. Students know exactly where a learning objective begins and where it ends. And in the Seventh Edition, we have separated the review questions at the end of each chapter and placed them after the appropriate summary point. Students can answer the questions that relate to the material they have just read. Likewise, the **Grademaker Study Guide and Workbook** is organized by learning objective, with different types of review questions for each objective. Students can divide the material in each chapter into manageable chunks, read it, review it, and practice it—without losing it!

WE INTEGRATE TECHNOLOGY IN A MEANINGFUL WAY

From the beginning, we have integrated new technologies into our **Integrated Learning System** in a meaningful way. The Seventh Edition continues this tradition by adding new and exciting content to our technology materials. We have also enhanced and refined popular media supplements to bring concepts alive in the classroom. Managers and workers explain why certain marketing strategies achieve glowing success and others failed. Other marketers speak about how their new product development process works or how they penetrated the global marketplace. Media concept applications, such as these, create higher levels of comprehension and interest among your students.

XTRA! CD-ROM

Our new **Xtra! CD-ROM** is like no other. We have included extra content modules on competitive intelligence, multicultural marketing, and broken brands. In a brand new video feature, each chapter has an "Ask the Author" segment in which one of the authors responds to frequently asked questions about the marketing topics discussed in the given chapter. For Xtra!, we have revised the **Marketing Planning Worksheets** to make them easier to use, plus we have created new exhibit worksheets for the tables and diagrams in the text. Students can print out the worksheets, and following the instructions on the sheet, fill in the diagram or table. They can then check their recall of important topics using the actual text exhibit. Other self-assessment tools include a ten-question quiz for each chapter that contains questions similar to what they will see on exams and in the **Grademaker Study and Workbook**. To help students decide whether or not they need additional review, an abridged chapter from the Grademaker is also on Xtra! And lastly, Xtra! features a copy of the **PowerPoint™ presentation.**

FRESH INTERNET ACTIVITIES AND REAL-TIME EXAMPLES

Despite the technology bust of 2000, the Internet is here to stay and continues to be a powerful resource for teaching and learning. Each chapter of *Marketing* contains numerous examples of the Internet's role in marketing, designated throughout the text by the icon in the margin. In addition, we regularly offer opportunities for students to use the Internet to further their study of chapter content. **On Line** activities with URLs appear in the margins throughout each chapter and are tied to either organizations mentioned in the text or the concepts being discussed. For example, in Chapter 5, students will read about how gender marketing is influencing the video game industry, which is beginning to develop new games based on popular female characters like Barbie and Nancy Drew aimed at capturing female customers. The On-Line activity below allows students to explore this trend in greater detail.

Because each activity calls for student effort and feedback, you can use these mini-exercises as additional assignments or quizzing opportunities. We have kept the best exercises from the Sixth Edition and added ninety new ones. Knowing how fast the Internet changes, we have a made a concerted effort to create exercises and direct students to sites that have staying power and that will not become obsolete by the end of the semester.

Links to all URLs in the book are located on the text's Internet site at **http://lamb.swlearning.com.**

GameGirlz

What kind of games are available at the Game-Girlz Web site? How do the games "for" girls differ from the games "for" boys at GameSpot?

http://www.gamegirlz.com

http://www.gamespot.com

On Line

WHAT MAKES *MARKETING 7E* SO POPULAR WITH STUDENTS?

Nearly every chapter has multiple technology assignments in the **Review It** section. Questions that contain a technology component are identified with the on-line icon. For example, after reviewing strategy concepts in Chapter 2, students are sent to the Web for the following activity:

> **④ Explain the components of a situation analysis.** In the situation (or SWOT) analysis, the firm should identify its internal strengths (S) and weaknesses (W) and also examine external opportunities (O) and threats (T). When examining external opportunities and threats, marketing managers must analyze aspects of the marketing environment in a process called environmental scanning. The six most often studied macroenvironmental forces are social, demographic, economic, technological, political and legal, and competitive. During the situation analysis, it is crucial that the marketer identify a competitive advantage and establish that it is a sustainable competitive advantage.
>
> 4.1 Competition in the private courier sector is fierce. UPS and FedEx dominate, but other companies, such as Airborne, Emery, and even the United States Postal Service, still have a decent chunk of the express package delivery market. Perform a mini-situation analysis on one of the companies listed below by stating one strength, one weakness, one opportunity, and one threat. You may want to consult the following Web sites as you build your grid:
>
> United Parcel Service (UPS) **http://www.ups.com**
>
> FedEx **http://www.fedex.com**
>
> Airborne **http://www.airborne.com**
>
> Emery **http://www.emeryworldwide.com**
>
> USPS **http://www.usps.gov**

In addition to the numerous Internet assignments throughout the book, we continue to offer students access to the InfoTrac database maintained by the Gale Research Group. InfoTrac contains over 14 million articles from over 3,800 sources dating back to 1980. Students can use InfoTrac to connect with the real world of marketing through refereed academic journals, business and popular magazines and newspapers, and a vast array of government publications.

With so many articles and publications at the students' disposal, they could get lost in research. So we have created guided exercises to help them develop their research and critical reading skills. For instance, in Chapter 18, after students review the government regulations that affect pricing, they can do the following exercise:

InfoTrac exercises like this one can be found throughout the text to either guide an original research project or provide structured reading exercise.

> 2.1 **INFOTRAC COLLEGE EDITION** What kind of factors can push a respectable firm to enter a price-fixing arrangement with a competitor? Using InfoTrac (**http://www.infotrac-college.com**), read about the price-fixing scandals that rocked the art auction industry or the Hollywood movie studios and Blockbuster Video during 2001 and 2002. If there are more current scandals, read a selection of articles on a particular industry. Then compile a list of business practices and pricing issues that are present in the reports of each scandal. Is each scandal unique, or are there overlapping characteristics? What conclusion can you draw about price fixing from the articles you read? How does the federal government deal with price fixing?

E-commerce changes at the speed of light. We completely rewrite Chapter 19, Internet Marketing, with each edition to explain the dynamic world of e-commerce. The latest marketing innovations, technology shifts, dot com success and failures, are covered like no other text. We don't neglect the traditional companies but explain how many of these firms are morphing to "bricks and clicks." Our Internet Marketing chapter is located at the text's Web site at **http://lamb.swlearning.com** and contains all of the features of our print chapters with the added bonus of direct links to company examples and sources of information.

When we debuted **Who Wants to Be a Marketer?** with the Sixth Edition, we did not anticipate how popular it would become. Developed by John Drea of Western Illinois University, this exciting supplement to the Seventh Edition of *Marketing* by Lamb, Hair, and McDaniel is an in-class, computer-based game. **Who Wants to Be a Marketer?** is a fun and exciting way to review terminology and concepts with students. This easy-to-use game only requires Microsoft PowerPoint™ and a method to display the screen to the entire class (such as a data projector). **Who Wants to Be a Marketer?** has two rounds of fifty original questions per each chapter, for a total of 2,100 questions! **Who Wants to Be a Marketer?** is only available for adopters of *Marketing* by Lamb, Hair, and McDaniel.

WE OFFER A ROBUST COMPREHENSIVE WEB SITE

Lamb, Hair, and McDaniel's Web site contains a wide array of supplementary products for instructors to use to enhance their course material and presentations, and for guiding students down the path to a clear understanding of the concepts presented within the text. It also offers Web pages dedicated to students' needs and geared toward helping them succeed. The instructor's site includes: a sample chapter from the Test Bank and the Grademaker Study Guide, the entire Instructor Manual, "Great Ideas in Teaching Marketing," the entire PowerPoint™ presentation with hyperlinks in viewable and printable formats, case updates for all the end-of-chapter and end-of-part cases (one update per case per semester), "Who Wants to Be a Marketer?", and a features archive of boxes and vignettes from the Sixth Edition. The abundant student materials include:

- ◉ The **Interactive Study Center** contains materials for every chapter of *Marketing, 7e*: chapter summary points; crossword puzzles of marketing terminology; Internet Applications which contain **On Line** margin activities plus **Use It** and **Review It** items from the text that have an Internet component; and interactive quizzes with a self-assessment for each chapter.

- ◉ A downloadable set of **PowerPoint™ slides** and the order form for the Grademaker Study Guide and Workbook, plus an abridged sample chapter from the study guide can be found on the Student Resources page.

- ◉ **Chapter 19** on Internet Marketing.

- ◉ The **Marketing Plan Project** features a new small business every semester. Students can read the case and develop a marketing plan for a real company struggling with various marketing issues. In conjunction with questions keyed to every chapter, instructors can use the **Marketing Plan Project** as a comprehensive case. Without the questions, the case provides the basis for a student project, which can be submitted at its completion to the profiled company via the publisher as part of the **Marketing Plan Project** Contest. Guidelines and contest rules appear on the **Marketing Plan Project** page at **http://lamb.swlearning.com**.

- ◉ To help students get started in the field of marketing, the Lamb, Hair, and McDaniel Web site features **Your Marketing Career**. This valuable tool presents information on a variety of marketing careers and includes helpful advice and a multitude of resources for starting a marketing career. A self-assessment tool, career listings with compensation ranges, a features-advantages-benefits model to help students determine job fit, a list of resources for job prospecting, information on how to write a résumé, and a pre-interview checklist are only some of the many career materials available at **Your Marketing Career**.

- ◉ **Career Exersites** are unique Internet activities designed to help students use the Web as a career research tool. Developed specifically for each chapter, the exersites give students resources for researching a marketing career in a field related to the chapter content. For example, the exersite for Chapter 8 (Decision Support Systems and Marketing Research) lists useful Web sites for exploring a career in marketing research with an activity to help build career skills.

- ◉ **Infotrac Exercises** allow students to read marketing news without having to cull through the plethora of business periodicals to find it. Each article consists of current news relating to the chapter topics. Discussion questions follow the article to help students apply what they know to the situation presented.

What Makes *Marketing 7e* so Popular with Instructors?

Our Integrated Learning System™

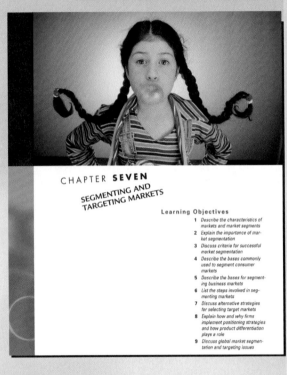

CHAPTER **SEVEN**
SEGMENTING AND
TARGETING MARKETS

Learning Objectives

1 Describe the characteristics of markets and market segments
2 Explain the importance of market segmentation
3 Discuss criteria for successful market segmentation
4 Describe the bases commonly used to segment consumer markets
5 Describe the bases for segmenting business markets
6 List the steps involved in segmenting markets
7 Discuss alternative strategies for selecting target markets
8 Explain how and why firms implement positioning strategies and how product differentiation plays a role
9 Discuss global market segmentation and targeting issues

Still Shaky? Here's a Tip.

Studying for comprehensive exams doesn't have to be a chore. Form a study group. Photocopy the *Marketing 7e* glossary and cut it into strips, one term per strip. Put all strips into a large bowl. Divide into teams and draw out one strip at a time. Quiz the opposing team and then read the correct answer. You can do the same with the summary sections at the end of each chapter. You can tabulate points, but you'll all win!

All of our new and exciting content is anchored by the cornerstone of our text, our fully **Integrated Learning System**. The text and all major supplements are organized around the learning objectives that appear at the beginning of each chapter, so *Marketing 7e* is both easy to teach from and to learn.

A numbered icon like the one shown in the margin identifies each objective in each chapter and appears next to its related material throughout the text, Instructor's Manual, Test Bank, and Study Guide. In other words, every learning objective links the text, Study Guide, Test Bank, and all components of the Instructor's Manual. The system is illustrated on the inside front cover of the text.

(1)

Chapter learning objectives are the linchpin of the **Integrated Learning System**. They provide a structure for your lesson plans–everything you need to assure complete coverage of each objective icon. Do you want to stress more on learning objective 4, Chapter 13, "Discuss nonstore retailing techniques?" No problem. Go to the Instructor's Manual, objective 4, Chapter 13, and you'll find supplemental material. Do you want to emphasize the same objective on an exam? In every chapter in the Test Bank, questions are organized by type and level of difficulty. Now you can test on objective 4 by type of question and degree of difficulty. This value-driven system for you, the instructor, delivers what it promises–full integration.

The integrated system also delivers value for students as they prepare for exams. The learning objective icons identify all the material in the text and Study Guide that relate to each specific learning objective. Students can easily check their grasp of each objective by reading the text sections, reviewing the corresponding summary section, answering the Study Guide questions for that objective, and returning to the appropriate text sections for further review when they have difficulty with any of the questions. Students can quickly identify all material relating to an objective by simply looking for the learning objective icon. And every chapter still concludes with a detailed study tip to help students master marketing concepts.

Our Text Pedagogy Excites and Reinforces Learning

Pedagogical features are meant to reinforce learning, but that doesn't mean that they have to be boring. We have created teaching tools within the text itself that will excite student interest as well as teach.

- **Cross-Functional Connections:** No marketer is an island. Marketing professionals work with every functional area of the company. The **Cross-Functional Connections** that open every part explore the give and take between marketing and all other business functions. Solutions to the topical questions are provided at the end of each part so that students can test their understanding of how marketing is integrated with the other functions of business.

◎ **Opening Vignettes, Revisited at Chapter Conclusions:** Each chapter begins with a new, current, real-world story about a marketing decision or situation facing a company. A special section before the **Review It** chapter summary called **Connect It** answers the teaser questions posed in the opening vignette and helps illustrate how the chapter material relates to the real world of marketing.

◎ **Use It:** Students are often heard to comment, "Yes, I can use this information when I graduate and get into my career, but what take-away value can I get right now?" **Use It** addresses this concern by covering a topic related to the chapter that the student can put to work today. For example, in Chapter 4 (Developing a Global Vision), **Use It** tells students how to find a job overseas and also offers tips on changing money abroad.

◎ **Define It:** Key terms appear in boldface in the text, with definitions in the margins, making it easy for students to check their understanding of key definitions. A complete alphabetical list of key terms appears at the end of each chapter as a study checklist called **Define It**, with page citations for easy reference.

◎ **Review It:** Each chapter ends with **Review It**, a summary that distills the main points of the chapter. Chapter summaries are organized around the learning objectives so that students can use them as a quick check on their achievement of learning goals. Discussion questions and activities are under the learning objective to which they pertain.

◎ **Writing Questions:** To help students improve their writing skills, we have included writing exercises with the **Review It** questions at the end of each chapter. These exercises are marked with the icon shown here. The writing questions are designed to be brief so that students can accomplish writing assignments in a short time and grading time is minimized.

◎ **End of Chapter Team Activities:** The ability to work collaboratively is key to success in today's business world. End-of-chapter team activities, identified by the icon shown here, give students opportunities to learn to work together by engaging in consensus building and problem solving.

◎ **Apply It–Application for Entrepreneurs:** These short scenarios prompt students to apply marketing concepts to small business and entrepreneurial settings. Each scenario ends with provocative questions to aid student analysis and comprehension.

◎ **Try It–Entrepreneurship Case:** All chapters contain **Try It**, an entrepreneurship case with questions to help work through problems facing real small business companies today.

All components of our comprehensive support package have been developed to help you prepare lectures and tests as quickly and easily as possible. We provide a wealth of information and activities beyond the text to supplement your lectures, as well as teaching aids in a variety of formats to fit your own teaching style.

INNOVATIVE AND VALUABLE INSTRUCTOR SUPPLEMENTS

INSTRUCTOR RESOURCE CD-ROM

Managing your classroom resources is now easier than ever. The new Instructor Resource CD-ROM contains all key instructor supplements–Instructor's Manual, Test Bank, and PowerPoint™.

POWERPOINT™ CD-ROM

To take full advantage of the new features of the *Marketing 7e* PowerPoint™ presentation, you'll want to use the customizable PowerPoint™ CD-ROM. Many of the 1,000 full-color images provided with *Marketing 7e*, contain valuable teaching notes to help guide you through your lecture. In addition, hyperlinks to the **On-Line** activities in the chapter margins are embedded in each chapter of slides so that you can maximize your use of these activities during class time. Short thirty-second television ads from recent Super Bowl broadcasts are embedded in the slide presentation and are only viewable through the PowerPoint™ CD-ROM. All you need is Windows to run the PowerPoint™ viewer and an LCD panel for classroom display.

TRIPLE OPTION VIDEO PACKAGE

The video package to accompany *Marketing 7e* is the most comprehensive in our history. We provide you with three options for video use: Each chapter has a combination of thirty-second clips (short) embedded in the instructor's PowerPoint™ CD-ROM presentation, two- to four-minute clips (medium) for classroom viewing, and a ten- to fifteen-minute clip (long) for both classroom viewing and home viewing via the new video CD-ROM. There are forty short clips, twenty-one medium clips, and seventeen long segments.

The short clips consist of television ads that were originally broadcast during the **Super Bowl** games. The medium clips have been pulled from **CNN**'s news footage archives and show how marketing principles operate in the world of big business. And the long clips are excerpted footage from various episodes of the thirty-minute **Small Business School (SBS)** program broadcast nationwide on PBS.

Each chapter has a designated **SBS** segment as the lead segment for that chapter, but because the **SBS** programs cover all aspects of business, **SBS** segments raise more issues than just those presented in the assigned chapter. For example, the lead segment for Chapter 1 is on Wahoo's Fish Taco, a uniquely Californian restaurant, but the content in the Wahoo's Fish Taco segment also relates to material in Chapter 5 (Consumer Decision Making), Chapter 7 (Segmenting and Targeting Markets), Chapter 13 (Retailing), and Chapter 15 (Advertising and Public Relations). The rich **SBS** videos will help reinforce what you've learned by showing you people who are doing marketing every day–and not according to thematic units. The multifaceted **SBS** videos give you maximum flexibility in how you use the videos, and combined with the short and medium option videos, the possibilities are endless!

A VALUE-BASED INSTRUCTOR'S MANUAL LIKE NO OTHER, THE CORE OF OUR INTEGRATED LEARNING SYSTEM™

Our Instructor's Manual is the core of our **Integrated Learning System**. For the Seventh Edition of *Marketing*, we have made our popular Instructor's Manual even more valuable for new and experienced instructors alike. Here is a list of the new features that will reduce class preparation time:

- Suggested syllabi for twelve- and sixteen-week terms.
- A pedagogy grid for each chapter briefly laying out 1) all the options the professor has in the chapter and 2) what key points in the chapter each feature addresses. The features included on the grid are the opening vignette, the boxed features, **Use It**, **Apply It**, **Try It**, and each video option.
- Three suggested lesson plans for each chapter: a lecture lesson plan, a small-group-work lesson plan, and a video lesson plan.

We have retained the proven features like the detailed chapter outline, lists of support material, supplemental articles, additional class activities, and solutions for all **Review It**, **Apply It**, and **Try It** and part cases in the book. Our manual is truly "one-stop shopping" for instructors teaching any size of marketing course.

COMPREHENSIVE TEST BANK AND WINDOWS TESTING SOFTWARE

To complete the **Integrated Learning System**, our enhanced Test Bank is organized around the learning objectives. It is available in print and new Windows software formats (ExamView testing software).

With ExamView, you can choose to prepare tests that cover all learning objectives or emphasize those you feel are most important. This updated Test Bank is one of the most comprehensive on the market, with over 3,300 true/false, multiple-choice, scenario, and essay questions. Our testing database, combined with the ease of ExamView, takes the pain out of exam preparation.

WEBTUTOR™ ADVANTAGE

WebTutor™ Advantage puts you ahead of the game in providing on-line course management for instructors and on-line learning for students. It contains all of the interactive study guide components that you could ever want and many valuable technology-oriented additions you never thought you'd get! **WebTutor™ Advantage** also contains e-lectures—this valuable student resource combines the robust PowerPoint™ presentation with narration. **WebTutor™ Advantage** also contains the Small Business School digitized videos and pedagogy, "Ask the Authors" video segments, and the "Who Wants to Be a Marketer?" game.

WebTUTOR™ Advantage

OTHER OUTSTANDING SUPPLEMENTS

Transparency Acetates: To supplement the PowerPoint™ presentation, 250 transparency acetates are available. They include figures and diagrams from the text, as well as synopses of important text content. Images are tied to the **Integrated Learning System** through the Instructor's Manual lecture outlines. Transparencies and their discussion prompts appear within the learning objective content where they apply. In addition, if you need more acetates than the 250 in our package, our PowerPoint™ presentation is available in printable format on the instructor's resource page of the Lamb, Hair, and McDaniel Web site (**http://lamb.swlearning. com**). View the slides and create your own acetates tailored to your particular course needs.

Handbook for New Instructors: This helpful booklet was specifically designed for instructors preparing to teach their first course in principles of marketing. It provides helpful hints on developing a course outline, lecturing, testing, giving feedback, and assigning projects.

Great Ideas in Teaching Marketing: We have moved Great Ideas to our instructor's resource page on the Lamb, Hair, and McDaniel Web site. In this way, we can regularly add to our collection of teaching ideas without having to wait for the next edition of Marketing. Submissions will be collected, organized, and presented on-line to keep Great Ideas a dynamic and up-to-date teaching resource. For Great Ideas, go to **http://lamb.swlearning.com.**

INNOVATIVE AND VALUABLE STUDENT SUPPLEMENTS

Marketing 7e provides an excellent vehicle for learning the fundamentals. For students to gain a true understanding of marketing, however, it's best if they can apply the principles they are learning in the classroom. And it's best if they have study aids that address their particular learning style. Our student supplements meet the needs of a variety of learning styles from visual to auditory, from hands-on to abstract conceptualization.

THE GRADEMAKER STUDY GUIDE AND WORKBOOK

The **Grademaker Study Guide and Workbook** has been greatly updated for the Seventh Edition). As part of the **Integrated Learning System**, the study guide questions are linked to the learning objectives by numbered icons. A student having difficulty with the material found in Chapter 5, Learning Objective 2, can quickly go to this Learning Objective in the Grademaker and find numerous questions and aids to master that material. Every chapter includes application questions in a variety of formats to help students to master concepts. Study guide questions are designed to be similar in type and difficulty level to the Test Bank questions. By careful review of the Grademaker, students can dramatically improve their test scores. Each Grademaker chapter opens with a self-assessment pre-test to help students identify areas where they need the most review, followed by chapter outlines with definitions, vocabulary practice, true/false, multiple choice, agree/disagree, and essay questions. Two new sections have been created for this edition of the Grademaker: marketing scenarios and marketing applications. Each scenario presents a marketing situation and is followed by a series of questions that ask students to evaluate the situation presented. The new applications require students to put marketing concepts to work, such as in the creation of a print advertisement for the chapter on Advertising and Public Relations (Chapter 15).

XTRA! CD-ROM

As described above, **Xtra! CD-ROM** is like no other interactive CD that has ever accompanied *Marketing*. Videos, exhibit worksheets, supplemental content modules, quizzes, and PowerPoint™ slides are the powerful Xtra! study tools we have created especially for this CD. Xtra! is free with every new copy of *Marketing 7e*. It is the most powerful electronic learning tool ever created for marketing students.

VIDEO CD-ROM

Video brings marketing concepts alive like no other format. Unfortunately, today's time-pressed instructors and students rarely have the space in the tightly-packed syllabus to dedicate to watching lengthy videos. Our video CD-ROM contains all seventeen of the **Small Business School** videos (the long segments described in the **Watch It** at the end of each chapter) and can be packaged with *Marketing*. Pedagogy created specifically for each video segment helps students experience how marketing concepts are in use in some of the country's most successful small businesses.

CADOTTE: EXPERIENCE MARKETING AT THE MARKETPLACE

This simulation will challenge students to make tough marketing decisions in a competitive, fast-paced market where the customers are demanding and the competition is working hard to increase market share. Theory comes alive as students learn to manage a new business venture, increase profit, improve customer satisfaction, and capture dominant market share.

ACKNOWLEDGEMENTS

This book could not have been written and published without the generous expert assistance of many people. First we wish to thank Julie Baker, The University of Texas at Arlington, for her contributions to several chapters. Glenn Voss did an excellent job in updating the Internet chapter. We would also like to recognize and thank Vicky Crittenden, Boston College, and Bill Crittenden, Northeastern University, for contributing the Cross-Functional Connections that open each part. Vicky also did and excellent job on the Critical Thinking cases and Marketing Miscues. We must also thank Jeffrey Gleich for contributing all of the new Entrepreneurship cases and Erika Matulich, University of Tampa, for her contributions to Chapter 2.

We also wish to thank each of the following persons for their work on the best supplement package that is available today. Our gratitude goes out to: Susan Peterson of Scottsdale Community College for her tremendous revision of the Instructor Manual and her detailed update of the Study Guide; Thomas and Betty Pritchett of Kennesaw State University for revising our comprehensive Test Bank and for writing the quizzes that appear in other parts of the package; Deborah Baker of Texas Christian University revised the PowerPoint™ presentation and added the wonderful teaching notes, hyperlinks, and videos to her already complete slide presentation; Jeffery Gleich for the excellent video teaching notes; and John Drea of Western Illinois University who created the fun classroom review game, "Who Wants to Be a Marketer?"

Our secretaries and administrative assistants, Fran Eller at TCU, Susan Sartwell at LSU, and RoseAnn Reddick at UTA, typed the manuscript, provided important quality control, and helped keep the project (and us) on schedule. Their dedication, hard work, and support were exemplary.

Our deepest gratitude goes to the team at Thomson Learning that has made this text a market leader. Jamie Gleich Bryant, our developmental editor, and Amy McGuire, our production editor, made this text a reality. A special thanks goes to Steve Hazelwood, our acquisitions editor, and Melissa Acuña, our Publisher, for their suggestions and support.

Finally, we are particularly indebted to our reviewers:

MEET THE AUTHORS

CHARLES W. LAMB, JR.
TEXAS CHRISTIAN UNIVERSITY

Charles W. Lamb, Jr., is the M.J. Neeley Professor of Marketing, M.J. Neeley School of Business, Texas Christian University. He served as chair of the department of marketing from 1982 to 1988 and again from 1997 to the present. He is currently serving as president-elect of the Academy of Marketing Science.

Lamb has authored or co-authored more than a dozen books and anthologies on marketing topics and over 150 articles that have appeared in academic journals and conference proceedings.

In 1997, he was awarded the prestigious Chancellor's Award for Distinguished Research and Creative Activity at TCU. This is the highest honor that the university bestows on its faculty. Other key honors he has received include the M.J. Neeley School of Business Research Award, selection as a Distinguished Fellow of the Academy of Marketing Science and a Fellow of the Southwestern Marketing Association.

Lamb earned an associate degree from Sinclair Community College, a bachelor's degree from Miami University, an MBA from Wright State University, and a doctorate from Kent State University. He previously served as assistant and associate professor of marketing at Texas A & M University.

JOSEPH F. HAIR, JR.
LOUISIANA STATE UNIVERSITY

Joseph Hair is Alvin C. Copeland Endowed Chair of Franchising and Director, Entrepreneurship Institute, Louisiana State University. Previously, Hair held the Phil B. Hardin Chair of Marketing at the University of Mississippi. He has taught graduate and undergraduate marketing and marketing research courses.

Hair has authored 27 books, monographs, and cases and over 60 articles in scholarly journals. He also has participated on many university committees and has chaired numerous departmental task forces. He serves on the editorial review boards of several journals.

He is a member of the American Marketing Association, Academy of Marketing Science, Southern Marketing Association, and Southwestern Marketing Association.

Hair holds a bachelor's degree in economics, a master's degree in marketing, and a doctorate in marketing, all from the University of Florida. He also serves as a marketing consultant to businesses in a variety of industries, ranging from food and retailing to financial services, health care, electronics, and the U.S. Departments of Agriculture and Interior.

CARL MCDANIEL
UNIVERSITY OF TEXAS, ARLINGTON

Carl McDaniel is a professor of marketing at the University of Texas–Arlington, where he has been chairman of the marketing department since 1976. He has been an instructor for more than 20 years and is the recipient of several awards for outstanding teaching. McDaniel has also been a district sales manager for Southwestern Bell Telephone Company. Currently, he serves as a board member of the North Texas Higher Education Authority.

In addition to Marketing, McDaniel also has co-authored numerous textbooks in marketing and business. McDaniel's research has appeared in such publications as the Journal of Marketing, Journal of Business Research, Journal of the Academy of Marketing Science, and California Management Review.

McDaniel is a member of the American Marketing Association, Academy of Marketing Science, Southern Marketing Association, Southwestern Marketing Association, and Western Marketing Association.

Besides his academic experience, McDaniel has business experience as the co-owner of a marketing research firm. Recently, McDaniel served as senior consultant to the International Trade Centre (ITC), Geneva, Switzerland. The ITC's mission is to help developing nations increase their exports. He has a bachelor's degree from the University of Arkansas and his master's degree and doctorate from Arizona State University.

PART 1

The World of Marketing

CROSS-FUNCTIONAL BUSINESS SYSTEMS: PUTTING THE CUSTOMER AT THE CENTER

Businesses today are faced with many changes and expectations. Technology has become a driving force in all decisions—whether they are corporate-wide strategic decisions or decisions as to where to place media funds. Businesses are forced to adapt, very quickly, to a new way of doing business via technological innovations. The speed of change in today's business world has led to functional-level management becoming empowered to make decisions that will help give their companies a competitive edge in a rapidly evolving, digitized marketplace.

With strategic decisions being made quickly by functional-level managers, it is imperative that all departments have a customer focus. This focus needs to be reflected in the daily activities of all employees, regardless of the areas in which they work—from accounting, finance, and manufacturing to human resources and marketing. A customer focus that permeates every facet of the organization does not come easily, however, nor has it always been implemented successfully.

Historically, three levels formed a "hierarchy of strategy" within a company: corporate strategy, business strategy, and functional strategy. The corporate and business-level strategies were supported by the individual functional strategies that brought together the various activities necessary to gain the desired competitive advantage. Traditionally, each functional area performs specialized portions of the organization's tasks. For example, the functional-level marketing strategy resolves questions concerning what products deliver customer satisfaction and value, what price to charge, how to distribute products, and what type of marketing communication activities will produce the desired impact. On the other hand, the functional-level manufacturing strategy decides what products should be manufactured and at what production rate, and how to make the products (e.g., labor or capital intensive). Since such functional activities require expertise in only one functional area, managers have traditionally been trained to manage "vertically."

Such vertical activities have led to the creation of corporate silos in business. An employee working in a silo generally does not understand the importance of his or her processes in providing the final product or service to the customer. Such vertical activities have resulted in departments comprised of functional specialists who have tended to talk only with each other. For example, marketers talk to other marketing folks, operational discussions take place on the shop floor among manufacturing engineers, development team members talk within their R&D groups, and financial analysts and accountants talk with one another.

Individual functional-level strategies resulting from such departmentalization are the center of much intraorganizational conflict. For example, conflict between the marketing group and the production schedule is common. Marketing tends to want output increased or decreased immediately. But the production schedule, once made, is often seen as very inflexible.

The effective formulation and implementation of a customer-focused strategy, however, depend upon functional groups working in partnership with one another. Crossing functional boundaries is referred to as managing "horizontally" and requires a significant level of coordination among business functions. For example, it is imperative that marketing managers take a keen interest in financial issues and that operational managers have a better understanding of the firm's customers.

Today's business environment has put considerable pressure on functional groups to work together more harmoniously. We see a dramatic rush to get products into the marketplace at a much faster rate than ever before. At the same time, customers are much more demanding about what they want in these products. The bottom line is that customers want customized products delivered immediately. Companies such as General Electric, Hewlett-Packard, and Ford have dedicated considerable time and resources to understanding and implementing high levels of cross-functional integration (often referred to as *internal partnering*).

In General Electric's entry-level Financial Management Program, trainees work in various jobs throughout the world during the first two years of employment. Members of this program change jobs every six months. While each change generally brings a new geographic location, it definitely brings a new cross-functional perspective on GE's businesses. Unfortunately, successful cross-functional interactions in most companies do not come easy and are often mired in conflict. Reasons for conflict between and among functional areas include divergent personalities, physical separation, data differences, and suboptimal reward systems.

Marketing people tend to be extroverted and interact easily with others, while R&D and manufacturing people are frequently introverted and work well with individual work processes and output. In addition to having different personalities, marketers and their product management colleagues in R&D and manufacturing often are housed in different locations. This is surprising when one thinks about the overlap all three groups have on a company's product.

The marketing department is typically located in the company's headquarters—which may be in the heart of a major business district, with sales located strategically close to customers. We often see the company's manufacturing group located in low-wage areas, low-rent districts, and close to suppliers. The manufacturing group may even be located in a different country. It becomes too easy for each department to "do its own thing," particularly if the groups are separated by language differences as well as time zones.

Another major source of conflict between marketing and its R&D and manufacturing counterparts is the type of data collected and used in decision making. Technical specialists in R&D and manufacturing have a difficult time understanding the lack of "hard" data that marketers work with. It is difficult to mesh marketing's attitudinal data with data on cycle times or tensile strength. For example, while marketing's forecasts are rarely 100 percent accurate, manufacturing can usually determine the precise costs associated with production processes.

Not surprisingly, marketing's reward system based on increased sales is often in direct conflict with manufacturing and R&D's reward systems that are driven by cost reduction. Marketing's ability to increase sales may be driven by offering consumers

depth in the product line. Unfortunately, increased depth of the line leads to more changeover in the production lines, which in turn drives up the cost of production.

A major challenge for marketers has been the development of mechanisms for reducing conflict between the marketing department and other business functions. Because of closer working relationships among human resources and information technology professionals, two major facilitating mechanisms have emerged: cross-functional teams and an information technology infrastructure.

To illustrate this functional integration, we can look at Hewlett-Packard's team approach to all of its product development. From concept to market entry, teams of engineers, marketers, manufacturers, financiers, and accountants bring together traditionally functional-level information into a cohesive program for product introduction at Hewlett-Packard. All information is shared across functional groups, and reports are prepared regularly that include details regarding interactions among functions.

Recognition of the customer's role in the organization and empowering employees are both necessary for success in today's business environment. Rapidly changing technology has made the cross-functional communication process much easier. Teamwork and an information technology infrastructure, in an environment that encourages and rewards better communication among all business functions, will ultimately result in a more satisfied, loyal customer.

Questions

1. What is the overlap among marketing, manufacturing, finance, accounting, and human resources? What does each of these functions do that results in this overlap?

2. Why is cross-functional coordination necessary to have a customer-oriented firm?

3. What roles do teamwork and technology play in cross-functional coordination?

CHAPTER **ONE**

AN OVERVIEW OF MARKETING

Learning Objectives

1 Define the term marketing

2 Describe four marketing management philosophies

3 Discuss the differences between sales and market orientations

4 Describe the marketing process

5 Describe several reasons for studying marketing

In 1994, Amilya Antonetti began to talk seriously about breaking into the $4.7 billion U.S. laundry-detergent market. Industry veterans told her she had to be joking. "They all laughed hysterically," Antonetti recalls. "They'd say, 'Honey, have you ever heard of Clorox? Have you ever heard of Tide? There's no place for you here.'"

Time and again, buyers for grocery stores told Antonetti that none of *their* customers would be interested in the hypoallergenic cleansing products she began developing after learning that her infant son's health problems were aggravated by the chemicals in standard brands. After one such conversation, Antonetti came close to admitting defeat. Then she did an about-face, marched right back into the guy's office, and declared, "I have one more thing to say to you: I *am* your customer."

Convinced that there were others out there like her, Antonetti did her own market research by haunting grocery-store aisles. She spent hours talking with female shoppers, she says, "Asking and asking and asking, What is it here that's missing?" She persuaded a retired soap buyer for Safeway to put her in touch with formulators. Then in late 1995, she and her lawyer husband, Dennis Karp, sold their home, secured $120,000 in loans from the Small Business Administration, and set up shop as SoapWorks in northern California's San Leandro.

It was a long haul, but five years later, grocery-store buyers were no longer laughing. And now Antonetti has shelf space in 2,500 stores from California to Florida. She generated revenues of $5 million in 1999. And she owes her success to the very customers that grocery-store buyers claimed did not exist. "There was very clearly a niche that was not being served," says Antonetti, who has boldly enlisted would-be customers in her sales effort. "If a mom comes in here and asks, 'Why are you not at my store?' I tell her, 'Look, your store already knows about me. I've already talked with every major chain. If you want us to be in your store, you need to talk to your store manager.'"

That's just what happened with Joellen Sutterfield, a fashion-industry executive who credits SoapWorks products with reducing the skin rashes she has suffered all her life. Sutterfield boasts that she hectored Safeway store managers for more than a year before they finally placed their first $50,000 SoapWorks order. "Now," Sutterfield says, "I'm working on the manager at the Whole Foods Market in San Ramon."

At Trader Joe's, SoapWorks has found a "cult following," says product manager Annette Davidson. A SoapWorks customer herself, Davidson says store managers at the 131-store chain reported such "huge demand" from customers that she decided to stock an expanded product line. Indeed, Antonetti's customers have become such apostles for SoapWorks, it's as if she's mixed a marketing ingredient into her formula.

But the secret to SoapWorks' customer-driven marketing scheme isn't solely in the suds. What really makes it work is Antonetti's demonstrated allegiance to her customers, who are smitten as much by what SoapWorks stands for as by what's inside the bottle.

"Our customers fit into a niche that was not being served by Tide and Cheer and All," says Antonetti. A black binder chock-full of customers' letters and e-mail messages attests to that. A few gripes do jump out from the correspondence: laundry powder left undissolved and weak grease-cutting agents. But most of the missives read like this: "After meeting you in Children's Hospital, we began using the products you gave us, and they are wonderful. We no longer need to leave the house after cleaning, and we all breathe much easier." Another writer credits SoapWorks laundry and bar soap with ridding them all of "painful, dry, flaky skin." Then there are those who simply seem smitten with Antonetti: "Thank you for caring about me and my children."

Now that she's gained a foothold in the market, Antonetti is more aggressively taking on the mainstream competition. She has a new label with a much bigger brand name and bold-colored bubbles. She's also formulating a more upscale product line based on cold-processed whole-leaf aloe.[1]

Amilya's initial motivation to go into the laundry-detergent business was based on her infant son's health needs. Describe her philosophy of business.

On Line

SoapWorks

How does SoapWorks use its Web site to connect with its market? What indications do you have that this is a customer-oriented company?

http://www.soapworks.com

What Is Marketing?

Define the term *marketing*

marketing
The process of planning and executing the conception, pricing, promotion, and distribution of ideas, goods, and services to create exchanges that satisfy individual and organizational goals.

What does the term *marketing* mean to you? Many people think it means the same as personal selling. Others think marketing is the same as personal selling and advertising. Still others believe marketing has something to do with making products available in stores, arranging displays, and maintaining inventories of products for future sales. Actually, marketing includes all of these activities and more.

Marketing has two facets. First, it is a philosophy, an attitude, a perspective, or a management orientation that stresses customer satisfaction. Second, marketing is a set of activities used to implement this philosophy. The American Marketing Association's definition encompasses both perspectives: "**Marketing** is the process of planning and executing the conception, pricing, promotion, and distribution of ideas, goods, and services to create exchanges that satisfy individual and organizational goals."[2]

The Concept of Exchange

exchange
The idea that people give up something to receive something they would rather have.

Exchange is the key term in the definition of marketing. The concept of **exchange** is quite simple. It means that people give up something to receive something they would rather have. Normally, we think of money as the medium of exchange. We "give up" money to "get" the goods and services we want. Exchange does not require money, however. Two persons may barter or trade such items as baseball cards or oil paintings.

An exchange can take place only if the following five conditions exist:

1. There must be at least two parties.
2. Each party has something that might be of value to the other party.
3. Each party is capable of communication and delivery.
4. Each party is free to accept or reject the exchange offer.
5. Each party believes it is appropriate or desirable to deal with the other party.[3]

Exchange will not necessarily take place even if all these conditions exist. They are, however, necessary for exchange to be possible. For example, you may place an advertisement in your local newspaper stating that your used automobile is for sale at a certain price. Several people may call you to ask about the car, some may test-drive it, and one or more may even make you an offer. All five conditions are necessary for an exchange to exist. But unless you reach an agreement with a buyer and actually sell the car, an exchange will not take place. Notice that marketing can occur even if an exchange does not occur. In the example just discussed, you would have engaged in marketing even if no one bought your used automobile.

Marketing Management Philosophies

Describe four marketing management philosophies

production orientation
A philosophy that focuses on the internal capabilities of the firm rather than on the desires and needs of the marketplace.

Four competing philosophies strongly influence an organization's marketing activities. These philosophies are commonly referred to as production, sales, market, and societal marketing orientations.

Production Orientation

A **production orientation** is a philosophy that focuses on the internal capabilities of the firm rather than on the desires and needs of the marketplace. A production orientation means that management assesses its resources and asks these questions: "What can we do best?" "What can our engineers design?" "What is easy to produce, given our equipment?" In the case of a service organization, managers ask, "What services are most convenient for the firm to offer?" and "Where do our talents lie?" Some have referred to this orientation as a *Field of Dreams* orientation, referring to the movie line, "If we build it, they will come." The furniture industry is infamous for its disregard of customers and for its slow cycle times. This has always been a production-oriented industry.

There is nothing wrong with assessing a firm's capabilities; in fact, such assessments are major considerations in strategic marketing planning (see Chapter 2). A production orientation falls short because it does not consider whether the goods and services that the firm produces most efficiently also meet the needs of the marketplace. Sometimes what a firm can best produce is exactly what the market wants. For example, the research and development department of 3M's commercial tape division developed and patented the adhesive component of Post-it Notes a year before a commercial application was identified. In other situations, as when competition is weak or demand exceeds supply, a production-oriented firm can survive and even prosper. More often, however, firms that succeed in competitive markets have a clear understanding that they must first determine what customers want and then produce it, rather than focus on what company management thinks should be produced.

Sales Orientation

A **sales orientation** is based on the ideas that people will buy more goods and services if aggressive sales techniques are used and that high sales result in high profits. Not only are sales to the final buyer emphasized but intermediaries are also encouraged to push manufacturers' products more aggressively. To sales-oriented firms, marketing means selling things and collecting money.

The fundamental problem with a sales orientation, as with a production orientation, is a lack of understanding of the needs and wants of the marketplace. Sales-oriented companies often find that, despite the quality of their sales force, they cannot convince people to buy goods or services that are neither wanted nor needed.

sales orientation
The idea that people will buy more goods and services if aggressive sales techniques are used and that high sales result in high profits.

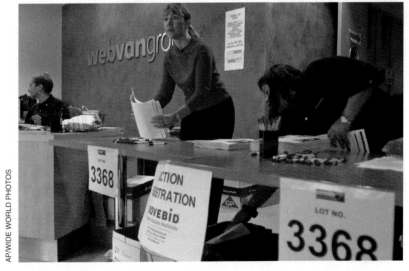

ON LINE

Some sales-oriented firms simply lack understanding of what is important to their customers. Many so-called dot-com businesses that came into existence in the late 1990s are no longer around. Some experts have predicted that 95 to 98 percent of the dot-coms will go out of business.[4] Most of those that did focused on the technology rather than the customer.

Kimberly Knickle couldn't have been happier when she signed up with online grocer Streamline.com. With two kids and a job, the $30 a month extra was worth it. Streamline installed a refrigerator in her garage to make deliveries when she wasn't home, picked up the dry cleaning, delivered stamps, and dropped off parcel shipments. The best part was the customer service. When something went wrong, Streamline instantly credited her account. She could always get someone on the phone. As the company gained a larger customer base, however, Knickle's enthusiasm turned sour. The deliveries became inconsistent, telephone customer service put her on hold more often, and the company overcharged her several times. The big blow came when it revamped its Web site: In the past, she could place an order for thirty items quickly, but the company switched to a new system that checked inventory in real time,

AP/WIDE WORLD PHOTOS

Workers prepare registration forms for bidders atop front lobby tables, which themselves were available for purchase, at the liquidation of on-line grocer Webvan Group. After churning through $830 million in two years, the company was forced into bankruptcy. Despite having mastered its supply chain and supplying great service, Webvan was not able to generate enough revenue to stay in business.

slowing down the interface tremendously. "The grocery store is two minutes away," Knickle says. "In 25 minutes, I could get two-thirds of my shopping done at the store. This was supposed to make my life easier."[5]

Market Orientation

The **marketing concept** is a simple and intuitively appealing philosophy. It states that the social and economic justification for an organization's existence is the satisfaction of customer wants and needs while meeting organizational objectives. It is based on an understanding that a sale does not depend on an aggressive sales force, but rather on a customer's decision to purchase a product. What a business thinks it produces is not of primary importance to its success. Instead, what customers think they are buying—the perceived value—defines a business. The marketing concept includes the following:

- Focusing on customer wants and needs so that the organization can distinguish its product(s) from competitors' offerings

- Integrating all the organization's activities, including production, to satisfy these wants

- Achieving long-term goals for the organization by satisfying customer wants and needs legally and responsibly

The marketing concept recognizes that there is no reason why customers should buy one organization's offerings unless they are in some way better at serving the customers' wants and needs than those offered by competing organizations.

Customers have higher expectations and more choices than ever before. This means that marketers have to listen more closely than ever before.[6] They also have to anticipate needs, to solve problems before they start, to provide service that wows, and to offer responses to mistakes

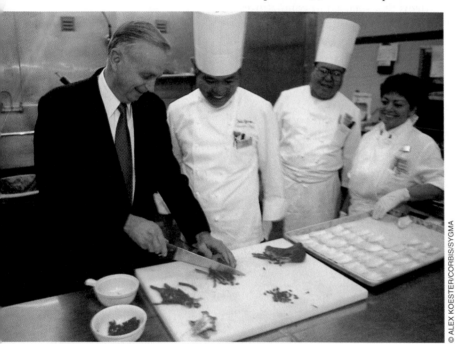

Adopting a market orientation requires top-management leadership and involvement. Bill Marriott knows this, so each year he travels widely visiting the company's hotels to ensure that every Marriott delivers superior customer value.

that more than make up for the original error.[7] For example, Netpulse Communications provides Internet connections to health clubs allowing exercisers to surf the Web or check their e-mail while they are working out. Netpulse uses a monitoring system to diagnose problems remotely. So, if a janitor accidentally disconnects a power cord, a service representative can call the club and ask them to plug the machine back in. Nine times out of ten Netpulse reports a problem to the club before anyone there is even aware of it.[8]

Firms that adopt and implement the marketing concept are said to be market oriented. Achieving a **market orientation** involves obtaining information about customers, competitors, and markets; examining the information from a total business perspective; determining how to deliver superior customer value; and implementing actions to provide value to customers.[9] It also entails establishing and maintaining mutually rewarding relationships with customers.

Today, companies of all types are adopting a market orientation. Bill Marriott, Marriott International's CEO, logs an average of 150,000 travel miles each year visiting the company's hotels, inspecting them, and talking to employees at all levels in the organization. Burton Snowboards became the best-known brand in one of the world's fastest-growing sports by identifying its most important customers, figuring out the product that those customers want, and then designing it. Almost every day

Burton staffers visit with some of the 300 professional riders worldwide who advise the company. These conversations take place on the slopes and on the phone. If one of them has a suggestion or a problem, a Burton employee calls back within twenty-four hours. Riders help develop virtually every Burton product.[10]

Understanding your competitive arena and competitors' strengths and weaknesses is a critical component of market orientation. This includes assessing what existing or potential competitors might be intending to do tomorrow as well as what they are doing today. Western Union failed to define its competitive arena as telecommunications, concentrating instead on telegraph services, and was eventually outflanked by fax technology. Had Western Union been a market-oriented company, its management might have better understood the changes taking place, seen the competitive threat, and developed strategies to counter the threat.[11]

Western Union

Has Western Union rebounded from its failure to define its competitive arena as telecommunications? Evaluate the company's Web site to find out. Against whom does Western Union seem to be competing in the twenty-first century?

http://www.westernunion.com

On Line

Societal Marketing Orientation

One reason a market-oriented organization may choose not to deliver the benefits sought by customers is that these benefits may not be good for individuals or society. This philosophy, called a **societal marketing orientation**, states that an organization exists not only to satisfy customer wants and needs and to meet organizational objectives but also to preserve or enhance individuals' and society's long-term best interests. Marketing products and containers that are less toxic than normal, are more durable, contain reusable materials, or are made of recyclable materials is consistent with a societal marketing orientation. Duracell and Eveready battery companies have reduced the levels of mercury in their batteries and will eventually market mercury-free products. Turtle Wax car wash products and detergents are biodegradable and can be "digested" by waste treatment plants. The company's plastic containers are made of recyclable plastic, and its spray products do not use propellants that damage the ozone layer in the earth's upper atmosphere.

societal marketing orientation
The idea that an organization exists not only to satisfy customer wants and needs and to meet organizational objectives but also to preserve or enhance individuals' and society's long-term best interests.

Differences Between Sales and Market Orientations

Discuss the differences between sales and market orientations

The differences between sales and market orientations are substantial. Exhibit 1.1 compares the two orientations in terms of five characteristics: the organization's focus, the firm's business, those to whom the product is directed, the firm's primary goal, and the tools used to achieve those goals.

The Organization's Focus

Personnel in sales-oriented firms tend to be "inward looking," focusing on selling what the organization makes rather than making what the market wants. Many of the historic sources of competitive advantage—technology, innovation, economies of scale—allowed companies to focus their efforts internally and prosper. Today, many successful firms derive their competitive advantage from an external, market-oriented focus. A market orientation has helped companies such as Boeing, Dell

COURTESY OF TURTLE WAX, INC.

Although Turtle Wax is not founded upon a societal marketing orientation in the same way as, say, the Sierra Club, the company still communicates to its customers that it is concerned about the environment. This placement on the Turtle Wax Web site reminds customers that the company included societal concerns in its corporate philosophy.

Exhibit 1.1 Differences Between Sales and Market Orientations

	What is the organization's focus?	What business are you in?	To whom is the product directed?	What is your primary goal?	How do you seek to achieve your goal?
Sales Orientation	Inward, upon the organization's needs	Selling goods and services	Everybody	Profit through maximum sales volume	Primarily through intensive promotion
Market Orientation	Outward, upon the wants and preferences of customers	Satisfying customer wants and needs and delivering superior value	Specific groups of people	Profit through customer satisfaction	Through coordinated marketing and interfunctional activities

Computer, Hewlett-Packard, and Southwest Airlines outperform their competitors. A sales orientation has led to the demise of many firms including Streamline.com, the Digital Entertainment Network, and Urban Box Office. As one technology industry analyst put it, "no one has ever gone to a Web site because they heard there was great Java running."[12] Former Kmart Corporation CEO Charles Conaway adds that, "anyone who loses their focus on the customer is in for ruin . . . it's just a matter of when it catches up with you."[13] Ironically, Kmart filed for Chapter 11 bankruptcy protection less than seventeen months after Conaway's remark was quoted in *Business Week*. One industry analyst concluded that "they [Kmart] need to define themselves more clearly and know who their customer is."[14] Another stated that "it focused on going up against Wal-Mart products and prices, but didn't consider the customer."[15] It does not appear that Conaway was following his own advice. Today, key issues in developing competitive advantage include creating customer value, maintaining customer satisfaction, and building long-term relationships.

Customer Value

customer value
The ratio of benefits to the sacrifice necessary to obtain those benefits.

Customer value is the ratio of benefits to the sacrifice necessary to obtain those benefits. The automobile industry illustrates the importance of creating customer value. To penetrate the fiercely competitive luxury automobile market, Lexus adopted a customer-driven approach, with particular emphasis on service. Lexus stresses product quality with a standard of zero defects in manufacturing. The service quality goal is to treat each customer as one would treat a guest in one's home, to pursue the perfect person-to-person relationship, and to strive to improve continually. This pursuit has enabled Lexus to establish a clear quality image and capture a significant share of the luxury car market.

Customer value is not simply a matter of high quality. A high-quality product that is available only at a high price will not be perceived as a good value, nor will bare-bones service or low-quality goods selling for a low price. Instead, customers value goods and services that are of the quality they expect and that are sold at prices they are willing to pay. Value can be used to sell a Mercedes Benz as well as a $3 Tyson frozen chicken dinner.

Value also stretches beyond quality and price to include customized options and fast delivery. Dell Computer Corporation encourages shoppers to customize products to their liking on its Web sites. By one count, customers can choose from among more than 25,000 different computer configurations. General Motors has introduced a build-to-order system that allows customers to custom design cars on-line for delivery in as few as four days.[16]

Marketers interested in customer value

- *Offer products that perform:* This is the bare minimum requirement. Consumers have lost patience with shoddy merchandise.

Zane's Cycles

What evidence of a market orientation do you see on Zane's Cycles' Web site? How does the company demonstrate its commitment to the customer?

http://www.zanescycles.com

On Line

- *Give consumers more than they expect:* Christopher Zane, owner of Zane's Cycles, one of the ten largest bicycle shops in the United States, suggests removing the bar rather than raising it. Zane's Cycles offers lifetime free service, lifetime parts warranties, and ninety-day price protection. The price protection plan is important to demonstrate to customers that they are getting free lifetime parts and services along with the lowest price available for the brands and models that they buy.[17]

- *Avoid unrealistic pricing:* E-marketers are leveraging Internet technology to redefine how prices are set and negotiated. With lower costs, e-marketers can often offer lower prices than their brick-and-mortar counterparts. The enormous popularity of auction sites such as eBay and Amazon.com and the customer-bid model used by Priceline illustrate that on-line customers are interested in bargain prices. Many are not willing to pay a premium for the convenience of examining the merchandise and taking it home with them.

- *Give the buyer facts:* Today's sophisticated consumer wants informative advertising and knowledgeable salespeople. A study by Andersen Consulting (now Accenture) revealed that Web sites that don't provide enough information are among the top ten things that "irk" Internet shoppers most.[18]

- *Offer organization-wide commitment in service and after-sales support:* People fly Southwest Airlines because the airline offers superior value. Although passengers do not get assigned seats or meals (just peanuts or crackers) when they use the airline, its service is reliable and friendly and costs less than most major airlines. All Southwest employees are involved in the effort to satisfy customers. Pilots tend to the boarding gate when their help is needed and ticket agents help move luggage. One reservation agent flew from Dallas to Tulsa with a frail, elderly woman whose son was afraid she couldn't handle the change of planes by herself on her way to St. Louis.

According to a Datamonitor study, "U.S. on-line businesses lose more than $6 billion in potential e-commerce sales annually due to lack of customer service at their Web sites."[19] Another recent report revealed that while 38 percent of studied companies responded to customer e-mails in six hours or less, a whopping 24 percent sent no response at all![20] Service quality is explored in more detail in Chapter 11.

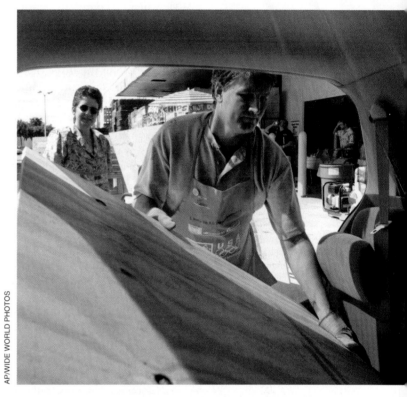

AP/WIDE WORLD PHOTOS

Customer-intimate companies achieve great success by building longtime relationships with their customers. Home Depot is an industry benchmark in customer satisfaction. Here, employee Juan Cruz loads plywood for a customer preparing her home against an impending hurricane.

Customer Satisfaction

Customer satisfaction is the feeling that a product has met or exceeded the customer's expectations. Keeping current customers satisfied is just as important as attracting new ones and a lot less expensive. Firms that have a reputation for delivering high levels of customer satisfaction do things differently from their competitors. Top management is obsessed with customer satisfaction, and employees throughout the organization understand the link between their job and satisfied customers. The culture of the organization is to focus on delighting customers rather than on selling products. John Chambers, chief executive of Cisco Systems, advises managers to "make your customers the center of your culture."[21] One way

customer satisfaction
The feeling that a product has met or exceeded the customer's expectations.

Volvo

How does Volvo use its Web site to maintain customer relations? Do you think Volvo has a sales or a market orientation? What evidence do you have to support your conclusion?

http://www.volvocars.com

On Line

that Cisco does this is by directly linking employee compensation programs to customer satisfaction study results.[22]

Staples, the office supply retailer, offers great prices on its paper, pens, fax machines, and other office supplies, but its main strategy is to grow by providing customers with the best solutions to their problems. Its approach is to emulate customer-intimate companies like Home Depot and Airborne Express. These companies do not pursue one-time transactions: They cultivate relationships.

Building Relationships

Attracting new customers to a business is only the beginning. The best companies view new customer attraction as the launching point for developing and enhancing a long-term relationship. Companies can expand market share in three ways: attracting new customers, increasing business with existing customers, and retaining current customers. Building relationships with existing customers directly addresses two of the three possibilities and indirectly addresses the other.

relationship marketing
A strategy that entails forging long-term partnerships with customers.

Relationship marketing is a strategy that entails forging long-term partnerships with customers. It begins with developing a clear understanding of who your customers are, what they value, what they want to buy, and how they prefer to interact with you and be served by you.[23] Companies then build relationships with customers by offering value and providing customer satisfaction. They are rewarded with repeat sales and referrals that lead to increases in sales, market share, and profits. Costs also fall because serving existing customers is less expensive than attracting new ones.

Lee Iacocca, former president of both Ford and Chrysler, says that if you "take care of your customers, everything else will fall into place. You have to understand your customers, and you have to follow them. You have to change as your customers' lives change."[24]

The Internet is an effective tool for generating relationships with customers because of its ability to interact with the customer. With the Internet, companies can use e-mail for fast customer service, discussion groups for building a sense of community, and database tracking of buying habits for customizing products.[25]

Customers also benefit from stable relationships with suppliers. Business buyers have found that partnerships with their suppliers are essential to producing high-quality products while cutting costs. Customers remain loyal to firms that provide them greater value and satisfaction than they expect from competing firms.

Most successful relationship marketing strategies depend on customer-oriented personnel, effective training programs, employees with authority to make decisions and solve problems, and teamwork.

Customer-Oriented Personnel For an organization to be focused on building relationships with customers, employees' attitudes and actions must be customer oriented. An employee may be the only contact a particular customer has with the firm. In that customer's eyes, the employee is the firm. Any person, department, or division that is not customer oriented weakens the positive image of the entire organization. For example, a potential customer who is greeted discourteously may well assume that the employee's attitude represents the whole firm.

The Role of Training Leading marketers recognize the role of employee training in customer service and relationship building. Of *Fortune*'s 100 best companies to work for, fifty-three offer on-site university courses and ninety-one have tuition reimbursement programs.[26] It is no coincidence that the public companies on this list such as Southwest Airlines and Cisco Systems perform much better than other firms in their respective industries. All new employees at Disneyland and Walt Disney World must attend Disney University, a special training program for Disney employees. They must first pass Traditions 1, a daylong course focusing on the Disney philosophy and operational procedures. Then they go on to specialized training. Similarly, McDonald's has Hamburger University. At American Express's Quality University, line employees and managers learn how to treat customers. There is an extra payoff for companies such as Disney and McDonald's that train their employees to be customer oriented. When employees make their customers happy, the employees are more likely to derive satisfaction from their jobs. Having contented workers who are committed to their jobs leads to better customer service and greater employee retention.

Disney

Disney training stretches beyond the bounds of its own organizational structures. Visit the Disney site listed below and search the site for information on the Disney Institute and its professional programs. What are the major themes of these programs? View a sample agenda to find out. What does this tell you about Disney's business philosophy?

http://disney.go.com

On Line

Empowerment In addition to training, many marketing-oriented firms are giving employees more authority to solve customer problems on the spot. The term used to describe this delegation of authority is **empowerment**. Employees develop ownership attitudes when they are treated like part-owners of the business and are expected to act the part. These employees manage themselves, are more likely to work hard, account for their own performance and the company's, and take prudent risks to build a stronger business and sustain the company's success. FedEx customer service representatives are trained and empowered to resolve customer problems. Although the average FedEx transaction costs only $16, the customer service representatives are empowered to spend up to $100 to resolve a customer problem.

empowerment
Delegation of authority to solve customers' problems quickly—usually by the first person that the customer notifies regarding a problem.

After John Yokoyama, owner of Pike Place Fish in Seattle's historic Farmer's Market, committed to empowering his employees, his cost of doing business dropped from 77 percent to 54 percent—a 43 percent increase in gross profit. Yokoyama attributes this success to each individual in the company taking personal responsibility for company profitability. "They like to win. They take it personally. They set new records nearly every month."[27]

Empowerment gives customers the feeling that their concerns are being addressed and gives employees the feeling that their expertise matters. The result is greater satisfaction for both customers and employees.

Teamwork Many organizations, such as Southwest Airlines and Walt Disney World, that are frequently noted for delivering superior customer value and providing high levels of customer satisfaction assign employees to teams and teach them team-building skills. **Teamwork** entails collaborative efforts of people to accomplish common objectives. Job performance, company performance, product value, and customer satisfaction all improve when people in the same department or work group begin supporting and assisting each other and emphasize cooperation instead of competition. Performance is also enhanced when people in different areas of responsibility such as production and sales or sales and service practice teamwork, with the ultimate goal of delivering superior customer value and satisfaction.

teamwork
Collaborative efforts of people to accomplish common objectives.

The Firm's Business

As Exhibit 1.1 illustrates, a sales-oriented firm defines its business (or mission) in terms of goods and services. A market-oriented firm defines its business in terms of the benefits its customers seek. People who spend their money, time, and energy expect to receive benefits, not just goods and services. This distinction has enormous implications.

Because of the limited way it defines its business, a sales-oriented firm often misses opportunities to serve

Empowering employees not only boosts job satisfaction, it boosts customer satisfaction. Each FedEx World Service Center customer service representative has the authority to send $100 to resolve a customer's complaint on the spot. FedEx World Service Center customer service representatives are trained and empowered to resolve customer problems.

customers whose wants can be met through only a wide range of product offerings instead of specific products. For example, in 1989, 220-year-old Britannica had estimated revenues of $650 million and a worldwide sales force of 7,500. Just five years later, after three consecutive years of losses, the sales force had collapsed to as few as 280 representatives. How did this respected company sink so low? Britannica managers saw that competitors were beginning to use CD-ROM to store huge masses of information but chose to ignore the new computer technology, as well as an offer to team up with Microsoft.

It's not hard to see why parents would rather give their children an encyclopedia on a compact disc instead of a printed one. The CD-ROM versions were either given away or sold by other publishers for under $400. A full thirty-two-volume set of *Encyclopaedia Britannica* weighs about 120 pounds, costs a minimum of $1,500, and takes up four and one-half feet of shelf space. If Britannica had defined its business as providing information instead of publishing books, it might not have suffered such a precipitous fall.

 Adopting a "better late than never" philosophy, Britannica has made its complete thirty-two-volume set available free on the Internet. The company no longer sells door-to-door and hopes to return to profitability by selling advertising on its Web site.

Answering the question "What is this firm's business?" in terms of the benefits customers seek, instead of goods and services, has at least three important advantages:

- It ensures that the firm keeps focusing on customers and avoids becoming preoccupied with goods, services, or the organization's internal needs.

- It encourages innovation and creativity by reminding people that there are many ways to satisfy customer wants.

- It stimulates an awareness of changes in customer desires and preferences so that product offerings are more likely to remain relevant.

Market orientation and the idea of focusing on customer wants do not mean that customers will always receive everything they want. It is not possible, for example, to profitably manufacture and market automobile tires that will last for 100,000 miles for $25. Furthermore, customers' preferences must be mediated by sound professional judgment as to how to deliver the benefits they seek. As one adage suggests, "People don't know what they want—they only want what they know." Consumers have a limited set of experiences. They are unlikely to request anything beyond those experiences because they are not aware of benefits they may gain from other potential offerings. For example, before the Internet, many people thought that shopping for some products was boring and time consuming, but could not express their need for electronic shopping.

Those to Whom the Product Is Directed

A sales-oriented organization targets its products at "everybody" or "the average customer." A market-oriented organization aims at specific groups of people (see again Exhibit 1.1). The fallacy of developing products directed at the average user is that relatively few average users actually exist. Typically, populations are characterized by diversity. An average is simply a midpoint in some set of characteristics. Because most potential customers are not "average," they are not likely to be attracted to an average product marketed to the average customer. Consider the market for shampoo as one simple example. There are shampoos for oily hair, dry hair, and dandruff. Some shampoos remove the gray or color hair. Special shampoos are marketed for infants and elderly people. There is even shampoo for people with average or normal hair (whatever that is), but this is a fairly small portion of the total market for shampoo.

A market-oriented organization recognizes that different customer groups want different features or benefits. It may therefore need to develop different goods, services, and promotional appeals. A market-oriented organization carefully analyzes the market and divides it into groups of people who are fairly similar in terms of selected characteristics. Then the organization develops marketing programs that will bring about mutually satisfying exchanges with one or more of those groups.

Paying attention to the customer isn't exactly a new concept. Back in the 1920s, General Motors began designing cars for every lifestyle and pocketbook. This was a breakthrough for an industry that had been largely driven by production needs ever since Henry Ford promised any color as long as it was black. The story about SoapWorks at the beginning of this chapter also illustrates the importance of identifying the needs of specific groups of people and tailoring marketing efforts to satisfy selected groups. Chapter 7 thoroughly explores the topic of analyzing markets and selecting those that appear to be most promising to the firm.

The Firm's Primary Goal

As Exhibit 1.1 illustrates, a sales-oriented organization seeks to achieve profitability through sales volume and tries to convince potential customers to buy, even if the seller knows that the customer and product are mismatched. Sales-oriented organizations place a higher premium on making a sale than on developing a long-term relationship with a customer. In contrast, the ultimate goal of most market-oriented organizations is to make a profit by creating customer value, providing customer satisfaction, and building long-term relationships with customers. The exception is so-called nonprofit organizations that exist to achieve goals other than profits. Nonprofit organizations can and should adopt a market orientation. Nonprofit organization marketing is explored further in Chapter 11.

Tools the Organization Uses to Achieve Its Goals

Sales-oriented organizations seek to generate sales volume through intensive promotional activities, mainly personal selling and advertising. In contrast, market-oriented organizations recognize that promotion decisions are only one of four basic marketing mix decisions that have to be made: product decisions, place (or distribution) decisions, promotion decisions, and pricing decisions. A market-oriented organization recognizes each of these four components as important. Furthermore, market-oriented organizations recognize that marketing is not just a responsibility of the marketing department. Interfunctional coordination means that skills and resources throughout the organization are needed to deliver superior customer service and value.

A Word of Caution

This comparison of sales and market orientations is not meant to belittle the role of promotion, especially personal selling, in the marketing mix. Promotion is the means by which organizations communicate with present and prospective customers about the merits and characteristics of their organization and products. Effective promotion is an essential part of effective marketing. Salespeople who work for market-oriented organizations are generally perceived by their customers to be

AP/WIDE WORLD PHOTOS

A market-oriented organization recognizes that customer groups and their wants vary, so it creates products and services to address these differences. *Grace* magazine embodies the full-fashioned lifestyle with features and columns that highlight relevant fashion, beauty, and style tips for larger women. But while fashion features are definitely geared to the 68 percent of American women size twelve and up, the rest of the magazine is far more general interest.

problem solvers and important links to supply sources and new products. Chapter 16 examines the nature of personal selling in more detail.

The Marketing Process

4

Describe the marketing process

Marketing managers are responsible for a variety of activities that together represent the marketing process. These include the following:

- Understanding the organization's mission and the role marketing plays in fulfilling that mission.
- Setting marketing objectives.
- Gathering, analyzing, and interpreting information about the organization's situation, including its strengths and weaknesses as well as opportunities and threats in the environment.
- Developing a marketing strategy by deciding exactly which wants and whose wants the organization will try to satisfy (target market strategy) and by developing appropriate marketing activities (the marketing mix) to satisfy the desires of selected target markets (the "Global Perspectives" box in this chapter describes an effort to enter a new target market). The marketing mix combines product, distribution, promotion, and pricing strategies in a way that creates exchanges that satisfy individual and organizational goals. The marketing mix is examined in detail in Chapter 2.

GLOBAL PERSPECTIVES

Powering into Europe

Coca-Cola Company sees the fragmented and fast-growing European sports-drink market as an important opportunity, which is why the company is investing $40 million to $50 million to launch Powerade in Europe. It is Coke's biggest marketing push in Europe in six years. "There is an open field in Europe. It's not like the United States," says Keith Pardy, director of strategic marketing for Coca-Cola West Europe.

Sports drinks command an even higher premium in Europe than in the United States, where the market is well established. A 500-milliliter bottle of a sports drink costs between 90 pence and £1 ($1.31–$1.45) in Britain, for example, compared with about 75 pence for the same size bottle of Coke or Pepsi.

Moreover, Coke believes Europeans aged 13 to 29, the target market for Powerade, increasingly are making sports a bigger part of their lives. Coke says its new Powerade drink increases endurance

during exercise by combining the benefits of a sports drink with the energy boost of drinks such as Red Bull, made by a closely held Austrian company. The formula in Europe is the same as in the new vitamin-B–enhanced U.S. Powerade, but the taste is slightly different because of certain European regulations on ingredients, Mr. Pardy says. The look is the same as in the United States, with a futuristic letter "P" logo.

As in the United States, Coke is marketing Powerade to the likes of surfers and skateboarders. Posters to be placed in gyms across Europe as part of the advertising campaign for Powerade will allude to "extreme sports" challenges, for example. But the company hopes the drink will eventually transcend its original use, and that European youths will begin drinking sports beverages more generally, as youths do in the United States.

"We want to grow the market in Europe to the point where you'll use it whenever you need en-

durance, beyond sports occasions," Mr. Pardy says.

Powerade will be launched in Britain, Ireland, France, Germany, Spain, Sweden, Turkey, Italy, Poland, Hungary, and Greece. The drink, which will be sold in citrus, orange, and vivid-blueberry flavor, will be distributed first through vending machines in gyms, sports centers, and soccer stadiums before moving to convenience stores and supermarkets.

Advertising for the drink will span billboards, television commercials, sponsorships with sports figures, the Internet, and direct mail. Most of the advertising will be directed at a male audience, as the sports-drink market is generally skewed more toward men in Europe.[28]

Describe Coke's target market strategy for Powerade in Europe. Explain the marketing mix that the company plans to employ.

- Implementing the marketing strategy.
- Designing performance measures.
- Periodically evaluating marketing efforts, and making changes if needed.

These activities and their relationships form the foundation on which the rest of the book is based. The table of contents at the beginning shows the order in which the activities are described. Exhibit 2.1 in Chapter 2 illustrates their interrelationships.

Why Study Marketing?

Now that you understand the meaning of the term *marketing*, why it is important to adopt a marketing orientation, and how organizations implement this philosophy, you may be asking, "What's in it for me?" or "Why should I study marketing?" These are important questions, whether you are majoring in a business field other

Describe several reasons for studying marketing

ETHICS IN MARKETING

A Red Light for Green Marketing?

After a decade of designing products to appeal to environmentally friendly sensibilities, many companies have concluded that "green" sales pitches don't sell. Some 41 percent of consumers say they don't buy green products because they fear the products won't work as well, according to market researchers RoperASW, which conducts an annual "Green Gauge" consumer-marketing poll.

Shoppers will pay for convenience far more readily than for ideology. In June 2001, after 70 percent of baby-food shoppers said they would prefer the convenience of plastic jars, Gerber Products Company switched from glass to No. 7 plastic, which can't be recycled. Few complained about environmental effects.

These days, bottles of water, disposable mops and heavy-duty plastic plates—all items that end up in landfills—are top sellers. Recycling rates for plastic soda bottles are about a third of what they were in 1995, while the number of single-serve bottles on the shelves more than doubled to 18 billion in 2000. New York Mayor Michael Bloomberg knows the environment is so far off voters' radar screens that he proposed to cut out all metal, glass, and plastic re-

cycling service in the city to save $57 million.

These days, only 29 percent of shoppers have recently bought a product because advertising on the label claimed it was environmentally safe or biodegradable, according to polls by RoperASW. Those who do tend to be younger and wealthier, but their ranks appear to be shrinking. Marketers have seen it coming ever since Ben & Jerry's discontinued "Rainforest Crunch" in 1997, citing slumping sales. The ice cream flavor had been introduced nationwide on Earth Day in 1990, touting conservation and nuts from rainforest trees.

Some marketers still successfully sell environmentally-friendly products, but increasingly they are doing so by playing down or skirting the green message. Personal "wellness" and safety is today's marketing fashion. Seventh Generation, a brand of natural household products, recently changed its slogan from "products for a healthy planet" to "safer for you and the environment."

"If talking about product safety is the path to get into a conversation with customers about the environment, then we haven't lost the authenticity of our mission," says

Jeffrey Hollender, Seventh Generation's president.

Some environmentalists blame consumers' waning demand for green products on confusion engendered by inconsistent eco-labeling. The "chasing arrows" recycling logo, for example, appears on the bottom of foam coffee cups, even though consumers can't readily recycle them anywhere in the United States.

The "Energy Star" labeling program launched by the Environmental Protection Agency (EPA) has been considerably more successful, says green-marketing consultant Jacquelyn Ottman. The EPA and industry together tightly control which products can carry the Energy Star logo, which signals energy efficiency. And, even though some Energy Star products carry a higher price tag, the program pitches energy cost savings over the long haul. "Customers will pay the premium when the benefits justify the price," says Ms. Ottman.[29]

Why do you think that consumers have lost interest in environmentally-friendly or "green" products? Do you agree with Gerber Products Company's decision to switch from glass to plastic? Explain your reasons.

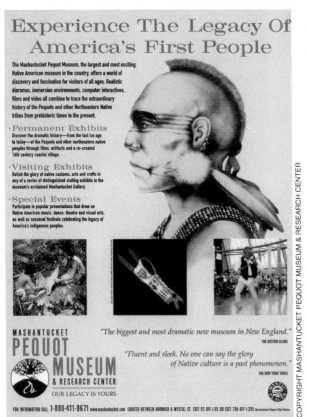

COPYRIGHT MASHANTUCKET PEQUOT MUSEUM & RESEARCH CENTER

Businesses are not the only entities that conduct marketing activities. Not-for-profit organizations like the Pequot Museum and Research Center provide career opportunities in marketing as well.

than marketing (such as accounting, finance, or management information systems) or a nonbusiness field (such as journalism, economics, or agriculture). There are several important reasons to study marketing: Marketing plays an important role in society, marketing is important to businesses, marketing offers outstanding career opportunities, and marketing affects your life every day.

Marketing Plays an Important Role in Society

The total population of the United States exceeds 280 million people. Think about how many transactions are needed each day to feed, clothe, and shelter a population of this size. The number is huge. And yet it all works quite well, partly because the well-developed U.S. economic system efficiently distributes the output of farms and factories. A typical U.S. family, for example, consumes 2.5 tons of food a year. Marketing makes food available when we want it, in desired quantities, at accessible locations, and in sanitary and convenient packages and forms (such as instant and frozen foods).

Marketing Is Important to Businesses

The fundamental objectives of most businesses are survival, profits, and growth. Marketing contributes directly to achieving these objectives. Marketing includes the following activities, which are vital to business organizations: assessing the wants and satisfactions of present and potential customers, designing and managing product offerings, determining prices and pricing policies, developing distribution strategies, and communicating with present and potential customers.

All businesspeople, regardless of specialization or area of responsibility, need to be familiar with the terminology and fundamentals of accounting, finance, management, and marketing. People in all business areas need to be able to communicate with specialists in other areas. Furthermore, marketing is not just a job done by people in a marketing department. Marketing is a part of the job of everyone in the organization. As David Packard of Hewlett-Packard put it: "Marketing is far too important to be left only to the marketing department." Marketing is not a department so much as a companywide orientation.[30] Therefore, a basic understanding of marketing is important to all businesspeople.

Marketing Offers Outstanding Career Opportunities

Between a fourth and a third of the entire civilian workforce in the United States performs marketing activities. Marketing offers great career opportunities in such areas as professional selling, marketing research, advertising, retail buying, distribution management, product management, product development, and wholesaling. Marketing career opportunities also exist in a variety of nonbusiness organizations, including hospitals, museums, universities, the armed forces, and various government and social service agencies. (See Chapter 11.)

As the global marketplace becomes more challenging, companies all over the world and of all sizes are going to have to become better marketers. For a comprehensive look at career opportunities in marketing and a variety of other useful information about careers, please visit our Web site at **http://lamb.swlearning.com**.

Marketing Affects Your Life Every Day

Marketing plays a major role in your everyday life. You participate in the marketing process as a consumer of goods and services. About half of every dollar you spend pays for marketing costs, such as marketing research, product development, packaging, transportation, storage, advertising, and sales expenses. By developing a better understanding of marketing, you will become a better-informed consumer. You will better understand the buying process and be able to negotiate more effectively with sellers. Moreover, you will be better prepared to demand satisfaction when the goods and services you buy do not meet the standards promised by the manufacturer or the marketer.

Looking Ahead

This book is divided into twenty-one chapters organized into seven major parts. The chapters are written from the marketing manager's perspective. Each chapter begins with a brief list of learning objectives followed by a brief story about a marketing situation faced by a firm or industry. At the end of each of these opening vignettes, thought-provoking questions link the story to the subject addressed in the chapter. Your instructor may wish to begin chapter discussions by asking members of your class to share their views about the questions.

The examples of global marketing highlighted in most chapters will help you understand that marketing takes place all over the world, between buyers and sellers in different countries. These and other global marketing examples throughout the book, marked with the icon shown in the margin, are intended to help you develop a global perspective on marketing.

Marketing ethics is another important topic selected for special treatment throughout the book. Chapters include highlighted stories about firms or industries that have faced ethical dilemmas or have engaged in practices that some consider unethical. Questions are posed to focus your thinking on the key ethical issues raised in each story.

Entrepreneurial insights are highlighted with icons. Every chapter also includes an application case related to small business. This material illustrates how entrepreneurs and small businesses can use the principles and concepts discussed in the book.

End-of-chapter materials begin with a final comment on the chapter-opening vignette called "Connect It." This is followed by a summary of the major topics ("Review It"), with discussion and writing questions (writing questions are identified with the icon in the margin) related to the topics. The questions include specific Internet and team activities, which are identified by appropriate icons. The on-line icon is also placed throughout the text to identify examples relating to technology. Another section, "Apply It," with discussion questions, is next, followed by a detailed ethics exercise called "Think About It." Then comes "Try It," a longer entrepreneurship case, and "Watch It," a section describing the different videos that supplement the chapter. Immediately following "Watch It" are the sections "Flip It," "Click It," and "Spin It," which let you know what additional learning opportunities are available in your study guide, on the *Marketing* Web site, and on your Xtra! CD-ROM.

Marketing 7e is also supported by InfoTrac College Edition. Several chapters throughout the book will give you the opportunity to refine your research skills through exercises specifically designed for InfoTrac. These exercises will be flagged by the icon at the left. All these features are intended to help you develop a more thorough understanding of marketing and enjoy the learning process.

The remaining chapters in Part 1 introduce you to the activities involved in developing a marketing plan, the dynamic environment in which marketing decisions must be made, ethics and social responsibility, and global marketing. Part 2 covers consumer decision making and buyer behavior; business marketing; the concepts of positioning, market segmentation, and targeting; and the nature and uses of marketing research and decision support systems. Parts 3 through 6 examine the elements of the marketing mix—product, distribution, promotion, and pricing. Part 7 contains three chapters. The first examines Internet marketing; the second focuses on customer relationship management; and the final chapter introduces integrated direct marketing, or one-to-one marketing.

CONNECT IT

Look back at the story at the beginning of this chapter about Amilya Antonetti's company SoapWorks. You should now find the assignment at the end of the story fairly easy. Amilya's initial motivation to enter the laundry-detergent market was based on her need to find a hypoallergenic product that would not aggravate her son's condition. She was unable to find such a product on the market and began developing her own. She tried to sell these products to grocery-store buyers but was rejected. At this point, we would describe Amilya's philosophy as sales oriented. "I need the product so others must need it. My job is to convince people to buy." But then Amilya began doing marketing research asking shoppers, "What is it here that's missing?" This reflects a market orientation. Amilya wanted to find out if other mothers wanted hypoallergenic laundry detergents. She also recognized that her products were not for everybody, but rather for specific groups of people with unique needs. Her success is directly related to identifying an unfulfilled need in the marketplace and developing products to satisfy that need.

USE IT

Lisa Imm, age 25, an assistant marketing manager at Commtouch, Inc., a global provider of Web-based e-mail, was looking to change fields—from database marketing to Internet marketing. But she had no idea how her current skills would transfer. Bottom line: She needed to network, and fast.

She didn't hit the party circuit or attend career fairs. Instead, she joined the e-mail list for Silicon Valley Web Grrls (www.webgrrls.com), a networking group for women who work in the technology sector. "I instantly had access to more than 1,000 people without physically having to meet them," Imm says. "The list is my virtual Rolodex."

Imm used the network not only to tap into what jobs were available but also to get valuable advice when she was considering offers: "People wrote back saying, 'I wouldn't work for that company, and this is why.' It was like having 100 personal recruiters and career counselors." A month after gathering information from the Web Grrls community and other sources, Imm landed her job.

What's her advice for others looking to take advantage of the power of a cyber-schmooze? First, be sure to join a group with credentials: "You can refer to the group on your résumé. Many times in an interview people will say, 'Wow! I've used that group too!' It's a great conversation starter." Also, give as generously as you receive. "If you don't respond to people when you've got the advice that they need, then you won't get much out of it."[31]

REVIEW IT

(1) **Define the term *marketing*.** The ultimate goal of all marketing activity is to facilitate mutually satisfying exchanges between parties. The activities of marketing include the conception, pricing, promotion, and distribution of ideas, goods, and services.

1.1 What is the AMA? What does it do? How do its services benefit marketers? **http://www.marketingpower.com**

1.2 **INFOTRAC COLLEGE EDITION** Log on to InfoTrac at **http://www.infotrac-college.com** and conduct a keyword search for "marketing." Read a couple of the articles. Based on what you have learned in this chapter, how do these articles describe or relate to marketing?

(2) **Describe four marketing management philosophies.** The role of marketing and the character of marketing activities within an organization are strongly influenced by its philosophy and orientation. A production-oriented organization focuses on the internal capabilities of the firm rather than on the desires and needs of the marketplace. A sales orientation is based on the beliefs that people will buy more products if aggressive sales techniques are used and that high sales volumes produce high profits. A market-oriented organization focuses on satisfying customer wants and needs while meeting organizational objectives. A societal marketing orientation goes beyond a market orientation to include the preservation or enhancement of individuals' and society's long-term best interests.

2.1 **WRITING** Your company president has decided to restructure the firm to make it more market oriented. She is going to announce the changes at an upcoming meeting. She has asked you to prepare a short speech outlining the general reasons for the new company orientation.

2.2 Donald E. Petersen, former chairman of the board of Ford Motor Company, remarked, "If we aren't customer driven, our cars won't be either." Explain how this statement reflects the marketing concept.

2.3 Give an example of a company that might be successfully following a production orientation. Why might a firm in this industry be successful following such an orientation?

(3) **Discuss the differences between sales and market orientations.** First, sales-oriented firms focus on their own needs; market-oriented firms focus on customers' needs and preferences. Second, sales-oriented companies consider themselves to be deliverers of goods and services, whereas market-oriented companies view themselves as satisfiers of customers. Third, sales-oriented firms direct their products to everyone; market-oriented firms aim at specific segments of the population. Fourth, although the primary goal of both types of firms is profit, sales-oriented businesses pursue maximum sales volume through intensive promotion, whereas market-oriented businesses pursue customer satisfaction through coordinated activities.

3.1 A friend of yours agrees with the adage "People don't know what they want—they only want what they know." Write your friend a letter expressing the extent to which you think marketers shape consumer wants.

3.2 **WRITING** Your local supermarket's slogan is "It's your store." However, when you asked one of the stock people to help you find a bag of chips, he told you it was not his job and that you should look a littler harder. On your way out, you noticed a sign with an address for complaints. Draft a letter explaining why the supermarket's slogan will never be credible unless the employees carry it out.

(4) **Describe the marketing process.** The marketing process includes understanding the organization's mission and the role marketing plays in fulfilling that mission, setting marketing objectives, scanning the environment, developing a marketing strategy by selecting a target market strategy, developing and implementing a marketing mix, implementing the strategy, designing performance measures, and evaluating marketing efforts and making changes if needed. The marketing mix combines product, distribution (place), promotion, and pricing strategies in a way that creates exchanges satisfying to individual organizational objectives.

4.1 **TEAM ON LINE** Form a small group of three or four members. Suppose you and your colleagues all work for an up-and-coming gourmet coffee company that has several stores, mostly in large cities across the United States. Your team has been assigned the task of assessing whether the company should begin marketing on the Internet. Each member has been assigned to visit three or four Internet sites for ideas. Some possibilities are:

- Toys 'R' Us at **http://www.toysrus.com**
- Wal-Mart at **http://www.wal-mart.com**
- Godiva chocolates at **http://www.godiva.com**
- Levi Strauss at **http://www.levi.com**

Use your imagination and look up others. As you can see, many companies are easy to find, as long as you can spell their names. Typically, you would use the following: **http://www.companyname.com**

Has Internet marketing helped the companies whose sites you visited? If so, how? What factors should your company consider before committing to Internet activity? Prepare a three- to five-minute presentation to give to your class.

⑤ **Describe several reasons for studying marketing.** First, marketing affects the allocation of goods and services that influence a nation's economy and standard of living. Second, an understanding of marketing is crucial to understanding most businesses. Third, career opportunities in marketing are diverse, profitable, and expected to increase significantly during the coming decade. Fourth, understanding marketing makes consumers more informed.

5.1 Write a letter to a friend or family member explaining why you think that a course in marketing will help you in your career in some field other than marketing.

DEFINE IT

customer satisfaction 11	marketing concept 8	societal marketing
customer value 10	market orientation 8	orientation 9
empowerment 13	production orientation 6	teamwork 13
exchange 6	relationship marketing 10	
marketing 6	sales orientation 7	

APPLY IT

Application for Entrepreneurs

Lisa King enjoyed working as a camp counselor during the summer. She started about the time she entered high school and continued through college. She even took a job at a camp the summer after graduating from college. She rationalized that this "internship," developing the camp yearbook, would help prepare her for a job in advertising.

As the summer passed, Lisa spent more time thinking about "what she was going to do when she grew up," as she liked to put it. Her thoughts always seemed to return to camping.

Lisa finally decided that she would like to open a small retail store specializing in camping supplies. The more she thought about it, the better she liked the idea.

She finally got up enough nerve to call her father, Tom, to discuss the idea. Tom's first response was, "Have you prepared a written plan?"

Lisa remembered preparing a marketing plan in her first class in marketing at the University of Miami. She asked her father to FedEx the text to her.

With financial backing from Tom, Lisa and her sister Jill opened Santorini Camping Supply the following fall. They picked the name Santorini because it was their favorite place in the Greek isles and, as Jill put it, "We just like the name."

On the first day the store was open, a customer asked Lisa if Santorini's guaranteed the products it sold. Lisa proudly replied, "Every product that is purchased from Santorini Camping Supply has a lifetime guarantee. If at any time you are not satisfied with one of our products, you can return it to the store for a full refund or exchange."

Questions

1. What marketing management philosophy is Santorini's expressing? Why have you reached this conclusion?

2. Do you think a lifetime guarantee for this kind of product is too generous? Why or why not?

3. Do you think this policy will contribute to success or to bankruptcy?

4. Suggest other customer service policies that might be appropriate for Santorini Camping Supply.

THINK ABOUT IT

Ethics Exercise

In today's business environment, ethics are extrememly important. In recent years, there have been numerous scandals and trials that stem from a lack of ethical judgment. For example, Adelphia Communications Corporation, which was the fourth largest cable television provider in the United States, declared bankruptcy, was under federal scrutiny for inflating numbers and making undisclosed loans to its major shareholders, and saw its principals arrested for fraud. The former CEO of Tyco International was charged with tax evasion and making secret deals with underlings. In 2002, over 150 firms revised their earnings reports, signaling that perhaps their accounting methods were questionable. And who can forget the catastrophic collapse of Enron and the guilty verdict against the most venerated accounting firm in the United States, Arthur Andersen, LLP?

Although some might say that these occurrences are the work of a few bad apples spoiling the bunch, it is clear that ethical decision making plays a very important role in a company's success and prosperity. For this reason, we are including an ethical exercise in every chapter. A brief scenario will present you with a situation in which the right thing to do may or may not be crystal clear, and you will need to decide the ethical way out of the dilemma. To help you with these decisions, we will always refer you back to the AMA's Code of Ethics, found on-line at **http://www.marketingpower.com**. This will give you a resource for the exercise and will also help reinforce the ethical standards that marketers should uphold.

Review the "Ethics in Marketing" story on page 17. How does the AMA Code of Ethics relate to this story? Discuss whether Gerber's decision to switch to plastic jars is consistent or inconsistent with the AMA Code of Ethics.

TRY IT

Entrepreneurship Case

Politzer & HANEY: Banking on Small Business

When Karen Prest, an analyst at Newton, MA-based Meridien Research, started conducting her research on whether banks were delivering services for small businesses, she expected the results to give banks a failing grade. "I went in as a skeptic," she says. "I was convinced by my own research. I saw how much banks are now focusing on small businesses. The study proved that small businesses are more and more in the limelight."

There was reason for her surprise. For years, there has been a lot of talk about banks going after the small-business marketplace. The U.S. Census Bureau defines a small business as one with fewer than five hundred employees. Ralph Dangelmaier, president of Massachusetts-based Politzer & HANEY, estimates that in his market there are between five and six million small businesses paying more than ten million people. Prest considers that a lucrative marketplace with a lot of untapped opportunity.

According to James Van Dyke, research director at Jupiter Media Metrix Inc., in San Francisco, banks have generally struggled with the small business

Still Shaky? Here's a Tip.

Use your textbook more like a notebook and less like a reference book. The margins are a great place for writing questions on content you don't understand, highlighting important concepts, and adding examples to help you remember the material. Writing in your book makes it a more comprehensive resource for marketing and a better study tool.

market, in part because it has been easier to see profits in large businesses. In addition, segmentation has been a challenge. Recently, banks have begun to recognize small business as a distinct, separate, and vastly underserved segment. In the past, banks have ignored the small business marketing, considering it too costly to serve and unable to provide a viable source of revenue to the bank. Technology has helped shift this thinking.

When technology proved that services could be accomplished securely over the Internet, the banking industry experienced somewhat of an epiphany. Web-based products have proliferated and enabled banks to target small businesses profitably. Some banks have long provided computer-based banking products. Politzer & HANEY has successfully offered DOS-based cash management products since the late 1980s. Windows-based products were launched in the 1990s and met with less success. But the bank's greatest success in this area has occurred since its creation of Web-based products.

From the late 1980s to the mid-1990s, Politzer & HANEY's products were used in about ten thousand small businesses. In the three to four years since its Internet-based products have been on the market, that penetration has gone to between fifty and sixty thousand companies. One report in 2001 estimated that of the six million small businesses, there's been a 1 percent penetration of small businesses using Web-based products, with penetration expected to climb to 20 to 30 percent.

Why have banks had such difficulty entering the small business market? One key reason is that banking products have not been tailored to fit the size of small business finances. This made the cash management process too expensive for the banks trying to service small business accounts. The Internet has changed that dramatically, and not only from the perspective of product offering. The Internet has affected service delivery as well. Dangelmaier says, "With the Internet, the dynamics change. Businesses can go right to the Web site. There's no cost to place software. There's standard browser technology. The cost of distribution is low, and the vendors have tuned in to this. There are hundreds of options for packaging the products, and we work with banks to help them package our cash management products for their customers."

Questions

1. Describe the shift in marketing management philosophy banks have had to make in order to serve small business.

2. Describe at least two steps in the marketing process that Politzer & HANEY took in order to help banks better serve potential small business customers.

3. Describe the major change in the marketing environment that has made it possible for banks to profitably serve small business clients.

WATCH IT

At the end of every chapter, "Watch It" will tell you about the different video options that accompany the text and support the chapter content. Each chapter will have a combination of thirty-second clips (short) embedded in the instructor's PowerPoint presentation, two- to four-minute clips (medium) for classroom viewing, and a ten- to fifteen-minute clip (long) for classroom viewing and available on a separate video CD-ROM. The short clips contain television ads that were originally broadcasted during Super Bowl games. The medium clips include CNN's news footage showing how marketing principles operate in the world of business. And the long clips are excerpts from various episodes of the thirty-minute Small Business School (SBS) program nationally broadcasted on PBS.

Because the SBS program covers all aspects of business, SBS segments raise more issues that just those presented in a single chapter. For example, the lead segment for Chapter 1 about Wahoo's Fish Taco, a uniquely Californian restaurant, also relates to material in Chapter 5 (Consumer Decision Making), Chapter 7 (Segmenting and Targeting Markets), Chapter 13 (Retailing), and Chapter 15 (Advertising and Public Relations). The rich SBS videos will help reinforce what you've learned by introducing you to people who are doing marketing every day—and not according to thematic units.

Read the descriptions and get ready to watch it!

Short

How can an advertisement convey a company's marketing focus? Watch the 30-second television spots on Lipton, OfficeDepot, and Dodge that are embedded in the Chapter 1 PowerPoint presentation found on your PowerPoint CD-ROM. Evaluate each ad based on the overview of marketing you just read.

Medium

Smaller banks are maximizing their marketing orientation through innovative customer service, and as a result, they are enjoying higher stock valuations on Wall Street. Watch the CNN clip for Chapter 1 and make a list of the ways that Commerce Bank is implementing the marketing concept.

Long

To give you insight into Chapter 1, Small Business School will introduce you to a company that shows the marketing concept in action. You'll meet two men who are building a chain of surfer food joints called Wahoo's Fish Taco. The restaurant, started by three brothers, Wing Lam, Ed Lee, and Ming Lee, has won numerous awards and has a return-on-investment that is off the charts. Step into the master class to see how the marketing concept is thriving in small business.

FLIP IT

 To learn more about the study opportunities available in your Study Guide, read the "Flip It" section at the end of each chapter. Each study guide chapter includes vocabulary review, study test questions, Internet activities, marketing applications and scenarios, and more. To help you determine the concepts you most need to review, you can perform a self-assessment by completing the pretest at the beginning of each study guide chapter. Can you explain the four marketing management philosophies? What about listing the steps in the marketing process? Check out your *Grademaker Study Guide* and find out.

CLICK IT

The *Marketing* Web site is rich with materials to help you review and master marketing concepts. Check your knowledge with the free quizzes, practice key terms using the crossword puzzles, or review key concepts using the PowerPoint slides. The "Use It" about Web Grrls and "Review It" questions 1.1, 1.2, and 4.1 are loaded in the *Marketing* Web site's Chapter 1 content. Go to **http://lamb.swlearning.com**, read the material, and follow the convenient links.

SPIN IT

 An Xtra! *CD-ROM* accompanies every new copy of *Marketing 7e* and is loaded with review opportunities and supplemental material. In addition to the quiz on the Web site, there's another quiz on your Xtra! CD-ROM. You can also quiz yourself using the worksheets for Exhibit 1.1 and see the videos of the authors answering frequently asked questions about marketing management philosophies such as "Are production firms ever successful?" Spin your Xtra! CD to find out.

CHAPTER **TWO**
STRATEGIC PLANNING FOR COMPETITIVE ADVANTAGE

Learning Objectives

1 Understand the importance of strategic marketing and know a basic outline for a marketing plan

2 Develop an appropriate business mission statement

3 Describe the criteria for stating good marketing objectives

4 Explain the components of a situation analysis

5 Identify sources of competitive advantage

6 Identify strategic alternatives and describe tools used to help select alternatives

7 Discuss target market strategies

8 Describe the elements of the marketing mix

9 Explain why implementation, evaluation, and control of the marketing plan are necessary

10 Identify several techniques that help make strategic planning effective

Coach, Inc., has been very successful over the past six years in transforming itself from a stodgy leather-goods company into a hip fashion brand. The turn-around began in the mid-1990s, a time when the company's handbags were heavy, unadorned leather that commanded a loyal customer base mainly because of their reputation for quality. However, sales were showing signs of slowing. Many retailers were offering young shoppers lightweight fabric bags. Gucci and Prada were popular, drawing off Coach customers on the high end, and knockoffs of the luxury bags were eroding Coach's following at the low end.

There was also a problem with Coach's quality: It was almost too good. Women would buy a Coach bag, and it would last so long that they would never replace it. And because Coach rarely offered new styles, even its most loyal customers hardly had a reason to visit its stores. The company's strategy was to introduce mixed-material bags, a more fun image, and a wider array of styles and products.

The first new style to be introduced was the "Neo" handbag that was a not-too-radical departure from the Coach tradition, but lighter, slimmer and made from a mix of leather and a neoprene-like fabric. It was also more functional, with more inside pockets. Shoppers loved the new look. Two years later came the "Hamptons" collection, including bags, sneakers, and scarves. In February of 2001 came the most visible departure from the boring days of monotone leather: the "Signature" collection. The logo pattern of C's, in fabric and leather, has been very successful.

The company also changed the supply chain, switching manufacturing from mostly company-run factories to independent facilities. The outside factories were able to move faster to catch fashion trends and could work in materials other than leather.

Coach has been responsive to customer needs and wants. When research showed that shoppers found a particular handbag uncomfortable, the company changed the design and sales increased fourfold. On another occasion, when the company learned that shoppers complained that a certain style tipped over when set down, a few inches were added to the bottom to make it more stable.

Image is an important part of Coach's strategy. The company avoids styles that might sell for a season but contribute nothing to the brand's long-term image. In 2001, Coach's head designer pulled camouflage at the last minute—and did not shed a tear when the look flamed out. He also resisted when department store buyers told him he would miss out by not offering faux leather—another short rage.

At its stores, Coach tailors merchandise and presentation to the customer demographics at a particular location. In a conservative region of the Midwest, for example, trendy products would be found in the back of the store; in New York, they are more likely to be out front. Coach's factory stores carry some older styles that were popular decades ago.

Coach's marketing strategy has resulted in increased sales and growth for the company. Here is an example of how one customer responded to the changes Coach made: Belle Hernandez, a thirty-year-old financial analyst in Los Angeles, had been a loyal Coach shopper in the early 1990s, but her visits trailed off in the late 1990s. She stopped because the styles seemed to be the same. In the fall of 2001, she was looking for a small red handbag and noticed one in a Coach ad. When she visited a Coach store, she was impressed with the store's new look, and now shops there about twice a month.[1]

What are the elements of Coach's marketing strategy? How would you describe Coach's competitive advantage? What type of strategic alternative (based on the strategic opportunity matrix) did Coach use to improve sales and growth?

The Nature of Strategic Planning

1

Understand the importance of strategic marketing and know a basic outline for a marketing plan

strategic planning
The managerial process of creating and maintaining a fit between the organization's objectives and resources and evolving market opportunities.

Strategic planning is the managerial process of creating and maintaining a fit between the organization's objectives and resources and the evolving market opportunities. The goal of strategic planning is long-run profitability and growth. Thus, strategic decisions require long-term commitments of resources.

A strategic error can threaten a firm's survival. On the other hand, a good strategic plan can help protect and grow the firm's resources. For instance, if the March of Dimes had decided to focus on fighting polio, the organization would no longer exist. Most of us view polio as a conquered disease. The March of Dimes survived by making the strategic decision to switch to fighting birth defects.

Strategic marketing management addresses two questions: What is the organization's main activity at a particular time? How will it reach its goals? Here are some examples of strategic decisions:

- The decision of Sears to buy Lands' End, a successful clothing catalog and on-line retail business, for $1.9 billion. The move could upgrade Sears' image and increase its presence in the catalog business and on the Internet. Lands' End clothing will enjoy greater retail distribution in Sears stores.[2]

- PepsiCo's introduction of a blue, berry-flavored version of its flagship Pepsi brand, and Coca-Cola's introduction of Vanilla Coke.[3]

- Kmart Corporation's decision to file for Chapter 11 bankruptcy and close almost three hundred stores in 2002, potentially jeopardizing its exclusive relationship with profitable brands such as Martha Stewart, Disney, and Joe Boxer.[4]

- S. C. Johnson's introduction of Shout Color Catchers, a laundry sheet for the washer that collects loose dyes and prevents clothes from bleeding color onto other laundry items.[5]

AP/WIDE WORLD PHOTOS

Strategic planning is critical to business success. Coca-Cola rolled out Vanilla Coke on the soft drink's 116th birthday. The new flavor was launched, appropriately, at the Vanilla Bean Café in Pomfret, Connecticut. The café's owner, Barry Jessurun, is pictured unloading the truck carrying the first order of Vanilla Coke.

All these decisions have affected or will affect each organization's long-run course, its allocation of resources, and ultimately its financial success. In contrast, an operating decision, such as changing the package design for Post's cornflakes or altering the sweetness of a Kraft salad dressing, probably won't have a big impact on the long-run profitability of the company.

How do companies go about strategic marketing planning? How do employees know how to implement the long-term goals of the firm? The answer is a marketing plan.

What Is a Marketing Plan?

planning
The process of anticipating future events and determining strategies to achieve organizational objectives in the future.

marketing planning
Designing activities relating to marketing objectives and the changing marketing environment.

marketing plan
A written document that acts as a guidebook of marketing activities for the marketing manager.

Planning is the process of anticipating future events and determining strategies to achieve organizational objectives in the future. **Marketing planning** involves designing activities relating to marketing objectives and the changing marketing environment. Marketing planning is the basis for all marketing strategies and decisions. Issues such as product lines, distribution channels, marketing communications, and pricing are all delineated in the **marketing plan**. The marketing plan is a written document that acts as a guidebook of marketing activities for the marketing manager. In this chapter, you will learn the importance of writing a marketing plan and the types of information contained in a marketing plan.

Why Write a Marketing Plan?

By specifying objectives and defining the actions required to attain them, a marketing plan provides the basis by which actual and expected performance can be compared. Marketing can be one of the most expensive and complicated business components, but it is one of the most important business activities. The written marketing plan provides clearly stated activities that help employees and managers understand and work toward common goals.

Writing a marketing plan allows you to examine the marketing environment in conjunction with the inner workings of the business. Once the marketing plan is written, it serves as a reference point for the success of future activities. Finally, the marketing plan allows the marketing manager to enter the marketplace with an awareness of possibilities and problems.

Coke

Pepsi

How are Coke and Pepsi using their Web sites to promote their new flavors? Do you see hints of any future strategies the companies might implement? Where?

http://www.coke.com

http://www.pepsi.com

On Line

Marketing Plan Elements

Marketing plans can be presented in many different ways. Most businesses need a written marketing plan because the scope of a marketing plan is large and can be complex. Details about tasks and activity assignments may be lost if communicated orally. Regardless of the way a marketing plan is presented, some elements are common to all marketing plans. These include defining the business mission and objectives, performing a situation analysis, delineating a target market, and establishing components of the marketing mix. Exhibit 2.1 shows these elements, which are also described further below. Other elements that may be included in a plan are budgets, implementation timetables, required marketing research efforts, or elements of advanced strategic planning. An example of a thumbnail marketing plan sketch appears in Exhibit 2.2.

Writing the Marketing Plan

The creation and implementation of a complete marketing plan will allow the organization to achieve marketing objectives and succeed. However, the marketing plan is only as good as the information it contains and the effort, creativity, and thought that went into its creation. Having a good marketing information system and a wealth of competitive intelligence (covered in Chapter 8) is critical to a thorough and accurate situation analysis. The role of managerial intuition is also important in the creation and selection of marketing strategies. Managers must weigh any information against its accuracy and their own judgment when making a marketing decision.

Note that the overall structure of the marketing plan (Exhibit 2.1) should not be viewed as a series of sequential planning steps. Many of the marketing plan elements are decided on simultaneously and in conjunction with one another. Similarly, the summary sample marketing plan (Exhibit 2.2) does not begin to cover the intricacies and detail of a full marketing plan. Further, every marketing plan has a different content, depending on the organization, its mission, objectives, targets, and marketing mix components. Visualize how the marketing plan in Exhibit 2.2 would differ if the firm offered only wireless communication connectivity services (not the physical products). How would the plan differ if the target market consisted of *Fortune* 500 firms with large sales forces instead of executives?

The marketing plan outline in Exhibit 2.7 (pages 47–49) is an expanded set of questions that can guide the formulation of a marketing plan. However, this outline should not be regarded as the only correct format for a marketing plan.

Exhibit 2.1

Elements of a Marketing Plan

Many organizations have their own distinctive format or terminology for creating a marketing plan. Every marketing plan should be unique to the firm for which it was created. Remember that although the format and order of presentation should be flexible, the same types of questions and topic areas should be covered in any marketing plan.

As you can see by the extent of the marketing plan outline in Exhibit 2.7, creating a complete marketing plan is not a simple or quick effort. However, it can be instructive to create summary marketing plans such as the sample summary plan shown in Exhibit 2.2 to get a quick idea of what a firm's marketing strategy is all about.

Exhibit 2.2

Sample Summary Marketing Plan

Business Mission	Ultracel is in the business of providing advanced communications technology and communications convenience to mobile users.
Marketing Objective	To achieve 20 percent, in dollar volume, of the wireless telephone market by year-end, 2004.
Situation Analysis	
Strengths	Well-funded organization, highly skilled workforce with low turnover, excellent relationships with suppliers, product differential and sustainable competitive advantage of patented color screen and Internet connectivity.
Weaknesses	Company name not well known, small firm with no manufacturing cost advantages, no long-term contracts with distributors, inexperience in the wireless communications market.
Opportunities	Explosive growth of wireless phone users, worldwide acceptance of cellular technology, newly expanded digital networks.
Threats	Heavy competition; technology is incompatible with current analog systems; not everyone can afford the systems, potential governmental regulation.
Target Market Selection	Young, mobile executives in North America and Europe, with incomes over $200,000 per year; frequent travelers; computer-dependent individuals.
Marketing Mix	
Product	Personal digital telephone. Brand name: Ultracel-4000. Features: simultaneous voice/data communication, Internet access, operation within buildings, linkups to data subscription and e-mail services, computer data storage, color screen, lightweight, 500-hour battery, 3-year unlimited warranty on parts and labor, 24-hour technical support, leather or titanium carrying case.
Place	Available through electronics retailers, upscale computer retailers, or via Web order company direct; products transported via airplane and temperature-controlled motor carrier.
Promotion	Fifty manufacturer's representatives for selling force, with 25 percent commissions; advertising in print media, Internet Web sites, cable television, and outdoor billboards; sales promotion in the form of introductory product rebates, technology trade shows; public relations efforts to news media and sponsorship of world-championship sporting events.
Price	Retail price of $299; assuming mild price sensitivity and future price wars. Lease option available; corporate discounts of 20 percent for volume purchases.
Implementation	First quarter: Complete marketing research on price, design promotional campaign, sign contracts with manufacturer's reps. Second quarter: Public relations campaign, product introduction at trade shows, rollout of advertising. Third quarter: Test market international markets.

Defining the Business Mission

The foundation of any marketing plan is the firm's **mission statement**, which answers the question, "What business are we in and where are we going?" Business mission definition profoundly affects the firm's long-run resource allocation, profitability, and survival. The mission statement is based on a careful analysis of benefits sought by present and potential customers and analysis of existing and anticipated environmental conditions. The firm's long-term vision, embodied in

Develop an appropriate business mission statement

mission statement
The firm's long-term vision based on a careful analysis of benefits sought by present and potential customers and analysis of existing and anticipated environmental conditions.

marketing myopia
Defining a business in terms of goods and services rather than in terms of the benefits that customers seek.

the mission statement, establishes boundaries for all subsequent decisions, objectives, and strategies. The American Marketing Association's mission statement is shown in Exhibit 2.3.

A mission statement should focus on the market or markets the organization is attempting to serve rather than on the good or service offered. Otherwise, a new technology may quickly make the good or service obsolete and the mission statement irrelevant to company functions. Business mission statements that are stated too narrowly suffer from **marketing myopia**—defining a business in terms of goods and services rather than in terms of the benefits that customers seek. In this context, *myopia* means narrow, short-term thinking. For example, Frito-Lay defines its mission as being in the snack-food business rather than in the corn chip business. The mission of sports teams is not just to play games but to serve the interests of the fans. AT&T does not sell telephones or long-distance services; it markets communications technology.

Alternatively, business missions may be stated too broadly. "To provide products of superior quality and value that improve the lives of the world's consumers" is probably too broad a mission statement for any firm except Procter & Gamble. Care must be taken when stating what business a firm is in. The mission statement of the ASPCA Animal Poison Control Center says that the organization is dedicated to "helping animals exposed to potentially hazardous substances by providing 24-hour veterinary diagnostic and treatment recommendations. The Center is committed to protecting and improving the lives of animals through toxicology educational programs and nontraditional research."[6] By correctly stating the business mission in terms of the benefits that customers seek, the foundation for the marketing plan is set. Many companies are focusing on designing more appropriate mission statements because these statements are frequently displayed on the World Wide Web.

strategic business unit (SBU)
A subgroup of a single business or collection of related businesses within the larger organization.

The organization may need to define a mission statement and objectives for a **strategic business unit (SBU)**, which is a subgroup of a single business or collection of related businesses within the larger organization. A properly defined SBU should have a distinct mission and specific target market, control over its resources, its own competitors, and plans independent of the other SBUs in the organization. Thus, a large firm such as Kraft General Foods may have marketing plans for each of its SBUs, which include breakfast foods, desserts, pet foods, and beverages.

Setting Marketing Plan Objectives

 3

Describe the criteria for stating good marketing objectives

Before the details of a marketing plan can be developed, goals and objectives for the plan must be stated. Without objectives, there is no basis for measuring the success of marketing plan activities. For example, in 2001, Hewlett-Packard's net income was $408 million—an 89 percent one-year growth rate. Sales and the number of employees also grew during this period. Sounds great, doesn't it?

Exhibit 2.3

American Marketing Association's Mission Statement

The American Marketing Association is an international professional organization for people involved in the practice, study, and teaching of marketing. Our principal roles are:

- To always understand and satisfy the needs of marketers so as to provide them with products and services that will help them be better marketers.
- To empower marketers through information, education, relationships, and resources that will enrich their professional development and careers.
- To advance the thought, application, and ethical practice of marketing.

SOURCE: http://www.marketingpower.com/about/ama/mission/, May 20, 2002.

Exhibit 2.4

Examples of Marketing Objectives

Poorly Stated Objectives	Well-Stated Objectives
Our objective is to be a leader in the industry in terms of new-product development.	Our objective is to spend 12 percent of sales revenue between 2003 and 2004 on research and development in an effort to introduce at least five new products in 2004.
Our objective is to maximize profits.	Our objective is to achieve a 10 percent return on investment during 2003, with a payback on new investments of no longer than four years.
Our objective is to better serve customers.	Our objective is to obtain customer satisfaction ratings of at least 90 percent on the 2003 annual customer satisfaction survey, and to retain at least 85 percent of our 2003 customers as repeat purchasers in 2004.
Our objective is to be the best that we can be.	Our objective is to increase market share from 30 percent to 40 percent in 2003 by increasing promotional expenditures by 14 percent.

Actually, these figures failed to meet objectives, and in 2002, H-P executives were denied their bonuses.[7]

A **marketing objective** is a statement of what is to be accomplished through marketing activities. To be useful, stated objectives should meet several criteria. First, objectives should be realistic, measurable, and time specific. It is tempting to state that the objective is "to be the best marketer of ferret food." However, what is "best" for one firm might be sales of one million pounds of ferret food per year, and to another firm, "best" might mean dominant market share. It may also be unrealistic for start-up firms or new products to command dominant market share, given other competitors in the marketplace. Finally, by what time should the goal be met? A more realistic objective would be "To achieve 10 percent dollar market share in the specialty pet food market within twelve months of product introduction."

Second, objectives must also be consistent and indicate the priorities of the organization. Specifically, objectives flow from the business mission statement to the rest of the marketing plan. Exhibit 2.4 shows some well-stated and poorly stated objectives. Notice how well they do or do not meet the above criteria.

Carefully specified objectives serve several functions. First, they communicate marketing management philosophies and provide direction for lower-level marketing managers so that marketing efforts are integrated and pointed in a consistent direction. Objectives also serve as motivators by creating something for employees to strive for. When objectives are attainable and challenging, they motivate those charged with achieving the objectives. Additionally, the process of writing specific objectives forces executives to clarify their thinking. Finally, objectives form a basis for control; the effectiveness of a plan can be gauged in light of the stated goals.

marketing objective
A statement of what is to be accomplished through marketing activities.

Conducting a Situation Analysis

Explain the components of a situation analysis

SWOT analysis
Identifying internal strengths (S) and weaknesses (W) and also examining external opportunities (O) and threats (T).

Before specific marketing activities can be defined, marketers must understand the current and potential environment that the product or service will be marketed in. A situation analysis is sometimes referred to as a **SWOT analysis;** that is, the firm should identify its internal strengths (S) and weaknesses (W) and also examine external opportunities (O) and threats (T).

When examining internal strengths and weaknesses, the marketing manager should focus on organizational resources such as production costs, marketing skills, financial resources, company or brand image, employee capabilities, and available technology. For example, a potential weakness for AirTran Airways (formerly ValuJet) is the age of its airplane fleet, which could indicate an image of danger or low quality. Other weaknesses include high labor turnover rates and limited flights. A potential strength is the low operating costs of the airline, which translate into lower prices for consumers. Another issue to consider in this section of the marketing plan is the historical background of the firm—its sales and profit history.

When examining external opportunities and threats, marketing managers must analyze aspects of the marketing environment. This process is called **environmental scanning**—the collection and interpretation of information about forces, events, and relationships in the external environment that may affect the future of the organization or the implementation of the marketing plan. Environmental scanning helps identify market opportunities and threats and provides guidelines for the design of marketing strategy. The six most often studied macroenvironmental forces are social, demographic, economic, technological, political and legal, and competitive. These forces are examined in detail in Chapter 3. For example, H&R Block, a tax preparation service, benefits from complex changes in tax codes that motivate citizens to have their tax returns prepared by a professional. Alternatively, tax-simplification or flat-tax plans would allow people to easily prepare their own returns.

environmental scanning
Collection and interpretation of information about forces, events, and relationships in the external environment that may affect the future of the organization or the implementation of the marketing plan.

Competitive Advantage

Identify sources of competitive advantage

Performing a SWOT analysis allows firms to identify their competitive advantage. A **competitive advantage** is a set of unique features of a company and its products that are perceived by the target market as significant and superior to the competition. It is the factor or factors that cause customers to patronize a firm and not the competition. There are three types of competitive advantages: cost, product/service differentiation, and niche strategies.

competitive advantage
The set of unique features of a company and its products that are perceived by the target market as significant and superior to the competition.

Cost Competitive Advantage

Cost leadership can result from obtaining inexpensive raw materials, creating an efficient scale of plant operations, designing products for ease of manufacture, controlling overhead costs, and avoiding marginal customers. DuPont, for example, has an exceptional cost competitive advantage in the production of titanium dioxide. Technicians created a production process using low-cost feedstock, giving DuPont a 20 percent cost advantage over its competitors. The cheaper feedstock technology is complex and can be accomplished only by investing about $100 million and several years of testing time. Having a **cost competitive advantage** means being the low-cost competitor in an industry while maintaining satisfactory profit margins.

cost competitive advantage
Being the low-cost competitor in an industry while maintaining satisfactory profit margins.

A cost competitive advantage enables a firm to deliver superior customer value. Chaparral Steel, for example, is the leading low-cost U.S. steel producer because it uses only scrap iron and steel and a very efficient continuous-casting process to make new steel. In fact, Chaparral is so efficient that it is the only U.S. steel producer that ships to Japan.

Sources of Cost Competitive Advantages

Costs can be reduced in a variety of ways.

experience curves
Curves that show costs declining at a predictable rate as experience with a product increases.

- *Experience curves:* **Experience curves** tell us that costs decline at a predictable rate as experience with a product increases. The experience curve effect encompasses a broad range of manufacturing, marketing, and administrative costs. Experience curves reflect learning by doing, technological advances, and economies of scale. Firms like Boeing and Texas Instruments use historical experience curves as a basis for predicting and setting prices. Experience curves allow management to forecast costs and set prices based on anticipated costs as opposed to current costs.

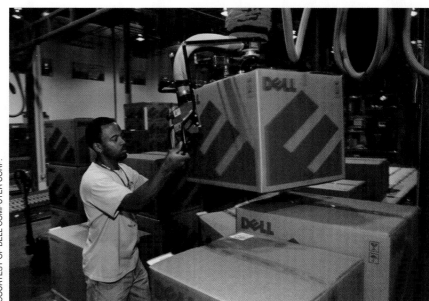

- *Efficient labor:* Labor costs can be an important component of total costs in low-skill, labor-intensive industries such as product assembly and apparel manufacturing. Many U.S. manufacturers such as Nike, Levi Strauss, and Liz Claiborne have gone offshore to achieve cheaper manufacturing costs. Many American companies are also outsourcing activities such as data entry and other labor-intensive jobs.

- *No-frills goods and services:* Marketers can lower costs by removing frills and options from a product or service. Southwest Airlines, for example, offers low fares but no seat assignments or meals. Low prices give Southwest a higher load factor and greater economies of scale, which, in turn, mean even lower prices such as Southwest's "Friends Fly Free" promotions.

- *Government subsidies:* Governments may provide assistance to target industries with grants and interest-free loans. Government assistance enabled Japanese semiconductor manufacturers to become global leaders.

- *Product design:* Cutting-edge design technology can help offset high labor costs. BMW is a world leader in designing cars for ease of manufacture and assembly. Reverse engineering—the process of disassembling a product piece by piece to learn its components and clues as to the manufacturing process—can also mean savings. Reverse engineering a low-cost competitor's product can save research and design costs. Japanese engineers have reversed many products, such as computer chips, coming out of Silicon Valley.

- *Reengineering:* Reengineering to make firms more efficient often leads to downsizing or layoffs of employees. Reeingineering can also mean pruning product lines, closing obsolete factories, and renegotiating contracts with suppliers. General Motors, for example, demanded a 15 percent average price reduction from suppliers during its reengineering.

- *Production innovations:* Production innovations such as new technology and simplified production techniques help lower the average cost of production. Technologies such as computer-aided design and computer-aided manufacturing (CAD/CAM) and increasingly sophisticated robots help companies like Boeing, Ford, and General Electric reduce their manufacturing costs.

- *New methods of service delivery:* Medical expenses have been substantially lowered by the use of outpatient surgery and walk-in clinics. Airlines, such as American, are lowering reservation and ticketing costs by encouraging passengers to use the Internet to book flights and by promoting "ticketless travel."

Building competitive advantage from a strong product or service results in a longer lasting advantage that is attractive to top managers. Dell Computer blends production innovation, efficient labor, and product design into a cost competitive advantage that fully supports the build-to-order business model it follows. A strong, long-lasting product, and service competitive advantage is the outcome, and it provides the company with superior performance results.

Product/Service Differentiation

Because cost competitive advantages are subject to continual erosion, product/service differentiation tends to provide a longer lasting competitive advantage. The durability of this strategy tends to make it more attractive to many

product/service differentiation
The provision of something that is unique and valuable to buyers beyond simply offering a lower price than the competition's.

niche competitive advantage
The advantage achieved when a firm seeks to target and effectively serve a small segment of the market.

sustainable competitive advantage
An advantage that cannot be copied by the competition.

top managers. **Product/service differentiation** exists when a firm provides something unique that is valuable to buyers beyond simply offering a low price. Examples include brand names (Lexus), a strong dealer network (Caterpillar Tractor for construction work), product reliability (Maytag appliances), image (Neiman Marcus in retailing), or service (FedEx). A great example of a company that has a strong product/service competitive advantage is Dell Computer. Dell takes orders straight from customers and builds each customer's personal computer to demand. This means that the customers get exactly what they want. Dell also gives its customers fast, convenient service that other companies can't match, including three-day delivery of PCs with all their custom software preloaded. No other computer company can do what Dell does.[8]

Niche Competitive Advantage

A **niche competitive advantage** seeks to target and effectively serve a single segment of the market (see Chapter 7). For small companies with limited resources that potentially face giant competitors, niching may be the only viable option. A market segment that has good growth potential but is not crucial to the success of major competitors is a good candidate for developing a niche strategy.

Many companies using a niche strategy serve only a limited geographic market. Buddy Freddy's is a very successful restaurant chain but is found only in Florida. Migros is the dominant grocery chain in Switzerland. It has no stores outside that small country.

Block Drug Company uses niching by focusing its product line on tooth products. It markets Polident to clean false teeth, Poligrip to hold false teeth, and Sensodyne toothpaste for persons with sensitive teeth. The Orvis Company manufactures and sells everything that anyone might ever need for fly fishing. Orvis is a very successful nicher.

Building Tomorrow's Competitive Advantage

The key to having a competitive advantage is the ability to sustain that advantage. A **sustainable competitive advantage** is one that cannot be copied by the competition. Dell Computer, discussed earlier, is a good example of a company that has a sustainable competitive advantage. Others include Rolex (high-quality watches), Nordstrom department stores (service), and Southwest Airlines (low price). In contrast, when Datril was introduced into the pain-reliever market, it was touted as being exactly like Tylenol, only cheaper. Tylenol responded by lowering its price, thus destroying Datril's competitive advantage and ability to remain on the market. In this case, low price was not a sustainable competitive advantage. Without a competitive advantage, target customers don't perceive any reason to patronize an organization instead of its competitors. The "Ethics in Marketing" box describes what is happening in the pharmaceutical industry as drugmakers use drugstores' patient lists to gain competitive advantage.

COURTESY OF TRAVELOCITY

Travelocity's advantage was noteworthy enough for its parent company, Sabre, to buy the experimental venture back from shareholders in 2002. The pioneering on-line travel company is succeeding in a market where many newer entrants, like Orbitz and Expedia, are increasing the level of competition.

How Drugmakers Use Pharmacies to Push Pricey Pills

Drugstores across the country have been calling and mailing letters to thousands of their customers suggesting that they use certain prescription medications. This practice is part of a wave of precision-targeted marketing by pharmaceutical makers who pay drugstores for the service. To compile lists of names, addresses, and phone numbers, the stores scour their data banks for people with prescriptions for a particular drug. Typically, these people are not asked for permission to use their personal data and don't know that the information will be used. For example, Eli Lilly paid Eckerd Drugs to send diabetes patients letters promoting an alternative treatment, but not mentioning that the new drug was almost twice as costly. The letters say, in small print at the bottom, that the mailings were funded through a grant from Lilly.

The retailers say the letters and phone calls are not marketing promotions, a designation that could subject them to stricter regulation. Rather, the companies call them "patient education," "patient compliance," or "disease management" programs. The purpose, they say, is to improve the health of patients by sending them refill reminders when they are past due or contacting them about new and better medical therapies.

Most of what the drug companies are doing with the drugstores helps protect the franchises of their premium-priced medicines. The pressure on major drug companies to increase sales has never been so great. They are losing billions of dollars in sales to generic competition at a time when a dry spell in company labs means few discoveries are generating new sales.

However, in a number of lawsuits, some pharmacy customers argue that the letters and phone calls invade their privacy. The lawsuits—against Walgreen Company, the Eckerd division of JCPenney, and the Good Neighbor association of independent pharmacists—charge that the companies access personal prescription information for financial gain without obtaining customer permission. Walgreen and Eckerd acknowledge using prescription records to contact their customers on behalf of the drugmakers but say they don't disclose the names to anyone outside their companies. A Good Neighbor spokesman says that the association does not engage in these programs, but that member pharmacies may contract directly with the companies.

Another problem is that pharmacists do not just sell drugs; they also provide advice and guidance on taking drugs. If a drugstore company is compensated to push particular drugs, that advice could be compromised. "The professional ethical standard is that we should not put ourselves in a position that allows our independent judgment to be potentially conflicted," says Jesse Vivian, a pharmacist and lawyer who teaches at Wayne State University in Detroit.

The drugstore chains typically receive between 85¢ and $1.50 for each letter they mail and between $2.00 and $3.50 for each phone call to a patient, industry officials say. Some contracts call for pharmacy chains to contact several hundred thousand patients as many as three or four times during the contract period, generally one year. In addition, some contracts entitle the pharmacies to rebates on drug prices for their services. Despite mounting legal challenges and efforts by regulators to limit the practice, drugstores continue to call and mail letters.[9]

Do you think the drugstores' practice of sending letters and making phone calls to their customers is ethical? Defend your answer.

The notion of competitive advantage means that a successful firm will stake out a position unique in some manner from its rivals. Imitation of competitors indicates a lack of competitive advantage and almost ensures mediocre performance. Moreover, competitors rarely stand still, so it is not surprising that imitation causes managers to feel trapped in a seemingly endless game of catch-up. They are regularly surprised by the new accomplishments of their rivals.

Companies need to build their own competitive advantages rather than copy a competitor. The sources of tomorrow's competitive advantages are the skills and assets of the organization. Assets include patents, copyrights, locations, and equipment and technology that are superior to those of the competition. Skills are functions such as customer service and promotion that the firm performs better than its competitors. Travelocity, for example, is known for its ease of on-line travel reservations. Marketing managers should continually focus the firm's skills and assets on sustaining and creating competitive advantages.

Remember, a sustainable competitive advantage is a function of the speed with which competitors can imitate a leading company's strategy and plans. Imitation requires a competitor to identify the leader's competitive advantage, determine how it is achieved, and then learn how to duplicate it.

Strategic Directions

The end result of the SWOT analysis and identification of a competitive advantage is to evaluate the strategic direction of the firm. Selecting a strategic alternative is the next step in marketing planning.

Strategic Alternatives

To discover a marketing opportunity, management must know how to identify the alternatives. One method for developing alternatives is Ansoff's strategic opportunity matrix (see Exhibit 2.5), which matches products with markets. Firms can explore these four options:

6

Identify strategic alternatives and describe tools used to help select alternatives

market penetration
A marketing strategy that tries to increase market share among existing customers.

- *Market penetration:* A firm using the **market penetration** alternative would try to increase market share among existing customers. If Kraft General Foods started a major campaign for Maxwell House coffee, with aggressive advertising and cents-off coupons to existing customers, it would be following a penetration strategy. McDonald's sold the most Happy Meals in history with a promotion that included Ty's Teeny Beanie Babies. Customer databases, discussed in Chapters 8 and 21, help managers implement this strategy.

market development
A marketing strategy that entails attracting new customers to existing products.

- *Market development:* **Market development** means attracting new customers to existing products. Ideally, new uses for old products stimulate additional sales among existing customers while also bringing in new buyers. McDonald's, for example, has opened restaurants in Russia, China, and Italy and is eagerly expanding into Eastern European countries. Coca-Cola and Pepsi have faster growth in their new foreign markets than at home. In the nonprofit area, the growing emphasis on continuing education and executive development by colleges and universities is a market development strategy. Another example of market development can be found in the "Global Perspectives" box.

product development
A marketing strategy that entails the creation of marketable new products; the process of converting applications for new technologies into marketable products.

- *Product development:* A **product development** strategy entails the creation of new products for present markets. Nike, the famous maker of athletic shoes, has introduced sleek ergonomic running watches, a high-altitude wrist compass, and a portable heart-rate monitor. These new offerings are targeted at athletes who want to time their daily jog and monitor how fast their heart is beating. The company has formed a new division called Techlab to develop the sports-technology products, which will have Nike's trademark swoosh and come in shades like "fire warm," "green leaf," and "cool sparkle."[10]

  Managers following the product development strategy can rely on their extensive knowledge of the target audience. They usually have a good feel for what customers like and dislike about current products and what existing needs are not being met. In addition, managers can rely on established distribution channels.

Exhibit 2.5

Ansoff's Strategic Opportunity Matrix

	Present Product	New Product
Present Market	**Market penetration:** McDonald's sells more Happy Meals with Disney movie promotions.	**Product development:** McDonald's introduces salad shakers and McWater.
New Market	**Market development:** McDonald's opens restaurants in China.	**Diversification:** McDonald's introduces line of children's clothing.

- *Diversification:* **Diversification** is a strategy of increasing sales by introducing new products into new markets. For example, LTV Corporation, a steel producer, diversified into the monorail business. Sony practiced a diversification strategy when it acquired Columbia Pictures; although motion pictures are not a new product in the marketplace, it was a new product for Sony. Coca-Cola manufactures and markets water-treatment and water-conditioning equipment, which has been a very challenging task for the traditional soft drink company. A diversification strategy can be risky when a firm is entering unfamiliar markets. On the other hand, it can be very profitable when a firm is entering markets with little or no competition.

diversification
A strategy of increasing sales by introducing new products into new markets.

Selecting a Strategic Alternative

Selecting which alternative to pursue depends on the overall company philosophy and culture. The choice also depends on the tool used to make the decision. Companies generally have one of two philosophies about when they expect profits. They either pursue profits right away or first seek to increase market share and then pursue profits. In the long run, market share and profitability are compatible goals. Many companies have long followed this credo: Build market share, and profits will surely follow. Michelin, the tire producer, consistently sacrifices short-term profits to achieve market share. On the other hand, IBM stresses profitability and stock valuation over market share, quality, and customer service. As you can see, the same strategic alternative may be viewed entirely differently by different firms.

A number of tools exist to help managers select a strategic alternative. The most common of these tools are in matrix form. The portfolio matrix is described in more detail.

GLOBAL PERSPECTIVES

Designing Products around Customer Needs

Brother Industries, Ltd., in Nagoya, Japan, has just introduced a phone music service that allows Japanese mobile phone users to download one of 4,800 tunes when a call arrives. The service also provides karaoke to be downloaded into cellphones, so that pictures and words come out on the screen.

This new service is an example of how Brother has been devising products for over sixty-seven years. Brother's strategy is, simply, to satisfy customers. The result is world-class products to support small businesses—including its first sewing machines, typewriters, printers, and electronic labeling systems. For the past six years, the company has held the top share of the U.S. facsimile market. Now, it is aiming to expand beyond its traditional market of small business and home offices and sell more to corporations. Brother has already

set up special solution teams in Europe for more customers in larger corporations.

Key to Brother's success is its approach to product development. Instead of finding a use for technology developed in its laboratories, the company follows a system it calls Brother Value Chain Management. This system starts with finding out what customers want, a process it calls the "demand chain," and then figures out ways to meet these needs—the "concurrent chain." Finally, it delivers the products in the supply chain. Its customer research focuses on how products feel for users. Once Brother gathers customer data, it designs products to meet the needs of its target market. Often this research leads the company to provide customers with multifunctional equipment—like a cost-saving fax, copier, tele-

phone, scanner, and printer all in one unit.

Another key to satisfying customers in the future is through what the company calls "humanware," which is a successor to the hard- and software that have dominated the marketplace over the last century. For example, sewing machines in the past were all manual; now they have microchip "brains" that make them more efficient and more pleasurable to use. By exchanging computerized embroidery patterns over the Internet, people on different sides of an ocean can share the same pattern and get their machines to stitch it automatically.[11]

What is Brother's competitive advantage? If you were to write a mission statement for Brother, what would it be?

Portfolio Matrix

Recall that large organizations engaged in strategic planning may create strategic business units. Each SBU has its own rate of return on investment, growth potential, and associated risk. Management must find a balance among the SBUs that yields the overall organization's desired growth and profits with an acceptable level of risk. Some SBUs generate large amounts of cash, and others need cash to foster growth. The challenge is to balance the organization's "portfolio" of SBUs for the best long-term performance.

To determine the future cash contributions and cash requirements expected for each SBU, managers can use the Boston Consulting Group's portfolio matrix. The **portfolio matrix** classifies each SBU by its present or forecasted growth and market share. The underlying assumption is that market share and profitability are strongly linked. The measure of market share used in the portfolio approach is *relative market share,* the ratio between the company's share and the share of the largest competitor. For example, if firm A has a 50 percent share and the competitor has 5 percent, the ratio is 10 to 1. If firm A has a 10 percent market share and the largest competitor has 20 percent, the ratio is 0.5 to 1.

Exhibit 2.6 is a hypothetical portfolio matrix for a large computer manufacturer. The size of the circle in each cell of the matrix represents dollar sales of the SBU relative to dollar sales of the company's other SBUs. The following categories are used in the matrix:

- *Stars:* A **star** is a market leader and growing fast. For example, computer manufacturers have identified subnotebook and handheld models as stars. Star SBUs usually have large profits but need a lot of cash to finance rapid growth. The best marketing tactic is to protect existing market share by reinvesting earnings in product improvement, better distribution, more promotion, and production

portfolio matrix
A tool for allocating resources among products or strategic business units on the basis of relative market share and market growth rate.

star
In the portfolio matrix, a business unit that is a fast-growing market leader.

Exhibit 2.6

Portfolio Matrix for a Large Computer Manufacturer

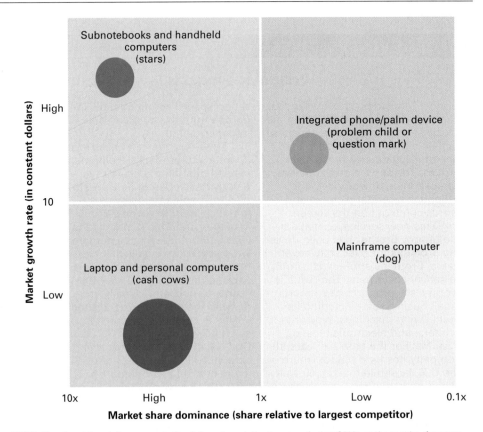

NOTE: The size of the circle represents the dollar sales relative to sales of other SBUs on the matrix—for example, 10x means sales are ten times greater than those of the next largest competitor.

efficiency. Management must strive to capture most of the new users as they enter the market.

- *Cash cows:* A **cash cow** is an SBU that usually generates more cash than it needs to maintain its market share. It is in a low-growth market, but the product has a dominant market share. Personal computers and laptops are categorized as cash cows in Exhibit 2.6. The basic strategy for a cash cow is to maintain market dominance by being the price leader and making technological improvements in the product. Managers should resist pressure to extend the basic line unless they can dramatically increase demand. Instead, they should allocate excess cash to the product categories where growth prospects are the greatest. For instance, the Clorox Company owns **KINGSFORD**® charcoal, the **GLAD**® brand of products, **FRESH STEP**®, **SCOOP AWAY**® and other pet litters, **BLACK FLAG**® pest control products, **BRITA**® water filtration systems, and **K.C. MASTERPIECE**® barbeque sauce, among others. Traditionally, the company's cash cow has been **CLOROX**® bleach, which owns the lion's share of a low-growth market. The Clorox Company has been highly successful in stretching the **CLOROX**® line to include scented chlorine bleach, as well as **CLOROX 2**®, a chlorine-free bleach for colored clothing. Another example is Heinz, which has two cash cows: ketchup and Weight Watchers frozen dinners.

- *Problem children:* A **problem child**, also called a **question mark**, shows rapid growth but poor profit margins. It has a low market share in a high-growth industry. Problem children need a great deal of cash. Without cash support, they eventually become dogs. The strategy options are to invest heavily to gain better market share, acquire competitors to get the necessary market share, or drop the SBU. Sometimes a firm can reposition the products of the SBU to move them into the star category.

- *Dogs:* A **dog** has low growth potential and a small market share. Most dogs eventually leave the marketplace. In the computer manufacturer example, the mainframe computer has become a dog. Other examples include Jack-in-the-Box shrimp dinners, Warner-Lambert's Reef mouthwash, and Campbell's Red Kettle soups. Frito-Lay has produced several dogs, including Stuffers cheese-filled snacks, Rumbles granola nuggets, and Toppels cheese-topped crackers—a trio irreverently known as Stumbles, Tumbles, and Twofers. The strategy options for dogs are to harvest or divest.

After classifying the company's SBUs in the matrix, the next step is to allocate future resources for each. The four basic strategies are to

- *Build:* If an organization has an SBU that it believes has the potential to be a star (probably a problem child at present), building would be an appropriate goal. The organization may decide to give up short-term profits and use its financial resources to achieve this goal. Procter & Gamble built Pringles from a money loser to a record profit maker.

- *Hold:* If an SBU is a very successful cash cow, a key goal would surely be to hold or preserve market share so that the organization can take advantage of the very positive cash flow. Bisquick has been a prosperous cash cow for General Mills for over two decades.

- *Harvest:* This strategy is appropriate for all SBUs except those classified as stars. The basic goal is to increase the short-term cash return without too much concern for the long-run impact. It is especially worthwhile when more cash is needed from a cash cow with long-run prospects that are unfavorable because of a low market growth rate. For instance, Lever Brothers has been harvesting Lifebuoy soap for a number of years with little promotional backing.

Cash cows generate more cash that they need to maintain their market share. CLOROX® is a cash cow. It has a 60 percent market share and has successfully introduced numerous scents as well as a chlorine-free bleach for colored clothes.

cash cow
In the portfolio matrix, a business unit that usually generates more cash than it needs to maintain its market share.

problem child (question mark)
In the portfolio matrix, a business unit that shows rapid growth but poor profit margins.

dog
In the portfolio matrix, a business unit that has low growth potential and a small market share.

What Clorox' Bleach does for whites...

Clorox 2' does for colors.

Now in three wonderful scents.

- *Divest:* Getting rid of SBUs with low shares of low-growth markets is often appropriate. Problem children and dogs are most suitable for this strategy. Procter & Gamble dropped Cincaprin, a coated aspirin, because of its low growth potential.

Describing the Marketing Strategy

marketing strategy
The activities of selecting and describing one or more target markets and developing and maintaining a marketing mix that will produce mutually satisfying exchanges with target markets.

Discuss target market strategies

market opportunity analysis (MOA)
The description and estimation of the size and sales potential of market segments that are of interest to the firm and the assessment of key competitors in these market segments.

Marketing strategy involves the activities of selecting and describing one or more target markets and developing and maintaining a marketing mix that will produce mutually satisfying exchanges with target markets.

Target Market Strategy

A market segment is a group of individuals or organizations that share one or more characteristics. They therefore may have relatively similar product needs. For example, parents of newborn babies need products such as formula, diapers, and special foods. The target market strategy identifies the market segment or segments on which to focus. This process begins with a **market opportunity analysis (MOA)**—the description and estimation of the size and sales potential of market segments that are of interest to the firm and the assessment of key competitors in these market segments. After the firm describes the market segments, it may target one or more of them. There are three general strategies for selecting target markets. Target market(s) can be selected by appealing to the entire market with one marketing mix, concentrating on one segment, or appealing to multiple market segments using multiple marketing mixes. The characteristics, advantages, and disadvantages of each strategic option are examined in Chapter 7. Target markets could be smokers who are concerned about white teeth (the target of Topol toothpaste), people concerned about sugar and calories in their soft drinks (Diet Pepsi), or college students needing inexpensive about-town transportation (Yamaha Razz scooter).

Any market segment that is targeted must be fully described. Demographics, psychographics, and buyer behavior should be assessed. Buyer behavior is covered in Chapters 5 and 6. If segments are differentiated by ethnicity, multicultural aspects of the marketing mix should be examined. A comprehensive module on multicultural marketing is on your Xtra! CD-ROM. If the target market is international, it is especially important to describe differences in culture, economic and technological development, and political structure that may affect the marketing plan. Global marketing is covered in more detail in Chapter 4.

Describe the elements of the marketing mix

marketing mix
A unique blend of product, distribution, promotion, and pricing strategies designed to produce mutually satisfying exchanges with a target market.

four Ps
Product, place, promotion, and price, which together make up the marketing mix.

The Marketing Mix

The term **marketing mix** refers to a unique blend of product, distribution, promotion, and pricing strategies designed to produce mutually satisfying exchanges with a target market. Distribution is sometimes referred to as place, thus giving us the **four Ps** of the marketing mix: product, place, promotion, and price. The marketing manager can control each component of the marketing mix, but the strategies for all four components must be blended to achieve optimal results. Any marketing mix is only as good as its weakest component. For example, the first pump toothpastes were distributed over cosmetic counters and failed. Not until pump toothpastes were distributed the same way as tube toothpastes did the products succeed. The best promotion and the lowest price cannot save a poor product. Similarly, excellent products with poor distribution, pricing, or promotion will likely fail.

Successful marketing mixes have been carefully designed to satisfy target markets. At first glance, McDonald's and Wendy's may appear to have roughly identical marketing mixes because they are both in the fast-food hamburger business.

However, McDonald's has been most successful with targeting parents with young children for lunchtime meals, whereas Wendy's targets the adult crowd for lunches and dinner. McDonald's has playgrounds, Ronald McDonald the clown, and children's Happy Meals. Wendy's has salad bars, carpeted restaurants, and no playgrounds.

Variations in marketing mixes do not occur by chance. Astute marketing managers devise marketing strategies to gain advantages over competitors and best serve the needs and wants of a particular target market segment. By manipulating elements of the marketing mix, marketing managers can fine-tune the customer offering and achieve competitive success.

Product Strategies

Typically, the marketing mix starts with the product "P." The heart of the marketing mix, the starting point, is the product offering and product strategy. It is hard to design a distribution strategy, decide on a promotion campaign, or set a price without knowing the product to be marketed.

The product includes not only the physical unit but also its package, warranty, after-sale service, brand name, company image, value, and many other factors. A Godiva chocolate has many product elements: the chocolate itself, a fancy gold wrapper, a customer satisfaction guarantee, and the prestige of the Godiva brand name. We buy things not only for what they do (benefits) but also for what they mean to us (status, quality, or reputation).

Products can be tangible goods such as computers, ideas like those offered by a consultant, or services such as medical care. Products should also offer customer value. Product decisions are covered in Chapters 9 and 10, and services marketing is detailed in Chapter 11.

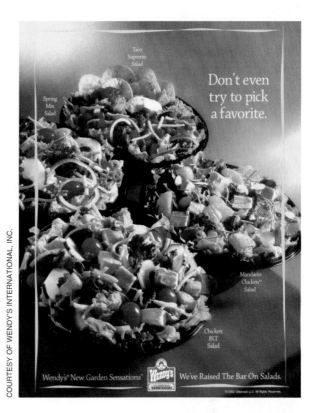

Although competing in the saturated fast-food industry, Wendy's does an excellent job of differentiating itself through its product mix. Rather than cater to families with young children, Wendy's tailors its offerings to meet the needs and wants of the adult lunch crowd. Its salad offerings are part of this strategy.

Distribution (Place) Strategies

Distribution strategies are concerned with making products available when and where customers want them. Would you rather buy a kiwi fruit at the twenty-four-hour grocery store within walking distance or fly to Australia to pick your own? A part of this place "P" is physical distribution, which involves all the business activities concerned with storing and transporting raw materials or finished products. The goal of distribution is to make sure products arrive in usable condition at designated places when needed. Distribution strategies are covered in Chapters 12 and 13.

Promotion Strategies

Promotion includes personal selling, advertising, sales promotion, and public relations. Promotion's role in the marketing mix is to bring about mutually satisfying exchanges with target markets by informing, educating, persuading, and reminding them of the benefits of an organization or a product. A good promotion strategy, like using the Dilbert character in a national promotion strategy for Office Depot, can dramatically increase sales. Good promotion strategies do not guarantee success, however. Despite massive promotional campaigns, the movies *Titan A.E.* and *Pearl Harbor* had disappointing box-office returns. Each element of the promotion "P" is coordinated and managed with the others to create a promotional blend or mix. These integrated marketing communications activities are

Do ad spending and massive promotional campaigns make a difference at the box office? All the hype surrounding the release of *Pearl Harbor*, from the U.S. premiere aboard the U.S.S. *John C. Stennis* aircraft carrier, to the Japanese premiere in the Tokyo Dome (packed with 30,000 moviegoers), could not deliver the desired box office receipts.

described in Chapters 14, 15, and 16. Technology-driven aspects of promotional marketing are covered in Chapters 19, 20, and 21.

Pricing Strategies

Price is what a buyer must give up to obtain a product. It is often the most flexible of the four marketing mix elements—the quickest element to change. Marketers can raise or lower prices more frequently and easily than they can change other marketing mix variables. Price is an important competitive weapon and is very important to the organization because price multiplied by the number of units sold equals total revenue for the firm. Pricing decisions are covered in Chapters 17 and 18.

Following Up the Marketing Plan

Implementation

Implementation is the process that turns marketing plans into action assignments and ensures that these assignments are executed in a way that accomplishes the plans' objectives. Implementation activities may involve detailed job assignments, activity descriptions, timelines, budgets, and lots of communication. Although implementation is essentially "doing what you said you were going to do," many organizations repeatedly experience failures in strategy implementation. Brilliant marketing plans are doomed to fail if they are not properly implemented. These detailed communications may or may not be part of the written marketing plan. If they are not part of the plan, they should be specified elsewhere as soon as the plan has been communicated.

Evaluation and Control

After a marketing plan is implemented, it should be evaluated. **Evaluation** entails gauging the extent to which marketing objectives have been achieved during the specified time period. Four common reasons for failing to achieve a marketing objective are unrealistic marketing objectives, inappropriate marketing strategies in the plan, poor implementation, and changes in the environment after the objective was specified and the strategy was implemented.

Once a plan is chosen and implemented, its effectiveness must be monitored. **Control** provides the mechanisms for evaluating marketing results in light of the plan's goals and for correcting actions that do not help the organization reach those goals within budget guidelines. Firms need to establish formal and informal control programs to make the entire operation more efficient.

Perhaps the broadest control device available to marketing managers is the **marketing audit**—a thorough, systematic, periodic evaluation of the goals, strategies, structure, and performance of the marketing organization. A marketing audit helps management allocate marketing resources efficiently. It has four characteristics:

* *Comprehensive:* The marketing audit covers all the major marketing issues facing an organization and not just trouble spots.

9
Explain why implementation, evaluation, and control of the marketing plan are necessary

implementation
The process that turns marketing plans into action assignments and ensures that these assignments are executed in a way that accomplishes the plans' objectives.

evaluation
Gauging the extent to which the marketing objectives have been achieved during the specified time period.

control
Provides the mechanisms for evaluating marketing results in light of the plan's goals and for correcting actions that do not help the organization reach those goals within budget guidelines.

marketing audit
A thorough, systematic, periodic evaluation of the goals, strategies, structure, and performance of the marketing organization.

- *Systematic:* The marketing audit takes place in an orderly sequence and covers the organization's marketing environment, internal marketing system, and specific marketing activities. The diagnosis is followed by an action plan with both short-run and long-run proposals for improving overall marketing effectiveness.

- *Independent:* The marketing audit is normally conducted by an inside or outside party who is independent enough to have top management's confidence and to be objective.

- *Periodic:* The marketing audit should be carried out on a regular schedule instead of only in a crisis. Whether it seems successful or is in deep trouble, any organization can benefit greatly from such an audit.

Although the main purpose of the marketing audit is to develop a full profile of the organization's marketing effort and to provide a basis for developing and revising the marketing plan, it is also an excellent way to improve communication and raise the level of marketing consciousness within the organization. It is a useful vehicle for selling the philosophy and techniques of strategic marketing to other members of the organization.

Effective Strategic Planning

Effective strategic planning requires continual attention, creativity, and management commitment:

- Strategic planning is not an annual exercise, in which managers go through the motions and forget about strategic planning until the next year. It should be an ongoing process because the environment is continually changing and the firm's resources and capabilities are continually evolving.

- Sound strategic planning is based on creativity. Managers should challenge assumptions about the firm and the environment and establish new strategies. For example, major oil companies developed the concept of the gasoline service station in an age when cars needed frequent and rather elaborate servicing. They held on to the full-service approach, but independents were quick to respond to new realities and moved to lower-cost self-service and convenience-store operations. The majors took several decades to catch up.

- Perhaps the most critical element in successful strategic planning is top management's support and participation. For example, Michael Anthony, CEO of Brookstone, Inc. and the Brookstone buying team, rack up hundreds of thousands of frequent flyer miles searching the world for manufacturers and inventors of unique products that can be carried in its retail stores, catalogs, and Internet site. Anthony has codeveloped some of these products and has also been active in remodeling efforts for Brookstone's 250 permanent and seasonal stores.

(10)
Identify several techniques that help make strategic planning effective

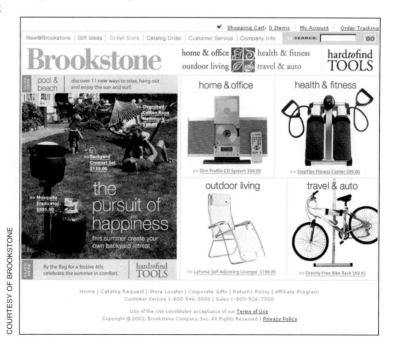

In the late twentieth century, the Internet constituted a new business strategy. Brookstone responded by opening a Web-based storefront to supplement its retail stores and catalog business.

COURTESY OF BROOKSTONE

Look back at the story about Coach, Inc. Coach has used several marketing strategy elements to increase its sales. Product strategies include redesigning its handbags to be more in tune with current styles, coming out with new designs each fashion season, and adding other products such as shoes and scarves to its line. Distribution strategies—in the context of the supply chain—were changed so that manufacturing was done in independent facilities rather than company-owned factories. At its stores, Coach tailors the merchandise and presentation to the demographics of the locale. Also, it replaced its conservative, "stodgy" image with a more fun, up-to-date image.

The foundation of Coach's competitive advantage is a stylish product of top quality. Coach also is responsive to its customers' needs and designs and revises products based on customer input.

The strategic alternative that most closely describes Coach's growth strategy is product development—the creation of new products for present markets.

How do the elements of a marketing plan apply to you personally? Put yourself in the situation of looking for a new job. In this scenario, you are marketing yourself. Let's look at the pieces of a marketing plan to see how to plan for your own marketing.

First, what is your mission? Are you looking only for part-time or temporary experience to enhance your résumé, or a career stepping-stone, or a full-time, long-term career choice? This mission will help set the stage for the rest of your plan. Next, what are your objectives? Do you need to find a job within the next thirty days, or are you more flexible? Are there specific job activities that you would like to perform? These job activities could be stated in the objectives portion of your résumé. Be sure the objectives are very specific; general objectives are of little use to you or an employer.

It's now time for your SWOT analysis. Be very honest in your self-assessment of weakness and strengths because these issues often come up during job interviews. What about opportunities and threats in the marketplace? Who is your competition? Do you have a competitive advantage? Consider any special leadership skills, international travel, computer experience, team projects, communications efforts, and other attributes. Any competitive advantage you possess should be noted in the cover letter of your résumé and your job interview.

What is your target market? Are you only looking for jobs with big, established organizations or small entrepreneurial firms? Companies in a particular industry? Do you have any geographic preferences? When you figure out your target, compile a list of firms that meet your requirements and describe them. The more you know about your target market potential employers, the more prepared you will be in an interview.

You are the product. How can you best present yourself? Think of your own packaging with regard to dress, appearance, mannerisms, and speech. What about place? Are you willing to travel or relocate? Or do you need an employer close to home? How will you travel to the employer? Is telecommuting an option? How will you promote yourself? A carefully constructed cover letter, résumé, business card, and personal Web site can all help communicate your skills to a potential employer. Think carefully about pricing issues, including salary, commission, bonuses, overtime, flexible time, insurance, and other benefits. What is a fair price for you? What is a normal price for a company of that size in that industry to offer?

Have you set up an implementation plan for applying to companies? Contacting them for potential interviews? Working on your wardrobe and interviewing skills? Remember to send thank you notes for your interviews as a control measure. When job offers come in, how will you evaluate them? If job offers don't come in, can you find out why and control for those aspects?

As you can see, marketing plan elements can apply to marketing an organization or an individual. And writing down a marketing plan can greatly assist in the search for the perfect strategy or job!

I. Business Mission

- What is the mission of the firm? What business is it in? How well is its mission understood throughout the organization? Five years from now, what business does it wish to be in?
- Does the firm define its business in terms of benefits its customers want rather than in terms of goods and services?

II. Objectives

- Is the firm's mission statement able to be translated into operational terms regarding the firm's objectives?
- What are the stated objectives of the organization? Are they formally written down? Do they lead logically to clearly stated marketing objectives? Are objectives based on sales, profits, or customers?
- Are the organization's marketing objectives stated in hierarchical order? Are they specific so that progress toward achievement can be measured? Are the objectives reasonable in light of the organization's resources? Are the objectives ambiguous? Do the objectives specify a time frame?
- Is the firm's main goal to maximize customer satisfaction or to get as many customers as possible?

III. Situation Analysis (SWOT Analysis)

- Has one or more competitive advantages been identified in the SWOT analysis?
- Are these advantages sustainable against the competition?

A. Internal Strengths and Weaknesses

- What is the history of the firm, including sales, profits, and organizational philosophies?
- What is the nature of the firm and its current situation?
- What resources does the firm have (financial, human, time, experience, asset, skill)?
- What policies inhibit the achievement of the firm's objectives with respect to organization, resource allocation, operations, hiring, training, and so on?

B. External Opportunities and Threats

- *Social:* What major social and lifestyle trends will have an impact on the firm? What action has the firm been taking in response to these trends?
- *Demographics:* What impact will forecasted trends in the size, age, profile, and distribution of population have on the firm? How will the changing nature of the family, the increase in the proportion of women in the workforce, and changes in the ethnic composition of the population affect the firm? What action has the firm taken in response to these developments and trends? Has the firm reevaluated its traditional products and expanded the range of specialized offerings to respond to these changes?
- *Economic:* What major trends in taxation and income sources will have an impact on the firm? What action has the firm taken in response to these trends?
- *Political, Legal, and Financial:* What laws are now being proposed at international, federal, state, and local levels that could affect marketing strategy and tactics? What recent changes in regulations and court decisions affect the firm? What political changes are taking place at each government level? What action has the firm taken in response to these legal and political changes?
- *Competition:* Which organizations are competing with the firm directly by offering a similar product? Which organizations are competing with the firm indirectly by securing its prime

prospects' time, money, energy, or commitment? What new competitive trends seem likely to emerge? How effective is the competition? What benefits do competitors offer that the firm does not? Is it appropriate for the firm to compete?

- *Technological:* What major technological changes are occurring that affect the firm?
- *Ecological:* What is the outlook for the cost and availability of natural resources and energy needed by the firm? Are the firm's products, services, and operations environmentally friendly?

IV. Marketing Strategy

A. Target Market Strategy

- Are the members of each market homogeneous or heterogeneous with respect to geographic, sociodemographic, and behavioral characteristics?
- What are the size, growth rate, and national and regional trends in each of the organization's market segments?
- Is the size of each market segment sufficiently large or important to warrant a unique marketing mix?
- Are market segments measurable and accessible to distribution and communication efforts?
- Which are the high- or low-opportunity segments?
- What are the evolving needs and satisfactions being sought by target markets?
- What benefits does the organization offer to each segment? How do these benefits compare with benefits offered by competitors?
- Is the firm positioning itself with a unique product? Is the product needed?
- How much of the firm's business is repeat versus new business? What percentage of the public can be classified as nonusers, light users, or heavy users?
- How do current target markets rate the firm and its competitors with respect to reputation, quality, and price? What is the firm's image with the specific market segments it seeks to serve?
- Does the firm try to direct its products only to specific groups of people or to everybody?
- Who buys the firm's products? How does a potential customer find out about the organization? When and how does a person become a customer?
- What are the major objections given by potential customers as to why they do not buy the firm's products?
- How do customers find out about and decide to purchase the product? When and where?
- Should the firm seek to expand, contract, or change the emphasis of its selected target markets? If so, in which target markets, and how vigorously?
- Could the firm more usefully withdraw from some areas where there are alternative suppliers and use its resources to serve new, unserved customer groups?
- What publics other than target markets (financial, media, government, citizen, local, general, and internal) represent opportunities or problems for the firm?

B. Marketing Mix

- Does the firm seek to achieve its goal chiefly through coordinated use of marketing activities (product, distribution, promotion, and pricing) or only through intensive promotion?
- Are the objectives and roles of each element of the marketing mix clearly specified?

(continued)

1. Product
   - What are the major product/service offerings of the firm? Do they complement each other, or is there unnecessary duplication?
   - What are the features and benefits of each product offering?
   - Where are the firm and each major product in the life cycle?
   - What are the pressures among various target markets to increase or decrease the range and quality of products?
   - What are the major weaknesses in each product area? What are the major complaints? What goes wrong most often?
   - Is the product name easy to pronounce? Spell? Recall? Is it descriptive, and does it communicate the benefits the product offers? Does the name distinguish the firm or product from all others?
   - What warranties are offered with the product? Are there other ways to guarantee customer satisfaction?
   - Does the product offer good customer value?
   - How is customer service handled? How is service quality assessed?

2. Place/Distribution
   - Should the firm try to deliver its offerings directly to customers, or can it better deliver selected offerings by involving other organizations? What channel(s) should be used in distributing product offerings?
   - What physical distribution facilities should be used? Where should they be located? What should be their major characteristics?
   - Are members of the target market willing and able to travel some distance to buy the product?
   - How good is access to facilities? Can access be improved? Which facilities need priority attention in these areas?
   - How are facility locations chosen? Is the site accessible to the target markets? Is it visible to the target markets?
   - What are the location and atmosphere of retail establishments? Do these retailers satisfy customers?
   - When are products made available to users (season of year, day of week, time of day)? Are these times most appropriate?

3. Promotion
   - How does a typical customer find out about the firm's products?
   - Does the message the firm delivers gain the attention of the intended target audience? Does it address the wants and needs of the target market, and does it suggest benefits or a means for satisfying these wants? Is the message appropriately positioned?
   - Does the promotion effort effectively inform, persuade, educate, and remind customers about the firm's products?
   - Does the firm establish budgets and measure effectiveness of promotional efforts?

   a. Advertising
      - Which media are currently being used? Has the firm chosen the types of media that will best reach its target markets?
      - Are the types of media used the most cost-effective, and do they contribute positively to the firm's image?
      - Are the dates and times the ads will appear the most appropriate? Has the firm prepared several versions of its advertisements?
      - Does the organization use an outside advertising agency? What functions does the ad agency perform for the organization?
      - What system is used to handle consumer inquiries resulting from advertising and promotions? What follow-up is done?

   b. Public Relations
      - Is there a well-conceived public relations and publicity program? Does the program have the ability to respond to bad publicity?
      - How is public relations normally handled by the firm? By whom? Have those responsible nurtured working relationships with media outlets?
      - Is the firm using all available public relations avenues? Is an effort made to understand each of the publicity outlet's needs and to provide each with story types that will appeal to its audience in readily usable forms?
      - What does the annual report say about the firm and its products? Who is being effectively reached by this vehicle? Does the benefit of the publication justify the cost?

   c. Personal Selling
      - How much of a typical salesperson's time is spent soliciting new customers as compared to serving existing customers?
      - How does the sales force determine which prospect will be called on and by whom? How is the frequency of contacts determined?
      - How is the sales force compensated? Are there incentives for encouraging more business?
      - How is the sales force organized and managed?
      - Has the sales force prepared an approach tailored to each prospect?
      - Has the firm matched sales personnel with the target market characteristics?
      - Is there appropriate follow-up to the initial personal selling effort? Are customers made to feel appreciated?
      - Can database or direct marketing be used to replace or supplement the sales force?

   d. Sales Promotion
      - What is the specific purpose of each sales promotion activity? Why is it offered? What does it try to achieve?
      - What categories of sales promotion are being used? Is sales promotion directed to the trade, the final consumer, or both?
      - Is the effort directed at all the firm's key publics or restricted to only potential customers?

4. Price
   - What levels of pricing and specific prices should be used?

- What mechanisms does the firm have to ensure that the prices charged are acceptable to customers?
- How price sensitive are customers?
- If a price change is put into effect, how will the number of customers change? Will total revenue increase or decrease?
- Which method is used for establishing a price: going rate, demand oriented, or cost based?
- What discounts are offered, and with what rationale?
- Has the firm considered the psychological dimensions of price?
- Have price increases kept pace with cost increases, inflation, or competitive levels?
- How are price promotions used?
- Do interested prospects have opportunities to sample products at an introductory price?
- What methods of payment are accepted? Is it in the firm's best interest to use these various payment methods?

V. Implementation, Evaluation, and Control

- Is the marketing organization structured appropriately to implement the marketing plan?
- What specific activities must take place? Who is responsible for these activities?
- What is the implementation timetable?
- What other marketing research is necessary?
- What will be the financial impact of this plan on a one-year projected income statement? How does projected income compare with expected revenue if the plan is not implemented?
- What are the performance standards?
- What monitoring procedures (audits) will take place and when?
- Does the firm seem to be trying to do too much or not enough?
- Are the core marketing strategies for achieving objectives sound? Are the objectives being met, and are the objectives appropriate?
- Are enough resources (or too many resources) budgeted to accomplish the marketing objectives?

REVIEW IT

(1) Understand the importance of strategic marketing and know a basic outline for a marketing plan. Strategic marketing planning is the basis for all marketing strategies and decisions. The marketing plan is a written document that acts as a guidebook of marketing activities for the marketing manager. By specifying objectives and defining the actions required to attain them, a marketing plan provides the basis on which actual and expected performance can be compared.

Although there is no set formula for a marketing plan or a single correct outline, basic factors that should be covered include stating the business mission, setting objectives, performing a situation analysis of internal and external environmental forces, selecting target market(s), delineating a marketing mix (product, place, promotion, and price), and establishing ways to implement, evaluate, and control the plan.

1.1 Your cousin wants to start his own business, and he is in a hurry. He has decided not to write a marketing plan because he thinks that preparing such a document would take too long. He says he doesn't need a formal proposal because he has already received funding from your uncle. Explain why it is important for him to write a plan anyway.

1.2 **WRITING** After graduation, you decide to take a position as the marketing manager for a small snack-food manufacturer. The company, Shur Snak, is growing, and this is the first time that the company has ever employed a marketing manager. Consequently, there is no marketing plan in place for you to follow. Outline a basic marketing plan for your boss to give her an idea of the direction you want to take the company.

(2) Develop an appropriate business mission statement. The mission statement is based on a careful analysis of benefits sought by present and potential customers and analysis of existing and anticipated environmental conditions. The firm's long-term vision, embodied in the mission statement, establishes boundaries for all subsequent decisions, objectives, and strategies. A mission statement should focus on the market or markets the organization is attempting to serve rather than on the good or service offered.

2.1 **ON LINE** How can a new company best define its business mission statement? Can you find examples of good and bad mission statements on the Internet? How might you improve the bad ones?

2.2 Thinking back to question 1.2, write a business mission statement for Shur Snak. What elements should you include? Evaluate the mission statement you wrote against some of those you found on-line in question 2.1.

(3) **Describe the criteria for stating good marketing objectives.** Objectives should be realistic, measurable, and time specific. Objectives must also be consistent and indicate the priorities of the organization.

3.1 Building on our Shur Snak example, imagine that your boss has stated that the marketing objective of the company is to do the best job of satisfying the needs and wants of the customer. Explain that although this objective is admirable, it does not meet the criteria for good objectives. What are these criteria? What is a specific example of a better objective for Shur Snak?

(4) **Explain the components of a situation analysis.** In the situation (or SWOT) analysis, the firm should identify its internal strengths (S) and weaknesses (W) and also examine external opportunities (O) and threats (T). When examining external opportunities and threats, marketing managers must analyze aspects of the marketing environment in a process called environmental scanning. The six most often studied macroenvironmental forces are social, demographic, economic, technological, political and legal, and competitive. During the situation analysis, it is crucial that the marketer identify a competitive advantage and establish that it is a sustainable competitive advantage.

4.1   Competition in the private courier sector is fierce. UPS and FedEx dominate, but other companies, such as Airborne, Emery, and even the United States Postal Service, still have a decent chunk of the express package delivery market. Perform a mini-situation analysis on one of the companies listed below by stating one strength, one weakness, one opportunity, and one threat. You may want to consult the following Web sites as you build your grid:

United Parcel Service (UPS)   **http://www.ups.com**

FedEx   **http://www.fedex.com**

Airborne   **http://www.airborne.com**

Emery   **http://www.emeryworldwide.com**

USPS   **http://www.usps.gov**

(5) **Identify sources of competitive advantage.** A competitive advantage is a set of unique features of a company and its products that are perceived by the target market as significant and superior to the competition. There are three types of competitive advantages: cost, product/service differentiation, and niche strategies. Sources of cost competitive advantages include experience curves, efficient labor, no-frills goods and services, government subsidies, product design, reengineering, product innovations, and new methods of service delivery. Produce/service differentiation exists when a firm provides something unique that is valuable to buyers beyond just low price. Niche competitive advantages come from targeting unique segments with specific needs and wants. The goal of all these sources of competitive advantage is to be sustainable.

5.1 Break into small groups and discuss examples (at least two per person) of the last few products you have purchased. What specific strategies were used to achieve competitive advantage? Is that competitive advantage sustainable against the competitors?

(6) **Identify strategic alternatives and describe tools used to help select alternatives.** The strategic opportunity matrix can be used to help management develop strategic alternatives. The four options are market penetration, product development, market development, and diversification. The portfolio matrix is a method of determining the profit potential and investment requirements of a firm's SBUs by classifying them as stars, cash cows, problem children, or dogs and then determining appropriate resource allocations for each.

6.1 Based on your SWOT analysis, decide what the strategic growth options are for the company you chose in question 4.1. Also, decide where your company's products fit in the Boston Consulting Group matrix.

(7) Discuss target market strategies. The target market strategy identifies which market segment or segments to focus on. This process begins with a market opportunity analysis (MOA), which describes and estimates the size and sales potential of market segments that are of interest to the firm. In addition, an assessment of key competitors in these market segments is performed. After the market segments are described, one or more may be targeted by the firm. The three strategies for selecting target markets are appealing to the entire market with one marketing mix, concentrating on one segment, or appealing to multiple market segments using multiple marketing mixes.

7.1 You are given the task of deciding the marketing strategy for a transportation company. How do the marketing mix elements change when the target market is (a) low-income workers without personal transportation, (b) corporate international business travelers, or (c) companies with urgent documents or perishable materials to get to customers?

(8) Describe the elements of the marketing mix. The marketing mix (or four Ps) is a blend of product, distribution (place), promotion, and pricing strategies designed to produce mutually satisfying exchanges with a target market. The starting point of the marketing mix is the product offering. Products can be tangible goods, ideas, or services. Distribution strategies are concerned with making products available when and where customers want them. Promotion includes personal selling, advertising, sales promotion, and public relations. Price is what a buyer must give up to obtain a product and is often the easiest to change of the four marketing mix elements.

8.1   Choose three or four other students and make up a team. Create a marketing plan to increase enrollment in your school. Describe the four marketing mix elements that make up the plan.

(9) Explain why implementation, evaluation, and control of the marketing plan are necessary. Before a marketing plan can work, it must be implemented; that is, people must perform the actions in the plan. The plan should also be evaluated to see if it has achieved its objectives. Poor implementation can be a major factor in a plan's failure. Control provides the mechanisms for evaluating marketing results in light of the plan's goals and for correcting actions that do not help the organization reach those goals within budget guidelines.

9.1 Have your school enrollment marketing plan team (from question 8.1) develop a plan to implement, evaluate, and control the marketing strategy.

9.2 INFOTRAC COLLEGE EDITION Using InfoTrac and the *Wall Street Journal*'s archive at **http://wsj.com**, trace the history of Kimberly-Clark's marketing plan and strategy for Cottonelle Fresh Rollwipes (premoistened toilet paper). Once you have a basic understanding of the product development and launch history, evaluate the plan set in motion by Kimberly-Clark. Does the company consider the product (and hence the plan) a success? Has the product been well received in the market? Are competitors moving in to take away market share with their own versions? Write a brief report giving a two-sentence synopsis of the product history and then describing what went right with the plan and what went wrong (if anything). If you identify flaws in the plan, say what the company could have done to avoid those problems.

10 **Identify several techniques that help make strategic planning effective.** First, management must realize that strategic planning is an ongoing process and not a once-a-year exercise. Second, good strategic planning involves a high level of creativity. The last requirement is top management's support and cooperation.

10.1 What techniques can make your school-enrollment marketing plan more effective?

DEFINE IT

cash cow 41
competitive advantage 34
control 44
cost competitive advantage 34
diversification 39
dog 41
environmental scanning 34
evaluation 44
experience curves 34
four Ps 42
implementation 44
market development 38

market opportunity analysis (MOA) 42
market penetration 38
marketing audit 44
marketing mix 42
marketing myopia 32
marketing objective 33
marketing plan 28
marketing planning 28
marketing strategy 42
mission statement 31
niche competitive advantage 36
planning 28

portfolio matrix 40
problem child (question mark) 41
product development 38
product/service differentiation 36
star 40
strategic business unit (SBU) 32
strategic planning 28
sustainable competitive advantage 36
SWOT analysis 33

APPLY IT

Application for Entrepreneurs

 Providing security for VIPS—ranging from government officials to movie stars—when they appear in public, typically means deploying protective barriers such as concrete walls or Plexiglas shields. A new product aims to replace those obstructive protection devices. Ibis Technologies, a three-year-old company in Butler, Pennsylvania, has developed an Instantaneous Personal Protection System (IPPS). The IPPS is a cross between an aircraft ejection seat and a car air bag. In less time than the ear can register the sound of gunfire, the IPPS surrounds the intended victim with a bullet-proof shield. This new security device can sit on the floor next to a VIP or terrorist target, or it can be used as a security guard in a busy lobby, disguised as a set of decorative planters.[12]

How does the IPPS work? A radar-sensor detects incoming objects (such as bullets or knives) and triggers an inflating air bag. The bullet-proof material traps the projectile like a baseball glove folding around a ball. In demonstrations, the shield has deployed quickly enough to survive assaults from .22-caliber through .44-caliber magnum rounds, submachine guns, shotgun blasts at close range, and knife-wielding attackers. Its detection range is about 150 feet. The device can also be fired by radio control.[13] The fully installed system weighs 400 pounds.

The IPPS technology can be extended to other applications, such as protecting vehicles and securing windows on buildings. A key challenge will be the ability to detect electronic signals that might set off the system accidentally, such as cellular phones or aircraft radar. Despite these challenges, Ibis Technologies Corporation has been selected as a top technology stock pick by hedge fund manager Jeffrey Puglisi.[14]

Questions

1. What is an appropriate mission statement for Ibis Technologies?

2. What specific objective would you suggest the company try to achieve?

3. What are the strengths, weaknesses, opportunities, and threats in this situation?

4. Does Ibis Technologies have a competitive advantage? Is it sustainable?

5. What strategic growth options can Ibis Technologies pursue?

6. Where do Ibis Technologies and its IPPS fit on strategic matrix tools?

7. What should the target market be? Why?

8. What are the elements of the marketing mix? Describe a brief strategy for each of the four Ps.

THINK ABOUT IT

Ethics Exercise

Abercrombie & Fitch, a retail clothing chain based in New Albany, Ohio, launched a line of thong underwear for pre-teen girls. Words like "eye candy" and "wink wink" were printed on the front of the skimpy underwear that some argued would fit girls aged five to ten. Abercrombie is known for its provocative ads and sexually oriented catalogs. Supporters of the strategy claim that producing thong-style underwear for the age ten to sixteen crowd is a good move; critics think that the line is tasteless and that marketing it to young girls is contemptuous.

Questions

1. Is marketing adult-styled undergarments to a younger audience unethical?

2. Would Abercrombie have been in the spotlight had the sexy words been omitted from the product?

3. What does the AMA Code of Ethics have to say about using sex to market products to adult consumers? To younger consumers? Read the code at **http://www.marketingpower.com** and then write a brief paragraph on how the code relates to this situation.

TRY IT

Entrepreneurship Case
A Noodé for a New Generation

When Seth Ratner launched Noodé (pronounced "newday") in spring 2001, it was with a very clearly articulated marketing strategy—and a hefty first year sales goal of $1.7 million. Nine months after rollout, Ratner's plan seems to be working quite well: His skin care company and product line had already topped the $1 million mark and showed no signs of slowing.

Formerly of Zirh Skin Nutrition, a male skin care line that was acquired by Shisheido in 2000, Ratner recognized an underserved market in young people ages fifteen to twenty-nine, a group he named "Generation Me." A combination of Generation X and Generation Y, Generation Me had long been ignored by the more-recognized skin care companies, which tended to make products to help older consumers fight wrinkles and recondition aging skin. No serious conservatively priced, high-end skin care solutions existed for young skin problems, such as oily skin, combination skin, and acne. That is, until Noodé.

Noodé's twelve-product line was developed by a group of dermatologists focusing on prevention and maintenance rather than repair. Although the products are serious skin care, their names all tie into the Generation Me market: Clean Me face wash, Scrub Me Gently facial scrub, Make Me Soft facial moisturizer, Help Me acne cream, Renew Me face peel, Make Me Moist body lotion, Rub Me massage oil, Wash Me Everywhere body wash, Scrub Me Harder body scrub, Heal and Protect Me face and body cream for calming and reducing redness, and the newest product, Shield Me sunscreen gel with SPF 15. Noodé intends to focus exclusively on skin care—and not branch out into cosmetics—in order to avoid losing the message of serious skin care.

So with only eleven products when the line was launched (Shield Me was added in Spring 2002), how did Noodé ring up so many sales in such a short period of time? The

NOODÉ SKINCARE LLC. 1-888-972-3477

starting point was zeroing in on the Generation Me market. Ratner wanted to identify what fifteen- to twenty-nine-year-olds wanted. He found that they are consumers concerned about "me" and want products exclusively for "me." Once the target market was clearly identified, Ratner built a product line to meet its needs and wants. That is why none of the flagship products contained sun protection. Generation Me likes to look tan, and Noodé products are geared toward a youthful market. The new Shield Me product seems to send a conflicting message, but the SPF 15 only gives enough protection not to burn during daily activities. Also appealing to the target market is the product packaging. Colorful products packaged in clear bottles with funky writing attract interest. Creamier products are sold in an innovative style of packaging referred to as a "tottle", which is a tube and a bottle combined, which prevents accidental discharge of the product.

Once the market and product were ready, Noodé introduced them in high-end retailers like Henri Bendel, Bloomingdale's, Fred Segal, and Nordstrom. The idea was to build relationships with stores, train store personnel, and make brochures, literature, and samples available to store customers. Noodé cosponsored a Teen Appreciation Day at Bloomingdale's during the 2001 back-to-school season with Ralph fragrances, Tony & Tina cosmetics, and *Lucky* magazine. Teens received free facials and makeovers during the event, which generated a month's worth of sales for Noodé in a single day. The cost of sponsorship was minimal.

Keeping promotion costs minimal has been a key tactic for Ratner. Rather than roll out his new product and company with a pricey national advertising campaign, he chose to use catalog inserts, postcards, in-store support combined with a heavy sampling program, and store events like the Teen Appreciation Day. Low promotion costs help Noodé make the most of its pricing strategy. Price points range from $15 for the Rub Me and Scrub Me products to $20 for the Help Me acne product.

In a market full of high-priced products aimed at older consumers, Noodé is certainly poised to be a long-term success. Noodé brings together a fun, cool skin care line (that's still serious and effective) with the niche market it's designed to serve.

Questions

1. Based on what you have read in the case, outline a rudimentary SWOT analysis for Noodé.

2. Describe Noodé's competitive advantage.

3. How is Noodé using the elements of the marketing mix to meet the needs and wants of Generation Me?

 WATCH IT

Short

To see how companies advertise their marketing strategies, watch the two H&R Block ads in your Chapter 2 PowerPoint presentation found on your PowerPoint CD-Rom. Think about the concepts of portfolio matrix as you watch.

Medium **VIDEO**

Marketing video game systems is becoming increasingly competitive, as Microsoft entered the arena with its Xbox. As you watch the CNN clip on the so-called video game wars, identify the concepts from the chapter that surface in the story. You may even want to do a very abbreviated marketing plan for Microsoft as it tries to increase its share of a competitive industry.

Long **SmallBusinessSchool** ▫
the Series on PBS stations and the Web

To give you insight into Chapter 2, Small Business School goes to New York City to visit the Nicole Miller Fashion House. Founded by Bud Konheim and Nicole Miller, this company gives us a perfect example of marketing strategy and the 4 Ps. Nicole Miller has a specific product, sold in well-chosen places, promoted with a clearly articulated message, and priced at a point that differentiates it without turning off potential customers.

What is Nicole Miller selling, for how much, and to whom? Step into the Master Class led by Konheim and Miller to see how they move ideas from mind to market to customer.

FLIP IT

 Flip to Chapter 2 in your *Grademaker Study Guide* for more review opportunities, including the pretest, vocabulary review, study test questions, marketing applications and scenarios, and more. Can you name the four Ps? Can you close your book and draw a portfolio matrix that depicts and describes the elements? If not, flip open your Study Guide to brush up.

CLICK IT

The *Marketing* Web site links you to all the Internet-based activities in this chapter, like "Review It" questions 2.1, 4.1, and 9.2, plus the On-Line exercises in the chapter margins. As a review, do the Chapter 2 quiz and crossword puzzle. You can also work the Career Exersite that shows you some Internet sites that can help you think strategically about your marketing career. Go to **http://lamb.swlearning.com**, read the material, and follow the links right from the site.

SPIN IT

Spin your Xtra! CD-ROM to find the supplemental content module on multicultural marketing. You can also test your understanding with the worksheets for exhibits 2.1, 2.5, and 2.6. In addition to the quiz on the Web site, there's another quiz on the Xtra! CD-ROM, plus video of the authors answering frequently asked questions about marketing strategy, such as "How can a company identify its own strengths, weaknesses, opportunities, and threats without being biased?" and "Are there really any implications of having a bad mission statement?"

CHAPTER **THREE**
THE MARKETING ENVIRONMENT AND MARKETING ETHICS

Learning Objectives

1 Discuss the external environment of marketing, and explain how it affects a firm

2 Describe the social factors that affect marketing

3 Explain the importance to marketing managers of current demographic trends

4 Explain the importance to marketing managers of multiculturalism and growing ethnic markets

5 Identify consumer and marketer reactions to the state of the economy

6 Identify the impact of technology on a firm

7 Discuss the political and legal environment of marketing

8 Explain the basics of foreign and domestic competition

9 Describe the role of ethics and ethical decisions in business

10 Discuss corporate social responsibility

Some things go out of fashion. That has been a hard lesson for Levi Strauss & Co., a company whose 501 blue jeans became famous in 1984 when a hunky model stripped them off in a laundromat for millions of admiring young women in Levi's television ads of the time.

"In the mid-80s, Levi's transformed the denim sector with that ad," says Sean Pillot de Chenecey, a youth-trend specialist at forecasting firm Captain Crikey in London. "But Levi's then committed the cardinal sin of becoming self-referential" by focusing too much on the 501 and not paying attention to changing tastes in threads. And while Levi's was stagnating, competitors such as Earl Jean and Diesel crowded the market with new products that seemed hipper to a generation stricken with chronic brand-attention-deficit disorder.

A sales decline at the closely held apparel maker began after a peak in 1996, when Levi's reported global sales of $7.1 billion, and has persisted ever since. Now the San Francisco-based company speaks of "slowing the decline" rather than boosting sales.

Levi's management readily admits it has made some mistakes. And instead of sloughing off the blame on a decline in the denim market, Levi's delivers a mea culpa: "We weren't selling in stores where young people shop. We weren't making the products they were interested in. We weren't branding our products in a famous way, and we weren't serving our customers well," says Robert Hanson, president of the Levi's brand in Europe, ticking off the four main reasons for Levi's recent hard times in Europe.

"We were responsible for the decline in the denim market," he adds.

Levi's is indeed the classic jeans maker, but some industry executives aren't as hard on the company and doubt it single-handedly brought on a decline in demand for denim. "Sometimes your products go out of fashion," says Alex Batchelor, managing director for Interbrand UK, a brand consultancy that is part of Omnicom Group.

But Levi's is making a concerted effort to come back. In the midst of a massive restructuring in which the company laid off thousands of workers and closed plants in the United States and Europe, Levi's is trying to put its best feet forward with new products and promotions.

In Levi's latest ad campaign in Europe, it promotes its "engineered" jeans, those with twisted seams designed to ergonomically fit both men and women.

After pushing the 501 for years, Levi's has developed a range of jeans in a bid to create a trickle-down effect: The company produces several high-end products, known as its red line and vintage lines, and also manufactures more basic models for mass consumption.

The company's retail plans mirror its product diversification in Europe. In what the company calls its "Icon" stores, the Levi's brand name is nowhere to be seen. Instead, the stores sell expensive vintage Levi's products alongside secondhand

books, vinyl albums, and custom-made shoes designed by local artisans.

In contrast, the company's heavily branded flagship stores offer themselves to the middle market and often adopt a more youthful approach. In department stores, Levi's introduced what it calls the advanced retail concept, which drapes jeans like spaghetti and displays Levi's products like fresh pasta and produce in a grocery store.

"Some we hang like spaghetti, others lie down like lasagna," Mr. Hanson says. He hopes the new presentation will have the jeans selling—as in the brand's glory days—like hot cakes.[1]

Changing tastes, fashion trends, and demographics all represent threats and/or opportunities to marketing managers. These are only a few factors in the external environment that can have an impact on a firm. Does the external environment affect the marketing mix of most companies? What other uncontrollable factors in the external environment might affect Levi's?

The External Marketing Environment

Discuss the external environment of marketing, and explain how it affects a firm

target market
A defined group most likely to buy a firm's product.

As you learned in Chapters 1 and 2, managers create a marketing mix by uniquely combining product, distribution, promotion, and price strategies. The marketing mix is, of course, under the firm's control and is designed to appeal to a specific group of potential buyers. A **target market** is a defined group that managers feel is most likely to buy a firm's product.

Over time, managers must alter the marketing mix because of changes in the environment in which consumers live, work, and make purchasing decisions. Also, as markets mature, some new consumers become part of the target market; others drop out. Those who remain may have different tastes, needs, incomes, lifestyles, and buying habits than the original target consumers.

Although managers can control the marketing mix, they cannot control elements in the external environment that continually mold and reshape the target market. Exhibit 3.1 shows the controllable and uncontrollable variables that affect the target market, whether it consists of consumers or business purchasers. The uncontrollable elements in the center of the diagram continually evolve and create changes in the target market. In contrast, managers can shape and reshape the marketing mix, depicted on the left side of the exhibit, to influence the target market.

Understanding the External Environment

Unless marketing managers understand the external environment, the firm cannot intelligently plan for the future. Thus, many organizations assemble a team of specialists to continually collect and evaluate environmental information, a process called environmental scanning. The goal in gathering the environmental data is to identify future market opportunities and threats.

For example, as technology continues to blur the line between personal computers, television, and compact disc players, a company like Sony may find itself

Exhibit 3.1 Effect of Uncontrollable Factors in the External Environment on the Marketing Mix competing against a company like Dell. Research shows that children would like to find more games bundled with computer software, while adults are more likely to desire various word-processing and business-related software. Is this information an opportunity or a threat to Dell marketing managers?

Environmental Management

  No one business is large or powerful enough to create major change in the external environment. Thus, marketing managers are basically adapters rather than agents of change. For example, despite the huge size of General Motors and Ford, these companies are continually challenged to meet the competitive push by the Japanese for an ever-growing share of the U.S. automobile market. Competition is basically an uncontrollable element in the external environment.

A firm is not always completely at the mercy of the external environment, however. Sometimes a firm can influence external events. For example, extensive lobbying by FedEx enabled it to acquire virtually all of the Japanese routes that it has sought. Japan had originally opposed new cargo routes for FedEx. The favorable decision was based on months of lobbying by FedEx at the White House, at several agencies, and in Congress for help in overcoming Japanese resistance. When a company implements strategies that attempt to shape the external environment within which it operates, it is engaging in **environmental management**.

The factors within the external environment that are important to marketing managers can be classified as social, demographic, economic, technological, political and legal, and competitive.

> **environmental management**
> When a company implements strategies that attempt to shape the external environment within which it operates.

Social Factors

Social change is perhaps the most difficult external variable for marketing managers to forecast, influence, or integrate into marketing plans. Social factors include our attitudes, values, and lifestyles. Social factors influence the products people buy, the prices paid for products, the effectiveness of specific promotions, and how, where, and when people expect to purchase products.

> **2**
> Describe the social factors that affect marketing

American Values

A *value* is a strongly held and enduring belief. During the United States' first 200 years, four basic values strongly influenced attitudes and lifestyles:

- *Self-sufficiency:* Every person should stand on his or her own two feet.
- *Upward mobility:* Success would come to anyone who got an education, worked hard, and played by the rules.
- *Work ethic:* Hard work, dedication to family, and frugality were moral and right.
- *Conformity:* No one should expect to be treated differently from everybody else.

These core values still hold for a majority of Americans today. A person's values are key determinants of what is important and not important, what actions to take or not to take, and how one behaves in social situations.

A person's values are typically formed through interaction with family, friends, and other influencers such as teachers, religious leaders, and politicians. The environment can also play a key role in shaping one's values. For example, people born during the Great Depression tend to be very conservative with money. People who came of age in the "hippie revolution" of the 1960s tend to be much less conservative with money.[2]

Values also influence our buying habits. Today's consumers are demanding, inquisitive, and discriminating. No longer willing to tolerate products that break down, they are insisting on high-quality goods that save time, energy, and often calories. U.S. consumers rank the characteristics of product quality as (1) reliability, (2) durability, (3) easy maintenance, (4) ease of use, (5) a trusted brand name, and (6) a low price. Shoppers are also concerned about nutrition and want to know what's in their food, and most are also environmentalists.

The Poverty of Time

Today, fewer consumers say that expensive cars, designer clothes, pleasure trips, and "platinum" credit cards are necessary components of a happy life. Instead, they put value on nonmaterial accomplishments, such as having control of their lives and being able to take a day off when they want.[3] Dual-career families have a **poverty of time**, with few hours to do anything but work and commute to work, handle family situations, do housework, shop, sleep, and eat. Of the people who say they don't have enough time, only 33 percent said that they were very happy with their lives.[4]

poverty of time
A lack of time to do anything but work, commute to work, handle family situations, do housework, shop, sleep, and eat.

A poverty of time means that people will decrease the amount of time spent doing things they dislike. That means doing less housework and home maintenance, and doing more dining out. It also means paying more attention to brand names—not in search of status, but to make buying decisions quicker and easier. Consumers on a constrained time budget will likely favor small shops over large ones, spend less time comparing prices, use technology to reduce transaction time, and patronize businesses that make life easier.[5]

No company has learned this better than Kinko's, the copy-shop empire. A few years ago, Kinko's noticed that busy customers in its stores didn't just want to do their photocopying and head home. They wanted to pop into a store, create a computer document, print it out, staple it, glue it, hole-punch it, and put it in a three-ring binder. In response, Kinko's has added computer workstations to many of its stores, along with sophisticated technical support and basic supplies that turn each of its copy centers into home offices away from home.

Today, 39 percent of Americans often spend leisure time getting ready for work.[6] Casual Fridays and home offices seem to be further blurring the boundaries between work and leisure. A recent survey noted that the leisure activity done most often was to spend time with the family.[7] There is little doubt that the value employees place on time versus money will continue to shift in favor of time. More employers will offer time off as an incentive. Aladdin Equipment, a Sarasota, Florida, maker of pool and spa replacement parts, achieved a 50 percent reduction in absenteeism and a 10 percent increase in productivity after it launched a four-and-one-half-day-a-week production schedule.[8] Perhaps the 7 percent annual growth in home-based self-employment is a backlash against the lack of quality of family time.[9]

Time-pressed individuals represent a tremendous marketing opportunity. Kinko's has made the most of opportunities to serve customers by transforming from a corner copy shop into a network of locations featuring additional services such as rental computers and sign and banner departments.

The Growth of Component Lifestyles

People in the United States today are piecing together **component lifestyles**. A lifestyle is a mode of living; it is the way people decide to live their lives. In other

component lifestyles
The practice of choosing goods and services that meet one's diverse needs and interests rather than conforming to a single, traditional lifestyle.

words, they are choosing products and services that meet diverse needs and interests rather than conforming to traditional stereotypes.

In the past, a person's profession—for instance, banker—defined his or her lifestyle. Today, a person can be a banker and also a gourmet, fitness enthusiast, dedicated single parent, and Internet guru. Each of these lifestyles is associated with different goods and services and represents a target audience. For example, for the gourmet, marketers offer cooking utensils, wines, and exotic foods through magazines like *Bon Appetit* and *Gourmet*. The fitness enthusiast buys Adidas equipment and special jogging outfits and reads *Runner* magazine. Component lifestyles increase the complexity of consumers' buying habits. The banker may own a BMW but change the oil himself or herself. He or she may buy fast food for lunch but French wine for dinner, own sophisticated photographic equipment and a low-priced home stereo, and shop for socks at Kmart or Wal-Mart and suits or dresses at Brooks Brothers.

The unique lifestyles of every consumer can require a different marketing mix. Sometimes blending products for a single target market can result in failure. To the bright young founders of WebTV, it looked like a home run: hook televisions up to the Net and tap into the vast market of couch potatoes curious about the World Wide Web. After burning through an estimated $50 million to advertise the new service, however, WebTV and partners Sony and Philips Electronics counted a disappointing fifty thousand subscribers. The problem was the wrong marketing message. Couch potatoes want to be better entertained, whereas computer users are content to explore the Internet using small PC screens.

The Changing Role of Families and Working Women

Component lifestyles have evolved because consumers can choose from a growing number of goods and services, and most have the money to exercise more options. The growth of dual-income families has resulted in increased purchasing power. Approximately 58 percent of all females between sixteen and sixty-five years old are now in the workforce, and female participation in the labor force is expected to grow to 63 percent by 2005.[10] Today, more than 9 million women-owned businesses in the United States generate $3.6 trillion in revenues.[11] The phenomenon of working women has probably had a greater effect on marketing than has any other social change.

As women's earnings grow, so do their levels of expertise, experience, and authority. Working-age women are not the same group businesses targeted thirty years ago. They expect different things in life—from their jobs, from their spouses, and from the products and services they buy.

The automotive industry has finally begun to realize the power of women in vehicle purchase decisions. Women are the principal buyers for 45 percent of all cars and trucks sold in the United States.[12] Saturn's advertising aims not only to attract women as customers, but also to woo them into the business. In an industry with a woefully small representation of women in sales, 16 percent of Saturn's sales staff are women, compared with 7 percent industry-wide. This has had a visible impact on sales to women. Even though about half of all automotive purchases are made by women, Saturn claims that women buy 64 percent of its cars.[13]

The growth in the number of working women has meant an increase in dual-career families. Although dual-career families typically have greater household incomes, they have less time for family activities (poverty of time). Their purchasing roles (which define the items traditionally bought by the man or the woman) are changing, as are their purchasing patterns.

In a recent survey, two-thirds to three-quarters of women said they are making many major economic decisions either independently or equally with a spouse. Few of the women said they left important marketplace decisions to others.[14]

Most importantly, as Exhibit 3.2 shows, cost is more prominent in decisions made by women, whereas quality is relatively more important to men. This

Exhibit 3.2

What's Important When You Shop		
	Women (%)	Men (%)
The quality of a product matters more than cost or other factors	48	54
The cost of an item is very critical to me	23	18

Women As Principal Decision Makers	
	All Women (%)
Set up, follow budget	64
Arrange travel	62
Purchase appliances	61
Purchase insurance	56
Invest in stocks, funds	50
Make a will	46
Buy a home	37

SOURCE: Christy Harvey, "A Guide to Who Holds the Purse Strings," *Wall Street Journal*, June 22, 2000, A14.

knowledge has important ramifications for managers creating a new marketing mix. Exhibit 3.2 also reveals where women act as principal decision makers.

When it comes to big-ticket, long-term items, women remain active in the decision-making process, though a plurality say they are more likely to make these decisions with a spouse. Life experience is an important factor in women's independence in long-term planning; married women over age fifty-five are more likely to make these decisions on their own than their younger counterparts are. Single women, of course, make more of their own decisions.[15]

More working women has meant an ever-increasing demand for time-saving devices and products, particularly for the kitchen. An increasingly popular way to preserve foods is irradiation. Irradiation, however, evokes the notion of nuclear weapons in the minds of some consumers. The "Ethics in Marketing" box explores how this new technology is being promoted in the marketplace.

Demographic Factors

Explain the importance to marketing managers of current demographic trends

demography
The study of people's vital statistics, such as their age, race and ethnicity, and location.

Another uncontrollable variable in the external environment—also extremely important to marketing managers—is **demography**, the study of people's vital statistics, such as their age, race and ethnicity, and location. Demographics are significant because the basis for any market is people. Demographic characteristics are strongly related to consumer buyer behavior in the marketplace. The vast wealth of America, and the resulting consumption of products and services, is reflected in the demographics of the United States versus the rest of the world (see Exhibit 3.3). This exhibit tells marketers many things. For example, the United States is growing much slower than the rest of the world. Faster growth, if it is coupled with rising incomes, means expanding markets. The longer life span of Americans suggests a growing market for products and services targeted toward the elderly. Read through the table and determine other implications for marketers.

We turn our attention now to a closer look at age groups, their impact, and the opportunities they present for marketers. The cohorts have been given the names of Generation Y, Generation X, and baby boomers. You will find that each cohort group has its own needs, values, and consumption patterns.

Irradiated Food by Any Other Name Might Be a Winner

The scene in the television commercial is straight out of Norman Rockwell, with a gray-haired woman pedaling her bicycle through quaint, sun-streaked streets.

This could be a spot for aspirin, or for orange juice. But as the woman makes her way home, to a barbecue with elderly friends and children, it becomes apparent that she isn't pushing a specific product. "SureBeam is much like milk pasteurization," says a homey voice-over. "It makes foods safer by helping to eliminate harmful bacteria."

And what is SureBeam? It happens to be one company's patented method of food irradiation. The thirty-second advertisement asks viewers to look for packages with the SureBeam seal. The "i" word is never mentioned—deliberately. Irradiation involves exposing foods to controlled levels of ionizing radiation, such as gamma rays, electron beams, and X-rays. The decades-old process kills most pathogens, including potentially deadly strains of *E. coli* bacteria. Currently, the technology is ap-

proved by the Food and Drug Administration for use on some foodstuffs like spices, fresh fruits, and vegetables as well as certain fresh meats. The agency is expected to broaden its approval to cover packaged foods like hot dogs.

But despite the FDA's blessing and the fact that the process might prevent some of the 5,000-plus food-safety-related deaths each year, many Americans frown upon the technology.

Irradiated foods are not radioactive. Still, consumer groups are divided on their safety. The National Consumers League, for instance, lauds irradiation as a valuable safety net; Public Citizen, on the other hand, contends that health-related issues loom. In any case, the amount of irradiated food on the shelves of U.S. grocery stores today is small.

SureBeam Corporation's ads are sure to fuel the debate. The company is based in San Diego. Its clients include Omaha Steaks and Huisken Meats, and it is working with food giant Kraft Foods Inc., which currently has no irradiated

food on the market. (A Kraft spokeswoman says the company is doing research with SureBeam "that could further enable us to improve the quality of our products.")

SureBeam has used the euphemism "electronic pasteurization" as part of its corporate logo and makes only scant reference to irradiation on its Web site and in other marketing materials. "There's no label that says, 'this product has been fumigated,' " says Andrew Hyncik, SureBeam's marketing director. "Why should we have to call attention to the fact that we've been irradiated?" A SureBeam spokesman says that "disinfestations" best describes the company's process for treating fruits and vegetables.[16]

Would you mind eating irradiated foods? Why or why not? Do you think that SureBeam's promotional campaign is deceptive? Should foods that have been irradiated be conspicuously labeled as such? What about fumigated veggies?

Exhibit 3.3

The Demographic Facts of Life*

United States		Planet Earth
283.5 million	Population	6.1 billion
3,717,796	Area, in square miles	51,789,516
15	Births per 1,000	22
9	Deaths per 1,000	9
120	Doubling time in years at current rate	51
337.8 million	Projected population, 2025	7.8 billion
7	Infant deaths per 1,000 live births	57
74 (male), 79 (female)	Life expectancy	64 (male), 68 (female)
21	Percent of population under age 15	31
13	Percent of population over age 65	7
74	Population per square mile	117
75	Percent urban	45
635 species	Endangered/threatened animals	5,205 species
447 species	Endangered/threatened plants	33,798 species
1,512 gallons	Daily water use per capita	465 gallons
59.4 barrels of oil equivalent	Energy use per capita	9.5 barrels of oil equivalent
1.3	Persons per motor vehicle	9
3	Percent of labor force in agriculture	49
19	Percent of labor force in industry	20
78	Percent of labor force in services	31
806	Televisions per 1,000 people	225

SOURCE: *Zero Population Growth (www.zpg.org).* *Data are for 2001.

Generation Y

Generation Y
People born between 1979 and 1994.

Those designated by demographics as **Generation Y** were born between 1979 and 1994. They are about sixty million strong, more than three times as large as Generation X. If this group of consumers does not like the mature brands of the baby boomers or Generation X, then marketers will be in trouble. Why? Simply because of the size of the Gen Y market. For example, baby boomers are into Lexus, Estee Lauder, L. L. Bean, and Coke. Gen Y-ers like Jeep Wrangler, Hard Candy, The North Face, and Mountain Dew.

Gen Y-ers, having grown up in an even more media-saturated, brand-conscious world than their parents, respond to ads differently and prefer to encounter those ads in different places. The marketers that capture Gen Y's attention do so by bringing their messages to the places these kids congregate, whether it's the Internet, a snowboarding tournament, or cable TV. The ads may be funny or disarmingly direct. What they don't do is suggest that the advertiser knows Gen Y better than these savvy consumers know themselves.

Generation Y is already driving the educational software and snowboard industries and soon will drive many others. Hawaiian Tropic, the nation's number three suntan lotion company, has dramatically increased its spring break promotions to Gen Y-ers at Panama City Beach, South Padre Island, and Daytona Beach.

For Generation Y, anyone can be a star. Everyone deserves to have his or her say. For young people, getting heard and becoming well known are not only easy, they seem natural. You can create your own Web site; make a movie with your own webcam or digital camera; post your thoughts, pictures, and writings on-line; even be on television. Part of the draw of reality TV shows like *Survivor* is that "real people" can become stars.[17]

Generation Y also loves customized products and services. Research found that 85 percent of those aged eighteen to twenty-four said they wished more products were customized to their unique tastes and needs. Only 62 percent of those sixty-five and older expressed similar feelings. The product categories in which Generation Y consumers wanted customized goods and services were (in rank order) clothes, shoes, travel planning, and computers and electronics.[18]

Companies are learning that they have to provide something unique and deeply personal to win loyalty. Winning consumer loyalty and repeat business is exactly what Wyndham Hotels seems to be doing with its mass customized guest recognition program, Wyndham By Request. Guests can join the free program by filling out a detailed preference form: Do you prefer foam or feather pillows? Sweet or salty snacks? A glass of Merlot or a cold Bud in the minifridge? Requests are automatically filled each time a customer reserves a room at any Wyndham property.

Generation X

Generation X
People born between 1965 and 1978.

Generation X—people born between 1965 and 1978—consists of 40 million consumers. It is the first generation of latchkey children—products of dual-career households or, in roughly half of the cases, of divorced or separated parents. Generation X began entering the workforce in the era of downsizing and downturn, so its members are likelier than the previous generation to be unemployed, underemployed, and living at home with Mom and Dad. Yet, as a generation that's been bombarded by multiple media since their cradle days, Gen X-ers are savvy and cynical consumers.

The members of Generation X don't mind indulging themselves. Among the young women of Generation X, 38 percent go to the movies in a given month, compared with 19 percent of the women who are now forty-five and older. The members of Generation X devote a larger-than-average share of their spending dollars to restaurant meals, alcoholic beverages, clothing, and electronic items such as televisions and stereos. They are more materialistic than past generations but have less hope of achieving their goals.

Travel companies, such as hotels, airlines, and car rental companies, that have spent the last thirty years marketing to baby boomers have discovered that Gen X-ers have vastly different preferences and interests from the older generation. To woo them, travel companies are creating unusual perks and unconventional gags in TV commercials. They're taping airfare promos to pizza boxes, teaching kickboxing classes in hotel fitness centers, and replacing buttoned-down restaurants with sweatshirt-casual bistros.

Starwood created an entire hotel chain for those customers, giving it the name W. Each hotel, where rooms go for about $300 a night, features contemporary designs, hip bars, and whimsical amenities such as gumball machines with Hot Tamale candies that make them magnets for young travelers, Starwood's vice president Guy Hensley says. And if they outgrow W's, Starwood hopes they'll switch to its more traditional Sheratons and Westins. "If we catch hold of the Generation X crowd now, they'll stay with us forever," says Hensley.[19]

Another example of creating a product specifically for Gen X-ers comes from Harley-Davidson. Harley-Davidson/Buell targeted the Buell "Blast" directly to Gen X-ers. This new model is a smaller, lighter, easier-handling, one-cylinder motorcycle, selling for under $4,500, and it was designed specifically for the male or female new rider or novice rider who is not yet ready for the traditionally heavier Harley-Davidson cruising or touring bikes.[20]

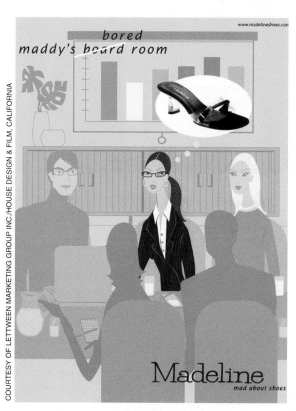

Generation X is not nearly as large as either Generation Y or the Baby Boom generation. Still, it represents a lucrative market, since its members spend a larger-than-average share of their incomes on restaurant meals, clothing, and electronics.

Baby Boomers: America's Mass Market

Almost 78 million **baby boomers** were born in the United States between 1946 and 1964, which created a huge market. The oldest are now over fifty-five, but they cling to their youth. One study found that baby boomers see themselves as continuing to be very active after they turn fifty. They won't even think of themselves as being senior citizens until after they turn sixty (39 percent) or seventy (42 percent).[21]

This group cherishes convenience, which has resulted in a growing demand for home delivery of items like large appliances, furniture, and groceries. In addition, the spreading culture of convenience explains the tremendous appeal of prepared take-out foods and the necessity of VCRs and cell phones.

Baby boomers' parents raised their children to think for and of themselves. Studies of child-rearing practices show that parents of the 1950s and 1960s consistently ranked "to think for themselves" as the number one trait they wanted to instill in their children.[22] Postwar affluence also allowed parents to indulge their children as never before. They invested in their children's skills by sending them to college. They encouraged their children to succeed in a job market that rewarded competitive drive more than cooperative spirit and individual skills more than teamwork.

In turn, the sheer size of the generation encouraged businesses to promote the emerging individuality of baby boomers. Even before the oldest baby boomers started earning their own living more than three decades ago, astute businesspeople saw the profits that come from giving millions of young people what they want. Businesses offered individualistic baby boomers a growing array of customized products and services—houses, cars, furniture, appliances, clothes, vacations, jobs, leisure time, and even beliefs.

baby boomers
People born between 1946 and 1964.

personalized economy
Delivering customized goods and services at a good value on demand.

The importance of individualism among baby boomers led to a **personalized economy**—a system that delivers customized goods and services at a good value on demand. Successful businesses in a personalized economy give customers what they want when they want it. To do this, they must know their customers extremely well. In fact, the intimacy between producer and consumer is exactly what makes an economy personalized.

As the age of today's average consumer moves toward forty, average consumption patterns are also changing. People in their early forties tend to focus on their families and finances. As this group grows in number, its members will buy more furniture from manufacturers like Lazy Boy, American Martindale, Baker, and Drexel-Heritage to replace the furniture they bought early in their marriages. The demand for family counselors and wellness programs should also increase. Additionally, discount investment brokers like Charles Schwab and E-trade and mutual funds like Fidelity and Dreyfus should profit. Because middle-aged consumers buy more reading materials than any other age group, the market for books and magazines should remain strong throughout the late 2000s. Women ages forty to sixty-four will be the largest age demographic group by the year 2010.[23] *More* magazine has been created to target this market. *More* promises features about fashion, beauty, and health, as well as pieces on married life after three decades. And all the models in *More*'s editorial pages are forty-plus.

Baby boomers are now in the nesting stage of their lives. Secure in their careers and generally stable, boomers are in their low-migration years. The fact that boomers are becoming homebodies, while other segments of the population are moving, means that boomers are not relocating to many of the nation's new economic "hot spots" (the Sunbelt states) that are attracting other segments of the population, such as newly arrived immigrants and Gen X-ers. Rather, boomers are returning to more "mature" (and often more pricey) regions of the country that they lived in when they were younger, such as New England and the eastern seaboard, the upper Midwest, the upper Rocky Mountains West and the Pacific Northwest.[24]

Older Consumers: Not Just Grandparents

As mentioned above, the oldest baby boomers have already crossed the fifty-five threshold that many demographers use to define the "mature market." Today's mature consumers are wealthier, healthier, and better educated than those of earlier generations. By 2005, 115 million consumers will be fifty years of age or older, making up 40 percent of the population.[25] Consumers in the mature market keep up with the times, are quite definite about their wants and needs, and have a series of unique behavior patterns. To summarize:

- They take frequent vacations.

- They eat out often—in both high-end and fast-food restaurants.

- They have specific needs with regard to banking and investment services, with definite differences between boomers and older consumers (those over sixty years old).

- They own computers, and they utilize them for a broad range of purposes.

- They are heavily into the Internet, including on-line shopping.

- They are somewhat light viewers of television (watching the major networks for news and entertainment, cable for education).[26]

Mature consumers are not happy with the way they are treated by marketers and advertisers. For the most part, they believe marketers and advertisers do not have their interests or needs in mind when developing products, designing packaging, and preparing advertising.

- More than half feel marketers do only a fair to poor job in considering their needs when they develop new products.

- Two out of five say marketers do only a fair to poor job in considering their needs when they develop packaging (as opposed to the 4 percent who feel they do an excellent job).
- And, most damaging to advertisers, almost half of boomers feel advertisers and their agencies ignore them in preparing their campaigns (4 percent are satisfied).[27]

Marketers who want to actively pursue the mature market must understand it. Aging consumers create some obvious opportunities. JCPenney's Easy Dressing clothes feature Velcro-fastened clothing for women with arthritis or other ailments who may have difficulty with zippers or buttons. Sales from the first Easy Dressing catalog were three times higher than expected. Chicago-based Cadaco offers a line of games with easy-to-read big print and larger game pieces. The series focuses on nostalgia by including Michigan rummy, hearts, poker, and bingo. Trivia buffs more familiar with Mitch Miller than Guns 'n' Roses can play Parker Brothers' "The Vintage Years" edition of *Trivial Pursuit*. The game, aimed at the sixty-plus crowd, poses questions covering the era from Charles Lindbergh to Dwight D. Eisenhower.

To persuade active retirees to move, the housing industry first renamed retirement developments, now often called "active-adult communities." Now, builders are also piling on amenities. Miami-based homebuilder Lennar Corporation has souped up its clubhouses in the past five years, adding restaurants, concierge services, computer labs, and gyms. In collaboration with a local university, Del Webb Corporation is building a several-thousand-square-foot educational center at Sun City Grand in Phoenix, where the company is based, that has classrooms, a lecture hall, a library, and a Starbucks.[28]

Growing Ethnic Markets

The United States is undergoing a new demographic transition: It is becoming a multicultural society. During this decade, the United States will shift further from a society dominated by whites and rooted in Western culture to a society characterized by three large racial and ethnic minorities: African Americans, U.S. Hispanics, and Asian Americans. All three minorities will grow in size and in share of the population, while the white majority declines as a percentage of the total. Native Americans and people with roots in Australia, the Middle East, the former Soviet Union, and other parts of the world will further enrich the fabric of U.S. society.

The labor force of the past was dominated by white men who are now retiring. Today's senior workers are equal parts women and men, and still overwhelmingly white. But in the entry-level jobs, a multicultural labor force is emerging. The proportion of non-Hispanic whites in the workforce in 2005 is estimated to be 74 percent, down from 77 percent in 1998.

Because so many white men are retiring, the non-Hispanic white labor force is growing slowly—by only 8 percent between 1994 and 2005. The number of Hispanic workers is growing much faster—by 36 percent—due to the continued immigration of young adults, higher birthrates, and relatively few retirees. These forces are also boosting the number of Asian workers—by 39 percent. The number of black workers is increasing too—by 15 percent, a rate slightly slower than the rate of growth of black adults in general (16.5 percent).[29]

Ethnic and Cultural Diversity

Multiculturalism occurs when all major ethnic groups in an area—such as a city, county, or census tract—are roughly equally represented. Because of its current demographic transition, the trend in the United States is toward greater multiculturalism.

4

Explain the importance to marketing managers of multiculturalism and growing ethnic markets

Read more about multicultural marketing in the supplemental module on your Xtra! CD.

multiculturalism
When all major ethnic groups in an area—such as a city, county, or census tract—are roughly equally represented.

On Line

San Francisco County is the most diverse county in the nation. The proportions of major ethnic groups are closer to being equal there than anywhere else. People of many ancestries have long been attracted to the area. Elsewhere, however, a careful examination of the statistics from the latest U.S. Census Bureau reveals that the nation's minority groups, especially Hispanics and Asians, are heavily clustered in selected regions and markets. Rather than witnessing the formation of a homogeneous national melting pot, we are seeing the creation of numerous mini-melting pots, while the rest of America remains much less diverse.[30]

In a broad swath of the country, the minority presence is still quite limited. As Exhibit 3.4 makes clear, America's racial and ethnic patterns have taken on distinctly regional dimensions. Hispanics dominate large portions of counties in a span of states stretching from California to Texas. Blacks are strongly represented in counties of the South as well as selected urban areas in the Northeast and Midwest. The Asian presence is relatively small and highly concentrated in a few scattered counties, largely in the West. And Native Americans are concentrated in select pockets in Oklahoma, the Southeast, the upper Midwest, and the West. Multiethnic counties are most prominent in California and the Southwest, with mixes of Asians and Hispanics, or Hispanics and Native Americans.[31]

Marketing Implications of Multiculturalism

In recent years the number of blacks, Hispanics, and Asians has grown explosively, and those groups now account for 79 million out of 284 million Americans. Collectively, they represent an estimated $1 trillion in annual spending power.[32] Hispanics are the fastest growing segment of the population. The diversity of the U.S. population is projected to stabilize around 2023, as the birthrates among minorities level off.

The marketer's task is more challenging in a diverse society because of differences in educational level and demand for goods and services. What's more, eth-

Exhibit 3.4

Micro Multiculturalism

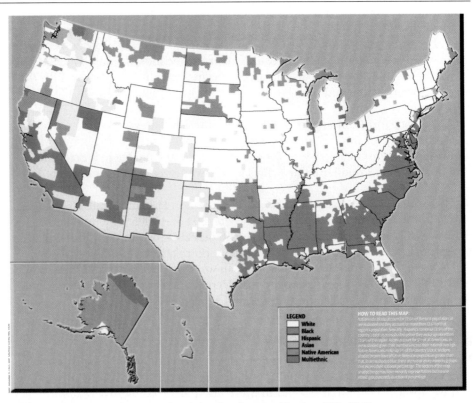

SOURCE: William Frey, "Micro Melting Pots," *American Demographics,* June 2001, 20–21.

nic markets are not homogeneous. There is not an African American market or a Hispanic market, any more than there is a white market. Instead, there are many niches within ethnic markets that require micro-marketing strategies. For example, African Eye, which offers women's designer fashions from Africa, attracted a thousand women to a fashion show at Prince Georges Plaza near Washington, D.C. The show featured the latest creations by Alfadi, a high-fashion Nigerian designer, who also hosted the show. African Eye's dresses and outfits blend African and Western influences and are priced at $50 to $600. Says Mozella Perry Ademiluyi, the president and cofounder of African Eye: "Our customer is professional, 30 to 65, has an income level of $30,000-plus and often is well-traveled. They don't just want to wear something that is African. They want something that is well-tailored, unique, and creative as well."[33]

Multicultural marketing has found great success on the Internet. Numerous sites, like iMinorities.com, provide information and services targeted toward a variety of minority groups.

Procter & Gamble has created a new "Multicultural Market Development Organization" to reach minority markets. Now, every six months, the firm sends out 4.5 million copies of its promotional magazine *Avanzando con tu Familia* (Getting ahead with your family). That's one copy for every two Hispanic households. Marketers have reworked the Spanish slogan for Cover Girl makeup, and product developers are creating new Secret deodorant scent names that they hope will appeal to Hispanic consumers. In addition, P&G's new line of Pampers diapers with "cloth-like backside" comes in boxes labeled in both English and Spanish.

Procter & Gamble isn't new to the Hispanic market. Cover Girl, which started using Latina models in 1993, added makeup shades aimed at Hispanic women a few years ago: darker shades for foundation and powder, and brighter colors for lipsticks and nail polish. P&G was also one of the first sponsors of *Sabado Gigante,* a Saturday variety show that has run on Spanish-language TV for fourteen years. P&G has been the top spender for Spanish advertising for many years.[34]

Another large company that has increased its emphasis on multicultural marketing is Sears, Roebuck and Company. Sears has around thirty stores nationwide located in urban areas with large Asian populations. Recently, the company recognized an opportunity to boost fall sales in those stores by forging a connection with the Asian Moon Festival.

The September holiday is a harvest-time celebration, similar to Thanksgiving, that is celebrated in many Asian countries. It coincides with the kickoff of retail's fall selling season (when Sears would be staging promotions, anyway), so a Moon Festival tie-in made sense. "We've had great success with it," says Gilbert Davila, Sears' vice president of multicultural and relationship marketing. "It's a good way for us to connect with the community."[35] Sears also does promotions tied to Black History Month in February and Mexican Independence Day in September.

For the Moon Festival, in addition to offering a free gift with any purchase over $10, the stores host a number of cultural events, such as performances by local dance troupes. The performances typically involve people dancing with— or in—large puppets representing animals or mythological creatures, as puppets are a traditional element in Asian culture.

The Asian market is a particular challenge for marketers because of the many different languages. Depending on the makeup of the surrounding communities, Sears advertises the Moon Festival in Mandarin, Cantonese, Vietnamese, or Korean; there are seven or eight stores in each language group, most of them in California. The programs staged in the stores are conducted in English, however. The ads run mainly in local Asian-language newspapers.

To learn more about multicultural marketing, read the supplemental module on your Xtra! CD.

The Internet Goes Multicultural

Since 1995, non-English-speaking Internet users have gone from less than 10 percent to as high as 50 percent, according to researcher Wired Digital. African Americans outpace all other segments—including the general market—for on-line adoption, according to Forrester Research.[36]

Today, approximately 40 percent of all African American households, 43 percent of Hispanic Americans, and 71 percent of Asian Americans are on-line.[37] During the holiday season in 2000, the average African American household spent $225 on on-line purchases, while Latino households spent $254—the same as white households. And Asian Americans outspent all other groups, with an average of $331 on e-commerce purchases during the same period.[38] In 2004, minorities are expected to spend an estimated $24.5 billion on-line.[39]

The huge growth in the multicultural on-line market has resulted in a proliferation of Web sites targeted to specific ethnic groups. Examples include AsianAvenue.com, a site for Asian Americans; StarMedia Network, which focuses on Latinos inside and outside the United States; and iMinorities, a job site for minorities. One of the more popular sites for African Americans is BlackPlanet.com, which averages 300 million page views per month.

African American portal BET.com recently partnered with Fannie Mae, the nation's largest source of funds to lenders for residential mortgages. The partnership is Fannie Mae's first major on-line marketing effort targeting minorities, even though Fannie Mae is very active in the on-line mortgage market. The multiyear partnership includes a newly created HomeCenter minisite on BET.com that's intended to simplify the home mortgage process. The HomeCenter offers practical tips, such as explaining the implications of different interest rates, and suggestions on how to evaluate, manage, and protect one's credit history. The information is geared to address concerns specific to African Americans.[40]

Economic Factors

Identify consumer and marketer reactions to the state of the economy

In addition to social and demographic factors, marketing managers must understand and react to the economic environment. The three economic areas of greatest concern to most marketers are the distribution of consumer income, inflation, and recession.

Rising Incomes

As disposable (or after-tax) incomes rise, more families and individuals can afford the "good life." Fortunately, U.S. incomes have continued to rise, although at a rather slow pace. After adjustment for inflation, median incomes in the United States rose less than 4 percent between 1980 and 2000.

Today, about two-thirds of all U.S. households earn a "middle-class" income. The rough boundaries for a middle-class income are $18,000, above poverty, to about $75,000, just short of wealth.[41] In 2001, almost half the households were in the upper end of the $18,000 to $75,000 range, as opposed to only a quarter in 1980. More than 10 percent of households now earn above $75,000.[42] As a result, Americans are buying more goods and services than ever before. For example, in raising a child to age seventeen, a middle-class family will spend over $124,000 in 2001 dollars. This new level of affluence is not limited to professionals or even individuals within specific age or education brackets. Rather, it cuts across all household types, well beyond what businesses traditionally consider to be markets for high-priced goods and services. This rising affluence stems primarily from the increasing number of dual-income families.

During the 2000s, many marketing managers are focusing on families with incomes over $35,000, because this group has the most discretionary income. The average American household has over $12,000 in discretionary income each year. Some marketers are concentrating their efforts on higher quality, higher priced goods and services. The Lexus automobile and American Airlines' "international class" service for business-class seats on transcontinental flights are examples of this trend.

Inflation

Inflation is a general rise in prices without a corresponding increase in wages, which results in decreased purchasing power. Fortunately, the United States has had a low rate of inflation for over a decade. The late 1990s and early 2000s have been marked by an inflation rate under 4 percent. The low rate of inflation is due to the tremendous productivity of the high-tech sector of the economy and the stability of the price of services. Both education and healthcare costs are rising much more slowly than in the past. The other good news is that the American economy grew at an annual rate of over 4 percent from 1997 to 2000.[43] These economic conditions benefit marketers, because real wages, and hence purchasing power, go up when inflation stays down. A significant increase in inflation almost always depresses real wages and the ability to buy more goods and services.

In times of low inflation, businesses seeking to increase their profit margins can do so only by increasing their efficiency. If they significantly increase prices, no one will purchase their goods or services.

In more inflationary times, marketers use a number of pricing strategies to cope. (See Chapter 18 for more on these strategies.) But in general, marketers must be aware that inflation causes consumers to either build up or diminish their brand loyalty. In one research session, a consumer panelist noted, "I used to use just Betty Crocker mixes, but now I think of either Betty Crocker or Duncan Hines, depending on which is on sale." Another participant said, "Pennies count now, and so I look at the whole shelf, and I read the ingredients. I don't really understand, but I can tell if it's exactly the same. So now I use this cheaper brand, and honestly, it works just as well." Inflation pressures consumers to make more economical purchases. Nevertheless, most consumers try hard to maintain their standard of living.

In creating marketing strategies to cope with inflation, managers must realize that, despite what happens to the seller's cost, the buyer is not going to pay more for a product than the subjective value he or she places on it. No matter how compelling the justification might be for a 10 percent price increase, marketers must always examine its impact on demand. Many marketers try to hold prices level as long as is practical.

Recession

A **recession** is a period of economic activity when income, production, and employment tend to fall—all of which reduce demand for goods and services. The slowdown in the high-tech sector, overextended consumer credit, and the terrorist attacks on America resulted in the economy slipping into a recession in 2001. The problems of inflation and recession go hand in hand, yet recession requires different marketing strategies:

- *Improve existing products and introduce new ones:* The goal is to reduce production hours, waste, and the cost of materials. Recessions increase the demand for goods and services that are economical and efficient, offer value, help organizations streamline practices and procedures, and improve customer service.

- *Maintain and expand customer services:* In a recession, many organizations postpone the purchase of new equipment and materials. Sales of replacement parts and other services may become an important source of income.

inflation
A general rise in prices without a corresponding increase in wages, which results in decreased purchasing power.

recession
A period of economic activity when income, production, and employment tend to fall—all of which reduce demand for goods and services.

- *Emphasize top-of-the-line products and promote product value:* Customers with less to spend will seek demonstrated quality, durability, satisfaction, and capacity to save time and money. High-priced, high-value items consistently fare well during recessions.

Technological and Resource Factors

6

Identify the impact of technology on a firm

basic research
Pure research that aims to confirm an existing theory or to learn more about a concept or phenomenon.

applied research
An attempt to develop new or improved products.

Sometimes new technology is an effective weapon against inflation and recession. New machines that reduce production costs can be one of a firm's most valuable assets. The power of a personal-computer microchip doubles about every eighteen months. The Pentium Pro, for example, introduced in 1995, contains 5.3 million transistors and performs three hundred million instructions per second (MIPS). The 886 chip, introduced in 2000, has fifteen million transistors and performs one thousand MIPS. Our ability, as a nation, to maintain and build wealth depends in large part on the speed and effectiveness with which we invent and adopt machines that lift productivity. For example, coal mining is typically thought of as unskilled, backbreaking labor. But visit Cyprus Amax Mineral Company's Twenty-mile Mine near Oak Creek, Colorado, and you will find workers with push-button controls who walk along massive machines that shear thirty-inch slices from an 850-foot coal wall. Laptop computers help miners track equipment breakdowns and water quality.

The United States excels at both basic and applied research. **Basic research** (or *pure research*) attempts to expand the frontiers of knowledge but is not aimed at a specific, pragmatic problem. Basic research aims to confirm an existing theory or to learn more about a concept or phenomenon. For example, basic research might focus on high-energy physics. **Applied research**, in contrast, attempts to develop new or improved products. The United States has dramatically improved its track record in applied research. For example, the United States leads the world in applying basic research to aircraft design and propulsion systems.

The huge investment in information technology has helped America hold down inflation, maintain economic growth, and effectively compete in world markets. Business purchases of information technology have been rising by 25 percent a year since the 1970s. MIT economics professor Erik Brynjolfsson says that hard-to-quantify innovations in the way companies do business are actually far more valuable than the hardware and software they've purchased. "More than $1 trillion in those intangibles has been built up over the past ten years."[44]

Information technology and the Internet have been the innovations driving increased productivity for the past decade. They will continue to do so in the foreseeable future. When Oracle wanted to boost operating margins, it automated such functions as office supply purchasing. That helped keep the workforce stable at 41,000 even as sales soared 30 percent. The company saved about $1 billion, and margins jumped from 20 percent to 33 percent.[45] Dell uses WebMethods software to act as a type of translator enabling instant communication between Dell's order management system and customers' procurement systems. By making it easier for corporate customers to use the Internet to place orders, Dell has dramatically reduced procurement errors and shaved approximately $5 million a year off its costs. Dell also uses TradeMatrix software to run its plants. This system allows Dell to see deep inside suppliers' business processes and vice versa. It tells suppliers which parts to get to which plant and when. TradeMatrix has saved Dell millions of dollars and has become a major competitive advantage. Dell's inventory averages one-tenth the average level of its rivals.[46] For more examples of how information technology and the Internet are boosting productivity, see Exhibit 3.5.

Sometimes, even though new technology is available, its effective utilization can be stymied by the external environment. Our "Global Perspectives" box details

Exhibit 3.5

Process	Example	Payoff
Innovation	Royal Dutch/Shell's "Game-Changer" teams use the Net to generate new business ideas.	New "Light Touch" oil discovery method found 30 million barrels
Collaboration	Ocean Spray's extranet assesses cranberry quality immediately and helps growers get better prices.	Growers get higher profits; Ocean Spray cuts waste and boosts productivity
Design	Honeywell uses the Net to help fashion a customized prototype of anything from a fan blade to a golf club head.	Design time cut from 6 months to 24 hours
Purchasing	Ford's AutoXchange creates massive on-line trading bazaar for its 30,000 suppliers.	Could save as much as $8 billion in first few years
Manufacturing	BP Amoco, using Net technology from Honeywell, can quickly identify plant inefficiencies.	Stems 2% per day productivity loss in Grangemouth, Scotland, refinery
Logistics	Cement maker Cemex uses Net-based truck dispatch system to speed deliveries to customers.	Cement delivered within 20 minutes, down from 3 hours
Marketing	Weyerhaeuser uses the Net to weed out its least valuable customers at Marshfield, Wisconsin, door plant.	Boosted the plant's return on net assets from –2% to 27% in a five-year period.
Service	GE Power Systems lets customers use the Net to compare the performance of its turbines against other GE turbines in the market.	Turbine productivity expected to rise by 1% to 2% annually.

SOURCE: "Working the Web," *Business Week*, February 14, 2000, 116.

how culture and tradition in Japan have slowed the use of the Internet and information technology.

Political and Legal Factors

Business needs government regulation to protect innovators of new technology, the interests of society in general, one business from another, and consumers. In turn, government needs business, because the marketplace generates taxes that support public efforts to educate our youth, protect our shores, and so on. The private sector also serves as a counterweight to government. The decentralization of power inherent in a private-enterprise system supplies the limitation on government essential for the survival of a democracy.

Discuss the political and legal environment of marketing

Every aspect of the marketing mix is subject to laws and restrictions. It is the duty of marketing managers or their legal assistants to understand these laws and conform to them, because failure to comply with regulations can have major consequences for a firm. Sometimes just sensing trends and taking corrective action before a government agency acts can help

The Internet Runs Headlong into Japan's Cultural Traditions

Japan's electronics manufacturers are rushing to capitalize on the popularity of the Internet, rolling out everything from Internet music players to digital cameras to Web-friendly computers. There's just one problem: Very little of the gear can be bought on-line in Japan.

The few exceptions come mostly from Sony Corporation. When it launched its PlayStation 2 video-game machine in Japan, enthusiastic buyers not only lined up for blocks in Akihabara, Tokyo's electronics district, they mobbed Sony's Web site. The site sold 380,000 PlayStation 2 units—nearly 40 percent of the total.

In the United States, electronic goods are readily sold on-line: Dell Computer Corporation says its dell.com Web site generates nearly 50 percent of its total sales, an average of $40 million a day as of year-end 1999. But it is going to be harder in Japan. That's partly for cultural reasons, industry insiders say: The Japanese tend to be pickier about what they buy and are reluctant to deal with merchants at a distance.

An even bigger obstacle is a major fortress of Old Japan: Each of the top electronics makers has a nationwide network of exclusive dealers, usually mom-and-pop stores long on the personal touch but short on information about up-to-date products.

Take a look at a typical store on Tokyo's Shinobazu Avenue, an outlet that is part of the 22,000-member Panasonic/National retail network. The dusty shelves are filled with 1950s hits—AM radios, space heaters. Asked about Will PC, a heavily advertised Panasonic computer, the aged owner says: "I'm sorry, is that a new product? I don't know anything about computers, since we don't stock any."

Manufacturers are reluctant to compete with these merchants, with whom they have long relationships. And small stores and big discounters would object to price cutting on direct sales via the Net.

All this explains an apparent paradox: Many electronics executives, who stand to win big on sales of Web-related products, dismiss Internet sales as a nonstarter. "We can't do it," says Akiyoshi Takano, president of Sanyo Electric Company's multimedia company, which sells such popular Web-related products as digital cameras.

But what about the success of PlayStation 2 on the Internet? Skeptics note that game fans knew all about the new PlayStation from advance publicity, so they had no need to test it out in the store. Still, many retailers are worried. "This sort of thing would have been unthinkable before now," says Takeo Higashikawa, the manager of a Sony-affiliated store. He thinks Sony was too "dry" and "American" in elbowing aside longtime retailers in favor of Internet sales. "What about the people who worked so hard over the years selling Sony's?" he wonders. Koichiro Katsurayama, a spokesman for Sony Computer Entertainment, says Sony gave retailers and its Web site equal treatment.

Many Japanese retailers are hoping the Internet will end up as a vehicle for only such specialty items. But a Sony managing director, Sunobu Horigome, says that's wishful thinking.[47]

Do you think e-commerce will ever be as popular in Japan as in the United States? What might Japanese manufacturers do to avoid clashes with Japanese retailers? Can you think of other countries where culture and tradition might hinder the development of e-commerce? What about in the United States?

---

avoid regulation. This didn't happen in the case of the tobacco industry. As a result, Joe Camel and the Marlboro Man are fading into the sunset along with other strategies used to promote tobacco products.

The challenge is not simply to keep the marketing department out of trouble, however, but to help it implement creative new programs to accomplish marketing objectives. It is all too easy for a marketing manager or sometimes a lawyer to say no to a marketing innovation that actually entails little risk. For example, an overly cautious lawyer could hold up sales of a desirable new product by warning that the package design could prompt a copyright infringement suit. Thus, it is important to have a thorough understanding of the laws established by the federal government, state governments, and regulatory agencies to control marketing-related issues.

Federal Legislation

Federal laws that affect marketing fall into several categories. First, the Sherman Act, the Clayton Act, the Federal Trade Commission Act, the Celler-Kefauver Antimerger Act, and the Hart-Scott-Rodino Act were passed to regulate the competitive environment. Second, the Robinson-Patman Act was designed to regulate pricing practices. Third, the Wheeler-Lea Act was created to control false advertising. These key pieces of legislation are summarized in Exhibit 3.6.

Exhibit 3.6

Primary U.S. Laws That Affect Marketing

Legislation	Impact on Marketing
Sherman Act of 1890	Makes trusts and conspiracies in restraint of trade illegal; makes monopolies and attempts to monopolize a misdemeanor.
Clayton Act of 1914	Outlaws discrimination in prices to different buyers; prohibits tying contracts (which require the buyer of one product to also buy another item in the line); makes illegal the combining of two or more competing corporations by pooling ownership of stock.
Federal Trade Commission Act of 1914	Creates the Federal Trade Commission to deal with antitrust matters; outlaws unfair methods of competition.
Robinson-Patman Act of 1936	Prohibits charging different prices to different buyers of merchandise of like grade and quantity; requires sellers to make any supplementary services or allowances available to all purchasers on a proportionately equal basis.
Wheeler-Lea Amendments to the FTC Act of 1938	Broadens the Federal Trade Commission's power to prohibit practices that might injure the public without affecting competition; outlaws false and deceptive advertising.
Lanham Act of 1946	Establishes protection for trademarks.
Celler-Kefauver Antimerger Act of 1950	Strengthens the Clayton Act to prevent corporate acquisitions that reduce competition.
Hart-Scott-Rodino Act of 1976	Requires large companies to notify the government of their intent to merge.

State Laws

State legislation that affects marketing varies. Oregon, for example, limits utility advertising to 0.5 percent of the company's net income. California has forced industry to improve consumer products and has also enacted legislation to lower the energy consumption of refrigerators, freezers, and air conditioners. Several states, including New Mexico and Kansas, are considering levying a tax on all in-state commercial advertising.

Regulatory Agencies

Although some state regulatory bodies more actively pursue violations of their marketing statutes, federal regulators generally have the greatest clout. The Consumer Product Safety Commission, the Federal Trade Commission, and the Food and Drug Administration are the three federal agencies most directly and actively involved in marketing affairs. These agencies, plus others, are discussed throughout the book, but a brief introduction is in order at this point.

The sole purpose of the **Consumer Product Safety Commission (CPSC)** is to protect the health and safety of consumers in and around their homes. The CPSC has the power to set mandatory safety standards for almost all products that consumers use (about fifteen thousand items). The CPSC consists of a five-member committee and about eleven hundred staff members, including technicians, lawyers, and administrative help. The commission can fine offending firms up to

Consumer Product Safety Commission (CPSC)
A federal agency established to protect the health and safety of consumers in and around their homes.

◀ ▶   On Line

Federal Trade Commission (FTC)
A federal agency empowered to prevent persons or corporations from using unfair methods of competition in commerce.

$500,000 and sentence their officers to up to a year in prison. It can also ban dangerous products from the marketplace.

The **Federal Trade Commission (FTC)** also consists of five members, each holding office for seven years. The FTC is empowered to prevent persons or corporations from using unfair methods of competition in commerce. It is authorized to investigate the practices of business combinations and to conduct hearings on antitrust matters and deceptive advertising. The FTC has a vast array of regulatory powers (see Exhibit 3.7). Nevertheless, it is not invincible. For example, the FTC had proposed to ban all advertising to children under age eight, to ban all advertising of the sugared products that are most likely to cause tooth decay to children under age twelve, and to require dental health and nutritional advertisements to be paid for by industry. Business reacted by lobbying to reduce the FTC's power. The two-year lobbying effort resulted in passage of the FTC Improvement Act of 1980. The major provisions of the act are as follows:

It bans the use of unfairness as a standard for industrywide rules against advertising. All the proposals concerning children's advertising were therefore suspended, because they were based almost entirely on the unfairness standard. It requires oversight hearings on the FTC every six months. This congressional review is designed to keep the commission accountable. Moreover, it keeps Congress aware of one of the many regulatory agencies it has created and is responsible for monitoring.

Businesses rarely band together to create change in the legal environment as they did to pass the FTC Improvement Act. Generally, marketing managers only react to legislation, regulation, and edicts. It is usually less costly to stay attuned to the regulatory environment than to fight the government. If marketers had toned down their hard-hitting advertisements to children, they might have avoided an

---

Exhibit 3.7

Powers of the Federal Trade Commission

Remedy	Procedure
Cease-and-Desist Order	A final order is issued to cease an illegal practice—and is often challenged in the courts.
Consent Decree	A business consents to stop the questionable practice without admitting its illegality.
Affirmative Disclosure	An advertiser is required to provide additional information about products in advertisements.
Corrective Advertising	An advertiser is required to correct the past effects of misleading advertising. (For example, 25 percent of a firm's media budget must be spent on FTC-approved advertisements or FTC-specified advertising.)
Restitution	Refunds are required to be given to consumers misled by deceptive advertising. According to a 1975 court-of-appeals decision, this remedy cannot be used except for practices carried out after the issuance of a cease-and-desist order.
Counteradvertising	The FTC proposed that the Federal Communications Commission permit advertisements in broadcast media to counteract advertising claims (also that free time be provided under certain conditions).

FTC inquiry altogether. The FTC also regulates advertising on the Internet as well as Internet abuses of consumer privacy (discussed in Chapter 8). The **Food and Drug Administration (FDA)**, another powerful agency, is charged with enforcing regulations against selling and distributing adulterated, misbranded, or hazardous food and drug products. In the last decade it took a very aggressive stance against tobacco products and may be turning its attention to the fast food industry.

Food and Drug Administration

What topics are currently receiving attention in FDA News? What effect has the attention had on market share?

http://www.fda.gov/

On Line

Competitive Factors

The competitive environment encompasses the number of competitors a firm must face, the relative size of the competitors, and the degree of interdependence within the industry. Management has little control over the competitive environment confronting a firm.

Food and Drug Administration (FDA)
A federal agency charged with enforcing regulations against selling and distributing adulterated, misbranded, or hazardous food and drug products.

⑧

Explain the basics of foreign and domestic competition

Competition for Market Share and Profits

As U.S. population growth slows, costs rise, and available resources tighten, firms find that they must work harder to maintain their profits and market share regardless of the form of the competitive market. Take, for example, the competition among airlines. To stop start-up Legend Airlines from starting operations at Dallas's Love Field, American Airlines sued the city of Dallas, the federal government, and the new airline itself. It also lobbied Congress, beseeched its frequent fliers, posted billboards around the city, and secretly paid for radio advertising from a "concerned citizens" group protesting expanded use of Dallas's close-in airport, Love Field. When none of that worked, American's parent, AMR Corporation, leased an asbestos-laden, abandoned terminal at Love Field—an airport it didn't even serve—just as the start-up, Legend Airlines, was negotiating for the same space. AMR said it needed more "office space"—fifteen miles from its headquarters. Legend nevertheless prevailed and in March 2000 began flying fifty-six-seat jets to Los Angeles and Washington, offering exclusively first-class seating, gourmet meals, and satellite TV, all for regular coach fare. Nevertheless, aggressive competition from American soon spelled the demise of Legend. A bankruptcy auction offered everything from leather seats to Styrofoam cups.

One of the greatest competitive battles in America is occurring in consumer package goods, and the two giants going toe-to-toe are Procter & Gamble and Unilever. Between 1996 and 2001, $52 billion Unilever and $40 billion P&G have been living in a parallel slow-growth universe. Since 1996, Unilever's sales have declined an average of 3.6 percent a year. P&G's have inched up 3.6 percent a year. Every market they compete in is barely growing, flat, or declining.

In this kind of environment, "it's a death struggle to incrementally gain share," says Burt Flickinger, a former P&G brand manager who now works as a consumer products consultant. P&G and Unilever have to slog it out for every fraction of every share in every category in every market where they compete. And that's a lot of slogging. Both companies own hundreds of the world's best-known brands—Crest, Pampers, Ivory (Procter & Gamble); Dove, Vaseline, Lipton (Unilever)—competing in some 140 countries. But perhaps the fiercest competition is taking place in the U.S. market for laundry detergent, where P&G's Tide and Unilever's Wisk have been locked in battle for more than thirty-five years.

In recent years, nobody has played this game better than Tide. While the rest of the industry stagnated, Tide's sales climbed by 41 percent, to $1.8 billion over the past five years. It now owns 40 percent of the market. Its strategy? First, Tide spends more than $100 million a year promoting its brand name by advertising on TV, billboards, subways, buses, magazines, and the Internet. It sponsors a NASCAR race car and youth soccer leagues. It holds nationwide publicity stunts, such as its

Competition is a driving force in the marketing environment, including laundry. Tide has become one of America's brand icons, in part by continually improving its product and increasing its market share. How competitive is the world of detergent? The formula for Tide is covered by 44 patents.

recent Dirtiest Kid in America contest. Tide has made itself an American brand icon—right up there with Coke and McDonald's.

But the real genius of Tide's strategy is its relentless stream of new and improved products. Each year P&G spends close to $2 billion on R&D, a large portion of which goes toward developing new formulations of Tide. There's Tide With Bleach, Tide Free (which has no fragrance), Tide WearCare (which purports to keep fabrics vibrant longer), and Tide Kick (whose package includes a nozzle to rub detergent directly into fabrics). In all, Tide has spawned more than sixty variations of itself.[48]

Global Competition

American Airlines, Unilever, and Procter & Gamble are savvy international competitors conducting business throughout the world. Many foreign competitors also consider the United States to be a ripe target market. Thus, a U.S. marketing manager can no longer worry about only domestic competitors. In automobiles, textiles, watches, televisions, steel, and many other areas, foreign competition has been strong. In the past, foreign firms penetrated U.S. markets by concentrating on price, but today the emphasis has switched to product quality. Nestlé, Sony, Rolls Royce, and Sandoz Pharmaceuticals are noted for quality, not cheap prices.

Global competition is discussed in much more detail in Chapter 4.

Ethical Behavior in Business

9

Describe the role of ethics and ethical decisions in business

ethics
The moral principles or values that generally govern the conduct of an individual.

morals
The rules people develop as a result of cultural values and norms.

Regardless of the intensity of the competition or the shifting external environment, firms must compete in an ethical manner. **Ethics** refers to the moral principles or values that generally govern the conduct of an individual or a group. Ethics can also be viewed as the standard of behavior by which conduct is judged. Standards that are legal may not always be ethical, and vice versa. Laws are the values and standards enforceable by the courts. Ethics consists of personal moral principles and values rather than societal prescriptions.

Defining the boundaries of ethicality and legality can be difficult. Often, judgment is needed to determine whether an action that may be legal is indeed ethical. For example, advertising liquor, tobacco, and X-rated movies in college newspapers is not illegal in many states, but is it ethical?

Morals are the rules people develop as a result of cultural values and norms. Culture is a socializing force that dictates what is right and wrong. Moral standards may also reflect the laws and regulations that affect social and economic behavior. Thus, morals can be considered a foundation of ethical behavior.

Morals are usually characterized as good or bad. "Good" and "bad" have different connotations, including "effective" and "ineffective." A good salesperson makes or exceeds the assigned quota. If the salesperson sells a new stereo or television set to a disadvantaged consumer—knowing full well that the person can't keep up the monthly payments—is the salesperson still a good one? What if the sale enables the salesperson to exceed his or her quota?

Another set of connotations for "good" and "bad" are "conforming" and "deviant" behaviors. A doctor who runs large ads for discounts on open-heart surgery would be considered bad, or unprofessional, in the sense of not conforming to the norms of the medical profession. "Bad" and "good" are also used to express the distinction between criminal and law-abiding behavior. And finally, the terms "good" and "bad" as defined by different religions differ markedly. A Muslim who eats pork would be considered bad, as would a fundamentalist Christian who drinks whiskey.

Morality and Business Ethics

 Today's business ethics actually consists of a subset of major life values learned since birth. The values businesspeople use to make decisions have been acquired through family, educational, and religious institutions.

Ethical values are situation specific and time oriented. Nevertheless, everyone must have an ethical base that applies to conduct in the business world and in personal life. One approach to developing a personal set of ethics is to examine the consequences of a particular act. Who is helped or hurt? How long lasting are the consequences? What actions produce the greatest good for the greatest number of people? A second approach stresses the importance of rules. Rules come in the form of customs, laws, professional standards, and common sense. Consider these examples of rules:

- Always treat others as you would like to be treated.

- Copying copyrighted computer software is against the law.

- It is wrong to lie, bribe, or exploit.

The last approach emphasizes the development of moral character within individuals. Ethical development can be thought of as having three levels:[49]

- *Preconventional morality,* the most basic level, is childlike. It is calculating, self-centered, and even selfish, based on what will be immediately punished or rewarded. Fortunately, most businesspeople have progressed beyond the self-centered and manipulative actions of preconventional morality.

- *Conventional morality* moves from an egocentric viewpoint toward the expectations of society. Loyalty and obedience to the organization (or society) become paramount. At the level of conventional morality, an ethical marketing decision would be concerned only with whether it is legal and how it will be viewed by others. This type of morality could be likened to the adage "When in Rome, do as the Romans do."

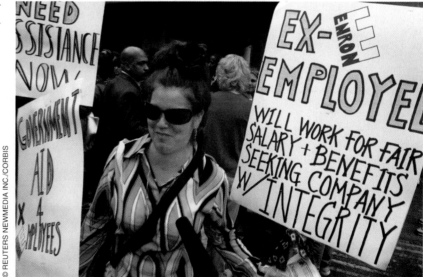

© REUTERS NEWMEDIA INC./CORBIS

- *Postconventional morality* represents the morality of the mature adult. At this level, people are less concerned about how others might see them and more concerned about how they see and judge themselves over the long run. A marketing decision maker who has attained a postconventional level of morality might ask, "Even though it is legal and will increase company profits, is it right in the long run? Might it do more harm than good in the end?"

Perhaps the most egregious example of unethical business practices in recent memory was the Enron scandal that extended to the company's auditing firm, the venerable Arthur Andersen. Thousands of employees were negatively—even detrimentally—affected by the scandal.

Ethical Decision Making

How do businesspeople make ethical decisions? There is no cut-and-dried answer. Some of the ethical issues managers face are shown in Exhibit 3.8. Studies show that the following factors tend to influence ethical decision making and judgments:[50]

- *Extent of ethical problems within the organization:* Marketing professionals who perceive fewer ethical problems in their organizations tend to disapprove more strongly of "unethical" or questionable practices than those who perceive more ethical problems. Apparently, the healthier the ethical environment, the greater is the likelihood that marketers will take a strong stand against questionable practices.

- *Top-management actions on ethics:* Top managers can influence the behavior of marketing professionals by encouraging ethical behavior and discouraging unethical behavior.

- *Potential magnitude of the consequences:* The greater the harm done to victims, the more likely it is that marketing professionals will recognize a problem as unethical.

- *Social consensus:* The greater the degree of agreement among managerial peers that an action is harmful, the more likely it is that marketers will recognize a problem as ethical.

- *Probability of a harmful outcome:* The greater the likelihood that an action will result in a harmful outcome, the more likely it is that marketers will recognize a problem as unethical.

- *Length of time between the decision and the onset of consequences:* The shorter the length of time between the action and the onset of negative consequences, the more likely it is that marketers will perceive a problem as unethical.

- *Number of people to be affected:* The greater the number of persons affected by a negative outcome, the more likely it is that marketers will recognize a problem as unethical.

Ethical Guidelines

Many organizations have become more interested in ethical issues. One sign of this interest is the increase in the number of large companies that appoint ethics officers—from virtually none five years ago to almost 25 percent of large corporations now. In addition, many companies of various sizes have developed a **code of ethics** as a guideline to help marketing managers and other employees make better decisions. In fact, a national study

code of ethics
A guideline to help marketing managers and other employees make better decisions.

Exhibit 3.8

Unethical Practices Marketing Managers May Have to Deal With

- Entertainment and gift giving
- False or misleading advertising
- Misrepresentation of goods, services, and company capabilities
- Lies told customers in order to get the sale
- Manipulation of data (falsifying or misusing statistics or information)
- Misleading product or service warranties
- Unfair manipulation of customers
- Exploitation of children and/or disadvantaged groups
- Stereotypical portrayals of women, minority groups, and senior citizens

- Invasion of customer privacy
- Sex-oriented advertising appeals
- Product or service deception
- Unsafe products or services
- Price deception
- Price discrimination
- Unfair remarks and inaccurate statements about competitors
- Smaller amounts of product in the same-size packages

found that 60 percent of the companies maintained a code of ethics, 33 percent offered ethics training, and 33 percent employed an ethics officer.[51] Some of the most highly praised codes of ethics are those of Boeing, Hewlett-Packard, Johnson & Johnson, and Norton Company.

Creating ethics guidelines has several advantages:

- It helps employees identify what their firm recognizes as acceptable business practices.

- A code of ethics can be an effective internal control on behavior, which is more desirable than external controls like government regulation.

- A written code helps employees avoid confusion when determining whether their decisions are ethical.

- The process of formulating the code of ethics facilitates discussion among employees about what is right and wrong and ultimately leads to better decisions.

University of British Columbia Centre for Applied Ethics

Research corporate codes of ethics through the Applied Ethics Resources page. Compare the codes of three companies. What common themes do you find?

http://www.ethics.ubc.ca/resources/business

On Line

Businesses, however, must be careful not to make their code of ethics too vague or too detailed. Codes that are too vague give little or no guidance to employees in their day-to-day activities. Codes that are too detailed encourage employees to substitute rules for judgment. For instance, if employees are involved in questionable behavior, they may use the absence of a written rule as a reason to continue behaving that way, even though their conscience may be saying no. The checklist in Exhibit 3.9 is an example of a simple but helpful set of ethical guidelines. Following the checklist will not guarantee the "rightness" of a decision, but it will improve the chances that the decision will be ethical.

 Although many companies have issued policies on ethical behavior, marketing managers must still put the policies into effect. They must address the classic "matter of degree" issue. For example, marketing researchers must often resort to deception to obtain unbiased answers to their research questions. Asking for a few minutes of a respondent's time is dishonest if the researcher knows the interview will last forty-five minutes. Not only must management post a code of ethics, but it must also give examples of what is ethical and unethical for each item in the code. Moreover, top management must stress to all employees the importance of adhering to the company's code of ethics. Without a detailed code of ethics and top management's support, creating ethical guidelines becomes an empty exercise. A recent survey of 2,300 employees of large corporations found that 75 percent had observed violations of the law or company standards in the previous twelve months.

Exhibit 3.9

Ethics Checklist

- Does the decision benefit one person or group but hurt or not benefit other individuals or groups? In other words, is my decision fair to all concerned?

- Would individuals or groups, particularly customers, be upset if they knew about my decision?

- Has important information been overlooked because my decision was made without input from other knowledgeable individuals or groups?

- Does my decision presume that my company is an exception to a common practice in this industry and that I therefore have the authority to break a rule?

- Would my decision offend or upset qualified job applicants?

- Will my decision create conflict between individuals or groups within the company?

- Will I have to pull rank or use coercion to implement my decision?

- Would I prefer to avoid the consequences of my decision?

- Did I avoid truthfully answering any of the above questions by telling myself that the risks of getting caught are low or that I could get away with the potentially unethical behavior?

On Line

Among other things, workers noted sexual harassment, conflicts of interest, employment discrimination, deceptive sales practices, unsafe working conditions, and environmental breaches. "People are not reporting misconduct because they are not encouraged to do so," says Richard Girgenti, a KPMG executive. The study found that nearly 75 percent of workers believed cynicism, low morale, and indifference were to blame for misconduct.[52] Many of these concerns have been addressed by the Professional Standards Committee of the American Marketing Association. The American Marketing Association's code of ethics is included on its Web site at **http://www.marketingpower.com.**

Corporate Social Responsibility

10

Discuss corporate social responsibility

corporate social responsibility
Business's concern for society's welfare.

pyramid of corporate social responsibility
A model that suggests corporate social responsibility is composed of economic, legal, ethical, and philanthropic responsibilities and that the firm's economic performance supports the entire structure.

Ethics and social responsibility are closely intertwined. Besides questioning tobacco companies' ethics, one might ask whether they are acting in a socially responsible manner when they promote tobacco. Are companies that produce low-cost handguns socially responsible in light of the fact that these guns are used in the majority of inner-city crimes? **Corporate social responsibility** is a business's concern for society's welfare. This concern is demonstrated by managers who consider both the long-range best interests of the company and the company's relationship to the society within which it operates.

One theorist suggests that total corporate social responsibility has four components: economic, legal, ethical, and philanthropic.[53] The **pyramid of corporate social responsibility**, shown in Exhibit 3.10, portrays economic performance as the foundation for the other three responsibilities. At the same time that it pursues profits (economic responsibility), however, a business is expected to obey the law (legal responsibility); to do what is right, just, and fair (ethical responsibilities); and to be a good corporate citizen (philanthropic responsibility). These four components are distinct but together constitute the whole. Still, if

Exhibit 3.10

Pyramid of Corporate Social Responsibility

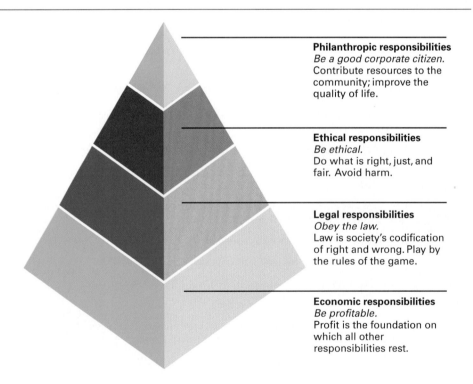

Philanthropic responsibilities
Be a good corporate citizen.
Contribute resources to the community; improve the quality of life.

Ethical responsibilities
Be ethical.
Do what is right, just, and fair. Avoid harm.

Legal responsibilities
Obey the law.
Law is society's codification of right and wrong. Play by the rules of the game.

Economic responsibilities
Be profitable.
Profit is the foundation on which all other responsibilities rest.

the company doesn't make a profit, then the other three responsibilities are moot.

Many companies are already working to make the world a better place to live. Consider these examples:

- Fetzer Vineyards of California has eliminated 91 percent of its waste since 1991 while sales have doubled. The winery grows grapes organically, relying on natural pest control.[54]

- Ben & Jerry's Ice Cream uses unbleached paper in its cartons and purchases only steroid-free milk.[55]

- The Entrepreneurs' Foundation, in Menlo Park, California, has sixty-one member companies that have each donated roughly $100,000 worth of stock for the purpose of addressing the needs of people in their community.[56]

- Abbott Laboratories funds free hearing examinations for the elderly at EarCare Clinics.[57]

- Target Stores gives 5 percent of its pretax earnings to charity.[58]

A current study ranked (in order) Home Depot, Johnson & Johnson, DaimlerChrysler, Anheuser-Busch, and McDonald's as having the highest level of social responsibility in America.[59] Yet, does being socially responsible create additional demand for the

Bob Nardelli, CEO of The Home Depot, working with associates on Habitat for Humanity build, Atlanta 2002

"Roll Up Your Sleeves and Join Me"

Volunteerism is something all of us at The Home Depot understand and embrace. It's been a part of our culture from the beginning. Collectively and individually, we have always returned to our communities a fair measure of what we have earned. We are 250,000 strong. We know we can make a difference. So can you. Volunteer in your community today.

Bob

Bob Nardelli

TEAMDEPOT
Building Better Communities

© 2002. Homer TLC. Inc.

company's goods and services? The answer is quite complex. In some cases, it is "yes," and in others, "no." For example, one factor is the issue on which the company focuses, such as health, education, or charitable giving and how this is perceived by the target market. Other factors are product/service quality and how the target market perceives the importance of social responsibility.[60]

Corporate social responsibility has become a part of American expectations. Bob Nardelli's Home Depot was ranked as having the highest level of social responsibility. Nardelli is pictured here working on a Habitat for Humanity house with Home Depot associates in Atlanta.

CONNECT IT

Look back at the story about Levi's. You should now understand that the external environment affects all firms and their marketing mixes. All of the other external variables, besides demographics and social factors, can influence Levi's sales. Political and legal factors may block the importation of Levi's into some countries. Changing labor laws can increase production costs. Boom periods and recessions can also affect sales.

Are you at the preconventional, conventional, or postconventional stage of ethical development? If you determine that you are at the preconventional level, you should begin striving for a more mature ethical outlook. This may mean taking an ethics course, reading a book on ethics, or engaging in a lot of introspection about yourself and your values. A person with preconventional ethics will probably have a difficult time succeeding in today's business world.

Ethics: A Part of Everyday Life

Realize that ethics plays a part in our lives every day. We all must answer questions such as these:

How do I balance the time and energy obligations of my work and my family?

How much should I pay my employees?

What should I do with the child of my husband's first marriage who is disrupting our new family?

How am I spending my money?

Should I "borrow" a copy of my friend's software?

If I know my employee is having troubles at home, should I treat her differently?

What should I do if I know a neighbor's child is getting into serious trouble?

How do I react to a sexist or racist joke?

Too many people make decisions about everyday questions without considering the underlying moral and ethical framework of the problems. They are simply swept along by the need to get through the day. Our challenge to you is to always think about the ethical consequences of your actions. Make doing so a habit.

Waiting for dramatic events before consciously tackling ethical considerations is like playing a sport only on the weekend. Just as a weekend warrior often ends up with pulled muscles and poor performance, people who seldom consider the ethical implications of daily activities won't have the coordination to work through the more difficult times in their lives. Don't let this happen to you.

Know Your Ethical Values

To get a better idea of your own level of ethical development, take an ethics test. Go to **http://www.worldbank.org/wbi/corpgov/eastasia/m5/m5selftest.htm**. Check your responses against those of others and read their comments. This test will give you better insight into yourself. A short discussion is provided after each question.

Work for a Socially Responsible Firm

When you enter the job market, make certain that you are going to work for a socially responsible organization. Ask a prospective employer how the company gives back to society. If you plan to work for a large company, check out Fortune's current list of America's most admired corporations. (It appears around March 1.)

If you plan to work for a multinational firm, examine *Fortune*'s list of the most globally admired corporations, which appears in October. The list is broken down by industry and includes ten to fifteen companies in each industry. Working for an ethical, socially responsible organization will make you proud of the place where you work.

REVIEW IT

(1) **Discuss the external environment of marketing and explain how it affects a firm.** The external marketing environment consists of social, demographic, economic, technological, political and legal, and competitive variables. Marketers generally cannot control the elements of the external environment. Instead, they must understand how the external environment is changing and the impact of change on the target market. Then marketing managers can create a marketing mix to effectively meet the needs of target customers.

1.1 What is the purpose of environmental scanning? Give an example.

1.2 Form six teams and make each one responsible for one of the uncontrollable elements in the marketing environment. Your boss, the company president, has asked each team to provide a one-year and a five-year forecast of tha major trends the firm will face. The firm is in the telecommunications equipment industry. It has no plans to become a telecommunications service provider like, for example, MCI and AT&T. Each team should use the library, the Internet, and other data sources to make its forecasts. Each team member should examine a minimum of one data source. The team should then pool its data and prepare its recommendation. A spokesperson for each team should present the findings to the class.

(2) Describe the social factors that affect marketing. Within the external environment, social factors are perhaps the most difficult for marketers to anticipate. Several major social trends are currently shaping marketing strategies. First, people of all ages have a broader range of interests, defying traditional consumer profiles. Second, changing gender roles are bringing more women into the workforce and increasing the number of men who shop. Third, a greater number of dual-career families has led to a poverty of time, creating a demand for timesaving goods and services.

2.1 Every country has a set of core values and beliefs. These values may vary somewhat from region to region of the nation. Identify five core values for your area of the country. Clip magazine advertisements that reflect these values and bring them to class.

(3) Explain the importance to marketing managers of current demographic trends. Today, several basic demographic patterns are influencing marketing mixes. Because the U.S. population is growing at a slower rate, marketers can no longer rely on profits from generally expanding markets. Marketers are also faced with increasingly experienced consumers among the younger generations, many of whom are "turned off" by traditional marketing mixes. And because the population is also growing older, marketers are offering more products that appeal to middle-aged and elderly markets.

3.1 Baby boomers in America are aging. Describe how this might affect the marketing mix for the following:
   a. Bally's Health Clubs
   b. McDonald's
   c. Whirlpool Corporation
   d. The state of Florida
   e. Target Stores

3.2 **WRITING** You have been asked to address a local Chamber of Commerce on the subject of "Generation Y." Prepare an outline for your talk.

3.3 How should Ford Motor Company market differently to Generation Y, Generation X, and baby boomers?

(4) Explain the importance to marketing managers of multiculturalism and growing ethnic markets. Multiculturalism occurs when all major ethnic groups in an area are roughly equally represented. Growing multiculturalism makes the marketer's task more challenging. America is not a melting pot but numerous mini-melting pots. Hispanics are the fastest growing segment of the population followed by African Americans. Many companies are now creating departments and committees to effectively target multicultural market segments. The heavy use of the Internet by minorities has resulted in the creation of many Web sites and portals tailored specifically for the needs of each group.

4.1 Explain how the Internet is having an impact on multicultural marketing.

4.2 **WRITING** Go to the library and look up a minority market such as the Hispanic market. Write a memo to your boss that details the many submarkets within this segment.

(5) Identify consumer and marketer reactions to the state of the economy. Marketers are currently targeting the increasing number of consumers with higher discretionary income by offering higher quality, higher priced goods and services. During a time of inflation, marketers generally attempt to maintain level pricing to avoid losing customer brand loyalty. During times of recession, many marketers maintain or reduce prices to counter the effects of decreased demand; they also concentrate on increasing production efficiency and improving customer service.

5.1 Explain how consumers' buying habits may change during a recessionary period.

5.2 ✎ **WRITING** Periods of inflation require firms to alter their marketing mix. Suppose a recent economic forecast expects inflation to be almost 10 percent during the next eighteen months. Your company manufactures hand tools for the home gardener. Write a memo to the company president explaining how the firm may have to alter its marketing mix.

(6) Identify the impact of technology on a firm. Monitoring new technology is essential to keeping up with competitors in today's marketing environment. The United States excels in basic research and, in recent years, has dramatically improved its track record in applied research. Information technology and the Internet have been driving increased U.S. productivity for the past decade. Without innovation, U.S. companies can't compete in global markets.

6.1 Give three examples of how technology has benefited marketers. Also, give several examples of how firms have been hurt by not keeping up with technological changes.

(7) Discuss the political and legal environment of marketing. All marketing activities are subject to state and federal laws and the rulings of regulatory agencies. Marketers are responsible for remaining aware of and abiding by such regulations. Some key federal laws that affect marketing are the Sherman Act, Clayton Act, Federal Trade Commission Act, Robinson-Patman Act, Wheeler-Lea Amendments to the FTC Act, Lanham Act, Celler-Kefauver Antimerger Act, and Hart-Scott-Rodino Act. The Consumer Product Safety Commission, the Federal Trade Commission, and the Food and Drug Administration are the three federal agencies most involved in regulating marketing activities.

7.1 The Federal Trade Commission and other governmental agencies have been both praised and criticized for their regulation of marketing activities. To what degree do you think the government should regulate marketing? Explain your position.

(8) Explain the basics of foreign and domestic competition. The competitive environment encompasses the number of competitors a firm must face, the relative size of the competitors, and the degree of interdependence within the industry. Declining population growth, rising costs, and shortages of resources have heightened domestic competition. Yet small firms that have an effective marketing mix continue to be able to compete with the giants. Meanwhile, dwindling international barriers are bringing in more foreign competitors and offering expanding opportunities for U.S. companies abroad.

8.1 Explain how the nature of competition is changing in America.

8.2 Might there be times when a company becomes too competitive? If so, what could be the consequences?

(9) Describe the role of ethics and ethical decisions in business. Business ethics may be viewed as a subset of the values of society as a whole. The ethical conduct of businesspeople is shaped by societal elements, including family, education, religion, and social movements. As members of society, businesspeople are morally obligated to consider the ethical implications of their decisions.

Ethical decision making is approached in three basic ways. The first approach examines the consequences of decisions. The second approach relies on rules and laws to guide decision making. The third approach is based on a theory of moral development that places individuals or groups in one of three developmental stages: preconventional morality, conventional morality, or postconventional morality.

Many companies develop a code of ethics to help their employees make ethical decisions. A code of ethics can help employees identify acceptable business practices, can be an effective internal control on behavior, can help employees avoid confusion when determining whether decisions are ethical, and can facilitate discussion about what is right and wrong.

9.1 **WRITING** Write a paragraph discussing the ethical dilemma in the following situation and identifying possible solutions: An insurance agent forgets to get the required signature from one of her clients who is buying an automobile insurance policy. The client acknowledges the purchase by giving the agent a signed personal check for the full amount. To avoid embarrassment and inconvenience, the agent forges the client's signature on the insurance application and sends it to the insurance company for processing.

(10) Discuss corporate social responsibility. Responsibility in business refers to a firm's concern for the way its decisions affect society. Social responsibility has four components: economic, legal, ethical, and philanthropic. These are intertwined, yet the most fundamental is earning a profit. If a firm does not earn a profit, the other three responsibilities are moot. Most businesspeople believe they should do more than pursue profits. Although a company must consider its economic needs first, it must also operate within the law, do what is ethical and fair, and be a good corporate citizen.

10.1 Describe at least three situations in which you would not purchase the products of a firm even though it is very socially responsible.

10.2 A firm's only responsibility to society is to earn a fair profit. Comment.

DEFINE IT

applied research 72
baby boomers 65
basic research 72
code of ethics 80
component lifestyles 60
Consumer Product Safety Commission (CPSC) 75
corporate social responsibility 82
demography 62

environmental management 59
ethics 78
Federal Trade Commission (FTC) 76
Food and Drug Administration (FDA) 77
Generation X 64
Generation Y 64
inflation 71

morals 78
multiculturalism 67
personalized economy 66
poverty of time 60
pyramid of corporate social responsibility 82
recession 71
target market 58

APPLY IT

Application for Entrepreneurs

Jeanette and Jeff Horowitz just inherited $175,000 from Jeanette's late Polish uncle, David Forski. The couple had always wanted to own a franchise and, after some initial investigation, have narrowed their choices down to two. The first is FASTSIGNS, the original retail sign franchise that has hundreds of locations and is found in virtually every state. Its advantages are business customers; standard business hours; a clean, attractive retail environment; national advertising support; and operational and marketing support.

Jeanette and Jeff's other opportunity is a Subway sandwich franchise, a highly rated sandwich system with over 13,000 restaurants. Its key advantages are a simple system with no cooking, low initial investment, quality products, and complete training and support.

Questions

1. What are some of the threats in the external environment that Jeanette and Jeff may face?

2. What factors in the external environment may create an opportunity for Jeff and Jeanette?

3. Go to **http://www.subway.com** and **http://www.fastsigns.com** and determine which franchise is more appealing to you. Why?

Ethics Exercise

Jane Barksdale has designed a line of clothing targeted toward Hispanic Americans. The items are sold only by catalog and on the Internet. She thinks that she can increase sales by publicizing that the firm is owned by a Hispanic American and all the employees are Hispanic Americans. She is not Hispanic American nor are most of the employees. She needs a high level of sales to pay her bank loan and remain in business.

Questions

1. Should she claim that she is Hispanic American?

2. Does the AMA Code of Ethics address this issue? Go to **http://www.marketingpower.com** and review the code. Then, write a brief paragraph on what the AMA Code of Ethics contains that relates to Jane Barksdale's dilemma.

TRY IT

Entrepreneurship Case

Identix: Shedding Light on Modern Security

Prior to the terrorist attacks against the United States on September 11, 2001, the high-tech field of biometrics—optical identification systems based on a person's biological features, such as eye patterns or fingerprints—probably seemed like something reserved for science fiction movies and top-secret government facilities. In fact, several companies were hard at work before the attacks developing biometrics applications for banking, travel, and civic identification validation. Chief among them is Identix (previously Visionics).

Formed in 1994 by Joseph Atick and other scientists and engineers, Identix was the first company to discover the proper algorithms for facial recognition. In 2001, Identix took in over $30 million of the $200 million market for biometrics technology in the United States. The total market value is expected to grow to $1 billion by 2004, and most predict Identix will lead the development of this nascent industry.

Sales of its most popular product, a facial recognition technology used in surveillance equipment called FaceIt, grew by 69 percent in 2001. For 2002, sales are expected to climb by 250 to 350 percent! The product is used in video surveillance and can scan for and authenticate specific faces within a crowd. The software that powers it can also improve the quality of a captured image, cut extraneous faces from a picture's background, and track a particular facial image over time.

Other Identix products are in hot demand as well—two from its Live Scan division, the TENPRINTER and FingerPrinter CMS, have been installed at forty-four airports, including those in Los Angeles, Boston, and Cincinnati. Orders are rising and should be boosted further by an FAA grant of $45 million to fund installation of biometrics products in U.S. airports. The company's products were also used at the 2002 Winter Olympic Games in Salt Lake City, Utah, and a recent deal with Honeywell will give its products vastly improved distribution potential, market visibility, and credibility.

Identix's products are also penetrating markets for use in systems used for involuntary identification in law enforcement. The U.S. Army uses a wearable, mobile version of FaceIt (it has a micro camera attached to an eyeglass) for its Digital Military Police program. Several civic police departments use another product, IBIS—an identification based information system—to photograph and scan fingerprints of subjects in the field. The IBIS remote data terminal can then verify identification information within minutes using a remote central database via wireless communication networks.

Though the advantages of increased security are apparent in times of crisis, many wonder if the increased proliferation of biometrics technology will lead to a compromise of personal privacy in the future, after the emotional aftershocks of the September 11th tragedies subside. Joseph Atick is on the record as saying that he is not working to create a national ID system, and that scanned images that don't match those on existing watch lists are immediately deleted from Identix's and Identix's customers' databases.

Americans' fear of privacy on the Internet is already a major social and economic concern, and concerns for privacy under conditions of surveillance or identification validation can only be expected to meet or exceed these already intense levels. In the latter case, however, the issue is one of concern for civil liberties more than one of techno phobia. Identix, therefore, needs to educate and address its customers, the government, and the public with regards to those concerns, or the market it has worked so hard to develop and lead might just disappear before its fiber-optic eyes.

Questions

1. Describe the technological, social, and political factors that are shaping the biometrics market.

2. How is Identix reacting to the above environmental conditions?

3. Does Identix appear to be acting in an ethical manner? Why or why not?

4. Explain why you support or oppose the implementation of biometrics-based security measures.

  WATCH IT

Short **SUPERBOWL**

The ad for GMC in Chapter 3's PowerPoint presentation on the PowerPoint CD-ROM illustrates how issues related to competition find their way into advertising. Consider the impact of demographic trends as you watch the three ads for Cadillac.

Medium **CNN VIDEO**

As you learned in the chapter, the political environment shapes the marketing environment in numerous ways. Riceland Farms had a large contract to sell rice to Iran, and on the point of shipment, the U.S. Government placed an embargo on Iran. Find out how Riceland Farms emerged from what could have been a devastating (even bankrupting) trade embargo. Other CNN clips that address the issues in Chapter 3 are the clips for Chapter 4 (on trade agreements), Chapter 6 (on coffee purchasing), Chapter 12 (on a Palestinian brewery), and Chapter 19 (on Internet gambling).

Long Small**BusinessSchool** ▣
the Series on PBS stations and the Web

To give you insight into Chapter 3, Small Business School will introduce you to Record Technologies, a company that blossomed just as its product was seemingly made obsolete. How could a company that makes vinyl LPs succeed in a digital world? By rigorously scanning its environment. Watch the segment and work the questions on the supplemental video CD-ROM.

FLIP IT

 Flip to Chapter 3 in your *Grademaker Study Guide* for more review opportunities, including the pretest, vocabulary review, study test questions, marketing applications and scenarios, and more. Can you draw the marketing environment? Can you close your book and list the uncontrollable factors in the external environment? Open your Study Guide to find out how much you know—or don't know.

CLICK IT

The *Marketing* Web site links you to all the Internet-based activities in this chapter, such as "Use It," "Apply It," and the On-line exercises in the chapter margins. As a review, do the Chapter 3 quiz and crossword puzzle. You can also work the Career Exersite that shows you what kind of marketing careers are available at the Food and Drug Administration (FDA) and Federal Trade Commission (FTC), federal agencies responsible for monitoring diverse marketing practices. Go to **http://lamb.swlearning.com**, read the material, and follow the links right from the site.

SPIN IT

Spin your Xtra! CD-ROM to find the supplemental content module on multicultural marketing. You can also test your understanding with the worksheets for Exhibits 3.1, 3.4, 3.5, 3.6, 3.7, 3.8, 3.9, and 3.10. In addition to the quiz on the Web site, there's another quiz on the Xtra! CD-ROM, plus video of the authors answering frequently asked questions about the marketing environment. Isn't it true that if you have a really great product, there is no need to worry about the external environment? Is it really that important for firms to be socially responsible? Spin your Xtra! CD and find out.

Still Shaky? Here's a Tip.

Create your own diagram of the marketing environment and compare it to the example in the chapter. Read a selection of business articles and list the factors at play in each of the articles you read. Visit the *Marketing* Web site at **http://lamb.swlearning.com** for a wealth of review and mastery activities.

CHAPTER **FOUR**
DEVELOPING A GLOBAL VISION

Learning Objectives

1 *Discuss the importance of global marketing*

2 *Discuss the impact of multi-national firms on the world economy*

3 *Describe the external environment facing global marketers*

4 *Identify the various ways of entering the global marketplace*

5 *List the basic elements involved in developing a global marketing mix*

6 *Discover how the Internet is affecting global marketing*

4

In brainstorming attractions for its new theme park in Japan, Universal Studios' American designers dreamed up a beast especially for the Japanese: a huge, primeval octopus purportedly hailing from the nearby harbor. Of course, they also envisioned the usual cast of characters from the Hollywood movie studio: E.T., Beetlejuice, and the Terminator. But the ambitious goal Universal set for its first theme park overseas was to rival the phenomenal success of Tokyo Disneyland, the best-attended theme park in the world. To do that, Universal knew it would have to match Disney's knack for making Americana palatable to the Japanese.

And that proved trickier than it sounds.

Descending from a line of silver-screen monsters that began with the Japanese-invented Godzilla, the "Octosaurus" would be a sure hit, Universal's park planners thought. Not so.

To the Japanese, monsters like Godzilla seem dated. Besides, octopuses are friendly, and also tasty. And why would a giant, primeval one be living in their hometown harbor? In the end, the sea monster was dumped, along with several samurai warriers and geisha dancers that had been inserted into entertainment scripts.

In its effort to replicate Disney's magic, Universal's team set into motion one of the most exhaustive attempts ever to mimic what the Japanese have done with everything from Buddhism to American baseball: subtly altering a foreign creation to make it uniquely their own.

"Tokyo Disneyland isn't an American experience. It's a totally Japanese experience," says Norman Elder, another member of the original Disney team in Japan and now head of Universal's marketing efforts here. "Ultimately, they have to embrace the park as their own."

It was in the United States, actually, that the Japanization of Universal began. By surveying Japanese visitors at Universal parks in Orlando and Los Angeles, Universal gradually drew a picture of what the Japanese did and didn't like about the U.S. parks. For example, cramped in their small homes, they swooned at expansive space. But accustomed to modest portions of food, many were turned off by the mountainous servings in the United States.

By mid-1999, a marketing survey in Japan had cataloged Japanese expectations for every aspect of Universal Studios Japan, from bathrooms to souvenir sales. One theme was clear, if a bit contradictory: Japanese wanted an authentic American experience, while expecting the park to cater to their own cultural preferences.

Searching for the right formula required painstaking attention to detail. Universal set up a test kitchen in Japan, where ten Japanese and U.S. chefs tested four thousand recipes to develop U.S.-style dishes with a touch of Japanese flavor. A seafood pizza and gumbo-style soup made the cut. A fried-shrimp concoction with colored rice crackers didn't. American tasters liked it. Japanese simply found it gross.

Julie Appelt, who was born and raised in Japan, and studied theater in the United States, was hired to ensure the shows and skits anchoring the park's entertainment didn't run afoul of Japanese sensibilities. American writers drafted scripts that were then translated into Japanese and given to a Japanese creative staff. There, cultural references and puns that Japanese wouldn't understand were stripped out.

In the final performances, English is used whenever possible. In a musical number based on the *Beetlejuice* movie, the main character banters away in Japanese while his sidekicks speak and sing in English. Snippets of Japanese and a Japanese stuntman were injected into a Wild West show to make the gunfight story more understandable to Japanese without ruining the effect of the U.S. performers.

Other features are uniquely Japanese. The nation's penchant for buying edible souvenirs inspired a 6,000-square-foot confection shop packed with Japanese sweets like dinosaur-shaped bean cakes. Restrooms include Japanese-style squat toilets. Even the park layout caters to the tendency of Japanese crowds to flow clockwise in an orderly manner, contrary to more-chaotic U.S. crowds that steer right.

And on the Jurassic Park water slide, millions of dollars were spent to widen the landing pond, redesign boat hulls, and install underwater wave-damping panels to reduce spray. Why? Many fastidious Japanese don't like to get wet, even on what's billed as one of the world's biggest water slides.[1]

Global marketers often face problems in the external environment that domestic marketers never encounter. Vastly different cultural values and ideas, for example, can present unique challenges as shown above. What are some other variables in the international external environment that can affect global marketers? Is it possible to market products the same way all over the world? Is globalization the wave of the future in international marketing?

Rewards of Global Marketing

1

Discuss the importance of global marketing

global marketing
Marketing that targets markets throughout the world.

global vision
Recognizing and reacting to international marketing opportunities, being aware of threats from foreign competitors in all markets, and effectively using international distribution networks.

Today, global revolutions are under way in many areas of our lives: management, politics, communications, technology. The word *global* has assumed a new meaning, referring to a boundless mobility and competition in social, business, and intellectual arenas. No longer just an option, **global marketing**—marketing that targets markets throughout the world—has become an imperative for business.

U.S. managers must develop a global vision not only to recognize and react to international marketing opportunities but also to remain competitive at home. Often a U.S. firm's toughest domestic competition comes from foreign companies. Moreover, a global vision enables a manager to understand that customer and distribution networks operate worldwide, blurring geographic and political barriers and making them increasingly irrelevant to business decisions. In summary, having a **global vision** means recognizing and reacting to international marketing opportunities, being aware of threats from foreign competitors in all markets, and effectively using international distribution networks.

Over the past two decades, world trade has climbed from $200 billion a year to over $7 trillion. Countries and companies that were never considered major players in global marketing are now important, some of them showing great skill.

Today, marketers face many challenges to their customary practices. Product development costs are rising, the life of products is getting shorter, and new technology is spreading around the world faster than ever. But marketing winners relish the pace of change instead of fearing it.

An example of a young company with a global vision that has capitalized on new technology is Ashtech in Sunnyvale, California. Ashtech makes equipment to capture and convert satellite signals from the U.S. government's Global Positioning System. Ashtech's chief engineer and his team of ten torture and test everything built by Ashtech—expensive black boxes of chips and circuits that use satellite signals to tell surveyors, farmers, mining machine operators, and others where they are with great accuracy. Over half of Ashtech's output is exported. Its biggest customer is Japan.

Adopting a global vision can be very lucrative for a company. Gillette, for example, gets about two-thirds of its revenue from its international division. About 70 percent of General Motors' profits come from operations outside the United States. Although Cheetos and Ruffles haven't done very well in Japan, the potato chip has been quite successful. PepsiCo's (owner of Frito-Lay) overseas snack business brings in more than $3.25 billion annually.

Pillsbury is reaping the rewards of having a global marketing strategy in India. Although wheat is still ground by hand at home in the vast majority of cases, Pillsbury is already the market leader in packaged flour.

Another company with a global vision is Pillsbury. The Pillsbury Doughboy is used in India to sell a product that the company had just about abandoned in America: flour. Pillsbury (owned by General Mills) has many higher margin products such as microwave pizzas in other parts of the world, but it discovered that in this tradition-bound market, it needed to push the basics.

Even so, selling packaged flour in India has been almost revolutionary, because most Indian housewives still buy raw wheat in bulk, clean it by hand, store it in huge metal hampers, and, every week, carry some to a neighborhood mill, or *chakki*, where it is ground between two stones.

To help reach those housewives, the Doughboy himself has gotten a makeover. In TV advertising, he presses his palms together and bows in the traditional Indian greeting. He speaks six regional languages.

Pillsbury is exploiting a potentially huge business. India consumes about sixty-nine million tons of wheat a year, second only to China. (The United States consumes about twenty-six million tons.) Much of India's wheat ends up as *roti*, a flat bread prepared on a griddle that accompanies almost every meal. In a nation where people traditionally eat with their hands, *roti* is the spoon. The blue Pillsbury flour package, which features the Doughboy hoisting a *roti,* has become the market leader in Bombay.

Global marketing is not a one-way street, whereby only U.S. companies sell their wares and services throughout the world. Foreign competition in the domestic market used to be relatively rare but now is found in almost every industry. In fact, in many industries the United States has lost significant market share to imported products. In electronics, cameras, automobiles, fine china, tractors, leather goods, and a host of other consumer and industrial products, U.S. companies have struggled at home to maintain their market shares against foreign competitors.

For the past two decades, U.S. companies often appeared to have difficulty competing with foreign rivals. Today, however, America has embarked on a new productivity boom. The United States has the highest productivity among all industrialized countries. The United States is the low-cost producer among industrialized nations, with unit labor costs rising more slowly than in either Japan or Germany. The value of goods manufactured annually by America's 380,000 manufacturing companies is more than 50 percent greater than what's turned out in Japan and a third larger than the combined output of France, Germany, and Britain.[2] Since the early 1990s, no major industrial nation's output has grown faster. American business is fully prepared to compete in the global marketplace.

Importance of Global Marketing to the United States

Many countries depend more on international commerce than the United States does. For example, France, Britain, and Germany all derive more than 19 percent of their gross domestic product from world trade, compared to about 12 percent for the United States. Nevertheless, the impact of international business on the U.S. economy is still impressive:

- The United States exports about a fifth of its industrial production and a third of its farm products.[3]
- One of every sixteen jobs in the United States is directly or indirectly supported by exports.
- U.S. businesses export over $500 billion in goods to foreign countries every year, and almost a third of U.S. corporate profits is derived from international trade and foreign investment.[4]
- Exports account for 20 percent of America's growth in economic activity.[5]
- The United States is the world's leading exporter of grain, selling more than $12 billion of this product a year to foreign countries, or about one-third of all agricultural exports.[6]
- Chemicals, office machinery and computers, automobiles, aircraft, and electrical and industrial machinery make up almost half of all nonagricultural exports.

These statistics might seem to imply that practically every business in the United States is selling its wares throughout the world, but nothing could be further from the truth. About 85 percent of all U.S. exports of manufactured goods are shipped by 250 companies; less than 10 percent of all manufacturing businesses, or around 25,000 companies, export their goods on a reg-ular basis.[7] Most small- and medium-sized firms are essentially nonparticipants in global trade and marketing. Only the very large multinational companies have seriously attempted to compete worldwide. Fortunately, more of the smaller companies are now aggressively pursuing international markets.

The Fear of Trade and Globalization

The protests in Seattle and Genoa during meetings of the World Trade Organization and the protests in New York during the convocation of the World Bank and the International Monetary Fund (the three organizations are discussed later in the chapter) showed that many people fear world trade and globalization. What do they fear? The negatives of global trade are as follows:

- Millions of Americans have lost jobs due to imports or production shifts abroad. Most find new jobs—that pay less.
- Millions of others fear losing their jobs, especially at those companies operating under competitive pressure.
- Employers often threaten to export jobs if workers do not accept pay cuts.
- Service and white-collar jobs are increasingly vulnerable to operations moving offshore.[8]

Mike Dolan, deputy director of Public Citizens' Global Trade Watch, speaks of a phenomenon he calls "downward harmonization"—the term is a takeoff on "harmonization," which refers to efforts by business to create global products and regulatory policies that make it easier to move production anywhere in the world and to create jobs in developing countries. But those jobs, Dolan says, often go to countries with the weakest laws governing labor, health and safety, and the environment—countries where corporations can pay substandard wages to employ workers in sweatshop conditions. Dolan's group has documented how the movement of jobs across borders compromises living standards for workers in industrialized countries, and how pressure from international regulators and from big companies has hurt efforts to regulate dangerous technologies and hazardous products in developing countries. Even human rights issues suffer—getting pushed off the agenda in favor of business-driven rights like copyright protection. "It's a lowering of consumer protection globally," says Dolan.[9]

Dolan and others are concerned that globalization is destroying national cultures, as when McDonald's changes the world's eating habits; that it is destroying the environment; and that poor countries are not participating in the new wealth globalization creates. These are the grievances voiced at protests when global organizations convene.

Successful global marketers have discovered that the path to profitability is through tailoring products to various tastes and desires. A Japanese salesclerk displays a package of flounder and spinach stew, a jar of white bait porridge, and a wild duck cream stew, all produced by America's leading baby-food maker, Gerber. The Japanese baby-food market has tripled in the past fifteen years, and more than four hundred infant entries jostle for spots on Japan's jam-packed supermarket shelves.

Benefits of Globalization

A closer look, however, reveals that globalization has been the engine that creates jobs and wealth. Benefits of global trade include:

- In China and the rest of East Asia, more people rose out of poverty between 1990 and 2000 than the entire population of the United States. The main reason was global trade.[10]
- In Africa, with its many developing economies, per capita income rose 3.6 percent per year during the 1990s, double the 1.8 percent of developed countries, and trade was the single biggest reason.[11]
- Productivity grows more quickly when countries produce goods and services in which they have a comparative advantage (discussed later in the chapter). Living standards can go up faster.
- Global competition and cheap imports keep down prices, so inflation is less likely to arrest economic growth.
- An open economy spurs innovation with fresh ideas from abroad.
- Export jobs often pay more than other jobs.[12]
- Relatively few American workers are in direct competition with workers from poorer countries. Most U.S. workers produce goods and services for industries

that face little cross-border competition such as healthcare and construction. Immigration has a much more direct impact on American wages than trade does.[13]

The Globalization Track Record

International trade now accounts for almost 20 percent of global gross domestic product, up from just 10 percent a decade ago.[14] Nations such as Hungary, Malaysia, and even China have made the leap into high-end manufacturing—improving living standards and offering better careers for many workers.

Other nations have not fared as well. The key to success is a government that makes the best use of inflows of foreign investment and know-how. That requires a track record of business-friendly policies to lure multinationals and domestic entrepreneurs alike to train workers, invest in modern technology, and nurture local suppliers and managers.

It also means paying more attention to basics such as solid governmental policies, good public education, a legal system that protects property rights, and a society where prosperity is widely shared. These are the kind of pro-growth policies that most of East Asia employed to develop from sweatshops in the 1960s and 1970s to industrial powers.[15]

The old Soviet bloc demonstrates how competition is dividing Eastern Europe into winners and losers. Hungary and Poland are thriving, while Romania, Bulgaria, and, to some extent, the Czech Republic are lagging. Different approaches to privatization help explain this divergence. The Czech Republic and Romania essentially issued shares in local factories to their citizens—a policy that seemed like a fair way to benefit the public. But that approach put insiders in charge of their enterprises. Hungary, instead, sold factories to both local businesspeople and multinationals. That accelerated the restructuring of the manufacturing sector.[16]

The Impact of Terrorism on Global Trade

The terrorist attacks on America on September 11, 2001, changed forever the way the world conducts business. The immediate impact was a shrinkage of global trade. Globalization will continue because the world's major markets are too vitally integrated for globalization to stop. Nevertheless, the process will be slower and costlier.

Companies are paying more for insurance and to provide security for overseas staff and property. Heightened border inspections slow movements of cargo, forcing companies to stock more inventory. Tighter immigration policies curtail the liberal inflows of skilled and blue-collar workers that allowed companies to expand while keeping wages in check. Meanwhile, greater concern about political risk is causing companies to greatly narrow their horizons when making new investments.[17] The impact of terrorism will lessen over time, but multinational firms will always, now, be on guard.

Multinational Firms

The United States has a number of large companies that are global marketers. Many of them have been very successful. A company that is heavily engaged in international trade, beyond exporting and importing, is called a **multinational corporation**. Multinational corporations move resources, goods, services, and skills across national boundaries without regard to the country in which the headquarters is located. The leading multinational firms in the world are listed in Exhibit 4.1.

A multinational corporation is more than a business entity, as the following paragraph explains:

Discuss the impact of multinational firms on the world economy

multinational corporation
A company that is heavily engaged in international trade, beyond exporting and importing.

Exhibit 4.1

The World's Largest Multinational
Corporations

Rank	Company Name	Country	Revenues ($ Millions)	Number of Employees
1	Wal-Mart Stores	U.S.	219,812.0	1,383,000
2	ExxonMobil	U.S.	191,581.0	87,000
3	General Motors	U.S.	177,260.0	365,000
4	BP	Britain	174,218.0	365,000
5	Ford Motor	U.S.	162,412.0	352,748
6	DaimlerChrysler	Germany	136,897.3	372,470
7	Royal Dutch/Shell Group	Brit./Neth.	135,211.0	91,000
8	General Electric	U.S.	125,913.0	310,000
9	Toyota Motor	Japan	120,814.4	246,702
10	Citigroup	U.S.	112,022.0	268,000
11	Mitsubishi	Japan	105,813.9	43,000
12	Mitsui	Japan	101,205.6	36,116
13	ChevronTexaco	U.S.	99,699.0	67,568
14	Total Fina Elf	France	94,311.9	122,025
15	Nippon Telegraph & Telephone	Japan	93,424.0	213,000
16	Itochu	Japan	91,176.6	36,529
17	Allianz	Germany	85,929.2	179,946
18	International Business Machines	U.S.	85,866.0	319,876
19	ING Group	Netherlands	82,999.1	113,143
20	Volkswagen	Germany	79,267.3	322,070
21	Siemens	Germany	77,358.9	484,000
22	Sumitomo	Japan	77,140.1	30,264
23	Philip Morris	U.S.	72,944.0	175,000
24	Marubeni	Japan	71,756.6	31,000
25	Verizon Communications	U.S.	67,190.0	247,000

SOURCE: "The World's Largest Corporations," *Fortune,* July 22, 2002, F-1.

The multinational corporation is, among other things, a private "government," often richer in assets and more populous in stockholders and employees than are some of the nation-states in which it carries on business. It is simultaneously a "citizen" of several nation-states, owing obedience to their laws and paying them taxes, yet having its own objectives and being responsive to a management located in a foreign nation. Small wonder that some critics see in it an irresponsible instrument of private economic power or of economic "imperialism" by its home country. Others view it as an international carrier of advanced management science and technology, an agent for the global transmission of cultures bringing closer the day when a common set of ideals will unite mankind.[18]

Many multinational corporations are enormous. For example, the sales of both ExxonMobil and General Motors are larger than the gross domestic product of all but twenty-two nations in the world. A multinational company may have several worldwide headquarters, depending on where certain markets or technologies are. Britain's APV, a maker of food-processing equipment, has a different headquarters for each of its worldwide businesses. ABB Asea Brown Boveri, the European electrical engineering giant based in Zurich, Switzerland, groups its thousands of products and services into fifty or so business areas. Each is run by a leadership team that crafts global business strategy, sets product development priorities, and decides where to make its products. None of the teams work out of Zurich headquarters;

they are scattered around the world. Leadership for power transformers is based in Germany, electric drives in Finland, and process automation in the United States.

Multinational Advantage

Large multinationals have several advantages over other companies. For instance, multinationals can often overcome trade problems. Taiwan and South Korea have long had an embargo against Japanese cars for political reasons and to help domestic carmakers. Yet Honda USA, a Japanese-owned company based in the United States, sends Accords to Taiwan and Korea. Another example is Germany's BASF, a major chemical and drug manufacturer. Its biotechnology research at home is challenged by the environmentally conscious Green movement. So BASF moved its cancer and immune-system research to Cambridge, Massachusetts.

Another advantage for multinationals is their ability to sidestep regulatory problems. When U.S. drugmaker SmithKline (now GlaxoSmithKline) and Britain's Beecham decided to merge, it was in part so they could avoid licensing and regulatory hassles in their largest markets. The merged company can say it's an insider in both Europe and the United States. "When we go to Brussels, we're a member state [of the European Union]," one executive explains. "And when we go to Washington, we're an American company."[19]

Multinationals can also shift production from one plant to another as market conditions change. When European demand for a certain solvent declined, Dow Chemical instructed its German plant to switch to manufacturing a chemical that had been imported from Louisiana and Texas. Computer models help Dow make decisions like these so it can run its plants more efficiently and keep costs down.

Multinationals can take a great idea in one part of their empire and leverage it around the world. Managers at chipmaker ST Microelectronics' Malaysian plant recently figured out a way to radically compress the assembly time for certain chips, from five days to five hours. Now the company plans to transfer the technique to its Moroccan plant.[20]

Finally, multinationals can often save a lot in labor costs, even in highly unionized countries. For example, Xerox started moving copier-rebuilding work to Mexico, where wages are much lower. Its union in Rochester, New York, objected because it saw that members' jobs were at risk. Eventually, the union agreed to change work styles and to improve productivity to keep the jobs at home.

Global Marketing Standardization

Traditionally, marketing-oriented multinational corporations have operated somewhat differently in each country. They use a strategy of providing different product features, packaging, advertising, and so on. However, Ted Levitt, a Harvard professor, described a trend toward what he referred to as "global marketing," with a slightly different meaning.[21] He contended that communication and technology have made the world smaller so that almost everyone everywhere wants all the things they have heard about, seen, or experienced. Thus, he saw the emergence of global markets for standardized consumer products on a huge scale, as opposed to segmented foreign markets with different products. In this book, global marketing is defined as individuals and organizations using a global vision to effectively market goods and services across national boundaries. To make the distinction, we can refer to Levitt's notion as **global marketing standardization**.

Global marketing standardization presumes that the markets throughout the world are becoming more alike. Firms practicing global marketing standardization produce "globally standardized products" to be sold the same way all over the world. Uniform production should enable companies to lower production and marketing costs and increase profits. However, research indicates that superior sales and profits do not necessarily follow from global standardization.[22]

Levitt cited Coca-Cola, Colgate-Palmolive, and McDonald's as successful global marketers. His critics point out, however, that the success of these three companies is really based on variation, not on offering the same product everywhere.

global marketing standardization
Production of uniform products that can be sold the same way all over the world.

McDonald's, for example, changes its salad dressings and provides self-serve espresso for French tastes. It sells bulgogi burgers in South Korea and falafel burgers in Egypt. It also offers different products to suit tastes in Germany (where it offers beer) and Japan (where it offers sake). Further, the fact that Coca-Cola and Colgate-Palmolive sell some of their products in more than 160 countries does not signify that they have adopted a high degree of standardization for all their products globally. Only three Coca-Cola brands are standardized, and one of them, Sprite, has a different formulation in Japan. Some Colgate-Palmolive products are marketed in just a few countries. Axion paste dishwashing detergent, for example, was formulated for developing countries, and La Croix Plus detergent was custom made for the French market. Colgate toothpaste is marketed the same way globally, although its advanced Gum Protection Formula is used in only twenty-seven nations.

Nevertheless, some multinational corporations are moving toward a degree of global marketing standardization. Eastman Kodak has launched a world brand of blank tapes for videocassette recorders. Procter & Gamble (P&G) calls its new philosophy "global planning." The idea is to determine which product modifications are necessary from country to country while trying to minimize those modifications. P&G has at least four products that are marketed similarly in most parts of the world: Camay soap, Crest toothpaste, Head and Shoulders shampoo, and Pampers diapers. However, the smell of Camay, the flavor of Crest, and the formula of Head and Shoulders, as well as the advertising, vary from country to country.

External Environment Facing Global Marketers

Describe the external environment facing global marketers

A global marketer or a firm considering global marketing faces problems, often due to the external environment, as many of the same environmental factors that operate in the domestic market also exist internationally. These factors include culture, economic and technological development, political structure and actions, demographic makeup, and natural resources.

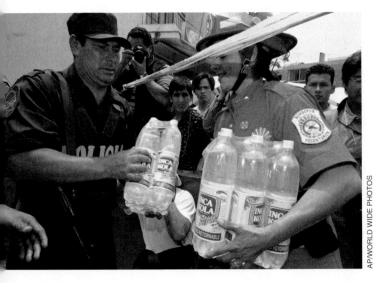

Culture

Central to any society is the common set of values shared by its citizens that determine what is socially acceptable. Culture underlies the family, the educational system, religion, and the social class system. The network of social organizations generates overlapping roles and status positions. These values and roles have a tremendous effect on people's preferences and thus on marketers' options. Inca Kola, a fruity, greenish-yellow carbonated drink, is the largest-selling soft drink in Peru. Despite being compared to "liquid bubble gum,"

Culture is a major factor marketers face when marketing products globally. Inca Kola, the largest selling soft drink in Peru, is a symbol of national heritage. Here a firefighter is delivering a case of the beverage to police engaged in a hostage stand-off.

the drink has become a symbol of national pride and heritage. The drink was invented in Peru and contains only fruit indigenous to the country. A local consumer of about a six-pack per day says, "I drink Inca Kola because it makes me feel like a Peruvian." He tells his young daughter, "This is our drink, not something invented overseas. It is named for your ancestors, the great Inca warriors."[23]

Culture may influence product preferences as in Inca Kola or influence the marketing mix in other ways. A U.S. luggage manufacturer found out that culture also affects thinking and perception. The company designed a new Middle East advertising campaign around the image of its luggage being carried on a magic flying carpet. A substantial part of a group in a marketing research study thought they were seeing advertising for Samsonite *carpets*. Green Giant learned that it could not use its Jolly Green Giant in parts of Asia where a green hat worn by a man signifies that he has an unfaithful wife.[24]

Business gift giving is common throughout the world. Yet culture can result in different interpretations of business gifts:

- Flowers are a well-recognized and appreciated gift in the United States, but in China, flowers can be interpreted as a symbol of death.

- A professional travel alarm clock is perfect for a U.S. businessperson who constantly travels. In China, however, clocks symbolize a severing of ties.

- In the United States, wrapping gifts with black or white paper is natural for fortieth birthdays and wedding celebrations. Although gifts in Japan should always be wrapped attractively in paper, black or white wrapping paper is used only for funerals.

- U.S. souvenirs such as electronic gadgets bearing a company logo are highly appreciated in the Middle East. It is important to understand, however, that gifts for wives are unacceptable in the Middle East, although gifts for children are allowed.

- While some alcohol-related corporate gifts are considered inappropriate in the United States, a good bottle of cognac is a much-appreciated business gift in Switzerland.

- In Argentina, business associates do not offer gifts to each other until a fairly close relationship has developed. Once it has, however, scarves, books, and music, in accordance with the recipient's tastes, are readily accepted.[25]

Language is another important aspect of culture. Marketers must take care in translating product names, slogans, production instructions, and promotional messages so as not to convey the wrong meaning. For example, Mitsubishi Motors had to rename its Pajero model in Spanish-speaking countries because the term describes a sexual activity. Toyota Motors' MR2 model dropped the number 2 in France because the combination sounds like a French swearword. The literal translation of Coca-Cola in Chinese characters means "bite the wax tadpole."

Each country has its own customs and traditions that determine business practices and influence negotiations with foreign customers. In many countries, personal relationships are more important than financial considerations. For instance, skipping social engagements in Mexico may lead to lost sales. Negotiations in Japan often include long evenings of dining, drinking, and entertaining, and only after a close personal relationship has been formed do business negotiations begin. The Japanese go through a very elaborate ritual when exchanging business cards. An American businesswoman was unaware of this important cultural tradition. She came into a meeting and tossed some of her business cards across the table at a group of stunned Japanese executives. One of them turned his back on her and walked out. The deal never went through.

Making successful sales presentations abroad requires a thorough understanding of the country's culture. Germans, for example, don't like risk and need strong reassurance. A successful presentation to a German client will emphasize three points: the bottom-line benefits of the product or service, that there will be strong service support, and that the product is guaranteed.[26] In southern Europe, it is an insult to show a price list. Without negotiating, you will not close the sale. The English want plenty of documentation for product claims and are less likely to simply accept the word of the sales representative. Scandinavian and Dutch companies are more likely to approach business transactions as Americans do than are companies in any other country.[27]

Fortunately, some habits and customs seem to be the same throughout much of the world. A study of 37,743 consumers from forty different countries found that 95 percent brushed their teeth daily.[28] Other activities that majorities worldwide engage in include reading a newspaper, listening to the radio, taking a shower, and washing their hair.

Economic and Technological Development

A second major factor in the external environment facing the global marketer is the level of economic development in the countries where it operates. In general, complex and sophisticated industries are found in developed countries, and more basic industries are found in less developed nations. Higher average family incomes are common in the more developed countries compared to the less developed markets. Larger incomes mean greater purchasing power and demand not only for consumer goods and services but also for the machinery and workers required to produce consumer goods.

To appreciate marketing opportunities (or lack of them), it is helpful to examine the five stages of economic growth and technological development: traditional society, preindustrial society, takeoff economy, industrializing society, and fully industrialized society.

The Traditional Society

traditional society
A society in the earliest stages of economic development, largely agricultural, with a social structure and value system that provide little opportunity for upward mobility.

Countries in the traditional stage are in the earliest phase of development. A **traditional society** is largely agricultural, with a social structure and value system that provide little opportunity for upward mobility. The culture may be highly stable, and economic growth may not get started without a powerful disruptive force. Therefore, introducing single units of technology into such a country is probably wasted effort. In Ghana, for instance, a tollway sixteen miles long and six lanes wide, intended to modernize distribution, does not connect to any city or village or other road.

The Preindustrial Society

preindustrial society
A society in the second stage of economic development, involving economic and social change and the emergence of a middle class with an entrepreneurial spirit.

The second stage of economic development, the **preindustrial society**, involves economic and social change and the emergence of a middle class with an entrepreneurial spirit. Nationalism may begin to rise, along with restrictions on multinational organizations. Countries like Madagascar and Uganda are in this stage. Effective marketing in these countries is very difficult because they lack the modern distribution and communication systems that U.S. marketers often take for granted. Peru, for example, did not establish a television network until 1975.

The Takeoff Economy

takeoff economy
A society in the third stage of economic development, involving a period of transition from a developing to a developed nation.

The **takeoff economy** is the period of transition from a developing to a developed nation. New industries arise and a generally healthy social and political climate emerges. Kenya and Vietnam have entered the takeoff stage. Although the political situation in Kenya is not considered particularly healthy, there are significant areas of economic growth. Oil exploration is increasing and Kenya is set to become the world's largest exporter of tea. In an effort to develop its economy, Vietnam now offers large tax breaks to foreign investors that promise jobs. Gold Medal Footware, headquartered in Taiwan, now employs five hundred young workers in Danang and hopes to increase the number to twenty-five hundred.

The Industrializing Society

The fourth phase of economic development is the **industrializing society**. During this era, technology spreads from sectors of the economy that powered the takeoff to the rest of the nation. Mexico, China, India, and Brazil are among the nations in this phase of development.

industrializing society
A society in the fourth stage of economic development, when technology spreads from sectors of the economy that powered the takeoff to the rest of the nation.

Countries in the industrializing stage begin to produce capital goods and consumer durable products. These industries also foster economic growth. As a result, a large middle class begins to emerge, and the demand for luxuries and services grows.

One of the fastest growing economies in the world today (about 7–8 percent per year) is China. This has resulted in per capita incomes quadrupling in only the last decade and a half. A population of 1.2 billion is producing a gross domestic product of over $1.4 trillion a year. This new industrial giant will be the world's largest manufacturing zone, the largest market for such key industries as telecommunications and aerospace, and one of the largest users of capital.

Rapidly growing large markets like China create enormous opportunities for American global marketers. One tempting market, for example, is the twenty-one million babies born in China each year. One-child families are the rule, so parents spare few expenses bringing up the baby. The Walt Disney Company is in department stores in a dozen or so Chinese cities with the Disney Babies line of T-shirts, rattles, and crib linens—all emblazoned with likenesses of baby Mickey Mouses and other characters.

The Fully Industrialized Society

The **fully industrialized society**, the fifth stage of economic development, is an exporter of manufactured products, many of which are based on advanced technology. Examples include automobiles, computers, airplanes, oil exploration equipment, and telecommunications gear. Britain, Japan, Germany, France, Canada, and the United States fall into this category.

fully industrialized society
A society in the fifth stage of economic development, a system based on the export of manufactured products, many of which are based on advanced technology.

The wealth of the industrialized nations creates tremendous market potential. Therefore, industrialized countries trade extensively. Also, industrialized nations usually ship manufactured goods to developing countries in exchange for raw materials like petroleum, precious metals, and bauxite.

Political Structure and Actions

Political structure is a third important variable facing global marketers. Government policies run the gamut from no private ownership and minimal individual freedom to little central government and maximum personal freedom. As rights of private property increase, government-owned industries and centralized planning tend to decrease. But rarely will a political environment be at one extreme or the other. India, for instance, is a republic with elements of socialism, monopoly capitalism, and competitive capitalism in its political ideology. Each year the Heritage Foundation publishes a ranking of countries according to their level of economic freedom. The Foundation considers fifty economic variables including banking and finance, trade policy, and regulation. The freest economies in order are Hong Kong, Singapore, Ireland, New Zealand, Luxembourg, the United States, the Netherlands, and Australia. The most repressed is North Korea.[29]

Many countries have changed from a centrally planned economy to a market-oriented one. Eastern European nations like Hungary and Poland have also been moving quickly with market reforms. Many of the reforms have increased foreign trade and investment. For example, in Poland, foreigners are now allowed to invest in all areas of industry, including agriculture, manufacturing, and trade. Poland even gives companies that invest in certain sectors some tax advantages.

Changes leading to market-oriented economies are not restricted to Eastern Europe and Russia. Many countries within Latin America are also attempting market reforms. Countries like Brazil and Mexico are reducing government control over many sectors of the economy. They are also selling state-owned companies to foreign and domestic investors and removing trade barriers that have protected their markets against foreign competition. Brazil has now overtaken Italy and Mexico to become the tenth largest automobile manufacturer in the world. India has recently opened up its market of nine hundred million consumers. Although India's per capita average income is quite low ($330), an estimated 250 million+ Indians have enough income to be considered middle class.

Actions by governments can either help or hinder competitors. Unfortunately, governments often do the latter. In a very unusual move, the government of Thailand has decided to launch a chain of more than three thousand Thai restaurants worldwide over the next five years, with the largest number, more than a thousand, slated for the United States. The restaurants, which will go by the names Elephant Jump for the fast-food branches, Cool Basil for the mid-priced restaurants, and Golden Leaf for the upscale eateries, are believed to be the first ever launched by a government.[30] These restaurants will compete with private restaurants around the world.

Another potential cloud on the horizon for some types of companies doing business abroad is the threat of nationalization, whereby a government takes over the ownership of certain industries or companies, such as airlines in Italy and Bull Computer in France, to infuse more capital into their development. Industries are also nationalized to allow domestic corporations to sell vital goods below cost. For example, for many years France has been supplying coal to users at a loss.

Legal Considerations

Closely related to and often intertwined with the political environment are legal considerations. Nationalistic sentiments of the French led to a law that requires pop music stations to play at least 40 percent of their songs in French (even though French teenagers love American and English rock and roll).

Many legal structures are designed to either encourage or limit trade. Here are some examples:

- *Tariff: a tax levied on the goods entering a country.* For example, the United States imposed a stiff tariff on steel imports in an effort to protect about five thousand U.S. jobs.

- *Quota: a limit on the amount of a specific product that can enter a country.* The United States has strict quotas for imported textiles, sugar, and many dairy products. Several U.S. companies have sought quotas as a means of protection from foreign competition. For example, Harley-Davidson convinced the U.S. government to place quotas on large motorcycles imported to the United States. These quotas gave the company the opportunity to improve its quality and compete with Japanese motorcycles.

- *Boycott: the exclusion of all products from certain countries or companies.* Governments use boycotts to exclude companies from countries with which they have a political dispute. Several Arab nations boycotted Coca-Cola because it maintained distributors in Israel.

- *Exchange control: a law compelling a company earning foreign exchange from its exports to sell it to a control agency, usually a central bank.* A company wishing to buy goods abroad must first obtain foreign currency exchange from the control agency. Generally, exchange controls limit the importation of luxuries. For instance, Avon Products drastically cut back new production lines and products in the Philippines because exchange controls prevented the company from converting pesos to dollars to ship back to the home office. The pesos had to be used in the Philippines. China restricts the amount of foreign currency each Chinese company is allowed to keep from its exports. Therefore, Chinese companies must usually get the government's approval to release funds before they can buy products from foreign companies.

- *Market grouping: also known as a common trade alliance; occurs when several countries agree to work together to form a common trade area that enhances trade opportunities.* The best-known market grouping is the European Union (EU), whose members are Austria, Belgium, Denmark, Finland, France, Germany, Greece, Ireland, Italy, Luxembourg, the Netherlands, Portugal, Spain, Sweden, and the United Kingdom. The EU, which was known as the European Community before 1994, has been evolving for more than four decades, yet until recently, many trade barriers existed among member nations.

- *Trade agreement: an agreement to stimulate international trade.* Not all government efforts are meant to stifle imports or investment by foreign corporations. The Uruguay Round of trade negotiations is an example of this. Likewise, China's most favored nation (MFN) status is considered a trade agreement. The largest Latin American trade agreement is **Mercosur,** which includes Brazil, Argentina, Chile, Bolivia, Uruguay, and Paraguay. The elimination of most tariffs among the trading partners has resulted in trade revenues of over $16 billion annually. The economic boom created by Mercosur will undoubtedly cause other nations to seek trade agreements on their own or enter Mercosur. The European Union, discussed on page 107, hopes to have a free-trade pact with Mercosur in the future.

Mercosur
The largest Latin American trade agreement, which includes Brazil, Argentina, Uruguay, and Paraguay.

Uruguay Round

The **Uruguay Round** is an agreement to dramatically lower trade barriers worldwide. Adopted in 1994, the agreement has been signed by 142 nations.[31] It is the most ambitious global trade agreement ever negotiated. The agreement has reduced tariffs by one-third worldwide. This, in turn, should raise global income by $235 billion annually. Perhaps most notable is the recognition of the new global realities. For the first time an agreement covers services, intellectual property rights, and trade-related investment measures such as exchange controls.

The Uruguay Round made several major changes in world trading practices:

Uruguay Round
An agreement to dramatically lower trade barriers worldwide; created the World Trade Organization.

- *Entertainment, pharmaceuticals, integrated circuits, and software:* The rules protect patents, copyrights, and trademarks for twenty years. Computer programs receive fifty years' protection and semiconductor chips receive ten years'. But many developing nations have a decade to phase in patent protection for drugs. France, which limits the number of U.S. movies and TV shows that can be shown, refused to liberalize market access for the U.S. entertainment industry.

- *Financial, legal, and accounting services:* Services came under International trading rules for the first time, creating a vast opportunity for these competitive U.S. industries. Now it is easier for managers and key personnel to be admitted to a country. Licensing standards for professionals, such as doctors, cannot discriminate against foreign applicants. That is, foreign applicants cannot be held to higher standards than domestic practitioners.

- *Agriculture:* Europe is gradually reducing farm subsidies, opening new opportunities for such U.S. farm exports as wheat and corn. Japan and Korea are beginning to import rice. But U.S. growers of sugar and citrus fruit have had their subsidies trimmed.

- *Textiles and apparel:* Strict quotas limiting imports from developing countries are being phased out, causing further job losses in the U.S. clothing trade. But retailers and consumers are the big winners, because quotas have added $15 billion a year to clothing prices.

- *A new trade organization:* The **World Trade Organization (WTO)** replaced the old **General Agreement on Tariffs and Trade (GATT)**, which was created in 1948. The old GATT contained extensive loopholes that enabled countries to avoid the trade-barrier reduction agreements—a situation similar to obeying the law only if you want to! Today, all WTO members must fully comply with all agreements under the Uruguay Round. The WTO also has an effective dispute settlement procedure with strict time limits to resolve disputes.

The service agreement under the Uruguay Round requires member countries to create adequate penalties against counterfeiting and piracy. China, which

World Trade Organization (WTO)
A trade organization that replaced the old General Agreement on Tariffs and Trade (GATT).

General Agreement on Tariffs and Trade (GATT)
Provided loopholes that enabled countries to avoid trade-barrier reduction agreements.

is joining the WTO, has done little to control its rampant piracy problems. The Chinese government estimates that counterfeit products with a total value of $16 billion are sold in the country each year.[32] Gillette estimates that a minimum of 25 percent of the firm's razor blades and Duracell batteries sold each year in China are fake. Procter & Gamble estimates that 20 percent of its products in China are fakes. The company has found products it doesn't even produce such as Head and Shoulders soap and Safeguard shampoo! Japan estimates that seven million of the eleven million motorcycles sold in China each year are fake Yamaha, Honda, and Suzuki machines.[33] The Chinese government is beginning to move more aggressively against counterfeiting with its admission to the WTO.

The trend toward globalization has brought to the fore several specific examples of the influence of political structures and legal considerations: the North American Free Trade Agreement, the Free Trade Agreement of the Americas, the Association of Southeast Asian Nations, the Asia-Pacific Economic Cooperation, and the European Union.

North American Free Trade Agreement

North American Free Trade Agreement (NAFTA)
An agreement between Canada, the United States, and Mexico that created the world's largest free-trade zone.

At the time it was instituted, the **North American Free Trade Agreement (NAFTA)** created the world's largest free-trade zone. Ratified by the U.S. Congress in 1993, the agreement includes Canada, the United States, and Mexico, with a combined population of 360 million and economy of $6 trillion.

Canada, the largest U.S. trading partner, entered a free-trade agreement with the United States in 1988. Thus, most of the new long-run opportunities for U.S. business under NAFTA have been in Mexico, America's third largest trading partner. Tariffs on Mexican exports to the United States averaged just 4 percent before the treaty was signed, and most goods entered the United States duty-free. Therefore, the main impact of NAFTA was to open the Mexican market to U.S. companies. When the treaty went into effect, tariffs on about half the items traded across the Rio Grande disappeared. The pact removed a web of Mexican licensing requirements, quotas, and tariffs that limited transactions in U.S. goods and services. For instance, the pact allowed U.S. and Canadian financial-services companies to own subsidiaries in Mexico for the first time in fifty years.

The real test of NAFTA is whether it can deliver rising prosperity on both sides of the Rio Grande. For Mexicans, NAFTA must provide rising wages, better benefits, and an expanding middle class with enough purchasing power to keep buying goods from the United States and Canada. As of 2001, that scenario was working. Between 1993 and 2001, U.S. exports to Mexico rose 170 percent, far above the 68 percent for overall U.S. exports. Mexican exports to the United States grew 241 percent during the same period.[34]

NAFTA, to date, has been very successful, displacing some workers but creating far more jobs than have been lost. For more information about NAFTA, see the Office of NAFTA & Inter-American Affairs at **http://www.mac.doc.gov/nafta**.

Free Trade Area of the Americas

Free Trade Agreement of the Americas (FTAA)
A regional trade agreement that, when signed, will create a regional trading zone encompassing 36 countries in North and South America.

The goal of **Free Trade Area of the Americas (FTAA)**, is to establish a free-trade zone similar to NAFTA throughout the Western Hemisphere. If created, FTAA would likely supplant Mercosur, a free-trade agreement between Brazil, Argentina, Uruguay and Paraguay. If ratified by all member nations, FTAA would become the largest trading zone in the world, consisting of 800 million people in thirty-four countries in both North and South America with a combined gross domestic product of $11 trillion![35] Similar to NAFTA, FTAA pledges to support trade "without barriers, without subsidies, without unfair practices, and with an increasing stream of productive investments."[36] Leaders from each of the thirty-four countries have agreed to finish FTAA negotiations by 2005. If that occurs, over the next decade nontariff barriers would be removed, tariffs would gradually be reduced to zero, rules for investing and financial markets would be standardized, and a process would be established to handle trade disputes.[37] For more information about FTAA, see **www.ftaa-alca.org**. For more information about Mercosur, see **http://www.mercosur.org/english/default.htm**.

Association of Southeast Asian Nations

The **Association of Southeast Asian Nations** (**ASEAN**) and the **Asia-Pacific Economic Cooperation** (**APEC**) are the two largest and most important regional trading groups in Asia. ASEAN is a trade agreement between Brunei Darussalam, Cambodia, Indonesia, Laos, Malaysia, Myanmar, the Philippines, Singapore, Thailand, and Vietnam. Together, these countries form a market of more than 330 million people. U.S. trade with ASEAN countries is sizable, exceeding $75 billion a year. In fact, the United States is ASEAN's largest trading partner, while the member nations of ASEAN are the United States' fifth largest trade group. ASEAN member countries have agreed to create an ASEAN free-trade area beginning in 2015 for the six original countries (Brunei Darussalam, Indonesia, Malaysia, the Philippines, Singapore, and Thailand) and in 2018 for newer member countries (Cambodia, Laos, Myanmar, and Vietnam).[38] For more information about ASEAN, see **http://www.aseansec.org**.

> **Association of Southeast Asian Nations (ASEAN)**
> A trade agreement among ten Asian nations.
>
> **Asia-Pacific Economic Cooperation (APEC)**
> A trade agreement that includes most ASEAN countries plus eleven other nations.

Asia-Pacific Economic Cooperation

The Asia-Pacific Economic Cooperation (APEC) is a broader agreement between Australia, Canada, Chile, People's Republic of China, Hong Kong, China, Japan, Korea, Mexico, New Zealand, Papua New Guinea, Peru, Russia, the United States, and all the members of ASEAN, except Cambodia, Laos, and Myanmar.[39] APEC's twenty-one member countries contain 2.5 billion people, account for 47 percent of all global trade, and have a combined gross domestic product of over $18 trillion. APEC countries agreed to begin reducing trade barriers in the year 2000, though it will take until 2020 for all trade barrier reductions to be completely phased in. For more information about APEC, see **http://www.apecsec.org.sg**.

European Union

In 1993, all twelve member countries of the European Community (EC) ratified the **Maastricht Treaty**. The treaty, named after the Dutch town where it was developed, set forth a plan to take the EC further toward economic, monetary, and political union. Officially called the Treaty on European Union, the document outlined plans for tightening bonds among the member states and creating a single market. The European Commission, which drafted the treaty, notes that Maastricht has created over two million new jobs.

> **Maastricht Treaty**
> An agreement among twelve countries of the European Community to pursue economic, monetary, and political union.

Although the heart of the treaty deals with developing a unified European market, Maastricht was also intended to increase integration among the European Union members in areas much closer to the core of national sovereignty. The treaty created a common currency and an independent central bank in 1999. The European Monetary Union (EMU) was launched on January 1, 1999, with Austria, Belgium, Finland, France, Germany, Ireland, Italy, Luxembourg, the Netherlands, Portugal, and Spain as members. Britain, Sweden, and Denmark chose not to join at the outset. Greece, which was too far from the EMU's stringent fiscal requirement to join at the start, joined later. A new European Central Bank was

In 2002, the euro became the currency of the EMU. The currency board pictured here shows the currencies of the EMU countries in euros. Read more about the impact of the euro in the Global Perspectives box in Chapter 17.

© AFP/CORBIS

also created along with an EMU currency called the euro. Together, the members of the EMU have a $6.4 trillion economy, the second largest in the world.

Common foreign, security, and defense policies are also goals, as well as European citizenship—whereby any European Union citizen can live, work, vote, and run for office anywhere in the member countries. The treaty standardized trade rules and coordinated health and safety standards. Duties, customs procedures, and taxes were also standardized. A driver hauling cargo from Amsterdam to Lisbon can now clear four border crossings by showing a single piece of paper. Before the Maastricht Treaty, the same driver would have carried two pounds of paper to cross the same borders. The overall goal is to end the need for a special product for each country—for example, a different Braun electric razor for Italy, Germany, France, and so forth. Goods marked GEC (goods for EC) can be traded freely, without being retested at each border. For more information about the Maastricht Treaty and the European Union, go to **http://europa.eu.int/index-en.htm**.

American businesses have recently been stung by aggressive antitrust actions taken by the European Commission, the European Union's executive branch. By EU law, the Commission must review any merger or acquisition involving any companies with significant revenues in the European Union. Thus, the Commission threatened to block AOL's acquisition of Time Warner unless Virgin Records was sold first. It was. The biggest action to date was denying the merger of General Electric with Honeywell, both U.S. firms. Even Jack Welch, the legendary General Electric CEO, could not persuade the European Commission to let the merger go through.[40]

Some economists have called the European Union the "United States of Europe." It is an attractive market, with 320 million consumers and purchasing power almost equal to that of the United States. But the European Union will probably never be a United States of Europe. For one thing, even in a united Europe, marketers will not be able to produce a single Europroduct for a generic Euroconsumer. With twelve different languages and individual national customs, Europe will always be far more diverse than the United States. Thus, product differences will continue. It will be a long time, for instance, before the French begin drinking the instant coffee that Britons enjoy. Preferences for washing machines also differ: British homemakers want front-loaders, and the French want top-loaders; Germans like lots of settings and high spin speeds; Italians like lower speeds. Even European companies that think they understand Euroconsumers often have difficulties producing "the right product." Atag Holdings NV, a diversified Dutch company whose main business is kitchen appliances, was confident it could cater to both the "potato" and "spaghetti" belts—marketers' terms for consumer preferences in northern and southern Europe. But Atag quickly discovered that preferences vary much more than that. For example, on its ovens, burner shape and size, knob and clock placement, temperature range, and colors vary greatly from country to country. Although Atag's kitchenware unit has lifted foreign sales to 25 percent of its total from 4 percent in the mid-1980s, it now believes that its range of designs and speed in delivering them, rather than the magic bullet of a Euro-product, will keep it competitive.[41]

An entirely different type of problem facing global marketers is the possibility of a protectionist movement by the European Union against outsiders. For example, European automakers have proposed holding Japanese imports at roughly their current 10 percent market share. The Irish, Danes, and Dutch don't make cars and have unrestricted home markets; they would be unhappy about limited imports of Toyotas and Datsuns. But France has a strict quota on Japanese cars to protect Renault and Peugeot. These local carmakers could be hurt if the quota is raised at all.

Interestingly, a number of big U.S. companies are already considered more "European" than many European companies. Coca-Cola and Kellogg's are considered classic European brand names. Ford and General Motors compete for the largest share of auto sales on the continent. IBM and Dell Computer dominate their markets. General Electric and AT&T are already strong all over Europe and have invested heavily in new manufacturing facilities throughout the continent.

Although many U.S. firms are well prepared to contend with European competition, the rivalry is perhaps more intense there than anywhere else in the world.

In the long run, it is questionable whether Europe has room for eight mass-market automakers, including Ford and GM, when the United States sustains just three. Similarly, an integrated Europe probably doesn't need twelve national airlines.

A global map of the regional trade agreements discussed in the preceding sections is depicted in Exhibit 4.2

Demographic Makeup

The three most densely populated nations in the world are China, India, and Indonesia. But that fact alone is not particularly useful to marketers. They also need to know whether the population is mostly urban or rural, because marketers may not have easy access to rural consumers. In Belgium about 90 percent of the population lives in an urban setting, whereas in Kenya almost 80 percent of the population lives in a rural setting. Belgium is thus the more attractive market.

Just as important as population is personal income within a country. The wealthiest countries in the world include Japan, the United States, Switzerland, Sweden, Canada, Germany, and several of the Arab oil-producing nations. At the other extreme are countries like Mali and Bangladesh, with a fraction of the per capita purchasing power of the United States. However, a low per capita income is not in itself enough reason to avoid a country. In countries with low per capita incomes, wealth is not evenly distributed. There are pockets of upper- and middle-class consumers in just about every country of the world. In some countries, such as India, the number of consumers is surprisingly large.

The most significant global economic news of the past decade is the rise of a global middle class. From Shekou, China, to Mexico City and countless cities in between, there are traffic jams, bustling bulldozers, and people hawking tickets to

Global Map of Regional Trade Agreements **Exhibit 4.2**

NAFTA (North American Free Trade Agreement) United States, Canada, and Mexico.

FTAA (Free Trade Area of the Americas) United States, Canada, Mexico, and all the countries in Central America and South America.

Maastricht Treaty of Europe Austria, Belgium, Denmark, Finland, France, Germany, Greece, Italy, Ireland, Luxembourg, The Netherlands, Portugal, Spain, Sweden, and the United Kingdom.

ASEAN Brunei Darussalam, Cambodia, Indonesia, Laos, Malaysia, Myanmar, the Philippines, Singapore, Thailand, and Vietnam.

APEC Australia, Canada, Chile, China, Hong Kong, Japan, Korea, Mexico, New Zealand, Papua New Guinea, Peru, Russia, the United States, and all members of ASEAN except Cambodia, Laos, and Myanmar.

various events. These are all signs of a growing middle class. In China, per capita incomes are rising rapidly. Developing countries, excluding Eastern Europe and the republics of the former Soviet Union, should grow about 4 percent annually over the next decade.

Growing economies demand professionals. In Asia, accountants, stock analysts, bankers, and even middle managers are in short supply. Rising affluence also creates demand for consumer durables such as refrigerators, VCRs, and automobiles. Companies like Procter & Gamble and Gillette offer an array of products at different price points to attract and keep customers as they move up the income scale. The percentage of the world's population that lives in industrialized nations has been declining since 1960, because industrialized nations have grown slowly and developing nations have grown rapidly. In this decade, more than 90 percent of the world's population growth will occur in developing countries and only 10 percent in the industrialized nations. The United Nations reports that in 2000, 79 percent of the world's population resided in developing countries—for example, Guinea, Bolivia, and Pakistan.

Natural Resources

A final factor in the external environment that has become more evident in the past decade is the shortage of natural resources. For example, petroleum shortages have created huge amounts of wealth for oil-producing countries such as Norway, Saudi Arabia, and the United Arab Emirates. Both consumer and industrial markets have blossomed in these countries. Other countries—such as Indonesia, Mexico, and Venezuela—were able to borrow heavily against oil reserves in order to develop more rapidly. On the other hand, industrial countries like Japan, the United States, and much of Western Europe experienced rampant inflation in the 1970s and an enormous transfer of wealth to the petroleum-rich nations. But during much of the 1990s, when the price of oil fell, the petroleum-rich nations suffered. Many were not able to service their foreign debts when their oil revenues were sharply reduced. The U.S. dependence on foreign oil will likely remain high.

Petroleum is not the only natural resource that affects international marketing. Warm climate and lack of water mean that many of Africa's countries will remain importers of foodstuffs. The United States, on the other hand, must rely on Africa for many precious metals. Japan depends heavily on the United States for timber and logs. A Minnesota company manufactures and sells a million pairs of disposable chopsticks to Japan each year. The list could go on, but the point is clear. Vast differences in natural resources create international dependencies, huge shifts of wealth, inflation and recession, export opportunities for countries with abundant resources, and even a stimulus for military intervention.

▌ Global Marketing by the Individual Firm

Identify the various ways of entering the global marketplace

A company should consider entering the global marketplace only after its management has a solid grasp of the global environment. Some relevant questions are "What are our options in selling abroad?" "How difficult is global marketing?" and "What are the potential risks and returns?" Concrete answers to these questions would probably encourage the many U.S. firms not selling overseas to venture into the international arena. Foreign sales could be an important source of profits.

Companies decide to "go global" for a number of reasons. Perhaps the most stimulating reason is to earn additional profits. Managers may feel that international sales will result in higher profit margins or more added-on profits. A second stimulus is that a firm may have a unique product or technological advantage not available to other international competitors. Such advantages should result in major business successes abroad. In other situations, management may have exclusive

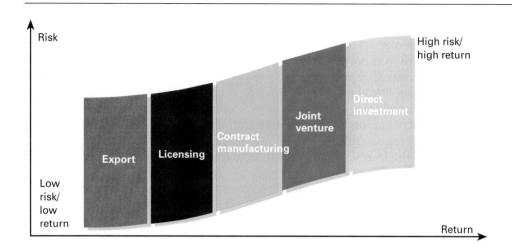

market information about foreign customers, marketplaces, or market situations not known to others. While exclusivity can provide an initial motivation for international marketing, managers must realize that competitors can be expected to catch up with the information advantage of the firm. Finally, saturated domestic markets, excess capacity, and potential for economies of scale can also be motivators to "go global." Economies of scale mean that average per-unit production costs fall as output is increased.

Many firms form multinational partnerships—called strategic alliances—to assist them in penetrating global markets; strategic alliances are examined in Chapter 6. Five other methods of entering the global marketplace are, in order of risk, export, licensing, contract manufacturing, the joint venture, and direct investment. (See Exhibit 4.3.)

Export

When a company decides to enter the global market, exporting is usually the least complicated and least risky alternative. **Exporting** is selling domestically produced products to buyers in another country. A company, for example, can sell directly to foreign importers or buyers. Exporting is not limited to huge corporations such as General Motors or 3M. Indeed, small companies account for 96 percent of all U.S. exporters, but only 30 percent of the export volume. The United States is the world's largest exporter. Many small businesses claim that they lack the money, time, or knowledge of foreign markets that exporting requires. The U.S. Department of Commerce is trying to make it easier for small businesses to begin exporting. The department has created a pilot program in which it has hired a private company to represent up to fifty small businesses at specific international trade fairs. For example, FTS, Inc., was hired to represent small firms at a trade show in Italy. The company handed out company brochures and other sales information to interested prospective Italian clients. Also, after the show was over, FTS gave each participating American company a list of potential Italian distributors for their products. Each American firm paid only $2,500 to be represented at the trade fair. For companies interested in exporting, the U.S. government stands ready to help in a variety of ways.

The U.S. Commercial Service within the Department of Commerce promotes itself as "Your Global Business Partner." It offers trade specialists in more than a hundred U.S. cities and eighty countries to help beginning exporters, as well as those already engaged in global marketing, increase their business. The primary services offered by the U.S. Commercial Service are marketing research, trade events, locating qualified buyers and partners, and global business consulting. These services are explained in more detail in Exhibit 4.4.

exporting
Selling domestically produced products to buyers in another country.

On Line

Recently, the U.S. Commercial Service launched a joint venture with IBM called BuyUSA.com. The Internet service offers one-on-one export counseling provided by the U.S. Commercial Service. In addition, the site provides Web-based sales leads to exporters. A U.S. exporter fills out a questionnaire on its product offerings and receives access to qualified foreign buyers. We suggest that you go to the Web site and take the BuyUSA tour and demo to learn more about how the U.S. Commercial Service aids American firms wanting to "go global." For those interested in international business, a nongovernmental Web site that offers links to hundreds of useful sites is available from the International Federation of International Trade Associations (**http://fita.org**).

Instead of selling directly to foreign buyers, a company may decide to sell to intermediaries located in its domestic market. The most common intermediary is the export merchant, also known as a **buyer for export**, which is usually treated like a domestic customer by the domestic manufacturer. The buyer for export assumes all risks and sells internationally for its own account. The domestic firm is involved only to the extent that its products are bought in foreign markets.

A second type of intermediary is the **export broker**, who plays the traditional broker's role by bringing buyer and seller together. The manufacturer still retains title and assumes all the risks. Export brokers operate primarily in agriculture and raw materials.

Export agents, a third type of intermediary, are foreign sales agents-distributors who live in the foreign country and perform the same functions as domestic manufacturers' agents, helping with international financing, shipping, and so on. The U.S. Department of Commerce has an agent-distributor service that helps about five thousand U.S. companies a year find an agent or distributor in virtually any country of the world. A second category of agents resides in the manufacturer's country but represents foreign buyers. This type of agent acts as a hired purchasing agent for foreign customers operating in the exporter's home market.

buyer for export
An intermediary in the global market that assumes all ownership risks and sells globally for its own account.

export broker
An intermediary who plays the traditional broker's role by bringing buyer and seller together.

export agent
An intermediary who acts like a manufacturer's agent for the exporter. The export agent lives in the foreign market.

Licensing

Another effective way for a firm to move into the global arena with relatively little risk is to sell a license to manufacture its product to someone in a foreign country. **Licensing** is the legal process whereby a licensor allows another firm to use its manufacturing process, trademarks, patents, trade secrets, or other proprietary knowledge. The licensee, in turn, pays the licensor a royalty or fee agreed on by both parties.

Because licensing has many advantages, U.S. companies have eagerly embraced the concept. For instance, Marvel Enterprises granted 4Kids Entertainment international licensing rights for X-Men-the-Movie, X-Men classic, Spider Man classic, the Fantastic Four, Silver Surfer, the Incredible Hulk, Avengers, Captain America, Iron Man, and Daredevil.

A licensor must make sure it can exercise the control over the licensee's activities needed to ensure proper quality, pricing, distribution, and so on. Licensing may also create a new competitor in the long run, if the licensee decides to void the license agreement. International law is often ineffective in stopping such actions. Two common ways of maintaining effective control over licensees are shipping one or more critical components from the United States or locally registering patents and trademarks to the U.S. firm, not to the licensee. Garment companies maintain control by delivering only so many labels per day; they also supply their own fabric and collect the scraps, and do accurate unit counts.

Franchising is a form of licensing that has grown rapidly in recent years. More than 350 U.S. franchisors operate more than thirty-two thousand outlets in foreign countries, bringing in sales of over $6 billion.[42] Over half of the international franchises are for fast-food restaurants and business services. New Horizons Computer Learning Centers has been franchising internationally since 1992. It now has

licensing
The legal process whereby a licensor agrees to let another firm use its manufacturing process, trademarks, patents, trade secrets, or other proprietary knowledge.

Exhibit 4.4

Assistance Provided by the U.S.
Commercial Service

Marketing Research

COUNTRY COMMERCIAL GUIDES

provide overviews for doing business in more than 120 countries with information on market conditions, best export prospects, financing, finding distributors, and legal and cultural issues.

INDUSTRY SECTOR ANALYSES

offer succinct international market information on specific industries that can help determine market potential, market size, and competitors for a firm's products and services.

INTERNATIONAL MARKET INSIGHTS

report on current conditions in specific country markets and identify upcoming opportunities for generating sales.

WEBCASTS

present market opportunities and insights on how to do business in specific countries. They are available on **http://www.usatrade.gov**.

FLEXIBLE MARKET RESEARCH

provides timely, customized, reliable answers to a company's inquiries about a market and its receptivity to its products and services.

Locating Qualified Buyers and Partners

MATCHMAKER TRADE DELEGATIONS

let managers meet face-to-face with qualified business prospects in two to four promising export markets. The program includes comprehensive country briefings, logistical support, and follow-up counseling.

INTERNATIONAL PARTNER SEARCHES

deliver detailed company information on up to five prescreened potential partners that have expressed an interest in a company's products and services.

GOLD KEY

arranges one-on-one appointments with carefully selected potential business partners in a targeted export market.

INTERNATIONAL COMPANY PROFILES

provide affordable, fast credit checks and background information on potential international buyers and other business partners.

TRADE OPPORTUNITY PROGRAM

provides daily worldwide trade leads from companies seeking to purchase or represent a firm's products or services. These leads are reviewed by our trade specialists and commercial officers.

GOLD KEY USA

helps international buyers locate the best U.S. suppliers. Counseling before and after business meetings is part of this service.

VIRTUAL MATCHMAKERS

give sales managers the opportunity to meet with groups of prescreened international business prospects and get answers to your market questions in an interactive video conference focusing on your industry.

VIDEO GOLD KEY

enables sales managers to meet with individual potential business partners throughout the world without leaving the United States. Available now in more than 100 U.S. and international locations.

Trade Events

COMMERCIAL NEWS USA

promotes a firm's products and services to more than 400,000 international buyers. A great way to reach a targeted audience eager to buy U.S. products and services, this magazine has a proven track record of high response rates and sales results.

SHOW TIME

provides in-depth counseling at major trade shows from a team of market and industry specialists who know the local and regional markets.

CATALOG EXHIBITIONS

showcase a firm's product and service literature in fast-growing export markets around the world.

SINGLE COMPANY PROMOTIONS

provide meeting space and carefully screened invitation lists to help a company present successful seminars featuring its products and services.

INTERNATIONAL BUYER PROGRAM

recruits and brings more than 125,000 international end-users and distributors to visit top U.S. trade shows. The Commercial Service helps organize meetings and provide matchmaking services and business counseling to help generate sales.

U.S. PAVILIONS

put your company in the best international trade shows with access to thousands of buyers. One-on-one matching at the show with potential buyers arranged by the commercial service's team of market and industry specialists can help generate sales and long-term business relationships at these high-volume shows.

Consulting

- Determine the best markets for a firm's products and services.

- Develop an effective export strategy.

- Evaluate international competitors.

- Identify and comply with legal and regulatory issues.

- Locate export financing.

- Settle disputes.

- Win contract bids.

- Learn about cultural and business protocol.

SOURCE: U.S. Commercial Service.

locations in forty-five countries. Most of the inquiries New Horizons receives about franchise opportunities come through the U.S. Commercial Service's Gold Key program (see Exhibit 4.4).[43]

Contract Manufacturing

Firms that do not want to become involved in licensing or to become heavily involved in global marketing may engage in **contract manufacturing**, which is private-label manufacturing by a foreign company. The foreign company produces a certain volume of products to specification, with the domestic firm's brand name on the goods. The domestic company usually handles the marketing. Thus, the domestic firm can broaden its global marketing base without investing in overseas plants and equipment. After establishing a solid base, the domestic firm may switch to a joint venture or direct investment.

Joint Venture

Joint ventures are similar to licensing agreements. In a **joint venture**, the domestic firm buys part of a foreign company or joins with a foreign company to create a new entity. A joint venture is a quick and relatively inexpensive way to go global and to gain needed expertise.[44] For example, Robert Mondavi Wineries entered into a joint venture with Baron Philippe de Rothschild, owner of Bordeaux's First Growth chateau, Mouton-Rothschild. They created a wine in California called Opus One. It was immediately established as the American vanguard of quality and price. Mondavi has entered other joint ventures with the Frescobaldi family in Tuscany and with Errazuriz in Chile. "We're doing these wines from around the world because they're going to come here anyway," he said. "The industry is going global, so we're going global, too."[45]

Recently, General Motors entered into a joint venture with Avtovaz, a Soviet-era auto manufacturer in Russia, to produce a car to be called the Chevrolet Niva. Russia is expected to be one of the top ten growth markets for cars during the first decade of the 2000s, and GM wants to be a player. The assembly and engineering will be done at low cost in Russia. GM is providing $333 million and technology. Avtovaz offers skilled workers and a distribution system.[46]

Joint ventures can be very risky. Many fail; others fall victim to a takeover, in which one partner buys out the other. In a survey of 150 companies involved in joint ventures that ended, three-quarters were found to have been taken over by Japanese partners. Gary Hamel, a professor at the London Business School, regards joint ventures as a race to learn: The partner that learns fastest comes to dominate the relationship and can then rewrite its terms.[47] Thus, a joint venture becomes a new form of competition.

Sometimes joint venture partners simply can't agree on management strategies and policies. For example, Procter & Gamble and its Vietnamese partner can't agree on what to do next in their unprofitable joint venture. Consumer-products giant P&G wants to inject more cash into the business; but because Phuong Dong Soap & Detergent, its state-owned partner, has said it's unable to provide the cash to match it, P&G has offered to buy out the Vietnamese stake. So far Phuong Dong has flatly refused to sell, and Ministry of Planning and Investment officials have described such an option as "impossible."[48]

Robert Mondavi Winery has a very agressive joint venture strategy. Opus One is the result of pairing with the premier French vintner Baron Philippe de Rothschild. The brand has been well received by American wine drinkers and hailed for its high quality.

COURTESY OF OPUS ONE

In a successful joint venture, both parties gain valuable skills from the alliance. In the General Motors–Suzuki joint venture in Canada, for example, both parties have contributed and gained. The alliance, CAMI Automotive, was formed to manufacture low-end cars for the U.S. market. The plant, run by Suzuki management, produces the Geo Metro/Suzuki Swift—the smallest, highest-gas-mileage GM car sold in North America—as well as the Geo Tracker/Suzuki Sidekick sport utility vehicle. Through CAMI, Suzuki has gained access to GM's dealer network and an expanded market for parts and components. GM avoided the cost of developing low-end cars and obtained models it needed to revitalize the lower end of its product line and its average fuel-economy rating. The CAMI factory may be one of the most productive plants in North America. There GM has learned how Japanese carmakers use work teams, run flexible assembly lines, and manage quality control.

Direct Investment

Active ownership of a foreign company or of overseas manufacturing or marketing facilities is **direct foreign investment**. Direct foreign investment by U.S. manufacturers is currently about $50 billion annually. Direct investors have either a controlling interest or a large minority interest in the firm. Thus, they have the greatest potential reward and the greatest potential risk.

Wal-Mart has now made direct investments in nine countries with more than 1,100 stores. International sales now top $32 billion.[49] Not all of its global investments have been successful. In Germany, Wal-Mart bought the twenty-one store Wertkauf hypermarket chain in 1997 and then seventy-four unprofitable and often decrepit Interspar stores in 1998. Problems in integrating and upgrading the stores resulted in at least $200 million in losses. Like all other German stores, Wal-Mart stores in Germany are required by law to close at 8 P.M. on weekdays and 4 P.M. on Saturdays, and they cannot open at all on Sundays. And costs are astronomical. Derek Rowe, an American brought over to supervise the $5 million renovation of the Dortmund store, estimated that construction costs in Germany are five times what they are in the United States.[50]

Now Wal-Mart seems to be turning the corner on its international operations. It is pushing operational authority down to country managers in order to respond better to local cultures. Wal-Mart enforces certain core principles such as "everyday low prices," but country managers handle their own buying, logistics, building design, and other operational decisions.

Direct investment by American companies in China has mushroomed. Today, direct investment there amounts to more than $8 billion, up from less than $200 million in 1989.[51] U.S. firms that have recently built manufacturing facilities in China include LaCrosse Footwear (winter boots), Lexmark (printers), Motorola (cell phones), Rubbermaid (cookware and storage products), Raleigh (bicycles), Cooper Tools (wrenches), Mattel Murray (Barbie doll playhouses), and Samsonite (luggage). These firms intend to sell not only to the 1.2 billion Chinese population but also to U.S. customers and the global market.

Sometimes firms make direct investments because they can find no suitable local partners. Also, direct investments avoid the communication problems and conflicts of interest that can arise with joint ventures. Other firms simply don't want to share their technology, which they fear may be stolen or ultimately used against them by creating a new competitor. Texas Instruments (TI) has historically been one of the latter companies. "TI was a technology company that hated to share anything," said Akira Ishikawa, senior vice president of TI's semiconductor group. "It wasn't in the culture to share or teach the most advanced semiconductor technologies. It was taboo. If you talked about that, you might be fired immediately."[52] Now TI has changed its attitude and entered into five Asian joint ventures. The reason was primarily to spread its financial risk.

A firm may make a direct foreign investment by acquiring an interest in an existing company or by building new facilities. It might do so because it has trouble transferring some resource to a foreign operation or getting that resource locally. One important resource is personnel, especially managers. If the local labor market is tight, the firm may buy an entire foreign firm and retain all its employees instead of paying higher salaries than competitors.

The United States is a popular place for direct investment by foreign companies. In 2002, the value of foreign-owned businesses in the United States was more than $475 billion.

direct foreign investment
Active ownership of a foreign company or of overseas manufacturing or marketing facilities.

The Global Marketing Mix

5

List the basic elements involved in developing a global marketing mix

To succeed, firms seeking to enter into foreign trade must still adhere to the principles of the marketing mix. Information gathered on foreign markets through research is the basis for the four Ps of global marketing strategy: product, place (distribution), promotion, and price. Marketing managers who understand the advantages and disadvantages of different ways of entering the global market and the effect of the external environment on the firm's marketing mix have a better chance of reaching their goals.

The first step in creating a marketing mix is developing a thorough understanding of the global target market. Often this knowledge can be obtained through the same types of marketing research used in the domestic market (see Chapter 8). However, global marketing research is conducted in vastly different environments. Conducting a survey can be difficult in developing countries, where telephone ownership is rare and mail delivery slow or sporadic. Drawing samples based on known population parameters is often difficult because of the lack of data. In some cities in South America, Mexico, and Asia, street maps are unavailable, streets are unidentified, and houses are unnumbered. Moreover, the questions a marketer can ask may differ in other cultures. In some cultures, people tend to be more private than in the United States and do not like to respond to personal questions on surveys. For instance, in France, questions about one's age and income are considered especially rude.

Product and Promotion

With the proper information, a good marketing mix can be developed. One important decision is whether to alter the product or the promotion for the global marketplace. Other options are to radically change the product or to adjust either the promotional message or the product to suit local conditions.

One Product, One Message

The strategy of global marketing standardization, which was discussed earlier, means developing a single product for all markets and promoting it the same way all over the world. For instance, Procter & Gamble uses the same product and promotional themes for Head and Shoulders in China as it does in the United States. The advertising draws attention to a person's dandruff problem, which stands out in a nation of black-haired people. Head and Shoulders is now the best-selling shampoo in China despite costing over 300 percent more than local brands. Buoyed by its success with Head and Shoulders, Procter & Gamble is using the same product and same promotion strategy with Tide detergent in China. It also used another common promotion tactic that it has found to be successful in the United States. The company spent half a million dollars to reach agreements with local washing machine manufacturers, which now include a free box of Tide with every new washer.

Metabolife International has devised five herbal medicine products for both the Chinese and the American markets. Both markets have a huge demand for herbal products, but their vastly different concepts of medicine have stymied companies that want to unlock both markets with one product. Until now, most dietary-supplement companies in the United States have hawked just one Chinese herb at a time. In China, however, herbs are almost always mixed together in formulas that are sold in a dizzying number of combinations depending on specific symptoms. A typical Chinese pharmacy, for example, offers dozens of herbal cold formulas depending on symptoms.

Metabolife selected five ailments—the common cold, arthritis, headache, premenstrual syndrome, and upset stomach—and asked a team of Chinese doctors to come up with one formula for each. Next, Metabolife researchers analyzed the formulas, identified the active ingredients, and put them in pill form. The result is a form of Chinese medicine called Chinac, which offers U.S. consumers a mixture of herbs similar to that found in medicine sold in China but without the variety found in a Chinese pharmacy. For example, the cold pill, called Immune Health Formula, is a mix of herbs aimed at relieving a typical winter flu.

But Metabolife figures Americans and Chinese are becoming more similar in their approach to herbal medicine. For Americans, Chinac offers a quick and easy entrée into what is for most consumers an unfamiliar field of medicine. For Chinese consumers, Metabolife may offer a welcome change to the confusing choices they face in a Chinese pharmacy.[53]

Global media—especially satellite and cable TV networks like CNN International, MTV Networks, and British Sky Broadcasting—make it possible to beam advertising to audiences unreachable a few years ago. "Eighteen-year-olds in Paris have more in common with eighteen-year-olds in New York than with their own parents," says William Roedy, director of MTV Europe. Almost all of MTV's advertisers run unified, English-language campaigns in the twenty-eight nations the firm reaches. The audiences "buy the same products, go to the same movies, listen to the same music, sip the same colas. Global advertising merely works on that premise."[54] Although teens throughout the world prefer movies above all other forms of television programming, they are closely followed by music videos, stand-up comedy, and then sports.

Even a one-product, one-message strategy may call for some changes to suit local needs, such as variations in the product's measurement units, package sizes, and labeling. Pillsbury, for example, changed the measurement unit for its cake mixes because adding "cups of" has no meaning in many developing countries. Also, in emerging economies, such as India, many people still buy a single cigarette rather than a package and one egg rather than a dozen. Hindustan Lever, a subsidiary of giant Lever Brothers, flooded the market with small packets of shampoo called sackets instead of bottles. The firm also markets toothpaste the same way. Now shampoo in sackets outsells traditional bottles. Hindustan now commands more than 70 percent of the market.[55]

Unchanged products may fail simply because of cultural factors. The game *Trivial Pursuit* failed in Japan. It seems that getting the answers wrong can be seen as a loss of face. Any type of war game tends to do very poorly in Germany, even though Germany is by far the world's biggest game-playing nation. A successful game in Germany has plenty of details and thick rulebooks. *Monopoly* remains the world's favorite board game; it seems to overcome all cultural barriers. The game is available in twenty-five languages, including Russian, Croatian, and Hebrew.

© GILLES BASSIGNAC/GETTY IMAGES/GETTY NEWS SERVICES

A one-product, one-message strategy does not work for all products. Parker Brothers' *Monopoly*, however, uses this strategy very successfully. A French Riviera version of the popular game debuted at the 2000 Cannes film festival. Depicted here is the Russian gameboard.

Product Invention

In the context of global marketing, product invention can be taken to mean either creating a new product for a market or drastically changing an existing product.

Mattel, Scrabble
Hasbro, Monopoly
Visit Mattel's Scrabble site and Hasbro's Monopoly site. Which game has more of an international presence on the Internet? Does this surprise you? Why?

http://www.mattelscrabble.com
http://www.monopoly.com

On Line

McDonald's

How does McDonald's alter its menu to suit specific cultural tastes? Visit at least seven country sites and record the different menu items you find.

http://www.mcdonalds.com

On Line

For the Japanese market, Nabisco had to remove the cream filling from its Oreo cookies because Japanese children thought they were too sweet. Ford thinks it can save billions on its product development costs by developing a single small-car chassis and then altering its styling to suit different countries. Campbell Soup invented a watercress and duck gizzard soup that is now selling well in China. It is also considering a cream of snake soup. Frito-Lay's most popular potato chip in Thailand is shrimp flavored. Dormont Manufacturing Company makes a simple gas hose that hooks up to deep-fat fryers and similar appliances. Sounds like something that could be sold globally, right? Wrong—in Europe differing national standards means that a different hose is required for each country. Minutiae such as the color of the plastic coating or how the end pieces should be attached to the rest of the hose and the couplings themselves create a myriad of design problems for Dormont Manufacturing.

Coca Cola's Thums Up cola outsells Coke by a four-to-one margin in India. In Turkey, Coke sells a pear-flavored drink, while in Germany it offers a berry drink. Now, Coke is developing soft drinks for tastes around the world.

Consumers in different countries use products differently. For example, in many countries, clothing is worn much longer between washings than in the United States, so a more durable fabric must be produced and marketed. For Peru, Goodyear developed a tire that contains a higher percentage of natural rubber and has better treads than tires manufactured elsewhere in order to handle the tough Peruvian driving conditions. Rubbermaid has sold millions of open-top wastebaskets in America; Europeans, picky about garbage peeking out of bins, wanted bins with tight lids that snap into place.

Product Adaptation

Another alternative for global marketers is to slightly alter a basic product to meet local conditions. Additional pizza toppings offered by Domino's in Japan include corn, curry, squid, and spinach. Japanese housewives couldn't fit American-size bottles of Joy dish soap on their shelves. Procter & Gamble changed the bottle to a compact cylinder that took less space. When Lewis Woolf Griptight, a British manufacturer of infant accessories such as pacifiers, came to the United States, it found subtle differences between United Kingdom and American parents. Elizabeth Lee, marketing manager, noted, "There are subtle differences, but many problems are the same. Whether a cup spills in America or in Madagascar or in the U.K., moms aren't going to like it," she said. "We didn't need to redo all the research to find out that people didn't want cups that spill, but we still had to do research on things like color and packaging."[56] The brand name "Kiddiwinks" is a British word for pacifiers. In the United States, the name was changed to "Binky" because of positive parental reactions in marketing research tests.

The French take great pride in their culture and architecture. McDonald's has become the focal point of French fears of economic globalization and the infringement of American pop culture on their Gallic traditions. McDonald's French branch claims that it is not global or American, but part of the French reality. Etienne Aussedat, McDonald's communications director in France, states, "Our restaurants are franchises and they are run by French businessmen. We buy our potatoes from farms in northern France, our beef from western France and our lettuces from Perpignan in southern France."[57] The concrete box restaurant design is being replaced by "de chez nous." Wooden structures made with trees from the Vosges Mountains in eastern France and façades that reflect traditional brasseries are now being built. The burgers feature "sauce à la moutarde," cantal cheese, and buns made by "La Boulangarie Française."

When products are defective, the way a corporation handles the situation varies from country to country. Consider the tainted milk story in the "Ethics in Marketing" box.

Pouring on the Apologies

Even in a country where apologies are an art form, Yumi Ito was taken aback by the gymnastics that two businessmen performed in her living room one Sunday.

Dressed in dark blue suits, the two men—employees of Japan's largest milk maker—literally prostrated themselves before her. Their heads touched the floor as they bowed over and over again to express remorse. The problem: Their company had produced a bad batch of milk that sickened Ms. Ito's one-and-a-half-year-old daughter. Their performance "was painful to watch," Ms. Ito said afterward, her recovered daughter jumping around beside her.

In a quintessentially Japanese show of corporate damage control, Snow Brand Milk Products Company put 2,000 employees into the streets—fully 13 percent of its workforce—to personally bow, scrape, apologize, and pay cash compensation to each of more than 14,000

people sickened by tainted milk from its factory in Osaka. About 180 victims were hospitalized.

The effort is remarkable even for Japan, where companies such as Snow Brand often send out employees to apologize for product flaws that in other countries might rate a replacement and a form letter. Yet Snow Brand executives say the crisis—heightened by criticism that senior officials were responding inadequately—demands extraordinary countermeasures. At stake was the fate of a conglomerate with $12.1 billion in annual sales of dairy products, wine, frozen pizzas, and other goods.

Noriaki Okuyama, a burly manager who plans ice-cream-sales strategy for eastern Japan, earnestly briefed the Snow Brand employees. His instructions: apologize first, then ask about the victim's health. After that, face the delicate issue of compensation. If possible, get a receipt for the

health-related expenses the customers are claiming. If that isn't possible, or if they get mad, back off and pay them anyway, he said. How much? "It's your judgment call," said Mr. Okuyama, sweat streaming down his brow. "If the amount is within 30,000 yen ($280), it should be OK." And don't talk back, no matter how angry the customer gets, Mr. Okuyama warned.

Then came questions: "What about pets?" asked a grizzled man in a gray suit. "Pets are the same as people," Mr. Okuyama replied. "We have to bear expenses for their sickness, too."[58]

Do you think that Snow Brand took the proper action? Can you imagine a U.S. manufacturer doing the same? Why or why not? Lawyers file thousands of product liability lawsuits in America each year. If U.S. companies followed the lead of Japanese firms in apologizing for defective products, might there be fewer lawsuits?

Only two years after the contaminated milk scandal that rocked Japan's Milk Products Company, company executives were forced to bow to the press again. This time the company was charged with allegedly passing off imported Australian beef as domestic in order to benefit from a government scheme to buy up homegrown beef as a precaution against mad cow disease.

AP/WORLD WIDE PHOTOS

Message Adaptation

Another global marketing strategy is to maintain the same basic product but alter the promotional strategy. Bicycles are mainly pleasure vehicles in the United States. In many parts of the world, however, they are a family's main mode of transportation. Thus, promotion in these countries should stress durability and efficiency. In contrast, U.S. advertising may emphasize escaping and having fun.

Harley-Davidson decided that its American promotion theme, "One steady constant in an increasingly screwed-up world," wouldn't appeal to the Japanese market. The Japanese ads combine American images with traditional Japanese ones: American riders passing a geisha in a rickshaw, Japanese ponies nibbling at a Harley motorcycle. Waiting lists for Harleys in Japan are now six months long.

A new campaign for ExxonMobil offers a fresh twist on message adaptation. The company wants the ads to carry the same look and feel regardless of the country in which they appear. To do this, ExxonMobil has produced five hours of commercial footage to be used as a library by local markets. As many as six different casts act out essentially the same story lines, with local markets picking which vignettes they want to use in their region. The company will use the footage to advertise its brands in a hundred countries. The campaign, which carries the tagline "We are drivers too," was tweaked to account for cultural differences. For example, the advertising agency asked actors to alternate using their right and left hands in scenes where they were eating food. In some regions, food is customarily eaten using only the right hand. ExxonMobil spent $150 million on the campaign.[59]

Global marketers find that promotion is a daunting task in some countries. For example, commercial television time is readily available in Canada but severely restricted in Germany. Until recently, marketers in Indonesia had only one subscription TV channel with few viewers (120,000 out of a nation of more than 200 million people). Because of this limited television audience, several marketers, such as the country's main Toyota dealer, had to develop direct-mail campaigns to reach their target markets.

Some cultures view a product as having less value if it has to be advertised. In other nations, claims that seem exaggerated by U.S. standards are commonplace. On the other hand, Germany does not permit advertisers to state that their products are "best" or "better" than those of competitors, a description commonly used in U.S. advertising. The hard-sell tactics and sexual themes so common in U.S. advertising are taboo in many countries. Procter & Gamble's advertisements for Cheer detergents were voted least popular in Japan because they used hard-sell testimonials. The negative reaction forced P&G to withdraw Cheer from the Japanese market. In the Middle East, pictures of women in print advertisements have been covered with censors' ink.

Language barriers, translation problems, and cultural differences have generated numerous headaches for international marketing managers. Consider these examples:

- A toothpaste claiming to give users white teeth was especially inappropriate in many areas of Southeast Asia, where the well-to-do chew betel nuts and black teeth are a sign of higher social status.

- Procter & Gamble's Japanese advertising for Camay soap nearly devastated the product. In one commercial, a man meeting a woman for the first time immediately compared her skin to that of a fine porcelain doll. Although the ad had worked in other Asian countries, the man came across as rude and disrespectful in Japan.

Pricing

Once marketing managers have determined a global product and promotion strategy, they can select the remainder of the marketing mix. Pricing presents some unique problems in the global sphere. Exporters must not only cover their production costs but also consider transportation costs, insurance, taxes, and tariffs. When deciding on a final price, marketers must also determine what customers are willing to spend on a particular product. Marketers also need to ensure that their foreign buyers will pay them. Because developing nations lack mass purchasing power, selling to them often poses special pricing problems. Sometimes a product can be simplified in order to lower the price. The firm must not assume that low-income countries are willing to accept lower quality, however. Although the nomads of the Sahara are very poor, they still buy expensive fabrics to make their clothing. Their survival in harsh conditions and extreme temperatures requires this expense. Additionally, certain expensive luxury items can be sold almost anywhere.

Companies must also be careful not to be so enthusiastic about entering a market that they use poor pricing strategies. Sales of Compaq computers have been growing very rapidly in China, but partially because the company (now owned by Hewlett-Packard) has been giving away computers against its will. Recently, a Chinese distributor failed to repay $32 million for computers that Compaq had extended on credit. Analysts say Compaq is now owed over $100 million by delinquent dealers and distributors in China.

 Also, money-back guarantees don't always work well in developing nations. Amway in China told customers that if they were not satisfied, they could bring the product (soap) back for a full refund, no questions asked—even if the bottles were empty. Some enterprising third parties began repackaging the soap and returning the empty bottles. Others just scoured empty bottles out of trash cans to seek refunds. When refunds mounted to $100,000 per day, Amway rescinded the policy, only to face angry distributors who marched into offices to complain. They felt they were entitled to the refunds. Amway offers the same guarantee worldwide—with very different results—so it was surprised by the Chinese reaction.[60]

Dumping

 Dumping is generally considered to be the sale of an exported product at a price lower than that charged for the same or a like product in the "home" market of the exporter. This practice is regarded as a form of price discrimination that can potentially harm the importing nation's competing industries. Dumping may occur as a result of exporter business strategies that include (1) trying to increase an overseas market share, (2) temporarily distributing products in overseas markets to offset slack demand in the home market, (3) lowering unit costs by exploiting large-scale production, and (4) attempting to maintain stable prices during periods of exchange rate fluctuations.

Historically, the dumping of goods has presented serious problems in international trade. As a result, dumping has led to significant disagreements among countries and diverse views about its harmfulness. Some trade economists view dumping as harmful only when it involves the use of "predatory" practices that intentionally try to eliminate competition and gain monopoly power in a market. They believe that predatory dumping rarely occurs and that antidumping enforcement is a protectionist tool whose cost to consumers and import-using industries exceeds the benefits to the industries receiving protection.

The Uruguay Round rewrote the international law on dumping. Now, under the agreement:

1. Dumping disputes are resolved by the World Trade Organization.

2. Dumping terms are specifically defined. For example, the "dumped price" must be at least 5 percent below the home market price before it is considered dumping.

3. At least 25 percent of the members of an industry must support its government filing a dumping complaint with the World Trade Organization. In other words, a government can't file a complaint if only one or two firms complain (unless they make up 25 percent of the industry).

Countertrade

Global trade does not always involve cash. Countertrade is a fast-growing way to conduct global business. In **countertrade**, all or part of the payment for goods or services is in the form of other goods or services. Countertrade is thus a form of barter (swapping goods for goods), an age-old practice whose origins have been traced back to cave dwellers. The U.S. Department of Commerce says that roughly 30 percent of all global trade is countertrade. In fact, both India and China have made billion-dollar government purchasing lists, with most of the goods to be paid for by countertrade.

One common type of countertrade is straight barter. For example, PepsiCo sends Pepsi syrup to Russian bottling plants and in payment gets Stolichnaya vodka, which is then marketed in the West. Another form of countertrade is the compensation agreement. Typically, a company provides technology and equipment for a

dumping
The sale of an exported product at a price lower than that charged for the same or a like product in the "home" market of the exporter.

countertrade
A form of trade in which all or part of the payment for goods or services is in the form of other goods or services.

plant in a developing nation and agrees to take full or partial payment in goods produced by that plant. For example, General Tire Company supplied equipment and know-how for a Romanian truck tire plant. In turn, General Tire sold the tires it received from the plant in the United States under the Victoria brand name. Pierre Cardin gives technical advice to China in exchange for silk and cashmere. In these cases, both sides benefit even though they don't use cash.

Atwood Richards is the world's largest company specializing in countertrade. When companies turn over unsold products to Atwood, they receive trade credits. The credits can be used to obtain other products and services Atwood has acquired—everything from hotel rooms and airline tickets to television advertising time, forklift trucks, carpeting, pulp, envelopes, steel castings, or satellite tracking systems.

Distribution

Solving promotional, price, and product problems does not guarantee global marketing success. The product still has to get adequate distribution. For example, Europeans don't play sports as much as Americans do, so they don't visit sporting-goods stores as often. Realizing this, Reebok started selling its shoes in about eight hundred traditional shoe stores in France. In one year, the company doubled its French sales. Harley-Davidson had to open two company-owned stores in Japan to get distribution for its Harley clothing and clothing accessories.

The Japanese distribution system is considered the most complicated in the world. Imported goods wind their way through layers of agents, wholesalers, and retailers. For example, a bottle of ninety-six aspirins costs about $20 because the bottle passes through at least six wholesalers, each of whom increases the selling price. As a result, the Japanese consumer pays the world's most exorbitant prices. These distribution channels seem to be based on historical and traditional patterns of socially arranged trade-offs, which Japanese officials claim are very hard for the government to change. Today, however, the system seems to be changing because of pressure from the Japanese consumer. Japanese shoppers are now placing low prices ahead of quality in their purchasing decisions. The retailer who can cut distribution costs and therefore the retail price gets the sale. For example, Kojima, a Japanese electronics superstore chain like the U.S. chains Circuit City and Best Buy, had to bypass General Electric's Japanese distribution partner Toshiba to import its merchandise at a good price. Toshiba's distribution system required refrigerators to pass through too many hands before they reached the retailer. Kojima went directly to GE headquarters in the United States and persuaded the company to sell it refrigerators, which were then shipped directly to Kojima. It is now selling GE refrigerators for about $800—half the price of a typical Japanese model.

Retail institutions in other countries also may differ from what a company is used to in its domestic market. The terms *department store* and *supermarket* may refer to types of retail outlets that are very different from those found in the United States. Japanese supermarkets, for example, are large multistory buildings that sell not only food but also clothing, furniture, and home appliances. Department stores are even larger outlets, but unlike their U.S. counterparts, they emphasize foodstuffs and operate a restaurant on the premises. For a variety of reasons, U.S.-type retail outlets do not exist or are impractical in developing countries. For instance, consumers may not have the storage space to keep food for several days. Refrigerators, when available, are usually small and do not allow for bulk storage. Attempting to build new retail outlets can be a frustrating battle. In Germany's Ruhr Valley, the discounter All Kauf SB-Warenhaus GmbH has struggled to build a store for fifteen years on land that it owns. Local authorities are blocking construction because they are afraid the store will hurt local retailers.

Europe's freight-rail system is a throwback to another era. No two countries use the same signaling systems or electric current for their trains. Trains in France and Britain run on the left side of dual-track lines, while those in the rest of Europe run on the right. Because France and Spain use two different gauges of track, trains crossing their shared border must stop to let each car be lifted so that its wheels can be changed.

In many developing nations, channels of distribution and the physical infrastructure are inadequate. To combat these problems, companies are using creative strategies. Colgate-Palmolive has introduced villagers in India to the concept of brushing teeth by rolling into villages with video vans that show half-hour infomercials on the benefits of toothpaste. The company received more than half of its revenue in that nation from rural areas in 2003. Until recently, the rural market was virtually invisible, due to a lack of distribution.

Certainly, not all global distribution is inefficient or primitive. United Parcel Service, through its wholly owned UPS Logistics Group, is embarking on an ambitious plan to dominate Asia's logistics business. UPS's new master plan envisions "superhubs" that will serve as single nodes for all incoming and outgoing goods.[61]

UPS Logistics recently opened a warehouse in Singapore, a joint venture with National Semiconductor Corporation. Every night at ten o'clock, the same unmarked truck goes past the tropical beaches of Malaysia on a two-hour journey south to the new warehouse. The cargo is also always the same: some of the most sophisticated semiconductors on earth, manufactured in a massive National Semiconductor plant outside Melaka. Most of the chips have a drop-dead delivery date of two or three days to factories throughout Asia, North America, and Europe, where they will eventually find their way into all manner of technology—from U.S. military aircraft to Japanese office equipment.

What distinguishes the 98,000-square-foot warehouse from others in the region is the invisible hand of custom-built software. In less than an hour, the incoming chips are bar coded, repackaged, and put aboard ships and planes. If an employee misdirects a box, the software shuts down a part of the system until the box is put in the correct slot or on the right conveyor belt.

The Impact of the Internet

In many respects "going global" is easier than it has ever been before. Opening an e-commerce site on the Internet immediately puts a company in the international marketplace. Sophisticated language translation software can make any site accessible to persons around the world. Global shippers such as UPS, FedEx, and DHL help solve international e-commerce distribution complexities. E4X, Inc., offers software to ease currency conversions. Sites that use E4X's software can post prices in U.S. dollars, then ask their customers what currency they wish to use for payment. If the answer is anything but dollars, E4X takes over the transaction and translates the price into any of twenty-two currencies, collects the payment from the customer, and pays the site in dollars, just as though it were any other transaction. Customers never realize they're dealing with a third party.[62]

Nevertheless, the promise of "borderless commerce" and the new "Internet economy" are still being restrained by the old brick-and-mortar rules, regulations, and habits. For example, Americans spend an average of $6,500 per year by credit card whereas Japanese spend less than $2,000. Many Japanese don't even have a credit card. So how do they pay for e-commerce purchases? 7-Eleven Japan, with over eight thousand convenience stores, has come to the rescue. eS-Books, the Japanese Web site partner of Yahoo! Japan, lets shoppers buy books and videos on the Internet, then specify to which 7-Eleven the merchandise is to be shipped. The buyer goes to that specific store and pays cash for the e-purchase.[63]

In Germany it is typically cheaper to buy books from Amazon.com in the United Kingdom rather than the local site. Why? Germany, France, and several

6

Discover how the Internet is affecting global marketing

Let's Buy It

What kind of deals can you find on LetsBuyIt.com? Would you be willing to buy a car this way? What about an appliance? A gift?

http://www.letsbuyit.com

On Line

other European states allow publishing cartels through which groups of book publishers can legally dictate retail prices to booksellers—both on-line and on the ground. *Galileo's Daughter,* a biography by Dava Sobel, for example, sells at the list price of 50.24 marks ($26.99) on Germany's Amazon.de; at Amazon.co.uk, it costs 40 percent less.[64]

The e-commerce site for the American clothing retailer Lands' End in Germany is not allowed to mention its unconditional refund policy because German retailers, which normally do not allow returns after fourteen days, sued and won a court ruling blocking mention of it.

Scandinavians, like the Japanese, are reluctant to use credit cards, the currency of the Internet, and the French have an *horreur* of revealing the private information that Net retailers ask for. French Web sites tend to be decidedly French. For example, FNAC, the largest French video, book, and music retailer, offers a daily "cultural newspaper" at its site.[65] A trendy Web site in France will have a black background, while bright colors and a geometrical layout give a site a German feel. Dutch surfers are keen on video downloads, and Scandinavians seem to have a soft spot for images of nature.[66]

Whatever their preferences in Web design, Europeans have shown themselves interested in saving money through Internet shopping. One of the hottest e-commerce sites in Europe, LetsBuyIt.com in Sweden, is about nothing but bargains.

CONNECT IT

Look back at the story about Universal Studios in Japan. Besides cultural factors, other uncontrollable variables in the global external environment include economic and technological, political, and demographic variables as well as natural resources.

Most products cannot be marketed exactly the same way all over the world. Different cultures, languages, levels of economic development, and distribution channels in global markets usually require either new products or modified products. Pricing, promotion, and distribution strategies must often be altered as well. There is no doubt that international markets will become even more important in the future.

USE IT

Study the Role of a Global Manager

As business becomes more global, chances are that you may become a global manager. Start learning right now what this means and if it's right for you. The life of a global manager can be hectic. One way to see if you might be cut out to be a global manager is to spend some time abroad. The ideal situation is to find a job overseas during the summer months. This experience will help you decide if you want to be a global manager. Also, it will look good on your résumé. One source of international jobs information is **http://www. internationaljobs.org/**.

Travel Abroad

Dene Harrington, senior relationship manager at Visa International in London, says: "We find that employers [worldwide] look favorably on people who have taken time out for traveling. They've shown that they're able to organize a trip, look after their security and finances. Experience of different cultures, confidence in meeting people, and self-reliance are very important skills in their future career, whatever that may be."[67]

STA Travel (**http://www.statravel.com**) with three hundred branches worldwide, specializes in student and youth travel. Students and those under age twenty-six with certain youth identification cards get discounts of up to a third off the published prices of airfares, hotels, city tours, around-the-world tickets, and overland tours.

Busabout (**http://www.busabout.com**) is a novel way for young travelers to explore Europe by road. Buses link seventy cities with service every one to two days in each direction allowing you the freedom to stop off for as long as you like along the way. The buses are nonsmoking and air-conditioned with an on-board guide to book your travel selections and accommodations as you go.

Hostels or budget hotels range from $12 to $22 a night. You decide when and where to start, stop off, or end the trip. Thus, you might buy a cheap "open-jaw" ticket (flying in to one city, departing from another). Arrive in Athens, for example, and return from London, or fly to Madrid and leave from Rome.

You can buy two types of passes at a 10 percent discount for students or those under twenty-six. A Consecutive Pass allows unlimited travel in the Busabout network, from two weeks to seven months. A Flexipass allows you to choose the number of traveling days within a time frame, ranging from ten days in two months to thirty days in four months.

A rail pass is another great way to get around Europe. Go to **http://railpass.com** for more information.

Changing Money Abroad

If you travel, work, or study abroad, you are going to need to change U.S. dollars into foreign currency. Making mistakes when changing money can cost you 10 to 20 percent of your bankroll. Here are a few tips about changing money abroad.

1. Know the exchange rate between U.S. dollars and the currencies of the countries you plan to visit before you go. Go to **http://www.cnnfn. com/markets/currencies** for the latest quotations. Keep up with the changing rates by reading *USA Today International* or the *International Herald Tribune* every day.

2. Avoid changing money at airports, train stations, and hotels. These places usually have the worst rates. Ask local people where they change money. Locals know where the best rates are.

3. Try to bargain with the clerk. Sometimes you can do better than the posted rate simply by asking.

4. Rather than making several small transactions, make one large exchange. This will often get you a better rate.

5. Don't change more than you will need. You'll pay another fee to change the foreign currency back to U.S. dollars.

6. Use a credit card. Typically, any major credit card will give you a better rate than a change booth or bank. Sometimes the spread is substantial, so minimize cash and use credit.

7. Traveler's checks usually have a worse exchange rate than cash. In other words, a $100 American Express traveler's check will give you less in exchange than a $100 bill. If your traveler's checks are lost or stolen, however, they will be replaced, so the peace of mind is usually worth the added expense.

8. Use your American ATM card to withdraw cash at foreign money machines. If your card is part of a global network, such as Cirrus or Plus, you may be able to withdraw money for a nominal fee at a reasonable exchange rate.

REVIEW IT

(1) **Discuss the importance of global marketing.** Businesspeople who adopt a global vision are better able to identify global marketing opportunities, understand the nature of global networks, and compete against foreign competition in domestic markets.

    1.1 What is meant by "having a global vision"? Why is it important?

    1.2 Isolationists have suggested that America would be much better off economically and politically if we just "built a wall" around the country and didn't deal with outsiders. Do you agree? Why or why not?

(2) **Discuss the impact of multinational firms on the world economy.** Multinational corporations are international traders that regularly operate across national borders. Because of their vast size and financial, technological, and material resources, multinational corporations have a great influence on the world economy. They have the ability to overcome trade problems, save on labor costs, and tap new technology.

2.1 Rubbermaid, the U.S. manufacturer of kitchen products and other household items, is considering moving to global marketing standardization. What are the pros and cons of this strategy?

2.2 Do you believe that multinationals are beneficial or harmful to developing nations? Why? What could foreign governments do to make them more beneficial?

3 **Describe the external environment facing global marketers.** Global marketers face the same environmental factors as they do domestically: culture, economic and technological development, political structure and actions, demography, and natural resources. Cultural considerations include societal values, attitudes and beliefs, language, and customary business practices. A country's economic and technological status depends on its stage of industrial development: traditional society, preindustrial society, takeoff economy, industrializing society, or fully industrialized society. The political structure is shaped by political ideology and such policies as tariffs, quotas, boycotts, exchange controls, trade agreements, and market groupings. Demographic variables include population, income distribution, and growth rate.

3.1 Many marketers now believe that teenagers in the developed countries are becoming "global consumers." That is, they all want and buy the same goods and services. Do you think this is true? If so, what has caused the phenomenon?

3.2 Renault and Peugeot dominate the French market but have no presence in the U.S. market. Why do you think that this is true?

3.3 **WRITING** Suppose that you are the marketing manager for a consumer-products firm that is about to undertake its first expansion abroad. Write a memo for your staff reminding them of the role culture will play in the new venture. Give examples.

3.4 **WRITING** Suppose that your state senator has asked you to contribute a brief article to her constituents' newsletter that answers the question, "Will there ever be a 'United States of Europe'?" Write a draft of your article, and include reasons why or why not.

3.5 **TEAM** Divide into six teams. Each team will be responsible for one of the following industries: entertainment; pharmaceuticals; computers and software; financial, legal, or accounting services; agriculture; and textiles and apparel. Interview one or more executives in each of these industries to determine how the Uruguay Round and NAFTA have affected and will affect their organizations. If a local firm cannot be contacted in your industry, use the library and the Internet to prepare your report.

3.6 What are the major barriers to international trade? Explain how government policies may be used to either restrict or stimulate global marketing.

3.7 Explain the impact of the Uruguay Round.

4 **Identify the various ways of entering the global marketplace.** Firms use the following strategies to enter global markets, in descending order of risk and profit: direct investment, joint venture, contract manufacturing, licensing, and export.

4.1 Candartel, an upscale manufacturer of lamps and lampshades in America, has decided to "go global." Top management is having trouble deciding how to develop the market. What are some market entry options for the firm?

4.2 Explain how the U.S. Commercial Service can help companies wanting to enter the international market.

4.3 What are some of the advantages and potential disadvantages of entering a joint venture?

5 **List the basic elements involved in developing a global marketing mix.** A firm's major consideration is how much it will adjust the four Ps—product, promotion, place (distribution), and price—within each country. One strategy is to use one product and one promotion message worldwide. A second strategy is to create new products for global markets. A third strategy is to keep the product basically the same but alter the promotional message. A fourth strategy is to slightly alter the product to meet local conditions.

5.1 The sale of cigarettes in many developed countries either has peaked or is declining. However, the developing markets represent major growth markets. Should U.S. tobacco companies capitalize on this opportunity?

5.2 Describe at least three situations where an American company might want to keep the product the same but alter the promotion. Also, give three examples where the product must be altered.

6 **Discover how the Internet is affecting global marketing.** Simply opening a Web site can open the door for international sales. International carriers, like UPS, can help solve logistics problems. Language translation software can help an e-commerce business become multilingual. Yet cultural differences and old-line rules, regulations, and taxes hinder rapid development of e-commerce in many countries.

6.1 Describe how "going global" via the Internet presents opportunities and challenges.

6.2 Give several examples of how culture may hinder "going global" via the Internet.

DEFINE IT

Asia-Pacific Economic
   Cooperation (APEC) 107
Association of Southeast
   Asian Nations (ASEAN)
   107
buyer for export 112
contract manufacturing 114
countertrade 121
direct foreign investment
   115
dumping 121
export agent 112
export broker 112

exporting 111
Free Trade Area of the
   Americas (FTAA) 106
fully industrialized society
   103
General Agreement on Tar-
   iffs and Trade (GATT) 105
global marketing 94
global marketing standardization 99
global vision 94
industrializing society 103
joint venture 114

licensing 112
Maastricht Treaty 107
Mercosur 105
multinational corporation
   97
North American Free Trade
   Agreement (NAFTA) 106
preindustrial society 102
takeoff economy 102
traditional society 102
Uruguay Round 105
World Trade Organization
   (WTO) 105

APPLY IT

Application for Entrepreneurs

Larry and Laurie Walther own a shop in Taos, New Mexico, that sells fine rugs crafted by Native Americans. They have expanded their business beyond Taos via direct mail. In fact, they have discovered a growing market in the United Kingdom. It seems that Europeans, particularly the English, French, and Germans, have an ongoing love affair with Native American culture. Larry and Laurie are now considering a direct-mail campaign to Germany. The typical American receives about 350 direct-mail pieces per year, whereas a German household gets fewer than 70. Also, Germany has 40 percent more people than the United Kingdom.

Yet, marketing to Germans by direct mail is different. Most buyers don't use credit cards when purchasing by mail. One German law dictates the size of free samples that can be distributed; another says that advertising mail cannot be camouflaged as a personal letter. Privacy laws restrict the preparation of finely targeted U.S.-style mailing lists. Mail carriers have to obey "no advertising" stickers that many Germans affix to their mailboxes.

Questions

1. Should Larry and Laurie attempt to enter the German market? Why or why not?
2. What can be done to overcome the credit card problem?

THINK ABOUT IT

Ethics Exercise

Moore Electronics sells automated lighting for airport runways. The government of an Eastern European country has offered Moore a contract to provide equipment for the fifteen major airports in the ocuntry. The official in charge of awarding the contract, however, is demanding a 5 percent kickback. He told Moore to build this into the contract price so that there would be no cost to Moore. Without the kickback, Moore loses the contract. Such kickbacks are considered a normal way of doing business in this country.

Questions

1. What should Moore do?
2. Does the AMA Code of Ethics address this issue? Go to **http://www.marketingpower .com** and review the code. Then write a brief paragraph on what the AMA Code of Ethics contains that relates to Moore's dilemma.

TRY IT

Entrepreneurship Case

Israel: A Ray of Light in the Global Optics Industry

 Though it's some 20,000 miles away from Silicon Valley, Israel has managed to produce its own version of the high-tech wonderland. The Internet revolution, biotechnology, and, yes, optics are driving the economy of this tiny country of just 6.4 million people. Today, there are some 50 optical start-ups around Israel. On a per capita basis, that would equate to about 2,200 optical companies in the United States.

Three major factors drive this growth: an inherent entrepreneurial attitude bred in Israel, world-class research universities, and funding through the venture capital community. The result has been a set of research-intensive companies that give a glimpse of how optical systems may be shaped over the next few years. The ultimate hope of many is to produce an Israeli-based optical powerhouse—a goal that so far has eluded many Israeli entrepreneurs.

The optical market here has all of the key ingredients for long-term growth—research and development, funding, and experience. There are more engineers per capita in Israel than anywhere else in the world. Israel, for example, has about 140 engineers per 10,000 employees versus roughly 70 engineers within the United States.

Many of those engineers and doctoral students are doing their research in Israel's world-class universities. Israel has been able to develop renowned research institutions like the Technion, Ben Gurion University, and Tel Aviv University. Homegrown talent is particularly important because of the strong connection between optical research and commercial optical products.

Most new optical companies are looking to leverage Israel's R&D skills to develop components or subsystems. Carriers currently are less willing to risk their networks on a start-up than they might have been in 2001—particularly a start-up that might be long on R&D but short on marketing and selling to a traditional telco (telecom company). For a carrier to purchase a system from an Israeli start-up takes "some guts," says Doron Nevo, a principal with an optics company called Kilolambda.

Ron Shilon certainly knows what Nevo is talking about. The CEO of Flexlight Networks, a supplier of passive-optical-network (PON) subsystems, has a simple explanation of why Flexlight is going after the subsystem market. "It's just too difficult for small start-ups, located 10,000 miles away, to pitch the carriers directly," he says.

And if past record is any indication of the future, many of the companies will look to cash out early, a problem that Tzvi Marom, president and CEO of BATM, a manufacturer of optical switches, laments. "We have not been able to build an optical industry here as much as we've built a collection of individual companies," says Marom, "Behind someone who sells products from Japan, for example, are zillions of companies supporting them." In Israel, Marom says, entrepreneurs have become so infatuated with the fast exit that there is no opportunity to craft those larger companies.

Instead, Israel has become a sort of start-up production line, generating high-tech start-ups that are subsequently acquired by the Nortels, Ciscos, and Lucents of the world. Then again, that may not be such a bad position after all.

Questions

1. Why have Israeli firms turned to the global marketplace to sell their products? Describe the global visions, and the responses to them, that drive that decision.

2. How have Israeli firms used their strengths to capture opportunities in the global marketplace for their optics products? What elements of the internal environment drive the development of their globally oriented optics industry?

3. What method of entering the global marketplace have the Israeli optics firms chosen? Do you think their choice makes the most sense? Why or why not?

WATCH IT

Short

To see how global marketing influences advertising, watch the Jumpman, Levi's, and Nike ads on the *Marketing* PowerPoint CD-ROM. When watching the ads, think about what makes them suitable or unsuitable for global marketing, and what global strategy they could support.

Medium

Trade agreements are proliferating around the world, but still some regions are having difficulty competing in certain regions. For example, because Europe does not have a trade agreement with Latin American countries, it is unable to secure coffee at as competitive a price as the United States, which does have a trade agreement with Latin America. Watch the CNN clip for this chapter to see how trade agreements translate into competitive advantage.

Long
the Series on PBS stations and the Web

To give you insight into Chapter 4, Small Business School will introduce you to Automated Food Systems, maker of the machinery that produces 95 percent of the 2.5 billion corn dogs consumed in the United States each year. In fact, this quintessentially American food is consumed throughout the world, and foreign companies that sell corn-dog type foods also produce them on Automated Food machines. Watch the segment and work the questions on the supplemental video CD-ROM.

FLIP IT

 Flip to Chapter 4 in your *Grademaker Study Guide* for more review opportunities, including the pretest, vocabulary review, study test questions, marketing applications, and much, much more. Do you know the major trade agreements? Can you close your book and list the ways a firm can enter the global marketplace? Open your Study Guide to find out how much you know—or don't know.

CLICK IT

The *Marketing* Web site links you to all the Internet-based activities in this chapter, like "Use It" and the On-Line exercises in the chapter margins. As a review, do the Chapter 4 quiz and crossword puzzle. You can also work the Career Exersite that shows you different types of global marketing careers. Or, review the main concepts in the PowerPoint presentation for Chapter 4. Go to **http://lamb.swlearning.com**, read the material, and follow the links right from the site.

SPIN IT

Spin your Xtra! CD-ROM to test your understanding of global marketing by completing the worksheets for exhibits 4.2, 4.3, and 4.4. If your instructor has assigned a marketing plan project, worksheets on Xtra! can help you organize your work. In addition to the quiz on the Web site, there's another quiz on the Xtra! CD-ROM, plus video of the authors answering frequently asked questions about global marketing, such as "Is global marketing only important to large multinational corporations?" and "What is the best way to enter global marketing?" Spin your Xtra! CD and find out.

Still Shaky? Here's a Tip.

Work out any Discussion and Writing Questions that your professor didn't assign as homework. Visit your professor or TA during office hours to check your answers.

MARKETING MISCUES

Kmart's Blue Lights Are in the Red, and There's Nothing Special about It

Is there anything special about Kmart anymore? Do consumers know what Kmart and its brands stand for? Does Kmart have an image in the retail marketplace? Answers to these questions were crucial to Kmart's long-term survival as the company entered into Chapter 11 bankruptcy proceedings in early 2002. Kmart's case was the largest retail bankruptcy filing in U.S. history, as well as the sixth-largest bankruptcy case in U.S. history.

More than a hundred years ago, Sebastian Kresge opened his first five-and-dime store in Michigan. This store was the first of what would come to be known as the S. S. Kresge Company. The company's business philosophy was to offer products that consumers needed at prices they could afford. In doing so, management expected that customers would keep returning. The company thought it had found the key to customer loyalty.

Unfortunately for Kresge, another retailing guru would soon enter the picture. In 1962, when Kresge launched the Kmart concept, Sam Walton was setting in motion the debut of Wal-Mart. Kmart never expected that the retailing showdown with Wal-Mart would ultimately result in Kmart's appearance in bankruptcy court. For forty years, it battled Wal-Mart, and in the end, Kmart had lost. What went wrong?

According to market analysts, Kmart made a series of strategic and tactical blunders. Strategically, Kmart failed to differentiate itself as a retailer. Instead of carving a niche for itself in the retail industry, it became boxed in between two different, yet similar, discount retailers—Wal-Mart and Target Corporation. Wal-Mart, with its "always low prices," solidly established itself as the low-price leader. With reasonably low prices, but not as low as Wal-Mart, Target became known as the trendy discounter by focusing on fashionable merchandise. Tactically, Kmart's blunders left shoppers with less than pleasant shopping experiences. Customers cited in-store concerns such as poor customer service, long checkout lines, inconsistent price marking, dingy stores, empty shelves, and old merchandise as issues that led to Kmart's downfall.

Some would say that this downfall should not have come as a surprise to Kmart management, employees, and customers. Kmart appeared to have focused solely on its competition and what they were doing rather than focusing on its customers and what they wanted. In the end, Kmart could not differentiate itself from Wal-Mart because it could not price below it. Nor could Kmart sway Target customers because it appeared unable to provide the in-store experience that made customers feel chic as they purchased discounted clothing.

At the time of its bankruptcy filing, Kmart was the third largest retailer in the United States, with 2,100 stores across the United States and Puerto Rico. While Kmart was filing Chapter 11, Wal-Mart boasted sales of $200 billion, with growth rates of 15 to 20 percent, and Target's 1,055 stores posted record sales revenue of $37 billion. With competition like this, there was doubt as to whether Kmart could rectify its past strategic missteps and differentiate itself in the retail marketplace. Could Kmart devise a unique and compelling strategy that would leave the company's fractured image behind? Or, should Kmart's blue lights be turned off forever?

Questions

1. Is this an example of poor strategy formulation or poor strategy implementation?

2. Describe Kmart's marketing mix in the years leading up to 2002.

3. Did Kmart have a market orientation?

CRITICAL THINKING CASE

Hewlett-Packard's CoolTown Puts Everyone and Everything on the Web

While the business world has focused on the merger between Hewlett-Packard Company (**http://www.hp.com**) and Compaq Computer Corporation, techno wizards at Hewlett-Packard Laboratories in Palo Alto, California, are spending their time conducting a living experiment. Dubbed "CoolTown," the experiment attempts to bridge the physical and virtual worlds and showcases HP's product offerings in building this bridge. Given HP's complex product line that has led to an unclear image in the marketplace, the jury is still out as to whether CoolTown will be successful at conveying the company's vision for the future in this wireless era.

The Company

Hewlett-Packard Company was founded in 1939 by Bill Hewlett and Dave Packard. Hewlett and Packard believed that HP existed to invent the "useful and significant." To them, the term *useful* meant contributions that would free businesses and consumers to focus on what mattered most to them. The term *significant* was indicative of HP's vow not only to make a profit but to also make a difference. The bottom line is that HP will help create a world where technology works for the consumer and not vice versa. Consistent with this vision is the set of corporate objectives, referred to as "The HP Way." The company's objectives focus on seven major areas: profit, customers, fields of interest, growth, company people, management, and citizenship.

At the beginning of the twenty-first century, HP is listed in the top twenty of the *Fortune* 500. Carly Fiorina is CEO, the company has almost ninety thousand employees, and company revenue is around $45 billion. Product offerings include printers, personal computers, servers, wireless devices, software, and consulting services. The company refers to its vision as service-centric computing, meaning that information technologies are delivered, managed, and purchased as services. To fulfill this vision, HP's strategy focuses on three key areas of invention: (1) enabling intelligent, connected devices and environment, (2) enabling an always-on Internet infrastructure, and (3) enabling a new generation of applications delivered as e-services.

When Fiorina took the helm in 1999, she envisioned a reinvention of HP. At that time, HP had a major market niche with its printers but was lackluster in the remainder of its markets. Many felt that the company was not only old-fashioned but also resistant to change. In a major move to reinvent HP, Fiorina spearheaded the merger with Compaq Computer. The merger could be a major step toward HP becoming a technology solutions provider.

Marketing Deficiencies

Although the merger between HP and Compaq may take the company in the technology solutions direction, some are concerned about the longer term implications of HP's weak marketing. HP is not known for its ability to tell a compelling story in the marketplace. Its image as a stodgy, old company is not expected to fare well in the new age economy. While boasting a strong product line, the company has not been able to excite the marketplace. With expectations of 45 percent annual growth and market share of $80 billion by 2004, the company will have to rectify its marketing deficiencies to remain competitive and meet its goals.

CoolTown

In June 2001, HP launched CoolTown. This project, which was developed at HP Laboratories, is a mock city that allows users to experience life in a technological environment. The goal of CoolTown is to make this futuristic environment transparent to the user. CoolTown visitors can experience how wireless technologies will change their lives.

Four components work in sync to make CoolTown functional: the Internet, handheld electronics, wireless networks, and computer intelligence. Combining these ingredients, users can see what a typical wireless day would be like. Examples include a CoolTown bookstore that recognizes customers and recommends new books, a CoolTown bus line that pinpoints bus location so that the rider does not get to the bus stop too early or too late, a CoolTown conference room where the speaker can control the projector remotely, and the CoolTown museum where a visitor can purchase products on-line as they are being viewed at the exhibit. Basically, CoolTown allows smart devices to link to other smart devices that are using the same language.

Of course, all of the technology employed in CoolTown is HP technology. The Coolbase Appliance Server is an embedded server from HP, Coolkit enables developers to build applications to run on

Cool-base, E-Squirt allows mobile phones or PDAs to direct e-services to other devices, and Beacons are handheld devices that broadcast to other wireless units (for example, PDAs and phones). Naturally, when HP customers are touring the CoolTown showroom, HP's Jornada handheld computers are used to navigate through the experience.

CoolTown, in conjunction with HP's Mobile E-Services Bazaar, has allowed HP to tap into new markets. Rather than focus on internal uses for CoolTown products, HP now can partner with wireless application engineers who can use HP products when they develop e-services for their customers. Additionally, the hope is that the CoolTown experience will interest customers in purchasing HP's consulting services to help with the wireless integration process.

HP as Net Innovator

While the Hewlett-Packard Company of the twenty-first century sees itself as an innovator, this image is very different from the stodgy company it became during the late twentieth century. It is unlikely that today's marketplace would identify HP on its short list of Internet innovators. Can HP compete with the likes of Microsoft, Oracle, and Sun Microsystems? How can HP merge its engineering expertise with a marketing message that will change its image in the customer's mindset?

Questions

1. What is HP's core business? How did the company build on this core business?

2. Does HP's success depend on its engineering prowess or its marketing expertise?

3. Describe the component parts of CoolTown and explain how these integrated parts could be used in everyday life. How does CoolTown help HP change its image in the marketplace?

4. Is the "new" HP consistent with the company's original reason for being in existence (to invent the "useful and significant")? Why or why not?

MARKETING PLANNING ACTIVITIES

Throughout the rest of this book, these end-of-part marketing planning activities will help you build a strategic marketing plan for a company of your choosing. To help you complete your plan, use the Marketing Planning Worksheets on your Xtra! CD-ROM. If you need a company for the basis of your work, follow the "Marketing Plan Project" link on the *Marketing* Web site (**http://lamb.swlearning.com**).

The World of Marketing

In the world of marketing, many different types of goods and services are offered to many different markets. Throughout this text, you will construct a marketing plan for your chosen company. Writing a marketing plan will give you a full depth of understanding for your company, its customers, and its marketing mix elements. The company you choose should be one that interests you, such as the manufacturer of your favorite product, a local business where you would like to work, or even a business you would like to start yourself to satisfy an unmet need or want. Despite recent troubles in the dot-com sector, you may also consider the Internet portion of marketing. Most firms have two options for implementing Internet marketing: starting an Internet business that is wholly operated in the e-marketing world or creating an Internet component of a marketing plan for a traditional, existing business. Both Internet opportunities require careful strategic marketing planning in order for the venture to succeed.

For electronic sources of information, search on the Electric Library at **http://www.elibrary.com** or the Internet Public Library at **http://www.ipl.org**. Another excellent source of information is the Sales and Marketing Executives Marketing Library at **http://www.sell.org**.

For some general help on business plans and marketing plans, visit **http://www.bplans.com** or **http://www.businessplans.org**. Before you begin, you will need to learn about the Internet as a business space. **Looksmart.com** has a category called "Internet Business" that you may find helpful both as a starting point and as you progress through the e-marketing planning activities. Another very useful site is **http://www.emarketer.com**. You should also refer to Exhibit 2.7 for additional marketing plan checklist items (Part I: Business Mission; Part II: Objectives; and Part III: Situation Analysis).

The first part of strategic planning deals with the world of marketing and involves stating your business mission with a marketing orientation, setting objectives, finding a differential advantage, and performing an assessment of strengths, weaknesses, opportunities, and threats. Use the following exercises to guide you through the first part of your strategic marketing plan:

1. Describe your chosen company. How long has it been in business, or when will it start business? Who are the key players? Is the company small or large? Does it offer a good or service? What are the strengths and weaknesses of this company? What are the orientation and organizational culture? List all the ways that your company follows the marketing concept. Can

your company satisfy the needs and wants of customers and still be profitable, legal, and socially responsible?

2. What should be the business mission of your company? Write the mission statement, keeping in mind the benefits offered to customers rather than the product or service sold. If you are starting the on-line arm of a traditional store, should you make any changes to the company's overall mission statement? For fun, visit the mission statement generator at **http://unitedmedia.com/comics/dilbert/games/index.html**, which may help illustrate how *not* to write your business mission statement.

3. Set marketing objectives for your chosen company. Make sure the objectives fit the criteria for good objectives. List at least three specific, measurable objectives for your company. Be sure these objectives relate to the mission statement and include a time frame.

4. Scan the marketing environment. Identify opportunities and threats to your chosen company in areas such as technology, the economy, the political and legal environment, and competition. Is your competition foreign, domestic, or both? Also, identify opportunities and threats based on possible market targets, including social factors, demographic factors, and multicultural issues.

5. Assume your company is or will be marketing globally. How should your company enter the global marketplace? How will international issues affect your firm?

6. Does your chosen business have a differential or competitive advantage? If it does not, there is no point in marketing the product. Can you create a sustainable advantage with skills, resources, or elements of the marketing mix? Begin your SWOT analysis with an analysis of the primary strength by asking, "What is the key differential or competitive advantage of my firm?" If you have an Internet offering, consider what advantages are gained by operating in the Internet space. What are other keys to the potential success of your company? What other strengths can your firm capitalize on?

7. Continue the SWOT analysis by taking an honest look at the weaknesses of your firm. What are the disadvantages to operating in the Internet space? How can you overcome them? You might want to enlist the help of a friend to act as a consultant who can give an unbiased opinion. Are there any ethical problems in the organization?

8. Identify any ethical issues that could affect your chosen firm. What steps should be taken to handle these issues? How should your company integrate corporate social responsibility into the plan? Describe how your company will handle

privacy concerns. In addition to suggestions for philanthropic responsibilities, write up a brief code of ethics for your firm. To see other codes of ethics, go to **http://csep.iit.edu/codes/**.

9. The last part of the SWOT analysis seeks to identify opportunities and threats in the external marketing environment by performing environmental scanning.

   a. To learn more about demographic, ethnic, and social trends that could affect your firm, investigate data from the U.S. Census Bureau at **http://www.census.gov**.

   b. To learn more about economic factors that could influence the strategies of your firm, visit the U.S. Economic and Statistics Administration at **http://www.esa.doc.gov** or the Bureau of Economic Analysis at **http://www.bea.doc.gov**.

   c. Be sure to look for computer and Internet usage statistics and think about whether they are a positive indicator for the target market you have selected. The resources at **http://cyberatlas.internet.com** and **http://acnielsen.com/products/reports/netwatch** can help. Determine which emerging technologies will have an impact on your company. Are these technological developments opportunities or threats?

   d. Understand how political and legal factors may influence your marketing decisions at **http://www.lawguru.com**. You may also wish to investigate the Web sites of federal government agencies that regulate your firm and industry. The Federal Trade Commission is at **http://www.ftc.gov**. The Federal Communications Commission is at **http://www.fcc.gov**. The Food and Drug Administration is at **http://www.fda.gov**. The Consumer Product Safety Commission is at **http://www.cpsc.gov**. The Better Business Bureau is at **http://www.bbb.org**. The Internal Revenue Service is at **http://www.irs.gov**. From here you can download all kinds of required and helpful forms.

   e. Identify your key competitors. A simple "yellow pages" (**http://bigbook.com**) listing of firms in the same business category can start your search. For on-line competitors, try **http://www.bizrate.com**. For more specific information on a competitor, investigate **http://www.companiesonline.com**.

   f. Competition often comes from companies that are working on the same exact market as yours. That is especially true in the Internet space. After you search for your direct competition, look for and think about what other companies are positioned to execute a similar business strategy for your target market.

Determine if there are any players who might be able to develop technology more quickly or reach your target customers more effectively than you.

g. If you choose an Internet presence, your product or service will be visible to a global community. Therefore, it is important to assess the international marketplace as well. A listing of international chambers of commerce is at **http://www.worldchambers.com** and the CIA World Factbook is at **http://www.cia.gov/cia/publications/factbook/index.html**.

10. Is there a key factor or assumption that you are using when performing your SWOT analysis? What would happen if this key factor or assumption did not exist?

CROSS-FUNCTIONAL CONNECTIONS SOLUTIONS

Questions

1. What is the overlap among marketing, manufacturing, finance, accounting, and human resources? What does each of these functions do that results in this overlap?

   The overlap among all functional areas within a firm lies in providing the final product or service to the consumer. Each functional area contributes in different ways to delivering the desired product to the end customer. Marketing, manufacturing, finance, accounting, and human resources work from the idea that the customer is most important and that the goal is to produce a product that meets the changing needs of consumers. Marketing and manufacturing tend to come into direct contact with the company's customers and products. Finance, accounting, and human resources tend to work on the periphery and may never come into contact with the physical aspects of the product and may never meet the end-user of the product or service. However, working together and utilizing each area's expertise and knowledge result in an integrated production process that aims to satisfy the customer.

2. Why is cross-functional coordination necessary in order to have a customer-oriented firm?

   Historically, everyone assumed that the customer belonged to the marketing department. We know now that this is not true. Everyone in the organization must understand the customer's wants and needs in order to satisfy these needs. Without the customer, there would be no need for an organization. For example, no customers would mean no products to develop or manufacture, no accounts receivable, and no need for employees.

   From the customer's perspective, good or bad products belong to the entire company—not just one particular function. Customers will not keep coming back if the company produces only low-quality merchandise—even if the marketing group has some of the best marketers in the world. Likewise, a high-quality product will not be successful in the marketplace if the product is positioned inaccurately, advertised inappropriately, priced too high or too low, or not available in the right outlets. Therefore, it is imperative that the business functions work together to send the same message to the marketplace.

3. What roles do teamwork and technology play in cross-functional coordination?

   Technology has created a digitized marketplace in which business decisions have to be made quickly in order for the firm to remain competitive. Customer demands increase in this fast-paced market, making it necessary for all functional areas to work together to deliver products to a market quickly. In working as a team, functional areas partner in the production/ delivery process, sharing relevant information with one another, as well as eliminating wasted time spent when working independently in departments.

Suggested Readings

Bryant Avey, "Building a People-Center Culture in the D-Age," *Chief Executive,* September 1999, 10.

Charles H. Noble, "Building the Strategy Implementation Network," *Business Horizons,* November–December 1999, 19–28.

PART 2

Analyzing Marketing Opportunities

CROSS-FUNCTIONAL CONNECTIONS

INFORMATION INTEGRATION TO SATISFY CUSTOMER WANTS AND NEEDS

Understanding customers is at the heart of the information-gathering process. Whether it is determining individual buying behavior, sharpening the company's target marketing skills, or understanding competitive actions, information is the key to success. The traditional perception of information gathering is that it is the "job" of the marketing department. However, many companies have come to realize that the market belongs to the entire company—making it everyone's responsibility to understand the marketplace.

Kellogg USA has focused extensively on improving the focus of its research efforts. The company's strategy involves better cross-functional acquisition and dissemination of market research information. The ultimate goal is to use the information to help move new and improved products into the marketplace much more quickly. In its attempt to increase profits, the company has discarded its traditional product development process that was housed in marketing. Now, the company utilizes cross-functional teams comprised of business functional areas, food technologists, and engineers in its product development efforts. Kellogg's marketers no longer take sole responsibility for the collection and use of information. While these different groups now work in tandem in developing products at Kellogg, the historical debate surrounding type of data continues in many companies.

This information debate between marketing and other functions centers on the qualitative versus quantitative format of functional data. The data collected by marketers are perceived to be qualitative, abstract data when compared to the quantitative data utilized by other functional areas. It has been difficult to get engineers and accountants to understand that marketing data provide statistically valid information that is important in making company-wide decisions.

Aside from the need for a general cross-functional sharing of data, there are five major areas in which information gathering and dissemination processes need to be formally integrated across functions:

1. Benchmarking studies
2. Customer teaming
3. Customer satisfaction studies
4. Data-mining
5. Forecasting

Benchmarking is the process of comparing a firm's performance in various activities with the performance of other companies that have completed similar activities. A benchmarking study could focus on cross-company comparisons of purchasing processes, inventory management, product development cycles, hiring practices, payroll processes, and order fulfillment. Gathering information on a firm's competitors during a benchmarking study involves an extensive amount of secondary research. Recently, cross-functional "shadow teams" have been formed to assist in better benchmarking of competitive activities. These shadow teams integrate internal information with all externally available information on specific competitors.

The Ford Motor Company was an early pioneer of the use of benchmarking. In the early 1980s, the company found itself at a competitive disadvantage compared to many foreign automobile manufacturers. Ford executives recognized that remaining competitive would demand a steep reduction in costs. One benchmarking study focused upon reducing the number of employees in the accounts payable department. Using information gained in a benchmarking study of its competitors, Ford was able to decrease its accounts payable staff by more than one-half. The study involved both primary and secondary research-areas in which marketers have extensive training. Similarly, many of the creative aspects (e.g., Six Sigma, Workout) of Jack Welch's tenure at General Electric were the result of benchmarking studies of competing and noncompeting companies.

Many companies are now *teaming* employees with customers in an attempt to bring the customer into the organization. Site visits are one popular way of better understanding needs and/or watching how a finished product is utilized in the business process. These visits involve team members from across various functions. For example, someone from research and development might visit a customer in order to observe in-use practices. Drawing from the on-site visit, the R&D employee could utilize these observations in adapting the product to the customer's needs within the select business framework. Tellabs, a telecommunications company that develops voice and data transmission products, teams its marketers and R&D engineers with customers in an attempt to reduce the risks inherent in new product development.

Additionally, Kodak attempts to gain a better understanding of how customers use its film by sending manufacturing employees to visit with professional users of its film products. Kodak is dependent upon accurate marketplace information in understanding both the customers' buying processes and their actual usage of Kodak products.

Customer satisfaction is driven by issues related to the firm's operational functions (for example, inventory management, capital budgeting), the firm's operational capabilities (for example, technology, procedures), as well as the firm's product mix. Therefore, a valid *customer satisfaction study* should gather information that can be shared with manufacturing (regarding satisfaction with speed of delivery), research and development (regarding satisfaction with product quality), human resources (regarding satisfaction with complaint handling), and finance/accounting (regarding satisfaction with credit policies). As such, all of these functional areas need to have input into the design of such studies.

The digital age has led to considerable *data-mining*. E-commerce capabilities have allowed companies to gather and analyze customer information in a matter of minutes, rather than having to wait for results from months-long data gathering processes. This use of technology is where considerable cross-functional interactions must occur. Companies such as DoubleClick, Kozmo, and AltaVista gather and store a wealth of consumer information—information that has to be effectively disseminated to the appropriate individuals.

Forecasting crosses the boundaries of multiple business functions. For example, marketing may offer a discount on a particular price. The impact of this price discount is felt, simultaneously, in many functional areas. A key functional partner in a price discount is manufacturing. The production plan will have to accommodate the expected increase in product sales and the oftentimes below-average product sales immediately after the discount period. While price is easy for marketers to change, manufacturing's plans cannot be changed overnight. The impact of a price change may be felt in the company's production schedule, the level of finished goods inventory, and the availability of raw materials. Unfortunately, marketing's ability to make price changes quickly has been the cause of much conflict between marketing and manufacturing.

Much of a firm's financial planning is driven by the company's sales forecast. Marketing has historically had a reputation of being too optimistic in its projections. As a result, financial planners have been known to take the sales forecast with "a grain of salt," and planning has often evolved around a lower than predicted level of sales. Marketing, then, looks at financial planners as too conservative and as basing their plans on internal data that are not driven by the marketplace.

Predicting worldwide demand has become a forecasting challenge for many companies. With help from a software program, Eastman Chemical Corporation utilizes cross-functional teams to predict demand across its supply chain. Not only is the company now able to make precise forecasts, but the program allows the dissemination of these real-time forecasts over the corporate intranet. This enables the synchronization of production and inventory with customer demand.

Marketplace information is a key driver in all decisions made by a company. Therefore, it is imperative that all functional areas participate in the gathering and dissemination of information. The importance of information is reflected in a new executive position, chief knowledge officer, that is now being staffed in many companies. Without a doubt, success in today's global environment is dependent upon all functional areas understanding the firm's customers and competitors.

Questions

1. Why has information historically been perceived as "owned" by the marketing department?
2. What data differences exist across functions?
3. What is the job of a chief knowledge officer?

Check It Out

For articles and exercises on the material in this part, and for other great study aids, visit the *Marketing* Web site at

http://lamb.swlearning.com

CHAPTER **FIVE**
CONSUMER DECISION MAKING

Learning Objectives

1 Explain why marketing managers should understand consumer behavior

2 Analyze the components of the consumer decision-making process

3 Explain the consumer's post-purchase evaluation process

4 Identify the types of consumer buying decisions and discuss the significance of consumer involvement

5 Identify and understand the cultural factors that affect consumer buying decisions

6 Identify and understand the social factors that affect consumer buying decisions

7 Identify and understand the individual factors that affect consumer buying decisions

8 Identify and understand the psychological factors that affect consumer buying decisions

Observing changes in consumer behavior is often a risky task involving picking up on a small blip on a marketer's radar that over time becomes more and more obvious. But in the wake of the terrorist attacks on September 11, 2001, consumer behavior in the United States changed, if only briefly, sending marketers scrambling overnight to adjust marketing campaigns.

In the days following the terrorist attacks, American consumers became less motivated by the need for prestige and self-expression. Instead consumers became focused on security, protection, friends, and family. For example, wealthy Americans who normally could be expected to purchase a luxury automobile were purchasing bulletproof and bomb-resistant SUVs. Wal-Mart customers bought guns, ammunition, gas cans, and televisions. Survival companies saw sales of gas masks and bomb shelters surge. And long-distance phone calls increased 100 percent as Americans checked in with loved ones.

In addition, Americans put materialism aside as a wave of volunteerism and patriotism swept the nation. During the first week after the attacks, Americans from all walks of life donated more than $325 million and 500,000 units of blood to relief efforts. Red, white, and blue became a fashion statement overnight as retailers struggled to meet the surging demand for U.S. flags. And firefighters and police officers replaced business tycoons as our national heroes.

Marketers had tough decisions to make. How do you promote products in the wake of a national tragedy? When will consumers be ready to think about new cars, computers, or movies? Should we take advantage of the nation's patriotic zeal, or will it be seen as opportunistic? Without the luxury of time to study consumer behavior, marketers waded in slowly with mixed results.

In the beginning, many companies simply chose to run sentimental ads honoring the victims and their families or encouraging Americans to get back to normal by shopping and dining out. Hollywood decided to err on the side of caution and pulled several war films scheduled for fall release. Automobile manufacturers, unable to afford slow sales, began running commercials designed to appeal to the nation's sense of patriotic duty. Microsoft decided to stick with plans to launch Windows XP in New York City with enthusiasm after changing the product's marketing slogan from "You Can Fly" to "Yes You Can."

During this time, manufacturers saw an increase in demand for U.S.-made products. The greeting card industry saw a surge in sales. Parents purchased cap guns and GI Joe dolls for their children. Consumers bought comfort food like Campbell's soup and read magazines like *Real Simple* and *Country Living*.[1]

Then Americans began to return to a sense of normalcy. And as they did, marketers began trying to understand what the new normal would be. What do you think? Did the events of September 11, 2001, change American culture, or did they just cause a dramatic blip in consumer behavior? What motivates consumers today? What factors affect their buying decisions? Questions like these will be considered as you read this chapter on the consumer decision-making process and its influences.

The Importance of Understanding Consumer Behavior

Explain why marketing managers should understand consumer behavior

consumer behavior
Processes a consumer uses to make purchase decisions, as well as to use and dispose of purchased goods or services; also includes factors that influence purchase decisions and product use.

Consumers' product and service preferences are constantly changing. In order to address this constant state of flux and to create a proper marketing mix for a well-defined market, marketing managers must have a thorough knowledge of consumer behavior. **Consumer behavior** describes how consumers make purchase decisions and how they use and dispose of the purchased goods or services. The study of consumer behavior also includes an analysis of factors that influence purchase decisions and product use.

Understanding how consumers make purchase decisions can help marketing managers in several ways. For example, if a manager knows through research that gas mileage is the most important attribute for a certain target market, the manufacturer can redesign the product to meet that criterion. If the firm cannot change the design in the short run, it can use promotion in an effort to change consumers' decision-making criteria. For example, an automobile manufacturer can advertise a car's maintenance-free features and sporty European style while downplaying gas mileage.

The Consumer Decision-Making Process

Analyze the components of the consumer decision-making process

consumer decision-making process
A five-step process used by consumers when buying goods or services.

When buying products, consumers generally follow the **consumer decision-making process** shown in Exhibit 5.1: (1) need recognition, (2) information search, (3) evaluation of alternatives, (4) purchase, and (5) postpurchase behavior. These five steps represent a general process that moves the consumer from recognition of a product or service need to the evaluation of a purchase. This process is a guideline for studying how consumers make decisions. It is important to note that this guideline does not assume that consumers' decisions will proceed in order through all of the steps of the process. In fact, the consumer may end the process at any time; he or she may not even make a purchase. Explanations as to why a consumer's progression through these steps may vary are offered at the end of the chapter in the section on the types of consumer buying decisions. Before addressing this issue, we will describe each step in the process in greater detail.

Need Recognition

need recognition
Result of an imbalance between actual and desired states.

The first stage in the consumer decision-making process is need recognition. **Need recognition** occurs when consumers are faced with an imbalance between actual and desired states. For example, do you often feel thirsty after strenuous exercise? Has a television commercial for a new sports car ever made you wish you could buy it? Need recognition is triggered when a consumer is exposed to either an internal or an external **stimulus**. Hunger and thirst are *internal stimuli;* the color of an automobile, the design of a package, a brand name mentioned by a friend, an advertisement on television, or cologne worn by a stranger are considered *external stimuli.*

stimulus
Any unit of input affecting one or more of the five senses: sight, smell, taste, touch, hearing.

A marketing manager's objective is to get consumers to recognize an imbalance between their present status and their preferred state. Advertising and sales promotion often provide this stimulus. Surveying buyer preferences provides marketers with information about consumer wants and needs that can be used to tailor products and services. For example, Procter & Gamble frequently surveys consumers regarding their wants and needs. P&G recently used the Internet to test market its new Crest Whitestrips home-bleaching kit. The test revealed that 80 percent of potential buyers were women between the ages of thirty-five and fifty-four, identifying the best target market for the product. The company was then able to fine-tune its marketing plan before launching the product nationwide.[2] In

Exhibit 5.1

Consumer Decision-Making Process

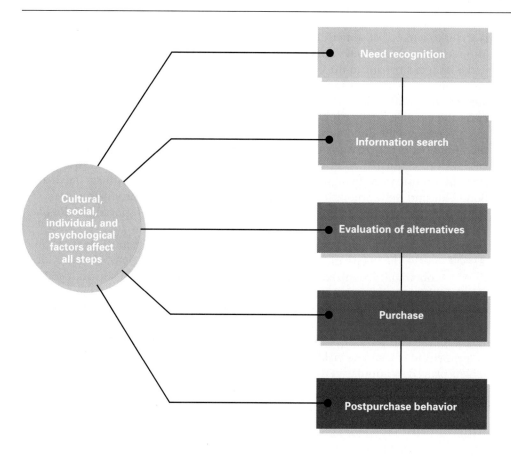

another example of how far P&G will go to learn about market trends, the company recently began videotaping consumers at home in its own version of reality TV to learn things about them that surveys do not reveal.[3]

Marketing managers can create wants on the part of the consumer. A **want** exists when someone has an unfulfilled need and has determined that a particular good or service will satisfy it. Young children may want toys, video games, and baseball equipment to meet their innate need to play and learn new skills. Teenagers may want compact discs, fashionable sneakers, and wide-leg jeans to fulfill their need of belonging. A want can be for a specific product or it can be for a certain attribute or feature of a product. For instance, adults may want ready-to-eat meals, drive-through dry cleaning service, and catalog shopping to fulfill their need for convenience. Older consumers may want goods and services that offer convenience, comfort, and security. Remote-controlled appliances, home deliveries, speaker phones, and motorized carts are all designed for comfort and convenience. A personal transmitter that can signal an ambulance or the police in an emergency offers security for older consumers.

Another way that marketers create new products and services is by observing trends in the marketplace. For example, as baby boomers become grandparents, marketers have created a whole industry around fulfilling their need to be involved in the lives of their grandchildren. Today, hospitals offer grandparenting classes to explain the theory behind new approaches to child care and to teach grandparents how to help parents while avoiding conflicts. Retailers encourage new grandparents to register so that their friends can plan baby showers to help them stock up on grandparenting essentials. And travel agents have packages specifically designed for grandparents wanting to vacation with their grandchildren including new camps and resorts that cater to children and grandparents.[4]

want
Recognition of an unfulfilled need and a product that will satisfy it.

Consumers recognize unfulfilled wants in various ways. The two most common occur when a current product isn't performing properly and when the consumer is about to run out of something that is generally kept on hand. Consumers may also recognize unfulfilled wants if they become aware of a product whose features make it seem superior to the one currently used. Such wants are usually created by advertising and other promotional activities. For example, Dockers recently created the new Mobile Pant that offers professional men seven invisible pockets to carry their wallet, keys, cellphone, and PDA (personal digital assistant). The advertising campaign for the new pants is designed to create a need among professional men for a better way to carry their business paraphernalia without giving up their casual style.[5] Similarly, aware of the popularity of MP3s and consumers' desire to take their music with them, more than a dozen car stereo manufacturers such as Sonicblue and Kenwood have added MP3 capabilities to their products. Other companies are also hoping to fulfill consumer needs with small portable MP3 players such as the iPod by Apple Computers.[6]

GLOBAL Marketers selling their products in global markets must carefully observe the needs and wants of consumers in various regions. Unilever hit on an unrecognized need of European consumers when it introduced Persil Tablets, premeasured laundry detergent in tablet form. Though the tablets are more expensive than regular laundry detergents, Unilever found that European consumers considered laundry a chore and wanted the process as simple and uncomplicated as possible. Unilever launched the tablets as less messy and more convenient to consumers tackling the pile of dirty clothes on wash day. The laundry tablets proved so popular in the United Kingdom that Unilever's Persil brand edged ahead of rival Procter & Gamble's best-selling Ariel powder detergent.[7]

Information Search

After recognizing a need or want, consumers search for information about the various alternatives available to satisfy it. An information search can occur internally, externally, or both. An **internal information search** is the process of recalling information stored in the memory. This stored information stems largely from previous experience with a product. For instance, while traveling you encounter a restaurant belonging to a chain that you tried somewhere else. By searching your memory, you can probably remember whether the food was good and in your price range.

In contrast, an **external information search** seeks information in the outside environment. There are two basic types of external information sources: nonmarketing-controlled and marketing-controlled. A **nonmarketing-controlled information source** is not associated with marketers promoting a product. A friend might recommend an IBM personal computer because he or she bought one and likes it. Nonmarketing-controlled information sources include personal experience (trying or observing a new product); personal sources (family, friends, acquaintances, and coworkers); and public sources, such as Underwriters Laboratories, *Consumer Reports,* and other rating organizations. For instance, consumers rely heavily on doctor and pharmacist recommendations when buying over-the-counter medications, and many consumers buy an OTC drug for the first time because their pharmacist recommends it. A recent survey on new car purchases by Generation Y found these car buyers were almost twice as likely as older buyers to get information about new cars from friends and relatives. Car manufacturers would therefore be likely to focus their marketing strategy on generating enthusiasm for their models via word of mouth.[8]

internal information search
The process of recalling past information stored in the memory.

external information search
The process of seeking information in the outside environment.

nonmarketing-controlled information source
A product information source that is not associated with advertising or promotion.

Consumers rely on external nonmarketing controlled information when buying a variety of products. For example, consumers rely heavily on the recommendations of doctors and pharmacists before buying an over-the-counter medication.

On the other hand, a **marketing-controlled information source**, is biased toward a specific product, because it originates with marketers promoting that product. Marketing-controlled information sources include mass-media advertising (radio, newspaper, television, and magazine advertising), sales promotion (contests, displays, premiums, and so forth), salespeople, product labels and packaging, and the Internet. Many consumers, however, are wary about the information they receive from marketing-controlled sources, arguing that most marketing campaigns stress the attributes of the product and don't mention the faults. These sentiments tend to be stronger among better educated and higher income consumers. For instance, in spite of extensive advertising highlighting its philanthropic activities, Philip Morris Companies continues to have a poor reputation among consumers. In fact, after a recent survey revealed that an extensive image campaign had not changed consumer opinion about the company, Philip Morris decided to change its corporate name to Altria to shift the focus away from the Philip Morris brand and onto the company's other brands like Kraft Foods and Miller Beer. In another example, surveys showed that consumers were skeptical about quality assurance advertisements made by Bridgestone's Firestone Tires in the wake of the company's massive tire recall.[9]

The extent to which an individual conducts an external search depends on his or her perceived risk, knowledge, prior experience, and level of interest in the good or service. Generally, as the perceived risk of the purchase increases, the consumer enlarges the search and considers more alternative brands. For instance, assume you want to buy a digital camera. The decision is a relatively risky one due to the expense and the technical nature of the camera's features, so you are motivated to search for information about models, options, and capabilities. You may decide to compare attributes of many cameras because the value of the time expended in finding data will be less than the cost of buying the wrong camera.[10] In contrast, more than 60 percent of bar patrons don't know what they will drink until seconds before they place their order, challenging the marketers of alcoholic beverages to find ways of "educating" potential customers on the spot.[11]

A consumer's knowledge about the product or service will also affect the extent of an external information search. If the consumer is knowledgeable and well informed about a potential purchase, he or she is less likely to search for additional information. In addition, the more knowledgeable the consumer is, the more efficiently he or she will conduct the search process, thereby requiring less time to search.

Another closely related factor that affects the extent of a consumer's external search is confidence in one's decision-making ability. A confident consumer not only has sufficient stored information about the product but also feels self-assured about making the right decision. People lacking this confidence will continue an information search even when they know a great deal about the product. Consumers with prior experience in buying a certain product will have less perceived risk than inexperienced consumers. Therefore, they will spend less time searching and limit the number of products that they consider.

A third factor influencing the external information search is product experience. Consumers who have had a positive prior experience with a product are more likely to limit their search to only those items related to the positive experience. For example, many consumers are loyal to Honda automobiles, which enjoy low repair rates and consequently high customer satisfaction, and they often own more than one.

Product experience can also play a major role in a consumer's decision to make a high-risk purchase. For example, TiVo, the maker of personal video recorders, found that due to the expensive and complex nature of its product, advertising was only moderately effective in generating sales. Instead, personal experience is the most important factor in the decision to purchase a PVR.[12]

Finally, the extent of the search undertaken is positively related to the amount of interest a consumer has in a product. A consumer who is more interested in a product will spend more time searching for information and alternatives. For

marketing-controlled information source
A product information source that originates with marketers promoting the product.

example, suppose you are a dedicated runner who reads jogging and fitness magazines and catalogs. In searching for a new pair of running shoes, you may enjoy reading about the new brands available and spend more time and effort than other buyers in deciding on the right shoe.

The consumer's information search should yield a group of brands, sometimes called the buyer's **evoked set** (or **consideration set**), which are the consumer's most preferred alternatives. From this set, the buyer will further evaluate the alternatives and make a choice. Consumers do not consider all the brands available in a product category, but they do seriously consider a much smaller set. For example, there are dozens of brands of shampoos and close to two hundred types of automobiles available in the United States, yet most consumers seriously contemplate only about four shampoos and no more than five automobiles when faced with a purchase decision. Having too many choices can, in fact, confuse consumers and affect their decision to buy. In a recent survey, only 3 percent of customers who were presented with thirty varieties of jam made the decision to purchase. In contrast, 30 percent of shoppers who had only six choices made a purchase.[13]

Evaluation of Alternatives and Purchase

After getting information and constructing an evoked set of alternative products, the consumer is ready to make a decision. A consumer will use the information stored in memory and obtained from outside sources to develop a set of criteria. These standards help the consumer evaluate and compare alternatives. One way to begin narrowing the number of choices in the evoked set is to pick a product attribute and then exclude all products in the set that don't have that attribute. For instance, assume that John is thinking about buying a new notebook computer to replace his current desktop machine. He is interested in one with a large color active-matrix display, CD-RW drive, and a processor speed of at least 1.2 gigahertz, so he excludes all notebooks without these features.

Another way to narrow the number of choices is to use cutoffs, or minimum or maximum levels of an attribute that an alternative must pass to be considered. Suppose John still must choose from a wide array of notebook computers that have active-matrix screens, CD-RW drives, and 1.2-plus processor speeds. He then names another product attribute: price. Given the amount of money he has set aside for a new computer, John decides he cannot spend more than $2,500. Therefore, he can exclude all notebook computers priced above $2,500. A final way to narrow the choices is to rank the attributes under consideration in order of importance and evaluate the products based on how well they perform on the most important attributes. To reach a final decision, John would pick the most important attributes, such as processor speed and active display, weigh the merits of each, and then evaluate alternative notebook computers on those criteria.

If new brands are added to an evoked set, the consumer's evaluation of the existing brands in that set changes. As a result, certain brands in the original set may become more desirable. Suppose John sees two notebook computers priced at $1,999 and $2,199. At the time, he may judge the $2,199 notebook computer as too expensive and choose not to purchase it. However, if he then adds to his list of alternatives another notebook computer that is priced at $2,499, he may view the $2,199 one as less expensive and decide to purchase it.

The goal of the marketing manager is to determine which attributes have the most influence on a consumer's choice. Several attributes may collectively affect a consumer's evaluation of products. A single attribute, such as price, may not adequately explain how consumers form their evoked set. Moreover, attributes that the marketer thinks are important may not be very important to the consumer. For example, if you are buying a new car, you will first have to determine which cars are in your price range. But then you would also likely consider size, styling, and the reputation of the car manufacturer before making a final decision.

A brand name can also have a significant impact on a consumer's ultimate choice. In a recent on-line survey, Johnson & Johnson was found to have the best

---

evoked set (consideration set)
Group of brands, resulting from an information search, from which a buyer can choose.

corporate reputation among American companies, benefiting from its heritage as the premier maker of baby powder and shampoo. Respondents uniformly cited the familiarity and comfort they feel in using J&J products on their children. When faced with dozens of products on the drugstore shelf, consumers naturally gravitate toward J&J products. By providing consumers with a certain set of promises, brands in essence simplify the consumer decision-making process so consumers do not have to rethink their options every time they need something.[14]

Following the evaluation of alternatives, the consumer decides which product to buy or decides not to buy a product at all. If he or she decides to make a purchase, the next step in the process is an evaluation of the product after the purchase.

Postpurchase Behavior

When buying products, consumers expect certain outcomes from the purchase. How well these expectations are met determines whether the consumer is satisfied or dissatisfied with the purchase. For example, a person buys a used car with somewhat low expectations for the car's actual performance. Surprisingly, the car turns out to be one of the best cars she has ever owned. Thus, the buyer's satisfaction is high, because her fairly low expectations were exceeded. On the other hand, a consumer who buys a brand-new car would expect it to perform especially well. But if the car turns out to be a lemon, she will be very dissatisfied because her high expectations have not been met. Price often creates high expectations.

For the marketer, an important element of any postpurchase evaluation is reducing any lingering doubts that the decision was sound. This is particularly important because 75 percent of all consumers say they had a bad experience in the last year with a product or service they purchased.[15] When people recognize inconsistency between their values or opinions and their behavior, they tend to feel an inner tension called **cognitive dissonance**. For example, suppose a consumer spends half his monthly salary on a new TV entertainment system. If he stops to think how much he has spent, he will probably feel dissonance. Dissonance occurs because the person knows the purchased product has some disadvantages as well as some advantages. In the case of the entertainment system, the disadvantage of cost battles the advantage of technological superiority.

Consumers try to reduce dissonance by justifying their decision. They might seek new information that reinforces positive ideas about the purchase, avoid information that contradicts their decision, or revoke the original decision by returning the product. People who have just bought a new car often read more advertisements for the newly purchased car than for other cars in order to reduce dissonance. In some instances, people deliberately seek contrary information in order to refute it and reduce dissonance. Dissatisfied customers sometimes rely on word of mouth to reduce cognitive dissonance, by letting friends and family know they are displeased.

Marketing managers can help reduce dissonance through effective communication with purchasers. For example, a customer service manager may slip a note inside the package congratulating the buyer on making a wise decision. Postpurchase letters sent by manufacturers and dissonance-reducing statements in instruction booklets may help customers feel at ease with their purchase. Advertising that displays the product's superiority over competing brands or guarantees can also help relieve the possible

One way companies reduce the effects of cognitive dissonance is by offering comprehensive money-back guarantees or refund policies. Lands' End was a pioneer in this area and still offers a lifetime guarantee of all its merchandise.

3 Explain the consumer's post-purchase evaluation process

cognitive dissonance
Inner tension that a consumer experiences after recognizing an inconsistency between behavior and values or opinions.

COPYRIGHT LANDS' END, INC., 2002. USED WITH PERMISSION.

dissonance of someone who has already bought the product. Catalog merchant Lands' End, for example, offers consumers a no-questions-asked guarantee: If a product purchased through a Lands' End catalog does not work out, no matter what the reason, the company will provide a prompt, no-hassle refund or exchange. Hyundai Motor Company promotes its "Hyundai Advantage" warranty, which includes ten-year engine and transmission coverage, bumper-to-bumper coverage for five years or sixty-thousand miles, and five years of unlimited roadside assistance. Hyundai even promises limited reimbursement of lodging expenses incurred as a result of a breakdown.[16]

Types of Consumer Buying Decisions and Consumer Involvement

Identify the types of consumer buying decisions and discuss the significance of consumer involvement

involvement
The amount of time and effort a buyer invests in the search, evaluation, and decision processes of consumer behavior.

routine response behavior
The type of decision making exhibited by consumers buying frequently purchased, low-cost goods and services; requires little search and decision time.

All consumer buying decisions generally fall along a continuum of three broad categories: routine response behavior, limited decision making, and extensive decision making (see Exhibit 5.2). Goods and services in these three categories can best be described in terms of five factors: level of consumer involvement, length of time to make a decision, cost of the good or service, degree of information search, and the number of alternatives considered. The level of consumer involvement is perhaps the most significant determinant in classifying buying decisions. **Involvement** is the amount of time and effort a buyer invests in the search, evaluation, and decision processes of consumer behavior.

Frequently purchased, low-cost goods and services are generally associated with **routine response behavior**. These goods and services can also be called low-involvement products because consumers spend little time on search and decision before making the purchase. Usually, buyers are familiar with several different brands in the product category but stick with one brand. Consumers engaged in routine response behavior normally don't experience need recognition until they are exposed to advertising or see the product displayed on a store shelf. Consumers buy first and evaluate later, whereas the reverse is true for extensive decision making. A parent, for example, will not stand at the cereal shelf in the grocery store for twenty minutes thinking about which brand of cereal to buy

Exhibit 5.2

Continuum of Consumer Buying Decisions

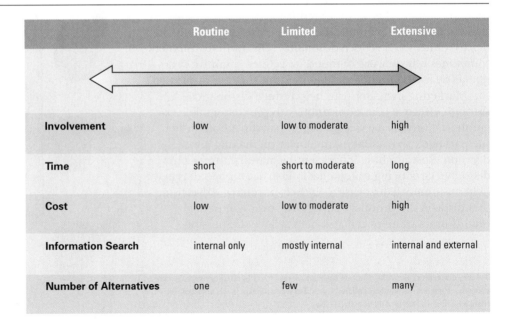

	Routine	Limited	Extensive
Involvement	low	low to moderate	high
Time	short	short to moderate	long
Cost	low	low to moderate	high
Information Search	internal only	mostly internal	internal and external
Number of Alternatives	one	few	many

for the children. Instead, he or she will walk by the shelf, find the family's usual brand, and put it into the cart.

Limited decision making typically occurs when a consumer has previous product experience but is unfamiliar with the current brands available. Limited decision making is also associated with lower levels of involvement (although higher than routine decisions) because consumers do expend moderate effort in searching for information or in considering various alternatives. Suppose the children's usual brand of cereal, Kellogg's Corn Flakes, is unavailable in the grocery store. Completely out of cereal at home, the parent now must select another brand. Before making a final selection, he or she may pull from the shelf several brands similar to Kellogg's Corn Flakes, such as Corn Chex and Cheerios, to compare their nutritional value and calories and to decide whether the children will like the new cereal.

Consumers practice **extensive decision making** when buying an unfamiliar, expensive product or an infrequently bought item. This process is the most complex type of consumer buying decision and is associated with high involvement on the part of the consumer. This process resembles the model outlined in Exhibit 5.1. These consumers want to make the right decision, so they want to know as much as they can about the product category and available brands. People usually experience cognitive dissonance only when buying high-involvement products. Buyers use several criteria for evaluating their options and spend much time seeking information. Buying a home or a car, for example, requires extensive decision making.

The type of decision making that consumers use to purchase a product does not necessarily remain constant. For instance, if a routinely purchased product no longer satisfies, consumers may practice limited or extensive decision making to switch to another brand. And people who first use extensive decision making may then use limited or routine decision making for future purchases. For example, a new mother may first extensively evaluate several brands of disposable diapers before selecting one. Subsequent purchases of diapers will then become routine.

Factors Determining the Level of Consumer Involvement

The level of involvement in the purchase depends on five factors: previous experience, interest, perceived risk, situation, and social visibility.

- *Previous experience:* When consumers have had previous experience with a good or service, the level of involvement typically decreases. After repeated product trials, consumers learn to make quick choices. Because consumers are familiar with the product and know whether it will satisfy their needs, they become less involved in the purchase. For example, consumers with pollen allergies typically buy the sinus medicine that has relieved their symptoms in the past.

- *Interest:* Involvement is directly related to consumer interests, as in cars, music, movies, bicycling, or electronics. Naturally, these areas of interest vary from one individual to another. Although some people have little interest in nursing homes, a person with elderly parents in poor health may be highly interested.

- *Perceived risk of negative consequences:* As the perceived risk in purchasing a product increases, so does a consumer's level of involvement. The types of risks that concern consumers include financial risk, social risk, and psychological risk. First, financial risk is exposure to loss of wealth or purchasing power. Because high risk is associated with high-priced purchases, consumers tend to become extremely involved. Therefore, price and involvement are usually directly related: As price increases, so does the level of involvement. For example, someone who is thinking of buying a home will normally spend much time and effort to find the right one. Second, consumers take social risks when they buy products that can affect people's social opinions of them (for example, driving an old, beat-up car or wearing unstylish clothes). Third, buyers undergo psychological risk if they feel that making the wrong decision might cause some concern or anxiety. For example, should a working parent hire a baby-sitter or enroll the child in a day-care center?

limited decision making
The type of decision making that requires a moderate amount of time for gathering information and deliberating about an unfamiliar brand in a familiar product category.

extensive decision making
The most complex type of consumer decision making, used when buying an unfamiliar, expensive product or an infrequently bought item; requires use of several criteria for evaluating options and much time for seeking information.

• *Situation:* The circumstances of a purchase may temporarily transform a low-involvement decision into a high-involvement one. High involvement comes into play when the consumer perceives risk in a specific situation. For example, an individual might routinely buy low-priced brands of liquor and wine. When the boss visits, however, the consumer might make a high-involvement decision and buy more prestigious brands.

• *Social visibility:* Involvement also increases as the social visibility of a product increases. Products often on social display include clothing (especially designer labels), jewelry, cars, and furniture. All these items make a statement about the purchaser and, therefore, carry a social risk.

Marketing Implications of Involvement

Marketing strategy varies according to the level of involvement associated with the product. For high-involvement product purchases, marketing managers have several responsibilities. First, promotion to the target market should be extensive and informative. A good ad gives consumers the information they need for making the purchase decision, as well as specifying the benefits and unique advantages of owning the product. For example, manufacturers of high-tech computers and peripheral equipment like scanners, printers, and modems run lengthy ads that detail technical information about such attributes as performance, resolution, and speed. To make the purchase decision easier, major automobile manufacturers now enable their customers to use virtual reality to test different combinations of colors, fabrics, hubcaps, and so forth. Customers can see the effect of different options using a touch screen to generate an image of the car after making their selections. They can even hear different configurations of stereo sound systems to select the one they like best.

Purchasing on-line involves added risk for many consumers, even in limited decision-making situations. To overcome the challenges of getting shoppers to complete purchases on-line, Landsend.com created a virtual three-dimensional model that customers can use to try on clothes. It also offers an on-line "personal shopper" to help customers identify items they might like. Purchase rates have been 26 percent higher among on-line shoppers who use the model and 80 percent higher among customers who use the personal shopper.[17]

For low-involvement product purchases, consumers may not recognize their wants until they are in the store. Therefore, in-store promotion is an important tool when promoting low-involvement products. Marketing managers have to focus on package design so the product will be eye-catching and easily recognized on the shelf. Examples of products that take this approach are Campbell's soups, Tide detergent, Velveeta cheese, and Heinz ketchup. In-store displays also stimulate sales of low-involvement products. A good display can explain the product's purpose and prompt recognition of a want. Displays of health and beauty aid items in supermarkets have been known to increase sales many times above normal. Coupons, cents-off deals, and two-for-one offers also effectively promote low-involvement items.

Linking a product to a higher-involvement issue is another tactic that marketing managers can use to increase the sales of a low-involvement product. For example, many food products are no longer just nutritious but also low in fat or cholesterol. Although packaged food may normally be a low-involvement product, reference to health issues raises the involvement level. To take advantage of

COURTESY OF STONYFIELD FARM

Although food products are generally considered low-involvement purchases, marketers can increase sales by linking high-involvement issues to their products. In this ad for Stonyfield Farm organic yogurts, the issue of children's health and welfare is elicited by the tag line "Earth to Mom."

aging baby boomers' interest in healthier foods, a recent advertisement from H.J. Heinz Company linked its ketchup with a growing body of research that suggests lycopene, an antioxidant found in tomatoes, can reduce the risk of prostate and cervical cancer.[18] Similarly, food products, such as Silk soy milk and Garden-burger meatless burgers, both of which contain soy protein, tout their health benefits in reducing the risk of coronary heart disease, preventing certain cancers, and reducing the symptoms of menopause. Soy-based products, long shunned in the United States for their taste, have seen their sales skyrocket as a result of these health claims.[19]

Factors Influencing Consumer Buying Decisions

The consumer decision-making process does not occur in a vacuum. On the contrary, underlying cultural, social, individual, and psychological factors strongly influence the decision process. They have an effect from the time a consumer perceives a stimulus through postpurchase behavior. Cultural factors, which include culture and values, subculture, and social class, exert the broadest influence over consumer decision making. Social factors sum up the social interactions between a consumer and influential groups of people, such as reference groups, opinion leaders, and family members. Individual factors, which include gender, age, family life-cycle stage, personality, self-concept, and lifestyle, are unique to each individual and play a major role in the type of products and services consumers want. Psychological factors determine how consumers perceive and interact with their environments and influence the ultimate decisions consumers make. They include perception, motivation, learning, beliefs, and attitudes. Exhibit 5.3 summarizes these influences.

Cultural Influences on Consumer Buying Decisions

The first major group of factors that influence consumer decision making are cultural factors. Cultural factors exert the broadest and deepest influence over a person's consumer behavior and decision making. Marketers must understand the way a people's culture and its accompanying values, as well as their subculture and social class, influence their buying behavior.

Identify and understand the cultural factors that affect consumer buying decisions

Culture and Values

Culture is the essential character of a society that distinguishes it from other cultural groups. The underlying elements of every culture are the values, language, myths, customs, rituals, and laws that shape the behavior of the culture, as well as the material artifacts, or products, of that behavior as they are transmitted from one generation to the next. Exhibit 5.4 lists some defining components of American culture.

Culture is pervasive. Cultural values and influences are the ocean in which individuals swim, and yet most are completely unaware that it is there. What people eat, how they dress, what they think and feel, and what language they speak are all dimensions of culture. It encompasses all the things consumers do without conscious choice because their culture's values, customs, and rituals are ingrained in their daily habits.

Culture is functional. Human interaction creates values and prescribes acceptable behavior for each culture. By establishing common expectations, culture gives order to society. Sometimes these expectations are coded into laws. For example, drivers in our culture must stop at a red light. Other times these expectations are

culture
The set of values, norms, attitudes, and other meaningful symbols that shape human behavior and the artifacts, or products, of that behavior as they are transmitted from one generation to the next.

Exhibit 5.3

Factors That Affect the Consumer
Decision-Making Process

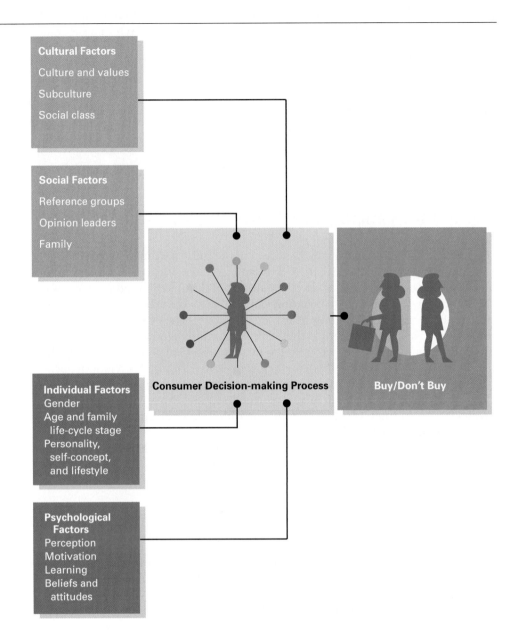

Cultural Factors
Culture and values
Subculture
Social class

Social Factors
Reference groups
Opinion leaders
Family

Individual Factors
Gender
Age and family
 life-cycle stage
Personality,
 self-concept,
 and lifestyle

**Psychological
 Factors**
Perception
Motivation
Learning
Beliefs and
 attitudes

Consumer Decision-making Process

Buy/Don't Buy

taken for granted. For example, grocery stores and hospitals are open twenty-four hours whereas bank lobbies are open only during bankers' hours.

Culture is learned. Consumers are not born knowing the values and norms of their society. Instead, they must learn what is acceptable from family and friends. Children learn the values that will govern their behavior from parents, teachers, and peers. As members of our society, they learn to shake hands when they greet someone, to drive on the right-hand side of the road, and to eat pizza and drink Coca-Cola.

Culture is dynamic. It adapts to changing needs and an evolving environment. The rapid growth of technology in today's world has accelerated the rate of cultural change. Television has changed entertainment patterns and family communication and has heightened public awareness of political and other news events. Automation has increased the amount of leisure time we have and, in some ways, has changed the traditional work ethic. Cultural norms will continue to evolve because of our need for social patterns that solve problems.

Exhibit 5.4

Components of American Culture

Component	Examples
Values	Success through hard work Emphasis on personal freedom
Language	English as the dominant language
Myths	Santa Claus delivers presents to good boys and girls on Christmas Eve. Abraham Lincoln walked a mile to return a penny.
Customs	Bathing daily Shaking hands when greeting new people Standard gratuity of 15 percent at restaurants
Rituals	Thanksgiving Day dinner Singing the "Star Spangled Banner" before baseball games Going to religious services on the appropriate day
Laws	Child labor laws Sherman Anti-Trust Act guarantees competition.
Material artifacts	Diamond engagement rings Beanie Babies

SOURCE: Adapted from *Consumer Behavior* by William D. Wells and David Prensky. Copyright © 1996 by John Wiley & Sons, Inc. Reprinted by permission of John Wiley & Sons, Inc. All Rights Reserved.

In the United States, rapid changes in diversity are causing major shifts in culture. For example, the growth of the Hispanic community is influencing American food, music, clothing, and entertainment. Additionally, African American culture has been embraced by the mainstream. In fact, when DaimlerChrysler wanted to update its image, the company began using actors with dark hair and brown skin whose ethnic background was hard to guess as a way to give the vehicles a more hip, urban image. The company's research found that all consumers, including whites, perceived multicultural actors as cool.[20]

The most defining element of a culture is its **values**—the enduring beliefs shared by a society that a specific mode of conduct is personally or socially preferable to another mode of conduct. People's value systems have a great effect on their consumer behavior. Consumers with similar value systems tend to react alike to prices and other marketing-related inducements. Values also correspond to consumption patterns. For example, Americans place a high value on convenience. This value has created lucrative markets for products such as breakfast bars, energy bars, and nutrition bars that allow consumers to eat on the go.[21] Values can also influence consumers' TV viewing habits or the magazines they read. For instance, people who strongly object to violence avoid crime shows, and those who oppose pornography do not buy *Hustler*. Core American values—those considered central to the American way of life—are presented in Exhibit 5.5.

The personal values of target consumers have important implications for marketing managers. When marketers understand the core values that underlie the attitudes that shape the buying patterns of America's consumers and how these values were molded by experiences, they can target their message more effectively. For example, the personal value systems of matures, baby boomers, Generation

value
The enduring belief that a specific mode of conduct is personally or socially preferable to another mode of conduct.

Exhibit 5.5

Core American Values

Success	Americans admire hard work, entrepreneurship, achievement, and success. Those achieving success in American society are rewarded with money, status, and prestige. For example, Bill Gates, once a nerdy computer buff, built Microsoft Computers into an internationally known giant. Gates is now one of the richest people in the world today.
Materialism	Americans value owning tangible goods. American society encourages consumption, ownership, and possession. Americans judge others based on their material possessions; for example, the type of car they own, where they live, and what type of clothes they wear.
Freedom	The American culture was founded on the principle of religious and political freedom. The U.S. Constitution and the Bill of Rights assure American citizens the right to life, liberty, and the pursuit of happiness. These freedoms are fundamental to the legal system and the moral fiber of American culture. The Internet, for example, is built on the principle of the right to free speech. Lawmakers who have attempted to limit the material available on the Internet have met with tough free-speech opponents.
Progress	Technological advances, as well as advances in medicine, science, health, and the quality of products and services, are important to Americans. Each year, for example, more than 25,000 new or improved consumer products are introduced on America's supermarket shelves.*
Youth	Americans are obsessed with youth and spend a good deal of time on products and procedures that make them feel and look younger. Americans spend millions each year on health and beauty aids, health clubs, and healthy foods. Media and advertising encourage the quest for youth by using young, attractive, slim models, such as those in ads from fashion designer Calvin Klein.
Capitalism	Americans believe in a free enterprise system characterized by competition and the chance for monetary success. Capitalism creates choices, quality, and value for Americans. Laws prohibit monopolistic control of a market and regulate free trade. Americans encourage small business success, such as that found by Apple Computer, Wal-Mart, and McDonald's, all of which started as small enterprises with a better idea that toppled the competition.

*Data obtained from the New Products Showcase and Learning Center, Ithaca, New York, Web site at **http://www.showlearn.com**, 1998.
SOURCE: From *Consumer Behavior* by William D. Wells and David Prensky. Copyright © 1996 John Wiley & Sons, Inc. Reprinted by permission of John Wiley & Sons, Inc. All Rights Reserved.

X-ers, and Generation Y-ers are quite different. The key to understanding *matures*, or everyone born before 1945, is recognizing the impact of the Great Depression and World War II on their lives. Facing these two immense challenges shaped a generation characterized by discipline, self-denial, financial and social conservatism, and a sense of obligation. Boomers, those individuals nurtured in the bountiful postwar period between 1945 and 1964, believe they are entitled to the wealth and opportunity that seemed endless in their youth. Generation X-ers are very accepting of diversity and individuality. They are also a very entrepreneurial-driven generation, ready to tackle life's challenges for themselves rather than as part of a crowd.[22] Gen Y-ers are more serious and socially conscious than Gen X-ers. Some of the defining events of their lives include Columbine, the O. J. Simpson trial, the Clinton impeachment, and the 2000 presidential election. They grew up with cable television, computers, debit cards, and cellphones, making them the most well connected generation to date—a fact that has important implications for word-of-mouth influence.[23]

Values represent what is most important in people's lives. Therefore, marketers watch carefully for shifts in consumers' values over time. For example, millions of Americans have acquired a passion for spirituality, as evidenced by the soaring sales of books with religious or spiritual themes and the popularity of television shows with similar themes. Similarly, after the September 11 terrorist attacks, when many people were fearful and concerned about self-protection, gun sales soared as did the sale of drugs to cure anthrax.

Understanding Culture Differences

GLOBAL Underlying core values can vary across cultures. Most Americans are more concerned about their health than their weight. But for many Brazilian women, being thin is more important than being healthy. In fact, a recent survey found that 75 percent of Brazilian women over the age of twenty who wanted to lose weight had taken prescription diet drugs for obesity even though less than one-third of the women were obese and the drugs presented the risk of side effects such as heart and lung damage. In contrast, most Chinese women do not place a high value on thinness and show little concern about being overweight.[24]

GLOBAL Without understanding a culture, a firm has little chance of selling products in it. Like people, products have cultural values and rules that influence their perception and use. Culture, therefore, must be understood before the behavior of individuals within the cultural context can be understood. Colors, for example, may have different meanings in global markets than they do at home. In China, white is the color of mourning and brides wear red. In the United States, black is for mourning and brides wear white. Recall from Chapter 4 that American designers at Universal Studios found they had much to learn about Japanese culture when planning a new theme park for Japan. Surveys showed that many of their original ideas to create Japanese attractions would not appeal to Japanese consumers who were hoping for an authentic American theme park that catered to their cultural differences. After extensive surveying and product testing, the result was a Universal Studios theme park with a more orderly clockwise layout, Japanese-style American food, and a Jurassic Park water slide designed to prevent riders from getting wet.[25]

GLOBAL Language is another important aspect of culture that global marketers must deal with. They must take care in translating product names, slogans, and promotional messages into foreign languages so as not to convey the wrong message. Consider the following examples of blunders made by marketers when delivering their message to Spanish-speaking consumers: General Motors discovered too late that Nova (the name of an economical car) literally means "doesn't go" in Spanish; Coors encouraged its English-speaking customers to "Turn it loose," but the phrase in Spanish means "Suffer from diarrhea"; and when Frank Perdue said, "It takes a tough man to make a tender chicken," Spanish speakers heard "It takes a sexually stimulated man to make a chicken affectionate."

As more companies expand their operations globally, the need to understand the cultures of foreign countries becomes more important. While marketers expanding into global markets generally adapt their products and business formats to the local culture, some fear that increasing globalization, as well as the proliferation of the Internet, will result in a homogeneous world culture of the future. U.S. companies in particular, they fear, are Americanizing the world by exporting bastions of American culture, such as McDonald's fast-food restaurants, Starbucks coffeehouses, Microsoft software, and American movies and entertainment. Read more about this issue in the "Global Perspectives" box.

THIS WILL BE A CREDIT LINE.

McDonald's has responded to cultural differences like no other company. Its Web site boasts: "If meeting the demands of local culture means adding to our regular menu, we'll do it." In Japan, the company introduced the Teriyaki McBurger, and in India, McDonald's serves meatless sandwiches.

Will Cultural Differences Survive a Global Economy?

Modern industry has established the world market. . . . All old-established national industries . . . are dislodged by new industries whose . . . products are consumed, not only at home, but in every quarter of the globe. In place of old wants . . . we find new wants, requiring for their satisfaction the products of distant lands and climes.

—Karl Marx and
Friedrich Engels
The Communist Manifesto

Although Karl Marx and Friedrich Engels wrote these words more than 150 years ago, this passage describes a present-day phenomenon in the world's cultures called *globalization*. Thirty years ago, most Chinese did not own televisions, refrigerators, or washing machines. But as economic reforms allowed more Western companies to offer their goods in China, ordinary people demanded these products. Today, 97 percent of Chinese in cities have televisions, and 88 percent have refrigerators and washing machines.

Globalization is not a new concept. Humans have been weaving commercial and cultural connections since the beginning of civilization. Today, computers, the Internet, cellular phones, cable television, and cheaper air transportation have accelerated and complicated these connections. Yet the basic dynamic remains the same: As people cross borders and oceans moving goods and services, their ideas move with them. And cultures change. The difference today is the speed at which these changes take place. Case in point: It took television thirteen years to acquire fifty million users; it took the Internet only five.

Everywhere, it seems, people are experiencing the fusion of cultures. London coffeehouses sell Italian espresso served by Algerian waiters while strains of the Beach Boys singing "I wish they all could be California girls . . ." can be

heard in the background. The classic American Barbie doll, once only available as a blond, now comes in some thirty national varieties, including, most recently, Austrian and Moroccan. At Hollywood High School in Los Angeles, the student body represents thirty-two different languages. Computer games fanatics in the United States play mah-jongg, an ancient Chinese game of strategy and luck, over the Internet against players from all over the world. *Cosmopolitan* magazine, the racy American fashion publication, is read by some 260,000 Chinese women every month. Adventurous diners in the midst of south Louisiana savor authentic Japanese sushi and join in karaoke singing. For about 100 rupees a month—about $2.34—slum-dwelling families in Mumbai (formerly Bombay) can surf more than fifty cable channels including Western imports such as TNT, MTV, CNN, and ESPN. McDonald's now has some twenty-five thousand restaurants worldwide, making the golden arches perhaps the most widely recognized trademark on the globe.

Not everyone is happy about the blending of cultures. Sociologists and anthropologists fear cultural cloning will result from what they regard as the "cultural assault" of ubiquitous Western multinationals such as McDonald's, Coca-Cola, Disney, Nike, MTV, and even the English language itself. Globalization has become a worrisome issue for many cultures. France worries about American films and television elbowing out French entertainment. Indians agonize that American junk food, television, films, blue jeans, pornography, and Christian missionaries will ruin traditional Indian values. Australians, in particular, have been phobically fearful of what they refer to as the remorseless march of American "cultural imperialism." In China, a recent book entitled *China Can Say No* became a best seller by admonishing Chinese who believe blindly in

anything foreign. Critics of globalization are convinced that Western, especially American, influences will pervade every culture, producing, as one observer terms it, one big "McWorld."

But not everyone is paranoid about cultural cloning. Proponents of globalization feel cultural change is inevitable and part of national evolution. For the most part, they contend, cultures take what they want from other cultures and adapt it to their needs. Tom Freston, CEO of MTV, contends that "kids today, outside of the U.S. in particular, travel with two passports. They have the international passport . . . that plugs them into what is going on with their peers around the world. So when you talk about action movies, sports stars, certain music stars like a Mariah Carey, certain kinds of clothing and styles, there is a homogeneity. But while that trend is going on, they have their other passport that is about their local world, which increasingly is more important to them." Hence, multinationals consistently adapt products and services to meet the needs of peoples in other lands. MTV tailors its music offerings in different countries to include local stars who sing in their own language. McDonald's outlets in India, where there are more than four hundred local languages and several very strict religions, serve mutton instead of beef and offer vegetarian menus acceptable to orthodox Hindus. Similarly, Revlon adapted the color palette and composition of its cosmetics to suit the Indian skin and climate.

Cultural change, supporters say, is a reality, not a choice. They believe that cultures won't become more uniform, but instead both old and new will tend to transform each other. Globalization won't mean just more television sets or Nike shoes, but rather a common destiny shaped by humanity.[26]

On Line

Subculture

A culture can be divided into subcultures on the basis of demographic characteristics, geographic regions, national and ethnic background, political beliefs, and religious beliefs. A **subculture** is a homogeneous group of people who share elements of the overall culture as well as cultural elements unique to their own group. Within subcultures, people's attitudes, values, and purchase decisions are even more similar than they are within the broader culture. Subcultural differences may result in considerable variation within a culture in what, how, when, and where people buy goods and services.

In the United States alone, countless subcultures can be identified. Many are concentrated geographically. People belonging to the Mormon religion, for example, are clustered mainly in Utah; Cajuns are located in the bayou regions of southern Louisiana. Hispanics are more predominant in those states that border Mexico, whereas the majority of Chinese, Japanese, and Koreans are found in the Pacific region of the United States.

Other subcultures are geographically dispersed. For example, computer hackers, people who are hearing or visually impaired, Harley-Davidson bikers, military families, university professors, and gays may be found throughout the country. Yet they have identifiable attitudes, values, and needs that distinguish them from the larger culture. For instance, Nokia Corporation sells phones that flash or vibrate for people with hearing problems while other companies, such as Nike and Pfizer, have aired commercials featuring people with various disabilities.[27] Similarly, Burger King has had good results in Chicago targeting people who work unusual hours and crave dinner-type food in the morning by advertising and offering burgers in the morning instead of waiting until 10:30 A.M. like most of its competitors.[28]

If marketers can identify subcultures, they can then design special marketing programs to serve their needs. According to the U.S. Census Bureau, the Hispanic population is the largest and fastest growing subculture, increasing at a rate of four times that of the general population. To tap into this large and growing segment, marketers have been spending a larger percentage of their marketing budgets advertising to Hispanics. Companies like Procter & Gamble, Anheuser-Busch, Hershey Foods, and Chuck E. Cheese all have Hispanic marketing campaigns, as do major league sports teams like the Texas Rangers and the Dallas Mavericks. The campaigns often feature both English and Spanish advertising and appeal to cultural pride.[29]

Other companies have been successful in targeting much smaller subcultures that are often overlooked. For example, Shaklee Corporation, a multilevel marketing company, has targeted subcultures such as the Amish, Mennonites, and Hasidic Jews. To recruit salespeople in these subcultures, Shaklee caters to their special needs. For example, Amish and Mennonite salespeople can earn a "bonus buggy" instead of the more traditional new car. To accommodate Hasidic customers, Shaklee toughened standards on their kosher products.[30]

Social Class

The United States, like other societies, does have a social class system. A **social class** is a group of people who are considered nearly equal in status or community

subculture
A homogeneous group of people who share elements of the overall culture as well as unique elements of their own group.

social class
A group of people in a society who are considered nearly equal in status or community esteem, who regularly socialize among themselves both formally and informally, and who share behavioral norms.

esteem, who regularly socialize among themselves both formally and informally, and who share behavioral norms.

A number of techniques have been used to measure social class, and a number of criteria have been used to define it. One view of contemporary U.S. status structure is shown in Exhibit 5.6.

As you can see from Exhibit 5.6, the upper and upper middle classes comprise the small segment of affluent and wealthy Americans. The upper social classes are more likely than other classes to contribute something to society—for example, by volunteer work or active participation in civic affairs. In terms of consumer buying patterns, the affluent are more likely to own their own home and purchase new cars and trucks and are less likely to smoke. The very rich flex their financial muscles by spending more on owned vacation homes, vacations and cruises, and housekeeping and gardening services. The most affluent consumers are more likely to attend art auctions and galleries, dance performances, operas, the theater, museums, concerts, and sporting events.[31]

The majority of Americans today define themselves as middle class, regardless of their actual income or educational attainment. This phenomenon is most likely due to the fact that working-class Americans tend to aspire to the middle-class lifestyle while some of those who do achieve affluence may downwardly aspire to respectable middle-class status as a matter of principle.[32] Attaining goals and achieving status and prestige are important to middle-class consumers. People falling into the middle class live in the gap between the haves and the have-nots. They aspire to the lifestyle of the more affluent but are constrained by the economic realities and cautious attitudes they share with the working class.

The working class is a distinct subset of the middle class. Interest in organized labor is one of the attributes most common among the working class. This group is more likely to rate job security as the most important reason for taking a job.[33] The working-class person depends heavily on relatives and the community for economic and emotional support. The emphasis on family ties is one sign of the group's intensely local view of the world. They like the local news far more than do middle-class audiences who favor national and world coverage. They are also more likely to vacation closer to home.

Exhibit 5.6

U.S. Social Class

Upper Classes		
Capitalist class	1%	People whose investment decisions shape the national economy; income mostly from assets, earned or inherited; university connections
Upper middle class	14%	Upper-level managers, professionals, owners of medium-sized businesses; college-educated; family income nearly twice national average
Middle Classes		
Middle class	33%	Middle-level white-collar, top-level blue-collar; education past high school typical; income somewhat above national average
Working class	32%	Middle-level blue-collar, lower-level white-collar; income slightly below national average
Lower Classes		
Working poor	11–12%	Low-paid service workers and operatives; some high school education; below mainstream in living standard but above poverty line
Underclass	8–9%	People who are not regularly employed and who depend primarily on the welfare system for sustenance; little schooling; living standard below poverty line

SOURCE: Adapted from Richard P. Coleman, "The Continuing Significance of Social Class to Marketing," *Journal of Consumer Research,* December 1983, p. 267; Dennis Gilbert and Joseph A. Kahl, *The American Class Structure: A Synthesis* (Homewood, IL: Dorsey Press, 1982), ch. 11.

Lifestyle distinctions between the social classes are greater than the distinctions within a given class. The most significant separation between the classes is the one between the middle and lower classes. It is here that the major shift in lifestyles appears. Members of the lower class typically fall at or below the poverty level in terms of income. This social class has the highest unemployment rate, and many individuals or families are subsidized through the welfare system. Many are illiterate, with little formal education. Compared to more affluent consumers, lower-class consumers have poorer diets and typically purchase much different types of foods when they shop.

Social class is typically measured as a combination of occupation, income, education, wealth, and other variables. For instance, affluent upper-class consumers are more likely to be salaried executives or self-employed professionals with at least an undergraduate degree. Working-class or middle-class consumers are more likely to be hourly service workers or blue-collar employees with only a high school education. Educational attainment, however, seems to be the most reliable indicator of a person's social and economic status (see Exhibit 5.7). Those with college degrees or graduate degrees are more likely to fall into the upper classes, while those people with some college experience but no degree fall closest to traditional concepts of the middle class.

Marketers are interested in social class for two main reasons. First, social class often indicates which medium to use for advertising. Suppose an insurance company seeks to sell its policies to middle-class families. It might advertise during the local evening news because middle-class families tend to watch more television than other classes do. If the company wants to sell more policies to upscale individuals, it might place a print ad in a business publication like the *Wall Street Journal*. The Internet, long the domain of more educated and affluent families, is becoming an important advertising outlet for advertisers hoping to reach blue-collar workers and homemakers. As the middle class rapidly adopts the medium, marketers are having to do more research to find out which Web sites will reach their audience.[34]

Second, knowing what products appeal to which social classes can help marketers determine where to best distribute their products. For example, a survey of consumer spending in the Washington, D.C. area reveals a stark contrast between Brie-eaters and Velveeta-eaters. The buyers of Brie, the soft and savory French cheese, are concentrated in the upscale neighborhoods of Northwest D.C. and the western suburbs of Montgomery County, Maryland, and Fairfax County, Virginia, where most residents are executives, white-collar professionals, or politicians. Brie fans tend to be college-educated professionals with six-figure incomes and an activist spirit. In contrast, aficionados of Velveeta, processed cheese marketed by Kraft, are concentrated in the middle-class, family-filled suburbs of Prince George's County and the predominantly black D.C. neighborhoods. Velveeta buyers tend to be married with children, high school educated, and employed at modestly paying service and blue-collar jobs.[35]

Exhibit 5.7

Social Class and Education

Percentage of adults in self-identified social classes who have a bachelor's degree or higher

Social Class	Percent
Lower	8
Working	12
Middle	34
Upper	61

SOURCE: "The New Working Class," *American Demographics*, January 1998, 51–55.

Social Influences on Consumer Buying Decisions

6

Identify and understand the social factors that affect consumer buying decisions

reference group
A group in society that influences an individual's purchasing behavior.

primary membership group
A reference group with which people interact regularly in an informal, face-to-face manner, such as family, friends, or fellow employees.

secondary membership group
A reference group with which people associate less consistently and more formally than a primary membership group, such as a club, professional group, or religious group.

aspirational reference group
A group that someone would like to join.

norm
A value or attitude deemed acceptable by a group.

Most consumers are likely to seek out the opinions of others to reduce their search and evaluation effort or uncertainty, especially as the perceived risk of the decision increases. Consumers may also seek out others' opinions for guidance on new products or services, products with image-related attributes, or products where attribute information is lacking or uninformative. Specifically, consumers interact socially with reference groups, opinion leaders, and family members to obtain product information and decision approval.

Reference Groups

All the formal and informal groups that influence the buying behavior of an individual are that person's **reference groups**. Consumers may use products or brands to identify with or become a member of a group. They learn from observing how members of their reference groups consume, and they use the same criteria to make their own consumer decisions.

Reference groups can be categorized very broadly as either direct or indirect (see Exhibit 5.8). Direct reference groups are face-to-face membership groups that touch people's lives directly. They can be either primary or secondary. **Primary membership groups** include all groups with which people interact regularly in an informal, face-to-face manner, such as family, friends, and coworkers. In contrast, people associate with **secondary membership groups** less consistently and more formally. These groups might include clubs, professional groups, and religious groups.

Consumers also are influenced by many indirect, nonmembership reference groups that they do not belong to. **Aspirational reference groups** are those that a person would like to join. To join an aspirational group, a person must at least conform to the norms of that group. (**Norms** are the values and attitudes deemed acceptable by the group.) Thus, a person who wants to be elected to public office may begin to dress more conservatively, as other politicians do. He or she may go to many of the restaurants and social engagements that city and business leaders attend and try to play a role that is acceptable to voters and other influential people. Similarly, teenagers today may dye their hair, experiment with body piercing and tattoos, and carry around copies of "in" books so that their peers will perceive them as well read.[36]

Exhibit 5.8

Types of Reference Groups

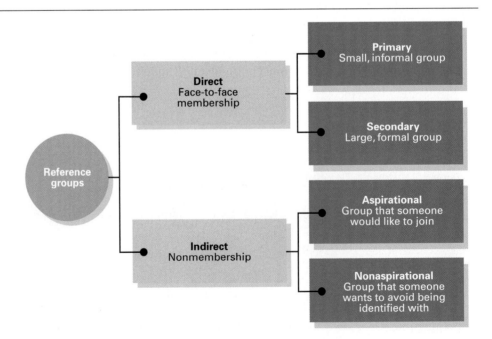

Nonaspirational reference groups, or dissociative groups, influence our behavior when we try to maintain distance from them. A consumer may avoid buying some types of clothing or car, going to certain restaurants or stores, or even buying a home in a certain neighborhood in order to avoid being associated with a particular group.

nonaspirational reference group
A group with which an individual does not want to associate.

The activities, values, and goals of reference groups directly influence consumer behavior. For marketers, reference groups have three important implications: (1) they serve as information sources and influence perceptions; (2) they affect an individual's aspiration levels; and (3) their norms either constrain or stimulate consumer behavior. For example, Teenage Research Unlimited, an Illinois research firm devoted to uncovering what's cool in the teen market, recently identified four loose groups of today's teens based on their interests in clothes, music, and activities. Tracking these groups reveals how products become cool and how groups influence the adoption of cool products by other groups. According to Teenage Research Unlimited, a trend or fad often starts with "Edge" teens who have the most innovative tastes. These teens are on the cutting edge of fashion and music, and they wear their attitude all over their bodies in the form of tattoos, body piercing, studded jewelry, or colored tresses. Certain fads embraced by Edgers will spark an interest in the small group of teens called "Influencers," who project the look other teens covet. Influencers also create their own trends like rap music, baggy jeans, and pro sports clothes. Once a fad is embraced and adopted by Influencers, the look becomes cool and desirable. "Conformers" and "Passives" comprise the majority of the teen population, but they will not embrace a fad until it gets its seal of approval from the Influencers.[37]

Understanding the effect of reference groups on a product is important for marketers as they track the life cycle of their products. Retailer Abercrombie & Fitch noticed it was beginning to lose its target audience of college students when its stores began attracting large numbers of high school students trying to be more like the college students. To solve the problem, A&F created its Hollister store chain specifically for high school students.[38]

GLOBAL In Japan, companies have long relied on the nation's high school girls to give them advice during product testing. Fads that catch on among teenage girls often become big trends throughout the country and among Japanese consumers in general. Food manufacturers frequently recruit Tokyo schoolgirls to sample potato chip recipes or chocolate bars. Television networks survey high school girls to fine-tune story lines for higher ratings on prime-time shows. Other companies pay girls to keep diaries of what they buy. In 1995, Warner-Lambert hired high school girls to help choose a new gum flavor. After extensive chewing and comparing, the girls settled on a flavor that became Trickle, now Japan's best-selling bubble gum.[39]

© PETER M. WILSON/CORBIS

Japanese teenage girls have long provided the marketing litmus test companies need before launching new products. Perhaps their success in this area is due to the fact that they are caught in a pivotal clash between a tradition of collectivism and a growing sense of individualism.

Opinion Leaders

Reference groups frequently include individuals known as group leaders, or **opinion leaders**—those who influence others. Obviously, it is important for marketing managers to persuade such people to purchase their goods or services. Many products and services that are integral parts of Americans' lives today got their initial boost from opinion leaders. For example, VCRs and sport utility vehicles were embraced by opinion leaders well ahead of the general public. Exhibit 5.9 lists some products and services for which individuals often seek the advice of an opinion leader before purchasing.

Opinion leaders are often the first to try new products and services out of pure curiosity. They are typically self-indulgent, making them more likely to explore unproven but intriguing products and services. Technology companies have

opinion leader
An individual who influences the opinions of others.

Exhibit 5.9

Words of Wisdom: Opinion Leaders'
Consumer Clout Extends Far Beyond
Their Own Purchases

	Average Number of People to Whom Opinion Leaders Recommended Products* in the Past Year	Millions of Recommendations Made
Restaurant	5.0	70
Vacation destination	5.1	44
TV Show	4.9	45
Car	4.1	29
Retail store	4.7	29
Clothing	4.5	24
Consumer electronics	4.5	16
Office equipment	5.8	12
Stock, mutual fund, CD, etc.	3.4	12

*Among those who recommended the product at all
SOURCE: Roper Starch Worldwide, Inc., New York, NY. Adapted from "Maximizing the Market with Influentials," *American Demographics*, July 1995, p. 42.

found that teenagers, because of their willingness to experiment, are key opinion leaders for the success of new technologies. For example, text messaging, which had its beginning with teenagers, has gained widespread appeal. Thus, many technology companies see creating a buzz among teens as a critical part of their marketing programs.[40]

Opinion leadership is a casual, face-to-face phenomenon and usually inconspicuous, so locating opinion leaders can be a challenge. Thus, marketers often try to create opinion leaders. They may use high school cheerleaders to model new fall fashions or civic leaders to promote insurance, new cars, and other merchandise. Revatex, the maker of JNCO jeans, sponsors extreme-sports athletes who appeal to the teen market. It also gives free clothes to trendsetters among teens in the hopes they will influence others to purchase the brand. JNCO outfits big-name DJs in the rave scene, as well as members of hip, alternative bands favored by the teen crowd. Similarly, the Web site of New York retailer Alloy Online (**www.alloyonline.com**) offers style tips, quizzes on topics like "What is your ideal guy type?" and gossip about teen idols like Britney Spears; it encourages teens to offer feedback about their likes and dislikes in a section called "Dig or Dis."[41] The "Ethics in Marketing" box questions how much marketers should target teenagers.

On a national level, companies sometimes use movie stars, sports figures, and other celebrities to promote products, hoping they are appropriate opinion leaders. Nike, for example, signed golf superstar Tiger Woods as a spokesperson for its products. The company hopes that consumers will see an affinity between the values that Woods represents and the values that Nike represents—earned success,

Targeting Teens at School

As we have discussed in this chapter, marketers study consumers, identify unmet needs, develop products and services to meet those needs, and find a way to sell the products to those consumers. That sounds simple, but the process is not always without critics.

For example, soft drink manufacturers know that teenagers are the biggest consumers of their products. They also know that most soft drink consumers develop brand loyalty in their teen years, so it is critical to the manufacturers' long-term success to convince teens to choose their brand. Therefore, Coca-Cola and PepsiCo spend millions of dollars marketing their products to teens. To this point, the behavior of Coca-Cola and PepsiCo is no different from that of any other successful marketing company.

But what happens when soft drink companies target high schools for product distribution? Given the amount of time teens spend at schools, that is a logical choice. But parents, teachers, and legislators are becoming increasingly concerned over the practice.

Here are a few reason why. First, according to new statistics from the Centers for Disease Control, American high school students are three times as likely to be overweight than they were twenty years ago. Looking to explain the increase, some people point to the greater availability of soft drinks and junk foods on school campuses. Others say the increase cannot be blamed on soft drinks and junk food alone and that the increased consumption of all types of food and the decline in exercise are to blame. Still other critics blame soft drinks for tooth decay, and one study even linked soft drink consumption to fractured bones in high school girls.

Second, other critics are concerned about the commercialization of our schools. In most cases, soft drinks are sold in schools through exclusive agreements, which give the soft drink company high visibility. In return, the schools are able to use profits from a percentage of the sales to fund student programs. Because so many schools need the funding, critics say, the schools are unable to turn down the offers and, in some cases, feel the need to promote soft drink sales in spite of health concerns.

In response to criticism, the Coca-Cola Company recently announced that it would no longer encourage the exclusive agreements and would look for less commercial ways to benefit the schools. But the contracts are made not by the Coca-Cola Company, but by its bottlers, many of which have continued the practice in spite of Coca-Cola's announcement because they are proud of their relationships with the schools and because of increased competition from PepsiCo. PepsiCo says it doesn't encourage the practice of exclusive contracts but that it will bid on them when asked.[42]

So what do you think? Should Coca-Cola and PepsiCo be able to target teens at school? What if the companies reduced the number of soft drinks in machines and added more water and juice options since both companies offer those products? What are the advantages and disadvantages of targeting teens in school? We will continue to explore the controversial topic of marketing in schools in the "Ethics in Marketing" box in Chapter 9 (see page 299).

---

discipline, hard work, achievement, and integrity. Nike also believes that the quality of Woods's golf game will be associated with the quality and value of its products. One year after Woods began appearing in ads and on the fairway with Nike's new line of golf balls, the company's market share tripled.[43]

The effectiveness of celebrity endorsements depends largely on how credible and attractive the spokesperson is and how familiar people are with him or her. Endorsements are most likely to succeed if an association between the spokesperson and the product can be reasonably established. For example, comedian Bill Cosby failed as an endorser for financial products but succeeded with such products as Kodak cameras and Jell-O gelatin. Consumers could not mentally link Bill Cosby with serious investment decisions but could associate him with leisure activities and everyday consumption. Additionally, in the selection of a celebrity endorser, marketers must consider the broader meanings associated with the endorser. Although the endorser may have certain attributes that are desirable for endorsing the product, he or she may also have other attributes that are inappropriate.

A marketing manager can also try to use opinion leaders through group sanctioning or referrals. For example, some companies sell products endorsed by the American Heart Association or the American Cancer Society. The Arthritis Foundation and McNeil Consumer Products formed an alliance to launch the Arthritis Foundation line of pain relievers, which quickly jumped to the number one selling position in the over-the-counter arthritis segment. Marketers also seek endorsements from schools, churches, cities, the military, and fraternal organizations as a form of group opinion leadership. Salespeople often ask to use opinion leaders' names as a means of achieving greater personal influence in a sales presentation.

Family

socialization process
How cultural values and norms are passed down to children.

The family is the most important social institution for many consumers, strongly influencing values, attitudes, self-concept—and buying behavior. For example, a family that strongly values good health will have a grocery list distinctly different from that of a family that views every dinner as a gourmet event. Moreover, the family is responsible for the **socialization process**, the passing down of cultural values and norms to children. Children learn by observing their parents' consumption patterns, and so they will tend to shop in a similar pattern.

Decision-making roles among family members tend to vary significantly, depending on the type of item purchased. Family members assume a variety of roles in the purchase process. *Initiators* are the ones who suggest, initiate, or plant the seed for the purchase process. The initiator can be any member of the family. For example, Sister might initiate the product search by asking for a new bicycle as a birthday present. *Influencers* are those members of the family whose opinions are valued. In our example, Mom might function as a price-range watchdog, an influencer whose main role is to veto or approve price ranges. Brother may give his opinion on certain makes of bicycles. The *decision maker* is the member of the family who actually makes the decision to buy or not to buy. For example, Dad or Mom is likely to choose the final brand and model of bicycle to buy after seeking further information from Sister about cosmetic features such as color and imposing additional criteria of his or her own, such as durability and safety. The *purchaser* (probably Dad or Mom) is the one who actually exchanges money for the product. Finally, the *consumer* is the actual user—Sister, in the case of the bicycle.

Marketers should consider family purchase situations along with the distribution of consumer and decision-maker roles among family members. Ordinary marketing views the individual as both decision maker and consumer. Family marketing adds several other possibilities: Sometimes more than one family member or all family members are involved in the decision; sometimes only children are involved in the decision; sometimes more than one consumer is involved; and sometimes the decision maker and the consumer are different people. Exhibit 5.10 represents the patterns of family purchasing relationships that are possible.

Children can have great influence over the purchase decisions of their parents. In many families, with both parents working and short on time, children are

Exhibit 5.10

Relationships among Purchasers and Consumers in the Family

		Purchase Decision Maker		
		Parent(s) Only	Child/Children Only	Some or All Family Members
Consumer	Parent(s)	golf clubs cosmetics wine	Mother's Day card	Christmas gifts minivan
	Child/ Children	diapers breakfast cereal	candy small toys	bicycle
	Some Family Members	videos long-distance phone service	children's movies	computers sports events
	All Family Members	clothing life insurance	fast-food restaurant	swim club membership vacations

SOURCE: From "Pulling the Family's Strings" by Robert Boutillier, *American Demographics*, August 1993. ©1993 PRIMEDIA Intertec, Stamford, CT. Reprinted with permission.

encouraged to participate. In addition, children in single-parent households become more involved in family decisions at an earlier age. Children are especially influential in decisions about food and eating out. Therefore, food companies listen closely to what children want. Children also are more interested in entertainment than food. Therefore, McDonald's and Burger King spend about $4 billion annually on toys for their kid meals; Quaker Oatmeal now features hidden treasures; Heinz ketchup is available in funky purple; and Parkay margarine comes in shocking pink and electric blue. Both the ketchup and the margarine come in squeezable bottles designed to allow small hands to design pictures. Promotions for food products aimed at children include a Web site that illustrates how to build a fort with french fries and books that teach children to count using Cheerios, M&Ms, and Oreos.[44] Children influence purchase decisions for many more products and services than food. Even though they are usually not the actual purchasers of such items, children often participate in decisions about toys, clothes, vacations, recreation, automobiles, and many other products.

GameGirlz
What kind of games are available at the GameGirlz Web site? How do the games "for" girls differ from the games "for" boys at GameSpot?
http://www.gamegirlz.com
http://www.gamespot.com

On Line

Individual Influences on Consumer Buying Decisions

A person's buying decisions are also influenced by personal characteristics that are unique to each individual, such as gender; age and life-cycle stage; and personality, self-concept, and lifestyle. Individual characteristics are generally stable over the course of one's life. For instance, most people do not change their gender, and the act of changing personality or lifestyle requires a complete reorientation of one's life. In the case of age and life-cycle stage, these changes occur gradually over time.

(7)
Identify and understand the individual factors that affect consumer buying decisions

Gender

Physiological differences between men and women result in different needs, such as health and beauty products. Just as important are the distinct cultural, social, and economic roles played by men and women and the effects that these have on their decision-making processes. For instance, when asked what features they would want on their next vehicle, Generation Y men yearn for more gadget and performance-oriented options, such as turbo-diesel or turbo-charged gas engines, run-flat tires, and high-intensity headlights. Generation Y women, on the other hand, prefer features that provide organization, practicality, and convenience, such as a wet storage area, power rear seats, cargo area dividers, and heated/cooled cup holders.[45]

 Men and women also shop differently. Studies show that men and women share similar motivations in terms of where to shop—that is, seeking reasonable prices, merchandise quality, and a friendly, low-pressure environment—but they don't necessarily feel the same about shopping in general. Most women enjoy shopping; their male counterparts claim to dislike the experience and shop only out of necessity. Further, men desire simple shopping experiences, stores with less variety, and convenience. Stores that are easy to shop in, are near home or office, or have knowledgeable personnel appeal more to men than to women.[46] The Internet appeals to men who find its ease of use a more enjoyable way to shop for clothing and gifts. Many Internet retailers are designing their sites to attract male gift buyers. Banana Republic's Web site prompts customers purchasing gifts to choose a price range. The site then returns five to six different suggestions. To help out its male shoppers, intimate apparel retailer Victoria's Secret lets women create password-protected wish lists and then zap them to their significant others to ensure there's no mistaking colors or sizes.[47]

Trends in gender marketing are influenced by the changing roles of men and women in society. For instance, as women around the world are working and earning

As the proportion of children in the U.S. population swells, this market segment is becoming increasingly important to marketers wanting to influence the kids that influence their parents' purchasing habits. Heinz's colored ketchups in the E-Z Squirt bottles are designed to do just that.

more, many industries are attracting new customers by marketing to women. The video game industry, which has traditionally targeted eighteen- to twenty-two-year-old men with games featuring guns and explosions, is beginning to develop new games based on popular female characters like Barbie and Nancy Drew aimed at capturing female customers. In South Korea, major credit card companies are now targeting working women by offering credit card benefits attractive to women such as discounts at department and bridal stores and disfigurement insurance for plastic surgery.[48]

The changing roles of women are also forcing companies that have traditionally targeted women to develop new strategies. Revlon stopped using glamorous supermodels to promote its products because it felt traditional "Cindy Crawford" ads "conveyed a man's view of women, not a woman's."[49] The company attempted to modernize its image by using new unknown models in ads highlighting universal truths about being a woman, such as a woman checking her reflection in the frozen food section of the grocery store. But the campaign did not work, and after seven months Revlon began using well-known models again with the new positioning statement "Be Unforgettable." The focus of the new campaign was on product benefits and promoting the Revlon brand name. It is often difficult for marketers to know how to respond as gender roles evolve and change.

Age and Family Life-Cycle Stage

The age and family life-cycle stage of a consumer can have a significant impact on consumer behavior. How old a consumer is generally indicates what products he or she may be interested in purchasing. Consumer tastes in food, clothing, cars, furniture, and recreation are often age related; for example, the favorite magazines for preteens aged eight to twelve include *Sports Illustrated for Kids*, *Nickelodeon*, and *Ranger Rick*. But as these consumers become teenagers their tastes in magazines diverge in favor of sports titles for boys and fashion/lifestyle titles for girls.[50]

Related to a person's age is his or her place in the family life cycle. As Chapter 7 explains in more detail, the *family life cycle* is an orderly series of stages through which consumers' attitudes and behavioral tendencies evolve through maturity, experience, and changing income and status. Marketers often define their target markets in terms of family life cycle, such as "young singles," "young married with children," and "middle-aged married without children." For instance, young singles spend more than average on alcoholic beverages, education, and entertainment. New parents typically increase their spending on health care, clothing, housing, and food and decrease their spending on alcohol, education, and transportation. Households with older children spend more on food, entertainment, personal care products, and education, as well as cars and gasoline. After their children leave home, spending by older couples on vehicles, women's clothing, health care, and long-distance calls typically increases. For instance, the presence of children in the home is the most significant determinant of the type of vehicle that's driven off the new car lot. Parents are the ultimate need-driven car consumers, requiring larger cars and trucks to haul their children and all their belongings. It comes as no surprise then that for all households with children, sport utility vehicles rank either first or second among new-vehicle purchases followed by minivans.[51]

Marketers should also be aware of the many nontraditional life-cycle paths that are common today and provide insights into the needs and wants of such consumers as divorced parents, lifelong singles, and childless couples. Three decades ago, traditional families comprised of married couples with children under eighteen accounted for nearly a majority of U.S. households. Today, traditional families make up only 23 percent of all households, while people living alone or with nonfamily members represent more than 30 percent. Furthermore, according to the U.S. Census Bureau, the number of single-mother households grew by 25 percent over the last decade. The shift toward more single-parent households is part of a broader societal change that has put more women on the career track. Although many marketers continue to be wary of targeting nontraditional families, Charles Schwab targeted single mothers in a recent advertising campaign featuring Sarah

Ferguson, the Duchess of York and a divorced mom; the idea was to appeal to single mothers' heightened awareness of the need for financial self-sufficiency.[52]

Personality, Self-Concept, and Lifestyle

Each consumer has a unique personality. **Personality** is a broad concept that can be thought of as a way of organizing and grouping how an individual typically reacts to situations. Thus, personality combines psychological makeup and environmental forces. It includes people's underlying dispositions, especially their most dominant characteristics. Although personality is one of the least useful concepts in the study of consumer behavior, some marketers believe that personality influences the types and brands of products purchased. For instance, the type of car, clothes, or jewelry a consumer buys may reflect one or more personality traits. Personality traits like those listed in Exhibit 5.11 may be used to describe a consumer's personality.

Self-concept, or self-perception, is how consumers perceive themselves. Self-concept includes attitudes, perceptions, beliefs, and self-evaluations. Although self-concept may change, the change is often gradual. Through self-concept, people define their identity, which in turn provides for consistent and coherent behavior.

Self-concept combines the **ideal self-image** (the way an individual would like to be) and the **real self-image** (how an individual actually perceives himself or herself). Generally, we try to raise our real self-image toward our ideal (or at least narrow the gap). Consumers seldom buy products that jeopardize their self-image. For example, someone who sees herself as a trendsetter wouldn't buy clothing that doesn't project a contemporary image.

Human behavior depends largely on self-concept. Because consumers want to protect their identity as individuals, the products they buy, the stores they patronize, and the credit cards they carry support their self-image. No other product quite reflects a person's self-image as much as the car he or she drives. For example, in a consumer survey conducted by Nissan, many consumers expressed dislike for family sedans like the Honda Accord and Toyota Camry, stating that, "they would buy one for their mothers, but not for themselves."[53] Likewise, Mitsubishi found that car buyers did not want to sacrifice a youthful image of themselves just because they have new responsibilities in life. Thus, advertising for the Montero sport utility vehicle and the Eclipse Spyder positions these vehicles as "spirited cars for spirited people" and encourages would-be car buyers to experience the exhilaration of driving stylish, exciting cars.

By influencing the degree to which consumers perceive a good or service to be self-relevant, marketers can affect consumers' motivation to learn about, shop for, and buy a certain brand. Marketers also consider self-concept important because it helps explain the relationship between individuals' perceptions of themselves and their consumer behavior.

An important component of self-concept is *body image*, the perception of the attractiveness of one's own physical features. For example, individuals who have

Bally Total Fitness

Does Bally Total Fitness use its Web site as a means to connect with consumers via their body image? Do the content and design of the site surprise you? Why or why not?

http://www.ballyfitness.com

On Line

personality
A way of organizing and grouping the consistencies of an individual's reactions to situations.

self-concept
How consumers perceive themselves in terms of attitudes, perceptions, beliefs, and self-evaluations.

ideal self-image
The way an individual would like to be.

real self-image
The way an individual actually perceives himself or herself.

Exhibit 5.11

Some Common Personality Traits

- Adaptability
- Need for affiliation
- Aggressiveness
- Need for achievement
- Ascendancy
- Autonomy
- Dominance

- Deference
- Defensiveness
- Emotionalism
- Orderliness
- Sociability
- Stability
- Self-confidence

Although fitness is categorized most closely as a physiological need, it can also be considered a self-esteem need, particularly the prestigious health club memberships that it often entails. Even during recession, members will not sacrifice expensive memberships because to do so would be a subtle admission of financial difficulties.

cosmetic surgery often experience significant improvement in their overall body image and self-concept. Moreover, a person's perception of body image can be a stronger reason for weight loss than either good health or other social factors.[54] With the median age of Americans rising, many companies are introducing products and services aimed at aging baby boomers who are concerned about their age and physical appearance. Sales of hair-coloring products for men, for instance, have more than doubled over the last decade, and television and print advertisements aimed at getting men to dye the gray out of their hair have tripled. Similarly, many companies including PepsiCo with Tropicana juices and Pfizer with its Viagra product are repositioning their products to focus on lifestyle. Bank of America is featuring Harley-riding seniors in its advertisements for its private-bank marketing campaign, and high-end anti-aging creams are flying off department store shelves. Finally marketers are also seeing boomers respond to products aimed at younger audiences. For instance, new Starwood "W" Hotels, designed and advertised to attract a young, hip crowd, are attracting large numbers of boomers.[55]

lifestyle
A mode of living as identified by a person's activities, interests, and opinions.

Personality and self-concept are reflected in lifestyle. A **lifestyle** is a mode of living, as identified by a person's activities, interests, and opinions. *Psychographics* is the analytical technique used to examine consumer lifestyles and to categorize consumers. Unlike personality characteristics, which are hard to describe and measure, lifestyle characteristics are useful in segmenting and targeting consumers. Lifestyle and psychographic analysis explicitly addresses the way consumers outwardly express their inner selves in their social and cultural environment.

Many companies now use psychographics to better understand their market segments. For many years, marketers selling products to mothers conveniently assumed that all moms were fairly homogeneous and concerned about the same things—the health and well-being of their children—and that they could all be reached with a similar message. But recent lifestyle research has shown that there are traditional, blended, and nontraditional moms, and companies like Procter & Gamble and Pillsbury are using strategies to reach these different types of mothers. Psychographics is also effective with other segments. Hyundai Motors targets customers it calls "Kids & Cul-De-Sacs." These consumers are up-scale, suburban families with a median household income of $68,900 who tend to shop on-line and visit Disney theme parks. Another major target for Hyundai is "Bohemian Mix," professionals aged twenty-five to forty-four with a median income of $38,500 who are likely to shop at the Gap, watch *Face the Nation*, and read *Elle* magazine.[56] Psychographics and lifestyle segmentation are discussed in more detail in Chapter 7.

Psychological Influences on Consumer Buying Decisions

8

Identify and understand the psychological factors that affect consumer buying decisions

An individual's buying decisions are further influenced by psychological factors: perception, motivation, learning, and beliefs and attitudes. These factors are what consumers use to interact with their world. They are the tools consumers use to recognize their feelings, gather and analyze information, formulate thoughts and opinions, and take action. Unlike the other three influences on consumer behavior, psychological influences can be affected by a person's environment because they are applied on specific occasions. For example, you will perceive different stimuli and process these stimuli in different ways depending on whether you are sitting in class concentrating on the instructor, sitting outside of class talking to friends, or sitting in your dorm room watching television.

Perception

The world is full of stimuli. A stimulus is any unit of input affecting one or more of the five senses: sight, smell, taste, touch, hearing. The process by which we select, organize, and interpret these stimuli into a meaningful and coherent picture is called **perception**. In essence, perception is how we see the world around us and how we recognize that we need some help in making a purchasing decision.

People cannot perceive every stimulus in their environment. Therefore, they use **selective exposure** to decide which stimuli to notice and which to ignore. A typical consumer is exposed to more than 250 advertising messages a day but notices only between eleven and twenty.

The familiarity of an object, contrast, movement, intensity (such as increased volume), and smell are cues that influence perception. Consumers use these cues to identify and define products and brands. The shape of a product's packaging, such as Coca-Cola's signature contour bottle, for instance, can influence perception. Color is another cue, and it plays a key role in consumers' perceptions. Packaged foods manufacturers use color to trigger unconscious associations for grocery shoppers who typically make their shopping decisions in the blink of an eye. Red, for instance, used on packages of Campbell's soups and SunMaid raisins, is associated with prolonged and increased eating. Green is associated with environmental goodness and healthy, low-fat foods. Health Choice entrées and Snack-Wells cookies use green. Premium products, like Sheba cat food and Ben & Jerry's ice cream, use black and gold on their packaging to convey their use of superior ingredients.[57] The shape and look of a product's packaging can also influence perception. Ivory Soap recently began packaging about one-third of its product in special packaging based on the original late nineteenth-century design. The company hopes to take advantage of a consumer trend toward simplifying life by emphasizing the brand's heritage and image of purity.[58]

What is perceived by consumers may also depend on the stimuli's vividness or shock value. Graphic warnings of the hazards associated with a product's use are perceived more readily and remembered more accurately than less vivid warnings or warnings that are written in text. "Sexier" ads excel at attracting the attention of younger consumers. Companies like Calvin Klein and Guess use sensuous ads to "cut through the clutter" of competing ads and other stimuli to capture the attention of the target audience. Similarly, Benetton ads use shock value by portraying taboo social issues, from racism to homosexuality.

Two other concepts closely related to selective exposure are selective distortion and selective retention. **Selective distortion** occurs when consumers change or distort information that conflicts with their feelings or beliefs. For example, suppose a consumer buys a Chrysler. After the purchase, if the consumer receives new information about a close alternative brand, such as a Ford, he or she may distort the information to make it more consistent with the prior view that the Chrysler is better than the Ford. Business travelers who fly often may distort or discount information about airline crashes because they must use air travel constantly in their jobs. People who smoke and have no plans to quit may distort information from medical reports and the Surgeon General about the link between cigarettes and lung cancer.

Selective retention is remembering only information that supports personal feelings or beliefs. The consumer forgets all information that may be inconsistent. After reading a pamphlet that contradicts one's political beliefs, for instance, a person may forget many of the points outlined in it.

Which stimuli will be perceived often depends on the individual. People can be exposed to the same stimuli under identical conditions but perceive them very

perception
The process by which people select, organize, and interpret stimuli into a meaningful and coherent picture.

selective exposure
The process whereby a consumer notices certain stimuli and ignores others.

selective distortion
A process whereby a consumer changes or distorts information that conflicts with his or her feelings or beliefs.

selective retention
A process whereby a consumer remembers only that information that supports his or her personal beliefs.

differently. For example, two people viewing a TV commercial may have different interpretations of the advertising message. One person may be thoroughly engrossed by the message and become highly motivated to buy the product. Thirty seconds after the ad ends, the second person may not be able to recall the content of the message or even the product advertised.

Marketing Implications of Perception

Marketers must recognize the importance of cues, or signals, in consumers' perception of products. Marketing managers first identify the important attributes, such as price or quality, that the targeted consumers want in a product and then design signals to communicate these attributes. For example, consumers will pay more for candy wrapped in expensive-looking foil packages. But shiny labels on wine bottles signify less expensive wines; dull labels indicate more expensive wines. Marketers also often use price as a signal to consumers that the product is of higher quality than competing products. Gibson Guitar Corporation briefly cut prices on many of its guitars to compete with Japanese rivals Yamaha and Ibanez but found instead that it sold more guitars when it charged more for them. Consumers perceived that the higher price indicated a better quality instrument.[59]

Of course, brand names send signals to consumers. The brand names of Close-Up toothpaste, DieHard batteries, and Caress moisturizing soap, for example, identify important product qualities. Names chosen for search engines and sites on the Internet, such as Yahoo!, Amazon.com, CDNow, and Excite, are intended to convey excitement, intensity, and vastness. Companies might even change their names to send a message to consumers. As today's electric utility companies increasingly enter nonregulated markets to sell power, natural gas, and other energy-related products and services, they are finding their old company names may hold some negative perceptions with consumers. Consequently, many are shaking their stodgy "Power & Light & Electric" names in favor of those that let consumers know they are not just about electricity anymore, such as Reliant Energy, Entergy, and Cinergy.

Consumers also associate quality and reliability with certain brand names. Companies watch their brand identity closely, in large part because a strong link has been established between perceived brand value and customer loyalty. Brand names that consistently enjoy high perceived value from consumers include Kodak, Disney, National Geographic, Mercedes-Benz, and Fisher-Price. Naming a product after a place can also add perceived value by association. Brand names using the words Santa Fe, Dakota, or Texas convey a sense of openness, freedom, and youth, but products named after other locations might conjure up images of pollution and crime.

Marketing managers are also interested in the *threshold level of perception:* the minimum difference in a stimulus that the consumer will notice. This concept is sometimes referred to as the "just-noticeable difference." For example, how much would Sony have to drop the price of a VCR before consumers recognized it as a bargain—$25? $50? or more? One study found that the just-noticeable difference in a stimulus is about a 20 percent change. For example, consumers will likely notice a 20 percent price decrease more quickly than a 15 percent decrease. This marketing principle can be applied to other marketing variables as well, such as package size or loudness of a broadcast advertisement.[60]

Another study showed that the bargain-price threshold for a name brand is lower than that for a store brand. In other words, consumers perceive a bargain more readily when stores offer a small discount on a name-brand item than when they offer the same discount on a store brand; a larger discount is needed to achieve a similar effect for a store brand.[61] Researchers also found that for low-cost grocery items, consumers typically do not see past the second digit in the price. For instance, consumers do not perceive any real difference between two comparable cans of tuna, one priced at $1.52 and the other at $1.59, because they ignore the last digit.[62]

Besides changing such stimuli as price, package size, and volume, marketers can change the product or attempt to reposition its image. Realtors, for example, have changed a property's address to enhance its image. In fact, one San Francisco real estate company almost lost a major deal when one of its potential clients refused to move into an office whose address was 444 Market Street because of the association of the number four with death in the Chinese community. The company saved the deal by renovating the lobby to include a new entrance and changing the building's address to One Front Street.[63] But marketers must be careful when adding features. How many new services will discounter Target Stores need to add before consumers perceive it as a full-service department store? How many sporty features will General Motors have to add to a basic two-door sedan before consumers start perceiving it as a sports car?

Marketing managers who intend to do business in global markets should be aware of how foreign consumers perceive their products. For instance, in Japan, product labels are often written in English or French, even though they may not translate into anything meaningful. But many Japanese associate foreign words on product labels with the exotic, the expensive, and high quality.

Marketers have often been suspected of sending advertising messages subconsciously to consumers in what is known as *subliminal perception*. The controversy began in 1957 when a researcher claimed to have increased popcorn and Coca-Cola sales at a movie theater after flashing "Eat popcorn" and "Drink Coca-Cola" on the screen every five seconds for 1/300th of a second, although the audience did not consciously recognize the messages. Almost immediately consumer protection groups became concerned that advertisers were brainwashing consumers, and this practice was pronounced illegal in California and Canada. Although the researcher later admitted to making up the data and scientists have been unable to replicate the study since, consumers are still wary of hidden messages that advertisers may be sending.

Motivation

By studying motivation, marketers can analyze the major forces influencing consumers to buy or not buy products. When you buy a product, you usually do so to fulfill some kind of need. These needs become motives when aroused sufficiently. For instance, suppose this morning you were so hungry before class that you needed to eat something. In response to that need, you stopped at McDonald's for an Egg McMuffin. In other words, you were motivated by hunger to stop at McDonald's. **Motives** are the driving forces that cause a person to take action to satisfy specific needs.

Why are people driven by particular needs at particular times? One popular theory is **Maslow's hierarchy of needs**, shown in Exhibit 5.12, which arranges needs in ascending order of importance: physiological, safety, social, esteem, and self-actualization. As a person fulfills one need, a higher level need becomes more important.

The most basic human needs are *physiological*—that is the needs for food, water, and shelter. Because they are essential to survival, these needs must be satisfied first. Ads showing a juicy hamburger or a runner gulping down Gatorade after a marathon are examples of appeals to satisfy the physiological needs of hunger and thirst.

Safety needs include security and freedom from pain and discomfort. Marketers often exploit consumers' fears and anxieties about safety to sell their products. For example, aware of the aging population's health fears, the retail medical imaging centers AmeriScan and HealthScreen America advertise that they offer consumers a full body scan for early detection of health problems such as coronary disease and cancer.[64] On the other hand, some companies or industries advertise to allay consumer fears. For example, in the wake of the September 11 terrorist attacks, the airline industry found itself having to conduct an image campaign to reassure consumers about the safety of air travel.[65]

After physiological and safety needs have been fulfilled, *social needs*—especially love and a sense of belonging—become the focus. Love includes acceptance by one's peers, as well as sex and romantic love. Marketing managers probably appeal more to

motive
A driving force that causes a person to take action to satisfy specific needs.

Maslow's hierarchy of needs
A method of classifying human needs and motivations into five categories in ascending order of importance: physiological, safety, social, esteem, and self-actualization.

Exhibit 5.12

Maslow's Hierarchy of Needs

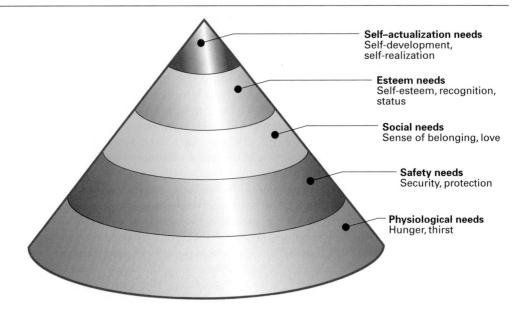

Self–actualization needs
Self-development,
self-realization

Esteem needs
Self-esteem, recognition,
status

Social needs
Sense of belonging, love

Safety needs
Security, protection

Physiological needs
Hunger, thirst

this need than to any other. Ads for clothes, cosmetics, and vacation packages suggest that buying the product can bring love. The need to belong is also a favorite of marketers, especially those marketing products to teens. Shoes and clothing brands such as Nike, adidas, Tommy Hilfiger, Gap, JNCO, and Abercrombie & Fitch score high with teenagers as "cool" brands. Teens who wear these labels feel and look like they belong to the in-crowd.

Love is acceptance without regard to one's contribution. Esteem is acceptance based on one's contribution to the group. *Self-esteem needs* include self-respect and a sense of accomplishment. Esteem needs also include prestige, fame, and recognition of one's accomplishments. Mont Blanc pens, Mercedes-Benz automobiles, and Neiman-Marcus stores all appeal to esteem needs. Most high-end spas and health clubs appeal to consumers' self-esteem needs. Like exclusive country clubs, clubs such as Chicago's East Bank Club are designed to make members feel proud of their commitment to fitness while also giving them a sense of social accomplishment. In fact, the clubs can be so effective that even during an economic recession, patrons will not give up their membership because to do so would be a public admission of financial problems.[66]

Asian consumers, in particular, are strongly motivated by status and appearance. Asians are always conscious of their place in a group, institution, or society as a whole. The importance of gaining social recognition turns Asians into some of the most image-conscious consumers in the world. Status-conscious Asians will not hesitate to spend freely on premium brands, such as BMW, Mercedes-Benz, and the best Scotch whiskey and French cognac. Indeed, marketers of luxury products such as Gucci, Louis Vuitton, and Prada find that demand for their products is so strong among image-conscious consumers that their sales are generally unaffected by economic downturns. In some cases, companies have been able to make up for sluggish European and U.S. sales by raising prices and volume in Asia.[67]

The highest human need is *self-actualization*. It refers to finding self-fulfillment and self-expression, reaching the point in life at which "people are what they feel they should be." Maslow felt that very few people ever attain this level. Even so, advertisements may focus on this type of need. For example, American Express ads convey the message that acquiring its card is one of the highest attainments in life. Similarly, Microsoft appealed to consumers' needs for self-actualization when it chose "Yes, You Can" as the Windows XP slogan.[68] And the U.S. Armed Forces' slogan urges young people to "Be all that you can be."

Even children must satisfy more than just the basic physiological and safety needs. Mattel's Barbie doll, for instance, fulfills a fundamental need that all girls share by playing out what it might be like in the grown-up world. Through Barbie, girls dream of achievement, glamour, romance, adventure, and nurturing. These dreams touch on many timeless needs, ranging from pride and success to belonging and love. Mattel zeros in on these core needs and addresses them with different Barbie products. Over the years, Barbie has been a teacher, a fashion model, a girlfriend, a dentist, an astronaut, a sister, and a veterinarian, to name a few.[69]

Learning

Almost all consumer behavior results from **learning**, which is the process that creates changes in behavior through experience and practice. It is not possible to observe learning directly, but we can infer when it has occurred by a person's actions. For example, suppose you see an advertisement for a new and improved cold medicine. If you go to the store that day and buy that remedy, we infer that you have learned something about the cold medicine.

There are two types of learning: experiential and conceptual. *Experiential learning* occurs when an experience changes your behavior. For example, if you try the new cold medicine when you get home and it does not relieve your symptoms, you may not buy that brand again. *Conceptual learning*, which is not learned through direct experience, is the second type of learning. Assume, for example, that you are standing at a soft drink machine and notice a new diet flavor with an artificial sweetener. Because someone has told you that diet beverages leave an aftertaste, you choose a different drink. You have learned that you would not like this new diet drink without ever trying it.

Reinforcement and repetition boost learning. Reinforcement can be positive or negative. If you see a vendor selling frozen yogurt (stimulus), buy it (response), and find the yogurt to be quite refreshing (reward), your behavior has been positively reinforced. On the other hand, if you buy a new flavor of yogurt and it does not taste good (negative reinforcement), you will not buy that flavor of yogurt again (response). Without positive or negative reinforcement, a person will not be motivated to repeat the behavior pattern or to avoid it. Thus, if a new brand evokes neutral feelings, some marketing activity, such as a price change or an increase in promotion, may be required to induce further consumption. Learning theory is helpful in reminding marketers that concrete and timely actions are what reinforce desired consumer behavior.

Repetition is a key strategy in promotional campaigns because it can lead to increased learning. Most marketers use repetitious advertising so that consumers will learn what their unique advantage is over the competition. Generally, to heighten learning, advertising messages should be spread over time rather than clustered together.

A related learning concept useful to marketing managers is stimulus generalization. In theory, **stimulus generalization** occurs when one response is extended to a second stimulus similar to the first. Marketers often use a successful, well-known brand name for a family of products because it gives consumers familiarity with and knowledge about each product in the family. Such brand-name families spur the introduction of new products and facilitate the sale of existing items. Jell-O frozen pudding pops rely on the familiarity of Jell-O gelatin; Clorox laundry detergent relies on familiarity with Clorox bleach; and Ivory shampoo relies on familiarity with Ivory soap. Microsoft recently entered the video game industry, hoping that the Microsoft brand would guarantee sales for the Xbox. Initial response to the Xbox has been strong based on Microsoft's reputation, but the company will have to work hard to make real progress in an industry dominated by other brand giants Sony and Nintendo.[70] Branding is examined in more detail in Chapter 9.

Another form of stimulus generalization occurs when retailers or wholesalers design their packages to resemble well-known manufacturers' brands.

learning
A process that creates changes in behavior, immediate or expected, through experience and practice.

stimulus generalization
A form of learning that occurs when one response is extended to a second stimulus similar to the first.

Such imitation often confuses consumers, who buy the imitator thinking it's the original. U.S. manufacturers in foreign markets have sometimes found little, if any, brand protection. In South Korea, Procter & Gamble's Ivory soap competes head-on with the Korean brand Bory, which has an almost identical logo on the package. Consumers dissatisfied with Bory may attribute their dissatisfaction to Ivory, never realizing that Bory is an imitator. Counterfeit products are also produced to look exactly like the original. For example, counterfeit Levi's jeans made in China are hot items in Europe, where Levi Strauss has had trouble keeping up with demand. The knockoffs look so much like the real thing that unsuspecting consumers don't know the difference—until after a few washes, when the belt loops fall off and the rivets begin to rust.

stimulus discrimination
A learned ability to differentiate among similar products.

The opposite of stimulus generalization is **stimulus discrimination**, which means learning to differentiate among similar products. Consumers usually prefer one product as more rewarding or stimulating. For example, some consumers prefer Coca-Cola and others prefer Pepsi; many insist they can taste a difference between the two brands.

With some types of products—such as aspirin, gasoline, bleach, paper towels—marketers rely on promotion to point out brand differences that consumers would otherwise not recognize. This process, called *product differentiation,* is discussed in more detail in Chapter 7. Usually, product differentiation is based on superficial differences. For example, Bayer tells consumers that it's the aspirin "doctors recommend most."

Beliefs and Attitudes

belief
An organized pattern of knowledge that an individual holds as true about his or her world.

Beliefs and attitudes are closely linked to values. A **belief** is an organized pattern of knowledge that an individual holds as true about his or her world. A consumer may believe that Sony's camcorder makes the best home videos, tolerates hard use, and is reasonably priced. These beliefs may be based on knowledge, faith, or hearsay. Consumers tend to develop a set of beliefs about a product's attributes and then, through these beliefs, form a *brand image*—a set of beliefs about a particular brand. In turn, the brand image shapes consumers' attitudes toward the product.

attitude
A learned tendency to respond consistently toward a given object.

An **attitude** is a learned tendency to respond consistently toward a given object, such as a brand. Attitudes rest on an individual's value system, which represents personal standards of good and bad, right and wrong, and so forth; therefore, attitudes tend to be more enduring and complex than beliefs.

 For an example of the nature of attitudes, consider the differing attitudes of consumers around the world toward the practice of purchasing on credit. Americans have long been enthusiastic about charging goods and services and are willing to pay high interest rates for the privilege of postponing payment. To many European consumers, doing what amounts to taking out a loan—even a small one—to pay for anything seems absurd. Germans especially are reluctant to buy on credit. Italy has a sophisticated credit and banking system well suited to handling credit cards, but Italians prefer to carry cash, often huge wads of it. Although most Japanese consumers have credit cards, card purchases amount to less than 1 percent of all consumer transactions. The Japanese have long looked down on credit purchases but acquire cards to use while traveling abroad.[71]

If a good or service is meeting its profit goals, positive attitudes toward the product merely need to be reinforced. If the brand is not succeeding, however, the marketing manager must strive to change target consumers' attitudes toward it. Changes in attitude tend to grow out of an individual's attempt to reconcile long-held values with a constant stream of new information. This change can be accomplished in three ways: changing beliefs about the brand's attributes, changing the relative importance of these beliefs, and adding new beliefs.

Changing Beliefs about Attributes

The first technique is to turn neutral or negative beliefs about product attributes into positive ones. For example, many consumers believe that it is easier and cheaper to take traditional film to be developed than it is to print their own digital photos. To change this belief, Sony Corporation has begun setting up kiosks in retail outlets that let consumers print their digital photos. The kiosks eliminate the need for consumers to purchase their own high-quality printer. Eastman Kodak and Hewlett-Packard are also developing special printers to allow retailers to offer photo printing as well.[72] Similarly, companies like Sageport and It's Never 2 Late are trying to change senior citizens' belief that computers are too complicated for them to learn. Sageport offers seniors an appliance that gives them Internet access without the confusion of operating a PC, and It's Never 2 Late is adapting software and hardware with larger type, fewer options, and more graphics to make it easier for seniors to use a PC.[73]

Changing beliefs about a service can be more difficult because service attributes are intangible. Convincing consumers to switch hairstylists or lawyers or to go to a mall dental clinic can be much more difficult than getting them to change brands of razor blades. Image, which is also largely intangible, significantly determines service patronage. For example, Tomra, a Norwegian recycling giant, hopes to increase the number of Americans who recycle by changing their perception that recycling is an unsavory chore. By building new rePlanet recycling kiosks in communities as an alternative to neighborhood recycling centers, Tomra is offering Americans a clean, convenient, service-oriented way to be responsible citizens.[74] Service marketing is explored in detail in Chapter 11.

Changing the Importance of Beliefs

The second approach to modifying attitudes is to change the relative importance of beliefs about an attribute. For years, consumers have known that bran cereals are high in natural fiber. The primary belief associated with this attribute is that the fiber tends to act as a mild, natural laxative. Today, however, cereal marketers promote the high fiber content of bran cereals as a possible factor in preventing certain types of cancer, vastly increasing the importance of this attribute in the minds of consumers. Similarly, the makers of Xenical, a weight-loss prescription drug, recently began marketing the medication in China, the world's second most obese nation. Most Chinese consumers place little importance on weight loss because they believe the problem is cosmetic. Therefore, to be successful in China, marketers will have to convince the Chinese and their doctors that obesity is a serious health issue that requires a medical solution.[75] You will read more about this topic in Chapter 7's "Global Perspectives" box.

Marketers can also emphasize the importance of some beliefs over others. For example, DaimlerChrysler's Jeep unit positions it as being rugged but promotes its luxury features. The newest Grand Cherokees have even more off-road capability, but very few owners ever take them off-road. Luxury features include a climate-control system with infrared beams that track drivers' and passengers' skin temperature to automatically adjust air conditioning and heat, his and her key rings that remember settings for power seats and mirrors, a system to reprogram radio stations for different drivers, and many other comforts.

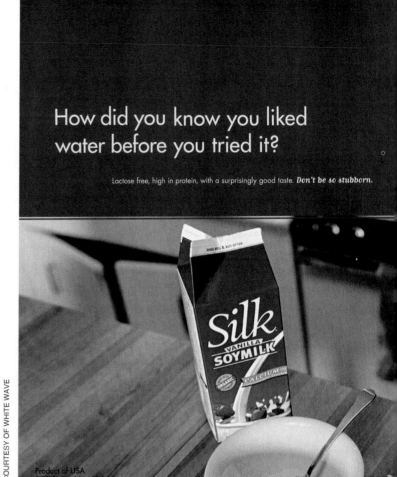

How did you know you liked water before you tried it?

Lactose free, high in protein, with a surprisingly good taste. *Don't be so stubborn.*

COURTESY OF WHITE WAVE

In order to increase sales, a company must change negative attitudes about its product held by those who are not buying it. One way to accomplish this is to change the beliefs about the product's attributes, such as taste. This ad for Silk soy milk does just that with its catchy question, and the follow up, "Don't be so stubborn."

Adding New Beliefs

The third approach to transforming attitudes is to add new beliefs. Although changes in consumption patterns often come slowly, cereal marketers are betting that consumers will eventually warm up to the idea of cereal as a snack. A print ad for Ralston Purina's Cookie-Crisp cereal features a boy popping the sugary nuggets into his mouth while he does his homework. Boxes of Kellogg's Cracklin' Oat Bran boast that the cereal tastes like oatmeal cookies and makes "a great snack . . . anytime." Similarly, commercials for Quaker Oats 100% Natural cereal promote eating it straight from the box. James River Corporation, the manufacturer of Dixie paper products, is also attempting to add new beliefs about the uses of its paper plates and cups with an advertising campaign aimed at positioning its product as a "home cleanup replacement." New commercials pitch Dixie paper plates as an alternative to washing dishes after everyday meals.[76]

U.S. companies attempting to market their goods overseas may need to help consumers add new beliefs about a product in general. Coca-Cola and PepsiCo have both found it challenging to sell their diet cola brands to consumers in India partly because diet foods of any kind are a new concept there, a country where malnutrition was widespread not too many years ago. Indians also have deep-rooted attitudes that anything labeled "diet" is meant for a sick person, such as a diabetic. As a general rule, most Indians are not diet-conscious, preferring food prepared in the traditional manner that tastes good. Indians are also suspicious of the artificial sweeteners used in diet colas. India's Health Ministry has required warning labels on cans and bottles of Diet Coke and Diet Pepsi saying "Not Recommended for Children."[77]

CONNECT IT

Reflecting on the chapter material, you should now be able to see how cultural, social, individual, and psychological factors affect the consumer decision-making process. Purchase decisions are influenced by many factors, from opinion leaders to peer groups. Individuals have unique values and opinions based upon the environment in which they have grown up. Marketers hoping to reach different segments must understand each segment's needs and wants, as well as the influnces that shape them, vary. Consumer behavior is a fascinating and often intricate process. An appreciation of consumer behavior and the factors that influence it will help you identify target markets and design effective marketing mixes.

USE IT

Find Product Ratings

Consumer Reports Online (**http://www. consumerreports.org**) is your one-stop source for information on hundreds of products you might be interested in purchasing, such as cars and trucks, appliances, electronics, household products, home office equipment, money and investing, health and food products, personal products, and leisure activities. The section on cars and trucks, for instance, offers a wealth of advice for those thinking of buying a new or used car, or seeking safety and maintenance tips. The site includes comparison ratings, reliability reports, negotiation advice, a personal car selector, information on car equipment and accessories, as well as exclusive ratings on auto-buying Web sites. Consumers Union, publisher of *Consumer Reports,* is a nonprofit consumer advocacy group with over sixty years of product testing. The group doesn't accept any outside advertising or support from product manufacturers, so the information you find is as unbiased as possible, but you have to pay for it as a subscriber.

Find the Best Price

Narrowed down your purchase decision to a single brand or a small set of alternative brands? Now find the best price on the Web with the use of a "shopping bot," a search engine that will systematically search the Web to find the lowest price from on-line retailers and auction sites. Visit CNET Shopper at **http://www.cnet.com** to search for the lowest price on computer systems and accessories, cameras, handheld personal assistants, software, and games. Or visit ShopBest.com (**http://www.shopbest.com**) for a shopping bot that can find the best price for an even broader selection of merchandise. ShopBest.com offers over twenty shopping departments, including apparel, computer hardware and software, art, furniture, music, movies, housewares, and toys.

REVIEW IT

1 **Explain why marketing managers should understand consumer behavior.** Consumer behavior describes how consumers make purchase decisions and how they use and dispose of the products they buy. An understanding of consumer behavior reduces marketing managers' uncertainty when they are defining a target market and designing a marketing mix.

1.1 The type of decision making a consumer uses for a product does not necessarily remain constant. Why? Support your answer with an example from your own experience.

2 **Analyze the components of the consumer decision-making process.** The consumer decision-making process begins with need recognition, when stimuli trigger awareness of an unfulfilled want. If additional information is required to make a purchase decision, the consumer may engage in an internal or external information search. The consumer then evaluates the additional information and establishes purchase guidelines. Finally, a purchase decision is made.

2.1 Visit Carpoint's Web site at **http://carpoint.msn.com/home/New.asp**. How does the site assist consumers in the evaluation stage of choosing a new car? Develop your own hypothetical evoked set of three or four car models and present your comparisons. Which vehicle attributes would be most important in your purchase decision?

3 **Explain the consumer's postpurchase evaluation process.** Consumer postpurchase evaluation is influenced by prepurchase expectations, the prepurchase information search, and the consumer's general level of self-confidence. Cognitive dissonance is the inner tension that a consumer experiences after recognizing a purchased product's disadvantages. When a purchase creates cognitive dissonance, consumers tend to react by seeking positive reinforcement for the purchase decision, avoiding negative information about the purchase decision, or revoking the purchase decision by returning the product.

3.1 Recall an occasion when you experienced cognitive dissonance about a purchase. In a letter to a friend, describe the event and explain what you did about it.

4 **Identify the types of consumer buying decisions and discuss the significance of consumer involvement.** Consumer decision making falls into three broad categories. First, consumers exhibit routine response behavior for frequently purchased, low-cost items that require very little decision effort; routine response behavior is typically characterized by brand loyalty. Second, consumers engage in limited decision making for occasional purchases or for unfamiliar brands in familiar product categories. Third, consumers practice extensive decision making when making unfamiliar, expensive, or infrequent purchases. High-involvement decisions usually include an extensive information search and a thorough evaluation of alternatives. In contrast, low-involvement decisions are characterized by brand loyalty and a lack of personal identification with the product. The main factors affecting the level of consumer involvement are previous experience, interest, perceived risk of negative consequences (financial, social, and psychological), situation, and social visibility.

4.1 Describe the three categories of consumer decision-making behavior. Name typical products for which each type of consumer behavior is used.

(5) **Identify and understand the cultural factors that affect consumer buying decisions.** Cultural influences on consumer buying decisions include culture and values, subculture, and social class. Culture is the essential character of a society that distinguishes it from other cultural groups. The underlying elements of every culture are the values, language, myths, customs, rituals, laws, and the artifacts, or products, that are transmitted from one generation to the next. The most defining element of a culture is its values—the enduring beliefs shared by a society that a specific mode of conduct is personally or socially preferable to another mode of conduct. A culture can be divided into subcultures on the basis of demographic characteristics, geographic regions, national and ethnic background, political beliefs, and religious beliefs. Subcultures share elements of the overall culture as well as cultural elements unique to their own group. A social class is a group of people who are considered nearly equal in status or community esteem, who regularly socialize among themselves both formally and informally, and who share behavioral norms.

5.1 **WRITING** You are a new marketing manager for a firm that produces a line of athletic shoes to be targeted to the college student subculture. In a memo to your boss, list some product attributes that might appeal to this subculture and the steps in your customers' purchase processes, and recommend some marketing strategies that can influence their decision.

(6) **Identify and understand the social factors that affect consumer buying decisions.** Social factors include such external influences as reference groups, opinion leaders, and family. Consumers seek out others' opinions for guidance on new products or services and products with image-related attributes or because attribute information is lacking or uninformative. Consumers may use products or brands to identify with or become a member of a reference group. Opinion leaders are members of reference groups who influence others' purchase decisions. Family members also influence purchase decisions; children tend to shop in similar patterns as their parents.

6.1 Family members play many different roles in the buying process: initiator, influencer, decision maker, purchaser, and consumer. In your family, name who might play each of these roles in the purchase of a dinner at Pizza Hut, a summer vacation, Froot Loops breakfast cereal, an Abercrombie & Fitch sweater, golf clubs, an Internet service provider, and a new car.

(7) **Identify and understand the individual factors that affect consumer buying decisions.** Individual factors that affect consumer buying decisions include gender; age and family life-cycle stage; and personality, self-concept, and lifestyle. Beyond obvious physiological differences, men and women differ in their social and economic roles that affect consumer buying decisions. How old a consumer is generally indicates what products he or she may be interested in purchasing. Marketers often define their target markets in terms of consumers' life-cycle stage, following changes in consumers' attitudes and behavioral tendencies as they mature. Finally, certain products and brands reflect consumers' personality, self-concept, and lifestyle.

7.1 Assume you are involved in the following consumer decision situations: (a) renting a video to watch with your roommates, (b) choosing a fast-food restaurant to go to with a new friend, (c) buying a popular music compact disc, (d) buying jeans to wear to class. List the individual factors that would influence your decision in each situation and explain your responses.

⑧ Identify and understand the psychological factors that affect consumer buying decisions. Psychological factors include perception, motivation, learning, values, beliefs, and attitudes. These factors allow consumers to interact with the world around them, recognize their feelings, gather and analyze information, formulate thoughts and opinions, and take action. Perception allows consumers to recognize their consumption problems. Motivation is what drives consumers to take action to satisfy specific consumption needs. Almost all consumer behavior results from learning, which is the process that creates changes in behavior through experience. Consumers with similar beliefs and attitudes tend to react alike to marketing-related inducements.

8.1 *ON LINE* How do beliefs and attitudes influence consumer behavior? How can negative attitudes toward a product be changed? How can marketers alter beliefs about a product? Give some examples of how marketers have changed negative attitudes about a product or added or altered beliefs about a product.

8.2 *INFOTRAC COLLEGE EDITION* How can nonmarketing periodicals help you understand consumer behavior? Using InfoTrac (**http://www.infotrac-college.com**), research articles from such publications as the *Journal of Psychology, Journal of American Ethnic History, Psychology Today, Race and Class, Working Women, Society,* and others. Select and read three articles that explore different topics (i.e., do not select three articles on psychology). Then, make a list of factors you think could affect consumer purchasing behavior. Include with each factor a way marketers could use this information to their benefit.

DEFINE IT

Application for Entrepreneurs

Deli Depot is a new franchise opportunity offering cold and hot sandwiches, soup, chili, yogurt, pies, and cookies. It is positioned to compete with Subway and similar sandwich restaurants. Its unique advantages include special sauces on sandwiches, supplementary menu items like soup and pies, and quick delivery within specified zones.

The franchise package offered to franchisees includes information on the factors that typically influence consumers' selection of casual restaurants. These selection factors, in order from most important to least important, include food taste, food variety, value for the money, restaurant reputation, friendliness of employees, and convenience of location.

Robert Powell and a group of investors purchased the right to all franchise locations in the Atlanta metropolitan area. His group estimates that five units can be opened successfully in the first year and that a total of thirty can be opened in the first five years.

Because this is a new franchise, potential customers must first be made aware of Deli Depot and then be convinced to try it. Over the long run, a loyal customer base must be established to make each Deli Depot a success.

Questions

1. Are Deli Depot's unique advantages strong enough to attract customers from Subway and other sandwich competitors? Why or why not?

2. Are all the important customer selection factors for sandwich restaurants included in the list? Do you agree with the importance rankings? Explain your answers.

3. How can Robert and his group make potential customers aware of the new Deli Depot locations and menu selections?

4. How can Robert and his group convince individuals who try Deli Depot to become regular customers?

Ethics Exercise

EyeOnU operates a Web filter service for public schools and libraries to protect students from inappropriate material on the Internet. Like the industry as a whole, the company's market share has been stagnant for the past two years. Looking for new sources of revenue, the company is considering selling the data it has collected about student surfing habits to marketers trying to learn more about students' behavior on the Web. The data is anonymous but privacy advocates are concerned about the precedent of selling information about children to marketers

Questions

1. What should EyeOnU do? Should it protect the student's data, or should it take the opportunity to create new revenues?

2. Does the AMA Code of Ethics address this issue? Go to **http://www.marketingpower.com** and review the code. Then, write a brief paragraph on how the AMA Code of Ethics relates to EyeOnU's dilemma.

Entrepreneurship Case

Bucking the Trend: Is 'Family' the Next Theme Restaurant?

In 1995, attorney and real estate investor Stephen Waite sparked a revitalization in Albany, New York, when he opened his Big House Brewing Company in a century-old vacant downtown building. The extremely successful restaurant and pub set off a chain reaction of development and improvement projects that have transformed downtown Albany into a very different place, especially after five o'clock. In 2002, Waite hoped to leverage his experience downtown to create an entirely new type of restaurant concept, this time in Clifton Park, an Albany suburb.

Although financiers were not terribly eager to underwrite the Big House in 1995, Waite and his new business partner, Eric Shilling, are having much less trouble garnering support for their idea this time around. The pair wants to create a family-friendly restaurant with miniature golf in the summer and outdoor ice skating in the winter, plus clowns and magicians the whole year round. Providing recreational activities in conjunction with family dining is not a new trend: Places like Chuck E. Cheese and Dave & Buster's have been doing it for years. But what Waite and Shilling know will set their establishment apart is the fact that it is a unique facility. The restaurant menu will incorporate dishes made with locally grown products, like local apples. Having dishes that are indigenous to the area will set the restaurant apart from the bevy of national chain restaurants and attractions that make up the American suburban landscape. In fact, the location of the new complex is not near any strip mall or commercial area. The proposed site is a wooded six-acre site near the community sports complex and local schools.

Waite and Shilling's whole project is bucking the trend of locating chains near other chains to drive traffic, forecasting that people are getting tired of chains. In fact, there is some evidence that Americans are getting tired of the sameness that pervades their culture. And even companies once thought of as innovators, like Hard Rock Café and The Gap, are struggling to some degree as consumers' attentions fade. Some former innovators, like Planet Hollywood, are now defunct. In some cases, consumers have stayed away because they are weary of the theme; in some cases it's because consumers demand higher quality than the theme restaurants provide. Amex conducted a series of seminars that examined consumer dining trends. Panelists included people from the marketing research discipline and chefs and owners of major restaurants. One trend identified by Barbara Caplan of Yankelovitch Partners, a national marketing research firm, was that of authenticity. Bobby Flay, popular chef and owner of the Mesa Grill and Bob in New York City, added to that by stating that consumers want an experience. But do theme restaurants provide that experience consumers seek?

With ten consecutive years of growth, the National Restaurant Association looked to top $408 billion in sales for 2002. And despite the hard times at many theme-based retailers (not just restaurants), Waite and Shilling are not alone in looking for the next successful theme. McDonald's opened its second-largest outlet in Columbus, Ohio's Easton Town Center in 2002. Not just a restaurant, this McDonald's includes an interactive miniature drive-thru for kids, a karaoke booth for customers to record CDs, a separate area where adults can eat, a merchandise area where customers can purchase McDonald's apparel and souvenirs, and a McTreat Center that sells ice cream treats, cookies, pastries, and imported Lavazza specialty coffee.

Although family-oriented dining is not new, it may very well be the new trend in theme restaurants. And even though Waite and Shilling want their family entertainment venue to be distinct from the chains in the nearby area, they are already looking at turning their idea into a regional chain, should it be as successful as they anticipate. Rick Sampson, the president of the New York State Restaurant Association, an Albany-based trade group, thinks that the popularity of themes is here to stay. "When the Hard Rock (Café) started off, they only had a couple," notes Sampson. "Their popularity made them what they are today."

Questions

1. What type of consumer buying decision best describes dining at Waite and Shilling's new family restaurant and entertainment complex? Is it different than the decision made to dine at McDonald's new Edu-Tainment restaurant? At a regular McDonald's restaurant? How?

2. List the factors that would influence a consumer to spend his or her dining budget at a family entertainment-themed restaurant. Include cultural, social, individual, and psychological factors on your list.

3. What influences on consumer decision making do you think are contributing to the declining performance of once-popular theme chains, like Hard Rock Café, The Gap, the Disney Store, the Warner Bros. Store, and so forth? Based on the factors you identify, do you think that opening a new theme restaurant is wise? Why or why not?

WATCH IT

Short

On your dedicated PowerPoint CD-ROM, you will find various ads that illustrate consumer decision-making. Ads from Budweiser, Monster, and Radio Shack are examples of how marketers dealt with the terrorist attacks of September 11. Ads from McDonald's and Charles Schwab illustrate other issues working in the consumer buying process.

Medium **VIDEO**

How important is perception in driving consumer behavior? In the early 2000's, while the media was reporting economic decline, consumers were still spending as they had in previous years because they felt that personally, things weren't so bad. So is perception or reality the more important factor in assessing consumer behavior? Watch the CNN clip and decide for yourself. The CNN clip for chapter 18 on the yacht boom also illustrates consumer behavior concepts.

Long
the Series on PBS stations and the Web

To give you insight into Chapter 5, Small Business School will introduce you to Cowgirl Enterprises and its founder, Donna Baase. Baase invented Cowgirl Cream in her kitchen, and now the company sells a full line of skin products to a certain type of woman. What type? Well, a cowgirl. Watch the segment and work the questions on the supplemental video CD-ROM.

 FLIP IT

Flip to Chapter 5 in your *Grademaker Study Guide* for more review opportunities, including the pretest, vocabulary review, Internet activities, study test questions, and consumer behavior scenarios. Do you know the major factors that influence consumer behavior? Can you close your book and diagram the consumer decision-making process? Open you Study Guide to find out how much you know—or don't know.

 CLICK IT

The *Marketing* Web site links you to all the Internet-based activities in this chapter, like "Use It," "Review It" Questions 2.1 and 8.2, and the On-Line exercises in the chapter margins. As a review, do the Chapter 5 quiz and crossword puzzle. You can also work the Career Exersite that shows you different resources for marketing careers in the area of consumer behavior. Or review the main concepts in the PowerPoint presentation for Chapter 5. Go to **http://lamb.swlearning.com**, read the material, and follow the links right from the site.

CHAPTER **SIX**

BUSINESS MARKETING

Learning Objectives

1 Describe business marketing

2 Describe the role of the Internet in business marketing

3 Discuss the role of relationship marketing and strategic alliances in business marketing

4 Identify the four major categories of business market customers

5 Explain the North American Industry Classification System

6 Explain the major differences between business and consumer markets

7 Describe the seven types of business goods and services

8 Discuss the unique aspects of business buying behavior

General Motors Corporation has spent the past several years weaving together a web of alliances and joint ventures to build its Asian presence. Now, the No. 1 automaker is trying to show it can turn this sprawling network into a real competitive advantage.

With profits in its home market slumping, GM is under pressure to make its Asian strategy deliver. So far, the results haven't been very encouraging. The most they can tout is that, combined with the sales of its alliance partners, GM's share of the Asian market is more than 16 percent, second only to Toyota Motor Corporation. "Cooperation between GM and our alliance partners is still in its infancy," says Asia chief Rudy Schlais. Though some of GM's Asian relationships date back decades, GM didn't devote much attention to them until recently. But after years of trying without much success to crack Asian markets on its own, GM now is counting on its partners to help. For example, in Japan GM has given up trying to sell large numbers of its U.S. or European models after years of trying without success. Instead, GM will begin selling the Chevrolet Cruze mini-SUV, a vehicle designed and built by Suzuki. GM and its allies hope that together they will be able to build a successful distribution network.

GM offers its partners the chance to lower parts costs thanks to volume discounts and big savings on costly research into future technologies. Already, they are winning deeper discounts from suppliers thanks to their larger buying power. But the Japanese companies, which rely more heavily on suppliers for engineering, are reluctant to adopt GM's approach for all their buying. Fuji officials say they don't expect to buy more than 30 percent of their parts through GM's system, for fear of compromising the uniqueness of their vehicles.

GM is finding out that sharing across regions and between independent companies is often complex. Though GM insists that minority-stake alliance deals avoid much of the pain and tension of a full-blown merger, the partners' independence can complicate efforts to cooperate. Take GM's $650 million plant in Thailand. On paper, the factory looks like a model for 21st century globalization. Located in a low-wage country, the factory is flexible enough to build everything from small Zafira minivans for European customers to sports cars for Italy's Fiat SpA, GM's European ally, to Asia-bound pickup trucks for Isuzu.

On the ground, things aren't so neat. Consider a slight rippling in the paint known as "orange peel." Engineers from Fuji wanted it reduced to a minimum on the Zafiras they will sell in Japan, since Japanese consumers expect a near-flawless paint job. But GM's Opel European unit didn't want orange peel eliminated entirely, since minor imperfections in the sheet metal are more obvious to the eye where the paint is smooth.

Though the factory employs the latest in GM's quality-control techniques, Opel insisted on an extra round of inspections to make sure the Zafiras it is getting are up to European standards. After passing that test, along with a test drive over a bumpy track designed to expose latent squeaks and rattles, Fuji submits them to another, even more thorough, once-over by quality checkers looking for defects that might put off picky buyers in Japan.[1]

What motivated General Motors to form strategic alliances and joint ventures with Asian automakers? What does GM bring to these relationships? What do the partners have to contribute?

What Is Business Marketing?

Describe business marketing

business marketing
The marketing of goods and services to individuals and organizations for purposes other than personal consumption.

Business marketing is the marketing of goods and services to individuals and organizations for purposes other than personal consumption. The sale of an overhead projector to your college or university is an example of business marketing. Business products include those that are used to manufacture other products, become part of another product, aid the normal operations of an organization, or are acquired for resale without any substantial change in form. The key characteristic distinguishing business products from consumer products is intended use, not physical characteristics. A product that is purchased for personal or family consumption or as a gift is a consumer good. If that same product, such as a microcomputer or a cellular telephone, is bought for use in a business, it is a business product.

Business Marketing on the Internet

Describe the role of the Internet in business marketing

It is hard to imagine that commercial use of the Internet began as recently as the mid-1990s.[2] In 1995, those commercial Web sites that did exist were static. Only a few had data-retrieval capabilities. Frames, tables, and styles were not available. Security of any sort was rare, and streaming video did not exist. In early 1995, the entire Internet could have been stored on fewer than fifty compact discs.[3]

What a difference a few years have made! Today, Dell Computer sells over $1 million worth of computer equipment every day on the Internet, and IBM purchases over $6 billion of goods and services annually through Internet transactions. The worldwide purchase of business goods and services runs into the trillions of dollars annually. Cost savings just from purchasing goods and services on-line are estimated to exceed $2 trillion annually.[4]

Business marketing on the Internet offers tremendous opportunities for firms to increase efficiency, reduce costs, improve customer service, create one-to-one relationships, introduce new products, and expand markets. One study, sponsored by Cisco Systems, reported that over 80 percent of all U.S. companies with five thousand or more employees have some form of Internet presence.[5]

COURTESY OF CARRIER CORP.

One company that has successfully deployed its e-business initiative is Carrier, maker of air conditioners. Particularly noteworthy is how the company's Brazilian division used the Internet to increase sales, inventory turns, and customer satisfaction, all while decreasing delivery times.

Two Success Stories

Carrier Corporation and the resins division of General Electric Company illustrate the opportunities for businesses to use the Internet to reduce costs, streamline order processing, and enhance customer service and satisfaction.

At Carrier, the world's largest manufacturer of air conditioners, company officials claim to have reduced costs by $100 million annually by buying and selling on the Internet.[6] Carrier now sells over $1 billion worth of products through the company's Web site. International sales and service results have been particularly remarkable.

The time required for Brazilian customers to place an order with Carrier and get confirmation has gone from six days to six minutes. Inventory turnover has increased from seventeen to twenty-four times per year. And 77 percent of the Brazilian customers report that they are "satisfied" or "highly satisfied" with the service they are receiving.[7] A similar initiative in Korea has resulted in 50 percent of all sales passing through the Web site and orders being delivered in eighteen days compared to thirty-three days in the past.[8]

In 1997, General Electric's resins division launched an e-commerce site that was affectionately named GEPolymerland. Employees thought it sounded like a magical place, like Disneyland or Never-Never Land. It has produced what some might call magical results. Sales made through the Web site increased twelve-fold from 1999 to 2000 and grew from $1.2 billion in 1999 to $3 billion in 2001.[9]

GE's goals for the site are reducing costs and helping customers streamline their buying. Since 95 percent of on-line orders go straight into GEPolymerland's information-management system without human intervention, the site cuts GE's costs and speeds up orders. There are savings on customer service costs, too. Answering a technical question by telephone might cost $80, but if the customer accesses the same information using a search tool, the cost is only 50 cents.[10]

GEPolymerland

Is GEPolymerland just an e-commerce site, or is it also a virtual community? Visit the site and see what it offers beyond on-line ordering of resins.

http://www.gepolymerland

On Line

Potential Unrealized

Carrier and GE's resins division were both successful marketers before they created easy-to-use Web sites. Putting the operations on-line didn't require changing fundamental business relationships: The Web sites were just a way to make the firms more efficient.

Most business buying and selling is done off-line. One recent study found that only 18 percent of business marketers with an on-line presence sell on-line at all. Another study found that corporate purchasing agents make a mere 20 percent of purchases on-line. As one person put it, "if you are buying a stapler, you have no problems clicking around on-line. If you're buying fifteen thousand staplers, you want to talk to someone."[11] What are the 82 percent of business marketers that have a presence on the Internet but are not selling goods and services offering? Most provide product information and promotion. Some answer questions. Others provide contact and ordering information. Business Internet marketing represents trillions of dollars of sales potential per year. It has currently reached only a fraction of its potential.

Benefits of Business Marketing on the Internet

As many examples in this book demonstrate, companies that use the Internet effectively gain clear advantages. These include:

1. *Lower prices:* Competition among on-line vendors leads to lower prices for business buyers.

2. *Greater selection of products and vendors:* The Web makes it possible for corporate purchasing agents to find numerous vendors for almost any product.

3. *Access to customer and product sales data:* Companies can develop customer lists and learn their buying characteristics. They can also immediately learn which products are selling best.

4. *Around-the-clock ordering and customer service:* Company Web sites provide extensive product information for prospective customers around the world on a "24/7" basis, thereby expanding markets and facilitating more transactions— without hiring additional personnel. Customers themselves decide how much information they require by clicking on site links. Well-designed sites offer solutions to customer problems and make product suggestions.

5. *Lower costs:* Cost savings are a major benefit of e-commerce. These can take many forms, from distribution savings to staff reductions and lower costs of purchasing supplies. Carrier used the Web to cut costs by $100 million. GEPolymerland.com contributed substantially to General Electric's $1 billion in cost savings in 2001.

Covisint

How many trading partners does Covisint boast? Check the Web site to find out. Read Covisint's latest newsletter, specifically the metrics column (various measurements Covisint makes to track its progress). Check back at the end of the semester to see what progress has been made.

http://www.covisint.com

On Line

6. *Customized products:* The Internet is revolutionizing product design and manufacturing. No longer do companies have to design and build products well in advance of the sale, basing product decisions on market research. They can use the Internet to take orders for products tailored to customer specifications. Dell Computers was one of the first to allow computer buyers to configure their ideal computer from menus at Dell's Web site. Even though Dell's build-to-order procedures were remarkably efficient when customers phoned in all their orders, the Web has increased its efficiency and profitability. Warehouses receive supply orders via Internet messages every two hours instead of daily faxes. Suppliers know about the company's inventory and production plans and get feedback on their performance in meeting shipping deadlines.

Many business marketers now realize that the Internet is a valuable tool for expanding markets and better serving customers. Exhibit 6.1 identifies seven Internet sites that contain important information for firms interested in competing in foreign markets. Exhibit 6.2 provides examples of popular Internet sites that cater to small businesses.

Exhibit 6.1

An Internet Guide to Small-Business Exporting

One of the easiest ways to delve into exporting is to utilize the Internet. Visit these sites, which offer valuable resources as well as links to additional information.

http://www.exim.gov   The Export-Import Bank of the United States was established to aid in financing and to facilitate U.S. exports.

http://www.exporthotline.com   Export Hotline contains thousands of market research reports, a trade library, and a variety of other resources focused on all aspects of global trade and investment.

http://www.fita.org   Trade associations are invaluable resources on exporting. Visit the Federation of International Trade Associations Web site to take advantage of all of its resources, including a network of three hundred thousand companies belonging to three hundred international trade associations in North America.

http://www.ita.doc.gov   The International Trade Administration of the U.S. Department of Commerce is "dedicated to helping U.S. businesses compete in the global marketplace." It offers many resources to encourage, assist, and advocate U.S. exports.

http://www.sba.gov   The U.S. Small Business Administration offers a wealth of basic information and resources, including various export support programs. It provides financial, technical, and management assistance to help Americans start, run, and help their businesses grow.

http://www.tradecompass.com   Trade Compass offers news, information, and sophisticated database products that help companies and individuals navigate the far reaches of trade, importing, exporting, sales, marketing, logistics, research, and e-business in today's global marketplace.

SOURCE: Based on information from Christopher Farrell and Edith Updike, "So You Think the World Is Your Oyster," *Business Week*, June 9, 1997, p. ENT8.

Exhibit 6.2

Internet Sites Specifically for Small Businesses

http://www.allbusiness.com AllBusiness provides entrepreneurs with the knowledge and tools to start, manage, and grow their business. The site links to hundreds of how-to articles and provides expert answers to questions.

http://www.bcentral.com Microsoft bCentral offers small-business solutions such as assistance in establishing an on-line business presence, enhancing sales or services, or managing business operations. The site also contains practical tips, advice, and links to how-to articles.

http://office.com Office.com offers practical information on how to start or run a business and how to transform an existing company into an e-business. Users access over five hundred databases for news that affects their companies or industries. Office.com is one of the ten most visited business Web sites on the Internet.

http://www.quicken.com/small_business/ This site offers information on starting, running, and growing a small business. It also provides links to a variety of other Quicken sites that are useful to small-business owners and managers.

Relationship Marketing and Strategic Alliances

As Chapter 1 explained, relationship marketing is the strategy that entails seeking and establishing ongoing partnerships with customers. Relationship marketing has become an important business marketing strategy as customers have become more demanding and competition has become more intense. Building long-term relationships with customers offers companies a way to build competitive advantage. For example, the FedEx Powership program includes a series of automated shipping, tracking, and invoicing systems that save customers time and money while solidifying their loyalty to FedEx. This produces a win-win situation. FedEx has a satisfied loyal customer, and the customer saves time and money shipping products to their customers.

Discuss the role of relationship marketing and strategic alliances in business marketing

Strategic Alliances

A **strategic alliance**, sometimes called a *strategic partnership*, is a cooperative agreement between business firms. Strategic alliances can take the form of licensing or distribution agreements, joint ventures, research and development consortia, and partnerships. They may be between manufacturers, manufacturers and customers, manufacturers and suppliers, and manufacturers and channel intermediaries.

Business marketers form strategic alliances to leverage what they have (technology, financial resources, access to markets) by combining these assets with those of other firms. Sometimes the alliance partners' assets are complementary. For example, UPS has developed strategic alliances with Ford, Nike, and Daimler-Chrysler to employ its information-technology expertise to track shipments and handle on-line orders. Ford uses UPS to track the more than four million cars and trucks it produces annually. Dealers log onto an Internet site to find out exactly where their orders are in the distribution system, much the way customers already can track UPS packages on the Internet using a tracking number.[12]

Some strategic alliances are formed to achieve economies of scale. General Motors, Ford, DaimlerChrysler, Nissan Motor Company, and Renault SA created an Internet automobile parts exchange, called Covisint, that is expected to account for

strategic alliance (strategic partnership)
A cooperative agreement between business firms.

Strategic alliances are at the heart of business marketing. Nobody knows this better than UPS. Its alliance with Office Depot makes UPS services available to the multitude of businesspeople that shop the supply superstore.

keiretsu
A network of interlocking corporate affiliates.

$300 billion in sales per year.[13] Covisint officials claim that the exchange will benefit small suppliers because they will have access to advanced technology that will provide them with faster and better access to buyers. Covisint officials also say smaller firms will be able to improve profit margins by reducing inventory and saving time.[14]

Relationships in Other Cultures

Although the terms "relationship marketing" and "strategic alliances" are fairly new, and popularized mostly by American business executives and educators, the concepts have long been familiar in other cultures. Businesses in countries such as Mexico, China, Japan, Korea, and much of Europe rely heavily on personal relationships. Chapter 20 explores customer relationship management in detail.

In Japan, for example, the basis of exchange between firms is personal relationships that are developed through what is called *amae*, or indulgent dependency. *Amae* is the feeling of nurturing concern for, and dependence upon, another. Reciprocity and personal relationships contribute to *amae*. Relationships between companies can develop into a **keiretsu**—a network of interlocking corporate affiliates. Within a keiretsu, executives may sit on the boards of their customers or their suppliers. Members of a keiretsu trade with each other whenever possible and often engage in joint product development, finance, and marketing activity. For example, the Toyota Group keiretsu includes fourteen core companies and another 170 that receive preferential treatment. Toyota holds an equity position in many of these 170 member firms and is represented on many of their boards of directors.

Many American firms have found that the best way to compete in Asian countries is to form relationships with Asian firms. For example, Fuji-Xerox markets copiers in Japan and other Asian countries. Whirlpool has spent over $200 million buying controlling interests in competing firms in China and in India. The "Global Perspectives" box in this chapter describes a strategic alliance between General Motors and Shanghai Automotive to create a "Farmer Car" for rural residents of China.

Major Categories of Business Customers

Identify the four major categories of business market customers

The business market consists of four major categories of customers: producers, resellers, governments, and institutions.

Producers

The producer segment of the business market includes profit-oriented individuals and organizations that use purchased goods and services to produce other products, to incorporate into other products, or to facilitate the daily operations of the organization. Examples of producers include construction, manufacturing, transportation, finance, real estate, and food service firms. In the United States there are over thirteen million firms in the producer segment of the business market. Some of these firms are small and others are among the world's largest businesses.

Individual producers often buy large quantities of goods and services. Companies like General Motors spend more than $70 billion annually—more than the gross domestic product of Ireland, Portugal, Turkey, or Greece—on such business products as steel, metal components, and tires.

Shanghai Auto and GM to Market Farmer's Car

Under a new agreement, Shanghai Automotive, one of China's biggest auto companies, will license GM technology to build a cheap, bare-bones combination pickup-delivery truck designed specifically for the country's farmers.

With nearly one billion consumers and a fast-growing network of national highways, China boasts an auto market expected to be the biggest in the world someday. The rural focus, however, is a major shift for GM and Shanghai Automotive, which so far have focused on catering to the country's white-collar urban workers. The two already make Buick sedans, which sell for around $40,000, and will soon begin regular production of a new, more affordable compact car, the Sail, priced around $10,000.

But with almost every major auto maker in the world competing to sell cars to the few Chinese urbanites who can afford them, sales of the Buicks haven't lived up to expectations, and some auto analysts say the new compact car could also face a lukewarm reception. In fact, total car sales in Chinese cities grew just 6 percent last year, less than half the rate of rural auto sales, initial figures show.

The new Farmer's Car, as it is currently called, is based on GM's Corsa Combo and will be sold under Shanghai Auto's brand, retailing for about $7,000. Shanghai Auto and GM are betting the car will be a hit among China's 800 million rural inhabitants, a huge group of consumers mostly overlooked by foreign investors because of their skimpy earnings and frugal lifestyle.

For now, that is the biggest stumbling block the new car faces. Though living standards in the countryside have leapt in the past decade, rural dwellers remain the country's lowest earners, making less than $300 a year on average. And with grain and some produce prices falling, that figure is unlikely to rise significantly during the next few years.

Shanghai Auto is so confident in the rural car that it recently bought an unprofitable government auto company in coastal Jiangsu province, where it will produce the new Combo. Already, dozens of executives from Shanghai GM, the joint venture, are being lent to the Combo factory, where they plan to retool the outdated plant using GM's Corsa platform. Plans call for the car to use some parts, possibly including the engine made at Shanghai GM's plant here, a $1.5 billion facility that now makes Buicks, family wagons, and, soon, the new Sail compact car.

Though China has a handful of auto companies that make simple pickup trucks for farmers, Shanghai Auto and GM are the first two major concerns to step into the vast countryside market. If the Combo proves successful, auto analysts say, that could change quickly. "This is a part of the market that hasn't registered on most companies' radar screens, but given the sheer number of farmers out there, these vehicles could end up dominating the market," says Yale Zhang, a Beijing executive with industry consultant Automotive Resources Asia.[15]

Do you think the first product of the Shanghai Auto/GM alliance, the Farmer's Car, will be successful? What are the benefits to each company in establishing such a partnership? The disadvantages?

Resellers

The reseller market includes retail and wholesale businesses that buy finished goods and resell them for a profit. A retailer sells mainly to final consumers; wholesalers sell mostly to retailers and other organizational customers. There are approximately 1.5 million retailers and five hundred thousand wholesalers operating in the United States. Consumer-product firms like Procter & Gamble, Kraft General Foods, and Coca-Cola sell directly to large retailers and retail chains and through wholesalers to smaller retail units. Retailing and wholesaling are explored in detail in Chapters 12 and 13.

Business product distributors are wholesalers that buy business products and resell them to business customers. They often carry thousands

© ANDY SACKS/TONY STONE IMAGES

The producer segment of the business market includes manufacturing, like this globe production line, as well as construction, finance, transportation, real estate, and others.

On Line

of items in stock and employ sales forces to call on business customers. Businesses that wish to buy a gross of pencils or a hundred pounds of fertilizer typically purchase these items from local distributors rather than directly from manufacturers such as Empire Pencil or Dow Chemical.

Governments

A third major segment of the business market is government. Government organizations include thousands of federal, state, and local buying units. They make up what may be the largest single market for goods and services in the world.

Contracts for government purchases are often put out for bid. Interested vendors submit bids (usually sealed) to provide specified products during a particular time. Sometimes the lowest bidder is awarded the contract. When the lowest bidder is not awarded the contract, strong evidence must be presented to justify the decision. Grounds for rejecting the lowest bid include lack of experience, inadequate financing, or poor past performance. Bidding allows all potential suppliers a fair chance at winning government contracts and helps ensure that public funds are spent wisely.

Federal Government

Name just about any good or service and chances are that someone in the federal government uses it. The U.S. federal government is the world's largest customer.

Although much of the federal government's buying is centralized, no single federal agency contracts for all the government's requirements, and no single buyer in any agency purchases all that the agency needs. We can view the federal government as a combination of several large companies with overlapping responsibilities and thousands of small independent units.

One popular source of information about government procurement is *Commerce Business Daily*. Until recently, businesses hoping to sell to the federal government found the document unorganized, and it often arrived too late to be useful. The new on-line version (**http://www.cbd-net.com**) is more timely and lets contractors find leads using keyword searches. *Doing Business with the General Services Administration, Selling to the Military*, and *Selling to the U.S. Air Force* are other examples of publications designed to explain how to do business with the federal government.

State, County, and City Government

Selling to states, counties, and cities can be less frustrating for both small and large vendors than selling to the federal government. Paperwork is typically simpler and more manageable than it is at the federal level. On the other hand, vendors must decide which of the over eighty-two thousand government units are likely to buy their wares. State and local buying agencies include school districts, highway departments, government-operated hospitals, and housing agencies.

Institutions

The fourth major segment of the business market is institutions that seek to achieve goals other than the standard business goals of profit, market share, and return on investment. This segment

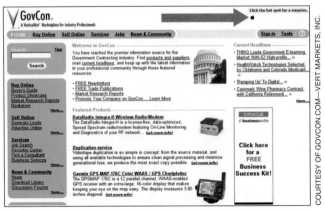

COURTESY OF GOVCON.COM—VERT MARKETS, INC.

For doing business with the federal government, there is no better on-line resource than govcon. com. Users can check industry news, consult government databases, and view active contracts.

includes schools, hospitals, colleges and universities, churches, labor unions, fraternal organizations, civic clubs, foundations, and other so-called nonbusiness organizations.

The North American Industry Classification System

The **North American Industry Classification System (NAICS)** is an industry classification system introduced in 1997 to replace the standard industrial classification system (SIC). NAICS (pronounced *nakes*) is an all-new system for classifying North American business establishments. The system, developed jointly by the United States, Canada, and Mexico, provides a common industry classification system for the North American Free Trade Association (NAFTA) partners. Goods- or service-producing firms that use identical or similar production processes are grouped together.

NAICS is an extremely valuable tool for business marketers engaged in analyzing, segmenting, and targeting markets. Each classification group is relatively homogeneous in terms of raw materials required, components used, manufacturing processes employed, and problems faced. The more digits in a code, the more homogenous the group is. Therefore, if a supplier understands the needs and requirements of a few firms within a classification, requirements can be projected for all firms in that category. The number, size, and geographic dispersion of firms can also be identified. This information can be converted to market potential estimates, market share estimates, and sales forecasts. It can also be used for identifying potential new customers. NAICS codes can help identify firms that may be prospective users of a supplier's goods and services.

Exhibit 6.3 (on page 194) provides an overview of NAICS. Exhibit 6.4 (on page 195) illustrates the six-digit classification system for two of the twenty NAICS economic sectors: manufacturing and information. The hierarchical structure of NAICS allows industry data to be summarized at several levels of detail. To illustrate:

- The first two digits designate a major economic sector such as agriculture (11) or manufacturing (31–33).

- The third digit designates an economic subsector such as crop production or apparel manufacturing.

- The fourth digit designates an industry group, such as grain and oil seed farming or fiber, yarn, and thread mills.

- The fifth digit designates the NAICS industry, such as wheat farming or broadwoven fabric mills.

- The sixth digit, when used, identifies subdivisions of NAICS industries that accommodate user needs in individual countries.[16]

For a complete listing of all NAICS codes, see **http://www.census.gov/epcd/www/naics.html**.

Explain the North American Industry Classification System

North American Industry Classification System (NAICS)
A detailed numbering system developed by the United States, Canada, and Mexico to classify North American business establishments by their main production processes.

Business versus Consumer Markets

The basic philosophy and practice of marketing are the same whether the customer is a business organization or a consumer. Business markets do, however, have characteristics different from consumer markets. Exhibit 6.5 on page 196 summarizes the main differences between business and consumer markets.

Explain the major differences between business and consumer markets

Exhibit 6.3

NAICS Two-Digit Codes and Corresponding Economic Sectors

NAICS Code	Economic Sector
11	Agriculture, forestry, and fishing
21	Mining
22	Utilities
23	Construction
31–33	Manufacturing
43	Wholesale trade
44–45	Retail trade
47–48	Transportation
51	Information
52	Finance and insurance
53	Real estate and rental and leasing
56	Professional and technical services
57	Management and support services
56	Professional and technical services
57	Management and support services
61	Education services
62	Health and social assistance
71	Arts, entertainment, and recreation
72	Food services, drinking places, and accommodations
81	Other services, except public administration
93	Public administration
98	Estates and trusts
99	Nonclassifiable

Exhibit 6.4

Examples of NAICS Hierarchy

| NAICS Level | Example 1 | | Example 2 | |
	NAICS Code	Description	NAICS Code	Description
Sector	31–33	Manufacturing	51	Information
Subsector	334	Computer and electronic product manufacturing	513	Broadcasting and telecommunications
Industry group	3346	Manufacturing and reproduction of magnetic and optical media	5133	Telecommunications
Industry	33461	Manufacturing and reproduction of magnetic and optical media	51332	Wireless telecommunications carriers, except satellite
U.S. industry	334611	Reproduction of software	513321	Paging

SOURCE: U.S. Census Bureau, "New Code System in NAICS," **http://www.census.gov/epcd/www/naics.html.**

Demand

Consumer demand for products is quite different from demand in the business market. Unlike consumer demand, business demand is derived, inelastic, joint, and fluctuating.

Derived Demand

The demand for business products is called **derived demand** because organizations buy products to be used in producing their customers' products. For example, the market for CPUs, hard drives, and CD-ROMs is derived from the demand for personal computers. These items are only valuable as components of computers. Demand for these items rises and falls with the demand for PCs.

Because demand is derived, business marketers must carefully monitor demand patterns and changing preferences in final consumer markets, even though their customers are not in those markets. Moreover, business marketers must carefully monitor their customers' forecasts, because derived demand is based on expectations of future demand for those customers' products.

Some business marketers not only monitor final consumer demand and customer forecasts but also try to influence final consumer demand. Aluminum producers use television and magazine advertisements to point out the convenience and recycling opportunities that aluminum offers to consumers who can choose to purchase soft drinks in either aluminum or plastic containers.

Inelastic Demand

The demand for many business products is inelastic with regard to price. *Inelastic demand* means that an increase or decrease in the price of the product will not significantly affect demand for the product. This will be discussed further in Chapter 17.

The price of a product used in the production of or as part of a final product is often a minor portion of the final product's total price. Therefore, demand for

derived demand
The demand for business products.

Characteristic	Business Market	Consumer Market
Demand	Organizational	Individual
Purchase volume	Larger	Smaller
Number of customers	Fewer	Many
Location of buyers	Geographically concentrated	Dispersed
Distribution structure	More direct	More indirect
Nature of buying	More professional	More personal
Nature of buying influence	Multiple	Single
Type of negotiations	More complex	Simpler
Use of reciprocity	Yes	No
Use of leasing	Greater	Lesser
Primary promotional method	Personal selling	Advertising

the final consumer product is not affected. If the price of automobile paint or spark plugs rose significantly, say, 200 percent in one year, do you think the number of new automobiles sold that year would be affected? Probably not.

Joint Demand

joint demand
The demand for two or more items used together in a final product.

Joint demand occurs when two or more items are used together in a final product. For example, a decline in the availability of memory chips will slow production of microcomputers, which will in turn reduce the demand for disk drives. One of the largest markets for Caterpillar diesel engines is over-the-road, heavy-duty truck manufacturers. A recent decline in sales of the behemoth trucks has led to fewer engines being purchased.[17]

Fluctuating Demand

multiplier effect (accelerator principle)
Phenomenon in which a small increase or decrease in consumer demand can produce a much larger change in demand for the facilities and equipment needed to make the consumer product.

The demand for business products—particularly new plants and equipment—tends to be more unstable than the demand for consumer products. A small increase or decrease in consumer demand can produce a much larger change in demand for the facilities and equipment needed to make the consumer product. Economists refer to this phenomenon as the **multiplier effect** (or **accelerator principle**).

Cummins Engine Company, a producer of heavy-duty diesel engines, uses sophisticated surface grinders to make parts. Suppose Cummins is using twenty surface grinders. Each machine lasts about ten years. Purchases have been timed so two machines will wear out and be replaced annually. If the demand for engine parts does not change, two grinders will be bought this year. If the demand for parts declines slightly, only eighteen grinders may be needed and Cummins won't replace the worn ones. However, suppose in the next year demand returns to previous levels plus a little more. To meet the new level of demand, Cummins will need to replace the two machines that wore out in the first year, the two that wore out in the second year, plus one or more additional machines. The multiplier effect works this way in many industries, producing highly fluctuating demand for business products.

Purchase Volume

Business customers buy in much larger quantities than consumers. Just think how large an order Kellogg typically places for the wheat bran and raisins used to manufacture Raisin Bran. Imagine the number of tires that DaimlerChrysler buys at one time.

Number of Customers

Business marketers usually have far fewer customers than consumer marketers. The advantage is that it is a lot easier to identify prospective buyers, monitor current customers' needs and levels of satisfaction, and personally attend to existing customers. The main disadvantage is that each customer becomes crucial—especially for those manufacturers that have only one customer. In many cases, this customer is the U.S. government. The success or failure of one bid can make the difference between prosperity and bankruptcy. In 2001, after five years of development, testing, and politicking, the Pentagon awarded Lockheed Martin a multidecade contract to build three thousand jet fighter airplanes.[18] Boeing Aircraft Company, the only other bidder on the $200 billion contract, immediately announced plans for substantial layoffs.

AP /WIDE WORLD PHOTOS.

Winning major contracts, particularly high-volume ones, is definitely a reason to cheer. Lockheed Martin employees celebrate after the announcement that the company won the U.S. Defense Department contract to build the Joint Striker Fighter aircraft.

Location of Buyers

Business customers tend to be much more geographically concentrated than consumers. For instance, more than half the nation's business buyers are located in New York, California, Pennsylvania, Illinois, Ohio, Michigan, and New Jersey. The aircraft and microelectronics industries are concentrated on the West Coast, and many of the firms that supply the automobile manufacturing industry are located in and around Detroit.

Distribution Structure

Many consumer products pass through a distribution system that includes the producer, one or more wholesalers, and a retailer. However, because of many of the characteristics already mentioned, channels of distribution are typically shorter in business marketing. Direct channels, where manufacturers market directly to users, are much more common.

Many businesses that market directly to users are discovering that the Internet offers great potential for reaching new and existing customers domestically and around the world, while reducing costs to both buyers and sellers. Several examples of the expanding potential of the Internet are cited in this chapter.

Nature of Buying

Unlike consumers, business buyers usually approach purchasing rather formally. Businesses use professionally trained purchasing agents or buyers who spend their entire career purchasing a limited number of items. They get to know the items and the sellers well. Some professional purchasers earn the designation of Certified Purchasing Manager (CPM) after participating in a rigorous certification program.

Nature of Buying Influence

Typically, more people are involved in a single business purchase decision than in a consumer purchase. Experts from fields as varied as quality control, marketing, and finance, as well as professional buyers and users, may be grouped in a buying center (discussed later in this chapter).

Type of Negotiations

Consumers are used to negotiating price on automobiles and real estate. In most cases, however, American consumers expect sellers to set the price and other conditions of sale, such as time of delivery and credit terms. In contrast, negotiating is common in business marketing. Buyers and sellers negotiate product specifications, delivery dates, payment terms, and other pricing matters. Sometimes these negotiations occur during many meetings over several months. Final contracts are often very long and detailed.

Use of Reciprocity

reciprocity
A practice where business purchasers choose to buy from their own customers.

Business purchasers often choose to buy from their own customers, a practice known as **reciprocity**. For example, General Motors buys engines for use in its automobiles and trucks from Borg Warner, which in turn buys many of the automobiles and trucks it needs from GM. This practice is neither unethical nor illegal unless one party coerces the other and the result is unfair competition. Reciprocity is generally considered a reasonable business practice. If all possible suppliers sell a similar product for about the same price, doesn't it make sense to buy from those firms that buy from you?

Use of Leasing

Consumers normally buy products rather than lease them. But businesses commonly lease expensive equipment such as computers, construction equipment and vehicles, and automobiles. Leasing allows firms to reduce capital outflow, acquire a seller's latest products, receive better services, and gain tax advantages.

The lessor, the firm providing the product, may be either the manufacturer or an independent firm. The benefits to the lessor include greater total revenue from leasing compared to selling and an opportunity to do business with customers who cannot afford to buy.

Primary Promotional Method

Business marketers tend to emphasize personal selling in their promotion efforts, especially for expensive items, custom-designed products, large-volume purchases, and situations requiring negotiations. The sale of many business products requires a great deal of personal contact. Personal selling is discussed in more detail in Chapter 16.

Types of Business Products

Business products generally fall into one of the following seven categories, depending on their use: major equipment, accessory equipment, raw materials, component parts, processed materials, supplies, and business services.

7

Describe the seven types of business goods and services

Major Equipment

Major equipment includes such capital goods as large or expensive machines, mainframe computers, blast furnaces, generators, airplanes, and buildings. (These items are also commonly called **installations**.) Major equipment is depreciated over time rather than charged as an expense in the year it is purchased. In addition, major equipment is often custom-designed for each customer. Personal selling is an important part of the marketing strategy for major equipment because distribution channels are almost always direct from the producer to the business user.

major equipment (installations)
Capital goods such as large or expensive machines, mainframe computers, blast furnaces, generators, airplanes, and buildings.

Accessory Equipment

Accessory equipment is generally less expensive and shorter-lived than major equipment. Examples include portable drills, power tools, microcomputers, and fax machines. Accessory equipment is often charged as an expense in the year it is bought rather than depreciated over its useful life. In contrast to major equipment, accessories are more often standardized and are usually bought by more customers. These customers tend to be widely dispersed. For example, all types of businesses buy microcomputers.

Local industrial distributors (wholesalers) play an important role in the marketing of accessory equipment because business buyers often purchase accessories from them. Regardless of where accessories are bought, advertising is a more vital promotional tool for accessory equipment than for major equipment.

accessory equipment
Goods, such as portable tools and office equipment, that are less expensive and shorter-lived than major equipment.

raw materials
Unprocessed extractive or agricultural products, such as mineral ore, lumber, wheat, corn, fruits, vegetables, and fish.

component parts
Either finished items ready for assembly or products that need very little processing before becoming part of some other product.

Raw Materials

Raw materials are unprocessed extractive or agricultural products—for example, mineral ore, lumber, wheat, corn, fruits, vegetables, and fish. Raw materials become part of finished products. Extensive users, such as steel or lumber mills and food canners, generally buy huge quantities of raw materials. Because there is often a large number of relatively small sellers of raw materials, none can greatly influence price or supply. Thus, the market tends to set the price of raw materials, and individual producers have little pricing flexibility. Promotion is almost always via personal selling, and distribution channels are usually direct from producer to business user.

Component Parts

Component parts are either finished items ready for assembly or products that need very little processing before becoming part of some other product. The Caterpillar diesel engines used in heavy-duty trucks that were mentioned earlier in this chapter are component parts. Other examples include spark plugs, tires, and electric motors for automobiles. A special feature of component

© INDEX STOCK IMAGERY / GARY CONNER

Raw materials constitute a large part of business purchasing. Buyers typically order raw materials, such as lumber and steel, in large quantity.

OEM
The acronym OEM stands for original equipment manufacturer. OEMs buy business goods that they incorporate into the products that they produce for eventual sale to other producers or to consumers.

parts is that they can retain their identity after becoming part of the final product. For example, automobile tires are clearly recognizable as part of a car. Moreover, because component parts often wear out, they may need to be replaced several times during the life of the final product. Thus, there are two important markets for many component parts: the original equipment manufacturer (OEM) market and the replacement market.

Many of the business features listed earlier in Exhibit 6.5 characterize the **OEM** market. The difference between unit costs and selling prices in the OEM market is often small, but profits can be substantial because of volume buying.

The replacement market is composed of organizations and individuals buying component parts to replace worn-out parts. Because components often retain their identity in final products, users may choose to replace a component part with the same brand used by the manufacturer—for example, the same brand of automobile tires or battery. The replacement market operates differently from the OEM market, however. Whether replacement buyers are organizations or individuals, they tend to demonstrate the characteristics of consumer markets that were shown in Exhibit 6.5. Consider, for example, an automobile replacement part. Purchase volume is usually small and there are many customers, geographically dispersed, who typically buy from car dealers or parts stores. Negotiations do not occur, and neither reciprocity nor leasing is usually an issue.

Manufacturers of component parts often direct their advertising toward replacement buyers. Cooper Tire & Rubber, for example, makes and markets component parts—automobile and truck tires—for the replacement market only. General Motors and other car makers compete with independent firms in the market for replacement automobile parts.

Processed Materials

processed materials
Products used directly in manufacturing other products.

Processed materials are products used directly in manufacturing other products. Unlike raw materials, they have had some processing. Examples include sheet metal, chemicals, specialty steel, lumber, corn syrup, and plastics. Unlike component parts, processed materials do not retain their identity in final products.

Most processed materials are marketed to OEMs or to distributors servicing the OEM market. Processed materials are generally bought according to customer specifications or to some industry standard, as is the case with steel and lumber. Price and service are important factors in choosing a vendor.

Supplies

supplies
Consumable items that do not become part of the final product.

Supplies are consumable items that do not become part of the final product—for example, lubricants, detergents, paper towels, pencils, and paper. Supplies are normally standardized items that purchasing agents routinely buy. Supplies typically have relatively short lives and are inexpensive compared to other business goods. Because supplies generally fall into one of three categories—maintenance, repair, or operating supplies—this category is often referred to as MRO items.

Competition in the MRO market is intense. Bic and Paper Mate, for example, battle for business purchases of inexpensive ballpoint pens.

Business Services

business services
Expense items that do not become part of a final product.

Business services are expense items that do not become part of a final product. Businesses often retain outside providers to perform janitorial, advertising, legal, management consulting, marketing research, maintenance, and other services. Hiring an outside provider makes sense when it costs less than hiring or assigning an employee to perform the task and when an outside provider is needed for particular expertise.

Business Buying Behavior

As you probably have already concluded, business buyers behave differently from consumers. Understanding how purchase decisions are made in organizations is a first step in developing a business selling strategy. Business buying behavior has five important aspects: buying centers, evaluative criteria, buying situations, business ethics, and customer service.

Discuss the unique aspects of business buying behavior

Buying Centers

A **buying center** includes all those persons in an organization who become involved in the purchase decision. Membership and influence vary from company to company. For instance, in engineering-dominated firms like Bell Helicopter, the buying center may consist almost entirely of engineers. In marketing-oriented firms like Toyota and IBM, marketing and engineering have almost equal authority. In consumer goods firms like Procter & Gamble, product managers and other marketing decision makers may dominate the buying center. In a small manufacturing company, almost everyone may be a member.

The number of people involved in a buying center varies with the complexity and importance of a purchase decision. The composition of the buying group will usually change from one purchase to another and sometimes even during various stages of the buying process. To make matters more complicated, buying centers do not appear on formal organization charts.

For example, even though a formal committee may have been set up to choose a new plant site, it is only part of the buying center. Other people, like the company president, often play informal yet powerful roles. In a lengthy decision-making process, such as finding a new plant location, some members may drop out of the buying center when they can no longer play a useful role. Others whose talents are needed then become part of the center. No formal announcement of "who is in" and "who is out" is ever made.

buying center
All those persons in an organization who become involved in the purchase decision.

Roles in the Buying Center

As in family purchasing decisions, several people may play a role in the business purchase process:

- *Initiator:* the person who first suggests making a purchase.

- *Influencers/evaluators:* people who influence the buying decision. They often help define specifications and provide information for evaluating options. Technical personnel are especially important as influencers.

- *Gatekeepers:* group members who regulate the flow of information. Frequently, the purchasing agent views the gatekeeping role as a source of his or her power. A secretary may also act as a gatekeeper by determining which vendors get an appointment with a buyer.

- *Decider:* the person who has the formal or informal power to choose or approve the selection of the supplier or brand. In complex situations, it is often difficult to determine who makes the final decision.

- *Purchaser:* the person who actually negotiates the purchase. It could be anyone from the president of the company to the purchasing agent, depending on the importance of the decision.

- *Users:* members of the organization who will actually use the product. Users often initiate the buying process and help define product specifications.

An example illustrating these basic roles is shown in Exhibit 6.6.

Exhibit 6.6

Buying-Center Roles for
Computer Purchases

Role	Illustration
Initiator	Division general manager proposes to replace company's computer network.
Influencers/evaluators	Corporate controller's office and vice president of data processing have an important say about which system and vendor the company will deal with.
Gatekeepers	Corporate departments for purchasing and data processing analyze company's needs and recommend likely matches with potential vendors.
Decider	Vice president of administration, with advice from others, selects vendor the company will deal with and system it will buy.
Purchaser	Purchasing agent negotiates terms of sale.
Users	All division employees use the computers.

Implications of Buying Centers for the Marketing Manager

Successful vendors realize the importance of identifying who is in the decision-making unit, each member's relative influence in the buying decision, and each member's evaluative criteria. Successful selling strategies often focus on determining the most important buying influences and tailoring sales presentations to the evaluative criteria most important to these buying-center members.

For example, Loctite Corporation, the manufacturer of Super Glue and industrial adhesives and sealants, found that engineers were the most important influencers and deciders in adhesive and sealant purchase decisions. As a result, Loctite focused its marketing efforts on production and maintenance engineers.

Evaluative Criteria

Business buyers evaluate products and suppliers against three important criteria: quality, service, and price—in that order.

Quality

In this case, quality refers to technical suitability. A superior tool can do a better job in the production process, and superior packaging can increase dealer and consumer acceptance of a brand. Evaluation of quality also applies to the salesperson and the salesperson's firm. Business buyers want to deal with reputable salespeople and companies that are financially responsible. Quality improvement should be part of every organization's marketing strategy.

Service

Almost as much as they want satisfactory products, business buyers want satisfactory service. A purchase offers several opportunities for service.

The entire
industry is about
to accelerate.
Welcome
to the world of
COVISINT.

Introducing a faster, more efficient way to
communicate, collaborate, buy, sell, trade and share information—business to business.
Buyer to supplier. Up and down the supplier chain.
Through product development. From any company. Anywhere. Anytime. In real time.
Being developed for the automotive world.
DaimlerChrysler, Ford Motor Company, General Motors, Nissan, and Renault
are moving the world's largest industry to the fast lane.
Stay tuned. And buckle your seat belt.

www.covisint.com

A global business exchange

© COURTESY OF COVISINT

One way that business buyers evaluate products and suppliers is by looking at the service the prospect provides. Covisint advertises itself as a more efficient way to conduct business with other businesses.

Suppose a vendor is selling heavy equipment. Prepurchase service could include a survey of the buyer's needs. After thorough analysis of the survey findings, the vendor could prepare a report and recommendations in the form of a purchasing proposal. If a purchase results, postpurchase service might consist of installing the equipment and training those who will be using it. Postsale services may also include maintenance and repairs. Another service that business buyers seek is dependability of supply. They must be able to count on delivery of what was ordered when it is scheduled to be delivered. Buyers also welcome services that help them sell their finished products. Services of this sort are especially appropriate when the seller's product is an identifiable part of the buyer's end product.

Price

Business buyers want to buy at low prices—at the lowest prices, under most circumstances. However, a buyer who pressures a supplier to cut prices to a point where the supplier loses money on the sale almost forces shortcuts on quality. The buyer also may, in effect, force the supplier to quit selling to him or her. Then a new source of supply will have to be found.

Buying Situations

Often business firms, especially manufacturers, must decide whether to make something or buy it from an outside supplier. The decision is essentially one of economics. Can an item of similar quality be bought at a lower price elsewhere? If not, is manufacturing it in-house the best use of limited company resources? For example, Briggs & Stratton Corporation, a major manufacturer of four-cycle engines, might be able to save $150,000 annually on outside purchases by spending $500,000 on the equipment needed to produce gas throttles internally. Yet Briggs & Stratton could also use that $500,000 to upgrade its carburetor assembly line, which would save $225,000 annually. If a firm does decide to buy a product instead of making it, the purchase will be a new buy, a modified rebuy, or a straight rebuy.

New Buy

A **new buy** is a situation requiring the purchase of a product for the first time. For example, suppose a manufacturing company needs a better way to page managers while they are working on the shop floor. Currently, each of the several managers has a distinct ring, for example, two short and one long, that sounds over the plant intercom whenever he or she is being paged by anyone in the factory. The company decides to replace its buzzer system of paging with handheld wireless radio technology that will allow managers to communicate immediately with the department initiating the page. This situation represents the greatest opportunity for new vendors. No long-term relationship has been established for this product, specifications may be somewhat fluid, and buyers are generally more open to new vendors.

new buy
A situation requiring the purchase of a product for the first time.

If the new item is a raw material or a critical component part, the buyer cannot afford to run out of supply. The seller must be able to convince the buyer that the seller's firm can consistently deliver a high-quality product on time.

Modified Rebuy

A **modified rebuy** is normally less critical and less time-consuming than a new buy. In a modified-rebuy situation, the purchaser wants some change in the original good or service. It may be a new color, greater tensile strength in a component part, more respondents in a marketing research study, or additional services in a janitorial contract.

Because the two parties are familiar with each other and credibility has been established, buyer and seller can concentrate on the specifics of the modification. But in some cases, modified rebuys are open to outside bidders. The purchaser uses this strategy to ensure that the new terms are competitive. An example would be the manufacturing company buying radios with a vibrating feature for managers who have trouble hearing the ring over the factory noise. The firm may open the bidding to examine the price/quality offerings of several suppliers.

Straight Rebuy

A **straight rebuy** is a situation vendors prefer. The purchaser is not looking for new information or other suppliers. An order is placed and the product is provided as in previous orders. Usually, a straight rebuy is routine because the terms of the purchase have been agreed to in earlier negotiations. An example would be the manufacturing company previously cited purchasing additional radios for new managers from the same supplier on a regular basis.

One common instrument used in straight-rebuy situations is the purchasing contract. Purchasing contracts are used with products that are bought often and in high volume. In essence, the purchasing contract makes the buyer's decision making routine and promises the salesperson a sure sale. The advantage to the buyer is a quick, confident decision and, to the salesperson, reduced or eliminated competition.

Suppliers must remember not to take straight-rebuy relationships for granted. Retaining existing customers is much easier than attracting new ones.

Business Ethics

The ethics of business buyer and seller relationships are often scrutinized and sometimes criticized by superiors, associates, other prospective suppliers, the general public, and the news media. Lockheed Martin Corporation, mindful of the key problems often faced by professional buyers and sellers, developed the ethical principles shown in the "Ethics in Marketing" box.

Customer Service

Business marketers are increasingly recognizing the benefits of developing a formal system to monitor customer opinions and perceptions of the quality of customer service. Companies like McDonald's, L.L. Bean, and Lexus build their strategies not only around products but also around a few highly developed service skills. Many firms are finding new ways to enhance customer service through technology. Business marketers are leading the way in adoption of new media technologies such as on-line services and CD-ROMs. For example, Honeywell has an on-line store that sells measurement and control instruments directly to corporate buyers. Honeywell's Industrial Store

---

modified rebuy
A situation where the purchaser wants some change in the original good or service.

straight rebuy
A situation in which the purchaser reorders the same goods or services without looking for new information or investigating other suppliers.

The Code of Ethics at Lockheed Martin

The booklet, *Setting the Standard*, has been adopted by the Lockheed Martin Board of Directors as this company's Code of Ethics and Business Conduct, and summarizes the virtues and principles that are to guide actions in the global marketplace. The code deals both with "doing things right" and with "the right thing to do" so as to maintain personal and institutional integrity.

While maintaining sensitivity to the diverse social and cultural settings in which the company conducts business, Lockheed Martin aims to set the standard for ethical conduct at all of its localities throughout the world. The company strives to achieve this through behavior in accordance with six virtues: honesty, integrity, respect, trust, responsibility, and citizenship.

THE CODE

Honesty:
to be truthful in all our endeavors; to be honest and forthright with one another and with our customers, communities, suppliers, and shareholders.

Integrity:
to say what we mean, to deliver what we promise, and to stand for what is right.

Respect:
to treat one another with dignity and fairness, appreciating the diversity of our workforce and the uniqueness of each employee.

Trust:
to build confidence through teamwork and open, candid communication.

Responsibility:
to speak up—without fear of retribution—and report concerns in the workplace, including violations of laws, regulations, and company policies, and seek clarification and guidance whenever there is doubt.

Citizenship:
to obey all the laws of the countries in which we do business and to do our part to make the communities in which we live and work better.[19]

(**http://www.industrialstore.honeywell.com**) carries instruments used by industries ranging from refineries and chemicals to metal, mining, oil, gas, food, and pharmaceuticals. Prospective customers can get quotes and place orders on-line twenty-four hours per day, seven days per week. Orders are quickly filled by the company's order management system. W. W. Grainger (**http://www.grainger.com**) sells about 20 percent of its $9 million per month sales on-line outside of normal business hours. Management believes that its electronic commerce business would grow more if its customer base of plant managers and janitors were more computer literate. Grainger is addressing the problem with workshops for customers.[20]

CONNECT IT

Look back at the story about General Motors at the beginning of the chapter. You now know that a strategic alliance is a cooperative agreement between business firms.

GM was motivated to form strategic alliances and joint ventures with Asian automakers to offset weak profits in the United States and to increase its share of the Asian market. GM has tried for several years to "crack" the Asian market on its own, but has not been very successful.

GM helps the Asian automakers by providing financial resources, technology, and lower parts costs. The Asian partners have access to markets through existing distribution networks. They also have a better understanding of local markets and customer buying behaviors.

Explore the Possibilities

Starting a business at home is one of the easiest ways to become self-employed. Using the Home Office Association of America (HOAA) Web site (**http://www.hoaa.com**) for ideas, choose a possible business opportunity that interests you and that has business marketing possibilities. Then explore both the HOAA site and the American Association of Home-Based Businesses Web site (**http://www.aahbb.org**) to learn more about how to set up your business.

Learn from an Entrepreneur

What does it really take to become an entrepreneur? Find out by interviewing a local entrepreneur or researching an entrepreneur you've read about in this chapter or in the business press. Get answers to the following questions, as well as any others you'd like to ask:

- How did you develop your vision for the company?
- What are the most important entrepreneurial characteristics that helped you succeed?
- Where did you learn the business skills you needed to run and grow the company?
- How did you research the feasibility of your idea? Prepare your business idea?
- What were the biggest challenges you had to overcome?
- Where did you obtain financing for the company?
- How do you market your products and services to other businesses?
- What are the most important lessons you learned by starting this company?
- What advice do you have for would-be entrepreneurs?

REVIEW IT

(1) Describe business marketing. Business marketing provides goods and services that are bought for use in business rather than for personal consumption. Intended use, not physical characteristics, distinguishes a business product from a consumer product.

1.1 **WRITING** As the marketing manager for Huggies diapers made by Kimberly-Clark, you are constantly going head-to-head with Pampers, produced by rival Procter & Gamble. You are considering unlocking the potential of the business market to increase your share of the disposable diaper market, but how? Write an outline of several ways you could transform this quintessentially consumer product into a successful business product as well.

(2) Describe the role of the Internet in business marketing. The rapid expansion and adoption of the Internet have made business markets more competitive than ever before. The number of business buyers and sellers using the Internet is rapidly increasing. Firms are seeking new and better ways to expand markets and sources of supply, increase sales and decrease costs, and better serve customers. With the Internet, every business in the world is potentially a local competitor.

2.1 **ON LINE** How could you use the Web site **http://www.business2business.on.ca** to help define a target market and develop a marketing plan?

2.2 **ON LINE** Reconsider question 1.1. How could you use the Internet in your business marketing of Huggies diapers?

(3) Discuss the role of relationship marketing and strategic alliances in business marketing. Relationship marketing entails seeking and establishing long-term alliances or partnerships with customers. A strategic alliance is a cooperative agreement between business firms. Firms form alliances to leverage what they do well by partnering with others who have complementary skills.

3.1 Why is relationship or personal selling the best way to promote in business marketing?

4 **Identify the four major categories of business market customers.** Producer markets consist of for-profit organizations and individuals that buy products to use in producing other products, as components of other products, or in facilitating business operations. Reseller markets consist of wholesalers and retailers that buy finished products to resell for profit. Government markets include federal, state, county, and city governments that buy goods and services to support their own operations and serve the needs of citizens. Institutional markets consist of very diverse nonbusiness institutions whose main goals do not include profit.

4.1 Understanding businesses is key to business marketing. Use Info-Trac (**http://www.infotrac-college.com**) to learn more about a variety of industries. Publications like *Manufacturing Automation, Computer Weekly, Power Generation Technology & Markets,* and *Biotech Equipment Update* can give you insights into many business marketing concepts. Research the industrial publications to find an article on a business marketer that interests you. Write a description of the company using as many concepts from the chapter as possible. What major category or categories of business market customers does this firm serve?

5 **Explain the North American Industry Classification System.** The NAICS provides a way to identify, analyze, segment, and target business and government markets. Organizations can be identified and compared by a numeric code indicating business sector, subsector, industry group, industry, and country industry. NAICS is a valuable tool for analyzing, segmenting, and targeting business markets.

5.1 Explain how a marketer can use the Web site **http://www.census. gov/epcd/www/naics.html** to convert SIC data to the NAICS.

6 **Explain the major differences between business and consumer markets.** In business markets, demand is derived, price-inelastic, joint, and fluctuating. Purchase volume is much larger than in consumer markets, customers are fewer in number and more geographically concentrated, and distribution channels are more direct. Buying is approached more formally using professional purchasing agents, more people are involved in the buying process, negotiation is more complex, and reciprocity and leasing are more common. And, finally, selling strategy in business markets normally focuses on personal contact rather than on advertising.

6.1 How might derived demand affect the manufacturing of an automobile?

6.2 Your boss has just asked you, the company purchasing manager, to buy new computers for an entire department. Since you have just recently purchased a new home computer, you are well-educated about the various products available. How will your buying process for the company differ from your recent purchase for yourself?

7 **Describe the seven types of business goods and services.** Major equipment includes capital goods, such as heavy machinery. Accessory equipment is typically less expensive and shorter-lived than major equipment. Raw materials are extractive or agricultural products that have not been processed. Component parts are finished or near-finished items to be used as parts of other products. Processed materials are used to manufacture other products. Supplies are consumable and not used as part of a final product. Business services are intangible products that many companies use in their operations.

7.1 In small groups, brainstorm examples of companies that feature the products in different business categories. (Avoid examples already listed in the chapter.) Compile a list of ten specific business products including at least one in each category. Then match up with another group. Have each group take turns naming a product and have the other group identify its appropriate category. Try to resolve all discrepancies by discussion. Some identified products might appropriately fit into more than one category.

(8) **Discuss the unique aspects of business buying behavior.** Business buying behavior is distinguished by five fundamental characteristics. First, buying is normally undertaken by a buying center consisting of many people who range widely in authority level. Second, business buyers typically evaluate alternative products and suppliers based on quality, service, and price—in that order. Third, business buying falls into three general categories: new buys, modified rebuys, and straight rebuys. Fourth, the ethics of business buyers and sellers are often scrutinized. Fifth, customer service before, during, and after the sale plays a big role in business purchase decisions.

8.1 **WRITING** A colleague of yours has sent you an e-mail seeking your advice as he attempts to sell a new voice-mail system to a local business. Send him a return e-mail describing the various people who might influence the customer's buying decision. Be sure to include suggestions for dealing with the needs of each of these individuals.

8.2 Intel Corporation supplies microprocessors to Hewlett-Packard for use in its computers. Describe the buying situation in this relationship, keeping in mind the rapid advance of technology in this industry.

DEFINE IT

accessory equipment 199
business marketing 186
business services 200
buying center 200
component parts 199
derived demand 195
joint demand 196
keiretsu 190
major equipment
    (installations) 199

modified rebuy 204
multiplier effect (accelerator
    principle) 196
new buy 203
North American Industry
    Classification System
    (NAICS) 193
OEM 200
processed materials 200
raw materials 199

reciprocity 198
straight rebuy 204
strategic alliance (strategic
    partnership) 189
supplies 200

APPLY IT

Application for Entrepreneurs

 Dan White is an independent video producer whose biggest client is the State of Illinois Agricultural Department. Although this account is big enough to support the entire business, Dan has developed other lines of business to eliminate the risks involved with having only one customer. Dan has also landed a sizable account through a high school friend who is the vice president of Good Hands Insurance. This also happens to be the company that underwrites Dan's life insurance. Additionally, Dan is hired to work on various projects for large production companies. Dan generated this business through long-term relationships built by working on projects for the state of Illinois.

As Dan prepares his business plan for the upcoming year, he is contemplating several strategic changes. Because of the increasing speed at which the video industry is evolving, Dan has observed two important trends. First, he is finding it increasingly difficult to own the latest video equipment that his customers are demanding. Second, Dan's clients are not able to keep up with the recent developments in the industry and would be willing to pay more for his expertise. Dan is looking into a lease for new equipment, and he is contemplating increasing the price of his services.

Questions

1. What two-digit NAICS code would you assign to Dan's business? For a complete list of all NAICS codes, see **http://www.census.gov/epcd/www/naics.html**.

2. Is Dan's choice to use Good Hands Insurance ethical? Why or why not?

3. How can Dan use the inelasticity of demand to his advantage?

4. Would you advise Dan to lease or buy the new equipment? Why?

THINK ABOUT IT

Ethics Exercise

Cameron Stock, purchasing manager for Goalie Keepaway, a sports equipment manufacturer, is responsible for buying $5 million of component parts and supplies every year. He has a preferred list of certified suppliers, many of which are awarded a large percentage of this business annually. Cameron has been offered an all-expense paid weekend for two in Las Vegas as a Christmas present from a major supplier with whom he has done business for close to a decade. Over this time, Cameron has built a very good relationship with the vendor.

Questions

1. Would it be legal and ethical for Cameron Stock to accept this gift?

2. How is this addressed in the AMA Code of Ethics? Go to the AMA Web site at **http://www.marketingpower.com** and reread the Code of Ethics. Write a brief paragraph summarizing where the AMA stands on the issue of supplier gifts.

TRY IT

Intrapreneurship Case

W. W. Grainger: Moving Maintenance to the Internet Space

For more than seventy years, W. W. Grainger has kept the manufacturing and other labor-intensive industries on their collective feet by supplying the much-needed parts that help keep the machinery and operations running. From tape to electric motors, from chemicals to industrial-strength mops, and from lubricating fluids to lightbulbs, Grainger lists seventy thousand parts in its legendary seven-pound red catalog. In the $220 billion maintenance, repair, and operating supplies (MRO) market, this Chicago-based company has staked its claim to a $5 billion piece. It has shipped its catalog to purchasing and procurement officers in manufacturing and office-related environments for over seventy years, and has always enjoyed the reputation of being America's premier industrial supplier of replacement and supplemental parts. An Old Economy stalwart, Grainger is the kind of company that many would have predicted would have trouble with the dawning of widespread adoption of the Internet. Using Net storefronts, Grainger's suppliers would be able to sell directly to its customers, and its New Economy competition would be able to move faster, having built completely Internet-focused business models. Grainger, however, has adapted in a way few Old Economy companies have, and its successful entrepreneurship in the Internet space has quieted doubters and reaffirmed its position as the nation's leader in the MRO market.

To battle inefficiencies in its order taking and fulfillment process, Grainger looked to the Internet for a viable solution that would allow it to move quicker and offer more parts and more value-added services to its customer base. Grainger.com sells the complete Grainger catalog of parts. Search functions allow customers to drastically reduce the time needed to leaf through the standard catalog for parts. The site also shows real-time inventory status of those parts and greatly simplifies the process of placing large orders. The success of the initiative is reflected in the fact that the average order placed on-line is twice as large as traditional orders, and customers who buy primarily on-line spend

20 percent more over the course of the year than those ordering through the old red catalog.

Perhaps what has contributed to Grainger's success on the Internet is that its Web site is well laid out, intuitive to navigate, and void of unwanted clutter like annoying and intrusive banner ads. There is a simplicity in browsing Grainger's on-line catalog, placing an order, and searching for parts and service information that is not normally found on business-to-consumer Internet retail sites. Grainger knows its buyers are people who know what they want, who are probably repeat customers, and who will buy based on cost or quality alone. Branding and advertising are not likely to sway the industrial purchasing manager whose job it is to find the most cost-effective and reliable parts, regardless of looks, style, or presentation. That is not to say that there is no place for branding in business-to-business marketing. Quite the opposite. Functionality rules in that market, and purchasers are judged on whether they save money or procure reliable parts (not parts that represent any great style). So instead of differentiating their parts based on style or self-image, business-to-business marketers brand their products to convey images of performance, endurance, or low cost.

Grainger has taken a fresh approach to the art of business-to-business messaging. Instead of taking the traditional approach of showing a picture of a product in the center of the page and filling the surrounding space with text heralding the product's superiority, Grainger borrowed a technique generally reserved for business-to-consumer marketers.

Grainger is not worried about its Web business cannibalizing its existing paper catalog business. In fact, it has made the on-line ordering and fulfillment process so efficient and accurate that it is much more cost-effective than filling orders the old way. Don Bielinsky, the Grainger group president, envisions and hopes for a time when over 50 percent of all Grainger orders are placed and filled through the digital medium. Only those who are too slow or too small to conduct business on the Internet would place orders through the paper catalog, and in a world of cheap PCs and available free Internet access, those types of customers are rapidly dwindling.

Questions

1. List the benefits Grainger has enjoyed by moving its business on-line.

2. How would you classify the types of business products Grainger sells? To what business market does it sell?

3. How has Grainger adopted consumer-style promotions to improve its business marketing?

WATCH IT

Short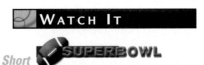

The FedEx ad on your dedicated PowerPoint CD-ROM shows how important business services are to companies in defraying costs and improving efficiencies. The ad uses humor to convey its message.

Medium **VIDEO**

Companies dictating business practices to suppliers is all too common in today's business environment. Although often this arrangement is to the detriment of the supplier, sometimes it is to the supplier's benefit. Such is the case with the Conservation Company, which works to create sustainable farming practices in the coffee industry and raise the standard of living of coffee producers and coffee producing countries. Compare what you see in the CNN clip for

Chapter 6 with what you discover at the Wal-Mart supplier Web page from the "On-Line" activity on page 395. Decide if you think how involved companies should be in their suppliers' affairs.

Long

To give you insight into Chapter 6, Small Business School will introduce you to the Souto family, owners of Rowland Roasters and its trademark brand of coffee, Café Pilon. When the Souto family immigrated to the United States from Cuba, it had to start over with nothing. Watch how this dynamic family rebuilt its business and grew it into a multimillion dollar enterprise that sells almost exclusively to other businesses.

FLIP IT

Flip to chapter 6 in your *Grademaker Study Guide* for more review opportunities, including the pretest, vocabulary review, Internet activities, study test questions, and business marketing scenarios. Do you know what distinguishes consumer products from business products? And can you list the four major categories of business market customers? Close your book and describe the seven types of business goods and services. Can't? Then flip open your Study Guide to brush up.

CLICK IT

The *Marketing* Web site links you to all the Internet-based activities in this chapter, like "Use It," "Review It" questions 2.1, 4.1, and 5.1, "Apply It," and the On-Line exercises in the chapter margins. As a review, do the Chapter 6 quiz and crossword puzzle. You can also work the Career Exersite that shows you different resources for careers in the area of business marketing. Or review the main concepts in the PowerPoint presentation for Chapter 6. Go to **http://lamb.swlearning.com**, read the material, and follow the links right from the site.

SPIN IT

Spin your Xtra! CD-ROM to test your understanding of business marketing by completing the worksheets for exhibits 6.1, 6.2, and 6.6. If your instructor has assigned a marketing plan project, worksheets on Xtra! can help you organize your work. In addition to the quiz on the Web site, there's another quiz on the Xtra! CD-ROM, plus video of the authors answering frequently asked questions about business marketing, such as "How can demand for business products be both derived and widely fluctuating?" and "What is an extranet?"

Still Shaky? Here's a Tip.

Find a study partner and have him or her quiz you using the end-of-chapter materials and the quizzes on your Xtra! CD-ROM. Try to give the rationale for each of your answers.

CHAPTER **SEVEN**

SEGMENTING AND TARGETING MARKETS

Learning Objectives

1 Describe the characteristics of markets and market segments

2 Explain the importance of market segmentation

3 Discuss criteria for successful market segmentation

4 Describe the bases commonly used to segment consumer markets

5 Describe the bases for segmenting business markets

6 List the steps involved in segmenting markets

7 Discuss alternative strategies for selecting target markets

8 Explain how and why firms implement positioning strategies and how product differentiation plays a role

9 Discuss global market segmentation and targeting issues

Hair care in the United States is a $45 billion industry. Hair care for kids under age twelve makes up approximately $5 billion of that market. Therefore, servicing only kids excludes nearly 90 percent of the market, and thus does not appear to represent a viable market segment. Furthermore, stylists have traditionally avoided this market because the customers tend to wiggle and wail and may even bite the hand that shears them.

However, the kids' haircutting industry is growing. Since 1995, at least four new children's haircutting chains have opened around the country. They join established kids' salons such as Cartoon Cuts, a $4.5 billion, sixteen-unit outfit whose first facility opened in Fairfax, Virginia, in 1991, and $2 million-plus Kids' Hair, Inc., which launched the first of ten stores in 1992 in Edina, Minnesota. The growth spurt is similar to that of children's specialty retail stores like GapKids and Gymboree, which emerged in the mid-1980s to take advantage of baby boomers' lavish spending on their kids.

Most of the new kids' haircutting chains began as regional enterprises, but many have plans to expand. One exception is Cool Cuts, whose founder from the start envisioned a national chain with hundreds of outlets. The company uses computer systems to capture point-of-sale customer data to learn each potential location's socioeconomic makeup. These data, combined with

sophisticated mapping that superimposes spending habits on demographic and economic data such as median home values, household income, and number and ages of children, allow the company to pinpoint the most lucrative spots for new sites.

While the chains have similarities— all claim to have superior customer service and consistent offerings—each one has its own variation on the kids theme. Cool Cuts, for example, divides its waiting area into two sides. For kids age six and under, a gated-in play space is stocked with Legos and videos such as *Barney* and *Sesame Street*. For older children there is an area stocked with Nintendo 64 stations. Kid Snips sells toys and splashes whimsical jungle creatures on its walls. Stylists at Cartoon Cuts wash as well as cut their customers' hair, dousing the suds with hoses that project from the trunks of green fiberglass elephants. For the most part, though, kids' salons make use of universal elements. Crayons, toys, and videos entertain waiting customers. Televisions (with or without VCRs) and video game systems are placed at cutting stations.

Specialty chairs—a rocket ship, a jeep, a racecar—or standard salon chairs outfitted with booster seats are the furniture of choice. Stylists blow bubbles and offer balloons and lollipops or small prizes.

The child is not the only customer in this niche, however. Parents are customers too. For example, at Snip-its, there are no crayons or toys. Nor are there the specialty chairs that are typically found at kids' salons. Instead, each station has either a child-sized salon chair or a standard salon chair (for older kids and lap sitters), as well a big cushy "parents" chair, which allows moms and dads to instruct the stylist without feeling they are in the way. Treehouse bills itself as a family destination, cutting the hair of little ones, their teenage siblings, and adults, and offering family packages.[1]

Based on this story, how would you define market segmentation and targeting? What type of targeting strategy are kids' hair salons using? Do you think the kids' market is a viable segment for salons to target? Explain your answer. This chapter will help you answer these questions and more.

On Line

Snip-its

How many market segments can you identify as being targeted by the Snip-its Web site? What about the Cartoon Cuts' and Kid's Cuts' (Cookie Cutter) sites? If you were a kid, where would you want to go to get your hair cut? If you were a parent, where would you want to take you child for a haircut?

http://www.snipits.com

http://www.cartoon-cuts.com

http://www.kidscuts.com

Market Segmentation

1

Describe the characteristics of markets and market segments

market
People or organizations with needs or wants and the ability and willingness to buy.

market segment
A subgroup of people or organizations sharing one or more characteristics that cause them to have similar product needs.

market segmentation
The process of dividing a market into meaningful, relatively similar, and identifiable segments or groups.

The term *market* means different things to different people. We are all familiar with the supermarket, stock market, labor market, fish market, and flea market. All these types of markets share several characteristics. First, they are composed of people (consumer markets) or organizations (business markets). Second, these people or organizations have wants and needs that can be satisfied by particular product categories. Third, they have the ability to buy the products they seek. Fourth, they are willing to exchange their resources, usually money or credit, for desired products. In sum, a **market** is (1) people or organizations with (2) needs or wants and with (3) the ability and (4) the willingness to buy. A group of people or an organization that lacks any one of these characteristics is not a market.

Within a market, a **market segment** is a subgroup of people or organizations sharing one or more characteristics that cause them to have similar product needs. At one extreme, we can define every person and every organization in the world as a market segment because each is unique. At the other extreme, we can define the entire consumer market as one large market segment and the business market as another large segment. All people have some similar characteristics and needs, as do all organizations.

From a marketing perspective, market segments can be described as somewhere between the two extremes. The process of dividing a market into meaningful, relatively similar, and identifiable segments or groups is called **market segmentation**. The purpose of market segmentation is to enable the marketer to tailor marketing mixes to meet the needs of one or more specific segments.

Exhibit 7.1 illustrates the concept of market segmentation. Each box represents a market consisting of seven persons. This market might vary as follows: one homogeneous market of seven people, a market consisting of seven individual segments, a market composed of two segments based on gender, a market composed of three age segments, or a market composed of five age and gender market segments. Age and gender and many other bases for segmenting markets are examined later in this chapter.

The Importance of Market Segmentation

2

Explain the importance of market segmentation

Until the 1960s, few firms practiced market segmentation. When they did, it was more likely a haphazard effort than a formal marketing strategy. Before 1960, for example, the Coca-Cola Company produced only one beverage and aimed it at the entire soft drink market. Today, Coca-Cola offers over a dozen different products to market segments based on diverse consumer preferences for flavors and calorie and caffeine content. Coca-Cola offers traditional soft drinks, energy drinks (such as Power Ade), flavored teas, fruit drinks (Fruitopia), and water (Dasani).

Market segmentation plays a key role in the marketing strategy of almost all successful organizations and is a powerful marketing tool for several reasons. Most importantly, nearly all markets include groups of people or organizations with different product needs and preferences. Market segmentation helps marketers define customer needs and wants more precisely. Because market segments differ in size and potential, segmentation helps decision makers more accurately define marketing objectives and better allocate resources. In turn, performance can be better evaluated when objectives are more precise.

Chico's, a successful women's fashion retailer, thrives by marketing to women aged thirty-five to fifty-five who like to wear comfortable, yet stylish clothing. It sells private-label clothing that comes in just a few nonjudgmental sizes: zero (regular sizes 4–6), one (8–10), two (10–12), and three (14–16). The Chico's look, built mainly around wash-and-wear fabrics, is loose and colorful. Prices are mod-

Exhibit 7.1

Concept of Market Segmentation

No market segmentation

Fully segmented market

Market segmentation
by gender: M, F

Market segmentation
by age group: 1, 2, 3

Market segmentation
by gender and age group

erate, ranging from $20 to $150. Chico's has developed a loyal base of customers and is a fast-growing retailer.[2]

Criteria for Successful Segmentation

Marketers segment markets for three important reasons. First, segmentation enables marketers to identify groups of customers with similar needs and to analyze the characteristics and buying behavior of these groups. Second, segmentation provides marketers with information to help them design marketing mixes specifically matched with the characteristics and desires of one or more segments. Third, segmentation is consistent with the marketing concept of satisfying customer wants and needs while meeting the organization's objectives.

To be useful, a segmentation scheme must produce segments that meet four basic criteria:

- *Substantiality:* A segment must be large enough to warrant developing and maintaining a special marketing mix. This criterion does not necessarily mean that a segment must have many potential customers. Marketers of custom-designed homes and business buildings, commercial airplanes, and large computer systems typically develop marketing programs tailored to each potential customer's needs. In most cases, however, a market segment needs many potential customers to make commercial sense. In the 1980s, home banking failed because not enough people owned personal computers. Today, a larger number of people own computers, and home banking is a growing industry.

- *Identifiability and measurability:* Segments must be identifiable and their size measurable. Data about the population within geographic boundaries, the

Discuss criteria for successful market segmentation

number of people in various age categories, and other social and demographic characteristics are often easy to get, and they provide fairly concrete measures of segment size. Suppose that a social service agency wants to identify segments by their readiness to participate in a drug and alcohol program or in prenatal care. Unless the agency can measure how many people are willing, indifferent, or unwilling to participate, it will have trouble gauging whether there are enough people to justify setting up the service.

- *Accessibility:* The firm must be able to reach members of targeted segments with customized marketing mixes. Some market segments are hard to reach—for example, senior citizens (especially those with reading or hearing disabilities), individuals who don't speak English, and the illiterate.

- *Responsiveness:* As Exhibit 7.1 illustrates, markets can be segmented using any criteria that seem logical. Unless one market segment responds to a marketing mix differently from other segments, however, that segment need not be treated separately. For instance, if all customers are equally price-conscious about a product, there is no need to offer high-, medium-, and low-priced versions to different segments.

 ## Bases for Segmenting Consumer Markets

Describe the bases commonly used to segment consumer markets

segmentation bases (variables)
Characteristics of individuals, groups, or organizations.

Marketers use **segmentation bases,** or **variables,** which are characteristics of individuals, groups, or organizations, to divide a total market into segments. The choice of segmentation bases is crucial because an inappropriate segmentation strategy may lead to lost sales and missed profit opportunities. The key is to identify bases that will produce substantial, measurable, and accessible segments that exhibit different response patterns to marketing mixes.

Markets can be segmented using a single variable, such as age group, or several variables, such as age group, gender, and education. Although it is less precise, single-variable segmentation has the advantage of being simpler and easier to use than multiple-variable segmentation. The disadvantages of multiple-variable segmentation are that it is often harder to use than single-variable segmentation; usable secondary data are less likely to be available; and as the number of segmentation bases increases, the size of individual segments decreases. Nevertheless, the current trend is toward using more rather than fewer variables to segment most markets. Multiple-variable segmentation is clearly more precise than single-variable segmentation.

Consumer goods marketers commonly use one or more of the following characteristics to segment markets: geography, demographics, psychographics, benefits sought, and usage rate.

Geographic Segmentation

geographic segmentation
Segmenting markets by region of a country or the world, market size, market density, or climate.

Geographic segmentation refers to segmenting markets by region of a country or the world, market size, market density, or climate. Market density means the number of people within a unit of land, such as a census tract. Climate is commonly used for geographic segmentation because of its dramatic impact on residents' needs and purchasing behavior. Snowblowers, water and snow skis, clothing, and air-conditioning and heating systems are products with varying appeal, depending on climate.

Consumer goods companies take a regional approach to marketing for four reasons. First, many firms need to find new ways to generate sales because of sluggish and intensely competitive markets. Second, computerized checkout stations with scanners enable retailers to assess accurately which brands sell best in their region. Third, many packaged-goods manufacturers are introducing new regional brands intended to appeal to local preferences. Fourth, a more regional approach

Bringing Science to Weight Loss in China

On a recent afternoon, five chubby teenagers, two women of normal build, and a man with a potbelly came to the Sino-Japanese Friendship Hospital. They are asked about their eating habits, then step on a high-tech scale connected to a computer, which calculates body mass and prints out an elaborate diet and exercise regimen. Each person also leaves the hospital with a bottle of a weight-loss drug called Xenical.

"I feel more secure seeing a doctor. At least there's less of a chance of getting cheated," says Cai Shuang, an eighteen-year old in baggy denim shorts and high tops who says she has tried several weight-loss pills advertised on television.

This is the kind of customer Roche Holding AG, the Swiss maker of Xenical, is hoping will help it conquer China's booming market in weight-loss products. China has hundreds of weight-loss treatments ranging from "slimming soups" to a traditional herb laxative, *dahuang*, derived from the rhubarb plant. As with the rest of China's pharmaceutical industry, shams and scams abound, piracy is rampant, claims are overblown, and regulation is minimal—a situation that has led many foreign drugmakers to target the country.

Roche is hoping to bring science to the business of weight loss in China. Its patented Xenical, which works by blocking fat absorption and was introduced in China in January 2001, is the first prescription weight-loss drug approved by the Chinese government: All other weight-loss products are labeled "health products" and cannot be sold in hospitals or prescribed by doctors. Roche has set up high-end hospital clinics in major cities and trained doctors at each one. It is counting on the doctors to help sell patients on the benefits of Xenical.

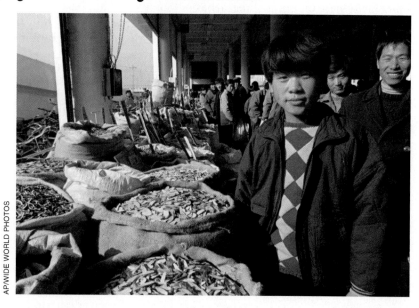

AP/WIDE WORLD PHOTOS

As China's economy is growing, obesity is becoming a serious national health problem. Western pharmaceutical companies are trying to bring science to China's weight loss market, but they are having difficulty penetrating a market that is comfortable self-prescribing traditional medicines, like those pictured here, without consulting a physician.

Roche, as well as other drug companies, face cultural hurdles in China. Many Chinese have some knowledge of traditional medicine and feel comfortable prescribing for themselves instead of seeing a doctor. Also, most Chinese people see weight as more of a cosmetic than a health issue, as do many doctors. Furthermore, it is not clear that Chinese consumers want to go to hospitals for their dieting advice. Many state-run hospitals have outdated facilities and require hours-long waits.

China ranks second after the United States in terms of the number of obese people, which numbers about seventy million. Over the past ten years, consumption of meat, fast food, and soft drinks in the country has increased with incomes. A generation that can still remember malnutrition and famine now worries about diseases like diabetes, hypertension, and the obesity that facilitates both. However, unlike in the United States, where many people understand basic nutrition and exercise, China is awash in ignorance. And the rapid pace of change in people's lives means that they are still eating as they used to even though they are no longer engaged in the physical labor they once were.

While Roche will not reveal actual numbers, it says sales of Xenical in China are growing between 30 percent and 50 percent a month and that it is targeting $12 million in sales in 2001.[3]

What cultural differences do manufacturers of obesity drugs like Roche have to contend with in China? Do you think China will continue to be a lucrative market segment for makers of obesity drugs to target? Explain your answer.

---

allows consumer goods companies to react more quickly to competition. For example, Cracker Barrel, a restaurant known in the South for home-style cooking, is altering its menu outside its core southern market to reflect local tastes. Customers in upstate New York can order Reuben sandwiches, and those in Texas can get eggs with salsa. Miller Lite developed the "Miller Lite True to Texas" marketing program, a statewide campaign targeting Texas beer drinkers. The "Global Perspectives" box provides another example of geographic market segmentation.

Demographic Segmentation

Marketers often segment markets on the basis of demographic information because it is widely available and often related to consumers' buying and consuming behavior. Some common bases of **demographic segmentation** are age, gender, income, ethnic background, and family life cycle. The discussion here provides some important information about the main demographic segments.

Age Segmentation

Attracting children is a popular strategy for many companies because they hope to instill brand loyalty early. Furthermore, children influence a great deal of family consumption. There are three subsegments in the children's market: young children (under age nine), tweens (ages nine to twelve), and teens (ages twelve to nineteen).

The U.S. Census projects there will be more than thirty-eight million children under age nine in the United States in 2005. High-end playthings like luxurious playhouses and BMW skateboards are gaining in popularity with children.[4] Nickelodeon, once simply a television network for kids, now publishes three magazines for this target market: *Nickelodeon*, an entertainment and humor book; *Rugrats Comic Adventures*, a comic book spun off from the popular TV show; and *Crayola Kids*, aimed at kids and their parents.[5] Older children, dubbed "tweens," number about twenty million and have an estimated spending power of $20 billion.[6] Tweens desire to be kids, but also want some of the fun and glamour of being a teenager.[7] Many retailers, such as Limited Too and abercrombie, are targeting tweens by selling clothing that is similar in style to the more teen- and young adult–oriented stores Limited and Abercrombie & Fitch. Teens, sometimes referred to as Generation Y, number thirty-two million, and represent approximately $153 billion in spending power. Teens spend most of their money on cloth-

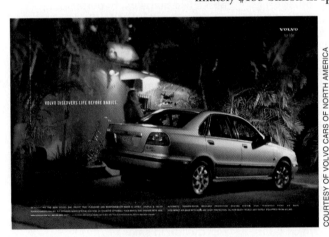

Age segmentation can clearly define your target, but it can also be restrictive. Volvo has broken out of its older, family image by launching a new ad campaign with ads like the one pictured. The goal is to attract youthful Gen X-ers to a brand most typically associated with family life.

ing, entertainment, and food. Teens can be loyal to companies that reach them, and they seem to prefer smaller, niche brands, such as Burton Snowboards, Femme Arsenal (a cosmetics firm), and Razor USA (markets push scooters and apparel).[8] The dairy industry is trying to make drinking milk cool among teenagers by selling sixteen-ounce bottles of milk in vending machines decorated with large pictures of the famous "Got Milk?" ads featuring skateboarder Tony Hawk or members of the Backstreet Boys band wearing milk mustaches.[9]

Other age segments are also appealing targets for marketers. The approximately fifty-eight million people classified as young adults, between twenty and thirty-four years of age, are being targeted by many beer, wine, and spirits companies. For example, Bacardi Ltd. hired a young marketing team to develop ads for Dewars Scotch. The team dropped the "mixability" angle stressed in previous ads and revived the famous Dewars profiles campaign, showing adventure-seeking twenty-five- to thirty-four-year olds. The campaign appeals to Generation X by focusing on people following their dreams and not just evoking money and success.[10] The computer-literate Gen X-ers also are a large and viable market for the Internet.

The baby boom generation, born between 1946 and 1964, comprises the largest age segment—about 30 percent of the entire U.S. population. Many in this group are approaching (or past) fifty years of age and are continuing to lead active, fully involved lifestyles. Now that many in this group are in or headed toward their fifties, they are changing the way people look at aging, which presents an opportunity for brands to reposition themselves and to be more lifestyle oriented. Starwood Hotels, for instance, designed its W chain to appeal to a young, hip crowd. But the company has been surprised at how much the hotels are attracting baby boomers.[11] Walgreen is opening many new drugstores in Sun Belt states, such as Florida, Texas, California, and Arizona, because that is where the baby boomers will retire and prescription sales will soar.[12]

Seniors (aged sixty-five and over) are especially attracted to companies that build relationships by taking the time to get to know them and their preferences. As an example, older customers say they prefer catalog shopping to retail outlets because of dissatisfaction with customer service at retail stores. People of this age group are more likely than most to have the combination of free time, money, and health that lets them pursue leisure-time activities, especially education and travel. Boston-based Elderhostel, a large education organization for older adults, enrolled 250,000 students last year in about ten thousand courses worldwide. And travelers fifty-five and older took nearly a third of the trips made within the United States in 1999.[13] In addition, though the senior audience may be coming on-line later than their younger counterparts, it is a large audience—one that is driven by a desire to stay in touch and stay connected.[14]

Gender Segmentation

Marketers of products such as clothing, cosmetics, personal-care items, magazines, jewelry, and footwear commonly segment markets by gender. Men aged eighteen to forty-nine are the segment most likely to purchase goods on-line. Many Internet companies have advertised to this group to build their brands and get exposure for their sites. For example, Blue Nile, one of the most successful on-line jewelry retailers, targets men who dislike jewelry stores, even though most of the jewelry it sells is for women.[15] However, brands that have traditionally been marketed to men, such as Gillette razors and Rogaine baldness remedy, are increasing their efforts to attract women. Computer and video game companies have traditionally targeted young men, but Interactive Digital Software Association, a trade group, found that women are buying just as much game software as men. As a result, more game companies and Web sites are focusing their marketing efforts on girls and women.[16] Conversely, "women's" products such as cosmetics, household products, and furniture are also being marketed to men. About 35 percent of the buyers of Tommy Hilfiger's beauty-care products are young men, who buy items such as Tommy's Remote Control Hair gel and Juiced Up orange-scented soap.[17] Rodale, Inc., is bringing out a new magazine for teenage boys called MH-18, which focuses on teen boys' lifestyles.[18]

© L. CLARKE/CORBIS

Gender segmentation can be a tricky, yet profitable, form of segmentation, particularly for companies that launch unique product offerings for each gender. One such example is video games. Once marketers discovered that girls and women buy as much game software as boys and men, more companies began to focus marketing efforts on both genders—and with great success.

Income Segmentation

Income is a popular demographic variable for segmenting markets because income level influences consumers' wants and determines their buying power. Many markets are segmented by income, including the markets for housing, clothing, automobiles, and food. For example, wholesale clubs Costco and Sam's Club appeal to different income segments. Costco attracts more upscale customers with warehouse prices for gourmet foods and upscale brands like Waterford crystal, Raymond Weil watches, and Ralph Lauren clothing. Sam's Club, on the other hand, originally focused more on members' business needs, offering bulk packages of the kinds of items sold in Wal-Mart's discount stores and supercenters. Sam's Club is now trying to win more upscale customers by adding items like jewelry and gourmet food.[19]

Ethnic Segmentation

Many companies are segmenting their markets by ethnicity. The three largest ethnic markets are the African American, Hispanic American, and Asian American. These three groups collectively are projected to make up one-third of the country's population by 2010, and have a combined buying power of more than $1 trillion. Ethnic communities also make up significant portions of many major metropolitan areas, including New York, Chicago, Los Angeles, and Miami.[20]

African Americans African Americans are the largest minority group in the United States, and their population is expected to grow to more than forty-five million by 2020. They spend more than whites on luxury items such as cars, clothing, and home furnishings. Consequently, a number of companies market specifically to African Americans. Coca-Cola runs television ads featuring as-yet-undiscovered black music artists like Tyrese and Ja Rule before they hit the big time.[21] As part of its sponsorship of the National Association of Black Journalists convention, DaimlerChrysler AG offers a "Ride & Drive" program that provides cars to attendees so that they can visit local attractions.[22] The Internet is of growing importance as a medium to reach the African American consumer. While Net use among this group lags behind that of the white population (28 percent of blacks versus 37 percent of whites), African Americans who are on-line are younger, more affluent, and better educated than African Americans who do not use the Internet. In addition, nearly 30 percent intend to place orders on-line, compared with 21 percent of the general population.[23] Web sites such as **http://www.netnoir.com** and **http://www.afronet.com** attract thousands of African Americans with news, information, entertainment, and products of interest to their audiences.

Hispanic Americans The U.S. Hispanic population numbers more than thirty million, accounting for more than 11 percent of the total population. By 2050, Hispanic Americans will comprise almost a quarter of the population. This group also has substantial buying power, estimated to be between $273 billion and $445 billion.[24]

Companies are increasingly directing marketing efforts at Hispanic Americans. Gateway, the computer manufacturer, launched a marketing program that included TV and radio ads in Spanish, a toll-free number for Spanish-speaking clients, and representatives in sales, customer service, and tech support who are fluent in the language.[25] Hormel has developed a family of Mexican brands, including salsas, peppers, juices, and chiles, called Herdez, and its advertising highlights the line's authentic heritage.[26] Hallmark Cards has designed a line of greeting cards to commemorate the Mexican holiday, Cinco de Mayo.[27] Liz Claiborne launched Mambo, advertising it as the first-ever "Latino" scent for young Americans.[28]

Asian Americans Like Hispanic Americans, Asian Americans are a diverse group with thirteen submarkets. The five largest are Chinese, Filipino, Japanese, Asian Indian, and Korean. This fast-growing market of 10.2 million is younger and better educated than the general market and has the highest average household income in the United States.

Some entrepreneurs are building large enclosed malls that cater to Asian consumers. At the Aberdeen Centre near Vancouver, British Columbia, nearly 80 percent of the merchants are Chinese Canadians, as are 80 percent of the customers. The mall offers fashions made in Hong Kong, a shop for traditional Chinese medicines, and a theater showing Chinese movies. Kung fu martial arts demonstrations and Chinese folk dances are held in the mall on weekends.

Family Life-Cycle Segmentation

The demographic factors of gender, age, and income often do not sufficiently explain why consumer buying behavior varies. Frequently, consumption patterns among people of the same age and gender differ because they are in different stages of the family life cycle. The **family life cycle (FLC)** is a series of stages determined by a combination of age, marital status, and the presence or absence of children.

Traditional families—married couples with children younger than eighteen years—constituted just 23.5 percent of all U.S. households according to the 2000 census data. Such families represented 30.2 percent of households in 1980 and 45 percent in 1960.[29] Exhibit 7.2 on page 222 illustrates both traditional and contemporary FLC patterns and shows how families' needs, incomes, resources, and expenditures differ at each stage. The horizontal flow shows the traditional family life cycle. The lower part of the exhibit gives some of the characteristics and purchase patterns of families in each stage of the traditional life cycle. The exhibit also acknowledges that about half of all first marriages end in divorce. When young marrieds move into the young divorced stage, their consumption patterns often revert back to those of the young single stage of the cycle. About four out of five divorced persons remarry by middle age and reenter the traditional life cycle, as indicated by the "recycled flow" in the exhibit. Charles Schwab Corporation, the San Francisco financial-services firm, ran a television ad featuring Sarah Ferguson, the Duchess of York and a divorced mom. The ad shows Ferguson telling a bedtime story to a little girl, and the story ends with the importance of girls understanding their financial choices. Schwab is eager to reach single women because they have a heightened interest in financial strategies.[30]

Psychographic Segmentation

Age, gender, income, ethnicity, family life-cycle stage, and other demographic variables are usually helpful in developing segmentation strategies, but often they don't paint the entire picture. Demographics provides the skeleton, but psychographics adds meat to the bones. **Psychographic segmentation** is market segmentation on the basis of the following variables:

- *Personality:* Personality reflects a person's traits, attitudes, and habits. Porsche Cars North America understood well the demographics of the Porsche owner: a forty-something male college graduate earning over $200,000 per year. However, research discovered that this general demographic category included five personality types that more effectively segmented Porsche buyers. Exhibit 7.3 on page 223 describes the five segments. Porsche refined its marketing as a result of the study, and, after a previous seven-year slump, the company's U.S. sales rose 48 percent.[31]

- *Motives:* Marketers of baby products and life insurance appeal to consumers' emotional motives—namely, to care for their loved ones. Using appeals to economy, reliability, and dependability, carmakers like Subaru and Suzuki target customers with rational motives. Carmakers like Mercedes-Benz, Jaguar, and Cadillac appeal to customers with status-related motives.

- *Lifestyles:* Lifestyle segmentation divides people into groups according to the way they spend their time, the importance of the things around them, their beliefs, and socioeconomic characteristics such as income and education. For example, Harley-

This ad for State Farm clearly appeals to consumers' emotional motives by associating the purchase of life insurance with the caring and responsibility of parenting.

family life cycle (FLC)
A series of stages determined by a combination of age, marital status, and the presence or absence of children.

psychographic segmentation
Market segmentation on the basis of personality, motives, lifestyles, and geodemographics.

Ten good reasons for buying life insurance.

State Farm Understands Life.

COPYRIGHT STATE FARM MUTUAL AUTOMOBILE INSURANCE COMPANY 1996. USED BY PERMISSION.

Young single	Young married without children	Young married with children	Middle-aged married with children	Middle-aged married without children	Older married	Older unmarried
Few financial burdens	Better off financially than they will be in near future	Home purchasing at peak	Financial position still better	Home ownership at peak	Drastic cut in income	Drastic cut in income
Fashion opinion leaders	Highest purchase rate and highest average purchase of durables	Liquid assets low	More wives work	Most satisfied with financial position and money saved	Keep home	Special need for attention, affection, and security
Recreation-oriented	Buy: cars, refrigerators, stoves, sensible and durable furniture, vacations	Dissatisfied with financial position and amount of money saved	Some children get jobs	Interested in travel, recreation, self-education	Buy: medical appliances, medical care, products that aid health, sleep, and digestion	Buy: same medical and product needs as other retired group
Buy: basic kitchen equipment, basic furniture, cars, equipment for mating game, vacations		Interested in new products	Hard to influence with advertising	Make gifts and contributions		
		Like advertised products	High average purchase of durables	Not interested in new products		
		Buy: washers, dryers, televisions, baby food, chest rubs, cough medicine, vitamins, dolls, wagons, sleds, skates	Buy: new and more tasteful furniture, auto travel, unnecessary appliances, boats, dental services, magazines	Buy: vacations, luxuries, home improvements		

Davidson divides its customers into seven lifestyle segments, from "cocky misfits" who are most likely to be arrogant troublemakers, to "laid-back camper types" committed to cycling and nature, to "classy capitalists" who have wealth and privilege.[32]

geodemographic segmentation

Segmenting potential customers into neighborhood lifestyle categories.

• *Geodemographics:* **Geodemographic segmentation** clusters potential customers into neighborhood lifestyle categories. It combines geographic, demographic, and lifestyle segmentations. Geodemographic segmentation helps marketers develop marketing programs tailored to prospective buyers who live in small geographic regions, such as neighborhoods, or who have very specific lifestyle and demographic characteristics. Central Market, an upscale H-E-B Company food store that sells groceries and prepared foods, has several locations in

Exhibit 7.3

Taxonomy of Porsche Buyers

Type	% of All	Owners Description
Top Guns	27%	Driven, ambitious types. Power and control matter. They expect to be noticed.
Elitists	24%	Old-money blue bloods. A car is just a car, no matter how expensive. It is not an extension of personality.
Proud Patrons	23%	Ownership is an end in itself. Their car is a trophy earned for hard work, and who cares if anyone sees them in it?
Bon Vivants	17%	Worldly jet setters and thrill seekers. Their car heightens the excitement in their already passionate lives.
Fantasists	9%	Walter Mitty types. Their car is an escape. Not only are they uninterested in impressing others with it, they also feel a little guilty about owning one.

Texas, and the merchandise mix varies according to the location. In Fort Worth there is a strong Western influence, so the company installed a smoker at that store to smoke beef and poultry—something its other stores do not have. The Hispanic market is strong in San Antonio and Fort Worth, so those stores stock a wide selection of fresh and dried peppers, avocados, and tomatoes.[33]

Psychographic variables can be used individually to segment markets or be combined with other variables to provide more detailed descriptions of market segments. One combination approach is the Claritas PRIZM Lifestyle software program that divides Americans into sixty-two "clusters," or consumer types, all with catchy names. The clusters combine basic demographic data such as age, ethnicity, and income with lifestyle information, such as magazine and sports preferences, taken from consumer surveys. For example, the "Kids and Cul-de-Sacs" group are upscale, suburban families with a median household income of $68,900 who tend to shop on-line and visit Disney theme parks. The "Bohemian Mix" cluster are professionals aged twenty-five to forty-four with a median income of $38,500 who are likely to shop at The Gap, and read *Elle* magazine. The program also predicts to which neighborhoods across the country the clusters are likely to gravitate. Using PRIZM, Hyundai chose zip codes with a high percentage of promising clusters and sent test-drive offers only to those areas (instead of blanketing entire cities with the offer). In those markets, Hyundai not only increased the number of people showing up for a test-drive but also increased its sales and cut its costs per vehicle sold in half.[34] You will read more about Claritas in Chapter 21.

Benefit Segmentation

Benefit segmentation is the process of grouping customers into market segments according to the benefits they seek from the product. Most types of market segmentation are based on the assumption that this variable and customers' needs are related. Benefit segmentation is different because it groups potential customers on

benefit segmentation
The process of grouping customers into market segments according to the benefits they seek from the product.

the basis of their needs or wants rather than some other characteristic, such as age or gender. The snack-food market, for example, can be divided into six benefit segments, as shown in Exhibit 7.4.

Customer profiles can be developed by examining demographic information associated with people seeking certain benefits. This information can be used to match marketing strategies with selected target markets. Procter & Gamble introduced Pampers Rash Guard, a diaper designed to combat diaper rash. To attract time-pressed consumers, Tops Friendly Markets supermarket chain is building stores half the size of some existing ones and emphasizing efficient shopping by locating carry-out foods near the front of the store and similar features.[35]

Usage-Rate Segmentation

usage-rate segmentation
Dividing a market by the amount of product bought or consumed.

Usage-rate segmentation divides a market by the amount of product bought or consumed. Categories vary with the product, but they are likely to include some combination of the following: former users, potential users, first-time users, light or irregular users, medium users, and heavy users. Segmenting by usage rate enables marketers to focus their efforts on heavy users or to develop multiple marketing mixes aimed at different segments. Because heavy users often account for a sizable portion of all product sales, some marketers focus on the heavy-user segment.

80/20 principle
A principle holding that 20 percent of all customers generate 80 percent of the demand.

The **80/20 principle** holds that 20 percent of all customers generate 80 percent of the demand. Although the percentages usually are not exact, the general idea often holds true. For example, in the fast-food industry, the heavy user accounts for only one of five fast-food patrons, but makes about 60 percent of all visits to fast-food restaurants. Using this definition, the heavy user (who is most

Exhibit 7.4 Lifestyle Segmentation of the Snack-Food Market

	Nutritional Snackers	Weight Watchers	Guilty Snackers	Party Snackers	Indiscriminate Snackers	Economical Snackers
% of Snackers	22%	14%	9%	15%	15%	18%
Lifestyle Characteristics	Self-assured, controlled	Outdoorsy, influential, venturesome	Highly anxious, isolated	Sociable	Hedonistic	Self-assured, price-oriented
Benefits Sought	Nutritious, without artificial ingredients, natural	Low in calories, quick energy	Low in calories, good tasting	Good to serve guests, served with pride, go well with beverages	Good tasting, satisfies hunger	Low in price, best value
Consumption Level of Snacks	Light	Light	Heavy	Average	Heavy	Average
Type of Snacks Usually Eaten	Fruits, vegetables, cheese	Yogurt, vegetables	Yogurt, cookies, crackers, candy	Nuts, potato chips, crackers, pretzels	Candy, ice cream, cookies, potato chips, pretzels, popcorn	No specific products
Demographics	Better educated, have younger children	Younger, single	Younger or older, female, lower socio-economic status	Middle-aged, nonurban	Teenager	Have large family, better educated

Are Brewers Using the Internet to Target Underage Drinkers?

Reluctantly nudged into the on-line world, major brewers are finding the Web offers a new way to win brand loyalty—especially among the young adult males who drank more than half of the 2.7 billion cases of beer sold in the United States in 2000. "We want to get that one-on-one time," says Tony Ponturo, vice president of marketing for Anheuser-Busch Companies, the brewer of Budweiser. "If [consumers] are on the Budweiser.com site and interacting with your site, that is something special and different. They will feel some loyalty to you."

Brewers are also adding features to their sites that have less to do with beer and more to do with the lifestyle of beer drinkers. For example, Miller and Budweiser offer on-line fantasy race-car leagues. Miller created a "beer pager" on its site that allows a user to send a message to a group of friends and track their responses. There are also concert promotions, interactive chats with sports stars, and on-line sweepstakes.

As the sites try to be more hip and youth-oriented, some public-health advocates worry that the on-line campaigns will increasingly attract underage drinkers. Beer companies, like other manufactur-ers of consumer products, strive to make a connection with consumers as early as possible. That requires a delicate balancing act of trying not to appeal to underage drinkers while still targeting the twenty-one-and-over crowd.

"We take great care to ensure people visiting our site are twenty-one and older," says Francine Katz, vice president of consumer affairs for Anheuser-Busch. "Our site is intended for adults." She notes that all visitors to the Budweiser site must enter a date of birth before being granted access to the site—a standard feature on beer Web pages.

But skeptics say the warning screen requiring a date of birth may actually attract underage drinkers because it suggests the site is taboo. In addition, the age screen is based on the honor sys-tem—there is no way to verify whether the user is entering his or her real date of birth.

The addition of games, con-cert promotions, and other pop culture to beer Web sites will inevitably lead to an increase in visits from teenagers, believes Kathryn Montgomery, the presi-dent of the Center for Media Education, a nonprofit organiza-tion that promotes television and Internet safeguards for children. She notes, "The whole nature of the Web creates new opportunities to make the products more fun and exciting and the site more about play than traditional adver-tising. I think there is an ulterior motive, one that is hard for us to prove, but it appears targeted at young people. [Youths who see the beer sites] connect consuming alcohol with having a lot of fun. It is very playful. There is no discus-sion of consequences."

George Hacker, director of the Alcohol Policies Project of the Center for Science in the Public Interest, says Coors Brewing Com-pany is the only major brewer to operate a Web site devoid of the glitzy promotions that might attract underage users. "The Internet rep-resents another means for beer to be in young kids' faces," says Hacker. "There are so many young people in the [on-line] audience that any standards brewers hold relating to targeting young people are worthless."[37]

Discuss the ethical implications of the beer industry's design and use of Web sites to promote alco-holic products. Do you think the beer industry is targeting children with its sites? Explain your answer.

---

often a single male) accounted for roughly $66 billion of the $110 billion the National Restaurant Association said was spent on fast food in 1999.[36]

Developing customers into heavy users is the goal behind many frequency/loyalty programs like the airlines' frequent flyer programs. Many supermarkets have also designed loyalty programs that reward the heavy-user segment with deals available only to them, such as in-store coupon dispensing systems, loyalty card programs, and special price deals on selected merchandise.

The "Ethics in Marketing" box describes how the brewing industry's use of the Internet to market beer to heavy users may also attract those who are too young to drink.

Bases for Segmenting Business Markets

The business market consists of four broad segments: producers, resellers, institu-tions, and government (for a detailed discussion of the characteristics of these segments, see Chapter 6). Whether marketers focus on only one or on all four of these segments, they are likely to find diversity among potential customers. Thus,

Describe the bases for seg-menting business markets

Home Depot

Does Home Depot's Web site reflect the same type of business and consumer segmentation it implements in its physical stores? (Each store has special areas for contractors.) Explain what you find.

http://www.homedepot.com

 On Line

further market segmentation offers just as many benefits to business marketers as it does to consumer-product marketers.

Company Characteristics

Company characteristics, such as geographic location, type of company, company size, and product use, can be important segmentation variables. Some markets tend to be regional because buyers prefer to purchase from local suppliers, and distant suppliers may have difficulty competing in terms of price and service. Therefore, firms that sell to geographically concentrated industries benefit by locating close to their markets.

Segmenting by customer type allows business marketers to tailor their marketing mixes to the unique needs of particular types of organizations or industries. Many companies are finding this form of segmentation to be quite effective. For example, Home Depot, one of the largest do-it-yourself retail businesses in the United States, has targeted professional repair and remodeling contractors in addition to consumers.

Volume of purchase (heavy, moderate, light) is a commonly used basis for business segmentation. Another is the buying organization's size, which may affect its purchasing procedures, the types and quantities of products it needs, and its responses to different marketing mixes. Banks frequently offer different services, lines of credit, and overall attention to commercial customers based on their size.

Many products, especially raw materials like steel, wood, and petroleum, have diverse applications. How customers use a product may influence the amount they buy, their buying criteria, and their selection of vendors. For example, a producer of springs may have customers that use the product in applications as diverse as making machine tools, bicycles, surgical devices, office equipment, telephones, and missile systems.

Buying Processes

Many business marketers find it helpful to segment customers and prospective customers on the basis of how they buy. For example, companies can segment some business markets by ranking key purchasing criteria, such as price, quality, technical support, and service. Atlas Corporation developed a commanding position in the industrial door market by providing customized products in just four weeks, which was much faster than the industry average of twelve to fifteen weeks. Atlas's primary market is companies with an immediate need for customized doors.

The purchasing strategies of buyers may provide useful segments. Two purchasing profiles that have been identified are satisficers and optimizers. **Satisficers** contact familiar suppliers and place the order with the first one to satisfy product and delivery requirements. **Optimizers** consider numerous suppliers (both familiar and unfamiliar), solicit bids, and study all proposals carefully before selecting one.

The personal characteristics of the buyers themselves (their demographic characteristics, decision style, tolerance for risk, confidence level, job responsibilities, etc.) influence their buying behavior and thus offer a viable basis for segmenting some business markets. IBM computer buyers, for example, are sometimes characterized as being more risk averse than buyers of less expensive computers that perform essentially the same functions. In advertising, therefore, IBM stressed its reputation for high quality and reliability.

satisficers
Business customers who place an order with the first familiar supplier to satisfy product and delivery requirements.

optimizers
Business customers who consider numerous suppliers, both familiar and unfamiliar, solicit bids, and study all proposals carefully before selecting one.

Customer Relationship

More and more, companies are beginning to go beyond the traditional segmentation variables by focusing on the type of relationship they have with their customers. For example, Cable & Wireless, a British telephone company, had traditionally segmented customers based on size. This meant that a *Fortune* 500 organization would have priority over a midsize customer, even if the midsize client accounted for more business. Recently, the company reevaluated this method and began using other factors, such as revenue generated by each customer, and how cost-effective and efficient it is for Cable & Wireless to serve particular customers.[38]

The Chapman Group, a Columbia, Maryland, company that specializes in sales and marketing process improvement, has designed a segmentation strategy based on types of relationships companies have with their customers. They developed three segments of relationships: client accounts, customer accounts, and buyer accounts. Clients collaborate with the organization on attaining mutual goals of profitability. They appreciate support, consistently offer profitable revenue, and have reasonable expectations of services for the prices they pay. They are willing to work on teams and expand relationships between both organizations. Customers are less interested in building a relationship network, are indifferent about mutual profitability, want most goods and services for lower-than-market prices, and are more costly to service. Buyers focus on price only. Value, relationships, and services typically do not offset pricing differences in this segment. Companies using this segmentation strategy can then offer different service approaches for each segment.[39]

Steps in Segmenting a Market

The purpose of market segmentation, in both consumer and business markets, is to identify marketing opportunities. Exhibit 7.5 traces the steps below in segmenting a market. Note that steps 5 and 6 are actually marketing activities that follow market segmentation (steps 1 through 4).

List the steps involved in segmenting markets

1. *Select a market or product category for study:* Define the overall market or product category to be studied. It may be a market in which the firm already competes, a new but related market or product category, or a totally new one. For instance, Anheuser-Busch closely examined the beer market before introducing Michelob Light and Bud Light. Anheuser-Busch also carefully studied the market for salty snacks before introducing the Eagle brand.

2. *Choose a basis or bases for segmenting the market:* This step requires managerial insight, creativity, and market knowledge. There are no scientific procedures for selecting segmentation variables. However, a successful segmentation scheme must produce segments that meet the four basic criteria discussed earlier in this chapter.

3. *Select segmentation descriptors:* After choosing one or more bases, the marketer must select the segmentation descriptors. Descriptors identify the specific segmentation variables to use. For example, if a company selects demographics as

Steps in Segmenting a Market and Subsequent Activities   **Exhibit 7.5**

1 Select a market or product category for study.

2 Choose a basis or bases for segmenting the market.

3 Select segmentation descriptors.

4 Profile and analyze segments.

5 Select target markets.

6 Design, implement, and maintain appropriate marketing mixes.

a basis of segmentation, it may use age, occupation, and income as descriptors. A company that selects usage segmentation needs to decide whether to go after heavy users, nonusers, or light users.

4. *Profile and analyze segments:* The profile should include the segments' size, expected growth, purchase frequency, current brand usage, brand loyalty, and long-term sales and profit potential. This information can then be used to rank potential market segments by profit opportunity, risk, consistency with organizational mission and objectives, and other factors important to the firm.

5. *Select target markets:* Selecting target markets is not a part of but a natural outcome of the segmentation process. It is a major decision that influences and often directly determines the firm's marketing mix. This topic is examined in greater detail later in this chapter.

6. *Design, implement, and maintain appropriate marketing mixes:* The marketing mix has been described as product, distribution, promotion, and pricing strategies intended to bring about mutually satisfying exchange relationships with target markets. Chapters 9 through 18 explore these topics in detail.

Strategies for Selecting Target Markets

7

Discuss alternative strategies for selecting target markets

target market
A group of people or organizations for which an organization designs, implements, and maintains a marketing mix intended to meet the needs of that group, resulting in mutually satisfying exchanges.

So far this chapter has focused on the market segmentation process, which is only the first step in deciding whom to approach about buying a product. The next task is to choose one or more target markets. A **target market** is a group of people or organizations for which an organization designs, implements, and maintains a marketing mix intended to meet the needs of that group, resulting in mutually satisfying exchanges. The three general strategies for selecting target markets—undifferentiated, concentrated, and multisegment targeting—are illustrated in Exhibit 7.6. Exhibit 7.7 illustrates the advantages and disadvantages of each targeting strategy.

Exhibit 7.6

Three Strategies for Selecting Target Markets

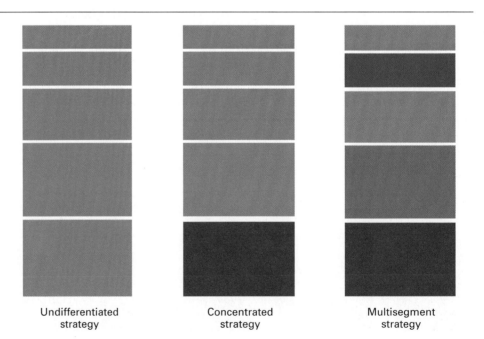

Undifferentiated strategy   Concentrated strategy   Multisegment strategy

Exhibit 7.7

Targeting Strategy	Advantages	Disadvantages
Undifferentiated Targeting	• Potential savings on production/marketing costs • Company more susceptible to competition	• Unimaginative product offerings
Concentrated Targeting	• Concentration of resources • Can better meet the needs of a narrowly defined segment • Allows some small firms to better compete with larger firms • Strong positioning	• Segments too small, or changing • Large competitors may more effectively market to niche segment
Multisegment Targeting	• Greater financial success • Economies of scale in production/marketing	• High costs • Cannibalization

Undifferentiated Targeting

A firm using an **undifferentiated targeting strategy** essentially adopts a mass-market philosophy, viewing the market as one big market with no individual segments. The firm uses one marketing mix for the entire market. A firm that adopts an undifferentiated targeting strategy assumes that individual customers have similar needs that can be met with a common marketing mix.

The first firm in an industry sometimes uses an undifferentiated targeting strategy. With no competition, the firm may not need to tailor marketing mixes to the preferences of market segments. Henry Ford's famous comment about the Model T is a classic example of an undifferentiated targeting strategy: "They can have their car in any color they want, as long as it's black." At one time, Coca-Cola used this strategy with a single product and a single size of its familiar green bottle. Marketers of commodity products, such as flour and sugar, are also likely to use an undifferentiated targeting strategy.

One advantage of undifferentiated marketing is the potential for saving on production and marketing. Because only one item is produced, the firm should be able to achieve economies of mass production. Also, marketing costs may be lower when there is only one product to promote and a single channel of distribution. Too often, however, an undifferentiated strategy emerges by default rather than by design, reflecting a failure to consider the advantages of a segmented approach. The result is often sterile, unimaginative product offerings that have little appeal to anyone.

Another problem associated with undifferentiated targeting is that it makes the company more susceptible to competitive inroads. Hershey lost a big share of the candy market to Mars and other candy companies before it changed to a multisegment targeting strategy. Coca-Cola forfeited its position as the leading seller of cola drinks in supermarkets to Pepsi-Cola in the late 1950s, when Pepsi began offering several sizes of containers.

You might think a firm producing a standard product like toilet tissue would adopt an undifferentiated strategy. However, this market has industrial segments and consumer segments. Industrial buyers want an economical, single-ply product sold in boxes of a hundred rolls. The consumer market demands a more versatile product in smaller quantities. Within the consumer market, the product is differentiated with designer print or no print, cushioned or noncushioned, and

undifferentiated targeting strategy
Marketing approach that views the market as one big market with no individual segments and thus requires a single marketing mix.

Charleston Gardens

What segmentation strategy does Charleston Gardens employ on its Web site? Why do you think as you do?

http://www.charlestongardens.com

 On Line

concentrated targeting strategy
A strategy used to select one segment of a market for targeting marketing efforts.

niche
One segment of a market.

economy priced or luxury priced. Fort Howard Corporation, the market share leader in industrial toilet paper, does not even sell to the consumer market.

Concentrated Targeting

With a **concentrated targeting strategy**, a firm selects a market **niche** (one segment of a market) for targeting its marketing efforts. Because the firm is appealing to a single segment, it can concentrate on understanding the needs, motives, and satisfactions of that segment's members and on developing and maintaining a highly specialized marketing mix. Some firms find that concentrating resources and meeting the needs of a narrowly defined market segment is more profitable than spreading resources over several different segments.

 For example, Starbucks became successful by focusing on a group of consumers that wanted gourmet coffee products. America Online (AOL) became one of the worlds' leading Internet providers by targeting Internet newcomers. By making the Internet interface easy to use, AOL was able to attract millions of people who otherwise might not have subscribed to an on-line service.[40] The City University of Hong Kong is restructuring its entire focus and transforming its programs into an e-business curriculum.[41]

Small firms often adopt a concentrated targeting strategy to compete effectively with much larger firms. For example, Enterprise Rent-A-Car rose to number one in the car rental industry by catering to people with cars in the shop. It has now expanded into the airport rental market.

Some firms, on the other hand, use a concentrated strategy to establish a strong position in a desirable market segment. Porsche, for instance, targets an upscale automobile market through "class appeal, not mass appeal."

Concentrated targeting violates the old adage "Don't put all your eggs in one basket." If the chosen segment is too small or if it shrinks because of environmental changes, the firm may suffer negative consequences. For instance, OshKosh B'Gosh, Inc., was highly successful selling children's wear in the 1980s. It was so successful, however, that the children's line came to define OshKosh's image to the extent that the company could not sell clothes to anyone else. Attempts at marketing older children's clothing, women's casual clothes, and maternity wear were all abandoned. Recognizing it was in the children's-wear business, the company expanded into products such as kids' shoes, children's eyewear, and plush toys.

A concentrated strategy can also be disastrous for a firm that is not successful in its narrowly defined target market. Before Procter & Gamble introduced Head and Shoulders shampoo, several small firms were already selling antidandruff shampoos. Head and Shoulders was introduced with a large promotional campaign, and the new brand captured over half the market immediately. Within a year, several of the firms that had been concentrating on this market segment went out of business.

AP/WIDE WORLD PHOTOS

Starbucks deploys a very concentrated marketing strategy by focusing on gourmet coffee drinkers. How serious is the company about its strategy? Senior Vice President Mary Williams, pictured here, slurps more than three hundred cups of coffee a day. She is in charge of coffee tasting, buying, and education for the company.

Multisegment Targeting

A firm that chooses to serve two or more well-defined market segments and develops a distinct marketing mix for each has a **multisegment targeting strategy**. Stouffer's, for example, offers gourmet entrées for one segment of the frozen dinner market and Lean Cuisine for another. Hershey offers premium candies like Golden Almond chocolate bars, packaged in gold foil, that are marketed to an adult audience. Another chocolate bar, called RSVP, is targeted toward consumers who crave the taste of Godiva chocolates at the price of a Hershey bar.

multisegment targeting strategy
A strategy that chooses two or more well-defined market segments and develops a distinct marketing mix for each.

Cosmetics companies seek to increase sales and market share by targeting multiple age and ethnic groups. Maybelline and Cover Girl, for example, market different lines to teenage women, young adult women, older women, and African American women. Mattel targets multiple markets with its Barbie doll. To make Barbie relevant to older girls, the brand has a new logo, new packaging, and an expanded product line of books and trendy apparel. Other new items include an electronic Barbie scrapbook to keep voice-recorded secrets and activity sets for fingernails and make-your-own lip-gloss. To target preteen girls, the company is introducing Barbie dolls with strands of hair studded with rhinestones, street-fashion clothing, and a first ever Barbie belly button.[42]

AP/WIDE WORLD PHOTOS

Mattel targets multiple markets with its Barbie doll. In an attempt to appeal to today's generation of young girls, the company rolled out "Generation" dolls. Traditional Barbies now share shelf space with the new line, which includes a doll with a nose ring and one with a butterfly tattoo on her stomach.

Sometimes organizations use different promotional appeals, rather than completely different marketing mixes, as the basis for a multisegment strategy. Beer marketers such as Adolph Coors and Anheuser-Busch advertise and promote special events targeted toward African American, Hispanic American, and Asian American market segments. The beverages and containers, however, do not differ by ethnic market segment.

Multisegment targeting offers many potential benefits to firms, including greater sales volume, higher profits, larger market share, and economies of scale in manufacturing and marketing. Yet it may also involve greater product design, production, promotion, inventory, marketing research, and management costs. Before deciding to use this strategy, firms should compare the benefits and costs of multisegment targeting to those of undifferentiated and concentrated targeting.

ON LINE

Another potential cost of multisegment targeting is **cannibalization**, which occurs when sales of a new product cut into sales of a firm's existing products. In many cases, however, companies prefer to steal sales from their own brands rather than lose sales to a competitor. Also, in today's fast-paced world of Internet business, some companies are willing to cannibalize existing business to build new business. Bank One launched WingspanBank.com as a freestanding all-Internet bank that would be free to poach Bank One's customers. Likewise, the pet-supply chain Petsmart spun off its on-line venture, Petsmart.com, as a separate company.

cannibalization
A situation that occurs when sales of a new product cut into sales of a firm's existing products.

Positioning

The development of any marketing mix depends on **positioning**, a process that influences potential customers' overall perception of a brand, product line, or organization in general. **Position** is the place a product, brand, or group of products occupies in consumers' minds relative to competing offerings. Consumer goods marketers are particularly concerned with positioning. Procter & Gamble, for example, markets eleven different laundry detergents, each with a unique position, as illustrated in Exhibit 7.8 on page 232.

8
Explain how and why firms implement positioning strategies and how product differentiation plays a role

positioning
Developing a specific marketing mix to influence potential customers' overall perception of a brand, product line, or organization in general.

position
The place a product, brand, or group of products occupies in consumers' minds relative to competing offerings.

Use the Internet to see how the positionings of the detergents listed in Exhibit 7.8 are reflected on their Web sites.

 On Line

Exhibit 7.8

Positioning of Procter & Gamble Detergents

Brand	Positioning	Market Share
Tide	Tough, powerful cleaning	31.1%
Cheer	Tough cleaning and color protection	8.2%
Bold	Detergent plus fabric softener	2.9%
Gain	Sunshine scent and odor-removing formula	2.6%
Era	Stain treatment and stain removal	2.2%
Dash	Value brand	1.8%
Oxydol	Bleach-boosted formula, whitening	1.4%
Solo	Detergent and fabric softener in liquid form	1.2%
Dreft	Outstanding cleaning for baby clothes, safe for tender skin	1.0%
Ivory Snow	Fabric and skin safety on baby clothes and fine washables	0.7%
Ariel	Tough cleaner, aimed at Hispanics	0.1%

Positioning assumes that consumers compare products on the basis of important features. Marketing efforts that emphasize irrelevant features are therefore likely to misfire. For example, Crystal Pepsi and a clear version of Coca-Cola's Tab failed because consumers perceived the "clear" positioning as more of a marketing gimmick than a benefit.

Effective positioning requires assessing the positions occupied by competing products, determining the important dimensions underlying these positions, and choosing a position in the market where the organization's marketing efforts will have the greatest impact. For example, Ford Motor Company styled the new Taurus models with conventional lines and installed new high-tech protection features. It positioned the Taurus as a safe, family sedan, based on marketing research that revealed consumers view safety as a top priority in automobiles.

As the previous example illustrates, **product differentiation** is a positioning strategy that many firms use to distinguish their products from those of competitors. The distinctions can be either real or perceived. Tandem Computer designed machines with two central processing units and two memories for computer systems that can never afford to be down or lose their databases (for example, an airline reservation system). In this case, Tandem used product differentiation to create a product with very real advantages for the target market. However, many everyday products, such as bleaches, aspirin, unleaded regular gasoline, and some soaps, are differentiated by such trivial means as brand names, packaging, color, smell, or "secret" additives. The marketer attempts to convince consumers that a particular brand is distinctive and that they should demand it over competing brands.

Some firms, instead of using product differentiation, position their products as being similar to competing products or brands. Artificial sweeteners advertised as tasting like sugar or margarine tasting like butter are two examples.

product differentiation
A positioning strategy that some firms use to distinguish their products from those of competitors.

Perceptual Mapping

Perceptual mapping is a means of displaying or graphing, in two or more dimensions, the location of products, brands, or groups of products in customers' minds. For example, after several years of decreasing market share and the perception of teenagers that Levi's were not "cool," Levi Strauss has developed a number of youth-oriented fashions, ranging from oddly cut jeans to nylon pants that unzip into shorts. It has also introduced apparel appealing to adults by extending the Dockers and Slates casual-pants brands.[43] The perceptual map in Exhibit 7.9 shows Levi's dozens of brands and subbrands, from cheap basics to high-priced fashion.

perceptual mapping
A means of displaying or graphing, in two or more dimensions, the location of products, brands, or groups of products in customers' minds.

Positioning Bases

Firms use a variety of bases for positioning, including the following:

- *Attribute:* A product is associated with an attribute, product feature, or customer benefit. Rockport shoes are positioned as an always comfortable brand that is

Exhibit 7.9

Perceptual Map and Positioning Strategy for Levi Strauss Products

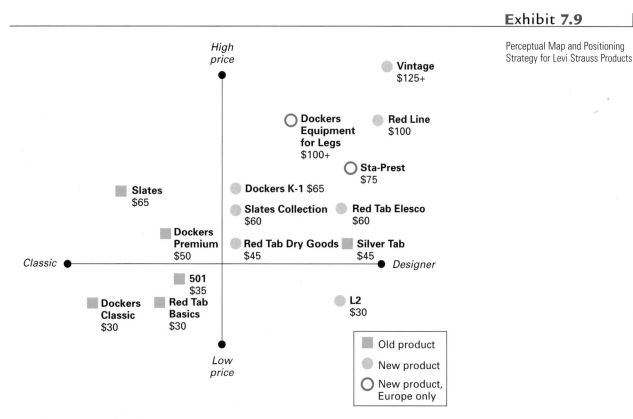

SOURCE: Nina Munk, "How Levi's Trashed a Great American Brand," *Fortune,* April 12, 1999, p. 84.

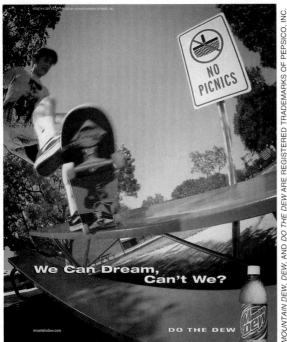

We Can Dream, Can't We?

mountaindew.com   DO THE DEW

Companies often use a mix of positioning bases to reach their target audience. Mountain Dew is one of these products. This ad combines the elements of youth, outdoor fun, and even irreverence.

available in a range of styles from working shoes to dress shoes.

- *Price and quality:* This positioning base may stress high price as a signal of quality or emphasize low price as an indication of value. Neiman Marcus uses the high-priced strategy; Wal-Mart has successfully followed the low-price and value strategy. The mass merchandiser Target has developed an interesting position based on price and quality. It is an "upscale discounter," sticking to low prices but offering higher quality and design than most discount chains.

- *Use or application:* AT&T telephone service advertising emphasized communicating with loved ones using the "Reach Out and Touch Someone" campaign. Stressing uses or applications can be an effective means of positioning a product with buyers. Kahlúa liqueur used advertising to point out 228 ways to consume the product.

- *Product user:* This positioning base focuses on a personality or type of user. Zale Corporation has several jewelry store concepts, each positioned to a different user. The Zale stores cater to middle-of-the-road consumers with traditional styles. Its Gordon's stores appeal to a slightly older clientele with a contemporary look. Guild is positioned for the more affluent fifty-plus consumer.

- *Product class:* The objective here is to position the product as being associated with a particular category of products; for example, positioning a margarine brand with butter.

- *Competitor:* Positioning against competitors is part of any positioning strategy. The Avis rental car positioning as number two exemplifies positioning against specific competitors.

It is not unusual for a marketer to use more than one of these bases. The AT&T "Reach Out and Touch Someone" campaign that stressed use also emphasized the relatively low cost of long-distance calling. Mountain Dew positioned its soft drink to the youth market as a thirst-quenching drink that is associated with teens having fun outdoors.

Repositioning

repositioning
Changing consumers' perceptions of a brand in relation to competing brands.

Sometimes products or companies are repositioned in order to sustain growth in slow markets or to correct positioning mistakes. **Repositioning** is changing consumers' perceptions of a brand in relation to competing brands. One of the most successful product repositioning campaigns ever was the National Pork Board's repositioning of pork as "the other white meat." In the late 1980s, when consumers became more health-conscious, pork producers were making changes in response to the demand for a leaner, higher quality product, but few people knew about it. While poultry sales were increasing, sales of pork products declined by more than 20 percent. The Pork Board launched the "Pork: The Other White Meat" campaign, which highlighted pork's conve-

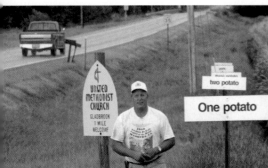

When the Pork Board launched the "Pork: The Other White Meat" campaign, it saw pork consumption rise to the point where pork is now the most eaten meat in the world. Building on this success, a new campaign has been developed in which ads repeat old adages, then unexpectedly drop in the word "Pork." Pictured here: "One potato, two potato, three potato, pork."

nience and nutritional benefits. By 1996, almost 90 percent of consumers surveyed recognized the slogan—up from 64 percent four years earlier. In 2000, new print, television, and Internet campaigns were introduced, and the slogan was named the fifth most memorable tag line in contemporary advertising by Northwestern University. Since the start of the campaign, pork production has increased nearly 40 percent, and pork is now the most eaten meat in the world.[44] Another company that has capitalized on the trend of health-consciousness in an effort to target baby boomers is Johnson & Johnson. The company repositioned St. Joseph baby aspirin as a low-dose aspirin for adults who want to reduce the risk of heart attack and stroke.[45]

Chapter 4 discussed the trend toward global market standardization, which enables firms like Coca-Cola, Colgate-Palmolive, McDonald's, and Nike to market similar products using similar marketing strategies in many different countries. This chapter has also discussed the trend toward targeting smaller, more precisely

United States Department of Agriculture

Review Exhibit 7.4 on the snack-food market. Then, visit the USDA Web site for an article on the snack-food market in Shanghai. Do the segments seem all that different? If you were a manufacturer of cheese popcorn, how would you penetrate the Shanghai snack market? A manufacturer of caramels?

http://www.fas.usda.gov/info/agexporter/1997/shangsnk.html

On Line

Global Issues in Market Segmentation and Targeting

defined markets.

The tasks involved in segmenting markets, selecting target markets, and designing, implementing, and maintaining appropriate marketing mixes (described in Exhibit 7.5) are the same whether the marketer has a local perspective or a global vision. The main difference is the segmentation variables commonly used. Countries are commonly grouped using such variables as per capita gross domestic product, geography, religion, culture, or political system.

Some firms have tried to group countries or customer segments around the world using lifestyle or psychographic variables. So-called Asian yuppies in places like Singapore, Hong Kong, Japan, and South Korea have substantial spending power and exhibit purchase and consumption behavior similar to that of their better-known counterparts in the United States. In this case, firms may be able to use a global market standardization approach.

 Recall from Chapter 4 that Metabolife International has introduced a line of Chinese herb formulas designed to treat five common ailments, such as the common cold and upset stomach. The line, called Chinac, is being marketed to both American and Chinese consumers. For Americans, Chinac offers an easy way to access what is for most consumers an unfamiliar field of medicine. For Chinese, Chinac may offer a welcome change to the numerous and confusing choices they face in a traditional Chinese pharmacy.[46]

9
Discuss global market segmentation and targeting issues

CONNECT IT

As you read at the beginning of this chapter, market segmentation refers to the process of dividing a market into meaningful, relatively similar, and identifiable segments or groups. Targeting is selecting one or more market segments for which an organization designs, implements, and maintains distinctive marketing mixes. Most of the hair salons discussed in

(continued)

the opening story are using a niche tartgeting strategy. They are attempting to appeal to one segment of the market: children. (One salon in the story, Treehouse, also targets parents, so it is using a multisegmentation strategy.) The kids' market would appear to violate one of the criteria for successful segmentation—substantiality—because it represents only 10 percent of the total hair care market. For individual salons in specific geographic locations, however, this niche is proving to be profitable, probably because few salons in those locations target kids.

Use It

The principles of positioning discussed in this chapter do not apply solely to products that you buy. Many people position themselves in different "marketplaces" based on how they present themselves through the clothing they choose, the hairstyles they wear, and the activities they engage in. For example, a young woman may position herself in the dating market by wearing short skirts, sporting a trendy hairstyle, and spending time at night clubs. Another woman may dress modestly, wear a conservative hairstyle, and attend single events at her church. These two women are positioning themselves to attract different kinds of men.

Apply what you have learned in this chapter about positioning by developing a written strategy for a female friend who is interviewing for a job in two different industries: banking and advertising. How would you suggest this friend dress and wear her hair for each of the two interviews? What activities should she stress on her résumé for the bank interview and the advertising agency interview? How would you advise a male friend?

Review It

(1) Describe the characteristics of markets and market segments. A market is composed of individuals or organizations with the ability and willingness to make purchases to fulfill their needs or wants. A market segment is a group of individuals or organizations with similar product needs as a result of one or more common characteristics.

1.1 Mercedes-Benz is thinking about advertising its cars to college students. Do you think that college students are a viable potential market for Mercedes? Why or why not?

1.2 *ON LINE* How are visitors to the following Web site segmented when seeking relevant job openings? Try this search engine and report your results: **http://www.careermag.com**.

(2) Explain the importance of market segmentation. Before the 1960s, few businesses targeted specific market segments. Today, segmentation is a crucial marketing strategy for nearly all successful organizations. Market segmentation enables marketers to tailor marketing mixes to meet the needs of particular population segments. Segmentation helps marketers identify consumer needs and preferences, areas of declining demand, and new marketing opportunities.

2.1 Describe market segmentation in terms of the historical evolution of marketing.

(3) Discuss criteria for successful market segmentation. Successful market segmentation depends on four basic criteria: (1) a market segment must be substantial and have enough potential customers to be viable; (2) a market segment must be identifiable and measurable; (3) members of a market segment must be accessible to marketing efforts; and (4) a market segment must respond to particular marketing efforts in a way that distinguishes it from other segments.

3.1   **WRITING**   Refer to the story about kids' hair salons at the beginning of the chapter. As a marketing consultant for a chain of hair salons, you have been asked to evaluate the kids' market as a potential segment for the chain to target. Write a memo to your client discussing your evaluation of the kids' segment in terms of the four criteria for successful market segmentation.

(4) **Describe the bases commonly used to segment consumer markets.** Five bases are commonly used for segmenting consumer markets. Geographic segmentation is based on region, size, density, and climate characteristics. Demographic segmentation is based on age, gender, income level, ethnicity, and family life-cycle characteristics. Psychographic segmentation includes personality, motives, and lifestyle characteristics. Benefits sought is a type of segmentation that identifies customers according to the benefits they seek in a product. Finally, usage segmentation divides a market by the amount of product purchased or consumed.

4.1   **WRITING**   Choose magazine ads for five different consumer products. For each ad, write a description of what you think the demographic characteristics of the targeted market are.

4.2   **ON LINE**   Investigate how Delta Airlines (**http://www.delta.com**) uses its Web site to cater to its market segments.

(5) **Describe the bases for segmenting business markets.** Business markets can be segmented on three general bases. First, businesses segment markets based on company characteristics, such as customers' geographic location, type of company, company size, and product use. Second, companies may segment customers based on the buying processes those customers use. Third, companies are increasingly basing market segmentation on the type of relationship they have with their customers.

5.1   **WRITING**   Choose five ads from business publications such as the *Wall Street Journal, Fortune,* and *Business Week.* For each ad, write a description of how you think the company has segmented its business market.

(6) **List the steps involved in segmenting markets.** Six steps are involved when segmenting markets: (1) selecting a market or product category for study; (2) choosing a basis or bases for segmenting the market; (3) selecting segmentation descriptors; (4) profiling and evaluating segments; (5) selecting target markets; and (6) designing, implementing, and maintaining appropriate marketing mixes.

6.1   **WRITING**   Write a letter to the president of your bank suggesting ideas for increasing profits and enhancing customer service by improving segmentation and targeting strategies.

(7) **Discuss alternative strategies for selecting target markets.** Marketers select target markets using three different strategies: undifferentiated targeting, concentrated targeting, and multisegment targeting. An undifferentiated targeting strategy assumes that all members of a market have similar needs that can be met with a single marketing mix. A concentrated targeting strategy focuses all marketing efforts on a single market segment. Multisegment targeting is a strategy that uses two or more marketing mixes to target two or more market segments.

7.1   **TEAM**   Form a team with two or three other students. Create an idea for a new product. Describe the segment (or segments) you are going to target with the product, and explain why you chose the targeting strategy you did.

8 **Explain how and why firms implement positioning strategies and how product differentiation plays a role.** Positioning is used to influence consumer perceptions of a particular brand, product line, or organization in relation to competitors. The term *position* refers to the place that the offering occupies in consumers' minds. To establish a unique position, many firms use product differentiation, emphasizing the real or perceived differences between competing offerings. Products may be differentiated on the basis of attribute, price and quality, use or application, product user, product class, or competitor.

8.1 Choose a product category (e.g., blue jeans), and identify at least three different brands and their respective positioning strategies. How is each position communicated to the target audience?

9 **Discuss global market segmentation and targeting issues.** The key tasks in market segmentation, targeting, and positioning are the same regardless of whether the target market is local, regional, national, or multinational. The main differences are the variables used by marketers in analyzing markets and assessing opportunities and the resources needed to implement strategies.

9.1 Find an article in a business newspaper or magazine that describes how a U.S. company is marketing its products in another country. Create a chart that compares the U.S. marketing mix elements with the same elements for the other country. You may also wish to consult foreign periodicals to see how multinational companies advertise their products in other countries.

DEFINE IT

benefit segmentation 223
cannibalization 231
concentrated targeting
  strategy 230
demographic segmentation
  218
80/20 principle 224
family life cycle (FLC) 221
geodemographic segmenta-
  tion 222
geographic segmentation
  216
market 214

market segment 214
market segmentation 214
multisegment targeting
  strategy 231
niche 230
optimizers 226
perceptual mapping 233
position 231
positioning 231
product differentiation 233
psychographic segmenta-
  tion 221
repositioning 234

satisficers 226
segmentation bases (vari-
  ables) 216
target market 228
undifferentiated targeting
  strategy 229
usage-rate segmentation
  224

APPLY IT

Application for Entrepreneurs

Judy Brown has always loved working with animals. She has experience in pet grooming, boarding, and in-home pet sitting. Judy wants to open a full-service business utilizing her skills that is uniquely positioned in relation to the traditional pet grooming/boarding businesses that operate in the town where she lives. Customers that use these current pet services deliver their pets to the firms and later pick them up. Most are open between 9 A.M. and 6 P.M. from Monday through Friday.

Judy lives in a midsize city that is close to a major airport. Many high-tech companies are located in or near her city, so there are a large number of men and women in managerial and information-technology positions who must travel frequently as part of their jobs. A lot of families have pets, so Judy thinks there is a market for pet-related services, despite the current competition.

Questions

1. How should Judy segment the market for pet services?

2. What targeting strategy should Judy use to start her business? Should this strategy change as her business prospers and grows?

3. How should Judy position her pet services business against her competition?

THINK ABOUT IT

Ethics Exercise

Tobacco companies are frequently criticized for targeting potential customers below the legal age to purchase and use their products. Critics cite Joe Camel and the Marlboro man as images meant to make smoking appealing to young people. If tobacco companies are actually following this particular demographic targeting strategy, most would agree that it is unethical if not illegal.

Questions

1. Is marketing tobacco products to younger consumers unethical?

2. Many are beginning to argue that fast-food companies, such as McDonald's and Burger King, are knowingly marketing unhealthy food to consumers. Is it unethical for fast-food companies to market kids' meals to children?

3. What does the AMA Code of Ethics have to say about marketing unhealthy or harmful products to consumers, particularly children and young adults? Go to the AMA Web site at **http://www.marketingpower.com** to review the code. Write a brief paragraph summarizing where the AMA stands on this important issue.

TRY IT

Entrepreneurship Case

Segmenting the On-line Market: The Case of eBay

When Pam Omidyar dreamed of a place where she could meet, talk, and trade with other collectors of Pez candy dispensers, her computer-programming and soon-to-be husband, Pierre Omidyar, immediately set to work on developing the software that would enable such interaction on-line. Together, in September 1995, they launched eBay.com, and within five short years it was one of the most recognizable brand names on the Internet. From its humble beginnings as a niche Web site, it has become the premier Internet auction showcase. eBay's 4,300 categories include everything from tie-dyed Grateful Dead Beanie Babies to bubblegum cards to nearly new Ferraris and even fine jewelry. Once you find what you're looking for, you can haggle for it in one of the four million daily auctions.

eBay positions itself as a folksy and friendly facilitator of an on-line community that caters to traders with varying tastes and preferences, but the original idea was to service one type of collector in a single geographic area—Pam and Pierre's neighborhood in San Francisco. The Omidyars' customer-focused strategy led to such a high degree of customer satisfaction that awareness of the site quickly spread through the entire Bay area. High customer loyalty, repeat usage, and very strong word-of-mouth advertising (*viral marketing*) fueled eBay's growth. eBay is unique in that it has equal appeal to the occasional Internet surfer, the nostalgic trader, the fanatic trader, the small business in search of used or inexpensive equipment, and those who simply love the thrill of the deal.

In trying to nurture its growing enterprise, eBay's entrepreneurial management team was faced with many marketing challenges that it still grapples with today:

- Attracting users who are accustomed to trading in traditional venues such as auction houses, estate sales, and flea markets
- Convincing Internet users to execute transactions on-line
- Organizing many specific product categories into a much smaller number of broad categories and corresponding market segments
- Developing a marketing mix to reach multiple targets

The first step for eBay was to build a killer product. eBay focuses on delivering a first-class user experience by providing frequent content and auction updates. The site's help areas are customized for either experienced or new users, and detailed collector news and information are available. The second step was developing a pricing schedule to satisfy its broad spectrum of users. Transactions can be executed for as little as twenty-five cents for the seller of a Pez dispenser, but eBay can claim as much as a 5 percent commission on the selling price of an expensive item like a diamond necklace. Under the direction of Senior Vice President of Marketing Brian Swette, the company rethought its past strategy of restricting on-line promotions to its own Web site and has accomplished prolific distribution on the World Wide Web. eBay has struck deals to gain presence on major entry portals like AOL, shopping verticals like MySimon.com, and destination sites like AutoTrader.com.

The final component of the marketing mix, promotion, was the most complex to address. At first glance, eBay has only one product—the on-line auction forum—that it sells to traders and consumers. To that end, eBay has remained faithful to its grassroots marketing effort in the off-line world. It has also maintained its presence at trade and collector shows of all kinds in order to evangelize the benefits of auctioning on-line. A closer look at what transpires at the site, however, reveals that eBay is the auction utility of choice for a range of collectors so stratified that on any one day a browser at eBay can encounter auctions for coins, clothes, model airplanes, or more controversial and hence discouraged items like hate-group materials, used underwear, or a human kidney. The challenge for eBay, therefore, is not so much that it has so many different consumers, but that each one of its consumers has very different needs. With that in mind, eBay has chosen to divide markets using a variety of segmentation strategies. It has employed demographic, psychographic, geodemographic, benefit, and usage-rate segmentation techniques to better understand and serve customer needs across a broad range in each.

In order to effectively promote the site to its eclectic audience, eBay developed a complex and comprehensive print advertising campaign aimed at several targets. Working with the advertising agency of Ogilvy & Mather, eBay decided to avoid mass print media and use niche publications. This way, the company could reach an audience that would be more captive at the point of exposure to the advertisement. Unique messaging and advertising copy was developed for campaigns deployed in twelve different vertical markets. Across those twelve markets, eBay selected seventy-five specialty magazines for their highly tailored advertisements. eBay still supports this strategy today. Although segmenting its market into multiple niches was a demanding and complex initiative, it has clearly been a successful tactic.

Currently, over ten million registered users buy and sell one of 450,000 new items posted to the auction site every day. Customers range from infrequent traders to traders who use eBay regularly to generate personal profit streams. eBay has special services such as My eBay and Mister Lister for frequent users and has gone so far as to build a Business Exchange area where it caters to needs of small businesses. Customers can participate in local auctions specific to their geographic region, bid on items whose proceeds go directly to one of many charities, or sign up for eBay magazine. Chat rooms, an on-line library of articles organized by collection category, and eBay's own newsletter all provide information to enhance and empower the customer's trading experience. eBay's success has inspired a proliferation of copycat auction sites, but none enjoys the customer base or widespread brand recognition of the original.

Questions

1. What types of segmentation does eBay use?

2. Does eBay use an undifferentiated, a niche, or a multiple targeting strategy? Discuss the range of tactics eBay uses to reach its target market.

3. Explain the tools eBay has developed for usage-rate segmentation and consider how eBay might use those tools to enhance its profitability.

4. How did eBay tackle the marketing challenges it faced as it grew from an entrepreneurial venture to a multimillion-dollar operation?

5. Describe eBay's target market.

 WATCH IT

Short

The Kellogg's ad on your dedicated PowerPoint CD-ROM illustrates the concepts of usage-rate segmentation. The series of six Mlife ads taken together are a wonderful example of demographic segmentation. After watching the full series, identify which market segments the company is targeting with each ad.

Medium

As the multi-racial population grows, identifying distinct market segments based on race will become increasingly difficult. CNN reported on the growth of the self-identified multi-racial population after the 2000 census. Watch the clip and consider the implications of multi-racial market segments on marketing practices.

Long
the Series on PBS stations and the Web

To give you insight into Chapter 7, Small Business School will take you to Le Travel Store in San Diego. This specialty retail shop has been serving a unique and specific group of customers for over twenty years. Bill and Joan Keller, owners of the store, will show you how identifying your market segment—and targeting it well—can lead to success.

 FLIP IT

Flip to Chapter 7 in your *Grademaker Study Guide* for more review opportunities, including the pretest, vocabulary review, Internet activities, study test questions, and segmentation scenarios. Can you explain why market segmentation is important? What are the most common bases that marketers use to segment markets? Don't know? Then you need to review with your Grademaker.

CLICK IT

The *Marketing* Web site links you to all the Internet-based activities in this chapter, like "Review It" questions 1.2 and 4.2, and the On-Line exercises in the chapter margins. As a review, do the Chapter 7 quiz and crossword puzzle. And don't forget the Career Exersite that shows you different resources if you'd like to incorporate segmenting and targeting markets into your marketing career. Review the main concepts in the PowerPoint presentation for Chapter 7, too. Go to **http://lamb.swlearning. com**, read the material, and follow the links right from the site.

Still Shaky? Here's a Tip.

The list of key terms on page 238 can be a valuable study aid. Write down the definition of each term on a separate piece of paper and without consulting the margin terms in the chapter. Cement your understanding by also writing an example if possible.

SPIN IT

Spin your Xtra! CD-ROM and test your understanding of market segmentation by completing the worksheets for Exhibits 7.2, 7.5, 7.6, and 7.7. If your instructor has assigned a marketing plan project, worksheets on Xtra! can help you organize your work. In addition to the quiz on the Web site, there's another quiz on the Xtra! CD-ROM, plus video of the authors answering frequently asked questions about target marketing, such as "How do firms choose NOT to target certain markets?" and "Could you explain perceptual mapping in more detail?"

CHAPTER **EIGHT**

DECISION SUPPORT SYSTEMS AND MARKETING RESEARCH

Learning Objectives

1 Explain the concept and purpose of a marketing decision support system

2 Define marketing research and explain its importance to marketing decision making

3 Describe the steps involved in conducting a marketing research project

4 Discuss the profound impact of the Internet on marketing research

5 Discuss the growing importance of scanner-based research

6 Explain the concept of competitive intelligence

In many ways, it's a common marketing situation: A manufacturer faces dwindling sales of a venerable product due to a shrinking core market; an ancillary market holds some promise, but its growth potential is hindered by pricing issues. In other ways, it's almost unique: Most of the people who buy the product do so because they have to, not because they want to; and most of them have no idea what the product is used for.

Then there's the product itself: duck stamps. Known in official parlance as Migratory Bird Hunting and Conservation Stamps, duck stamps are a required annual purchase for duck hunters. (Most hunters say they have little idea of what duck stamp fees are used for. They just know that you have to buy a stamp if you want to hunt ducks.) But the number of hunters is decreasing, and though the stamps are sought after by collectors, their hefty price (last year's stamp was $15) makes accumulating them an expensive proposition for the garden-variety philatelist. "We needed to find a way to reach a new audience, to broaden our market, as with any product," says Margaret Wendy, manager of sales and marketing, Federal Duck Stamp Office, Department of the Interior, U.S. Fish and Wildlife Service, Washington, D.C.

Initially, the idea was to focus the marketing campaign on the stamps themselves, their beauty, and the value of collecting them. But in focus groups conducted during the development of the campaign by The Ball Group, a Lancaster, Pennsylvania–based research and advertising firm, the stamps themselves weren't enough to make the sale. "The collecting aspect was of minimal interest," says Wes Ball, the firm's president.

Focus groups were held in cities around the country, two groups per city, one with environmentally active people and the other with people who were not environmentally active but who were not predisposed against environmental issues. (In addition, a telephone survey with a random national sample was conducted to determine awareness of the Duck Stamp program and to gauge interest and participation in environmental issues.)

Thanks to new strategies based upon the marketing research, hunters and stamp collectors won't be the only ones making an annual duck stamp purchase.

"We discovered a huge contingent who are concerned about the environment, especially air and water quality, and they believed that wetlands are a primary water filter for us, and felt that [up to] a $30 contribution was not only attractive but one that they would actively support again and again. We had people say, 'Now that I know about this I'll contribute money every year,'" Ball says.[1]

What are the various techniques for conducting marketing research? Should managers always do marketing research before they make a decision? How does marketing research relate to decision support systems? We will explore all these topics and others in Chapter 8.

On Line

U.S. Fish and Wildlife Service

How well is the government marketing duck stamps over the Internet? Does the U.S. Fish and Wildlife Service Web site reflect the desire to market the stamps to environmental groups?

http://www.fws.gov
http://www.duckstamp.com

Marketing Decision Support Systems

1

Explain the concept and purpose of a marketing decision support system

marketing information
Everyday information about developments in the marketing environment that managers use to prepare and adjust marketing plans.

decision support system (DSS)
An interactive, flexible computerized information system that enables managers to obtain and manipulate information as they are making decisions.

Accurate and timely information is the lifeblood of marketing decision making. Good information can help maximize an organization's sales and efficiently use scarce company resources. To prepare and adjust marketing plans, managers need a system for gathering everyday information about developments in the marketing environment—that is, for gathering **marketing information**. The system most commonly used these days for gathering marketing information is called a *marketing decision support system.*

A marketing **decision support system (DSS)** is an interactive, flexible computerized information system that enables managers to obtain and manipulate information as they are making decisions. A DSS bypasses the information-processing specialist and gives managers access to useful data from their own desks.

These are the characteristics of a true DSS:

- *Interactive:* Managers give simple instructions and see immediate results. The process is under their direct control; no computer programmer is needed. Managers don't have to wait for scheduled reports.

- *Flexible:* A DSS can sort, regroup, total, average, and manipulate the data in various ways. It will shift gears as the user changes topics, matching information to the problem at hand. For example, the CEO can see highly aggregated figures, and the marketing analyst can view very detailed breakouts.

- *Discovery-oriented:* Managers can probe for trends, isolate problems, and ask "what if" questions.

- *Accessible:* Managers who aren't skilled with computers can easily learn how to use a DSS. Novice users should be able to choose a standard, or default, method of using the system. They can bypass optional features so they can work with the basic system right away while gradually learning to apply its advanced features.

As a hypothetical example of how a DSS can be used, consider Renee Smith, vice president and manager of new products for Central Corporation. To evaluate sales of a recently introduced product, Renee can "call up" sales by the week, then by the month, breaking them out at her option by, say, customer segments. As she works at her desktop computer, her inquiries can go in several directions, depending on the decision at hand. If her train of thought raises questions about monthly sales last quarter compared to forecasts, she can use her DSS to analyze problems immediately. Renee might see that her new product's sales were significantly below forecasts. Were her forecasts too optimistic? She compares other products' sales to her forecasts and finds that the targets were very accurate. Was something wrong with the product? Is her sales department getting insufficient leads, or is it not putting leads to good use? Thinking a minute about how to examine that question, she checks ratios of leads converted to sales, product by product. The results disturb her. Only 5 percent of the new product's leads generated orders, compared to the company's 12 percent all-product average. Why? Renee guesses that the sales force is not supporting the new product vigorously enough. Quantitative information from the DSS could perhaps provide more evidence to back that suspicion. But already having enough quantitative knowledge to satisfy herself, the VP acts on her intuition and experience and decides to have a chat with her sales manager.

database marketing
The creation of a large computerized file of customers' and potential customers' profiles and purchase patterns.

Perhaps the fastest-growing use of DSSs is for **database marketing**, which is the creation of a large computerized file of customers' and potential customers' profiles and purchase patterns. It is usually the key tool for successful micromarketing, which relies on very specific information about a market (see Chapter 21).

The Role of Marketing Research

Marketing research is the process of planning, collecting, and analyzing data relevant to a marketing decision. The results of this analysis are then communicated to management. Marketing research plays a key role in the marketing system. It provides decision makers with data on the effectiveness of the current marketing mix and also with insights for necessary changes. Furthermore, marketing research is a main data source for both management information systems and DSS.

Marketing research has three roles: descriptive, diagnostic, and predictive. Its *descriptive* role includes gathering and presenting factual statements. For example, what is the historic sales trend in the industry? What are consumers' attitudes toward a product and its advertising? Its *diagnostic* role includes explaining data. For instance, what was the impact on sales of a change in the design of the package? Its *predictive* function is to address "what if" questions. For example, how can the researcher use the descriptive and diagnostic research to predict the results of a planned marketing decision?

Management Uses of Marketing Research

Marketing research can help managers in several ways. It improves the quality of decision making and helps managers trace problems. Most important, sound marketing research helps managers focus on the paramount importance of keeping existing customers, aids them in better understanding the marketplace, and alerts them to marketplace trends. Marketing research helps managers gauge the perceived value of their goods and services as well as the level of customer satisfaction.

marketing research
The process of planning, collecting, and analyzing data relevant to a marketing decision.

AP/WIDE WORLD PHOTOS

Marketing research can help managers in several ways. For example, research revealed which brands of plumbing fixtures were traditional to New York City. This helped the Brooklyn Home Depot's store manager Rich Kantor to arrange his small pilot store designed to meet the needs of urban communities.

Improving the Quality of Decision Making

Managers can sharpen their decision making by using marketing research to explore the desirability of various marketing alternatives. For example, despite the growing popularity of cruise ships—nearly six million North American passengers boarded U.S.-based ships in 2001—cruises still get only a tiny slice of Americans' vacation time. Just 5 percent of people who take vacations longer than five days and are willing to spend $1,000 per person take cruises.[2] Royal Caribbean Cruise Lines liked the tremendous potential in the cruising market. Its job was to find a way to woo those people who wouldn't be caught dead on a cruise ship. The classic objections that people raise to vacationing on a cruise ship have not changed in nearly twenty years. Marketing research found that people worry about feeling trapped; they'd rather participate in activities than sit in a pool lounge all day long; they don't like having to eat in an elegant dining room, seven nights in a row, and share a table with strangers; and they don't like having to eat at a set time. In other words, they want options.

Royal Caribbean tackled those objections. That's how *Voyager of the Sea* ended up with an in-line skating track, a kids-only pool, a rock-climbing wall, an English pub, a Johnny Rockets restaurant, and a roulette wheel so big that gamblers can ride around its rim as if it were a carousel. To date, the ship has been very successful at attracting first-time cruisers.

Tracing Problems

Another way managers use marketing research is to find out why a plan backfires. Was the initial decision incorrect? Did an unforeseen change in the external environment cause the plan to fail? How can the same mistake be avoided in the future?

Keebler introduced Sweet Spots, a shortbread cookie with a huge chocolate drop on it. It has had acceptable sales and is still on the market, but only after the company used marketing research to overcome several problems. Soon after the cookie's introduction, Keebler increased the box size from 10 ounces at $2.29 to 15 ounces at $3.19. Demand immediately fell. Market research showed that Sweet Spots were now considered more of a luxury than an everyday item. Keebler lowered the price and went back to the 10-ounce box. Even though Sweet Spots originally was aimed at upscale adult females, the company also tried to appeal to kids. In subsequent research, Keebler found that the package graphics appealed to mothers but not to children.[3]

Focusing on the Paramount Importance of Keeping Existing Customers

An inextricable link exists between customer satisfaction and customer loyalty. Long-term relationships don't just happen but are grounded in the delivery of service and value by the firm. Customer retention pays big dividends for organizations. Powered by repeat sales and referrals, revenues and market share grow. Costs fall because firms spend less money and energy attempting to replace defectors. Steady customers are easy to serve because they understand the modus operandi and make fewer demands on employees' time. Increased customer retention also drives job satisfaction and pride, which lead to higher employee retention. In turn, the knowledge employees acquire as they stay longer increases productivity. A Bain & Company study estimates that a 5 percent decrease in the customer defection rate can boost profits by 25 to 95 percent.[4]

The ability to retain customers is based on an intimate understanding of their needs. This knowledge comes primarily from marketing research. For example, British Airways recast its first-class transatlantic service based on detailed marketing research. Most airlines stress top-of-the-line service in their transatlantic first-class cabins, but British Air's research found that most first-class passengers simply want to sleep. British Air now gives premium flyers the option of dinner on the ground, before takeoff, in the first-class lounge. Then, once on board, they can slip into British Air pajamas, put their heads on real pillows, slip under blankets, and enjoy an interruption-free flight. On arrival at their destination, first-class passengers can have breakfast, use comfortable dressing rooms and showers, and even have their clothes pressed before they set off. These changes in British Air's first-class service were driven strictly by marketing research.

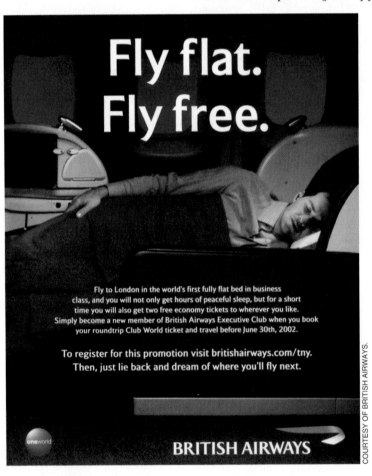

Fly to London in the world's first fully flat bed in business class, and you will not only get hours of peaceful sleep, but for a short time you will also get two free economy tickets to wherever you like. Simply become a new member of British Airways Executive Club when you book your roundtrip Club World ticket and travel before June 30th, 2002.

To register for this promotion visit britishairways.com/tny. Then, just lie back and dream of where you'll fly next.

BRITISH AIRWAYS

COURTESY OF BRITISH AIRWAYS.

British Airways refined its First Class service based on marketing research that revealed that travelers often wanted to sleep during long-haul flights. The company further applied this information to create the world's first fully flat bed in business class (Club World) as shown above.

Understanding the Ever-Changing Marketplace

Marketing research also helps managers understand what is going on in the marketplace and take advantage of opportunities. Historically, marketing research has been practiced for as long as marketing has existed. The early Phoenicians carried out market demand studies as they traded in the various ports of the Mediterranean Sea. Marco Polo's diary indicates he was performing a marketing research function as he traveled to China. There is even evidence that the Spanish systematically conducted "market surveys" as they explored the New World, and there are examples of marketing research conducted during the Renaissance.

 Today, Internet marketing research can help companies quickly and efficiently understand what is happening in the marketplace. For example, Women.com, an on-line community site that offers editorial content and e-commerce services, has surveyed visitors for several years but recently boosted its research efforts. The surveys are designed to discover visitors' demographic and psychographic profiles for the network's internal use, as well as to share with advertisers.

Along with collecting basic demographic data, the site also asks visitors about their e-commerce habits (whether they've shopped for or purchased anything on-line recently, for instance), their feelings about privacy on the Internet, and value and attitudinal questions, such as whether they agree or disagree with statements like "I'm usually the first in my peer group to try something new." Such information provides a picture of the person on the other side of the computer that goes beyond her average age and income, says Regina Lewis, director of research for Women.com Networks, Inc. Understanding whether visitors are more risk oriented, family focused, or career minded helps Women.com set the right tone when talking to visitors, Lewis says, and has resulted in page redesigns.[5]

Steps in a Marketing Research Project

Virtually all firms that have adopted the marketing concept engage in some marketing research because it offers decision makers many benefits. Some companies spend millions on marketing research; others, particularly smaller firms, conduct informal, limited-scale research studies. For example, when Eurasia restaurant, serving Eurasian cuisine, first opened along Chicago's ritzy Michigan Avenue, it drew novelty seekers. But it turned off the important business lunch crowd, and sales began to decline. The owner surveyed several hundred businesspeople working within a mile of the restaurant. He found that they were confused by Eurasia's concept and wanted more traditional Asian fare at lower prices. In response, the restaurant altered its concept; it hired a Thai chef, revamped the menu, and cut prices. The dining room was soon full again.

Whether a research project costs $200 or $2 million, the same general process should be followed. The marketing research process is a scientific approach to decision making that maximizes the chance of getting accurate and meaningful results. Exhibit 8.1 on page 250 traces the steps: (1) identifying and formulating the problem/opportunity, (2) planning the research design and gathering primary data, (3) specifying the sampling procedures, (4) collecting the data, (5) analyzing the data, (6) preparing and presenting the report, and (7) following up.

The research process begins with the recognition of a marketing problem or opportunity. As changes occur in the firm's external environment, marketing managers are faced with the questions, "Should we change the existing marketing mix?" and, if so, "How?" Marketing research may be used to evaluate product, promotion, distribution, or pricing alternatives. In addition, it is used to find and evaluate new market opportunities.

For example, more than twenty million babies have been born in the United States since 1995, forming the largest generation since the baby boomers. More impressive than their numbers, though, is their wealth. The increase in single-parent and dual-earner households means kids are making shopping decisions

Describe the steps involved in conducting a marketing research project

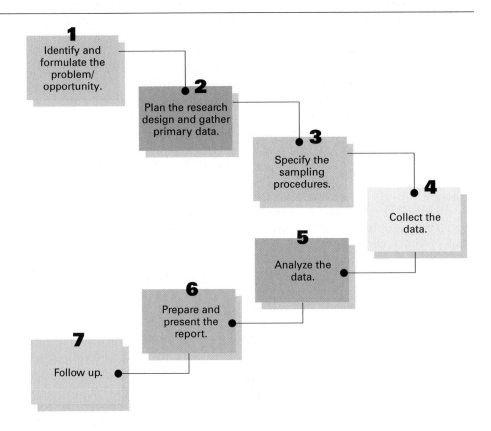

once left to mom. Combining allowance, earnings, and gifts, kids fourteen and under will directly spend an estimated $23 billion this year, and they will influence the spending of another $200 billion.

For savvy marketers, these statistics represent opportunity. Marketing research can home in and clarify where the best opportunities lie. Walt Disney, for example, is launching a twenty-four-hour kids' radio network based on its marketing research. Sometimes research can lead to unexpected results requiring creative uses of the marketing mix. General Motors recently completed an analysis of "backseat consumers," that is, children between five and fifteen years of age. Marketing research discovered that parents often let their children play a tie-breaking role in deciding what car to purchase. Marketing managers, armed with this information, launched several programs. GM purchased the inside cover of *Sports Illustrated for Kids,* a magazine targeted to boys from eight to fourteen years old. The ad featured a brightly colored two-page spread for the Chevy Venture minivan, a vehicle targeted toward young families. GM also sent the minivan into malls and showed Disney movies on a VCR inside the van.

The GM story illustrates an important point about problem/opportunity definition. The **marketing research problem** is information oriented. It involves determining what information is needed and how that information can be obtained efficiently and effectively. The **marketing research objective**, then, is to provide insightful decision-making information. This requires specific pieces of information needed to answer the marketing research problem. Managers must combine this information with their own experience and other information to make a proper decision. In the GM scenario, the marketing research objective was to determine what role, if any, backseat consumers play in a family's decision to purchase an automobile. In contrast, the **management decision problem** is action oriented. Management problems tend to be much broader in scope and far more general, whereas marketing research problems must be more narrowly defined and specific if the research effort is to be successful. Sometimes several research studies must be conducted to solve a broad management problem. Once GM determined that children

marketing research problem
Determining what information is needed and how that information can be obtained efficiently and effectively.

marketing research objective
The specific information needed to solve a marketing research problem; the objective should be to provide insightful decision-making information.

management decision problem
A broad-based problem that requires marketing research in order for managers to take proper actions.

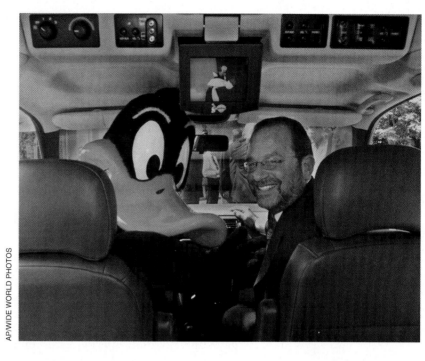

GM continues to reap the benefits of its marketing research revealing how important kids are in the family decision-making process. In 2000, the company introduced the Warner Bros. Edition Chevy Venture minivan. This model includes a built-in child's restraining seat, a video player, and an on-going package called VentureTainment!

AP/WIDE WORLD PHOTOS

within this target market played a tiebreaker role, the question became one of what should be done to influence the tiebreakers. GM used marketing research to determine that direct advertising to children in the target market and mall promotions would be the best form of promotion.

Secondary Data

A valuable tool throughout the research process but particularly in the problem/opportunity identification stage is **secondary data**—data previously collected for any purpose other than the one at hand. Secondary information originating within the company includes documents such as annual reports, reports to stockholders, product testing results perhaps made available to the news media, and house periodicals composed by the company's personnel for communication to employees, customers, or others. Often this information is incorporated into a company's internal database.

Innumerable outside sources of secondary information also exist, principally in the forms of government (federal, state, and local) departments and agencies that compile and publish summaries of business data. Trade and industry associations also publish secondary data. Still more data are available in business periodicals and other news media that regularly publish studies and articles on the economy, specific industries, and even individual companies. The unpublished summarized secondary information from these sources corresponds to internal reports, memos, or special-purpose analyses with limited circulation. Economic considerations or priorities in the organization may preclude publication of these summaries. Most of the sources listed above can be found on the Internet.

Secondary data save time and money if they help solve the researcher's problem. Even if the problem is not solved, secondary data have other advantages. They can aid in formulating the problem statement and suggest research methods and other types of data needed for solving the problem. In addition, secondary data can pinpoint the kinds of people to approach and their locations and serve as a basis of comparison for other data. The disadvantages of secondary data stem mainly from a mismatch between the researcher's unique problem and the purpose for which the secondary data were originally gathered, which are typically different. For example, a major consumer-products manufacturer wanted to determine the market potential for a fireplace log made of coal rather than compressed wood by-products. The researcher found plenty of secondary data about total wood consumed as fuel, quantities consumed in each state, and types of wood burned. Secondary data were also available about consumer attitudes and purchase patterns of wood by-product fireplace logs. The wealth of secondary data provided the researcher with many insights into the artificial log market. Yet nowhere was there any information that would tell the firm whether consumers would buy artificial logs made of coal.

The quality of secondary data may also pose a problem. Often secondary data sources do not give detailed information that would enable a researcher to assess their quality or relevance. Whenever possible, a researcher needs to address these

secondary data
Data previously collected for any purpose other than the one at hand.

important questions: Who gathered the data? Why were the data obtained? What methodology was used? How were classifications (such as heavy users versus light users) developed and defined? When was the information gathered?

The New Age of Secondary Information: The Internet

Gathering secondary data, while necessary in almost any research project, has traditionally been a tedious and boring job. The researcher often had to write to government agencies, trade associations, or other secondary data providers and then wait days or weeks for a reply that might never come. Often, one or more trips to the library were required and the researcher might find that needed reports were checked out or missing. With the rapid development of the Internet and World Wide Web in the last few years, however, much of the drudgery associated with the collection of secondary data has been eliminated.

Finding Secondary Data on the Internet

If you know the address of a particular Web site that contains the secondary data that you are searching for, you can type a description of what you are looking for directly into your Web browser (Netscape Navigator and Microsoft Internet Explorer are the dominant browsers).

Search Engines Sites such as AltaVista, Excite, and Google have become popular with researchers looking for information on the Web. These organizations offer what are called *search engines* that scan the Web looking for sites on a designated topic. Each search engine uses its own indexing system to locate relevant information. All of them allow users to enter one or more keywords that will initiate a search of the databases of Web sites for all occurrences of those words. They then return listings that allow users to go immediately to the sites described.

Remember that the Internet is a self-publishing medium. Your visits to search engines will yield files with a wide range of quality from a variety of sources. Try out multiple sites when you are investigating a topic.

Directories In addition to search engines, you can use subject directories on the Web to explore a subject. There are two basic types of directories: (1) academic and professional directories, often created and maintained by subject experts to support the needs of researchers, and (2) commercial portals, which cater to the general public and are competing for traffic. Directories depend upon people to compile their listings.

- *Academic and professional directories* are created by librarians or subject experts and tend to be associated with libraries and academic institutions. These collections are created to enhance the research process and help users find high-quality sites of interest. A careful selection process is applied, and links to the selected resources are usually annotated. These collections are often created to serve an institution's constituency but may be useful to any researcher. As a rule, these sites do not generate income or carry advertising. INFOMINE, from the University of California, is an example of an academic directory.

- *Commercial portals* are created to generate income and serve the general public. These services link to a wide range of topics and often emphasize entertainment, commerce, hobbies, sports, travel, and other interests not necessarily covered by academic directories. These sites seek to draw traffic in order to support advertising. As a part of this goal, the directory is offered in conjunction with a number of additional customer services. Yahoo! is an example of a commercial portal.

The lines between directories and search engines are blurring. Directories are present at some search engine sites, and sometimes their contents are searched along with content from the general Web. For example, AltaVista offers the LookSmart directory; Infoseek shares the screen with the directory at the Go Network; Excite has its own directory; and Lycos offers the directory contents from the Netscape Open Directory. Directory results are sometimes placed before search results to steer users to the directory's content. This can be a useful way of getting at substantive content relating to your query. Most subject directories offer a search engine mechanism to query the database.

Sites of Interest to Marketing Researchers A number of Web sites are accessed daily by marketing researchers in search of information. These sites offer an incredible variety of information. A list of those used most often is shown in Exhibit 8.2 on pages 254–255.

Periodical, Newspaper, and Book Databases

Several excellent periodical, newspaper, and book databases are available to researchers. Some can be directly accessed via the Internet and others through your local library's Web site. A list of these databases is shown in Exhibit 8.3 on page 256.

Internet Discussion Groups and Special Interest Groups as Sources of Secondary Data

A primary means of communicating with other professionals and special interest groups on the Internet is through newsgroups. With an Internet connection and newsreader software, you can visit any newsgroup supported by your service provider. If your service provider does not offer newsgroups or does not carry the group in which you are interested, you can find one of the publicly available newsgroup servers that does carry the group you would like to read.

Newsgroups function much like bulletin boards for a particular topic or interest. A newsgroup is established to focus on a particular topic. Readers stop by that newsgroup to read messages left by other people, post responses to others' questions, and send rebuttals to comments with which they disagree. Generally, there is some management of the messages to keep discussions within the topic area and to remove offensive material. However, readers of a newsgroup are free to discuss any issue and communicate with anyone in the world that visits that newsgroup. Images and data files can be exchanged in newsgroups, just as they can be exchanged via e-mail.

With over 250,000 newsgroups currently in existence and more being added every day, there is a newsgroup for nearly every hobby, profession, and lifestyle. Newsgroup messages look like e-mail messages. They contain a subject title, author, and a message body. Unlike normal e-mail messages, though, newsgroup messages are threaded discussions. This means that any reply to a previous message will appear linked to that message. Therefore, you can follow a discussion between two or more people by starting at the original message and following the links (or threads) to each successive reply. You can send images, sound files, and video clips attached to your message for anyone to download and examine.

Planning the Research Design and Gathering Primary Data

Good secondary data can help researchers conduct a thorough situation analysis. With that information, researchers can list their unanswered questions and rank them. Researchers must then decide the exact information required to answer the questions. The **research design** specifies which research questions must be answered, how and when the data will be gathered, and how the data will be analyzed. Typically, the project budget is finalized after the research design has been approved.

newsgroups
Function like bulletin boards on the Internet. They are established to focus on a particular topic.

research design
Specifies which research questions must be answered, how and when the data will be gathered, and how the data will be analyzed.

Organization	URL	Description
American Demographics/ Marketing Tools	http://www.marketingtools.com	Searches the full text of all of *American Demographics* and *Marketing Tools.*
American Marketing Association	http://www.ama.org	Searches all of the AMA's publications by using keywords.
BLS Consumer Expenditure Surveys	http://stats.bls.gov/esxprod.htm	Provides information on the buying habits of consumers, including data on their expenditures, income, and consumer credit.
Bureau of Economic Analysis	http://.bea.gov	Provides a wide range of economic statistics.
Bureau of Transportation Statistics	http://www.bts.gov	Comprehensive source for a wide range of statistics on transportation.
Centers for Disease Control and Prevention	http://www.cdc.gov/nchs	As the federal government's principal vital and health statistical agency, the National Center for Health Statistics has a lot to offer. The NCHS, a subdivision of the Centers for Disease Control and Prevention, maintains data on vital events, health status, lifestyle and exposure to unhealthy influences, the onset and diagnosis of illness and disability, and the use of health care.
Cyberatlas	http://www.cyberatlas.com	Viewers can browse the latest research compiled from several reputable firms, including Media Metrix, Greenfield Online, Intelliquest, and Inteco. The geography page fills you in on surveys about on-line populations around the world. There's also a generous section on e-commerce that breaks out research in different markets, like advertising, finance, and retail. Peek into the stats toolbox for a mother lode of lists on everything from weekly usage data to the top-ten banner ads.
The Dismal Scientist	http://www.dismal.com	An authoritative site offering timely economic information, with comprehensive data and analysis at the metro, state, and national levels. There's also data and analyses of global issues, including situations facing Asia, South America, and Europe. Visitors can rank states and metro areas on more than 100 economic, socioeconomic, and demographic categories.
Easy Analytic Software	http://www.easidemographics.com	Easy Analytic Software, a New York City-based developer and marketer of demographic data, offers demographic site reports, or three-ring studies, including current estimates for population and households. Each three-ring study offers census estimates for race, ethnicity, age distribution, income distribution, and weather data. The site also offers one million pages of demographic reports for all zip codes, counties, metropolitan areas, cities, sectional centers, television markets, states, and other geographies.
EconData	http://www.econdata.net	A premier site for researchers interested in economics and demographics. There is a tremendous number of links to government, private, and academic data sources. Check out the top-ten data sources list.
Economic Research Service, Department of Agriculture	http://www.ers.usda.gov	Provides a wide range of agricultural statistics.
Encyclopedia Britannica	http://www.britannica.com	Entire 32-volume encyclopedia is available free on-line.

Organization	URL	Description
Equifax National Decision Systems	http://www.equifax.com/biz/index.shtml	Provides access to a wide range of secondary data on many topics. Most must be purchased.
ESRI	http://www.esribis.com	On ESRI Business Information Solutions' site, users can type in their zip codes to get a snapshot of the dominant profile type in their town. Population figures are available for the zips, as are percentages for race and gender. Median household income, average home values, and average rent are also presented.
Find/SVP	http://www.findsvp.com	Offers consulting and research services. Claims to offer access to the largest private information center in the United States.
Harris Info Service	http://www.harrisinfo.com	Offers business-to-business data on American manufacturers and key decision makers.
Marketing Research Association	http://www.MRA-net.org	Analyzes causes and solutions of "declining respondent cooperation"; links to research suppliers.
Mediamark Research	http://www.mediamark.com/mri/docs/toplinereports.html	Marketers and researchers looking for demographic data on magazines, cable TV, or 53 different product or service categories can find it at Top-Line Reports site. Top-Line Reports breaks down cable TV networks according to viewers' age, gender, median age, and income. Magazines are listed by total audience, circulation, readers per copy, median age, and income.
Nielsen Media Research	http://www.nielsen-netratings.com	Course on Internet audience information. Researchers can find data and Internet growth and user patterns.
Office of Research & Statistics, SSA	http://www.ssa.gov/statistics/fast_facts/2002/index.html	Provides a range of government statistics.
Pcensus for Windows	http://www.tetrad.com	Provides detailed information about the population of metropolitan areas.
Population Reference Bureau	http://www.prb.org/prb	Source of demographic information on population issues.
Service Intelligence	http://www.serviceintelligence.com	The site has an area devoted to customer stories of unpleasant experiences with airlines, banks, restaurants, and other service businesses. It's not all bad news, though—"hero" stories are also included.
Strategic Mapping	http://www.stratmap.org	Offers an extensive selection of geographic files, includes detailed geography for the entire United States.
U.S. Census Bureau	http://www.census.gov	Very useful source of virtually all census data.
U.S. Demography	http://www.ciesin.org	Excellent source of U.S. demographic information.
USA Data	http://www.usadata.com	Provides access to consumer lifestyle data on a local, regional, or national basis.
World Opinion	http://www.worldopinion.com	Perhaps the premier site for the marketing research industry; thousands of marketing research reports available.

Exhibit 8.3

Full-Text Periodical, Newspaper, and Book Databases Used by Marketing Researchers

Source	Description
ABI/Inform Global	Updated monthly; provides bibliographic information and abstracts for approximately 1,000 journals in business and management. Includes full-text entries for approximately 520 journals. Among the major marketing journals now included in full-text format are *Journal of Marketing; JMR: Journal of Marketing Research;* and *Journal of the Academy of Marketing Science.*
Dow Jones Interactive	Includes full-text news and articles from over 3,400 sources including newspapers from around the world, as well as information on companies, industries, stocks, bonds, mutual funds, and foreign exchange rates; updated daily.
Electric Library	Contains over 5 million full-text documents in all subject areas. Content is updated daily and includes an archive of up to twelve years. Covers six separate media types: newspapers and news wires, periodicals, TV and radio program transcripts, literature and reference books, photos, and maps.
Lexis-Nexis	The Lexis-Nexis database contains 2.5 billion searchable documents. Each week, 14.7 million new documents are added. It includes 18,871 news and business sources. Lexis-Nexis is the largest business information service. It offers access to thousands of worldwide newspapers, magazines, trade journals, industry newsletters, tax and accounting information, financial data, public records, legislative data, and company information.
Periodical Abstracts Research II (PAR)	Covers current affairs, business, industry news, cultural events, editorial material, and general interest topics from more than 1,800 general and academic periodicals. Includes full-text articles from more than 600 journals. Full-text coverage began in 1992; updated monthly. Marketing journals are not heavily indexed in this database, but those that are available full-text include *Direct Marketing; Journal of Consumer Affairs;* and *Sales & Marketing Management.*

primary data
Information collected for the first time. Can be used for solving the particular problem under investigation.

Sometimes research questions can be answered by gathering more secondary data; otherwise, primary data may be needed. **Primary data**, or information collected for the first time, can be used for solving the particular problem under investigation. The main advantage of primary data is that they will answer a specific research question that secondary data cannot answer. For example, suppose Pillsbury has two new recipes for refrigerated dough for sugar cookies. Which one will consumers like better? Secondary data will not help answer this question. Instead, targeted consumers must try each recipe and evaluate the tastes, textures, and appearances of each cookie. Moreover, primary data are current and researchers know the source. Sometimes researchers gather the data themselves rather than assign projects to outside companies. Researchers also specify the methodology of the research. Secrecy can be maintained because the information is proprietary. In contrast, secondary data are available to all interested parties for relatively small fees.

Gathering primary data is expensive; costs can range from a few thousand dollars for a limited survey to several million for a nationwide study. For instance, a nationwide, fifteen-minute telephone interview with one thousand adult males can cost $50,000 for everything, including a data analysis and report. Because primary data gathering is so expensive, firms commonly cut back on the number of interviews to save money. Larger companies that conduct many research projects use another cost-saving technique. They piggyback studies, or gather data on two different projects using one questionnaire. The drawback is that answering questions about, say, dog food and gourmet coffee may be confusing to respondents. Piggybacking also requires a longer interview (sometimes a half hour or longer), which

Do convenience polls qualify as bona fide survey research? The woman pictured here is casting a poll vote in a survey asking Australians whether they should cut constitutional ties with Britain (Country) or retain Queen Elizabeth as Australia's constitutional monarch (Queen).

tires respondents. The quality of the answers typically declines, with people giving curt replies and thinking, "When will this end!" A lengthy interview also makes people less likely to participate in other research surveys.[6]

Nevertheless, the disadvantages of primary data gathering are usually offset by the advantages. It is often the only way of solving a research problem. And with a variety of techniques available for research—including surveys, observations, and experiments—primary research can address almost any marketing question.

Survey Research

The most popular technique for gathering primary data is **survey research**, in which a researcher interacts with people to obtain facts, opinions, and attitudes. Exhibit 8.4 summarizes the characteristics of traditional forms of research.

In-Home Personal Interviews Although in-home personal interviews often provide high-quality information, they tend to be very expensive because of the interviewers' travel time and mileage costs. Therefore, they are rapidly disappearing from the marketing researcher's survey toolbox.

survey research
The most popular technique for gathering primary data in which a researcher interacts with people to obtain facts, opinions, and attitudes.

Characteristics of Traditional Forms of Survey Research   **Exhibit 8.4**

Characteristic	In-Home Personal Interviews	Mall Intercept Interviews	Central-Location Telephone Interviews	Self-Administered and One-Time Mail Surveys	Mail Panel Surveys	Executive Interviews	Focus Groups
Cost	High	Moderate	Moderate	Low	Moderate	High	Low
Time span	Moderate	Moderate	Fast	Slow	Relatively slow	Moderate	Fast
Use of interviewer probes	Yes	Yes	Yes	No	Yes	Yes	Yes
Ability to show concepts to respondent	Yes (also taste tests)	Yes (also taste tests)	No	Yes	Yes	Yes	Yes
Management control over interviewer	Low	Moderate	High	n/a	n/a	Moderate	High
General data quality	High	Moderate	High to moderate	Moderate to low	Moderate	High	Moderate
Ability to collect large amounts of data	High	Moderate	Moderate to low	Low to moderate	Moderate	Moderate	Moderate
Ability to handle complex questionnaires	High	Moderate	High if computer-aided	Low	Low	High	Low

Mall Intercept Interviews The **mall intercept interview** is conducted in the common areas of shopping malls or in a market research office within the mall. It is the economy version of the door-to-door interview with personal contact between interviewer and respondent, minus the interviewer's travel time and mileage costs. To conduct this type of interview, the research firm rents office space in the mall or pays a significant daily fee. One drawback is that it is hard to get a representative sample of the population.

However, an interviewer can also probe when necessary—a technique used to clarify a person's response. For example, an interviewer might ask, "What did you like best about the salad dressing you just tried?" The respondent might reply, "Taste." This answer doesn't provide a lot of information, so the interviewer could probe by saying, "Can you tell me a little bit more about taste?" The respondent then elaborates: "Yes, it's not too sweet, it has the right amount of pepper, and I love that hint of garlic."

Mall intercept interviews must be brief. Only the shortest ones are conducted while respondents are standing. Usually, researchers invite respondents to their office for interviews, which are still rarely over fifteen minutes long. The researchers often show respondents concepts for new products or a test commercial or have them taste a new food product. The overall quality of mall intercept interviews is about the same as telephone interviews.

Marketing researchers are applying computer technology in mall interviewing. The first technique is **computer-assisted personal interviewing**. The researcher conducts in-person interviews, reads questions to the respondent off a computer screen, and directly keys the respondent's answers into the computer. A second approach is **computer-assisted self-interviewing**. A mall interviewer intercepts and directs willing respondents to nearby computers. Each respondent reads questions off a computer screen and directly keys his or her answers into a computer. The third use of technology is fully automated self-interviewing. Respondents are guided by interviewers or independently approach a centrally located computer station or kiosk, read questions off a screen, and directly key their answers into the station's computer.

computer-assisted personal interviewing
An interviewing method in which the interviewer reads the questions from a computer screen and enters the respondent's data directly into the computer.

computer-assisted self-interviewing
An interviewing method in which a mall interviewer intercepts and directs willing respondents to nearby computers where the respondent reads questions off a computer screen and directly keys his or her answers into a computer.

central-location telephone (CLT) facility
A specially designed phone room used to conduct telephone interviewing.

Telephone Interviews Compared to the personal interview, the telephone interview costs less and may provide the best sample of any traditional survey procedure. Most telephone interviewing is conducted from a specially designed phone room called a **central-location telephone (CLT) facility**. A phone room has many phone lines, individual interviewing stations, sometimes monitoring equipment, and headsets. The research firm typically will interview people nationwide from a single location.

Many CLT facilities offer computer-assisted interviewing. The interviewer reads the questions from a computer screen and enters the respondent's data directly into the computer. The researcher can stop the survey at any point and immediately print out the survey results. Thus, a researcher can get a sense of the project as it unfolds and fine-tune the research design as necessary. An on-line interviewing system can also save time and money because data entry occurs as the response is recorded rather than as a separate process after the interview. Hallmark Cards found that an interviewer administered a printed questionnaire for its Shoebox Greeting cards in twenty-eight minutes. The same questionnaire administered with computer assistance took only eighteen minutes.

Mail Surveys Mail surveys have several benefits: relatively low cost, elimination of interviewers and field supervisors, centralized control, and actual or promised anonymity for respondents (which may draw more candid responses). Some researchers feel that mail questionnaires give the respondent a chance to reply more thoughtfully and to check records, talk to family members, and so forth. A disadvantage is that mail questionnaires usually produce low response rates.

Low response rates pose a problem because certain elements of the population tend to respond more than others. The resulting sample may therefore not represent the surveyed population. For example, the sample may have too many retired people and too few working people. In this instance, answers to a question about attitudes toward Social Security might indicate a much more favorable overall view of the system than is actually the case. Another serious problem with mail surveys is that no one probes respondents to clarify or elaborate on their answers.

Mail panels like those operated by Market Facts, National Family Opinion Research, and NPD Research offer an alternative to the one-shot mail survey. A mail panel consists of a sample of households recruited to participate by mail for a given period. Panel members often receive gifts in return for their participation. Essentially, the panel is a sample used several times. In contrast to one-time mail surveys, the response rates from mail panels are high. Rates of 70 percent (of those who agree to participate) are not uncommon.

Executive Interviews Marketing researchers use **executive interviews** to conduct the industrial equivalent of door-to-door interviewing. This type of survey involves interviewing businesspeople, at their offices, concerning industrial products or services. For example, if Dell wanted information regarding user preferences for different features that might be offered in a new line of computer printers, it would need to interview prospective user-purchasers of the printers. It is appropriate to locate and interview these people at their offices.

executive interviews
A type of survey that involves interviewing businesspeople at their offices concerning industrial products or services.

This type of interviewing is very expensive. First, individuals involved in the purchase decision for the product in question must be identified and located. Sometimes lists can be obtained from various sources, but more frequently screening must be conducted over the telephone. A particular company is likely to have individuals of the type being sought, but locating those people within a large organization can be expensive and time-consuming. Once a qualified person is located, the next step is to get that person to agree to be interviewed and to set a time for the interview. This is not as hard as it might seem because most professionals seem to enjoy talking about topics related to their work.

Finally, an interviewer must go to the particular place at the appointed time. Long waits are frequently encountered; cancellations are not uncommon. This type of survey requires the very best interviewers because they are frequently interviewing on topics that they know very little about. Executive interviewing has essentially the same advantages and disadvantages as in-home interviewing.

Focus Groups A **focus group** is a type of personal interviewing. Often recruited by random telephone screening, seven to ten people with certain desired characteristics form a focus group. These qualified consumers are usually offered an incentive (typically $30 to $50) to participate in a group discussion. The meeting place (sometimes resembling a living room, sometimes featuring a conference table) has audiotaping and perhaps videotaping equipment. It also likely has a viewing room with a one-way mirror so that clients (manufacturers or retailers) may watch the session. During the session, a moderator, hired by the research company, leads the group discussion.

focus group
Seven to ten people who participate in a group discussion led by a moderator.

Focus groups are much more than question-and-answer interviews. Market researchers draw a distinction between "group dynamics" and "group interviewing." The interaction provided in **group dynamics** is essential to the success of focus-group research; this interaction is the reason for conducting group rather than individual research. One of the essential postulates of group-session usage is the idea that a response from one person may become a stimulus for another, thereby generating an interplay of responses that may yield more information than if the same number of people had contributed independently.

group dynamics
Group interaction essential to the success of focus-group research.

Because of the group dynamics of focus groups, researchers can uncover more information than in a single interview. Here people are tasting cookies while a food scientist takes notes. Later they will conduct a focus group regarding the cookies.

© DANA WHITE/PHOTOEDIT

Focus groups are occasionally used to brainstorm new product ideas or to screen concepts for new products. Ford Motor Company, for example, asked consumers to drive several automobile prototypes. These "test drivers" were then brought together in focus groups. During the discussions, consumers complained that they were scuffing their shoes because the rear seats lacked foot room. In response, Ford sloped the floor underneath the front seats, widened the space between the seat adjustment tracks, and made the tracks in the Taurus and Sable models out of smooth plastic instead of metal.

A new system by Focus Vision Network allows client companies and advertising agencies to view live focus groups in Chicago, Dallas, Boston, and fifteen other major cities. For example, the private satellite network lets a General Motors researcher observing a San Diego focus group control two cameras in the viewing room. The researcher can get a full-group view or a close-up, zoom, or pan the participants. The researcher can also communicate directly with the moderator using an ear receiver. Ogilvy & Mather (a large New York advertising agency whose clients include StarKist Sea Foods, Seagram's, MasterCard, and Burger King) has installed the system.

 The newest development in qualitative research is the on-line or cyber focus group. A number of organizations are currently offering this new means of conducting focus groups. The process is fairly simple.

- The research firm builds a database of respondents via a screening questionnaire on its Web site.

- When a client comes to a firm with a need for a particular focus group, the firm goes to its database and identifies individuals who appear to qualify. It sends an e-mail message to these individuals, asking them to log on to a particular site at a particular time scheduled for the group. The firm pays them an incentive for their participation.

- The firm develops a discussion guide similar to the one used for a conventional focus group.

- A moderator runs the group by typing in questions on-line for all to see. The group operates in an environment similar to that of a chat room so that all participants see all questions and all responses.

- The firm captures the complete text of the focus group and makes it available for review after the group has finished.

Many advantages are claimed for cyber groups. Cyber Dialogue, a marketing research company specializing in cyber groups, lists the following benefits of on-line focus groups on its Web site:

- *Speed:* Typically, focus groups can be recruited and conducted, with delivery of results, within five days of client approval.

- *Cost effectiveness:* Off-line focus groups incur costs for facility rental, air fare, hotel, and food. None of these costs is incurred with on-line focus groups.

- *Broad geographic scope:* In a given focus group, you can speak to people in Boise, Idaho, and Miami, Florida, at the same time.

- *Accessibility:* On-line focus groups give you access to individuals who otherwise might be difficult to recruit (e.g., business travelers, doctors, mothers with infants).

- *Honesty:* From behind their screen names, respondents are anonymous to other respondents and tend to talk more freely about issues that might create inhibitions in a face-to-face group.

Cyber Dialogue charges $3,000 for its focus groups. This compares very favorably to a cost in the range of $7,000 without travel costs for conventional focus groups. Unfortunately, no systematic evaluation comparing on-line focus groups and conventional focus groups has been done at this time.

Open-Ended Questions	Closed-Ended Questions	Scaled-Response Question
1. What advantages, if any, do you think ordering from a mail-order catalog offers compared to shopping at a local retail outlet? (*Probe:* What else?)	**Dichotomous** 1. Did you heat the Danish product before serving it? Yes . . . . .1 No 2	Now that you have used the rug cleaner, would you say that you . . . *(Circle one.)* Would definitely buy it . . . . .1 Would probably buy it . . . . .2 Might or might not buy it . . . . .3 Probably would not buy it . . . . .4 Definitely would not buy it 5
2. Why do you have one or more of your rugs or carpets professionally cleaned rather than having you or someone else in the household clean them?	2. The federal government doesn't care what people like me think. Agree . . . . .1 Disagree 2	
3. What is there about the color of the eye shadow that makes you like it the best?	**Multiple choice** 1. I'd like you to think back to the last footwear of any kind that you bought. I'll read you a list of descriptions and would like for you to tell me which category they fall into. *(Read list and circle proper category.)* Dress and/or formal . . . . .1 Casual . . . . .2 Canvas/trainer/gym shoes . . . . .3 Specialized athletic shoes . . . . .4 Boots 5	
	2. In the last three months, have you used Noxzema skin cream . . . (Circle all that apply.) As a facial wash .1 For moisturizing the skin . . . . .2 For treating blemishes . . . . .3 For cleansing the skin . . . . .4 For treating dry skin . . . . .5 For softening skin . . . . .6 For sunburn . . . . .7 For making the facial skin smooth 8	

Questionnaire Design

All forms of survey research require a questionnaire. Questionnaires ensure that all respondents will be asked the same series of questions. Questionnaires include three basic types of questions: open-ended, closed-ended, and scaled-response (see Exhibit 8.5). An **open-ended question** encourages an answer phrased in the respondent's own words. Researchers get a rich array of information based on the respondent's frame of reference. In contrast, a **closed-ended question** asks the respondent to make a selection from a limited list of responses. Traditionally, marketing researchers separate the two-choice question (called *dichotomous*) from the many-item type (often called *multiple choice*). A **scaled-response question** is a closed-ended question designed to measure the intensity of a respondent's answer.

Closed-ended and scaled-response questions are easier to tabulate than open-ended questions because response choices are fixed. On the other hand, unless the researcher designs the closed-ended question very carefully, an important choice may be omitted.

For example, suppose a food study asked this question: "Besides meat, which of the following items do you normally add to a taco that you prepare at home?"

open-ended question
An interview question that encourages an answer phrased in the respondent's own words.

closed-ended question
An interview question that asks the respondent to make a selection from a limited list of responses.

scaled-response question
A closed-ended question designed to measure the intensity of a respondent's answer.

Avocado	1	Olives (black/green)	6
Cheese (Monterey Jack/cheddar)	2	Onions (red/white)	7
Guacamole	3	Peppers (red/green)	8
Lettuce	4	Pimento	9
Mexican hot sauce	5	Sour cream	0

The list seems complete, doesn't it? However, consider the following responses: "I usually add a green, avocado-tasting hot sauce"; "I cut up a mixture of lettuce and spinach"; "I'm a vegetarian; I don't use meat at all. My taco is filled only with guacamole." How would you code these replies? As you can see, the question needs an "other" category.

A good question must also be clear and concise, and ambiguous language must be avoided. Take, for example, the question "Do you live within ten minutes of here?" The answer depends on the mode of transportation (maybe the person walks), driving speed, perceived time, and other factors. Instead, respondents should see a map with certain areas highlighted and be asked whether they live in one of those areas.

Designing and interpreting scaled-response questions can be particularly difficult in global marketing research. A researcher must fully understand cultural differences, as the "Global Perspectives" box explains.

Clarity also implies using reasonable terminology. A questionnaire is not a vocabulary test. Jargon should be avoided, and language should be geared to the target audience. A question such as "What is the level of efficacy of your preponderant dishwasher powder?" would probably be greeted by a lot of blank stares. It would be much simpler to say "Are you (1) very satisfied, (2) somewhat satisfied, or (3) not satisfied with your current brand of dishwasher powder?"

Stating the survey's purpose at the beginning of the interview also improves clarity. The respondents should understand the study's intentions and the inter-

GLOBAL PERSPECTIVES

Culture Complicates Global Marketing Research

Except in very unusual circumstances, customer interviews should always be conducted in the local language by local interviewers. That would include even those interviews conducted with respondents who speak English well. Few people are as at ease or articulate in a second or third language as they are in their own mother tongue. By forcing respondents to speak a foreign language, you are, from the outset, limiting their ability to express their opinions and needs clearly and articulately.

Even something as straightforward as a scaled-response question should be given careful thought. It is best to utilize rating scales that make the most sense to the given population. For example, Americans may be very comfortable giving performance ratings using an A–F "school grade" system. That scale, however, is meaningless to Germans, who are more familiar with a 1–6 rating scale, with 1 indicating the best performance and 6 indicating the worst performance. And of course the Japanese wouldn't understand our letter grades at all—they generally use a 100-point scale for these purposes. You may even find that different populations use the same rating scales differently. For example, Germans may consistently give lower grades than Italians, while Italians may consistently rate every attribute as more important than Spaniards. These differences need to be factored in during the analysis phase.

Cultural differences can also surface with an issue like participation incentives. The first question is, "Are cash incentives appropriate in this market?" In Japan, for example, incentives for businesspeople often take the form of a gift, rather than cash. Sometimes it is better to offer gift certificates to major department stores as incentives. Charitable donations might also be an option.[7]

Americans, Australians, and the English all speak a common language. Therefore, cultural considerations are not important when designing and interpreting a marketing research study. Do you agree or disagree? Why? Door-to-door interviewing is almost nonexistent anymore in the United States. Do you think this is a worldwide trend? Why or why not? If a person in the United States and another person in Beijing, responding to the same questionnaire (the only difference being that one is in English and one is in Mandarin), both give something a "6" rating, do their responses really mean the same thing? Isn't a "6" always a "6" on a scale of 1–7?

viewer's expectations. Sometimes, of course, to get an unbiased response, the interviewer must disguise the true purpose of the study. If an interviewer says, "We're conducting an image study for American National Bank" and then proceeds to ask a series of questions about the bank, chances are the responses will be biased. Many times respondents will try to provide answers that they believe are "correct" or that the interviewer wants to hear.

Finally, to ensure clarity, the interviewer should avoid asking two questions in one; for example, "How did you like the taste and texture of the Pepperidge Farm coffee cake?" This should be divided into two questions, one concerning taste and the other texture.

A question should also be unbiased. A question such as "Have you purchased any quality Black & Decker tools in the past six months?" biases respondents to think of the topic in a certain way (in this case, to link quality and Black & Decker tools). Questions can also be leading: "Weren't you pleased with the good service you received last night at the Holiday Inn?" (The respondent is all but instructed to say yes.) These examples are quite obvious; unfortunately, bias is usually more subtle. Even an interviewer's clothing or gestures can create bias.

Often getting people to answer a questionnaire is not easy. One innovative approach that ties research to gaming is thriving on the Internet. The "Ethics in Marketing" box discusses this new approach to data gathering.

Observation Research

In contrast to survey research, **observation research** depends on watching what people do. Specifically, it can be defined as the systematic process of recording the behavioral patterns of people, objects, and occurrences without questioning or communicating with them. A market researcher using the observation technique witnesses and records information as events occur or compiles evidence from records of past events. Carried a step further, observation may involve watching people or phenomena and may be conducted by human observers or machines. Examples of these various observational situations are shown in Exhibit 8.6 on page 264.

Two common forms of people-watching-people research are mystery shoppers and one-way mirror observations. **Mystery shoppers** are researchers posing as customers who gather observational data about a store (i.e., are the shelves neatly stocked?) and collect data about customer/employee interactions. In the latter case, of course, there is communication between the mystery shopper and the employee. The mystery shopper may ask, "How much is this item?" "Do you have this in blue?" or "Can you deliver this by Friday?" The interaction is not an interview, and communication occurs only so that the mystery shopper can observe the actions and comments of the employee. Mystery shopping is, therefore, classified as an observational marketing research method even though communication is often involved. Conducted on a continuous basis, mystery shopping can motivate and recognize service performance. Used as a benchmark, mystery shopping can pinpoint strengths and weaknesses for training operations and policy refinements.

observation research
A research method that relies on three types of observation: people watching people, people watching an activity, and machines watching people.

mystery shoppers
Researchers posing as customers who gather observational data about a store.

Find the Monkey and You Get to Fill Out a Questionnaire

Not all Internet sites have fallen on hard times. Sites like FreeLotto.com, Flipside.com, and TreeLoot.com are continuing to grow at a rapid pace. By offering free gifts, prizes, coupons, or big cash winnings, gaming and sweepstakes sites are able to sign up game players and get them to divulge their names, addresses, and, in some cases, hobbies, interests, and buying patterns. The sites then use the information to sell advertisers targeted e-mail lists or space in a daily e-mail message to players.

That is gold to advertisers who want to get better results by targeting their ads to specific users. Ford Motor Company, for example, could put ads in e-mails sent to users who indicated they might buy a car in the next twelve months. Or a credit card company could offer a new card with a bigger limit to someone who plans to buy a computer.

"It's market research disguised as a game," says analyst Jim Magahad of PC Data Corporation, a research firm in Reston, Virginia. "And the information they are getting is very valuable."

To lure players to those games, sites have come up with some pretty catchy campaigns. One of the most memorable approaches is TreeLoot's "Punch the Monkey" banner ad that has run for almost the past two years. The ad invites Web surfers to try to knock out a monkey zooming across a banner at the top of their screen. If you can click on the elusive monkey, you win $20 in credits that can be exchanged for discounts at Web retailers or other prizes—and you get linked to TreeLoot's Web site, where you can play the site's money-tree game to win more credits.

FreeLotto runs a daily lotto drawing that has $11 million in cash prizes available to be won each day. Players must provide a valid e-mail and postal address and the name that will be on the check if they win. While choosing lottery numbers, users answer questions about interests in travel or any plans to buy a computer, car, or house. Plus, to submit their lotto numbers for the daily drawing, the players must click on one of several featured ads.

"It's direct mail without the postage, and the consumer does your daily entry—what could be better?" asks FreeLotto's chief executive Kevin Aronin.

Further, Jim Magahad of PC Data says the proliferation of Internet use among a broader population has helped boost the use of these sites. Gaming sites were the fastest-growing segment of the Internet last year, according to PC Data, and that is largely due to the willingness of people to give out information about themselves for the chance to win big.

"Now you have Middle America on-line—it's not just the affluent—and Middle America loves lotto," says Magahad.

Privacy concerns have largely been a moot point for the companies. Most promise not to disclose information without the players' consent, but the players, who volunteer the information, generally agree to let it be used.[8]

Are FreeLotto and TreeLoot really conducting marketing research? Is it ethical to require game participants to answer questions about purchase plans as a requirement to continue in the game? Is it ethical for a marketing research company to sell names, addresses, and question responses to companies? What if the respondent consents? Do you see any privacy issues here?

Exhibit 8.6

Observational Situations

Situation	Example
People watching people	Observers stationed in supermarkets watch consumers select frozen Mexican dinners; the purpose is to see how much comparison shopping people do at the point of purchase.
People watching phenomena	Observer stationed at an intersection counts traffic moving in various directions.
Machines watching people	Movie or videotape cameras record behavior as in the people-watching-people example above.
Machines watching phenomena	Traffic-counting machines monitor traffic flow.

One interesting observation situation is toy-testing day camp. Pictured here, Fama Ana tries on a pair of "spy glasses" at Durcell Toy Testing Camp. In one week, over one thousand children in fifteen U.S. cities test twenty-five different toys while marketers look on.

© MICHAEL GREENLAR/THE IMAGE WORKS

At the Fisher-Price Play Laboratory, children are invited to spend twelve sessions playing with toys. Toy designers watch through one-way mirrors to see how children react to Fisher-Price's and other makers' toys. Fisher-Price, for example, had difficulty designing a toy lawn mower that children would play with. A designer, observing behind the mirror, noticed the children's fascination with soap bubbles. He then created a lawn mower that spewed soap bubbles. It sold over a million units in the first year.

Experiments

An **experiment** is a method a researcher can use to gather primary data. The researcher alters one or more variables—price, package design, shelf space, advertising theme, advertising expenditures—while observing the effects of those alterations on another variable (usually sales). The best experiments are those in which all factors are held constant except the ones being manipulated. The researcher can then observe that changes in sales, for example, result from changes in the amount of money spent on advertising.

Holding all other factors constant in the external environment is a monumental and costly, if not impossible, task. Such factors as competitors' actions, weather, and economic conditions are beyond the researcher's control. Yet market researchers have ways to account for the ever-changing external environment. Mars, the candy company, was losing sales to other candy companies. Traditional surveys showed that the shrinking candy bar was not perceived as a good value. Mars wondered whether a bigger bar sold at the same price would increase sales enough to offset the higher ingredient costs. The company designed an experiment in which the marketing mix stayed the same in different markets but the size of the candy bar varied. The substantial increase in sales of the bigger bar quickly proved that the additional costs would be more than covered by the additional revenue. Mars increased the bar size—and its market share and profits.

experiment
A method a researcher uses to gather primary data.

Specifying the Sampling Procedures

Once the researchers decide how they will collect primary data, their next step is to select the sampling procedures they will use. A firm can seldom take a census of all possible users of a new product, nor can they all be interviewed. Therefore, a firm must select a sample of the group to be interviewed. A **sample** is a subset from a larger population.

Several questions must be answered before a sampling plan is chosen. First, the population, or **universe**, of interest must be defined. This is the group from which the sample will be drawn. It should include all the people whose opinions, behavior, preferences, attitudes, and so on are of interest to the marketer. For example, in a study whose purpose is to determine the market for a new canned dog food, the universe might be defined to include all current buyers of canned dog food.

After the universe has been defined, the next question is whether the sample must be representative of the population. If the answer is yes, a probability sample is needed. Otherwise, a nonprobability sample might be considered.

sample
A subset from a large population.

universe
The population from which a sample will be drawn.

Probability Samples

A **probability sample** is a sample in which every element in the population has a known statistical likelihood of being selected. Its most desirable feature is that scientific rules can be used to ensure that the sample represents the population.

probability sample
A sample in which every element in the population has a known statistical likelihood of being selected.

random sample
A sample arranged in such a way that every element of the population has an equal chance of being selected as part of the sample.

nonprobability sample
Any sample in which little or no attempt is made to get a representative cross section of the population.

convenience sample
A form of nonprobability sample using respondents who are convenient or readily accessible to the researcher—for example, employees, friends, or relatives.

One type of probability sample is a **random sample**—a sample arranged in such a way that every element of the population has an equal chance of being selected as part of the sample. For example, suppose a university is interested in getting a cross section of student opinions on a proposed sports complex to be built using student activity fees. If the university can acquire an up-to-date list of all the enrolled students, it can draw a random sample by using random numbers from a table (found in most statistics books) to select students from the list. Common forms of probability and nonprobability samples are shown in Exhibit 8.7.

Nonprobability Samples

Any sample in which little or no attempt is made to get a representative cross section of the population can be considered a **nonprobability sample**. A common form of a nonprobability sample is the **convenience sample**, which uses respondents who are convenient or readily accessible to the researcher—for instance, employees, friends, or relatives.

Exhibit 8.7

Types of Samples

Probability Samples	
Simple Random Sample	Every member of the population has a known and equal chance of selection.
Stratified Sample	Population is divided into mutually exclusive groups (such as gender or age); then random samples are drawn from each group.
Cluster Sample	Population is divided into mutually exclusive groups (such as geographic areas); then a random sample of clusters is selected. The researcher then collects data from all the elements in the selected clusters or from a probability sample of elements within each selected cluster.
Systematic Sample	A list of the population is obtained—i.e., all persons with a checking account at XYZ Bank—and a *skip interval* is obtained by dividing the sample size by the population size. If the sample size is 100 and the bank has 1,000 customers, then the skip interval is 10. The beginning number is randomly chosen within the skip interval. If the beginning number is 8, then the skip pattern would be 8,18, 28, ...
Nonprobability Samples	
Convenience Sample	The researcher selects the easiest population members from which to obtain information.
Judgment Sample	The researcher's selection criteria are based on personal judgment that the elements (persons) chosen will likely give accurate information.
Quota Sample	The researcher finds a prescribed number of people in several categories—i.e., owners of large dogs versus owners of small dogs. Respondents are not selected on probability sampling criteria.
Snowball Sample	Additional respondents are selected on the basis of referrals from the initial respondents. This method is used when a desired type of respondent is hard to find—i.e., persons who have taken round-the-world cruises in the last three years. This technique employs the old adage "Birds of a feather flock together."

Nonprobability samples are acceptable as long as the researcher understands their nonrepresentative nature. Because of their lower cost, nonprobability samples are the basis of much marketing research.

Types of Errors

Whenever a sample is used in marketing research, two major types of error may occur: measurement error and sampling error. **Measurement error** occurs when there is a difference between the information desired by the researcher and the information provided by the measurement process. For example, people may tell an interviewer that they purchase Coors beer when they do not. Measurement error generally tends to be larger than sampling error.

Sampling error occurs when a sample somehow does not represent the target population. Sampling error can be one of several types. Nonresponse error occurs when the sample actually interviewed differs from the sample drawn. This error happens because the original people selected to be interviewed either refused to cooperate or were inaccessible. For example, people who feel embarrassed about their drinking habits may refuse to talk about them.

Frame error, another type of sampling error, arises if the sample drawn from a population differs from the target population. For instance, suppose a telephone survey is conducted to find out Chicago beer drinkers' attitudes toward Coors. If a Chicago telephone directory is used as the *frame* (the device or list from which the respondents are selected), the survey will contain a frame error. Not all Chicago beer drinkers have a phone, and many phone numbers are unlisted. An ideal sample (for example, a sample with no frame error) matches all important characteristics of the target population to be surveyed. Could you find a perfect frame for Chicago beer drinkers?

Random error occurs when the selected sample is an imperfect representation of the overall population. Random error represents how accurately the chosen sample's true average (mean) value reflects the population's true average (mean) value. For example, we might take a random sample of beer drinkers in Chicago and find that 16 percent regularly drink Coors beer. The next day we might repeat the same sampling procedure and discover that 14 percent regularly drink Coors beer. The difference is due to random error.

measurement error
An error that occurs when there is a difference between the information desired by the researcher and the information provided by the measurement process.

sampling error
An error that occurs when a sample somehow does not represent the target population.

frame error
An error that occurs when a sample drawn from a population differs from the target population.

random error
An error that occurs when the selected sample is an imperfect representation of the overall population.

Collecting the Data

Marketing research field service firms collect most primary data. A **field service firm** specializes in interviewing respondents on a subcontracted basis. Many have offices throughout the country. A typical marketing research study involves data collection in several cities, requiring the marketer to work with a comparable number of field service firms. To ensure uniformity among all subcontractors, detailed field instructions should be developed for every job. Nothing should be open to chance; no interpretations of procedures should be left to subcontractors.

Besides conducting interviews, field service firms provide focus-group facilities, mall intercept locations, test product storage, and kitchen facilities to prepare test food products. They also conduct retail audits (counting the amount of a product sold off retail shelves).

field service firm
A firm that specializes in interviewing respondents on a subcontracted basis.

Analyzing the Data

After collecting the data, the marketing researcher proceeds to the next step in the research process: data analysis. The purpose of this analysis is to interpret and draw conclusions from the mass of collected data. The marketing researcher tries to organize and analyze those data by using one or more techniques common to marketing research: one-way frequency counts, cross-tabulations, and more sophisticated statistical analysis. Of these three techniques, one-way

Exhibit 8.8

Hypothetical Cross-Tabulation between Gender and Brand of Microwave Popcorn Purchased Most Frequently

| Brand | Purchase by Gender | |
	Male	Female
Orville Reddenbacher	31%	48%
T.V. Time	12	6
Pop Rite	38	4
Act Two	7	23
Weight Watchers	4	18
Other	8	0

cross-tabulation
A method of analyzing data that lets the analyst look at the responses to one question in relation to the responses to one or more other questions.

frequency counts are the simplest. One-way frequency tables record the responses to a question. For example, the answers to the question "What brand of microwave popcorn do you buy most often?" would provide a one-way frequency distribution. One-way frequency tables are always done in data analysis, at least as a first step, because they provide the researcher with a general picture of the study's results.

A **cross-tabulation**, or "cross-tab," lets the analyst look at the responses to one question in relation to the responses to one or more other questions. For example, what is the association between gender and the brand of microwave popcorn bought most frequently? Hypothetical answers to this question are shown in Exhibit 8.8. Although the Orville Reddenbacher brand was popular with both males and females, it was more popular with females. Compared with women, men strongly preferred Pop Rite, whereas women were more likely than men to buy Weight Watchers popcorn.

Researchers can use many other more powerful and sophisticated statistical techniques, such as hypothesis testing, measures of association, and regression analysis. A description of these techniques goes beyond the scope of this book but can be found in any good marketing research textbook. The use of sophisticated statistical techniques depends on the researchers' objectives and the nature of the data gathered.

Preparing and Presenting the Report

After data analysis has been completed, the researcher must prepare the report and communicate the conclusions and recommendations to management. This is a key step in the process. If the marketing researcher wants managers to carry out the recommendations, he or she must convince them that the results are credible and justified by the data collected.

Researchers are usually required to present both written and oral reports on the project. Today, the written report is no more than a copy of the PowerPoint slides used in the oral presentation. Both reports should be tailored to the audience. They should begin with a clear, concise statement of the research objectives, followed by a complete, but brief and simple, explanation of the research design or methodology employed. A summary of major findings should come next. The conclusion of the report should also present recommendations to management.

Most people who enter marketing will become research users rather than research suppliers. Thus, they must know what to notice in a report. As with many other items we purchase, quality is not always readily apparent. Nor does a high price guarantee superior quality. The basis for measuring the quality of a marketing research report is the research proposal. Did the report meet the objectives established in the proposal? Was the methodology outlined in the proposal followed? Are the conclusions based on logical deductions from the data analysis? Do the recommendations seem prudent, given the conclusions?

Following Up

The final step in the marketing research process is to follow up. The researcher should determine why management did or did not carry out the recommendations in the report. Was sufficient decision-making information included? What could have been done to make the report more useful to management? A good rapport between the product manager, or whoever authorized the project, and the market researcher is essential. Often they must work together on many studies throughout the year.

The Profound Impact of the Internet on Marketing Research

In many ways, the Internet has turned the world of marketing research upside-down. Old ways of conducting some types of research may soon seem as quaint as a steam-engine train. New techniques and new ways of conducting traditional marketing research are coming on-line in increasing numbers every day. By 2005, Internet marketing research will account for about 50 percent of all marketing research revenue in the United States.[9]

There are several reasons for the success of Internet marketing research:

- It allows for better and faster decision making through much more rapid access to business intelligence.

- It improves the ability to respond quickly to customer needs and market shifts.

- It makes follow-up studies and longitudinal research much easier to conduct and more fruitful.

- It slashes labor- and time-intensive research activities (and associated costs), including mailing, telephone solicitation, data entry, data tabulation, and reporting.[10]

Advantages of Internet Surveys

The huge growth in the popularity of Internet surveys is the result of the many advantages offered by the Internet. The specific advantages of Internet surveys are related to many factors:

Discuss the profound impact of the Internet on marketing research

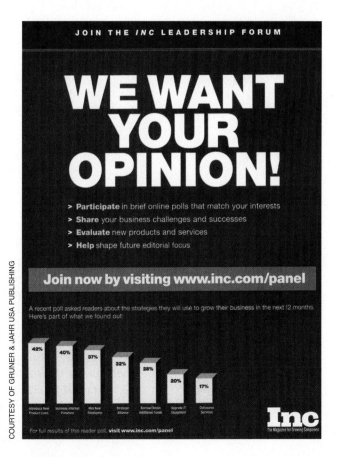

The Internet is becoming a powerful tool in marketing research as more and more Americans get on-line. *Inc. Magazine* is one of a growing number of companies turning to the Internet to gather data about customers and their opinions.

- *Rapid development, real-time reporting:* Internet surveys can be broadcast to thousands of potential respondents simultaneously. Respondents complete surveys simultaneously; then results are tabulated and posted for corporate clients to view as the returns arrive. The result: survey results can be in a client's hands in significantly less time than would be required for traditional surveys.

- *Dramatically reduced costs:* The Internet can cut costs by 25 to 40 percent and provide results in half the time it takes to do traditional telephone surveys. Data-collection costs account for a large proportion of any traditional market research budget. Telephone surveys are labor-intensive efforts incurring training, telecommunications, and management costs. Electronic methods eliminate these completely. While costs for traditional survey techniques rise proportionally with the number of interviews desired, electronic solicitations can grow in volume with little increase in project costs.

- *Personalized questions and data:* Internet surveys can be highly personalized for greater relevance to each respondent's own situation, thus speeding the response process. Respondents enjoy a personalized survey because they are asked to answer only pertinent questions, can pause and resume the survey as needed, and can see previous responses and correct inconsistencies.

- *Improved respondent participation:* Busy respondents may be growing increasingly intolerant of "snail mail" or telephone-based surveys. Internet surveys take half as much time to complete as phone interviews, can be accomplished at the respondent's convenience (after work hours), and are much more stimulating and engaging. Graphics, interactivity, links to incentive sites and real-time summary reports make the interview enjoyable. The result? Much higher response rates.

- *Contact with the hard-to-reach:* Certain groups—doctors, high-income professionals, top management in Global 2000 firms—are among the most surveyed on the planet and the most difficult to reach. Many of these groups are well represented on-line. Internet surveys provide convenient anytime/anywhere access that makes it easy for busy professionals to participate.[11]

The rapid growth of Internet survey research is a result of the mushrooming number of Americans on-line—the current estimate being more than 50 percent. This in turn has meant that researchers are finding that on-line and off-line research results are the same. For example, America Online's (AOL) Digital Marketing Services (DMS), an on-line research organization, has done a number of surveys with both on-line and off-line samples. DMS's clients include IBM, Eastman Kodak, and Procter & Gamble. In well over a hundred side-by-side comparisons of on-line and off-line studies, both techniques led clients to the same business decisions.[12] The guidance from both sets of data was the same.

Internet Samples

Internet samples may be classified as unrestricted, screened, or recruited.[13] In an **unrestricted Internet sample**, anyone who desires can complete the questionnaire. It is fully self-selecting and probably representative of nothing except Web surfers. The problem is exacerbated if the same Internet user can access the questionnaire repeatedly. For example, *InfoWorld*, a computer user magazine, decided to conduct its Readers Choice survey for the first time on the Internet. The results were so skewed by repeat voting for one product that the entire survey was publicly abandoned and the editor asked for readers' help to avoid the problem again. A simple solution to repeat respondents is to lock respondents out of the site after they have filled out the questionnaire.

Screened Internet samples adjust for the unrepresentativeness of the self-selected respondents by imposing quotas based on some desired sample characteristics. These are often demographic characteristics such as gender, income, and geographic region, or product-related criteria such as past purchase behavior, job

unrestricted Internet sample
A survey in which anyone with a computer and modem can fill out the questionnaire.

screened Internet sample
An Internet sample with quotas based on desired sample characteristics.

responsibilities, or current product use. The applications for screened samples are generally similar to those for unrestricted samples.

Screened sample questionnaires typically use a branching or skip pattern for asking screening questions to determine whether the full questionnaire should be presented to a respondent. Some Web survey systems can make immediate market segment calculations that first assign a respondent to a particular segment based on screening questions and then select the appropriate questionnaire to match the respondent's segment.

Alternatively, some Internet research providers maintain a "panel house" that recruits respondents who fill out a preliminary classification questionnaire. This information is used to classify respondents into demographic segments. Clients specify the desired segments, and the respondents who match the desired demographics are permitted to fill out the questionnaires of all clients who specify that segment.

Recruited Internet samples are used for targeted populations in surveys that require more control over the makeup of the sample. Respondents are recruited by telephone, mail, e-mail, or in person. After qualification, they are sent the questionnaire by e-mail or are directed to a Web site that contains a link to the questionnaire. At Web sites, passwords are normally used to restrict access to the questionnaire to the recruited sample members. Since the makeup of the sample is known, completions can be monitored, and the participation rate can be improved by sending follow-up messages to those who do not complete the questionnaire.

Recruited samples are ideal in applications that already have a database from which to recruit the sample. For example, a good application would be a survey that used a customer database to recruit respondents for a purchaser satisfaction study.

recruited Internet sample
A sample in which respondents are prerecruited and must qualify to participate. They are then e-mailed a questionnaire or directed to a secure Web site.

Other Uses of the Internet by Marketing Researchers

The Internet revolution in marketing research has had an impact on more than just the way surveys are conducted. The management of the research process and the dissemination of information have also been greatly enhanced by the Internet. Several key areas have been affected by the Internet:

- *The distribution of requests for proposals (RFPs) and proposals:* Companies can now quickly and efficiently send RFPs to a select e-mail list of research suppliers. In turn, research suppliers can develop proposals and e-mail them back to clients. A process that used to take days using snail mail now occurs in a matter of hours.

- *Collaboration between the client and the research supplier in the management of a research project:* Now a researcher and client may both be looking at a proposal, RFP, report, or some type of statistical analysis at the same time on their respective computer screens while discussing it over the telephone. This is very powerful and efficient. Changes in the sample size, quotas, and other aspects of the research plan can be discussed and made immediately.

- *Data management and on-line analysis:* Clients can access their survey via the research supplier's secure Web site and monitor the data gathering in real time. The client can use sophisticated tools to actually do data analysis as the survey develops. This real-time analysis may result in changes in the questionnaire, sample size, or the types of respondents being interviewed. The research supplier and the client become partners in "just-in-time" marketing research.

- *Publication and distribution of reports:* Reports can be published to the Web directly from programs such as PowerPoint and all the latest versions of leading word-processing, spreadsheet, and presentation software packages. This means that results are available to appropriate managers worldwide on an almost instantaneous basis. Reports can be searched for the content of interest using the same Web browser used to view the report.

- *Viewing of oral presentations of marketing research surveys by widely scattered audiences:* By placing oral presentations on password-protected Web sites, managers throughout the world can see and hear the actual client presentation. This saves time and money by avoiding the need for the managers to travel to a central meeting site.[14]

Discuss the growing importance of scanner-based research

scanner-based research
A system for gathering information from a single group of respondents by continuously monitoring the advertising, promotion, and pricing they are exposed to and the things they buy.

IRI's BehaviorScan product allows IRI to track individual household purchases over time. Participants in the household panel present an ID card at the checkout of a scanner-equipped grocery store.

BehaviorScan
A scanner-based research program that tracks the purchases of three thousand households through store scanners.

InfoScan
A scanner-based sales-tracking service for the consumer packaged-goods industry.

Scanner-Based Research

Scanner-based research is a system for gathering information from a single group of respondents by continuously monitoring the advertising, promotion, and pricing they are exposed to and the things they buy. The variables measured are advertising campaigns, coupons, displays, and product prices. The result is a huge database of marketing efforts and consumer behavior. Scanner-based research is bringing ever closer the Holy Grail of marketing research: an accurate, objective picture of the direct causal relationship between different kinds of marketing efforts and actual sales.

The two major scanner-based suppliers are Information Resources. Inc. (IRI) and the A. C. Nielsen Company. Each has about half the market. However, IRI is the founder of scanner-based research.

IRI's first product is called **BehaviorScan**. A household panel (a group of three thousand long-term participants in the research project) has been recruited and maintained in each BehaviorScan town. Panel members shop with an ID card, which is presented at the checkout in scanner-equipped grocery stores and drugstores, allowing IRI to track electronically each household's purchases, item by item, over time. It uses microcomputers to measure TV viewing in each panel household and can send special commercials to panel member television sets. With such a measure of household purchasing, it is possible to manipulate marketing variables, such as TV advertising or consumer promotions, or to introduce a new product and analyze real changes in consumer buying behavior.

IRI's most successful product is **InfoScan**—a scanner-based sales-tracking service for the consumer packaged-goods industry. Retail sales, detailed consumer purchasing information (including measurement of store loyalty and total grocery basket expenditures), and promotional activity by manufacturers and retailers are monitored and evaluated for all bar-coded products. Data are collected weekly from more than thirty-one thousand supermarkets, drugstores, and mass merchandisers.[15]

When Should Marketing Research Be Conducted?

When managers have several possible solutions to a problem, they should not instinctively call for marketing research. In fact, the first decision to make is whether to conduct marketing research at all.

Some companies have been conducting research in certain markets for many years. Such firms understand the characteristics of target customers and their likes and dislikes about existing products. Under these circumstances, further research would be repetitive and waste money. Procter & Gamble, for example, has extensive knowledge of the coffee market. After it conducted initial taste tests with Folgers Instant Coffee, P&G went into national distribution without further research. Consolidated Foods Kitchen of Sara Lee followed the same strategy with its frozen croissants, as did Quaker Oats with Chewy Granola Bars. This tactic, however, does not always work. P&G marketers thought they understood the pain reliever market thoroughly, so they bypassed market research for Encaprin aspirin in capsules. Because it lacked a distinct competitive advantage over existing products, however, the product failed and was withdrawn from the market.

Managers rarely have such great trust in their judgment that they would refuse more information if it were available and free. But they might have enough confidence that they would be unwilling to pay very much for the information or to wait a long time to receive it. The willingness to acquire additional decision-making information depends on managers' perceptions of its quality, price, and timing. Of course, if perfect information were available—that is, the data conclusively showed which alternative to choose—decision makers would be willing to pay more for it than for information that still left uncertainty. In summary, research should be undertaken only when the expected value of the information is greater than the cost of obtaining it.

Competitive Intelligence

Derived from military intelligence, competitive intelligence is an important tool for helping a firm overcome a competitor's advantage. Specifically, competitive intelligence can help identify the advantage, play a major role in determining how the advantage was achieved, and then provide insights on how it was achieved.

Competitive intelligence (CI) is the creation of a system that helps managers assess their competitors and their vendors in order to become a more efficient and effective competitor. Intelligence is analyzed information. It becomes decision-making intelligence when it has implications for the organization. For example, a primary competitor may have plans to introduce a product with performance standards equal to ours but with a 15 percent cost advantage. The new product will reach the market in eight months. This intelligence has important decision-making and policy consequences for management. Competitive intelligence and environmental scanning (where management gathers data about the external environment—see Chapter 2) combine to create marketing intelligence. Marketing intelligence is then used as input into a marketing decision support system.

6

Explain the concept of competitive intelligence

competitive intelligence (CI)
An intelligence system that helps managers assess their competition and vendors in order to become more efficient and effective competitors.

Advantages of Competitive Intelligence

Competitive intelligence is one of the hottest areas in marketing today. Firms like General Motors, Ford, GTW, AT&T, Motorola, and many others have large, well-established CI units. The Ford Taurus came about after Ford engineers, aided by CI, examined competitors' cars and incorporated the best features into one auto.

Competitive intelligence helps managers assess their competition and their vendors, which, in turn, means fewer surprises. Competitive intelligence allows managers to predict changes in business relationships, identify marketplace opportunities, guard against threats, forecast a competitor's strategy, discover new or potential competitors, learn from the success or failure of others, learn about new technologies that can affect the company, and learn about the impact of government regulations on the competition. In summary, CI promotes effective and efficient decision making, which should lead to greater profitability. Sheena Sharp, principal, Sharp Information Research, says: "CI gives the company the competitive advantage of foresight and allows it to learn today what will be discovered by others tomorrow."[16]

Several years ago NutraSweet's patent on the artificial sweetener *aspartame* was expiring, and the company faced potential disaster. Management was afraid that chemical and food companies would move into the market. NutraSweet analyzed competitors' prices, customer relations, expansion plans, and advertising campaigns. The company used the information to cut costs, improve service, and preserve most of its market. "We maintained over 80 percent of our market," said NutraSweet's Robert E. Flynn. He said that CI practices are worth $50 million a year to his company.

Sources of Competitive Intelligence

The Internet and its databases are a great source of CI. A CI researcher can use Internet databases to answer these and other questions:

- What articles were written about this market?
- What companies are associated with this product group?
- What patents have been filed for this technology?
- What are the major magazines or texts in this industry?
- What are the chances that I will find something in print on the target company?
- How many companies are in the same industry as the target company?
- Who are the reporters studying this industry?
- How can I be updated on industry and company events without having to constantly request the information?
- How can I compile a list of the leading experts in the industry and the key institutions they are associated with?

Non-computer-based sources of CI can be found in a variety of areas:

- A company's salespeople, who can directly observe and ask questions about the competition.
- Experts with in-depth knowledge of a subject or activity.
- CI consultants, who can use their knowledge and experience to gather needed information quickly and efficiently.
- Government agencies, a valuable source of all types of data.
- Uniform Commercial Code (UCC) filings, a system that identifies goods that are leased or pledged as collateral. This is an excellent source for learning about a company's latest additions to plant assets.
- Suppliers, a group that may offer information on products shipped to a competitor.
- Periodicals, a good source for timely articles on successes, failures, opportunities, and threats.
- The Yellow Pages, which often provide data on number of competitors, trading areas, and special offerings.
- Trade shows, official gatherings where competitors display their latest offerings.

This list is not exhaustive but it does provide an idea of how CI can be gathered.

CD

Read more about competitive intelligence in the supplemental module on your Xtra! CD-ROM.

CONNECT IT

Look back at the story about duck stamps at the beginning of this chapter. A company can use survey research, observations, or experiments to conduct marketing research.

Unless a company has extensive knowledge, based on research, of the problem at hand, it should probably conduct marketing research. Yet managers should also be reasonably sure that the cost of gathering the information will be less than the value of the data gathered.

Key marketing data often come from a company's own decision support system, which continually gathers data from a variety of sources and funnels the information to decision makers. They then manipulate the data to make better decisions. DSS data are often supplemented by marketing research information.

As a consumer, you participate in shaping consumer products by the choices you make and the products and services you buy. You can become a better consumer by actively participating in marketing surveys and learning more about the products you buy.

Participate in Marketing Research Surveys

All of us get tired of telephone solicitations where people try to sell us everything from new carpet to chimney cleaning. Recognize that marketing research surveys are different. A true marketing research survey will *never* involve a sales pitch nor

will the research firm sell your name to a database marketer. The purpose of marketing research is to build better goods and services for you and me. If you help out such researchers, you ultimately help yourself. The Council for Marketing and Opinion Research (CMOR) is an organization of hundreds of marketing research professionals that is dedicated to preserving the integrity of the research industry. If you receive a call from someone who tries to sell you something under the guise of marketing research, get the name and address of the organization. Call CMOR at 1 (800) 887-CMOR and report the abuse.

REVIEW IT

1 **Explain the concept and purpose of a marketing decision support system.** A decision support system (DSS) makes data instantly available to marketing managers and allows them to manipulate the data themselves to make marketing decisions. Four characteristics make DSSs especially useful to marketing managers: They are interactive, flexible, discovery oriented, and accessible. Decision support systems give managers access to information immediately and without outside assistance. They allow users to manipulate data in a variety of ways and to answer "what if" questions. And, finally, they are accessible to novice computer users.

1.1 In the absence of company problems, is there any reason to develop a marketing DSS?

1.2 Explain the difference between marketing research and a DSS.

2 **Define marketing research and explain its importance to marketing decision making.** Marketing research is a process of collecting and analyzing data for the purpose of solving specific marketing problems. Marketers use marketing research to explore the profitability of marketing strategies. They can examine why particular strategies failed and analyze characteristics of specific market segments. Managers can use research findings to help keep current customers. Moreover, marketing research allows management to behave proactively, rather than reactively, by identifying newly emerging patterns in society and the economy.

2.1 The task of marketing is to create exchanges. What role might marketing research play in the facilitation of the exchange process?

2.2 Marketing research has traditionally been associated with manufacturers of consumer goods. Today, however, an increasing number of organizations, both profit and nonprofit, are using marketing research. Why do you think this trend exists? Give some examples of specific reasons why organizations might use marketing research.

2.3 WRITING Write a reply to the following statement: "I own a restaurant in the downtown area. I see customers every day whom I know on a first-name basis. I understand their likes and dislikes. If I put something on the menu and it doesn't sell, I know that they didn't like it. I also read the magazine *Modern Restaurants*, so I know what the trends are in the industry. This is all of the marketing research I need to do."

2.4 Give an example of (a) the descriptive role of marketing research, (b) the diagnostic role, and (c) the predictive function of marketing research.

3 **Describe the steps involved in conducting a marketing research project.** The marketing research process involves several basic steps. First, the researcher and the decision maker must agree on a problem statement or set of research objectives. The researcher then creates an overall research design to specify how primary data will be gathered and analyzed. Before collecting data, the researcher decides whether the group to be interviewed will be a probability or nonprobability sample. Field service firms are often hired to carry out data collection. Once data have been collected, the researcher analyzes them using statistical analysis. The researcher then prepares and presents oral and written reports, with conclusions and recommendations, to management. As a final step, the researcher determines whether the recommendations were implemented and what could have been done to make the project more successful.

3.1 Critique the following methodologies and suggest more appropriate alternatives:

a. A supermarket was interested in determining its image. It dropped a short questionnaire into the grocery bag of each customer before putting in the groceries.

b. To assess the extent of its trade area, a shopping mall stationed interviewers in the parking lot every Monday and Friday evening. Interviewers walked up to people after they had parked their cars and asked them for their zip codes.

c. To assess the popularity of a new movie, a major studio invited people to call a 900 number and vote yes, they would see it again, or no, they would not. Each caller was billed a $2 charge.

3.2 **WRITING** You have been charged with determining how to attract more business majors to your school. Write an outline of the steps you would take, including the sampling procedures, to accomplish the task.

3.3 Why are secondary data sometimes preferable to primary data?

3.4 Discuss when focus groups should and should not be used.

3.5 **TEAM** Divide the class into teams of eight persons. Each group will conduct a focus group on the quality and number of services that your college is providing to its students. One person from each group should be chosen to act as moderator. Remember, it is the moderator's job to facilitate discussion, not to lead the discussion. These groups should last approximately forty-five minutes. If possible, the groups should be videotaped or recorded. Upon completion, each group should write a brief report of its results. Consider offering to meet with the dean of students to share the results of your research.

4 **Discuss the profound impact of the Internet on marketing research.** The Internet has vastly simplified the secondary data search process, placing more sources of information in front of researchers than ever before. Internet survey research is surging in popularity. Internet surveys can be created rapidly and reported in real time. They are also relatively inexpensive and can easily be personalized. Often researchers can use the Internet to contact respondents who are difficult to reach by other means. The Internet can also be used to distribute research proposals and reports and to facilitate collaboration between the client and the research supplier. Clients can access real-time data and analyze the information as the collection process continues.

4.1 **ON LINE** Use the Internet and a Web browser, such as Lycos or Yahoo!, and type "marketing research." You will then have thousands of options. Pick a Web site that you find interesting and report on its content to the class.

4.2 Why has the Internet been of such great value to researchers seeking secondary data?

⑤ Discuss the growing importance of scanner-based research. A scanner-based research system enables marketers to monitor a market panel's exposure and reaction to such variables as advertising, coupons, store displays, packaging, and price. By analyzing these variables in relation to the panel's subsequent buying behavior, marketers gain useful insight into sales and marketing strategies.

5.1 Why has scanner-based research been seen as "the ultimate answer" for marketing researchers? Do you see any disadvantages of this methodology?

5.2 Detractors claim that scanner-based research is like "driving a car down the road looking only in the rearview mirror." What does this mean? Do you agree?

⑥ Explain the concept of competitive intelligence. Competitive intelligence (CI) is the creation of an intelligence system that helps managers assess their competition and their vendors in order to become more efficient and effective competitors. Intelligence is analyzed information, and it becomes decision-making intelligence when it has implications for the organization.

By helping managers assess their competition and vendors, CI leads to fewer surprises. CI allows managers to predict changes in business relationships, guard against threats, forecast a competitor's strategy, and develop a successful marketing plan.

The Internet and databases accessed via the Internet offer excellent sources of CI. Company personnel, particularly sales and service representatives, are usually good sources of CI. Many companies require their salespersons to routinely fill out CI reports. Other external sources of CI include experts, CI consultants, government agencies, UCC filings, suppliers, newspapers and other publications, Yellow Pages, and trade shows.

6.1 Why do you think that CI is so hot in today's environment?

6.2 Prepare a memo to your boss at United Airlines and outline why the organization needs a CI unit.

6.3 Form a team with three other students. Each team must choose a firm in the PC manufacturing industry and then go to the Web site of the firm and acquire as much CI as possible. Each team will then prepare a five-minute oral presentation on its findings.

DEFINE IT

APPLY IT

Application for Entrepreneurs

 Bill and Mary Osborn hit it lucky with dot-com stocks. At the age of thirty-nine, they have amassed $5.2 million from astutely playing the stock market. They cashed out before the dot-com crash, and now they are ready to pursue their dream.

The Osborns have always wanted to live in Colorado and have dreamed of owning a small hotel. Mary hit upon the idea of doing both—that is, building a hotel in Colorado that they could manage. Initial research uncovered the following information.

When asked which two or three things are most important in choosing a hotel for a vacation, Americans put nonsmoking rooms first (40 percent). Twenty-four-hour access to food (36 percent), quality in-room amenities such as coffeemakers and hair dryers (34 percent), athletic facilities (31 percent), and "good evening facilities" (26 percent) are next. Vacationers rank supervised activities for children much higher than business travelers (10 percent versus 3 percent).

Overnight business travelers, who traveled in the past year, in contrast, focus on things that will make their trip more productive. Like vacationers, they rate nonsmoking rooms tops (46 percent). But they put quality in-room amenities (39 percent) and transportation to the airport (32 percent) next. And, while they cite many of the same things as vacationers as being important, they put a much higher priority on some things, particularly in-room connections for computer, fax, and on-line access (21 percent, seventeen points higher than vacationers), being able to earn airline miles (15 percent, eight points higher), and frequent guest programs (14 percent, five points higher).

Questions

Use the Internet to help determine the following:

1. What price range should be offered?

2. Where in Colorado should the hotel be built?

3. Should the hotel cater primarily to business or vacation travelers?

4. What amenities and features should the hotel offer?

5. Should Mary and Bill consider becoming a franchisee?

THINK ABOUT IT

Ethics Exercise

John Michael Smythe owns a small marketing research firm in Cleveland, Ohio, which employs seventy-five people. Most employees are sole breadwinners in their families. John's firm has not fared well for the past two years and is on the verge of bankruptcy. The company recently surveyed over 2,500 people in Ohio about new car purchase plans for the Ohio Department of Economic Development. Because the study identified many hot prospects for new cars, a new car dealer has offered John $8,000 for the names and phone numbers of people saying they are "likely" or "very likely" to buy a new car within the next twelve months. John needs the money to avoid laying off a number of employees.

Questions

1. Should John Smythe sell the names?

2. Does the AMA Code of Ethics address this issue? Go to **http://www.marketingpower. com** and review the code. Then, write a brief paragraph on what the AMA Code of Ethics contains that relates to John Smythe's dilemma.

Entrepreneursip Case

Cool and How to Find It: Look-Look

COURTESY LOOK-LOOK, INC.

You can't always believe what you hear, particularly in the fast-moving world of youth trends. That is, unless you listen to Sharon Lee and DeeDee Gordon, founders of Look-Look, the most accurate information resource on the global youth culture. The pair founded the company in 1999, determined to find whatever makes the cultural spider-sense tingle—music, shoes, clothes, games, makeup, food, and technology. Lee and Gordon took Look-Look on-line in 2000, and the company has quickly risen to be the paragon of trend forecasting in the youth market. How?

When Sharon Lee needs to know what's cool, she taps into a network of experts the CIA would envy. It's a Web-linked weave of nearly ten-thousand volunteers and part-timers, aged fourteen to thirty, recruited over several years at clubs and hangouts around the country, from New York to Los Angeles and points in between, to report on their world.

Look-Look's multilevel database is populated with thousands of prescreened recruits who log on to answer surveys and polls, register opinions, and communicate for points that can lead to cash, digital cameras, and other techie toys. Some of the recruits, armed with digital cameras, can photograph their world, then upload the pictures, send e-mail reports, and use Look-Look's Intranet message boards. The young field agents might snap anything from a rave to their bedroom walls. Look-Look relies on "early adopters" and "influencers" to provide the layers of information that traditional research only skims.

Look-Look is a cool seeker, paid by major marketers to get the first bead on what's next on the horizon. With a cool seeker's expertise, even the most staid company can be on the razor's edge: Look-Look ferreted out the then-uncharted popularity of under-a-dollar stores, fold-up scooters, and over-the-shoulder bags.

Cornerstone Promotion, a Look-Look rival, was behind Microsoft's successful launch of the Xbox video-gaming system. "Seventy kids got units," said Cornerstone's president. "They were plugged into the local clubs and set up gaming parties with music giveaways from our record label clients. They'd do it in campus rec centers or at night clubs or on radio shows." By the time Xbox made its debut, "we created a huge frenzy." Microsoft was no longer stodgy compared to Sega or PlayStation.

In addition to youth market environmental scanning, a client might ask Look-Look to check the coolness quotient of a product. After the small army is canvassed with on-line polls and surveys, the results are arranged into categories. "The turnaround," says Lee, "can be as little as forty-eight hours." Look-Look categorizes information into ten channels: fashion, entertainment, technology, activities, eating and drinking, health and beauty, mood of culture (how kids feel about life), spirituality, city guide, and Look Out (a "best of" findings in a snapshot). The information is put through rigorous paces. "Methodology is crucial, especially with the quantity and quality of the sample," says Lee. "We can take a sample of 300 or thousands. That's up to Gallup standards."

To ensure the most accurate information, Look-Look steers away from focus groups because peer pressure is a factor at this age; teens are more likely to bend to pressure and follow the leader of a peer group. One-on-one interviews are, therefore, preferred. They keep the responses truer and uninfluenced by external pressures. To get to cool, Look-Look has to keep its sources cool.

And what is cool, anyway? Says Lee, "For young people now it's pure raw emotion—it's anything that inspires you to think 'I want that because it fits me so well.' It can be a person, a product, a place, anything." according to Que Gaskins, the chief marketing officer of Ad*itive, a multicultural marketing firm, cool really starts with the "what if" factor: " 'What if I wore that hat or that jersey?' Then you give it your own twist, the way African American males sport Asian tattoos or middle-class white kids wear dreadlocks or corn-rows. But there's just no formula for cool."

"Cool burns out so fast that by the time companies know it's cool, it's not cool anymore," says Lee. "The old-time corporate methodology was to treat it like the annual report for shareholders—going out and testing a sample size of a few hundred people, then retesting it again the next year. But a year in youth culture is like a year in dog years."

Still, cool is as hard to pin down as a weather forecast for next week. But the real arbiters of cool are those who can afford to lead. "Ultimately," says Gaskins, "the future of cool belongs to whoever has the most buying power."

Questions

1. What is Look-Look offering businesses that traditional market research firms cannot offer?

2. Describe the role of the Internet in youth trend spotting. Do you think a research firm can accurately forecast youth trends without an on-line component to its research plan?

3. Go to Look-Look's Web site at **http://www.look-look.com** and check out some of the free information in each category. How accurate do you find the information? Have you seen any of these trends in your city or region, or among your friends and classmates?

4. Make a list of products or companies that you think could benefit from Look-Look's form of predictive market research. Next to each item, write a brief reason why and how you think cool seeking would benefit the company or product.

 WATCH IT

Short

It's not often that marketing research topics are depicted in advertisements. The two ads for Quiznos in the Chapter 8 PowerPoint presentation on the *Marketing* PowerPoint CD-ROM spoof research validity.

Medium

Staying abreast of current trends is difficult enough without trying to forecast what will be popular in the future. One researcher takes candid shots of people throughout Tokyo, and then uploads them to the Web so that clients can view the pictures. Watch this cool hunter in action in the CNN clip for Chapter 8.

Long

To give you insights into Chapter 8, Small Business School will take you the Specialty Cheese Company in Lowell, Wisconsin. Vickie and Paul Scharfman develop new products, avoid product bombs, and transform an old business into a thriving company, all through marketing research.

 FLIP IT

Flip to Chapter 8 in your *Grademaker Study Guide* for more review opportunities, including the pretest, vocabulary review, Internet activities, study test questions, and marketing research scenarios. Can you explain why market research is so important? Can you close your book and outline the marketing research process? Can't? Then you need to review with your *Grademaker*.

CLICK IT

The *Marketing* Web site links you to all the Internet-based activities in this chapter, like "Review It" question 6.3, "Apply It," and the On-Line exercises in the chapter margins. As a review, do the Chapter 8 quiz and crossword puzzle. And don't forget the Career Exersite that shows you different resources if you're interested in a career in marketing research. Review the main concepts in the PowerPoint presentation for Chapter 8, too. Go to **http://lamb.swlearning.com**, read the material, and follow the links right from the site.

SPIN IT

Spin your Xtra! CD-ROM to find out more about competitive intelligence in the supplemental content module. Then test your understanding of marketing research by completing the worksheets for exhibits 8.1, 8.4, 8.6, and 8.7. If your instructor has assigned a marketing plan project, worksheets on Xtra! can help you organize your work. In addition to the quiz on the Web site, there's another quiz on the Xtra! CD-ROM, plus video of the authors answering frequently asked quesitons about marketing research, such as "Are there ever conflicts between marketing researchers and product managers?" and "What is the difference between qualitative and quantitative research?"

Still Shaky? Here's a Tip.

Review your class notes. Do they give you enough information? If they are lacking, visit your campus study center to learn how to take good notes.

MARKETING MISCUES

Metricom's Ricochet Fails to Rebound

In 1995, Metricom, Inc., introduced a wireless data service that it promised would replicate a desktop in the field. Ten years after its 1985 start as a company focused on developing technology to enable utilities to check meters remotely, Metricom was the first company to offer reliable wireless access and expected to be way ahead of the wireless pack. Six years, and millions of dollars later, the company went bankrupt. What was to blame? Flawed marketing.

The Product

Metricom, Inc., based in Los Gatos, California, offered both a product (Ricochet modem) and a service (Microcellular Data Network). The Ricochet wireless modem, which sold for about $350, was a small black box that plugged into the serial port of a computer. The modem was equipped with a rechargeable battery and came with a power adapter/charger. The Ricochet technology provided wireless data speeds up to 128 kilobits per second.

Metricom's Microcellular Data Network consisted of Ricochet transmitter repeater radios installed on existing poles (e.g., light poles) less than half a mile apart in market areas where Metricom had decided to do business. Because the transmitters were placed on existing infrastructure, Metricom had to obtain permission from landlords or city offices to install them. Once the transmitters were installed in a given city, a Ricochet modem could be used.

By 2001, the company offered high-speed wireless service in fifteen market areas in the United States. These included fifteen major cities: Atlanta, Baltimore, Dallas, Denver, Detroit, Houston, Los Angeles, Minneapolis, New York, Philadelphia, Phoenix, San Diego, San Francisco, Seattle, and Washington, D.C. Reseller partners included WorldCom, Inc., Juno Online, GoAmerica, Aether Systems, Wireless Web-Connect!, and IP communications.

The Promotion

Why didn't customers buy the Ricochet system? Analysts and industry observers claim that a weak marketing program was to blame for Metricom's demise. While the market did not fault Metricom's products, the rest of the company's marketing mix received considerable criticism. The lack of overall market coverage (only a few cities) and the length of time it took to roll out to new cities were problems. Furthermore, at $80 a month, Metricom's mobile access cost three times as much as dial-up services and was not price-competitive with local cable providers and phone-company DSLs.

The company's advertising campaign was considered confusing, especially for a product that could, itself, be confusing to potential users. Metricom advertised its Ricochet wireless system in markets as they opened. The advertising used two characters, Rico and Chet, a spy duo who obtained top set information off the Internet while in their car.

Possibly the most important problem, however, was that Metricom may have targeted the wrong market segment. With a small change in its pricing model, the company could have offered wireless technology to homes and offices within its access cities. Why didn't the company realize that business users would need Internet access from more than fifteen cities, but that there were millions of home and office users in the markets within the company's network?

Questions

1. Where did Metricom go wrong?
2. How important was the target market to Metricom's success?

CRITICAL THINKING CASE

Square Two: On Par with Female Golfers' Needs

As a supplier of low-priced yet high-quality golf clubs for men and women since 1974, Square Two golf has always targeted the budget-minded segment of new golf equipment buyers. The golf equipment industry has changed markedly, and the game's surge in popularity has pushed the market for golf equipment and supplies to almost $2.5 billion per year. Fighting for survival among traditional golf giants such as Taylor-Made, Titleist, Ping, and Callaway, Square Two Golf has used a crafty positioning and segmentation strategy to fortify its business.

Having long ago identified differentiation as the key to its survival, Square Two determined that the best way to grow its business would be to turn its attention to a very specific segment of the golf equipment market. During the past several years, the number of female golfers in the United States surged past five million, or almost 20 percent of the country's total participants. The average female player has a household income of $70,000. In light of these environmental factors, the company undertook a gradual repositioning initiative that aligned it almost exclusively with the women's game.

The company's first major step was its launch of a national television ad campaign in 1999. Set in a golf shop, the ads featured a woman who informed viewers that buying the latest in women's golf technology does not have to be prohibitively expensive. Doug Buffington, the company's chief operating officer, affirms that the ad's message reinforces Square Two's unique selling proposition: supplying women with more choices of affordable golf equipment using patented technology than better-known brands. Buffington also notes that the ads communicate the products' value and inspire viewers to ask store representatives what the differences are between Square Two's clubs and those made by the competition. The advertising spots led Square Two to its first year of profitability.

Not resting on his laurels, Buffington initiated a deal in June 2001 to acquire a leading women's golf shoe manufacturer, Lady Fairway, in order to extend Square Two's product lines. That deal inspired the chairman of Nancy Lopez Golf, a maker of high-end women's clubs named after the eponymous Hall of Fame golfer, to approach Square Two with a similar acquisition deal. Since the Nancy Lopez line would complement Square Two's existing line of affordable clubs, thus enabling it to serve the entire women's market at multiple price levels, Square Two agreed.

The Lopez line caters to the more affluent golfer, so there is little chance that one line will cannibalize the other. Moreover, both companies have a strong history of targeting women, and their deal opens new and improved distribution channels. Though costs of marketing the new lines initially hurt the Square Two's bottom line, the acquisitions have led to increased revenues, and stronger positioning promises to increase profitability in the future.

Buffington's repositioning strategy culminated in June 2001 with the public announcement that Square Two changed its corporate name to Women's Golf Unlimited (WGU). The new company oversees the development and marketing of its two club brands, Square Two Golf and Nancy Lopez Golf, and its shoe, apparel, and accessories brand, Lady Fairway. The synergies, however, are not limited to product development. Retail outlets carrying the new company's three product lines can offer their customers a one-stop source for all of their equipment needs.

Square Two's repositioning effort proved to be extremely insightful. Critics may point out that although women represent 20 percent of the golfing population, they only account for 15 percent of the market's $2.5 billion in spending. Critics may also cite the statistic that shows the number of female golfers has slightly decreased from 5.8 million to 5.1 million in the last couple of years. Both facts are true, but one of the reasons many female golfers may have left the game is that equipment manufacturers have not sufficiently met their unique needs. WGU, however, manufactures golf clubs and supporting equipment designed to meet the needs of women's smaller bodies and swing speeds, while providing pleasing aesthetics.

That is where WGU sees a huge opportunity. It has the potential to use its knowledge of and sensitivity towards the women's market to motivate female players to spend proportionately to their share of the total market's population. It is an untapped market value of well over $100 million.

Questions

1. Does the group of consumers to which WGU targets its products satisfy the definition of a market, a market segment, or both? Explain.

2. Discuss the importance of market segmentation strategy to WGU.

3. Describe the positioning strategy for WGU as an organization.

4. Describe the positioning for each of the two golf club brands that WGU markets.

MARKETING PLANNING ACTIVITIES

To complete all seven activities, use the Part 2 Marketing Planning Worksheets on your *Xtra!* CD-ROM. If you need a company for the basis of your work, follow the "Marketing Plan Project" link on the *Marketing* Web site (**http://lamb.swcollege.com**).

Analyzing Marketing Opportunities

For continued general assistance on business plans and marketing plans, visit **http://www.bplans.com** or **http://www.businessplans.org**. For electronic sources of information, search the Electric Library at **http://www.elibrary.com** or the Internet Public Library at **http://www.ipl.org**. Another excellent source of information is the Sales and Marketing Executives Marketing Library at **http://www.sell.org**. You should also refer to Exhibit 2.7 for additional marketing plan checklist items (Part IV.A: Target Market Strategy).

The next step in preparing a marketing plan for the company you have chosen is to get a thorough understanding of the marketing opportunities in terms of marketing to customers. Investigate Internet opportunities, with a special focus on potential customers. Try to understand both consumer and business decision making because Internet business can be built to serve either market. In fact, most experts predict that the business-to-business sector of the Internet will be several times larger than the business-to-consumer sector. Knowing how to perform marketing research to find out more about both customers and competitors is key for any strategic marketing plan.

Use the following exercises to guide you through the second part of your strategic marketing plan:

1. Identify the NAIC code for your chosen company's industry. Perform a brief industry analysis (from U.S. *Industrial Outlook*, for example) of your firm's industry, based on the NAIC code. You can find SIC codes at **http://www.wave.net/upg/immigration/sic_index.html**. These codes will help you perform further research. For example, register with the free site **http://www.zapdata.com** and get market analyses and profiles for your firm and industry. The Statistical Data Locators site (**http://www.ntu.edu.sg/library/stat/statdata.htm**) is a good collection of statistical and economic sources from countries and regions outside the United States.

2. To whom does your company market (consumer, industrial, government, not-for-profit, or a combination of targets)? Within each market, are there specific segments or niches that your company can concentrate on? If so, which one(s) would you focus on and why? What are the factors used to create these segments? What are the Internet capabilities in those markets? If you try to encourage those segments to access your product or service via the Internet, will that change which segments are most important to your business? How? What are the factors used to create these segments? Which segments should your company focus on and why? A resource indicating segment-specific resources is available at **http://www.awool.com/**. Additionally, the U.S. Census Bureau has a number of databases you can access with statistics for different marketing segments at **http://www.census.gov**. You can also look at the unique challenges of business-to-business e-marketing at **www.clickz.com**.

3. Describe your company's target market segment(s). Use demographics, psychographics, geographics, economic factors, size, growth rates, trends, NAIC codes, and any other appropriate descriptors. What role does the Internet play in your target market's life? How is the target market for your Internet business different from that of a traditional business in your market?

4. Describe the decision-making process that customers go through when purchasing your company's product or service. What are the critical factors that influence this purchase-behavior process? How will this decision making affect your e-marketing focus and your market offering? If you have a brick-and-mortar presence, will you encourage any existing customers to shop online? Why?

5. Using the list of key differential advantages described in the first part of your marketing plan, create a series of positioning grids, using two factors as dimensions (see Exhibit 7.9 for example). Then plot the list of key competitors identified earlier onto these positioning grids. Is your company too close to a key competitor? Are there spaces where the consumer's needs and wants are unsatisfied? Check out the concepts and models used by Positioning Strategies at **http://www.positioning.com** to increase your understanding of positioning strategies. Consider how the Internet changes what factors are important to success in your market space. Is technology the most important factor for your firm, or are there other ways for you to differentiate from and beat your competition?

6. Are there any critical issues you must explore with primary marketing research before you can implement your marketing plan? These might include items such as customer demand, purchase intentions, customer perceptions of product quality, price perceptions, and reaction to critical promotion. List some critical research questions and decide which form of research you would use. Design a brief Internet customer satisfaction survey that you could place on your Web site. Use the "Survey Wiz" at **http://psych.fullerton.edu/mbirnbaum/programs/surveyWiz.HTM** to help you with your questionnaire. Also check out Insight Express at **http://www.insightexpress.com**.

7. What type of competitive intelligence will you need to gather in order to monitor your market space? How can analyzing the job offerings, mission or "about us" statements, products and services descriptions, or other general information on your competitors' Web sites help you figure out their strategic direction? What areas of a Web site could you scan to gather competitive information? Perhaps you will need to select a clipping service. Go to **http://www.looksmart.com** and search for "News Clipping Services." For an excellent compilation of competitive intelligence tools, go to **http://www.fuld.com/i3/index.html**.

CROSS-FUNCTIONAL CONNECTIONS SOLUTIONS

Questions

1. Why has information historically been perceived as "owned" by the marketing department?

   There are probably a few general answers to this question. One is that because the information is referred to as "marketing research" rather than "market" or "marketplace," it automatically denotes that it is part of the marketing department. Also, the research has traditionally been conducted by the marketing department—reinforcing the notion that the marketing department owns it. Additionally, prior to the 1990s, the marketing department was the only formal link between the company and the customer. Because a primary focus of marketing research is the customer, it was always owned by the marketing department.

2. What data differences exist across functions?

   The historical data debate between marketing and other business functions centers on the qualitative versus quantitative format of the data. The data collected by marketers are perceived to be "touchy-feely" data in contrast to the "hard" data utilized by other functional areas. In addition to unit sales and competitive offerings, marketing data look at customers' perceptions—something very "soft" when compared to other functional data. For example, manufacturing can cite exact production output, cost, and cycle data, and R&D has precise specifications for tensile strength, electrical usage, and battery power. Add accounting data with their general accounting standards to the "hard" data side of the picture, and it's not surprising that data differences cause cross-functional conflict within a firm.

3. What is the job of a chief knowledge officer?

   The chief knowledge officer is a company executive who manages institutional learning. CKOs are responsible for integrating internal and external knowledge into their companies. In addition to monitoring this information, the CKO creates and propagates new knowledge based on industry observations, best practices, and benchmarking studies. The CKO shares the collected knowledge with all members of the firm, thereby providing them with consistently important and relevant information.

Suggested Readings

James A. Cook, "Web Browser Brings Product Demand into Focus," *Logistics Management and Distribution*, May 1999, 67–70.

Alex Taylor III, "Kellogg Cranks Up Its Idea Machine," *Fortune*, July 5, 1999, 181–182.

PART 3

Product Decisions

BLURRING FUNCTIONAL LINES IN SPEED-TO-MARKET INITIATIVES

Marketing focuses upon a company's products/services from a *demand-side* perspective. Via marketing research methods, marketers determine current and future wants and needs. Once these wants and needs are determined, marketing then expects the research and development group to develop a device that will satisfy customer demands. When developed, the expectation is that the manufacturing group will produce the device. The device becomes a true product with the development of a marketing program that adds value to customers.

Manufacturing and R&D typically view products from a *supply-side* perspective; in this framework, however, new product conception is the job of the R&D group for design, with the device then produced by the manufacturing group. The supply-side role of marketing is getting the marketplace to want the product. From this perspective, marketing is the functional group that tells the marketplace about the product's performance but has no input as to what actually goes into the product.

Many businesspeople have suggested that whether a company or product is driven by a demand-side or a supply-side focus is dependent upon the nature of the product. For example, highly technological products such as components of a computer would be based more on supply-side thinking. Prior to the development of products such as Intel components (which make computers function better) or PCMCIA cards by SystemSoft Corporation (which allow computers to communicate via a modem), consumers probably did not have sufficient knowledge to ask for such component parts. Consumer products (such as snack foods or personal-care products), however, appear to be better examples of demand-side concepts.

Demand-side versus supply-side thinking has resulted in three major areas of conflict between marketing and R&D/manufacturing: managing variety, managing availability, and managing reliability. Generally, marketing wants a large variety of high-quality products for customers to choose from and will promise the shortest delivery time necessary to get the order. On the flip side, R&D and manufacturing prefer fewer models so that they can devote attention to a smaller number of projects—resulting in high quality—without holding too many products in inventory.

Research and development and manufacturing functional groups have become quite efficient at working together—using processes referred to as "design-factory fit," "concurrent engineering," "design for manufacturability and assembly," and "early manufacturing involvement." Basically, all of these concepts refer to advance linkage between a product's design and its manufacturing needs so that the manufacturing group will be ready to make the product once it has been designed. Companies have been quite successful at implementing these concepts. Ryobi Group, a Japanese manufacturer of products such as power tools and power equipment, utilized design for manufacturability and assembly in the development of a new engine for handheld power equipment. The company successfully included its marketing group in the new product development process by receiving input with respect to customers' desired product features.

The efficient coordinating processes developed on the technical side of business have been meshed with customers' demands for high-quality, highly customized products that can be delivered immediately. Such expectations are in direct contrast to traditional thinking. Traditionally, companies made standardized products available immediately, with customers understanding that customization would result in delays in delivery. Today's marketplace is increasingly demanding that companies compete on both time and customization.

The key to providing customized products quickly is a multidisciplinary approach to business. Marketplace demands of immediacy and customization have focused attention on marketing, R&D, and manufacturing. Traditionally, products were conceptualized by one function, given to another function to produce, and then handed over to another function to sell. However, competing on time in the new product development process does away with linear product development. Now, the expectation is that the final product is high quality and has moved through the company's functional processes in at least half the time of the traditional linear process.

Xerox has become a leader in utilizing cross-functional teams to both improve product quality and speed new products to market. Harley-Davidson uses cross-functional teams from concept to market. Implementing the cross-functional team approach helped save the company from possible demise in the latter half of the twentieth century. The general idea is that a company can design a product that satisfies customers' demands while simultaneously designing a product that is quicker and easier to assemble. This type of design and assembly requires a high level of coordination among marketing, R&D, and manufacturing.

Boeing refers to this type of coordination as "paperless design." The design of the Boeing 777 utilized teams from R&D, manufacturing, marketing, customers, and finance—with all team members interacting to assemble an airplane on a computer system that allowed them to model the airplane and iron out bugs long before the major expense of building a prototype.

Manufacturers also have focused on meeting customization and speed-to-market demands with "modularization." With modular components, some of a product's component parts fit in all, or most, of the company's products. Many of the power tools made by Black & Decker are made with modular components. The modularity reduces the number of individual parts, allowing the firm to quickly customize the product beyond its core architecture. However, modularization does increase the time and cost of (re)designing products. Thus, marketing, manufacturing, and finance have to work closely with R&D to demonstrate the long-term payoff of modularization.

The finance and accounting areas have also been particularly thorny areas concerning both new and existing products. Financial managers often complain that marketers are not held to the same financial standards as the rest of the company, particularly when rolling out a new product. In turn, marketers feel the need to justify each expenditure—even though the payback on marketing allocations, such as advertising, is not immediate and/or always easily discernible. This type of friction, referred to as "creative friction" at Harley-Davidson, between market-

ing and finance/accounting can slow the development cycle and be in direct conflict with the speed-to-market initiatives the company may be taking. Product innovator 3M has been at the forefront of using management accounting tools to integrate customer value and shareholder value.

Typically, we think of new products in terms of tangible items, but cross-functional coordination is particularly important in the introduction and delivery of a new or existing service. Since the production and marketing of a service happen simultaneously, it is imperative that these two functions are closely integrated. The 1990s' focus on customer service, which will no doubt be an even greater issue in the twenty-first century, has added another function to this marketing-production coupling—human resources.

Employees are at the heart of customer service. The front-line employee plays a pivotal role in delivering high-quality service. A service provider's profitability and growth objectives are driven by customer loyalty, which is in turn driven by customer satisfaction, which is the direct result of human interaction with the service provider.

Whether it is developing a new product/service or managing the existing product line or service offerings, cross-functional teamwork is necessary for company-wide success. Successful interaction between marketing and all other business functions is imperative for competitive advantage in today's rapidly changing marketplace.

Questions

1. What is the difference between the demand-side perspective and the supply-side perspective to doing business? Is either perspective more appropriate?

2. What are some of the popular business terms used to describe cross-functional integration?

3. Why are employees (whether in marketing or not) at the heart of customer service?

CHAPTER **NINE**

PRODUCT CONCEPTS

Learning Objectives

1 *Define the term* product

2 *Classify consumer products*

3 *Define the terms* product item, product line, *and* product mix

4 *Describe marketing uses of branding*

5 *Describe marketing uses of packaging and labeling*

6 *Discuss global issues in branding and packaging*

7 *Describe how and why product warranties are important marketing tools*

In the summer of 1999, Design Continuum's parking lot could have doubled as a Texas barbecue cook-off. However, the consultants at the Boston product design company were researching a new product for Coleman, the company known for its lanterns and camping stoves. Coleman was about to introduce the first gas grill in its hundred-year history. While grills do not pose a difficult engineering problem, the marketing of a Coleman backyard grill was a challenge. Coleman has a successful brand name, but it had never produced anything besides camping products. "If you know the Coleman brand, it's radical to propose having a backyard grill," noted Mark Prince, Continuum's director of marketing. "They were taking the brand into new territory." Moreover, Coleman had no branding guide to help designers.

The Continuum team examined years of Coleman catalogs to try and define what made the Coleman brand unique. It found several things that Coleman products had in common, including their weight and their signature green enamel finish. The design team tried a few radical ideas, including a design for a grill that resembled a Coleman lantern. But customer surveys found that customers preferred the sturdy, traditional designs that Coleman was known for. People expected the new grills to carry on the Coleman heritage, which meant reliable and durable products.

The challenge was to translate this heritage into a new product category. The Continuum/Coleman team decided to create not the most advanced grill in the industry, but one that had the unique aspects of the Coleman brand: weight and the green enamel color. "When you see this grill in Home Depot, you don't say, 'Wow, that's better than anything I've seen,'" Prince says. "You look at it and say it's a Coleman."

To introduce the product, Coleman used its connections with stores like Home Depot and Sears to persuade them to carry the new grills, priced in the $300 to $500 range. A print ad campaign ran in outdoor-enthusiast magazines. The company also sponsored cook-offs at Nascar events. The grill got a public relations boost from *Consumer Reports*, which gave it one of its highest ratings.

The new line of grills captured 4 percent of the market and was one of the most successful launches in Sunbeam's (Coleman's parent company) history. In fact, the new grills have helped attract people to the entire Coleman brand.[1]

Explain how Coleman's new grill fits into the company's product mix. Why do you think that Coleman was so successful with its new grill? What other new products might Coleman be successful with? We will answer these questions and more in Chapter 9.

What Is a Product?

1

Define the term *product*

product
Everything, both favorable and unfavorable, that a person receives in an exchange.

The product offering, the heart of an organization's marketing program, is usually the starting point in creating a marketing mix. A marketing manager cannot determine a price, design a promotion strategy, or create a distribution channel until the firm has a product to sell. Moreover, an excellent distribution channel, a persuasive promotion campaign, and a fair price have no value with a poor or inadequate product offering.

A **product** may be defined as everything, both favorable and unfavorable, that a person receives in an exchange. A product may be a tangible good like a pair of shoes, a service like a haircut, an idea like "don't litter," or any combination of these three. Packaging, style, color, options, and size are some typical product features. Just as important are intangibles such as service, the seller's image, the manufacturer's reputation, and the way consumers believe others will view the product.

To most people, the term *product* means a tangible good. However, services and ideas are also products. (Chapter 11 focuses specifically on the unique aspects of marketing services.) The marketing process identified in Chapter 1 is the same whether the product marketed is a good, a service, an idea, or some combination of these.

Types of Consumer Products

2

Classify consumer products

business product (industrial product)
A product used to manufacture other goods or services, to facilitate an organization's operations, or to resell to other customers.

consumer product
A product bought to satisfy an individual's personal wants.

Products can be classified as either business (industrial) or consumer products, depending on the buyer's intentions. The key distinction between the two types of products is their intended use. If the intended use is a business purpose, the product is classified as a business or industrial product. As explained in Chapter 6, a **business product** is used to manufacture other goods or services, to facilitate an organization's operations, or to resell to other customers. A **consumer product** is bought to satisfy an individual's personal wants. Sometimes the same item can be classified as either a business or a consumer product, depending on its intended use. Examples include lightbulbs, pencils and paper, and computers.

We need to know about product classifications because business and consumer products are marketed differently. They are marketed to different target markets and tend to use different distribution, promotion, and pricing strategies.

Chapter 6 examined seven categories of business products: major equipment, accessory equipment, component parts, processed materials, raw materials, supplies, and services. The current chapter examines an effective way of categorizing consumer products. Although there are several ways to classify them, the most popular approach includes these four types: convenience products, shopping products, specialty products, and unsought products (see Exhibit 9.1). This approach classifies products according to how much effort is normally used to shop for them.

Convenience Products

convenience product
A relatively inexpensive item that merits little shopping effort.

A **convenience product** is a relatively inexpensive item that merits little shopping effort—that is, a consumer is unwilling to shop extensively for such an item. Candy, soft drinks, combs, aspirin, small hardware items, dry cleaning, and car washes fall into the convenience product category.

Consumers buy convenience products regularly, usually without much planning. Nevertheless, consumers do know the brand names of popular convenience products, such as Coca-Cola, Bayer aspirin, and Right Guard deodorant. Convenience products normally require wide distribution in order to sell sufficient quantities to meet profit goals.

Exhibit 9.1

Classification of Consumer Products

Shopping Products

A **shopping product** is usually more expensive than a convenience product and is found in fewer stores. Consumers usually buy a shopping product only after comparing several brands or stores on style, practicality, price, and lifestyle compatibility. They are willing to invest some effort into this process to get the desired benefits.

There are two types of shopping products: homogeneous and heterogeneous. Consumers perceive *homogeneous* shopping products as basically similar—for example, washers, dryers, refrigerators, and televisions. With homogeneous shopping products, consumers typically look for the lowest-priced brand that has the desired features.

In contrast, consumers perceive *heterogeneous* shopping products as essentially different—for example, furniture, clothing, housing, and universities. Consumers often have trouble comparing heterogeneous shopping products because the prices, quality, and features vary so much. The benefit of comparing heterogeneous shopping products is "finding the best product or brand for me"; this decision is often highly individual.

Specialty Products

When consumers search extensively for a particular item and are very reluctant to accept substitutes, that item is a **specialty product**. Fine watches, Rolls Royce automobiles, expensive stereo equipment, gourmet restaurants, and highly specialized forms of medical care are generally considered specialty products.

Marketers of specialty products often use selective, status-conscious

shopping product
A product that requires comparison shopping because it is usually more expensive than a convenience product and is found in fewer stores.

specialty product
A particular item that consumers search extensively for and are very reluctant to accept substitutes.

With homogeneous products such as stoves, consumers typically buy the lowest-priced brand that has the desired features.

© GETTY IMAGES/PHOTODISC

advertising to maintain their product's exclusive image. Distribution is often limited to one or a very few outlets in a geographic area. Brand names and quality of service are often very important.

Unsought Products

unsought product
A product unknown to the potential buyer or a known product that the buyer does not actively seek.

A product unknown to the potential buyer or a known product that the buyer does not actively seek is referred to as an **unsought product**. New products fall into this category until advertising and distribution increase consumer awareness of them.

Some goods are always marketed as unsought items, especially needed products we do not like to think about or care to spend money on. Insurance, burial plots, encyclopedias, and similar items require aggressive personal selling and highly persuasive advertising. Salespeople actively seek leads to potential buyers. Because consumers usually do not seek out this type of product, the company must go directly to them through a salesperson, direct mail, or direct-response advertising.

Product Items, Lines, and Mixes

Define the terms *product item, product line,* and *product mix*

product item
A specific version of a product that can be designated as a distinct offering among an organization's products.

product line
A group of closely related product items.

product mix
All products that an organization sells.

Rarely does a company sell a single product. More often, it sells a variety of things. A **product item** is a specific version of a product that can be designated as a distinct offering among an organization's products. Gillette's MACH 3 razor is an example of a product item (see Exhibit 9.2).

A group of closely related product items is a **product line**. For example, the column in Exhibit 9.2 titled "Blades and Razors" represents one of Gillette's product lines. Different container sizes and shapes also distinguish items in a product line. Diet Coke, for example, is available in cans and various plastic containers. Each size and each container are separate product items.

An organization's **product mix** includes all the products it sells. All Gillette's products—blades and razors, toiletries, writing instruments, and lighters—constitute its product mix. Each product item in the product mix may require a separate marketing strategy. In some cases, however, product lines and even entire product mixes share some marketing strategy components. Nike promoted all of its product items and lines with the theme "Just Do It."

Organizations derive several benefits from organizing related items into product lines, including the following:

Exhibit 9.2

Gillette's Product Lines
and Product Mix

	Width of the Product Mix			
	Blades and Razors	**Toiletries**	**Writing Instruments**	**Lighters**
Depth of the Product Lines	MACH 3	Series	Paper Mate	Cricket
	Sensor	Adorn	Flair	S.T. Dupont
	Trac II	Toni		
	Atra	Right Guard		
	Swivel	Silkience		
	Double-Edge	Soft and Dri		
	Lady Gillette	Foamy		
	Super Speed	Dry Look		
	Twin Injector	Dry Idea		
	Techmatic	Brush Plus		

- *Advertising economies:* Product lines provide economies of scale in advertising. Several products can be advertised under the umbrella of the line. Campbell's can talk about its soup being "m-m-good" and promote the entire line.

- *Package uniformity:* A product line can benefit from package uniformity. All packages in the line may have a common look and still keep their individual identities. Again, Campbell's soup is a good example.

- *Standardized components:* Product lines allow firms to standardize components, thus reducing manufacturing and inventory costs. For example, many of the components Samsonite uses in its folding tables and chairs are also used in its patio furniture. General Motors uses the same parts on many automobile makes and models.

- *Efficient sales and distribution:* A product line enables sales personnel for companies like Procter & Gamble to provide a full range of choices to customers. Distributors and retailers are often more inclined to stock the company's products if it offers a full line. Transportation and warehousing costs are likely to be lower for a product line than for a collection of individual items.

- *Equivalent quality:* Purchasers usually expect and believe that all products in a line are about equal in quality. Consumers expect that all Campbell's soups and all Mary Kay cosmetics will be of similar quality.

Marriott

Does Marriott use its product lines to organize its Web site? How so? Compare the sites for the different hotels listed on the site. What conclusions can you draw about Marriott's product mix based on what you see at the various sites?

http://www.marriott.com

On Line

Product mix width (or breadth) refers to the number of product lines an organization offers. In Exhibit 9.2, for example, the width of Gillette's product mix is four product lines. **Product line depth** is the number of product items in a product line. As shown in Exhibit 9.2, the blades and razors product line consists of ten product items; the toiletries product line also includes ten product items.

Firms increase the *width* of their product mix to diversify risk. To generate sales and boost profits, firms spread risk across many product lines rather than depend on only one or two. Firms also widen their product mix to capitalize on established reputations. By introducing new product lines, Kodak capitalized on its image as a leader in photographic products. Kodak's product lines now include film, processing, still cameras, movie cameras, paper, and chemicals. Limited, Inc., a company that mostly comprises women's apparel stores (Limited, Limited Too, Victoria's Secret) developed a line of makeup under the Victoria's Secret brand.

Firms increase the *depth* of product lines to attract buyers with different preferences, to increase sales and profits by further segmenting the market, to capitalize on economies of scale in production and marketing, and to even out seasonal sales patterns. Marriott International has fourteen different lodging brands that are divided into three groups. The full-service group includes flagship Marriott, upscale Renaissance Hotels and Resorts, and Marriott Conference Centers. The select service group includes Courtyard, Spring Hill Suites, and Fairfield Inn. The extended stay group includes Residence Inn and ExecuStay.

Adjustments to Product Items, Lines, and Mixes

Over time, firms change product items, lines, and mixes to take advantage of new technical or product developments or to respond to changes in the environment. They may adjust by modifying products, repositioning products, or extending or contracting product lines.

Product Modification

Marketing managers must decide if and when to modify existing products. **Product modification** changes one or more of a product's characteristics:

- *Quality modification:* change in a product's dependability or durability. Reducing a product's quality may let the manufacturer lower the price and appeal to target

product mix width
The number of product lines an organization offers.

product line depth
The number of product items in a product line.

product modification
Changing one or more of a product's characteristics.

EVERY KID GOES THROUGH STAGES. FORTUNATELY, SO DO OUR NEW BRUSHES.

COURTESY THE GILLETTE COMPANY

Oral-B's Stages toothbrushes represent a functional modification to adult toothbrushes. Numerous colors and designs of a single stage toothbrush would be a style modification.

markets unable to afford the original product. On the other hand, increasing quality can help the firm compete with rival firms. Increasing quality can also result in increased brand loyalty, greater ability to raise prices, or new opportunities for market segmentation. Inexpensive ink-jet printers have improved in quality to the point that they produce photo-quality images. These printers are now competing with camera film. To appeal to a more upscale market, Robert Mondavi Winery introduced a high-end wine called Twin Oaks to prestige restaurants and hotels. This wine is positioned as a higher quality wine than the one Mondavi sells in supermarkets.

- *Functional modification:* change in a product's versatility, effectiveness, convenience, or safety. Oral-B introduced Stages toothbrushes, a line of toothbrushes for children. For example, Stage 2, designed for toddlers, has an easy-to-grip handle and a narrow brush that makes it easier to reach all teeth.[2] Lea & Perrins offers its steak sauce in a value-priced squeeze bottle with a "no mess, stay clean" cap.

- *Style modification:* aesthetic product change, rather than a quality or functional change. Pontiac modified the style of its Aztec car based on focus-group results after initial sales were weak. The original two-tone color scheme that featured gray trim was replaced by a monochromatic color scheme, and the small wheels were replaced with sixteen-inch cast aluminum wheels. A spoiler was also added to soften some of the car's sharp lines.[3] Clothing and auto manufacturers also commonly use style modifications to motivate customers to replace products before they are worn out. **Planned obsolescence** is a term commonly used to describe the practice of modifying products so that those that have already been sold become obsolete before they actually need replacement. Some argue that planned obsolescence is wasteful; some claim it is unethical. Marketers respond that consumers favor style modifications because they like changes in the appearance of goods like clothing and cars. Marketers also contend that consumers, not manufacturers and marketers, decide when styles are obsolete.

planned obsolescence
The practice of modifying products so those that have already been sold become obsolete before they actually need replacement.

Repositioning

Repositioning, as Chapter 7 explained, involves changing consumers' perceptions of a brand. For example, Tommy Hilfiger started out as a company offering classic, preppy clothing. During the 1990s, Hilfiger was repositioned as a hipper, more urban brand to appeal to a younger audience. During 2001, to combat decreasing sales and to regain its core market, Hilfiger once again repositioned itself and returned to its clean-cut image.[4]

GLOBAL Changing demographics, declining sales, or changes in the social environment often motivate firms to reposition established brands. The Japanese cosmetics company Shiseido changed the positioning of its cosmetics from masking products to products to enhance women's inner beauty. Based on this repositioning, the company introduced a new skin-care line that has helped to attract a younger audience (twenty-five- to thirty-year olds) than its traditional market of women aged thirty to forty-five.[5]

Product Line Extensions

product line extension
Adding additional products to an existing product line in order to compete more broadly in the industry.

A **product line extension** occurs when a company's management decides to add products to an existing product line in order to compete more broadly in the industry. Minute Maid has added two calcium-fortified juices—Premium Home-

Squeezed Style orange juice and Ruby Red Grapefruit Blend—to attract health-conscious baby boomers.[6] Jolly Rancher launched Fruit Chews to compete in the chewy candy product category.[7] Procter & Gamble has developed numerous extensions of its Tide laundry detergent, including Tide with Bleach, Tide Free (which has no fragrance), Tide WearCare (which claims to keep fabrics brighter longer), and Tide Kick (whose package has a nozzle to rub detergent directly into fabrics).[8]

The story in the "Global Perspectives" box illustrates how Coca-Cola and Procter & Gamble expanded their beverage lines to respond to consumer needs in developing countries.

Unilever

Can Unilever delete anything from its product lines? Visit the company's product category pages on its "Brands" Web page to see the number of existing products and new products planned. Write a proposal for contracting one of Unilever's product lines.

http://www.unilever.com

On Line

Product Line Contraction

Does the world really need thirty-one varieties of Head and Shoulders shampoo? Or fifty-two versions of Crest? Black & Decker has decided the answer is no. The company has deleted a number of household products—Dustbusters, SnakeLight flashlights, and toaster ovens—and is concentrating on power tools. Symptoms of product line overextension include the following:

- Some products in the line do not contribute to profits because of low sales or cannibalize sales of other items in the line.

- Manufacturing or marketing resources are disproportionately allocated to slow-moving products.

- Some items in the line are obsolete because of new product entries in the line or new products offered by competitors.

Three major benefits are likely when a firm contracts overextended product lines. First, resources become concentrated on the most important products. Second, managers no longer waste resources trying to improve the sales and profits of poorly performing products. Third, new product items have a greater chance of being successful because more financial and human resources are available to manage them.

©TERRI MILLER/E-VISUAL COMMUNICATIONS, INC.

Product extensions enable a company to compete more broadly in an industry. Coca-Cola's Minute Maid was successful building upon its original Premium orange juice brand with Premium Blends, which mix orange juice with cranberry, passion fruit, strawberry and banana, or tangerine juice. Other product extensions include Minute Maid Coolers, Minute Maid Smoothies, and Minute Maid Frozen Fruit Bars, among others.

Branding

The success of any business or consumer product depends in part on the target market's ability to distinguish one product from another. Branding is the main tool marketers use to distinguish their products from the competition's.

A **brand** is a name, term, symbol, design, or combination thereof that identifies a seller's products and differentiates them from competitors' products. A **brand name** is that part of a brand that can be spoken, including letters (GM, YMCA), words (Chevrolet), and numbers (WD-40, 7-Eleven). The elements of a brand that cannot be spoken are called the **brand mark**—for example, the well-known Mercedes-Benz and Delta Airlines symbols.

Benefits of Branding

Branding has three main purposes: product identification, repeat sales, and new-product sales. The most important purpose is *product identification*. Branding allows marketers to distinguish their products from all others. Many brand names are familiar to consumers and indicate quality.

Describe marketing uses of branding

brand
A name, term, symbol, design, or combination thereof that identifies a seller's products and differentiates them from competitors' products.

brand name
That part of a brand that can be spoken, including letters, words, and numbers.

brand mark
The elements of a brand that cannot be spoken.

Drinks for Developing Countries

In the spring of 2001, Coca-Cola Company conducted a clinical test of a special drink on children in Gabarone, Botswana. The beverage looked and tasted like the company's Hi-C orange-flavored drink, but this drink contained twelve vitamins and minerals chronically lacking in the diets of people in developing countries. The test was part of "Project Mission," a continuing research and development effort aimed at creating a drink to help fight diseases like anemia, blindness, and other afflictions that are common in poorer parts of the world. At the end of eight weeks, results of the test showed that levels of iron and zinc in the children's blood had grown. Some parents said their children, whose diets consist mostly of cornmeal and rice, had more energy and had become more attentive at school. The new drink, to be called Vitango, could help Coke increase sales at a time when growth of carbonated beverages is slowing.

After its launch, Vitango will put Coca-Cola in direct competition with Procter & Gamble Company, which has a similar drink that is already being sold. P&G launched its product, Nutristar, in late 2001 in Venezuela after years of research and development and clinical tests. A powdered drink that contains eight vitamins and five minerals, Nutristar is sold at most food stores in flavors like mango and passion fruit. So far, the drink is doing well. Available also at McDonald's, Nutristar is the chosen beverage with about half the Happy Meals the restaurants sell. Nutristar is also being sampled in schools.

While the market for such drinks is limited, they are meant to offer Coke and P&G a chance to attempt the role of good corporate citizen at a time when being perceived as such is increasingly important for U.S. multinational firms. Coke has high hopes for Vitango in Africa and Latin America, where its products already reach some of the most remote areas. A second clinical test, to determine how well Vitango's nutrients are absorbed into the bloodstream, was just finished in Peru.

"Micronutrient" deficiencies, or a lack of vitamins and minerals such as vitamin A, iron, and zinc, are believed to afflict about two billion children around the world. With vitamin pills costly to distribute and pill-taking regimes hard to enforce, fortification of foods offers the most promising prospects for combating some deficiencies.

Coke's Project Mission began in April 2000, when a group of marketing and innovation executives visited the company's operations in Ecuador. Local managers there were looking for a less obtru-sive way to advance the Coca-Cola name in secondary schools than through bottle-cap contests that promoted sales of cola. With economic conditions in the country deteriorating, children were poorly nourished and inattentive in class. In developing the beverage, Coke found out that a powdered version of Hi-C sold to restaurants appealed to consumer groups tested in South Africa. With that information, the company put together a "worldwide nutrition advisory board" to create a combination of vitamins and minerals that would be absorbed well and whose taste would not be too strong. Powder, liquid, and even carbonated forms of the beverage were developed. Concerned with water quality in Africa, Coke wants to sell the beverage there in a ready-to-drink form. The beverage is not intended to replace drinking milk or juice, but as a supplement that augments a healthy diet.[9]

Would you consider Vitango to be a product modification for Coca-Cola? If so, what type of modification does it represent? What type of branding strategy does Coca-Cola appear to be using with Vitango? Do you think that this brand name would be successful in other countries? Support your answer.

---

brand equity
The value of company and brand names.

The term **brand equity** refers to the value of company and brand names. A brand that has high awareness, perceived quality, and brand loyalty among customers has high brand equity. A brand with strong brand equity is a valuable asset. As the "Ethics in Marketing" box shows, however, concerns have been raised about the way some companies attempt to build brand equity.

global brand
A brand where at least 20 percent of the product is sold outside its home country or region.

The term **global brand** has been used to refer to brands where at least 20 percent of the product is sold outside their home country or region. "A strong global brand acts as an ambassador when companies enter new markets or offer new products." It also helps guide corporate strategy decisions by indicating which new ideas fit within the brand concept and which do not.[11] Yum Brands (formerly Tricon Global Restaurants), which owns Pizza Hut, KFC, and Taco Bell, is a good example of a company that has developed strong global brands. Yum believes that it has to adapt its restaurants to local tastes and different cultural and political climates. In Japan, for instance, KFC sells tempura crispy strips. In northern England, KFC focuses on gravy and potatoes, while in Thailand it offers rice with soy or sweet chili sauce. In China, the company re-

Lesson Plans

It's hard to resist a large group of consumers that is always looking for the Next Big Thing and is a guaranteed captive audience seven to eight hours a day, five days a week, nine months of the year. While advertising to kids under eighteen is tricky enough, reaching them at school takes marketers even further into an ethical gray area.

Teenage Research Unlimited, a marketing research firm based in Northbrook, Illinois, estimates that U.S. teens, ages twelve to nineteen, spent a total of about $155 billion in 2000. While no statistic exists for the total amount spent by corporations each year on in-school marketing programs, Milwaukee-based Center for the Analysis of Commercialism in Education (CACE), a nonprofit academic group dedicated to tracking marketing in U.S. schools, reports that the last decade has seen a 395 percent increase in the number of stories on the subject published or broadcast in the U.S. media.

Despite the increased media attention, in-school marketing programs are nearly irresistible—for the administration as well as the marketers—because of the money that goes to the school above and beyond what local communities and state and federal governments provide. For example, programs to help students with special needs often lack sufficient funds, and the money from marketing agreements can be a boost to districts seeking to fill this void.

Soft drink vending machines in schools are among the most common, and the most controversial, types of in-school marketing agreements. The machines may generate hundreds of thousands of dollars a year in extra revenue for the schools that have them, but they have in the past increased concerns of parents and others about the mix of marketing and education. For example, in 1998, a Georgia high school senior wore a Pepsi-branded t-shirt on the school-designated "Coke Day." The result was a day's suspension—and nationwide publicity, including a number of editorials decrying corporate America's involvement in the classroom. (The principal ultimately withdrew the suspension and cleared his [the student's] record.)

More recently, the machines have been targeted because of the lack of nutritional value in carbonated drinks. One thing that soft drink marketers have done to address these concerns has been to make sure a variety of beverages, such as fruit juice and water, are available in school vending machines. However, the move does not make many nutritionists happy. They note that many juice drinks found in vending machines are high in calories, low on nutrition, and not much healthier for kids than soft drinks.

Another education-based program is Pizza Hut's Book It. This program is positioned as a teacher's aid, and awards certificates to students in elementary schools who complete reading assignments. "We are not marketing to kids, but providing a literacy curriculum to teachers," says Patty Sullivan, director of public relations for Pizza Hut. Since the Book It program's creation in 1985, Pizza Hut has given away $178 million in pizza to schoolchildren. The program has also probably generated additional revenue for the company, assuming that family and friends accompanying the awardee make additional purchases. Meanwhile, the program has escaped much of the criticism that has been leveled at other in-school marketing programs. Indeed, the U.S. Department of Education has granted Book It several Certificates of Recognition, citing it as a model educational partnership between a corporation and schools.[10]

Is in-school marketing ethical? Do you think that there is a difference between types of in-school marketing (for example, vending machines versus the Book It program)? Explain your answers.

cruits employees who balance an understanding of the Chinese mind-set with Western business training.[12] Exhibit 9.3 lists the world's ten most valuable brands.

What constitutes a good brand name? Most effective brand names have several of the following features:

- Is easy to pronounce (by both domestic and foreign buyers)
- Is easy to recognize
- Is easy to remember
- Is short
- Is distinctive, unique
- Describes the product
- Describes product use
- Describes product benefits
- Has a positive connotation

Tide

How does Tide use its Web site to maintain customer relationships? To build its brand?

http://www.tide.com

 ◀ ▶   **On Line**

Exhibit 9.3

The World's Ten Most Valuable Brands

Rank	Brand	2001 Brand Value ($ billions)	Country of Ownership
1	Coca-Cola	68.9	U.S.
2	Microsoft	65.1	U.S.
3	IBM	52.8	U.S.
4.	GE	42.4	U.S.
5	Nokia	35.0	Finland
6	Intel	34.7	U.S.
7	Disney	32.6	U.S.
8	Ford	30.1	U.S.
9	McDonald's	25.3	U.S.
10	AT&T	22.8	U.S.

SOURCE: Gerry Khermouch, Stanley Holmes, and Moon Ihlwan, "The Best Global Brands," *Business Week*, August 6, 2001, 50–57.

- Reinforces the desired product image
- Is legally protectable in home and foreign markets of interest

Obviously, no brand exhibits all of these characteristics. The most important issue is that the brand can be protected for exclusive use by its owner.

The best generator of *repeat sales* is satisfied customers. Branding helps consumers identify products they wish to buy again and avoid those they do not. **Brand loyalty**, a consistent preference for one brand over all others, is quite high in some product categories. Over half the users in product categories such as cigarettes, mayonnaise, toothpaste, coffee, headache remedies, photographic film, bath soap, and ketchup are loyal to one brand. Brand identity is essential to developing brand loyalty.

The third main purpose of branding is to *facilitate new-product sales*. Company and brand names like those listed in Exhibit 9.3 are extremely useful when introducing new products.

brand loyalty
A consistent preference for one brand over all others.

Procter & Gamble has an extensive Web presence to support its complete slate of brands. In 2000, the company launched the pg.com network, touting it as "the one place where all our brands hang out together."

where's the one place all our brands hang out together?

introducing the **PG.com** network

The new pg.com lets you **do more**, **learn more** and **get more** from P&G and our brands than ever before...

Discover the surprising number of online resources our brands have to offer.

Try and buy products before they're available in stores.

Share your ideas for improving our products and creating new ones.

and coming soon... Take advantage of new tools to help manage your P&G shareholders account.

w w w . p g . c o m

© THE PROCTER & GAMBLE COMPANY. USED BY PERMISSION.

The Internet provides firms a new alternative for generating brand awareness, promoting a desired brand image, stimulating new and repeat brand sales, and enhancing brand loyalty and building brand equity. A number of packaged-goods firms, such as Procter & Gamble, Campbell's soup, and Gerber, have a presence on-line. Tide.com offers a useful feature called Stain Detective, a digital tip sheet on how to remove almost any substance from almost any fabric. Reflect.com lets women mix and match various options to create their own "brands" of makeup, perfume, and other beauty-care products.[13]

Branding Strategies

Firms face complex branding decisions. As Exhibit 9.4 illustrates, the first decision is whether to brand at all. Some firms actually use the lack of a brand name as a selling point. These unbranded products are called generic products. Firms that decide to brand their products may choose to follow a policy of using manufacturers' brands, private (distributor) brands, or both. In either case, they must then decide among a policy of individual branding (different brands for different products), family branding (common names for different products), or a combination of individual branding and family branding.

Generic Products versus Branded Products

A **generic product** is typically a no-frills, no-brand-name, low-cost product that is simply identified by its product category. (Note that a generic product and a brand name that becomes generic, such as cellophane, are not the same thing.) Generic products have captured significant market shares in some product categories, such as canned fruits, canned vegetables, and paper products. These unbranded products are frequently identified only by black stenciled lettering on white packages.

The main appeal of generics is their low price. Generic grocery products are usually 30 to 40 percent less expensive than manufacturers' brands in the same product category and 20 to 25 percent less expensive than retailer-owned brands.

generic product
A no-frills, no-brand-name, low-cost product that is simply identified by its product category.

Major Branding Decisions **Exhibit 9.4**

```
                    Brand                          No brand

        Manufacturer's                          Private brand
           brand

Individual brand    Family brand    Combination      Individual brand    Family brand    Combination
Examples:           Examples:       (family          Example: McClark's   Examples:       (family and
Tide, Cheer         General Electric, and individual) Restaurant          IGA, Kroger     individual)
                    RCA             Example: Kellogg's Bar-B-Cue Sauce                     Example:
                                    Rice Krispies                                         Sears-Kenmore
```

Pharmaceuticals are another product category where generics have made inroads. When patents on successful pharmaceutical products expire, low-cost generics rapidly appear on the market. For example, when the patent on Merck's popular antiarthritis drug Clinoril expired, sales declined by 50 percent almost immediately.

Manufacturers' Brands versus Private Brands

manufacturer's brand
The brand name of a manufacturer.

The brand name of a manufacturer—such as Kodak, Lazy Boy, and Fruit of the Loom—is called a **manufacturer's brand**. Sometimes "national brand" is used as a synonym for "manufacturer's brand." This term is not always accurate, however, because many manufacturers serve only regional markets. Using "manufacturer's brand" more precisely defines the brand's owner.

private brand
A brand name owned by a wholesaler or a retailer.

A **private brand**, also known as a private label or store brand, is a brand name owned by a wholesaler or a retailer. Hunt Club (a JCPenney brand), Sam's American Choice (Wal-Mart), and IGA (Independent Grocers' Association) are all private brands. Private brands now account for over 20 percent of sales at all U.S. mass merchandisers, drugstores, and supermarkets. At some stores, the penetration is much higher: At Target, for example, more than 50 percent of the merchandise is exclusive to the store. And across the board, store brands are growing faster than national brands.[14] Marketing experts predict that private labels will make up as much as 30 percent of grocery sales within five years—particularly as big supermarkets continue to consolidate.[15]

Exhibit 9.5 illustrates key issues that wholesalers and retailers should consider in deciding whether to sell manufacturers' brands or private brands. Many firms, such as JCPenney, Kmart, and Safeway, offer a combination of both. In fact, JCPenney and Sears have turned their low-priced, private-label jeans into some of the

Exhibit 9.5

Comparing Manufacturers' and Private Brands from the Reseller's Perspective

Key Advantages of Carrying Manufacturers' Brands	Key Advantages of Carrying Private Brands
• Heavy advertising to the consumer by manufacturers like Procter & Gamble helps develop strong consumer loyalties.	• A wholesaler or retailer can usually earn higher profits on its own brand. In addition, because the private brand is exclusive, there is less pressure to mark the price down to meet competition.
• Well-known manufacturers' brands, such as Kodak and Fisher-Price, can attract new customers and enhance the dealer's (wholesaler's or retailer's) prestige.	• A manufacturer can decide to drop a brand or a reseller at any time or even to become a direct competitor to its dealers.
• Many manufacturers offer rapid delivery, enabling the dealer to carry less inventory.	• A private brand ties the customer to the wholesaler or retailer. A person who wants a Die-Hard battery must go to Sears.
• If a dealer happens to sell a manufacturer's brand of poor quality, the customer may simply switch brands and remain loyal to the dealer.	• Wholesalers and retailers have no control over the intensity of distribution of manufacturers' brands. Wal-Mart store managers don't have to worry about competing with other sellers of Sam's American Choice products or Ol' Roy dog food. They know that these brands are sold only in Wal-Mart and Sam's Wholesale Club stores.

most popular brands around, thanks to hip marketing campaigns that feature rock bands, Web sites, and imagery targeted at teens.

Individual Brands versus Family Brands

Many companies use different brand names for different products, a practice referred to as **individual branding**. Companies use individual brands when their products vary greatly in use or performance. For instance, it would not make sense to use the same brand name for a pair of dress socks and a baseball bat. Procter & Gamble targets different segments of the laundry-detergent market with Bold, Cheer, Dash, Dreft, Era, Gain, Ivory Snow, Oxydol, Solo, and Tide. Marriott International also targets different market segments with Courtyard by Marriott, Residence Inn, and Fairfield Inn.

In contrast, a company that markets several different products under the same brand name is using a **family brand**. Sony's family brand includes radios, television sets, stereos, and other electronic products. A brand name can only be stretched so far, however. Do you know the differences among Holiday Inn, Holiday Inn Express, Holiday Inn Select, Holiday Inn Sunspree Resort, Holiday Inn Garden Court, and Holiday Inn Hotel & Suites? Neither do most travelers.

Cobranding

Cobranding entails placing two or more brand names on a product or its package. There are three types of cobranding. *Ingredient branding* identifies the brand of a part that makes up the product. Examples of ingredient branding are Intel (a microprocessor) in a personal computer, such as Dell, or a premium leather interior (Coach) in an automobile (Lincoln). *Cooperative branding* occurs when two brands receiving equal treatment (in the context of an advertisement) borrow on each other's brand equity. A promotional contest jointly sponsored by Ramada Inns, American Express, and Continental Airlines is an example of cooperative branding. Guests at Ramada who paid with an American Express card were automatically entered in the contest and were eligible to win more than a hundred getaways for two at any Ramada in the continental United States and round-trip airfare from Continental.[16] Finally, there is *complementary branding*, where products are advertised or marketed together to suggest usage, such as a spirits brand (Seagram's) and a compatible mixer (7-Up).

Cobranding is a useful strategy when a combination of brand names enhances the prestige or perceived value of a product or when it benefits brand owners and users. Toyota Motor's luxury division introduced a Platinum version of its Lexus brand. For a premium of as much as 10 percent above the base sticker prices, buyers get upgraded paint, leathers and accessories, and a free two-year subscription to the $300-a-year American Express Platinum Card. Both companies say that the Platinum Series models will reinforce their brands while delivering added value.[17]

Cobranding may be used to increase a company's presence in markets in which it has little or no market share. For example, Disney is attempting to increase its share of the food and beverage market by developing cobranding deals with Minute Maid for an eighteen-variety line of Disney Xtreme! Coolers based on Mickey and Friends and with Kellogg for cobranded cereals.[18]

European firms have been slower to adopt cobranding than U.S. firms have. One reason is that European customers seem to be more skeptical than U.S. customers about trying

Kellogg's
Disney

How are Kellogg's and Disney promoting their cobranding of cereals on their company Web sites? Does one of the two companies benefit more than the other from the arrangement? If so, which one? How?

http://www.kelloggs.com
http://www.disney.com

On Line

individual branding
Using different brand names for different products.

family brand
Marketing several different products under the same brand name.

cobranding
Placing two or more brand names on a product or its package.

On Line

Post Cereal
Quaker Oats

Ingredient branding can enhance the prestige and value of a brand. Cookies and candies are some common ingredients that appear in other products, like cereal and ice cream. Visit the Post Cereal and Quaker Oats Web sites to see how each company has incorporated ingredient branding into marketing strategy. What ingredients is each company using in its products? Do you think the cobranded products you find have increased value over a plain product (i.e., a product without a branded ingredient)?

http://www.postcereal.com
http://www.quakeroats.com

new brands. European retailers also typically have less shelf space than their U.S. counterparts and are less willing to give new brands a try.

Trademarks

A **trademark** is the exclusive right to use a brand or part of a brand. Others are prohibited from using the brand without permission. A **service mark** performs the same function for services, such as H&R Block and Weight Watchers. Parts of a brand or other product identification may qualify for trademark protection. Some examples are

- Shapes, such as the Jeep front grille and the Coca-Cola bottle
- Ornamental color or design, such as the decoration on Nike tennis shoes, the black-and-copper color combination of a Duracell battery, Levi's small tag on the left side of the rear pocket of its jeans, or the cutoff black cone on the top of Cross pens
- Catchy phrases, such as Prudential's "Own a piece of the rock," Merrill Lynch's "We're bullish on America," and Budweiser's "This Bud's for you"
- Abbreviations, such as Bud, Coke, or The Met
- Sounds, such as General Electric Broadcasting Company's ship's bell clock sound and the MGM lion's roar.

The Trademark Revision Act of 1988 allows organizations to register trademarks based on a bona fide intention to use them (normally, within six months following the issuance of the trademark) for ten years. To renew the trademark, the company must prove it is using it. Rights to a trademark last as long as the mark is used. Normally, if the firm does not use it for two years, the trademark is considered abandoned, and a new user can claim exclusive ownership of the mark.

In November 1999, legislation went into effect that explicitly applies trademark law to the on-line world. This law includes financial penalties for those who violate trademarked products or who register an otherwise trademarked term as a domain name.[19]

Companies that fail to protect their trademarks face the possibility that their product names will become generic. A **generic product name** identifies a product by class or type and cannot be trademarked. Former brand names that were not sufficiently protected by their owners and were subsequently declared to be generic product names by U.S. courts include aspirin, cellophane, linoleum, thermos, kerosene, monopoly, cola, and shredded wheat.

Companies like Rolls Royce, Cross, Xerox, Levi Strauss, Frigidaire, and McDonald's aggressively enforce their trademarks. Rolls Royce, Coca-Cola, and Xerox even run newspaper and magazine ads stating that their names are trademarks and should not be used as descriptive or generic terms. Some ads threaten lawsuits against competitors that violate trademarks.

Despite severe penalties for trademark violations, trademark infringement lawsuits are not uncommon. One of the major battles is over brand names that closely resemble another brand name. Donna Karan filed a lawsuit against Donnkenny Inc., whose Nasdaq trading symbol—DNKY—was too close to Karan's DKNY trademark.

Companies must also contend with fake or unauthorized brands, such as fake Levi's jeans, Microsoft software, Rolex watches, Reebok and Nike footwear, and Louis Vuitton handbags. Sales of copycat golf clubs, such as Big Bursa, a knockoff of Callaway's popular Big Bertha, are growing.

In Europe, you can sue counterfeiters only if your brand, logo, or trademark is formally registered. Until recently, formal registration was required in each country in which a company sought protection. A company can now register its trademark in all European Union (EU) member countries with one application.

Packaging

Packages have always served a practical function—that is, they hold contents together and protect goods as they move through the distribution channel. Today, however, packaging is also a container for promoting the product and making it easier and safer to use.

Packaging Functions

The three most important functions of packaging are to contain and protect products, promote products, and facilitate the storage, use, and convenience of products. A fourth function of packaging that is becoming increasingly important is to facilitate recycling and reduce environmental damage.

(5)

Describe marketing uses of packaging and labeling

Containing and Protecting Products

The most obvious function of packaging is to contain products that are liquid, granular, or otherwise divisible. Packaging also enables manufacturers, wholesalers, and retailers to market products in specific quantities, such as ounces.

Physical protection is another obvious function of packaging. Most products are handled several times between the time they are manufactured, harvested, or otherwise produced and the time they are consumed or used. Many products are shipped, stored, and inspected several times between production and consumption. Some, like milk, need to be refrigerated. Others, like beer, are sensitive to light. Still others, like medicines and bandages, need to be kept sterile. Packages protect products from breakage, evaporation, spillage, spoilage, light, heat, cold, infestation, and many other conditions.

Promoting Products

Packaging does more than identify the brand, list the ingredients, specify features, and give directions. A package differentiates a product from competing products and may associate a new product with a family of other products from the same manufacturer. Welch's repackaged its line of grape juice–based jams, jellies, and juices to unify the line and get more impact on the shelf.

Packages use designs, colors, shapes, and materials to try to influence consumers' perceptions and buying behavior. For example, marketing research shows that health-conscious consumers are likely to think that any food is probably good for them as long as it comes in green packaging. Two top brands of low-fat foods—SnackWell's and Healthy Choice—use green packaging. Sunsweet Growers, appealing to baby boomers' interest in health foods, used the theme "Be good to yourself" on new packages for its line of prune products.[20]

Packaging has a measurable effect on sales. Quaker Oats revised the package for Rice-a-Roni without making any other changes in marketing strategy and experienced a 44 percent increase in sales in one year.

Facilitating Storage, Use, and Convenience

Wholesalers and retailers prefer packages that are easy to ship, store, and stock on shelves. They also like packages that protect products, prevent spoilage or breakage, and extend the product's shelf life.

Consumers' requirements for storage, use, and convenience cover many dimensions. Consumers are constantly seeking items that are easy to handle, open, and reclose, although some consumers want packages that are tamperproof or childproof. Consumers also want reusable and disposable packages. Surveys conducted by *Sales & Marketing Management* magazine revealed that consumers dislike—and avoid buying—leaky ice cream boxes, overly heavy or fat vinegar bottles,

Pringles invented the innovative tube package that has become as much a part of the product as the chip itself. New packaging ideas, however, are crucial to Pringles in the twenty-first century. Why? The patent on the package just expired, and rivals are quickly entering the market with their own version of the chip tube.

immovable pry-up lids on glass bottles, key-opener sardine cans, and hard-to-pour cereal boxes. Such packaging innovations as zipper tear strips, hinged lids, tab slots, screw-on tops, and pour spouts were introduced to solve these and other problems. H.J. Heinz Company developed a new container for ketchup designed to fit the hands of children and encourage extra squeezing, which facilitates use for this target market.[21] Miracle-Gro's new packages have pictures on the front of the plants for which the products are formulated, so gardeners can more easily identify which product best fits their needs.[22]

Some firms use packaging to segment markets. For example, a C&H sugar carton with an easy-to-pour, re-closable top is targeted to consumers who don't do a lot of baking and are willing to pay at least twenty cents more for the package. Different-size packages appeal to heavy, moderate, and light users. Salt is sold in package sizes ranging from single serving to picnic size to giant economy size. Campbell's soup is packaged in single-serving cans aimed at the elderly and singles market segments. Beer and soft drinks are similarly marketed in various package sizes and types. Packaging convenience can increase a product's utility and, therefore, its market share and profits. Guinness Bass Import is testing a packaged-draft system that allows consumers to drink nitrogenated Guinness Stout right out of the bottle. This package could win converts among consumers who prefer to drink beer straight from the bottle and in nightclubs that offer beer only in bottles rather than in a glass or on draft.[23]

The Internet will soon give consumers more packaging options. Indeed, the Internet may significantly change the purpose and appearance of packaging. Packaging for products sold on the Internet will be more under the customer's control and will be customized by consumers to fit their needs. Some designers are already offering to personalize, for a fee, packages such as wine bottle labels.[24]

Facilitating Recycling and Reducing Environmental Damage

One of the most important packaging issues today is compatibility with the environment.

Some firms use their packaging to target environmentally concerned market segments. Brocato International markets shampoo and hair conditioner in bottles that are biodegradable in landfills. Procter & Gamble markets Sure Pro and Old Spice in "eco-friendly" pump-spray packages that do not rely on aerosol propellants. Other firms that have introduced pump sprays include S. C. Johnson (Pledge furniture polish) and Reckitt & Coleman Household Products (Woolite rug cleaner).

Labeling

An integral part of any package is its label. Labeling generally takes one of two forms: persuasive or informational. **Persuasive labeling** focuses on a promotional theme or logo, and consumer information is secondary. Price Pfister developed a new, persuasive label—featuring a picture of a faucet, the brand name, and the logo—with the goal of strengthening brand identity and becoming known as a brand instead of as a manufacturer. Note that the standard promotional claims—such as "new," "improved," and "super"—are no longer very persuasive. Consumers have been saturated with "newness" and thus discount these claims.

persuasive labeling
A type of package labeling that focuses on a promotional theme or logo and consumer information is secondary.

© THE PROCTER & GAMBLE COMPANY. USED BY PERMISSION.

Informational labeling, in contrast, is designed to help consumers make proper product selections and lower their cognitive dissonance after the purchase. Sears attaches a "label of confidence" to all its floor coverings. This label gives such product information as durability, color, features, cleanability, care instructions, and construction standards. Most major furniture manufacturers affix labels to their wares that explain the products' construction features, such as type of frame, number of coils, and fabric characteristics. The Nutritional Labeling and Education Act of 1990 mandated detailed nutritional information on most food packages and standards for health claims on food packaging. An important outcome of this legislation has been guidelines from the Food and Drug Administration for using terms like *low fat, light, reduced cholesterol, low sodium, low calorie,* and *fresh.*

Universal Product Codes

The **universal product codes (UPCs)** that appear on most items in supermarkets and other high-volume outlets were first introduced in 1974. Because the numerical codes appear as a series of thick and thin vertical lines, they are often called *bar codes.* The lines are read by computerized optical scanners that match codes with brand names, package sizes, and prices. They also print information on cash register tapes and help retailers rapidly and accurately prepare records of customer purchases, control inventories, and track sales. The UPC system and scanners are also used in single-source research (see Chapter 8).

Food and Drug Administration

Just what does the label on your snack foods say? What about your makeup? Go to the Food and Drug Administration's Web site to read the exact requirements for labeling various products. Pick a product and report back to the class.

http://www.fda.gov

On Line

informational labeling
A type of package labeling designed to help consumers make proper product selections and lower their cognitive dissonance after the purchase.

universal product codes (UPCs)
A series of thick and thin vertical lines (bar codes), readable by computerized optical scanners, that represent numbers used to track products.

Global Issues in Branding and Packaging

International marketers must address several concerns regarding branding and packaging.

6

Discuss global issues in branding and packaging

Branding

 When planning to enter a foreign market with an existing product, a firm has three options for handling the brand name:

- *One brand name everywhere:* This strategy is useful when the company markets mainly one product and the brand name does not have negative connotations in any local market. The Coca-Cola Company uses a one-brand-name strategy in 195 countries around the world. The advantages of a one-brand-name strategy are greater identification of the product from market to market and ease of coordinating promotion from market to market.

- *Adaptations and modifications:* A one-brand-name strategy is not possible when the name cannot be pronounced in the local language, when the brand name is owned by someone else, or when the brand name has a negative or vulgar connotation in the local language. The Iranian detergent "Barf," for example, might encounter some problems in the U.S. market.

- *Different brand names in different markets:* Local brand names are often used when translation or pronunciation problems occur, when the marketer wants the brand to appear to be a local brand, or when regulations require localization. Gillette's Silkience hair conditioner is called Soyance in France and Sientel in Italy. The adaptations were deemed to be more appealing in the local markets. Coca-Cola's Sprite brand had to be renamed Kin in Korea to satisfy a government prohibition on the unnecessary use of foreign words. Snuggle fabric softener is called FaFa in Japan, Cajoline in France, and other cuddly names elsewhere in the world.

Coca-Cola uses a one-brand-name strategy in 195 countries around the world. Its product and positive image are recognizable almost everywhere.

Packaging

 Three aspects of packaging that are especially important in international marketing are labeling, aesthetics, and climate considerations. The major *labeling* concern is properly translating ingredient, promotional, and instructional information on labels. In Eastern Europe, packages of Ariel detergent are printed in fourteen languages, from Latvian to Lithuanian. Care must also be employed in meeting all local labeling requirements. Several years ago, an Italian judge ordered that all bottles of Coca-Cola be removed from retail shelves because the ingredients were not properly labeled. Labeling is also harder in countries like Belgium and Finland, which require it to be bilingual.

Package *aesthetics* may also require some attention. The key is to stay attuned to cultural traits in host countries. For example, colors may have different connotations. Red is associated with witchcraft in some countries, green may be a sign of danger, and white may be symbolic of death. Aesthetics also influence package size. Soft drinks are not sold in six-packs in countries that lack refrigeration. In some countries, products like detergent may be bought only in small quantities because of a lack of storage space. Other products, like cigarettes, may be bought in small quantities, and even single units, because of the low purchasing power of buyers.

On the other hand, simple visual elements of the brand, such as a symbol or logo, can be a standardizing element across products and countries. For example, when Scott Paper wanted to establish a global brand identity for its product line, it used a single brand mark for all product lines that had the flexibility to accommodate such variables as country-specific product names.

Extreme *climates* and long-distance shipping necessitate sturdier and more durable packages for goods sold overseas. Spillage, spoilage, and breakage are all more important concerns when products are shipped long distances or frequently handled during shipping and storage. Packages may also have to ensure a longer product life if the time between production and consumption lengthens significantly.

Product Warranties

(7)

Describe how and why product warranties are important marketing tools

warranty
A confirmation of the quality or performance of a good or service.

express warranty
A written guarantee.

implied warranty
An unwritten guarantee that the good or service is fit for the purpose for which it was sold.

Just as a package is designed to protect the product, a **warranty** protects the buyer and gives essential information about the product. A warranty confirms the quality or performance of a good or service. An **express warranty** is a written guarantee. Express warranties range from simple statements—such as "100 percent cotton" (a guarantee of quality) and "complete satisfaction guaranteed" (a statement of performance)—to extensive documents written in technical language. In contrast, an **implied warranty** is an unwritten guarantee that the good or service is fit for the purpose for which it was sold. All sales have an implied warranty under the Uniform Commercial Code.

Congress passed the Magnuson-Moss Warranty–Federal Trade Commission Improvement Act in 1975 to help consumers understand warranties and get action from manufacturers and dealers. A manufacturer that promises a full warranty must meet certain minimum standards, including repair "within a reasonable time and without charge" of any defects and replacement of the merchandise or a full refund if the product does not work "after a reasonable number of attempts" at repair. Any warranty that does not live up to this tough prescription must be "conspicuously" promoted as a limited warranty.

CONNECT IT

Look back at the chapter-opening story about Coleman's new outdoor gas grill. The grill represents both a new product item and a new product line for Coleman. Coleman's success with the grill is likely due to consumers' familiarity with the Coleman brand and the perception that the company offers good-quality products. High brand equity helps companies introduce new products because consumers trust the brand. Also, although the grill was the first home-use product Coleman developed, consumers may have perceived that if Coleman makes good camping stoves, it would probably also make a good outdoor gas grill. Based on that logic, Coleman might be successful with charcoal grills, grill accessories, or backyard lanterns.

USE IT

As a student, you are required to hand in written assignments, such as papers and group projects. Have you ever thought about these class projects as a product that you exchange for a grade? Maybe not, but some of the product concepts discussed in this chapter are as applicable to class projects as they are to products. One of the most applicable product concepts in this context is that of packaging. Think about the four functions of packaging, and how they might apply to class projects. How could you more effectively package your class projects to contain and protect the project? As a tool for promotion, packaging is not only important for identification purposes, but also serves the critical function of differentiating your project from the competition (other students' projects). It is also important to facilitate storage, use, and convenience of the project for your customer— the instructor! What are some things you could do to make your project more convenient for the instructor to read and to grade? Finally, packaging facilitates recycling. How might you facilitate the environmental recycling of your project?

REVIEW IT

(1) **Define the term *product*.** A product is anything, desired or not, that a person or organization receives in an exchange. The basic goal of purchasing decisions is to receive the tangible and intangible benefits associated with a product. Tangible aspects include packaging, style, color, size, and features. Intangible qualities include service, the retailer's image, the manufacturer's reputation, and the social status associated with a product. An organization's product offering is the crucial element in any marketing mix.

1.1 Form a team of four or five. Have the team determine what the tangible and intangible benefits are for a computer, a tube of toothpaste, a beauty salon, and a dentist.

(2) **Classify consumer products.** Consumer products are classified into four categories: convenience products, shopping products, specialty products, and unsought products. Convenience products are relatively inexpensive and require limited shopping effort. Shopping products are of two types: homogeneous and heterogeneous. Because of the similarity of homogeneous products, they are differentiated mainly by price and features. In contrast, heterogeneous products appeal to consumers because of their distinct characteristics. Specialty products possess unique benefits that are highly desirable to certain customers. Finally, unsought products are either new products or products that require aggressive selling because they are generally avoided or overlooked by consumers.

2.1 **TEAM** Break into groups of four or five. Have the members of the group classify each of the following products into the category (convenience, shopping, specialty, unsought) that they think fits best from their perspective as consumers (i.e., if they were buying the product): Coca-Cola (brand), car stereo, winter coat, pair of shoes, life insurance, blue jeans, fast-food hamburgers, shampoo, canned vegetables, frozen pizza.

(3) **Define the terms *product item, product line*, and *product mix*.** A product item is a specific version of a product that can be designated as a distinct offering among an organization's products. A product line is a group of closely related products offered by an organization. An organization's product mix includes all the products it sells. Product mix width refers to the number of product lines an organization offers. Product line depth is the number of product items in a product line. Firms modify existing products by changing their quality, functional characteristics, or style. Product line extension occurs when a firm adds new products to existing product lines.

3.1 **WRITING** A local civic organization has asked you to give a luncheon presentation about planned obsolescence. Rather than pursuing a negative approach by talking about how businesses exploit customers through planned obsolescence, you have decided to talk about the benefits of producing products that do not last forever. Prepare a one-page outline of your presentation.

3.2 **ON LINE** What is the product mix offered at Web site **http://www.rubbermaid.com**?

(4) **Describe marketing uses of branding.** A brand is a name, term, or symbol that identifies and differentiates a firm's products. Established brands encourage customer loyalty and help new products succeed. Branding strategies require decisions about individual, family, manufacturers', and private brands.

4.1 **WRITING** A local supermarket would like to introduce its own brand of paper goods (i.e., paper towels, facial tissue, etc.) to sell alongside its current inventory. The company has hired you to generate a report outlining the advantages and disadvantages of doing so. Write the report.

(5) **Describe marketing uses of packaging and labeling.** Packaging has four functions: containing and protecting products; promoting products; facilitating product storage, use, and convenience; and facilitating recycling and reducing environmental damage. As a tool for promotion, packaging identifies the brand and its features. It also serves the critical function of differentiating a product from competing products and linking it with related products from the same manufacturer. The label is an integral part of the package, with persuasive and informational functions. In essence, the package is the marketer's last chance to influence buyers before they make a purchase decision.

5.1 **WRITING** Find a product at home that has a distinctive package. Write a paragraph evaluating that package based on the four functions of packaging discussed in the chapter.

(6) **Discuss global issues in branding and packaging.** In addition to brand piracy, international marketers must address a variety of concerns regarding branding and packaging, including choosing a brand name policy, translating labels and meeting host-country labeling requirements, making packages aesthetically compatible with host-country cultures, and offering the sizes of packages preferred in host countries.

6.1 **ON LINE** List the countries to which Levi Strauss & Company markets through the Web site **http://www.levi.com**. How do the product offerings differ between the U.S. and European selections?

7 Describe how and why product warranties are important marketing tools. Product warranties are important tools because they offer consumers protection and help them gauge product quality.

7.1 INFOTRAC COLLEGE EDITION Learn more about how product warranties are handled worldwide. Using InfoTrac (**http://infotrac-college.com**), run a keyword search for "warranty" or "guarantee" and a country of interest. For example, search for "warranty" and "Germany" or "guarantee" and "Mexico." Write a paragraph about what you discover.

DEFINE IT

brand 297	generic product name 304	product line extension 296
brand equity 298	global brand 298	product mix 294
brand loyalty 300	implied warranty 308	product mix width 295
brand mark 297	individual branding 303	product modification 295
brand name 297	informational labeling 307	service mark 304
business product (industrial product) 292	manufacturer's brand 302	shopping product 293
cobranding 303	persuasive labeling 306	specialty product 293
consumer product 292	planned obsolescence 296	trademark 304
convenience product 292	private brand 302	universal product code (UPC; bar code) 307
express warranty 308	product 292	unsought product 294
family brand 303	product item 294	warranty 308
generic product 301	product line 294	
	product line depth 295	

APPLY IT

Application for Entrepreneurs

 The Baker family owns one of the largest catfish farms in central Texas and is known for raising the sweetest catfish in the area. After graduating from college with a degree in marketing, Frank Baker returned to the farm with lots of ideas for new ways to cash in on the farm's reputation. At the time, the family allowed the butcher at the local supermarket to use the Baker name on their catfish. In central Texas, eating Baker Farms catfish was a sign of status. Frank, eager to put his degree to work, convinced his family that they could make money off their name by selling their catfish products already packaged to supermarkets. After hearing the idea, the family quickly met to formulate a plan to begin selling Baker Farms catfish.

Questions

1. What type of product is the Baker family selling? List your reasons.

2. What type of branding is the Baker family using? List your reasons.

3. How should Baker Farms catfish be packaged?

4. Assuming that the Baker family wishes to reposition their catfish products, what would be an optimal strategy?

THINK ABOUT IT

Ethics Exercise

A product that a potential buyer knows about but that he or she is not actively seeking is called an unsought product. Is the marketing of unsought products unethical? Discuss your answer in terms of the AMA Code of Ethics, found at **http://www.marketingpower.com**.

Entrepreneurship Case

Maps à la Carte

A love of maps combined with some computer savvy may have translated into a viable business for two Massachusetts entrepreneurs. Ed McNierney and Bill Everett, both former executives at Kodak Company's software subsidiary in Billerica, Massachusetts, launched Maps à la Carte's Topozone.com Web site in November 1999. Founded in 1999, Maps à la Carte is a Digital Cartographic Business Partner with the U.S. Geological Survey.

Topographic maps are used extensively by hikers, hunters, surveyors, and geologists. The maps contain information such as elevation, positioning, and landmarks and are produced by the U.S. Geological Survey. Unfortunately, these sixty thousand different maps do not fit together when users try to move from map to map. For example, some maps are curved at the edges, while others are rectangles, and they may even come in different scales. McNierney and Everett were able to solve such problems with Topozone.com.

Targeting the more than fifty million outdoor recreation enthusiasts (both McNierney and Everett are avid outdoorsmen), the Topozone.com site is the first interactive, seamless U.S. topographic map site on the Web. Prior to this on-line capability, outdoor recreation enthusiasts had to use paper and CD-ROM topographic maps to plan their outdoor adventures. Map giant DeLorme Publishing Company offers topographic maps on CD-ROMs, and Maptech, Inc., includes topographic maps on its site. DeLorme's CD-ROMs sell for around $100, however, and Maptech, with its emphasis on nautical areas, has tended to target boaters rather than hikers. Therefore, U.S. Geological Survey and industry experts suggest that Topozone. com, with its high quality and extensive site search tools, is the map industry leader.

Within six months of launch, the Topozone.com site was averaging around 150,000 visitors a month. In addition to outdoor enthusiasts, the site was reaching beyond the intended target market. Visitors included genealogists, hobbyists, and cemetery associations. Additionally, the site won About.com's "1999 Best of the Net" award and was designated as the number one on-line geography site, replacing MapQuest.

While Maps à la Carte's new product offering appeared to be a huge success, company executives were not experiencing overnight wealth. With a good product service idea that was lauded by many, the company was not charging consumers to print out screen maps. By June 2000, the company had made only $50,000 in revenue from advertising and licensing fees. Maps à la Carte licensed its Topozone.com topographic map content to leading Web sites such as MapQuest.com, Trails.com, GreatLodge.com, ALLOUTDOORS.com, and Points-Beyond.com, and the company was offering banner advertising opportunities.

To make money on this new product venture, McNierney and Everett developed a business model wherein they would give away the topographic map data and sell consumers the software that allowed users to make full use of the better quality maps available at Topozone.com. To work within this new product development business model, Maps à la Carte sold almost 20 percent of the company to Navitrak, a Canadian mapping company, in June 2000 for approximately $1 million. Navitrak is a wireless navigation technology company specializing in the development and manufacture of personal navigation devices. Along with this 20 percent acquisition, the companies will work together to further develop topographic mapping systems for the outdoor recreation market.

As entrepreneurs, McNierney and Everett developed and introduced a product that satisfied a need of outdoor enthusiasts and others. With a major investment by Navitrak, the two must focus upon extending the product concept into new markets and/or product extensions. With the fast pace of change and development in Internet-related offerings and a slew of potential competitors, McNierney and Everett have to move quickly.

Questions

1. What type of product does Topozone.com offer?

2. Should Maps à la Carte consider a branding strategy?

3. Should Maps à la Carte combine with Navitrak in a cobranding strategy? What would be the benefits of cobranding?

WATCH IT

Short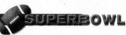

The *Marketing* PowerPoint CD-ROM has four ad videos in the Chapter 9 slide presentation. The concepts of homogeneous shopping products, product line, cobranding, private brands, and warranty are illustrated in ads for AOL/WebMD, Kenmore, Chrysler, and Radio Shack. While watching the ads, write about the concepts you see in each ad.

Medium

What makes a product organic, and what does hypoallergenic actually mean? The CNN clips for Chapter 9 address products and issues relating to standardizing the organic claim.

Long

To give you insight into Chapter 9, Small Business School will take you to Fluker Cricket Farms in Baton Rouge, Louisiana. Richard Fluker started the business when he couldn't find bait before going fishing. Now his product line includes gourmet snacks! Watch the segment and see how real businesspeople are working with the concepts of product item, line, and mix.

FLIP IT

 Flip to Chapter 9 in your *Grademaker Study Guide* for more review opportunities, including the pretest, vocabulary review, Internet activities, study test questions, and a marketing application based on product concepts. Can you describe branding? Do you know the difference between product lines, items, and mixes? If you're not quite sure, then you need to review with your *Grademaker*.

CLICK IT

The *Marketing* Web site links you to all the Internet-based activities in this chapter, like "Review It" questions 3.2, 6.1, and 7.1 and the On-Line exercises in the chapter margins. As a review, do the Chapter 9 quiz and crossword puzzle. And don't forget the Career Exersite that shows you different resources if you're interested in a brand management or other product-related career. Review the main concepts in the PowerPoint presentation for Chapter 9, too. Go to **http://lamb.swcollege.com**, read the material, and follow the links right from the site.

SPIN IT

Spin your Xtra! CD-ROM to test your understanding of the product concepts in the chapter by completing the worksheets for exhibits 9.1, 9.4, and 9.5. If your instructor has assigned a marketing plan project, worksheets on Xtra! can help you organize your work. In addition to the quiz on the Web site, there's another quiz on the Xtra! CD-ROM, plus video of the authors answering frequently asked questions about product concepts: 1. "If a product falls into one of the four types discussed in the text, does it stay in that category as long as it is on the market?" and 2. "Is planned obsolescence always due to style changes?" Spin your Xtra! CD and find out.

Still Shaky? Here's a Tip.

Pick up a recent copy of the *Wall Street Journal* at a newsstand or library and read several articles in the Marketplace section (section B). What product issues are facing the companies you read about? Make two lists: one of marketing concepts you read about and one of product topics.

CHAPTER **TEN**

DEVELOPING AND MANAGING PRODUCTS

Learning Objectives

1 *Explain the importance of developing new products and describe the six categories of new products*

2 *Explain the steps in the new-product development process*

3 *Explain why some products succeed and others fail*

4 *Discuss global issues in new-product development*

5 *Explain the diffusion process through which new products are adopted*

6 *Explain the concept of product life cycles*

Every carmaker in the world is trying to figure out how to use the Internet to streamline the new-product development process, which traditionally can take four to six years and cost billions of dollars for a major launch. The Chrysler Group has reason to be trying harder than the rest. The company is losing money, and the Germans have arrived from the parent company to supervise a turnaround.

Part of Chrysler's answer to the pressure it faces is FastCar. The project is still in the early stages, but two hundred workstations at Chrysler's Auburn Hills, Michigan, headquarters have been tied into the Web-based system.

FastCar allows the company to link the flow of information from at least six major information systems that until now have not been able to communicate seamlessly—finance has had its system, engineering had a different one, purchasing relied on a third, and so on. There were even smaller, largely secret "shadow" systems. Because each arm of Chrysler had spent huge sums of money building information systems that suited its individual needs, headquarters could never force all of the departments onto one centrally controlled system. So far, the various arms of Chrysler are communicating over the Internet only in designing a large car for the 2004 model year.

The sheer scale and complexity of the auto industry are daunting for even the most intrepid Net maven. The rule of thumb is that any given car has roughly 12,000 moving parts. Chrysler has 50,000 different components that it draws upon internally. Every screw, bolt, and button has detailed specifications. When other variations are introduced (Do you want 16-inch or 17-inch tires? What color paint do you want?), there are billions of permutations for Chrysler vehicles. So, even though Net-based collaboration is old hat for some newer, smaller companies, it's an enormous undertaking for the auto industry.

The whole point of FastCar is to keep everyone working on the same design at the same time. As designers go through hundreds of variations, colleagues at other arms of Chrysler can understand what is changing in real time. In the past, if the designers changed something, engineers would have to catch up later to see what effect that would have on manufacturing; finance would have to reassess the costs; and quality control would have to reexamine its own issues. By then, the designers could be on to the next iteration.

Now FastCar offers everyone what Chrysler calls a "unified data model" or a "single point of truth" that they can see in three dimensions. The goal of FastCar is to move from theme selection to design completion to mass manufacturing within two years, roughly half the current industry standard.

FastCar is not aimed only at Chrysler's internal processes. Chrysler says FastCar will eventually work seamlessly with Covisint, an industry consortium set up with General Motors, Ford Motor, Renault, and Nissan. FastCar and Covisint fit together "like Lego blocks," the company says.

Using Covisint's standards, FastCar hopes to send e-mail messages to suppliers with hyperlinks to 3-D renderings of the parts or systems that are changing. Suppliers can use a personal computer or a laptop and don't need expensive workstations.

No one knows how fast the auto industry can migrate to Net-based systems. It is the most wrenching period of change since Henry Ford introduced the assembly line nearly ninety years ago. Aside from cutting the cost of each auto by as much as $1,500, moving to newer Internet-based systems should make the industry much more responsive to fashion trends. Chris Cedergren, managing director of Nextrend, a consultancy in Thousand Oaks, California, argues that to survive, an automaker will have to become more like a Calvin Klein or Ralph Lauren design house. "They have to be able to get a concept from the design studio to the dealer's showroom in eighteen months and do it for 30 to 35 percent less than it costs today," says Cedergren. If the FastCar project succeeds, that type of speed, savings, and flexibility could become standard operating procedure for an industry mired today in lags, costs, and rigidity.[1]

How has the Internet helped Chrysler to reduce the time it takes to design and develop a new car and at the same time dramatically reduce costs and increase flexibility? Could these processes be helpful to firms in other industries?

The Importance of New Products

1

Explain the importance of developing new products and describe the six categories of new products

New products are important to sustain growth and profits and to replace obsolete items. 3M Company introduces about five hundred new products each year. Of the products Corning, Inc., sold in 2000, 84 percent had been introduced within the past four years. [2] As Exhibit 10.1 illustrates, the number of new-product introductions rose rapidly throughout the 1970s, 1980s, and early- to mid-1990s. In the late 1990s, fewer new products were introduced annually. The decline in new-food-item introductions is particularly dramatic. What accounts for this reversal after twenty-five years of annual increases? The cost of new-product failures is a contributing factor. Others include the intense competitive pressure and rigorous financial scrutiny that marketers face from Wall Street analysts. [3] The decline in the U.S. economy in 2000 and 2001 also left many firms risk averse.

Categories of New Products

new product

A product new to the world, the market, the producer, the seller, or some combination of these.

The term **new product** is somewhat confusing because its meaning varies widely. Actually, the term has several "correct" definitions. A product can be new to the world, to the market, to the producer or seller, or to some combination of these. There are six categories of new products:

- *New-to-the-world products* (also called *discontinuous innovations*): These products create an entirely new market. The telephone, television, computer, and facsim-

---

☐**Exhibit 10.1**

New-Product Introductions, 1964–2000

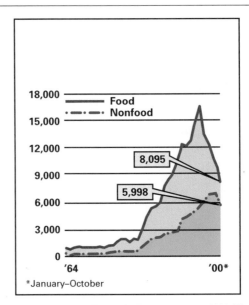

SOURCE: Gary Strauss, "Squeezing New from Old," *USA Today*, January 4, 2000, B1.

ile machine are commonly cited examples of new-to-the-world products. New-to-the-world products represent the smallest category of new products.

- *New product lines:* These products, which the firm has not previously offered, allow it to enter an established market. Heinz Frozen Foods introduced a new product line called Boston Market Home Style following a ten-year licensing deal with Boston Chicken, Inc. The new line anchors the premium end of three Heinz lines that include Budget Gourmet (a value product line) and Smart Ones (a nutritionally oriented product line).

- *Additions to existing product lines:* This category includes new products that supplement a firm's established line. Examples of product line additions include Tide detergent in tablet form, Downey Wrinkle Releaser fabric softener, and Yoplait's Go-Gurt, packaged in kid-friendly Popsicle-style tubes.[4] Kimberly-Clark has added a moistened version of toilet paper to its Cottonelle line.[5]

- *Improvements or revisions of existing products:* The "new and improved" product may be significantly or slightly changed. For example, Breyers Soft 'n Creamy! ice cream "scoops right out without bending the spoon." Anyone who has ever sat around for fifteen minutes waiting for a half-gallon of ice cream to thaw would certainly agree that this is a product improvement. Another type of revision is package improvement. The Heinz EZ Squirt Ketchup bottle is short, is made from easy-to-squeeze plastic, and has a needle-shaped nozzle that lets small hands use it to decorate food.[6] Most new products fit into the revision or improvement category.

- *Repositioned products:* These are existing products targeted at new markets or market segments. The bottle for Beefeater gin was totally redesigned in an effort to appeal to a younger, more upscale market.[7] Dippity-Do, the "green colored goo" that has been marketed to adult women since 1965, is being repositioned to target teen buyers, according to managers at White Rain, the corporate parent.[8]

- *Lower-priced products:* This category refers to products that provide performance similar to competing brands at a lower price. Hewlett-Packard Laser Jet 3100 is a scanner, copier, printer, and fax machine combined. This new product is priced lower than many conventional color copiers and much lower than the combined price of the four items purchased separately. The so-called e-machines that have been introduced for under $500 also fit into this category of new product!

Sometimes a product's claim to be safer than an existing product raises ethical issues, as the "Ethics in Marketing" box discusses.

Introduce Your Kids To Their First No Brainer.

Cold Remedy A.

OR

Cold Remedy B.

New Breathe Right Nasal Strips relieve your child's nasal congestion without drugs of any kind. So now, you both can rest a little easier.

Breathe Right. Right Now.

COURTESY OF CNS INC.

Into what category of new products do you think the Breathe Right Nasal Strip falls? It could possibly fall into more than one: additions to existing product lines and repositioned products. How?

The New-Product Development Process

The management and technology consulting firm Booz, Allen, & Hamilton has studied the new-product development process for over thirty years. Analyzing five major studies undertaken during this period, the firm has concluded that the companies most likely to succeed in developing and introducing new products are those that take the following actions:

2

Explain the steps in the new-product development process

Less Toxins, Great Taste

Vector Tobacco Ltd. recently introduced a new cigarette called Omni, with the slogan, "Reduced carcinogens, premium taste." The ad says that Omni was created to "significantly" cut levels of chemicals that are the "major causes of lung cancer" in smokers. "Now there's actually a reason to change brands," it says.

The tobacco in the Omni cigarette is treated with a combination of chemicals, including palladium, a metal most commonly found in the catalytic converters of cars. Vector says that the treatment, combined with a new, carbon-filled filter, has resulted in a cigarette that tastes as good as competitors' brands but has lower levels of a number of toxic and cancer-causing compounds.

Vector says that its palladium catalyst reduces various cancer-causing compounds known as polycyclic aromatic hydrocarbons, or PAHs, by 15 to 60 percent. It also cuts down on a tobacco-specific nitrosamine, known as NNK, that is considered an especially potent lung carcinogen. Levels of another nitrosamine, however, aren't reduced. The filter removes nearly all the benzene from the cigarette's smoke and also makes significant cuts in other chemicals, Vector scientist Robert Bereman says.

Vector acknowledges there is no scientific proof that these reductions will make its cigarettes any less dangerous than the average Marlboro or Camel. It has yet to complete any human or animal tests of the effects of smoking the new cigarettes. In an open letter to be published in magazines and newspapers, Vector's chief executive, Bennett S. LeBow, writes that "there is no such thing as a safe cigarette, and we do not encourage anyone to smoke." But, he adds: "We strongly believe that if you do smoke, Omni is the best alternative."

"We're doing what we have to do to do the right thing," Mr. LeBow says. "If we have this technology, we have to come out with it. I wouldn't be able to sleep at night if I were sitting on this."

Vector's strategy already is drawing fire from antismoking activists, public-health experts and some of its larger rivals in the cigarette business, who say the ads are misleading. "Everything is designed to imply that this cigarette is safer, with Vector having no proof whatsoever that this is the case," says Matthew L. Myers, president of the Campaign for Tobacco-Free Kids, a Washington advocacy group. "That has the potential to cause serious harm to consumers."

The whole notion of a less hazardous cigarette is controversial. Proponents say it would be wrong not to try to reduce the harm caused by smoking, which contributes to more than 400,000 deaths a year in the United States. But some anti-tobacco activists worry that the newfangled cigarettes will discourage smokers from quitting and possibly entice nonsmokers to light up.[9]

Is Omni a new product? If so, what category of new product does it fit into? Are Vector's claims for Omni legal and ethical?

- Make the long-term commitment needed to support innovation and new-product development
- Use a company-specific approach, driven by corporate objectives and strategies, with a well-defined new-product strategy at its core
- Capitalize on experience to achieve and maintain competitive advantage
- Establish an environment—a management style, organizational structure, and degree of top-management support—conducive to achieving company-specific new-product and corporate objectives

Most companies follow a formal new-product development process, usually starting with a new-product strategy. Exhibit 10.2 traces the seven-step process, which is discussed in detail in this section. The exhibit is funnel-shaped to highlight the fact that each stage acts as a screen. The purpose is to filter out unworkable ideas.

New-Product Strategy

new-product strategy
A plan that links the new-product development process with the objectives of the marketing department, the business unit, and the corporation.

A **new-product strategy** links the new-product development process with the objectives of the marketing department, the business unit, and the corporation. A new-product strategy must be compatible with these objectives, and in turn, all three objectives must be consistent with one another.

A new-product strategy is part of the organization's overall marketing strategy. It sharpens the focus and provides general guidelines for generating, screening, and evaluating new-product ideas. The new-product strategy specifies the roles

Exhibit 10.2

New-Product Development Process

1 New-product strategy

2 Idea generation

3 Idea screening

4 Business analysis

5 Development

6 Test marketing

7 Commercialization

New product

that new products must play in the organization's overall plan and describes the characteristics of products the organization wants to offer and the markets it wants to serve.

Idea Generation

New-product ideas come from many sources, including customers, employees, distributors, competitors, research and development (R&D), and consultants.

- *Customers:* The marketing concept suggests that customers' wants and needs should be the springboard for developing new products. Thermos, the vacuum bottle manufacturer, provides an interesting example of how companies tap customers for ideas. The company's first step in developing an innovative home barbecue grill was to send ten members of its interdisciplinary new-product team into the field for about a month. Their assignment was to learn all about people's cookout needs and to invent a product to meet them. In various cities including Boston, Los Angeles, and Columbus, Ohio, the team conducted focus groups, visited people's homes, and even videotaped barbecues.

- *Employees:* Marketing personnel—advertising and marketing research employees, as well as salespeople—often create new-product ideas because they analyze and are involved in the marketplace. The very successful introduction of Post-it

Notes started with an employee's idea. In 1974, the R&D department of 3M's commercial tape division developed and patented the adhesive component of Post-it Notes. However, it was a year before an employee of the commercial tape division, who sang in a church choir, identified a use for the adhesive. He had been using paper clips and slips of paper to mark places in hymn books. But the paper clips damaged his books, and the slips of paper fell out. The solution, as we now all know, was to apply the adhesive to small pieces of paper and sell them in packages.

- *Distributors:* A well-trained sales force routinely asks distributors about needs that are not being met. Because they are closer to end users, distributors are often more aware of customer needs than are manufacturers. The inspiration for Rubbermaid's litter-free lunch box, named Sidekick, came from a distributor. The distributor suggested that Rubbermaid place some of its plastic containers inside a lunch box and sell the box as an alternative to plastic wrap and paper bags.

- *Competitors:* No firms rely solely on internally generated ideas for new products. A big part of any organization's marketing intelligence system should be monitoring the performance of competitors' products. One purpose of competitive monitoring is to determine which, if any, of the competitors' products should be copied.

There is plenty of information about competitors on the World Wide Web. For example, AltaVista (**http://www.altavista.digital.com**) is a powerful index tool that can be used to locate information about products and companies. Fuld & Company's competitive intelligence guide provides links to a variety of market intelligence sites.

- *Research and development:* R&D is carried out in four distinct ways. Basic research is scientific research aimed at discovering new technologies. Applied research takes these new technologies and tries to find useful applications for them. **Product development** goes one step further by converting applications into marketable products. *Product modification* makes cosmetic or functional changes in existing products. Many new-product breakthroughs come from R&D activities. Pert Plus, Procter & Gamble's combination shampoo and conditioner, was invented in the laboratory. So was Take Heart, a new product line from Quaker Oats, that includes an ingredient called Reducol, which has been found to lower the level of low-density lipoprotein or LDL, cholesterol.[10]

- *Consultants:* Outside consultants are always available to examine a business and recommend product ideas. Examples include the Weston Group; Booz, Allen, & Hamilton; and Management Decisions. Traditionally, consultants determine whether a company has a balanced portfolio of products and, if not, what new-product ideas are needed to offset the imbalance. For instance, an outside consultant conceived Airwick's highly successful Carpet Fresh carpet cleaner.

Creativity is the wellspring of new-product ideas, regardless of who comes up with them. A variety of approaches and techniques have been developed to stimulate creative thinking. The two considered most useful for generating new-product ideas are brainstorming and focus-group exercises. The goal of **brainstorming** is to get a group to think of unlimited ways to vary a product or solve a problem. Group members avoid criticism of an idea, no matter how ridiculous it may seem. Objective evaluation is postponed. The sheer quantity of ideas is what matters. As noted in Chapter 8, an objective of focus-group interviews is to stimulate insightful comments through group interaction. Focus groups usually consist of seven to ten people. Sometimes consumer focus groups generate excellent new-product ideas—for example, Cycle dog food, Stick-Up room deodorizers, Dustbuster vacuum cleaners, and Wendy's salad bar. In the industrial market, machine tools, keyboard designs, aircraft interiors, and backhoe accessories have evolved from focus groups.

product development
A marketing strategy that entails the creation of marketable new products; the process of converting applications for new technologies into marketable products.

brainstorming
The process of getting a group to think of unlimited ways to vary a product or solve a problem.

Idea Screening

After new ideas have been generated, they pass through the first filter in the product development process. This stage, called **screening**, eliminates ideas that are inconsistent with the organization's new-product strategy or are obviously inappropriate for some other reason. The new-product committee, the new-product department, or some other formally appointed group performs the screening review. General Motors' Advanced Portfolio Exploration Group (APEx) knows that only one out of every twenty new car concepts developed by the group will ever become a reality. That's not a bad percentage. In the pharmaceutical business, one new product out of five thousand ideas is not uncommon.[11] Most new-product ideas are rejected at the screening stage.

Concept tests are often used at the screening stage to rate concept (or product) alternatives. A **concept test** evaluates a new-product idea, usually before any prototype has been created. Typically, researchers get consumer reactions to descriptions and visual representations of a proposed product.

Concept tests are considered fairly good predictors of success for line extensions. They have also been relatively precise predictors of success for new products that are not copycat items, are not easily classified into existing product categories, and do not require major changes in consumer behavior—such as Betty Crocker Tuna Helper, Cycle dog food, and Libby Fruit Float. However, concept tests are usually inaccurate in predicting the success of new products that create new consumption patterns and require major changes in consumer behavior—such as microwave ovens, videocassette recorders, computers, and word processors.

Business Analysis

New-product ideas that survive the initial screening process move to the **business analysis** stage, where preliminary figures for demand, cost, sales, and profitability are calculated. For the first time, costs and revenues are estimated and compared. Depending on the nature of the product and the company, this process may be simple or complex.

The newness of the product, the size of the market, and the nature of the competition all affect the accuracy of revenue projections. In an established market like soft drinks, industry estimates of total market size are available. Forecasting market share for a new entry is a bigger challenge.

Analyzing overall economic trends and their impact on estimated sales is especially important in product categories that are sensitive to fluctuations in the business cycle. If consumers view the economy as uncertain and risky, they will put off buying durable goods like major home appliances, automobiles, and homes. Likewise, business buyers postpone major equipment purchases if they expect a recession.

These questions are commonly asked during the business analysis stage:

- What is the likely demand for the product?

- What impact would the new product probably have on total sales, profits, market share, and return on investment?

- How would the introduction of the product affect existing products? Would the new product cannibalize existing products?

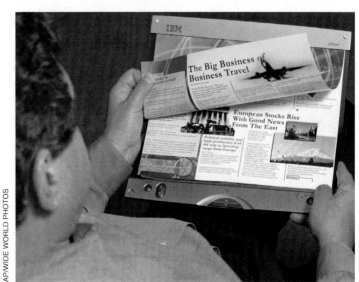

New product development is the lifeblood of many companies. IBM is working on a flexible panel/e-newspaper device that will allow users to download news services through wireless access.

AP/WIDE WORLD PHOTOS

- Would current customers benefit from the product?
- Would the product enhance the image of the company's overall product mix?
- Would the new product affect current employees in any way? Would it lead to hiring more people or reducing the size of the workforce?
- What new facilities, if any, would be needed?
- How might competitors respond?
- What is the risk of failure? Is the company willing to take the risk?

Answering these and related questions may require studies of markets, competition, costs, and technical capabilities. But at the end of this stage, management should have a good understanding of the product's market potential. This full understanding is important because costs increase dramatically once a product idea enters the development stage.

Development

development
The stage in the product development process in which a prototype is developed and a marketing strategy is outlined.

In the early stage of **development**, the R&D department or engineering department may develop a prototype of the product. During this stage, the firm should start sketching a marketing strategy. The marketing department should decide on the product's packaging, branding, labeling, and so forth. In addition, it should map out preliminary promotion, price, and distribution strategies. The technical feasibility of manufacturing the product at an acceptable cost should also be thoroughly examined.

The development stage can last a long time and thus be very expensive. Crest toothpaste was in the development stage for ten years. It took eighteen years to develop Minute Rice, fifteen years to develop the Polaroid Colorpack camera, fifteen years to develop the Xerox copy machine, and fifty-five years to develop television. Gillette spent six years developing the MACH 3 razor.

simultaneous product development
A team-oriented approach to new-product development.

The development process works best when all the involved areas (R&D, marketing, engineering, production, and even suppliers) work together rather than sequentially, a process called **simultaneous product development.** This approach allows firms to shorten the development process and reduce costs. With simultaneous product development, all relevant functional areas and outside suppliers participate in all stages of the development process. Rather than proceeding through highly structured stages, the cross-functional team operates in unison. Involving key suppliers early in the process capitalizes on their specialized knowledge and enables them to design and develop critical component parts.

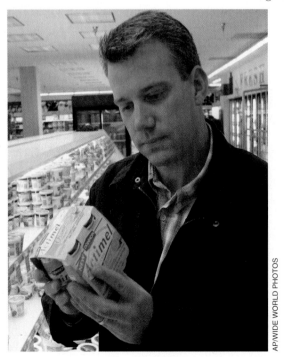

The Internet is a useful tool for implementing simultaneous product development. On the Net, multiple partners from a variety of locations can meet regularly to assess new-product ideas, analyze markets and demographics, and review cost information. Ideas judged to be feasible can quickly be converted into new products. For example, Procter & Gamble has created an autonomous idea laboratory called Corporate New Ventures. Its mission is to encourage ideas for products and put the best ideas into speedy production. Corporate New Ventures has $250 million in seed money and reports directly to top management. The story at the beginning of this chapter about the Chrysler Group of DaimlerChrysler using the Internet to connect various groups both inside and outside the company illustrates the value of the Internet in simultaneous product development efforts.

AP/WIDE WORLD PHOTOS

Dannon chose to test market its successful European product Actimel in Colorado before rolling out the bacteria-loaded dairy product nationwide. Test marketing for two years allowed the company to refine its marketing strategy and determine customer reaction.

Laboratory tests are often conducted on prototype models during the development stage. User safety is an important aspect of laboratory testing, which actually subjects products to much more severe treatment than is expected by end users. The Consumer Product Safety Act of 1972 requires manufacturers to conduct a "reasonable testing program" to ensure that their products conform to established safety standards.

Many products that test well in the laboratory are also tried out in homes or businesses. Examples of product categories well suited for such use tests include human and pet food products, household cleaning products, and industrial chemicals and supplies. These products are all relatively inexpensive, and their performance characteristics are apparent to users. For example, at the W. K. Kellogg Institute for Food and Nutrition Research, cross-functional teams of employees spend their days cooking, eating, and comparing notes. Management believes that creativity comes from diversity, so researchers with unusual backgrounds are recruited. The Institute employs people from twenty-two different countries. The company is quite pleased with the results produced by the Institute. In one month, researchers generated sixty-five new product ideas and ninety-four new packaging ideas.[12]

Most products require some refinement based on the results of laboratory and use tests. General Mills tested various package prototypes of Go-Gurt with mothers and their children. "If you could squeeze it, push it, pump it, peel it, or sip it, we tried it."[13] A second stage of development often takes place before test marketing.

What can you find out on the Internet about current test marketing? Use the Google search engine and type in "Test Marketing."
http://www.google.com

On Line

Test Marketing

After products and marketing programs have been developed, they are usually tested in the marketplace. **Test marketing** is the limited introduction of a product and a marketing program to determine the reactions of potential customers in a market situation. Test marketing allows management to evaluate alternative strategies and to assess how well the various aspects of the marketing mix fit together. Quaker Oats test marketed the Take Heart line of food products including ready-to-eat cereals, snack bars, and fruit juice beverages in selected markets in the New York State area before introducing the line nationwide.[14] Even established products are test marketed to assess new marketing strategies. One-dollar bottles of chocolate, strawberry, and coffee-flavored milk, distributed through vending machines, were offered in schools in Texas, California, Massachusetts, Nebraska, and Florida to assess this alternative distribution strategy. Initial weekly sales ran about two hundred bottles per machine.[15]

The cities chosen as test sites should reflect market conditions in the new product's projected market area. Yet no "magic city" exists that can universally represent market conditions, and a product's success in one city doesn't guarantee that it will be a nationwide hit. When selecting test market cities, researchers should therefore find locations where the demographics and purchasing habits mirror the overall market. The company should also have good distribution in test cities. Moreover, test locations should be isolated from the media. If the TV stations in a particular market reach a very large area outside that market, the advertising used for the test product may pull in many consumers from outside the market. The product may then appear more successful than it really is. Exhibit 10.3 on page 324 provides a useful checklist of criteria for selecting test markets.

The High Costs of Test Marketing

Test marketing frequently takes one year or longer, and costs can exceed $1 million. Some products remain in test markets even longer. McDonald's spent twelve years developing and testing salads before introducing them. Despite the cost, many firms believe it is a lot better to fail in a test market than in a national introduction.

Because test marketing is so expensive, some companies do not test line extensions of well-known brands. For example, because the Folgers brand is well

test marketing
The limited introduction of a product and a marketing program to determine the reactions of potential customers in a market situation.

Exhibit 10.3

In choosing a test market, many criteria need to be considered, especially the following:
Similarity to planned distribution outlets
Relative isolation from other cities
Availability of advertising media that will cooperate
Diversified cross section of ages, religions, cultural-societal preferences, etc.
No atypical purchasing habits
Representative population size
Typical per capita income
Good record as a test city, but not overly used
Not easily "jammed" by competitors
Stability of year-round sales
No dominant television station; multiple newspapers, magazines, and radio stations
Availability of research and audit services
Availability of retailers that will cooperate
Freedom from unusual influences, such as one industry's dominance or heavy tourism

known, Procter & Gamble faced little risk in distributing its instant decaffeinated version nationally. Consolidated Foods Kitchen of Sara Lee followed the same approach with its frozen croissants. Other products introduced without being test marketed include General Foods' International Coffees, Quaker Oats' Chewy Granola Bars and Granola Dipps, and Pillsbury's Milk Break Bars.

The high cost of test marketing is not just financial. One unavoidable problem is that test marketing exposes the new product and its marketing mix to competitors before its introduction. Thus, the element of surprise is lost. Several years ago, for example, Procter & Gamble began testing a ready-to-spread Duncan Hines frosting. General Mills took note and rushed to market with its own Betty Crocker brand, which now is the best-selling brand of ready-to-spread frosting. Competitors can also sabotage or "jam" a testing program by introducing their own sales promotion, pricing, or advertising campaign. The purpose is to hide or distort the normal conditions that the testing firm might expect in the market.

Alternatives to Test Marketing

Many firms are looking for cheaper, faster, safer alternatives to traditional test marketing. In the early 1980s, Information Resources, Inc., pioneered one alternative: single-source research using supermarket scanner data (discussed in Chapter 8). A typical supermarket scanner test costs about $300,000. Another alternative to traditional test marketing is **simulated (laboratory) market testing**. Advertising and other promotional materials for several products, including the test product, are shown to members of the product's target market. These people are then taken to shop at a mock or real store, where their purchases are recorded. Shopper behavior, including repeat purchasing, is monitored to assess the product's likely performance under true market conditions. Research firms offer simulated market tests for $25,000 to $100,000, compared to $1 million or more for full-scale test marketing.

On-Line Test Marketing

Despite these alternatives, most firms still consider test marketing essential for most new products. The high price of failure simply prohibits the widespread introduction of most new products without testing. Many firms are finding that the Internet offers a fast, cost-effective way to conduct test marketing.

Procter & Gamble is an avid proponent of using the Internet as a means for gauging customer demand for potential new products. The company reportedly conducts 40 percent of its product tests and other studies on-line and hopes to cut its $140 million annual research budget in half by shifting efforts to the Internet.[16]

Many products that are not available in grocery stores or drugstores can be sampled or purchased from P&G's corporate Web site **http://PG.com**. Crest Whitestrips provides an illustration.

In August 2000, when P&G brand manager Val Bogdan-Powers was ready to launch Crest Whitestrips, a new home tooth-bleaching kit, management wasn't sure that consumers would be willing to pay the proposed $44 retail price. She then began an eight-month campaign offering the strips exclusively on P&G's **http://whitestrips.com**. TV spots and magazine ads were run to promote the on-line sale. In eight months, 144,000 whitening kits were sold on-line. The product was introduced in retail outlets in 2001, and $50 million worth of kits were sold in the first three months at the $44 per kit price.[17]

Other consumer goods firms that have recently begun on-line test marketing include General Mills and Quaker Oats. Other sites have appeared that offer consumers prototype products developed by all sizes of firms.

Commercialization

The final stage in the new-product development process is **commercialization**, the decision to market a product. The decision to commercialize the product sets several tasks in motion: ordering production materials and equipment, starting production, building inventories, shipping the product to field distribution points, training the sales force, announcing the new product to the trade, and advertising to potential customers. "Our goal," says Bruce Thompson, senior vice president of product development and engineering at Sea Ray Boats, "is to deliver to the customer what they want even before they need it."[18]

The time from the initial commercialization decision to the product's actual introduction varies. It can range from a few weeks for simple products that use existing equipment to several years for technical products that require custom manufacturing equipment.

The total cost of development and initial introduction can be staggering. Gillette spent $750 million developing MACH 3, and the first-year marketing budget for the new three-bladed razor was $300 million.

Johnson & Johnson

How important are new products to Johnson & Johnson? Go to its Web site to find out. How many innovations do you recognize?

http://www.jnj.com

On Line

simulated (laboratory) market testing
The presentation of advertising and other promotion materials for several products, including a test product, to members of the product's target market.

commercialization
The decision to market a product.

3

Explain why some products succeed and others fail

For some products, a well-planned Internet campaign can provide new-product information for people who are looking for the solutions that a particular new product offers. Attempting to reach customers at the point in time when they need a product is much more cost-effective and efficient than communicating with a target market that may eventually have a need for the product.

Despite the high cost of developing and testing new products, a large proportion of all new-product introductions fail. Products fail for a number of reasons. One common reason is that they simply do not offer any discernible benefit compared to existing products. Another commonly cited factor in new-product failures is a poor match between product features and customer desires. For example, there are telephone systems on the market with over seven hundred different functions, although the average user is happy with just ten functions. Other reasons for failure include overestimation of market size, incorrect positioning, a price too high or too low, inadequate distribution, poor promotion, or simply an inferior product compared to those of competitors.

Failure can be a matter of degree. Absolute failure occurs when a company cannot recoup its development, marketing, and production costs. The product actually loses money for the company. A relative product failure results when the product returns a profit but fails to achieve sales, profit, or market share goals.

High costs and other risks of developing and testing new products do not stop many companies, such as Rubbermaid, Colgate-Palmolive, Campbell's Soup, 3M Company, and Procter & Gamble, from aggressively developing and introducing new products.

The most important factor in successful new-product introduction is a good match between the product and market needs—as the marketing concept would predict. Successful new products deliver a meaningful and perceivable benefit to a sizable number of people or organizations and are different in some meaningful way from their intended substitutes. Firms that routinely experience success in new-product introductions tend to share the following characteristics:

- A history of carefully listening to customers
- An obsession with producing the best product possible
- A vision of what the market will be like in the future
- Strong leadership
- A commitment to new-product development
- A project-based team approach to new-product development
- Getting every aspect of the product development process right.[19]

Global Issues in New-Product Development

4

Discuss global issues in new-product development

Increasing globalization of markets and of competition provides a reason for multinational firms to consider new-product development from a worldwide perspective. A firm that starts with a global strategy is better able to develop products that are marketable worldwide. In many multinational corporations, every product is developed for potential worldwide distribution, and unique market requirements are built in whenever possible. Procter & Gamble introduced Pampers Phases into global markets within one month of introducing the product in the United States. P&G's goal was to have the product on the shelf in ninety countries within one year. The objective was to establish brand loyalty among dealers and consumers before foreign competitors could react.

Some global marketers design their products to meet regulations and other key requirements in their major markets and then, if necessary, meet smaller markets' requirements country by country. Nissan develops lead-country car models that, with minor changes, can be sold in most markets. For the remaining markets, Nissan provides other models that can readily be adapted. With this approach, Nissan has been able to reduce the number of its basic models from forty-eight to eighteen.

Some products, however, have little potential for global market penetration without modification. Russia and China represent two huge automobile markets but not at prevailing international prices. General Motors, Ford Motor Company, Fiat, Renault, and others are working with Russian partners to produce cars that can retail for $15,000 or less.[20] GM, Toyota, and Volkswagen AG are focusing on China.[21] You may recall from Chapter 6 that GM and Shanghai Auto Industry Corporation have formed a strategic alliance to develop and market a "Farmer's Car" targeted at rural Chinese consumers.

We often hear about how popular American products are in foreign countries. Recently, U.S. companies such as Levi Strauss, Coca-Cola, RJR Nabisco, and Nike have been finding that products popular in foreign markets can become hits in the United States. An example is Häagen-Dazs new ice cream flavor *dulce de leche* originally introduced in Buenos Aires in 1997. The brand is named after a caramelized milk drink that is popular in Argentina. *Dulce de leche* became an instant success in Argentina. The brand has since been introduced in the United States, and sales are increasing at over 25 percent per month.

Other companies are applying a new twist on the popular international business aphorism, "think global, act local." Coca-Cola CEO Douglas N. Daft calls "think local, act local" a plan that gives country managers more autonomy in new-product development.[22] The idea has resulted in seven new brands of energy drinks, waters, and teas being introduced in various Asian countries recently. More are planned to diversify beyond colas.

Results are impressive. Approximately 90 percent of Coca-Cola's worldwide sales come from traditional brands such as Coke and Sprite. In Japan, it's more like one-third. Xing Mu (Smart), a Coca-Cola brand, has become the fourth-most-popular carbonated soft drink in China in just four years.[23]

Coca-Cola also follows a one product–one message strategy in some markets. It markets Powerade, an American brand of sport drink, the same way in Europe as in the United States. It also markets a popular European rehydrating, after-exercise drink called Aquarius.[24]

© MICHAEL NEWMAN/PHOTOEDIT

Insights for new products are coming increasingly from around the world. An Argentine success, Häagen-Dazs's *dulce de leche,* is gaining popularity in the United States where in-store displays promote the new flavor.

©AFP/CORBIS

Coca-Cola is a company that seems to need little help with global penetration of its product. In fact, despite adapting its product formula and product mix to various cultures, Coke is one of the world's most recognized brands.

The Spread of New Products

Managers have a better chance of successfully marketing products if they understand how consumers learn about and adopt products. A person who buys a new product never before tried may ultimately become an **adopter**, a consumer who was happy enough with his or her trial experience with a product to use it again.

Diffusion of Innovation

An **innovation** is a product perceived as new by a potential adopter. It really doesn't matter whether the product is "new to the world" or some other category of new product. If it is new to a potential adopter, it is an innovation in this context. **Diffusion** is the process by which the adoption of an innovation spreads.

(5)
Explain the diffusion process through which new products are adopted

adopter
A consumer who was happy enough with his or her trial experience with a product to use it again.

innovation
A product perceived as new by a potential adopter.

diffusion
The process by which the adoption of an innovation spreads.

Five categories of adopters participate in the diffusion process:

- *Innovators:* the first 2.5 percent of all those who adopt the product. Innovators are eager to try new ideas and products, almost as an obsession. In addition to having higher incomes, they are more worldly and more active outside their community than noninnovators. They rely less on group norms and are more self-confident. Because they are well educated, they are more likely to get their information from scientific sources and experts. Innovators are characterized as being venturesome.

- *Early adopters:* the next 13.5 percent to adopt the product. Although early adopters are not the very first, they do adopt early in the product's life cycle. Compared to innovators, they rely much more on group norms and values. They are also more oriented to the local community, in contrast to the innovators' worldly outlook. Early adopters are more likely than innovators to be opinion leaders because of their closer affiliation with groups. The respect of others is a dominant characteristic of early adopters.

- *Early majority:* the next 34 percent to adopt. The early majority weighs the pros and cons before adopting a new product. They are likely to collect more information and evaluate more brands than early adopters, therefore extending the adoption process. They rely on the group for information but are unlikely to be opinion leaders themselves. Instead, they tend to be opinion leaders' friends and neighbors. The early majority is an important link in the process of diffusing new ideas because they are positioned between earlier and later adopters. A dominant characteristic of the early majority is deliberateness.

- *Late majority:* the next 34 percent to adopt. The late majority adopts a new product because most of their friends have already adopted it. Because they also rely on group norms, their adoption stems from pressure to conform. This group tends to be older and below average in income and education. They depend mainly on word-of-mouth communication rather than on the mass media. The dominant characteristic of the late majority is skepticism.

- *Laggards:* the final 16 percent to adopt. Like innovators, laggards do not rely on group norms. Their independence is rooted in their ties to tradition. Thus, the past heavily influences their decisions. By the time laggards adopt an innovation, it has probably been outmoded and replaced by something else. For example, they may have bought their first black-and-white TV set after color television was already widely diffused. Laggards have the longest adoption time and the lowest socioeconomic status. They tend to be suspicious of new products and alienated from a rapidly advancing society. The dominant value of laggards is tradition. Marketers typically ignore laggards, who do not seem to be motivated by advertising or personal selling.

Exhibit 10.4 illustrates the diffusion of three familiar products throughout the United States. Virtually every household is equipped with one or more color televisions. Note that some product categories, such as monochrome televisions, may never be adopted by 100 percent of the population. The adopter categories refer to all of those who will eventually adopt a product, not the entire population.

Product Characteristics and the Rate of Adoption

Five product characteristics can be used to predict and explain the rate of acceptance and diffusion of a new product:

- *Complexity:* the degree of difficulty involved in understanding and using a new product. The more complex the product, the slower is its diffusion. For instance, before many of their functions were automated, 35mm cameras were used primarily by hobbyists and professionals. The cameras were just too complex for most people to learn to operate.

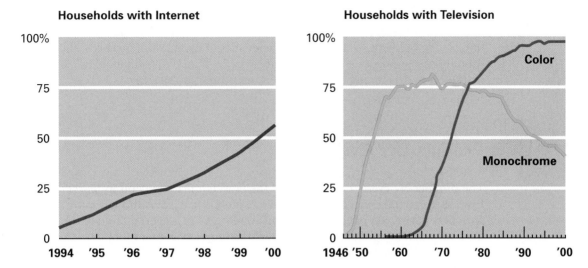

Households with Internet

Households with Television

- *Compatibility:* the degree to which the new product is consistent with existing values and product knowledge, past experiences, and current needs. Incompatible products diffuse more slowly than compatible products. For example, the introduction of contraceptives is incompatible in countries where religious beliefs discourage the use of birth control techniques.

- *Relative advantage:* the degree to which a product is perceived as superior to existing substitutes. For example, because it reduces cooking time, the microwave oven has a clear relative advantage over a conventional oven.

- *Observability:* the degree to which the benefits or other results of using the product can be observed by others and communicated to target customers. For instance, fashion items and automobiles are highly visible and more observable than personal-care items.

- *"Trialability":* the degree to which a product can be tried on a limited basis. It is much easier to try a new toothpaste or breakfast cereal than a new automobile or microcomputer. Demonstrations in showrooms and test-drives are different from in-home trial use. To stimulate trials, marketers use free-sampling programs, tasting displays, and small package sizes.

Marketing Implications of the Adoption Process

Two types of communication aid the diffusion process: *word-of-mouth communication* among consumers and communication from marketers to consumers. Word-of-mouth communication within and across groups speeds diffusion. Opinion leaders discuss new products with their followers and with other opinion leaders. Marketers must therefore ensure that opinion leaders have the types of information desired in the media that they use. Suppliers of some products, such as professional and health-care services, rely almost solely on word-of-mouth communication for new business.

The second type of communication aiding the diffusion process is *communication directly from the marketer to potential adopters.* Messages directed toward early adopters should normally use different appeals than messages directed toward the early majority, the late majority, or the laggards. Early adopters are more important than innovators because they make up a larger group, are more socially active, and are usually opinion leaders.

As the focus of a promotional campaign shifts from early adopters to the early majority and the late majority, marketers should study the dominant characteristics, buying behavior, and media characteristics of these target markets. Then they should revise messages and media strategy to fit. The diffusion model helps guide marketers in developing and implementing promotion strategy.

Product Life Cycles

6

Explain the concept of product life cycles

product life cycle (PLC)
A concept that provides a way to trace the stages of a product's acceptance, from its introduction (birth) to its decline (death).

product category
All brands that satisfy a particular type of need.

The **product life cycle (PLC)** is one of the most familiar concepts in marketing. Few other general concepts have been so widely discussed. Although some researchers have challenged the theoretical basis and managerial value of the PLC, most believe it has great potential as a marketing management tool.

The product life cycle is a concept that provides a way to trace the stages of a product's acceptance, from its introduction (birth) to its decline (death). As Exhibit 10.5 shows, a product progresses through four major stages: introduction, growth, maturity, and decline. Note that the product life cycle illustrated does not refer to any one brand; rather, it refers to the life cycle for a product category or product class. A **product category** includes all brands that satisfy a particular type of need. Product categories include passenger cars, cigarettes, soft drinks, and coffee. When we trace the product life cycle of a product such as DVD players, we are including the aggregate sales of all brands of DVD players, not just a single brand.

The time a product spends in any one stage of the life cycle may vary dramatically. Some products, such as fad items, move through the entire cycle in weeks. Others, such as electric clothes washers and dryers, stay in the maturity stage for decades. Exhibit 10.5 illustrates the typical life cycle for a consumer durable good, such as a washer or dryer. In contrast, Exhibit 10.6 illustrates typical life cycles for styles (such as formal, business, or casual clothing), fashions (such as miniskirts or stirrup pants), and fads (such as leopard-print clothing). Changes in a product, its uses, its image, or its positioning can extend that product's life cycle.

Exhibit 10.5

Four Stages of the Product Life Cycle

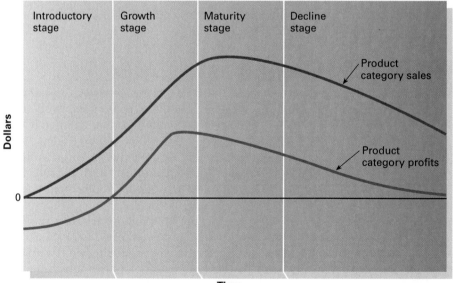

Exhibit 10.6

Product Life Cycles for Styles, Fashions, and Fads

Style	Fashion	Fad

The product life cycle concept does not tell managers the length of a product's life cycle or its duration in any stage. It does not dictate marketing strategy. It is simply a tool to help marketers forecast future events and suggest appropriate strategies. Look at Exhibit 10.7 on page 332. What conclusions can you draw about the product life cycle of DVD players based on four and a half years of sales data?

Introductory Stage

The **introductory stage** of the product life cycle represents the full-scale launch of a new product into the marketplace. Computer databases for personal use, room-deodorizing air-conditioning filters, and wind-powered home electric generators are all product categories that have recently entered the product life cycle. A high failure rate, little competition, frequent product modification, and limited distribution typify the introduction stage of the PLC.

Marketing costs in the introductory stage are normally high for several reasons. High dealer margins are often needed to obtain adequate distribution, and incentives are needed to get consumers to try the new product. Advertising expenses are high because of the need to educate consumers about the new product's benefits. Production costs are also often high in this stage, as product and manufacturing flaws are identified and corrected and efforts are undertaken to develop mass-production economies.

As Exhibit 10.5 illustrates, sales normally increase slowly during the introductory stage. Moreover, profits are usually negative because of R&D costs, factory tooling, and high introduction costs. The length of the introductory phase is largely determined by product characteristics, such as the product's advantages over substitute products, the educational effort required to make the product known, and management's commitment of resources to the new item. A short introductory period is usually preferred to help reduce the impact of negative earnings and cash flows. As soon as the product gets off the ground, the financial burden should begin to diminish. Also, a short introduction helps dispel some of the uncertainty as to whether the new product will be successful.

Promotion strategy in the introductory stage focuses on developing product awareness and informing consumers about

introductory stage
The full-scale launch of a new product into the marketplace.

COURTESY AMERIFIT NUTRITION, INC.

Styles, fashions, and fads tend to follow different product life cycles. Based on what you see in Exhibits 10.5 and 10.6, what is the life cycle for Vitaballs, a new vitamin infused bubblegum? Do you think it will be adopted by the mainstream? If so, how quickly?

Exhibit 10.7

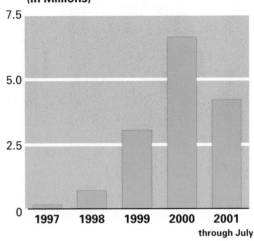

**Annual Sales of DVD Players
(in Millions)***

SOURCE: Marten Peers, "For Now, At Least, DVD Sales Are Soaring As Prices Drop," *Wall Street Journal*, September 11, 2001, B4. Reprinted by permission of the *Wall Street Journal.* ©2001. Dow Jones & Company, Inc. All rights reserved worldwide. 2001. Dow Jones & Company, Inc. Data supplied by NPD Intellect Market Tracking.

the product category's potential benefits. At this stage, the communication challenge is to stimulate primary demand—demand for the product in general rather than for a specific brand. Intensive personal selling is often required to gain acceptance for the product among wholesalers and retailers. Promotion of convenience products often requires heavy consumer sampling and couponing. Shopping and specialty products demand educational advertising and personal selling to the final consumer.

Growth Stage

growth stage
The second stage of the product life cycle when sales typically grow at an increasing rate, many competitors enter the market, large companies may start acquiring small pioneering firms, and profits are healthy.

If a product category survives the introductory stage, it advances to the **growth stage** of the life cycle. In this stage, sales typically grow at an increasing rate, many competitors enter the market, and large companies may start to acquire small pioneering firms. Profits rise rapidly in the growth stage, reach their peak, and begin declining as competition intensifies. Emphasis switches from primary demand promotion (for example, promoting personal digital assistants [PDAs]) to aggressive brand advertising and communication of the differences between brands (for example, promoting Casio versus Palm and Visor).

Distribution becomes a major key to success during the growth stage, as well as in later stages. Manufacturers scramble to sign up dealers and distributors and to build long-term relationships. Without adequate distribution, it is impossible to establish a strong market position.

Maturity Stage

maturity stage
A period during which sales increase at a decreasing rate.

A period during which sales increase at a decreasing rate signals the beginning of the **maturity stage** of the life cycle. New users cannot be added indefinitely, and sooner or later the market approaches saturation. Normally, this is the longest stage of the product life cycle. Many major household appliances are in the maturity stage of their life cycles.

For shopping products and many specialty products, annual models begin to appear during the maturity stage. Product lines are lengthened to appeal to additional market segments. Service and repair assume more important roles as manufacturers strive to distinguish their products from others. Product design changes tend to become stylistic (How can the product be made different?) rather than functional (How can the product be made better?).

As prices and profits continue to fall, marginal competitors start dropping out of the market. Dealer margins also shrink, resulting in less shelf space for mature items, lower dealer inventories, and a general reluctance to promote the product. Thus, promotion to dealers often intensifies during this stage in order to retain loyalty.

Heavy consumer promotion by the manufacturer is also required to maintain market share. Consider these well-known examples of competition in the maturity stage: the "cola war" featuring Coke and Pepsi, the "beer war" featuring Anheuser-Busch's Budweiser brands and Philip Morris's Miller brands, and the "burger wars" pitting leader McDonald's against challengers Burger King and Wendy's.

Another characteristic of the maturity stage is the emergence of "niche marketers" that target narrow, well-defined, underserved segments of a market. Starbucks Coffee targets its gourmet line at the only segment of the coffee market that is growing: new, younger, more affluent coffee drinkers.

Decline Stage

A long-run drop in sales signals the beginning of the **decline stage**. The rate of decline is governed by how rapidly consumer tastes change or substitute products are adopted. Many convenience products and fad items lose their market overnight, leaving large inventories of unsold items, such as designer jeans. Others die more slowly, like citizen band (CB) radios, black-and-white console television sets, and nonelectronic wristwatches.

Some firms have developed successful strategies for marketing products in the decline stage of the product life cycle. They eliminate all nonessential marketing expenses and let sales decline as more and more customers discontinue purchasing the products. Eventually, the product is withdrawn from the market.

Management sage Peter Drucker says that all companies should practice "organized abandonment," which entails reviewing every product, service, and policy every two or three years and asking the critical question, "If we didn't do this already, would we launch it now?" Would we introduce the product, service, or policy now? If the answer is no, it's time to begin the abandonment process.[25]

Implications for Marketing Management

The product life cycle concept encourages marketing managers to plan so that they can take the initiative instead of reacting to past events. The product life cycle is especially useful as a predicting or forecasting tool. Because products pass through distinctive stages, it is often possible to estimate a product's location on the curve using historical data. Profits, like sales, tend to follow a predictable path over a product's life cycle.

McDonald's

What is McDonald's doing to successfully compete in the maturity stage?

http://www.mcdonalds.com

On Line

AP/WIDE WORLD PHOTOS

Coffee is an example of a product in the maturity stage where niche marketers have emerged. Starbucks, for example, targets its gourmet products at newer, younger, more affluent coffee drinkers.

decline stage
A long-run drop in sales.

Exhibit 10.8   Typical Marketing Strategies during the Product Life Cycle

Marketing Mix Strategy	Product Life Cycle Stage			
	Introduction	Growth	Maturity	Decline
Product Strategy	Limited number of models; frequent product modifications	Expanded number of models; frequent product modifications	Large number of models	Elimination of unprofitable models and brands
Distribution Strategy	Distribution usually limited, depending on product; intensive efforts and high margins often needed to attract wholesalers and retailers	Expanded number of dealers; intensive efforts to establish long-term relationships with wholesalers and retailers	Extensive number of dealers; margins declining; intensive efforts to retain distributors and shelf space	Unprofitable outlets phased out
Promotion Strategy	Develop product awareness; stimulate primary demand; use intensive personal selling to distributors; use sampling and couponing for consumers	Stimulate selective demand; advertise brand aggressively	Stimulate selective demand; advertise brand aggressively; promote heavily to retain dealers and customers	Phase out all promotion
Pricing Strategy	Prices are usually high to recover development costs (see Chapter 17)	Prices begin to fall toward end of growth stage as result of competitive pressure	Prices continue to fall	Prices stabilize at relatively low level; small price rises are possible if competition is negligible

Exhibit 10.8 briefly summarizes some typical marketing strategies during each stage of the product life cycle. Exhibit 10.9 shows the relationship between the adopter categories and stages of the product life cycle. Note that the various categories of adopters first buy products in different stages of the product life cycle. Almost all sales in the maturity and decline stages represent repeat purchasing.

Exhibit 10.9

Relationship between the Diffusion Process and the Product Life Cycle

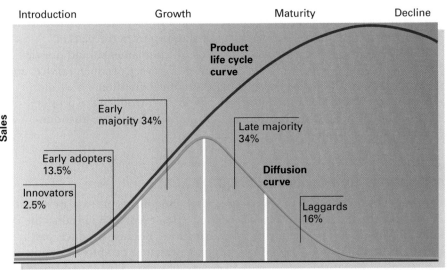

Diffusion curve: **Percentage of total adoptions by category**
Product life cycle curve: **Time**

CONNECT IT

Look back at the story at the beginning of this chapter about how the Chrysler Group is using the Internet to streamline the new-product development process. You now know that involving design, production, finance, and other areas including outside suppliers in the new-product development process is called simultaneous product development. The process reduces product development time by keeping everyone up-to-date on design and development changes and allows a stamping engineer, for example, to watch what is happening so that he or she can make sure the company's stamping plants (where multistory-high presses stamp sheets

of metal) can actually make the body that designers select.[26]

The Internet has been particularly helpful to Chrysler because the industry is very complex. Web technology has linked areas within the company that must communicate with one another and that previously had been using different information systems. In addition, the Covisint system will help coordinate activities with suppliers. Other firms such as Procter & Gamble are also using the Internet to implement simultaneous product development processes.

USE IT

Stay Informed

To keep current with the changing trends and new products in the financial-services industry, arm yourself with information. A banking Web site that will help you make informed decisions is **http://www.bankrate.com**. It has a How-to section that teaches the basics of banking and helps you calculate your payment on loans. The site's collection of interest rate information covers everything from car loans to money market accounts and enables you to compare rates from financial institutions in all fifty states. You can also check the fees different banks charge for their services and compare them to on-line banking service charges.

Locate Lenders

More and more financial institutions are expanding their lending to entrepreneurs and small-business

owners. The following Web sites help start-ups and small businesses find financing:

- **http://quicken.com and http://intuit.com** Both of these sites offer numerous tools for small business and personal finance. Lending Tree offers access to several financial institutions through its site. You can fill out a single loan application at its Web site, **http://lendingtree.com**, and you will receive quotes from various lenders.

- **http://www.icba.org** The Web site of the Independent Community Bankers of America provides leads to all U.S. community banks.

- **http://www.Yahoo.com** This site links to various sources of financial information, news, and advice.

REVIEW IT

(1) Explain the importance of developing new products and describe the six categories of new products. New products are important to sustain growth and profits and to replace obsolete items. New products can be classified as new-to-the-world products (discontinuous innovations), new product lines, additions to existing product lines, improvements or revisions of existing products, repositioned products, or lower cost products. To sustain or increase profits, a firm must introduce at least one new successful product before a previous product advances to the maturity stage and profit levels begin to drop. Several factors make it more important than ever for firms to consistently introduce new products: shortened product life cycles, rapidly changing technology and consumer priorities, the high rate of new-product failures, and the length of time needed to implement new-product ideas.

1.1 How many new products can you identify ? Visit the supermarket and make a list of at least fifteen items with the word "New" on the label. Include on your list anything that looks like a new product. Next to each item on your list, write the category of new product that best describes the item. Share your results with the class.

(2) Explain the steps in the new-product development process. First, a firm forms a new-product strategy by outlining the characteristics and roles of future products. Then new-product ideas are generated by customers, employees, distributors, competitors, and internal R&D personnel. Once a product idea has survived initial screening by an appointed screening group, it undergoes business analysis to determine its potential profitability. If a product concept seems viable, it progresses into the development phase, in which the technical and economic feasibility of the manufacturing process is evaluated. The development phase also includes laboratory and use testing of a product for performance and safety. Following initial testing and refinement, most products are introduced in a test market to evaluate consumer response and marketing strategies. Finally, test market successes are propelled into full commercialization. The commercialization process involves starting up production, building inventories, shipping to distributors, training a sales force, announcing the product to the trade, and advertising to consumers.

2.1 List the advantages of simultaneous product development.

2.2 WRITING You are a marketing manager for Nike. Your department has come up with the idea of manufacturing a baseball bat for use in colleges around the nation. Assuming you are in the business analysis stage, write a brief analysis based on the questions in the "Business Analysis" section of the chapter.

2.3 What are the major disadvantages to test marketing, and how might they be avoided?

2.4 ON LINE How could information from customer orders at **http://www.pizzahut.com** help the company's marketers plan new-product developments?

2.5 ON LINE How is customer input affecting the development of Baked Lay's potato chips? Go to **http://www.fritolay.com** to find out.

(3) Explain why some products succeed and others fail. The most important factor in determining the success of a new product is the extent to which the product matches the needs of the market. Good matches are frequently successful. Poor matches are not.

3.1 TEAM In small groups, brainstorm ideas for a new wet-weather clothing line. What type of product would potential customers want and need? Prepare and deliver a brief presentation to your class.

(4) Discuss global issues in new-product development. A marketer with global vision seeks to develop products that can easily be adapted to suit local needs. The goal is not simply to develop a standard product that can be sold worldwide. Smart global marketers also look for good product ideas worldwide.

4.1 GLOBAL ON LINE Visit **http://pg.com** and look at the brands it offers around the world. What conclusions can you draw about Procter & Gamble's global new-product development strategy?

(5) Explain the diffusion process through which new products are adopted. The diffusion process is the spread of a new product from its producer to ultimate adopters.

Adopters in the diffusion process belong to five categories: innovators, early adopters, the early majority, the late majority, and laggards. Product characteristics that affect the rate of adoption include product complexity, compatibility with existing social values, relative advantage over existing substitutes, visibility, and "trialability." The diffusion process is facilitated by word-of-mouth communication and communication from marketers to consumers.

5.1 Describe some products whose adoption rates have been affected by complexity, compatibility, relative advantage, observability, and/or "trialability."

5.2 What type of adopter behavior do you typically follow? Explain.

(6) **Explain the concept of product life cycles.** All product categories undergo a life cycle with four stages: introduction, growth, maturity, and decline. The rate at which products move through these stages varies dramatically. Marketing managers use the product life cycle concept as an analytical tool to forecast a product's future and devise effective marketing strategies.

6.1 *INFOTRAC COLLEGE EDITION* ON LINE Place the personal computer on the product life cycle curve, and give reasons for placing it where you did. Use InfoTrac (**http://www.infotrac-college.com**) to consult publications like *Technology Review, Computer World,* and *Computer Weekly* to help support your position.

DEFINE IT

adopter 327
brainstorming 320
business analysis 321
commercialization 325
concept test 321
decline stage 333
development 322
diffusion 327

growth stage 332
innovation 327
introductory stage 331
maturity stage 332
new product 316
new-product strategy 318
product category 330
product development 320

product life cycle (PLC) 330
screening 321
simulated (laboratory) market testing 325
simultaneous product development 322
test marketing 323

APPLY IT

Application for Entrepreneurs

Joyce Strand went to the oven to remove the newest batch of beef jerky that she would later sell to the Frontenac Central Store. To her surprise, she had turned the oven up too high, and the beef jerky had dried to a crisp. Although the texture was much different, the jerky still had its unmistakable taste. Joyce decided to take it to the Central Store anyway and let the customers decide. The new snack became a huge success in the snack-food section of the store. Because of her recent success, Joyce began experimenting with different tastes and textures of snack foods that she sells at the Central Store. Realizing that innovation can be very profitable, Joyce now actively looks for new ways to please her customers.

Questions

1. How might Joyce ensure that proper attention is paid to developing new products?

2. What factors should she be aware of that might lead to product failure?

Ethics Exercise

One source of new product ideas is competitors. Steven Fischer recently joined Frankie and Alex Specialty Products as a brand manager. His new boss told him, "We don't have a budget for new product development. We just monitor our competitors' new product introductions and offer "knock-offs" or copies of any that look like they will be successful."

Questions

1. Is this practice ethical?
2. Does the AMA Code of Ethics address this issue? Go to **http://www.marketingpower. com** and review the code. Then, write a brief paragraph on what the AMA Code of Ethics contains that relates to knock-off products.

TRY IT

COURTESY OF THE VALVOLINE COMPANY

Entrepreneurship Case

Valvoline: Coming to a Pep Rally Near You

Be prepared for surprises at Valvoline's research and development lab in Lexington, Kentucky. You might picture lab director Fran Lockwood poring over bottles of colored fluids or frowning over mathematical equations. But recently, she was touching up a picture she'd drawn on the wall by her desk with a can of black Spirit Foam.

The foam, a decorative spray that will not drip, was developed by Lockwood's crew of scientists. Lockwood had drawn a pumpkin, a lopsided one with two bats—not birds, she insisted—flying overhead. She wasn't happy with the way the eyes on the pumpkin had turned out.

This is not what you'd expect from the top scientist at Valvoline, a chemist who runs a $4.9 million lab. But then, Spirit Foam isn't the kind of product you'd expect from a company like Valvoline, the world's oldest premium motor-oil brand.

During three years of research, testing, and tweaking, Lockwood's scientists revved up their creative engines to create Spirit Foam. Valvoline is taking the product, its first non-automotive invention brought to market in its 108-year history, for a test-drive at Wal-Mart stores across the nation.

Analysts are applauding Valvoline's move, one the company's competitors have also made in recent years. Pennzoil–Quaker State introduced Glass Chalk, a chalk that can be used to write on glass, about two years ago, and its Medo division makes air fresheners for the home. Industry observers think it is time Valvoline stepped out, too.

"They're pretty well-known, so it makes sense for them to spin into other products to take advantage of that," says Mike Beall of Davenport & Company LLC in Richmond, Virginia. "It's clever of them to try it. They have the maturity to carry it out."

Spirit Foam has sold beyond the company's expectations. The product contributed about $500,000 in profits to the company in September 2001, its first month on the shelf. Wal-Mart quickly asked Valvoline to move the product out of testing mode and into full production.

According to Jim O'Brien, the company's president, Valvoline wanted its first steps out of its motor oil box to be made with a product that would easily capture the public's attention: "We wanted to prove that we can call on customers we don't normally call on and be welcomed in, and have an audience."

O'Brien says that while the motor oil market will be a profitable market for Valvoline for many years, it is growing at only 1 to 2 percent per year. Valvoline's 2001 fiscal year wasn't great for the company. For the year, operating income climbed only slightly, from $78 million to $81 million, while sales and revenues improved from $1.07 billion to $1.09 billion.

Plans for other products are already in the works. Lockwood has formed a strategic group dedicated to exploring new project areas, and she plans to have a new product idea every year.

"We're not going to leave our core business to chase a few whiffs," O'Brien says. "We were feeling around outside the box, but we're not jumping out. This is more of an evolution than a revolution."

Questions

1. How you think Spirit Foam's characteristics will affect its rate of adoption?

2. What advantages does Valvoline have when introducing a new product into a new marketplace?

3. Why is a new product like Spirit Foam so important to Valvoline's future? What kind of marketing strategy is Valvoline following?

4. To what category of new products does Spirit Foam belong? Why is this an advantage for Valvoline? Explain.

WATCH IT

Short

The *Marketing* PowerPoint CD-ROM has five ad videos in the Chapter 10 slide presentation. The concepts of new products are illustrated by ads for Pizza Hut's new Pizzone, Ruffles 3D, and Cool Relief Tums. Watch how companies advertise a product in the mature stage of the PLC in the Tylenol ad.

Medium

New products are often in the news, but do you know how companies launch new products using trade shows? Visit a technology trade show in the CNN news clip for Chapter 10.

Long

To give you insights into Chapter 10, Small Business School will take you to Karsten Manufacturing, creators and makers of Ping golf clubs. What started out to be a club banned by the Professional Golf Association has become the industry standard. When Karsten Solheim invented the now-famous putter, the innovation did not take off quite as well as he had hoped. Step into the SBS Master Class to learn more about product development and diffusion of innovation.

FLIP IT

 Flip to Chapter 10 in your *Grademaker Study Guide* for more review opportunities, including the pretest, vocabulary review, study test questions, and a marketing application based on product concepts. Can you describe the product life cycle? Do you know which marketing mix strategies work best at each point in the product life cycle? What about the diffusion of innovation? If you're unsure, then pick up your *Grademaker* and review.

CLICK IT

The *Marketing* Web site links you to all the Internet-based activities in this chapter, like the "Use It," "Review It" questions 2.4, 2.5, 4.1, and 6.1, and the On-Line exercises in the chapter margins. As a review, do the Chapter 10 quiz and crossword puzzle. And don't forget the Career Exersite that gives you resources for exploring product-development career opportunities. Review the main concepts in the PowerPoint presentation for Chapter 10, too. Go to **http://lamb.swlearning.com**, read the material, and follow the links right from the site.

SPIN IT

Spin your Xtra! CD-ROM to test your understanding of the new-product development concepts in the chapter by completing the worksheets for Exhibits 10.2, 10.3, 10.5, 10.6, 10.8, and 10.9. If your instructor has assigned a marketing plan project, worksheets on Xtra! can help you organize your work. In addition to the quiz on the Web site, there's another quiz on the Xtra! CD-ROM, plus video of the authors answering frequently asked questions about new products and product diffusion, such as "Why do so many new products fail?" and "Why is such a small proportion of the new products introduced each year 'new-to-the-world' products?"

CHAPTER **ELEVEN**
SERVICES AND NONPROFIT ORGANIZATION MARKETING

Learning Objectives

1 *Discuss the importance of services to the economy*

2 *Discuss the differences between services and goods*

3 *Describe the components of service quality and the gap model of service quality*

4 *Develop marketing mixes for services*

5 *Discuss relationship marketing in services*

6 *Explain internal marketing in services*

7 *Discuss global issues in services marketing*

8 *Describe nonprofit organization marketing*

In the summer of 1996, Yellow Freight Systems began implementing a marketing strategy that would help to transform the company from a long-haul carrier into something completely different: a carrier that offered multiple services and that was built around unprecedented customer service. Today, Yellow is a different company. It still transports primarily big, heavy freight (minimum one hundred pounds). But the one-dimensional long-haul approach is gone and so is the complacency that resulted from long years of regulation in the trucking industry. No more telling customers, "Sorry, we can't do that." Instead, the new approach is "Yes, we can."

In an attempt to offer one-stop shopping, Yellow has added a variety of services, including regional and expedited shipping, to satisfy a broader range of transportation needs. The old Yellow gave customers a rough estimate of when a shipment would arrive. It might show up then, or it might not. The new Yellow is faster, more precise, and more profitable. It has gone from being a company in the trucking business to being a company that recognizes it is in the service business.

For a long time, Yellow's focus was on operational efficiency. Employees monitored how much freight moved through the network daily, how full the trailers were, and other internal measures. While Yellow was a model of efficiency, it had no idea whether its customers were satisfied. The new focus of the company became how to best satisfy customer needs. To that end, the company conducts over six hundred surveys with different customers each month to determine what will satisfy customers. For example, the research made a compelling case for dramatically improving reliability: Customers who said that they would use Yellow again and recommend it to others had received good service.

Those who had not were less loyal. While this was a fairly obvious lesson for a traditional service provider, it was a critical one for a company that was trying to become customer-centric.

Yellow's Exact Express service epitomizes the company's commitment to customers. Introduced in 1998, it was Yellow's first expedited, time-definite, guaranteed service. Everyone involved, from the customer representative to the driver, is committed to doing what it takes to satisfy the customer's needs—even if that means using an outside air-cargo partner to meet a deadline. Exact Express has a good track record—deliveries arrive when they are supposed to arrive 98 percent of the time. It is Yellow's most expensive and most profitable service, growing with double-digit increases every year.

One of the main reasons Yellow has been able to expand and improve service is its state-of-the-art technology. Since 1994, the company has spent about $80 million a year on its highly integrated information systems. The technology has led to significant changes in virtually every stage of the business. For example, it has influenced how orders get processed and relayed from the call centers to the terminals, how the dispatchers assign drivers for pickups and deliveries, and how the dock workers load and unload trailers. When repeat customers call 1-800-GO-YELLOW, the system automatically opens a customer profile that corresponds to the caller's phone number. The representative instantly knows where the customer's company is located; what type of loading dock it has; the size, weight, and contents of previous shipments; previous shipping destinations; and who has signed for deliveries. If a customer calls back in the future with

an identical shipping order, the entire process then takes about fifteen seconds.

Each dock worker is equipped with a wireless mobile data terminal designed to speed up the loading and unloading process. The dock supervisor also has access to the incoming and outgoing freight at his computer station. If he notices that a truck is running behind, he can dispatch a second employee and a forklift to speed things up. The old system was inflexible: one employee per trailer. The central dispatch office can track the day's shipping activity on a map of the United States, and identify service failures in the making and work with the terminals to devise solutions.

Yellow's defect rate is down from 40 percent in 1996 to 5 percent today, and its on-time performance (excluding weather delays) is in the high nineties. The number of customers surveyed who said they would recommend Yellow has doubled since 1997. And in an industry where profit margins are typically slim, the company continues to create promising sources of revenue, including Transportation.com, a logistics service for small- and medium-sized businesses.[1]

How does a service, such as trucking, differ from goods—for example, soft drinks, automobiles, or blue jeans? Contrast Yellow's service mix before and after 1996. Which components of service quality improved as a result of Yellow's concern with satisfying its customers? We will answer these questions and more in Chapter 11.

The Importance of Services

1

Discuss the importance of
services to the economy

service
The result of applying human or
mechanical efforts to people or
objects.

A **service** is the result of applying human or mechanical efforts to people or objects. Services involve a deed, a performance, or an effort that cannot be physically possessed. Today, the service sector substantially influences the U.S. economy. The service sector accounts for 76 percent of the U.S. gross domestic product and 79 percent of employment.[2] The demand for services is expected to continue. According to the Bureau of Labor Statistics, service occupations will be responsible for all net job growth through the year 2005, as can be seen in Exhibit 11.1. Much of this demand results from demographics. An aging population will need nurses, home health care, physical therapists, and social workers. Two-earner families need child-care, housecleaning, and lawn-care services. Also increasing will be the demand for information managers, such as computer engineers and systems analysts. There is also a growing market for service companies worldwide. U.S. service exports are expected to reach $650 billion by 2010—about the same value as current U.S. exports of farm and manufactured goods.[3]

The marketing process described in Chapter 1 is the same for all types of products, whether they are goods or services. Many ideas and strategies discussed throughout this book have been illustrated with service examples. In many ways, marketing is marketing, regardless of the product's characteristics. In addition, although a comparison of goods and services marketing can be beneficial, in reality it is hard to distinguish clearly between manufacturing and service firms. Indeed, many manufacturing firms can point to service as a major factor in their success. For example, maintenance and repair services offered by the manufacturer are important to buyers of copy machines. Nevertheless, services have some unique characteristics that distinguish them from goods, and marketing strategies need to be adjusted for these characteristics.

How Services Differ from Goods

2

Discuss the differences between services and goods

Services have four unique characteristics that distinguish them from goods. Services are intangible performances, they are produced and consumed simultaneously, they have greater variability in inputs and outputs than goods, and they are perishable.

☐Exhibit 11.1   Service-Producing Industries and Job Growth

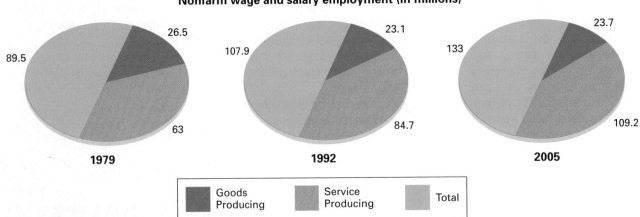

Nonfarm wage and salary employment (in millions)

	1979	1992	2005
26.5 / 89.5 / 63	23.1 / 107.9 / 84.7	23.7 / 133 / 109.2	

Goods Producing   Service Producing   Total

SOURCE: *Arlington Star Telegram*, September 2, 1996, B9.

Services Are Intangible Performances

The basic difference between services and goods is that services are intangible performances. Because of their **intangibility**, they cannot be touched, seen, tasted, heard, or felt in the same manner that goods can be sensed. Services cannot be stored and are often easy to duplicate.

Evaluating the quality of services before or even after making a purchase is harder than evaluating the quality of goods because, compared to goods, services tend to exhibit fewer search qualities. A **search quality** is a characteristic that can be easily assessed before purchase—for instance, the color of an appliance or automobile. At the same time, services tend to exhibit more experience and credence qualities. An **experience quality** is a characteristic that can be assessed only after use, such as the quality of a meal in a restaurant or the actual experience of a vacation. A **credence quality** is a characteristic that consumers may have difficulty assessing even after purchase because they do not have the necessary knowledge or experience. Medical and consulting services are examples of services that exhibit credence qualities.

These characteristics also make it harder for marketers to communicate the benefits of an intangible service than to communicate the benefits of tangible goods. Thus, marketers often rely on tangible cues to communicate a service's nature and quality. For example, Travelers' Insurance Company's use of the umbrella symbol helps make tangible the benefit of protection that insurance provides.

The facilities that customers visit, or from which services are delivered, are a critical tangible part of the total service offering. Messages about the organization are communicated to customers through such elements as the decor, the clutter or neatness of service areas, and the staff's manners and dress. The Sheraton Hotel chain is replacing its outdated shag carpeting and flowered bedspreads with pin stripes and sleigh beds. Its goal is to restore a reputation for reliability and comfort and to avoid scaring off travelers with tacky accommodations. The new design will feature clubby library-like furnishings and practical amenities like ergonomic desk chairs and two-line phones. The remodeling is also a part of the strategy followed by Sheraton's parent company, Starwood Hotels & Resorts Worldwide, to differentiate the company's hotel brands aesthetically. For example, it wants its Sheratons to attract conservative business travelers, while its Westin Hotels are targeting younger, hipper, and somewhat richer overnighters.[4]

Services Are Produced and Consumed Simultaneously

Goods are produced, sold, and then consumed. In contrast, services are often sold, produced, and consumed at the same time. In other words, their production and consumption are inseparable activities. This means that, because consumers must be present during the production of services like haircuts or surgery, they are actually involved in the production of the services they buy. That type of consumer involvement is rare in goods manufacturing.

Simultaneous production and consumption also means that services normally cannot be produced in a centralized location and consumed in decentralized locations, as goods typically are. Services are also inseparable from the perspective of the service provider. Thus, the quality of service that firms are able to deliver depends on the quality of their employees.

intangibility
The inability of services to be touched, seen, tasted, heard, or felt in the same manner that goods can be sensed.

search quality
A characteristic that can be easily assessed before purchase.

experience quality
A characteristic that can be assessed only after use.

credence quality
A characteristic that consumers may have difficulty assessing even after purchase because they do not have the necessary knowledge or experience.

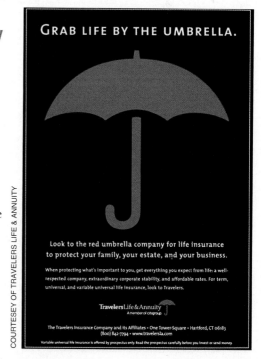

GRAB LIFE BY THE UMBRELLA.

Look to the red umbrella company for life insurance to protect your family, your estate, and your business.

When protecting what's important to you, get everything you expect from life: a well-respected company, extraordinary corporate stability, and affordable rates. For term, universal, and variable universal life insurance, look to Travelers.

Travelers Life & Annuity
A member of citigroup

The Travelers Insurance Company and Its Affiliates • One Tower Square • Hartford, CT 06183
(800) 842-7794 • www.travelersla.com

Variable universal life insurance is offered by prospectus only. Read the prospectus carefully before you invest or send money.

COURTESEY OF TRAVELERS LIFE & ANNUITY

To communicate the benefits of intangible services, marketers often rely on concrete symbols. The umbrella symbol used by Travelers Insurance signifies protection. This helps give the company's service substance.

National Amusements
AMC Theatres

Do National Amusements and AMC Theatres use their Web sites to combat the perishability of movie tickets? What about sites like MovieTickets.com?

http://www.nationalamusements.com

http://www.amctheatres.com

http://www.movietickets.com

 On Line

Services Have Greater Variability

One great strength of McDonald's is consistency. Whether customers order a Big Mac and french fries in Fort Worth, Tokyo, or Moscow, they know exactly what they are going to get. This is not the case with many service providers. Because services have greater variability of inputs and outputs, they tend to be less standardized and uniform than goods. For example, physicians in a group practice or barbers in a barber shop differ within each group in their technical and interpersonal skills. A given physician's or barber's performance may even vary depending on time of day, physical health, or some other factor. Because services tend to be labor-intensive and production and consumption are inseparable, consistency and quality control can be hard to achieve.

Standardization and training help increase consistency and reliability. Limited-menu restaurants like Pizza Hut and KFC offer customers high consistency from one visit to the next because of standardized preparation procedures. Another way to increase consistency is to mechanize the process. Banks have reduced the inconsistency of teller services by providing automated teller machines (ATMs). Automatic coin receptacles on toll roads have replaced human collectors.

Services Are Perishable

Services are perishable, which means that they cannot be stored, warehoused, or inventoried. An empty hotel room or airplane seat produces no revenue that day. The revenue is lost. Yet service organizations are often forced to turn away full-price customers during peak periods.

One of the most important challenges in many service industries is finding ways to synchronize supply and demand. The philosophy that some revenue is better than none has prompted many hotels to offer deep discounts on weekends and during the off-season and has prompted airlines to adopt similar pricing strategies during off-peak hours. Car rental agencies, movie theaters, and restaurants also use discounts to encourage demand during nonpeak periods.

Service Quality

Describe the components of service quality and the gap model of service quality

reliability
The ability to perform a service dependably, accurately, and consistently.

responsiveness
The ability to provide prompt service.

assurance
The knowledge and courtesy of employees and their ability to convey trust.

Because of the four unique characteristics of services, service quality is more difficult to define and measure than is the quality of tangible goods. Business executives rank the improvement of service quality as one of the most critical challenges facing them today.

Research has shown that customers evaluate service quality by the following five components:[5]

- *Reliability:* the ability to perform the service dependably, accurately, and consistently. Reliability is performing the service right the first time. This component has been found to be the one most important to consumers.

- *Responsiveness:* the ability to provide prompt service. Examples of responsiveness include calling the customer back quickly, serving lunch fast to someone who is in a hurry, or mailing a transaction slip immediately. The ultimate in responsiveness is offering service twenty-four hours a day, seven days a week. For example, customer service representatives answer calls round the clock at Relocation Management Resources, Inc., which arranges all the details of transporting household goods for companies that are relocating their employees. Even the company's president invites customers to call his cellphone at all hours.[6]

- *Assurance:* the knowledge and courtesy of employees and their ability to convey trust. Skilled employees who treat customers with respect and make customers feel that they can trust the firm exemplify assurance.

- **Empathy:** caring, individualized attention to customers. Firms whose employees recognize customers, call them by name, and learn their customers' specific requirements are providing empathy. Union Square Hospitality Group, owner of several popular New York City restaurants, will return items customers have left behind by messenger or FedEx so that the customers do not have to return to retrieve their belongings.[7]

- **Tangibles:** the physical evidence of the service. The tangible parts of a service include the physical facilities, tools, and equipment used to provide the service, such as a doctor's office or an ATM, and the appearance of personnel.

    Overall service quality is measured by combining customers' evaluations for all five components.

The Gap Model of Service Quality

A model of service quality called the **gap model** identifies five gaps that can cause problems in service delivery and influence customer evaluations of service quality.[8] These gaps are illustrated in Exhibit 11.2:

- *Gap 1:* the gap between what customers want and what management thinks customers want. This gap results from a lack of understanding or a misinterpretation

empathy
Caring, individualized attention to customers.

tangibles
The physical evidence of a service, including the physical facilities, tools, and equipment used to provide the service.

gap model
A model identifying five gaps that can cause problems in service delivery and influence customer evaluations of service quality.

Exhibit 11.2

Gap Model of Service Quality

SOURCE: A. Parasuraman, Valarie A. Zeithaml and Leonard L. Berry, "A Conceptual Model of Service Quality and Its Implications for Future Research," *Journal of Marketing,* 49 (Fall) 1985, 41–50.

Evaluate your last Internet purchase according to gaps 4 and 5. How could the company bridge those gaps?

◀ ▶   On Line

of the customers' needs, wants, or desires. A firm that does little or no customer satisfaction research is likely to experience this gap. An important step in closing gap 1 is to keep in touch with what customers want by doing research on customer needs and customer satisfaction. Every year, Susquehanna Health System, recipient of the 1999 Global Best Practices Awards in the category of Exceeding Customer Expectations, looks at its own as well as national surveys of patient statisfaction to determine what patients really want.[9]

- *Gap 2:* the gap between what management thinks customers want and the quality specifications that management develops to provide the service. Essentially, this gap is the result of management's inability to translate customers' needs into delivery systems within the firm. For example, Kentucky Fried Chicken once rated its managers' success according to "chicken efficiency," or how much chicken they threw away at the end of the night. Consumers who came in late at night would either have to wait for chicken to be cooked or settle for chicken several hours old. The "chicken efficiency" measurement did not take customers into account.

- *Gap 3:* the gap between the service quality specifications and the service that is actually provided. If both gaps 1 and 2 have been closed, then gap 3 is due to the inability of management and employees to do what should be done. Poorly trained or poorly motivated workers can cause this gap. Management needs to ensure that employees have the skills and the proper tools to perform their jobs. Other techniques that help to close gap 3 are training employees so they know what management expects and encouraging teamwork.

- *Gap 4:* the gap between what the company provides and what the customer is told it provides. This is clearly a communication gap. It may include misleading or deceptive advertising campaigns promising more than the firm can deliver or doing "whatever it takes" to get the business. To close this gap, companies need to create realistic customer expectations through honest, accurate communication about what the firms can provide.

- *Gap 5:* the gap between the service that customers receive and the service they want. This gap can be positive or negative. For example, if a patient expects to wait twenty minutes in the physician's office before seeing the physician but waits only ten minutes, the patient's evaluation of service quality will be high. However, a forty-minute wait would result in a lower evaluation.

When any one or more of these gaps are large, service quality is perceived as low. As the gaps shrink, service quality improves. The Ritz-Carlton is a company that excels in closing gaps to offer superior service quality—so much so that it has twice won the Baldrige National Quality Award. This hotel firm puts potential employees through a comprehensive screening process to match their skills with positions for which they are naturally inclined. The Ritz-Carlton also sponsors one of the most thorough training programs in the business world. Its frontline employees undergo three-hundred hours of training their first year and one-hundred and twenty hours per year thereafter. They learn how all the areas in the hotel work together to provide customer satisfaction. They also learn about the company's vision and the high service standards Ritz-Carlton aims to achieve with each guest experience. When they first report to their jobs, they are paired with a trainer, who is an experienced

© STEVE DUNWELL/CORBIS

Ritz-Carlton works hard to close any gaps in service its customers might experience. The Baldrige National Quality Award winner trains its employees to give superior service in one of the most thorough training programs in the business world.

coworker. Ritz-Carlton employees are authorized to spend up to $2,000 on the spot to make sure a customer's needs are met. For example, a couple mentioned to their bellhop in passing that they were on their honeymoon. He sent them champagne and flowers, creating a lasting, positive impression. The company also recognizes and rewards employee contributions by listing them in its weekly newsletter, by paying spot cash bonuses, and by mentioning great acts of service during each hotel's daily morning meeting.[10]

Marketing Mixes for Services

Services' unique characteristics—intangibility, simultaneous production and consumption, variability, and perishability—make marketing more challenging. Elements of the marketing mix (product, distribution, promotion, and pricing) need to be adjusted to meet the special needs created by these characteristics.

Develop marketing mixes for services

Product (Service) Strategy

The development of "product" strategy in services marketing requires planning focused on the service process.[11] Four types of processing occur:

- *People processing* takes place when the service is directed at a customer. Examples are transportation services, hairstyling, health clubs, and dental and health care.

- *Possession processing* occurs when the service is directed at customers' physical possessions. Examples are lawn care, car repair, dry cleaning, and veterinary services.

- *Mental stimulus processing* refers to services directed at people's minds. Examples are entertainment, spectator sports events, theater performances, and education.

- *Information processing* describes services that use technology or brainpower directed at a customer's assets. Examples are insurance, banking, and consulting.

Because customers' experiences and involvement differ for each of these types of services, marketing strategies may also differ. For example, people processing services require customers to enter the *service factory*, which is a physical location, such as an aircraft, a physician's office, or a hair salon. In contrast, possession processing services typically do not require the presence of the customer in the service factory; the customer may simply leave the car at the garage for repairs, for example. Marketing strategies for the former would therefore focus more on an attractive, comfortable physical environment and employee training on employee-customer interaction issues than would strategies for the latter.

Dry cleaning is an example of possession processing services. These types of services require less focus on attractive physical environments and customer service training than people processing services like hairdressers and airlines.

Core and Supplementary Services

The service offering can be viewed as a bundle of activities that includes the **core service**, which is the most basic benefit the customer is buying, and a group of **supplementary services** that support or enhance the core service. Exhibit 11.3 on page 350 illustrates these concepts for FedEx. The core service is overnight transportation and delivery of packages, which involves possession processing. The supplementary services, some of which involve information processing, include problem solving, advice and information, billing statements, and order taking.

In many service industries, the core service becomes a commodity as competition increases. Thus, firms usually emphasize supplementary services to create a

core service
The most basic benefit the consumer is buying.

supplementary services
A group of services that support or enhance the core service.

Exhibit 11.3

Core and Supplementary Services
for FedEx

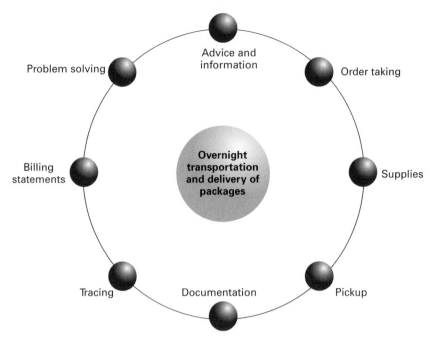

SOURCE: From *Services Marketing,* 3rd ed., by Christopher H. Lovelock, © 1996. Reprinted by permission of Prentice-Hall, Inc., Upper Saddle River, NJ.

mass customization
A strategy that uses technology to deliver customized services on a mass basis.

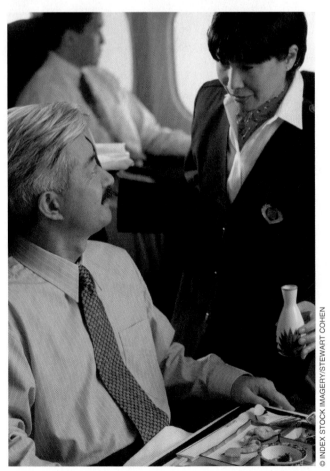

Making services more personalized is the goal of mass customization. Serving passengers when they want to eat, rather than when the airline wants to serve, is an example of this.

competitive advantage. Virgin Atlantic, Malaysia Airlines, and Japan Airlines provide complimentary limo service to and from the airport. Virgin's chauffeurs check in passengers en route. In some cities, United Airlines delivers passengers' luggage to their hotels so that they can go straight to business meetings.[12] On the other hand, some firms are positioning themselves in the marketplace by greatly reducing supplementary services. For example, Microtel Inn is an amenity-free hotel concept known as "fast lodging." These low-cost hotels have one- and two-bedroom accommodations and a swimming pool, but no meeting rooms or other services.

Mass Customization

An important issue in developing the service offering is whether to customize or standardize it. Customized services are more flexible and respond to individual customers' needs. They also usually command a higher price. The traditional law firm, which treats each case differently according to the client's situation, offers customized services. Standardized services are more efficient and cost less. Unlike the traditional law firm, for example, Hyatt Legal Services offers low-cost, standardized service "packages" for those with uncomplicated legal needs, such as drawing up a will or mediating an uncontested divorce.

Instead of choosing to either standardize or customize a service, a firm may incorporate elements of both by adopting an emerging strategy called **mass customization**. Mass customization uses technology to deliver customized services on a mass basis, which results in giving each customer whatever she or he asks for.

For example, a feature on Lands' End Web site allows women to define their figures on-line, receive advice on what swimsuits will flatter their shapes, and mix and match more than 216 combinations of colors and styles. Several airlines are designing services to cater to travelers' individual needs and preferences. Some will serve dinner to passengers when they want to eat it, rather than when the airline wants to serve it. More airlines are offering video-on-demand systems, which let passengers start or stop their movie anytime they want. British Airlines predicts that there will be airline seats that will read passengers' shapes and program their seat-position preferences into smart cards.[13]

The Service Mix

Most service organizations market more than one service. For example, Chem-Lawn offers lawn care, shrub care, carpet cleaning, and industrial lawn services. Each organization's service mix represents a set of opportunities, risks, and challenges. Each part of the service mix should make a different contribution to achieving the firm's goals. To succeed, each service may also need a different level of financial support.

Designing a service strategy therefore means deciding what new services to introduce to which target market, what existing services to maintain, and what services to eliminate. For example, to increase membership, AAA added financial services, credit cards, and travel perks. Organic, a San Francisco-based company that designs Web sites for clients, has set up two new service divisions: Organic Communications, a full-service public relations department; and Organic Logistics, which helps clients to figure out how to get products ordered on-line into customers' hands.[14]

Distribution Strategy

Distribution strategies for service organizations must focus on such issues as convenience, number of outlets, direct versus indirect distribution, location, and scheduling. A key factor influencing the selection of a service provider is convenience. Therefore, service firms must offer convenience. American Airlines, for example, invested millions of dollars developing the SABRE reservation system to make the reservation process more convenient for independent travel agents. This system is one of the most widely used reservation systems in the industry and is the engine that powers Travelocity.

An important distribution objective for many service firms is the *number of outlets* to use or the number of outlets to open during a certain time. Generally, the intensity of distribution should meet, but not exceed, the target market's needs and preferences. Having too few outlets may inconvenience customers; having too many outlets may boost costs unnecessarily. Intensity of distribution may also depend on the image desired. Having only a few outlets may make the service seem more exclusive or selective.

The next service distribution decision is whether to distribute services to end users *directly* or *indirectly* through other firms. Because of the intangible nature of services, many service firms have to use direct distribution or franchising. Examples include legal, medical, accounting, and personal-care services. The newest form of direct distribution is the Internet. Most of the major airlines are now using on-line services to sell tickets directly to consumers, which results in lower distribution costs for the airline companies. Merrill Lynch offers Merrill Lynch OnLine, an Internet-based service that connects clients with company representatives. Other firms with standardized service packages have developed indirect channels using independent intermediaries. For example, Bank of America is offering teller services and loan services to customers in small satellite facilities located in Albertson's grocery stores in Texas.

The *location* of a service most clearly reveals the relationship between its target market strategy and distribution strategy. Reportedly, Conrad Hilton claimed that the three most important factors in determining a hotel's success are "location, location, and location." An interesting location trend has started in the banking industry. In the past few years, banks aggressively directed customers away from branches and toward ATMs and the Internet. In a recent about-face, banks are trying to entice customers back into the branches. For example, Washington Mutual, Inc., based in Seattle, is designing new branches and remodeling old ones to resemble a Gap store. Each branch employs a concierge who greets customers. Tellers and managers in khakis and casual shirts walk the floor offering traditional bank services as well as products such as insurance and mutual funds. Customers can also buy products such as colorful calculators, pens, and piggy banks.[15]

For time-dependent service providers like airlines, physicians, and dentists, scheduling is often a more important factor. Scheduling is sometimes the most important factor in a customer's choice of airline.

Promotion Strategy

Consumers and business users have more trouble evaluating services than goods because services are less tangible. In turn, marketers have more trouble promoting intangible services than tangible goods. Here are four promotion strategies they can try:

AP/WIDE WORLD PHOTOS

Using real customers can be a successful promotion strategy. One of the more successful of recent memory has been Jared Fogle, spokesperson for Subway. When Subway executives heard that Fogle went from 425 pounds to 180 pounds eating their product, they put him in a TV commercial.

- *Stressing tangible cues:* A tangible cue is a concrete symbol of the service offering. To make their intangible services more tangible, hotels turn down the bedcovers and put mints on the pillows. Insurance companies use symbols like rocks, blankets, umbrellas, and hands to help make their intangible services appear tangible. Merrill Lynch uses a bull to help give its services substance.

- *Using personal information sources:* A personal information source is someone consumers are familiar with (such as a celebrity) or someone they know or can relate to personally. Celebrity endorsements are sometimes used to reduce customers' perceived risk in choosing a service. Service firms may also seek to simulate positive word-of-mouth communication among present and prospective customers by using real customers in their ads.

- *Creating a strong organizational image:* One way to create an image is to manage the evidence, including the physical environment of the service facility, the appearance of the service employees, and the tangible items associated with a service (like stationery, bills, and business cards). For example, McDonald's has created a strong organizational image with its Golden Arches, relatively standardized interiors, and employee uniforms. Another way to create an image is through branding. MCI Communications has grown by creating and promoting brands in the commodity business of common-carrier long-distance service. An example of an MCI brand is 1-800-COLLECT.

- *Engaging in postpurchase communication:* Postpurchase communication refers to the follow-up activities that a service firm might engage in after a customer transaction. Postcard surveys, telephone calls, brochures, and various other types of follow-up show customers that their feedback matters and their patronage is appreciated.

Price Strategy

Considerations in pricing a service are similar to the pricing considerations to be discussed in Chapters 17 and 18. However, the unique characteristics of services present two special pricing challenges.

First, in order to price a service, it is important to define the unit of service consumption. For example, should pricing be based on completing a specific service task (cutting a customer's hair), or should it be time based (how long it takes to cut a customer's hair)? Some services include the consumption of goods, such as food and beverages. Restaurants charge customers for food and drink rather than the use of a table and chairs. Some transportation firms charge by distance; others charge a flat rate.

Second, for services that are composed of multiple elements, the issue is whether pricing should be based on a "bundle" of elements or whether each element should be priced separately. A bundled price may be preferable when consumers dislike having to pay "extra" for every part of the service (for example, paying extra for baggage or food on an airplane), and it is simpler for the firm to administer. For instance, MCI offered a basic communications package that included thirty minutes of telephone time, five hours of Internet access, a personal number that could route calls to several locations, and a calling card all for one price. Alternatively, customers may not want to pay for service elements they do not use. Many furniture stores now have "unbundled" delivery charges from the price of the furniture. Customers who wish to can pick up the furniture at the store, saving on the delivery fee.

Marketers should set performance objectives when pricing each service. Three categories of pricing objectives have been suggested:[16]

- *Revenue-oriented pricing* focuses on maximizing the surplus of income over costs. A limitation of this approach is that determining costs can be difficult for many services.

- *Operations-oriented pricing* seeks to match supply and demand by varying prices. For example, matching hotel demand to the number of available rooms can be achieved by raising prices at peak times and decreasing them during slow times.

- *Patronage-oriented pricing* tries to maximize the number of customers using the service. Thus, prices vary with different market segments' ability to pay, and methods of payment (such as credit) are offered that increase the likelihood of a purchase.

A firm may need to use more than one type of pricing objective. In fact, all three objectives probably need to be included to some degree in a pricing strategy, although the importance of each type may vary depending on the type of service provided, the prices that competitors are charging, the differing ability of various customer segments to pay, or the opportunity to negotiate price. For customized services (for example, legal services and construction services), customers may also have the ability to negotiate a price.

E*Trade
Ameritrade
Schwab

Compare the pricing for services on the largest Internet financial Web sites. How can you account for the great differences in price for essentially the same service?

http://www.etrade.com

http://www.ameritrade.com

http://www.schwab.com

On Line

Relationship Marketing in Services

Many services involve ongoing interaction between the service organization and the customer. Thus, they can benefit from relationship marketing, the strategy described in Chapter 1, as a means of attracting, developing, and retaining customer relationships. The idea is to develop strong loyalty by creating satisfied customers who will buy additional services from the firm and are unlikely to switch to a competitor. Satisfied customers are also likely to engage in positive word-of-mouth communication, thereby helping to bring in new customers.

Many businesses have found that it is more cost-effective to hang on to the customers they have than to focus only on attracting new ones. A bank executive, for example, found that increasing customer retention by 2 percent can have the same effect on profits as reducing costs by 10 percent.

Discuss relationship marketing in services

Services that purchasers receive on a continuing basis (for example, cable TV, banking, insurance) can be considered membership services. This type of service naturally lends itself to relationship marketing. When services involve discrete transactions (for example, a movie theater, a restaurant, public transportation), it may be more difficult to build membership-type relationships with customers. Nevertheless, services involving discrete transactions may be transformed into membership relationships using marketing tools. For example, the service could be sold in bulk (for example, a theater series subscription or a commuter ticket on public transportation). Or a service firm could offer special benefits to customers who choose to register with the firm (for example, loyalty programs for hotels, airlines, and car rental firms). The service firm that has a more formalized relationship with its customers has an advantage because it knows who its customers are and how and when they use the services offered.[17]

It has been suggested that relationship marketing can be practiced at three levels:[18]

- *Level 1:* The firm uses pricing incentives to encourage customers to continue doing business with it. Examples include the frequent flyer programs offered by many airlines and the free or discounted travel services given to frequent hotel guests. This level of relationship marketing is the least effective in the long term because its price-based advantage is easily imitated by other firms.

- *Level 2:* This level of relationship marketing also uses pricing incentives but seeks to build social bonds with customers. The firm stays in touch with customers, learns about their needs, and designs services to meet those needs. 1-800-FLOWERS, for example, developed an on-line Gift Reminder Program. Customers who reach the company via its Web site can register unlimited birthdays, anniversaries, or other special occasions. Five days before each occasion and at their request, 1-800-FLOWERS sends them an e-mail reminder. Level 2 relationship marketing has a higher potential for keeping the firm ahead of the competition than does level 1 relationship marketing.

- *Level 3:* At this level, the firm again uses financial and social bonds but adds structural bonds to the formula. Structural bonds are developed by offering value-added services that are not readily available from other firms. Hertz's #1 Club Gold program allows members to call and reserve a car, board a courtesy bus at the airport, tell the driver their name, and get dropped off in front of their car. Hertz also starts up the car and turns on the air conditioning or heat, depending on the temperature. Marketing programs like this one have the strongest potential for sustaining long-term relationships with customers.

Internal Marketing in Service Firms

(6)

Explain internal marketing in services

internal marketing
Treating employees as customers and developing systems and benefits that satisfy their needs.

Services are performances, so the quality of a firm's employees is an important part of building long-term relationships with customers. Employees who like their jobs and are satisfied with the firm they work for are more likely to deliver superior service to customers. In other words, a firm that makes its employees happy has a better chance of keeping its customers coming back. Studies show that replacing an employee costs roughly 1.5 times a year's pay. Also, companies with highly committed employees have been found to post sharply higher shareholder returns.[19] Thus, it is critical that service firms practice **internal marketing**, which means treating employees as customers and developing systems and benefits that satisfy their needs. Internal marketing involves the following activities: competing for talent, offering a vision, training employees, stressing teamwork, giving employees more freedom to make decisions, measuring and rewarding good service performance, and knowing employees' needs.[20]

Companies have instituted a wide variety of programs designed to satisfy employees. Some companies are trying to retain happy employees by offering concierges who run errands to help ease the lives of time-strapped, stressed-out workers.[21] Marriott International set up a twenty-four-hour hotline to answer questions from employees having personal and family problems.[22] These examples illustrate how service firms can invest in their most important resource—their employees.

Global Issues in Services Marketing

The international marketing of services is a major part of global business, and the United States has become the world's largest exporter of services. Competition in international services is increasing rapidly, however.

To be successful in the global marketplace, service firms must first determine the nature of their core product. Then the marketing mix elements (additional services, pricing, promotion, distribution) should be designed to take into account each country's cultural, technological, and political environment.

Because of their competitive advantages, many U.S. service industries have been able to enter the global marketplace. U.S. banks, for example, have advantages in customer service and collections management. The field of construction and engineering services offers great global potential; U.S. companies have vast experience in this industry, so economies of scale are possible for machinery and materials, human resource management, and project management. The U.S. insurance industry has substantial knowledge about underwriting, risk evaluation, and insurance operations that it can export to other countries. American hotel chains also have great potential for globalization, as the "Global Perspectives" box on the next page illustrates.

7

Discuss global issues in services marketing

Nonprofit Organization Marketing

A **nonprofit organization** is an organization that exists to achieve some goal other than the usual business goals of profit, market share, or return on investment. Nonprofit organizations share important characteristics with private-sector service firms. Both market intangible products. Both often require the customer to be present during the production process. Both for-profit and nonprofit services vary greatly from producer to producer and from day to day, even from the same producer. Neither for-profit nor nonprofit services can be stored in the way that tangible goods can be produced, saved, and sold at a later date.

Few people realize that nonprofit organizations account for over 20 percent of the economic activity in the United States. The cost of government, the predominant form of nonprofit organization, has become the biggest single item in the American family budget—more than housing, food, or health care. Together,

8

Describe nonprofit organization marketing

nonprofit organization
An organization that exists to achieve some goal other than the usual business goals of profit, market share, or return on investment.

Exporting Management Savvy

Using little more than a desktop computer, a telephone, and his experience as a hotel manager, Rajiv Bhatia helps other hotel operators across the globe help their guests enjoy their stay. Mr. Bhatia, who works for Cendant Corporation, a company that has 130 hotel properties in eighty countries, is one of a growing number of U.S. "knowledge workers," professionals whose management skills in service industries like lodging are in increasing demand as franchisers expand abroad. Born in India, schooled in Brussels, and trained in hotels in Ireland, India, and Manhattan, he is the kind of professional more likely to be recruited in America than anywhere else because he is a well-educated immigrant who is comfortable working across national boundaries.

What Mr. Bhatia does for hotels, others are doing for McDonald's, Hertz, Kinko's, and Ace Hardware. Essentially, they export management and technical assistance to overseas service providers. This assistance, including sales of data processing, marketing, research, and legal services, generated fees and other commissions totaling about $18 billion in 2000—nearly a fourth of the trade surplus in services.

Exported U.S. services, which totaled $255 billion in 2000 aren't enough to offset the U.S. trade deficit in goods, which grew to $345 billion in the same time period. But the service surplus may be more long lasting, as countries that currently outsell U.S. producers of merchandise spend their profits on services offered by U.S. companies in return.

Mr. Bhatia offers many forms of assistance. For example, Premesh Patel, director of information technology for Days Inn in South Africa, needs help downloading the chain's Web page onto a compact disc. A request comes from Curacao for the Travelodge chain's sleepy-bear logo, which the hotel needs for promotional flyers.

A more urgent problem comes from Mexico. Workers in Los Cabos are on strike, and refuse to let guests into a hotel. Angered guests are threatening to sue the chain for the cost of their ruined vacations. Working the phone and fax machine over the next twenty-four hours, Mr. Bhatia helps the hotel's owner, who is in Mexico City, direct the staff on the ground in Los Cabos. Several dozen guests are moved to another wing of the hotel, where strikers can't restrict their access. Rooms are found for three other guests at a hotel nearby. Complaints and refunds are kept to a minimum.

Mexico, which has a $2.7 billion annual deficit trading services with the United States, is where Mr. Bhatia makes his biggest contribution to the U.S. trade balance, as the principal manager for all of Days Inn properties in Mexico. With nine motels in operation or under construction there, Mexico is where Days Inn has its largest network outside the United States and Canada. Mr. Bhatia keeps tabs on construction of a new hotel in Mexico City's trendy Condesa neighborhood, by checking out prospective franchisees to avoid becoming a partner with an investor with ties to drug trafficking. He also conducts management seminars in Mexico several times a year, and hosts a steady stream of young hotel managers training in New Jersey.

By building its Mexican presence, Cendant leverages the value of its brands in the United States, because it draws more Mexican guests into its motels. William Hanley, Mr. Bhatia's boss at Cendant, notes that "The best advertisement for our brand at home is a successful property in Mexico."[23]

Explain the advantages to Cendant of having hotels all over the world. What marketing elements might it have to adjust in different countries?

---

federal, state, and local governments collect tax revenues that amount to more than a third of the U.S. gross domestic product. Moreover, they employ nearly one of every five nonagricultural civilian workers. In addition to government entities, nonprofit organizations include hundreds of thousands of private museums, theaters, schools, and churches.

What Is Nonprofit Organization Marketing?

nonprofit organization marketing
The effort by nonprofit organizations to bring about mutually satisfying exchanges with target markets.

Nonprofit organization marketing is the effort by nonprofit organizations to bring about mutually satisfying exchanges with target markets. Although these organizations vary substantially in size and purpose and operate in different environments, most perform the following marketing activities:

- Identify the customers they wish to serve or attract (although they usually use another term, such as *clients, patients, members,* or *sponsors)*

- Explicitly or implicitly specify objectives

- Develop, manage, and eliminate programs and services

- Decide on prices to charge (although they use other terms, such as *fees, donations, tuition, fares, fines,* or *rates*)

- Schedule events or programs, and determine where they will be held or where services will be offered

- Communicate their availability through brochures, signs, public service announcements, or advertisements

Often, the nonprofit organizations that carry out these functions do not realize they are engaged in marketing.

PETA

What do you think are the marketing objectives of PETA? Visiting its Web site may help you find the answers. Are there conflicting objectives? Objectives that surprise you?

http://www.peta.org

On Line

Unique Aspects of Nonprofit Organization Marketing Strategies

Like their counterparts in business organizations, nonprofit managers develop marketing strategies to bring about mutually satisfying exchanges with target markets. However, marketing in nonprofit organizations is unique in many ways—including the setting of marketing objectives, the selection of target markets, and the development of appropriate marketing mixes.

Objectives

In the private sector, the profit motive is both an objective for guiding decisions and a criterion for evaluating results. Nonprofit organizations do not seek to make a profit for redistribution to owners or shareholders. Rather, their focus is often on generating enough funds to cover expenses. The Methodist Church does not gauge its success by the amount of money left in offering plates. The Museum of Science and Industry does not base its performance evaluations on the dollar value of tokens put into the turnstile.

Most nonprofit organizations are expected to provide equitable, effective, and efficient services that respond to the wants and preferences of multiple constituencies. These include users, payers, donors, politicians, appointed officials, the media, and the general public. Nonprofit organizations cannot measure their success or failure in strictly financial terms.

The lack of a financial "bottom line" and the existence of multiple, diverse, intangible, and sometimes vague or conflicting objectives make prioritizing objectives, making decisions, and evaluating performance hard for nonprofit managers. They must often use approaches different from the ones commonly used in the private sector. For example, Planned Parenthood has devised a system for basing salary increases on how employees perform in relation to the objectives they set each year.

Target Markets

Three issues relating to target markets are unique to nonprofit organizations:

- *Apathetic or strongly opposed targets:* Private-sector organizations usually give priority to developing those market segments that are most likely to respond to particular offerings. In contrast, nonprofit organizations must often target those who are apathetic about or strongly opposed to receiving their services, such as vaccinations, family-planning guidance, help for problems of drug or alcohol abuse, and psychological counseling.

- *Pressure to adopt undifferentiated segmentation strategies:* Nonprofit organizations often adopt undifferentiated strategies (see Chapter 7) by default. Sometimes they fail to recognize the advantages of targeting, or an undifferentiated approach may appear to offer economies of scale and low per capita costs. In other instances, nonprofit organizations are pressured or required to serve the maximum number of people by targeting the average user. The problem with developing services targeted at the average user is that there are few "average" users. Therefore, such strategies typically fail to fully satisfy any market segment.

- *Complementary positioning:* The main role of many nonprofit organizations is to provide services, with available resources, to those who are not adequately served by private-sector organizations. As a result, the nonprofit organization must often complement, rather than compete with, the efforts of others. The positioning task is to identify underserved market segments and to develop marketing programs that match their needs rather than to target the niches that may be most profitable. For example, a university library may see itself as complementing the services of the public library, rather than as competing with it.

Product Decisions

There are three product-related distinctions between business and nonprofit organizations:

- *Benefit complexity:* Rather than simple product concepts, like "Fly the friendly skies" or "We earn money the old-fashioned way," nonprofit organizations often market complex behaviors or ideas. Examples include the need to exercise or eat right, not to drink and drive, and not to smoke tobacco. The benefits that a person receives are complex, long term, and intangible and therefore are more difficult to communicate to consumers.

- *Benefit strength:* The benefit strength of many nonprofit offerings is quite weak or indirect. What are the direct, personal benefits to you of driving fifty-five miles per hour, donating blood, or asking your neighbors to contribute money to a charity? In contrast, most private-sector service organizations can offer customers direct, personal benefits in an exchange relationship.

- *Involvement:* Many nonprofit organizations market products that elicit very low involvement ("Prevent forest fires" or "Don't litter") or very high involvement ("Join the military" or "Stop smoking"). The typical range for private-sector goods is much narrower. Traditional promotional tools may be inadequate to motivate adoption of either low- or high-involvement products.

Distribution Decisions

A nonprofit organization's capacity for distributing its service offerings to potential customer groups when and where they want them is typically a key variable in determining the success of those service offerings. For example, most state land-grant universities offer extension programs throughout their state to reach the general public. Many large universities have one or more satellite campus locations to provide easier access for students in other areas. Some educational institutions also offer classes to students at off-campus locations via interactive video technology.

The extent to which a service depends on fixed facilities has important implications for distribution decisions. Obviously, services like rail transit and lake fishing can be delivered only at specific points. Many nonprofit services, however, do not depend on special facilities. Counseling, for example, need not take place in agency offices; it may occur wherever counselors and clients can meet. Probation services, outreach youth programs, and educational courses taught on commuter trains are other examples of deliverable services.

Promotion Decisions

Many nonprofit organizations are explicitly or implicitly prohibited from advertising, thus limiting their promotion options. Most federal agencies fall into this category. Other nonprofit organizations simply do not have the resources to retain advertising agencies, promotion consultants, or marketing staff. However, nonprofit organizations have a few special promotion resources to call on:

- *Professional volunteers:* Nonprofit organizations often seek out marketing, sales, and advertising professionals to help them develop and implement promotion strategies. In some instances, an advertising agency donates its services in exchange for potential long-term benefits. One advertising agency donated its services to a major symphony because the symphony had a blue-ribbon board of directors. Donated services create goodwill, personal contacts, and general awareness of the donor's organization, reputation, and competency.

Advertising Council
What are the most compelling PSAs on the Ad Council site at the moment?
http://www.adcouncil.org

On Line

- *Sales promotion activities:* Sales promotion activities that make use of existing services or other resources are increasingly being used to draw attention to the offerings of nonprofit organizations. Sometimes nonprofit charities even team up with other companies for promotional activities. For example, in a number of large cities including Dallas, Chicago, and Denver, local charities lined up retailers such as Crate & Barrel and Polo Ralph Lauren to offer 20 percent discounts for a limited time to shoppers who purchased a special $50 card from the charity. To get the discount, the shopper simply showed the participating store the card.[24]

- *Public service advertising:* A **public service advertisement (PSA)** is an announcement that promotes a program of a federal, state, or local government or of a nonprofit organization. Unlike a commercial advertiser, the sponsor of the PSA does not pay for the time or space. Instead, it is donated by the medium. The Advertising Council has developed PSAs that are some of the most memorable advertisements of all time. For example, Smokey the Bear reminded everyone to be careful not to start forest fires.

public service advertisement (PSA)
An announcement that promotes a program of a federal, state, or local government or of a nonprofit organization.

Sometimes for-profit firms offer charitable cause–related promotions, such as the one described in the "Ethics in Marketing" box, that may raise ethical concerns.

Pricing Decisions

Five key characteristics distinguish the pricing decisions of nonprofit organizations from those of the profit sector:

- *Pricing objectives:* The main pricing objective in the profit sector is revenue or, more specifically, profit maximization, sales maximization, or target return on

---

ETHICS IN MARKETING

All for the Cause

Modern-day "cause marketing" goes back to 1974 and the inception of the Ronald McDonald House Charities. Since then, the trend has been building steadily. The 1980s saw Pizza Hut, Lens-Crafters, and Home Depot launch nationwide drives to benefit charities. In the 1990s, many major retail, automotive, and cosmetic companies embraced a variety of causes, from child and family issues to breast cancer.

The trend isn't simply a case of corporate consciousness-raising; consumers are increasingly demanding that corporations "give back." According to a joint study by branding and communications firm Cone and research firm Roper Starch Worldwide, nearly two-thirds of Americans now say cause marketing should be a standard

business practice. Roughly the same fraction agree that, all else being equal, they would be likely to switch brands or retailers to those associated with a good cause.

Dan Cunningham, chief chokolada (yes, that's his official title) of Dan's Chocolates, needed to convince the nation that fresh chocolate, shipped within seven days of manufacture from his Madison, Wisconsin, factory, is better than chocolate found lingering on retail shelves. So he devised "The Great Chocolate Challenge," the first nationwide chocolate tasting party.

For ten days in April, he offered the first ten thousand visitors to his site a six-piece chocolate sampler for a $1 donation to charity. Dan's paid about $3 million for the Challenge: $1 million to make

and ship the chocolate, and another $2 million on radio ads in seven cities. The company also placed banners on the Blue Mountain Arts Web site.

The result? The campaign quadrupled orders and site traffic, and almost ten percent of "Challengers" became return customers. "We did more business in the month of May than we did the entire first quarter," says Ted Richardson, Dan's chief marketing officer. Though it's hard to separate the impact of Mother's Day from the promotion, no one's arguing with the $50,000 that Dan's donated to charity at the end of the Challenge.[25]

Is it ethical to use donations to charity to increase sales?

How my lust for salad spun out of control.

Paul Newman

Yes, I'm a certified nut about salad. One Christmas, I concocted a batch of my ding-dong drop-dead dressing — the most virgin of olive oils, vintage wine vinegar and the freshest of herbs and spices to give it a kick. I went door to door passing out bottles to friends and neighbors. Couple of weeks later they were attacking the house looking for more. So...it was either bottle it up or never answer the door.

NEWMAN'S OWN®
Paul Newman donates all his profits to charity.

Over $125 million donated to thousands of charities since 1982.

www.newmansown.com
©2002 Newman's Own Inc.

COURTESY OF NEWMAN'S OWN

As you read in the "Ethics in Marketing" box, cause-related marketing can be a controversial marketing technique because not all companies are as scrupulous as they should be about their intentions. A company like Newman's Own, however, which donates all after-tax profits to charity, is clear in its mission. By not profiting from using causes as a marketing tool, its motives are beyond reproach.

sales or investment. Many nonprofit organizations must also be concerned about revenue. Often, however, nonprofit organizations seek to either partially or fully defray costs rather than to achieve a profit for distribution to stockholders. Nonprofit organizations also seek to redistribute income—for instance, through taxation and sliding-scale fees. Moreover, they strive to allocate resources fairly among individuals or households or across geographic or political boundaries.

- *Nonfinancial prices:* In many nonprofit situations, consumers are not charged a monetary price but instead must absorb nonmonetary costs. The importance of those costs is illustrated by the large number of eligible citizens who do not take advantage of so-called free services for the poor. In many public assistance programs, about half the people who are eligible don't participate. Nonmonetary costs consist of the opportunity cost of time, embarrassment costs, and effort costs.

- *Indirect payment:* Indirect payment through taxes is common to marketers of "free" services, such as libraries, fire protection, and police protection. Indirect payment is not a common practice in the profit sector.

- *Separation between payers and users:* By design, the services of many charitable organizations are provided for those who are relatively poor and largely paid for by those who are better off financially. Although examples of separation between payers and users can be found in the profit sector (such as insurance claims), the practice is much less prevalent.

- *Below-cost pricing:* An example of below-cost pricing is university tuition. Virtually all private and public colleges and universities price their services below full cost.

CONNECT IT

Look back at the story about Yellow Freight Systems at the beginning of this chapter. After reading the chapter, you should know the answers to the questions posed at the end of the story. A service, such as trucking, differs from goods in four basic characteristics. Compared to goods, services are intangible performances, are produced and consumed simultaneously, have greater variability, and are perishable. Yellow's service before 1996 was narrowly focused on long-haul trucking. After 1996, it broadened its service mix to offer one-stop shopping for shipping. Yellow's concern with satisfying its customers helped the company to improve the reliability, responsiveness, and assurance components of service quality.

Have you ever wanted to provide feedback to your college or university about the quality of the services that you, as a student, receive? Choose a department or function within your college or university (for example, the registrar, advising office, bursar, financial-aid office) with which you have had a negative service quality experience. Write a letter to the department/function and suggest ways it can improve its service quality. Use what you have learned about the components of service quality (tangibles, reliability, responsiveness, empathy, and assurance) to help you think about what needs to be improved. You may also use the gap model of service quality to guide your thoughts and suggestions about how to make improvements. For example, you might suggest that a department needs to conduct research to find out what kind of service students expect.

REVIEW IT

1 **Discuss the importance of services to the economy.** The service sector plays a crucial role in the U.S. economy, employing about three-quarters of the workforce and accounting for more than 70 percent of the gross domestic product.

1.1 What services does the Web site **http://www.travelweb.com** offer? How do visitors use the Special Offer List?

2 **Discuss the differences between services and goods.** Services are distinguished by four characteristics. Services are intangible performances in that they lack clearly identifiable physical characteristics, making it difficult for marketers to communicate their specific benefits to potential customers. The production and consumption of services occur simultaneously. Services are variable because their quality depends on such elements as the service provider, individual consumer, location, and so on. Finally, services are perishable in the sense that they cannot be stored or saved. As a result, synchronizing supply with demand is particularly challenging in the service industry.

2.1 Assume that you are a manager of a bank branch. Write a list of the implications of intangibility for your firm.

3 **Describe the components of service quality and the gap model of service quality.** Service quality has five components: reliability (ability to perform the service dependably, accurately, and consistently), responsiveness (providing prompt service), assurance (knowledge and courtesy of employees and their ability to convey trust), empathy (caring, individualized attention), and tangibles (physical evidence of the service).

The gap model identifies five key discrepancies that can influence customer evaluations of service quality. When the gaps are large, service quality is low. As the gaps shrink, service quality improves. Gap 1 is found between customers' expectations and management's perceptions of those expectations. Gap 2 is found between management's perception of what the customer wants and specifications for service quality. Gap 3 is found between service quality specifications and delivery of the service. Gap 4 is found between service delivery and what the company promises to the customer through external communication. Gap 5 is found between customers' service expectations and their perceptions of service performance.

3.1 Analyze a recent experience that you have had with a service business (for example, hairdresser, movie theater, dentist, restaurant, car repair) in terms of your expectations and perceptions about each of the five components of service quality.

4 **Develop marketing mixes for services.** "Product" (service) strategy issues include what is being processed (people, possessions, mental stimulus, information), core and supplementary services, customization versus standardization, and the service mix or portfolio. Distribution decisions involve convenience, number of outlets, direct versus indirect distribution, and scheduling. Stressing tangible cues, using personal sources of information, creating strong organizational images, and engaging in postpurchase communication are effective promotion strategies. Pricing objectives for services can be revenue oriented, operations oriented, patronage oriented, or any combination of the three.

4.1 Form a team with at least two other classmates, and come up with an idea for a new service. Develop a marketing mix strategy for the new service.

5 **Discuss relationship marketing in services.** Relationship marketing in services involves attracting, developing, and retaining customer relationships. There are three levels of relationship marketing: Level 1 focuses on pricing incentives; level 2 uses pricing incentives and social bonds with customers; and level 3 uses pricing, social bonds, and structural bonds to build long-term relationships.

5.1 For the new service developed for question 4.1, have the members of the team discuss how they would implement a relationship marketing strategy.

6 **Explain internal marketing in services.** Internal marketing means treating employees as customers and developing systems and benefits that satisfy their needs. Employees who like their jobs and are happy with the firm they work for are more likely to deliver good service. Internal marketing activities include competing for talent, offering a vision, training employees, stressing teamwork, giving employees freedom to make decisions, measuring and rewarding good service performance, and knowing employees' needs.

6.1 WRITING Choose a service firm with which you do a lot of business. Write a memo to the manager explaining the importance of internal marketing and outlining the factors internal marketing includes.

7 **Discuss global issues in services marketing.** The United States has become the world's largest exporter of services. Although competition is keen, the United States has a competitive advantage because of its vast experience in many service industries. To be successful globally, service firms must adjust their marketing mix for the environment of each target country.

7.1 What issues would you have to think about in going global with the new service that you developed in the questions above? How would you change your marketing mix to address those issues?

8 **Describe nonprofit organization marketing.** Nonprofit organizations pursue goals other than profit, market share, and return on investment. Nonprofit organization marketing facilitates mutually satisfying exchanges between nonprofit organizations and their target markets. Several unique characteristics distinguish nonbusiness marketing strategy, including a concern with services and social behaviors rather than manufactured goods and profit; a difficult, undifferentiated, and in some ways marginal target market; a complex product that may have only indirect benefits and elicit very low involvement; a short, direct, immediate distribution channel; a relative lack of resources for promotion; and prices only indirectly related to the exchange between the producer and the consumer of services.

8.1 TEAM Form a team with two or three classmates. Using the promotion strategies discussed in the nonprofit section of this chapter, develop a promotion strategy for your college or university.

APPLY IT

Application for Entrepreneurs

 Amanda Jocobs has decided she wants to start a marketing consulting business. She has been able to generate solid financial backing for her venture because she has already developed an outstanding reputation as a creative and successful marketer. Thus, start-up resources are not a large problem. Amanda will target small companies with her services. Her business will be located in a medium-sized community not far from a large city.

Questions

1. How can Amanda make her service tangible for potential clients?

2. What can Amanda do to ensure she will offer a quality service to her clients?

3. What marketing strategies can Amanda use to help her develop long-term relationships with her clients?

THINK ABOUT IT

Ethics Exercise

Web sites such as Oncology.com, cancerpage.com and CancerSource.com offer cancer patients sophisticated medical data and advice in exchange for personal data that is then sold to advertisers and business partners and used by the Web sites to create products to sell back to patients. Some argue that cancer patients visiting these sites are willingly exchanging their personal information for the sites' medical information. Others would contend that this kind of exchange is unethical.

Questions

1. Is this practice ethical?

2. Does the AMA Code of Ethics have anything to say about this issue? Go to **http://www.marketingpower.com** and review the code. Then, write a brief paragraph on what the AMA Code of Ethics contains that relates to this scenario.

TRY IT

Entrepreneurship Case
Closing the Digital Divide in the Inner City

 Entering the new millennium, there were more than 350,000 unfilled technology jobs. In the Chicago area alone, there were 18,000 technology positions to be filled. To satisfy this demand for technology professionals, Leslie Beller resigned from Jobs for Youth in 1999 and founded the Inner City Computer Stars Foundation. Start-up funds came from two investors at the Chicago Mercantile Exchange ($15,000) and a December 1999 fund-raiser ($50,000). Largely known as i.c.stars, the

Chicago-based not-for-profit organization is focused upon closing the so-called digital divide.

Closing the digital divide is about making sure information is available to everyone, not just a few select groups. Disenfranchised groups in the technology revolution include minorities, females, the poor, and the disabled. Beller's organization, i.c.stars, is a technology training program that focuses upon inner-city, primarily African American and Latino youth. The goal is to prepare eighteen to twenty-four-year-olds for the technology, telecommunications, and Internet industry workplace.

As a nonprofit organization, Beller has two very different target markets: (1) inner-city youth who will participate in the technology training program and (2) the investment community that will provide funding for the program (and eventually jobs for the trained youth).

The technology training program is an intensive three-month program that includes a cost-of-living stipend for the participant. The first month focuses upon topics such as HTML, Java, and project management. During the second month, participants develop and execute their own Web sites, which are hosted at the **http://www.icstars.org** portal. In the third month, the participants work with paying clients on Web-related projects. The objective, at the end of the third month, is to place program participants in webmaster or IT professional positions. The first program began in June 2000 with ten inner-city youth from the south and west sides of Chicago and from uptown Chicago.

Targeting the Chicago investment community, i.c.stars hopes to raise $1 million to keep the organization operational. The organization plans to accomplish this via a not-for-profit road show where various aspects of i.c.stars are presented and described. Unlike traditional not-for-profit fundraising efforts that target foundations, the road show targets angel investors, venture capital groups, and corporations with a real-time presentation of the organization. The road show allows i.c.stars to operate as a dot-com company in its fundraising. Investors can sign up to participate in the organization's activities at the road show Web site, **http://www.iccapital.org**. The key selling point in the road show is the opportunity to gain social equity in the future of the Chicago community.

Business Plan

i.c.stars' five-year business plan calls for the organization to eventually generate revenue through placement fees and production contracts. To be financially stable within five years, i.c.stars has the following timetable:

- Years 1 and 2:   Perfect the three-month training program model
- Years 2 and 3:   Serve the Chicago community and technology market
- Years 3 and 4:   Create an i.c.stars consulting service around the organization's core competencies of assessment, diversity/workplace culture training, IT leadership training, and project management
- Year 5:   Financial stability through training programs

Continued Success

i.c.stars has lined up an impressive group of corporate sponsors. Groups such as William Blair & Company, closerlook.com, Lante Corporation, Blue-Meteor, and Expedior, as well as many angel investors, have contributed to i.c.stars' success to date. Beller, however, has to continue developing such sponsorship relationships if she wants to accomplish her five-year plan and achieve the long-term goal of not only financial stability but the crossing of the digital divide between technology and minority groups.

Questions

1. What is i.c.stars' product?

2. What is unique about the i.c.stars' marketing strategy?

3. Does i.c.stars face any pricing issues?

4. What does Beller need to do to continue building sponsorship relationships?

Short

The *Marketing* PowerPoint CD-ROM has eleven videos in the Chapter 11 slide presentation. Watch the six public service announcements (PSAs) and decide which you think are the most compelling—those on drugs and terrorism, or one of the four nonsmoking campaign ads. Then watch ads for the United Way to observe nonprofit organization marketing and for Visa to see how promotion strategies work in the service mix.

Medium

Is it possible to transform a product into a service? Watch the CNN clip for Chapter 11 and see how Marvel Comics and others have extended their comic book brands (like Superman, Spiderman, and the Hulk) to the big screen.

Long SmallBusinessSchool
the Series on PBS stations and the Web

To give you insight into Chapter 11, Small Business School will take you inside the Texas Jet terminal at Meacham Field in Fort Worth, Texas. When Reed Pigman realized he couldn't compete with other private jet companies on price, he decided that he was really in a service business. Watch the segment to discover very innovative ways of approaching this market.

FLIP IT

 Flip to Chapter 11 in your *Grademaker Study Guide* for more review opportunities, including the pretest, vocabulary review, Internet activities, study test questions, and an application exercise based on services marketing. Do services really differ from goods? How do you develop a marketing mix for service businesses? If you don't know, then flip open your *Grademaker* and review.

CLICK IT

 The *Marketing* Web site links you to all the Internet-based activities in this chapter, like "Review It" question 1.1 and the On-Line exercises in the chapter margins. As a review, do the Chapter 11 quiz and crossword puzzle. And don't forget the Career Exersite that gives you resources for exploring marketing career opportunities in the service industry and the nonprofit sector. Review the main concepts in the PowerPoint presentation for Chapter 11, too. Go to **http://lamb.swlearning.com**, read the material, and follow the links right from the site.

SPIN IT

 Spin your Xtra! CD-ROM to test your understanding of the service marketing concepts in the chapter by completing the worksheets for Exhibits 11.2 and 11.4. If your instructor has assigned a marketing plan project, worksheets on Xtra! can help you organize your work. In addition to the quiz on the Web site, there's another quiz on the Xtra! CD-ROM, plus video of the authors answering frequently asked questions about service marketing topics, such as "It is really meaningful to distinguish between goods and services firms?"

Still Shaky? Here's a Tip.

Take advantage of all the review opportunities on the Marketing Web site at **http://lamb. swlearning.com**. Write up a list of questions you have about concepts you don't understand and visit your professor or TA during office hours.

MARKETING MISCUES

Did Moxi Digital Stop to Consider Demand?

A home entertainment revolution was on the horizon if one believed Steve Perlman, the founder of Moxi Digital, Inc. A relatively new Palo Alto, California, company, formerly known as Rearden Steel Technology, Moxi Digital was seeking to dominate the home entertainment market by seamlessly integrating a home's television, stereo, and computer. The company's revolutionary product, the Moxi Media Center, was unveiled in January 2002. At the time, however, there were rumors that potential demand might be uncertain and that the company might not have the cash flow to survive.

The Moxi Media Center was five products in one: a digital cable/satellite receiver, a digital music jukebox, a personal video recorder, a DVD player, and a cable/DSL modem. With these five products, the Moxi had three main capabilities: (1) a navigation system to reduce the number of clicks to find items, (2) secure multiformatted video and music playback, and (3) storage and organization of music tracks. The Moxi was similar in appearance to a videocassette recorder, sat on the television, and had a remote control. Beyond appearances, the Moxi was a technological breakthrough that allowed any television or personal computer in the house to receive entertainment and data. Interestingly, the product's name was not related to any technological aspect of the product market. "Moxi" came from the word *moxie,* meaning gumption, excitement, and spunk.

Total U.S. consumer electronics sales were expected to be almost $96 billion by the end of 2002. Included in these estimates were sales of multi-use products such as a cellphone and MP3 combination and a digital voice recorder box combined with direct broadcast satellite, as well as increased sales of DVD players, digital cameras, and mobile electronics. Nevertheless, industry experts were skeptical as to whether a product such as the Moxi that could truly be classified as a disruptive technology would generate much demand. With the Moxi selling to consumers at more than $400, the company would need to do considerable market education to generate demand at the break-even level.

In fact, market acceptance of the Moxi appeared questionable. Would consumers who were only beginning to adjust to the potential of digital entertainment accept, much less adopt, such state-of-the-art technology? Did consumers see a need to network their televisions, computers, stereos, and MP3 players? Or were consumers happy with their current arrangement of separate entertainment devices? Additionally, did the typical American household own the entertainment equipment necessary to make the Moxi useful?

In addition to these market-oriented questions, several company-related concerns had arisen. Moxi Digital would not actually manufacture the media center. Rather, it would offer the designs for free to consumer electronics manufacturers. Thus, the company would rely on intermediaries to fulfill the product's offerings. Would Moxi Digital, along with the necessary and numerous intermediaries, be able to deliver what it promised? More important, however, would the company, which had raised almost $70 million in funding, run out of money before the product even hit the market? There were sincere questions as to whether Moxi Digital could turn its dreams into reality. Was the Moxi Media Center an expensive product idea that was too advanced for the marketplace to adopt quickly enough to warrant funneling more dollars into the invention?

Questions

1. How is the Moxi a disruptive technology?

2. What can a company do to prevent such elaborate investments that do not result in bringing a product to market?

The Segway Human Transporter

A product code-named after Ginger Rogers and a media frenzy about an invention bigger than the Internet set the stage for DEKA Research and Development Corporation's Segway human transporter (Segway HT; http://www.segway.com). But was the buzz about the product too much? Did it create expectations beyond the product's capabilities? Was it too early? Was the buzz leak really an accident? Will the Segway HT change the transportation marketplace? Just as important, what is the market for this new product?

DEKA Research and Development Corporation

Founded in 1982 by Dean Kamen, DEKA focuses on the product market of radical technologies, with a mission to foster innovations that enhance quality of life. Though technically a research and development group, DEKA has the capabilities to take a product from concept to low-volume manufacturing runs. Based in Manchester, New Hampshire, the company remains relatively small and employs about two hundred engineers, technicians, and machinists.

Kamen is a well-known inventor and entrepreneur, holding more than 150 U.S. and foreign patents. His innovative, scientific achievements have resulted in numerous awards and public recognition. *Smithsonian* magazine labeled him "the Pied Piper of technology" and the *New York Times* called him "a new kind of hero for American youth." He is the recipient of the Kilby Award (for extraordinary contributions to society), the Heinz Award in Technology, and the National Medal of Technology.

Innovative health-care products resulting from Kamen's inventions are numerous. His infusion devices gained immediate and international recognition. The market for these devices was huge, prompting Kamen to found AutoSyringe, Inc., to manufacture and market the products. The company's wearable infusion pump gained rapid acceptance in chemotherapy, neonatology, and endocrinology. AutoSyringe also produced and marketed the first insulin pump for diabetics. Eventually, Kamen sold AutoSyringe, Inc., to Baxter International Corporation and then went on to start DEKA.

Since its inception, DEKA has worked closely with several large companies in the health-care industry. Major corporate partners include Baxter Healthcare Corporation, Davol, Inc., and Johnson & Johnson. DEKA designs and develops products for its corporate partners. For Baxter Healthcare Corporation, DEKA developed a relatively small, light-weight peritoneal dialysis machine that allows greater mobility for the user. In conjunction with Davol, Inc., DEKA developed a one-system irrigation pump for common medical procedures such as laparoscopy, arthroscopy, and hysteroscopy. Various companies within Johnson & Johnson (Cordis Corporation, THERAKOS, and Independence Technology) have used DEKA's medical innovations. DEKA and Cordis introduced the first intravascular stent to reduce artery blockage, and DEKA and THERAKOS developed the most advanced and innovative technology used to treat cutaneous T-cell lymphoma. DEKA and Independence Technology are working together to develop and market a product similar to a wheelchair that can climb stairs, raise the user to eye level, and traverse uneven terrain.

Introducing the Segway Human Transporter

The Segway HT, referred to as a disruptive technology, could soon hit the sidewalks, streets, and hallways of a few cities and businesses. This new-age people mover has been described as a cross between a rotary lawn mower and a scooter or a large weed whacker that a person can stand on. This description is somewhat deceptive, however, in that the Segway HT is not as straightforward as a rotary lawn mower, scooter, or weed whacker. It has three personal computers' worth of computer technology, dual-motored wheels, five solid-state gyroscopes, tubeless and flat-resistant lightweight tires, and handlebars for balance. The product does not have a brake, engine, throttle, gearshift, or steering wheel. It works with human equilibrium by responding to movements. Leaning forward on the Segway HT causes it to accelerate, and leaning backward causes it to stop. Basically, the gyroscopes act like the inner ear, the computer acts like a brain, the motors act like muscles, and the wheels act like feet.

Product specifications include a maximum speed of 5 to 17 miles per hour depending upon settings and terrain, a battery charge of 17 miles on flat surfaces, one hour of charge for two hours of operation, a passenger load of 250 pounds, a weight of 65 to 80 pounds, and a cost of $3,000 for the consumer model and $8,000 for the industrial model.

Bringing the Segway HT to market has not been without obstacles. One of the earliest problems was raised by the Church of Christ, Scientist, which owns the rights to anything referring to Ginger Rogers. Another obstacle is that the federal government must determine whether the product should be classified as a motor vehicle. If it is not a motor vehicle, the

Segway HT will likely fall under the auspices of the Consumer Product Safety Commission.

Empowering Pedestrians

DEKA has no mass-market experience, yet it has developed a product that could change the way pedestrians get from point A to point B. Early product-related buzz prompted mixed opinions. While people who had seen or tried the Segway HT were enthusiastic about its potential for success, others were skeptical of its ability to make it to market. The bottom line—would the practicalities of manufacturing and marketing the invention keep it out of consumer hands?

Questions

1. Why is the Segway HT considered a disruptive technology? Is it really just a high-end toy?

2. Can DEKA make the transition from inventing to selling?

3. How can DEKA garner a portion of the $300 billion transportation industry? Who are likely the purchasers of this latest product?

4. Is the Segway HT a consumer product or a business-to-business product?

MARKETING PLANNING ACTIVITIES

To complete all nine activities, use the Part 3 Marketing Planning Worksheets on your Xtra! CD-ROM. If you need a company for the basis of your work, follow the "Marketing Plan Project" link on the *Marketing* Web site (**http://lamb.swlearning.com**).

Product Decisions

For continued general assistance on business plans and marketing plans, visit **http://www.bplans.com** or **http://www.businessplans.org**. For electronic sources of information, search on the Electric Library at **http://wwws.elibrary.com/** or the Internet Public Library at **http://www.ipl.org/**. Another excellent source of information is the Sales and Marketing Executives Marketing Library at **http://www.sell. org/**. You should also refer to Exhibit 2.7 for additional marketing plan checklist items (Part IV.B.1.: Marketing Mix—Product).

In the first part of your strategic marketing plan, you stated your business mission and objectives and performed a detailed SWOT analysis. In the second part of the plan, you identified and described target market segments and described their buying behaviors and decision-making processes. In addition, you identified sources of competitive intelligence and determined whether any further marketing research would be needed before the marketing plan could be implemented.

The next stage of the strategic planning process involves defining the elements of the marketing mix: product, place, promotion, and pricing strategies. This third part of the planning process will focus on product and service components. Be sure that the strategies recommended here match the needs and wants of the target audience(s) you identified earlier.

Use the following exercises to guide you through the third part of your strategic marketing plan:

1. How would you classify the offering to your customers? Is it a consumer product? A business-to-business product? A good or a service? Both? How does this classification change the focus of your marketing plan? Is your product unique enough to be patented? Check with the U.S. Patent and Trademark Office at **http://www.uspto.gov**.

2. Place your company's offerings into a product portfolio. Consider the broader impact of marketing a product item within a line or mix. Factors to consider include price, image, complementary products, distribution relationship, and the like. Are there any special product features that selling on the Internet would allow you to add or force you to take away?

3. Does your chosen company have a brand name and brand mark? If not, design both. If so, evaluate the ability of the brand name and mark to communicate effectively to the target market. Is strong branding more or less important in an Internet environment? Why? What makes branding so important? If your firm needs to hire a professional branding company, look for "Naming and Branding Marketing Firms" on **http://www.looksmart. com**. Of particular importance are firms that can translate your brand name into other languages and check for negative implications. Try translations yourself at **http://www.iTools.com/research-it/ research-it.html**. You can also try to generate brand names made up of random syllables or test a brand name's meaning at **http://www. nomina.net/**.

What will your company's Internet address be? To see what URLs are available, go to **http:// www.companyname.com** and try some out.

Should your URL be the same as your company's name? Why or why not? What happens if a customer mistypes your name? Should you register under alternative spellings?

4. Is the product packaged and labeled? How should it be packaged and why? Do the package and the label design match other communications tools? How is this an opportunity to communicate with your customers?

5. Evaluate warranties or guarantees offered by your firm, including product return policies. How will customers return products they purchased from the Web site? Design the parameters for warranties and return policies. Should your return policy be stricter on-line than off-line? Why or why not?

6. Place your company's product in the appropriate stage of the product life cycle. What are the implications of being in this stage? Would the product life cycle be lengthened, shortened, or not affected by selling your product or service on-line? Would selling your offering on the Internet make it seem earlier on the product life cycle to your customers? Why?

7. What categories of adopters are likely to buy your company's product? Is the product diffusing slowly or quickly through the marketplace? Why?

What elements of the diffusion process can you control to make sure your offering diffuses more quickly throughout the adopter categories and marketplace in general? Will positive word-of-mouth communication be easier or harder to generate on-line?

8. What service aspects are provided with the product? List specific examples of how you can incorporate all five elements of service quality into your offering. What tactics can you define that would minimize any potential service quality gaps? How is customer service handled? What elements of service quality can your firm focus on? What impact would selling on the Internet have on your customer service operation?

9. With whom should your chosen company practice relationship marketing? Marketing on the Internet is particularly vulnerable to breakdowns in client relationships. Which sorts of bonds should be stressed in the relationship marketing strategy? How can your company "touch" its customers differently on-line than off-line? Are there advantages to on-line customer service? Disadvantages?

CROSS-FUNCTIONAL CONNECTIONS SOLUTIONS

Functional Lines Blur in Speed to Market

Questions

1. What is the difference between the demand-side perspective and the supply-side perspective to doing business? Is either perspective more appropriate?

The demand-side perspective focuses upon determining, via marketing research, the customer's wants and needs. Products/services are then developed that satisfy these wants and needs. Once they are developed, marketing adds the finishing touches by positioning the products/services in such a manner that the customers recognize that the products/services will fulfill their demands. Demand-side starts with the customer and ends with the customer, with marketing and the other business functions working in the middle.

The supply-side perspective takes the position that engineers should develop and manufacture leading-edge products. Once a product is developed and manufactured, marketing then introduces the product to the customer by telling the customer about the product's performance. Supply-side

tends to start with the research and development group; then it moves to the manufacturing group and then to marketing, after which it eventually ends with the customer.

As marketers, we believe that the demand-side perspective is the better approach to doing business. However, some argue that the supply-side perspective is more appropriate for high-technology products—that if we waited for the customer, we would not yet have call-waiting, microwave ovens, or video games.

2. What are some of the popular business terms used to describe cross-functional integration?

design-factory fit

concurrent engineering

design for manufacturability and assembly

early manufacturing involvement

paperless design

modularization

3. Why are all employees (whether involved in marketing or not) at the heart of customer service?

A customer generally does not work directly with the marketing department when purchasing a product or service. Instead, the customer may be asking questions of someone on the store floor who was hired to stock shelves, work the cash register, or sweep the floor. The responses that customers receive from these employees tend to represent the customer's image of the company. Also, when a customer calls to check on the status of a repair, the customer is speaking with someone who may have been hired to answer the telephone. Nevertheless, this receptionist is the customer's first contact within the organization and provides a lasting impression of the way the company treats its customers. The way all employees treat the customer becomes intermingled with the product's quality and can drive the customer's perception of quality either up or down.

Suggested Readings

Donald Gerwin, "Team Empowerment in New Product Development," *Business Horizons,* July/August 1999, 29–36.

Avan R. Jassawalla and Hemant C. Sashittal, "Cross-Functional Dynamics in New Product Development," *Research Technology Management,* January/February 2000, 46–49.

PART 4

Distribution Decisions

CROSS-FUNCTIONAL COLLABORATION IN MANAGING DISTRIBUTION

To achieve customer satisfaction, the company must have the right product at the right place at the right time (and at the right price). The need for cross-functional coordination in developing and producing a high-quality product is clear. Getting the product to the consumer at the right place and time is also a result of considerable interaction among marketing and its internal and external partners. Once the product is designed, developed, and produced, marketing and its partners must get the product from the factory to the end user using the best methods. The giant retailer Wal-Mart has based much of its competitive success on its ability to get the right products in the right stores at the right time—products that are then sold to customers via the company's helpful, friendly sales staff.

Considerable costs are associated with getting a high-quality product out the door, and manufacturing has been a key marketing partner in making the delivery process successful. Advanced manufacturing systems (AMS) have been developed that not only reduce costs (ultimately affecting the price charged to the customer) but also allow faster product delivery. Two popular advanced manufacturing systems are just-in-time (JIT) and electronic data interchange (EDI).

A JIT manufacturing system allows the production of a product as needed, instead of producing for stock. Ultimately, such a manufacturing system can change the channel structure by eliminating a channel intermediary. Customers may be able to receive products directly from the manufacturer rather than having to receive the product via a distribution channel. The absence of a channel intermediary not only makes products available quickly, but it also results in fewer channel members and, in turn, decreased costs—the ultimate in efficient operations. However, marketing must make sure that the change makes the channel structure not only more efficient but also more effective. That is, marketing has to determine if the channel intermediary provides a service that will otherwise be unavailable if the product is shipped directly to the customer from the manufacturer.

The use of EDI can significantly increase the efficiency of operations between the shop floor and distribution of the product. EDI permits the exchange of information electronically—using data collected at the point of sale and transmitted automatically to the manufacturing department. This allows manufacturing to know the exact number of available units at any point in time, enabling the manufacturing group to time its production and delivery to meet the customer's specific needs. Eli Lilly Canada is a health-care company that must be able to trace its product movements from the time of manufacture to the point of customer delivery. The company uses a wireless data communication process to track this movement. Its radio frequency–based warehouse management system was implemented by a cross-functional team comprised of manufacturing, technology, and marketing experts.

In some instances, retail sales data transmitted electronically to the manufacturing group start the machines on the shop floor. Such quick response to channel needs can dramatically reduce the time from order entry to delivery. Benetton, the Italian clothing company, uses its retail data to actually schedule specific factories that make its clothes. Such enterprise-wide integrated systems are revolutionizing the retail industry. Retailers are now able to electronically assimilate and transmit inventory data for individual stores, as well as information as to what products are selling at what price in what market.

Many companies have seen the cycle time from order entry to delivery cut in half due to direct (and immediate) interactions between channel members and the manufacturing function in a firm. This reduction in cycle time also allows retailers to reduce the amount of inventory they need to warehouse, which in turn lowers cost and, ultimately, price. British Airways Engineering has focused on the maintenance and repair side of its organization in order to provide better turnaround times for its customers. The company's Sonic Project has allowed the organization to provide greater customer satisfaction through a better understanding of the fleet repair cycle. Historically, items for repair would slowly pass through all stages of the repair process—a process that could take as long as fifty to sixty days. Today, the average cycle time, is down to fourteen days, much to customers' delight.

As these examples illustrate, operational efficiencies in linking marketing's distribution to manufacturing's production processes are the result of well-thought-out cross-functional plans. Such plans have to be developed in conjunction with both marketing and manufacturing functional groups. Benefits to consumers appear in both dollar savings and improved customer service.

One important aspect of the channel of distribution is the actual delivery of the company's products. The equipment used to make deliveries is an important factor. Decisions regarding the type of transportation equipment—from aircraft to rail cars—receive considerable input from both the marketing and the finance/accounting groups. For example, marketing might prefer that its perishable product be delivered by air to avoid any spoilage. From a cost-effectiveness viewpoint, however, the financial group might determine that the product should be shipped by truck—that the costs associated with any spoiled product would be offset by the savings from shipping by truck instead of air. The two functional groups have to balance customer demands with the relative costs of shipment. The manufacturing group must be involved as well, to ensure that appropriate and cost-effective packaging is used for the transportation method ultimately selected.

FedEx exemplifies the type of company that has been able to balance external market considerations with internal cost-effectiveness. The company has experienced great marketplace success with its guaranteed overnight delivery. At the heart of its overnight delivery system is a company-owned fleet of airplanes that operates out of the company's hub in Memphis, Tennessee. Additionally, the company's delivery vans are equipped with computers so that individual shipments can be traced throughout the distribution process. This extensive network of distribution required input from marketing as to what it would take to become an industry leader and from finance/accounting as to the costs associated with owning a fleet of airplanes and installing computers in delivery vans.

A functional department that cannot be overlooked in a company's distribution process is the human resources department. This is particularly important for a service provider (such as FedEx or a hospital emergency room) since the people are the ones who actually make the logistical process work appropriately. An interesting aspect of a service provider is that production and delivery of the company's product (service) take place simultaneously. Therefore, functional integration has to occur at the point of delivery. The customer's perception of quality delivery is determined by the actual tasks performed as well as by the way employees talk, look, and act. This makes it imperative that marketing and human resources work together to hire and train the right people.

Coordination between marketing and other business functions is necessary to get a high-quality, competitively priced product or service to the end user in a timely manner. Companies such as UPS and FedEx that compete for the same customers have become experts at developing channel systems that utilize all functional components of the organization in getting the right product/service to the right customer at just the right time.

Technology is a powerful force behind improvements in distribution. In the future, more and more companies will be combining cross-functional skills with information technology infrastructures to better serve customers.

Questions

1. What are some of the popular advanced manufacturing systems, and how do they interact with marketing?

2. What is an enterprise-wide integrated distribution system? What is marketing's role in such a system?

3. How do production and delivery happen simultaneously in the service sector? What other functional areas are important partners in the service arena?

CHAPTER **TWELVE**

MARKETING CHANNELS AND SUPPLY CHAIN MANAGEMENT

Learning Objectives

1 Explain what a marketing channel is and why intermediaries are needed

2 Define the types of channel intermediaries and describe their functions and activities

3 Describe the channel structures for consumer and business-to-business products and discuss alternative channel arrangements

4 Define supply chain management and discuss its benefits

5 Discuss the issues that influence channel strategy

6 Explain channel leadership, conflict, and partnering

7 Describe the logistical components of the supply chain

8 Discuss new technology and emerging trends in supply chain management

9 Discuss channels and distribution decisions in global markets

10 Identify the special problems and opportunities associated with distribution in service organizations

How does a traditional grocery store profitably compete head-to-head with Wal-Mart Supercenters? Leadership at the H-E-B Grocery Company believes excellence in supply chain management is one key.

In the early 1990s when Wal-Mart began opening its combination grocery and general merchandise stores, grocery companies were forced to look at their own strengths and weaknesses to determine the best strategy to compete. Some companies decided to concede price to Wal-Mart and to compete instead with customer service. Others decided to cut services to the bare bones and compete on price. H-E-B Grocery Company decided that with excellence in supply chain management it could compete successfully with Wal-Mart without sacrificing low prices or customer service.

To meet this goal, leadership groups from every aspect of the supply chain work as a team to reduce supply chain costs and to increase customer service. For starters, in addition to negotiating lower prices, managers in H-E-B's procurement office communicate directly with suppliers to ensure reliable just-in-time delivery to the company's stores and warehouses. The procurement department also works closely with suppliers to develop more efficient product packaging. For example, produce is shipped in green plastic containers that can be used to display products in the stores. The new packaging improves product quality by reducing damage during shipping and handling and saves time in the stores by dramatically reducing the need for product handling. Finally, the new packaging reduces waste because the packages can be returned to the vendor and used again.

Order processing is handled using advanced computer technology. Store management sends daily orders to the warehouse electronically using a handheld computer system. The system saves time and paper at both the store and warehouse levels. In addition, order information is simultaneously shared with suppliers including H-E-B's own manufacturing units, which then begin production to replenish the company's inventory. The combination of supplier relations and advanced technology enables H-E-B to operate effectively with lean inventories without sacrificing the company's ability to have the right products on store shelves at the right time.

Another critical part of H-E-B's supply chain is the company's state-of-the-art warehouse and distribution centers, which are designed to increase accuracy and reduce time by minimizing product handling and delivery times. Every product in the warehouse system is tracked with radio frequency technology, making it easy for an order selector to find a specific product at any time. Warehouses are organized according to the layout of the company's retail stores. Therefore, when order selectors build a pallet to ship to a store, items are unpacked in the order they are displayed. Finally, each pallet is scanned to confirm that the order is correct before it is loaded onto a truck.

When an order is ready to ship to the store, H-E-B's distribution team uses computer technology to plan deliveries based on mileage, order size, and traffic patterns. In fact, the company has a strategic alliance with Houston's Metro system that gives dispatchers real-time traffic information so that drivers can avoid being caught in traffic delays.

Distribution centers are also strategically placed throughout H-E-B's market area to allow for same-day deliveries.

Finally, the company is investing in a new fleet of alternative fuel trucks. By using cleaner burning fuel, the company is able to save money through lower fuel costs and a reduction in maintenance requirements.

The result of all this attention to detail is the largest privately owned grocery company in the United States. Today, H-E-B operates more than 275 stores, twelve manufacturing plants, and four warehouse and distribution centers throughout Texas and Mexico. How has technology enabled H-E-B to become the largest privately owned grocery company in the United States? What other factors have helped H-E-B become a leader in its field? As you read the following chapter, you will learn more about how supply chain management adds competitive advantage to companies of all kinds.

Marketing Channels

1

Explain what a marketing channel is and why intermediaries are needed

marketing channel (channel of distribution)
A set of interdependent organizations that ease the transfer of ownership as products move from producer to business user or consumer.

channel members
All parties in the marketing channel that negotiate with one another, buy and sell products, and facilitate the change of ownership between buyer and seller in the course of moving the product from the manufacturer into the hands of the final consumer.

supply chain
The connected chain of all of the business entities, both internal and external to the company, that perform or support the logistics function.

The term *channel* is derived from the Latin word *canalis*, which means canal. A marketing channel can be viewed as a large canal or pipeline through which products, their ownership, communication, financing and payment, and accompanying risk flow to the consumer. Formally, a **marketing channel** (also called a **channel of distribution**) is a business structure of interdependent organizations that reach from the point of product origin to the consumer with the purpose of moving products to their final consumption destination. Marketing channels facilitate the physical movement of goods through the supply chain, representing "place" in the marketing mix (product, price, promotion, and place) and encompassing the processes involved in getting the right product to the right place at the right time.

Many different types of organizations participate in marketing channels. **Channel members** (also called *intermediaries, resellers,* and *middlemen*) negotiate with one another, buy and sell products, and facilitate the change of ownership between buyer and seller in the course of moving the product from the manufacturer into the hands of the final consumer. An important aspect of marketing channels is the joint effort of all channel members to create a continuous and seamless supply chain. The **supply chain** is the connected chain of all of the business entities, both internal and external to the company, that perform or support the marketing channel functions. As products move through the supply chain, channel members facilitate the distribution process by providing specialization and division of labor, overcoming discrepancies, and providing contact efficiency.

Providing Specialization and Division of Labor

According to the concept of specialization and division of labor, breaking down a complex task into smaller, simpler ones and allocating them to specialists will create greater efficiency and lower average production costs. Manufacturers achieve economies of scale through the use of efficient equipment capable of producing large quantities of a single product.

Marketing channels can also attain economies of scale through specialization and division of labor by aiding producers who lack the motivation, financing, or expertise to market directly to end users or consumers. In some cases, as with most consumer convenience goods, such as soft drinks, the cost of marketing directly to millions of consumers—taking and shipping individual orders—is prohibitive. For this reason, producers hire channel members, such as wholesalers and retailers, to do what the producers are not equipped to do or what channel members are better prepared to do. Channel members can do some things more efficiently than producers because they have built good relationships with their customers. Therefore, their specialized expertise enhances the overall performance of the channel.

Overcoming Discrepancies

Marketing channels also aid in overcoming discrepancies of quantity, assortment, time, and space created by economies of scale in production. For example, assume that Pillsbury can efficiently produce its Hungry Jack instant pancake mix only at a rate of 5,000 units in a typical day. Not even the most ardent pancake fan could consume that amount in a year, much less in a day. The quantity produced to achieve low unit costs has created a **discrepancy of quantity**, which is the difference between the amount of product produced and the amount an end user wants to buy. By storing the product and distributing it in the appropriate amounts, marketing channels overcome quantity discrepancies by making products available in the quantities that consumers desire.

Mass production creates not only discrepancies of quantity but also discrepancies of assortment. A **discrepancy of assortment** occurs when a consumer does not have all of the items needed to receive full satisfaction from a product. For pancakes

discrepancy of quantity
The difference between the amount of product produced and the amount an end user wants to buy.

discrepancy of assortment
The lack of all the items a customer needs to receive full satisfaction from a product or products.

to provide maximum satisfaction, several other products are required to complete the assortment. At the very least, most people want a knife, fork, plate, butter, and syrup. Others might add orange juice, coffee, cream, sugar, eggs, and bacon or sausage. Even though Pillsbury is a large consumer-products company, it does not come close to providing the optimal assortment to go with its Hungry Jack pancakes. To overcome discrepancies of assortment, marketing channels assemble in one place many of the products necessary to complete a consumer's needed assortment.

A **temporal discrepancy** is created when a product is produced but a consumer is not ready to buy it. Marketing channels overcome temporal discrepancies by maintaining inventories in anticipation of demand. For example, manufacturers of seasonal merchandise, such as Christmas decorations, are in operation all year even though consumer demand is concentrated during certain months of the year.

Furthermore, because mass production requires many potential buyers, markets are usually scattered over large geographic regions, creating a **spatial discrepancy**. Often global, or at least nationwide, markets are needed to absorb the outputs of mass producers. Marketing channels overcome spatial discrepancies by making products available in locations convenient to consumers. For example, automobile manufacturers overcome spatial discrepancies by franchising dealerships close to consumers.

temporal discrepancy
A situation that occurs when a product is produced but a customer is not ready to buy it.

spatial discrepancy
The difference between the location of a producer and the location of widely scattered markets.

Providing Contact Efficiency

The third need fulfilled by marketing channels is a way to provide contact efficiency. Consider your extra costs if supermarkets, department stores, and shopping centers or malls did not exist. Suppose you had to buy your milk at a dairy and your meat at a stockyard. Imagine buying your eggs and chicken at a hatchery and your fruits and vegetables at various farms. You would spend a great deal of time, money, and energy just shopping for a few groceries. Supply chains simplify distribution by cutting the number of transactions required to get products from manufacturers to consumers and making an assortment of goods available in one location.

Consider the example illustrated in Exhibit 12.1 on page 378. Four consumers each want to buy a television set. Without a retail intermediary like Circuit City, television manufacturers JVC, Zenith, Sony, Toshiba, and RCA would each have to make four contacts to reach the four buyers who are in the target market, totaling twenty transactions. However, when Circuit City acts as an intermediary between the producer and consumers, each producer only has to make one contact, reducing the number of transactions to nine. Each producer sells to one retailer rather than to four consumers. In turn, consumers buy from one retailer instead of from five producers.

Channel Intermediaries and Their Functions

Intermediaries in a channel negotiate with one another, facilitate the change of ownership between buyers and sellers, and physically move products from the manufacturer to the final consumer. The most prominent difference separating intermediaries is whether or not they take title to the product. *Taking title* means they own the merchandise and control the terms of the sale—for example, price and delivery date. Retailers and merchant wholesalers are examples of intermediaries who take title to products in the marketing channel and resell them. **Retailers** are firms that sell mainly to consumers. Retailers will be discussed in more detail in Chapter 13.

Merchant wholesalers are those organizations that facilitate the movement of products and services from the manufacturer to producers, resellers, governments, institutions, and retailers. All merchant wholesalers take title to the goods they sell, and most of them operate one or more warehouses where they receive goods, store them, and later reship them. Customers are mostly small- or moderate-sized retailers, but merchant wholesalers also market to manufacturers and institutional clients.

Define the types of channel intermediaries and describe their functions and activities

retailer
A channel intermediary that sells mainly to consumers.

merchant wholesaler
An institution that buys goods from manufacturers and resells them to businesses, government agencies, and other wholesalers or retailers and that receives and takes title to goods, stores them in its own warehouses, and later ships them.

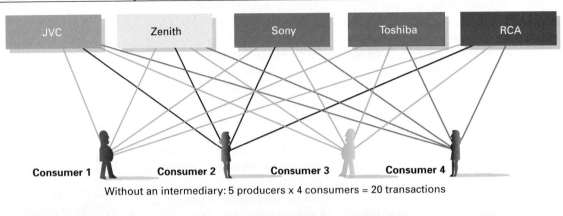

Without an intermediary: 5 producers x 4 consumers = 20 transactions

With an intermediary: 5 producers + 4 consumers = 9 transactions

agents and brokers
Wholesaling intermediaries who do not take title to a product but facilitate its sale from producer to end user by representing retailers, wholesalers, or manufacturers.

Other intermediaries do not take title to goods and services they market but do facilitate the exchange of ownership between sellers and buyers. **Agents and brokers** simply facilitate the sale of a product from producer to end user by representing retailers, wholesalers, or manufacturers. Title reflects ownership, and ownership usually implies control. Unlike wholesalers, agents or brokers only facilitate sales and generally have little input into the terms of the sale. They do, however, get a fee or commission based on sales volume.

Variations in channel structures are due in large part to variations in the numbers and types of wholesaling intermediaries. Generally, product characteristics, buyer considerations, and market conditions determine the type of intermediary the manufacturer should use. Product characteristics that may dictate a certain type of wholesaling intermediary include whether the product is standardized or customized, the complexity of the product, and the gross margin of the product. Buyer considerations affecting wholesaler choice include how often the product is purchased and how long the buyer is willing to wait to receive the product. Market characteristics determining the wholesaler type include how many buyers are in the market and whether they are concentrated in a general location or are widely dispersed. Exhibit 12.2 shows these determining factors. For example, a manufacturer that produces only a few engines a year for space rockets will probably use an agent or broker to sell its product. In addition, the handful of customers that need the product are most likely concentrated near rocket launching sites, again making an agent or broker more practical. On the other hand, a book publisher that prints thousands of books and has many widely dispersed customers with year-round demand for its product will probably use a merchant wholesaler.

Channel Functions Performed by Intermediaries

Retailing and wholesaling intermediaries in marketing channels perform several essential functions that make the flow of goods between producer and buyer possible. The three basic functions that intermediaries perform are summarized in Exhibit 12.3.

Exhibit 12.2

Factor	Merchant Wholesalers	Agents or Brokers
Nature of Product	Standard	Nonstandard, custom
Technicality of Product	Complex	Simple
Product's Gross Margin	High	Low
Frequency of Ordering	Frequent	Infrequent
Time between Order and Receipt of Shipment	Buyer desires shorter lead time	Buyer satisfied with long lead time
Number of Customers	Many	Few
Concentration of Customers	Dispersed	Concentrated

SOURCE: Reprinted by permission of the publisher. From Donald M. Jackson and Michael F. D'Amico, "Products and Markets Served by Distributors and Agents," 27–33 in *Industrial Marketing Management.* Copyright 1989 by Elsevier Science Inc.

Transactional functions involve contacting and communicating with prospective buyers to make them aware of existing products and explain their features, advantages, and benefits. Intermediaries in the supply chain also provide *logistical* functions. **Logistics** is a term borrowed from the military that describes the process of strategically managing the efficient flow and storage of raw materials,

logistics
The process of strategically managing the efficient flow and storage of raw materials, in-process inventory, and finished goods from point of origin to point of consumption.

Exhibit 12.3

Type of Function	Description
Transactional Functions	**Contacting and promoting:** Contacting potential customers, promoting products, and soliciting orders **Negotiating:** Determining how many goods or services to buy and sell, type of transportation to use, when to deliver, and method and timing of payment **Risk taking:** Assuming the risk of owning inventory
Logistical Functions	**Physically distributing:** Transporting and sorting goods to overcome temporal and spatial discrepancies **Storing:** Maintaining inventories and protecting goods **Sorting:** Overcoming discrepancies of quantity and assortment by *Sorting out:* Breaking down a heterogeneous supply into separate homogeneous stocks *Accumulation:* Combining similar stocks into a larger homogeneous supply *Allocation:* Breaking a homogeneous supply into smaller and smaller lots ("breaking bulk") *Assortment:* Combining products into collections or assortments that buyers want available at one place
Facilitating Function	**Researching:** Gathering information about other channel members and consumers **Financing:** Extending credit and other financial services to facilitate the flow of goods through the channel to the final consumer

in-process inventory, and finished goods from point of origin to point of consumption. Logistical functions include transporting, storing, sorting out, accumulating, allocating, and assorting products into either homogeneous or heterogeneous collections. For example, grading agricultural products typifies the sorting-out process while consolidation of many lots of grade A eggs from different sources into one lot illustrates the accumulation process. Supermarkets or other retailers perform the assorting function by assembling thousands of different items that match their customers' desires. Similarly, while large companies typically have direct channels, many small companies depend on wholesalers to champion and distribute their products. For example, small beverage manufacturers like Jones Soda, Honest Tea, and Energy Brands depend on wholesalers to distribute their products in a marketplace dominated by large competitors like Coca-Cola and Pepsi.[1]

The third basic channel function, *facilitating*, includes research and financing. Research provides information about channel members and consumers by getting answers to key questions: Who are the buyers? Where are they located? Why do they buy? Financing ensures that channel members have the money to keep products moving through the channel to the ultimate consumer.

A single company may provide one, two, or all three functions. Consider Kramer Beverage Company, a Coors beer distributor. As a beer distributor, Kramer provides transactional, logistical, and facilitating channel functions. Sales representatives contact local bars and restaurants to negotiate the terms of the sale, possibly giving the customer a discount for large purchases, and arrange for delivery of the beer. At the same time, Kramer also provides a facilitating function by extending credit to the customer. Kramer merchandising representatives, meanwhile, assist in promoting the beer on a local level by hanging Coors beer signs and posters. Kramer also provides logistical functions by accumulating the many types of Coors beer from the Coors manufacturing plant in Golden, Colorado, and storing them in its refrigerated warehouse. When an order needs to be filled, Kramer then sorts the beer into heterogeneous collections for each particular customer. For example, the local Chili's Grill & Bar may need two kegs of Coors, three kegs of Coors Light, and two cases of Killian's Red in bottles. The beer will then be loaded onto a refrigerated truck and transported to the restaurant. Upon arrival, the Kramer delivery person will transport the kegs and cases of beer into the restaurant's refrigerator and may also restock the coolers behind the bar.

Although individual members can be added to or deleted from a channel, someone must still perform these essential functions. They can be performed by producers, end users, or consumers, channel intermediaries such as wholesalers and retailers, and sometimes nonmember channel participants. For example, if a manufacturer decides to eliminate its private fleet of trucks, it must still have a way to move the goods to the wholesaler. This task may be accomplished by the wholesaler, which may have its own fleet of trucks, or by a nonmember channel participant, such as an independent trucking firm. Nonmembers also provide many other essential functions that may at one time have been provided by a channel member. For example, research firms may perform the research function; advertising agencies, the promotion function; transportation and storage firms, the physical distribution function; and banks, the financing function.

Channel Structures

3

Describe the channel structures for consumer and business-to-business products and discuss alternative channel arrangements

A product can take many routes to reach its final consumer. Marketers search for the most efficient channel from the many alternatives available. Marketing a consumer convenience good like gum or candy differs from marketing a specialty good like a Mercedes-Benz. The two products require very different distribution channels. Likewise, the appropriate channel for a major equipment supplier like Boeing Aircraft would be unsuitable for an accessory equipment producer like

Black & Decker. To illustrate the differences in typical marketing channels for consumer and business-to-business products like these, the next sections discuss the structures of marketing channels for each product type. Alternative channel structures are also discussed.

What kind of marketing channel functions can be performed over the Internet? Why do you think so?

On Line

Channels for Consumer Products

Exhibit 12.4 illustrates the four ways manufacturers can route products to consumers. Producers use the **direct channel** to sell directly to consumers. Direct marketing activities—including telemarketing, mail-order and catalog shopping, and forms of electronic retailing like on-line shopping and shop-at-home television networks—are a good example of this type of channel structure. For example, home computer users can purchase Dell computers directly over the telephone or directly from Dell's Internet Web site. There are no intermediaries. Producer-owned stores and factory outlet stores—like Sherwin-Williams, Polo Ralph Lauren, Oneida, and West Point Pepperel—are other examples of direct channels. Farmers' markets are also direct channels. Direct marketing and factory outlets are discussed in more detail in Chapter 13.

At the other end of the spectrum, an *agent/broker channel* involves a fairly complicated process. Agent/broker channels are typically used in markets with many small manufacturers and many retailers that lack the resources to find each other. Agents or brokers bring manufacturers and wholesalers together for negotiations, but they do not take title to merchandise. Ownership passes directly to one or more wholesalers and then to retailers. Finally, retailers sell to the ultimate consumer of the product. For example, a food broker represents buyers and sellers of grocery products. The broker acts on behalf of many different producers and negotiates the sale of their products to wholesalers that specialize in foodstuffs. These wholesalers in turn sell to grocers and convenience stores.

Most consumer products are sold through distribution channels similar to the other two alternatives: the retailer channel and the wholesaler channel. A *retailer channel* is most common when the retailer is large and can buy in large quantities

direct channel
A distribution channel in which producers sell directly to consumers.

Marketing Channels for Consumer Products   **Exhibit 12.4**

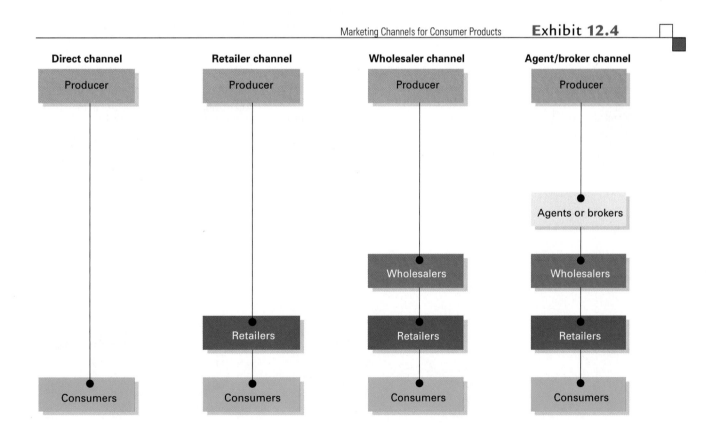

Direct channel	Retailer channel	Wholesaler channel	Agent/broker channel
Producer	Producer	Producer	Producer
			Agents or brokers
		Wholesalers	Wholesalers
	Retailers	Retailers	Retailers
Consumers	Consumers	Consumers	Consumers

directly from the manufacturer. Wal-Mart, Sears, and car dealers are examples of retailers that often bypass a wholesaler. A *wholesaler channel* is frequently used for low-cost items that are frequently purchased, such as candy, cigarettes, and magazines. For example, M&M/Mars sells candies and chocolates to wholesalers in large quantities. The wholesalers then break these quantities into smaller quantities to satisfy individual retailer orders.

Channels for Business-to-Business and Industrial Products

As Exhibit 12.5 illustrates, five channel structures are common in business-to-business and industrial markets. First, direct channels are typical in business-to-business and industrial markets. For example, manufacturers buy large quantities of raw materials, major equipment, processed materials, and supplies directly from other manufacturers. Manufacturers that require suppliers to meet detailed technical specifications often prefer direct channels. The direct communication required between DaimlerChrysler and its suppliers, for example, along with the tremendous size of the orders, makes anything but a direct channel impractical. The channel from producer to government buyers is also a direct channel. Since much of government buying is done through bidding, a direct channel is attractive. Dell Computer Corporation, for example, the top seller of desktop computers to federal, state, and local government agencies in the United States, sells the computers through direct channels.[2]

Companies selling standardized items of moderate or low value often rely on *industrial distributors.* In many ways, an industrial distributor is like a supermarket for organizations. Industrial distributors are wholesalers and channel members that buy and take title to products. Moreover, they usually keep inventories of their products and sell and service them. Often small manufacturers cannot afford to employ their own sales force. Instead, they rely on manufacturers' representatives or selling agents to sell to either industrial distributors or users.

Increasingly, companies are using the Internet to create more direct and efficient business-to-business channels. Industry analysts predict that more than $5.7 trillion in business-to-business commerce will be conducted on-line by 2004. Currently, three major forms of business-to-business ex-

---

☐ Exhibit 12.5   Channels for Business-to-Business and Industrial Products changes are taking place on the Internet. The first and smallest sector is made up of new Internet companies that have been developed to link buyers and sellers. These companies act as agents and charge a service fee. A second form of marketplace has been developed by existing companies looking for a way to drop the intermediary from the supply chain. For example, the Worldwide Retail Exchange is a marketplace created by more than fifty major retailers including Target, JCPenney, and Safeway. Retailers use the exchange to make purchases that in the past would have required telephone, fax, or face-to-face sales calls. Retailers using the exchange estimate they have saved approximately 15 percent in their purchasing costs. Finally, the third type of Internet marketplace is a "private exchange." Private exchanges allow companies to automate their supply chains while sharing information only with select suppliers. Ace Hardware and Hewlett-Packard, for example, use private exchanges to manage their inventory supplies.[3]

Alternative Channel Arrangements

Rarely does a producer use just one type of channel to move its product. It usually employs several different or alternative channels, which include multiple channels, nontraditional channels, and strategic channel alliances.

Multiple Channels

When a producer selects two or more channels to distribute the same product to target markets, this arrangement is called **dual distribution** (or **multiple distribution**). For example, Whirlpool sells its washers, dryers, and refrigerators directly to home and apartment builders and contractors, but it also sells these same appliances to retail stores that sell to consumers. Avon, which has traditionally sold its products only through a company sales force, has launched a new cosmetic line with JCPenney. The venture into retail, called "Avon Centers," is part of an overall strategy to update Avon's image.[4] Similarly, Dell Computer recently made a radical departure from its direct channel sales model by testing retail kiosks in shopping malls

dual distribution (multiple distribution)
The use of two or more channels to distribute the same product to target markets.

COURTESY OF BECOMING

as a way to increase its market share of personal home computers. The company has also tried selling computers directly to home users through cable shopping channels.[5] Multiple channels may also be employed by producers with unique second brands. For example, the Walt Disney Company routinely releases first-run animated films to movie theaters and then releases a sequel directly to the home-video market. Such sequels as *Aladdin and the King of Thieves* and *Beauty and the Beast: The Enchanted Christmas* follow up its theater blockbusters.

Adding a new supply chain can renew a company's image. Such is the case with Avon, the leading company in direct selling, which broke its own mold with the launch of beComing, the company's first brand distributed exclusively in retail outlets.

Nontraditional Channels

Often nontraditional channel arrangements help differentiate a firm's product from the competition. For example, manufacturers may decide to use nontraditional channels such as the Internet, mail-order channels, or infomercials, to sell products instead of going through traditional retailer channels. Although nontraditional channels may limit a brand's coverage, they can give a producer serving a niche market a way to gain market access and customer attention without having to establish channel intermediaries. Nontraditional channels can also provide another avenue of sales for larger firms. For example, a London publisher has begun

Why Just Collapse The Supply Chain When You Can Flatten The Competition?

Rockwell Automation can link your manufacturing operations to your business goals.

e-Manufacturing isn't a new way to make a product. It's the advanced way to link your resources together to achieve significantly greater efficiencies.

Rockwell Automation integrated plant-floor architecture, with seamless connectivity to your information systems, can enable your enterprise for build-to-order production and nonstop operation. Helping you gain the flexibility to adjust to changing market conditions.

By creating an e-Manufacturing strategy, which links your manufacturing environment to your business environment, you share critical information across your enterprise. And synchronize your supply chain.

e-Manufacturing solutions from Rockwell Automation, your Complete Automation™ provider. Helping you build a streamlined model of competitive strength. For more information, visit our web site **www.rockwellautomation.com**.

Rockwell Automation

Copyright © 2002 Rockwell Automation. All rights reserved. AD 8.5CE006-ERP

COURTESY OF ROCKWELL AUTOMATION

strategic channel alliance
A cooperative agreement between business firms to use the other's already established distribution channel.

Supply chain management is the key to competitiveness, and numerous companies market tools to help other businesses manage their supply chains effectively. Rockwell Automation is one such solutions provider, helping companies share critical production information across the business enterprise.

selling short stories through a vending machine in the London Underground. Instead of the traditional book format, the stories are printed like folded maps making them an easy-to-read alternative for commuters.[6]

Strategic Channel Alliances

Producers often form **strategic channel alliances**, which enable the producers to use another manufacturer's already-established channel. Alliances are used most often when the creation of marketing channel relationships may be too expensive and time-consuming. Amazon and Circuit City have a multiyear agreement to expand the selection of electronics available on Amazon.com. Under the agreement, Amazon.com customers have the option of purchasing items from Amazon's inventory of electronic items or from the broader selection offered by Circuit City. The arrangement benefits both companies: It allows Amazon.com to deepen its selection without increasing its own inventory expense, and it increases sales for Circuit City. Similarly, Amazon.com and Target formed an alliance involving the customer service and distribution operations for Target.com. The deal increases Target's online selection of books, music, and entertainment while adding clothing, jewelry, and other products to Amazon's selection.[7]

Strategic channel alliances are proving to be more successful for growing businesses than mergers and acquisitions. This is especially true in global markets where cultural differences, distance, and other barriers can prove challenging. For example, Heinz has a strategic alliance with Kagome, one of Japan's largest food companies. The companies are working together to find ways to reduce operating costs while expanding both brands' market presence globally.[8]

---

④
Define supply chain management and discuss its benefits

supply chain management
A management system that coordinates and integrates all of the activities performed by supply chain members into a seamless process, from the source to the point of consumption, resulting in enhanced customer and economic value.

Supply Chain Management

In today's sophisticated marketplace, many companies are turning to supply chain management for competitive advantage. The goal of **supply chain management** is to coordinate and integrate all of the activities performed by supply chain members into a seamless process from the source to the point of consumption, ultimately giving supply chain managers "total visibility" of the supply chain both inside and outside the firm. The philosophy behind supply chain management is that by visualizing the entire supply chain, supply chain managers can maximize strengths and efficiencies at each level of the process to create a highly competitive, customer-driven supply system that is able to respond immediately to changes in supply and demand.

An important element of supply chain management is that it is completely customer driven. In the mass-production era, manufacturers produced standardized products that were "pushed" down through the supply channel to the consumer. In contrast, in today's marketplace, products are being driven by customers, who expect to receive product configurations and services matched to their unique needs. For example, Dell only builds computers according to its customers' precise specifications, such as the amount of RAM memory; type of monitor, modem, or CD drive; and amount of hard disk space. Similarly, car companies offer customers the option to customize even economy-priced cars. For less than $20,000, customers can order a Mitsubishi Lancer with spoilers and flashy colors or a Mazda Protégé with a faster engine, special transmission, and 280-watt MP3 sound system. The focus is on pulling products into the marketplace and partnering with members of the supply chain to enhance customer value. Customizing an automobile is now possible because of new supply chain relationships between the automobile manufacturers and the after-market auto-parts industry.[9]

Nash Finch
What role does Nash Finch play in the supply chain?
http://www.nashfinch.com

On Line

This reversal of the flow of demand from a "push" to a "pull" has resulted in a radical reformulation of both market expectations and traditional marketing, production, and distribution functions. Through the channel partnership of suppliers, manufacturers, wholesalers, and retailers along the entire supply chain who work together toward the common goal of creating customer value, supply chain management allows companies to respond with the unique product configuration and mix of services demanded by the customer. Today, supply chain management plays a dual role: first, as a *communicator* of customer demand that extends from the point of sale all the way back to the supplier, and second, as a *physical flow process* that engineers the timely and cost-effective movement of goods through the entire supply pipeline.[10]

Accordingly, supply chain managers are responsible for making channel strategy decisions, coordinating the sourcing and procurement of raw materials, scheduling production, processing orders, managing inventory, transporting and storing supplies and finished goods, and coordinating customer service activities. Supply chain managers are also responsible for the management of information that flows through the supply chain. Coordinating the relationships between the company and its external partners, such as vendors, carriers, and third-party companies, is also a critical function of supply chain management. Because supply chain managers play such a major role in both cost control and customer satisfaction, they are more valuable than ever. In fact, average salaries for supply chain graduates have increased more than 25 percent in spite of the recent recession.[11]

In summary, supply chain managers are responsible for directing raw materials and parts to the production department and the finished or semifinished product through warehouses and eventually to the intermediary or end user. Above all, supply chain management begins and ends with the customer. Instead of forcing into the market a product that may or may not sell quickly, supply chain managers react to actual customer demand. By doing so, they minimize the flow of raw materials, finished product, and packaging materials at every point in the supply chain, resulting in lower costs and increased customer value. Exhibit 12.6 on page 386 depicts the supply chain process.

Benefits of Supply Chain Management

Supply chain management is a key means of differentiation for a firm and a critical component in marketing and corporate strategy. Companies that focus on supply chain management commonly report lower inventory, transportation, warehousing, and packaging costs; greater supply chain flexibility; improved customer service; and higher revenues. Research has shown a clear relationship between supply chain performance and profitability. Leaders in supply chain management report a 5 percent increase in revenue due to reducing supply chain costs, a 65 percent increase in supply chain flexibility, and an 18 percent improvement in cash flow.[12]

Dreyer's ice cream has built its success on its logistics system. The company recently invested $150 million in a new fleet of trucks, manufacturing centers, additional employees, and a computerized delivery system that enables dispatchers to design delivery routes around sales volume, mileage, traffic patterns, road tolls, and a store's hours of operation. As a return on its investment, the company has experienced a 33 percent increase in sales accounts, eliminated more than 42,000 unnecessary stops, saved $11 million

AP/WIDE WORLD PHOTOS

Dreyer's Ice Cream's successful logistics systems starts with its state-of-the-art manufacturing facility. The return on investment the company experienced subsequent to its supply chain upgrades was extremely impressive.

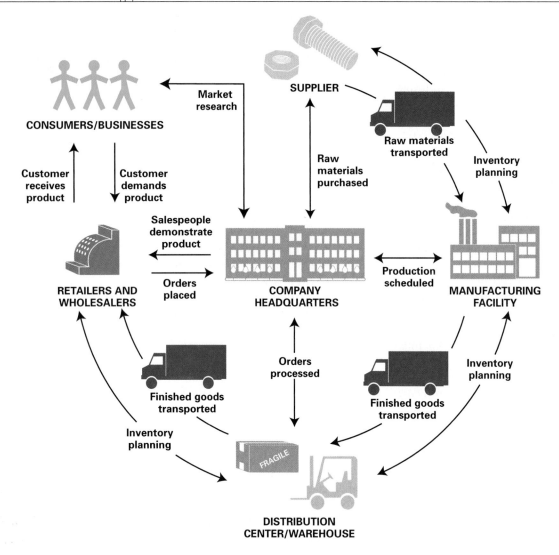

in gas and labor hours, and increased its net income by 150 percent between 1999 and 2000. In fact, the system provides such strong customer service capability and cost savings that nearly one-third of Dreyer's revenue comes from deals to distribute its competitors' brands such as Häagen-Dazs and Ben & Jerry's.[13] On a more individual level, one materials analyst for a company that produces seat belts reported that when her company began focusing on supply chain management, it shortened her workweek by fifteen to twenty hours and reduced her inventory costs by 75 percent.[14]

◼◼◼ Making Channel Strategy Decisions

Discuss the issues that influence channel strategy

Devising a marketing channel strategy requires several critical decisions. Supply chain managers must decide what role distribution will play in the overall marketing strategy. In addition, they must be sure that the channel strategy chosen is consistent with product, promotion, and pricing strategies. In making these decisions, marketing managers must analyze what factors will influence the choice of channel and what level of distribution intensity will be appropriate.

Factors Affecting Channel Choice

Supply chain managers must answer many questions before choosing a marketing channel. The final choice depends on the analysis of several factors, which often interact. These factors can be grouped as market factors, product factors, and producer factors.

Market Factors

Among the most important market factors affecting the choice of distribution channel are target customer considerations. Specifically, supply chain managers should answer the following questions: Who are the potential customers? What do they buy? Where do they buy? When do they buy? How do they buy? Additionally, the choice of channel depends on whether the producer is selling to consumers or to industrial customers. Industrial customers' buying habits are very different from those of consumers. Industrial customers tend to buy in larger quantities and require more customer service. Consumers usually buy in very small quantities and sometimes do not mind if they get no service at all, as in a discount store.

The geographic location and size of the market are also important to channel selection. As a rule, if the target market is concentrated in one or more specific areas, then direct selling through a sales force is appropriate. When markets are more widely dispersed, intermediaries would be less expensive. The size of the market also influences channel choice. Generally, a very large market requires more intermediaries. For instance, Procter & Gamble has to reach millions of consumers with its many brands of household goods. It needs many intermediaries, including wholesalers and retailers.

Product Factors

Products that are more complex, customized, and expensive tend to benefit from shorter and more direct marketing channels. These types of products sell better through a direct sales force. Examples include pharmaceuticals, scientific instruments, airplanes, and mainframe computer systems. On the other hand, the more standardized a product is, the longer its distribution channel can be and the greater the number of intermediaries that can be involved. For example, the formula for chewing gum is about the same from producer to producer, with the exception of flavor and shape. Chewing gum is also very inexpensive. As a result, the distribution channel for gum tends to involve many wholesalers and retailers.

The product's life cycle is also an important factor in choosing a marketing channel. In fact, the choice of channel may change over the life of the product. For example, when photocopiers were first available, they were typically sold by a direct sales force. Now, however, photocopiers can be found in several places, including warehouse clubs, electronics superstores, and mail-order catalogs. As products become more common and less intimidating to potential users, producers tend to look for alternative channels. Gatorade was originally sold to sports teams, gyms, and fitness clubs. As the drink became more popular, mainstream supermarket channels were added, followed by convenience stores and drugstores. Now Gatorade can be found in vending machines and even in some fast-food restaurants.

Another factor is the delicacy of the product. Perishable products like vegetables and milk have a relatively short life span. Fragile

Vending machines are becoming a popular way to sell everything from boxer shorts to cameras. Kodak teamed up with Maytag to roll out thousands of camera-and-film vending machines by the end of 2003. Kodak wants to satisfy instant cravings for a must-have snapshot in places like amusement parks, ski resorts, and the beach.

products like china and crystal require a minimum amount of handling. Therefore, both require fairly short marketing channels.

Producer Factors

Several factors pertaining to the producer itself are important to the selection of a marketing channel. In general, producers with large financial, managerial, and marketing resources are better able to use more direct channels. These producers have the ability to hire and train their own sales force, warehouse their own goods, and extend credit to their customers. Smaller or weaker firms, on the other hand, must rely on intermediaries to provide these services for them. Compared to producers with only one or two product lines, producers that sell several products in a related area are able to choose channels that are more direct. Sales expenses then can be spread over more products.

A producer's desire to control pricing, positioning, brand image, and customer support also tends to influence channel selection. For instance, firms that sell products with exclusive brand images, such as designer perfumes and clothing, usually avoid channels in which discount retailers are present. Manufacturers of upscale products, such as Gucci (handbags) and Godiva (chocolates), may sell their wares only in expensive stores in order to maintain an image of exclusivity. Many producers have opted to risk their image, however, and test sales in discount channels. Levi Strauss expanded its distribution to include JCPenney and Sears. JCPenney is now Levi Strauss's biggest customer.

Levels of Distribution Intensity

Organizations have three options for intensity of distribution: intensive distribution, selective distribution, or exclusive distribution (see Exhibit 12.7).

Intensive Distribution

intensive distribution
A form of distribution aimed at having a product available in every outlet where target customers might want to buy it.

Intensive distribution is a form of distribution aimed at maximum market coverage. The manufacturer tries to have the product available in every outlet where potential customers might want to buy it. If buyers are unwilling to search for a product (as is true of convenience goods and operating supplies), the product

Exhibit 12.7

Intensity of Distribution Levels

Intensity Level	Distribution Intensity Objective	Number of Intermediaries in Each Market	Examples
Intensive	Achieve mass-market selling; popular with health and beauty aids and convenience goods that must be available everywhere	Many	Pepsi-Cola, Frito-Lay potato chips, Huggies diapers, Alpo dog food, Crayola crayons
Selective	Work closely with selected intermediaries who meet certain criteria; typically used for shopping goods and some specialty goods	Several	Donna Karan clothing, Hewlett-Packard printers, Burton snowboards, Aveda aromatherapy products
Exclusive	Work with a single intermediary for products that require special resources or positioning; typically used for specialty goods and major industrial equipment	One	BMW cars, Rolex watches, Subway franchise

must be very accessible to buyers. A low-value product that is purchased frequently may require a lengthy channel. For example, candy is found in almost every type of retail store imaginable. It is typically sold to retailers in small quantities by a food or candy wholesaler. The Wrigley Company could not afford to sell its gum directly to every service station, drugstore, supermarket, and discount store. The cost would be too high.

Most manufacturers pursuing an intensive distribution strategy sell to a large percentage of the wholesalers willing to stock their products. Retailers' willingness (or unwillingness) to handle items tends to control the manufacturer's ability to achieve intensive distribution. For example, a retailer already carrying ten brands of gum may show little enthusiasm for one more brand.

Selective Distribution

Selective distribution is achieved by screening dealers and retailers to eliminate all but a few in any single area. Because only a few are chosen, the consumer must seek out the product. For example, when Heeling Sports Ltd. launched Heelys, thick-soled sneakers with a wheel embedded in each heel, the company hired a group of forty teens to perform Heelys exhibitions in targeted malls, skate parks, and college campuses across the country to create demand. Then the company made the decision to avoid large stores like Target and FAO Schwarz and to distribute the shoes only through selected mall retailers and skate and surf shops in order to position the product as "cool and kind of irreverent."[15]

selective distribution
A form of distribution achieved by screening dealers to eliminate all but a few in any single area.

Selective distribution strategies often hinge on a manufacturer's desire to maintain a superior product image so as to be able to charge a premium price. DKNY clothing, for instance, is sold only in select retail outlets, mainly full-price department stores. Likewise, premium pet food brands such as Hill's Pet Nutrition and Ralston-Purina's ProPlan are distributed chiefly through specialty pet food stores and veterinarians, rather than mass retailers like Wal-Mart, so that a premium price can be charged. Procter & Gamble, which purchased rival premium pet food brand Iams, recently expanded Iams's selective distribution strategy to include mass retailer Target. The strategy could jeopardize Iams's high-price strategy and disenfranchise the breeders and veterinarians who have been the brand's primary source of strength over the years.[16]

Exclusive Distribution

The most restrictive form of market coverage is **exclusive distribution**, which entails only one or a few dealers within a given area. Because buyers may have to search or travel extensively to buy the product, exclusive distribution is usually confined to consumer specialty goods, a few shopping goods, and major industrial equipment. Products such as Rolls Royce automobiles, Chris-Craft power boats, and Pettibone tower cranes are distributed under exclusive arrangements. Sometimes exclusive territories are granted by new companies (such as franchisers) to obtain market coverage in a particular area. Limited distribution may also serve to project an exclusive image for the product.

exclusive distribution
A form of distribution that establishes one or a few dealers within a given area.

Retailers and wholesalers may be unwilling to commit the time and money necessary to promote and service a product unless the manufacturer guarantees them an exclusive territory. This arrangement shields the dealer from direct competition and enables it to be the main beneficiary of the manufacturer's promotion efforts in that geographic area. With exclusive distribution, channels of communication are usually well established because the manufacturer works with a limited number of dealers rather than many accounts.

Exclusive distribution has been part of retailing for years. Toys are often made exclusively for certain retailers and cannot be found elsewhere. Exclusive distribution may also take place within a retailer's store rather than a geographic area—for example, when a retailer agrees not to sell a manufacturer's competing brands. Radio Shack, for instance, has prospered in recent years by offering electronics manufacturers exclusivity within its stores. When Sprint Corporation was looking for a retail base from which to sell its new wireless phone network, Radio Shack offered to make Sprint its exclusive national wireless provider. The agreement helped Sprint become the leader in digital personal communications services, selling more wireless phones than rivals Best Buy, Circuit City, and Sears. Radio Shack cut similar exclusive distribution deals with HP-Compaq Computers, satellite television provider DirecTV, and RCA for audio and video equipment.[17]

Managing Channel Relationships

6

Explain channel leadership, conflict, and partnering.

A marketing channel is more than a set of institutions linked by economic ties. Social relationships play an important role in building unity among channel members. A critical aspect of supply chain management, therefore, is managing the social relationships among channel members to achieve synergy. The basic social dimensions of channels are power, control, leadership, conflict, and partnering.

Channel Power, Control, and Leadership

channel power

The capacity of a particular marketing channel member to control or influence the behavior of other channel members.

channel control

A situation that occurs when one marketing channel member intentionally affects another member's behavior.

channel leader (channel captain)

A member of a marketing channel that exercises authority and power over the activities of other channel members.

Channel power is a channel member's capacity to control or influence the behavior of other channel members. **Channel control** occurs when one channel member affects another member's behavior. To achieve control, a channel member assumes channel leadership and exercises authority and power. This member is termed the **channel leader**, or **channel captain**. In one marketing channel, a manufacturer may be the leader because it controls new-product designs and product availability. In another, a retailer may be the channel leader because it wields power and control over the retail price, inventory levels, and postsale service.

The exercise of channel power is a routine element of many business activities in which the outcome is often more efficient operations and cost savings. For instance, grain has traditionally been stored and transported by an inefficient system controlled by unrelated small-town grain elevators. In a new trend, more than 150 large, high-speed elevators have been opened, making the system faster and more cost-efficient. The new elevators are capable of loading twice as many cars in half the time of the traditional elevators. As a result, the new system has lowered transportation costs, making U.S. grain more competitive globally and enabling farmers to make higher profits.[18]

Channel Conflict

channel conflict

A clash of goals and methods between distribution channel members.

Inequitable channel relationships often lead to **channel conflict**, which is a clash of goals and methods among the members of a distribution channel. In a broad context, conflict may not be bad. Often it arises because staid, traditional channel members refuse to keep pace with the times. Removing an outdated intermediary may result in reduced costs for the entire supply chain.

Conflicts among channel members can be due to many different situations and factors. Oftentimes, conflict arises because channel members have conflicting goals. For instance, athletic footwear retailers want to sell as many shoes as possible in order to maximize profits, regardless of whether the shoe is manufactured by Nike, adidas, or Saucony. But the Nike manufacturer wants a certain sales volume and market share in each market.

Conflict can also arise when channel members fail to fulfill expectations of other channel members—for example, when a franchisee does not follow the rules set down by the franchiser, or when communications channels break down between channel members. As another example, if a manufacturer reduces the length of warranty coverage and fails to communicate this change to dealers, then conflict may occur when dealers make repairs with the expectation that they will be reimbursed by the manufacturer. Further, ideological differences and different perceptions of reality can also cause conflict among channel members. For instance, retailers may believe "the customer is always right" and offer a very liberal return policy. Wholesalers and manufacturers may feel that people "try to get something for nothing" or don't follow product instructions carefully. Their differing views of allowable returns will undoubtably conflict with those of retailers.

Conflict within a channel can be either horizontal or vertical. **Horizontal conflict** occurs among channel members on the same level, such as two or more different wholesalers or two or more different retailers, that handle the same manufacturer's brands. This type of channel conflict is found most often when manufacturers practice dual or multiple distribution strategies. For instance, there was considerable channel conflict after computer manufacturers began distributing their computers beyond the traditional computer resellers and to discount stores, department stores, warehouse clubs, and giant electronic superstores, such as Circuit City and Comp-USA. Horizontal conflict can also occur when channel members on the same level feel they are being treated unfairly by the manufacturer. For example, the American Booksellers Association, a group representing small independent booksellers, filed a lawsuit against bookstore giants Barnes & Noble and Borders, claiming they had violated antitrust laws by using their buying power to demand "illegal and secret" discounts from publishers. These deals, the association contended, put independent booksellers at a serious competitive disadvantage.[19]

Many regard horizontal conflict as healthy competition. Much more serious is **vertical conflict**, which occurs between different levels in a marketing channel, most typically between the manufacturer and wholesaler or the manufacturer and retailer. Producer-versus-wholesaler conflict occurs when the producer chooses to bypass the wholesaler and deal directly with the consumer or retailer. For example, conflict arose when several producers agreed to Wal-Mart's request to deal with it directly, bypassing intermediaries altogether.

Dual distribution strategies can also cause vertical conflict in the channel. For example, high-end fashion designers have traditionally sold their products through luxury retailers such as Neiman Marcus and Saks Fifth Avenue. Interested in increasing sales and gaining additional presentation control, many designers such as Giorgio Armani, Donna Karan, and Louis Vuitton have begun opening their own boutiques in the same shopping centers that are anchored by Neiman Marcus and Saks Fifth Avenue stores. As a result, the department stores are seeing a huge decline in revenue.[20] Similarly, manufacturers that are experimenting with selling to customers directly over the Internet are also creating conflict with their traditional retailing intermediaries. For example, Baby Jogger worked closely with retailers to build a business with $15 million in sales. But when numerous look-alike products began appearing on the market, the company decided to try to increase sales by selling directly to consumers on the Internet. Angry retailers responded by promoting other brands. Recognizing how important the retailers were to its success, Baby Jogger halted Internet sales in 2001.[21]

Producers and retailers may also disagree over the terms of the sale or other aspects of the business relationship. When Procter & Gamble introduced "everyday low pricing" to its retail channel members, a strategy designed to standardize wholesale prices and eliminate most trade promotions, many retailers retaliated. Some cut the variety of P&G sizes they carried or eliminated marginal brands. Others moved P&G brands from prime shelf space to less visible shelves.

Channel Partnering

Regardless of the locus of power, channel members rely heavily on one another. Even the most powerful manufacturers depend on dealers to sell their products; even the most powerful retailers require the products provided by suppliers. In sharp contrast to the adversarial relationships of the past between buyers and sellers,

horizontal conflict
A channel conflict that occurs among channel members on the same level.

vertical conflict
A channel conflict that occurs between different levels in a marketing channel, most typically between the manufacturer and wholesaler or between the manufacturer and retailer.

**channel partnering
(channel cooperation)**
The joint effort of all channel members to create a supply chain that serves customers and creates a competitive advantage.

contemporary management thought emphasizes the development of close working partnerships among channel members. **Channel partnering**, or **channel cooperation**, is the joint effort of all channel members to create a supply chain that serves customers and creates a competitive advantage. Channel partnering is vital if each member is to gain something from other members. By cooperating, retailers, wholesalers, manufacturers, and suppliers can speed up inventory replenishment, improve customer service, and reduce the total costs of the marketing channel.

Channel alliances and partnerships help supply chain managers create the parallel flow of materials and information required to leverage the supply chains' intellectual, material, and marketing resources. The rapid growth in channel partnering is due to new enabling technology and the need to lower costs. A comparison between companies that approach the marketplace unilaterally and those that engage in channel cooperation and form partnerships is detailed in Exhibit 12.8.

Collaborating channel partners meet the needs of consumers more effectively by ensuring that the right products are available at the right time and for a lower cost, thus boosting sales and profits. Forced to become more efficient, many companies are turning formerly adversarial relationships into partnerships. For example, when all three branches of the U.S. and British militaries went shopping for more than three thousand new stealth fighter jets, long-time rivals in the defense industry had to work together to win the $200 billion contract. If the project is successful, the Joint Strike Fighter jet will be the first plane adapted to meet the needs of all three branches of the U.S. and British militaries. To meet that goal, Lockheed Martin, BAE Systems, and Northrop Grumman will have to work as partners. According to the partnership, Lockheed Martin will design and oversee the project, BAE Systems will be responsible for major subassembly, and Northrop Grumman will build the central fuselage and design its radar and stealth systems.[22]

Managing the Logistical Components of the Supply Chain

 Describe the logistical components of the supply chain

Now that you are familiar with the structure and strategy of marketing channels and the role of supply chain management, it is important to also understand the physical means through which products move through the supply chain. As men-

Exhibit 12.8

Transaction- versus Partnership-Based Firms

	Transaction-Based	Partnership-Based
Relationships between Manufacturer and Supplier	• Short-term • Adversarial • Independent • Price more important	• Long-term • Cooperative • Dependent • Value-added services more important
Number of Suppliers	Many	Few
Level of Information Sharing	Minimal	High
Investment Required	Minimal	High

SOURCE: David Frederick Ross, *Competing Through Supply Chain Management: Creating Market-Winning Strategies Through Supply Chain Partnerships* (New York: Chapman & Hall, 1998), 61.

tioned earlier, supply chain management coordinates and integrates all of the activities performed by supply chain members into a seamless process. The supply chain consists of several interrelated and integrated logistical components: (1) sourcing and procurement of raw materials and supplies, (2) production scheduling, (3) order processing, (4) inventory control, (5) warehousing and materials-handling, and (6) transportation. These components are shown in Exhibit 12.9.

Integrating and linking all of the logistics components of the supply chain is the **logistics information system**. Today's supply chain logisticians are at the forefront of information technology, which is not just a functional affiliate of supply chain management. Rather it is the enabler, the facilitator, the linkage that connects the various components and partners of the supply chain into an integrated whole. Electronic data interchange, on-board computers, satellite and cellular communications systems, materials-handling and warehouse-management software, enterprise-wide systems solutions, and the Internet are among the information enablers of successful supply chain management.

The **supply chain team**, in concert with the logistics information system, orchestrates the movement of goods, services, and information from the source to the consumer. Supply chain teams typically cut across organizational boundaries, embracing all parties who participate in moving the product to market. The best supply chain teams also move beyond the organization to include the external participants in the chain, such as suppliers, transportation carriers, and third-party logistics suppliers. Members of the supply chain communicate, coordinate, and cooperate extensively.

Today's corporate supply chain logisticians have become so efficient that the U.S. Marine Corps is now consulting with companies like Wal-Mart, United Parcel Service, and Unilever to improve its own supply chain efficiency. The Marine Corps's goal is to reduce the time it takes to deliver supplies to the front lines from one week to twenty-four hours and lower costs by cutting inventories in half.[23]

Sourcing and Procurement

One of the most important links in the supply chain is that between the manufacturer and the supplier. Purchasing professionals are on the front lines of supply

logistics information system
Information technology that integrates and links all of the logistics functions of the supply chain.

supply chain team
An entire group of individuals who orchestrate the movement of goods, services, and information from the source to the consumer.

Exhibit 12.9

Integrated Logistical Components of the Supply Chain

chain management. Purchasing departments plan purchasing strategies, develop specifications, select suppliers, and negotiate price and service levels.

The goal of most sourcing and procurement activities is to reduce the costs of raw materials and supplies. Purchasing professionals have traditionally relied on tough negotiations to get the lowest price possible from suppliers of raw materials, supplies, and components. Perhaps the biggest contribution purchasing can make to supply chain management, however, is in the area of vendor relations. Companies can use the purchasing function to strategically manage suppliers in order to reduce the total cost of materials and services. Through enhanced vendor relations, buyers and sellers can develop cooperative relationships that reduce costs and improve efficiency with the aim of lowering prices and enhancing profits. By integrating suppliers into their companies' businesses, purchasing managers have become better able to streamline purchasing processes, manage inventory levels, and reduce overall costs of the sourcing and procurement operations.

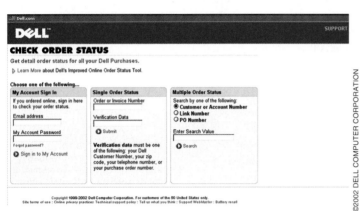

©2002 DELL COMPUTER CORPORATION

Build-to-order computers are more than commonplace today, thanks to the direct selling model of Dell Computer. The company allows customers to track their orders throughout manufacturing and shipping.

Production Scheduling

In traditional mass-market manufacturing, production begins when forecasts call for additional products to be made or inventory control systems signal low inventory levels. The firm then makes a product and transports the finished goods to its own warehouses or those of intermediaries, where the goods wait to be ordered by retailers or customers. Production scheduling based on pushing a product down to the consumer obviously has its disadvantages, the most notable being that companies risk making products that may become obsolete or that consumers don't want in the first place.

In a customer "pull" manufacturing environment, which is growing in popularity, production of goods or services is not scheduled until an order is placed by the customer specifying the desired configuration. As you read in Chapter 11, this process, known as **mass customization**, or **build-to-order**, uniquely tailors mass-market goods and services to the needs of the individuals who buy them. Companies as diverse as BMW, Dell Computer, Levi Strauss, Mattel, and a slew of Web-based businesses are adopting mass customization to maintain or obtain a competitive edge.

As more companies move toward mass customization—and away from mass marketing—of goods, the need to stay on top of consumer demand is forcing manufacturers to make their supply chains more flexible. Flexibility is critical to a manufacturer's success when dramatic swings in demand occur. For example, automobile manufacturers such as Honda and Toyota have been modifying their assembly plants to make it easier to shift production based on demand. As a result, the companies can move new models into production in only a few months to keep up with the frequently changing tastes of consumers.[24]

Just-in-Time Manufacturing

mass customization (build-to-order)

A production method whereby products are not made until an order is placed by the customer; products are made according to customer specifications.

just-in-time production (JIT)

A process that redefines and simplifies manufacturing by reducing inventory levels and delivering raw materials just when they are needed on the production line.

GLOBAL An important manufacturing process common today among manufacturers is just-in-time manufacturing. Borrowed from the Japanese, **just-in-time production (JIT)**, sometimes called *lean production*, requires manufacturers to work closely with suppliers and transportation providers to get necessary items to the assembly line or factory floor at the precise time they are needed for production. For the manufacturer, JIT means that raw materials arrive at the assembly line in guaranteed working order "just in time" to be installed, and finished products are generally shipped to the customer immediately after completion. For the supplier,

JIT means supplying customers with products in just a few days, or even a few hours, rather than weeks. For the ultimate consumer, JIT means lower costs, shorter lead times, and products that more closely meet the consumer's needs. For example, Zara, a European clothing manu-facturer and retailer, has begun using the JIT process to ensure that its stores are stocked with the latest fashion trends. Using its salespeople to track which fashions are selling fastest, the company can increase production of hot items and ship them to its stores in just a few days. Because Zara stores do not maintain large inventories, they can respond quickly to fashion trends and offer their products for less, giving Zara a distinct advantage over more traditional retailers like Gap that place orders months in advance.[25]

JIT benefits manufacturers most by reducing their raw materials inventories. For example, at Dell Computer's Texas plant, computer components often are de-livered just minutes before they are needed. Chips, boards, and drives are kept in trucks backed into bays located fifty feet from the beginning of the production line. On average, Dell takes only about a week from buying parts to selling them as a fin-ished product. Similarly, Customized Transportation, Inc., works with General Mo-tors to coordinate delivery of interior door panels at the moment they are needed for production. CTI also helps GM manage its supply chain by issuing purchase or-ders, buying the raw materials from vendors, assembling the components, and packaging them for delivery.[26]

Additionally, JIT shortens lead times—the time it takes to get parts from a sup-plier after an order has been placed. Manufacturers also enjoy better relationships with suppliers and can decrease their production and storeroom costs. Because there is little safety stock, and therefore no margin for error, the manufacturer cannot afford to make a mistake. As a result, a manufacturer using JIT must be sure it receives high-quality parts from all vendors, be confident that the supplier will meet all delivery commitments, and have a crisis management plan to handle any disruptions. Finally, JIT tends to reduce the amount of paperwork.

Order Processing

The order is often the catalyst that sets the supply chain in motion, especially in the build-to-order environments of leading computer manufacturers such as Dell. The **order processing system** processes the requirements of the customer and sends the information into the supply chain via the logistics information system. The order goes to the manufacturer's warehouse. If the order is in stock, the order is filled and arrangements are made to ship it. If the order is not in stock, it trig-gers a replenishment request that finds its way to the factory floor.

The role of proper order processing in providing good service cannot be overemphasized. As an order enters the system, management must monitor two flows: the flow of goods and the flow of information. Often the best-laid plans of marketers can get entangled in the order processing system. Obviously, good com-munication among sales representatives, office personnel, and warehouse and shipping personnel is essential to correct order processing. Shipping incorrect merchandise or partially filled orders can create just as much dissatisfaction as stockouts or slow deliveries. The flow of goods and information must be continu-ally monitored so that mistakes can be corrected before an invoice is prepared and the merchandise shipped.

Order processing is becoming more automated through the use of computer technology known as **electronic data interchange (EDI)**. The ba-sic idea of EDI is to replace the paper documents that usually accompany business transactions, such as purchase orders and invoices, with electronic trans-mission of the needed information. A typical EDI message includes all the informa-tion that would traditionally be included on a paper invoice such as product code, quantity, and transportation details. The information is usually sent via private net-works, which are more secure and reliable than the networks used for standard

Wal-Mart
Is EDI a requirement for Wal-Mart suppliers? Go to Wal-Mart's Web site and read the "Supplier Information" pages. Does selling to Wal-Mart seem worth the effort? Why or why not?
http://www.walmartstores.com

On Line

order processing system
A system whereby orders are en-tered into the supply chain and filled.

electronic data interchange (EDI)
Information technology that re-places the paper documents that usually accompany business trans-actions, such as purchase orders and invoices, with electronic transmission of the needed infor-mation to reduce inventory levels, improve cash flow, streamline op-erations, and increase the speed and accuracy of information transmission.

e-mail messages. Most importantly, the information can be read and processed by computers, significantly reducing costs and increasing efficiency.[27] Companies that use EDI can reduce inventory levels, improve cash flow, streamline operations, and increase the speed and accuracy of information transmission. EDI is also believed to create a closer relationship between buyers and sellers.

It should not be surprising that retailers have become major users of EDI. For Wal-Mart, Target, and the like, logistics speed and accuracy are crucial competitive tools in an overcrowded retail environment. Many big retailers are helping their suppliers acquire EDI technology so that they can be linked into the system. EDI works hand in hand with retailers' *efficient consumer response* programs, which are designed to have the right products on the shelf, in the right styles and colors, through improved inventory, ordering, and distribution techniques. (See Chapter 13 for more discussion of retailers' use of EDI techniques.)

Inventory Control

Closely interrelated with the procurement, manufacturing, and ordering processes is the **inventory control system**—a method that develops and maintains an adequate assortment of materials or products to meet a manufacturer's or a customer's demands.

Inventory decisions, for both raw materials and finished goods, have a big impact on supply chain costs and the level of service provided. If too many products are kept in inventory, costs increase—as do risks of obsolescence, theft, and damage. If too few products are kept on hand, then the company risks product shortages and angry customers, and ultimately lost sales. For example, due to negative sales projections, many retailers cut back on orders for Christmas 2001 because they were afraid of having to discount huge end-of-year inventories. As a result, several companies including Garnet Hill and Lands' End lost sales due to inventory shortages on popular new items. Manufacturers like Panasonic were unable to alleviate the retailers' problems because they too were carrying lean inventories.[28] The goal of inventory management, therefore, is to keep inventory levels as low as possible while maintaining an adequate supply of goods to meet customer demand.

Managing inventory from the supplier to the manufacturer is called **materials requirement planning** (**MRP**), or **materials management**. This system also encompasses the sourcing and procurement operations, signaling purchasing when raw materials, supplies, or components will need to be replenished for the production of more goods. The system that manages the finished goods inventory from manufacturer to end user is commonly referred to as **distribution resource planning** (**DRP**). Both inventory systems use various inputs, such as sales forecasts, available inventory, outstanding orders, lead times, and mode of transportation to be used, to determine what actions must be taken to replenish goods at all points in the supply chain. Demand in the system is collected at each level in the supply chain, from the retailer back up the chain to the manufacturer. With the use of electronic data interchange, the information can be transmitted much faster to meet the quick-response needs of today's competitive marketplace.[29] Exhibit 12.10 provides an example of inventory replenishment using DRP from the retailer to the manufacturer.

Just-in-time manufacturing processes have had a significant impact on reducing inventory levels. Since JIT requires supplies to be delivered at the time they are needed on the factory floor, little inventory is needed. With JIT the purchasing firm can reduce the amount of raw materials and parts it keeps on hand by ordering more often and in smaller amounts. And lower inventory levels due to JIT can give firms a competitive edge through the flexibility to halt production of existing products in favor of those gaining popularity with consumers. Savings also come from having less capital tied up in inventory and from the reduced need for storage facilities.

Warehousing and Materials-Handling

Supply chain logisticians oversee the constant flow of raw materials from suppliers to manufacturer and finished goods from the manufacturer to the ultimate consumer.

inventory control system
A method of developing and maintaining an adequate assortment of materials or products to meet a manufacturer's or a customer's demand.

materials requirement planning (MRP) (materials management)
An inventory control system that manages the replenishment of raw materials, supplies, and components from the supplier to the manufacturer.

distribution resource planning (DRP)
An inventory control system that manages the replenishment of goods from the manufacturer to the final consumer.

Exhibit 12.10

Inventory Replenishment Example

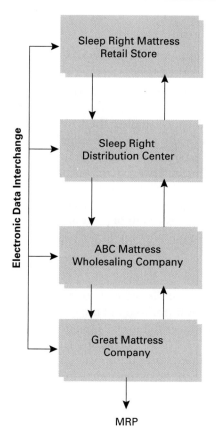

Sleep Right is planning a promotion on the Great Mattress Company's Gentle Rest mattress. Sales forecast is for fifty units to be sold. Sleep Right has ten open Gentle Rest orders with its distribution center. New mattresses must be delivered in two weeks in time for the promotion.

Sleep Right's Distribution Center is electronically notified of the order of fifty new Gentle Rest mattresses. It currently has twenty Gentle Rest mattresses in inventory and begins putting together the transportation plans to deliver these to the Sleep Right Store. Delivery takes one day. It orders forty new mattresses from its mattress wholesaler to make up the difference.

ABC Mattress Wholesaling Company is electronically notified of Sleep Right DC's order of forty new Gentle Rest mattresses. It currently does not have any of these in stock but electronically orders forty from the Great Mattress Company's factory. Once it receives the new mattresses, it can have them delivered to the Sleep Right DC in two days.

The Great Mattress Company electronically receives ABC's order and forwards it to the factory floor. Production of a new mattress takes twenty minutes. The total order of forty mattresses can be ready to be shipped to ABC in two days. Delivery takes one day. Raw material supplies for this order are electronically requested from Great Mattress's supply partners, who deliver the needed materials just-in-time to its stitching machines.

Although JIT manufacturing processes may eliminate the need to warehouse many raw materials, manufacturers may often keep some safety stock on hand in the event of an emergency, such as a strike at a supplier's plant or a catastrophic event that temporarily stops the flow of raw materials to the production line. Likewise, the final user may not need or want the goods at the same time the manufacturer produces and wants to sell them. Products like grain and corn are produced seasonally, but consumers demand them year-round. Other products, such as Christmas ornaments and turkeys, are produced year-round, but consumers do not want them until autumn or winter. Therefore, management must have a storage system to hold these products until they are shipped.

Storage is what helps manufacturers manage supply and demand, or production and consumption. It provides time utility to buyers and sellers, which means that the seller stores the product until the buyer wants or needs it. Even when products are used regularly, not seasonally, many manufacturers store excess products in case the demand surpasses the amount produced at a given time. Storing additional product does have disadvantages, however, including the costs of insurance on the stored product, taxes, obsolescence or spoilage, theft, and warehouse operating costs. Another drawback is opportunity costs—that is, the opportunities lost because money is tied up in stored product instead of being used for something else.

Because businesses are focusing on cutting supply chain costs, the warehousing industry is also changing to better serve its customers. For example, many warehouses are putting greater emphasis on more efficient unloading and reloading layouts and customized services that move merchandise through the warehouse faster, often in the same day. They also are investing in services using sophisticated tracking technology such as materials-handling systems.[30]

A **materials-handling system** moves inventory into, within, and out of the warehouse. Materials-handling includes these functions:

materials-handling system
A method of moving inventory into, within, and out of the warehouse.

- Receiving goods into the warehouse or distribution center
- Identifying, sorting, and labeling the goods
- Dispatching the goods to a temporary storage area
- Recalling, selecting, or picking the goods for shipment (may include packaging the product in a protective container for shipping)

The goal of the materials-handling system is to move items quickly with minimal handling. With a manual, nonautomated materials-handling system, a product may be handled more than a dozen times. Each time it is handled, the cost and risk of damage increase; each lifting of a product stresses its package. Consequently, most manufacturers today have moved to automated systems. Scanners quickly identify goods entering and leaving a warehouse through bar-coded labels affixed to the packaging. Automatic storage and retrieval systems automatically store and pick goods in the warehouse or distribution center. Automated materials-handling systems decrease product handling, ensure accurate placement of product, and improve the accuracy of order picking and the rates of on-time shipment.

Transportation

Transportation typically accounts for 5 to 10 percent of the price of goods.[31] Supply chain logisticians must decide which mode of transportation to use to move products from supplier to producer and from producer to buyer. These decision are, of course, related to all other logistics decisions. The five major modes of transportation are railroads, motor carriers, pipelines, water transportation, and airways. Supply chain managers generally choose a mode of transportation on the basis of several criteria:

- *Cost:* The total amount a specific carrier charges to move the product from the point of origin to the destination
- *Transit time:* The total time a carrier has possession of goods, including the time required for pickup and delivery, handling, and movement between the point of origin and the destination
- *Reliability:* The consistency with which the carrier delivers goods on time and in acceptable condition
- *Capability:* The ability of the carrier to provide the appropriate equipment and conditions for moving specific kinds of goods, such as those that must be transported in a controlled environment (for example, under refrigeration)
- *Accessibility:* A carrier's ability to move goods over a specific route or network
- *Traceability:* The relative ease with which a shipment can be located and transferred

The mode of transportation used depends on the needs of the shipper, as they relate to these six criteria. Exhibit 12.11 compares the basic modes of transportation on these criteria.

In many cases, especially in a JIT manufacturing environment, the transportation network replaces the warehouse or eliminates the expense of storing inventories as goods are timed to arrive the moment they're needed on the assembly line or for shipment to customers. In fact, Toyota is so committed to JIT that is has no parts warehouses in the United States. Instead, it works closely with its suppliers to make sure that parts will be delivered on time even during a crisis. For example, Continental Teves, Inc., supplies Toyota with German-made steering sensors for its Sequoia SUV. Traditionally, the parts were flown from Germany and delivered to Toyota when they were needed for installation. Following the September 11 terrorist attacks, however, Continental decided to begin shipping the parts via ship to ensure that Toyota will receive shipments on time even if U.S. airspace is shut down. Although the change will increase Continental's costs, the company decided it was necessary to meet Toyota's needs.[32]

Exhibit 12.11

Criteria for Ranking Modes of Transportation

	Highest				Lowest
Relative Cost	Air	Truck	Rail	Pipe	Water
Transit Time	Water	Rail	Pipe	Truck	Air
Reliability	Pipe	Truck	Rail	Air	Water
Capability	Water	Rail	Truck	Air	Pipe
Accessibility	Truck	Rail	Air	Water	Pipe
Traceability	Air	Truck	Rail	Water	Pipe

Trends in Supply Chain Management

Several technological advances and business trends are affecting the job of the supply chain manager today. Three of the most outstanding trends are advanced computer technology, outsourcing of logistics functions, and electronic distribution.

8

Discuss new technology and emerging trends in supply chain management

Advanced Computer Technology

Advanced computer technology has boosted the efficiency of logistics dramatically with tools such as automatic identification systems (auto ID) using bar coding and radio frequency technology, communications technology, and supply chain software systems that help synchronize the flow of goods and information with customer demand. Amazon.com's state-of-the-art distribution centers, for instance, use sophisticated order picking systems that utilize computer terminals to guide workers through the picking and packing process. Radio frequency technology, which uses radio signals that work with scanned bar codes identifying products, directs Amazon's workers to the exact locations in the warehouse where the product is stored. Warehouse management software examines pick rates, location, and picking and storage patterns, and builds combinations of customer orders for shipping. After installing these supply chain technology tools, Amazon saw a 70 percent improvement in operational efficiency.[33]

One of the major goals of technology is to bring up-to-date information to the supply chain manager's

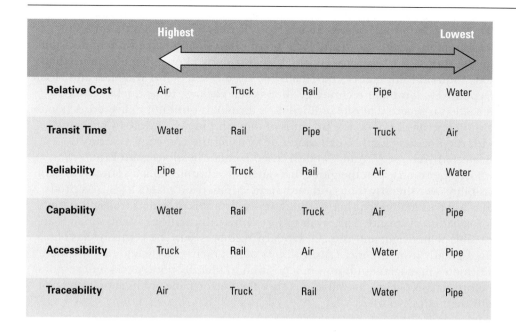

© DAVID SAMUEL ROBBI/CORBIS SYGMA

Matt Spangler and others are pictured here picking orders from the media cage at Amazon.com's Seattle distribution center. Amazon's command of the supply chain has translated into increased sales and customer satisfaction, but the company is still struggling to turn a profit.

desk. The transportation system has long been referred to as a "black hole," where products and materials fall out of sight until they reappear some time later in a plant, store, or warehouse. Now carriers have systems that track freight, monitor the speed and location of carriers, and make routing decisions on the spur of the moment. For instance, Roadway Express handles more than sixty thousand shipments a day, many for large retailers like Wal-Mart and Home Depot. New computer technology allows each package to be tracked from the minute it is received at one of Roadway's terminals until it is delivered. Anxious customers can check on the progress of their shipment anytime by checking with the Roadway Express call center or by using the company's password-protected Web site.[34] And, Swedish-based communications giant Ericsson, whose operations span the globe, uses specialized supply chain software to gain visibility over the fifty thousand outbound shipments it makes a year. As products leave its manufacturing facilities, transportation providers transmit status information at specified intervals to Ericsson's information system, which is accessible to management using a standard Web browser. The company has benefited greatly from the increased visibility of shipments the system has provided. Ericsson's management is now in a position to identify bottlenecks and respond before a crisis occurs, as well as measure the performance of its supply chain at different checkpoints.[35]

Outsourcing Logistics Functions

outsourcing (contract logistics)
A manufacturer's or supplier's use of an independent third party to manage an entire function of the logistics system, such as transportation, warehousing, or order processing.

External partners are becoming increasingly important in the efficient deployment of supply chain management. **Outsourcing**, or **contract logistics**, is a rapidly growing segment of the distribution industry in which a manufacturer or supplier turns over the entire function of buying and managing transportation or another function of the supply chain, such as warehousing, to an independent third party. Many manufacturers are turning to outside partners for their logistics expertise in an effort to focus on the core competencies that they do best. Partners create and manage entire solutions for getting products where they need to be, when they need to be there. Logistics partners offer staff, an infrastructure, and services that reach consumers virtually anywhere in the world. Because a logistics provider is focused, clients receive service in a timely, efficient manner, thereby increasing customers' level of satisfaction and boosting their perception of added value to a company's offerings. The trend is so strong that the supply chain outsourcing industry is expected to generate almost $1.8 billion in revenue by the year 2005.[36]

Third-party contract logistics allow companies to cut inventories, locate stock at fewer plants and distribution centers, and still provide the same service level or even better. The companies then can refocus investment on their core business. Recall from Chapter 6 that Ford Motor Company decided to use third-party logistics provider UPS Worldwide Logistics Group to manage the delivery of Ford, Lincoln, and Mercury cars and trucks in the United States, Canada, and Mexico. The companies say they expect the alliance will reduce the time it takes to move vehicles from Ford's plants to dealers and customers by up to 40 percent. The alliance will also provide Web-based information systems that allow Ford and its dealers to track individual vehicle status from production through final delivery.[37]

Many firms are taking outsourcing one step further by allowing business partners to take over the final assembly of their product or its packaging in an effort to reduce inventory costs, speed up delivery, or meet customer requirements better. Ryder Truck Lines assembles and packages twenty-two different combinations of shrink-wrapped boxes that contain the ice trays, drawers, shelves, doors, and other accessories for the various refrigerator models Whirlpool sells. Similarly, outsourcing firm, StarTek, Inc., packages and ships products for Microsoft, provides technical support to customers of AOL Time Warner, and maintains AT&T communication systems.[38]

Electronic distribution has become a viable channel for numerous products, from financial services to postage to software. The IRS is also realizing gains by accepting tax returns online.

Electronic Distribution

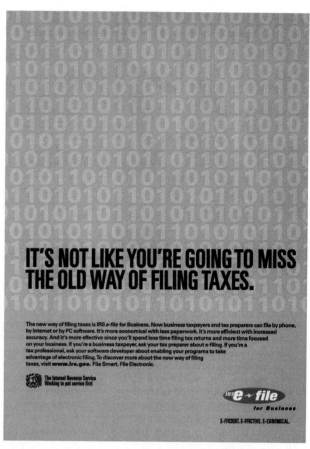

Electronic distribution is the most recent development in the logistics arena. Broadly defined, **electronic distribution** includes any kind of product or service that can be distributed electronically, whether over traditional forms such as fiber-optic cable or through satellite transmission of electronic signals. For instance, instead of buying and installing software from stores, computer users increasingly can purchase software over the Internet and download it electronically to their personal computers or rent the same software from Internet services that have the program available for use on their servers. For example, Intuit, Inc., allows people to fill out their tax returns on its Web site rather than buying its TurboTax software.[39] Postage stamps can now be purchased on-line through E-Stamp, which uses a silver-dollar size "vault" attached to the purchaser's computer to keep track of postage purchases.[40] Similarly, on-line ticket companies and movie theaters have recently developed the technology to sell tickets to sporting events, concerts, and movies via the Internet; consumers can print the tickets at home on a standard computer printer.[41]

Hollywood movie studios are getting ready to deliver their products directly to consumers through digital pipelines.[42] Consumers can already download digital files of their favorite music, movies, and television shows to be played on their computers, portable players, and televisions, often without paying for the file. This controversial form of electronic distribution is discussed in the "Ethics in Marketing" box.

electronic distribution
A distribution technique that includes any kind of product or servive that can be distributed electronically, whether over traditional forms such as fiber optic cable or through satellite transmission of electronic signals.

Channels and Distribution Decisions for Global Markets

With the surging popularity of free-trade agreements and treaties, such as the European Union and the North American Free Trade Agreement (NAFTA) over the past decade, global marketing channels and management of the supply chain have become increasingly important to U.S. corporations that export their products or manufacture abroad.

9

Discuss channels and distribution decisions in global markets

Developing Global Marketing Channels

Executives should recognize the unique cultural, economic, institutional, and legal aspects of each market before trying to design marketing channels in foreign countries. Manufacturers introducing products in global markets face a tough decision: what type of channel structure to use. Specifically, should the product be marketed directly, mostly by company salespeople, or through independent foreign intermediaries, such as agents and distributors? Using company salespeople generally provides more control and is less risky than using foreign intermediaries. However, setting up a sales force in a foreign country also entails a greater commitment, both financially and organizationally.

Video Piracy

As discussed in the chapter, new Internet and computer technology has been largely responsible for advances in supply chain management. However, the new technology and the Internet are also creating serious supply chain problems for the entertainment industry. For example, the invention of MP3 music files, which can be swapped on the Internet and burned onto compact discs, had a dramatic effect on traditional music sales. The music industry was forced to sue Napster, the leading music file swapping Web site, which eventually filed for bankruptcy, for copyright infringement and to develop both new distribution channels and new technologies to prevent music swapping.

Similarly, new technology now allows consumers to make and swap digital copies of television shows and movies. For instance, digital video recorders (DVRs) allow consumers to record their favorite television shows and movies via traditional cable, broadcast, satellite, and Internet connections. With DVRs, consumers can watch their favorite programs when it is convenient and even pause live programming. As adoption of the technology increases, DVRs could have an impact on television advertising sales and program scheduling. The industry is more concerned, however, about SonicBlue's introduction of ReplayTV 4000, which not only enables consumers to automatically skip commercials but also allows them to send copies over the Internet to other Replay users.

Consumers can also obtain copies of their favorite movies and television shows by going on-line with one of two popular software programs that make it easy to swap video files on the Internet—Morpheus and Kazaa. With more than forty million users between the two, experts say that more than one million users are downloading copies of their favorite television shows and movies at any given time. Available downloads include every *Simpsons* episode ever recorded, film classics such as *Breakfast at Tiffany's,* and episodes of HBO's *The Sopranos* and *Sex in the City.* Finally, digital video cameras with FireWire are even making it easy to share copies of movies currently being shown in theaters.

All of these new technologies are leading to a dramatic increase in video piracy. Movie theaters around the globe are reporting heavy losses as a result. In fact, the Motion Picture Association of America claims that consumers illegally copy 350,000 films a day on the Internet. Other piracy experts put the number closer to a million a day. What's more, experts predict the trend will grow as technology improves and Internet speed increases.

To protect its product, the television industry has sued SonicBlue, claiming that ReplayTV 4000 illegally jeopardizes the industry's two main revenue sources: advertising and subscription fees. SonicBlue claims that copyright laws give consumers a "fair use" right to share—an argument the courts rejected in the Napster trial. Further, the company contends that it is creating innovative products that give consumers more control over

how they use entertainment. The film industry has also sued StreamCast Networks, the distributor of Morpheus, for copyright infringement. StreamCast argues that the software enables people to share home movies and films that are in the public domain.

Regardless of the outcome of these lawsuits, the entertainment industry is examining the future of its distribution channels. Television studios are looking for a way to use electronic tags within a broadcast to prevent copying and are asking the federal government to require that all television sets, receivers, and computers be capable of reading the tags. For the tags to be effective, the studios would have to cease all nondigital broadcasts—a move that could eliminate free television, forcing consumers to use a cable or satellite company for program access.

In contrast, in an effort to satisfy consumers, MGM, Sony, Paramount, Universal, and Warner Brothers studios have started a joint venture called Moviefly to provide consumers with a secure, reliable way to "rent" movies on the Internet. Of course, if successful, the joint venture would eliminate cable and satellite companies from the pay-per-view distribution channel.[43]

What other distribution options does the entertainment industry have? Will new technology give the industry a way to protect its products, or will the industry be forced to reinvent the way it operates? How do you think television programs and movies will be distributed in the future?

Marketers should be aware that channel structures and types abroad may differ from those of channels in the United States. For instance, the more highly developed a nation is economically, the more specialized its channel types. Therefore, a marketer wishing to sell in Germany or Japan will have several channel types to choose from. Conversely, developing countries like India, Ethiopia, and Venezuela have limited channel types available; there are typically few mail-order channels, vending machines, or specialized retailers and wholesalers.

 Marketers must also be aware that many foreign countries have "gray" marketing channels, in which products are distributed through unauthorized channel intermediaries. It is estimated that sales of coun-

Challenges and Opportunities in China

Thanks to the Internet, new technology, and international trade agreements, global supply chains are bringing the world's businesses closer together. Today, large multinational corporations and small businesses alike look to markets around the world for their sourcing and procurement needs. Critics argue that this trend is widening the gap between the nations that have and those that do not. Proponents counter that globalization has brought education and economic development to developing nations and lower prices to the world's markets. Either way, both sides agree that globalization is here to stay. One development that global supply chain managers are watching closely is China's admission into the World Trade Organization (WTO).

For the many companies hoping to market their products to the world's largest market, opportunities abound. So do challenges for supply chain managers since China does not function as a single market but as hundreds, each with its own unique trade barriers. For example, each province and municipality has its own tariffs and trade restrictions. Transportation is particularly difficult. Not only is infra-

structure questionable outside urban areas but many provinces also have their own government-controlled transportation companies and outside transportation companies are not welcome. As a result, cargo must be unloaded and reloaded at each border crossing within the country. In fact, current supply chain costs in China are typically 30 to 40 percent of wholesale prices, compared to 5 to 20 percent in the United States.

On the other hand, China's participation in the WTO will secure the opening of additional markets to Chinese exports. With the greater availability of cheap Chinese goods, companies everywhere, including those already doing business with Chinese companies, may see lower sourcing and procurement costs. This should be good for consumers, but for emerging economies like India and Thailand, the competition could be deadly. Therefore, many companies are tightening up operations and focusing on quality to improve their ability to compete against the cheaper Chinese products. One such company is Bajaj Auto, a motorcycle manufacturer in New Delhi. Bajaj has expanded operations to take advantage of

economies of scale, invested heavily in R&D to stay on the cutting edge, and put its finances in order so that it can take advantage of future growth opportunities.

Supply chain managers will have to manage relationships with their Chinese supply chain partners closely to protect company interests from design piracy. For example, one of Black & Decker's Chinese sources turned around and competed head-to-head with Black & Decker in Germany using the American company's own design. The Japanese motorcycle manufacturers Yamaha, Honda, and Suzuki have also had problems with Chinese companies stealing their designs.

In the end, experts agree that China's participation in world markets will make the global economy more competitive, ultimately benefiting consumers. In the meantime, global supply chain managers will have to monitor developments around the world, particularly in Asia.[45]

What other global supply chain challenges and opportunities do you see in working with China? Will China's participation in world markets strengthen globalization, or will it have a negative impact?

---

terfeit luxury items like Prada handbags and Big Bertha golf clubs have reached almost $2 billion a year. The new fakes are harder to detect and hit the market almost instantly. For instance, a fake Christian Dior saddlebag was available just weeks after the original arrived on retailers' shelves. Similarly, Chinese companies are producing so many knockoffs of Yamaha, Honda, and Suzuki motorcycles that the Japanese companies are seeing a drop in sales. What's more, many companies are getting so good at design piracy that they are beginning to launch their own new products.[44] The "Global Perspectives" box provides more details on the impact of supply chain globalization.

 The Internet has also proved to be a way for pirates to circumvent authorized distribution channels, especially in the case of popular prescription drugs. In recent years, the U.S. Customs Service has seized millions of dollars worth of prescription drugs, most of which were purchased from foreign Internet sites. Some were seized because they had not been approved for use in the United States, others because they did not comply with U.S. labeling laws. Most sites offer just a handful of the most popular drugs, such as Viagra and the diet drug Xenical; consumers can get the drugs after obtaining the approval of a doctor who is affiliated with the site and who never sees the patient.

Global Logistics and Supply Chain Management

As global trade becomes a more decisive factor in success or failure for firms of all sizes, a well-thought-out global logistics strategy becomes more important.

One of the most critical global logistical issues for importers of any size is coping with the legalities of trade in other countries. Shippers and distributors must be aware of the permits, licenses, and registrations they may need to acquire and, depending on the type of product they are importing, the tariffs, quotas, and other regulations that apply in each country. This multitude of different rules is why multinational companies like Eastman Kodak are so committed to working through the World Trade Organization to develop a global set of rules and to encourage countries to participate. Other goals for these companies include reducing trade barriers such as tariffs. As these barriers fall, the flow of merchandise across borders is increasing as more companies are sourcing from multiple countries. For instance, a Kodak camera sold in France may have been assembled there, but the camera mechanism probably came from China and the film from the United States.[46]

The presence of different rules hasn't slowed the spread of supply chain globalization, however. In spite of the added costs associated with importing and exporting goods, many companies are looking to other countries for their sourcing and procurement needs. For example, Applica, Inc., a U.S. maker of small appliances, is committed to using technology to improve its relationships with suppliers in Mexico. The company has linked its suppliers directly to sales data from Wal-Mart stores to help manage production and inventory costs.[47]

Transportation can also be a major issue for companies dealing with global supply chains. Uncertainty regarding shipping usually tops the list of reasons why companies, especially smaller ones, resist international markets. Even companies that have scored overseas successes often are vulnerable to logistical problems. Large companies have the capital to create global logistics systems, but smaller companies often must rely on the services of carriers and freight forwarders to get their products to overseas markets.

In some instances, poor infrastructure makes transportation dangerous and unreliable. And the process of moving goods across the borders of even the most industrialized nations can still be complicated by government regulations. For example, NAFTA was supposed to improve the flow of goods across the continent, but moving goods across the border still requires approvals from dozens of government agencies, broker intervention, and hours spent at border checks. Shipping companies like Ryder are working to make the process easier. Currently, Ryder operates a cross-border facility in San Antonio to help clients like General Motors and Xerox with customs and logistics costs. The company also is part of a pilot project to automate border crossings with technology similar to that of an E-Z pass. The new system sends and receives short-range radio signals containing information on the load to toll booths, weigh stations, and border crossings. If the cargo meets requirements, the truck or train receives a green light to go ahead. Questionable cargo is set aside for further inspection. Transportation industry experts believe the system could reduce delivery times by more than three hours.[48]

10

Identify the special problems and opportunities associated with distribution in service organizations

Channels and Distribution Decisions for Services

The fastest-growing part of our economy is the service sector. Although distribution in the service sector is difficult to visualize, the same skills, techniques, and strategies used to manage inventory can also be used to manage service inventory—for instance, hospital beds, bank accounts, or airline seats. The quality of the planning and execution of distribution can have a major impact on costs and customer satisfaction.

One thing that sets service distribution apart from traditional manufacturing distribution is that, in a service environment, production and consumption are simultaneous. In manufacturing, a production setback can often be remedied by using safety stock or a faster mode of transportation. Such substitution is not possible with a service. The benefits of a service are also relatively intangible—that is, you can't normally see the benefits of a service, such as a doctor's physical exam. But a consumer can normally see the benefits provided by a product—for example, a vacuum cleaner removing dirt from the carpet.

Because service industries are so customer oriented, customer service is a priority. Service distribution focuses on three main areas:

- *Minimizing wait times:* Minimizing the amount of time customers wait in line to deposit a check, wait for their food at a restaurant, or wait in a doctor's office for an appointment is a key factor in maintaining the quality of service. People tend to overestimate the amount of time they spend waiting in line, researchers report, and unexplained waiting seems longer than explained waits. To reduce anxiety among waiting customers, some restaurants give patrons pagers that allow them to roam around or go to the bar. Banks sometimes install electronic boards displaying stock quotes or sports scores. Car rental companies reward repeat customers by eliminating their waits altogether.[49] Airports have designed comfortable sitting areas with televisions and children's play areas for those waiting to board planes. Some service companies are using sophisticated technology to further ease their customers' waiting time. Similarly, many hotels are experimenting with electronic check-in kiosks. Travelers can insert their credit cards to check in upon arrival to receive their room key, get directions and print maps to area restaurants and attractions, and print out their hotel bills.[50]

- *Managing service capacity:* For product manufacturers, inventory acts as a buffer, enabling them to provide the product during periods of peak demand without extraordinary efforts. Service firms don't have this luxury. If they don't have the capacity to meet demand, they must either turn down some prospective customers, let service levels slip, or expand capacity. For instance, at tax time a tax preparation firm may have so many customers desiring its services that it has to either turn business away or add temporary offices or preparers. Popular restaurants risk losing business when seating is unavailable or the wait is too long.

- *Improving service delivery:* Like manufacturers, service firms are now experimenting with different distribution channels for their services. Choosing the right distribution channel can increase the times that services are available (such as using the Internet to disseminate information and services 24/7) or add to customer convenience (like pizza delivery, walk-in medical clinics, or a dry cleaner located in a supermarket). The airline industry has found that using the Internet for ticket sales both reduces distribution costs and raises the level of customer service by making it easier for customers to plan their own travel. Cruise lines, on the other hand, have found that travel agents add value by helping customers sort through the abundance of information and complicated options available when booking a cruise.[51]

Does your bank deliver any of its services on-line? Visit its Web site to find out. Which on-line services would you be inclined to use? Are there any that you would definitely *not* use? Why not?

On Line

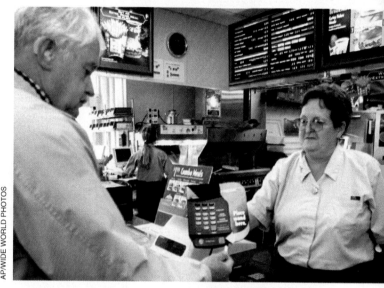

AP/WIDE WORLD PHOTOS

Modeled after successful programs like ExxonMobil's Speedpass, McDonald's is testing a program to minimize the time customers spend at the register. Customers run a small wand over the electronic reader to pay for food they order. People can load the wand electronically with dollars by using a credit or debit card. Reduced time paying for food means that McDonald's can sell hamburgers almost as fast as customers can order them.

The Internet is fast becoming an alternative channel for delivering services. Consumers can now purchase plane tickets, plan a vacation cruise, reserve a hotel room, pay bills, purchase mutual funds, and receive electronic newspapers in cyberspace. Insurance giant Allstate, for instance, now sells auto and home insurance directly to consumers in some states through the Internet in addition to its traditional network of agents. The effort reduces costs so that Allstate can stay competitive with rival insurance companies Progressive and Geico that already target customers directly.[52] Similarly, several new residential real estate Web sites are making it easier for customers to shop for a new home on the Web. Traditionally, the only way for customers to gain access to realtors' listings was to work through a real estate agent who would search the listings and then show customers homes that met their requirements. The new companies offer direct access to the listings, enabling customers to review properties for sale on their own, and choose which ones they would like to visit.[53]

CONNECT IT

As you complete this chapter, you should be able to see how marketing channels operate and how supply chain management is necessary to move goods from the manufacturer to the final consumer. Companies can choose from several different marketing channels to sell their products. For example, as the opening story discussed, H-E-B is using supply chain concepts and technology to compete successfully with giants like Wal-Mart. This strategy has made H-E-B the largest privately owned grocery distribution company in the United States.

USE IT

Buy Your Textbooks through a Direct Marketing Channel

 Save money and valuable loafing or study time by buying your textbooks from on-line textbook sellers, such as Big Words (**bigwords.com**), **ecampus.com**, or **VarsityBooks. com.** These sites provide students with the right textbooks, at the right price, right in time for classes to begin. And, instead of having to wait in line at the bookstore with your course curriculum, you can zap your book list to any of the cyber-bookstores that work with your school and then have them delivered directly to your dorm room. Since approximately nine out of ten of the fifteen million students enrolled in higher-education institutions use the Internet, buying textbooks on-line is a natural fit.

Have a Product You Want to Sell on the Web?

Specialized Web sites can help you set up an e-commerce site with minimal effort and cost. Sites such as **BizLand.com**, **Big-step.com**, and **Go2Net** help small-business owners create e-commerce Web sites where purchases can be accepted on-line with a credit card. BizLand's site, for instance, provides free on-line storefronts and shopping carts, custom domain names, e-mail, business promotional tools, site monitoring, plus lots more. Easy-to-use software helps merchants build and maintain catalogs of products and services to sell over the Internet. The sites are becoming very popular; Bizland's membership swelled to over 500,000 small-business owners from all 50 states plus 150 countries in just one year.

1 **Explain what a marketing channel is and why intermediaries are needed.** A marketing channel is a business structure of interdependent organizations that reach from the point of product origin to the consumer with the purpose of physically moving products to their final consumption destination, representing "place" in the marketing mix and encompassing the processes involved in getting the right product to the right place at the right time. Members of a marketing channel create a continuous and seamless supply chain that performs or supports the marketing channel functions. Channel members provide economies to the distribution process in the form of specialization and division of labor; overcoming discrepancies in quantity, assortment, time, and space; and providing contact efficiency.

1.1 Your family runs a specialty ice cream parlor, Graeter's, that manufactures its own ice cream in small batches and sells it only in pint-sized containers. Recently, someone not affiliated with the company sent six pints of its ice cream to Oprah Winfrey, who proclaimed on her national TV show that it was the best ice cream she had ever eaten. Immediately after the broadcast, orders came flooding in, overwhelming your small-batch production schedule and your rudimentary distribution system. The company's shipping manager thinks she can handle it, but you disagree. List the reasons why you need to restructure your supply chain.[54]

2 **Define the types of channel intermediaries and describe their functions and activities.** The most prominent difference separating intermediaries is whether or not they take title to the product. Retailers and merchant wholesalers take title, but agents and brokers do not. Retailers are firms that sell mainly to consumers. Merchant wholesalers are those organizations that facilitate the movement of products and services from the manufacturer to producers, resellers, governments, institutions, and retailers. Agents and brokers do not take title to the goods and services they market, but do they facilitate the exchange of ownership between sellers and buyers. Channel intermediaries perform three basic types of functions. Transactional functions include contacting and promoting, negotiating, and risk taking. Logistical functions performed by channel members include physical distribution, storing, and sorting functions. Finally, channel members may perform facilitating functions, such as researching and financing.

2.1 Discuss the reasons intermediaries are important to the distribution of most goods. What important functions do they provide?

3 **Describe the channel structures for consumer and business-to-business products and discuss alternative channel arrangements.** Marketing channels for consumer and business-to-business products vary in degree of complexity. The simplest consumer-product channel involves direct selling from producers to consumers. Businesses may sell directly to business or government buyers. Marketing channels grow more complex as intermediaries become involved. Consumer-product channel intermediaries include agents, brokers, wholesalers, and retailers. Business-product channel intermediaries include agents, brokers, and industrial distributors. Marketers often use alternative channel arrangements to move their products to the consumer. With dual distribution or multiple distribution, they choose two or more different channels to distribute the same product. Nontraditional channels help differentiate a firm's product from the competitor's or provide a manufacturer with another avenue for sales. Finally, strategic channel alliances are arrangements that use another manufacturer's already established channel.

3.1 Describe the most likely marketing channel structure for each of these consumer products: candy bars, Tupperware products, nonfiction books, new automobiles, farmers' market produce, and stereo equipment. Now, construct alternative channels for these same products.

3.2 INFOTRAC COLLEGE EDITION Dell Computer successfully uses a direct channel to sell computers and equipment it manufactures to consumers over the telephone and Internet. How has Dell affected traditional computer retailers with brick-and-mortar buildings? How have other computer manufacturers, such as Compaq and IBM, countered Dell's competitive advantage in its direct channel? Use Info-Trac (**http://www.infotrac-college.com**) to search for articles on this topic. You may also need to consult your campus library's databases on companies and articles to search for this information.

3.3 **WRITING** You have been hired to design an alternative marketing channel for a firm specializing in the manufacturing and marketing of novelties for college student organizations. In a memo to the president of the firm, describe how the channel operates.

3.4 **WRITING** Building on question 1.1, determine a new channel structure for Graeter's. Write a proposal to present to your key managers.

④ **Define supply chain management and discuss its benefits.** Supply chain management coordinates and integrates all of the activities performed by supply chain members into a seamless process from the source to the point of consumption. The responsibilities of a supply chain manager include developing channel design strategies, managing the relationships of supply chain members, sourcing and procurement of raw materials, scheduling production, processing orders, managing inventory and storing product, and selecting transportation modes. The supply chain manager is also responsible for managing customer service and the information that flows through the supply chain. The benefits of supply chain management include reduced costs in inventory management, transportation, warehousing, and packaging; improved service through techniques like time-based delivery and make-to-order; and enhanced revenues, which result from such supply chain–related achievements as higher product availability and more customized products

4.1 Discuss the benefits of supply chain management. How does the implementation of supply chain management result in enhanced customer value?

⑤ **Discuss the issues that influence channel strategy.** When determining marketing channel strategy, the supply chain manager must determine what market, product, and producer factors will influence the choice of channel. The manager must also determine the appropriate level of distribution intensity. Intensive distribution is distribution aimed at maximum market coverage. Selective distribution is achieved by screening dealers to eliminate all but a few in any single area. The most restrictive form of market coverage is exclusive distribution, which entails only one or a few dealers within a given area.

5.1 Decide which distribution intensity level—intensive, selective, or exclusive—is used for each of the following products, and explain why: Rolex watches, Land Rover sport utility vehicles, M&Ms, special edition Barbie dolls, Crest toothpaste.

5.2 **TEAM** Now that you have a basic channel structure for Graeter's (from question 3.4), form a team of three to four students and list the market, product, and producer factors that will affect your final channel structure.

⑥ **Explain channel leadership, conflict, and partnering.** Power, control, leadership, conflict, and partnering are the main social dimensions of marketing channel relationships. Channel power refers to the capacity of one channel member to control or influence other channel members. Channel control occurs when one channel member intentionally affects another member's behavior. Channel leadership is the exercise of authority and power. Channel conflict occurs when there is a clash of goals and methods among the members of a distribution channel. Channel conflict can be either horizontal, among channel members at the same level, or vertical, among channel members at different levels of the channel. Channel partnering is the joint effort of all channel members to create a supply chain that serves customers and creates a competitive advantage. Collaborating channel partners meet the needs of consumers more effectively by ensuring that the right products reach shelves at the right time and at a lower cost, boosting sales and profits.

6.1 Procter & Gamble and Wal-Mart are key partners in a shared supply chain. P&G is one of Wal-Mart's biggest suppliers, and Wal-Mart provides extremely detailed scanner data about customer purchases of P&G products. Wal-Mart recently began selling its own brand of Sam's Choice laundry detergent in bright orange bottles alongside P&G's Tide but for a greatly reduced price. What do you think will be the impact of this new product on what has been a stable channel relationship?

(7) Describe the logistical components of the supply chain. The logistics supply chain consists of several interrelated and integrated logistical components: (1) sourcing and procurement of raw materials and supplies, (2) production scheduling, (3) order processing, (4) inventory control, (5) warehousing and materials-handling, and (6) transportation. Integrating and linking all of the logistics functions of the supply chain is the logistics information system. Information technology connects the various components and partners of the supply chain into an integrated whole. The supply chain team, in concert with the logistics information system, orchestrates the movement of goods, services, and information from the source to the consumer. Supply chain teams typically cut across organizational boundaries, embracing all parties who participate in moving product to market. Procurement deals with the purchase of raw materials, supplies, and components according to production scheduling. Order processing monitors the flow of goods and information (order entry and order handling). Inventory control systems regulate when and how much to buy (order timing and order quantity) Warehousing provides storage of goods until needed by the customer while the materials-handling system moves inventory into, within, and out of the warehouse. Finally, the major modes of transportation include railroads, motor carriers, pipelines, waterways, and airways.

7.1 Discuss the impact of just-in-time production on the entire supply chain. Specifically, how does JIT affect suppliers, procurement planning, inventory levels, mode of transportation selected, and warehousing? What are the benefits of JIT to the end consumer?

7.2 Assume that you are the supply chain manager for a producer of expensive, high-tech computer components. Identify the most suitable method(s) of transporting your product in terms of cost, transit time, reliability, capability, accessibility, and traceability. Now, assume you are the supply chain manager for a producer of milk. How does this change your choice of transportation?

(8) Discuss new technology and emerging trends in supply chain management. Several trends are emerging that affect the job of today's supply chain manager. Technology and automation are bringing up-to-date distribution information to the decision maker's desk. Technology is also linking suppliers, buyers, and carriers for joint decision making, and it has created a new electronic distribution channel. Many companies are saving money and time by outsourcing third-party carriers to handle some or all aspects of the distribution process.

8.1 Visit the Web site of Menlo Logistics at **http://www.menlolog.com**. What logistics functions can this third-party logistics supplier provide? How does its mission fit in with the supply chain management philosophy?

8.2 *INFOTRAC COLLEGE EDITION* Use InfoTrac (**http://www.infotrac-college.com**) to locate the following article in the June 12, 2000 issue of *Computerworld* magazine: "Filling Orders a Hot E-Business: Companies Race to Offer Logistics Services" by Julia King. Read the article and write a summary of the implications of Internet commerce for the U.S. transportation and logistics industries.

(9) Discuss channels and distribution decisions in global markets. Global marketing channels are becoming more important to U.S. companies seeking growth abroad. Manufacturers introducing products in foreign countries must decide what type of channel structure to use—in particular, whether the product should be marketed through direct channels or through foreign intermediaries. Marketers should be aware that channel structures in foreign markets may be very different from those they are accustomed to in the United States. Global distribution expertise is also emerging as an important skill for supply chain managers as many countries are removing trade barriers.

9.1   INFOTRAC COLLEGE EDITION   How are transportation and logistics issues handled around the world? To find out, consult the *Transportation Journal* using Info-Trac (**http://www.infotrac-college.com**). Create a grid comparing at least two countries according to standard procedures, particular challenges faced, and creative solutions to problems they have encountered.

(10) **Identify the special problems and opportunities associated with distribution in service organizations.** Managers in service industries use the same skills, techniques, and strategies to manage logistics functions as managers in goods-producing industries. The distribution of services focuses on three main areas: minimizing wait times, managing service capacity, and improving service delivery.

10.1   WRITING   Assume that you are the marketing manager of a hospital. Write a report indicating the distribution functions that concern you. Discuss the similarities and dissimilarities of distribution for services and for goods.

DEFINE IT

APPLY IT

Application for Entrepreneurs

ENTREPRENEUR   Boudreaux has owned and operated a small spice-manufacturing business in south Louisiana for about ten years. Boudreaux has also experimented with preparing and selling several sauces, mostly for meats and salads. For the most part, the firm has sold its products locally, but on occasion, distributors have signed contracts to sell Boudreaux's products regionally. Boudreaux's most recent product—a spicy Cajun mayonnaise—has been a huge success locally, and several inquiries have come from large distributors about the possibilities of selling the mayonnaise regionally and perhaps nationally. No research has been conducted to determine the level or scope of demand for the mayonnaise. Also, it has been packaged and sold in only a twelve-ounce bottle. The red-and-white label just says "Boudreaux's Cajun Mayonnaise" and lists the major ingredients.

Questions

1. What should Boudreaux do to help the firm decide how best to market the new Cajun mayonnaise?

2. Should Boudreaux sign a contract with one of the distributors to sell the Cajun mayonnaise, or should his firm try to sell the product directly to one or more of the major supermarket chains?

THINK ABOUT IT

Ethics Exercise

Wholesome Snacks Inc., the maker of a variety of cookies and crackers, has just created a new vitamin-packed cookie. The new cookie has the potential to combat many of the health issues caused by malnutrition in children throughout poverty stricken parts of the world. To date, however, many of the larger third world markets have resisted opening distribution channels to Wholesome's products. Wholesome realizes that its new cookie could also help open the door for the company to sell its less nutritious products in these markets. Therefore, the company is offering the new cookie at a low cost to government relief programs in exchange for long sought after distribution channels. The company feels the deal is good for business, but the countries feel it is corporate bullying.

Questions

1. What do you think about Wholesome's idea for opening a new distribution channel?

2. Does the AMA Code of Ethics address this issue? Go to **http://www.marketingpower. com** and review the code. Then, write a brief paragraph stating what the AMA Code of Ethics contains that relates to distribution channels in developing nations.

TRY IT

Entrepreneurship Case
CarsDirect.com: Driving Car Buyers to the Internet

CarsDirect.com is heating up the new car industry. The country's first direct broker of cars on the Internet has sent automakers, on-line-buying services, and dealer groups scrambling to control the growing number of customers going on-line to shortcut the traditional process of shopping for new and used vehicles. The Internet start-up sparked a flurry of copycat Web sites dedicated to the direct-to-consumer purchase of cars, like CarOrder.com, DriveOff.com, Carpoint.com, and Greenlight.com. But several have now gone out of business.

Backed by Michael Dell's personal investment firm, CarsDirect.com was conceived by Bill Gross, chairman of Idealab, a venture incubator that has also launched other Internet businesses, such as eToys, Tickets.com, and Cooking.com. After becoming frustrated with his own efforts at buying an auto on-line, Gross realized that current Internet options for car buying were not only inadequate but did nothing to leverage available technology on behalf of the consumer. At the time of his search, on-line car sites functioned only as lead generators for local dealers, requiring him to close the sale of his car the old-fashioned way: haggling at the dealership with the untrustworthiest of people—a car salesperson.

His vision, CarsDirect.com, sells cars entirely through the Internet, allowing consumers to bypass traditional car dealers in their negotiations. As a car broker, CarsDirect.com offers Web buyers a car at a fixed price based on recent average selling prices. Then,

CarsDirect.com works through its network of existing dealers to get the car at that price. Since CarsDirect.com doesn't hold franchise agreements with any car manufacturers, consumers enjoy an impartial and unbiased shopping experience as well as an unrivaled selection. In contrast, buying cars the old-fashioned way makes consumers travel from car dealer to car dealer looking for the models they are interested in or the best price.

Car buyers visiting CarsDirect.com can research a car by searching the site's extensive database, which provides objective information on price, performance, and options for more than 2,500 different makes and models—virtually every production vehicle available in the United States. CarsDirect.com's research tools let buyers compare the features of vehicles and see in seconds the manufacturer's suggested retail price, the invoice, and, most importantly, the price CarsDirect.com can get for them. If a consumer wants to buy, payment is arranged completely on-line to close the deal. Financing options are provided through CarsDirect.com's financial partner Bank One, one of the nation's largest banks and a major automotive lender. Then, the buyer can arrange for delivery of the vehicle at home or the office or pick it up from a local automotive retailer.

With on-line auto sales expected to exceed 5 percent of total sales soon, there are still big hurdles ahead for car brokers like CarsDirect.com. General Motors, for instance, recently warned its 7,700 dealers to cease and desist from using on-line car-buying sites like CarsDirect.com. The largest obstacle, however, is the myriad of state franchise laws that protect car dealers and restrict direct sales of automobiles. Car brokers have found that no two states' franchise laws are the same, and many include rules that are arcane or impractical. Texas, the nation's second biggest automotive market, has the most restrictive dealer-protection laws in the country. There, only state-licensed dealers can sell cars. Brokering of cars to consumers by anyone other than a dealer is strictly prohibited. As a result, car brokers have had to redesign their direct-sales model around Texas laws. CarsDirect.com, for instance, currently does not offer cars to residents of Texas. Often, instead of trying to bypass dealers, Internet car brokers are forming alliances with dealers or reworking their strategies to become more dealer-friendly to comply with state law.

Questions

1. Explain how CarsDirect.com fits into the channel structure for car retailing to consumers.

2. How has CarsDirect.com's selling model caused channel conflict?

3. Visit CarsDirect.com's Web site at **http://www.carsdirect.com**. Give examples of how its Web site simplifies the car-buying process for consumers.

  WATCH IT

Short SUPERBOWL

The *Marketing* PowerPoint CD-ROM has two ad videos in the Chapter 12 slide presentation. An eTrade ad shows how companies advertise products with electronic distribution. What do you think is the issue illustrated by the Columbia TriStar ad?

Medium CNN VIDEO

Distribution is a key issue for a Palestinian Brewery. Watch the CNN clip on Taybeh Beer and identify ways that Taybeh can overcome the serious obstacles that it faces. Issues related to the concepts in Chapters 3 and 4 are also presented in the Taybeh segment. You may want to review the clip from Chapter 11, this time focusing on how companies are essentially changing the "place" in the marketing mix for Spiderman, Batman, and others.

To give you insight into Chapter 12, Small Business School will take you back to Karsten Manufacturing in Phoenix, Arizona, to see how this company manages its supply chain. Although you will see the same segment you viewed for Chapter 10, this time concentrate on issues like channel structure, channel relationships, and the logistical components of Karsten's supply chain.

FLIP IT

Flip to Chapter 12 in your *Grademaker Study Guide* for more review opportunities, including the pretest, vocabulary review, Internet activities, study test questions, and an application exercise based on marketing channel concepts. Can you close your book and diagram the various channel structures discussed in the book? Do you know the issues that marketers must consider when determining a channel strategy? If not, then pick up your *Grademaker* and review.

CLICK IT

The *Marketing* Web site links you to all the Internet-based activities in this chapter, like the "Use It," "Review It" questions 3.2, 8.1, 8.2, and 9.1, and the On-Line exercises in the chapter margins. As a review, do the Chapter 12 quiz and crossword puzzle. And don't forget the Career Exersite that gives you resources for exploring marketing career opportunities in supply chain management. Review the main concepts in the PowerPoint presentation for Chapter 12, too. Go to **http://lamb.swlearning.com**, read the material, and follow the links right from the site.

SPIN IT

Spin your Xtra! CD-ROM to test your understanding of the service marketing concepts in the chapter by completing the worksheets for Exhibits 12.1 through 12.7, 12.9, and 12.11. If your instructor has assigned a marketing plan project, worksheets on Xtra! can help you organize your work. In addition to the quiz on the Web site, there's another quiz on the Xtra! CD-ROM, plus video of the authors answering frequently asked questions about supply chain management topics, such as "What factors should be considered when deciding the best channels of distribution?" and "Why should management be concerned about supply chain management?"

Still Shaky? Here's a Tip.

In the margin next to each paragraph or section in the chapter, write the question that the section answers. For example, "What discrepancies do marketing channels aid in overcoming?" could go on page 376. Once you have questions throughout the chapter, you can quiz yourself by using a blank piece of paper to cover the content. To check yourself, reveal each paragraph after you have answered the corresponding question.

CHAPTER **THIRTEEN**

RETAILING

Learning Objectives

1 *Discuss the importance of retailing in the U.S. economy*

2 *Explain the dimensions by which retailers can be classified*

3 *Describe the major types of retail operations*

4 *Discuss nonstore retailing techniques*

5 *Define franchising and describe its two basic forms*

6 *List the major tasks involved in developing a retail marketing strategy*

7 *Discuss the challenges of expanding retailing operations into global markets*

8 *Describe future trends in retailing*

Target, it seems, is right on target. With sales of $29 billion annually and approximately a thousand stores in forty-six states, Target strives to be the best place to buy high-quality merchandise at low prices in surroundings that make shopping fun. With that goal in mind, Target has successfully branded itself as the fashionable place to buy discount.

Unlike its discount competitors, Target seeks an affluent, educated clientele. Therefore, the chain doesn't sell the cheapest products possible or use advertising gimmicks. Instead Target draws on its department store roots to offer customers quality, stylish merchandise at low prices. Eighty percent of the chain's apparel merchandise is private-label knockoffs of the more expensive brands found in traditional department stores like Marshall Field's or Nordstrom. In addition, the stores also carry exclusive branded products such as household accessories by Michael Graves and Todd Oldham and apparel for juniors by Mossimo. Target's merchandising strategy of offering upscale items is carried over in its new Super Target combination general merchandise and grocery stores, where customers can buy gourmet food items such as fresh sushi, Starbucks coffee, and Dean & Deluca cooking oils. Being so narrowly focused on the type of products its customers want has helped the chain to consistently meet customer expectations.

Another important part of Target's success has been the company's advertising and promotions campaign. The current campaign, which presents a "bull's eye world" on television and in fashion magazines, is more about fun and fashion than price. It also has made Target's logo a cultural icon. For instance, when Target was a sponsor of CBS's *Survivor* series, customers everywhere recognized the logo on the parachute that appeared in almost every episode. But most importantly the campaign's print and television ads make consumers want to shop at Target.

Target's management also applies consistency and discipline to store presentation. Target customers often cite cleanliness, attractive displays, and availability of merchandise as reasons they like to shop there. As one customer commented, "I'm just drawn to Target. Something about that place makes me want to spend money."

Finally, in spite of the discount nature of the stores, Target operates under the mentality that customers are guests. The staff treats customers courteously and will even drop what they are doing to help a customer locate an item. The same focus on customer service led Target to create both its popular Club Wedd bridal registry and The Lullaby Club baby registry.[1]

So what's next? How will Target continue to grow sales and open new stores in an increasingly tight market? What has made the chain stand out from its competitors? How does a retailer's target market determine its merchandise selection? What factors are involved in developing a store's atmosphere? This chapter seeks to answer these questions and many more by discussing retailers' important role in moving products and services to the ultimate consumer. We begin with a discussion of the role of retailing and the ways in which retail operations can be classified, followed by a description of the decisions involved in developing a retail marketing strategy.

On Line

Target Stores

How does Target use its Web site to reach the niche it seeks to occupy? Compare Target's site to those of Wal-Mart and Sears. Are the sites as differentiated as the stores?

http://www.target.com

http://www.walmart.com

http://www.sears.com

The Role of Retailing

1

Discuss the importance of retailing in the U.S. economy

retailing
All the activities directly related to the sale of goods and services to the ultimate consumer for personal, nonbusiness use.

Retailing—all the activities directly related to the sale of goods and services to the ultimate consumer for personal, nonbusiness use—has enhanced the quality of our daily lives. When we shop for groceries, hair styling, clothes, books, and many other products and services, we are involved in retailing. The millions of goods and services provided by retailers mirror the needs and styles of U.S. society.

Retailing affects all of us directly or indirectly. The retailing industry is one of the largest employers; over 1.6 million U.S. retailers employ more than twenty million people, or nearly one out of every five workers. At the store level, retailing is still considered a mom-and-pop business. Almost nine out of ten retail companies employ fewer than twenty employees and, according to the National Retail Federation, 95 percent of all retailers operate just one store.[2]

The U.S. economy is heavily dependent on retailing. Retailers ring up over $3.18 trillion in sales annually, almost a third of the gross domestic product (GDP).[3] Although most retailers are quite small, a few giant organizations dominate the industry, most notably Wal-Mart, whose annual U.S. sales alone account for about 5 percent of all retail sales. Who are these giants? Exhibit 13.1 lists the ten largest U.S. retailers.

Classification of Retail Operations

2

Explain the dimensions by which retailers can be classified

A retail establishment can be classified according to its ownership, level of service, product assortment, and price. Specifically, retailers use the latter three variables to position themselves in the competitive marketplace. (As noted in Chapter 7, positioning is the strategy used to influence how consumers perceive one product in relation to all competing products.) These three variables can be combined in several ways to create distinctly different retail operations. Exhibit 13.2 lists the major types of retail stores discussed in this chapter and classifies them by level of service, product assortment, price, and gross margin.

Ownership

independent retailers
Retailers owned by a single person or partnership and not operated as part of a larger retail institution.

chain stores
Stores owned and operated as a group by a single organization.

franchise
The right to operate a business or to sell a product.

Retailers can be broadly classified by form of ownership: independent, part of a chain, or franchise outlet. Retailers owned by a single person or partnership and not operated as part of a larger retail institution are **independent retailers**. Around the world, most retailers are independent, operating one or a few stores in their community. Local florists, shoe stores, and ethnic food markets typically fit this classification.

Chain stores are owned and operated as a group by a single organization. Under this form of ownership, many administrative tasks are handled by the home office for the entire chain. The home office also buys most of the merchandise sold in the stores.

Franchises are owned and operated by individuals but are licensed by a larger supporting organization. Franchising combines the advantages of independent ownership with those of the chain store organization. Franchising is discussed in more detail later in the chapter.

Level of Service

The level of service that retailers provide can be classified along a continuum, from full service to self-service. Some retailers, such as exclusive clothing stores, offer high levels of service. They provide alterations, credit, delivery, consulting, liberal return policies, layaway, gift wrapping, and personal shopping. Discount stores

Exhibit 13.1

Ten Largest U.S. Retailers

2000 Rank	Company	Retailing Formats	2001 Revenues (in billions)	2001 Number of Stores
1	**Wal-Mart** Bentonville, Arkansas	Discount stores, super-centers, and warehouse clubs	$219.8	4,414
2	**The Home Depot** Atlanta, Georgia	Home centers	$53.6	1,348
3	**Kroger** Cincinnati, Ohio	Supermarkets and convenience stores	$50.1	3,534
4	**Sears, Roebuck** Hoffman Estates, Illinois	Department stores, catalogs, home centers, and specialty	$41.1	2,960
5	**Target Corporation*** Minneapolis, Minnesota	Discount stores and department stores	$39.4	1,381
6	**Albertson's** Boise, Idaho	Supermarkets	$37.9	2,400
7	**Kmart**[†] Troy, Michigan	Discount stores and supercenters	$37.0	2,150
8	**Costco** Issaquah, Washington	Warehouse clubs	$34.8	369
9	**Safeway** Pleasanton, California	Supermarkets	$34.3	1,773
10	**JCPenney** Plano, Texas	Department stores, catalogs, and drugstores	$32.0	3,770

* Renamed Target Corporation in January 2000; formerly was Dayton Hudson Corporation.
[†] Kmart declared bankruptcy in 2002, so future figures will most likely drastically differ.
SOURCE: STORES, July 2002, **http://www.stores.org**. Sales figures include international sales.

usually offer fewer services. Retailers like factory outlets and warehouse clubs offer virtually no services.

Product Assortment

The third basis for positioning or classifying stores is by the breadth and depth of their product line. Specialty stores—for example, Hallmark card stores, Lady Foot Locker, and TCBY yogurt shops—have the most concentrated product assortments, usually carrying single or narrow product lines but in considerable depth. On the other end of the spectrum, full-line discounters typically carry broad assortments of merchandise with limited depth. For example, Target carries automotive supplies, household cleaning products, and pet food. However, Target may carry only four or five brands of canned dog food; a supermarket may carry as many as twenty.

Exhibit 13.2

Types of Stores and Their
Characteristics

Type of Retailer	Level of Service	Product Assortment	Price	Gross Margin
Department store	Moderately high to high	Broad	Moderate to high	Moderately high
Specialty store	High	Narrow	Moderate to high	High
Supermarket	Low	Broad	Moderate	Low
Convenience store	Low	Medium to narrow	Moderately high	Moderately high
Drugstore	Low to moderate	Medium	Moderate	Low
Full-line discount store	Moderate to low	Medium to broad	Moderately low	Moderately low
Discount specialty store	Moderate to low	Medium to broad	Moderately low to low	Moderately low
Warehouse clubs	Low	Broad	Low to very low	Low
Off-price retailer	Low	Medium to narrow	Low	Low
Restaurant	Low to high	Narrow	Low to high	Low to high

Other retailers, such as factory outlet stores, may carry only part of a single line. Liz Claiborne, a major manufacturer of women's clothing, sells only certain items of its own brand in its many outlet stores. Discount specialty stores like Home Depot or Toys "R" Us carry a broad assortment in concentrated product lines, such as building and home supplies or toys.

Price

Price is a fourth way to position retail stores. Traditional department stores and specialty stores typically charge the full "suggested retail price." In contrast, discounters, factory outlets, and off-price retailers use low prices as a major lure for shoppers.

gross margin
The amount of money the retailer makes as a percentage of sales after the cost of goods sold is subtracted.

The last column in Exhibit 13.2 shows the typical **gross margin**—how much the retailer makes as a percentage of sales after the cost of goods sold is subtracted. The level of gross margin and the price level generally match. For example, a traditional jewelry store has high prices and high gross margins. A factory outlet has low prices and low gross margins. Markdowns on merchandise during sale periods and price wars among competitors, in which stores lower prices on certain items in an effort to win customers, cause gross margins to decline. When Wal-Mart entered the grocery business in a small Arkansas community, a fierce price war ensued. By the time the price war was in full swing, the price of a quart of milk had plummeted by more than 50 percent (below the price of a pint) and a loaf of bread sold for only 9¢, prices at which no retailer could make a profit.

Major Types of Retail Operations

Traditionally, there have been several distinct types of retail stores, with each offering a different product assortment, type of service, and price level, according to its customers' shopping preferences.

In a recent trend, however, retailers are experimenting with alternative formats that make it harder to classify them. For instance, supermarkets are expanding their nonfood items and services, discounters are adding groceries, drugstores are becoming more like convenience stores, and department stores are experimenting with smaller stores.[4] Nevertheless, many stores still fall into the basic types.

Describe the major types of retail operations

Department Stores

Housing several departments under one roof, a **department store** carries a wide variety of shopping and specialty goods, including apparel, cosmetics, housewares, electronics, and sometimes furniture. Purchases are generally made within each department rather than at one central checkout area. Each department is treated as a separate buying center to achieve economies in promotion, buying, service, and control. Each department is usually headed by a **buyer**, a department head who not only selects the merchandise for his or her department but may also be responsible for promotion and for personnel. For a consistent, uniform store image, central management sets broad policies about the types of merchandise carried and price ranges. Central management is also responsible for the overall advertising program, credit policies, store expansion, customer service, and so on.

Large independent department stores are rare today. Most are owned by national chains. Among the largest U.S. department store chains are Sears, Target Corporation, JCPenney, Federated Department Stores, and May Department Stores. All operate more than one chain of retail stores, from discount chains to upscale clothiers. Two newer department store chains are Dillard's, based in Little Rock, Arkansas, and Nordstrom, with corporate headquarters in Seattle. Dillard's is known for its distribution expertise; Nordstrom offers innovative customer service. Both of these growing chains have a very promising future.

In recent years, consumers have become more cost conscious and value oriented. Specialty retailers like The Gap, discounters, catalog outlets, and even on-line Internet shopping alternatives are offering superior merchandise selection and presentation, sharper pricing, and greater convenience to take sales away from department stores. They have also been quicker to adopt new technology and invest in labor-saving strategies. In addition, their leaner cost structure translates into lower prices for the customer. Meanwhile, manufacturers like Liz Claiborne, Bass, Calvin Klein, and Polo/Ralph Lauren have opened outlet stores of their own and more discount stores such as Wal-Mart and Target have upgraded their apparel assortments, taking more sales away from department stores.

department store
A store housing several departments under one roof.

buyer
A department head who selects the merchandise for his or her department and may also be responsible for promotion and personnel.

Recent trends in retailing are making it increasingly difficult to classify retailers, as stores are crossing into each other's domains. This woman is purchasing computer software in her grocery store.

© ALAN LEVENSON/GETTY IMAGES/STONE

Department store managers are using several strategies to preserve their market share. One is to reposition department stores as specialty outlets. They are dividing departments into miniboutiques, each featuring a distinct fashion taste, as specialty stores do. For example, many upscale department stores feature Donna Karan and Liz Claiborne boutiques within their stores. Department stores are also enhancing customer service to shift the focus away from price. Services include complimentary alterations, longer store hours, personalized attention, after-sale follow-up, and personal wardrobe planning. And a few department store chains like Bloomingdale's and Macy's are also experimenting with smaller, alternative formats.[5] Finally, department stores are expanding, remodeling, and revitalizing to show off new merchandising directions and to reflect the growth in their marketing areas.

Specialty Stores

specialty store
A retail store specializing in a given type of merchandise.

Specialty store formats allow retailers to refine their segmentation strategies and tailor their merchandise to specific target markets. A **specialty store** is not only a type of store but also a method of retail operations—namely, specializing in a given type of merchandise. Examples include children's clothing, men's clothing, candy, baked goods, gourmet coffee, sporting goods, and pet supplies. A typical specialty store carries a deeper but narrower assortment of specialty merchandise than does a department store. Generally, specialty stores' knowledgeable sales clerks offer more attentive customer service. The format has become very powerful in the apparel market and other areas. In fact, according to recent studies, consumers buy more clothing from specialty stores than from any other type of retailer.[6] The Disney Store, Gadzooks, Williams-Sonoma, Foot Locker, and Tower Records are examples of successful chain specialty retailers.

Consumers usually consider price to be secondary in specialty outlets. Instead, the distinctive merchandise, the store's physical appearance, and the caliber of the staff determine its popularity. For example, Chico's, a national retail chain, has grown quickly by offering quality, private-label clothing for baby boomer women. The moderately priced clothing is styled to be loose, colorful, and low maintenance. Salesclerks focus on salesmanship, helping customers put together outfits and offering advice on which styles look best.[7] Because of their attention to the customer and limited product line, manufacturers often favor introducing new products in small specialty stores before moving on to larger retail and department stores.

Small specialty stores also provide a low-risk testing ground for many new products. Nike, for instance, often uses athletic footwear retailer Foot Locker as its venue for new shoe introductions. As an example, Nike introduced its $130 Tuned Air running shoe exclusively at Foot Locker shoe outlets. While the arrangement protected Foot Locker from price competition from other retailers, allowing it to charge full retail price, it also created an image of exclusivity for Nike.[8]

MARK RICHARDS/PHOTOEDIT

Sephora is a specialty cosmetics store that supplements its boutique format with in-store kiosks where customers can consult the company's Web site for items not in the store.

supermarket
A large, departmentalized, self-service retailer that specializes in food and some nonfood items.

Supermarkets

U.S. consumers spend about a tenth of their disposable income in **supermarkets**—large, departmentalized, self-service retailers that specialize in food and some nonfood items.

A decade ago, industry experts predicted the decline of the supermarket industry, whose slim profit margins of just 1 to 2 percent of sales left it vulnerable. These experts originally felt that supermarkets would merely need an ever-growing customer base to sustain volume and compensate for low margins. Although the population continued to grow, albeit at less than 1 percent a year on average, supermarkets still experienced declining sales. As a result, experts were forced to examine not only population trends but also demographic and lifestyle changes of consumers. They discovered several trends affecting the supermarket industry.

For example, as dual-income and single-parent families increase, consumers are eating out more or are too busy to prepare meals at home. According to the U.S. Department of Agriculture, Americans spent only about two-thirds of their food money in retail grocery stores, compared with a third spent for food away from home. In comparison, Americans spent over three-fourths of their food money in grocery stores in 1950.[9] The growth in the away-from-home food market has been driven by the entry of more women into the workforce and their need for convenience and time-saving products. Working couples need one-stop shopping, and the increasing number of affluent customers are willing to pay for specialty and prepared foods.

As stores seek to meet consumer demand for one-stop shopping, conventional supermarkets are being replaced by bigger *superstores*, which are usually twice the size of supermarkets. Superstores meet the needs of today's customers for convenience, variety, and service. Superstores offer one-stop shopping for many food and nonfood needs, as well as many services—including pharmacies, flower shops, salad bars, in-store bakeries, takeout food sections, sit-down restaurants, health food sections, video rentals, dry-cleaning services, shoe repair, photo processing, and banking. Some even offer family dentistry or optical shops. This tendency to offer a wide variety of nontraditional goods and services under one roof is called **scrambled merchandising**. Canada's largest supermarket chain Loblaw exemplifies this trend: Along with dry cleaning, a liquor store, a coffee shop, a pharmacy, and a banking center, it also offers video-game and cellphone sales outlets and leases space to a clothing chain and a fitness club complete with a sauna, tanning beds, and day-care center. Loblaw's ancillary services aim to attract today's time-strapped customers by providing one-stop shopping.[10]

A recent trend in supermarket diversification is the addition of store-owned gas stations. The gas stations are not only a new revenue source for the supermarkets and a convenience for customers, but they also attract customers to the location by offering lower prices than can usually be found at a traditional gas station. Experts expect the trend will continue and that by the year 2005 supermarkets will account for 15 percent of overall gasoline sales.[11]

Another demographic trend affecting supermarkets is expanding ethnicity. Over the next fifty years, nonwhite ethnic groups will constitute the fastest-growing segments of the American population. According to the U.S. Census Bureau, the most pronounced population growth will be seen among Hispanics, Asian Americans, and African Americans. If current trends in shopping patterns among ethnic groups continue, these demographic changes promise to have a vast impact on supermarket retailers. For example, both African American and Hispanic households now outspend white American households on weekly grocery shopping. In terms of shopping habits, African Americans and Hispanics tend to be conservative, looking for products and brands they know and trust and patronizing stores that reliably meet their needs. It will also be increasingly important for supermarkets to tailor their stores' product mix to reflect the demographics of the population they serve.[12]

Many supermarket chains are tailoring marketing strategies to appeal to specific consumer segments to help them stand out in an increasingly competitive marketplace. Most notable is the shift toward *loyalty marketing programs* that reward loyal customers carrying frequent shopper cards with discounts or gifts. Once scanned at the checkout, frequent shopper cards help supermarket retailers electronically track shopper's buying habits. Sixty percent of customers who shop at the 110 stores operated by South Carolina–based Piggly Wiggly, for instance, carry the Pig's Favorite loyalty card. Customers use their card each time they shop to get special discounts on items. Piggly Wiggly also uses consumer purchase data stored in its database to determine customer preferences. If management sees that a customer buys flowers regularly, then it sends that customer a coupon redeemable in its floral department.[13]

scrambled merchandising
The tendency to offer a wide variety of nontraditional goods and services under one roof.

drugstore
A retail store that stocks pharmacy-related products and services as its main draw.

convenience store
A miniature supermarket, carrying only a limited line of high-turnover convenience goods.

discount store
A retailer that competes on the basis of low prices, high turnover, and high volume.

full-line discount stores
A retailer that offers consumers very limited service and carries a broad assortment of well-known, nationally branded "hard goods."

Drugstores

Drugstores stock pharmacy-related products and services as their main draw. Consumers are most often attracted to a drugstore by its pharmacy or pharmacist, its convenience, or because it honors their third-party prescription drug plan. Drugstores also carry an extensive selection of over-the-counter (OTC) medications, cosmetics, health and beauty aids, seasonal merchandise, specialty items such as greeting cards and a limited selection of toys, and some nonrefrigerated convenience foods. As competition has increased from mass merchandisers and supermarkets with their own pharmacies, as well as from direct-mail prescription services, drugstores have been adding value-added services such as twenty-four-hour operations and drive-through pharmacies.

Demographic trends in the United States look favorable for the drugstore industry. As the baby boom population continues to age, they will spend an increasing percentage of their disposable income on health care and wellness. This is good news for the drugstore industry, as the average sixty-year-old purchases fifteen prescriptions per year, nearly twice as many as the average thirty-year-old. Because baby boomers are attentive to their health and keenly sensitive about their looks, the increased traffic at the pharmacy counter in the future should also spur sales in other traditionally strong drugstore merchandise categories, most notably over-the-counter drugs, vitamins, and health and beauty aids.[14]

Convenience Stores

A **convenience store** can be defined as a miniature supermarket, carrying only a limited line of high-turnover convenience goods. These self-service stores are typically located near residential areas and are open twenty-four hours, seven days a week. Convenience stores offer exactly what their name implies: convenient location, long hours, fast service. However, prices are almost always higher at a convenience store than at a supermarket. Thus, the customer pays for the convenience.

From the mid-1970s to the mid-1980s, hundreds of new convenience stores opened, many with self-service gas pumps. Full-service gas stations fought back by closing service bays and opening miniature stores of their own, selling convenience items like cigarettes, sodas, and snacks. Supermarkets and discount stores also wooed customers with one-stop shopping and quick checkout. To combat the gas stations' and supermarkets' competition, convenience store operators have changed their strategy. They have expanded their offerings of nonfood items with video rentals, health and beauty aids, upscale sandwich and salad lines, and more fresh produce. Some convenience stores are even selling Pizza Hut and Taco Bell products prepared in the store.

Discount Stores

A **discount store** is a retailer that competes on the basis of low prices, high turnover, and high volume. Discounters can be classified into four major categories: full-line discount stores, discount specialty stores, warehouse clubs, and off-price discount retailers.

Full-Line Discount Stores

Compared to traditional department stores, **full-line discount stores** offer consumers very limited service and carry a much broader assortment of well-known, nationally branded "hard goods," including housewares, toys, automotive parts, hardware, sporting goods, and garden items, as well as clothing, bedding, and linens. Some even carry limited nonperishable food items, such as soft drinks, canned goods, and potato chips. As with department stores, national chains dominate the discounters. Full-line discounters are often called mass merchandisers. **Mass merchandising** is the retailing strategy whereby retailers use moderate to low prices on large quantities of merchandise and lower service to stimulate high turnover of products.

  Wal-Mart is the largest full-line discount organization in terms of sales. With over four thousand stores, Wal-Mart has expanded rapidly by locating on the outskirts of small towns and absorbing business for miles around. Much of Wal-Mart's success has been attributed to its merchandising foresight, cost consciousness, efficient communication and distribution systems, and involved, motivated employees. Wal-Mart is credited with pioneering the retail strategy of "everyday low pricing," a strategy now widely copied by retailers the world over. Besides expanding throughout all fifty states and Puerto Rico, Wal-Mart has expanded globally into Mexico, Canada, Brazil, Argentina, China, Germany, Korea, and, the United Kingdom.[15] Wal-Mart has also become a formidable retailing giant in on-line shopping, concentrating on toys and electronics. With tie-ins to its stores across the country, Wal-Mart is expected to introduce millions of customers to on-line shopping with in-store kiosks linking to the site and the ability to handle returns and exchanges from Internet sales at its physical stores.[16]

A hybrid of the full-line discounter is the hypermarket, a concept adapted from the Europeans. The flashy **hypermarket** format combines a supermarket and full-line discount store in a space ranging from 200,000 to 300,000 square feet. Although they have enjoyed widespread success in Europe, where consumers have fewer retailing choices, hypermarkets have been much less successful in the United States. Most Europeans still need to visit several small stores just for their food needs, which makes hypermarkets a good alternative. Americans, on the other hand, can easily pick among a host of stores that offer large selections of merchandise. According to retailing executives and analysts, American customers have found hypermarkets to be too big. Both Wal-Mart's Hypermart USA and Kmart's American Fare hypermarket formats never got beyond the experimental stage.

Similar to a hypermarket, but only half the size, is the **supercenter**, which combines groceries and general merchandise goods with a wide range of services including pharmacy, dry cleaning, portrait studios, photo finishing, hair salons, optical shops, and restaurants—all in one location. For supercenter operators like Wal-Mart, food is a customer magnet that sharply increases the store's overall volume, while taking customers away from traditional supermarkets. Wal-Mart now operates over 900 supercenters and plans to keep opening them at a rate of more than 150 a year for the near future. Although Target has been the last major discounter to embrace the supercenter concept, it recently doubled the number of Super Target stores and is investing in the development of private-label grocery products.[17]

 Supercenters are also threatening to push Europe's traditional small and medium-sized food stores into extinction. Old-fashioned corner stores and family businesses are giving way to larger chains that offer food, drugs, services, and general merchandise all in one place. Many European countries are passing legislation to make it more difficult for supercenters to open. In France, for example, laws were passed that banned authorizations for new supercenters over 1,000 square meters (10,800 square feet). Belgium and Portugal have passed similar bans. In Britain and the Netherlands, areas outside towns and cities are off limits to superstores. By imposing planning and building restrictions for large stores, these countries are trying to accommodate environmental concerns, movements to revive city centers, and the worries of small shopkeepers.

An increasingly popular variation of off-price retailing at full-line discount stores is *extreme-value retailing*, the most notable examples being Dollar General and Family Dollar. Extreme-value retailers have grown in popularity as major discounters continue to shift toward the supercenter format, broadening their customer base and increasing their offerings of higher priced goods aimed at higher income consumers. This has created an opening for extreme-value retailers to entice shoppers from the low-income segment. Low- and fixed-income customers are drawn to

mass merchandising
A retailing strategy using moderate to low prices on large quantities of merchandise and lower service to stimulate high turnover of products.

hypermarket
A retail store that combines a supermarket and full-line discount store in a space ranging from 200,000 to 300,000 square feet.

supercenter
A retail store that combines groceries and general merchandise goods with a wide range of services.

extreme-value retailers, whose stores are located within their communities. Extreme-value retailers also build smaller stores (a typical store is about the size of one department in a Wal-Mart superstore) with a narrower selection of merchandise emphasizing day-to-day necessities. Rock-bottom prices are also key to their success. With the average transaction under $10, extreme-value retailers have found low price to be far more critical to building traffic and loyalty than any other retailing format.[18]

Specialty Discount Stores

Another discount niche includes the single-line **specialty discount stores**—for example, stores selling sporting goods, electronics, auto parts, office supplies, and toys. These stores offer a nearly complete selection of single-line merchandise and use self-service, discount prices, high volume, and high turnover to their advantage. Specialty discount stores are often termed **category killers** because they so heavily dominate their narrow merchandise segment. Examples include Toys "R" Us in toys, Circuit City and Best Buy in electronics, Staples and Office Depot in office supplies, Home Depot in home improvement supplies, IKEA in home furnishings, and Bed, Bath & Beyond in kitchen and bath accessories.

  Toys "R" Us was the first category killer, offering a giant selection of toys, usually over fifteen thousand different items per store, at prices usually 10 to 15 percent less than competitors'. When Toys "R" Us came on the retail scene, department stores were generally limiting their toy assortments to the Christmas season. Toys "R" Us offered a broad assortment of inventory all year long. Additionally, the playing field was scattered with many small toy chains or mom-and-pop stores. With its bright warehouse-style stores, Toys "R" Us gobbled up market share, and many small toy stores failed and department stores eliminated their toy departments. The Toys "R" Us chain—currently an $11.3 billion company with more than 1,500 stores worldwide—now commands about a quarter of the U.S. retail toy business. Toys "R" Us first went international in 1984 with stores in Canada and Singapore. Since then, the company has opened over 492 stores in more than two dozen foreign countries, the most recent being Japan. Toys "R" Us has also expanded its category-killer retailing concept to include over 200 Kids "R" Us children's clothing stores and 148 Babies "R" Us product stores. In addition, the company's Web site garnered more than $180 million in sales last year thanks in part to an alliance with Amazon.com. The company plans to build on its momentum by also enhancing its Web sites for Babies "R" Us and Imaginarium.com.[19]

Other specialty segments have followed the lead of Toys "R" Us, hoping to build similar retailing empires in highly fragmented mom-and-pop markets. For instance, the home improvement industry was once dominated by professional builders and small hardware stores that offered basic staple products. Similarly, prior to the creation of Petsmart and Petco pet supplies chains, the pet industry was dominated by thousands of independent neighborhood pet stores. Another industry that was very fragmented was the office products industry. As more people began to work from home, replacing their typewriters with personal computers and purchasing fax machines, the local stationery store, with its limited selection of paper and writing materials, quickly became obsolete. The industry is now dominated by Office Depot, Staples, and OfficeMax, each stocking some five to seven thousand different types of products. Category-dominant retailers like these serve their customers by offering a large selection of merchandise, stores that make shopping easy, and low prices every day, which eliminates the need for time-consuming comparison shopping.

Warehouse Membership Clubs

Warehouse membership clubs sell a limited selection of brand-name appliances, household items, and groceries. These are usually sold in bulk from warehouse outlets on a cash-and-carry basis to members only. Individual members of warehouse clubs are charged low or no membership fees. Currently, the leading stores in this category are Wal-Mart's Sam's Club, Costco, and BJ's Wholesale Club.

Warehouse clubs have had a major impact on supermarkets. With 90,000 square feet or more, warehouse clubs offer 60 to 70 percent general merchandise and health- and beauty-care products, with grocery-related items making up the difference. Warehouse club members tend to be more educated and more affluent and have a larger household than regular supermarket shoppers. These core customers use warehouse clubs to stock up on staples; then they go to specialty outlets or food stores for perishables.

Fierce competition is commonplace in the warehouse club industry. Common practices include price slashing, selling below cost, locating outlets to compete directly with each other, and sometimes hiring away rivals' employees to get an edge in local markets. In one recent battle, Sam's Club has been targeting Costco's more affluent clientele. Costco, with annual revenues more than twice those of Sam's Club, dedicates approximately 25 percent of its inventory to high-end products like TaylorMade golf clubs and Coach handbags to attract wealthier customers who tend to spend more per visit. In an effort to beat Costco at its own game, Sam's Club has not only expanded its selection of fresh food, wine, and branded products, but has also begun holding promotional diamond and fine jewelry sales to draw customers.[20]

Off-Price Retailers

An **off-price retailer** sells at prices 25 percent or more below traditional department store prices because it pays cash for its stock and usually doesn't ask for return privileges. Off-price retailers buy manufacturers' overruns at cost or even less. They also absorb goods from bankrupt stores, irregular merchandise, and unsold end-of-season output. Nevertheless, much off-price retailer merchandise is first-quality, current goods. Because buyers for off-price retailers purchase only what is available or what they can get a good deal on, merchandise styles and brands often change monthly. Today there are hundreds of off-price retailers, the best known being T. J. Maxx, Ross Stores, Marshall's, HomeGoods, and Tuesday Morning.

Factory outlets are an interesting variation on the off-price concept. A **factory outlet** is an off-price retailer that is owned and operated by a manufacturer. Thus, it carries one line of merchandise—its own. Each season, from 5 to 10 percent of a manufacturer's output does not sell through regular distribution channels because it consists of closeouts (merchandise being discontinued), factory seconds, and canceled orders. With factory outlets, manufacturers can regulate where their surplus is sold, and they can realize higher profit margins than they would by disposing of the goods through independent wholesalers and retailers. Factory outlet malls typically locate in out-of-the-way rural areas or near vacation destinations. Most are situated at least thirty miles from urban or suburban shopping areas so that manufacturers don't alienate their department store accounts by selling the same goods virtually next door at a discount.

Several manufacturers reaping the benefits of outlet mall popularity include Liz Claiborne, J. Crew, and Calvin Klein clothiers; West Point Pepperel textiles; Oneida silversmiths; and Dansk kitchenwares. Top-drawer department stores—including Saks Fifth Avenue and Neiman Marcus—have also opened outlet stores to sell hard-to-move merchandise. Dillard Department Stores has opened a series of clearance centers to make final attempts to move merchandise that failed to sell in the department store. To move their clearance items, Nordstrom's operates Nordstrom Rack and Boston's Filene's has Filene's Basement.

As outlet malls have gained in popularity, however, they are beginning to act less and less like traditional outlets in which manufacturers sold surplus or damaged goods. For instance, some manufacturers such as The Gap, Brooks Brothers, Ann Taylor, and Donna Karan now make lower-quality lines specifically for their outlet stores. Outlet store centers are also becoming less sensitive toward department stores that carry their brands at full retail price and are choosing to compete

off-price retailer
A retailer that sells at prices 25 percent or more below traditional department store prices because it pays cash for its stock and usually doesn't ask for return privileges.

factory outlet
An off-price retailer that is owned and operated by a manufacturer.

with regional malls by adding high-end amenities and entertainment to draw customers. For instance, Silver Sands Factory Stores in Destin, Florida, offers shoppers a two-level, 30,000-square-foot family entertainment center with activities for both children and adults. Similarly, Carlsbad Company Stores' outlet center in Carlsbad, California, features a sculpture garden, state-of-the-art fountain, and bright airy rest rooms designed for easy use by shoppers with bags and families with small children.[21]

Restaurants

Restaurants straddle the line between retailing establishments and service establishments. Restaurants do sell tangible products, food and drink, but they also provide a valuable service for consumers in the form of food preparation and food service. Most restaurants could even fall into the definition of a specialty retailer given that most concentrate their menu offerings on a distinctive type of cuisine—for example, Olive Garden Italian restaurants, Starbucks coffeehouses, Popeye's Fried Chicken, and Pizza Hut pizza restaurants.

As a retailing institution, restaurants must deal with many of the same issues as a more traditional retailer, such as personnel, distribution, inventory management, promotion, pricing, and location. Restaurants and food-service retailers run the spectrum from those offering limited service and inexpensive food, such as fast-food chains or the local snack bar or coffeehouse, to those that offer sit-down service and moderate to high prices, such as the likes of the Outback Steakhouse & Saloon chain or a local trendy Italian bistro.

Eating out is an important part of Americans' daily activities and is growing in strength. According to the National Restaurant Association, more than 54 billion meals are eaten in restaurants or cafeterias annually. This means that Americans consume an average of 4.2 commercially prepared meals per week. Food away from home accounts for about 25 percent of the household food budget for lower income families and as much as 50 percent for those with higher incomes. The trend toward eating out has been fueled by the increase in working mothers and dual-income families who have more money to eat out and less time to prepare meals at home. Money spent on food away from home is expected to grow from 46 percent of household food budgets in 2002 to 53 percent by 2010.[22]

The restaurant industry is one of the most entrepreneurial of businesses and one of the most competitive. Because barriers to entering the restaurant industry are low, the opportunity appeals to many people. The risks, however, are great. About 50 percent of all new restaurants fail within the first year of operation. Restaurants face competition not only from other restaurants but also from the consumer who can easily choose to cook at home. Competition has fostered innovation in the restaurant industry, such as Pizza Hut's introduction of The Edge pizza, to the ever-changing menus at fast-food restaurants. Seeking out and targeting underserved distribution niches is another way restaurants are competing with one another to reach consumers. Fast-food operators are increasingly looking to provide service at locations such as hospitals, airports, schools, and highway rest stops. Companies like Subway, Dunkin' Donuts, and Church's Fried Chicken also are partnering with branded service stations to offer customers one-stop shopping. These partnerships save money on leases, lure more customers, and foster innovation.

More restaurants are now competing directly with supermarkets by offering takeout and delivery in an effort to capture more of the home meal replacement market. Eatzi's Market & Bakery, for instance, is a cross between a gourmet grocery store and an upscale delicatessen where chefs behind counters cook, bake, and prepare meals. Eatzi's now has markets in Dallas, Houston, Atlanta, and Rockville, Maryland, where its chefs create over 100 ready-to-go entrees, 75 cheeses, 50 breads, and 125 desserts, and even fresh sushi. Consumers can even purchase wine, flowers, and cigars to complement their prepared meal.[23]

Nonstore Retailing

The retailing methods discussed so far have been at the origin in-store methods, in which customers must physically shop at stores. In contrast, **nonstore retailing** is shopping without visiting a store. Because consumers demand convenience, non-store retailing is currently growing faster than in-store retailing. The major forms of nonstore retailing are automatic vending, direct retailing, direct marketing, and electronic retailing.

nonstore retailing
Shopping without visiting a store.

Automatic Vending

A low-profile yet important form of retailing is **automatic vending**, the use of machines to offer goods for sale—for example, the cola, candy, or snack vending machines found in college cafeterias and office buildings. Vending is the most pervasive retail business in the United States, with about six million vending machines selling $30 billion annually. Food and beverages account for about 85 percent of all sales from vending machines. Due to the convenience, consumers are willing to pay higher prices for products from a vending machine than for the same products in traditional retail settings.[24]

automatic vending
The use of machines to offer goods for sale.

Retailers are constantly seeking new opportunities to sell via vending. For example, United Artists Theaters offer moviegoers the option of purchasing hot popcorn, Tombstone pizza, Kraft macaroni-and-cheese, and chicken fingers from a vending machine instead of waiting in line at the concession stand.[25] Many vending machines today also sell nontraditional kinds of merchandise, such as videos, toys, stickers, and sports cards. Vending machines in college libraries sell computer diskettes, pens and highlighters, and other office-type supplies. Tourists can purchase film and disposable cameras from vending machines in many popular destinations. And Joe Boxer underwear can be purchased with a credit card from vending machines in selected department stores.

Automatic vending is being used to sell everything from hot french fries to prescription medication. In Australia, you can even order a Coke from a vending machine using your mobile phone.

Of course, vending machines are also an important tool in the ongoing cola wars between Coca-Cola and Pepsi. Both companies are constantly looking for new ways to improve vending machine sales. For example, Pepsi recently introduced new vending machines that allow customers to pay with a credit card for a soft drink. Coca-Cola is working on a new vending machine for workplaces. By using radio frequency identification to bill customers directly for their purchases, the machines would eventually allow Coca-Cola to offer loyalty awards to its vending machine customers.[26]

Direct Retailing

In **direct retailing**, representatives sell products door-to-door, office-to-office, or at home sales parties. Companies like Avon, Mary Kay Cosmetics, The Pampered Chef, Usbourne Books, and World Book Encyclopedia depend on these techniques. Even personal computers are now being sold through direct retailing methods. Hand Technologies, based in Austin, Texas, sells computers using a team of consultants to sell computer products via demonstrations in the home and local

direct retailing
The selling of products by representatives who work door-to-door, office-to-office, or at home parties.

seminars for schools and families. The company targets new users of technology who need more support when they purchase, set up, and learn about computers and the Internet. The company now has over one thousand part-time consultants to sell personal computers directly to the customer.[27]

Most direct retailers seem to favor party plans these days in lieu of door-to-door canvassing. Party plans call for one person, the host, to gather as many prospective buyers as possible. The parties are generally part social gathering, part shopping, and part entertainment. For instance, at a Pampered Chef kitchen show, the party starts with a cooking demonstration that is designed to showcase many of the products offered for sale. Following the demonstration, the guests are treated to food and refreshments while they visit with one another and make their purchases.[28] Similarly, when young mothers shop for their children at house parties held by Orient Express, the chance to meet and talk with other young mothers is as much a part of the agenda as the purchases.

The sales of direct retailers have suffered as women have entered the workforce. Working women are not home during the day and have little time to attend selling parties. Although most direct sellers like Avon and Tupperware still advocate the party plan method, the realities of the marketplace have forced them to be more creative in reaching their target customer. Direct sales representatives now hold parties in offices, parks, and even parking lots. Others hold informal gatherings where shoppers can drop in at their convenience or offer self-improvement classes. Many direct retailers are also turning to direct mail, telephone, or more traditional retailing venues to find new avenues to their customers and increase sales. Avon, for instance, has begun opening cosmetic kiosk counters, called Avon Beauty Centers, in malls and strip centers. Direct retailers are also experimenting with the Internet to reach more buyers and increase sales. Amway recently launched an entirely new on-line spin-off, called Quixtar.com. Customers access the site using referral numbers unique to each of the Amway reps, which ensures that the reps earn commissions. Avon, Tupperware, and Mary Kay have followed Amway's lead by setting up Internet retail sites. At Avon's site, individual reps have created home pages that link from Avon's home page so that the sale will still go through them.[29]

In response to the decline in U.S. sales, many direct retailers are exploring opportunities in other countries. For example, Mary Kay, Avon, and Amway have started successful operations in China by adapting their business models to China's laws. Mary Kay agents in China do not purchase and resell the products but are paid a sales commission instead. The company also changed its slogan from "God First, Family Second, Career Third," to "Faith First, Family Second, Career Third."[30]

Direct Marketing

direct marketing (direct-response marketing)
Techniques used to get consumers to make a purchase from their home, office, or other nonretail setting.

Direct marketing, sometimes called **direct-response marketing**, refers to the techniques used to get consumers to make a purchase from their home, office, or other nonretail setting. Those techniques include direct mail, catalogs and mail order, telemarketing, and electronic retailing. Shoppers using these methods are less bound by traditional shopping situations. Time-strapped consumers and those who live in rural or suburban areas are most likely to be direct-response shoppers because they value the convenience and flexibility that direct marketing provides.

Direct Mail

Direct mail can be the most efficient or the least efficient retailing method, depending on the quality of the mailing list and the effectiveness of the mailing piece. According to the Direct Marketing Association, direct mail generated $580 billion in revenue in 2001. With direct mail, marketers can precisely target their customers according to demographics, geographics, and even psychographics. Good mailing lists come from an internal database or are available from list brokers for about $35 to $150 per thousand names. For example, a Los Angeles computer software manufacturer selling programs for managing medical records may buy a list of all the physicians in the area. The software manufacturer may then design a direct-mail piece explaining the benefits of its system and send the piece to each physician. Today, direct mailers are even using videocassettes in place of letters and brochures to deliver their sales message to consumers.

Direct mailers are becoming more sophisticated in targeting the "right" customers. Using statistical methods to analyze census data, lifestyle and financial information, and past-purchase and credit history, direct mailers can pick out those most likely to buy their products. For example, a direct marketer like Dell Computer might use this technique to target 500,000 people with the right spending patterns, demographics, and preferences. Without it, Dell could easily mail millions of solicitations annually. Some solicitations may be targeted to only ten thousand of the best prospects, saving the company millions in postage while still preserving sales.

Catalogs and Mail Order

Consumers can now buy just about anything through the mail, from the mundane like books, music, and polo shirts to the outlandish, such as the $5 million diamond-and-ruby-studded bra available through the Victoria's Secret catalog. Although women make up the bulk of catalog shoppers, the percentage of male catalog shoppers has recently soared. As changing demographics have shifted more of the shopping responsibility to men, they are viewing shopping via catalog, mail order, and the Internet as more sensible than a trip to the mall.

Successful catalogs are usually created and designed for highly segmented markets. Sears, whose catalog sales had dropped off, replaced its "big book" with a collection of more successful specialty catalogs targeted to specific market segments. Certain types of retailers are also using mail order to good effect. For example, computer manufacturers have discovered that mail order is a lucrative way to sell computers to home and small-business users, evidenced by the huge successes of Dell Computer and Gateway. Dell has used its direct business model to become a $31.8 billion company that is ranked number one in global market share.[31] Dell began shifting its sales to the Internet in the late 1990s and now sells over $50 million worth of computers and computer equipment on-line every day.

Improved customer service and quick delivery policies have boosted consumer confidence in mail order. L.L. Bean and Lands' End are two catalog companies known for their excellent customer service. Shoppers may order twenty-four hours a day and return any merchandise for any reason for a full refund. Other successful mail-order catalogs—including Spiegel, Talbots, Frontgate, and Lillian Vernon—target hardworking, home-oriented baby boomers who don't have time to visit or would rather not visit a retail store. To remain competitive and save time for customers, catalog companies are building computer databases containing customer information so they do not have to repeatedly give their addresses, credit card information, and so on. They also are working with overnight shippers such as UPS and FedEx to speed up deliveries. Indeed, some products can be ordered as late at 12:30 A.M. and still arrive the same day by 10:30 A.M.

Telemarketing

Telemarketing is the use of the telephone to sell directly to consumers. It consists of outbound sales calls, usually unsolicited, and inbound calls—that is, orders through toll-free 800 numbers or fee-based 900 numbers.

Outbound telemarketing is an attractive direct-marketing technique because of rising postage rates and decreasing long-distance phone rates. Skyrocketing field

telemarketing
The use of the telephone to sell directly to consumers.

sales costs have also put pressure on marketing managers to use outbound tele-marketing. Searching for ways to keep costs under control, marketing managers are discovering how to pinpoint prospects quickly, zero in on serious buyers, and keep in close touch with regular customers. Meanwhile, they are reserving expensive, time-consuming, in-person calls for closing sales. The large number of outbound telemarketing calls, however, has led many states to pass laws establishing "do not call" lists of consumers who do not want to receive unsolicited phone calls. Although those in the industry insist that these lists help them by eliminating non-buyers, this trend could have a long-term effect on telemarketing sales.

Inbound telemarketing programs, which use 800 and 900 numbers, are mainly used to take orders, generate leads, and provide customer service. Inbound 800 telemarketing has successfully supplemented direct-response TV, radio, and print advertising for more than twenty-five years. The more recently introduced 900 numbers, which customers pay to call, are gaining popularity as a cost-effective way for companies to target customers. One of the major benefits of 900 numbers is that they allow marketers to generate qualified responses. Although the charge may reduce the total volume of calls, the calls that do come are from customers who have a true interest in the product.

Electronic Retailing

Electronic retailing includes the twenty-four-hour, shop-at-home television networks and on-line retailing.

Shop-at-Home Networks

The shop-at-home television networks are specialized forms of direct-response marketing. These shows display merchandise, with the retail price, to home viewers. Viewers can phone in their orders directly on a toll-free line and shop with a credit card. The shop-at-home industry has quickly grown into a billion-dollar business with a loyal customer following. Shop-at-home networks have the capability of reaching nearly every home that has a television set.

The best-known shop-at-home networks are the Home Shopping Network and the QVC (Quality, Value, Convenience) Network. Home shopping networks attract a broad audience through diverse programming and product offerings and are now adding new products to appeal to more affluent audiences. For instance, on QVC, cooking programs attract both men and women, fashion programs attract mostly women, and the NFL Team Shop attracts primarily men. Since it began broadcasting, the channel has sold everything from Sony electronics to Bugs Bunny to Gucci. In 2000, the company shipped more than 79 million packages worldwide and had a customer file of approximately 20 million people in four countries accounting for its $3.5 billion in sales.[32]

On-line Retailing

For years, shopping at home meant looking through catalogs and then placing an order over the telephone. For many people today, however, it now means turning on a computer, surfing retail Web sites, and selecting and ordering products on-line with the click of a mouse. **On-line retailing**, or *e-tailing*, is a type of shopping available to consumers with personal computers and access to the Internet. According to Nielsen Reports, 60 percent of Americans had Internet access either at home or in the workplace in 2001.[33]

On-line retailing has exploded in the last several years as consumers have found this type of shopping convenient and, in many instances, less costly. Consumers can shop without leaving home, choose from a wide selection of merchants, use shopping comparison services to search the Web for the best price, and then have the items delivered to their doorsteps. As a result, on-line shopping continues to grow at a rapid pace. In fact, according to the National Retail Federation, e-retailers' sales increased by more than 45 percent in 2001 to $65 billion.[34] On-line

on-line retailing
A type of shopping available to consumers with personal computers and access to the Internet.

retailing is also increasing in popularity outside the United States. Read more about e-tailing worldwide in the "Global Perspectives" box.

Original Web-based retailers, like Amazon.com and CDNow, pioneered on-line retailing, selling merchandise more cheaply and conveniently than their brick-and-mortar competition. Both companies have continued to grow and prosper by offering outstanding customer service. Today, CDNow offers customers more than 500,000 CDs, videos, DVDs, and digital music downloads with forty-eight-hour delivery.[35] Similarly, Amazon.com, which opened for business in 1995 with a mission to transform book buying into the fastest, easiest, and most enjoyable shopping experience possible, has grown into a $3.12 billion company selling a combination of both new and used items, ranging from books and electronics to toys and hardware. Amazon has customers in more than 220 countries around the world.[36]

Most traditional retailers have now jumped on the Internet bandwagon, allowing shoppers to purchase the same merchandise found in their stores from their Web site. On-line retailing also fits well with traditional catalog companies, such as Lands' End and Eddie Bauer that already have established distribution networks. In a drastic turnabout in its retail strategy, computer software retailer Egghead recently closed all of its brick-and-mortar stores, moved its entire business onto the Web, and added ".com" to the end of its name. Software purchased at the company's site, **http://www.egghead.com**, can be downloaded directly to the purchaser's computer.

As the popularity of on-line retailing grows, it is becoming critical that retailers be on-line and that their stores, Web sites, and catalogs be integrated. Customers expect to find the same brands, products, and prices whether they purchase online, on the phone, or in a store. Therefore, retailers are increasingly using in-store kiosks to help tie the channels together for greater customer service. Retailer

---

On-line Retailing Growing Worldwide

Consumers around the world are embracing on-line retailing. In fact, in 2001 about 54 percent of Internet users worldwide used the Internet to gather information about products and services, and 27 percent purchased on-line. What's more, analysts predict that the number of on-line shoppers will double in the next few years.

According to a recent survey, the items most commonly purchased on-line are books, CDs, videos, and computer games. Books are the number one best seller everywhere except Brazil and Canada where music tops the list. British and French shoppers like to purchase food and beverages online, and flowers are popular purchases in Switzerland. Swiss and Spanish shoppers purchase more financial services on-line than customers in other foreign countries. Almost 60 percent of on-line shoppers have purchased from an on-line retailer in another country.

The main reason they do so is that the product is not available in their country, but finding a product at a lower price in another country also persuades some shoppers to go international.

So what should a retailer know about global on-line retailing? First, having a multichannel approach to retailing is important. Customers worldwide want the option of shopping on-line. Second, contrary to the belief that on-line shoppers are a unique audience, given Internet access, the same customers who shop in stores are buying on-line. Third, consumers expect the same product selection and customer service on-line that they receive in stores. And finally, customers will push retailers to make their Web site work the way they want it to work.

In addition, retailers interested in global on-line retailing can learn by studying the success of global on-line retailers like Amazon.com.

Amazon.com is the most popular place to shop on-line in the United States, United Kingdom, Canada, Italy, and Australia. In 2001, company sales in the United Kingdom, Germany, France, and Japan grew 81 percent, and more than 29 percent of total company sales were to international customers. The top reasons given for shopping at Amazon.com by customers everywhere are product selection, competitive prices, ease-of-use, product availability, and delivery speed.[37]

As Internet usage around the world increases, so will the number of on-line shoppers. How do you think that will affect traditional retailers? Will they learn to operate in the cyberworld, or will they try to compete against their on-line counterparts? Do you think the Internet will create a truly global retail marketplace?

and cataloger Williams-Sonoma, for example, recently linked its store gift registry to its Web site, allowing brides to see who has bought what in real time. Banana Republic stores in New York and Santa Monica, California, have kiosks where customers can order items that aren't on the shelves. Kiosks are even more popular among retailers that target younger, more computer-oriented customers. For example, Van's operates eight skate parks, which are a combination retail store, entertainment venue, and alternative sports arena. In addition to the skating rink, each park has a lounge area where customers can hang out, watch customized videos, and surf Van's Web site at a bank of kiosks. Each kiosk not only offers a complete selection of Van's footwear, apparel, and accessories, but also includes a full-service pro shop that sells over five hundred skateboards, bicycles, helmets, and other equipment and an information center with the latest tour, special event, and contest information.[38]

A relatively new phenomenon in on-line retailing is the success of auctions run by Internet companies like eBay and Amazon.com. With close to two million items for sale each day, ranging from antique clocks to car stereos, eBay leads the trend in cyberspace auctions. Internet auction services, like eBay, run the Web service and collect a token listing fee, plus a commission of 1 to 5 percent when a sale is completed. Recently, eBay announced a new joint venture with Sotheby's to offer fine art, rare coins, sports collectibles, jewelry, and antiques on-line. Each item carries a stamp of authenticity from Sotheby's or one of the 2,800 art and antiques dealers worldwide who have signed exclusive agreements with Sotheby's. The deal is a boost to eBay's fine arts and antiques division and will allow Sotheby's to continue on-line sales without the overhead expense of managing its own site.[39]

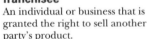

Franchising

⑤

Define franchising and describe its two basic forms

franchiser
The originator of a trade name, product, methods of operation, and so on, that grants operating rights to another party to sell its product.

franchisee
An individual or business that is granted the right to sell another party's product.

A *franchise* is a continuing relationship in which a franchiser grants to a franchisee the business rights to operate or to sell a product. The **franchiser** originates the trade name, product, methods of operation, and so on. The **franchisee**, in return, pays the franchiser for the right to use its name, product, or business methods. A franchise agreement between the two parties usually lasts for ten to twenty years, at which time the agreement can be renewed if both parties are agreeable.

To be granted the rights to a franchise, a franchisee usually pays an initial, one-time franchise fee. The amount of this fee depends solely on the individual franchiser, but it generally ranges from $5,000 to $150,000. In addition to this initial franchise fee, the franchisee is expected to pay weekly, biweekly, or monthly royalty fees, usually in the range of 3 to 7 percent of gross revenues. The franchisee may also be expected to pay advertising fees, which usually cover the cost of promotional materials and, if the franchise organization is large enough, regional or national advertising. A McDonald's franchise, for example, costs an initial $45,000 per store plus a monthly fee based upon the restaurant's sales performance and base rent. In addition, a new McDonald's franchisee can expect start-up costs for equipment and pre-opening expenses to range from $444,800 to $742,150. The size of the restaurant facility, area of the country, inventory, selection of kitchen equipment, signage, and style of decor and landscaping affect new restaurant costs.[40] While the dollar amount will vary depending on the type of franchise, fees such as these are typical for all major franchisers, including Burger King, Jani-King, Athlete's Foot, and Subway.

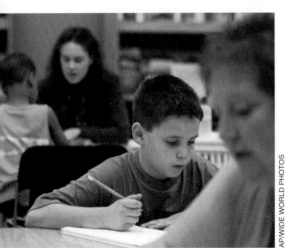

AP/WIDE WORLD PHOTOS

Franchising is most thought of with respect to restaurants, but some of the most successful franchises of late are not even food related. Sylvan Learning Systems is an example. To learn more about Sylvan, do the On-Line activity at the top of this page.

Franchising is not new. General Motors has used this approach since 1898, and Rexall drugstores, since 1901. Today, there are over half a million franchised establishments in the United States, with combined sales approaching $1 trillion, or about 40 percent of all retail trade. Although franchised restaurants attract most of those dollars, hundreds of retail and service franchises, such as Alphagraphics Printshops, Mail Boxes, Etc., and Sylvan Learning Systems, also are thriving. Indeed, there are over 320,000 franchises in seventy-five industries. Industries expected to see real growth in franchising include home repair, business support services, automotive repairs, hair salons, children's services, and telecommunications.[41] Exhibit 13.3 lists some facts about some of the largest and best-known U.S. franchisers.

Two basic forms of franchises are used today: product and trade name franchising and business format franchising. In *product and trade name franchising*, a dealer agrees to sell certain products provided by a manufacturer or a wholesaler. This approach has been used most widely in the auto and truck, soft drink bottling, tire, and gasoline service industries. For example, a local tire retailer may hold a franchise to sell Michelin tires. Likewise, the Coca-Cola bottler in a particular area is a product and trade name franchisee licensed to bottle and sell Coca-Cola's soft drinks.

Largest U.S. Franchisers **Exhibit 13.3**

Franchiser	Type of Business	Total Units	Initial Investment
McDonald's Corporation Oak Brook, Illinois	Fast food	Franchised units: 18,361 Company-owned units: 5,262	$444,800–$742,150
Southland Corporation (7-Eleven) Dallas, Texas	Convenience stores	Franchised units: 15,572 Company-owned units: 2,666	Not available
Subway Sandwiches & Salads Milford, Connecticut	Fast food	Franchised units: 13,537 Company-owned units: 2	$66,200–$175,000
Burger King Corporation Miami, Florida	Fast food	Franchised units: 7,495 Company-owned units: 758	$73,000–$511,000
KFC Corporation Louisville, Kentucky	Fast food	Franchised units: 3,255 Company-owned units: 1,759	Not available
Pizza Hut, Inc. Dallas, Texas	Pizza	Franchised units: 4,200 Company-owned units: 2,800	Not available
Tandy Corporation Fort Worth, Texas	Consumer electronics	Franchised units: 6,779 Company-owned units: 1,890	$60,000+
Jani-King International Dallas, Texas	Janitorial, cleaning services	Franchised units: 7,700 Company-owned units: 35	$5,500–$80,000
Taco Bell Corporation Dallas, Texas	Fast food	Franchised units: 4,600 Company-owned units: 3,044	$200,000+
International Dairy Queen Minneapolis, Minnesota	Ice cream, fast food	Franchised units: 5,347 Company-owned units: NA	Not available

SOURCE: Franchise Opportunities Guide Online, International Franchise Association, Washington, D.C., **http://www.franchise.org**.

Business format franchising is an ongoing business relationship between a franchiser and a franchisee. Typically, a franchiser "sells" a franchisee the rights to use the franchiser's format or approach to doing business. This form of franchising has rapidly expanded since the 1950s through retailing, restaurant, food-service, hotel and motel, printing, and real estate franchises. Fast-food restaurants like McDonald's, Wendy's, and Burger King use this kind of franchising, as do other companies such as Hyatt Corporation, Unocal Corporation, and ExxonMobil Corporation. To be eligible to be a Domino's Pizza franchisee, you must have worked in a Domino's pizza store for at least one year. The company believes that after working in an existing location, you will have a better understanding of the company and its values and standards. Then potential franchisees must participate in a series of career development, franchise orientation, presentation skills, and franchise development programs.[42]

 Like other retailers, franchisers are seeking new growth abroad. Hundreds of U.S. franchisers have begun international expansion and are actively looking for foreign franchisees to open new locations. KFC operates approximately five thousand restaurants in the United States and 6,000 abroad in more than eighty countries around the world including Japan, Australia, China, Indonesia, and Saudi Arabia. An additional one thousand overseas locations are planned for the near future. KFC's parent company attributes the franchise's success to its ability to adapt to local cultures and tastes without losing control of quality and brand image.[43] The International Franchise Association now lists over fifty national franchise organizations in countries from Argentina to Zimbabwe.

Franchisers usually allow franchisees to alter their business format slightly in foreign markets. For example, some McDonald's franchisees in Germany sell beer, and in Japan they offer food items that appeal to Japanese tastes, such as steamed dumplings, curry with rice, and roast pork cutlet burgers with melted cheese. McDonald's franchisees in India serve mutton instead of beef because most Indians are Hindu, a religion whose followers believe cows are a sacred symbol of the source of life. The menu also features rice-based Vegetable Burgers made with peas, carrots, red pepper, beans, and Indian spices as well as Vegetable McNuggets. But, in spite of menu differences, McDonald's foreign franchisees still maintain the company's standards of service and cleanliness.

Retail Marketing Strategy

6

List the major tasks involved in developing a retail marketing strategy

Retailers must develop marketing strategies based on overall goals and strategic plans. Retailing goals might include more traffic, higher sales of a specific item, a more upscale image, or heightened public awareness of the retail operation. The strategies that retailers use to obtain their goals might include a sale, an updated decor, or a new advertisement. The key tasks in strategic retailing are defining and selecting a target market and developing the retailing mix to successfully meet the needs of the chosen target market.

Defining a Target Market

The first and foremost task in developing a retail strategy is to define the target market. This process begins with market segmentation, the topic of Chapter 7. Successful retailing has always been based on knowing the customer. Sometimes retailing chains flounder when management loses sight of the customers the stores should be serving. For example, during the 1990s The Gap built a retail empire by offering updated, casual classics like white shirts and khaki pants that appealed to everyone from high school through middle age. But the company began losing customers in 1999 when it shifted toward trendier fashions with a limited appeal.

Analysts blame the chain's problems on losing focus and touch with its customers.[44]

Target markets in retailing are often defined by demographics, geographics, and psychographics. For instance, Bluefly.com, a discount fashion e-tailer, targets women who are in their thirties, have a higher-than-average income, read fashion magazines, and favor high-end designers. By understanding who its customer are, the company has been able to tailor its Web site to appeal specifically to its audience. The result is a higher sales rate than most e-tailers.[45]

Determining a target market is a prerequisite to creating the retailing mix. For example, Target's merchandising approach for sporting goods is to match its product assortment to the demographics of the local store and region. The amount of space devoted to sporting goods, as well as in-store promotions, also varies according to each store's target market. Similarly, Ann Taylor caters to working women in their thirties and forties—a group of customers notoriously pressed for time. Consequently, its stores offer a one-stop wardrobe solution with color-coordinated blouses, sweaters, skirts, and trousers that make it easy to create a wardrobe with just a few purchases.[46]

Choosing the Retailing Mix

Retailers combine the elements of the retailing mix to come up with a single retailing method to attract the target market. The **retailing mix** consists of six Ps: the four Ps of the marketing mix (product, place, promotion, and price) plus presentation and personnel (see Exhibit 13.4).

The combination of the six Ps projects a store's image, which influences consumers' perceptions. Using these impressions of stores, shoppers position one store against another. A retail marketing manager must make sure that the store's positioning is compatible with the target customers' expectations. As discussed at the beginning of the chapter, retail stores can be positioned on three broad dimensions: service provided by store personnel, product assortment, and price. Management should use everything else—place, presentation, and promotion—to fine-tune the basic positioning of the store.

retailing mix
A combination of the six Ps— product, place, promotion, price, presentation, and personnel—to sell goods and services to the ultimate consumer.

Exhibit 13.4

The Retailing Mix

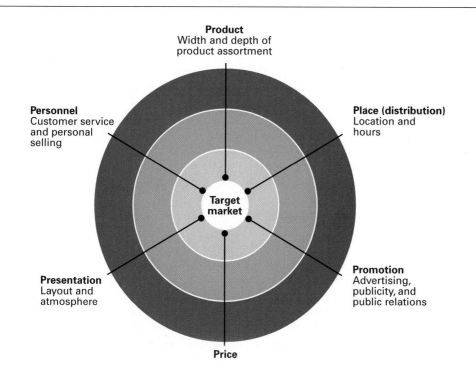

Product
Width and depth of product assortment

Personnel
Customer service and personal selling

Place (distribution)
Location and hours

Target market

Presentation
Layout and atmosphere

Promotion
Advertising, publicity, and public relations

Price

The Product Offering

product offering
The mix of products offered to the consumer by the retailer; also called the *product assortment* or *merchandise mix.*

The first element in the retailing mix is the **product offering**, also called the *product assortment* or *merchandise mix.* Retailers decide what to sell on the basis of what their target market wants to buy. They can base their decision on market research, past sales, fashion trends, customer requests, and other sources. A new technology, called *analytics,* uses complex mathematical models to help retailers make better product mix decisions. Early adopters of the technology, such as Dillard's, are using analytics to determine which products to stock at what price, how to manage markdowns, and how to advertise to draw target customers.[47]

Developing a product offering is essentially a question of the width and depth of the product assortment. *Width* refers to the assortment of products offered; *depth* refers to the number of different brands offered within each assortment. Price, store design, displays, and service are important to consumers in determining where to shop, but the most critical factor is merchandise selection. This reasoning also holds true for on-line retailers. Amazon.com, for instance, has ambitious plans to build the world's biggest on-line department store so that shoppers can get whatever they want with one click on their Web browsers. As with a traditional department store or mass merchandiser, Amazon offers considerable width in its product assortment with millions of different items, including books, music, toys, videos, tools and hardware, health and beauty aids, electronics, and software. Conversely, on-line specialty retailers, such as Garden.com, CDNow, and Blockbuster's Reel.com, focus on a single category of merchandise, hoping to attract loyal customers with a larger depth of products at lower prices and better customer service. Many on-line retailers purposely focus on single product line niches that could never garner enough foot traffic to support a traditional brick-and-mortar store. Mustardstore.com, for instance, offers 660 different gourmet mustards, while Fridgedoor.com sells 1,500 different types of refrigerator magnets to collectors.[48]

After determining what products will satisfy target customers' desires, retailers must find sources of supply and evaluate the products. When the right products are found, the retail buyer negotiates a purchase contract. The buying function can either be performed in-house or be delegated to an outside firm. The goods must then be moved from the seller to the retailer, which means shipping, storing, and stocking the inventory. The trick is to manage the inventory by cutting prices to move slow goods and by keeping adequate supplies of hot-selling items in stock. As in all good systems, the final step is to evaluate the entire process to seek more efficient methods and eliminate problems and bottlenecks.

One of the more efficient new methods of managing inventory and streamlining the way products are moved from supplier to distributor to retailer is called *efficient consumer response (ECR).* At the heart of ECR is *electronic data interchange (EDI),* the computer-to-computer exchange of information, at every stage of the supply chain. In a full implementation of ECR, products are scanned at the retail store when purchased, which updates the store's inventory lists. Headquarters then polls the stores to retrieve the data needed to produce an order. The vendor confirms the order, shipping date, and delivery time, then ships the order and transmits the invoice electronically. The item is received at the warehouse, scanned into inventory, and then sent to the store. The invoice and receiving data are reconciled, and payment via an electronic transfer of funds completes the process.

Many retailers are experimenting with or have successfully implemented ECR and EDI. Calendar Club, a mall-based kiosk retailer of calendars, uses ECR and EDI to get the right products at its kiosks, some of which sell more than one thousand calendars a day for the 120 days a year they are open. Calendar Club developed an ECR replenishment solution that allows the company to pick, pack, and ship unique replenishment orders for each kiosk every night.[49]

private-label brands
Brands that are designed and developed using the retailer's name.

As margins drop and competition intensifies, retailers are becoming ever more aware of the advantages of **private brands**, or those brands that are designed and developed using the retailer's name. Because the cost of goods typically makes up between 70 and 85 percent of a retailer's expenses, eliminating intermediaries can shave costs. As a result, prices of private-label goods are typically lower than for national brands, giving customers greater value. Private-label branding is not new. For decades, Sears has fashioned its Kenmore, Craftsman, and DieHard brands into household names. Lately, Wal-Mart has begun rolling out its own private-label brands, such as White Cloud paper products, Spring Valley nutritional supplements, Sam's American Choice laundry detergent, EverActive alkaline batteries, and EverStart auto batteries, with much success. Its Ol' Roy dog food and Sam's American Choice garden fertilizer are now the best-selling brands in their categories. As the nation's largest retailer, Wal-Mart's foray into private labels worries many brand marketers, such as Procter & Gamble, which manufactures Tide laundry detergent. Whereas Wal-Mart was once its biggest customer, the giant retailer is transforming itself into P&G's biggest competitor with the introduction of Sam's American Choice laundry soap that sells for 25 to 30 percent lower. And while Wal-Mart's private labels may not steal significant sales away from popular brands like Tide, in the long run smaller second- and third-tier brands that don't bring consumers to the shelves may have a difficult time surviving.[50]

Promotion Strategy

Retail promotion strategy includes advertising, public relations and publicity, and sales promotion. The goal is to help position the store in consumers' minds. Retailers design intriguing ads, stage special events, and develop promotions aimed at their target markets. For example, today's grand openings are a carefully orchestrated blend of advertising, merchandising, goodwill, and glitter. All the elements of an opening—press coverage, special events, media advertising, and store displays—are carefully planned.

Retailers' advertising is carried out mostly at the local level, although retail giants like Sears and JCPenney can advertise nationally. Local advertising by retailers usually provides specific information about their stores, such as location, merchandise, hours, prices, and special sales. In contrast, national retail advertising generally focuses on image. For example, Target has used its "sign of the times" advertising campaign to effectively position itself as the "chic place to buy cheap."

Target's advertising campaign also takes advantage of cooperative advertising, another popular retail advertising practice. Traditionally, marketers would pay retailers to feature their products in store mailers, or a marketer would develop a TV campaign for the product and simply tack on several retailers' names at the end. But Target's advertising makes use of a more collaborative trend in cooperative advertising by integrating products such as Tide laundry detergent, Tums antacids, or Coca-Cola into the actual campaign.[51] Another common form of cooperative advertising involves promotion of exclusive products. For instance, Kmart's advertising campaign for its Martha Stewart product line has the dual role of promoting the products and attracting customers to the store.

Many retailers are forgoing media advertising these days in favor of direct-mail or frequent shopper programs. Direct-mail and catalog programs are luring many retailers, which hope they will prove to be a cost-effective means of increasing brand loyalty and spending by core customers. Nordstrom, for example, mails catalogs featuring brand-name and private-brand clothing, shoes, and accessories to target the shop-at-home crowd. Home repair outlets such as Lowe's and Home Depot have also used direct mail, often around holidays when people have time off to complete needed repairs. Restaurants and small retailers have successfully used frequent diner or frequent shopper programs for years. Now many retail chains, like The Gap, Victoria's Secret, and Eddie Bauer, are offering frequent shopper programs with perks ranging from gift certificates to special "members only" sale prices. For example, customers with a Victoria's Secret Angel credit card are offered monthly specials on store merchandise, including items that generally are not put on sale to the public.

The Proper Location

The retailing axiom "location, location, location" has long emphasized the importance of place to the retail mix. The location decision is important first because the retailer is making a large, semipermanent commitment of resources that can reduce its future flexibility. Second, the location will affect the store's future growth and profitability.

Site location begins by choosing a community. Important factors to consider are the area's economic growth potential, the amount of competition, and geography. For instance, retailers like T. J. Maxx, Wal-Mart, and Toys "R" Us build stores in areas where the population is growing. Often these large retailers will build stores in new communities that are still under development. On the other hand, while population growth is an important consideration for fast-food restaurants, most also look for an area with other fast-food restaurants because being located in clusters helps to draw customers for each restaurant. Finally, for many retailers geography remains the most important factor in choosing a community. For example, Starbucks coffee looks for densely populated urban communities for its stores, Talbots looks for locations near upper-class neighborhoods, and Buckle stores look for locations in small, underserved cities.

After settling on a geographic region or community, retailers must choose a specific site. In addition to growth potential, the important factors are neighborhood socioeconomic characteristics, traffic flows, land costs, zoning regulations, and public transportation. A particular site's visibility, parking, entrance and exit locations, accessibility, and safety and security issues are other variables contributing to site selection success. Additionally, a retailer should consider how its store would fit into the surrounding environment. Retail decision makers probably would not locate a Dollar General store next door to a Neiman Marcus department store.

One final decision about location faces retailers: whether to have a freestanding unit or to become a tenant in a shopping center or mall.

Freestanding Stores An isolated, freestanding location can be used by large retailers like Wal-Mart, Kmart, or Target and sellers of shopping goods like furniture and cars because they are "destination" stores, or those stores consumers will purposely plan to visit. In other words, customers will seek them out. An isolated store location may have the advantages of low site cost or rent and no nearby competitors. On the other hand, it may be hard to attract customers to a freestanding location, and no other retailers are around to share costs.

Freestanding units are increasing in popularity as retailers strive to make their stores more convenient to access, more enticing to shop, and more profitable. Freestanding sites now account for more than half of the millions of square feet of retail construction starts in the United States as more and more retailers are deciding not to locate in pedestrian malls. Perhaps the greatest reason for developing a freestanding site is greater visibility. Retailers often feel they get lost in huge centers and malls, but freestanding units can help stores develop an identity with shoppers. The ability to grow at faster rates through freestanding buildings has also propelled the surge toward stand-alone units. Retailers like The Sports Authority, Linens & Things, and Bed, Bath & Beyond often choose to be freestanding in order to achieve their expansion objectives. An aggressive expansion plan may not allow time to wait for shopping centers to be built. Similarly, drugstore chains like Walgreens and Rite-Aid have been aggressively relocating their existing mall and shopping center stores to freestanding sites, especially street corner sites for drive-through accessibility.

Shopping Centers The tremendous boom in shopping centers began after World War II, as the U.S. population started migrating to the suburbs. The first shopping centers were *strip centers*, typically located along a busy street. They usually included a supermarket, a variety store, and perhaps a few specialty stores. Essentially unplanned business districts, these strip centers remain popular.

Next, the small *community shopping centers* emerged, with one or two small department store branches, more specialty shops, one or two restaurants, and several apparel stores. These centers offer a broader variety of shopping, specialty, and convenience goods, provide large off-street parking lots, and usually include 75,000 to 300,000 square feet of retail space.

Finally, along came the huge *regional malls,* generally offering 400,000 to 800,000 square feet of shopping space. Regional malls are either entirely enclosed or roofed to allow shopping in any weather. Many are landscaped with trees, fountains, sculptures, and the like to enhance the shopping environment. They have acres of free parking. The *anchor stores* or *generator stores* (JCPenney, Sears, or major department stores) are usually located at opposite ends of the mall to create heavy foot traffic. Las Vegas's Fashion Show Mall takes the concept to the extreme. When renovations are completed, the mall will span two million square feet with eight anchor stores including Neiman Marcus, Lord & Taylor, and Nordstrom.[52]

According to shopping center developers, *lifestyle centers* are now emerging as the newest generation of shopping centers offering time-pressed consumers a more convenient alternative to malls. These new open-air shopping centers are targeted to upper-income shoppers with an aversion for "the mall" and seek to create an atmosphere that is part neighborhood park and part urban shopping center. Lifestyle centers generally feature approximately 300,000 square feet of upscale retail space occupied by trendy restaurants and specialty retailers like Pottery Barn and Williams-Sonoma. Other attractions include expensive landscaping and convenient parking. Developers expect that there will be more than fifty lifestyle centers around the country by 2004.[53]

Locating in a community shopping center or regional mall offers several advantages. First, the facilities are designed to attract shoppers. Second, the shopping environment, anchor stores, and "village square" activities draw customers. Third, ample parking is available. Fourth, the center or mall projects a unified image. Fifth, tenants also share the expenses of the mall's common area and promotions for the whole mall. Finally, malls can target different demographic groups. Some malls are considered upscale; others are aimed at people shopping for bargains.

Locating in a shopping center or mall does have disadvantages. These include expensive leases, the chance that common promotion efforts will not attract customers to a particular store, lease restrictions on merchandise carried and hours of operation, the anchor stores' domination of the tenants' association, and the possibility of having direct competitors within the same facility. Consumers have also become more pressed for time in recent years and have decreased the number of visits and the time they spend in malls in favor of more convenient stand-alone stores and neighborhood centers. Faced with this trend, mall developers have improved the layout of many malls to make it more convenient for customers to shop. For instance, the RiverTown Crossings center in Grandville, Michigan, clusters competing stores, like Abercrombie Kids, GapKids, Gymboree, and other kids' clothing stores in one section of the mall to accommodate time-strapped parents.[54]

Retail Prices

Another important element in the retailing mix is price. It is important to understand that retailing's ultimate goal is to sell products to consumers and that the right price is critical in ensuring sales. Because retail prices are usually based on the cost of the merchandise, an essential part of pricing is efficient and timely buying.

Price is also a key element in a retail store's positioning strategy and classification. Higher prices often indicate a level of quality and help reinforce the prestigious image of retailers, as they do for Lord & Taylor, Saks Fifth Avenue, Gucci, Cartier, and Neiman Marcus. On the other hand, discounters and off-price retailers, such as Target and T. J. Maxx, offer a good value for the money. There are even stores, such as Dollar Tree, where everything costs shoppers one dollar. Dollar

Tree's single-price-point strategy is aimed at getting higher-income customers to make impulse purchases through what analysts call the "wow factor"—the excitement of discovering that an item costs only a dollar.[55]

A pricing trend among American retailers that seems to be here to stay is *everyday low pricing*, or EDLP. Introduced to the retail industry by Wal-Mart, EDLP offers consumers a low price all the time rather than holding periodic sales on merchandise. Even large retail giants, like Federated Department Stores, parent of Macy's and Bloomingdale's, have phased out deep discounts and sales in favor of lower prices every day. Similarly, The Gap reduced prices on denim jeans, denim shirts, socks, and other items to protect and broaden the company's share of the casual clothes market. Supermarkets such as Albertson's and Winn Dixie have also found success in EDLP.

Presentation of the Retail Store

The presentation of a retail store helps determine the store's image and positions the retail store in consumers' minds. For instance, a retailer that wants to position itself as an upscale store would use a lavish or sophisticated presentation.

The main element of a store's presentation is its **atmosphere**, the overall impression conveyed by a store's physical layout, decor, and surroundings. The atmosphere might create a relaxed or busy feeling, a sense of luxury or of efficiency, a friendly or cold attitude, a sense of organization or of clutter, or a fun or serious mood. For example, the look at Express stores is designed to make suburban shoppers feel as though they have just strolled into a Parisian boutique. Signage is often in French, and the background music has a European flair. Likewise, REI sporting-goods stores feature indoor rock-climbing walls, bike test trails, and rain rooms for testing outdoor gear.

More often these days retailers are adding an element of entertainment to their store atmosphere. The Nike Town store in Chicago looks more like a museum than a traditional retail store. The three-story space displays products amid life-size Michael Jordan statues and glassed-in relics like baseball legend Nolan Ryan's shoes. A History of Air exhibit explains the pockets of air on the bottom of some Nike shoes. A video theater plays Nike commercials and short films featuring Nike gear.

The layout of retail stores is a key factor in their success. Layout is planned so that all space in the store is used effectively, including aisles, fixtures, merchandise displays, and nonselling areas. Effective store layout ensures the customer's shopping ease and convenience, but it also has a powerful influence on customer traffic patterns and purchasing behavior. For instance, Kohl's is known for its unique circular store layout, which encourages customers to pass all of a store's departments to reach the checkout lanes. The stores are smaller than most department stores but have a wide aisle designed to allow plenty of room for customers and shopping carts. Each department is limited to five display racks on the main aisle. Displays are spaced widely apart and are set at varying heights so that a customer can see everything in the department, including wall displays, from the main aisle. To further enhance the store's clean crisp presentation, merchandise is displayed from light to dark, which research suggests is most pleasing to the eye. Finally, to encourage last-minute, impulse purchases, Kohl's displays low-cost items at the checkout register. The result

atmosphere
The overall impression conveyed by a store's physical layout, decor, and surroundings.

© DAVID SAMUEL ROBBINS/CORBIS

Retailers use the physical space of the store to entice customers to buy merchandise. REI encourages customers to try out the rock climbing wall at its flagship Seattle, Washington, store.

of the store layout is a $279 sales per square foot average (sales per square foot is a standard industry measurement).[56]

Layout also includes where products are placed in the store. Many technologically advanced retailers are using a technique called *market-basket analysis* to analyze the huge amounts of data collected through their point-of-purchase scanning equipment. The analysis looks for products that are commonly purchased together to help retailers remerchandise their stores to place products in the right places. Wal-Mart uses market-basket analysis to determine where in the store to stock products for customer convenience. Bananas are placed not only in the produce section but also in the cereal aisle. Kleenex tissues are in the paper-goods aisle and also mixed in with the cold medicines. Measuring spoons are in the housewares and also hanging next to Crisco shortening. During October, flashlights are not only in the hardware aisle but also with the Halloween costumes.[57]

These are the most influential factors in creating a store's atmosphere:

- *Employee type and density:* Employee type refers to an employee's general characteristics—for instance, neat, friendly, knowledgeable, or service oriented. Density is the number of employees per thousand square feet of selling space. A discounter like Kmart has a low employee density that creates a "do-it-yourself," casual atmosphere. In contrast, Neiman Marcus's density is much higher, denoting readiness to serve the customer's every whim. Too many employees and not enough customers, however, can convey an air of desperation and intimidate customers.

- *Merchandise type and density:* The type of merchandise carried and how it is displayed add to the atmosphere the retailer is trying to create. A prestigious retailer like Saks or Marshall Field's carries the best brand names and displays them in a neat, uncluttered arrangement. Discounters and off-price retailers may sell some well-known brands, but many carry seconds or out-of-season goods. Their merchandise may be stacked so high that it falls into the aisles, helping create the impression that "We've got so much stuff, we're practically giving it away."

- *Fixture type and density:* Fixtures can be elegant (rich woods), trendy (chrome and smoked glass), or consist of old, beat-up tables, as in an antiques store. The fixtures should be consistent with the general atmosphere the store is trying to create. The Gap creates a relaxed and uncluttered atmosphere by displaying its merchandise on tables and shelves, rather than on traditional pipe racks, allowing customers to see and touch the merchandise more easily. Adding technology as a fixture is a recent successful trend in coffee shops and lounges. The most popular examples include adding PCs to provide Internet access to customers and ultimately get them to remain in the store longer. E-Trade's flagship bank branch is technologically hip with computer workstations and flat-panel televisions tuned to financial networks instead of the traditional teller windows and doctor's-office-style waiting areas.[58]

- *Sound:* Sound can be pleasant or unpleasant for a customer. Classical music at a nice Italian restaurant helps create ambience, just as country-and-western music does at a truck stop. Music can also entice customers to stay in the store longer and buy more or eat quickly and leave a table for others. For instance, rapid music tends to make people eat more, chew less, and take bigger bites whereas slow music prompts people to dine more leisurely and eat less. Retailers can tailor their musical atmosphere to their shoppers' demographics and the merchandise they're selling. Music can control the pace of the store traffic, create an image, and attract or direct the shopper's attention. For example, Harrods in London features music by live harpists, pianists, and marching bagpipers to create different atmospheres in different departments. Coffee shops are also getting into the music business as are theme restaurants like Hard Rock Cafe, Planet Hollywood, Harley Davidson Cafe, and Rainforest Cafe, which turn

© RICHARD CUMMINS/CORBIS

This enormous frog sculpture crowns the entrance to the Rainforest Cafe in Chicago, Illinois. Coupled with the giant toadstools that flank the doors, the sculptures that decorate the outside of the restaurant create an impression of fun and whimsy.

eating a hamburger and fries into an experience. Au Bon Pain, Starbucks, and Victoria's Secret have all sold copies of their background music, hoping that the music will remind consumers of the feeling of being in their stores.

- *Odors:* Smell can either stimulate or detract from sales. The wonderful smell of pastries and breads entices bakery customers. Conversely, customers can be repulsed by bad odors such as cigarette smoke, musty smells, antiseptic odors, and overly powerful room deodorizers. If a grocery store pumps in the smell of baked goods, sales in that department increase threefold. Department stores have pumped in fragrances that are pleasing to their target market, and the response has been favorable. Not surprisingly, retailers are increasingly using fragrance as a key design element, as important as layout, lighting, and background music. Research suggests that people evaluate merchandise more positively, spend more time shopping, and are generally in a better mood when an agreeable odor is present. Retailers use fragrances as an extension of their retail strategy. The Rainforest Cafe, for instance, pumps fresh-flower extracts into its retail sections. Similarly, the Christmas Store at Disney World, which is open year-round, is infused with the scents of evergreen and spiced apple cider. Jordan's Furniture in Massachusetts and New Hampshire uses the scent of pine in its country-style sections to make the environment more interesting and encourage customers to linger longer.[59]

- *Visual factors:* Colors can create a mood or focus attention and therefore are an important factor in atmosphere. Red, yellow, and orange are considered warm colors and are used when a feeling of warmth and closeness is desired. Cool colors like blue, green, and violet are used to open up closed-in places and create an air of elegance and cleanliness. Some colors are better for display. For instance, diamonds appear most striking against black or dark blue velvet. The lighting can also have an important effect on store atmosphere. Jewelry is best displayed under high-intensity spotlights and cosmetics under more natural lighting. Many retailers have found that natural lighting, either from windows or skylights, can lead to increased sales. Outdoor lighting can also affect consumer patronage. Consumers often are afraid to shop after dark in many areas and prefer strong lighting for safety. The outdoor facade of the store also adds to its ambience and helps create favorable first impressions by shoppers. For example, on the top of the roof over the door at Cup o' Joe specialty coffee shop in Lennox Town Square, Columbus, Ohio, sits a twelve-foot-wide by six-foot-tall coffee mug. The coffee shop's designers used the exaggerated storefront to call attention to its site, which would have otherwise gotten lost amid its big-box neighbors Old Navy, Target, and an AMC Theater.[60]

Personnel and Customer Service

People are a unique aspect of retailing. Most retail sales involve a customer–salesperson relationship, if only briefly. When customers shop at a grocery store, the cashiers check and bag their groceries. When customers shop at a prestigious clothier, the salesclerks may help select the styles, sizes, and colors. They may also assist in the fitting process, offer alteration services, wrap purchases, and even offer a glass of champagne. Sales personnel provide their customers with the amount of service prescribed in the retail strategy of the store.

Retail salespeople serve another important selling function: They persuade shoppers to buy. They must therefore be able to persuade customers that what they are selling is what the customer needs. Salespeople are trained in two common selling techniques: trading up and suggestion selling. Trading up means persuading customers to buy a higher-priced item than they originally intended to buy. To avoid selling customers something they do not need or want, however, salespeople should take care when practicing trading-up techniques. Suggestion selling, a common practice among most retailers, seeks to broaden customers' original purchases with related items. For example, McDonald's cashiers may ask customers whether they would like a hot apple pie with their hamburger and fries. Suggestion selling and trading up should always help shoppers recognize true needs rather than sell them unwanted merchandise. To learn about problems retailers sometimes have with overzealous employees, read about racial profiling by retailers in the "Ethics in Marketing" box.

Providing great customer service is one of the most challenging elements in the retail mix because customer expectations for service are so varied. What customers expect in a department store is very different from their expectations for a discount store. Customer expectations also change. Ten years ago, shoppers wanted personal one-on-one attention. Today, most customers are happy to help themselves as long as they can easily find what they need. For example, Home Depot has always had a reputation for great customer service. Shoppers enjoy talking to the store's knowledgeable staff in the busy, do-it-yourself, warehouse atmosphere. But as store sales increased, the company began receiving customer feedback that the salespeople seemed too busy to help and the stores were too cluttered. To meet customers' new

ETHICS IN MARKETING

Racial Profiling in Retail

As discussed in the chapter, in most cases retailers rely on their salespeople to represent the company to the customer. Therefore, to make customers feel welcome and appreciated, retailers look for salespeople who are courteous and outgoing. But what if some customers don't feel welcome?

As racial profiling has become an important issue in the United States, many African Americans say they often feel unwelcome in retail stores and restaurants. According to a recent Gallup poll, 46 percent of African Americans feel they have been mistreated in stores or malls, and 39 percent feel they have been treated unfairly in restaurants. Whether or not the perception is reality, rumors of discrimination are harmful to a retailer, and if the perception is widespread, it can have a negative effect on business.

Why do so many African Americans feel unwelcome, and what can retailers do about it? One reason may be that many retail and restaurant owners hire off-duty police officers to provide security. Police officers are trained to be police officers, not salespeople.

They are not trained to believe the customer is always right, and they are not hired to help customers. Instead, they may be there to make customers feel safe or to prevent shoplifting. In other words, they are in the store to discourage wrongdoing. And if the officers believe that African Americans are more likely to cause trouble, they may watch African American customers more closely, thereby creating the customers' perception of being mistreated.

Several high-profile incidents of racial profiling involving off-duty police officers have been in the news. In one of the most blatant examples, an off-duty police officer who was working as a security guard at an Eddie Bauer warehouse sale confronted an African American teenager and accused him of stealing the shirt he was wearing. When the customer explained that he had purchased the shirt at the sale the previous day, the officer insisted that he remove the shirt and come back with the receipt to prove he had purchased it. The incident led to community outrage, a lawsuit, and an out-of-court settlement. Similarly, Dil-

lard's currently faces multiple lawsuits involving charges of racial profiling by off-duty police officers.

As a result of these incidents, Eddie Bauer and many other retailers have decided not to use off-duty police officers for store security. But to be fair, not all racial profiling accusations are the result of off-duty police officers. For instance, community activists in the Detroit area claim that civilian security guards at both Lord & Taylor and Kroger engage in racial profiling. In fact, all it takes for customers to feel mistreated is one salesperson who shadows or asks for additional identification from minority customers. Many large chains are following Eddie Bauer's lead and have started including diversity training in their employee orientation programs.[63]

What do you think? Can retailers prevent racial profiling in their stores? How important is it for retailers to be proactive about racial profiling? Is the risk of racial profiling by security justified by the fact that retailers lose almost $8.5 billion annually to shoplifters?

expectations, the company recently changed its store policy to free up staff time to help customers and has eliminated merchandise displays from the aisles.[61]

 Customer service is also critical for on-line retailers. On-line shoppers expect a retailer's Web site to be easy to use, products to be available, and returns to be simple. Therefore, customer-friendly retailers like Bluefly.com design their sites to give their customers the information they need such as what's new and what's on sale. Other companies like Amazon.com and LandsEnd.com offer product recommendations and personal shoppers. Many on-line retailers have also begun including a return envelope with all orders to make returns easier for the customer.[62]

Global Retailing

7

Discuss the challenges of expanding retailing operations into global markets

It is no accident that U.S. retailers are now testing their store concepts on a global basis. With the battle for market share among domestic retailers showing no sign of abating and growth prospects dismal, mature retailers are looking for growth opportunities in the growing consumer economies of other countries. American retailers have made quite an impact on the global market, as Exhibit 13.5 displays. Seven of the top ten global retailers are from the

Exhibit 13.5

Ranking of Global Retailers

Rank	Retailer	Country of Origin	Format	2000 Retail Sales ($ millions)
1	Wal-Mart	U.S.	Discount/Warehouse	191,329
2	Carrefour	France	Cash & Carry/Convenience/Discount/ Hypermarket/Supermarket	59,703
3	Kroger	U.S.	Convenience/Department/Discount/ Drug/Supermarket	49,000
4	Home Depot	U.S.	DIY/Specialty	45,738
5	Metra	Germany	Department/DIY/Hypermakret/ Specialty/Supermarket/Warehouse/ Mail Order	42,439
6	Ahold	Netherlands	Cash & Carry/Convenience/Discount/ Drug/Hypermarket	41,539
7	Kmart	U.S.	Discount	37,028
8	Albertson's	U.S.	Drug/Supermarket	36,762
9	Sears, Roebuck	U.S.	Department/Mail Order/Specialty	36,548
10	Target	U.S.	Department/Discount	36,362

SOURCE: Nation Retail Federation, "Top 200 Global Retailers 2001," Stores.org

United States, with Wal-Mart holding the top spot with sales about three times that of its nearest competitors.

Several events have made expansion across national borders more feasible. First, the spread of communication networks and mass media has homogenized tastes and product preferences to some extent around the world. As a result, the casual American lifestyle and the products that symbolize it, such as Levi's jeans and Nike sportswear, have become more appealing. Second, the lowering of trade barriers and tariffs has facilitated the expansion of American retailers to Mexico, Canada, and Europe. Last, high growth potential in underserved markets is also luring U.S. retailers abroad into Latin America, South America, and Asia. China contains a quarter of the world's population and only recently opened its markets to outside concerns. Although the majority of China's population still lacks adequate consumer spending power, projections call for the country's economy to eclipse all others in the next twenty-five years.

Before taking the plunge into the international retailing arena, the soundest advice retailers can heed is to do their homework (see Exhibit 13.6). Analysts from consulting firm Ernst & Young count among the prerequisites for going global a secure and profitable position domestically, a long-term perspective

---

Factors Used to Analyze Global Retail Markets **Exhibit 13.6**

- **Market size and economics:** Analyzing factors such as population and demographic trends, economics (including gross domestic product and consumer spending), and political trends that could make or break the success of a retailer in a foreign country. For instance, in China the central government has been urging middle-income Chinese to buy their own housing. For retailers, this means plenty of new apartments and homes to fill with more electronics, bigger refrigerators and kitchens for edibles, and roomier closets.

- **Infrastructure and distribution:** Building global supply chains and securing qualified labor can be particularly challenging in emerging markets. Expansion to Canada and Mexico is simpler logistically for U.S. retailers than transporting their stores across oceans. In many developing countries such as China, underdeveloped transportation infrastructures as well as few logistics providers pose daunting distribution challenges to retailers trying to stock products in stores.

- **Competition:** Assessing the current competitive landscape and how the retailer could bring innovations to the market. Compared to the United States, Mexico, for instance, is considered grossly understored; the country has less than 550 square feet of food and apparel stores per thousand people, compared to 20,000 square feet per thousand people in the United States. Similarly, Europe has a higher percentage of independent, mom-and-pop operations. The highly fragmented European market appears ripe for well-capitalized U.S. big-box retailers.

- **Operations:** Assessing how operational concerns, such as real estate, labor, and inventory, will affect the success of an overseas unit. For instance, labor laws vary drastically from country to country. Cultural differences also affect holidays, number of vacation days for employees, and hours of operation. U.S. retail stores are open an average of seventy hours a week whereas retail stores in Greece are open only about forty-six hours a week.

- **Financial and tax reporting:** Addressing issues such as currency fluctuations, the hedging of risks, and how a region's tax regime and incentives would fit in to a retailer's overall tax strategy. A lot of retailers are entering Brazil and Chile because their markets are open and their business economies and financial systems are more "Western-like."

- **Merchandise acceptability:** Conducting research to understand local consumer needs, preferences, and buying habits, and then reinventing the assortment to match the culture of the region. For instance, back-to-school sales occur in April in Japan, and August in Europe is a traditionally slow retailing month because most Europeans are on vacation. When IKEA came to the United States, it learned that it needed to offer larger beds, furniture with larger drawers, and different assortments of kitchen utensils.

- **Partnering capability:** Considering the availability of suitable partners in a desired country or region. Starbucks coffee typically picks distribution and supply partners before it decides on a country or region because poor strategic alliances or logistics partnering can make or break a retail operation.

SOURCE: From "Global Retailing '97," Ernst & Young special report for *Chain Store Age*, December 1997. Reprinted by permission from Chain Store Age. Copyright Lebhar-Friedman, Inc., 425 Park Avenue, NY, NY 10022.

because many foreign operations take a long time to set up and even longer to turn a profit, and a global strategy that meshes with the retailer's overall corporate strategy. Retailers should first determine what their core competency is, whether it be low prices, a distinctive fashion look, or excellent customer service, and determine whether this differentiation is what the local market wants. For instance, The Gap's international success is attributable to its allegiance to the "American casual" formula that made it so successful in its home market, including The Gap name. Similarly, wherever shoppers travel, they can reasonably expect to experience Wal-Mart's friendliness, the quality, service, and cleanliness of McDonald's.

In addition to keeping their core strengths when going global, retailers need to understand the cultural differences of new markets because the differences can affect almost every area of the retail mix. Differences in color, style, or taste preferences can affect a company's product choices. For example, lime green is a popular color on the sunny beaches of St. Tropez, but customers in northern Europe feel it leaves them looking sickly. Tight skirts are popular in France but not in countries like Holland where women often bicycle to work. Cultural differences also should be taken into consideration on all location, presentation, and promotion decisions. For instance, Canadian retailer Pop Shoppes failed in the United States because most U.S. consumers don't call soft drinks pop and therefore failed to understand what the store sold. Differences in supply chain, real estate, and employment costs can undermine a retailer's price strategy. And, as always, great customer service depends on a retailer's understanding of customer expectations.[64]

Trends in Retailing

(8)

Describe future trends in retailing

Predicting the future is always risky, but the use of entertainment to lure customers, a shift toward providing greater convenience to receive the patronage of today's precision shoppers, and the emergence of customer management programs to foster loyalty and enhance communications with a retailer's best customers are three of the more important trends for retailing's future.

Entertainment

Adding entertainment to the retail environment is one of the most popular strategies in retailing in recent years. Small retailers as well as national chains are using entertainment to set themselves apart from the competition.

Entertainment is not limited to music, videos, fashion shows, or guest appearances by soap opera stars or book authors. Entertainment includes anything that makes shoppers have a good time, stimulates their senses or emotions, and gets them into a store, keeps them there, and encourages them to buy and to keep coming back. The quiet, comfortable couches and cafes of bookstores and combination book and music retailers such as Barnes & Noble, Books-a-Million, Borders, and Media Play are entertaining as are the Gershwin tunes coming from the piano in a Nordstrom's atrium. Video screens and loud, energetic music capture the attention of many younger consumers. To attract affluent, young professionals, Brooks Brothers stores host in-store cocktail parties with margaritas, food, and store discounts. Similarly, many high-end retailers like Bergdorf Goodman are using exclusive trunk shows to attract affluent women in their thirties and forties to shop. Trunk shows also allow retailers to increase sales of full-price items.[65]

Convenience and Efficiency

Today's consumer is increasingly looking for ways to shop more quickly and efficiently. The trend not only reflects the increase in women working full- or part-time but also can be attributed to all consumers being more stretched for time. Consumers are visiting malls only about half as often as they used to, and the number of stores they visit when they get there is down substantially, too. According to a recent survey, 61 percent of shoppers said that convenience was the most important factor in deciding where to shop. Shoppers in the same study also indicated that they are shopping in only 1.9 stores per week, compared to 2.9 the year before.[66] Therefore, retailers must make sure that customers have a positive experience every time they shop.

Retailers must also learn to better manage the patronage experience. Consumers are no longer satisfied when a store merely meets their expectations. They desire delightful experiences brought about by retailers who anticipate consumers' expectations and go the extra mile to exceed them on a regular basis. Dimensions in which retailers can far exceed expectations include shopping assistance, the buying process, delivery and installation of the product, service after the sale, and disposal and renewal of the product.

Examples of ways this can be done include offering amenities such as pick-up service for shoppers who do not want to fight traffic, baby-sitting services, free drinks and refreshments during shopping, and preferred shopper parking spaces. For example, IGA supermarkets offer parents a child-care center where they can leave their kids while buying groceries. The play area includes computers, puzzles and crayons, television, and other entertainment activities. Drugstores are offering flu shots, cholesterol screenings, and in-store health clinics. In addition, retailers that maintain records of consumers' preferences in product features are able to offer individualized attention to consumers during product selection. Sales associates can preselect items that are most likely to be preferred by the customer. For example, the store's records may indicate that a consumer prefers a particular style of suit, leading the sales associate to show the consumer the new suits for the season in that style.

To improve customer service, many retailers are also implementing multichannel strategies. Retailers like Eddie Bauer and Talbots are using their catalogs and Web sites to familiarize customers with their merchandise selection and then offering special in-store incentives designed to entice customers to the store. Once inside the store, customers have access to catalogs and Web sites for purchasing items out-of-stock at the time of their visit.[67] Retailers that successfully integrate multiple channels are finding that doing so increases sales in each channel.

Experts predict that in the future retailers, especially supermarkets, will become true marketers rather than marketers that act as distribution centers. For instance, packaged goods and staples won't be sold in supermarkets. Instead, they will be delivered directly to consumers at home, within fifteen minutes of an order's placement, freeing shoppers to visit stores for things they enjoy buying—fresh produce, meats, and the fixings for a dinner party. Consumers who need staples would use hand scanners to record products' bar codes and update electronic shopping lists. Magazine ads would also carry bar codes so that consumers could scan pages to put new products on their lists. Already, Frigidaire has produced a concept model refrigerator that comes complete with a video screen and bar-code scanner, which consumers can use to reorder products by scanning their used-up container across the door. The scanner picks up the UPC and automatically reorders a fresh supply. The video screen also connects to the Internet, allowing consumers to check e-mail, pay bills, check their bank account, and shop on-line.[68]

Customer Management

Today, prime locations and unique merchandise are not the primary indicators of success they once were in the retail environment. Instead, retailers are recognizing that customer equity is one of the only ways to sustain true competitive advantage. Through customer management strategies, leading retailers are intensifying their

Entertainment in the retail environment is at its pinnacle in the Donna Karan New York boutique. Customers sit at a coffee bar while a grid of televisions provides the single screen for a fashion show broadcast.

efforts to identify, satisfy, retain, and maximize the value of their best customers. Enabled by database technology, these forward-focused retailers are employing strategies designed to capture customers' share of mind, wallet, and time. Using database technology to manage customer relationships is the topic of Chapters 20 and 21.

Emerging customer management strategies that retailers are embracing include customer relationship marketing, loyalty programs, and clienteling. Regardless of the strategy used, the intent is the same—to foster loyalty and develop an ongoing dialogue with a retailer's best customers. *Customer relationship marketing (CRM)* originated out of the need to more accurately target a fragmented customer base that was becoming increasingly more difficult to reach with mass advertising vehicles like television and newspapers. CRM is the topic of Chapter 20.

Armed with richer customer databases and the technology to gather and analyze customer and sales data, retailers are now taking active measures to develop loyalty programs that identify and reward their best customers. Sears' KidVantage program, for example, provides savings to members with young children. Similarly, specialty retailer Loehmann's, which offers women's designer apparel at discounted prices, uses data from its Insider Club to understand what customers are purchasing, when they are purchasing, and the type of events they prefer. In addition to periodic coupon and members-only savings, Insider Club members, currently 1.6 million strong, are notified of items and sales events. Loehmann's also launched a co-branded Insider Club Platinum Visa Card that provides a rebate on purchases.

Another approach to managing and building long-term relationships with best customers is *clienteling*. Saks Fifth Avenue, for example, strongly emphasizes personal contact with customers on the part of managers and sales associates. Associates collect and maintain detailed electronic client profiles that can be used to provide enhanced service. Sales associates are also encouraged to service clients across all departments so that the associates, already familiar with size and style preferences, can address clients' complete wardrobe needs as opposed to merely selling merchandise from their assigned department.

CONNECT IT

Think back now to the opening story about Target's phenomenal success as an upscale discounter. With sales growing exponentially, the chain's retailing strategy of providing quality, fashionable products at a low price in a fun atmosphere has proved to be a big hit with its core target market. Every element in Target's retailing mix, from merchandise assortment to price levels, service levels, atmosphere, and location, must be carefully considered to provide its customers with the products and shopping experience they are looking for. This is no easy feat for retailers, but finding the right combination can mean the difference between success and failure. And Target has indeed found success.

USE IT

Study Franchise Opportunities

Franchising offers an alternative to starting a business on your own. But which franchise is a good match for your interests and skills? Narrow the field of the thousands of different franchise opportunities by visiting the Franchise Handbook Online at **http://www.franchise1.com**. There you will find articles with checklists to help you thoroughly research a franchise and its industry, as well as a directory of franchise opportunities. Armed with this information, you can develop a questionnaire to evaluate a prospective franchise. Also visit the

International Franchise Association, a Washington, D.C., trade group, at **http://www.franchise.org** to find more information about franchising and learn if it's right for you.

Stop Junk Mail
If you are upset about junk mail, contact the Direct Marketing Association and have your name removed from mailing lists. The e-mail address is **http://www.the-dma.org**. You can also join an umbrella organization dedicated to stopping the flood of junk e-mail, intrusive telemarketing calls, and junk mail. One such organization is Stop the Junk Mail, found at **http://www.stopthejunkmail.com**.

REVIEW IT

1 **Discuss the importance of retailing in the U.S. economy.** Retailing plays a vital role in the U.S. economy for two main reasons. First, retail businesses contribute to our high standard of living by providing a vast number and diversity of goods and services. Second, retailing employs a large part of the U.S. working population—over twenty million people.

1.1 INFOTRAC COLLEGE EDITION   In order to fully appreciate the role retailing plays in the U.S. economy, it may be helpful to review a selection of press articles related to the retailing industry. Using InfoTrac (**http://www.infotrac-college.com**), run a keyword search for articles pertaining to retailing. Read a selection of articles, and report your findings to the class.

2 **Explain the dimensions by which retailers can be classified.** Many different kinds of retailers exist. A retail establishment can be classified according to its ownership, level of service, product assortment, and price. On the basis of ownership, retailers can be broadly differentiated as independent retailers, chain stores, or franchise outlets. The level of service retailers provide can be classified along a continuum of high to low. Retailers also classify themselves by the breadth and depth of their product assortments; some retailers have concentrated product assortments, whereas others have extensive product assortments. Last, general price levels also classify a store, from discounters offering low prices to exclusive specialty stores where high prices are the norm. Retailers use these latter three variables to position themselves in the marketplace.

2.1 TEAM WRITING   Form a team of three classmates to identify different retail stores in your city where pet supplies are sold. Include non-store forms of retailing as well, such as catalogs, the Internet, or the local veterinarian. Team members should divide up and visit all the different retailing outlets for pet supplies. Prepare a report describing the differences in brands and products sold at each of the retailing formats and the differences in store characteristics and service levels. For example, which brands are sold via mass merchandiser, independent specialty store, or other venue. Suggest why different products and brands are distributed through different types of stores.

3 **Describe the major types of retail operations.** The major types of retail stores are department stores, specialty retailers, supermarkets, drugstores, convenience stores, discount stores, and restaurants. Department stores carry a wide assortment of shopping and specialty goods, are organized into relatively independent departments, and offset higher prices by emphasizing customer service and decor. Specialty retailers typically carry a narrower but deeper assortment of merchandise, emphasizing distinctive products and a high level of customer service. Supermarkets are large self-service retailers that offer a wide variety of food products and some nonfood items. Drugstores are retail formats that sell mostly prescription and over-the-counter medications, health and beauty aids, cosmetics, and specialty items. Convenience stores carry a limited line of high-turnover convenience goods. Discount stores offer low-priced general merchandise and consist of four types: full-line discounters, discount specialty retailers, warehouse clubs, and off-price retailers. Finally, restaurants straddle the line between the retailing and services industries; whereas restaurants sell a product, food and drink, to final consumers, they can also be considered service marketers because they provide consumers with the service of preparing food and providing table service.

3.1 Discuss the possible marketing implications of the recent trend toward supercenters, which combine a supermarket and a full-line discount store.

3.2 Explain the function of warehouse clubs. Why are they classified as both wholesalers and retailers?

④ Discuss nonstore retailing techniques. Nonstore retailing, which is shopping outside a store setting, has three major categories. Automatic vending uses machines to offer products for sale. In direct retailing, the sales transaction occurs in a home setting, typically through door-to-door sales or party plan selling. Direct marketing refers to the techniques used to get consumers to buy from their homes or place of business. Those techniques include direct mail, catalogs and mail order, telemarketing, and electronic retailing, such as home shopping channels and on-line retailing using the Internet.

4.1 Go to the Gift Shop at on-line wine retailer Wine.com's Web site at **http://www.wine.com/**. How does this site help shoppers select gifts?

4.2 How much does the most powerful computer with the fastest modem, most memory, largest monitor, biggest hard drive, and all the available peripherals cost at **http://www.dell.com**? Then visit a store like Best Buy or Circuit City and price a comparable computer. How can you explain any price differences between the two retail operations? Explain any differences in features that you encountered. What conclusions can you draw from your research?

4.3 Why should retailers market their printed catalogs on-line? Look at Web site **http://www.catalogsite.com**.

⑤ Define franchising and describe its two basic forms. Franchising is a continuing relationship in which a franchiser grants to a franchisee the business rights to operate or to sell a product. Modern franchising takes two basic forms. In product and trade name franchising, a dealer agrees to buy or sell certain products or product lines from a particular manufacturer or wholesaler. Business format franchising is an ongoing business relationship in which a franchisee uses a franchiser's name, format, or method of business in return for several types of fees.

5.1 What advantages does franchising provide to franchisers as well as franchisees?

⑥ List the major tasks involved in developing a retail marketing strategy. Retail management begins with defining the target market, typically on the basis of demographic, geographic, or psychographic characteristics. After determining the target market, retail managers must develop the six variables of the retailing mix: product, promotion, place, price, presentation, and personnel.

6.1 Identify a successful retail business in your community. What marketing strategies have led to its success?

6.2 You want to convince your boss, the owner of a retail store, of the importance of store atmosphere. Write a memo citing specific examples of how store atmosphere affects your own shopping behavior.

⑦ Discuss the challenges of expanding retailing operations into global markets. With increased competition and slow domestic growth, mature retailers are looking for growth opportunities in the developing consumer economies of other countries. The homogenization of tastes and product preferences around the world, the lowering of trade barriers, and the emergence of underserved markets have made the prospects of expanding across national borders more feasible for many retailers. Retailers wanting to expand globally should first determine what their core competency is and determine whether this differentiation is what the local market wants. Retailers also need to skillfully make adjustments in product mix to meet local demands.

7.1 Your retail clothing company is considering expanding into Mexico. What information about the country and its customs should you collect before opening a store in Mexico?

8 **Describe future trends in retailing.** Three major trends are evident in retailing today. First, adding entertainment to the retail environment is one of the most popular strategies in retailing in recent years. Small retailers as well as national chains are using entertainment to set themselves apart from the competition. Second, retailers of the future will offer more convenience and efficiency to consumers as consumers become more precise on their shopping trips. Staples won't be sold in stores but instead will be delivered directly to the consumer, freeing shoppers to visit stores for products they enjoy buying. Advances in technology will make it easier for consumers to obtain the products they want. Last, more and more retailers are using the information they collect about their customers at the point of sale to develop customer management programs, including customer relationship marketing, loyalty programs, and clienteling.

8.1 *INFOTRAC* COLLEGE EDITION *WRITING* You have been asked to write a brief article about the way consumer demand for convenience and efficiency is influencing the future of retailing. Write the outline for your article. Once you have written your outline, use InfoTrac (**http://www.infrotrac-college.com**) to locate the article in *Business Credit* magazine titled, "Electronic Retailing: A Threat to Brick and Mortar Retailers?" by Keith Ackerman. How does your article differ? Is Ackerman's article still relevant?

APPLY IT

Application for Entrepreneurs

ENTREPRENEUR Ron Johnson is developing a retail strategy to open up his new athletic shoe and sports equipment store. He has decided to carry Nike and Converse as his two lines of athletic shoes. This will give him top-of-the-line merchandise (Nike) and a lower priced, high-quality alternative (Converse). He obtained permission from one of his former professors to hold brainstorming sessions in a couple of his classes. From these sessions, he identified the following evaluative criteria customers might use in selecting a particular athletic shoe to purchase: (1) attractiveness/style/color, (2) brand name, (3) comfort, (4) price, (5) endorsement, and (6) quality. He also determined that location, a friend's recommendation, brands carried, and store atmosphere are important in selecting a place to purchase athletic shoes.

Questions

1. What type of retailing strategy should Ron use?
2. Which elements of the retailing mix are relatively more important?
3. Should Ron incorporate a Web site into his retail strategy? Why or why not?

THINK ABOUT IT

Ethics Exercise

A–Z Grocery Company is well known for offering quality grocery products at the lowest prices in the market. When the company applied for a zoning change to build a new store in a middle-class neighborhood, several city council people objected because the company has no stores in low-income neighborhoods, where they argue the low prices are needed most. The company contends they cannot operate profitably in these neighborhoods because of higher security and operating costs.

Questions

1. Should low-cost retailers be required to locate near low-income customers? Why or why not?
2. Does the AMA Code of Ethics address this issue? Go to **http://www.marketingpower.com** and review the code. Then, write a brief paragraph on how the AMA Code of Ethics relates to retailing locations.

TRY IT

Entrepreneurship Case
Delia's Retails to Teens

Stephen Kahn knew he had a good idea for a new direct retailing business: sell funky clothes and accessories targeted to Sabrina-wannabe girls between the ages of ten and twenty-four. The problem was convincing financial backers that his idea was more than good—it was very lucrative. When he first presented his idea to venture capitalists, they scoffed at his business plan and refused to lend him money. Teens, they said, are an elusive group with limited financial resources and no access to credit cards. Moreover, teens are fickle, and the pace in teen fashion trends is often too fast for retailers to keep up.

Convinced that this overlooked niche had potential, Kahn, a former leveraged-buyout specialist and recent Yale grad, put up $100,000 of his own money and turned to family and friends for the other $1 million start-up capital he needed to print and mass mail his first catalog, called Delia's. Launched from a Brooklyn garage in 1993, Delia's startled Wall Street with its success, quickly becoming the nation's leading direct retailer of teen fashion.

Kahn's hunch about preteen and teenage girls, it turns out, was right on target. According to Teenage Research Unlimited, a consulting firm specializing in the teen market, young adults between the ages of twelve and nineteen spend an estimated $153 billion a year, or roughly $90 a week. Parents provide over half of their teens' incomes on an as-needed basis, with the rest coming from odd jobs, gifts, and allowances. Further, teens increasingly have access to their parents' credit cards and, in a growing number of cases, are acquiring their own credit cards with an adult sponsor. Parents are also setting up "digital on-line credit accounts" for their teens' on-line spending funded by their own credit cards. Not obligated to pay rent or other household expenses, most teens are free to spend their money on whatever they choose—accessories, CDs, and, most importantly, apparel. Additionally, buying decisions in teen apparel are being made at increasingly younger ages.

One of the most significant reasons for Delia's phenomenal success is the fact that it makes funky fashion accessible and affordable to preteen and teenage girls all across the nation. For young girls in rural and remote areas that lack options to buy cool clothes, Delia's serves as an equalizer of teen fashion. Now, teens in small midwestern or southern towns have the same fashion choices as their counterparts living in Los Angeles or New York. In schools all across the country, critiquing the latest Delia's catalog has become a lunchtime ritual.

After some fairly harrowing experiences with several suppliers early on, Kahn and partner Christopher Edgar, his ex-Yale University roommate, developed more of their own private-label merchandise in order to offer Delia's target market more unique clothing and accessories. More recent catalogs also attempt to target a slightly older demographic, aiming to be aspirational to preteens while not turning off older girls. The duo also weeded out suppliers that couldn't make consistent product and on-time shipments and opened their own warehousing facility to better control the fulfillment process and improve quality. These measures paid off for Delia's: Revenue hit $215 million in 2000, and its mailing list numbers more than 11 million. Not bad for a company that had sales of $150,000 just five years earlier.

Delia's has taken a multichannel approach to retailing. In addition to its successful direct-mail catalog, the company has opened some two dozen retail stores, operates several e-commerce sites. With virtually no advertising, the on-line store has attracted over 100,000 on-line buyers and more than five thousand catalog requests each day.

Questions

1. What type of retailer is Delia's?

2. Describe Delia's retailing strategy as best as you can in terms of product, price, place, promotion, people, and presentation.

3. Visit Delia's Web site at **http://www.delias.com**. How does it entertain and involve young girls in its brand? What is the focal point of the Web site?

Short

The *Marketing* PowerPoint CD-ROM has four video ad clips in the Chapter 13 slide presentation. The concepts of franchising, specialty retailing, discount stores, and direct retailing are illustrated in ads for Blockbuster, Office Depot, the NFL Store, and RadioShack.

Medium

How can retailers leverage the Internet when selling products that people are more comfortable buying in person, like bathing suits? CNN takes you to Lands' End so that you can see the creation of the company's virtual fitting room.

Long

To give you insight into Chapter 13, Small Business School goes to The Art Store in San Diego, California. Started by George Granoff, The Art Store has locations in several California cities and in New York City. Granoff, who lives in Boston, will take you inside the world of retail—and also inside a very targeted retail store. His market is so specific that you may be reminded of concepts from Chapter 7 regarding segmenting and targeting markets.

FLIP IT

Flip to Chapter 13 in your *Grademaker Study Guide* for more review opportunities, including the pretest, vocabulary review, Internet activities, study test questions, and an application exercise based on retailing concepts. Can you close your book and describe the major types of retail operations? Can you clearly explain to a friend who's not in the class how to classify retailers? Do you know the tasks involved in developing a retailing strategy? If not, then pick up your *Grademaker* and review.

CLICK IT

The *Marketing* Web site links you to all the Internet-based activities in this chapter, like the "Use It," "Review It" questions 4.1, 4.2, and 4.3, and the On-Line exercises in the chapter margins. As a review, do the Chapter 13 quiz and crossword puzzle. And don't forget the Career Exersite that gives you resources for exploring marketing career opportunities in retailing. Review the main concepts in the PowerPoint presentation for Chapter 13, too. Go to **http://lamb.swlearning.com**, read the material, and follow the links right from the site.

SPIN IT

Spin your Xtra! CD-ROM to test your understanding of the retailing concepts in the chapter by completing the worksheets for exhibits 13.2, 13.4, and 13.6. If your instructor has assigned a marketing plan project, worksheets on Xtra! can help you organize your work. In addition to the quiz on the Web site, there's another quiz on the Xtra! CD-ROM, plus video of the authors answering frequently asked questions about retailing topics, such as "How can small retailers compete with companies like Wal-Mart?"

MARKETING MISCUES

Jeremy's MicroBatch Ice Creams Gets Licked in Distribution

In October 2000, Jeremy's MicroBatch Ice Creams, Inc. discontinued operations. Founded in 1997 by Jeremy Kraus, a junior at the Wharton School of the University of Pennsylvania, the company and its guerrilla marketing techniques had drawn considerable attention. Kraus received two "entrepreneur of the year" awards, one from the Pennsylvania governor's office and the other from Mail Boxes, Etc. In the second annual Mail Boxes, Etc.'s "See Your Small Business on the Super Bowl Search," Kraus won $5,000 and the opportunity to feature his company's product in a $1.6 million television spot during the second quarter of the 1999 Super Bowl.

Kraus seemed to have everything going for him. In the company's initial public offering in February 2000, Kraus raised approximately $6 million. But, in October 2000, the company ran out of money after its marketing and distribution strategies failed. The collapse occurred despite attempts, in July 2000, to salvage the firm by replacing Kraus as CEO and revising its marketing efforts.

Jeremy's MicroBatch Ice Creams was inspired by successes in the microbrewery business. The company actually grew out of a business plan that Kraus had prepared for a class at Wharton. The idea was to make high-quality ice cream in limited quantities. The major points of Kraus's marketing plan included the following:

- *Target market:* Generation Y, teens, and twenty-somethings. The target market was comprised of consumers similar to the company's founder.
- *Product:* high-quality ice cream. Ice cream flavors included Vanilla Cream Stout (vanilla, cream stout swirl, chocolate-covered pretzels), Wired (vanilla with caffeine), Purple Passion Pills (purple mint, fudge swirl, chocolate-covered blue mint candies), Welcome to Tiramisu (tiramisu with espresso swirl, chocolate chunks, vanilla wafer cookies), Eve's Sinful Cider (apple cider, chunks of apple, apple swirl), Triple Espresso (coffee, espresso swirl, chocolate truffle chunks, chocolate-covered espresso beans), and Revenge of Chocolate Overload (chocolate, fudge swirl, chocolate truffle chunks, chocolate-covered almonds). Old flavors would be removed when new flavors were introduced, making each

product available for a limited time only. Production of the ice cream was outsourced.
- *Promotion:* an aggressive guerrilla marketing campaign. The company budgeted (and spent) $2.4 million for magazine ads, radio spots, posters, Internet ads, and its "Secret Service." The "Secret Service" was made up of a hundred part-time student employees who distributed free samples of the product in fifteen northeastern cities via the company's MicroBatch Mobiles.
- *Distribution:* supermarket chains. Jeremy's MicroBatch ice cream was available in over five thousand grocery stores, such as Roche Brothers, Stop & Shop, A&P Food Mart, Donelan's, Tedeschi, and Victory Markets, in New England, Colorado, Minnesota, Florida, Texas, and Arizona.
- *Price:* $3.29 to $3.59 per pint. The high price was intended to reinforce the company's positioning as a high-quality, limited edition ice cream product.

Unfortunately, Jeremy's MicroBatch Ice Creams made a couple of obvious distribution errors. First, the company failed to match its distribution strategy to where its target market would likely shop for specialty-flavored, pint-sized ice cream. The company was promoting its product on college campuses via its team of Secret Service salespeople, but it failed to secure distribution in outlets where these college students were likely to shop. Second, the company spent almost half of its 1999 revenues on slotting fees to grocery stores. It was battling for a limited quantity of freezer space, and larger competitors had deeper pockets to pay the supermarket chains for this space.

In September 2000, the company, under new leadership, decided to alter its distribution strategy and focus on placing MicroBatch freezers in coffeehouses, movie theaters, bookstores, and convenience stores, as well as opening Jeremy's MicroBatch Ice Creams retail shops. The strategy was never implemented, however, as the company went out of business in October 2000.

Questions

1. What was wrong with the initial distribution strategy at Jeremy's MicroBatch Ice Creams?

2. Were any other components of the marketing plan out of sync with the company's aspirations?

CRITICAL THINKING CASE

StreamCast Networks— A New Name in P2P Distribution

Probably one of the best-remembered names in peer-to-peer (P2P) file sharing will be Napster. Founded by Shawn Fanning in May 1999, Napster claimed to be the world's leading file-sharing community. Although Napster was the market leader and a pioneer in P2P file sharing, successful copyright infringement lawsuits by the music industry led to the downfall of the firm's business model. But these lawsuits did not lead to the overall demise of the practice of distributing media products via the Internet. In less than a year, over sixty million people downloaded Morpheus, a file-sharing program that enables users to distribute music and video over the Internet. Is it time for the entertainment industry to embrace this new method of distribution instead of fighting it through the court system?

Peer-to-Peer File Sharing

File sharing using personal computers has been around for many years. Historically, one person would download a file onto a disk and hand deliver the file to another person or another computer. The emergence of e-mail, however, changed this delivery process. Using e-mail attachments, users could share files by e-mailing the files to each other. The file-sharing revolution took on a whole new dimension, however, with the advent of video games such as *Diablo* (by Blizzard Entertainment) and companies like Napster. Suddenly, by stretching the capabilities of the Internet, a gamer could play *Diablo* against an unknown gamer and/or download music provided by an unknown person.

Unfortunately for these file sharers, the real world has not been as open to file sharing as they might have liked. Lawsuits charged that Napster had violated copyright laws by allowing users to use its centralized server to download and copy music. *Diablo* users, however, do not violate copyright laws because they have to buy the game from the manufacturer before playing on-line. With Napster, the file-sharing recipient used a centralized system, Napster, to obtain music without paying for it; with *Diablo*, the file-sharing recipient has paid for the right to play on-line by purchasing the game from Blizzard Entertainment.

The editors at the O'Reilly Network put together a directory of players in the P2P marketplace. Since the nature of P2P distribution is ill defined, the directory is divided into nineteen categories: (1) agents as peers, (2) collaboration, (3) development frameworks, (4) devices as peers, (5) distributed computation, (6) distributed objects, (7) distributed search engines, (8) file sharing, (9) gaming, (10) infrastructure, (11) Internet operating system, (12) licensed media distribution, (13) messaging frameworks, (14) metadata, (15) reputation and asset management, (16) security,

(17) servers/services as peers, (18) superdistribution, and (19) the writeable Web. The large number of categories appears to be indicative of the evolving nature of this new method of distribution. As StreamCast Networks demonstrates, the P2P model is a continually evolving distribution network.

StreamCast Networks, Inc.

According to the company's Web site (**http://www.streamcastnetworks.com**), StreamCast Networks, Inc., "is a leading global communications technology company that is revolutionizing Internet digital media distribution and communications via a unique software-driven solution that enables users to communicate with one another more efficiently on an unprecedented scale." The company offers two products: Morpheus and MusicCity.com. Morpheus is a P2P file-sharing program that allows users access to media content without utilizing a central server. The program is distributed free to users. MusicCity.com is a Web site that allows independent artists to showcase their music directly to the customer. Using the Morpheus P2P technology, users can listen to music and then have the option of purchasing it. StreamCast Networks, which is based in Tennessee, has two divisions. The Content Division is home to the company's two products. The Technology Division serves as the research and development arm of the company.

The Battle over Morpheus—Distributed Computing or Entertainment Piracy?

According to the Motion Picture Association of America, on-line users illegally copy films 350,000 times a day. These users are utilizing free file-sharing programs such as Morpheus. In addition to StreamCast Networks, other file-sharing companies include Grokster, based in the West Indies, and Kazaa, based in the Netherlands.

By late 2001, the Recording Industry Association of America and the Motion Picture Association of America had joined together and filed suit against these P2P companies, charging them with the theft of movies, music, and other copyrighted material. The suit charges that P2P file sharing is a copyright infringement and is not any different from the file sharing that was facilitated by Napster. StreamCast Networks, however, claims that it is really the users who are infringing upon copyright and not Morpheus because Morpheus does not operate a central server. The company insists that its Web site clearly warns against copyright infringement and says that it cannot control the use of Morpheus.

P2P could dramatically change the entertainment distribution process. In an industry that spends millions of dollars to produce one film, control of the distribution process is crucial to long-term profitability. Will P2P become a distribution partner, or will it remain an industry nemesis?

Questions

1. Describe the traditional models of distribution. Does P2P fit logically within the traditional framework?

2. What is the basis for the channel conflict?

3. What is the major difference between Morpheus and Napster?

4. Is Morpheus distributed computing or entertainment piracy?

MARKETING PLANNING ACTIVITIES

To complete all six activities, use the Part 4 Marketing Planning Worksheets on your Xtra! CD-ROM. If you need a company for the basis of your work, follow the "Marketing Plan Project" link on the *Marketing* Web site (**http://lamb.swlearning.com**).

Distribution Decisions

For continued general assistance on business plans and marketing plans, visit **http://www.bplans.com** or **http://www.businessplans.org**. For electronic sources of information, search the Electric Library at **http://www.elibrary.com** or the Internet Public Library at **http://www.ipl.org**. Another excellent source of information is the Sales and Marketing Executives Marketing Library at **http://www.sell.org**. You should also refer to Exhibit 2.7 for additional marketing plan checklist items (Part IV.B.2: Marketing Mix—Place/Distribution).

In the first part of your strategic marketing plan, you stated your business mission and objectives and performed a detailed SWOT analysis. In the second part of the plan you identified and described target market segments and identified sources of competitive intelligence and the need for further marketing research. Next, you began the process of defining the marketing mix, starting with the first component: product.

The next stage of the strategic planning process continues defining the elements of the marketing mix, and this section focuses on place, or distribution. Distribution is a key component of any business. For the e-business, distribution seems "invisible" to the consumer who may not care where your firm is located but wants the product delivered quickly and inexpensively. Creating a worldwide distribution system is an additional challenge to the marketer.

Use the following exercises to guide you through the distribution part of your strategic marketing plan:

1. Discuss the implications of dual/multiple distribution. If your firm sells through a major department store and its own catalog and then decides to have an on-line World Wide Web site or open its own store in a factory outlet, what will happen to channel relationships? To the final price offered to consumers? To promotional vehicles? Most e-marketers assume that a direct distribution channel, with no intermediaries, is the most efficient and least costly method for getting product offerings to customers. However, if you decide on a different distribution channel, you will also have to identify warehouses, fulfillment services, transportation firms, packing companies, and many other facilitating agencies. Does your firm have the capabilities to handle this, or should your firm invest in channel members to take over these tasks and functions? Check out the code of Internet Commerce Standards at **http://www.gii.com/standard/index.html**.

2. Decide what channel(s) your chosen company should be using. Describe the intermediaries involved and their likely behavior. What are the implications of these channels? Describe the conflict that might arise from having both an e-marketing offering and a brick-and-mortar offering. If distribution costs are different, will your firm set the same or different prices for end customers?

3. Which distribution intensity level would be best for your company's product? Justify your decision.

4. What physical distribution facilities will be needed to complete delivery of products and services to the buyer? Where should these facilities be located? Check out the Warehouse Location Simulation at **http://www.orie.cornell.edu/~jackson.whsloc.html**. How should the product be distributed? Justify your selection of transportation mode(s). What other types of channel facilitators will you require to get your product offering to your customers? Search under **http://www.looksmart.com** for either "Full Service Direct Marketing Firms" or "E-commerce Transaction Management Products."

5. What types of retail establishments might be used for your firm's product? Are they in locations convenient to the target customers? What is the atmosphere of each type of facility? How can you get the atmosphere of the brick-and-mortar offering to match the offering of your Web site?

6. If you have developed an Internet-based service, to what other Web sites might you "distribute" your service? How will working with these other Web sites help you reach your target audience? Are there other Web sites from which you might accept distribution deals that would make your product or service offering stronger? Explain how strategic distribution with other Web sites or services can give you a competitive advantage.

CROSS-FUNCTIONAL CONNECTIONS SOLUTIONS

Questions

1. What are some of the popular advanced manufacturing systems and how do they interact with marketing?

   Advanced manufacturing systems—which include just-in-time (JIT), manufacturing resources planning (MRP), and electronic data interchange (EDI)—allow a firm to compete on both time and quality. The systems enable firms to respond faster to customers' demands and to shorten the new-product production cycle. The systems allow firms to produce a large variety of high-quality products in a reduced cycle time. Consequently, such systems result in more timely deliveries.

2. What is an enterprise-wide integrated distribution system? What is marketing's role in such a system?

   Simply put, an enterprise-wide integrated distribution system brings together all aspects of the business in order to get products to customers in a timely manner. Such a system generally relies heavily upon automated exchanges among various channel parties. The marketing function's role in such a system is varied and may include channel selection strategies, automatic customer data transmission to the shop floor, wireless tracking of a customer's order, and/or customer satisfaction measures.

3. How do production and delivery happen simultaneously in the service sector? What other functional areas are important partners in the service arena?

   A unique characteristic of a service is its inseparability; that is, services are generally sold, produced, and consumed at the same time. Consumers must be present during the production and delivery of a service. For example, a consumer receives a haircut at the same time that the haircut is being produced. This inseparability means that the service cannot be produced in one location and delivered at another location. Thus, the quality of the service depends upon the quality of the employee—making human resources a very important cross-functional partner.

Suggested Readings

Alexander E. Ellinger, "Improving Marketing/Logistics Cross-Functional Collaborations in the Supply Chain," *Industrial Marketing Management,* January 2000, 85–96.

Perry A. Trunick, "New Demands for Tomorrow's Manager," *Transportation & Distribution,* December 1998, 18–19.

PART 5

Promotion Decisions

CROSS-FUNCTIONAL CONNECTIONS

UNDERSTANDING MARKETING COMMUNICATIONS' CONTRIBUTION TO FIRM VALUE

When purchasing a product or service, a customer does not think in terms of advertising, sales promotion, public relations, and personal selling, nor does he or she think in terms of marketing, manufacturing, accounting, finance, research and development, and human resources. Rather, the product or service received by the customer is the sum of all of the internal processes, just as the communications message is the sum of all of the communications vehicles available to the firm. It is the company's responsibility to make certain that the product/service received by the customer is consistent with the message that the customer has received via the firm's integrated marketing communications. For example, advertising for Priceline.com touts its ease of use. Therefore, when a potential customer attempts to buy something using Priceline.com, there should not be complicating features that make it difficult for the customer to buy products on-line.

Product quality is an issue that touches the heart of a firm's operational processes. Marketers love to tout a product's superior quality when communicating with potential customers. When a company's communications strategy focuses on promoting quality features, pressure is placed on R&D, manufacturing, and human resources to deliver quality. Unfortunately, features that signal quality to a scientist or an engineer in a manufacturing or R&D department may not readily translate to perceptions of quality by the customer.

If a firm's communications program entices the consumer to try a product or service, the product or service must then be consistent with the consumer's expectations of the quality. Too frequently, marketers have developed award-winning communications campaigns for a new product, only to see the product fail in the market due to inconsistency between what the communications program is conveying and what the product delivers.

The need for interaction between marketing and manufacturing does not stop with the product introduction campaign, however. At any point in a product's life cycle, marketing may decide to promote the product. For example, Colgate-Palmolive may decide to offer a price discount over a two- or three-week period, to advertise heavily, and/or to offer coupons in a freestanding insert for one of its bar soaps. From marketing's perspective, the hope is that a consumer will try the soap due to the heavy marketing communications effort (and keep using the product even after the communications effort has stopped).

Marketing at Colgate-Palmolive would need to work closely with manufacturing when planning such an extensive product promotion. Otherwise manufacturing will be producing the product at its traditional level, which will be inconsistent with marketing's promotional sales plan. An integrated marketing communications program that generates high demand for a product is only as good as the product's availability. That is, a well-orchestrated marketing campaign can create a powerful purchasing stimulus. But when manufacturing cannot meet demand, consumers consider competitive brands in order to satisfy the product want or need stimulated by the marketing communications program.

Advertising and promotional efforts tend to be a source of friction between marketing and financial managers. Oddly, advertising and promotional expenditures are generally viewed as cost elements rather than investments in the product or brand. Marketers view these expenditures as investments in building the business, much as companies invest in personnel in order to have a well-managed organization. Customer satisfaction and repeat business depend upon constant maintenance by the marketing department. In contrast, accountants often view advertising and promotional expenses as variable costs. Unfortunately, viewed as variable costs, advertising expenses are tied directly to sales increases and decreases, and marketing budgets are often cut when they are needed most.

Personal selling is a component of integrated marketing communications where considerable interaction among functions has been occurring and where expenses tend to be viewed as investments since human capital is involved. It is no longer sufficient for a salesperson to have good personal interaction skills to be successful. Now, salespeople have to possess intimate knowledge of the products they present to potential consumers. For example, a sales representative for South-Western College Publishing has to understand the topics covered in a particular textbook in order to talk knowledgeably to professors in the area. At Kele & Associates, a business-to-business supplier of building automation peripherals, sales and accounting collaborate to better understand national account profitability. The company understands that nurturing a current account is less expensive than identifying and developing new accounts.

At the same time, it is no longer sufficient for R&D engineers or manufacturing specialists to work only within their limited domains. Many firms are now insisting that R&D and manufacturing talk directly with customers. Not surprisingly, such an external emphasis is in direct contrast to the technical orientation of R&D and manufacturing employees. Additionally, it is often assumed that salespeople are more extroverted than R&D and manufacturing employees, who are considered to be inherently introverted. Firms such as Motorola and Intuit expect that their engineers will go on sales calls. These engineers may visit customers with a marketing person as part of a sales call or separately in order to watch the customer use the product. There seems to be no better way of developing and manufacturing innovative, cutting-edge products than to have the people who work directly with the product also work closely with the end user.

On the flip side of this, companies could consider including salespeople on cross-functional new-product development teams. Salespeople are the ones out in the field who see how customers use the company's products on a daily basis and hear what customers are saying about their preferences. They can bring the voice of the customer into the firm. Additionally, salespeople are great sources of competitive intelligence as they are often the first to hear (from a customer) about a competitor's new product.

The sales area is also beginning to work closely with the finance, accounting, and human resource groups with regard to compensation systems. Firms are beginning to move from sales objectives (volume and/or revenue) to financial objectives (profit). By linking sales commissions to profit-related objectives, firms stress the importance of understanding the firm's margin versus focusing solely on product revenue. Computer giants such as IBM and Hewlett-Packard follow a variable commission strategy that links a salesperson's commission to a product's profit margin.

While finance and accounting will generally be focused on the profit aspect of the salesperson's objectives, human resources will have to work closely with the salesperson to develop the most appropriate compensation system for the types of accounts in the salesperson's territory. Additionally, the human resources staff is trained in methods to help the salesperson clarify individual goals, regarding responsibilities and desired accomplishments, that will be consistent with company-wide strategic goals. In today's business environment of teamwork and cross selling, the human resources department may also be called upon to help interview and train potential sales personnel.

The clear linkage among finance, accounting, human resources, and marketing with regard to a firm's selling strategy is exemplified in IBM's focus on profits and customer satisfaction. As mentioned earlier, IBM follows a variable commission strategy that ties a salesperson's commission to margins on the company's products. Sixty percent of the commission is tied to profit margin. Interestingly, the other 40 percent of the commission is linked to customer satisfaction. Customer satisfaction is measured according to the customer's perception of how well its IBM sales team has helped it achieve its own company objectives.

A successful integrated marketing communications program requires that marketing work closely with R&D and manufacturing with regard to quality and availability. Simultaneously, marketing has to interact closely with finance, accounting, and human resources to establish appropriate goals and objectives for its marketing communications programs. It is the sum of the external messages and internal operations that produces a satisfied customer.

Questions

1. Why are the company's marketing communications of particular concern to R&D and manufacturing?

2. Why do financial managers view advertising and promotional expenditures as costs?

3. How has personal selling become functionally integrated?

CHAPTER FOURTEEN
INTEGRATED MARKETING COMMUNICATIONS

Learning Objectives

1 Discuss the role of promotion in the marketing mix

2 Discuss the elements of the promotional mix

3 Describe the communication process

4 Explain the goals and tasks of promotion

5 Discuss the AIDA concept and its relationship to the promotional mix

6 Describe the factors that affect the promotional mix

7 Discuss the concept of integrated marketing communications

In the five years since *Maxim* was first introduced to the United States, the publication with its formula of "sex, sports, beer, gadgets, clothes, and fitness" has upset the leaders in the men's magazine industry such as *Gentlemen's Quarterly* and *Esquire*. A newcomer in an industry that has recently seen ad revenues decline sharply, *Maxim* now sells 2.5 million copies each month—two and a half times as many as either *GQ* or *Esquire*. Its recent $115 million worth of advertising was more than *GQ* has and twice as much as *Esquire;* with statistics like these, *Maxim* joins the elite ranks of *Cosmo, Glamour,* and a handful of other established magazines.

How has *Maxim* realized such success while more seasoned marketers are experiencing sluggish ad sales and a declining subscriber base? *Maxim* uses an approach that emphasizes low entry costs, a proven editorial formula, and a guerrilla-style approach to marketing that is redefining the magazine industry. *Maxim* started by asking potential readers what they wanted. But instead of hosting traditional focus groups, the publishers felt they could get more information by going where men congregate. Using unofficial focus groups held at bars or sporting events in select U.S. cities, the publishers of *Maxim* gained invaluable knowledge about the needs of its target audience—males twenty-six to thirty-two years old. By giving its readers what they want, the magazine has seen unprecedented growth in its subscriber base. With an initial run of 250,000 copies, *Maxim* has had impressive gains in newsstand appeal, recently reaching one million in single-copy sales. The magazine regularly receives 35,000 to 50,000 blow-in subscription cards from each issue.

Maxim's strategy to becoming a success in the United States included keeping initial expenses low and incorporating a unique marketing mix. Instead of relying on traditional advertising, *Maxim* plans elaborate parties and other marketing events, then reaps the rewards of the free publicity and media coverage. Its first party, "Circus Maximus," was held on a closed-off Sunset Boulevard complete with a parade led by actress Jamie Presley riding on an elephant. Another promotional party took place at the Farmer's Daughter Motor Inn and included a performance by The Cult and motel rooms decorated in twenty-one exotic themes. The magazine also generated a great deal of public relations mileage from its annual "Hot 100 Women" special edition.

Maxim also knows the importance of on-line marketing. Statistics show that 76 percent of *Maxim*'s readers finish reading the magazine the first day they get it. So *Maxim* updates its Web site (**http://www.maximonline.com**) daily, offering interactive programs that include its *Maxim Challenge* football pool, games, and live chats with *Maxim* cover girls like actress Tara Reid. *Maxim* has also teamed up with other companies for cross-promotions that include joint parties with Smirnoff Ice in cities throughout the country and weekend getaways at the trendy W Hotel in ten cities.[1]

As you can see, *Maxim* places considerable emphasis on promotion in its marketing mix. What types of promotional tools are available to companies, and what factors influence the choice of tool? Why is consistent integrated marketing important to the promotional plan? These questions, and others, will be answered as you read this chapter.

1

Discuss the role of promotion in the marketing mix

promotion
Communication by marketers that informs, persuades, and reminds potential buyers of a product in order to influence an opinion or elicit a response.

promotional strategy
A plan for the optimal use of the elements of promotion: advertising, public relations, personal selling, and sales promotion.

differential advantage
One or more unique aspects of an organization that cause target consumers to patronize that firm rather than competitors.

The Role of Promotion in the Marketing Mix

Few goods or services, no matter how well developed, priced, or distributed, can survive in the marketplace without effective **promotion**—communication by marketers that informs, persuades, and reminds potential buyers of a product in order to influence their opinion or elicit a response.

Promotional strategy is a plan for the optimal use of the elements of promotion: advertising, public relations, personal selling, and sales promotion. As Exhibit 14.1 shows, the marketing manager determines the goals of the company's promotional strategy in light of the firm's overall goals for the marketing mix—product, place (distribution), promotion, and price. Using these overall goals, marketers combine the elements of the promotional strategy (the promotional mix) into a coordinated plan. The promotion plan then becomes an integral part of the marketing strategy for reaching the target market.

The main function of a marketer's promotional strategy is to convince target customers that the goods and services offered provide a differential advantage over the competition. A **differential advantage** is the set of unique features of a company and its products that are perceived by the target market as significant and superior to the competition. Such features can include high product quality, rapid delivery, low prices, excellent service, or a feature not offered by the competition. For example, Revlon ColorStay Lipcolor promises unsmeared lipstick all day long. By effectively communicating this differential advantage through advertising featuring model Cindy Crawford, Revlon can stimulate demand for its

Exhibit 14.1

Role of Promotion in the Marketing Mix

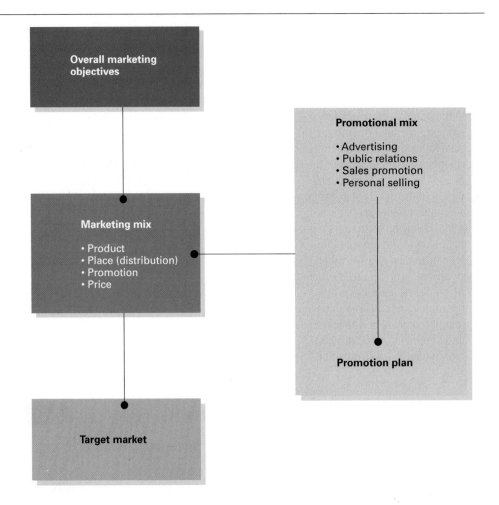

Revlon ColorStay Lipcolor promises unsmeared lipstick all day long. By effectively communicating this differential advantage through advertising, Revlon can stimulate demand for its smudge-free line of makeup.

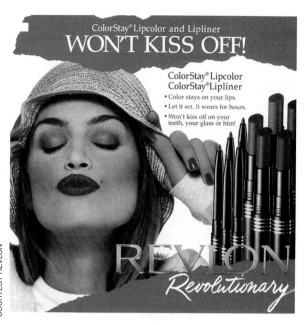

smudge-free line of makeup. Promotion is therefore a vital part of the marketing mix, informing consumers of a product's benefits and thereby positioning the product in the marketplace.

The Promotional Mix

Most promotional strategies use several ingredients—which may include advertising, public relations, sales promotion, and personal selling—to reach a target market. That combination is called the **promotional mix**. The proper promotional mix is the one that management believes will meet the needs of the target market and fulfill the organization's overall goals. The more funds allocated to each promotional ingredient and the more managerial emphasis placed on each technique, the more important that element is thought to be in the overall mix.

Advertising

Almost all companies selling a good or a service use some form of advertising, whether it be in the form of a multimillion-dollar campaign or a simple classified ad in a newspaper. **Advertising** is any form of paid communication in which the sponsor or company is identified. Traditional media—such as television, radio, newspapers, magazines, books, direct mail, billboards, and transit cards (advertisements on buses and taxis and at bus stops)—are most commonly used to transmit advertisements to consumers. With the increasing fragmentation of traditional media choices, marketers are sending their advertisements to consumers in many new and innovative ways, such as with interactive video technology located in department stores and supermarkets and through Internet Web sites and electronic mail.

One of the primary benefits of advertising is its ability to communicate to a large number of people at one time. Cost per contact, therefore, is typically very low. Advertising has the advantage of being able to reach the masses (for instance, through national television networks), but it can also be microtargeted to small groups of potential customers, such as television ads on a targeted cable network or through print advertising in a trade magazine.

Although the cost per contact in advertising is very low, the total cost to advertise is typically very high. This hurdle tends to restrict advertising on a national basis to only those companies that are financially able to do so. For instance, when Degree antiperspirant introduced its new line of clear gel products aimed at men, the company spent $25 to $30 million in media advertising alone.[2] Few small companies can match this level of spending for a national campaign. Chapter 15 examines advertising in greater detail.

 Many companies are including Internet advertising as a vital component in their marketing mix. Banner ads, viral marketing, and interactive promotions are all ways that marketers utilize the Internet to try and reach their target audience. But some consumers and lawmakers feel that privacy issues are being violated. Read about this issue in the "Ethics in Marketing" box.

Public Relations

Concerned about how they are perceived by their target markets, organizations often spend large sums to build a positive public image. **Public relations** is the

②
Discuss the elements of the promotional mix

promotional mix
The combination of promotional tools—including advertising, public relations, personal selling, and sales promotion—used to reach the target market and fulfill the organization's overall goals.

advertising
Impersonal, one-way mass communication about a product or organization that is paid for by a marketer.

public relations
The marketing function that evaluates public attitudes, identifies areas within the organization the public may be interested in, and executes a program of action to earn public understanding and acceptance.

You've Got Mail

Turn the computer on, check your e-mail, and more than likely you're bombarded with messages like "You can lose twenty pounds by the summer!" "Cut your mortgage payments in half!" and "Click here to find out how you can take the dream vacation of a lifetime!" Welcome to the Internet! You've got mail—now how do you get rid of it?

Some marketers have been making money by sending unwanted e-mail for years. It seems like the perfect way to reach hundreds, even thousands, with your marketing message. Research shows that e-mail users recently received an average of 1,465 messages during the year, and 571 of them were spam. These figures are expected to more than double to 3,846 messages, 1,479 of them junk, within four years. Spamming—sending out unsolicited advertise-

ments over a computer network to many addresses—annoys most consumers and is now coming under scrutiny from the government.

Just how do marketers get your e-mail address in the first place? Chat rooms, message boards, Internet directories, Web pages, and on-line shopping are prime "harvesting" sites for spammers. Other companies may sell their customer data lists. When Toysmart.com filed for bankruptcy, the company tried to sell its customer database—after promising customers it wouldn't share the information gathered on-line.

Some corporations are now making privacy a competitive advantage. Atlanta-based Internet provider EarthLink is proud of its Spaminator, which the company describes as a "state-of-the-art solution for removing unsolicited

e-mail from your mailbox before it gets to you." America Online, the nation's largest Internet provider, has been blocking mail from known spammers for years. Several states have passed laws limiting unsolicited mass commercial e-mail in an attempt to protect computer users from unwanted intrusions. Under many of the laws, unsolicited e-mail is prohibited or must contain opt-out instructions.

Unsolicited e-mail is a huge inconvenience to consumers. Companies that employ this practice should worry about consumer backlash. Marketers have an ethical and, in some states, legal obligation to keep consumers and their privacy concerns in mind.[3]

Is e-mail an effective marketing tool to use with college students? When does e-mail as a marketing tool become spamming?

---

marketing function that evaluates public attitudes, identifies areas within the organization the public may be interested in, and executes a program of action to earn public understanding and acceptance. Public relations helps an organization communicate with its customers, suppliers, stockholders, government officials, employees, and the community in which it operates. Marketers use public relations not only to maintain a positive image but also to educate the public about the company's goals and objectives, introduce new products, and help support the sales effort.

HBO, as part of its effort to add 20 percent to its subscriber base over a five-year period, created a ten-hour miniseries based on Stephen Ambrose's best-selling novel *Band of Brothers*. The story follows Easy Company's real-life journey from basic training to V-E Day. The made-for-television miniseries had all the elements of a Hollywood blockbuster: brand-name producers (Steven Spielberg and Tom Hanks), $120 million budget, stellar cast, and a marketing blitz that was one of HBO's most extensive to date. The marketing campaign included billboards, traditional advertising to promote the series, and a savvy public relations and publicity plan. A behind-the-scenes feature and tie-ins with AOL Time Warner, Inc., helped gain public exposure for the series. For example, *Band of Brothers* appeared prominently on the welcome screen, which is the first thing AOL's thirty million subscribers see when they log on. A separate Web site allowed visitors to "experience the war" through the latest Internet technology. TBS, Time Warner's cable TV network, featured a war movie every Monday night for eleven weeks, and the Turner Classic Movies cable TV channel ran a thirty-six-hour marathon of war films prior to the *Band of Brothers* debut. HBO also distributed student magazines, posters, and study guides to as many as three million tenth and eleventh graders—some of whom were also treated to school visits from Easy Company veterans. The miniseries was a critical and commercial success with 9.9 million viewers tuning in during its two-hour premiere.[4]

A solid public relations program can generate favorable **publicity**—public information about a company, good, or service appearing in the mass media as a news item. The organization generally is not identified as the source of the infor-

publicity
Public information about a company, good, or service appearing in the mass media as a news item.

mation. The soy industry received favorable publicity and an increase in sales after the Food and Drug Administration (FDA) approved a health claim for food labeling suggesting a link between soy protein and the reduced risk of coronary heart disease.[5] This incident underscores a peculiar reality of marketing: No matter how many millions are spent on advertising, nothing sells a product better than free publicity.

Although an organization does not pay for this kind of mass-media exposure, publicity should not be viewed as free. Preparing news releases, staging special events, and persuading media personnel to print or broadcast them costs money. During the year-and-a-half it took the FDA to approve the soy claim, meatless burger marketer Gardenburger was busy capitalizing on the pre-approval buzz on soy and readying a public relations plan to put its brand at the forefront should the FDA approve the claim. While the FDA was mulling its final decision, Gardenburger used interim packaging touting its soy burgers as "great-tasting and packed with soy protein" to spark interest among those who were hearing about soy's health attributes in the press. Gardenburger also provided footage of its factory lines to major media outlets. These tactics proved quite beneficial for the soy marketer: Seventy-five newspapers and one hundred television stations used Gardenburger's packaging and production line footage in their coverage of the soy story, reaching some thirty-five million consumers. Two months after the FDA's approval, Gardenburger's sales had risen 25 percent.[6] Public relations and publicity are examined further in Chapter 15.

Sales Promotion

Sales promotion consists of all marketing activities—other than personal selling, advertising, and public relations—that stimulate consumer purchasing and dealer effectiveness. Sales promotion is generally a short-run tool used to stimulate immediate increases in demand. Sales promotion can be aimed at end consumers, trade customers, or a company's employees. Sales promotions include free samples, contests, premiums, trade shows, vacation giveaways, and coupons. A major promotional campaign might use several of these sales promotion tools. For example, Motorola, a sponsor of a mountain bike event called "24 Hours of Adrenaline," teamed up recently with Canadian Future Shop to debut the Motorola Gear Grab. This promotion gave ten people twenty-four seconds to grab as much Motorola gear as they could in a Future Shop store. Contestants worked in pairs and used Motorola two-way radios so that one partner could provide the other with the name, description, and location of a Motorola product—including cellphones and messaging devices—within the store. Contestants were also eligible for a grand prize of various Motorola and mountain biking gear. Besides the Gear Grab, Motorola sponsored several mini–Gear Grabs during mountain bike event weekends in different cities.[7]

Often marketers use sales promotion to improve the effectiveness of other ingredients in the promotional mix, especially advertising and personal selling. Research shows that sales promotion complements advertising by yielding faster sales responses. Lever 2000 recently shifted some of its marketing dollars to focus more on sampling instead of traditional advertising. The company literally took to the streets to launch its Pure Rain Body Wash. The sampling program had samplers dressed in shower costumes and handing out product samples to consumers in different cities. During the program, consumers also were surveyed on shower-related questions such as "Which famous person would you most like to shower with?" Along with sampling, two transit stops were converted into shower stalls. In cities where ordinances prevented such conversions, tents were set up.[8] Sales promotion is discussed in more detail in Chapter 16.

Personal Selling

Personal selling is a purchase situation in which two people communicate in an attempt to influence each other. In this dyad, both the buyer and the seller have

Nabisco
Nabisco lists its promotions on its Web site. What do you think the advantages and disadvantages of this are? Visit the site to get more information.
http://www.nabiscoworld.com

On Line

sales promotion
Marketing activities—other than personal selling, advertising, and public relations—that stimulate consumer buying and dealer effectiveness.

personal selling
A purchase situation in which two people communicate in an attempt to influence each other.

specific objectives they wish to accomplish. The buyer may need to minimize cost or assure a quality product, for instance, while the salesperson may need to maximize revenue and profits.[9]

Traditional methods of personal selling include a planned presentation to one or more prospective buyers for the purpose of making a sale. Whether it takes place face-to-face or over the phone, personal selling attempts to persuade the buyer to accept a point of view or convince the buyer to take some action. For example, a car salesperson may try to persuade a car buyer that a particular model is superior to a competing model in certain features, such as gas mileage, roominess, and interior styling. Once the buyer is somewhat convinced, then the salesperson may attempt to elicit some action from the buyer, such as a test-drive or a purchase. Frequently, in this traditional view of personal selling, the objectives of the salesperson are at the expense of the buyer, creating a win-lose outcome.

More current notions on the subject of personal selling emphasize the relationship that develops between a salesperson and a buyer. This concept is more typical with business- and industrial-type goods, such as heavy machinery or computer systems, than with consumer goods. Relationship selling emphasizes a win-win outcome and the accomplishment of mutual objectives that benefits both buyer and salesperson in the long term. Rather than focusing on a quick sale, relationship selling attempts to create a long-term, committed relationship based on trust, increased customer loyalty, and a continuation of the relationship between the salesperson and the customer.[10] Personal selling and relationship selling are discussed in Chapter 16.

3

Describe the communication process

▋ Marketing Communication

Promotional strategy is closely related to the process of communication. As humans, we assign meaning to feelings, ideas, facts, attitudes, and emotions. **Communication** is the process by which we exchange or share meanings through a common set of symbols. When a company develops a new product, changes an old one, or simply tries to increase sales of an existing good or service, it must communicate its selling message to potential customers. Marketers communicate information about the firm and its products to the target market and various publics through its promotion programs. Nestlé Crunch, for example, set out to reverse a decline in sales by establishing a consistent brand message that emphasized the candy's "crunchy" personality and key attributes. The company then signed Los Angeles basketball star Shaquille O'Neal as its spokesperson because it felt his personality—confident, witty, and entertaining—matched the attributes of the candy bar. Nestlé promoted the relationship through special events and television commercials. In the first three months of the campaign, dollar volume of Nestlé Crunch was up 5.2 percent over the previous year.[11] Read Shaq's own words about the power of marketing and advertising in Exhibit 14.2.

Communication can be divided into two major categories: interpersonal communication and mass communication. **Interpersonal communication** is direct, face-to-face communication between two or more people. When communicating face-to-face, people see the other person's reaction and can respond almost immediately. A salesperson speaking directly with a client is an example of marketing communication that is interpersonal.

Mass communication refers to communicating a concept or message to large audiences. A great deal of marketing communication is directed to consumers as a whole, usually through a mass medium such as television or newspapers. When a company advertises, it generally does not personally know the people with whom it is trying to communicate. Furthermore, the company is unable to respond immediately to consumers' reactions to its message. Instead, the marketing manager

communication
The process by which we exchange or share meanings through a common set of symbols.

interpersonal communication
Direct, fact-to-face communication between two or more people.

mass communication
The communication of a concept or message to large audiences.

While on the outside looking in, I did not realize that marketing was so complicated. I never knew that a person, such as an athlete, could have such a powerful effect on peoples' thought processes and purchasing behavior. The use of a well-known athlete in marketing a product or service can have a great impact on the sales of that product or service. Look at Michael Jordan. Almost overnight most every kid either was wearing or wanted to wear Air Jordan shoes.

Why does this happen? Is it the appeal of a great athlete or is it great marketing? The answer is "none of the above." It's both. In my years as a professional basketball player, I have seen firsthand the dramatic appeal that athletes have for the fans and public in general. Top-name athletes are like E. F. Hutton—when they talk, people listen. But why do they listen? I believe they listen to us, the athletes, because we have credibility. The effectiveness of celebrity endorsements depends largely on how credible and attractive the spokesperson is and how familiar people are with him or her. Companies sometimes use sports figures and other celebrities to promote products hoping they are appropriate opinion leaders.

Because of an athlete's fame and fortune, or attraction, the athlete can often have the right credibility to be a successful spokesperson. The best definition of credibility that I could find was by James Gordon in his book, *Rhetoric of Western Thought.* He said that attraction "can come from a person's observable talents, achievements, occupational position or status, personality and appearance, and style."* That may be why a famous athlete's personality and position can help him or her communicate more effectively than a not-so-famous athlete.

Credibility is a positive force in the persuasive promotion used predominantly by cola marketers like Pepsi because of what I like to call "dreamful attraction." For example, when I was young, I dreamed that I was like Dr. J., the famous basketball player for the Philadelphia 76ers. I would take his head off a poster and put my head on it. I wanted to be Dr. J. That is dreamful attraction. The youth of today are no different. Just the other day a kid stopped me and told me that he wanted to be like me. He had a dreamful attraction. This dreamful attraction can help sell products. In my case, Pepsi, Spalding, Kenner, and Reebok are hoping that they are able to package properly and market whatever dreamful attraction I might have for their target audience—kids.

There are many ways to communicate to my target audience. I find that the most effective way for me is through television commercials. This avenue gives me a chance to express myself and show my real feelings about a message we are trying to communicate—either visually or vocally. I feel that I have what Clint Eastwood has—"Sudden Impaq." My impact is revealed through my sense of humor and my nonverbal communication.

Why does Shaq sell? Communication. Although the verbal communication in many of my commercials is slim, the impact is still there. This makes me believe even more in the quote that who you are can almost be as important as what you say. But if you can blend the two together—who you are and what you have to say—then imagine how much more successful the communication message can be in the marketing process. Andre Agassi's favorite quote from his Canon commercial is "Image is everything." If it is not everything, it is almost everything. If you have the right image, match it with the right product, and market it properly, then success should follow.

I have been involved in commercials and the marketing of products for only a short time, but I have learned a great deal. If there is one formula for success in selling products, it would be this: Marketing plus credibility and image plus effective communications equals increase in sales—hopefully.

Now, you can call me Dr. Shaq, M.E. (Marketing Expert).

*James Gordon, *Rhetoric of Western Thought,* (Dubuque, Iowa: Kendall-Hunt Publishing Co., 1976), 207.

must wait to see whether people are reacting positively or negatively to the mass-communicated promotion. Any clutter from competitors' messages or other distractions in the environment can reduce the effectiveness of the mass communication effort.

The Communication Process

Marketers are both senders and receivers of messages. As *senders*, marketers attempt to inform, persuade, and remind the target market to adopt courses of action compatible with the need to promote the purchase of goods and services. As *receivers*, marketers attune themselves to the target market in order to develop the appropriate messages, adapt existing messages, and spot new communication opportunities. In this way, marketing communication is a two-way, rather than one-way, process.[12] The two-way nature of the communication process is shown in Exhibit 14.3.

The Sender and Encoding

The **sender** is the originator of the message in the communication process. In an interpersonal conversation, the sender may be a parent, a friend, or a salesperson. For an advertisement or press release, the sender is the company or organization itself. For example, the International Olympics Committee and its television partner NBC were the senders of messages promoting the 2002 Winter Games in Salt Lake City to a younger target audience. To appeal to eighteen- to thirty-four-year-olds, the Winter Games promoted more of the extreme sports—the fast, gravity-defying, and often dangerous activities that have surged in popularity among American youth.[13]

Encoding is the conversion of the sender's ideas and thoughts into a message, usually in the form of words or signs. Thus, to promote the Winter Games, NBC might encode its Olympics messages into advertisements. In addition, an NBC sports announcer, covering other extreme sports events, might encode the promotional message into a sports update to the prospective audience watching the event.

A basic principle of encoding is that what matters is not what the source says but what the receiver hears. One way of conveying a message that the receiver will hear properly is to use concrete words and pictures. For example, one television commercial for the Winter Games featured skater Tara Lipinski gliding across the ice to classical music. "To some people," said the smooth voice-over, "the Winter Olympics looks like this. Others see it like this." On the word "this," Lipinski disappeared from the screen; with a crash of noise and techno music, she was replaced by images of crashing skiers, somersaulting freestylers, careening hockey players, soaring ski jumpers, and speeding lugers. The voice-over then read the tagline, "Something for everyone."[14]

Message Transmission

Transmission of a message requires a **channel**—a voice, radio, newspaper, or other communication medium. A facial expression or gesture can also serve as a channel.

sender
The originator of the message in the communication process.

encoding
The conversion of a sender's ideas and thoughts into a message, usually in the form of words or signs.

channel
A medium of communication—such as a voice, radio, or newspaper—for transmitting a message.

Exhibit 14.3 Communication Process

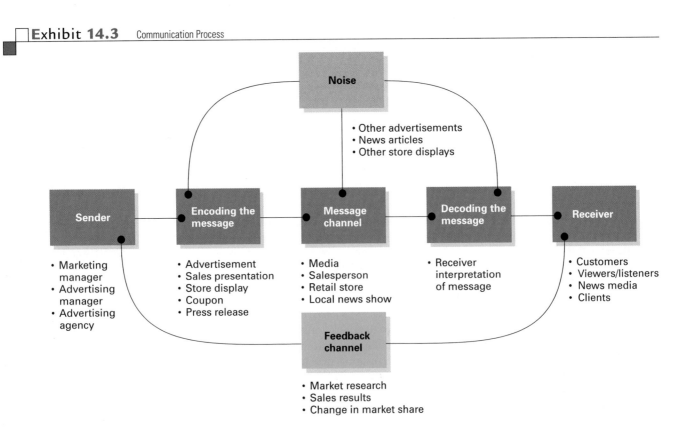

Reception occurs when the message is detected by the receiver and enters his or her frame of reference. In a two-way conversation such as a sales pitch given by a sales representative to a potential client, reception is normally high. In contrast, the desired receivers may or may not detect the message when it is mass communicated because most media are cluttered by **noise**—anything that interferes with, distorts, or slows down the transmission of information. In some media overcrowded with advertisers, such as newspapers and television, the noise level is high and the reception level is low. For example, competing network advertisements, other entertainment option advertisements, or other programming on the network itself might hamper reception of the Winter Games' television ads. Transmission can also be hindered by situational factors such as physical surroundings like light, sound, location, and weather; the presence of other people; or the temporary moods consumers might bring to the situation. Mass communication may not even reach all the right consumers. Some members of the target audience may have been watching television when advertisements for the Winter Games were shown, but others may not have been.

The Receiver and Decoding

Marketers communicate their message through a channel to customers, or **receivers**, who will decode the message. **Decoding** is the interpretation of the language and symbols sent by the source through a channel. Common understanding between two communicators, or a common frame of reference, is required for effective communication. Therefore, marketing managers must ensure a proper match between the message to be conveyed and the target market's attitudes and ideas.

Even though a message has been received, it will not necessarily be properly decoded—or even seen, viewed, or heard—because of selective exposure, distortion, and retention (refer to Chapter 5).[15] Even when people receive a message, they tend to manipulate, alter, and modify it to reflect their own biases, needs, knowledge, and culture. Factors that can lead to miscommunication include differences in age, social class, education, culture, and ethnicity. Further, because people don't always listen or read carefully, they can easily misinterpret what is said or written. In fact, researchers have found that a large proportion of both printed and televised communications are misunderstood by consumers. Bright colors and bold graphics have been shown to increase consumers' comprehension of marketing communication. Even these techniques are not foolproof, however. A classic example of miscommunication occurred when Lever Brothers mailed out samples of its then new dishwashing liquid, Sunlight, which contains real lemon juice. The package clearly stated that Sunlight was a household cleaning product. However, many people saw the word *sunlight,* the large picture of lemons, and the phrase "with real lemon juice" and thought the product was lemon juice.

Marketers targeting consumers in foreign countries must also worry about the translation and possible miscommunication of their promotional messages by other cultures. An important issue for global marketers is whether to standardize or customize the message for each global market in which they sell. For instance, when advertising the PT Cruiser in foreign markets, Daimler-Chrysler might choose to use the same commercials and selling points that it uses in the United States, or it might decide to develop unique ads for each country or culture. Read about how some global marketers have adapted their marketing mix to appeal to consumers in different cultures in the "Global Perspectives" box.

Feedback

In interpersonal communication, the receiver's response to a message is direct **feedback** to the source. Feedback may be verbal, as in saying "I agree," or nonverbal, as in nodding, smiling, frowning, or gesturing.

noise
Anything that interferes with, distorts, or slows down the transmission of information.

receiver
The person who decodes a message.

decoding
Interpretation of the language and symbols sent by the source through a channel.

feedback
The receiver's response to a message.

For the 2002 Winter Games in Salt Lake City, Utah, Olympic organizers (and broadcasters) chose to highlight the extreme sports. Czech athlete Ales Valenta is pictured here upside-down and mid-air during his gold-medal winning jump.

AP/WIDE WORLD PHOTOS

Conquering the World—Who's Buying?

When Pizza Express opened restaurants in Europe, the pizza chain had to modify its menu in Hungary, the Czech Republic, and Poland by adding local wines, beers, and some pasta items to attract consumers who were skeptical of a fast-food restaurant that served only pizza. When another U.S. company wanted to market a cosmetic product called "Mist Stick" in Europe, it found that the name would have been a bad idea in German-language countries. The name looks and sounds like the German equivalent of "piece of manure." When an American sales rep met with a Japanese company to discuss a business transaction, he made a $100,000 mistake by scribbling something on the back of the Japanese representative's business card. In Japan, it is customary to show a business card the same respect you would show a person.

Global marketing—being able to sell your products or services worldwide—is a huge undertaking. Marketing products or services overseas requires both cultural sensitivity and an understanding of the consumers in the market. For example, words in English may have a totally different meaning in other countries. American Motors once offered a model named Matador, evoking the glamorous image of a bullfighter—but the word also means "killer" in Spanish. Even the emotional and psychological properties associated with color used in logos, packaging, and other collateral marketing materials vary from culture to culture.

Another lesson global companies are learning is that you can't expect that the same formula that works in one country will work in another. Spiegel in Japan recently redesigned its clothing line to include straight-leg pants and stretchy shirts to better fit the Japanese shape. When Office Depot entered Japan, the superstore found that 20,000-square-foot stores with wide aisles and signage in English were too expensive to run (rent is twice as high in Japan as it is in America) and that

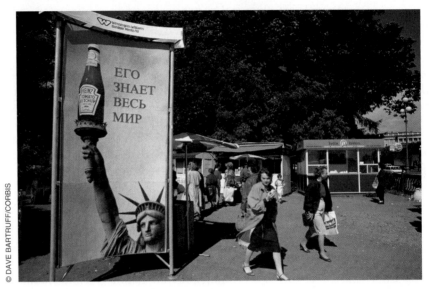

© DAVE BARTRUFF/CORBIS

Global marketers must pay attention to cultural differences, linguistic differences, and the attitudes of consumers in the given market. Heinz, however, was able to use a generally standardized approach because it discovered that teens around the world were more alike in their use of ketchup than they were different.

consumers were confused by the English-language signs and put off by the warehouse atmosphere.

One of the hottest debates among global marketing professionals is whether to customize or standardize promotional messages. Some believe the message should be tailored to each country or region to be most effective since different cultures perceive and react to promotional messages differently. Kodak, for example, favors a customized approach to advertising in China because consumer tastes and values vary between mainland China and the more progressive Taiwan and Hong Kong areas. Others believe marketers should develop one message, translate it into the language of each country, and deliver it to all target markets. They say consumers everywhere have the same basic needs and desires and can therefore be persuaded by universal appeals. For example, Heinz concluded from its research that teens around the world are really more alike in their use of ketchup than they are different. As a result, it rolled out a $50 million global advertising campaign to seventy-

five countries with only minor creative tweaks in the food the teens were pouring the ketchup over. Probably the best answer to this dilemma is to use a mixture of standardization and customization—standardize the message but pay attention to local differences when executing it. For example, Coca-Cola uses a standardized appeal when promoting cola, but it tailors the message to regional and international markets. All ads include the tagline "Coca-Cola. Enjoy," but the campaign's "Enjoy" melody has nineteen different versions in genres as varied as reggae, techno, hip-hop, and country depending on demographic and regional preferences.[16]

So what can marketers do as they enter new cultural markets? Taking time to research and define customer needs and learn how the market operates can go a long way in helping companies reach their global goals. What other type of research could marketers utilize when entering new countries? Can you think of other barriers, such as language, that could hinder a company's entry into another country?

Because mass communicators like NBC are often cut off from direct feedback, they must rely on market research or analysis of television ratings for indirect feedback. NBC might use such measurements as the percentage of television viewers who recognized, recalled, or stated that they were exposed to the Winter Games messages. Indirect feedback enables mass communicators to decide whether to continue, modify, or drop a message.

The Communication Process and the Promotional Mix

The four elements of the promotional mix differ in their ability to affect the target audience. For instance, promotional mix elements may communicate with the consumer directly or indirectly. The message may flow one way or two ways. Feedback may be fast or slow, a little or a lot. Likewise, the communicator may have varying degrees of control over message delivery, content, and flexibility. Exhibit 14.4 outlines differences among the promotional mix elements with respect to mode of communication, marketer's control over the communication process, amount and speed of feedback, direction of message flow, marketer's control over the message, identification of the sender, speed in reaching large audiences, and message flexibility.

From Exhibit 14.4, you can see that most elements of the promotional mix are indirect and impersonal when used to communicate with a target market, providing only one direction of message flow. For example, advertising, public relations, and

Characteristics of the Elements in the Promotional Mix **Exhibit 14.4**

	Advertising	**Public Relations**	**Sales Promotion**	**Personal Selling**
Mode of Communication	Indirect and nonpersonal	Usually indirect and nonpersonal	Usually indirect and nonpersonal	Direct and face-to-face
Communicator Control over Situation	Low	Moderate to low	Moderate to low	High
Amount of Feedback	Little	Little	Little to moderate	Much
Speed of Feedback	Delayed	Delayed	Varies	Immediate
Direction of Message Flow	One-way	One-way	Mostly one-way	Two-way
Control over Message Content	Yes	No	Yes	Yes
Identification of Sponsor	Yes	No	Yes	Yes
Speed in Reaching Large Audience	Fast	Usually fast	Fast	Slow
Message Flexibility	Same message to all audiences	Usually no direct control over message	Same message to varied target audiences	Tailored to prospective buyer

sales promotion are generally impersonal, one-way means of mass communication. Because they provide no opportunity for direct feedback, they cannot easily adapt to consumers' changing preferences, individual differences, and personal goals.

Personal selling, on the other hand, is personal, two-way communication. The salesperson is able to receive immediate feedback from the consumer and adjust the message in response. Personal selling, however, is very slow in dispersing the marketer's message to large audiences. Because a salesperson can only communicate to one person or a small group of persons at one time, it is a poor choice if the marketer wants to send a message to many potential buyers.

The Goals and Tasks of Promotion

4

Explain the goals and tasks of promotion

People communicate with one another for many reasons. They seek amusement, ask for help, give assistance or instructions, provide information, and express ideas and thoughts. Promotion, on the other hand, seeks to modify behavior and thoughts in some way. For example, promoters may try to persuade consumers to eat at Burger King rather than at McDonald's. Promotion also strives to reinforce existing behavior—for instance, getting consumers to continue to dine at Burger King once they have switched. The source (the seller) hopes to project a favorable image or to motivate purchase of the company's goods and services.

Promotion can perform one or more of three tasks: *inform* the target audience, *persuade* the target audience, or *remind* the target audience. Often a marketer will try to accomplish two or more of these tasks at the same time. Exhibit 14.5 lists the three tasks of promotion and some examples of each.

Informing

Informative promotion may seek to convert an existing need into a want or to stimulate interest in a new product. It is generally more prevalent during the early stages of the product life cycle. People typically will not buy a product service or support a nonprofit organization until they know its purpose and its benefits to them. Informative messages are important for promoting complex and technical products such as automobiles, computers, and investment services. Informative promotion is also important for a "new" brand being introduced into an "old"

Exhibit 14.5

Promotion Tasks and Examples

- **Informative promotion**
  Increasing the awareness of a new brand, product class, or product attribute
  Explaining how the product works
  Suggesting new uses for a product
  Building a company image

- **Persuasive promotion**
  Encouraging brand switching
  Changing customers' perceptions of product attributes
  Influencing customers to buy now
  Persuading customers to call

- **Reminder promotion**
  Reminding consumers that the product may be needed in the near future
  Reminding consumers where to buy the product
  Maintaining consumer awareness

product class—for example, a new brand of frozen pizza entering the frozen pizza industry, which is dominated by well-known brands like Kraft's DiGiorno and Schwan's Grocery Products' Red Baron. The new product cannot establish itself against more mature products unless potential buyers are aware of it, understand its benefits, and understand its positioning in the marketplace.

Persuading

Persuasive promotion is designed to stimulate a purchase or an action—for example, to drink more Coca-Cola or to use H&R Block tax services. Persuasion normally becomes the main promotion goal when the product enters the growth stage of its life cycle. By this time, the target market should have general product awareness and some knowledge of how the product can fulfill their wants. Therefore, the promotional task switches from informing consumers about the product category to persuading them to buy the company's brand rather than the competitor's. At this time, the promotional message emphasizes the product's real and perceived differential advantages, often appealing to emotional needs such as love, belonging, self-esteem, and ego satisfaction.

Persuasion can also be an important goal for very competitive mature product categories such as many household items, soft drinks, beer, and banking services. In a marketplace characterized by many competitors, the promotional message often encourages brand switching and aims to convert some buyers into loyal users. For example, to persuade new customers to switch their checking accounts, a bank's marketing manager may offer a year's worth of free checks with no fees.

Critics believe that some promotional messages and techniques can be too persuasive, causing consumers to buy products and services they really don't need.

A "new" brand being introduced into an "old" category, like Disney brand children's clothing, for example, can benefit from informative promotion. Explain the product's benefits and advantages in a way that will draw attention to it and help it compete against mature brands like HealthTex, Garanimals and McKids.

Reminding

Reminder promotion is used to keep the product and brand name in the public's mind. This type of promotion prevails during the maturity stage of the life cycle. It assumes that the target market has already been persuaded of the good's or service's merits. Its purpose is simply to trigger a memory. Crest toothpaste, Tide laundry detergent, Miller beer, and many other consumer products often use reminder promotion.

Promotional Goals and the AIDA Concept

Discuss the AIDA concept and its relationship to the promotional mix

AIDA concept
A model that outlines the process for achieving promotional goals in terms of stages of consumer involvement with the message; the acronym stands for *attention, interest, desire,* and *action.*

The ultimate goal of any promotion is to get someone to buy a good or service or, in the case of nonprofit organizations, to take some action (for instance, donate blood). A classic model for reaching promotional goals is called the **AIDA concept.**[17] The acronym stands for *attention, interest, desire,* and *action*—the stages of consumer involvement with a promotional message.

This model proposes that consumers respond to marketing messages in a cognitive (thinking), affective (feeling), and conative (doing) sequence. First, the promotion manager attracts a person's *attention* by (in personal selling) a greeting and approach or (in advertising and sales promotion) loud volume, unusual contrasts, bold headlines, movement, bright colors, and so on. Next, a good sales presenta-

What role can the Internet play in the AIDA concept? Consider Exhibit 14.6. Re-create the table by deciding how effective you think the Internet would be as an advertising tool to create attention, interest, desire, and action. Continue to evaluate the Internet as a public relations tool, sales promotion tool, and personal selling tool.

◀ ▶   On Line

tion, demonstration, or advertisement creates *interest* in the product and then, by illustrating how the product's features will satisfy the consumer's needs, arouses *desire*. Finally, a special offer or a strong closing sales pitch may be used to obtain purchase *action*.

The AIDA concept assumes that promotion propels consumers along the following four steps in the purchase-decision process:

1. *Attention:* The advertiser must first gain the attention of the target market. A firm cannot sell something if the market does not know that the good or service exists. Imagine that Acme Company, a pet food manufacturer, is introducing a new brand of cat food called Stripes, specially formulated for finicky cats. To increase the general awareness of its new brand, Acme heavily publicizes the introduction and places several ads on TV and in consumer magazines.

2. *Interest:* Simple awareness of a brand seldom leads to a sale. The next step is to create interest in the product. A print ad or TV commercial can't actually tell pet owners whether their cats will like Stripes. Thus, Acme might send samples of the new cat food to cat owners to create interest in the new brand.

3. *Desire:* Even though owners (and their cats) may like Stripes, they may not see any advantage over competing brands, especially if owners are brand loyal. Therefore, Acme must create brand preference by explaining the product's differential advantage over the competition. Specifically, Acme has to show that cats want to eat nothing else. Advertising at this stage claims that Stripes will satisfy "even the pickiest of the litter." Although pet owners may come to prefer Stripes to other brands, they still may not have developed the desire to buy the new brand. At this stage Acme might offer the consumer additional reasons to buy Stripes, such as easy-to-open, zip-lock packaging that keeps the product fresh; additional vitamins and minerals that healthy cats need; or feline taste-test results.

4. *Action:* Some members of the target market may now be convinced to buy Stripes but have yet to make the purchase. Displays in grocery stores, coupons, premiums, and trial-size packages can often push the complacent shopper into purchase.

Most buyers involved in high-involvement purchase situations pass through the four stages of the AIDA model on the way to making a purchase. The promoter's task is to determine where on the purchase ladder most of the target consumers are located and design a promotion plan to meet their needs. For instance, if Acme has determined that about half its buyers are in the preference or conviction stage but have not bought Stripes cat food for some reason, the company may mail cents-off coupons to cat owners to prompt them to buy.

The AIDA concept does not explain how all promotions influence purchase decisions. The model suggests that promotional effectiveness can be measured in terms of consumers progressing from one stage to the next. However, the order of stages in the model, as well as whether consumers go through all steps, has been much debated. For example, a purchase can occur without interest or desire, perhaps when a low-involvement product is bought on impulse. Regardless of the order of the stages or consumers' progression through these stages, the AIDA concept helps marketers by suggesting which promotional strategy will be most effective.[18]

AIDA and the Promotional Mix

Exhibit 14.6 depicts the relationship between the promotional mix and the AIDA model. It shows that, although advertising does have an impact in the later stages, it is most useful in gaining attention for goods or services. In contrast, personal selling reaches fewer people at first. Salespeople are more effective at creating customer interest for merchandise or a ser-

This cosmetics saleswoman at Clinique can create desire for her line of products by showing her potential customer how wonderful she looks after using them. Salespeople are very effective at creating desire, particularly in this type of situation.

©BOHEMIAN NOMAD PICTUREMAKERS/CORBIS

Exhibit 14.6

	Attention	Interest	Desire	Action
Advertising	Very effective	Very effective	Somewhat effective	Not effective
Public Relations	Very effective	Very effective	Very effective	Not effective
Sales Promotion	Somewhat effective	Somewhat effective	Very effective	Somewhat effective
Personal Selling	Somewhat effective	Very effective	Very effective	Very effective

When the Elements of Promotion Are Most Useful

vice and at creating desire. For example, advertising may help a potential computer purchaser gain knowledge and information about competing brands, but the salesperson in an electronics store may be the one who actually encourages the buyer to decide a particular brand is the best choice. The salesperson also has the advantage of having the computer physically there to demonstrate its capabilities to the buyer.

Public relations has its greatest impact in gaining attention for a company, good, or service. Many companies can attract attention and build goodwill by sponsoring community events that benefit a worthy cause such as antidrug and antigang programs. Such sponsorships project a positive image of the firm and its products into the minds of consumers and potential consumers. Good publicity can also help develop consumer desire for a product. When Hasbro's Tiger Electronics wanted to launch its new line of toys—robotic dogs—the company arranged for Iditarod winner Doug Swingley to deliver the first litter of Poo-Chis to New York's FAO Schwarz via his winning dogsled team. NBC's *Today Show* picked up the publicity stunt and more than a thousand robotic dogs were sold in the store's opening hours.[19] Book publishers push to get their titles on the best-seller lists of major publications, such as *Publishers Weekly* or the *New York Times*. Book authors also make appearances on talk shows and at bookstores to personally sign books and speak to fans. Similarly, movie marketers use prerelease publicity to raise the profile of their movies and to increase initial box-office sales. For example, most major motion picture studios have their own Web sites with multimedia clips and publicity photos of their current movies to attract viewers. Furthermore, movie promoters will include publicity gained from reviewers' quotes and Academy Award nominations in their advertising.

Sales promotion's greatest strength is in creating strong desire and purchase intent. Coupons and other price-off promotions are techniques used to persuade customers to buy new products. Frequent buyer sales promotion programs, popular among retailers, allow consumers to accumulate points or dollars that can later be redeemed for goods. Frequent buyer programs tend to increase purchase intent and loyalty and encourage repeat purchases. While many supermarket chains have developed loyalty programs patterned after the frequent flyer programs started by airlines, Safeway actually partnered with United Airlines to launch a program called "Grocery Miles." This program allows customers to earn frequent flyer miles for their supermarket purchases. To take part, customers must be members of United's Mileage Plus frequent flyer program and the Safeway Club. Then, once enrolled in Grocery Miles, shoppers earn 125 miles for every $250 they spend through a specified time period.[20]

Factors Affecting the Promotional Mix

Describe the factors that affect the promotional mix

Promotional mixes vary a great deal from one product and one industry to the next. Normally, advertising and personal selling are used to promote goods and services, supported and supplemented by sales promotion. Public relations helps develop a positive image for the organization and the product line. However, a firm may choose not to use all four promotional elements in its promotional mix, or it may choose to use them in varying degrees. The particular promotional mix chosen by a firm for a product or service depends on several factors: the nature of the product, the stage in the product life cycle, target market characteristics, the type of buying decision, funds available for promotion, and whether a push or a pull strategy will be used.

Nature of the Product

Characteristics of the product itself can influence the promotional mix. For instance, a product can be classified as either a business product or a consumer product (refer to Chapter 9). As business products are often custom-tailored to the buyer's exact specifications, they are often not well suited to mass promotion. Therefore, producers of most business goods, such as computer systems or industrial machinery, rely more heavily on personal selling than on advertising. Informative personal selling is common for industrial installations, accessories, and component parts and materials. Advertising, however, still serves a purpose in promoting business goods. Advertisements in trade media may be used to create general buyer awareness and interest. Moreover, advertising can help locate potential customers for the sales force. For example, print media advertising often includes coupons soliciting the potential customer to "fill this out for more detailed information."

In contrast, because consumer products generally are not custom-made, they do not require the selling efforts of a company representative who can tailor them to the user's needs. Thus, consumer goods are promoted mainly through advertising to create brand familiarity. Broadcast advertising, newspapers, and consumer-oriented magazines are used extensively to promote consumer goods, especially nondurables. Sales promotion, the brand name, and the product's packaging are about twice as important for consumer goods as for business products. Persuasive personal selling is important at the retail level for shopping goods such as automobiles and appliances.

The costs and risks associated with a product also influence the promotional mix. As a general rule, when the costs or risks of using a product increase, personal selling becomes more important. Items that are a small part of a firm's budget (supply items) or of a consumer's budget (convenience products) do not require a salesperson to close the sale. In fact, inexpensive items cannot support the cost of a salesperson's time and effort unless the potential volume is high. On the other hand, expensive and complex machinery, new buildings, cars, and new homes represent a considerable investment. A salesperson must assure buyers that they are spending their money wisely and not taking an undue financial risk.

Social risk is an issue as well. Many consumer goods are not products of great social importance because they do not reflect social position. People do not experience much social risk in buying a loaf of bread or a candy bar. However, buying some shopping products and many specialty products such as jewelry and clothing does involve a social risk. Many consumers depend on sales personnel for guidance and advice in making the "proper" choice.

Stage in the Product Life Cycle

The product's stage in its life cycle is a big factor in designing a promotional mix (see Exhibit 14.7). During the *introduction stage*, the basic goal of promotion is to inform the target audience that the product is available. Initially, the emphasis is on the general product class—for example, personal computer systems. This emphasis gradually changes to gaining attention for a specific brand, such as IBM, Apple, and Compaq. Typically, both extensive advertising and public relations inform the target audience of the product class or brand and heighten awareness levels. Sales promotion encourages early trial of the product, and personal selling gets retailers to carry the product.

When the product reaches the *growth stage* of the life cycle, the promotion blend may shift. Often a change is necessary because different types of potential buyers are targeted. Although advertising and public relations continue to be major elements of the promotional mix, sales promotion can be reduced because consumers need fewer incentives to purchase. The promotional strategy is to emphasize the product's differential advantage over the competition. Persuasive promotion is used to build and maintain brand loyalty to support the product during the growth stage. By this stage, personal selling has usually succeeded in getting adequate distribution for the product.

As the product reaches the *maturity stage* of its life cycle, competition becomes fiercer, and thus persuasive and reminder advertising are more strongly emphasized. Sales promotion comes back into focus as product sellers try to increase their market share.

All promotion, especially advertising, is reduced as the product enters the *decline stage*. Nevertheless, personal selling and sales promotion efforts may be maintained, particularly at the retail level.

Product Life Cycle and the Promotional Mix **Exhibit 14.7**

On Line

Target Market Characteristics

A target market characterized by widely scattered potential customers, highly informed buyers, and brand-loyal repeat purchasers generally requires a promotional mix with more advertising and sales promotion and less personal selling. Sometimes, however, personal selling is required even when buyers are well informed and geographically dispersed. Although industrial installations and component parts may be sold to extremely competent people with extensive education and work experience, salespeople must still be present to explain the product and work out the details of the purchase agreement.

Often firms sell goods and services in markets where potential customers are hard to locate. Print advertising can be used to find them. The reader is invited to call for more information or to mail in a reply card for a detailed brochure. As the calls or cards are received, salespeople are sent to visit the potential customers.

Type of Buying Decision

The promotional mix also depends on the type of buying decision—for example, a routine decision or a complex decision. For routine consumer decisions like buying toothpaste or soft drinks, the most effective promotion calls attention to the brand or reminds the consumer about the brand. Advertising and, especially, sales promotion are the most productive promotion tools to use for routine decisions.

If the decision is neither routine nor complex, advertising and public relations help establish awareness for the good or service. Suppose a man is looking for a bottle of wine to serve to his dinner guests. As a beer drinker, he is not familiar with wines, yet he has seen advertising for Sutter Home wine and has also read an article in a popular magazine about the Sutter Home winery. He may be more likely to buy this brand because he is already aware of it.

In contrast, consumers making complex buying decisions are more extensively involved. They rely on large amounts of information to help them reach a purchase decision. Personal selling is most effective in helping these consumers decide. For example, consumers thinking about buying a car usually depend on a salesperson to provide the information they need to reach a decision. Print advertising may also be used for high-involvement purchase decisions because it can often provide a large amount of information to the consumer.

Consumers making complex buying decisions often depend on the salesperson to provide important product information. Purchasing a car is one such example. Can you think of others?

Available Funds

Money, or the lack of it, may easily be the most important factor in determining the promotional mix. A small, undercapitalized manufacturer may rely heavily on free publicity if its product is unique. If the situation warrants a sales force, a financially strained firm may turn to manufacturers' agents, who work on a commission basis with no advances or expense accounts. Even well-capitalized organizations may not be able to afford the advertising rates of publications like *Better Homes and Gardens*, *Reader's Digest*, and the *Wall Street Journal*. The price of a high-profile advertisement in these media could support a salesperson for a year.

When funds are available to permit a mix of promotional elements, a firm will generally try to optimize its return on promotion dollars while minimizing the *cost per contact*, or the cost of reaching one member of the target market. In general, the cost per contact is very high for personal selling, public relations, and sales promotions like sampling and demonstrations. On the other hand, for the number of people national advertising reaches, it has a very low cost per contact.

Usually, there is a trade-off among the funds available, the number of people in the target market, the quality of communication needed, and the relative costs of the promotional elements. A company may have to forgo a full-page, color advertisement in *People* magazine in order to pay for a personal selling effort. Although the magazine ad will reach more people than personal selling, the high cost of the magazine space is a problem.

Push and Pull Strategies

The last factor that affects the promotional mix is whether a push or a pull promotional strategy will be used. Manufacturers may use aggressive personal selling and trade advertising to convince a wholesaler or a retailer to carry and sell their merchandise. This approach is known as a **push strategy** (see Exhibit 14.8). The wholesaler, in turn, must often push the merchandise forward by persuading the retailer to handle the goods. The retailer then uses advertising, displays, and other forms of promotion to convince the consumer to buy the "pushed" products. This concept also applies to services. For example, the Jamaican Tourism Board targets

push strategy
A marketing strategy that uses aggressive personal selling and trade advertising to convince a wholesaler or a retailer to carry and sell particular merchandise.

Push Strategy versus Pull Strategy **Exhibit 14.8**

pull strategy
A marketing strategy that stimulates consumer demand to obtain product distribution.

promotions to travel agencies, which, in turn, tell their customers about the benefits of vacationing in Jamaica.

At the other extreme is a **pull strategy**, which stimulates consumer demand to obtain product distribution. Rather than trying to sell to the wholesaler, the manufacturer using a pull strategy focuses its promotional efforts on end consumers or opinion leaders. For example, BriteSmile Professional Teeth Whitening Centers sent office merchandising displays to dentists across the country to create a buzz and generate demand for its after-care whitening maintenance products, such as the Sonicare sonic toothbrush, toothpaste, mouthwash, and mint gum.[21] As consumers begin demanding the product, the retailer orders the merchandise from the wholesaler. The wholesaler, confronted with rising demand, then places an order for the "pulled" merchandise from the manufacturer. Consumer demand pulls the product through the channel of distribution (see Exhibit 14.8). Heavy sampling, introductory consumer advertising, cents-off campaigns, and couponing are part of a pull strategy. For example, Smirnoff Ice sold almost eleven million cases in its first six months of national distribution. Contributing to those unprecedented numbers were extensive sampling, on-premise promotions, and $25 million in advertising.[22]

Rarely does a company use a pull or a push strategy exclusively. Instead, the mix will emphasize one of these strategies. For example, pharmaceutical companies generally use a push strategy, through personal selling and trade advertising, to promote their drugs and therapies to physicians. Sales presentations and advertisements in medical journals give physicians the detailed information they need to prescribe medication to their patients. Most pharmaceutical companies supplement their push promotional strategy with a pull strategy targeted directly to potential patients through advertisements in consumer magazines and on television.

Integrated Marketing Communications

7

Discuss the concept of integrated marketing communications

Ideally, marketing communications from each promotional mix element (personal selling, advertising, sales promotion, and public relations) should be integrated—that is, the message reaching the consumer should be the same regardless of whether it is from an advertisement, a salesperson in the field, a magazine article, or a coupon in a newspaper insert.

From the consumer's standpoint, a company's communications are already integrated. Consumers do not think in terms of the four elements of promotion: advertising, sales promotion, public relations, and personal selling. Instead, everything is an "ad." The only people who recognize the distinctions among these communications elements are the marketers themselves. Unfortunately, many marketers neglect this fact when planning promotional messages and fail to integrate their communication efforts from one element to the next. The most common rift typically occurs between personal selling and the other elements of the promotional mix.

integrated marketing communications (IMC)
The careful coordination of all promotional messages for a product or a service to assure the consistency of messages at every contact point where a company meets the consumer.

This unintegrated, disjointed approach to promotion has propelled many companies to adopt the concept of **integrated marketing communications (IMC)**. IMC is the careful coordination of all promotional messages—traditional advertising, direct marketing, interactive, public relations, sales promotion, personal selling, event marketing, and other communications—for a product or service to assure the consistency of messages at every contact point where a company meets the consumer.[23] Following the concept of IMC, marketing managers carefully work out the roles that various promotional elements will play in the marketing mix. Timing of promotional activities is coordinated, and the results of each campaign are carefully monitored to improve future use of the promotional mix tools. Typically, a marketing communications director is appointed who has overall responsibility for integrating the company's marketing communications.

Movie marketing campaigns benefit greatly from an IMC approach. Those campaigns that are most integrated generally have more impact and make a deeper impression on potential moviegoers, leading to higher box-office sales. New Line Cinema used an integrated marketing approach when it released the first installment of *The Lord of the Rings: The Fellowship of the Ring.* Excitement about the release of the film gathered momentum a full year in advance as the trailer was shown on the Internet (the trailer received sixty-two million hits the first week on-line). A partnership with Burger King gave consumers the opportunity to buy *The Fellowship of the Ring* glass goblets with the purchase of a Whopper sandwich value meal. Consumers could also buy a Burger King Big Kids Meal to receive one of nineteen premiums featuring characters from the movie. One hundred selected bookstores around the country sponsored lunchtime events featuring a twenty-minute video that included never-before-seen interviews, behind-the-scenes footage, and conversations with director Peter Jackson and other stars from the movie. The bookstores were also given in-store event kits to supplement the showing with a trivia contest, in-store readings by fans of favorite scenes, or other activities. Cobranded DVD players and VCR packages loaded with movie trailers, behind-the-scenes footage, and stickers hit shelves a couple of months before the movie premiered. Through an agreement with the New York Times Company, both the *Times* and NYTimes.com promoted the film. Praised by critics and audiences alike, *The Fellowship of the Ring* surpassed the $100 million mark on its opening weekend and was named the top movie of the year by *Entertainment Weekly* and *Rolling Stone.*[24]

AP/WIDE WORLD PHOTOS

Movies are often very successful at implementing integrated marketing campaigns. *The Lord of the Rings, Spiderman* and others were able to parlay huge box-office successes into merchandising successes—not to mention great anticipation for sequels.

The IMC concept of has been growing in popularity for several reasons. First, the proliferation of thousands of media choices beyond traditional television has made promotion a more complicated task. Instead of promoting a product just through mass-media options, like television and magazines, promotional messages today can appear in many varied sources. Further, the mass market has also fragmented—more selectively segmented markets and an increase in niche marketing have replaced the traditional broad market groups that marketers promoted to in years past. For instance, many popular magazines now have Spanish-language editions targeted toward America's growing Hispanic population. Finally, marketers have slashed their advertising spending in favor of promotional techniques that generate immediate sales responses and those that are more easily measured, such as direct marketing. Thus, the interest in IMC is largely a reaction to the scrutiny that marketing communications has come under and, particularly, to suggestions that uncoordinated promotional activity leads to a strategy that is wasteful and inefficient.[25]

CONNECT IT

The publishers of *Maxim* employ many different elements of the promotional mix to promote the magazine to its readers. Guerrilla marketing tactics, public relations, and publicity are important elements of their plan. *Maxim*'s integrated promotional plan conveys a consistent and clear message of the magazine's image and has been crucial to the company's success in the men's magazine industry. As you read the next two chapters, keep in mind that marketers try to choose the mix of promotional elements that will best promote their good or service. Rarely will a marketer rely on just one method of promotion.

REVIEW IT

(1) **Discuss the role of promotion in the marketing mix.** Promotion is communication by marketers that informs, persuades, and reminds potential buyers of a product in order to influence an opinion or elicit a response. Promotional strategy is the plan for using the elements of promotion—advertising, public relations, sales promotion, and personal selling—to meet the firm's overall objectives and marketing goals. Based on these objectives, the elements of the promotional strategy become a coordinated promotion plan. The promotion plan then becomes an integral part of the total marketing strategy for reaching the target market along with product, distribution, and price.

1.1 What is a promotional strategy? Explain the concept of a differential advantage in relation to promotional strategy.

(2) **Discuss the elements of the promotional mix.** The elements of the promotional mix include advertising, public relations, sales promotion, and personal selling. Advertising is a form of impersonal, one-way mass communication paid for by the source. Public relations is the function of promotion concerned with a firm's public image. Firms can't buy good publicity, but they can take steps to create a positive company image. Sales promotion is typically used to back up other components of the promotional mix by stimulating immediate demand. Finally, personal selling typically involves direct communication, in person or by telephone; the seller tries to initiate a purchase by informing and persuading one or more potential buyers.

2.1 WRITING   As the promotional manager for a new line of cosmetics targeted to preteen girls, you have been assigned the task of deciding which promotional mix elements—advertising, public relations, sales promotion, and personal selling—should be used in promoting it. Your budget for promoting the preteen cosmetics line is limited. Write a promotional plan explaining your choice of promotional mix elements given the nature of the product, the stage in the product life cycle, the target market characteristics, the type of buying decision, available funds, and the use of a pull or push strategy.

(3) **Describe the communication process.** The communication process has several steps. When an individual or organization has a message it wishes to convey to a target audience, it encodes that message using language and symbols familiar to the intended receiver and sends the message through a channel of communication. Noise in the transmission channel distorts the source's intended message. Reception occurs if the message falls within the receiver's frame of reference. The receiver decodes the message and usually provides feedback to the source. Normally, feedback is direct for interpersonal communication and indirect for mass communication.

3.1 Why is understanding the target market a crucial aspect of the communication process?

(4) Explain the goals and tasks of promotion. The fundamental goals of promotion are to induce, modify, or reinforce behavior by informing, persuading, and reminding. Informative promotion explains a good's or service's purpose and benefits. Promotion that informs the consumer is typically used to increase demand for a general product category or to introduce a new good or service. Persuasive promotion is designed to stimulate a purchase or an action. Promotion that persuades the consumer to buy is essential during the growth stage of the product life cycle, when competition becomes fierce. Reminder promotion is used to keep the product and brand name in the public's mind. Promotions that remind are generally used during the maturity stage of the product life cycle.

4.1 Why might a marketing manager choose to promote his or her product using persuasion? Give some current examples of persuasive promotion.

4.2 Choose a partner from class and go together to interview the owners or managers of several small businesses in your city. Ask them what their promotional objectives are and why. Are they trying to inform, persuade, or remind customers to do business with them? Also determine whether they believe they have an awareness problem or whether they need to persuade customers to come to them instead of to competitors. Ask them to list the characteristics of their primary market, the strengths and weaknesses of their direct competitors, and how they are positioning their store to compete. Prepare a report to present in class summarizing your findings.

(5) Discuss the AIDA concept and its relationship to the promotional mix. The AIDA model outlines the four basic stages in the purchase decision-making process, which are initiated and propelled by promotional activities: (1) attention, (2) interest, (3) desire, and (4) action. The components of the promotional mix have varying levels of influence at each stage of the AIDA model. Advertising is a good tool for increasing awareness and knowledge of a good or service. Sales promotion is effective when consumers are at the purchase stage of the decision-making process. Personal selling is most effective in developing customer interest and desire.

5.1 Discuss the AIDA concept. How do these different stages of consumer involvement affect the promotional mix?

(6) Describe the factors that affect the promotional mix. Promotion managers consider many factors when creating promotional mixes. These factors include the nature of the product, product life-cycle stage, target market characteristics, the type of buying decision involved, availability of funds, and feasibility of push or pull strategies. Because most business products tend to be custom-tailored to the buyer's exact specifications, the marketing manager may choose a promotional mix that relies more heavily on personal selling. On the other hand, consumer products are generally mass produced and lend themselves more to mass promotional efforts such as advertising and sales promotion. As products move through different stages of the product life cycle, marketers will choose to use different promotional elements. For example, advertising is emphasized more in the introductory stage of the product life cycle than in the decline stage. Characteristics of the target market, such as geographic location of potential buyers and brand loyalty, influence the promotional mix as does whether the buying decision is complex or routine. The amount of funds a firm has to allocate to promotion may also help determine the promotional mix. Small firms with limited funds may rely more heavily on public relations, whereas larger firms may be able to afford broadcast or print advertising. Last, if a firm uses a push strategy to promote the product or service, the marketing manager may choose to use aggressive advertising and personal selling to wholesalers and retailers. If a pull strategy is chosen, then the manager often relies on aggressive mass promotion, such as advertising and sales promotion, to stimulate consumer demand.

6.1 Explain the difference between a "pull" and a "push" promotional strategy. Under what conditions should each strategy be used?

6.2 Choose two companies, one a consumer-products company and the other an on-line retailer. Conduct some research on these two companies in terms of their promotional practices by observation (such as looking in magazines, the newspaper, television, Web site, etc.) and searching at your campus library. You may also use InfoTrac (**http://www.infotrac-college.com**) to locate any articles written on the promotional activities of the companies you select. Describe some of the types of promotions that these companies have engaged in during the last year—for example, ran television ads, sponsored an event, held a sweepstakes, or expanded sales force. To the best of your abilities, determine the objective of each promotion in relation to the AIDA model. For example, the objective of a magazine ad might be to gain attention or to create interest, while the objective of a coupon might be to stimulate the action of purchase. Also note if the companies' promotions are integrated or not.

6.3 Visit **http://www.teenresearch.com**. What research can this company offer about the size and growth of the teen market, the buying power of teenagers, and their buying habits? Why might these statistics be important to a company targeting teenagers in terms of marketing communications and promotion strategy?

7 **Discuss the concept of integrated marketing communications.** Integrated marketing communications is the careful coordination of all promotional messages for a product or service to assure the consistency of messages at every contact point where a company meets the consumer—advertising, sales promotion, personal selling, public relations, as well as direct marketing, packaging, and other forms of communication. Marketing managers carefully coordinate all promotional activities to ensure that consumers see and hear one message. Integrated marketing communications has received more attention in recent years due to the proliferation of media choices, the fragmentation of mass markets into more segmented niches, and the decrease in advertising spending in favor of promotional techniques that generate an immediate sales response.

7.1 Discuss the importance of integrated marketing communications. Give some current examples of companies that are and are not practicing IMC.

DEFINE IT

advertising 467
AIDA concept 477
channel 473
communication 470
decoding 473
differential advantage 466
encoding 472
feedback 473
integrated marketing communications (IMC) 484

interpersonal communication 470
mass communication 471
noise 473
personal selling 469
promotion 466
promotional mix 467
promotional strategy 466
publicity 468
public relations 467

pull strategy 484
push strategy 483
receiver 473
sales promotion 469
sender 472

APPLY IT

Application for Entrepreneurs

Be Safe is a small, independent business that markets child-proofing services to parents with small children and to day-care centers and home day-care providers. For a small fee,

Jill Sherman, the owner, will visit the customer's home or facility and point out areas that might be dangerous to small children, such as exposed electrical outlets, poisonous products and plants, or falling hazards. Jill also sells and installs safety items in homes and facilities to make them safer for children. Currently, most of her business comes through referrals or the Yellow Pages, but she would like to increase her business through some form of promotion, although her budget to do so will be small. She has noticed that many of her clients, especially new parents, don't know much about child safety in the home or about the products that can help prevent child injuries. Other clients, especially day-care centers, know about child safety but often install the wrong products or don't maintain a safe environment at all times, exposing children to danger.

Questions

1. What goals should Be Safe's promotional efforts try to achieve? How will these goals differ by target market?

2. How might the type of buying decision and the nature of this service influence the promotional mix?

3. Given Be Safe's small budget, what types of promotional methods would you suggest?

THINK ABOUT IT

Ethics Exercise

Integrated Marketing Solutions is a consumer products marketing services firm. Currently, the firm is handling the launch of a new book for one of its publishing clients. The campaign includes advance review copies for key book reviewers, "Coming Soon" posters for booksellers, an author book signing tour, and several television interviews. Everything has been produced and scheduled for release next week. Today, Jane Kershaw, the account executive, learned that in spite of numerous favorable reviews, the book review quoted on all of the promotional materials is fabricated.

Questions

1. What should Jane do?

2. What does the AMA Code of Ethics say about accuracy in promotional materials? Go to **http://www.marketingpower.com** and review the code. Then, write a brief paragraph describing how the AMA Code of Ethics relates to this issue.

TRY IT

Entrepreneurship Case

Nantucket Nectars: Blending Marketing Methods for a Juicy Success

After graduating from Brown University in the spring of 1989, college friends Tom First and Tom Scott moved to Nantucket Island, Massachusetts, determined to make it on their own and avoid the inevitable coat-and-tie corporate life. There, the two friends opened a boat-based delivery business in Nantucket Harbor to service the visiting yachts that came to the remote island in the warmer months. Having the summer of their lives, the pair delivered coffee, muffins, laundry, and other necessities to well-to-do island visitors and worked other odd jobs, such as shelling scallops, washing dogs, and pumping sewage, to earn money. Then Nantucket's ferocious winter kicked in, and their business slowed to a crawl.

One night during their first winter, the Toms started mixing fruit in a blender, trying to re-create a peach nectar that First had tasted during his travels to Spain. When they stumbled on some flavorful concoctions, their entrepreneurial spirits took over, and First and Scott decided to hand-bottle their juices in recycled wine bottles and sell them off

PHOTO COURTESY OF NANTUCKET NECTARS.

their boat when the yachts returned with the warmer weather. They called their juices Nantucket Nectars and sold two thousand bottles at $1 apiece the next summer. Encouraged by their initial sales, First and Scott decided to go into the juice business.

In the beginning, the pair targeted New England colleges close to Nantucket Island and Boston and the young adults there who would most likely be receptive to their anti-establishment and underdog image. They pitched a big purple tent at football games and other college events, handing out juice and T-shirts with the distinct Nantucket Nectars' logo. Their low-cost, grass-roots marketing early on helped position Nantucket Nectars as the youthful, natural, and independent alternative to larger juice and beverage companies.

They also stumbled upon an effective radio advertising campaign. After booking a recording session, the Toms never got around to actually writing a script for their ad. Instead, they persuaded the radio producer to just record them talking. First and Scott "shot the breeze" for a couple of hours, reminiscing about their early days as "Juice Guys," and then edited the conversation for a radio spot. What resulted was an off-the-cuff, down-to-earth radio ad that ended up winning an award for excellence in radio advertising.

Nantucket Nectars still prefers such homespun techniques to promote its many juice flavors. The company uses "mobile marketing squads" that drive purple Winnebagos to outdoor events frequented by the company's coveted consumers—eighteen- to thirty-five-year-olds. Members of the company's high-energy, purple-shirted juice squad hand out free samples of the company's flavorful juices to sports fans, marathoners, and concertgoers. Mobile squads will also swap any competitor's product for a new cold bottle of Nantucket Nectars.

To introduce its latest Squeezed Nectars line of juice teas and lemonades packaged in distinctive wide-mouthed glass canning jars, the company relied heavily on sampling and promotions to create a buzz. In addition, the Toms decided to invite their grandmothers to promote the new line. In radio spots, the grandmothers chat with Scott and First about a wide range of topics, but mostly about how lemonade was made long ago, reinforcing the idea that Nantucket Nectars' lemonades taste just like grandma's.

From its humble beginnings, Nantucket Nectars has grown to be a major player in the premium juice drink category with a loyal following. While "Juice Guys" First and Scott have had their share of bumps along the way, their once tiny company now employs over one hundred people, and revenues top $80 million. Their evolving juice lineup—fifty different flavors in all—are sold in about forty states and in Britain, France, Korea, the Caribbean, South and Central America, and Canada. The Toms still consider themselves the underdog in the premium juice industry. But no matter how much Nantucket Nectars grows, Scott says, he will always be looking for ways to change since the only way to succeed in this competitive environment is to be entrepreneurial.

Questions

1. What elements of the promotional mix does Nantucket Nectars utilize to promote its juice line?

2. Where would you place Nantucket Nectars in the product life cycle? How does this affect the company's choice of promotional mix elements?

3. Visit the company's Web site at **http://www.juiceguys.com**. Give examples of how its Web site conveys its folksy, down-to-earth image.

WATCH IT

Short

The *Marketing* PowerPoint CD-ROM has five video ad clips in the Chapter 14 slide presentation. After watching the three Pepsi ads, determine how consistent the marketing message was. What communication function do the Pontiac and Taco Bell ads convey?

Medium   **VIDEO**

When the outside auditor of McDonald's popular Monopoly givaway game was charged with fraud, the fast-food giant had a serious communication problem on its hands. Watch the clip on the scandal and determine how well McDonald's communicated with its customers during and after the game was compromised. This segment is also relevant for Chapter 15.

Long Small**Business**School ◘
the Series on PBS stations and the Web

To give you insight into Chapter 14, Small Business School introduces you to a company rescued from the ashes of a dying franchise by the innovation of one man and his plan for integrated marketing communications. Cloud 9 Shuttle is the result of John Hawkins turning a boring airport Super Shuttle franchise into a unique and exciting brand through a solid strategy and a well-communicated marketing message. Hawkins leads this Master Class, so join him for a lesson in integrated marketing communications.

 FLIP IT

 Flip to Chapter 14 in your *Grademaker Study Guide* for more review opportunities, including the pretest, vocabulary review, Internet activities, study test questions, and an application exercise based on IMC concepts. What is the role of promotion in the marketing mix? Can you close your book and diagram the communication process? What about describing the difference between push and pull strategies? If not, then pick up your *Grademaker* and review.

CLICK IT

 The *Marketing* Web site links you to all the Internet-based activities in this chapter, like the "Use It," "Review It" questions 6.2 and 6.3, and the On-Line exercises in the chapter margins. As a review, do the Chapter 14 quiz and crossword puzzle. And don't forget the Career Exersite that gives you resources for exploring marketing career opportunities in promotions. Review the main concepts in the PowerPoint presentation for Chapter 14, too. Go to **http://lamb.swlearning.com**, read the material, and follow the links right from the site.

SPIN IT

Spin your Xtra! CD-ROM to test your understanding of the promotion concepts in the chapter by completing the worksheets for exhibits 14.1 and 14.3 through 14.8. If your instructor has assigned a marketing plan project, worksheets on Xtra! can help you organize your work. In addition to the quiz on the Web site, there's another quiz on the Xtra! CD-ROM, plus video of the authors answering frequently asked questions about promotion topics, such as, "Which factors influence the promotional mix and how?" and "How do businesses tell customers about their products and services?"

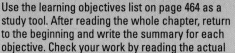

Still Shaky? Here's a Tip.

Use the learning objectives list on page 464 as a study tool. After reading the whole chapter, return to the beginning and write the summary for each objective. Check your work by reading the actual summary points on pages 486–488.

CHAPTER **FIFTEEN**

ADVERTISING AND PUBLIC RELATIONS

Learning Objectives

1 *Discuss the effects of advertising on market share and consumers*

2 *Identify the major types of advertising*

3 *Discuss the creative decisions in developing an advertising campaign*

4 *Describe media evaluation and selection techniques*

5 *Discuss the role of public relations in the promotional mix*

It's after midnight and the dance clubs are jumping—music is pulsating, lights are flashing, people are dancing, and the bar is littered with little silver and blue cans. Yes, Red Bull is in the house—and has absolutely no intention of leaving the party.

Red Bull, exported from Austria, has created and dominated the energy drink category with marketing savvy, guerrilla tactics, and unusual distribution methods. Dietrich Mateschitz, the owner of Red Bull International, created the caffeine-charged beverage in 1987, based on a popular health tonic he discovered in Thailand. After spreading into neighboring countries including Hungary, Slovenia, Germany, and Switzerland, Red Bull charged into the U.S. market, virtually creating the energy drink market and taking it by the horns.

Initially, Red Bull was the drink of choice for extreme athletes and all-night ravers, but the taurine-based energy drink has gained a larger following and can now be found on supermarket shelves in almost every state. According to Red Bull's Web site at (**http://www. redbull.com**), "Taurine is a conditionally essential amino acid, which naturally occurs in the body. But in times of extreme physical exertion, the body no longer produces the required amounts and a relative deficiency results." Hence, a need is identified and Red Bull races to fill it.

In less than three years, Red Bull has spawned a hot new beverage category and boosted sales from a base of $12 million to $42 million in 1998 and $75 million in 1999, according to Beverage Marketing Corporation. Now Coke, Anheuser-Busch, and Pepsi are looking to get a piece of the action, and some predict that sales of energy drinks in the United States could top $500 million in the next few years.

But with 70 percent of the market share, Red Bull executives feel confident that they can continue leading the category by employing the same marketing techniques that put them on the map in the first place.

The company's consistent strategy has been to "open up" a market by securing unusual distribution channels. Red Bull initially began its U.S. charge in Santa Monica, California, by piggybacking with established distributors that deliver a number of brands. As the drink became more popular, Red Bull narrowed its distribution methods by contacting smaller distributors and insisting that they sell only Red Bull. Otherwise, Red Bull sets up warehouses and hires college students to deliver its product. Results have been incredible—in a new market, Red Bull generally breaks even within the first three months and shows a profit after six.

Another tactic that Red Bull employs is hiring hip locals "who embody the spirit of Red Bull" in target areas to drive around in a Red Bull logoed car, hand out samples, and educate consumers about the product.

Sales teams also visit targeted on-site accounts—trendy nightclubs and bars. After an initial purchase of a few cases, Red Bull supplies the bar with a branded cooler and other POP (Point-of-Purchase) items. The sales teams also work to get the drink into convenience stores near colleges, gyms, health-food stores, and supermarkets.

While Red Bull relies heavily on sampling events at bars and nightclubs, alternative sports have proved to be a natural fit for the product. Red Bull underwrites a number of extreme sports competitions and sponsors about three dozen athletes like kayaker Tao Berman, who set a world record by paddling over a 98-foot waterfall. Another unique event Red Bull sponsors is a DJ Academy. The latest one, held in New York City and taught by such mix masters as MJ Cole and Shadow Boy, was offered to sixty aspiring DJs from around the world.

Once established in a market, Red Bull employs more traditional advertising. Current ads portray an animated bull character and carry the tag "Red Bull Gives You Wings." The ads run on late-night TV and on popular alternative radio shows.[1]

How do marketers like Red Bull decide what type of advertising message should be conveyed to prospective consumers? How do marketers decide which media to use? How do public relations and publicity benefit a marketer's promotional plan? Answers to these questions and many more will be found as you read through this chapter.

The Effects of Advertising

1

Discuss the effects of advertising on market share and consumers

Advertising is defined in Chapter 14 as any form of impersonal, paid communication in which the sponsor or company is identified. It is a popular form of promotion, especially for consumer packaged goods and services. Advertising spending increases annually, and estimated U.S. expenditures now exceed $240 billion per year.[2]

Although total advertising expenditures seem large, the industry itself is very small. Only about 284,000 people are employed in the advertising departments of manufacturers, wholesalers, and retailers and in the 13,000 or so advertising agencies.[3] This figure also includes people working in media services, such as radio and television, magazines and newspapers, and direct-mail firms.

The amount of money budgeted for advertising by some firms is staggering (see Exhibit 15.1). General Motors, Philip Morris, Procter & Gamble, Ford Motor, and Pfizer each spend over $2 billion annually on national advertising alone. That's over $6 million a day by each company. If sales promotion and public relations are included, this figure rises even higher. Over ninety additional companies spend over $200 million each.

Spending on advertising varies by industry. For example, the game and toy industry has one of the highest ratios of advertising dollars to sales. For every $1.00 of merchandise sold in the toy industry, about 12¢ to 15¢ is spent on advertising the toy to consumers. Book publishers spend roughly 27¢ on advertising for every $1.00 of book revenue. Other consumer goods manufacturers that spend heavily

Exhibit 15.1

Top Ten Leaders by U.S. Advertising Spending

Rank	Advertiser	Total U.S. Ad Spending In 2000 (in millions)	Average Ad Spending per Day in 2000
1	General Motors Corp., Detroit	$3,934.8	$10, 780, 273
2	Philip Morris, New York	$2,602.9	$7, 131,232
3	Procter & Gamble, Cincinnati	$2,363.5	$6,475,342
4	Ford Motor, Dearborn, Michigan	$2,345.2	$6,425,205
5	Pfizer, New York	$2,265.3	$6,206,301
6	PepsiCo, Purchase, New York	$2,100.7	$5,755,342
7	DaimlerChrysler, Auburn Hills, Michigan/Stuttgart, Germany	$1,984.0	$5,435,616
8	AOL Time Warner, New York	$1,770.1	$4,849,589
9	Walt Disney, Burbank, California	$1,757.5	$4,815,068
10	Verizon Communications, New York	$1,612.9	$4,418,904

SOURCE: Computed from data obtained from "100 Leaders by U.S. Advertising Spending," *Advertising Age,* September 24, 2001, s2.

on advertising in relation to total sales include sugar and confectionery products manufacturers, leather manufacturers, watchmakers, perfume and cosmetic manufacturers, detergent makers, and wine and liquor companies.[4]

Advertising and Market Share

Today's most successful brands of consumer goods, like Ivory soap and Coca-Cola, were built by heavy advertising and marketing investments long ago. Today's advertising dollars are spent on maintaining brand awareness and market share.

New brands with a small market share tend to spend proportionately more for advertising and sales promotion than those with a large market share, typically for two reasons. First, beyond a certain level of spending for advertising and sales promotion, diminishing returns set in. That is, sales or market share begins to decrease no matter how much is spent on advertising and sales promotion. This phenomenon is called the **advertising response function**. Understanding the advertising response function helps marketers use budgets wisely. A market leader like Johnson & Johnson's Neutrogena typically spends proportionately less on advertising than a newcomer like Jergens' Naturally Smooth Shave Minimizing Moisturizer brand. Jergens spends more on its brand to gain attention and increase market share. Neutrogena, on the other hand, spends only as much as is needed to maintain market share; anything more would produce diminishing benefits. Neutrogena has already captured the attention of the majority of its target market. It only needs to remind customers of its product.

The second reason that new brands tend to require higher spending for advertising and sales promotion is that a certain minimum level of exposure is needed to measurably affect purchase habits. If Jergens advertised Naturally Smooth Shave Minimizing Moisturizer in only one or two publications and bought only one or two television spots, it certainly would not achieve the exposure needed to penetrate consumers' perceptual defenses, gain attention, and ultimately affect purchase intentions. Instead, Naturally Smooth Shave Minimizing Moisturizer was advertised in many different media for a sustained time.

The Effects of Advertising on Consumers

Advertising affects consumers' daily lives, informing them about products and services and influencing their attitudes, beliefs, and ultimately their purchases. The average U.S. citizen is exposed to hundreds of advertisements a day from all types of advertising media. In the television medium alone, researchers estimate that the average viewer watches at least six hours of commercial television messages a week. In addition, that person would be exposed to countless print ads and promotional messages seen in other places.[5] Advertising affects the TV programs people watch, the content of the newspapers they read, the politicians they elect, the medicines they take, and the toys their children play with. Consequently, the influence of advertising on the U.S. socioeconomic system has been the subject of extensive debate among economists, marketers, sociologists, psychologists, politicians, consumerists, and many others.

While advertising cannot change consumers' deeply rooted values and attitudes, advertising may succeed in transforming a person's negative attitude toward a product into a positive one. For instance, serious or dramatic advertisements are more effective at changing consumers' negative attitudes. Humorous ads, on the other hand, have been shown to be more effective at shaping attitudes when consumers already have a positive image of the advertised brand.[6] For this reason, beer marketers often use humorous ads to communicate with their core market of young adults.

Advertising also reinforces positive attitudes toward brands. When consumers have a neutral or favorable frame of reference toward a product or brand,

advertising response function
A phenomenon in which spending for advertising and sales promotion increases sales or market share up to a certain level but then produces diminishing returns.

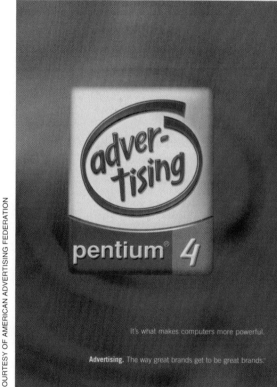

COURTESY OF AMERICAN ADVERTISING FEDERATION

adver-tising
pentium 4
It's what makes computers more powerful.
Advertising. The way great brands get to be great brands.

Advertising investments undeniably help build a brand. The American Advertising Federation reminds companies of this through its Great Brands campaign. Intel Corporation gave permission to modify their logo for use in this campaign.

advertising often positively influences them. When consumers are already highly loyal to a brand, they may buy more of it when advertising and promotion for that brand increase.[7] This is why market leaders like General Motors and Procter & Gamble spend billions of dollars annually to reinforce and remind their loyal customers about the benefits of their cars and household products.

Further, advertising can affect the way consumers rank a brand's attributes, such as color, taste, smell, and texture. For example, in years past, car ads emphasized such brand attributes as roominess, speed, and low maintenance. Today, however, car marketers have added safety to the list. Safety features like antilock brakes, power door locks, and air bags are now a standard part of the message in many carmakers' ads.

Major Types of Advertising

2
Identify the major types of advertising

institutional advertising
A form of advertising designed to enhance a company's image rather than promote a particular product.

product advertising
A form of advertising that touts the benefits of a specific good or service.

The firm's promotional objectives determine the type of advertising it uses. If the goal of the promotion plan is to build up the image of the company or the industry, **institutional advertising** may be used. In contrast, if the advertiser wants to enhance the sales of a specific good or service, **product advertising** is used.

Institutional Advertising

Advertising in the United States has historically been product oriented. However, modern corporations market multiple products and need a different type of advertising. Institutional advertising, or corporate advertising, promotes the corporation as a whole and is designed to establish, change, or maintain the corporation's identity. It usually does not ask the audience to do anything but maintain a favorable attitude toward the advertiser and its goods and services. Known around the world as a commercial airline manufacturer, the Boeing Company wanted to be as well known for its other products—especially in the areas of aerospace and communications. The company initiated its first-ever corporate campaign to shift the focus from airplane manufacturer to high-tech aerospace and communications expert. The campaign broke with three TV spots featuring shots of astronauts, the world spinning and rockets lifting off, and—significantly—satellites. The spots all used the tagline "*Boeing.* Forever new frontiers." [8] Boeing has dedicated $40 million of a $72 million global budget to advertise the strategic message of "tomorrow will be better because of something Boeing is doing or will be doing." [9]

 A form of institutional advertising called **advocacy advertising** is typically used to safeguard against negative consumer attitudes and to enhance the company's credibility among consumers who already favor its position. Often corporations use advocacy advertising to express their views on controversial issues. At other times, firms' advocacy campaigns react to criticism or blame, some in direct response to criticism by the media. Other advocacy campaigns may try to ward off increased regulation, damaging legislation, or an unfavorable outcome in a lawsuit. The tobacco companies have utilized "good citizen campaigns" in the United States and around the world in an effort to create a positive public image for themselves after losing several class-action suits and being accused of

COURTESY OF FORD MOTOR COMPANY

In one of the most compelling institutional ad campaigns of recent memory, Ford Chairman and CEO Bill Ford appears in several TV spots that communicate both the heritage and the vision of Ford. These ads are critical in the wake of several crises that befell the company under Jacques Nasser's tenure.

targeting children with their marketing campaigns. In an effort to improve public opinion, Philip Morris has been pouring $100 million a year into feel-good ads promoting corporate good deeds such as donations to food banks and shelters for battered women.[10]

Product Advertising

Unlike institutional advertising, product advertising promotes the benefits of a specific good or service. The product's stage in its life cycle often determines which type of product advertising is used: pioneering advertising, competitive advertising, or comparative advertising.

Pioneering Advertising

Pioneering advertising is intended to stimulate primary demand for a new product or product category. Heavily used during the introductory stage of the product life cycle, pioneering advertising offers consumers in-depth information about the benefits of the product class. Pioneering advertising also seeks to create interest. Microsoft used pioneering advertising to introduce its new Windows and Office software products. In a move to reposition the products as more "user-friendly," the software giant renamed its flagship products by adding "XP"—short for "Experience"—to the Windows and Office upgrades.[11] Microsoft's $200 million four-month launch phase kicked off with two fifteen-second TV teaser spots, plus one sixty-second and two thirty-second TV spots that featured the Madonna song "Ray of Light." The print, outdoor, TV, and on-line campaign carries the tagline "Yes, you can" and features XP's signature look—blue skies with white clouds over a green field. The goal of Microsoft's pioneering campaign was to convince PC users to buy the upgrade because of the more intuitive interfaces and abilities to work seamlessly and easily with digital photographs, music files, and video.[12]

Competitive Advertising

Firms use competitive or brand advertising when a product enters the growth phase of the product life cycle and other companies begin to enter the marketplace. Instead of building demand for the product category, the goal of **competitive advertising** is to influence demand for a specific brand. Often promotion becomes less informative and appeals more to emotions during this phase. Advertisements may begin to stress subtle differences between brands, with heavy emphasis on building recall of a brand name and creating a favorable attitude toward the brand. Automobile advertising has long used very competitive messages, drawing distinctions based on such factors as quality, performance, and image.

Comparative Advertising

Comparative advertising directly or indirectly compares two or more competing brands on one or more specific attributes. Some advertisers even use comparative advertising against their own brands. Products experiencing sluggish growth or those entering the marketplace against strong competitors are more likely to employ comparative claims in their advertising. For instance, comparative ads from pizza maker Papa John's claim its pizza beat Pizza Hut pizza in a blind taste test. The comparative television spot contrasts its sauce—using a glamour shot of vine-ripened tomatoes—with Pizza Hut's, depicted as thick red goo scooped from a plastic bag.[13] Another comparative spot depicts a sculptor creating statues out of tomato paste used by rivals. The spot then shows tomato sauce easily flowing from a Papa John's can.[14]

Before the 1970s, comparative advertising was allowed only if the competing brand was veiled and unidentified. In 1971, however, the Federal Trade Commission (FTC) fostered the growth of comparative

Pizza Hut
Papa John's
Can you find evidence of comparative advertising on either Pizza Hut's or Papa John's Web site?
http://www.pizzahut.com
http://www.papajohns.com

On Line

advocacy advertising
A form of advertising in which an organization expresses its views on controversial issues or responds to media attacks.

pioneering advertising
A form of advertising designed to stimulate primary demand for a new product or product category.

competitive advertising
A form of advertising designed to influence demand for a specific brand.

comparative advertising
A form of advertising that compares two or more specifically named or shown competing brands on one or more specific attributes.

advertising by saying that it provided information to the customer and that advertisers were more skillful than the government in communicating this information. Federal rulings prohibit advertisers from falsely describing competitors' products and allow competitors to sue if ads show their products or mention their brand names in an incorrect or false manner. For instance, Target Corporation initiated a legal challenge to force Kmart to discontinue its "Dare to Compare" in-store advertising program. The campaign boasted that Kmart's prices on certain items beat the prices at competing stores, including Target. Target provided an audit, which showed that 74 percent of the signage surveyed listed the wrong Kmart or Target price and compared items that the nearest Target didn't even sell. Target withdrew its motion for a temporary restraining order after Kmart permanently removed the "Dare to Compare" signage in all its U.S. stores.[15]

 FTC rules also apply to advertisers making false claims about their own products. Recently, a physicians' group filed false advertising complaints against the popular and long-lasting "milk mustache" ad campaign. The physicians said the ads, featuring sports figures like Kristi Yamaguchi and Mark McGwire, falsely claim to enhance sports performances. In response to the physicians' petition, a federal panel was formed to determine whether there was a scientific consensus regarding the range of benefits attributed to milk. The panel's report supported most of the physicians' complaints and was turned over to the FTC for investigation.[16] In a case against computer maker Gateway, the FTC required the company to reimburse customers after it charged them for an Internet access plan that was supposed to be free. Gateway offered one year of free Internet access as an incentive to buy Gateway Essential PCs, but customers found themselves paying $3.95 per hour for Net access. Similarly, Juno Online Services faced FTC charges for making it difficult to cancel free trials of its access plan and for not explaining hidden phone charges. Juno now must reimburse customers and disclose its access charges.[17]

Companies must be careful with comparative advertising approaches in other countries as well. Germany, Italy, Belgium, and France, for example, do not permit advertisers to claim that their products are best or better than competitors' products, which are common claims in the United States. In the Netherlands, car manufacturers cannot make claims in their advertising about the fuel consumption or environmental aspects of the car. Similarly, Lands' End ran afoul of a German law prohibiting lifetime guarantee claims, which happen to be one of Lands' End's guiding principles. The law is making it difficult for the direct retailer to sell its products and advertise its lifetime guarantee through the Internet and direct mail. In Italy, Absolut ran an ad claiming that it was the only vodka made from grain, which is perceived to produce a higher quality vodka than that made from potatoes. Rival distributor Aosta Company, noting that two of its products were made from grain, filed a complaint against Absolut's Italian distributor, Seagram Italia.[18] Although comparative advertising has been legal in Italy since 1999, ads cannot make unsubstantiated claims. So authorities ordered the campaign stopped and Seagram Italia had to pull all ads. Finally, in South Korea, where comparative advertising is banned, ads for the domestic search engine Empas proclaim, "Empas Is No. 1, Yahoo! Is No. 6," and "If you can't find it with Yahoo!, try Empas." Yahoo! filed a complaint with Korea's Fair Trade Commission requesting that the ads be stopped.[19]

In other countries, hard-hitting comparative advertising will not be effective because it offends cultural values. For example, Arabic culture generally encourages people not to compete with one another, and the sharing of wealth is common practice. Therefore, comparative advertising is not consistent with social values in these countries.[20] Japanese advertisers are also reluctant to use comparative advertising because it is considered confrontational and doesn't promote the respectful treatment of consumers or portray a company in a respectful light. Nevertheless, although the Japanese have traditionally favored soft-sell advertising approaches, consumers are witnessing a trend toward comparative ads.

Creative Decisions in Advertising

Advertisements that are seen on television, in magazines, and on the Internet are typically the result of an **advertising campaign**—a series of related advertisements focusing on a common theme, slogan, and set of advertising appeals. It is a specific advertising effort for a particular product that extends for a defined period of time. For example, XM Satellite Radio, the first subscription-based, digital-quality, satellite-transmitted radio service, developed an introductory advertising campaign around the theme "Radio to the Power of X." The company was attempting to persuade consumers to pay $10 a month for what has always been free. Launched in movie theaters followed by TV, the $100 million ad campaign featured musicians and objects crashing to earth, each highlighting a different genre of satellite programming. B. B. King, Snoop Dogg, and David Bowie made appearances as they tumbled toward the ground. Other spots showed records raining on kids in a parking lot and a truck driver caught in a storm of cellos, trombones, and pianos. At the end of each spot, an XM tuner cycled through the channels until it rested on the appropriate genre. The idea was to convey the endless variety of programming offered on XM Satellite Radio and to set XM apart from its competitor, Sirius.[21]

Before any creative work can begin on an advertising campaign, it is important to determine what goals or objectives the advertising should achieve. An **advertising objective** identifies the specific communication task that a campaign should accomplish for a specified target audience during a specified period. The objectives of a specific advertising campaign often depend on the overall corporate objectives and the product being advertised. For instance, Pacific Bell's main objective in a recent campaign was to emphasize the benefit of using its fiber DSL for Internet service over a cable line. Television commercials showed what happens when human beings are forced to share resources. Each spot is narrated by a resident of fictitious Laurel Lane, who says that everything in the neighborhood was just fine until "everyone started sharing the same cable line for Internet. That's when things on-line got slower and people started acting, well downright un-neighborly." The spot shows people trying to log on and getting frustrated because it's taking so long to get connected. Then all the residents of the neighborhood start to turn on one another. Two kids engage in a shouting match with an adult—the words "Web Hog" are painted on his house. An elderly woman sees a balloon float over her fence from next door and punctures it with her rake. An ice cream truck drives around the neighborhood with the words "Log off" spray-painted on the side. The commercial continues to document neighborhood atrocities until the payoff at the end that uses the tagline: "Don't share a cable line. Get Pacific Bell DSL. Always fast. Never shared." The commercials advertised the objective so successfully that they had to be discontinued because Pacific Bell got so many orders that it had trouble filling all of them.[22]

The DAGMAR approach (Defining Advertising Goals for Measured Advertising Results) is one method of setting objectives. According to this method, all advertising objectives should precisely define the target audience, the desired percentage change in some specified measure of effectiveness, and the time frame in which that change is to occur. For example, the objectives for an advertising campaign for Coca-Cola's revamped Powerade brand might be achieving a 15 percent increase in its share of the sports-drink market within eight months.

Once objectives are defined, creative work can begin on the advertising campaign. Advertising campaigns often follow the AIDA model, which was discussed in Chapter 14. Depending on where consumers are in the AIDA process, the creative development of an advertising campaign might focus on creating attention, arousing interest, stimulating desire, or ultimately leading to the action of buying the product. Specifically, creative decisions include identifying product benefits, developing and evaluating advertising appeals, executing the message, and evaluating the effectiveness of the campaign.

Discuss the creative decisions in developing an advertising campaign

advertising campaign
A series of related advertisements focusing on a common theme, slogan, and set of advertising appeals.

advertising objective
A specific communication task that a campaign should accomplish for a specified target audience during a specified period.

Identifying Product Benefits

A well-known rule of thumb in the advertising industry is "Sell the sizzle, not the steak"—that is, in advertising the goal is to sell the benefits of the product, not its attributes. An attribute is simply a feature of the product such as its easy-open package or special formulation. A benefit is what consumers will receive or achieve by using the product. A benefit should answer the consumer's question "What's in it for me?" Benefits might be such things as convenience, pleasure, savings, or relief. A quick test to determine whether you are offering attributes or benefits in your advertising is to ask "So?" Consider this example:

> *Attribute:* "Powerade's new line has been reformulated to combine the scientific benefits of sports drinks with B vitamins and to speed up energy metabolism." "So . . . ?"
> *Benefit:* "So, you'll satisfy your thirst with a great-tasting drink that will power you throughout the day."

Marketing research and intuition are usually used to unearth the perceived benefits of a product and to rank consumers' preferences for these benefits. Coke's rival, PepsiCo, has its own sports drink, Gatorade. Already positioned as *the* thirst-quencher, Gatorade's advertising touts its refueling benefits to serious athletes of mainstream sports.[23]

Developing and Evaluating Advertising Appeals

An **advertising appeal** identifies a reason for a person to buy a product. Developing advertising appeals, a challenging task, is typically the responsibility of the creative people in the advertising agency. Advertising appeals typically play off of consumers' emotions, such as fear or love, or address some need or want the consumer has, such as a need for convenience or the desire to save money.

Advertising campaigns can focus on one or more advertising appeals. Often the appeals are quite general, thus allowing the firm to develop a number of sub-themes or minicampaigns using both advertising and sales promotion. Several possible advertising appeals are listed in Exhibit 15.2.

Choosing the best appeal from those developed normally requires market research. Criteria for evaluation include desirability, exclusiveness, and believability. The appeal first must make a positive impression on and be desirable to the target market. It must also be exclusive or unique; consumers must be able to distinguish the advertiser's message from competitors' messages. Most important, the appeal should be believable. An appeal that makes extravagant claims not only wastes promotional dollars but also creates ill will for the advertiser.

The advertising appeal selected for the campaign becomes what advertisers call its **unique selling proposition**. The unique selling proposition usually becomes the campaign's slogan. Powerade's advertising campaign aimed at the nontraditional sports enthusiast carries the slogan "Very Real Power." This is also Powerade's unique selling proposition, implying that you can push yourself to the limit because the drink offers more "power" through carbonated fuel.[24]

Effective slogans often become so ingrained that consumers can immediately conjure up images of the product just by hearing the slogan. For example, most consumers can easily name the companies and products behind these memorable slogans or even hum the jingle that goes along with some of them: "Have it your way," "Tastes great, less filling," "Ring around the collar," and "Tum te Tum Tum." Advertisers often revive old slogans or jingles in the hope that the nostalgia will create good feelings with consumers. American Motors brought back Joe Isuzu after an eleven-year absence because research showed that during the initial four-year campaign the brand's awareness was at an all-time high. Maytag Corporation refreshed its campaign featuring its appliance pitchman by changing the actor who plays him—the second change since the ads originated in 1967. And Hershey

---

advertising appeal
A reason for a person to buy a product.

unique selling proposition
A desirable, exclusive, and believable advertising appeal selected as the theme for a campaign.

Exhibit 15.2

Common Advertising Appeals

Profit	Lets consumers know whether the product will save them money, make them money, or keep them from losing money
Health	Appeals to those who are body-conscious or who want to be healthy
Love or Romance	Is used often in selling cosmetics and perfumes
Fear	Can center around social embarrassment, growing old, or losing one's health; because of its power, requires advertiser to exercise care in execution
Admiration	Is the reason that celebrity spokespeople are used so often in advertising
Convenience	Is often used for fast-food restaurants and microwave foods
Fun and Pleasure	Are the key to advertising vacations, beer, amusement parks, and more
Vanity and Egotism	Are used most often for expensive or conspicuous items such as cars and clothing
Environmental Consciousness	Centers around protecting the environment and being considerate of others in the community

Foods' Kit Kat bar's ten-year old jingle "Gimme a Break" is so etched in consumers' minds that recently the agency hired a film crew to walk around and ask people on the street to sing the jingle for use in future spots.[25]

Executing the Message

Message execution is the way an advertisement portrays its information. In general, the AIDA (see Chapter 14) plan is a good blueprint for executing an advertising message. Any ad should immediately draw the reader's, viewer's, or listener's attention. The advertiser must then use the message to hold consumers' interest, create desire for the good or service, and ultimately motivate action—a purchase.

The style in which the message is executed is one of the most creative elements of an advertisement. Exhibit 15.3 lists some examples of executional styles used by advertisers. Executional styles often dictate what type of media is to be employed to convey the message. Scientific executional styles lend themselves well to print advertising where more information can be conveyed. On the other hand, demonstration and musical styles are more likely found in broadcast advertising.

COURTESY OF THE DIAL CORPORATION

Cleans the pocket that holds the wallet that holds the money you'll save.

Purex® gets clothes clean and smelling fresh for about half the price of more expensive brands. Don't waste money on dirt.

Although there are numerous appeals that could be successfully used to advertise laundry detergent, Purex has chosen the profit appeal in this print ad.

Exhibit 15.3

Ten Common Executional Styles
for Advertising

Slice-of-Life	Depicts people in normal settings, such as at the dinner table or in their car. McDonald's often uses slice-of-life styles showing youngsters munching french fries and Happy Meals on family outings.
Lifestyle	Shows how well the product will fit in with the consumer's lifestyle. As their Volkswagen Jetta moves through the streets of the French Quarter, the Gen X drivers plug in a techno music CD and marvel at how the rhythms of the world mimic the ambient vibe inside their vehicle.
Spokesperson/ Testimonial	Can feature a celebrity, company official, or typical consumer making a testimonial or endorsing a product. Sarah Michelle Gellar, star of *Buffy the Vampire Slayer*, endorses Maybelline cosmetics while country singer Shania Twain introduced Revlon's ColorStay Liquid Lip. Dell Computer founder Michael Dell touts his vision of the customer experience via Dell in television ads.
Fantasy	Creates a fantasy for the viewer built around use of the product. Carmakers often use this style to let viewers fantasize about how they would feel speeding around tight corners or down long country roads in their cars.
Humorous	Advertisers often use humor in their ads, such as Snickers' "Not Going Anywhere for a While" campaign featuring hundreds of souls waiting, sometimes impatiently, to get into heaven.
Real/Animated Product Symbols	Creates a character that represents the product in advertisements, such as the Energizer bunny, Starkist's Charlie the Tuna, or General Mills' longtime icon, Betty Crocker, redesigned for the new millennium.
Mood or Image	Builds a mood or image around the product, such as peace, love, or beauty. De-Beers ads depicting shadowy silhouettes wearing diamond engagement rings and diamond necklaces portray passion and intimacy while extolling that a "diamond is forever."
Demonstration	Shows consumers the expected benefit. Many consumer products use this technique. Laundry-detergent spots are famous for demonstrating how their product will clean clothes whiter and brighter. Fort James Corporation recently demonstrated in television commercials how its Dixie Rinse & ReUse disposable stoneware product line can stand up to the heat of a blowtorch and survive a cycle in a clothes washer.
Musical	Conveys the message of the advertisement through song. For example, Nike's recent ads depicting a marathoner's tortured feet, skier Picabo Street's surgery-scarred knee, and a surfer's thigh scarred by a shark attack while strains of Joe Cocker's "You Are So Beautiful" are heard in the background.
Scientific	Uses research or scientific evidence to give a brand superiority over competitors. Pain relievers like Advil, Bayer, and Excedrin use scientific evidence in their ads.

Injecting humor into an advertisement is a popular and effective executional style. Humorous executional styles are more often used in radio and television advertising than in print or magazine advertising where humor is less easily communicated. Humorous ads are typically used for lower risk, routine purchases such as candy, cigarettes, and soft drinks than for higher risk purchases or those that are

expensive, durable, or flamboyant.[26]
Anheuser-Busch's consistent humorous
approach to its Budweiser and Bud
Light advertising campaigns has been
credited with giving Bud a competitive
edge in an image-conscious category
that traditionally prefers upscale imports. Frogs, lizards, a ferret and, of
course, the "Whassup?" guys resonate
with the core twenty-one- to twenty-
seven-year-old target market and have
also secured a place in American pop
culture.[27] But the situation must be
considered before using a humorous
approach in advertising. After the September 11 terrorist attacks on the Pentagon and the World Trade Center,
many shell-shocked consumers felt that

AP/WIDE WORLD PHOTOS

some advertising campaigns were no longer appropriate. And participants in nationwide focus groups felt that marketers should consider using sentimental messages or even reviving nostalgic campaigns.[28]

Using a spokesperson is a common executional style (recall the Bill Ford ad on
page 496.). The Maytag Man may be the
most well-known spokesperson, revived
in the past decade by Gordon Jump, who
starred in the 1970's sit-com *WKRP in
Cincinnati*.

> **GLOBAL** Executional styles for foreign advertising are often quite different
from those we are accustomed to in the United States. Sometimes they are
sexually oriented or aesthetically imaginative. For example, European advertising avoids the direct-sell approaches common in U.S. ads and instead is more
indirect, more symbolic, and, above all, more visual. Nike, known in the United
States for "in-your-face" advertising and irreverent slogans such as "Just Do It," discovered that its brash advertising did not appeal to Europeans. A television commercial of Satan and his demons playing soccer against a team of Nike endorsers was a
hit in America. Many European stations refused to run it, however, saying it was too
scary and offensive to show in prime time, when kids were watching.[29]

> **GLOBAL** Japanese advertising is known for relying on fantasy and mood to sell
products. Ads in Japan notoriously lack the emphatic selling demonstrations found in U.S. advertising, limit the exposure of unique product features, and avoid direct comparisons to competitors' products. Japanese ads often
feature cartoon characters or place the actors in irrelevant situations. For example,
one advertisement promotes an insect spray while showing the actor having teeth
extracted at the dentist's office. One explanation of Japan's preference for soft-sell
advertising is cultural: Japanese consumers are naturally suspicious of someone who
needs to extol the virtues of a product. Additionally, unlike advertising agencies in
the United States, which consider working for competing companies to be unethical, Japan's larger ad agencies customarily maintain business relationships with
competing advertisers. Ads are less hard-hitting so as not to offend other clients.[30]

Postcampaign Evaluation

Evaluating an advertising campaign can be the most demanding task facing advertisers. How do advertisers know whether the campaign led to an increase in sales or
market share or elevated awareness of the product? Most advertising campaigns
aim to create an image for the good or service instead of asking for action, so their
real effect is unknown. So many variables shape the effectiveness of an ad that, in
many cases, advertisers must guess whether their money has been well spent. Despite this gray area, marketers spend a considerable amount of time studying advertising effectiveness and its probable impact on sales, market share, or awareness.

Testing ad effectiveness can be done either before or after the campaign. Before a campaign is released, marketing managers use pretests to determine the
best advertising appeal, layout, and media vehicle. After advertisers implement a

campaign, they often conduct tests to measure its effectiveness. Several monitoring techniques can be used to determine whether the campaign has met its original goals. Even if a campaign has been highly successful, advertisers still typically do a postcampaign analysis. They assess how the campaign might have been more efficient and what factors contributed to its success.

Media Decisions in Advertising

 4
Describe media evaluation and selection techniques

medium
The channel used to convey a message to a target market.

media planning
The series of decisions advertisers make regarding the selection and use of media, allowing the marketer to optimally and cost-effectively communicate the message to the target audience.

A major decision for advertisers is the choice of **medium**—the channel used to convey a message to a target market. **Media planning**, therefore, is the series of decisions advertisers make regarding the selection and use of media, allowing the marketer to optimally and cost-effectively communicate the message to the target audience.[31] Specifically, advertisers must determine which types of media will best communicate the benefits of their product or service to the target audience and when and for how long the advertisement will run.

Promotional objectives and the appeal and executional style of the advertising strongly affect the selection of media. It is important to understand that both creative and media decisions are made at the same time. Creative work cannot be completed without knowing which medium will be used to convey the message to the target market. For instance, creative planning will likely differ for an ad to be displayed on an outdoor billboard versus that placed in a print medium, such as a newspaper or magazine. In many cases, the advertising objectives dictate the medium and the creative approach to be used. For example, if the objective is to demonstrate how fast a product operates, a TV commercial that shows this action may be the best choice.

As mentioned at the beginning of this chapter, U.S. advertisers spend over $240 billion on media advertising annually. About 46 percent, or $110 billion, is spent in media monitored by national reporting services—newspapers, magazines, Yellow Pages, Internet, radio, television, and outdoor media. The remaining 54 percent, or $130 million, is spent on unmonitored media, such as direct mail, trade exhibits, cooperative advertising, brochures, coupons, catalogs, and special events.[32] Exhibit 15.4 breaks down the $110 billion spent in monitored advertising by media type. As you can see, more than 40 percent of every dollar spent in moni-

Exhibit 15.4

Domestic Advertising Spending in Monitored Media for 2000

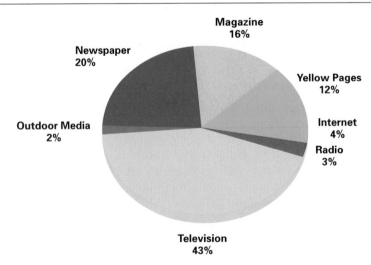

SOURCE: "Domestic Advertising Spending by Medium," *Advertising Age*, September 24, 2001, s12.

tored media goes toward purchasing time for TV ads. The nation's largest advertisers, such as those listed earlier in Exhibit 15.1, spend even more on television advertising—about 63¢ of every $1.00 spent in monitored media.[33]

Media Types

Advertising media are channels that advertisers use in mass communication. The seven major advertising media are newspapers, magazines, radio, television, outdoor media, Yellow Pages, and the Internet. Exhibit 15.5 summarizes the advantages and disadvantages of these major channels. In recent years, however, alternative media vehicles have emerged that give advertisers innovative ways to reach their target audience and avoid advertising clutter.

Exhibit 15.5

Advantages and Disadvantages of Major Advertising Media

Medium	Advantages	Disadvantages
Newspapers	Geographic selectivity and flexibility; short-term advertiser commitments; news value and immediacy; year-round readership; high individual market coverage; co-op and local tie-in availability; short lead time	Little demographic selectivity; limited color capabilities; low pass-along rate; may be expensive
Magazines	Good reproduction, especially for color; demographic selectivity; regional selectivity; local market selectivity; relatively long advertising life; high pass-along rate	Long-term advertiser commitments; slow audience buildup; limited demonstration capabilities; lack of urgency; long lead time
Radio	Low cost; immediacy of message; can be scheduled on short notice; relatively no seasonal change in audience; highly portable; short-term advertiser commitments; entertainment carryover	No visual treatment; short advertising life of message; high frequency required to generate comprehension and retention; distractions from background sound; commercial clutter
Television	Ability to reach a wide, diverse audience; low cost per thousand; creative opportunities for demonstration; immediacy of messages; entertainment carryover; demographic selectivity with cable stations	Short life of message; some consumer skepticism about claims; high campaign cost; little demographic selectivity with network stations; long-term advertiser commitments; long lead times required for production; commercial clutter
Outdoor media	Repetition; moderate cost; flexibility; geographic selectivity	Short message; lack of demographic selectivity; high "noise" level distracting audience
Internet	Fastest growing medium; ability to reach a narrow target audience; relatively short lead time required for creating Web-based advertising; moderate cost	Difficult to measure ad effectiveness and return on investment; ad exposure relies on "click-through" from banner ads; not all consumers have access to the Internet

cooperative advertising
An arrangement in which the manufacturer and the retailer split the costs of advertising the manufacturer's brand.

Newspapers

The advantages of newspaper advertising include geographic flexibility and timeliness. Because copywriters can usually prepare newspaper ads quickly and at a reasonable cost, local merchants can reach their target market almost daily. Because newspapers are generally a mass-market medium, however, they may not be the best vehicle for marketers trying to reach a very narrow market. For example, local newspapers are not the best media vehicles for reaching purchasers of specialty steel products or even tropical fish. These target consumers make up very small, specialized markets. Newspaper advertising also encounters a lot of distractions from competing ads and news stories; thus, one company's ad may not be particularly visible.

The main sources of newspaper ad revenue are local retailers, classified ads, and cooperative advertising. In **cooperative advertising**, the manufacturer and the retailer split the costs of advertising the manufacturer's brand. One reason manufacturers use cooperative advertising is the impracticality of listing all their dealers in national advertising. Also, co-op advertising encourages retailers to devote more effort to the manufacturer's lines.

Magazines

Compared to the cost of other media, the cost per contact in magazine advertising is usually high. The cost per potential customer may be much lower, however, because magazines are often targeted to specialized audiences and thus reach more potential customers. The types of products most frequently advertised in magazines include automobiles, apparel, computers, and cigarettes.

One of the main advantages of magazine advertising is its market selectivity. Magazines are published for virtually every market segment. For instance, *PC Week* is a leading computer magazine; *Working Mother* targets one of the fastest growing consumer segments; *Sports Illustrated* is a successful all-around sporting publication; *Marketing News* is a trade magazine for the marketing professional; *The Source* is a niche publication geared to young urbanites with a passion for hip-hop music.

Radio

Radio has several strengths as an advertising medium: selectivity and audience segmentation, a large out-of-home audience, low unit and production costs, timeliness, and geographic flexibility. Local advertisers are the most frequent users of radio advertising, contributing over three-quarters of all radio ad revenues. Like newspapers, radio also lends itself well to cooperative advertising.

Long merely an afterthought to many advertisers, radio advertising is enjoying a resurgence in popularity. As Americans become more mobile and pressed for time, other media such as network television and newspapers struggle to retain viewers and readers. Radio listening, however, has grown in step with population increases mainly because its immediate, portable nature meshes so well with a fast-paced lifestyle. The ability to target specific demographic groups is also a major selling point for radio stations, attracting advertisers who are pursuing narrowly defined audiences that are more likely to respond to certain kinds of ads and products. Moreover, radio listeners tend to listen habitually and at predictable times, with the most popular being "drive time," when commuters form a vast captive audience.[34]

Television

Because television is an audiovisual medium, it provides advertisers with many creative opportunities. Television broadcasters include network television, independent stations, cable television, and a relative newcomer, direct broadcast satellite television. ABC, CBS, NBC, and the Fox Network dominate network television, which reaches a wide and diverse market. Conversely, cable television and direct broadcast satellite systems, such as DirecTV and PrimeStar, offer consumers a multitude of channels devoted exclusively to particular audiences—for example, women, children, African Americans, nature lovers, senior citizens, Christians, Hispanics, sports fans, fitness enthusiasts. Because of its targeted channels, cable television is often characterized as "narrowcasting" by media buyers. More businesses are including cable buys in their marketing mix. For instance, Novell, a marketer of Internet software, found that consumers who were exposed to its ads several times on cable were more familiar with its story and had an increasingly favorable view of the company. Even better, viewers of its spots on cable were found to be more likely to buy or recommend a Novell product.[35]

Advertising time on television can be very expensive, especially for network stations and popular cable stations. First-run prime-time shows and special events command the highest rates. A thirty-second spot goes for about $445,000 on *Survivor*, for example, and for about $426,000 on *ER*. The same-length spot costs about $321,000 on the popular comedy *Will & Grace* and about $62,000 on *Buffy the Vampire Slayer*.[36] Spots during *Monday Night Football* cost about $330,000. Super Bowl spots are particularly expensive. One thirty-second spot during the 2001 Super Bowl telecast cost advertisers an average of $2.05 million.[37]

A relatively new form of television advertising is the **infomercial**, a thirty-minute or longer advertisement. Infomercials are an attractive advertising vehicle for many marketers because of the cheap air time and the relatively small production cost. Advertisers say the infomercial is an ideal way to present complicated information to potential customers, which other advertising vehicles typically don't allow time to do. Infomercials are rapidly gaining favor with some of the more mainstream marketers. In the last few years, several companies including AOL, Philips Electronics, Apple, Nissan, Mercedes, Nikon, and Microsoft have bought infomercial airtime. And a growing number of businesses are adding to the legitimacy of the medium by producing infomercials with a more polished look. For example, Callaway Golf used an infomercial to pitch its expensive new Rule 35 ball to upscale golfers. A higher production budget was established to allow for a lot of graphic detail with a rich feel to enhance the perceived quality of the product and the medium. Hollywood is even cashing in on infomercials. Universal Pictures recently released a thirty-minute infomercial for its Jurassic Park franchise hosted by E! Entertainment's Steve Kmetko. The actual offer—a boxed DVD/video set of the movie's first two installments—airs periodically during the glossy, behind-the-scenes footage, which includes interviews with the stars of the latest flick, *Jurassic Park III*. With the polished look of a behind-the-scenes special, it feels more like thirty minutes of programming than an infomercial.[38]

Outdoor Media

Outdoor or out-of-home advertising is a flexible, low-cost medium that may take a variety of forms. Examples include billboards, skywriting, giant inflatables, mini-billboards in malls and on bus stop shelters, signs in sports arenas, lighted moving signs in bus terminals and airports, and ads painted on the sides of cars, trucks, buses, or even water towers. Marketers have even begun utilizing the plywood scaffolding that often rings downtown construction sites. Manhattan's Times Square, with an estimated 1.5 million daily pedestrians and recent construction projects, for example, has been a popular area for outdoor advertising using scaffolding.[39]

Outdoor advertising reaches a broad and diverse market and is, therefore, ideal for promoting convenience products and services as well as directing consumers to local businesses. One of outdoor's main advantages over other media is that its exposure frequency is very high, yet the amount of clutter from competing ads is very low. Outdoor advertising also has the ability to be customized to local

Fox Network
ABC
What kind of advertising is done on the Fox Network's Web site? Compare this with the site for ABC. What differences do you notice? Why do you think a television network would choose not to sell ad space on its Web site?

http://www.fox.com
http://www.abc.com

On Line

infomercial
A thirty-minute or longer advertisement that looks more like a TV talk show than a sales pitch.

Outdoor advertising is becoming increasingly innovative and three-dimensional. Delta's living billboard is an example of how far you can go with outdoor media.

marketing needs. For these reasons, local business establishments, such as local services and amusements, retailers, public transportation, and hotels and restaurants, are the leading outdoor advertisers.[40]

After the loss of tobacco advertising (tobacco companies agreed to stop advertising in outdoor media as part of a 1998 settlement with states that had sued to recover money spent on treatment of smokers), outdoor advertising found a new market in emerging Internet companies. Rates went as high as $100,000 a month for certain positions in California during the height of the dot-com frenzy. But now that the dot-com spending boom is over and many of the Internet companies are defunct, the outdoor industry is looking to reposition itself for the future. Outdoor advertising categories on the rise include telecommunications with a heavy emphasis on wireless services, financial services, and packaged goods. Plus, dot-com advertising has not completely ended. Core technology companies like Oracle continue to rely heavily on outdoor advertising in Silicon Valley.[41]

Outdoor advertising continues to become more innovative. For instance, Absolut Vodka teamed up with Ikea furniture to produce a 19-by-49-foot billboard in Manhattan's SoHo district. The billboard shows a life-size studio apartment in the shape of an Absolut bottle that is filled with furniture from Ikea. The billboard is basically a fully furnished apartment with everything glued to the board and then turned on its side.[42]

The Internet

The World Wide Web and the Internet have undoubtedly shaken up the advertising world. With ad revenues approaching $6 billion in 2001, the Internet has established itself as a solid advertising medium.[43] On-line advertising has made significant gains since the early 1990s, and is making up an ever-larger portion of companies' total advertising budgets. By 2005, Internet advertising is expected to amount to exceed $25 billion and represent close to 10 percent of total media spending. Popular Internet sites and search engines, such as Netscape and Yahoo!, as well as on-line service providers like America Online, generally sell advertising space, called "banners," to marketers to promote their goods and services. Internet surfers click on these banners to be linked to more information about the advertised product or service.

Advertising executives and academicians have hotly debated the effectiveness of banner ads. Early research indicated that banner ads were generating response rates as high as 30 percent.[44] But other industry observers feel that banner ads have been largely ineffective, with low click-through rates and recall. Consumers today are more Web savvy and often ignore banner advertising, to the point where the click-through rate is less than 1 percent. Marketers are recognizing, however, that banner ads can build brand awareness, so banners are being produced that don't actually link to anything. Initial studies indicate that brand awareness increases by 5 percent and that the association between the brand and its tagline increases by an average of 16 percent with banner advertising.[45] With close to 60 percent of the U.S. population now on-line, marketers are looking for new approaches to on-line advertising. Some marketers are offering a variety of content-sponsorship deals, video ads that pop up in another window, and on-line and off-line cross-promotions. They are also developing new ad formats with big, hard-to-miss shapes. The new formats include the *skyscraper,* a tall, skinny oblong at the side of a Web page, and the *rectangle,* a box much larger than a banner. These new formats are large enough for marketers to include their entire message so that users don't have to click through to another site.[46]

Marketing on the Internet and World Wide Web is discussed in more detail in Chapter 19.

Alternative Media

To cut through the clutter of traditional advertising media, advertisers are creating new media vehicles to advertise their products, some ordinary and others quite innovative. Alternative media vehicles can include shopping carts in grocery stores, computer screen savers, CD-ROMs, interactive kiosks in department stores, and advertisements run before movies at the cinema and on rented videocassettes. In fact, just about anything can become a vehicle for displaying advertising. For instance, supermarkets are now testing "Flooranimation," ads on supermarket floors that will be animated with graphics and sounds. Unanimated floor ads are already in use, and research shows that static floor ads increase sales 15 percent to 30 percent. Marketers are hoping that with animation and sound, sales will increase even more.[47] Video Venue recently unveiled plans to install ten-inch, wireless, high-resolution screens at gas pumps to run six-minute cycles of full-motion video and sound ads. Marketers are hoping to capitalize on the four to six minutes it takes for consumers to pump gas and will advertise products available right there in the store.[48] Marketers are also looking for more innovative ways to reach captive and often bored commuters. For instance, subway systems are now showing ads via lighted boxes installed along tunnel walls. As a train passes through the tunnel, the passengers view the illuminated boxes, which create the same kind of illusion as a child's flip book, in which the images appear to move as the pages are flipped rapidly.[49]

As marketers keep looking for innovative ways to get noticed, some are using shocking images in their advertising in hopes of capturing attention. Read more about this issue in the "Ethics in Marketing" box.

Media Selection Considerations

An important element in any advertising campaign is the **media mix**, the combination of media to be used. Media mix decisions are typically based on several factors: cost per contact, reach, frequency, target audience considerations, flexibility of the medium, noise level, and the life span of the medium.

Cost per contact is the cost of reaching one member of the target market. Naturally, as the size of the audience increases, so does the total cost. Cost per contact enables an advertiser to compare media vehicles, such as television versus radio or magazine versus newspaper, or more specifically *Newsweek* versus *Time*. An advertiser debating whether to spend local advertising dollars for TV spots or radio spots could

media mix
The combination of media to be used for a promotional campaign.

cost per contact
The cost of reaching one member of the target market.

Lunch hour elevator passengers follow the stock market through a wireless Internet device installed by the elevator door. Otis Elevator, Captivate, and eBillboards are entering this alternative media space and bringing weather, news, sports, and stock market data to elevator riders in many of the largest cities in the United States.

AP/WIDE WORLD PHOTOS

Sex Sells—But at What Price?

Housewives in Scotland are plastering their kitchens with posters of the new Scottish beefcake hocking the virtues of Scottish beef. Print ads selling shoes show leather-clad dominatrix models. Lap dances seem to go hand in hand with liquor ads. Even yogurt is getting naughty with a television spot showing a woman—dressed in only a French maid's costume and a bad accent—spoon feeding the wholesome goodness to her husband. Yes, in the land of *Sex in the City* and political sex scandals, it seems anything goes. But are marketers pushing the envelope when it comes to using sex in advertising?

Since the 1950s, sex has been used to sell products like beer, cars, and jeans. But these days, sex is being used to peddle everything from tea to shampoo. Some marketers contend that ads with shock value may be the only way to reach a public desensitized by the likes of Howard Stern, *The Man Show,* and Jerry Springer. But many companies are crossing the line in their advertising and targeting a much younger audience. For example, Abercrombie & Fitch, a popular clothing line for teens, offered a "Naughty & Nice" catalog that caused four states to threaten legal action. The catalog featured "various models in states of undress, sex tips from porn star Jenna Jameson, and a cartoon of Santa and Mrs. Claus enjoying a little S&M." Similarly, Nike took its "Just Do It" slogan to a whole new level with sports bra ads showing nothing but breasts—some covered with hands, some bare.

But some ad campaigns are causing much more of a stir than companies bargained for. The French Connection has had several print and television spots banned by the United Kingdom's Advertising Standards Authority. Five employees lost their jobs at InfoUSA when the CEO found out they had approved an ad featuring "a blond woman wearing black leather, a mask, and a dog collar." And, after receiving a signed complaint from approximately forty-five high school librarians, *Seventeen* magazine pulled a Candie's fragrance ad featuring a young woman sitting on a sink with her legs wrapped suggestively around a male model.

Other countries are also cracking down on sexually explicit advertising. In France, advertising authorities have set up standards on how the body may be portrayed to sell products. Advertising watchdogs in Germany and Italy have denounced ads deemed humiliating to women, and the European Union is discussing whether to place more severe restrictions on television commercials aimed at children.[50]

Overall, ad professionals claim to have little respect for sexual appeals that are used just to get attention. But sexual imagery will be used to sell products as long as people keep buying. How far is too far in terms of sexually explicit advertising? Do marketers have a moral responsibility to the public when it comes to advertising? How might consumer backlash over an ad campaign adversely affect a company's corporate reputation?

---

reach
The number of target consumers exposed to a commercial at least once during a specific period, usually four weeks.

frequency
The number of times an individual is exposed to a given message during a specific period.

consider the cost per contact of each. The advertiser might then pick the vehicle with the lowest cost per contact to maximize advertising punch for the money spent.

Reach is the number of different target consumers who are exposed to a commercial at least once during a specific period, usually four weeks. Media plans for product introductions and attempts at increasing brand awareness usually emphasize reach. For example, an advertiser might try to reach 70 percent of the target audience during the first three months of the campaign. Reach is related to a medium's ratings, generally referred to in the industry as *gross ratings points*, or GRP. A television program with a higher GRP means that more people are tuning in to the show and the reach is higher. Accordingly, as GRP increases for a particular medium, so does cost per contact.

Because the typical ad is short-lived and because often only a small portion of an ad may be perceived at one time, advertisers repeat their ads so that consumers will remember the message. **Frequency** is the number of times an individual is exposed to a message during a specific period. Advertisers use average frequency to measure the intensity of a specific medium's coverage. For example, Coca-Cola might want an average exposure frequency of five for its Powerade television ads. That means that each of the television viewers who saw the ad saw it an average of five times. Exhibit 15.6 provides a glimpse at exposure and frequency rates for some of today's top brands.

Media selection is also a matter of matching the advertising medium with the product's target market. If marketers are trying to reach teenage females, they

Exhibit 15.6

Advertised Brand	Household Exposures (in millions)**	Number of Times Ad Aired
Burger King	285.8	57
JCPenney	181.6	31
Pontiac Grand Am	173.3	25
Boston Market	166.1	27
Ford autos and trucks	162.5	21
Honda Accord	152.4	23
Nissan Altima	150.7	14
AT&T	143.4	22
Wendy's	137.0	26
Miller Lite	131.8	12

*Advertisers getting the most exposure during prime-time TV on ABC, CBS, NBC, Fox, UPN, and WB networks
**One household might be exposed to several ads each day.
SOURCES: "Nielsen's Top TV Advertisers," *USA Today*, June 15, 1998, 8B; Nielsen Media Research, Monitor Plus Service.

might select *Seventeen* magazine. If they are trying to reach consumers over fifty years old, they may choose *Modern Maturity* magazine. A medium's ability to reach a precisely defined market is its **audience selectivity**. Some media vehicles, like general newspapers and network television, appeal to a wide cross section of the population. Others—such as *Brides, Popular Mechanics, Architectural Digest*, MTV, ESPN, and Christian radio stations—appeal to very specific groups. Viewer profiles for a sampling of popular cable networks are presented in Exhibit 15.7.

The *flexibility* of a medium can be extremely important to an advertiser. In the past, because of printing timetables, pasteup requirements, and so on, some magazines required final ad copy several months before publication. Therefore, magazine advertising traditionally could not adapt as rapidly to changing market conditions. While this is fast changing due to computer technology that creates electronic ad images and layouts, the lead time for magazine advertising is still considerably longer. Radio and Internet advertising, on the other hand, provide maximum flexibility. Usually, the advertiser can change a radio ad on the day it is aired, if necessary. Similarly, advertisements on the Internet can be changed in minutes with the click of a few buttons.

Noise level is the level of distraction to the target audience in a medium. For example, to understand a televised promotional message, viewers must watch and listen carefully. But they often watch television with others, who may well provide distractions. Noise can also be created by competing ads, as when a street is lined

audience selectivity
The ability of an advertising medium to reach a precisely defined market.

Exhibit 15.7

BET	Targeted to African Americans aged 18 to 49.
CNBC	*Business Day* viewers have a median household net worth of over $1 million; 98% are college educated; 80% use their computer daily; 69% connect to the Internet daily.
Discovery Channel	Appeals to adults aged 25 to 54 with household incomes over $75,000.
ESPN Classic	Delivers a higher concentration of men aged 18 to 49 than the ten most widely distributed cable networks.
House & Garden Television (HGTV)	Appeals strongly to men and women who own their own homes with incomes of $75,000 or more; most likely to be in professional or managerial position.
Lifetime Network	Top cable network aimed at working women.
MTV	Number one rated cable network for 12- to 24-year-olds; Watched by over 305 million households in 87 territories around the globe.

SOURCE: "2000 Cable Programming Guide," *Advertising Age*, June 5, 2000.

with billboards or when a television program is cluttered with competing ads. About two-thirds of a newspaper's pages are now filled with advertising. A recent Sunday issue of the *Los Angeles Times* contained over one thousand ads, not counting the small classifieds. Even more space is dedicated to ads in magazines. For example, 85 percent of the space in the February/March issue of *Brides* magazine is typically devoted to advertisements. In contrast, direct mail is a private medium with a low noise level. Typically, no other advertising media or news stories compete for direct-mail readers' attention.

Media have either a short or long life span. *Life span* means that messages can either quickly fade or persist as tangible copy to be carefully studied. For example, a radio commercial may last less than a minute. Listeners can't replay the commercial unless they have recorded the program. One way advertisers overcome this problem is by repeating radio ads often. In contrast, a magazine has a relatively long life span. A person may read several articles, put the magazine down, and pick it up a week later to continue reading. In addition, magazines often have a high pass-along rate. That is, one person will read the publication and then give it to someone else to read.

Media planners have traditionally relied upon the above factors for selecting an effective media mix, with reach, frequency, and cost often the overriding criteria. Some recent studies, however, question the reliance media planners have traditionally placed on reach and frequency. For instance, one recent study suggests that well-established brands with familiar messages may need fewer exposures to be effective, while newer brands or brands with unfamiliar messages may need more exposures to become familiar.[51]

Additionally, media planners have hundreds more media options today than they had forty years ago when network television reigned. For instance, there are over 1,600 television stations across the country. In the Los Angeles market alone, there are now seventy-nine radio stations, seven offering an "adult contemporary" format. The number of unique magazine titles has more than doubled over the last decade, with publications now targeting every target market possible.

Satellite television can now bring hundreds of channels into viewers' homes. The Internet provides media planners with even more targeted choices in which to send their messages. And alternative media choices are popping up in some very unlikely places. *Media fragmentation* is forcing media planners to pay as much attention to where they place their advertising, as to how often the advertisement is repeated. New research suggests evaluating reach along with frequency in assessing the effectiveness of advertising. That is, it may be more important to reach as many consumers in as many media vehicles as possible than to achieve a certain number of exposures in any one particular medium.[52] In evaluating reach versus frequency, therefore, the media planner ultimately must select an approach that is most likely to result in the ad being understood and remembered when a purchase decision is being made.

Advertising researchers are also discussing the qualitative factors that should be present during media selection. These qualitative factors include such things as attention to the commercial and the program, involvement, program liking, lack of distractions, and other audience behaviors that affect the likelihood that a commercial message is being seen and, hopefully, absorbed. While advertisers can advertise their product in as many media as possible and repeat the ad as many times as they like, the ad still may not be effective if the audience is not paying attention.[53] Recent research into audience attentiveness for television, for example, shows that the longer viewers stay tuned to a particular program, the more memorable they find the commercials. The study suggests that "holding power," is more important than ratings (the number of people tuning in to any part of the program) when selecting media vehicles, challenging the long-held assumption that the higher the rating of a program, the higher the cost to advertise during the program. For instance, the television program *ER*, which is one of the top-rated shows among twenty-five- to fifty-four-year-olds and costs over $400,000 for a thirty-second spot, measures relatively lower for holding power than the low-rated program *Candid Camera*, which ranks high in holding power, but costs only $55,000 for a thirty-second spot.[54]

Media Scheduling

After choosing the media for the advertising campaign, advertisers must schedule the ads. A **media schedule** designates the medium or media to be used (such as magazines, television, or radio), the specific vehicles (such as *People* magazine, *Friends* TV show, or Howard Stern's national radio program), and the insertion dates of the advertising.

There are three basic types of media schedules:

- Products in the latter stages of the product life cycle, which are advertised on a reminder basis, use a **continuous media schedule**. A continuous schedule allows the advertising to run steadily throughout the advertising period. Examples include Ivory soap, Coca-Cola, and Marlboro cigarettes.

- With a **flighted media schedule**, the advertiser may schedule the ads heavily every other month or every two weeks to achieve a greater impact with an increased frequency and reach at those times. Movie studios might schedule television advertising on Wednesday and Thursday nights, when moviegoers are deciding which films to see that weekend. A variation is the **pulsing media schedule**, which combines continuous scheduling with flighting. Continuous advertising is simply heavier during the

media schedule
Designation of the media, the specific publications or programs, and the insertion dates of advertising.

continuous media schedule
A media scheduling strategy in which advertising is run steadily throughout the advertising period; used for products in the latter stages of the product life cycle.

flighted media schedule
A media scheduling strategy in which ads are run heavily every other month or every two weeks, to achieve a greater impact with an increased frequency and reach at those times.

pulsing media schedule
A media scheduling strategy that uses continuous scheduling throughout the year coupled with a flighted schedule during the best sales periods.

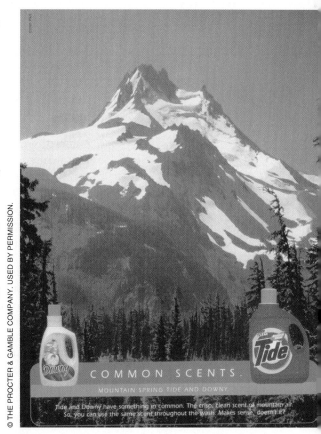

Laundry detergent is a product in the mature stage of the product life cycle. As such, companies like Procter & Gamble use a continuous media schedule to remind consumers to chose Tide over the competition. Compare this ad for Tide with the ad for Purex on page 501. Which do you find more compelling? Why?

best sale periods. A retail department store may advertise on a year-round basis but place more advertising during certain sale periods such as Thanksgiving, Christmas, and back-to-school.

- Certain times of the year call for a **seasonal media schedule**. Products like Contac cold tablets and Coppertone suntan lotion, which are used more during certain times of the year, tend to follow a seasonal strategy. Advertising for champagne is concentrated during the weeks of Christmas and New Year's, whereas health clubs concentrate their advertising in January to take advantage of New Year's resolutions.

New research comparing continuous media schedules versus flighted ones finds that continuous schedules for television advertisements are more effective than flighting in driving sales. The research suggests that it may be more important to get exposure as close as possible to the time when someone is going to make a purchase. For example, if a consumer shops on a weekly basis, the best time to reach that person is right before he or she shops. Therefore, the advertiser should maintain a continuous schedule over as long a period of time as possible.[55] Often called *recency planning*, this new theory of scheduling is now commonly used for scheduling television advertising for frequently purchased products, such as Coca-Cola or Tide detergent. Recency planning's main premise is that advertising works by influencing the brand choice of people who are ready to buy.[56]

Public Relations

5
Discuss the role of public relations in the promotional mix

Public relations is the element in the promotional mix that evaluates public attitudes, identifies issues that may elicit public concern, and executes programs to gain public understanding and acceptance. Like advertising and sales promotion, public relations is a vital link in a progressive company's marketing communication mix. Marketing managers plan solid public relations campaigns that fit into overall marketing plans and focus on targeted audiences. These campaigns strive to maintain a positive image of the corporation in the eyes of the public. Before launching public relations programs, managers evaluate public attitudes and company actions. Then they create programs to capitalize on the factors that enhance the firm's image and minimize the factors that could generate a negative image.

Many people associate public relations with publicity. *Publicity* is the effort to capture media attention—for example, through articles or editorials in publications or through human-interest stories on radio or television programs. Corporations usually initiate publicity through a press release that furthers their public relations plans. A company about to introduce a new product or open a new store may send press releases to the media in the hope that the story will be published or broadcast. Savvy publicity can often create overnight sensations. Artisan Entertainment hoped its independent film, *The Blair Witch Project,* would be its summer 1999 hit, but couldn't spend big-studio advertising dollars to advertise it. So Artisan turned to a public relations strategy to build excitement and curiosity about the film. The cornerstone of its strategy proved to be the film's Web site, which showed outtakes from unused footage, faked official documents, and interviews that suggested a police cover-up to build the legend of the Blair Witch. At the height of the campaign, the site was getting three million hits a day. Artisan also used "street" teams to distribute missing person fliers and stick figures. It also held film screenings on forty college campuses across the country. When the film finally opened after weeks of built-up suspense, it quickly became a hit, breaking attendance records and topping opening weekend numbers for such heavyweights as *Star Wars: The Phantom Menace.*[57]

Corporate donations and sponsorships can also create favorable publicity. When two high school seniors wanted to go to college in California, but couldn't afford the tuition, they set out to find corporate sponsors to pay for their education. The young entrepreneurs set up a Web site offering their services as "spokesguys" and posted photos of themselves wearing T-shirts and carrying surfboards inscribed with the message YOUR LOGO HERE. They got the attention of First USA, the country's largest Visa issuer, which decided to lend a hand. In exchange for the boys promoting fiscal responsibility to other college kids, First USA paid for their tuition and room and board. As a public relations investment, it's already paid off with the kind of publicity that money can't buy, including a story in the *New York Times*.[58]

Public relations departments may perform any or all of the following functions:

- *Press relations:* placing positive, newsworthy information in the news media to attract attention to a product, a service, or a person associated with the firm or institution

- *Product publicity:* publicizing specific products or services

- *Corporate communication:* creating internal and external messages to promote a positive image of the firm or institution

- *Public affairs:* building and maintaining national or local community relations

- *Lobbying:* influencing legislators and government officials to promote or defeat legislation and regulation

- *Employee and investor relations:* maintaining positive relationships with employees, shareholders, and others in the financial community

- *Crisis management:* responding to unfavorable publicity or a negative event

Major Public Relations Tools

Public relations professionals commonly use several tools, including new-product publicity, product placement, consumer education, event sponsorship, and issue sponsorship. A relatively new tool public relations professionals are using in increasing numbers is a Web site on the Internet. Although many of these tools require an active role on the part of the public relations professional, such as writing press releases and engaging in proactive media relations, many of these techniques create their own publicity.

New-Product Publicity

Publicity is instrumental in introducing new products and services. Publicity can help advertisers explain what's different about their new product by prompting free news stories or positive word of mouth about it. During the introductory period, an especially innovative new product often needs more exposure than conventional, paid advertising affords. Public relations professionals write press releases or develop videos in an effort to generate news about their new product. They also jockey for exposure of their product or service at major events, on popular television and news shows, or in the hands of influential people. When the Krispy Kreme doughnut chain opened an outlet in Phoenix, company officials arranged for the store's first customer to be Arizona's Maricopa County Sheriff Joe Arpaio, who is billed as "the toughest sheriff in America" and is known for making his prisoners wear pink underwear. Before television cameras, the famous sheriff ate his doughnut and declared, "These doughnuts are so good they should be illegal."[59]

Product Placement

Marketers can also garner publicity by making sure their products appear at special events or in movies or television shows. When NBC was looking for backing for the reality show *Lost*, a competitive race from the Gobi desert to the

BMW

Find out more about BMW films starring Clive Owen. Do these films, directed by award-winning directors, do a good job promoting BMW cars?

http://www.bmwfilms.com

On Line

Statue of Liberty, it found four corporations that were willing to fund six episodes. In exchange, Coca-Cola, Johnson & Johnson, Lowe's, and Marriott International secured much of the ad time and attained placement for their products in the series. For example, participants drank Dasani bottled water (a Coke product) and used survival items from crates imprinted with Lowe's logo.[60] And best-selling author Fay Weldon caused quite a stir in literary circles with her novel *The Bulgari Connection*. The Italian jewelry company reportedly paid an undisclosed amount of money to be prominently featured in the novel. Public relations experts predict that books are the next wave of product placement.[61] Product placement is also catching on in other countries. Read the "Global Perspectives" box to find out how marketers are placing their products in Chinese soap operas.

Companies reap invaluable product exposure through product placement, usually at a fraction of the cost of paid-for advertising. Often the fee for exposure is in merchandise. Fashion designer Georgio Armani, for example, uses celebrities to burnish his brand in the eyes of the public. Armani clothed Samuel L. Jackson for his role in the movie *Shaft*. The designer then marketed a line of *Shaft*-inspired clothes and featured Jackson in fashion shows in Milan, Italy. Armani also provides select Hollywood stars and celebrities like Ricky Martin and Lauryn Hill with free gowns and tuxedos for personal appearances.[62]

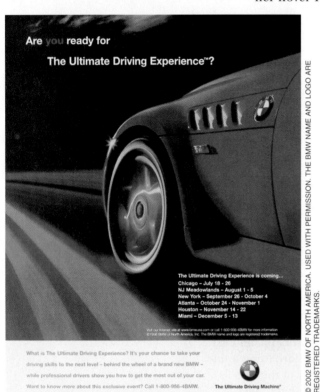

Are you ready for **The Ultimate Driving Experience™**?

The Ultimate Driving Experience is coming...
Chicago – July 18 - 26
NJ Meadowlands – August 1 - 5
New York – September 26 - October 4
Atlanta – October 24 - November 1
Houston – November 14 - 22
Miami – December 5 - 13

Visit our Internet site at www.bmwusa.com or call 1-800-956-4BMW for more information
©1998 BMW of North America, Inc. The BMW name and logo are registered trademarks.

What is The Ultimate Driving Experience? It's your chance to take your driving skills to the next level – behind the wheel of a brand new BMW – while professional drivers show you how to get the most out of your car. Want to know more about this exclusive event? Call 1-800-956-4BMW.

The Ultimate Driving Machine®

© 2002 BMW OF NORTH AMERICA. USED WITH PERMISSION. THE BMW NAME AND LOGO ARE REGISTERED TRADEMARKS.

Consumer education can not only influence the buying decision but can result in better, more loyal customers. BMW's instructional driving tour is a way to show off its car's capabilities to prospective purchasers and current owners without mounting expensive advertising campaigns.

Consumer Education

Some major firms believe that educated consumers are better, more loyal customers. Financial planning firms often sponsor free educational seminars on money management, retirement planning, and investing in the hope that the seminar participants will choose the sponsoring organization for their future financial needs. Likewise, computer hardware and software firms, realizing that many consumers feel intimidated by new technology and recognizing the strong relationship between learning and purchasing patterns, sponsor computer seminars and free in-store demonstrations. BMW of North America, for example, recently sponsored an instructional driving school for teenagers in thirteen major cities across the United States. Teens received a special four-hour training session that included driving techniques, accident avoidance skills, and traction aid tricks from a professional driver.[63]

Event Sponsorship

Public relations managers can sponsor events or community activities that are sufficiently newsworthy to achieve press coverage; at the same time, these events also reinforce brand identification. Sporting, music, and arts events remain the most popular choices of event sponsors, although many are now turning to more specialized events such as tie-ins with schools, charities, and other community service organizations. For example, NBC, Emap Petersen, Mountain Dew, Doritos, Toyota, Hasbro Interactive, the U.S. Marines, Ultimate Speed Stick, and Unionbay sponsored the Gravity Games extreme sporting event that competes with ESPN's highly successful X Games. Some 200,000 spectators, a large majority of them young males between the ages of twelve and twenty-four, descended on Providence, Rhode Island, for the eight-day festival. Sponsors gave away free samples, hosted extreme athlete autograph sessions and sports demonstrations, and organized alternative music concerts.[64]

Product Placement in Chinese Soap Opera

To the delight of marketers, soap is suddenly showing up on the set of China's popular soap opera *Love Talks*, one of the first television series in China engineered by advertisers. Set in a fictitious Shanghai ad agency, the soap opera features the budding romance between a veteran male account director and a novice account executive. The unique aspect of this show is the obvious placement of brand-name products visible throughout the show. For example, one scene shows the soap's star Qu Ying, rushing to work, leaving an important folder at home. The camera zooms in on the forgotten folder, which just happens to be sitting next to a big tube of Pond's Vaseline Intensive Care lotion. The scene then cuts to Ms. Qu in a cab where she is applying Maybelline lipstick, when she notices the missing folder—oh no! Quickly, she borrows a Motorola mobile phone from a handsome stranger in another car.

Marketers, such as Unilever, Motorola, Maybelline, Duracell, and General Electric, have already signed up as sponsors of *Love Talks*. Other brands, such as Braun and Nike, have also cashed in on sponsorships, promotion, and product placement opportunities with the Chinese soap opera. Show sponsorships cost $240,000 to $360,000. Television in China is still under strict government control, but shows such as *Love Talks* are demonstrating new opportunities for advertisers.

While paying to have a product appear in movies or television shows is old hat in the United States and other countries, the concept is revolutionary in China. Most commercials on Chinese state-run television are run in back-to-back, ten-minute-long "bricks," or segments. Due to the large number of commercials that run during each brick, it's difficult for any one advertiser to attract viewers' attention with just a thirty-second ad. Product placement, therefore, provides an innovative way for a product to get noticed. Advertisers are also attracted to the drama since its viewers represent a burgeoning middle class in the world's most populous country.

Love Talks, produced by United Media, now airs on 128 of China's 800 television stations. The show has been so popular with viewers that the production company has begun developing two more series—one about an architect's family life, called *Home*, and another about a modeling agency, called *Model*. The original *Love Talks* series has also been syndicated to broadcasters in Taiwan, Hong Kong, Thailand, Malaysia, and Singapore.[65]

Can you recall any name-brand products that you saw in a television series or a motion picture? How did this affect your perception of the brand?

Marketers can also create their own events tied around their product. The state of Hawaii recently organized its own mall touring event, titled "Experience Aloha: Hawaii on Tour," to promote the islands as a tourist destination. The tour traveled to twenty-two U.S. cities for weekend mall visits that included hula dancers, chefs cooking Hawaiian cuisine, lei-making demonstrations, and a virtual reality film simulating a helicopter ride over Hawaii's islands.[66]

Issue Sponsorship

Corporations can build public awareness and loyalty by supporting their customers' favorite issues. Education, health care, and social programs get the largest share of corporate funding. Firms often donate a percentage of sales or profits to a worthy cause that their target market is likely to favor. For example, the Gap hoped to break through the holiday advertising clutter by focusing on a simple theme of "Give your gift" reinforced by corporate donations. The company made donations to charities on behalf of the celebrities appearing in the commercials and print ads, including the singers Sheryl Crow and Alanis Morissette and the cast of *The Producers*.[67]

"Green marketing" has also become an important way for companies to build awareness and loyalty by promoting a popular issue. By positioning their brands as ecologically sound, marketers can convey concern for the environment and society as a whole. Burger King and McDonald's no longer use styrofoam cartons to package their burgers in an effort to decrease waste in landfills. In a similar effort, Toyota is working with the Japanese government to implement a program where people purchase "transportation" without owning a car. Consumers can buy access to

Toyota's electronic fleet of automobiles to travel for short distances. Thus, Toyota is both establishing itself as the leader in electronic-combustion automobiles and reducing a negative environmental impact.[68]

Internet Web Sites

 Public relations professionals are increasingly using their Internet Web sites as a vehicle to post news releases on products, product enhancements, strategic relationships, and financial earnings. Corporate press releases, technical papers and articles, and product news help inform the press, customers, prospects, industry analysts, stockholders, and others of the firm's products and services and their applications. The Web site can also be an open forum for new-product ideas, product improvements, and customer feedback. On-line reviews from opinion leaders and other consumers also help marketers sway shopping decisions in their favor. When Sony redesigned Playstation.com, it incorporated message boards where its game-playing community could post notes. Players discuss techie topics like "Desperately Seeking Playstation2," review and exchange tips on games, and even vote on lifestyle issues such as music and personal taste.[69]

Several marketers also use the Web to try new products and gather more consumer data. Through research, Volkswagen knew that 60 percent of its customers use the Internet. So, when the company wanted to attract a different, "funkier" audience for its new Beetle and test out new car colors, it employed a special on-line marketing promotion. Volkswagen made a limited-edition model of its Beetle available exclusively on-line, in two limited-edition colors: Vapor Blue and Reflex Yellow. The company got the word out about the promotion through traditional advertising methods. After experiencing print, TV, or radio advertisements, consumers signed up to learn more via e-mail. On being admitted to a special section of the VW site, consumers learned more about the car, viewed photos, checked the availability, picked a dealer, and considered financing and a purchase date. The on-line promotion was a huge success, and Volkswagen sold out of all four thousand limited-edition Beetles.[70]

Managing Unfavorable Publicity

Although the majority of marketers try to avoid unpleasant situations, crises do happen. Intel faced this reality after consumers became aware of an obscure flaw in its Pentium chip. In our free-press environment, publicity is not easily controlled, especially in a crisis. **Crisis management** is the coordinated effort to handle the effects of unfavorable publicity, ensuring fast and accurate communication in times of emergency.

A good public relations staff is perhaps more important in bad times than in good. Companies must have a communication policy firmly in hand before a disaster occurs, because timing is uncontrollable. When a promotional game scandal rocked McDonald's, the company found out just how important crisis management is. An employee of the agency that had handled promotion for McDonald's for over twenty-five years was arrested for stealing winning game pieces from McDonald's popular *Monopoly* and *Who Wants to Be a Millionaire* games and giving them to family and friends to redeem. Although McDonald's employees had no knowledge of the fraud and none were implicated in the scandal, several class-action lawsuits were filed against the company. McDonald's immediately initiated a recovery plan to minimize damage among its customer base. This included mass distribution of a letter, a newspaper ad, a TV ad, and a five-day instant win game in which McDonald's awarded $10 million in prizes to customers to make up for the prizes that had been wrongfully awarded.[71]

crisis management
A coordinated effort to handle the effects of unfavorable publicity or of another unexpected, unfavorable event.

A good public relations and crisis management plan helped steer the Walt Disney Company out of a public relations mess after it was twice forced to postpone the maiden voyage of its new cruise ship, *Disney Magic,* due to production delays. Forty cruises originally scheduled to begin sailing in March 1998 were canceled, forcing approximately ninety-six thousand potential travelers to change their plans. Because travelers who booked early were Disney's most enthusiastic fans, the company faced a public relations nightmare. To begin fixing the damage, Disney overnighted apologies to disappointed travelers, offering 50 percent discounts to those who had been inconvenienced twice and 25 percent discounts to those bumped once. Disney also offered full refunds to those who didn't rebook and covered any lost commissions for travel agents.[72] Similarly, Internet auctioneer eBay used effective crisis management to climb its way out of a public relations mess after a computer crash halted its bidding operations for twenty-two hours. The outage left nearly 2.3 million auctions stranded in the middle of bids, infuriating customers and sellers. To soothe users' frustrations, eBay sent messages apologizing for the disruption and promising to aggressively hire more computer-network experts. The company also refunded users' listing fees totaling close to $5 million.[73]

CONNECT IT

As you finish reading this chapter, think back to the opening story about how Red Bull created and continues to dominate the energy drink category with marketing savvy, guerrilla tactics, and unusual distribution methods. To advertise its products, Red Bull's promotional team went through the same creative steps as other marketers—from determining what appeal to use to choosing the appropriate executional style. Great effort was also expended in deciding which medium would best reach the desired target market. Public relations and publicity also played a significant role in the success Red Bull has achieved.

USE IT

Becoming a Media Expert
Find the perfect magazine to advertise your product or service. Visit the Media-Finder Web site at **http://www.mediafinder.com**. The site has a searchable database of thousands of magazines. Or visit Channel Seven at **http://www.channelseven.com** to find news and views on hot new advertising mediums.

Ticked Off about That Ad?
File a complaint with the Better Business Bureau. See which companies get the most complaints about their advertising at the Better Business Bureau's Web site at **http://www.bbb.org**. Want to avoid legal problems with your advertising campaign? Find detailed information about advertising law and Federal Trade Commission regulations at **http://www.advertisinglaw.com**.

How to Write a Press Release
Visit **http://www.press-release-writing.com** to learn the right way to get publicity for your product or service. This Web site offers sample press releases, templates, formatting suggestions, and basic information that should always be included. The service also helps you distribute your press release to thousands of different media outlets.

(1) Discuss the effects of advertising on market share and consumers. Advertising helps marketers increase or maintain brand awareness and, subsequently, market share. Typically, more is spent to advertise new brands with a small market share than to advertise older brands. Brands with a large market share use advertising mainly to maintain their share of the market. Advertising affects consumers' daily lives as well as their purchases. Although advertising can seldom change strongly held consumer attitudes and values, it may transform a consumer's negative attitude toward a product into a positive one. Additionally, when consumers are highly loyal to a brand, they may buy more of that brand when advertising is increased. Last, advertising can also change the importance of a brand's attributes to consumers. By emphasizing different brand attributes, advertisers can change their appeal in response to consumers' changing needs or try to achieve an advantage over competing brands.

1.1 Discuss the reasons why new brands with a smaller market share spend proportionately more on advertising than brands with a larger market share.

1.2 **TEAM** Form a three-person team. Divide the responsibility for getting newspaper advertisements and menus for several local restaurants. While you are at the restaurants to obtain copies of their menus, observe the atmosphere and interview the manager to determine what he or she believes are the primary reasons people choose to dine there. Pool your information and develop a table comparing the restaurants in terms of convenience of location, value for the money, food variety and quality, atmosphere, and so on. Rank the restaurants in terms of their appeal to college students. Explain the basis of your rankings. What other market segment would be attracted to the restaurants and why? Do the newspaper advertisements emphasize the most effective appeal for a particular restaurant? Explain.

(2) Identify the major types of advertising. Advertising is any form of nonpersonal, paid communication in which the sponsor or company is identified. The two major types of advertising are institutional advertising and product advertising. Institutional advertising is not product oriented; rather, its purpose is to foster a positive company image among the general public, investment community, customers, and employees. Product advertising is designed mainly to promote goods and services, and it is classified into three main categories: pioneering, competitive, and comparative. A product's place in the product life cycle is a major determinant of the type of advertising used to promote it.

2.1 At what stage in a product's life cycle are pioneering, competitive, and comparative advertising most likely to occur? Give a current example of each type of advertising.

(3) Discuss the creative decisions in developing an advertising campaign. Before any creative work can begin on an advertising campaign, it is important to determine what goals or objectives the advertising should achieve. The objectives of a specific advertising campaign often depend on the overall corporate objectives and the product being advertised. Once objectives are defined, creative work can begin on the advertising campaign. Creative decisions include identifying the product's benefits, developing possible advertising appeals, evaluating and selecting the advertising appeals, executing the advertising message, and evaluating the effectiveness of the campaign.

3.1 What is an advertising appeal? Give some examples of advertising appeals you have observed recently in the media.

3.2 **WRITING** Design a full-page magazine advertisement for a new brand of soft drink. The name of the new drink, as well as package design, is at your discretion. On a separate sheet, specify the benefits stressed or appeals made in the advertisement.

4 **Describe media evaluation and selection techniques.** Media evaluation and selection make up a crucial step in the advertising campaign process. Major types of advertising media include newspapers, magazines, radio, television, outdoor advertising such as billboards and bus panels, and the Internet. Recent trends in advertising media include fax, video shopping carts, computer screen savers, and cinema and video advertising. Promotion managers choose the advertising campaign's media mix on the basis of the following variables: cost per contact, reach, frequency, characteristics of the target audience, flexibility of the medium, noise level, and the life span of the medium. After choosing the media mix, a media schedule designates when the advertisement will appear and the specific vehicles it will appear in.

4.1 What are the advantages of radio advertising? Why is radio expanding as an advertising medium?

4.2 **WRITING** You are the advertising manager of a sailing magazine, and one of your biggest potential advertisers has questioned your rates. Write the firm a letter explaining why you believe your audience selectivity is worth the extra expense for advertisers.

4.3 Identify an appropriate media mix for the following products:

a. Chewing tobacco

b. *People* magazine

c. Weed-Eaters

d. Foot odor killers

e. "Drink responsibly" campaigns by beer brewers

5 **Discuss the role of public relations in the promotional mix.** Public relations is a vital part of a firm's promotional mix. A company fosters good publicity to enhance its image and promote its products. Popular public relations tools include new-product publicity, product placement, consumer education, event sponsorship, issue sponsorship, and Internet Web sites. An equally important aspect of public relations is managing unfavorable publicity in a way that is least damaging to a firm's image.

5.1 How can advertising and publicity work together? Give an example.

5.2 **WRITING** As the new public relations director for a sportswear company, you have been asked to set public relations objectives for a new line of athletic shoes to be introduced to the teen market. Draft a memo outlining the objectives you propose for the shoe's introduction and your reasons for them.

5.3 **WRITING** Reports have just surfaced that your company, a fast-food chain, sold contaminated food products that have made several people seriously ill. As your company's public relations manager, devise a plan to handle the crisis.

5.4 **WRITING** **INFOTRAC COLLEGE EDITION** The Ford/Firestone tire recall of 2000 was one of the biggest public relations nightmares of recent memory. How well did the companies handle the situation? Use InfoTrac (**http://www.infotrac-college.com**) to run a keyword search on "Ford public relations." Read a selection of the articles, and then write an analysis of CEO Jacques Nasser's performance in the face of this crisis. What did he do well? What could he have done better? Evaluate his solution to the problem. Has Ford recovered from the recall? What about Firestone?

DEFINE IT

advertising appeal 500	advertising response func-	audience selectivity 511
advertising campaign 499	tion 495	comparative advertising
advertising objective 499	advocacy advertising 497	497

APPLY IT

Application for Entrepreneurs

Quality of service is increasingly the basis for deciding where to do business. Customers are five times more likely to return to a particular business if they perceive that it is providing higher quality service than the competition.

The Student Copy Center is a local business competing with Kinko's and a couple of other national franchise copy centers. Its owner, Mack Bayles, just attended a Small Business Administration workshop on customer service. He learned that when people say they expect good customer service, they most often mean they want prompt and accurate service from friendly, knowledgeable, and courteous employees. The presenter also emphasized that all market segments, even the most price conscious, expect good customer service. Mack wants to use this knowledge to develop an effective advertising campaign.

Mack has no idea what his customers think about either his copy business or that of his competitors. He decides, therefore, to ask his customers to complete a brief survey while in his store. From his survey he learns that Student Copy Center is considered friendlier and more courteous than the major competitors but is rated lower on speed of service.

Questions

1. What should Mack do before developing his advertising campaign?

2. Should Mack use comparative ads? Explain your choice.

3. What advertising appeal would be most effective for Mack? Why?

4. Should Mack consider Internet advertising? If so, what kind?

THINK ABOUT IT

Ethics Exercise

Creative Advertising Agency has been asked to help its largest client improve its corporate image after a highly publicized product recall. The client requests a television advertisement highlighting the company's generous donation of products to low-income families. The only such donation the company has made, however, is a donation of the recalled products. The account executive fears promoting the donation could cause further consumer backlash, but the client continues to press for the spot.

Questions

1. Should Creative Advertising meet the client's expectations (i.e., create the promotional spot) or risk losing the account? Explain your reasoning.

2. What does the AMA Code of Ethics say about truth in advertising? Go to **http://www.marketingpower.com** and review the code. Then, write a brief paragraph describing how the AMA Code of Ethics relates to this issue.

Entrepreneurship Case

The Move from TV to TiVo

In the late 1990s, Silicon Graphics, Inc., employees Mike Ramsay and Jim Barton were working together on the *Full-Service Network Project* in Orlando, Florida, a joint venture between then Time Warner and Silicon Graphics to create the first large-scale interactive television system, when they hit upon an idea. They could build a system that would give viewers control over their television programming and their time, but with far greater intelligence and ease-of-use than anything previously designed at a price the average customer could afford.

Their idea was the genesis of TiVo, a revolutionary new service that puts viewers in control of their television-viewing experience in a way never before possible. TiVo's service uses an electronic device called a digital video recorder (DVR). Its newest set top box, the Series2, can digitally save up to 60 hours of television programs to its hard disk. But instead of punching in times and channels one at a time to record a show on a video cassette tape, like with a VCR, the DVR uses a telephone connection to download television program schedules that pop up on the TV screen. TiVo subscribers then click on any shows they want to select and digitally record them. What's more, the Series2 has the ability to deliver digital music and photo files, video party games, Internet radio, and broadband video.

With TiVo, viewers get more control than ever over what they want to watch on television. Subscribers can digitally record their favorite shows, creating and organizing their own programming schedule to watch when they want, not bound by the timetable of any network schedule. Some of TiVo's television network partners even allow subscribers to select shows as they are advertised in televised promotions. For instance, if a subscriber sees a promo for an upcoming show to be aired on Showtime, she can click the remote when a small icon appears in the corner of her television screen during the promo to automatically record it when the program is aired. No longer do viewers have to remember when the desired show will come on in order to watch it—TiVo records properly even if the network changes its schedule! TiVo can also automatically record subscribers' favorite shows every week or suggest other shows that they might want to see based on what they've recorded in the past.

Ranging in cost from $299 for the 40-hour version available for AT&T Broadband customers to $399 for the 60-hour version, the digital video recorders provide several features that are superior to a conventional VCR and its limited recording capabilities. During live programs, for example, viewers can pause during a broadcast while the DVR keeps recording. DVRs can also provide instant replay and slow motion features so avid sports fans will never miss a play again. Additionally, TiVo DVRs include a fast-forward button so viewers can bypass television commercials or catch up with live programming that they have paused.

TiVo, based in Alviso, California, currently has over 422,000 subscribers, with projections of continued growth. While analysts expect DVRs to take several years to reach the market penetration of the ubiquitous VCR, DVRs are projected to be in 14 million homes by 2005, possibly making them the fastest-growing consumer electronics product in history. If this prediction pans out, the impact on television from DVRs and TiVo-like services could be enormous. For instance, since TiVo subscribers can create their own programming schedule, prime time could become increasingly irrelevant as more shows get recorded for later viewing. Additionally, viewers armed with the ability to fast-forward through commercials will see less of them; analysts are estimating that the viewing of commercials will decrease by 50 percent by 2009 with increased market penetration of DVRs.

Not surprisingly, TiVo and DVRs have most advertising and television executives watching carefully to see how the technology emerges. TiVo believes its technology is actually an opportunity for advertisers to target their audiences more directly. Best Buy was the first consumer electronics retailer to work with TiVo to deliver customized advertising to TiVo subscribers. As an extension of their national "Go Mobile" advertising campaign,

Best Buy provided an electronic tag for commercials that appeared to TiVo subscribers. Simply clicking their remote control while the ads were on their television screen transported TiVo subscribers to a "Video Showcase" area where they could view innovative Best Buy branded entertainment.

For the TiVo portion of this campaign, Best Buy filmed an exclusive "behind the scenes" jam session with artist Sheryl Crow featuring two singles from her latest album. In addition to the Sheryl Crow content, TiVo viewers also saw branded entertainment vignettes that offered fun, tongue-in-cheek tips for achieving "Electronic Feng Shui" with Best Buy's mobile products. While viewers watched the Best Buy branded advertisement, TiVo paused the program they were watching so they could return immediately to the programming, whether live or recorded, without missing a moment of their show.

Another feature Best Buy took advantage of was TiVo's lead generation and request-for-information capabilities. To test this feature, Best Buy gave TiVo subscribers a chance to receive a free Sheryl Crow CD. Using their remote control, the first two thousand TiVo subscribers to opt-in received the CD from Best Buy.

Lastly, but perhaps most importantly, the feature that advertisers may look forward to the most is the ability to measure audience exposure in real time. For the first time ever, companies can accurately track their return-on-advertising. TiVo can provide deep information on how anonymous users interacted with the entertainment including when it was viewed and how often, giving brand marketers new tools for maximizing the effectiveness of their television campaigns.

For now, many in the entertainment industry have decided it's better to join than oppose digital video recording services. Entertainment giants like AOL Time Warner, DIRECTV, AT&T, RealNetworks, Blockbuster, Cox Communications, Showtime Networks, Home Box Office, and others have partnered with TiVo to develop programming and advertising solutions. Additionally, entertainment companies including Interscope Geffen A&M, New Line Cinema, Sony Pictures and PBS have partnered with TiVo to produce entertainment Showcases similar to the Best Buy campaign that will extend their advertising campaigns and appeal to the entertainment enthusiasts within TiVo's subscriber base.

Questions

1. If the majority of TiVo viewers fast-forward through commercials, advertisers will be essentially wasting the millions of dollars they spend on them. What solutions might you suggest to advertisers as TiVo gains in popularity?

2. How might TiVo and DVRs affect traditional television networks that rely on advertising revenue to support original programming?

3. How might the popularity of TiVo's service affect traditional media selection criteria like reach and frequency?

WATCH IT

Short

The *Marketing* PowerPoint CD-ROM has six video ad clips embedded in the Chapter 15 slide presentation. Ads for e*Trade, Chrysler, Monster, Roche, Dockers, and Goodyear illustrate the concepts of event sponsorship, institutional advertising, advocacy advertising, issue sponsorship, and executional styles. List all the concepts you see working in the ads, then identify the executional styles for each.

Medium **CNN VIDEO**

A new trend in advertising is called *advertainment*, or using entertainment as a medium for advertising. Several companies have put specialized movies on their Web sites as a means to pull customers to their sites. Perhaps the best known are the BMW films directed by Oscar-winning directors. Watch the CNN clip on Internet movies and evaluate advertainment.

Long   SmallBusinessSchool
          the Series on PBS stations and the Web

To give you insights into Chapter 15, Small Business School introduces you to Tere Zubizarreta, founder and CEO of Zubi Advertising. Based in Miami, Zubi Advertising specializes in creating advertising for the entire Hispanic American market. Tere Zubizarreta, also called Mama Zubi, knows how to sell everything from car wax to airline tickets to the men and women who grew up speaking Spanish at home, or who call Spanish their first language. Join Mama Zubi for a look inside the advertising world and the Hispanic target market.

FLIP IT

Flip to Chapter 15 in your *Grademaker Study Guide* for more review opportunities, including the pretest, vocabulary review, Internet activities, study test questions, and an application exercise based on advertising concepts. What are the major types of advertising? How do you decide where to advertise your message? Can you close your book and list several advertising appeals and executional styles? If not, then pick up your *Grademaker* and review.

CLICK IT

The *Marketing* Web site links you to all the Internet-based activities in this chapter, like the "Use It," "Review It" question 5.4, and the On-Line exercises in the chapter margins. As a review, do the Chapter 15 quiz and crossword puzzle. And don't forget the Career Exersite that gives you resources for exploring marketing career opportunities in advertising and public relations. Review the main concepts in the PowerPoint presentation for Chapter 15, too. Go to **http://lamb.swlearning.com**, read the material, and follow the links right from the site.

SPIN IT

Spin your Xtra! CD-ROM to test your understanding of the advertising concepts in the chapter by completing the worksheets for exhibits 15.2, 15.3, and 15.5. If your instructor has assigned a marketing plan project, worksheets on Xtra! can help you organize your work. In addition to the quiz on the Web site, there's another quiz on the Xtra! CD-ROM, plus video of the authors answering frequently asked questions about advertising topics, such as "How do businesses know how much to advertise?"

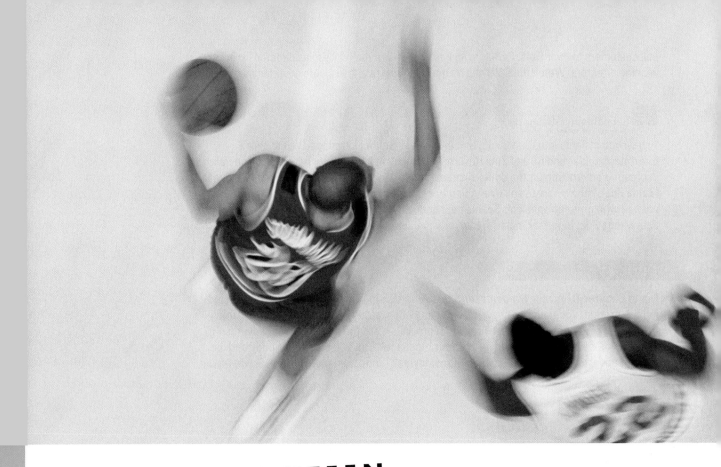

CHAPTER **SIXTEEN**

SALES PROMOTION AND PERSONAL SELLING

Learning Objectives

1 Define and state the objectives of sales promotion

2 Discuss the most common forms of consumer sales promotion

3 List the most common forms of trade sales promotion

4 Describe personal selling

5 Discuss the key differences between relationship selling and traditional selling

6 List the steps in the selling process

7 Describe the functions of sales management

How would you go about creating excitement and selling tickets for a basketball team with a 9–23 season? Well, if you're a dot-com entrepreneur named Mark Cuban, you employ a hard-charging sales culture to turn around what was one of basketball's most downtrodden franchises—the Dallas Mavericks. After pocketing $1.9 billion from Yahoo! for his audio-streaming business, Broadcast.com, Cuban bought the Mavericks for $280 million and set out to build another winner. His mission when he took over as owner was to turn a team that hadn't been to the playoffs in ten years into a champion—while dramatically increasing ticket sales and sponsorship revenues.

No small feat, but Cuban was confident that aggressive salesmanship could do the trick. After all, this formula had worked for both of his previous companies. Cuban realized early on that selling wasn't about taking something from somebody, but about helping someone. He believed that to be successful, salespeople have to understand their customers and solve their problems or meet their needs with a product or service. When Cuban first took over the Mavericks, the team had five full-time salespeople. Within one week, he hired thirty more. The team still has a sales force of thirty-five constantly calling prospective ticket buyers and corporate sponsors—and the effort is obviously working. Before the Mavericks stepped onto the court the first year Cuban bought the team, season ticket sales were up 70 percent, and corporate sponsorship revenue had increased about 30 percent. Twenty of their games sold out—three times the previous season's number—and the Mavericks made it to the playoffs.

But these results didn't come just from increasing the sales force. Cuban has instilled a sales culture fueled by enthusiasm in the Mavericks' salespeople. The office walls are covered by large motivational posters that read "12,000 Season Tickets or Bust," "Your Best Opportunity Is Today. Yesterday Has Already Passed," and a quote from Cuban himself, "Our #1 Priority Is Selling Season Tickets." Cuban also provides his sales staff with the motivation to succeed. As at many companies, incentive plans are based on deals that are closed, but Cuban doesn't stop there. He also rewards his sales force for the number of calls made each day—any rep who makes more than a hundred calls in one day gets a bonus. During the season, when ticket sales are not as heavy, the staff is divided up into teams and given group goals to hit for rewards.

Although the organization's biggest incentive is cash, salespeople also receive various other rewards for hard work, including a car wash service that regularly washes their vehicles, free drinks in the soda machine, and unexpected weekly gifts from in-kind trades with sponsors. Cuban believes these little motivators coupled with cash incentives are what keep his sales force working hard. And it's that dedicated, aggressive sales force that will keep the Mavericks center court. Cuban knows his team won't win every game, every time. So he's trained his salespeople to sell the entertainment aspect of Mavericks games. In fact, salespeople are not permitted to mention the team's won–loss record on sales calls because regardless of whether the team is winning or losing, fans have to be sold on the product—the games. Of course, selling Mavericks games isn't a problem anymore. With attendance up, TV ratings doubled, and a basketball team earning respect in a town that loves football, Cuban's aggressive sales style is definitely first string.[1]

What is the sales process, and why is it important to personal selling? What role does training play in a successful sales organization? What else besides compensation can sales managers use to motivate their salespeople? These questions and others about personal selling and sales management will be answered in the second part of this chapter after discussing the topic of sales promotion.

Sales Promotion

Define and state the objectives of sales promotion

In addition to using advertising, public relations, and personal selling, marketing managers can use sales promotion to increase the effectiveness of their promotional efforts. *Sales promotion* is marketing communication activities, other than advertising, personal selling, and public relations, in which a short-term incentive motivates consumers or members of the distribution channel to purchase a good or service immediately, either by lowering the price or by adding value.

Advertising offers the consumer a reason to buy; sales promotion offers an incentive to buy. Both are important, but sales promotion is usually cheaper than advertising and easier to measure. A major national TV advertising campaign may cost over $2 million to create, produce, and place. In contrast, a newspaper coupon campaign or promotional contest may cost only about half as much. It is also hard to calculate exactly how many people buy a product as a result of seeing a TV ad. With sales promotion, however, marketers know the precise number of coupons redeemed or the number of contest entries.

Sales promotion is usually targeted toward either of two distinctly different markets. **Consumer sales promotion** is targeted to the ultimate consumer market. **Trade sales promotion** is directed to members of the marketing channel, such as wholesalers and retailers. Sales promotion has become an important element in a marketer's integrated marketing communications program (see Chapter 14). Sales promotion expenditures have been steadily increasing over the last several years as a result of increased competition, the ever-expanding array of available media choices, consumers and retailers demanding more deals from manufacturers, and the continued reliance on accountable and measurable marketing strategies. In addition, product and service marketers that have traditionally ignored sales promotion activities, such as power companies and restaurants, have discovered the marketing power of sales promotion. In fact, *PROMO Magazine* estimates that promotion marketing in the United States now exceeds $100 billion a year.[2]

consumer sales promotion
Sales promotion activities targeting the ultimate consumer.

trade sales promotion
Sales promotion activities targeting a channel member, such as a wholesaler or retailer.

The Objectives of Sales Promotion

Sales promotion usually has more effect on behavior than on attitudes. Immediate purchase is the goal of sales promotion, regardless of the form it takes. Therefore, it seems to make more sense when planning a sales promotion campaign to target customers according to their general behavior. For instance, is the consumer loyal to your product or to your competitor's? Does the consumer switch brands readily in favor of the best deal? Does the consumer buy only the least expensive product, no matter what? Does the consumer buy any products in your category at all?

The objectives of a promotion depend on the general behavior of target consumers (see Exhibit 16.1). For example, marketers who are targeting loyal users of their product actually don't want to change behavior. Instead, they need to reinforce existing behavior or increase product usage. An effective tool for strengthening brand loyalty is the *frequent buyer program* that rewards consumers for repeat purchases. Other types of promotions are more effective with customers prone to brand switching or with those who are loyal to a competitor's product. A cents-off coupon, free sample, or eye-catching display in a store will often entice shoppers to try a different brand. Consumers who do not use the product may be enticed to try it through the distribution of free samples.

Once marketers understand the dynamics occurring within their product category and have determined the particular consumers and consumer behaviors they want to influence, they can then go about selecting promotional tools to achieve these goals.

Types of Consumers and Sales Promotion Goals **Exhibit 16.1**

Type of Buyer	Desired Results	Sales Promotion Examples
Loyal customers People who buy your product most or all of the time	Reinforce behavior, increase consumption, change purchase timing	• Loyalty marketing programs, such as frequent buyer cards or frequent shopper clubs • Bonus packs that give loyal consumers an incentive to stock up or premiums offered in return for proofs of purchase
Competitor's customers People who buy a competitor's product most or all of the time	Break loyalty, persuade to switch to your brand	• Sampling to introduce your product's superior qualities compared to their brand • Sweepstakes, contests, or premiums that create interest in the product
Brand switchers People who buy a variety of products in the category	Persuade to buy your brand more often	• Any promotion that lowers the price of the product, such as coupons, price-off packages, and bonus packs • Trade deals that help make the product more readily available than competing products
Price buyers People who consistently buy the least expensive brand	Appeal with low prices or supply added value that makes price less important	• Coupons, price-off packages, refunds, or trade deals that reduce the price of the brand to match that of the brand that would have been purchased

SOURCE: From *Sales Promotion Essentials*, 2nd ed., by Don E. Schultz, William A. Robinson, and Lisa A. Petrison. Reprinted by permission of NTC Publishing Group, 4255 Touhy Ave., Lincolnwood, IL 60048.

Tools for Consumer Sales Promotion

Marketing managers must decide which consumer sales promotion devices to use in a specific campaign. The methods chosen must suit the objectives to ensure success of the overall promotion plan. Popular tools for consumer sales promotion are coupons and rebates, premiums, loyalty marketing programs, contests and sweepstakes, sampling, and point-of-purchase promotion. Consumer sales promotion tools have also been easily transferred to on-line versions to entice Internet users to visit sites, purchase products, or use services on the Web.

Discuss the most common forms of consumer sales promotion

Coupons and Rebates

A **coupon** is a certificate that entitles consumers to an immediate price reduction when they buy the product. Coupons are a particularly good way to encourage product trial and repurchase. They are also likely to increase the amount of a product bought.

Coupon distribution has been steadily declining in recent years as packaged-goods marketers attempt to wean consumers off coupon clipping. Although

coupon
A certificate that entitles consumers to an immediate price reduction when they buy the product.

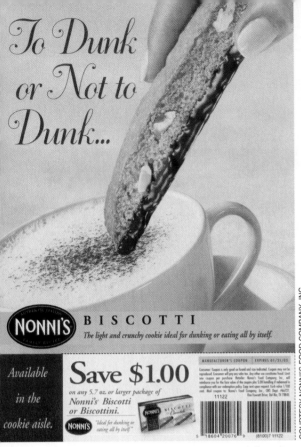

To Dunk or Not to Dunk...

NONNI'S BISCOTTI
The light and crunchy cookie ideal for dunking or eating all by itself.

Available in the cookie aisle.

MANUFACTURER'S COUPON   EXPIRES 01/31/03

Save $1.00
on any 5.7 oz. or larger package of Nonni's Biscotti or Biscottini.

NONNI'S "Ideal for dunking or eating all by itself."

Consumer: Coupon is only good on brand and size indicated. Coupon may not be reproduced. Consumer will pay any sales tax. Any other use constitutes fraud. Limit one coupon per purchase. Retailer: Nonni's Food Company, Inc. will reimburse you for the face value of this coupon plus 5.00¢ handling if redeemed in compliance with our redemption policy. Copy void upon request. Cash value 1/100 cent. Mail coupons to: Nonni's Food Company, Inc. CMS Dept #46477, One Fawcett Drive, Del Rio, TX 78840.

11122

5 18604 20076 9   (8100)7 11122

COURTESY NONNI'S FOOD COMPANY, INC.

rebate
A cash refund given for the purchase of a product during a specific period.

premium
An extra item offered to the consumer, usually in exchange for some proof of purchase of the promoted product.

Although coupons are a high-cost promotion alternative, they are still holding their own. Since coupons tend to be redeemed by customers who would have bought the product anyway, can you argue that coupons are really more of a loyalty marketing program? Why or why not?

approximately 248 billion coupons are distributed each year, only about 1.8 percent, or about 4.5 billion, are actually redeemed by consumers.[3] Part of the problem is that coupons are often wasted on consumers who have no interest in the product, such as pet food or feminine products coupons that reach the petless or men. This is due mainly to the typical distribution of coupons in mass-media newspaper Sunday inserts. Additionally, coupons are more likely to encourage repeat purchase by regular users, customers who would have purchased the product regardless, than to stimulate product trial by nonusers.

Because of their high cost and disappointing redemption rates, many marketers are reevaluating their use of coupons. By shortening the time the coupon can be redeemed, some marketers have increased redemption rates by creating a greater sense of urgency to redeem the coupon. Other marketers are deemphasizing their use of coupons in favor of everyday low pricing, while others are distributing single, all-purpose coupons that can be redeemed for several brands. In-store coupons are becoming more popular as they have proved more likely to affect customer buying decisions.

Instant coupons on product packages, coupons distributed from on-shelf coupon-dispensing machines, and electronic coupons issued at the checkout counter are achieving much higher redemption rates. Indeed, instant coupons are redeemed more than fifteen times more frequently than traditional newspaper coupons, indicating that consumers are making more in-store purchase decisions. As marketing tactics grow more sophisticated, coupons are no longer being viewed as a stand-alone tactic, but as an integral component of a larger promotional campaign. For example, Dr. Pepper/Seven Up kicked off its sponsorship of the Grammys with a "Sit On Your Can at the Grammys" under-the-cap game and included a 55¢ coupon on-pack to encourage buying the brand.[4]

Rebates are similar to coupons in that they offer the purchaser a price reduction; however, because the purchaser must mail in a rebate form and usually some proof of purchase, the reward is not as immediate. Traditionally used by food and cigarette manufacturers, rebates now appear on all types of products, from computers and software to film and baby seats. Consumers purchasing Earth's Best baby foods, for example, received a $2 rebate when they also bought the children's music CD "More Songs from Pooh Corner" by singer Kenny Loggins. In exchange, Earth's Best got to place its own coupons inside the Sony CD package.[5]

Manufacturers prefer rebates for several reasons. Rebates allow manufacturers to offer price cuts to consumers directly. Manufacturers have more control over rebate promotions because they can be rolled out and shut off quickly. Further, because buyers must fill out forms with their names, addresses, and other data, manufacturers use rebate programs to build customer databases. Perhaps the best reason of all to offer rebates is that although rebates are particularly good at enticing purchase, most consumers never bother to redeem them. Studies have found that as few as 2 percent of consumers eligible for rebates apply for them.[6]

Premiums

A **premium** is an extra item offered to the consumer, usually in exchange for some proof that the promoted product has been purchased. Premiums reinforce the consumer's purchase decision, increase consumption, and persuade nonusers to switch brands. Premiums like telephones, tote bags, and umbrellas are available when consumers buy cosmetics, magazines, bank services, rental cars, and so on. Probably the best example of the use of premiums is the McDonald's Happy Meal that rewards children with a small toy in the meal. The fast-food marketer's lucrative pacts with Ty, Inc., marketer of Beanie Babies, and Disney puts its Happy Meals in high demand with children. And recently, McDonald's teamed up with Toys "R" Us for a holiday program that made the most of cross-promotion for both companies. During the Christmas holidays, Happy Meals featured one of eight miniature premiums based on Paramus, the Toys "R" Us private-label plush line. The toys were poly-bagged with a miniature twenty-page version of the Big Toy Book, the chain's annual holiday megacircular. The mini-books contained $100 in Toys "R" Us coupons for McDonald's customers. The campaign marks the first time McDonald's has let a retailer tie into Happy Meals on such a grand scale.[7]

Premiums can also include more product for the regular price, such as two-for-the-price-of-one bonus packs or packages that include more of the product. Kellogg's, for instance, added two more pastries and waffles to its Pop Tarts and Eggo packages without increasing the price in an effort to boost market share lost to private-label brands and new competitors. The promotion was so successful the company decided to keep the additional product in its regular packaging.

Loyalty Marketing Programs

Loyalty marketing programs, or **frequent buyer programs**, reward loyal consumers for making multiple purchases. Popularized by the airline industry in the mid-1980s through frequent flyer programs, loyalty marketing enables companies to strategically invest sales promotion dollars in activities designed to capture greater profits from customers already loyal to the product or company.[8] One study concluded that if a company retains an additional 5 percent of its customers each year, profits will increase by at least 25 percent. What's more, improving customer retention by a mere 2 percent can decrease costs by as much as 10 percent.[9] The Phoenix Suns and Cleveland Cavaliers, for example, have both recently installed loyalty marketing programs that team officials say attracted seven thousand fans in the first month of the season.[10]

The objective of loyalty marketing programs is to build long-term, mutually beneficial relationships between a company and its key customers. Frequent shopper card programs offered by many supermarkets and other retailers have become so popular that almost half of all American households now belong to one. For example, Neiman Marcus created InCircle as a way to cater to its best customers. InCircle members can cash in points—one point is earned for each dollar spent—for a snake-skin-patterned Nokia phone cover, a trip to Los Angeles for a movie premiere with *InStyle* magazine, or a photo shoot with celebrity photographer Annie Leibovitz.[11] Through loyalty programs, shoppers receive discounts, alerts on new products, and other types of enticing offers. In

loyalty marketing program
A promotional program designed to build long-term, mutually beneficial relationships between a company and its key customers.

frequent buyer program
A loyalty program in which loyal consumers are rewarded for making multiple purchases of a particular good or service.

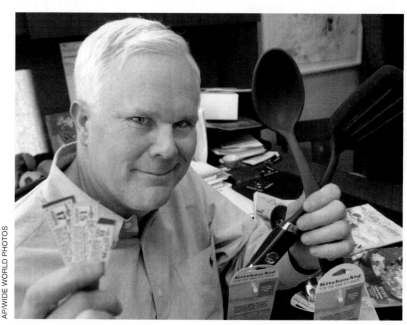

Although it seems that loyalty marketing programs are a recent trend, they date back quite a while. General Mills' Betty Crocker coupon program is entering its seventh decade and is among the longest-running loyalty marketing programs in the United States. Customers collect points from the packaging of General Mills products and then redeem the accumulated points for various products.

AP/WIDE WORLD PHOTOS

exchange, retailers are able to build customer databases that help them better understand customer preferences.

Contests and Sweepstakes

Contests and sweepstakes are generally designed to create interest in a good or service, often to encourage brand switching. *Contests* are promotions in which participants use some skill or ability to compete for prizes. A consumer contest usually requires entrants to answer questions, complete sentences, or write a paragraph about the product and submit proof of purchase. Winning a *sweepstakes*, on the other hand, depends on chance or luck, and participation is free. Sweepstakes usually draw about ten times more entries than contests do.

While contests and sweepstakes may draw considerable interest and publicity, generally they are not effective tools for generating long-term sales. To increase their effectiveness, sales promotion managers must make certain the award will appeal to the target market.[12] For example, Home & Garden Television Network's annual "Dream Home Giveaway" sweepstakes awards a fully furnished, custom-built home to one lucky viewer. The promotion is cosponsored by Sears, which stocks the home with Kenmore appliances, a Craftsman workshop, home fashions, lawn and garden equipment, and home electronics, and General Motors, which fills the garage with a new sport utility vehicle. The annual sweepstakes typically draws over four million entries.[13] But offering several smaller prizes to many winners instead of one huge prize to just one person often will increase the effectiveness of the promotion. A recent trend in sweepstakes is to combine on-pack and on-line promotions such as Kraft Foods' Game of Life (get the game piece on the packaging and check on-line to see if you're a winner). Such sweepstakes not only drive site traffic, but also save money on postage, seeding, and security. On-line sweepstakes can also require consumers to divulge information before entering—a plus for databases. And companies are offering extra entries as perks for supplying information. For example, Kellogg's "Be the Ultimate Pokémon Master" sweepstakes gave kids an extra entry for each e-card they sent to friends. And Gillette's launch of the Venus razor included an on-line sweepstakes offering extra entries for serving up friends' e-mail addresses.[14]

Sampling

sampling
A promotional program that allows the consumer the opportunity to try a product or service for free.

Consumers generally perceive a certain amount of risk in trying new products. Many are afraid of trying something they will not like (such as a new food item) or spending too much money and getting little reward. **Sampling** allows the customer to try a product risk-free. Sampling can increase retail sales by as much as 40 percent.[15] It is no surprise, therefore, that product sampling has increased 8.2 percent annually in recent years and that spending on sampling is projected to reach $1.8 billion by 2005.[16]

Sampling can be accomplished by directly mailing the sample to the customer, delivering the sample door-to-door, packaging the sample with another product, or demonstrating or sampling the product at a retail store. Recently, Ben & Jerry's Homemade wanted to get the word out about a new flavor of ice cream. The company deployed hot-air balloons to summer fairs and festivals in key markets and made

Distributing samples can often mitigate the risks consumers perceive in trying a new product. As part of its global marketing strategy, Starbucks has aggressively expanded into Asia. A woman in Hong Kong samples of cup of coffee from "Mercury Man," a Starbucks employee who walks around with a pot of coffee on his back.

© AFP/CORBIS

guerrilla visits to office buildings in thirteen cities. More than one million free scoops were served.[17]

Sampling at special events is a popular, effective, and high-profile distribution method that permits marketers to piggyback onto fun-based consumer activities—including sporting events, college fests, fairs and festivals, beach events, and chili cook-offs. To help demonstrate Sprint PCS wireless telecommunications products in Los Angeles, Sprint hired a local high school track team to run alongside Los Angeles Marathon competitors so that runners could call friends and family free while running. Sprint also supplied phones to moviegoers for free calls while waiting in line. Similarly, product sampling during tailgating at college and professional football stadiums allows marketers to reach anywhere from 10,000 to 50,000 consumers in a single afternoon. For example, H.J. Heinz is now testing products such as new barbecue sauces and ketchups to get immediate feedback about what consumers like and dislike about the products.[18]

Distributing samples to specific location types where consumers regularly meet for a common objective or interest, such as health clubs, churches, or doctors' offices, is one of the most efficient methods of sampling. What better way to get consumers to try a product than to offer a sample exactly when it is needed most? Marketers agree that companies must be much more precise in what, where, and how samples are delivered. If someone visits a health club regularly, chances are he or she is a good prospect for a health-food product or vitamin supplement. Health club instructors are handing out not only these products but also body wash, deodorant, and face cloths to sweating participants at the end of class, and makers of stain removers and hand cleansers are giving away samples in mall food courts and petting zoos. This method of distributing samples is working. In fact, one recent study found that sampling events produced an average 36 percent increase in sales soon afterward.[19]

Likewise, pharmaceutical companies offer free samples of new and expensive drugs as a tactic to entice doctors and consumers to become loyal to a product. Marketing practices for the pharmaceutical industry as a whole, however, are coming under increased scrutiny. Read about this issue in the "Ethics in Marketing" box.

Point-of-Purchase Promotion

Point-of-purchase (P-O-P) promotion includes any promotional display set up at the retailer's location to build traffic, advertise the product, or induce impulse buying. Point-of-purchase promotions include shelf "talkers" (signs attached to store shelves), shelf extenders (attachments that extend shelves so products stand out), ads on grocery carts and bags, end-aisle and floor-stand displays, television monitors at supermarket checkout counters, in-store audio messages, and audiovisual displays. One big advantage of P-O-P promotion is that it offers manufacturers a captive audience in retail stores. Another advantage is that between 70 and 80 percent of all retail purchase decisions are made in-store, so P-O-P promotions can be very effective. A recent study found that properly displayed P-O-P promotions boosted sales anywhere from 2 to 65 percent, depending on the brand and P-O-P mix. Signs such as header or riser cards increased weekly store sales 6 percent for one brand; base or case wraps boosted total sales 12 percent; standees, 2 percent; inflatable or mobile displays, 40 percent; and signs that advertised a brand's sports, movie, or charity tie-in, 65 percent.[20]

Corporations are cashing in on in-store purchasing decisions through more sophisticated P-O-P promotions. For example, MasterCard International sent 300,000 of its merchant and restaurant partners across the country P-O-P kits containing window clings, tent cards, employee buttons, register decals, coupons, and check presenter inserts customized by retail category. The promotion program, called Priceless P-O-P, awarded one cardholder five "prizes of a lifetime": an African safari, a visit from a celebrity chef, a behind-the-scenes tour of Space Center Houston, a trip to a racing school in England, and VIP passes to the My VH-1 Music Awards. MasterCard encouraged compliance among retailers with a mystery

point-of-purchase display
A promotional display set up at the retailer's location to build traffic, advertise the product, or induce impulse buying.

Pharmaceutical Sales—Just What the Doctor Ordered?

With free trips, expensive dinners, promotional gadgets, and hundreds of free drug samples, drug companies are waging an increasingly sophisticated campaign to win over doctors and patients, while keeping a $120 billion-a-year business growing. In recent years, the pharmaceutical industry has been highly criticized for its sales and marketing practices, and many physicians are concerned that the increasingly lavish spending on the part of drug companies is undermining the integrity of the profession. Of course, other doctors reject the idea that receiving gifts ranging from pens and note cards to free meals and travel would affect their prescribing habits.

Either way, pharmaceutical selling is quickly becoming a daily exercise in ethical judgment. Why? There's a fine line between the common practice of buying a prospect's time with a free meal and bribing doctors to prescribe a manufacturer's drug. Although some supporters of incentives and samples may feel bribery is too strong a word, a recent industry estimate shows that pharmaceutical promotional spending has reached nearly $14 billion. Add to this figure the fact that the collective pharmaceutical sales force has grown to more than 56,000 people and that equals one sales rep and approximately $100,000 for every

eleven practicing physicians in the United States. The explosion in the number of salespeople in the field—and the amount of funding used to promote their products—forces close examination of the pressures and influences drug reps may exert on doctors and the relationships between them.

While most physicians agree that pharmaceutical reps provide much-needed information and education through brochures, article reprints, and presentations, the sales push rarely stops there. Office visits are often followed by meals at expensive restaurants, meetings in exotic locales, and a deluge of promotional specialty items. Pfizer alone spends an estimated $85.7 million annually on promotional products like pens, coffee mugs, shirts, and umbrellas for reps to leave behind.

This is not a new phenomenon. Drugmakers have been "wining and dining" physicians for years—and this practice has aroused enough controversy to bring about periodic reviews by Congress and the American Medical Association (AMA). According to current guidelines in the AMA's Code of Ethics, doctors are supposed to limit gifts they receive from pharmaceutical companies to $100. However, both drug manufacturers and physicians can easily get around these guidelines. Doc-

tors are allowed to receive honoraria for "advising" drug companies for just a couple of hours. Training seminars held at vacation destinations, dinner parties with featured guest lecturers, and golf excursions are all ways to buy time with doctors. In fact, recent figures show that physicians received invitations to 225,000 pharmaceutical events in one year.

Although many doctors deny that the marketing practices employed by the pharmaceutical industry influence their prescription decisions, research shows the contrary. Studies have shown that after doctors participate in industry-sponsored events, they write more prescriptions and are more likely to prescribe expensive, brand-name medications than generic drugs.[21]

In the end, the fact remains that drug companies have every right to make a profit and will continue to find ways to increase sales. But at what price? Patients are the ones who are really paying—in the form of skyrocketing prescription costs—for every promotional item that's handed out, every honorarium given, and every dinner bought.

Should pharmaceutical companies be able to spend so much to entertain and provide gifts to physicians? How much is too much to spend on physicians in an attempt to market a particular drug?

---

shopper program that sent teams into stores to award $50 gift cards to store employees whenever they encountered a Priceless P-O-P. Five random participants won $2,500 gift cards, and the staff at the store that produced the grand-prize winner earned a Major League Baseball prize package.[22]

On-line Sales Promotion

On-line sales promotions have been booming in recent years due to the overwhelming popularity of the Internet. Marketers funneled some $926 million into on-line sales promotions in 1999 and close to $2 billion in 2000. Sales promotion on the Internet has proved to be effective and cost-efficient, generating response rates that are three to five times higher than their off-line counterparts. According to a recent survey of marketers, the most effective types of on-line sales promotions are free merchandise, sweepstakes, free shipping with purchases, and coupons.

Eager to boost traffic, Internet retailers have been busy giving away free services or equipment, such as personal computers, to lure consumers not only to their own Web site but to the Internet in general. For example, on-line toy retailer

RightStart.com waives shipping charges for orders over a certain amount. Wine.com routinely sends e-mail offering discounts on wine purchases to customers on its mailing list. Sega Enterprises gave away free Dreamcast video-game consoles, which list for $199, to customers who subscribed to its new Sega Web service for two years at $21.95 a month. The company is betting the giveaway will spur sales of its game software and help it tap into the expanding community of Internet game players. Sega also hopes to steal customers from market leaders Sony Corporation, which markets the PlayStation 2, and Nintendo.[23]

After several years of declining coupon distribution due to high cost and low redemption rates, many marketers have begun experimenting with distributing coupons on-line. One recent study found that nearly 30 percent of all Web surfers clip virtual coupons. Although e-coupons make up less than 1 percent of the 248 billion coupons distributed yearly in the United States, almost 57 percent of those who click on e-coupons or get them via e-mail redeem them, compared with the 1.2 percent of Sunday paper coupons that are redeemed. In addition, e-coupons can help marketers lure new customers. For example, Staples.com jumped from 23rd to 14th among retail Web sites with the most buyers through an e-coupon promotion that offered $25 off on purchases of $75 or more.[24]

On-line versions of loyalty programs are also popping up. Burger King is rewarding its loyal Whopper fans with the fast-food version of frequent flyer miles they can cash in on the Internet. In one program, customers were able to use points earned with fast-food purchases to bid on compact discs, tickets, and other rewards with on-line auctioneer eBay.[25]

Tools for Trade Sales Promotion

Whereas consumer promotions *pull* a product through the channel by creating demand, trade promotions *push* a product through the distribution channel (see Chapter 12). When selling to members of the distribution channel, manufacturers use many of the same sales promotion tools used in consumer promotions—such as sales contests, premiums, and point-of-purchase displays. Several tools, however, are unique to manufacturers and intermediaries:

- *Trade allowances:* A **trade allowance** is a price reduction offered by manufacturers to intermediaries such as wholesalers and retailers. The price reduction or rebate is given in exchange for doing something specific, such as allocating space for a new product or buying something during special periods. For example, a local dealer could receive a special discount for running its own promotion on GE telephones.

- *Push money:* Intermediaries receive **push money** as a bonus for pushing the manufacturer's brand through the distribution channel. Often the push money is directed toward a retailer's salespeople. LinoColor, the leading high-end scanner company, produces a Picture Perfect Rewards catalog filled with merchandise retailers can purchase with points accrued for every LinoColor scanner they sell.

List the most common forms of trade sales promotion

trade allowance
A price reduction offered by manufacturers to intermediaries, such as wholesalers and retailers.

push money
Money offered to channel intermediaries to encourage them to "push" products—that is, to encourage other members of the channel to sell the products.

The cover of the catalog features a wave runner that was brought to three industry trade shows and given away in a sweepstakes to one of the dealers who had visited all the product displays and passed a quiz. The program resulted in a 26 percent increase in LinoColor sales, and the manufacturer recruited thirty-two new dealers to carry the product line.[26]

- *Training:* Sometimes a manufacturer will train an intermediary's personnel if the product is rather complex—as frequently occurs in the computer and telecommunication industries. For example, if a large department store purchases an NCR computerized cash register system, NCR may provide free training so the salespeople can learn how to use the new system.

- *Free merchandise:* Often a manufacturer offers retailers free merchandise in lieu of quantity discounts. For example, a breakfast cereal manufacturer may throw in one case of free cereal for every twenty cases ordered by the retailer. Occasionally, free merchandise is used as payment for trade allowances normally provided through other sales promotions. Instead of giving a retailer a price reduction for buying a certain quantity of merchandise, the manufacturer may throw in extra merchandise "free" (that is, at a cost that would equal the price reduction).

- *Store demonstrations:* Manufacturers can also arrange with retailers to perform an in-store demonstration. Food manufacturers often send representatives to grocery stores and supermarkets to let customers sample a product while shopping. Cosmetic companies also send their representatives to department stores to promote their beauty aids by performing facials and makeovers for customers.

- *Business meetings, conventions, and trade shows:* Trade association meetings, conferences, and conventions are an important aspect of sales promotion and a growing, multibillion-dollar market. At these shows, manufacturers, distributors, and other vendors have the chance to display their goods or describe their services to customers and potential customers. A recent study reported that, on average, it costs 56 percent less to close a lead generated at an exhibition than a lead generated in the field—$625 versus $1,117.[27] Trade shows have been uniquely effective in introducing new products; they can establish products in the marketplace more quickly than can advertising, direct marketing, or sales calls. Companies participate in trade shows to attract and identify new prospects, serve current customers, introduce new products, enhance corporate image, test the market response to new products, enhance corporate morale, and gather competitive product information.

Trade promotions are popular among manufacturers for many reasons. Trade sales promotion tools help manufacturers gain new distributors for their products, obtain wholesaler and retailer support for consumer sales promotions, build or reduce dealer inventories, and improve trade relations. Car manufacturers annually sponsor dozens of auto shows for consumers. Many of the displays feature interactive computer stations where consumers enter vehicle specifications and get a printout of prices and local dealer names. In return, the local car dealers get the names of good prospects. The shows attract millions of consumers, providing dealers with increased store traffic as well as good leads.

AP/WIDE WORLD PHOTOS

Store demonstrations are not limited to trade sales promotion. The Bath and Body Works in Columbus, Ohio, gives customers free samples of massages, manicures, and sugar scrubs to create a stress-free shopping experience.

Personal Selling

Describe personal selling

As mentioned in Chapter 15, *personal selling* is direct communication between a sales representative and one or more prospective buyers in an attempt to influence each other in a purchase situation.

In a sense, all businesspeople are salespeople. An individual may become a plant manager, a chemist, an engineer, or a member of any profession and yet still have to sell. During a job search, applicants must "sell" themselves to prospective employers in an interview. To reach the top in most organizations, individuals need to sell ideas to peers, superiors, and subordinates. Most important, people must sell themselves and their ideas to just about everyone with whom they have a continuing relationship and to many other people they see only once or twice. Chances are that students majoring in business or marketing will start their professional careers in sales. Even students in nonbusiness majors may pursue a sales career.

Personal selling offers several advantages over other forms of promotion:

- Personal selling provides a detailed explanation or demonstration of the product. This capability is especially needed for complex or new goods and services.

- The sales message can be varied according to the motivations and interests of each prospective customer. Moreover, when the prospect has questions or raises objections, the salesperson is there to provide explanations. In contrast, advertising and sales promotion can only respond to the objections the copywriter thinks are important to customers.

- Personal selling can be directed only to qualified prospects. Other forms of promotion include some unavoidable waste because many people in the audience are not prospective customers.

- Personal selling costs can be controlled by adjusting the size of the sales force (and resulting expenses) in one-person increments. On the other hand, advertising and sales promotion must often be purchased in fairly large amounts.

- Perhaps the most important advantage is that personal selling is considerably more effective than other forms of promotion in obtaining a sale and gaining a satisfied customer.

Personal selling might work better than other forms of promotion given certain customer and product characteristics. Generally speaking, personal selling becomes more important as the number of potential customers decreases, as the complexity of the product increases, and as the value of the product grows (see Exhibit 16.2). When there are relatively few potential customers and the value of the good or service is relatively sufficient, the time and travel costs of personally visiting each prospect are justifiable. For highly complex goods, such as business jets or private communication systems, a salesperson is needed to determine the prospective customer's needs, explain the product's basic advantages, and propose the exact features and accessories that will meet the client's needs.

Exhibit 16.2

Comparison of Personal Selling and Advertising/Sales Promotion

Personal selling is more important if...	Advertising and sales promotion are more important if...
The product has a high value. It is a custom-made product. There are few customers. The product is technically complex. Customers are concentrated.	The product has a low value. It is a standardized product. There are many customers. The product is easy to understand. Customers are geographically dispersed.
Examples: insurance policies, custom windows, airplane engines	**Examples:** soap, magazine subscriptions, cotton T-shirts

5

Discuss the key differences between relationship selling and traditional selling

relationship selling (consultative selling)

A sales practice that involves building, maintaining, and enhancing interactions with customers in order to develop long-term satisfaction through mutually beneficial partnerships.

Relationship Selling

Until recently, marketing theory and practice concerning personal selling focused almost entirely on a planned presentation to prospective customers for the sole purpose of making the sale. Marketers were most concerned with making a one-time sale and then moving on to the next prospect. Whether the presentation took place face-to-face during a personal sales call or over the telephone (telemarketing), traditional personal selling methods attempted to persuade the buyer to accept a point of view or convince the buyer to take some action. Once the customer was somewhat convinced, then the salesperson used a variety of techniques in an attempt to elicit a purchase. Frequently, the objectives of the salesperson were at the expense of the buyer, creating a win-lose outcome. Although this type of sales approach has not disappeared entirely, it is being used less and less often by professional salespeople.

In contrast, modern views of personal selling emphasize the relationship that develops between a salesperson and a buyer. **Relationship selling**, or **consultative selling**, is a multistage process that emphasizes personalization and empathy as key ingredients in identifying prospects and developing them as long-term, satisfied customers. The old way was to sell a product, but with relationship selling, the objective is to build long-term branded relationships with consumers/buyers.[28] Thus, the focus is on building mutual trust between the buyer and seller through the delivery of anticipated, long-term, value-added benefits to the buyer.

We were there when you were a child of the '60s and when you became a parent of the '90s.

Relationship selling emphasizes personalization and empathy in the process of developing long-term customers. This ad for State Farm showcases the commitment of the company to its customers throughout their various life stages.

Relationship or consultative salespeople, therefore, become consultants, partners, and problem solvers for their customers. They strive to build long-term relationships with key accounts by developing trust over time. The emphasis shifts from a one-time sale to a long-term relationship in which the salesperson works with the customer to develop solutions for enhancing the customer's bottom line. Moreover, research has shown that a positive customer-salesperson relationship contributes to trust, increased customer loyalty, and the intent to continue the relationship with the salesperson.[29] Thus, relationship selling promotes a win-win situation for both buyer and seller.

The end result of relationship selling tends to be loyal customers who purchase from the company time after time. A relationship selling strategy focused on retaining customers costs a company less than if it were constantly prospecting and selling to new customers. Companies that focus on customer retention through high customer service gain 6 percent market share per year, while companies that offer low customer service lose 2 percent market share per year.[30] In fact, it costs businesses six times more to gain a new customer than to retain a current one.[31]

Relationship selling is more typical with selling situations for industrial-type goods, such as heavy machinery or computer systems, and services, such as airlines and insurance, than for consumer goods. For example, Kinko's has built a long-term business relationship with PeopleSoft. The software maker now gives many of its training and educational materials printing jobs to Kinko's—a deal worth close to $5 million in revenues. Kinko's has forged such a close relationship with the company that Kinko's representatives are even invited to sit in on internal planning meetings in PeopleSoft's human resources department at the company's headquarters.[32]

Exhibit 16.3 lists the key differences between traditional personal selling and relationship or consultative selling. These differences will become more apparent as we explore the personal selling process later in the chapter.

Exhibit 16.3

Key Differences between Traditional
Selling and Relationship Selling

Traditional Personal Selling	Relationship or Consultative Selling
Sell products (goods and services)	Sell advice, assistance, and counsel
Focus on closing sales	Focus on improving the customer's bottom line
Limited sales planning	Consider sales planning as top priority
Spend most contact time telling customers about product	Spend most contact time attempting to build a problem-solving environment with the customer
Conduct "product-specific" needs assessment	Conduct discovery in the full scope of the customer's operations
"Lone wolf" approach to the account	Team approach to the account
Proposals and presentations based on pricing and product features	Proposals and presentations based on profit-impact and strategic benefits to the customer
Sales follow-up is short term, focused on product delivery	Sales follow-up is long term, focused on long-term relationship enhancement

SOURCE: Robert M. Peterson, Patrick L. Schul, and George H. Lucas, Jr., "Consultative Selling: Walking the Walk in the New Selling Environment," National Conference on Sales Management, *Proceedings,* March 1996.

Steps in the Selling Process

Although personal selling may sound like a relatively simple task, completing a sale actually requires several steps. The **sales process**, or **sales cycle**, is simply the set of steps a salesperson goes through to sell a particular product or service. The sales process or cycle can be unique for each product or service, depending on the features of the product or service, characteristics of customer segments, and internal processes in place within the firm, such as how leads are gathered.

Some sales take only a few minutes, but others may take months or years to complete, especially when selling customized goods or services. The typical sale for Eastman Kodak's line of high-speed motion analysis cameras takes anywhere from nine to eighteen months to close.[33] On the other end of the spectrum, sales of its more basic cameras to retailers are generally more routine and may take only a few days. Whether a salesperson spends a few minutes or a few years on a sale, these are the seven basic steps in the personal selling process:

1. Generating leads
2. Qualifying leads
3. Approaching the customer and probing needs
4. Developing and proposing solutions
5. Handling objections
6. Closing the sale
7. Following up

List the steps in the selling process

sales process (sales cycle)
The set of steps a salesperson goes through in a particular organization to sell a particular product or service.

On Line

Like other forms of promotion, these steps of selling follow the AIDA concept discussed in Chapter 14. Once a salesperson has located a prospect with the authority to buy, he or she tries to get the prospect's attention. A thorough needs assessment turned into an effective sales proposal and presentation should generate interest. After developing the customer's initial desire (preferably during the presentation of the sales proposal), the salesperson seeks action in the close by trying to get an agreement to buy. Follow-up after the sale, the final step in the selling process, not only lowers cognitive dissonance (refer to Chapter 5) but also may open up opportunities to discuss future sales. Effective follow-up will also lead to repeat business in which the process may start all over again at the needs assessment step.

Traditional selling and relationship selling follow the same basic steps. What is different between the two selling methods is the relative importance placed on key steps in the process (see Exhibit 16.4). Traditional selling efforts are transaction oriented, focusing on generating as many leads as possible, making as many presentations as possible, and closing as many sales as possible. Minimal effort is placed on asking questions to identify customer needs and wants or matching these needs and wants to the benefits of the product or service. In contrast, the salesperson practicing relationship selling emphasizes an up-front investment in the time and effort needed to uncover each customer's specific needs and wants and matching to them, as closely as possible, the product or service offering. By doing the homework up front, the salesperson creates the conditions necessary for a relatively straightforward close.[34] Let's look at each step of the selling process individually.

Generating Leads

Initial groundwork must precede communication between the potential buyer and the salesperson. **Lead generation**, or **prospecting**, is the identification of those firms and people most likely to buy the seller's offerings. These firms or people become "sales leads" or "prospects."

 Sales leads can be secured in several different ways, most notably through advertising, trade shows and conventions, or direct-mail and telemarketing programs. Favorable publicity also helps to create leads. Company records of past client purchases are another excellent source of leads. Many sales professionals are also securing valuable leads from their firm's Internet Web site. For example, Ford Motor Company's drive to reach consumers on-line is paying off. Recently, the company's combination of Web sites and other on-line ventures sent an estimated half-million leads—60 percent of them in the United States—to its dealers.[35] In the future, more than half of all sales leads likely will come from the Internet.

Another way to gather a lead is through a **referral**—a recommendation from a customer or business associate. The advantages of referrals over other forms of prospecting include highly qualified leads, higher closing rates, larger initial transactions, and shorter sales cycles. Simply put, the salesperson and the company can earn more money in less time when prospecting using referrals. To increase the number of referrals they receive, some companies even pay or send small gifts to customers or suppliers who provide referrals. Research has suggested that one re-

lead generation (prospecting)
Identification of those firms and people most likely to buy the seller's offerings.

referral
A recommendation to a salesperson from a customer or business associate.

Exhibit 16.4

Key Selling Steps	Traditional Selling	Relationship/Consultative Selling
Generating leads	High	Low
Qualifying leads	Low	High
Approaching the customer and probing needs	Low	High
Developing and proposing solutions	Low	High
Handling objections	High	Low
Closing the sale	High	Low
Following up	Low	High

ferral is as valuable as up to twelve cold calls. However, although 80 percent of clients would be willing to give referrals, only 20 percent are ever asked.[36]

Networking is the related method of using friends, business contacts, coworkers, acquaintances, and fellow members in professional and civic organizations to find out about potential clients. Indeed, a number of national networking clubs have recently been started for the sole purpose of generating leads and providing valuable business advice. The networking clubs usually have between fifteen and thirty members in noncompeting business categories. During weekly breakfast or lunch meetings, each member is allowed to talk about the company he or she represents for an allotted period of time. Then members exchange lead cards. Research suggests that, on average, chapter members see an increase in business volume of between 16 and 25 percent after they've been with their group for three to six months.[37]

Before the advent of more sophisticated methods of lead generation, such as direct mail and telemarketing, most prospecting was done through **cold calling**— a form of lead generation in which the salesperson approaches potential buyers without any prior knowledge of the prospects' needs or financial status. Although this method is still used, many sales managers have realized the inefficiencies of having their top salespeople use their valuable selling time searching for the proverbial "needle in a haystack." Passing the job of cold calling to a lower-cost employee, typically an internal sales support person, allows salespeople to spend more time and use their relationship-building skills on prospects who have already been identified. Sales experts note that the days of cold calls and unannounced office visits have given way to referral-based and relationship selling.[38]

Qualifying Leads

When a prospect shows interest in learning more about a product, the salesperson has the opportunity to follow up, or qualify, the lead. Personally visiting unqualified prospects wastes valuable salesperson time and company resources. Often many leads go unanswered because salespeople are given no indication as to how qualified the leads are in terms of interest and ability to purchase. One study that surveyed four hundred marketers whose companies advertise in trade publications

networking
A process of finding out about potential clients from friends, business contacts, coworkers, acquaintances, and fellow members in professional and civic organizations.

cold calling
A form of lead generation in which the salesperson approaches potential buyers without any prior knowledge of the prospects' needs or financial status.

found that almost 40 percent of the leads generated went completely unanswered, most likely due to the fact that they were unqualified.[39]

Lead qualification consists of determining whether the prospect has three things:[40]

- *A recognized need:* The most basic criterion for determining whether someone is a prospect for a product is a need that is not being satisfied. The salesperson should first consider prospects who are aware of a need but should not discount prospects who have not yet recognized that they have one. With a little more information about the product, they may decide they do have a need for it. Preliminary interviews and questioning can often provide the salesperson with enough information to determine whether there is a need.

- *Buying power:* Buying power involves both authority to make the purchase decision and access to funds to pay for it. To avoid wasting time and money, the salesperson needs to identify the purchasing authority and the ability to pay before making a presentation. Organizational charts and information about a firm's credit standing can provide valuable clues.

- *Receptivity and accessibility:* The prospect must be willing to see the salesperson and be accessible to the salesperson. Some prospects simply refuse to see salespeople. Others, because of their stature in their organization, will see only a salesperson or sales manager with similar stature.

Often the task of lead qualification is handled by a telemarketing group or a sales support person who *prequalifies* the lead for the salesperson. Prequalification systems free sales representatives from the time-consuming task of following up on leads to determine need, buying power, and receptiveness. Prequalification systems may even set up initial appointments with the prospect for the salesperson. The result is more time for the sales force to spend in front of interested customers. Protocol, an integrated direct marketing services company, helps clients with follow-up by loading lead information into a high-yield database. Protocol contacts trade show attendees and qualifies them using a scripting process based on input from the company for which it is working. After qualification, Protocol distributes A- and B-level leads to the client.[41]

With more and more companies setting up Web sites on the Internet, qualifying on-line leads has also received some attention. The object of a company's Web site should be to get visitors to register, indicate what products they are interested in, and offer up some information on their time frame and resources. Leads from the Internet can then be prioritized (those indicating a short time frame, for instance, given a higher priority) and then transferred to salespeople. Often Web site visitors can be enticed to answer questions with offers of free merchandise or information. Enticing visitors to register also allows companies to customize future electronic interactions—for example, by giving prospects who visit the Web site their choice from a menu of products tailored specifically to their needs.[42]

Approaching the Customer and Probing Needs

Prior to approaching the customer, the salesperson should learn as much as possible about the prospect's organization and its buyers. This process, called the **preapproach**, describes the "homework" that must be done by the salesperson before contacting the prospect. This may include consulting standard reference sources, such as Moody's, Standard & Poor's, or Dun & Bradstreet, or contacting acquaintances or others who may have information about the prospect. Another preapproach task is to determine whether the actual approach should be a personal visit, a phone call, a letter, or some other form of communication.

During the sales approach, the salesperson either talks to the prospect or secures an appointment for a future time in which to probe the prospect further as to his or her needs. Relationship selling theorists suggest that salespeople should begin developing mutual trust with their prospect during the approach. Salespeo-

lead qualification
Determination of a sales prospect's (1) recognized need, (2) buying power, and (3) receptivity and accessibility.

preapproach
A process that describes the "homework" that must be done by a salesperson before he or she contacts a prospect.

ple should use the approach as a way of introducing themselves and their company and products. They must sell themselves before they can sell the product. Small talk that introduces sincerity and some suggestion of friendship is encouraged to build rapport with the prospect, but remarks that could be construed as insincere should be avoided.[43]

The salesperson's ultimate goal during the approach is to conduct a **needs assessment** to find out as much as possible about the prospect's situation. This involves interviewing the customer to determine his or her specific needs and wants and the range of options the customer has for satisfying them. The salesperson should be determining how to maximize the fit between what he or she can offer and what the prospective customer wants. As part of the needs assessment, the consultative salesperson must know everything there is to know about the following:[44]

- *The product or service:* Product knowledge is the cornerstone for conducting a successful needs analysis. The consultative salesperson must be an expert on his or her product or service, including technical specifications, the product's features and benefits, pricing and billing procedures, warranty and service support, performance comparisons with the competition, other customers' experiences with the product, and current advertising and promotional campaign messages.

- *Customers and their needs:* The salesperson should know more about customers than they know about themselves. That's the secret to relationship and consultative selling, where the salesperson acts not only as a supplier of products and services but also as a trusted consultant and adviser. The professional salesperson doesn't just sell products. He or she brings to each client business-building ideas and solutions to problems. For the customer, consulting a professional salesperson is like having another vital person on the team at no cost.

- *The competition:* The salesperson must know as much about the competitor's company and products as he or she knows about his or her own company. *Competitive intelligence* includes many factors: who the competitors are and what is known about them; how their products and services compare; advantages and disadvantages; and strengths and weaknesses.

- *The industry:* Knowing the industry involves active research on the part of the salesperson. This means attending industry and trade association meetings, reading articles published in industry and trade journals, keeping track of legislation and regulation that affect the industry, awareness of product alternatives and innovations from domestic and foreign competition, and having a feel for economic and financial conditions that may affect the industry.

Creating a *customer profile* during the approach helps salespeople optimize their time and resources. This profile is then used to help develop an intelligent analysis of the prospect's needs in preparation for the next step, developing and proposing solutions. Customer profile information is typically stored and manipulated using sales force automation software packages designed for use on laptop computers. Sales force automation software provides sales reps with a computerized and efficient method of collecting customer information for use during the entire sales process. Further, customer and sales data stored in a computer database can be easily shared among sales team members. The information can also be appended with industry statistics, sales or meeting notes, billing data, and other information that may be pertinent to the prospect or the prospect's company. The more salespeople know about their prospects, the better they can meet their needs.

Salespeople should wrap up their sales approach and need-probing mission by summarizing the prospect's need, problem, and interest. The salesperson should also get a commitment from the customer to some kind of action, whether it's reading promotional material or agreeing to a demonstration. This commitment helps qualify the prospect further and justify additional time invested by the salesperson. The salesperson should reiterate the action he or she promises to

needs assessment
A determination of the customer's specific needs and wants and the range of options the customer has for satisfying them.

take, such as sending information or calling back to provide answers to questions. The date and time of the next call should be set at the conclusion of the sales approach as well as an agenda for the next call in terms of what the salesperson hopes to accomplish, such as providing a demonstration or presenting a solution.[45]

Developing and Proposing Solutions

Once the salesperson has gathered the appropriate information about the client's needs and wants, the next step is to determine whether his or her company's products or services match the needs of the prospective customer. The salesperson then develops a solution, or possibly several solutions, in which the salesperson's product or service solves the client's problems or meets a specific need.

These solutions are typically presented to the client in the form of a sales proposal presented at a sales presentation. A **sales proposal** is a written document or professional presentation that outlines how the company's product or service will meet or exceed the client's needs. The **sales presentation** is the formal meeting in which the salesperson has the opportunity to present the sales proposal. The presentation should be explicitly tied to the prospect's expressed needs. Further, the prospect should be involved in the presentation by being encouraged to participate in demonstrations or by exposure to computer exercises, slides, video or audio, flipcharts, photographs, and so on.[46]

ON LINE Technology has become an important part of presenting solutions for many salespeople. Pen manufacturer BIC utilized the Internet to connect with its wholesale and convenience store customers. Before launching BIClink.com, BIC received 80 percent of its order volume by fax. Processing these orders was time-consuming, and the orders often were filled with errors. BIClink.com has eliminated the potential for errors and made it easier and faster to validate purchase order numbers, ship dates, case quantities, and pricing. When customers sign on (through a secure, password-protected system), the welcome screen is personalized with their company's name and the name of their BIC rep. On placing an order, customers receive both a hard copy and e-mail confirmation statement with the salesperson's name and contact information including e-mail, voice mail, phone, and fax numbers. The site has proved to be a success—in its first six weeks of operation, more than 50 percent of customers who previously ordered by fax began ordering on-line.[47]

Because the salesperson often has only one opportunity to present solutions, the quality of both the sales proposal and presentation can make or break the sale. Salespeople must be able to present the proposal and handle any customer objections confidently and professionally. For a powerful presentation, salespeople must be well prepared, use direct eye contact, ask open-ended questions, be poised, use hand gestures and voice inflection, focus on the customer's needs, incorporate visual elements that impart valuable information, know how to operate the audio/visual or computer equipment being used for the presentation, make sure the equipment works, and prac-

sales proposal
A formal written document or professional presentation that outlines how the salesperson's product or service will meet or exceed the prospect's needs.

sales presentation
A formal meeting in which the salesperson presents a sales proposal to a prospective buyer.

COURTESY OF BIC CONSUMER PRODUCTS, A DIVISION OF BIC USA INC.

Part of the selling process involves proposing solutions to resolve difficulties customers are having. BIC utilized the Internet to streamline the order process for its wholesale and convenience store customers. The result was BIClink.com.

tice, practice, practice.[48] Nothing dies faster than a boring presentation. If the salesperson doesn't have a convincing and confident manner, then the prospect will very often forget the information. Prospects take in body language, voice patterns, dress, and body type. Often customers are more likely to remember how salespeople present themselves than what salespeople say.

Handling Objections

Rarely does a prospect say "I'll buy it" right after a presentation. Instead, the prospect often raises objections or asks questions about the proposal and the product. The potential buyer may insist that the price is too high, that he or she does not have enough information to make a decision, or that the good or service will not satisfy the present need. The buyer may also lack confidence in the seller's organization or product.

One of the first lessons that every salesperson learns is that objections to the product should not be taken personally as confrontations or insults. Rather, a salesperson should view objections as requests for information. A good salesperson considers objections a legitimate part of the purchase decision. To handle objections effectively, the salesperson should anticipate specific objections such as concerns about price, fully investigate the objection with the customer, be wary of what the competition is offering, and, above all, stay calm. Before a crucial sales presentation with an important prospect, for example, Dell Computer salespeople anticipated that the customer would have doubts as to whether Dell's direct selling model would provide the same level of service and dedication as a reseller would. Being prepared helped Dell win the contract.[49]

Often the salesperson can use the objection to close the sale. If the customer tries to pit suppliers against each other to drive down the price, the salesperson should be prepared to point out weaknesses in the competitor's offer and stand by the quality in his or her own proposal.[50]

Closing the Sale

At the end of the presentation, the salesperson should ask the customer how he or she would like to proceed. If the customer exhibits signs that he or she is ready to purchase and all questions have been answered and objections have been met, then the salesperson can try to close the sale. Customers often give signals during or after the presentation that they are ready to buy or are not interested. Examples include changes in facial expressions, gestures, and questions asked. The salesperson should look for these signals and respond appropriately.

Closing requires courage and skill. Naturally, the salesperson wants to avoid rejection, and asking for a sale carries with it the risk of a negative answer. A salesperson should keep an open mind when asking for the sale and be prepared for either a yes or a no. Rarely is a sale closed on the first call. In fact, the typical salesperson averages about 765 sales calls a year, many of which are repeat calls to the same client in an attempt to make the sale.[51] Some salespeople may negotiate with large accounts for several years before closing a sale. As you can see, building a good relationship with the customer is very important. Often, if the salesperson has developed a strong relationship with the customer, only minimal efforts are needed to close a sale.

Negotiation often plays a key role in the closing of the sale. **Negotiation** is the process during which both the salesperson and the prospect offer special concessions in an attempt to arrive at a sales agreement. For example, the salesperson may offer a price cut, free installation, free service, or a trial order. Effective negotiators, however, avoid using price as a negotiation tool because cutting price directly affects a company's profitability. Because companies spend millions on advertising and product development to create value, when salespeople give in to price negotiations too quickly, it decreases the value of the product. Instead, effective salespeople should emphasize value to the customer, rendering price a

negotiation
The process during which both the salesperson and the prospect offer special concessions in an attempt to arrive at a sales agreement.

nonissue. Salespeople should also be prepared to ask for trade-offs and try to avoid giving unilateral concessions. If you're making only a 50 percent margin on a product, and you need at least a 60 percent margin, raise your prices or drop the product.[52] Moreover, if the customer asks for a 5 percent discount, the salesperson should ask for something in return, such as higher volume or more flexibility in delivery schedules.

More and more U.S. companies are expanding their marketing and selling efforts into global markets. Salespeople selling in foreign markets should tailor their presentation and closing styles to each market. Different personalities and skills will be successful in some countries and absolute failures in others. For instance, if a salesperson is an excellent closer and always focuses on the next sale, doing business in Latin America might be difficult. The reason is that in Latin America people want to take a long time building a personal relationship with their suppliers.[53] Read about other global dos and don'ts of selling in the "Global Perspectives" box.

Following Up

follow-up
The final step of the selling process, in which the salesperson ensures that delivery schedules are met, that the goods or services perform as promised, and that the buyers' employees are properly trained to use the products.

Unfortunately, many salespeople hold the attitude that making the sale is all that's important. Once the sale is made, they can forget about their customers. They are wrong. Salespeople's responsibilities do not end with making the sales and placing the orders. One of the most important aspects of their jobs is **follow-up**—the final step in the delivery process, in which they must ensure that delivery schedules are met, that the goods or services perform as promised, and that the buyers' employees are properly trained to use the products.

Whereas the traditional sales approach's extent of follow-up with the customer is generally limited to successful product delivery and performance, a basic goal of relationship selling is to motivate customers to come back, again and again, by developing and nurturing long-term relationships. Most businesses depend on repeat sales, and repeat sales depend on thorough and continued follow-up by the salesperson. Finding a new customer is far more expensive than retaining an existing customer. When customers feel abandoned, cognitive dissonance arises and repeat sales decline. Today, this issue is more pertinent than ever because customers are far less loyal to brands and vendors. Buyers are more inclined to look for the best deal, especially in the case of poor after-the-sale follow-up. More and more buyers favor building a relationship with sellers.

Automated e-mail follow-up marketing—a combination of sales automation and Internet technology—is enhancing customer satisfaction as well as bringing in more business for some marketers. Here's how it works: After the initial contact with a prospect, a software program automatically sends a series of personalized e-mail over a period of time. CollegeRecruiter.com is one company taking advantage of this technology. The company posts ads for businesses recruiting recent college graduates on its Web site and has seen phenomenal results from autoresponse marketing. Prospects start receiving a series of e-mails once they have visited the site and requested advertising rates. The first message goes out immediately. The next two go out in four to eleven days. From there, e-mails go out monthly. The average sale for CollegeRecruiter.com is $375, and the company gets $4,000 to $5,000 in additional sales from new customers each month just from the automated follow-ups.[54]

■ Sales Management

Describe the functions of sales management

There is an old adage in business that nothing happens until a sale is made. Without sales there is no need for accountants, production workers, or even a company president. Sales provide the fuel that keeps the corporate engines humming. Com-

Global Dos and Don'ts in Selling

Most large companies with operations on foreign soil are employing locals to sell their products—international buyers are often cold to Americans trying to peddle their wares. So the Americans who find themselves trying to sell internationally had better be prepared.

Most selling skills that are successful in America also will work overseas. However, knowing how to act in certain cultures can be the difference between closing the deal and losing a customer. Some things that Americans take for granted could easily cost them a deal overseas. A simple thumbs-up sign that we give everyday could offend a customer in another country. Here, from many international business experts, are some things to watch out for in various countries and regions around the world.

- **Arab countries:** Don't use your left hand to hold, offer, or receive materials because Arabs use their left hand to touch toilet paper. If you must use your left hand to write, apologize for doing so. Handshakes in Arab countries are a bit limp and last longer than typical American handshakes.

- **China:** Never talk business on the first meeting—it's disrespectful. Don't refuse tea during a business discussion. Always drink it, even if you're offered a dozen cups a day. Never begin to eat or drink before your host does. Also, printed materials presented to Chinese business leaders should be in black and white, because colors have great significance for the Chinese. The Chinese tend to be extremely meticulous, looking to create long-term relationships with a supplier before agreeing to buy anything. Chinese are more intradependent and tend to include more people in on a deal. Most deals in China are finalized in a social setting, either over drinks or dinner. Additionally, getting to know the businessperson's family will personalize and strengthen the relationship.

- **European countries:** Western and Eastern Europeans reshake hands whenever they're apart for even a short period of time, for example, lunch.

- **France:** Don't schedule a breakfast meeting—the French tend not to meet until after 10 A.M. Since the French knowledge of wine is far greater than that of most Americans, avoid giving wine or wine-related gifts to French clients. The French also prefer gifts that are of French origin.

- **Germany:** Don't address a business associate by his or her first name, even if you've known each other for years. Always wait for an invitation to do so. Also, breakfast meetings are unheard of here, too. Salespeople should expect a sober, rigid business climate and negotiations that lack flexibility and compromise.

- **Central and South America:** People here don't take the clock too seriously—scheduling more than two appointments in one day can prove disastrous. Latin Americans also tend to use a lighter, lingering handshake. Negotiations with Central and South American customers typically include a great deal of bargaining. Personal relationships are also important in Central and South America, so salespeople should make face-to-face contact with their clients during meetings and presentations.

- **Japan:** Don't bring up business on the golf course—always wait for your host to take the initiative. Don't cross your legs in Japan—showing the bottom of the foot is insulting. Japanese businesspeople shake hands with one firm gesture combined with a slight bow, which should be returned. Japanese prefer gifts from well-known American stores, such as Tiffany's or Saks Fifth Avenue. Also, the higher the position of the recipient, the more elaborately wrapped the gift should be.

- **Mexico:** Don't send a bouquet of red or yellow flowers as a gift—Mexicans associate those colors with evil spirits and death. Instead, send a box of premium chocolates. Including a small gift for the client's children creates a positive impression.

- **Vietnam:** When meeting a Vietnamese woman, wait for her to extend a hand first—she may simply nod or bow slightly, the most common form of greeting in Vietnam. Vietnamese do not like to be touched or patted on the back or shoulders in social situations.

- **Miscellaneous:** The thumbs-up gesture is considered offensive in the Middle East, rude in Australia, and a sign of "OK" in France. It's rude to cross your arms while facing someone in Turkey. In the Middle East don't ask, "How's the family?"—it's considered too personal. In most Asian countries, staring directly into a person's eyes is considered discourteous.[55]

---

panies like Cisco Systems, International Paper, and Johnson Controls, and several thousand other manufacturers would cease to exist without successful salespeople. Even companies like Procter & Gamble and Kraft General Foods that mainly sell consumer goods and use extensive advertising campaigns still rely on salespeople to move products through the channel of distribution. Thus, sales management is one of marketing's most critical specialties. Effective sales management stems from a highly success-oriented sales force that accomplishes its mission economically and efficiently. Poor sales management can lead to unmet profit objectives or even to the downfall of the corporation.

Just as selling is a personal relationship, so is sales management. Although the sales manager's basic job is to maximize sales at a reasonable cost while also maximizing profits, he or she also has many other important responsibilities and decisions:

1. Defining sales goals and the sales process

2. Determining the sales force structure

3. Recruiting and training the sales force

4. Compensating and motivating the sales force

5. Evaluating the sales force

Defining Sales Goals and the Sales Process

quota
A statement of the individual salesperson's sales objectives, usually based on sales volume alone but sometimes including key accounts (those with greatest potential), new accounts, repeat sales, and specific products.

Effective sales management begins with a determination of sales goals. Without goals to achieve, salesperson performance would be mediocre at best, and the company would likely fail. Like any marketing objective, sales goals should be stated in clear, precise, and measurable terms and should always specify a time frame for their fulfillment. Overall sales force goals are usually stated in terms of desired dollar sales volume, market share, or profit level. For example, a life insurance company may have a goal to sell $50 million in life insurance policies annually, to attain a 12 percent market share, or to achieve $1 million in profits. Individual salespeople are also assigned goals in the form of quotas. A **quota** is simply a statement of the salesperson's sales goals, usually based on sales volume alone but sometimes including key accounts (those with greatest potential), new accounts, repeat sales, and specific products.

Great sales managers focus not only on sales goals but also on the entire process that drives their sales organizations to reach those goals. Without a keen understanding of the sales process, a manager will never be successful—no matter how defined the sales goals or how great the sales reps. An important responsibility of the sales manager, therefore, is to determine the most effective and efficient sales process to follow in selling each different product and service. Although the basic steps of the sales process are the same as discussed earlier in the chapter (i.e., lead generation and qualification, approach and needs assessment, proposal creation and presentation, handling objections, closing, and follow-up), a manager must formally define the specific procedures salespeople go through to do their jobs—for example, where leads are generated, how they are qualified, what the best way is to approach potential clients, and what terms can be negotiated during closing. General Electric is one company that focuses on attracting, hiring, and keeping the right salespeople through continuous training and the development of an effective sales process for its sales force. GE has an excellent performance management program that gives an employee concrete goals to meet in order to receive a promotion. The company performs formal reviews three or four times a year and also provides an extensive product- and skills-training program that can last anywhere from one to two years. Salespeople are also rotated through up to five assignments before being placed in a permanent position to see what best suits the individual sales rep. When a GE rep finally makes a call, he or she is completely knowledgeable about the product being sold.[56]

Determining the Sales Force Structure

Because personal selling is so costly, no sales department can afford to be disorganized. Proper design helps the sales manager organize and delegate sales duties and provide direction for salespeople. Sales departments are most commonly organized by geographic regions, by product line, by marketing function performed (such as account development or account maintenance), by market or industry, or by individual client or account. The sales force for IBM could be organized into sales territories covering New England, the Midwest, the South, and the West Coast or could be organized into distinct groups selling personal computer systems and mainframe computer systems. IBM salespeople may also be assigned to a specific industry or market, for example, the telecommunications industry, or to key clients such as AT&T and Sprint.

Market- or industry-based structures and key account structures are gaining popularity in today's competitive selling environment, especially with the emphasis on relationship selling. Being familiar with one industry or market allows sales reps to become experts in their fields and thereby offer better solutions and service. Further, by organizing the sales force around specific customers, many companies hope to improve customer service, encourage collaboration with other arms of the company, and unite salespeople in customer-focused sales teams. Internet advertising solutions company DoubleClick, for example, realigned its 175 salespeople into six vertical industry channels: automotive, business, entertainment and youth, technology, women and health, and travel. Previously, DoubleClick salespeople sold Internet ad space in a variety of different categories. Now salespeople can focus on one category, get a better understanding of the sites with related subject matter, and consult with advertisers about their competition.[57]

Recruiting and Training the Sales Force

Sales force recruitment should be based on an accurate, detailed description of the sales task as defined by the sales manager. Aside from the usual characteristics such as level of experience or education, what traits should sales managers look for in applicants? One of the most important traits of top performers is ego strength, or having a strong, healthy self-esteem and the ability to bounce back from rejection. Great salespeople also have a sense of urgency and competitiveness that pushes their sales to completion. Moreover, they have a desire to persuade people and close the sale. Effective salespeople are also assertive; they have the ability to be firm in one-to-one negotiations, to lead the sales process, and to get their point across confidently, without being overbearing or aggressive. They are sociable, willing to take risks, and capable of understanding complex concepts and ideas. Additionally, great salespeople are creative in developing client solutions, and they possess empathy—the ability to place oneself in someone else's shoes. Not surprisingly, in a recent study of top salespeople, almost 95 percent claim their sales style is relationship oriented rather than transaction oriented.[58]

After the sales recruit has been hired and given a brief orientation, training begins. A new salesperson generally receives instruction in company policies and practices, selling techniques, product knowledge, industry and customer characteristics, and non-selling duties such as filling out sales and market information reports or using a sales automation computer program. Firms that sell complex products generally offer the most extensive

Motivating the sales force is one of the sales managers' toughest jobs. At Wal-Mart Home Office in Bentonville, Arkansas, associates attend a weekly sales meeting that brings executives, management, and associates together in an informal setting.

AP/WIDE WORLD PHOTOS

training programs. Pharmaceutical giant Merck, for example, takes a highly scientific approach to its market and trains its reps to understand the science of the medicine it sells so that they can maintain a peer-to-peer discussion with the physicians they call upon.[59]

Most successful sales organizations have learned that training is not just for newly hired salespeople. Instead, training is offered to all salespeople in an ongoing effort to hone selling skills and relationship building. In pursuit of solid salesperson-client relationships, training programs now seek to improve salespeople's consultative selling and listening skills and to broaden their product and customer knowledge. In addition, training programs stress the interpersonal skills needed to become the contact person for customers. Because negotiation is increasingly important in closing a sale, salespeople are also trained to negotiate effectively without risking profits. A recent international study predicts the corporate on-line learning market will soon surpass the $7 billion mark as more companies reevaluate the high cost of sending one or two employees to a central training classroom. Corel Corporation started an on-line training program to educate its own salespeople. The on-line training has been so successful that it recently was expanded to include customers using Corel products.[60]

Compensating and Motivating the Sales Force

Compensation planning is one of the sales manager's toughest jobs. Only good planning will ensure that compensation attracts, motivates, and retains good salespeople. Generally, companies and industries with lower levels of compensation suffer higher turnover rates, which increase costs and decrease effectiveness. Therefore, compensation needs to be competitive enough to attract and motivate the best salespeople. Firms sometimes take profit into account when developing their compensation plans. Instead of paying salespeople on overall volume, they pay according to the profitability achieved from selling each product. Still other companies tie a part of the salesperson's total compensation to customer satisfaction assessed through periodic customer surveys.

The three basic compensation methods for salespeople are commission, salary, and combination plans. A typical commission plan gives salespeople a specified percentage of their sales revenue. A **straight commission** system compensates the salesperson only when a sale is made. On the other end of the spectrum, a **straight salary** system compensates a salesperson with a stated salary regardless of sales productivity. Most companies, however, offer a compromise between straight commission and straight salary plans. A *combination system* offers a base salary plus an incentive—usually a commission or a bonus. Combination systems have benefits for both the sales manager and the salesperson. The salary portion of the plan helps the manager control the sales force; the incentive provides motivation. For the salesperson, a combination plan offers an incentive to excel while minimizing the extremely wide swings in earnings that may occur when the economy surges or contracts too much.

As the emphasis on relationship selling increases, many sales managers feel that tying a portion of a salesperson's compensation to a client's satisfaction with the salesperson and the company encourages relationship building. To determine this, sales managers can survey clients on a salesperson's ability to create realistic expectations and his or her responsiveness to customer needs.[61] At PeopleSoft, structure, culture, and strategies are built around customer satisfaction. Sales force compensation is tied to both sales quotas and a satisfaction metric that allows clients to voice their opinions on the service given.[62]

Although the compensation plan motivates a salesperson to sell, sometimes it is not enough to produce the volume of sales or the profit margin required by sales management. Sales managers, therefore, often offer rewards or incentives, such as recognition at ceremonies, plaques, vacations, merchandise, and pay raises or cash bonuses. For example, Lorry I. Lokey, president and CEO of Business Wire, invites

straight commission
A method of compensation in which the salesperson is paid some percentage when a sale is made.

straight salary
A method of compensation in which the salesperson receives a salary regardless of sales productivity.

employees from one of the company's twenty-six offices nationwide to join him on a free trip to a predetermined location, usually overseas. To qualify, employees must have celebrated their five-year anniversary with the company.[63] But, of course, the most popular incentives are cash rewards, used by 64 percent of sales organizations polled in a recent survey.[64] Rewards may help increase overall sales volume, add new accounts, improve morale and goodwill, move slow items, and bolster slow sales. They can be used to achieve long-term or short-term objectives, such as unloading overstocked inventory and meeting a monthly or quarterly sales goal.

Motivation also takes the form of effective sales leadership on the part of the sales manager. An effective sales manager is inspirational to his or her salespeople, encouraging them to achieve their goals through clear and enthusiastic communications. He or she has a clear vision and commitment to the mission of the organization and the ability to instill pride and earn the respect of employees. Effective sales leaders continuously increase their knowledge and skill base while also encouraging others to do so. A recent study that assessed the attributes of sales leaders found that the best sales leaders share a number of key personality traits (see Exhibit 16.5), such as a sense of urgency, openness to new ideas, and a desire to take risks. These traits separate motivational sales leaders from mere sales managers.

Evaluating the Sales Force

The final task of sales managers is evaluating the effectiveness and performance of the sales force. To evaluate the sales force, the sales manager needs feedback—that is, regular information from salespeople. Typical performance measures include sales volume, contribution to profit, calls per order, sales or profits per call, or percentage of calls achieving specific goals such as sales of products that the firm is heavily promoting.

Exhibit 16.5

Seven Key Leadership Traits of Effective Sales Leaders

Effective sales leaders . . .	
Are assertive	Assertive sales leaders know when and how to get tough and how to assert their authority.
Possess ego drive	Sales leaders with ego drive have the desire and ability to persuade their reps to take action.
Possess ego strength	Sales leaders with ego strength are able to make sure not only that they bounce back from rejection but also that their reps rebound, too.
Take risks	Risk-taking sales leaders are willing to go out on a limb in an effort to make a sale or enhance a relationship.
Are innovative	Innovative sales leaders stay open to new ideas and new ways of conducting business.
Have a sense of urgency	Urgent sales leaders understand that getting things done now is critical to winning and keeping business.
Are empathetic	Empathetic sales leaders help their reps grow by listening and understanding.

SOURCE: Table adapted from "The 7 Traits of Great Sales Leaders" by Geoffrey Brewer, *Sales & Marketing Management*, July 1997, 38–46. Reprinted with permission.

Performance information helps the sales manager monitor a salesperson's progress through the sales cycle and pinpoint where breakdowns may be occurring. For example, by knowing the number of prospects an individual salesperson has in each step of the sales cycle process and determining where prospects are falling out of the sales cycle, a manager can determine how effective a salesperson may be at lead generation, needs assessment, proposal generation, presenting, closing, and follow-up stages. This information can then tell a manager what sales skills may need to be reassessed or retrained. For example, if a sales manager notices that a sales rep seems to be letting too many prospects slip away after presenting proposals, it may mean he or she needs help with developing proposals, handling objections, or closing sales.

The Impact of Technology on Personal Selling

Will the increasingly sophisticated technology now available at marketers' fingertips eliminate the need for salespeople? Experts agree that a relationship between the salesperson and customer will always be necessary. Technology, however, can certainly help to improve that relationship.[65] Cellphones, laptops, pagers, e-mail, and electronic organizers allow salespeople to be more accessible to both clients and the company. Moreover, the Internet provides salespeople with vast resources of information on clients, competitors, and the industry. In fact, many companies are utilizing technology to stay more in touch with their own employees. For instance, IBM invited 320,000 employees to an electronic brainstorming session. A total of 52,600 employees logged on to the event to discuss issues of employee retention, work efficiency, quality, and teamwork.[66]

E-business, or buying, selling, marketing, collaborating with partners, and servicing customers electronically using the Internet, is also having a significant impact on personal selling. In 2002, almost 100 percent of large companies, more than 80 percent of medium-sized companies, and almost 50 percent of small companies were engaged in e-commerce.[67] Additionally, 85 percent of business respondents regard e-business as vital to their company's success.[68] For customers, the Web has become a powerful tool to get accurate and up-to-date information on products, pricing, and order status. The Internet also cost-effectively processes orders and services requests. Although on the surface the Internet might look like a threat to the job security of salespeople, the Web is actually freeing sales reps from tedious administrative tasks, like shipping catalogs, placing routine orders, or tracking orders. This leaves them more time to focus on the needs of their clients. At Carlson Wagonlit Travel, for instance, shifting sales of routine products like short-haul shuttle flights to the Web is freeing up travel agents to do more outbound selling to high-potential customers.[69]

CONNECT IT

As you think back to the opening story, recall how entrepreneur Mark Cuban turned the Dallas Mavericks basketball team around with an aggressive sales program. The sales force, which grew from five to thirty-five, was given clear sales objectives, strong motivation through an incentive plan and a culture that focused on success, and a proven sales process that emphasized building strong customer relationships. Moreover, salespeople were trained to sell the entertainment aspect of Mavericks games and not the team's win–loss record because regardless of whether the team is winning or losing, fans have to be sold on the product—the games. With this aggressive sales program, the Mavericks' attendance increased as did their TV ratings. An aggressive sales program is a very effective competitive tool for sales managers.

Get Free Product Samples On-line
Receive free samples of consumer products by registering on-line at **http://www.FreeSamples.com** and **http://www.StartSampling.com**. There you can choose from a variety of free products, such as beauty aids, pet food, and new food products. In exchange, you provide marketers with feedback on what you liked and didn't like about the product.

Sell Yourself
Go to Amazon.com and under the search engine type "selling yourself." Order one or more books available to improve your sell-ing skills. Also, consider a Dale Carnegie training course. For more information, go to **http://www.dale-carnegie.com/**.

Looking for a Sales Job?
Find job leads in the *Sales & Marketing Management* magazine careers section at **http://www.salesandmarketing.com**. Or visit popular employment site Monster.com (**http://www.monster.com**) and use its searchable database to search for sales opportunities in a specific geographic area. You can also post your résumé at these and a number of other employment sites.

REVIEW IT

1 **Define and state the objectives of sales promotion.** Sales promotion consists of those marketing communication activities, other than advertising, personal selling, and public relations, in which a short-term incentive motivates consumers or members of the distribution channel to purchase a good or service immediately, either by lowering the price or by adding value. The main objectives of sales promotion are to increase trial purchases, consumer inventories, and repeat purchases. Sales promotion is also used to encourage brand switching and to build brand loyalty. Sales promotion supports advertising activities.

1.1 **WRITING** You have recently been assigned the task of developing promotional techniques to introduce your company's new product, a Cajun chicken sandwich. Advertising spending is limited, so the introduction will include only some low-budget sales promotion techniques. Write a sales promotion plan that will increase awareness of your new sandwich and allow your customer base to try it risk-free.

2 **Discuss the most common forms of consumer sales promotion.** Consumer forms of sales promotion include coupons and rebates, premiums, loyalty marketing programs, contests and sweepstakes, sampling, and point-of-purchase displays. Coupons are certificates entitling consumers to an immediate price reduction when they purchase a product or service. Coupons are a particularly good way to encourage product trial and brand switching. Similar to coupons, rebates provide purchasers with a price reduction, although it is not immediate. To receive a rebate, consumers generally must mail in a rebate form with a proof of purchase. Premiums offer an extra item or incentive to the consumer for buying a product or service. Premiums reinforce the consumer's purchase decision, increase consumption, and persuade nonusers to switch brands. Rewarding loyal customers is the basis of loyalty marketing programs. Loyalty programs are extremely effective at building long-term, mutually beneficial relationships between a company and its key customers. Contests and sweepstakes are generally designed to create interest, often to encourage brand switching. Because consumers perceive risk in trying new products, sampling is an effective method for gaining new customers. Finally, point-of-purchase displays set up at the retailer's location build traffic, advertise the product, and induce impulse buying.

2.1 Discuss how different forms of sales promotion can erode or build brand loyalty. If a company's objective is to enhance customer loyalty to its products, what sales promotion techniques will be most appropriate?

2.2 What forms of consumer sales promotion might induce impulse purchases? What forms of sales promotion are more effective at persuading consumers to switch brands?

2.3 Form a three-person team. Go to the local grocery store and write down all of the forms of sales promotion you see, including company name, product being promoted, form of promotion, and objective. Also, make a note of the sales promotion's message or offer, such as "two-for-one" or "cents off." Create a table that lists this information; then rate the effectiveness of each one, in your opinion, on a scale from 1 to 5 where 1 is "poor" and 5 is "excellent." Present a summary of your findings to the class. What kind of conclusions can you draw about product type and promotion?

2.4 Visit the site **http://www.ci.cendant.com**. How does this company help on-line businesses conduct loyalty marketing programs? Present some examples.

2.5 Not everyone thinks supermarket shopper cards are a bargain. Go to **http://www.nocards.org**. and read several pages. Is the information on the site compelling? What do you think of shopper cards? You may want to use the Internet to research shopper cards in more detail before forming an opinion.

③ List the most common forms of trade sales promotion. Manufacturers use many of the same sales promotion tools used in consumer promotions, such as sales contests, premiums, and point-of-purchase displays. In addition, manufacturers and channel intermediaries use several unique promotional strategies: trade allowances, push money, training programs, free merchandise, store demonstrations, and meetings, conventions, and trade shows.

3.1 How does trade sales promotion differ from consumer sales promotion? How is it the same?

3.2 Form a team of three to five students. As marketing managers, you are in charge of selling Dixie cups. Design a consumer sales promotion plan and trade sales promotion plan for your product. Incorporate at least three different promotion tools into each plan. Share your results with the other teams in the class.

④ Describe personal selling. Personal selling is direct communication between a sales representative and one or more prospective buyers in an attempt to influence each other in a purchase situation. Broadly speaking, all businesspeople use personal selling to promote themselves and their ideas. Personal selling offers several advantages over other forms of promotion. Personal selling allows sales-people to thoroughly explain and demonstrate a product. Salespeople have the flexibility to tailor a sales proposal to the needs and preferences of individual customers. Personal selling is more efficient than other forms of promotion because salespeople target qualified prospects and avoid wasting efforts on unlikely buyers. Personal selling affords greater managerial control over promotion costs. Finally, personal selling is the most effective method of closing a sale and producing satisfied customers.

4.1 Discuss the role of personal selling in promoting products. What advantages does personal selling offer over other forms of promotion?

⑤ Discuss the key differences between relationship selling and traditional selling. Relationship selling is the practice of building, maintaining, and enhancing interactions with customers in order to develop long-term satisfaction through mutually beneficial partnerships. Traditional selling, on the other hand, is transaction focused. That is, the salesperson is most concerned with making one-time sales and moving on to the next prospect. Salespeople practicing relationship selling spend more time understanding a prospect's needs and developing solutions to meet those needs.

5.1 What are the key differences between relationship selling and traditional methods of selling? What types of products or services do you think would be conducive to relationship selling?

6 List the steps in the selling process. The selling process is composed of seven basic steps: (1) generating leads, (2) qualifying leads, (3) assessing approach and needs, (4) developing and proposing solutions, (5) handling objections, (6) closing the sale, and (7) following up.

6.1 You are a new salesperson for a well-known medical software company, and one of your clients is a large group of physicians. You have just arranged an initial meeting with the office manager. Develop a list of questions you might ask at this meeting to uncover the group's specific needs.

6.2 What does sales follow-up entail? Why is it an essential step in the selling process, particularly from the perspective of relationship selling? How does it relate to cognitive dissonance?

7 Describe the functions of sales management. Sales management is a critical area of marketing that performs several important functions. Sales managers set overall company sales goals and define the sales process most effective for achieving those goals. They determine sales force structure based on geographic, product, functional, or customer variables. Managers develop the sales force through recruiting and training. Sales management motivates the sales force through compensation planning, motivational tools, and effective sales leadership. Finally, sales managers evaluate the sales force through salesperson feedback and other methods of determining their performance.

7.1 *INFOTRAC COLLEGE EDITION*   ON LINE   Managing a sales force in today's e-business environment can be difficult, especially with the Internet perceived as a threat to job security. Use InfoTrac (**http://www.infotrac-college.com**) to locate an article in *Electronic News* titled, "Creating a Web-Savvy Sales Force" by Wally York. Read the article and list York's key elements. How does this tie in with what you read in the chapter?

7.2 *TEAM*   With two classmates, select a company or business near campus that has a sales force. Using York's article (from question 7.1) as a starting point, list all the things the company would need to do to create an e-savvy sales force.

7.3 *INFOTRAC COLLEGE EDITION*   Without revenue, a company cannot survive, and sales is the means to that end. How important is the effectiveness of a company's sales force? Use InfoTrac (**http://www.infotrac-college.com**) to run a keyword search for "sales force" or "sales force automation." Skim six to ten articles and write down all the automation tools (software and hardware) that you discover.

DEFINE IT

cold calling 541
consumer sales promotion 528
coupon 529
follow-up 546
frequent buyer program 531
lead generation (prospecting) 540
lead qualification 542
loyalty marketing program 531
needs assessment 543

negotiation 545
networking 541
point-of-purchase display 533
preapproach 542
premium 530
push money 535
quota 548
rebate 530
referral 540
relationship selling (consultative selling) 538

sales presentation 544
sales process (sales cycle) 539
sales proposal 544
sampling 532
straight commission 550
straight salary 550
trade allowance 535
trade sales promotion 528

Application for Entrepreneurs

Morgan's is a retail clothing store offering high-quality, reasonably priced merchandise. Its target markets include students at the local university and working individuals, primarily in the age range eighteen to thirty-five. The location is about three miles from the campus in an upscale strip center next to a small, local mall. For several years the owner has been using several student interns as part-time salespersons and assistant managers. He has been able to find good workers, but turnover is high and training new employees takes a lot of time. Also, his sales training has consisted mostly of asking new student interns to review the internship reports of former student employees. To reduce these problems, he has considered hiring a college graduate full-time and fewer part-time interns. The full-time employee should reduce turnover and the need for repeated training and be able to help him develop a better sales training approach. He pays the interns between $7 and $10 per hour, depending on their experience. College graduates would have to be paid between $27,000 and $30,000 per year plus benefits.

Questions

1. What factors must be considered in making this decision?
2. Should he hire a college graduate as a full-time employee? Why?

THINK ABOUT IT

Ethics Exercise

Bruce Jackson sells air conditioners for Comfort Heating and Air Conditioning. He is having a very good year and hopes to win the incentive trip his company awards the top salesperson each year. With one quarter in the year left to go, Bruce learns that another salesperson has slightly higher sales. He also learns that the other salesperson is exaggerating product benefits in his sales pitch but company officials seem to be looking the other way.

Questions

1. What should Bruce do?
2. Does the AMA Code of Ethics address this issue in its Code of Ethics? Go to **http://www.marketingpower.com** and review the code. Then, write a brief paragraph describing how the AMA Code of Ethics relates to this issue.

TRY IT

Entrepreneurship Case
Varsity Group: The Campus Bookstore Alternative

The U.S. market for educational textbooks is roughly an $8 billion industry, with U.S. college students spending $4-5 billion each year purchasing over seventy million textbooks needed for classes. With the industry averaging 7 percent annual growth, the marketing implications—and opportunities—can be huge, but so can the challenges. Varsity Group knows this probably better than most.

The company burst onto the college campus scene in 1998 ready to turn what is now a $10 billion-a-year campus store retail business on its ear by providing an on-line store where college students could buy their books and supplies at a discount. When the company first launched its on-line storefront, VarsityBooks.com, only about 1 percent of college textbooks were sold via the Web. But with close to 100 percent of college students using the Internet and over 70 percent logging on daily, the potential for Varsity Group and other on-line textbook retailers to make it big was enormous. On-line textbook retailers offered all the conveniences of Internet shopping, such as round-the-clock service and a wider selection than the campus bookstore could offer. And because Varsity Group had no brick-and-mortar storefront and few storage costs, it could sell some textbooks for as much as 40 percent less than traditional textbook sellers.

Initially, Varsity Group succeeded in the on-line textbook market because of its highly creative, albeit unusual, promotional tactics. Instead of putting its entire promotional budget into buying ads in the campus newspaper or on local radio stations, Varsity Group would recruit college students to help promote its Web site on college campuses and to persuade their classmates to purchase their textbooks from the company's Web site instead of at inconvenient campus bookstores where prices are higher. At one point, close to three thousand students on six hundred U.S. campuses signed on to become representatives for Varsity Group. Campus reps received hourly and commission-based wages and the freedom to execute their own campaigns. Lead campus reps enjoyed business cards, stock options, a PalmPilot, and a flexible budget. Student reps also attended biannual training programs to listen to speakers on marketing best practices, case studies, codes of conduct, and team management skills.

Some of the more interesting grassroots promotional and sales techniques to student reps used to promote VarsityBooks.com included sponsoring parties, dressing local bands in VarsityBooks.com t-shirts, and handing out candy bars, granola bars, and lollipops with VarsityBooks.com coupons. At Florida State University, campus reps used sidewalk chalk to pen messages such as "Smashing Savings" on sidewalks around campus. At Stanford University, Varsity reps passed out coupons at a nearby movie theater. Other reps distributed price comparison flyers for particular courses at classroom doorways.

Immediately, there was a high level of interest from students nationwide, forcing college bookstores to respond quickly and become more competitive on prices and improve their service levels. With these enhancements made at the nearby college bookstore, students could generally get their textbooks more quickly and easily on campus. Within two years, Varsity Group was changing its business model to address the new marketplace. Confident that there was still a role for an on-line campus bookstore, the company shifted its focus from selling textbooks directly to students to a more institutional approach that offered an on-line bookstore solution for private secondary schools and colleges. Rather than an army of student sales reps, Varsity Groups now employs an in-house sales force dedicated to the entire sales process.

For roughly six months out of the year, in-house account managers work to generate leads about educational institutions in need of a viable bookstore option. Managers are looking for the many smaller, private schools and colleges that are no longer able to underwrite the expense of an independent campus bookstore or that no longer want the hassle of managing one. Through its eduPartners program, Varsity Group enrolled over one hundred and forty such institutions in 2002.

Once account managers have identified schools that would be good candidates for the eduPartners program, senior sales representatives take over to complete the sales process. This includes visiting the campus and assessing the full needs of the potential client. This process can take anywhere from one month to one year, and schools that join typically start using VarsityBooks the following semester, so Varsity Group now has a sales cycle that could stretch to twelve months or longer. Since the target customer has changed from the student buying the book to the school providing the service of a bookstore, the sales force has taken a more consultative approach to its sales strategy. That is, the student reps spent a great deal of time in designing and implementing creative promotional strategies to attract student customers. Now, the in-house sales reps spend more time building relationships with Varsity Group's eduPartners, listening to their needs and developing solutions to match them: eduPartners receive a high level of service at a reasonable price and lose all the hassles of managing and financing a campus store.

Although Varsity Group has changed its sales strategy from a customer focus to an institutional focus, the company continues to look for unique market segments and opportunities by leveraging a novel approach in its marketing efforts. The student reps were the first way the company did this; being the first on-line bookstore solution for smaller schools is the current way the company is doing this.

Questions

1. What can you deduce about the textbook market from Varsity Group's new sales strategy?

2. What can you deduce about Varsity Group's promotional goals from the changes it has made to its business model?

3. You are a sales rep for Varsity Group and are working with potential clients, who are not entirely convinced that eduPartners will work for their campus. Anticipate objections that they may raise and address them positively. You may consult the Varsity-Books.com Web site at **http://www.varsitybooks.com** as a resource.

WATCH IT

Short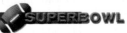

The *Marketing* PowerPoint CD-ROM has two video ad clips embedded in the Chapter 16 slide presentation. Identify the issues in the Pizza Hut and Ruffles ads that make them a good fit for this chapter.

Medium

Licensing is a popular way to expand the potential of a brand. This CNN clip takes you to a licensing trade show to see how cartoon characters are licensed and promoted. Is this a typical trade show? What brands (i.e., characters) do you recognize? Recall information from Chapter 4 as you view the clip.

Long   **SmallBusinessSchool** ◘
the Series on PBS stations and the Web

For Chapter 16, Small Business School takes us inside the world of Ann and Michael McGilvray, founders of AMCI. AMCI is a sales agency with over ninety sales reps covering twenty-two states. Have you ever bought a rubber bug? It may very well have been sold to the store where you bought it by Ann McGilvray or one of her reps. Let's see what the woman who has sold everything from greeting cards to glow-in-the-dark cockroaches has to say about personal selling and sales management. AMCI also offers a great example of sales management as well as marketing channels. So recall the material you learned about in Chapter 12 as you turn your attention to the AMCI Master Class.

FLIP IT

 Flip to Chapter 16 in your *Grademaker Study Guide* for more review opportunities, including the pretest, vocabulary review, Internet activities, study test questions, and an application exercise based on promotion and personal selling concepts. What are the objectives of sales promotion? Do you know the difference between traditional selling and relationship selling? If not, pick up your *Grademaker* and review.

CLICK IT

 The *Marketing* Web site links you to all the Internet-based activities in this chapter, like the "Use It," "Review It" questions 2.4, 2.5, 7.1, and 7.3, "Think About It," and the On-Line exercises in the chapter margins. As a review, do the Chapter 16 quiz and crossword puzzle. And don't forget the Career Exersite that shows you resources for exploring marketing career opportunities in personal selling. Review the main concepts in the PowerPoint presentation for Chapter 16, too. Go to **http://lamb.swlearning.com**, read the material, and follow the links right from the site.

MARKETING MISCUES

Duracell's Duck Is Turned Off

The Duracell division of The Gillette Company is a worldwide leader in the manufacturing and marketing of high-performance alkaline batteries; its Duracell Coppertop battery is one of the most popular alkaline batteries in the world. In June 2001, Duracell introduced an improved line of Duracell Coppertop alkaline batteries. In November 2001, the company announced the debut of "Mr. Quackers" as the star of a new television advertising campaign. By early 2002, however, the company had to stop running the ad. Battery competitor Energizer had accused Duracell of false and misleading advertising.

Founded in 1901, Gillette is a world-renowned consumer-products company. It operates in three major consumer businesses: grooming, portable power, and oral care. Skillful marketing and superior technology are hallmarks of Gillette's success. The company's vision focuses on building its brands by delivering consumer value faster and better than its competition. The company's success at achieving its vision is reflected in the fact that more than one billion people around the world use one or more Gillette products daily. All three of the company's major businesses within Gillette are world leaders in their markets.

With the proliferation of portable electronic devices, the premium battery market in the United States had become a $2.5 billion segment by 2001. The two market leaders were Duracell and Energizer. Though Energizer, long known for its Energizer bunny, held a sizable share of this premium segment, Duracell was, by far, the market share leader with almost 50 percent share of the U.S. alkaline battery market. Nevertheless, 75 percent of the world's battery consumers still used the less costly zinc carbon battery, a lower performing battery. Hence, a huge market opportunity existed if consumers could be persuaded to switch from zinc carbon to alkaline batteries.

Recognizing this vast market potential, both Duracell and Energizer decided to refocus their 2001 promotional efforts on their flagship brands. For Duracell, this meant focusing on the new and improved version of its flagship Coppertop brand, which incorporated the company's revolutionary M3 technology—more fuel, more efficiency, and more power. The battery line consisted of AA, AAA, C, D, and 9-volt sizes. Additionally, Duracell offered a line of specialty batteries for use in items such as cameras, hearing aids, and watches.

New York–based BBDO created "Mr. Quackers" to star in Duracell's new television advertising campaign for the improved battery. Mr. Quackers was a cute little robotic duck whose alkaline power outlasted that of three remote-controlled villains (Dr. Shred, The Incinerator, and The Black Widow) who were powered by heavy-duty batteries. The ad closed with the claim that Duracell Coppertop batteries lasted up to three times longer than heavy-duty or super heavy-duty batteries. The commercial, part of a $100 million global ad and marketing campaign, was targeted to air during prime-time, daytime, late-night, syndicated, cable, and Hispanic programming in North America.

With such an unassuming star in the ad, Gillette, Duracell, and BBDO were surprised when Energizer filed a lawsuit alleging false and misleading advertising. Gillette's ad touted the durability of its Duracell Coppertop battery over zinc. Energizer felt that the commercials led consumers to believe that only Duracell alkaline batteries were more durable than zinc batteries, when, in fact, all alkaline batteries (including those made by Energizer) outperform zinc batteries.

Questions

1. What were the goals of the "Mr. Quackers" ad?
2. Why was Duracell using this form of comparative advertising?

Philip Morris Companies, Inc., Changes Its Name to Altria Group

What's in a name? Can a new name change a company's image? Do people really think of Philip Morris when they are buying Altoids mints, Jell-O, Maxwell House coffee, Philadelphia cream cheese, or Kraft macaroni and cheese? Will a name change help Philip Morris clarify who and what the company is?

The Holding Company

Named in the nineteenth century after the company's founder, Philip Morris Companies, Inc., (**http://www.philipmorris.com**), is the world's largest producer and marketer of consumer package goods. With annual sales of almost $100 billion and a workforce of 178,000 people, the company is home to many well-known food products. Subsidiaries within the Philip Morris Companies include the following:

- *Kraft Foods North America:* Headquartered in Illinois, Kraft Foods North America is the largest packaged food company in the United Staes and Canada. The company offers beverages (coffee and soft drinks), breakfast cereals (Post), salad dressings, snacks, toppings (Dream Whip), cheese (Velveeta), condiments and sauces, confectioneries (Toblerone), dry desserts (D-Zerta), dry grocery products (Calumet), ethnic foods (Taco Bell grocery brand), meals/side dishes (Stove Top), dairy products (Breyer's), fresh pasta and sauces (Di-Giorno), processed meats (Oscar Mayer), pickles and sauerkraut (Claussen), and pizza (Tombstone).
- *Kraft Foods International:* Operating in over a hundred countries, Kraft Foods International is the largest food company based in the United States. The company offers many Kraft products, as well as products tailored specifically to individual countries. Brands include Gallito, Prince Polo, and Suchard (snacks); Frisco, Kool-Aid, and Tang (powdered soft drinks); Dairylea and Sottilette (cheese); El Caserio and Simenthal (convenient meals); Bird's, O'Boy, Royal, and Vegemite (grocery); Cerealitas, Club Social, and Trakinas (biscuits); Estreall and Maarud (salty snacks); and Carte Noire, Jacobs, Maxim, and Splendid (coffee).
- *Philip Morris U.S.A.:* As the leading U.S. cigarette manufacturer, the company develops, manufactures, and markets the following tobacco products: Marlboro, Virginia Slims, Benson & Hedges, Merit, Parliament, Alpine, Basic, Cambridge, Bristol, Bucks, Chesterfield, Collector's Choice, Commander, English Ovals, Lark, L&M, Saratoga, and Superslims.

- *Philip Morris International, Inc.:* This group is the world's leading international cigarette group. The company offers around eighty brands of cigarettes worldwide. Subsidiaries and affiliates of Philip Morris International are responsible for manufacturing, marketing, selling, and distributing the company's cigarette products. Latin American affiliates also offer a wide variety of food and beverage products under the Philip Morris International umbrella.

Altria Group

In an effort to separate the company's food businesses from its tobacco businesses, Philip Morris Companies has proposed to change the holding company's name to Altria Group. The company's subsidiaries, with considerable brand equity in both the business-to-business and consumer markets, will keep their current individual company names. The new name will not appear on any of the company's products.

The new name, Altria, comes from the Latin word *altus,* which means to reach higher. (Not all Latin scholars agree on the derivation of the word. One scholar observed that Altria could just as easily have come from the Latin word *altrix,* which means wet nurse.) Landor Associates, part of the Young & Rubicam division of the WPP Group, assisted in the selection of the new corporate name. The new name is intended to reflect the company's growth and diversification into consumer products and to underscore its efforts to achieve even stronger financial performance, all the while promoting a greater understanding of corporate social responsibility. The new corporate logo will be a square with multicolored squares within it.

Critics of the new name attribute the name change to an attempt to move away from the company's image as a tobacco company. Antismoking groups are concerned that if it succeeds in shedding its tobacco company image, the company will face less criticism from socially conscious groups, become more sought after for charitable support, and improve its recruiting efforts at top business schools. All the while, the company will still be producing and marketing its dominant tobacco products.

The name change is also attracting concern from two other companies. Altria Healthcare, a specialist in health-care accounting management and practice located in Alabama, is concerned that a tobacco and alcohol company is adopting a name identical to that of a health-care business. Likewise, The

Altira Group, a venture capital group based in Colorado, is bothered by the similarity in the two names. This is particularly worrisome since the Philip Morris Capital Corporation, which could someday be renamed Altria Corporation, is an investment firm like Altira.

Questions

1. Why is Philip Morris making this name change?
2. What are the possible positive and negative effects of the name change?

3. How can the new name, Altria, be used in the company's promotional efforts?
4. Should the company use the name Altria in conjunction with its subsidiaries? Why or why not?

MARKETING PLANNING ACTIVITIES

To complete all eleven activities, use the Part 5 Marketing Planning Worksheets on your Xtra! CD-ROM. If you need a company for the basis of your work, follow the "Marketing Plan Project" link on the *Marketing* Web site (**http://lamb.swlearning.com**).

Integrated Marketing Communications

For continued general assistance on business plans and marketing plans, visit **http://www.bplans.com** or **http://www.businessplans.org**. For electronic sources of information, search on the Electric Library at **http://wwws.elibrary.com** or the Internet Public Library at **http://www.ipl.org**. Another excellent source of information is the Sales and Marketing Executives Marketing Library at **http://www.sell.org**. You should also refer to Exhibit 2.7 for additional marketing plan checklist items (Part IV.B.3: Marketing Mix—Promotion).

You began your strategic marketing plan by stating your business mission and objectives and conducting a detailed SWOT analysis. In the second part of the plan, you identified and described target market segments and identified sources of competitive intelligence and the need for further marketing research. Next, you began the process of defining the marketing mix, starting with the components of product and distribution.

The next stage of the strategic planning process continues the task of defining the elements of the marketing mix, and this section focuses on promotions. If you are working with an electronic offering, integrating promotional communications seamlessly presents unique challenges for the marketer because Web-based strategies are so different from traditional media. Even so, it is important to consider all parts of the promotion mix, including advertising, public relations, sales promotion, and personal selling. An excellent on-line resource with many links to promotion sites is **http://advertising.utexas.edu/world**.

Use the following exercises to guide you through the promotions part of your strategic marketing plan:

1. Define your promotional objectives. What specific results do you hope to accomplish, and which promotional tools will be responsible? How will you use promotions to differentiate yourself from your competition? Remember that promotions cannot be directly tied to sales because too many other factors (competition, environment, price, distribution, product, customer service, company reputation, and so on) affect sales. State specific objectives that can be tied directly to the result of promotional activities—for example, number of people redeeming a coupon, share of audience during a commercial, percentage attitude change after a telemarketing campaign, or number of people calling a toll-free information hotline. Remember to have off-line promotions drive on-line traffic as well.

2. Design a promotional message or theme. Does this message inform, remind, persuade, or educate the target market? Make sure this message will work across both traditional and electronic media. How is your promotional message consistent with your branding? Is this message or slogan unique and important enough to be copyrighted? Check with the U.S. Copyright Office at **http://lcweb.loc.gov/copyright**.

3. Will you be designing and producing all your promotional tools in-house, or do you need to find an agency? What are the advantages of designing promotional tools in-house? Disadvantages? Try **http://www.agencyfinder.com** for assistance with your decision or investigate **http://pwr.com/creative** to find additional creative talent to enhance your own work.

4. Investigate different media placement rates (such as for a school newspaper, local newspaper, national newspaper, local radio station, local TV station, general or specialty interest magazine, local billboard, transit advertising, or the Internet). You can either call local media or consult *Standard Rate and Data Services (SRDS)*. Which media should your firm use? Which media can your firm afford? When should media be used? To request on-line media kits from both traditional and electronic media sources, go to the Kit Director at **http://www.mediadirector.com**. Additionally, you can register to get free advertising and rate information from **http://www.adratecard.com**, which provides information about radio, newspaper, magazine, television, outdoor, and Internet media rates and buying.

5. Do an Internet-only firm and a firm with an established brick-and-mortar presence have different advertising concerns? If so, what are they? Design the advertising for each medium selected in question 4. Do all advertising pieces carry a uniform theme and style? Is there sufficient information about benefits offered to consumers? Do customers have an option for obtaining further information?

6. List the public relations activities that your company should do. Be sure to make them consistent with your branding and other promotions. In addition, write a plan for handling bad publicity. Bad publicity travels at light speed over the Internet and is much more of a challenge to an e-marketer. Check out **http://urbanlegends.about.com** to see how misinformation can travel the Internet and cause public relations nightmares for companies. Think about using a news clipping service for your company (such as the one you hired to gather competitive intelligence earlier). For further public relations resources, visit **http://www.aboutpr.com**. Sharpspider helps companies with press submissions of all sorts (**http://www.sharpspider.com**).

7. Evaluate or create printed materials for your chosen company (such as data sheets, brochures, stationery, or rate cards). Does the literature suffi-

ciently answer questions? Provide enough information for further contact? Effectively promote product features and customer service? Note a competitive advantage?

8. Think about ways your promotions could turn a first-time customer or deal-hunter into a repeat, loyal customer. Which sales promotion tools should your company use? What trade shows could your firm attend? Search the *Eventline* database for trade shows appropriate to your firm. Order media kits and explore the feasibility and costs of attending those trade shows. For a listing of trade shows, go to **http://www.exhibitornet.com** and look for the directory of shows, or the Trade Show News Network at **http://www.tsnn.com**. What about on-line coupons? There are dozens of on-line coupon sites that you can find with any search engine. What about promotional products? Try **http://www.promotionalproducts.com** for help.

9. What other sales promotion tools could your firm use? What are the costs? What is the impact of using these methods on pricing?

10. Will you need a sales force? Identify and justify the best type (internal or external) and structure (product, customer, geographic, etc.) for your firm's sales force. You may find that in e-marketing, a sales force is more of a customer service and customer relations management tool. True selling activities may be limited to selling and buying on-line media space and links. In many circumstances, strategic partnerships and distribution deals have replaced traditional sales in the Internet space. What types of alliances and partnerships will you pursue? Will you work with other on-line firms, off-line firms, or both?

11. Explore the Internet to research your company, its competition, and the industry in general. How are advertising and promotion being handled in this medium?

CROSS-FUNCTIONAL CONNECTIONS SOLUTIONS

Understanding Marketing Communications' Contribution to Firm Value

Questions

1. Why is a company's marketing communications of particular concern to research and development and manufacturing?

Marketers have a tendency to refer to product quality in their communications with potential customers. However, it is not the marketing department that develops and produces the actual product. The R&D and manufacturing groups provide the physical product that marketing presents to customers. If a customer is dissatisfied with the product's quality, then it is typically the "hands-on" groups that are blamed for the low-quality product.

2. Why do financial managers view advertising and promotional expenditures as costs?

Financial managers believe there is a direct correlation between advertising and promotional expenditures and sales. In recognizing this relationship, financial managers view these expenditures as variable costs, thinking that one directly affects the other. Financial analysts are result oriented and ultimately will base their allocation of funds on whether or not the product is selling; they view an increase in sales as "money well spent." Unfortunately, viewing this relationship as such can be detrimental to the product; advertising budgets may be cut, based on low sales numbers, when they are needed most. These expenditures should be viewed as fixed costs, unrelated to sales increases or decreases.

3. How has personal selling become functionally integrated?

Personal selling has become functionally integrated in many ways. One major change in the salesperson's skill set has become the need to possess intimate knowledge of the products being presented to a customer. It is no longer sufficient to have great personal interacting skills—the salesperson has to clearly understand the products he or she is presenting. Another major area of integration has been the involvement of R&D and manufacturing in customer visits. Finance, accounting, and human resources are taking a much stronger role in the sales process with regard to compensation systems, cross selling, and teamwork.

Suggested Readings

Bob Donath, "Tell Bean Counters Your Variable Is Fixed," *Marketing News*, June 19, 2000, 14.

Erin Strout, "Planning to Profit from National Accounts," *Sales and Marketing Management*, October 1999, 107.

PART 6

Pricing Decisions

PRICING TO SATISFY BOTH INTERNAL AND EXTERNAL DEMANDS

Pricing is the one element of the marketing mix that is "owned" by multiple groups within a company. As such, there is considerable cross-functional input into the pricing decision process. Unfortunately, there is usually little agreement across functions as to the best price to give a particular product.

Marketing is interested in pricing to provide value to the customer, while meeting competitors' prices. Since costs determine the floor on prices, the accounting group has traditionally identified with a cost-plus pricing approach. Naturally, finance has a keen interest in the pricing process in relation to its targets for return on investment. The relationship between price and demand has downstream effects on the manufacturing process, bringing production capabilities into the pricing decisions—particularly in relation to the company's ability to produce the number of units needed to break even. Research and development pays close attention to the introductory price of the product since this is considered to be the point at which development costs are recouped. With all of these interested parties, it is hard to say if any one particular functional group is actually in charge of the final pricing decision!

The pricing decision must be viewed as an interactive process. There is a strong need for cross-functional interaction. For example, if marketing identifies an initial price as too high to capture customer interest, R&D and manufacturing must be consulted to see if product features, product materials, or assembly processes can be modified to decrease costs. Finance and accounting must be involved in reevaluating appropriate margins.

Probably one of the major breakthroughs in the cross-functional ownership of the pricing process has been activity-based costing (ABC). Just as marketing and manufacturing have long focused on product customization, ABC provides the capability to customize price. The method requires input from marketing, accounting, and manufacturing. Essentially, ABC uses cost drivers to assign costs. The process requires a clear market segmentation approach based on customer needs. Activity-based costing allows the company to determine what will have to be

done to satisfy customers' needs and assign a cost to each of these activities. In this way, firms can distinguish between the truly profitable customers and those who may purchase in volume but require so much work (activities) that they are actually unprofitable customers.

Marketers have long realized the importance of accounting information in the pricing process. Tactically, marketers have long recognized that accurate cost data are needed to make good pricing decisions, but traditional accounting methods were faulted for being too production oriented. However, it is this cost information that points to the lowest possible price that can be charged for a product without losing money on a per item basis (considering traditional accounting methods).

The activity-based system, however, goes beyond the cost of manufacturing and looks at how much it costs to maintain individual customer accounts. Ultimately, ABC allows marketers to price products/services to individual consumers based on the total cost to provide the product or service. From a marketer's perspective, for example, travel time to visit with a customer would be included as a cost and could be reflected in the price charged to that particular customer.

The conflict caused by pricing is especially evident in the sale of automobiles in the European Union. Due to government pricing regulations, it is often cheaper for customers to buy their cars from a dealer in another country. For example, an English consumer will spend considerably less money if he or she buys a car in another country and then registers it in England. However, a right-hand drive car may not be immediately available in the other country. In countries where most delivered cars are left-hand drive, the non-English dealer will probably have to order a right-hand drive car. In this situation implementing ABC might show that doing business with noncountry buyers is more expensive than dealers had realized.

Products such as CDs, software, and prescription medications do not fall easily within a traditional pricing process. The pricing of such products extends the pricing initiative into functional departments that include engineers and the legal department. It is very difficult to determine the actual costs involved in developing these types of products. Burning a new CD, making duplicates of software, or making one additional pill on the machine is unlikely to correlate with the price of the product. Instead, the human investment, time, and legal maneuvering involved in developing these types of products have to be considered. Production costs do not accurately reflect the firm's investment expenses.

Additionally, some products fall into the category of "better than, but not as good as" competitive products. Computer products and computer peripherals fall into this category. Such new products have to be priced higher than the "better than" competitive products and lower than the "not as good as" competitive products. Listening solely to accountants and their pure cost data might lead to a product being priced too close to the high-end competitor (with better capabilities) or too close to the low-end competitor (therefore not conveying the value added of the new product offering).

The marketing function is generally the driver in day-to-day price decisions. The speed at which price can change in response to competitive pressure is somewhat astounding. The price per gallon of gasoline at the local Mobil station may be $1.57 on Monday, $1.59 on Tuesday, and $1.53 on Wednesday. Such price changes can have an effect on the company's demand. Thus, pricing decisions must be coordinated with supply decisions. In the case of the Mobil station, there could also be an impact on the number of workers needed to service customers on any given day. Although marketers try to think about the overall organizational impact of their daily pricing decisions, minor changes can have a ripple effect throughout the organization. Price promotions are an example of the downstream effects of day-to-day pricing decisions.

A major objective of a price promotion campaign is stimulating increased demand for the firm's product. Studies show that the sales rate changes during and immediately after the campaign. Such fluctuating sales have a dual effect upon the manufacturer. For example, a Kroger store will increase the quantity ordered of liter bottles of Coca-Cola so that it will have inventory on hand during a promotional period. But the store may order more than it expects to sell during the promotional period so that it can

sell the discounted bottles at the regular price (i.e., greater margin) after the promotional period. This reduces normal delivery after the promotion and puts the Kroger store in the comfortable position of waiting until the next deal to repurchase.

This sort of buying behavior disrupts the production and delivery cycle and may mean having to ask employees to work extra shifts (thus increasing manufacturing costs due to overtime pay) to help meet demand. Decreased purchasing after the price promotion period has the opposite effect. Manufacturing may need to build excess inventory in order to maintain a stable production flow, thus driving up inventory costs.

The relative importance of marketing's internal partners in the pricing process relates closely to the product life cycle. Accounting, finance, and R&D have particular interests that appear to be addressed during the introductory stage of the life cycle. Manufacturing's interest in the pricing process seems more prevalent during the growth stage when the production facility is attempting to reach economies of scale. Once the product reaches maturity, all competitive manufacturers are operating with similar cost structures, and pricing is most clearly driven by the external environment. However, overall monitoring of product revenue is important throughout a product's life cycle.

Too many variables are at play in the pricing decision to say that the decision is the responsibility of any particular function. Rather, all functions have a need for functional-level input. However, it is safe to say that marketing has the broadest perspective on pricing since it is the function that looks at both internal cost issues and external demand pressures.

Questions

1. Should marketing play the lead role in coordinating the pricing decision? Explain why or why not.
2. How is activity-based costing more market oriented than traditional accounting methods?
3. What kinds of internal problems are caused by price promotions?

Check It Out

For articles and exercises on the material in this part, and for other great study aids, visit the *Marketing* Web site at

http://lamb.swlearning.com

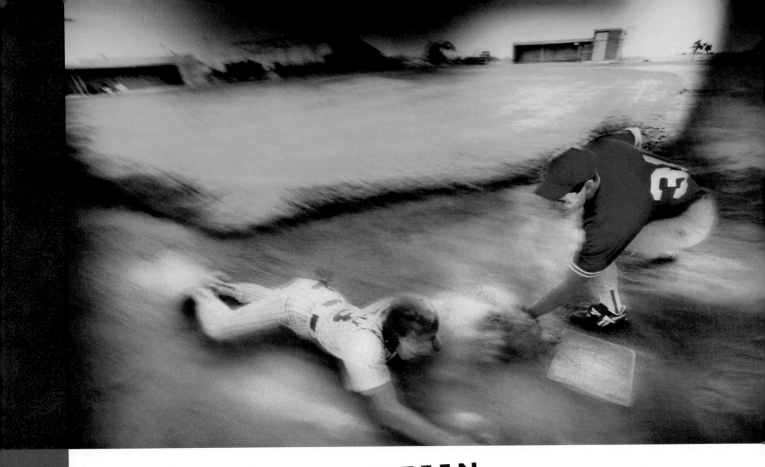

CHAPTER **SEVENTEEN**
PRICING CONCEPTS

Learning Objectives

1 Discuss the importance of pricing decisions to the economy and to the individual firm

2 List and explain a variety of pricing objectives

3 Explain the role of demand in price determination

4 Understand the concept of yield management systems

5 Describe cost-oriented pricing strategies

6 Demonstrate how the product life cycle, competition, distribution and promotion strategies, customer demands, the Internet and extranets, and perceptions of quality can affect price

Major League Baseball is banking on fan loyalty in a new way. It is charging a fee for searchable video highlights and live radio feeds of games broadcast over the Internet.

The Internet arm of Major League Baseball is streaming video highlights of nearly all games over the Net. The video is available on **Mlb.com** and individual team sites an hour after each game. Major League Baseball Advanced Media is using Virage, Inc.'s video-serving technology, which breaks up video clips pitch-by-pitch and makes them searchable. Fans can download the clips at 56 Kbps or 300 Kbps. Major League Baseball officials hope such capabilities will persuade fans to log on, even though they'll have to pay a small monthly fee, less than $10, for the video clip–search service.

Virage CEO Paul Lego says the service is worth the price. "It's the biggest video product on the Web today," he says. "There's no reason Internet content shouldn't be able to command the same types of deals as TV content."

That philosophy is extending to Internet radio broadcasts as well. Baseball cut a deal with RealNetworks, Inc., that ends free Internet radio broadcasts of major league games. The broadcasts cost $10 per year, though subscribers get a $10 gift certificate from Mlb.com's online store.

Ultimately, Major League Baseball wants to show live videocasts of games over the Net, says Bob Bowman, CEO of MLB Advanced Media, a company jointly owned by the thirty major league franchises, though he declined to predict a date. Baseball is prevented from televising local games on the Net under existing TV contracts. "Sports helped make the cable industry," Bowman says. "They're going to help make the Internet as well."[1]

Major League Baseball is counting on significant demand for its Internet video highlights. How are demand, costs, and profits related? Will the Internet have a major impact on pricing in general? What role are yield management systems playing in increased profitability? Can price influence the perceived quality of a product?

The Importance of Price

Discuss the importance of pricing decisions to the economy and to the individual firm

Price means one thing to the consumer and something else to the seller. To the consumer, it is the cost of something. To the seller, price is revenue, the primary source of profits. In the broadest sense, price allocates resources in a free-market economy. With so many ways of looking at price, it's no wonder that marketing managers find the task of setting prices a challenge.

What Is Price?

price
That which is given up in an exchange to acquire a good or service.

Price is that which is given up in an exchange to acquire a good or service. Price is typically the money exchanged for the good or service. It may also be time lost while waiting to acquire the good or service. Standing in long lines at the airport first to check in and then to get through the new security checkpoint procedures is a cost. In fact, these delays are one reason more people are selecting alternative modes of transportation for relatively short trips. Price might also include "lost dignity" for individuals who lose their jobs and must rely on charity to obtain food and clothing.

Consumers are interested in obtaining a "reasonable price." "Reasonable price" really means "perceived reasonable value" at the time of the transaction. One of the authors of this textbook bought a fancy European-designed toaster for about $45. The toaster's wide mouth made it possible to toast a bagel, warm a muffin, and, with a special $15 attachment, make a grilled sandwich. The author felt that a toaster with all these features surely must be worth the total price of $60. But after three months of using the device, toast burned around the edges and raw in the middle lost its appeal. The disappointed buyer put the toaster in the attic. Why didn't he return it to the retailer? Because the boutique had gone out of business, and no other local retailer carried the brand. Also, there was no U.S. service center. Remember, the price paid is based on the satisfaction consumers *expect* to receive from a product and not necessarily the satisfaction they *actually* receive.

Price can relate to anything with perceived value, not just money. When goods and services are exchanged, the trade is called *barter*. For example, if you exchange this book for a chemistry book at the end of the term, you have engaged in barter. The price you paid for the chemistry book was this textbook.

The Importance of Price to Marketing Managers

revenue
The price charged to customers multiplied by the number of units sold.

profit
Revenue minus expenses.

Prices are the key to revenues, which in turn are the key to profits for an organization. **Revenue** is the price charged to customers multiplied by the number of units sold. Revenue is what pays for every activity of the company: production, finance, sales, distribution, and so on. What's left over (if anything) is **profit**. Managers usually strive to charge a price that will earn a fair profit.

To earn a profit, managers must choose a price that is not too high or too low, a price that equals the perceived value to target consumers. If, in consumers' minds, a price is set too high, the perceived value will be less than the cost, and sales opportunities will be lost. Many mainstream purchasers of cars, sporting goods, CDs, tools, wedding gowns, and computers are buying "used or preowned" items to get a better deal. Pricing a new product too high may give some shoppers an incentive to go to a "preowned" or consignment retailer.[2]

Lost sales mean lost revenue. Conversely, if a price is too low, it may be perceived as a great value for the consumer, but the firm loses revenue it could have earned. Setting prices too low may not even attract as many buyers as managers might think. One study surveyed over two thousand shoppers at national chains around the country and found that over 60 percent intended to buy full-price items only.[3] Retailers that place too much emphasis on discounts may not be able to meet the expectations of full-price customers.

Trying to set the right price is one of the most stressful and pressure-filled tasks of the marketing manager, as trends in the consumer market attest:

- Confronting a flood of new products, potential buyers carefully evaluate the price of each one against the value of existing products.

- The increased availability of bargain-priced private and generic brands has put downward pressure on overall prices.

- Many firms are trying to maintain or regain their market share by cutting prices. For example, Dell has gained PC market share by aggressively cutting prices.

- With the general decline in consumer confidence after the terrorist attacks of 2001, some consumers have become more reluctant to spend.

 In the organizational market, where customers include both governments and businesses, buyers are also becoming more price sensitive and better informed. In the consumer market, consumers are using the Internet to make wiser purchasing decisions. Computerized information systems enable the organizational buyer to compare price and performance with great ease and accuracy. Improved communication and the increased use of telemarketing and computer-aided selling have also opened up many markets to new competitors. Finally, competition in general is increasing, so some installations, accessories, and component parts are being marketed like indistinguishable commodities.

Setting the right price on a product is extremely critical and so is a source of much stress for the marketing manager. Part of the reason is the continuous flood of new products that encourages shoppers to carefully compare prices.

Pricing Objectives

To survive in today's highly competitive marketplace, companies need pricing objectives that are specific, attainable, and measurable. Realistic pricing goals then require periodic monitoring to determine the effectiveness of the company's strategy. For convenience, pricing objectives can be divided into three categories: profit oriented, sales oriented, and status quo.

Profit-Oriented Pricing Objectives

Profit-oriented objectives include profit maximization, satisfactory profits, and target return on investment. A brief discussion of each of these objectives follows.

2

List and explain a variety of pricing objectives

Profit Maximization

Profit maximization means setting prices so that total revenue is as large as possible relative to total costs. (A more theoretically precise definition and explanation of profit maximization appear later in the chapter.) Profit maximization does not always signify unreasonably high prices, however. Both price and profits depend on the type of competitive environment a firm faces, such as whether it is in a monopoly position (being the only seller) or in a much more competitive situation. Also, remember that a firm cannot charge a price higher than the product's perceived value. Many firms do not have the accounting data they need for maximizing profits. It is easy to say that a company should keep producing and selling goods or services as long as revenues exceed costs. Yet it is often hard to set up an accounting system that can accurately determine the point of profit maximization.

Sometimes managers say that their company is trying to maximize profits—in other words, trying to make as much money as possible. Although this goal may sound impressive to stockholders, it is not good enough for planning. The statement

"We want to make all the money we can" is vague and lacks focus. It gives management license to do just about anything it wants to do.

Satisfactory Profits

 Satisfactory profits are a reasonable level of profits. Rather than maximizing profits, many organizations strive for profits that are satisfactory to the stockholders and management—in other words, a level of profits consistent with the level of risk an organization faces. In a risky industry, a satisfactory profit may be 35 percent. In a low-risk industry, it might be 7 percent. To maximize profits, a small-business owner might have to keep his or her store open seven days a week. However, the owner might not want to work that hard and might be satisfied with less profit.

Target Return on Investment

return on investment (ROI)
Net profit after taxes divided by total assets.

The most common profit objective is a target **return on investment (ROI)**, sometimes called the firm's return on total assets. ROI measures management's overall effectiveness in generating profits with the available assets. The higher the firm's return on investment, the better off the firm is. Many companies—including DuPont, General Motors, Navistar, ExxonMobil, and Union Carbide—use target return on investment as their main pricing goal.

Return on investment is calculated as follows:

$$\text{Return on investment} = \frac{\text{Net profits after taxes}}{\text{Total assets}}$$

Assume that in 2004 Johnson Controls had assets of \$4.5 million, net profits of \$550,000, and a target ROI of 10 percent. This was the actual ROI:

$$\text{ROI} = \frac{550,000}{4,500,000}$$

$$= 12.2 \text{ percent}$$

As you can see, the ROI for Johnson Controls exceeded its target, which indicates that the company prospered in 2004.

Comparing the 12.2 percent ROI with the industry average provides a more meaningful picture, however. Any ROI needs to be evaluated in terms of the competitive environment, risks in the industry, and economic conditions. Generally speaking, firms seek ROIs in the 10 to 30 percent range. For example, General Electric seeks a 25 percent ROI, whereas Alcoa, Rubbermaid, and most major pharmaceutical companies strive for a 20 percent ROI. In some industries such as the grocery industry, however, a return of under 5 percent is common and acceptable.

A company with a target ROI can predetermine its desired level of profitability. The marketing manager can use the standard, such as 10 percent ROI, to determine whether a particular price and marketing mix are feasible. In addition, however, the manager must weigh the risk of a given strategy even if the return is in the acceptable range.

Sales-Oriented Pricing Objectives

Sales-oriented pricing objectives are based either on market share or on dollar or unit sales. The effective marketing manager should be familiar with these pricing objectives.

Market Share

market share
A company's product sales as a percentage of total sales for that industry.

Market share is a company's product sales as a percentage of total sales for that industry. Sales can be reported in dollars or in units of product. It is very important to know whether market share is expressed in revenue or units because the results

Exhibit 17.1

Two Ways to Measure Market Share (Units and Revenue)

Company	Units Sold	Unit Price	Total Revenue	Unit Market Share	Revenue Market Share
A	1,000	$1.00	$1,000,000	50%	25%
B	200	4.00	800,000	10	20
C	500	2.00	1,000,000	25	25
D	300	4.00	1,200,000	15	30
Total	2,000		$4,000,000		

may be different. Consider four companies competing in an industry with 2,000 total unit sales and total industry revenue of $4 million (see Exhibit 17.1). Company A has the largest unit market share at 50 percent, but it has only 25 percent of the revenue market share. In contrast, company D has only a 15 percent unit share but the largest revenue share: 30 percent. Usually, market share is expressed in terms of revenue and not units.

Many companies believe that maintaining or increasing market share is an indicator of the effectiveness of their marketing mix. Larger market shares have indeed often meant higher profits, thanks to greater economies of scale, market power, and ability to compensate top-quality management. Conventional wisdom also says that market share and return on investment are strongly related. For the most part they are; however, many companies with low market share survive and even prosper. To succeed with a low market share, companies need to compete in industries with slow growth and few product changes—for instance, industrial component parts and supplies. Otherwise, they must vie in an industry that makes frequently bought items, such as consumer convenience goods.

The late 1990s and early 2000s proved that the conventional wisdom about market share and profitability isn't always reliable. Because of extreme competition in some industries, many market share leaders either did not reach their target ROI or actually lost money. Freightliner, DaimlerChrysler's U.S. heavy truck unit, aggressively fought for market share gains during the past decade. While Freightliner grew to become the market leader with a 36 percent market share, its profits suffered. In 2001, it had an estimated loss of $500 million. To cut costs, Freightliner plans to slash eight thousand jobs.[4] The airline, personal-computer, and food industries also had this problem. Procter & Gamble switched from market share to ROI objectives after realizing that profits don't automatically follow from a large market share. PepsiCo says its new Pepsi challenge is to be No. 1 in share of industry profit, not in share of sales volume.

Still, the struggle for market share can be all-consuming for some companies. For over a decade, Maxwell House and Folgers, the biggest U.S. coffee brands, have been locked in a struggle to dominate the market. Their weapons have been advertising, perpetual rounds of price cutting, and millions upon millions of cents-off coupons. At this point, Maxwell House, a unit of Kraft General Foods, has regained a few drops of market share that it had lost to Folgers, a unit of Procter & Gamble, earlier in the war. Maxwell House's strategy has been to advertise heavily (spending over $100 million a year) and to introduce new products that lure consumers with taste rather than price. Examples include ready-made coffee in refrigerator cartons and coffee syrup, both designed for consumers to pour and microwave as needed. Nevertheless, Folgers is still the nation's best-selling coffee, although the Kraft General Foods brands, which include Yuban and Sanka, account for a 35 percent market share. P&G has 32 percent of the U.S. coffee market.

Research organizations like A. C. Nielsen and Information Resources, Inc., provide excellent market share reports for many different industries. These reports enable companies to track their performance in various product categories over time.

Sales Maximization

Rather than strive for market share, sometimes companies try to maximize sales. A firm with the objective of maximizing sales ignores profits, competition, and the marketing environment as long as sales are rising.

If a company is strapped for funds or faces an uncertain future, it may try to generate a maximum amount of cash in the short run. Management's task when using this objective is to calculate which price–quantity relationship generates the greatest cash revenue. Sales maximization can also be effectively used on a temporary basis to sell off excess inventory. It is not uncommon to find Christmas cards, ornaments, and so on discounted at 50 to 70 percent off retail prices after the holiday season. In addition, management can use sales maximization for year-end sales to clear out old models before introducing the new ones.

Maximization of cash should never be a long-run objective because cash maximization may mean little or no profitability. Without profits, a company cannot survive.

Status Quo Pricing Objectives

status quo pricing
A pricing objective that maintains existing prices or meets the competition's prices.

Status quo pricing seeks to maintain existing prices or to meet the competition's prices. This third category of pricing objectives has the major advantage of requiring little planning. It is essentially a passive policy.

Often firms competing in an industry with an established price leader simply meet the competition's prices. These industries typically have fewer price wars than those with direct price competition. In other cases, managers regularly shop competitors' stores to ensure that their prices are comparable. Target's middle managers must visit competing Kmart stores weekly to compare prices and then make adjustments. In response to MCI WorldCom's claims that its long-distance service is overpriced, AT&T struck back with advertisements showing that its rates are essentially equal to competitors'. AT&T was attempting to convince target consumers that it follows a status quo pricing strategy.

The Demand Determinant of Price

Explain the role of demand in price determination

After marketing managers establish pricing goals, they must set specific prices to reach those goals. The price they set for each product depends mostly on two factors: the demand for the good or service and the cost to the seller for that good or service. When pricing goals are mainly sales oriented, demand considerations usually dominate. Other factors, such as distribution and promotion strategies, perceived quality, demands of large customers, the Internet, and stage of the product life cycle, can also influence price.

The Nature of Demand

demand
The quantity of a product that will be sold in the market at various prices for a specified period.

Demand is the quantity of a product that will be sold in the market at various prices for a specified period. The quantity of a product that people will buy depends on its price. The higher the price, the fewer goods or services consumers will demand. Conversely, the lower the price, the more goods or services they will demand.

This trend is illustrated in Exhibit 17.2(a), which graphs the demand per week for gourmet popcorn at a local retailer at various prices. This graph is called a *demand curve*. The vertical axis of the graph shows different prices of gourmet popcorn, measured in dollars per package. The horizontal axis measures the quantity of gourmet popcorn that will be demanded per week at each price. For example, at a price of $2.50, 50 packages will be sold per week; at $1.00, consumers will demand 120 packages—as the *demand schedule* in Exhibit 17.2(b) shows.

The demand curve in Exhibit 17.2 slopes downward and to the right, which indicates that more gourmet popcorn is demanded as the price is lowered. In other words, if popcorn manufacturers put a greater quantity on the market, then their hope of selling all of it will be realized only by selling it at a lower price.

One reason more is sold at lower prices than at higher prices is that lower prices bring in new buyers. This fact might not be so obvious with gourmet popcorn, but consider the example of steak. As the price of steak drops lower and lower, some people who have not been eating steak will probably start buying it rather than hamburger. With each reduction in price, existing customers may also buy extra amounts. Similarly, if the price of gourmet popcorn falls low enough, some people will buy more than they have bought in the past.

Supply is the quantity of a product that will be offered to the market by a supplier or suppliers at various prices for a specified period. Exhibit 17.3(a) on page 576 illustrates the resulting *supply curve* for gourmet popcorn. Unlike the falling demand curve, the supply curve for gourmet popcorn slopes upward and to the right. At higher prices, gourmet popcorn manufacturers will obtain more resources (popcorn, flavorings, salt) and produce more gourmet popcorn. If the price consumers are willing to pay for gourmet popcorn increases, producers can afford to buy more ingredients.

Output tends to increase at higher prices because manufacturers can sell more packages of gourmet popcorn and earn greater profits. The *supply schedule* in Exhibit 17.3(b) shows that at $2 suppliers are willing to place 110 packages of gourmet popcorn on the market, but that they will offer 140 packages at a price of $3.

supply
The quantity of a product that will be offered to the market by a supplier at various prices for a specified period.

Exhibit 17.2

Demand Curve and Demand Schedule for Gourmet Popcorn

(a) Demand curve

(b) Demand schedule

Price per package of gourmet popcorn ($)	Packages of gourmet popcorn demanded per week
3.00	35
2.50	50
2.00	65
1.50	85
1.00	120

☐ Exhibit 17.3

Supply Curve and Supply Schedule
for Gourmet Popcorn

(a) Supply curve

(b) Supply schedule

Price per package of gourmet popcorn ($)	Packages of gourmet popcorn supplied per week
3.00	140
2.50	130
2.00	110
1.50	85
1.00	25

How Demand and Supply Establish Prices

At this point, let's combine the concepts of demand and supply to see how competitive market prices are determined. So far, the premise is that if the price is X, then consumers will purchase Y amount of gourmet popcorn. How high or low will prices actually go? How many packages of gourmet popcorn will be produced? How many packages will be consumed? The demand curve cannot predict consumption, nor can the supply curve alone forecast production. Instead, we need to look at what happens when supply and demand interact—as shown in Exhibit 17.4.

At a price of $3, the public would demand only 35 packages of gourmet popcorn. However, suppliers stand ready to place 140 packages on the market at this price (data from the demand and supply schedules). If they do, they would create a surplus of 105 packages of gourmet popcorn. How does a merchant eliminate a surplus? It lowers the price.

At a price of $1, 120 packages would be demanded, but only 25 would be placed on the market. A shortage of 95 units would be created. If a product is in short supply and consumers want it, how do they entice the dealer to part with one unit? They offer more money—that is, pay a higher price.

Now let's examine a price of $1.50. At this price, 85 packages are demanded and 85 are supplied. When demand and supply are equal, a state called **price equilibrium** is achieved. A temporary price below equilibrium—say, $1.00—results in a shortage because at that price the demand for gourmet popcorn is greater than the available supply. Shortages put upward pressure on price. As long as demand and

price equilibrium
The price at which demand and supply are equal.

Exhibit 17.4

Equilibrium Price for Gourmet Popcorn

supply remain the same, however, temporary price increases or decreases tend to return to equilibrium. At equilibrium, there is no inclination for prices to rise or fall.

An equilibrium price may not be reached all at once. Prices may fluctuate during a trial-and-error period as the market for a good or service moves toward equilibrium. Sooner or later, however, demand and supply will settle into proper balance.

Elasticity of Demand

To appreciate demand analysis, you should understand the concept of elasticity. **Elasticity of demand** refers to consumers' responsiveness or sensitivity to changes in price. **Elastic demand** occurs when consumers buy more or less of a product when the price changes. Conversely, **inelastic demand** means that an increase or a decrease in price will not significantly affect demand for the product.

Elasticity over the range of a demand curve can be measured by using this formula:

$$\text{Elasticity } (E) = \frac{\text{Percentage change in quantity demanded of good A}}{\text{Percentage change in price of good A}}$$

If *E* is greater than 1, demand is elastic.
If *E* is less than 1, demand is inelastic.
If *E* is equal to 1, demand is unitary.

Unitary elasticity means that an increase in sales exactly offsets a decrease in prices, so total revenue remains the same.

Elasticity can be measured by observing these changes in total revenue:

If price goes down and revenue goes up, demand is elastic.
If price goes down and revenue goes down, demand is inelastic.
If price goes up and revenue goes up, demand is inelastic.
If price goes up and revenue goes down, demand is elastic.
If price goes up or down and revenue stays the same, elasticity is unitary.

elasticity of demand
Consumers' responsiveness or sensitivity to changes in price.

elastic demand
A situation in which consumer demand is sensitive to changes in price.

inelastic demand
A situation in which an increase or a decrease in price will not significantly affect demand for the product.

unitary elasticity
A situation in which total revenue remains the same when prices change.

Exhibit 17.5(a) shows a very elastic demand curve. Decreasing the price of a Sony VCR from $300 to $200 increases sales from 18,000 units to 59,000 units. Revenue increases from $5.4 million ($300 × 18,000) to $11.8 million ($200 × 59,000). The price decrease results in a large increase in sales and revenue.

Exhibit 17.5(b) shows a completely inelastic demand curve. The state of Nevada dropped its used-car vehicle inspection fee from $20 to $10. The state continued to inspect about 400,000 used cars annually. Decreasing the price (inspection fee) 50 percent did not cause people to buy more used cars. Demand is completely inelastic for inspection fees, which are required by law. Thus, it also follows that Nevada could double the original fee to $40 and double the state's inspection revenues. People won't quit buying used cars if the inspection fee increases—within a reasonable range.

Exhibit 17.6 presents the demand curve and demand schedule for three-ounce bottles of Spring Break suntan lotion. Let's follow the demand curve from the highest price to the lowest and examine what happens to elasticity as the price decreases.

Inelastic Demand

The initial decrease in the price of Spring Break suntan lotion, from $5.00 to $2.25, results in a decrease in total revenue of $969 ($5,075 − $4,106). When price and total revenue fall, demand is inelastic. The decrease in price is much greater than the increase in suntan lotion sales (810 bottles). Demand is therefore not very flexible in the price range $5.00 to $2.25.

When demand is inelastic, sellers can raise prices and increase total revenue. Often items that are relatively inexpensive but convenient tend to have inelastic demand.

Elastic Demand

In the example of Spring Break suntan lotion, shown in Exhibit 17.6, when the price is dropped from $2.25 to $1.00, total revenue increases by $679 ($4,785 − $4,106). An increase in total revenue when price falls indicates that demand is elastic. Let's measure Spring Break's elasticity of demand when the price drops from $2.25 to $1.00 by applying the formula presented earlier:

$$
\begin{aligned}
E &= \frac{\text{Change in quantity/(Sum of quantities/2)}}{\text{Change in price/(Sum of prices/2)}} \\
&= \frac{(4,785 - 1,825)/[(1,825 + 4,785)/2]}{(2.25 - 1)/[(2.25 + 1.00)/2]} \\
&= \frac{2,960/3,305}{1.25/1.63} \\
&= \frac{.896}{.767} \\
&= 1.17
\end{aligned}
$$

Because E is greater than 1, demand is elastic.

Factors That Affect Elasticity

Several factors affect elasticity of demand, including the following:

- *Availability of substitutes:* When many substitute products are available, the consumer can easily switch from one product to another, making demand elastic. The same is true in reverse: A person with complete renal failure will pay whatever is charged for a kidney transplant because there is no substitute.

- *Price relative to purchasing power:* If a price is so low that it is an inconsequential part of an individual's budget, demand will be inelastic. For example, if the price of salt doubles, consumers will not stop putting salt and pepper on their eggs because salt is cheap anyway.

Exhibit 17.5

Exhibit 17.6

Demand for Three-Ounce Bottles of
Spring Break Suntan Lotion

(b) Demand schedule

Price ($)	Quantity demanded	Total revenue (price × quantity)	Elasticity
5.00	1,015	$5,075 ●	Inelastic
2.25	1,825	4,106 ●	
1.00	4,785	4,785 ●	Elastic
0.75	6,380	4,785 ●	Unitary

- *Product durability:* Consumers often have the option of repairing durable products rather than replacing them, thus prolonging their useful life. If a person had planned to buy a new car and prices suddenly began to rise, he or she might elect to fix the old car and drive it for another year. In other words, people are sensitive to the price increase, and demand is elastic.

- *A product's other uses:* The greater the number of different uses for a product, the more elastic demand tends to be. If a product has only one use, as may be true of a new medicine, the quantity purchased probably will not vary as price varies. A person will consume only the prescribed quantity, regardless of price. On the other hand, a product like steel has many possible applications. As its price falls, steel becomes more economically feasible in a wider variety of applications, thereby making demand relatively elastic.

Examples of both elastic and inelastic demand abound in everyday life. For example, in May 1999, the cellphone rate in India was 16.8 rupees per minute. By

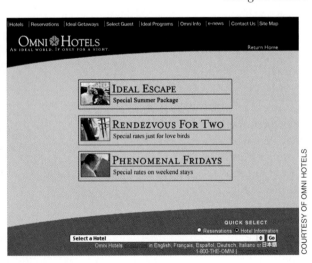
④

Understand the concept of yield management systems

yield management systems (YMS)
A technique for adjusting prices that uses complex mathematical software to profitably fill unused capacity by discounting early purchases, limiting early sales at these discounted prices, and overbooking capacity.

The new- and used-car industries have an inverse relationship to supply and demand. As the demand for new cars rises (such as with the zero percent financing deals after the September 11 terrorist attacks), demand for new cars increases, and supplies shrink. At the same time, when this occurs, the demand for used cars decreases, and used-car inventories swell. This puts manufacturers and their dealers (who often stock both new and used automobiles) in a delicate relationship.

November 2001, the rate had fallen to 4.5 rupees per minute. As a result, the number of cellphone subscribers rose from 1.7 million to 4.5 million.[5] Does this indicate elastic or inelastic demand for cellphone service? When car manufacturers began offering zero percent financing in 2001, sales of new vehicles jumped 35 percent over the same period a year earlier. Sales of so many new cars resulted in a huge surplus of used vehicles. When demand remains constant and supply increases, prices fall. In this case, the price of a used Lexus fell 12 percent from the price for a comparable vehicle a year earlier; the price of a used Chevrolet Tahoe fell 14 percent, and the price of used Ford F-series pickup trucks fell 11 percent.[6] This is simply supply and demand at work.

The Power of Yield Management Systems

When competitive pressures are high, a company must know when it can raise prices to maximize its revenues. More and more companies are turning to yield management systems to help adjust prices. First developed in the airline industry, **yield management systems (YMS)** use complex mathematical software to profitably fill unused capacity. The software employs techniques such as discounting early purchases, limiting early sales at these discounted prices, and overbooking capacity. YMS now are appearing in other services such as lodging, other transportation forms, rental firms, and even hospitals.[7]

Yield management systems are spreading beyond service industries as their popularity increases. The lessons of airlines and hotels aren't entirely applicable to other industries, however, because plane seats and hotel beds are perishable—if they go empty, the revenue opportunity is lost forever. So it makes sense to slash prices to move toward capacity if it's possible to do so without reducing the prices that other customers pay. Cars and steel aren't so perishable. Still, the capacity to make these goods is perishable. An underused factory or mill is a lost revenue opportunity. So it makes sense to cut prices to use up capacity if it's possible to do so while getting other customers to pay full price.

ProfitLogic has helped customers such as JCPenney, Gymboree, Ann Taylor, and the Gap determine the best markdown price. The software has boosted profit margins from 5 to 18 percent. KhiMetrics, used by Buy.com and others, analyzes dozens of factors such as a product's life cycle, competitors' prices, and past sales data at various price points before churning out a list of possible prices and calculating the best ones. New sales data are fed back into the formulae daily to refine the process. Systems such as this aren't cheap, however, costing from $200,000 to $500,000.[8]

Some companies, such as American Airlines and Omni Hotels, are creating their own YMS software. Omni Charm (Centralized Hotel Automated Revenue Management), created by Omni Hotels, predicts demand and indicates when to discount rooms and when to charge the maximum. Marriott, with a similar system, earns an additional estimated $400 million per year.[9]

Although yield management is being implemented across diverse and multiple industries, it is the hallmark of the travel industry. Often hotels like Omni offer different weekend specials each week to encourage the kind of spontaneous travel that will maximize company revenues.

The Cost Determinant of Price

Sometimes companies minimize or ignore the importance of demand and decide to price their products largely or solely on the basis of costs. Prices determined strictly on the basis of costs may be too high for the target market, thereby reducing or eliminating sales. On the other hand, cost-based prices may be too low, causing the firm to earn a lower return than it should. Nevertheless, costs should generally be part of any price determination, if only as a floor below which a good or service must not be priced in the long run.

The idea of cost may seem simple, but it is actually a multifaceted concept, especially for producers of goods and services. A **variable cost** is a cost that varies with changes in the level of output; an example of a variable cost is the cost of materials. In contrast, a **fixed cost** does not change as output is increased or decreased. Examples include rent and executives' salaries.

To compare the cost of production to the selling price of a product, it is helpful to calculate costs per unit, or average costs. **Average variable cost (AVC)** equals total variable costs divided by quantity of output. **Average total cost (ATC)** equals total costs divided by output. As the graph in Exhibit 17.7(a) shows, AVC and ATC are basically U-shaped curves. In contrast, average fixed costs (AFC) decline continually as output increases because total fixed costs are constant.

Marginal cost (MC) is the change in total costs associated with a one-unit change in output. Exhibit 17.7(b) shows that when output rises from seven to eight units, the change in total cost is from $640 to $750; therefore, marginal cost is $110.

All the curves illustrated in Exhibit 17.7(a) have definite relationships:

- AVC plus AFC equals ATC.

- MC falls for a while and then turns upward, in this case with the fourth unit. At that point diminishing returns set in, meaning that less output is produced for every additional dollar spent on variable input.

- MC intersects both AVC and ATC at their lowest possible points.

- When MC is less than AVC or ATC, the incremental cost will continue to pull the averages down. Conversely, when MC is greater than AVC or ATC, it pulls the averages up, and ATC and AVC begin to rise.

- The minimum point on the ATC curve is the least cost point for a fixed-capacity firm, although it is not necessarily the most profitable point.

Costs can be used to set prices in a variety of ways. The first two methods discussed here, markup pricing and formula pricing, are relatively simple. The other three—profit maximization pricing, break-even pricing, and target-return pricing—make use of the more complicated concepts of cost.

Markup Pricing

Markup pricing, the most popular method used by wholesalers and retailers to establish a selling price, does not directly analyze the costs of production. Instead, **markup pricing** uses the cost of buying the product from the producer, plus amounts for profit and for expenses not otherwise accounted for. The total determines the selling price.

A retailer, for example, adds a certain percentage to the cost of the merchandise received to arrive at the retail price. An item that costs the retailer $1.80 and is sold for $2.20 carries a markup of 40¢, which is a markup of 22 percent of the cost (40¢ ÷ $1.80). Retailers tend to discuss markup in terms of its percentage of the retail price—in this example, 18 percent (40¢ ÷ $2.20). The difference between the retailer's cost and the selling price (40¢) is the gross margin, as Chapter 13 explained.

5

Describe cost-oriented pricing strategies

variable cost
A cost that varies with changes in the level of output.

fixed cost
A cost that does not change as output is increased or decreased.

average variable cost (AVC)
Total variable costs divided by quantity of output.

average total cost (ATC)
Total costs divided by quantity of output.

marginal cost (MC)
The change in total costs associated with a one-unit change in output.

markup pricing
The cost of buying the product from the producer plus amounts for profit and for expenses not otherwise accounted for.

(a) Cost curves

(b) Cost schedule

	Total-cost data, per week			Average-cost data, per week			
(1) **Total** **product** **(Q)**	**(2)** **Total** **fixed cost** **(TFC)**	**(3)** **Total** **variable cost** **(TVC)**	**(4)** **Total** **cost** **(TC)**	**(5)** **Average** **fixed cost** **(AFC)**	**(6)** **Average** **variable** **cost** **(AVC)**	**(7)** **Average** **total cost** **(ATC)**	**(8)** **Marginal** **cost** **(MC)**
			$TC = TFC + TVC$	$AFC = \dfrac{TFC}{Q}$	$AVC = \dfrac{TVC}{Q}$	$ATC = \dfrac{TC}{Q}$	$(MC) = \dfrac{\text{change in TC}}{\text{change in Q}}$
0	$100	$ 0	$ 100	—	—	—	—
1	100	90	190	$100.00	$90.00	$190.00	$ 90
2	100	170	270	50.00	85.00	135.00	80
3	100	240	340	33.33	80.00	113.33	70
4	100	300	400	25.00	75.00	100.00	60
5	100	370	470	20.00	74.00	94.00	70
6	100	450	550	16.67	75.00	91.67	80
7	100	540	640	14.29	77.14	91.43	90
8	100	650	750	12.50	81.25	93.75	110
9	100	780	880	11.11	86.67	97.78	130
10	100	930	1,030	10.00	93.00	103.00	150

keystoning
The practice of marking up prices by 100 percent, or doubling the cost.

Markups are often based on experience. For example, many small retailers mark up merchandise 100 percent over cost. (In other words, they double the cost.) This tactic is called **keystoning**. Some other factors that influence markups are the merchandise's appeal to customers, past response to the markup (an implicit demand consideration), the item's promotional value, the seasonality of the goods, their fashion appeal, the product's traditional selling price, and competition. Most retailers avoid any set markup because of such considerations as promotional value and seasonality.

The biggest advantage of markup pricing is its simplicity. The primary disadvantage is that it ignores demand and may result in overpricing or underpricing the merchandise.

High profits from unhealthy products such as cigarettes can raise ethical questions. So can governments' addictions to cigarette revenue, as discussed in the "Ethics in Marketing" box.

Many Governments Are Hooked on Tobacco Revenue

Four million people will die this year from lung cancer and other smoking-related diseases, according to the World Health Organization. By 2030, the agency predicts, the annual loss of life will more than double, making cigarettes the leading cause of premature death around the globe, outstripping malaria, AIDS, and other scourges.

Yet, some countries make more money from a pack of smokes than do the tobacco companies. More than 70 percent of the average retail price of Marlboro cigarettes in the European Union goes into governments' pockets. In Brazil, the government's take is about 65 percent. Tobacco taxes account for about 6 percent of federal government tax revenue in Germany. For the roughly two dozen governments that still manufacture cigarettes, dependence on tobacco revenue can be even higher. China, whose government is the world's largest cigarette maker, derives about 13 percent of its annual income from tobacco sales and taxes.

All that can make governments reluctant to take aggressive action against smoking. In Japan, where the government owns two-thirds of the country's largest cigarette maker, Japan Tobacco, Inc., the Health Ministry dropped plans for specific targets to reduce tobacco use after complaints from tobacco interests.

Because smokers are hooked on cigarettes, they are less responsive to price increases than consumers of many other goods. That means that in the short to medium term, tax revenue would increase as consumption declines. In the United States, a 10 percent increase in cigarette prices translates into a 4 percent drop in consumption. In developing countries, where people have less disposable income, the World Bank estimates that a 10 percent price increase would reduce consumption by about 8 percent, on average.

A study by Teh-wei Hu, a health economist at the University of California at Berkeley, and Zhengzhong Mao, of the West China University of Medical Sciences, concludes that a 25 percent cigarette-tax increase in China would reduce consumption there by 4.57 billion packs and boost central-government revenue by 24.74 billion yuan.

Worldwide, the public-health benefits of tax increases would be significant, the World Bank says. A recent bank report estimates that a sustained 10 percent increase in the real price of cigarettes around the globe would prompt 40 million people to quit and deter many others from starting to smoke, saving about 10 million lives while, at the same time, boosting government revenue by an average of 7 percent.[10]

Should governments get out of the tobacco business? Why or why not? Do you think that the U.S. government should increase taxes on cigarettes 100 percent or more? Why or why not? Consider the 2002 tax increase in New York City. A more direct alternative is to ban smoking altogether. Is this feasible?

Profit Maximization Pricing

Producers tend to use more complicated methods of setting prices than distributors use. One is **profit maximization**, which occurs when marginal revenue equals marginal cost. You learned earlier that marginal cost is the change in total costs associated with a one-unit change in output. Similarly, **marginal revenue (MR)** is the extra revenue associated with selling an extra unit of output. As long as the revenue of the last unit produced and sold is greater than the cost of the last unit produced and sold, the firm should continue manufacturing and selling the product.

Exhibit 17.8 on page 584 shows the marginal revenues and marginal costs for a hypothetical firm, using the cost data from Exhibit 17.7(b). The profit-maximizing quantity, where MR = MC, is six units. You might say, "If profit is zero, why produce the sixth unit? Why not stop at five?" In fact, you would be right. The firm, however, would not know that the fifth unit would produce zero profits until it determined that profits were no longer increasing. Economists suggest producing up to the point where MR = MC. If marginal revenue is just one penny greater than marginal costs, it will still increase total profits.

profit maximization
A method of setting prices that occurs when marginal revenue equals marginal cost.

marginal revenue (MR)
The extra revenue associated with selling an extra unit of output or the change in total revenue with a one-unit change in output.

Break-Even Pricing

Now let's take a closer look at the relationship between sales and cost. **Break-even analysis** determines what sales volume must be reached before the company breaks even (its total costs equal total revenue) and no profits are earned.

The typical break-even model assumes a given fixed cost and a constant average variable cost. Suppose that Universal Sportswear, a hypothetical firm, has fixed

break-even analysis
A method of determining what sales volume must be reached before total revenue equals total costs.

Exhibit 17.8

Point of Profit Maximization

Quantity	Marginal Revenue (MR)	Marginal Cost (MC)	Cumulative Total Profit
0	—	—	—
1	$140	$ 90	$ 50
2	130	80	100
3	105	70	135
4	95	60	170
5	85	70	185
*6	80	80	185
7	75	90	170
8	60	110	120
9	50	130	40
10	40	150	(70)

*Profit maximization

costs of $2,000 and that the cost of labor and materials for each unit produced is 50¢. Assume that it can sell up to 6,000 units of its product at $1 without having to lower its price.

Exhibit 17.9(a) illustrates Universal Sportswear's break-even point. As Exhibit 17.9(b) indicates, Universal Sportswear's total variable costs increase by 50¢ every time a new unit is produced, and total fixed costs remain constant at $2,000 regardless of the level of output. Therefore, for 4,000 units of output, Universal Sportswear has $2,000 in fixed costs and $2,000 in total variable costs (4,000 units × 50¢), or $4,000 in total costs.

Revenue is also $4,000 (4,000 units × $1), giving a net profit of zero dollars at the break-even point of 4,000 units. Notice that once the firm gets past the break-even point, the gap between total revenue and total costs gets wider and wider because both functions are assumed to be linear.

The formula for calculating break-even quantities is simple:

$$\text{Break-even quantity} = \frac{\text{Total fixed costs}}{\text{Fixed cost contribution}}$$

Fixed cost contribution is the price minus the average variable cost. Therefore, for Universal Sportswear,

$$\text{Break-even quantity} = \frac{\$2,000}{(\$1.00 - 50¢)} = \frac{\$2,000}{50¢}$$

$$= 4,000 \text{ units}$$

(a) Break-even point

(b) Costs and revenues

Output	Total fixed costs	Average variable costs	Total variable costs	Average total costs	Average revenue (price)	Total revenue	Total costs	Profit or loss
500	$2,000	$0.50	$ 250	$4.50	$1.00	$ 500	$2,250	($1,750)
1,000	2,000	0.50	500	2.50	1.00	1,000	2,500	(1,500)
1,500	2,000	0.50	750	1.83	1.00	1,500	2,750	(1,250)
2,000	2,000	0.50	1,000	1.50	1.00	2,000	3,000	(1,000)
2,500	2,000	0.50	1,250	1.30	1.00	2,500	3,250	(750)
3,000	2,000	0.50	1,500	1.17	1.00	3,000	3,500	(500)
3,500	2,000	0.50	1,750	1.07	1.00	3,500	3,750	(250)
*4,000	2,000	0.50	2,000	1.00	1.00	4,000	4,000	(0)
4,500	2,000	0.50	2,250	.94	1.00	4,500	4,250	250
5,000	2,000	0.50	2,500	.90	1.00	5,000	4,500	500
5,500	2,000	0.50	2,750	.86	1.00	5,500	4,750	750
6,000	2,000	0.50	3,000	.83	1.00	6,000	5,000	1,000

*Break-even point

The advantage of break-even analysis is that it provides a quick estimate of how much the firm must sell to break even and how much profit can be earned if a higher sales volume is obtained. If a firm is operating close to the break-even point, it may want to see what can be done to reduce costs or increase sales. Moreover, in a simple break-even analysis, it is not necessary to compute marginal costs and marginal revenues because price and average cost per unit are assumed to be constant. Also, because accounting data for marginal cost and revenue are frequently unavailable, it is convenient not to have to depend on that information.

Break-even analysis is not without several important limitations. Sometimes it is hard to know whether a cost is fixed or variable. If labor wins a tough guaranteed-employment contract, are the resulting expenses a fixed cost? Are middle-level executives' salaries fixed costs? More important than cost determination is the fact that simple break-even analysis ignores demand. How does Universal Sportswear know it can sell 4,000 units at $1? Could it sell the same 4,000 units at $2 or even $5? Obviously, this information would profoundly affect the firm's pricing decisions.

Pricing competition was turned on its head with the introduction of the euro in 2002. Now consumers across the European Union can compare prices as never before, as explained in the "Global Perspectives" box.

The Euro Shines a Bright Light on Price Differentials across Europe

On the front page of the European edition of *The Guardian,* a British newspaper, is a small table showing the price of the newspaper in both dollars and euros (€) for over thirty countries, from Albania ($2) to Ukraine ($3.50). It comes as a surprise that readers in Greece and Portugal pay €1.67, in France €2.13, and in Finland and the Netherlands as much as €2.61. Before euro prices, such price differentials were hard to spot. Now they are glaring.

The price information on the front of *The Economist,* a British journal, tells a different story, with prices bunched closely around €4.30. In some markets that meant a small price cut, in others a tiny increase. The only euro-zone country where the price remains out of line is Greece, which joined the European Union's monetary union later than the other members and has relatively low prices for newspapers and magazines.

The Economist's managers decided as long as three years ago to equalize European prices as far as possible, believing that it was better to send a consistent price signal to customers than to price by market. Since then, the price has been capped in the more expensive markets and steadily increased in the cheaper ones to achieve the necessary convergence. The eventual common newsstand price of €4.35 was not aligned to the lowest euro-zone price because that would have been too costly; nor was it set

to match the highest one because that would have risked losing sales in cheaper markets. Like businesses all over Europe, *The Economist* had to make a judgment based on its knowledge of its customers and markets.

Such judgments are necessary because the greater transparency the single currency brings to prices will make a big difference to the way business is conducted. Simple economic theory suggests that savvy consumers now look across European markets and note where the price of a good or service is lowest. They then either purchase the good or service there, or they will use the information to prevail upon their more expensive local provider to bring the price down. The overall effect across dozens of sectors is deflationary. In the face of relentless downward pressure on prices, some businesses are struggling to maintain their profitability.

This deflationary pressure is applied not only by consumers but also by businesses to their own suppliers, thus reinforcing the trend. Big retailers are increasingly seeking to buy from manufacturers at a single euro price, whereas in the past they typically bought locally in each country where they trade. Manufacturers had been able to maintain price differentials because their customers found it difficult to compare prices. With the euro, it is now much easier.

Examples of big price differentials abound. Recently, a 10-kilome-

ter taxi ride in Lisbon was a quarter of the price of a similar journey in Luxembourg. A kilo of beef cost €15 in Paris, €21 in Amsterdam, and €9.90 in Madrid. A visit to the cinema in Dublin or Brussels cost €8, but in Athens moviegoers paid only €5.90 to see the same film. A 5-kilo jumbo pack of laundry detergent cost €9.80 in Brussels, but an extortionate €24.30 in Helsinki. And a packet of proprietary aspirin cost €3.70 in Athens, but €12.90 in Rome and Berlin.

How can such differences be justified? Some companies continue to cling to traditional explanations involving different local tax rates, varying transport costs, and so on. The truth is that until now manufacturers and retailers alike have deliberately (and mostly, though not always, legally) exploited the fact that consumers found it hard to make price comparisons. They have also used sophisticated ways of disguising their true prices from each other.[11]

If you were a manufacturer in the European Union, how would you handle different prices in different euro-zone countries? Do you think that the euro will be beneficial for European Union consumers? Why or why not? Do customs, such as the French preference for side-loading washing machines and the German preference for top-loaders, have any impact on pricing strategy?

Other Determinants of Price

6

Demonstrate how the product life cycle, competition, distribution and promotion strategies, customer demands, the Internet and extranets, and perceptions of quality can affect price

Other factors besides demand and costs can influence price. For example, the stages in the product life cycle, the competition, and the product distribution strategy, promotion strategy, and perceived quality can all affect pricing.

Stages in the Product Life Cycle

As a product moves through its life cycle (see Chapter 10), the demand for the product and the competitive conditions tend to change:

- *Introductory stage:* Management usually sets prices high during the introductory stage. One reason is that it hopes to recover its development costs quickly. In addition, demand originates in the core of the market (the customers whose needs ideally match the product's attributes) and thus is relatively inelastic. On the other hand, if the target market is highly price sensitive, management often finds it better to price the product at the market level or lower. For example, when Kraft General Foods brought out Country Time lemonade, it was priced like similar products in the highly competitive beverage market because the market was price sensitive.

- *Growth stage:* As the product enters the growth stage, prices generally begin to stabilize for several reasons. First, competitors have entered the market, increasing the available supply. Second, the product has begun to appeal to a broader market, often lower income groups. Finally, economies of scale are lowering costs, and the savings can be passed on to the consumer in the form of lower prices.

- *Maturity stage:* Maturity usually brings further price decreases as competition increases and inefficient, high-cost firms are eliminated. Distribution channels become a significant cost factor, however, because of the need to offer wide product lines for highly segmented markets, extensive service requirements, and the sheer number of dealers necessary to absorb high-volume production. The manufacturers that remain in the market toward the end of the maturity stage typically offer similar prices. Usually, only the most efficient remain, and they have comparable costs. At this stage, price increases are usually cost initiated, not demand initiated. Nor do price reductions in the late phase of maturity stimulate much demand. Because demand is limited and producers have similar cost structures, the remaining competitors will probably match price reductions.

- *Decline stage:* The final stage of the life cycle may see further price decreases as the few remaining competitors try to salvage the last vestiges of demand. When only one firm is left in the market, prices begin to stabilize. In fact, prices may eventually rise dramatically if the product survives and moves into the specialty goods category, as horse-drawn carriages and vinyl records have.

The Competition

Competition varies during the product life cycle, of course, and so at times it may strongly affect pricing decisions. Although a firm may not have any competition at first, the high prices it charges may eventually induce another firm to enter the market. Several Internet auto sellers, such as Autobytel.com, have sprung up in response to the perceived high profit margins earned by car dealers.

On the other hand, intense competition can sometimes lead to price wars. What pulls companies into such self-defeating price wars? Often they make the mistake of measuring their success by market share rather than by profitability—but something more is at play. Michael Marn, a partner at McKinsey, the worldwide management consulting company, who heads its pricing practice worldwide, says that price wars are often caused by companies misreading or misunderstanding competitors. Marn tells of one McKinsey client, a company that dominated the market for adhesive labels nationwide. After a small competitor built a tiny factory in southern Florida with no prospects for further expansion, the company reacted with a nationwide price cut of 15 to 20 percent and, says Marn, "gave away profitability for two years." Typically, concludes Marn, price wars are "overreactions to threats that either aren't there at all or are not as big as they seem."[12]

Make every dish forgettable.

REYNOLDS (R) POT LUX (TM) COOKWARE PRINT AD COURTESY OF REYNOLDS CONSUMER PRODUCTS, A BUSINESS OF ALCOA CONSUMER PRODUCTS.

Management usually sets prices higher during the introductory stage of the product life cycle. Still, it must be careful not to set the price too high that it turns customers off. With a product innovation like Reynold's PotLux disposable cookware, how do you think managers decide on a base price?

Competition can be a significant factor in pricing. Microsoft's Xbox and Sony's PlayStation are continuing to go head-to-head, much like Coke and Pepsi. Such intense competition has a definite impact on pricing, which in turn affects revenue.

One company recently took action to avoid a calamitous price war by outsmarting its competition. A company (call it Acme) heard that its competitor was trying to steal some business by offering a low price to one of its best customers. Instead of immediately cutting prices, Acme reps visited three of its competitor's best clients and said they figured the client was paying x, the same price that the competitor had quoted to Acme's own customer. Within days, the competitor had retracted its low-price offer to Acme's client. Presumably, the competitor had received calls from three angry clients asking for the same special deal.

Distribution Strategy

An effective distribution network can often overcome other minor flaws in the marketing mix.[13] For example, although consumers may perceive a price as being slightly higher than normal, they may buy the product anyway if it is being sold at a convenient retail outlet.

Adequate distribution for a new product can often be attained by offering a larger-than-usual profit margin to distributors. A variation on this strategy is to give dealers a large trade allowance to help offset the costs of promotion and further stimulate demand at the retail level.

Manufacturers have gradually been losing control within the distribution channel to wholesalers and retailers, which often adopt pricing strategies that serve their own purposes. For instance, some distributors are **selling against the brand**: They place well-known brands on the shelves at high prices while offering other brands—typically, their private-label brands, such as Craftsman tools, Kroger canned pears, or Cost Cutter paper towels—at lower prices. Of course, sales of the higher priced brands decline.

Wholesalers and retailers may also go outside traditional distribution channels to buy gray-market goods. As explained previously, distributors obtain the goods through unauthorized channels for less than they would normally pay, so they can sell the goods with a bigger-than-normal markup or at a reduced price. Imports seem to be particularly susceptible to gray marketing. Porsches, JVC stereos, and Seiko watches are among the brand-name products that have experienced this problem. Although consumers may pay less for gray-market goods, they often find that the manufacturer won't honor the warranty.

Manufacturers can regain some control over price by using an exclusive distribution system, by franchising, or by avoiding doing business with price-cutting discounters. Manufacturers can also package merchandise with the selling price marked on it or place goods on consignment. The best way for manufacturers to control prices, however, is to develop brand loyalty in consumers by delivering quality and value.

The Impact of the Internet and Extranets

The Internet, corporate networks, and wireless setups are linking people, machines, and companies around the globe—and connecting sellers and buyers as never before. This link is enabling buyers to quickly and easily compare products and prices, putting them in a better bargaining position. At the same time, the technology allows sellers to collect detailed data about customers' buying habits, preferences, and even spending limits so that they can tailor their products and prices. For a time, all of these developments raised hopes of a more efficient marketplace.

selling against the brand
Stocking well-known branded items at high prices in order to sell store brands at discounted prices.

Unfortunately, the promise of pricing efficiencies for Internet retailers and lower costs for consumers has run headlong into reality. Flawed pricing strategies have taken much of the blame for the continuing implosion of dot-coms. Too many merchants offered deep discounts that made profits all but impossible to achieve. Other e-retailers have felt the consumer backlash against price discrimination, as the Internet has given shoppers the ability to better detect price discrepancies and bargains. The dot-com survivors must now figure out if it is even possible to take advantage of the Internet's unique capabilities to set dynamic prices, which would better reflect a customer's willingness to pay more under different circumstances.

"Before the Internet existed, retail was a very competitive, difficult, low-margin business," says Austan Goolsbee, an economist at the University of Chicago. "With the advent of Internet retailers, there was a brief moment in which they and others believed they had broken the iron chain of low margins and high competition in retail by introducing the Internet. Now, retail on-line is starting to look like retail off-line—very competitive, profit margins squeezed. In all, a very tough place to be."[14]

Setting prices on the Internet was expected to offer retailers a number of advantages. To begin with, it would be far easier to raise or lower prices in response to demand, without the need for a clerk to run through a store with a pricing gun. On-line prices could be changed in far smaller increments—even by just a penny or two—as frequently as a merchant desired, making it possible to fine-tune pricing strategies.

But the real payoff was supposed to be better information on exactly how price-conscious customers are. For instance, knowing that customer A doesn't care whether an Oscar-nominated DVD in her shopping basket costs $21.95 or $25.95 would leave an enterprising merchant free to charge the higher price on the spot. By contrast, knowing that customer B is going to put author John Le Carré's latest thriller back on the shelf unless it's priced at $20, instead of $28, would open an opportunity for a bookseller to make the sale by cutting the price in real time.

The idea was to charge exactly what the market will bear. But putting this into practice on-line has turned out to be exceptionally difficult, in part because the Internet has also empowered consumers to compare prices to find out if other merchants are offering a better deal or if other consumers are getting a bigger break. And the Internet has also made it easier for consumers to complain.

For example, Amazon.com faced a problem when customers learned they had paid different prices for the same DVD movies as a result of a marketing test in which the retailer varied prices to gauge the effect on demand. After complaints from irate consumers, who learned from on-line chat boards that they had paid higher prices, Amazon announced it would refund the difference between the highest and lowest prices in the test.

While the Internet helps drive down prices by making it easier for consumers to shop for the best bargain, it also makes it possible for on-line merchants to monitor each other's prices—whether higher or lower—and to adjust them in concert without overtly colluding. As long as the number of retailers in a given market is relatively small, it is now much simpler for merchants to signal each other by changing prices for short periods—long enough for their competitors to notice, but not so long that consumers do. Airlines have long used on-line reservation systems to signal fare changes to each other.

"On-line markets may not be as cutthroat as is commonly expected," says Hal Varian, dean of the school of information management and systems at the University of California at Berkeley. "The only check on this upward drift in prices comes from competitive suppliers such as local [bricks-and-mortar] merchants who may find it more difficult to change prices so rapidly."[15] Recent research has supported the notion that on-line merchants can find ways to raise prices. One study looked at the on-line pricing of books at Amazon.com and its two closest competitors: Borders.com and Barnes & Noble.com. The researchers found that for over half the items studied, all three retailers charged virtually the same price, differing at

On Line

most by five cents. What's more, those prices were substantially higher than the lowest prices offered by other on-line retailers.[16] That runs against early conventional wisdom of Internet shopping—that consumers were only a click away from lower prices offered by a competing merchant.

On-line price-comparison engines, known as shopbots, were supposed to make it easy for consumers to find the lowest prices for any goods. But making effective use of competitive price information has been more difficult for consumers than retailers and economists originally thought. For one thing, price comparisons, which must include a range of shipping options and fees, state-based sales taxes, and any special offers from individual merchants, are far from straightforward. And the time it takes to look up the best prices for a collection of items—say, books or DVDs—can outweigh price savings of a dollar or two.

"Shopbots are tedious to use," says Karen Clay, a Carnegie Mellon economist, who notes that consumers also tend to be willing to pay more for goods from familiar on-line retailers. Since trying a new retailer always involves uncertainty as to whether goods will arrive on time, whether customer service is satisfactory, and even whether the merchant has honestly posted its prices, she says, "that uncertainty can easily outweigh what you could save by shopping somewhere else."[17]

One area where the Internet is having, and will continue to have, a major impact on pricing is the bargaining power between buyers and sellers. For example, a group of forty-plus retailers, with nearly three and a half times the buying power of Wal-Mart, have formed the WorldWide Retail Exchange. On the manufacturing side, Procter & Gamble, Kraft Foods, and others have invested more than $250 million to build business-to-business (B2B) megamarket Transora. Whatever the outcome of these markets, suppliers will soon be facing a world in which there are no more weak customers. Every buyer will wield Wal-Mart's bargaining power.[18]

As bargaining power evens out, companies are reaching price agreements more quickly and then disseminating this information throughout the channel of distribution. Manufacturers are creating private networks, or **extranets,** that link them with their suppliers and customers. These systems make it possible to get a precise handle on inventory, costs, and demand at any given moment—and, after bargaining with suppliers, adjust prices instantly. In the past, a significant cost, known as the "menu cost," was associated with changing prices. For a company with a large product line, it could take months for price adjustments to filter down to distributors, retailers, and salespeople. Streamlined networks reduce menu cost and time to near zero.

extranet
A private electronic network that links a company with its suppliers and customers.

Internet Auctions

The Internet auction business is huge. Part of the lure of buying on-line is that shoppers don't have to go to a flea market or use up a coveted weekend day or worry about the weather. Plus, bidding itself can be fun and exciting. A few of the most popular consumer auction sites are the following

- **http://www.auctions.amazon.com:** Links to Sotheby's for qualified sellers of high-end items.

- **http://www.ebay.com:** The most popular auction site.

- **http://www.auctions.yahoo.com:** Free listings and numerous selling categories including international auctions.

Even though consumers are spending billions on Internet auctions, B2B auctions are likely to be the dominant form in the future. FreeMarkets, Inc., a publicly traded B2B exchange based in Pittsburgh, has hosted on-line reverse auctions—in which suppliers bid for a factory's component order—involving $5.4 billion of transactions. Among the companies using FreeMarkets are Owens Corning, GlaxoSmithKline PLC, and Visteon Corporation, the auto-parts unit spun off by Ford Motor Company.[19] As an example of the benefits of using FreeMarkets.com, a company paid $175,000 for the last batch of plastic auto parts—before using auctions. This time, in thirty-three minutes of frenzied bidding by twenty-five competing suppliers, the price comes down to $118,000.[20]

FreeMarkets has quickly moved beyond selling metal and plastic parts and is auctioning tax preparation services, relocation services, temporary help, and other services. And it's just getting started. Ford, General Motors, and DaimlerChrysler have created an exchange called Covisint (competing with FreeMarkets) to buy huge quantities of parts (see Chapter 6); retailers have created the Worldwide Retail Exchange and Global Net Xchange; and dozens of similar services are running or in the works.

Recently, Whirlpool began holding on-line auctions. Participants bid on the price of the items that they would supply to Whirlpool, but with a twist: They had to include the date when Whirlpool would have to pay for the items. The company wanted to see which suppliers would offer the longest grace period before requiring payment. Five auctions held over five months helped Whirlpool uncover savings of close to $2 million and more than doubled the grace period.

Whirlpool's success is a sign that the B2B auction world is shifting from haggling over prices to niggling over parameters of the deal. Warranties, delivery dates, transportation methods, customer support, financing options, and quality have all become bargaining chips.

As demand for these auctions increases, so too has the number of tools that enable such electronic negotiations. In the past year, Ariba, B2eMarkets, BayBuilder, eBreviate, and Moai have all released products designed to make the process smoother. "Price-only auctions are dead," says Sarah Pfaff, co-founder and executive vice president of eBreviate, a California-based subsidiary of EDS. "Businesses can't afford to rely only on the lowest price."[21]

Promotion Strategy

Price is often used as a promotional tool to increase consumer interest. The weekly flyers sent out by grocery stores in the Sunday newspaper, for instance, advertise many products with special low prices. Crested Butte Ski Resort in Colorado tried a unique twist on price promotions. It made the unusual offer of free skiing between Thanksgiving and Christmas. Its only revenues were voluntary contributions from lodging and restaurant owners who benefited from the droves of skiers taking advantage of the promotion. Lodging during the slack period is now booked solid, and on the busiest days nine thousand skiers jam slopes designed for about sixty-five hundred. Crested Butte Resort no longer loses money during this time of the year.

Pricing can be a tool for trade promotions as well. For example, Levi's Dockers (casual men's pants) are very popular with white-collar men ages twenty-five to forty-five, a growing and lucrative market. Sensing an opportunity, rival pantsmaker Bugle Boy began offering similar pants at cheaper wholesale prices, which gave retailers a bigger gross margin than they were getting with Dockers. Levi Strauss had to either lower prices or risk its $400 million annual Docker sales. Although Levi Strauss intended its cheapest Dockers to retail for $35, it started selling Dockers to retailers for $18 a pair. Retailers could then advertise Dockers at a very attractive retail price of $25.

Demands of Large Customers

Large customers of manufacturers such as Wal-Mart, JCPenney, and other department stores often make specific pricing demands that the suppliers must agree to. Department stores are making greater-than-ever demands on their suppliers to cover the heavy discounts and markdowns on their own selling floors. They want suppliers to guarantee their stores' profit margins, and they insist on cash rebates if the guarantee isn't met. They are also exacting fines for violations of ticketing, packing, and shipping rules. Cumulatively, the demands are nearly wiping out profits for all but the very biggest suppliers, according to fashion designers and garment makers.

Few stores ask for stiffer margin guarantees than May's Lord & Taylor chain.[22] Makers of moderate-priced dresses say Lord & Taylor is the entry point for vendors hoping to do business with other May department store chains like Hecht's and Foley's. May sets the profitability bar high, insisting on a guaranteed profit margin as high as 48 percent in some cases, according to Beau Baker, former chief executive officer of Beau David, Inc., a small dress company.

In the past when a garment maker sold to a store, the two parties would agree on a retail price, and at the end of the season, the supplier would rebate some of the cost of markdowns. Discounts and markdowns were far rarer then than they are today: Department stores could afford plenty of sales help to push products. As stores cut labor costs, however, they came to rely on promotional markdowns and sales to move goods—with suppliers covering profit-margin shortfalls.

The Relationship of Price to Quality

When a purchase decision involves great uncertainty, consumers tend to rely on a high price as a predictor of good quality. Reliance on price as an indicator of quality seems to occur for all products, but it reveals itself more strongly for some items than for others.[23] Among the products that benefit from this phenomenon are coffee, stockings, aspirin, salt, floor wax, shampoo, clothing, furniture, perfume, whiskey, and many services. If the consumer obtains additional information—for instance, about the brand or the store—then reliance on price as an indicator of quality decreases.[24] In the absence of other information, people typically assume that prices are higher because the products contain better materials, because they are made more carefully, or, in the case of professional services, because the provider has more expertise. In other words, consumers assume that "You get what you pay for." One study has shown that some people believe "You get what you pay for" much more strongly than others; that is, some consumers tend to rely much more heavily on price as a quality indicator than others do.[25] In general, consumers tend to be more accurate in their price-quality assessments for nondurable goods (such as ice cream, frozen pizza, or oven cleaner) than for durable goods (such as coffeemakers, gas grills, or ten-speed bikes).[26] Knowledgeable merchants take these consumer attitudes into account when devising their pricing strategies. **Prestige pricing** is charging a high price to help promote a high-quality image. A successful prestige pricing strategy requires a retail price that is reasonably consistent with consumers' expectations.

prestige pricing
Charging a high price to help promote a high-quality image.

No one goes shopping at a Gucci's shop in New York and expects to pay $9.95 for a pair of loafers. In fact, demand would fall drastically at such a low price. Bayer aspirin would probably lose market share over the long run if it lowered its prices. A new mustard packaged in a crockery jar was not successful until its price was doubled.

Consumers also expect private or store brands to be cheaper than national brands. However, if the price difference between a private brand and a nationally distributed manufacturer's brand is *too* great, consumers tend to believe that the private brand is inferior. On the other hand, if the savings aren't big enough, there is little incentive to buy the private brand. One study of scanner data found that if the price difference between the national brand and the private brand was less than 10 percent, people tended not to buy the private brand. If the price difference was greater than 20 percent, consumers perceived the private brand to be inferior.[27]

The latest research on price-quality relationships focused on summer durable goods. The researchers first conducted a study to ascer-

COURTESY OF TIGI

Hair-care products benefit from the customer perception that higher prices mean higher quality. Salon products, like Bed Head and Paul Mitchell, convey the message of quality through high prices and exclusive distribution. In fact, customers may assume that the products are better because of the expertise of the hairdresser in whose salon the products are sold.

tain the dimensions of quality. These are (1) ease of use; (2) versatility (the ability of a product to perform more functions, e.g., special stitch types on sewing machines, or be more flexible, e.g., continuous temperature controls on microwave ovens); (3) durability; (4) serviceability (ease of obtaining quality repairs); (5) performance; and (6) prestige. The researchers found that when consumers focused on prestige and/or durability to assess quality, price was a strong indicator of perceived overall quality. Price was less important as an indicator of quality if the consumer was focusing on one of the other four dimensions of quality.[28]

CONNECT IT

Look back at the story at the beginning of this chapter on how Major League Baseball is charging fees for Internet video clips. Costs, revenues, and profits are directly related. Revenue minus costs equals profits. Profits can be increased by increasing revenues, lowering costs, or both. The Internet is already having a major impact on pricing. Consumers are finding better deals and making better decisions by comparing prices. Old-line manufacturers face the dilemma of competing directly with their channel members if the manufacturer sells through its own Web site.

Yield management systems will help boost revenues of not only service businesses but old-line manufacturers as well. This in turn will mean increased profits for the organization.

Price can have an impact on perceived quality, depending on a number of issues, such as the type of product, advertising, and the consumer's personality. For durable goods, price plays a key role in determining quality if consumers are focusing on prestige and/or durability as determinants of quality.

USE IT

If you want to save money on airline tickets or hotel rooms, give Priceline.com a try. No, you won't get an airline ticket from New York to Los Angeles for $100. But if you can be flexible, you should save some money. Priceline sells many of its tickets for about the same price as the twenty-one-day advance fare even when the flight is booked only two days prior to departure.

If you like checking out airlines' last-minute online travel deals but hate sifting through all those

weekly e-mails, here's a solution: Smarter Living (**http://www.smarterliving.com**) is a service that sorts through the special deals of twenty major airlines and sends them out weekly in a single electronic newsletter. Sign up free at its Web site. Also, try **Orbitz.com** for cheap airfares.

For good values on airline seats, also check out **http://www.cheaptickets.com**; for hotel rooms, try **http://www.hoteldiscounters.com** and **http://www.hotels.com**.

REVIEW IT

(1) **Discuss the importance of pricing decisions to the economy and to the individual firm.** Pricing plays an integral role in the U.S. economy by allocating goods and services among consumers, governments, and businesses. Pricing is essential in business because it creates revenue, which is the basis of all business activity. In setting prices, marketing managers strive to find a level high enough to produce a satisfactory profit.

1.1 Why is pricing so important to the marketing manager?

(2) **List and explain a variety of pricing objectives.** Establishing realistic and measurable pricing objectives is a critical part of any firm's marketing strategy. Pricing objectives are commonly classified into three categories: profit oriented, sales oriented, and status quo. Profit-oriented pricing is based on profit maximization, a satisfactory level of profit, or a target return on investment. The goal of profit maximization is to generate as much revenue as possible in relation to cost. Often, a more practical approach than profit maximization is setting prices to produce profits that will satisfy management and stockholders. The most common profit-oriented strategy is pricing for a specific return on investment relative to a firm's assets. The second type of pricing objective is sales oriented, and it focuses on either maintaining a percentage share of the market or maximizing dollar or unit sales. The third type of pricing objective aims to maintain the status quo by matching competitors' prices.

2.1 Give an example of each major type of pricing objective.

(3) **Explain the role of demand in price determination.** Demand is a key determinant of price. When establishing prices, a firm must first determine demand for its product. A typical demand schedule shows an inverse relationship between quantity demanded and price: When price is lowered, sales increase; and when price is increased, the quantity demanded falls. For prestige products, however, there may be a direct relationship between demand and price: The quantity demanded will increase as price increases.

Marketing managers must also consider demand elasticity when setting prices. Elasticity of demand is the degree to which the quantity demanded fluctuates with changes in price. If consumers are sensitive to changes in price, demand is elastic; if they are insensitive to price changes, demand is inelastic. Thus, an increase in price will result in lower sales for an elastic product and little or no loss in sales for an inelastic product.

3.1 Explain the role of supply and demand in determining price.

3.2 If a firm can increase its total revenue by raising its price, shouldn't it do so?

3.3 Explain the concepts of elastic and inelastic demand. Why should managers understand these concepts?

(4) **Understand the concept of yield management systems.** Yield management systems use complex mathematical software to profitably fill unused capacity. The software uses techniques such as discounting early purchases, limiting early sales at these discounted prices, and overbooking capacity. These systems are primarily used in service businesses and are substantially raising revenues.

4.1 Why are so many companies adopting yield management systems?

4.2 *INFOTRAC COLLEGE EDITION* How is yield management helping companies achieve competitive advantage? Use InfoTrac to find out (**http://www.infotrac-college.com**). Run a keyword search for "yield management" and read through the headlines to see what industries are profiled most often. Then read the article from *Computerworld* titled "Software Fills Trucks, Maximizes Revenue; Sitton Motor Lines Takes Lead in Applying Analysis Tool Outside the Travel Industry" by Matthew Schwartz. Answer the following questions:

- How is Sitton Motor Lines using yield management principles and software?
- Describe the implementation of the new software.
- What other industries are cited as good candidates for yield management?

(5) **Describe cost-oriented pricing strategies.** The other major determinant of price is cost. Marketers use several cost-oriented pricing strategies. To cover their own expenses and obtain a profit, wholesalers and retailers commonly use markup pricing: They tack an extra amount onto the manufacturer's original price. Another pricing technique is to maximize profits by setting price where marginal revenue equals marginal cost. Still another pricing strategy determines how much a firm must sell to break even and uses this amount as a reference point for adjusting price.

5.1 **WRITING** Your firm has based its pricing strictly on cost in the past. As the newly hired marketing manager, you believe this policy should change. Write the president a memo explaining your reasons.

5.2 Why is it important for managers to understand the concept of break-even points? Are there any drawbacks?

(6) Demonstrate how the product life cycle, competition, distribution and promotion strategies, customer demands, the Internet and extranets, and perceptions of quality can affect price. The price of a product normally changes as it moves through the life cycle and as demand for the product and competitive conditions change. Management often sets a high price at the introductory stage, and the high price tends to attract competition. The competition usually drives prices down because individual competitors lower prices to gain market share.

Adequate distribution for a new product can sometimes be obtained by offering a larger-than-usual profit margin to wholesalers and retailers. The Internet enables consumers to compare products and prices quickly and efficiently. Extranets help control costs and lower prices. Price is also used as a promotional tool to attract customers. Special low prices often attract new customers and entice existing customers to buy more. Demands of large customers can squeeze the profit margins of suppliers.

Perceptions of quality can also influence pricing strategies. A firm trying to project a prestigious image often charges a premium price for a product. Consumers tend to equate high prices with high quality.

6.1 **TEAM** Divide the class into teams of five. Each team will be assigned a different grocery store from a different chain. (An independent is fine.) Appoint a group leader. The group leaders should meet as a group and pick fifteen nationally branded grocery items. Each item should be specifically described as to brand name and size of the package. Each team will then proceed to its assigned store and collect price data on the fifteen items. The team should also gather price data on fifteen similar store brands and fifteen generics, if possible.

Each team should present its results to the class and discuss why there are price variations between stores, national brands, store brands, and generics.

As a next step, go back to your assigned store and share the overall results with the store manager. Bring back the manager's comments and share them with the class.

6.2 How does the stage of a product's life cycle affect price? Give some examples.

6.3 **ON LINE** Go back to Priceline.com. Can you research a ticket's price before purchasing it? What products and services are available for purchasing? How comfortable are you with naming your own price? Relate the supply and demand curves to customer-determined pricing.

Go to one of the Internet auction sites listed in this chapter. Report to the class on how the auction process works and the items being auctioned.

6.4 **INFOTRAC COLLEGE EDITION** How important is pricing when a company is entering new markets? The article in *Across the Board* titled "Is the Price Right?" by Peter Meyer can tell you. Print out the article using InfoTrac (**http://www.infotrac-college.com**) and then underline all of the chapter concepts that it discusses. What issues does the article address that the chapter does not? What issues does the chapter address that are not included in the article?

APPLY IT

Application for Entrepreneurs

Bernie Opinal has decided to wash windows in his neighborhood during spring break instead of heading to Daytona Beach with his buddies. Bernie lives with his parents in a neighborhood with homes typically in the 3,000- to 3,500-square-foot range. Bernie plans to hire his little brother Butch to help him. His plan is to clean every window inside and out, plus replace any missing caulking or weather-stripping at no extra charge. His estimated demand and associated costs are as follows:

Output	P	AR	MR	MC	AVC	ATC
0				—	—	—
1	$140.00			$31.00	$31.00	$54.00
2	130.00			28.00	29.50	41.00
3	120.00			31.00	30.00	37.67
4	110.00			34.00	31.00	36.75
5	100.00			37.00	32.20	36.80
6	90.00			40.00	33.50	37.33
7	80.00			43.00	34.86	38.14
8	70.00			46.00	36.25	39.13
9	60.00			49.00	37.67	40.22
10	50.00			52.00	39.10	41.40

Questions

1. What are the marginal revenue and average revenue at each price?

2. How many houses should Bernie contract with to maximize profits?

3. What is the total profit at profit maximization?

THINK ABOUT IT

Ethics Exercise

Advanced Bio Medics (ABM) has invented a new stem-cell based drug that will arrest even advanced forms of lung cancer. Development costs were actually quite low because the drug was an accidental discovery by scientists working on a different project. To stop the disease requires a regimen of taking one pill per week for twenty weeks. There is no substitute offered by competitors. ABM is thinking that it could maximize its profits by charging $10,000 per pill. Of course, many will die because they can't afford the medicine at this price.

Questions

1. Should ABM maximize its profits?

2. Does the AMA Code of Ethics address this issue? Go to **http://www. marketingpower.com** and review the code. Then, write a brief paragraph on what the AMA Code of Ethics contains that relates to ABM's dilemma.

TRY IT

Entrepreneurship Case

A Taste of Class

In 1987, JoAnn James left her job at a popular Cincinnati restaurant to start her own catering company, A Taste of Class (ATOC). Soon she found a partner, Ernie Block, and the company quickly grew to annual revenues of $250,000. Specializing in traditional American food, ATOC is an off-premise catering company that serves both the business and consumer markets.

JoAnn's son, Mark, joined the business while still in high school and worked there through college. He eventually bought out his mother's partner in 1993. Mark's first concern was to make sure that he did not alienate his customer base by implementing any changes to the basic formula that had made ATOC successful. But Mark had a goal of reaching $1 million in sales by his tenth year anniversary, so he knew that continuing to operate out of the existing location—an 800-square-foot kitchen with no office space—would not work in the long run.

By 2002, eight years into his plan, he was still $250,000 away from his goal. Although Mark has made great strides and has been very creative in growing his business by following common-sense marketing techniques, he has not implemented any formal marketing plan. About one-third of his business comes from corporate clients, one-third from weddings, and one-third from other special occasions.

ATOC has a traditional product mix: hot buffet, cold buffet, hot sit-down, breakfast buffet, box lunches, and drop-offs (hot and cold meals). The company can serve parties of twenty-five to ten thousand, all with only six full-time employees (i.e., cooks) and a small army of contract servers. On any given week, ATOC will have four to five caterings a day, with twenty to twenty-five each weekend day. Regular corporate clients include Delta Airlines, the United States Marine Corps, and Seagram's, and are supplemented with numerous individual clients.

Mark's menus are very straightforward (roast beef and gravy, green beans, lasagna, lemon chicken, etc.). He thinks that they may be too simplistic and not flowery enough. In fact, some employees want to incorporate more exotic, gourmet dishes into the company's offerings. Mark wants to stick to the company's core business, but he admits that the *language* used to describe his menus could be a bit more glamorous. Mark knows that his best value menu is his gourmet buffet (carved meat, sides, salads, and desserts), his best selling food items are on his hot buffet (roast beef and gravy, mashed potatoes, and green beans), and that his best return on investment is on hot buffet drop-offs (where he drops the food off at the client, who then returns ATOC's catering equipment). In fact, he knows that he makes a better return in general on parties for which ATOC does not provide the personnel.

Mark currently uses variable pricing: He tries to match his prices to what his prospective customers expect to pay. He has a base price for his standard menus. The base price is designed to attract the largest number of customers. He used to have tiered pricing, where an increase in the number of people to be served resulted in a per person reduction in the price of the meal. Printed menus indicated different prices for different sized groups. For example a dinner for five to ten people was priced more expensively than the same dinner for a party of 110. When the tiered prices were printed on the menu, Mark had limited flexibility in his pricing strategy. But after doing some competitive research, he discovered that it was mostly lower-end caterers that were using this pricing strategy. Mark still varies the price charged according to party size. He now does it at the bidding end, however, not on the printed menu. This gives him greater flexibility to achieve desired profit margins. When Mark first took over the daily operations of the business from Ernie

Block, he did not raise prices. In fact, the company saw its first price increases in nearly a decade in 2002. Still, ATOC's prices are about 5 to 10 percent below the market.

Questions

1. How can Mark keep prices low without communicating a low-end, average product?

2. How can he raise prices without alienating customers who have been trained over the years to expect a deal from ATOC?

3. If A Taste of Class was using an Activity Based Costing method of accounting, determine what specific business activities—areas such as accounting, food costs, food preparation, marketing, and administrative activities—would contribute to the cost of each individual sale.

4. Does a yield management system make sense for A Taste of Class? If so, how would it work?

 WATCH IT

Short SUPERBOWL

The *Marketing* PowerPoint CD-ROM includes two video ad clips embedded in the Chapter 17 slide presentation. While watching the ad for the NFL Store, determine what factors led to selecting the price that is advertised. Do the same for the Taco Bell ad. What pricing strategy is evoked?

Medium **CNN VIDEO**

Supply and demand affect all markets, and the same is true of the wine industry. Watch this CNN clip to see the effect of supply and demand and competition on the pricing of wines—and on the target market. You may want to review the clip from Chapter 6 on coffee farming practices as another example of variables that affect price.

Long SmallBusinessSchool ▣
the Series on PBS stations and the Web

For Chapter 17, Small Business School returns to Meacham Field in Fort Worth, Texas, and TexasJet. When you see the video this time, focus on the challenges Reed Pigman faced when he tried to compete with other private jet companies on price. Watch the segment and think about the kind of pricing strategy he is using for his jet service.

 FLIP IT

 Flip to Chapter 17 in your *Grademaker Study Guide* for more review opportunities, including the pretest, vocabulary review, Internet activities, study test questions, and an application exercise based on pricing concepts. How does demand determine product pricing? Can you describe cost-oriented pricing strategies? What about how various elements like the PLC, competition, and others affect the pricing of an offering? If you're a bit shaky, then pick up your *Grademaker* and review.

 CLICK IT

The *Marketing* Web site links you to all the Internet-based activities in this chapter, like the "Use It," "Review It" questions 4.2, 6.3, and 6.4, and the On-Line exercises in the chapter margins. As a review, do the Chapter 17 quiz and crossword puzzle. And don't forget the

Career Exersite that shows you resources for exploring marketing career opportunities in pricing. Review the main concepts in the PowerPoint presentation for Chapter 17, too. Go to **http://lamb.swlearning.com**, read the material, and follow the links right from the site.

CHAPTER **EIGHTEEN**
SETTING THE RIGHT PRICE

Learning Objectives

1 Describe the procedure for setting the right price

2 Identify the legal and ethical constraints on pricing decisions

3 Explain how discounts, geographic pricing, and other special pricing tactics can be used to fine-tune the base price

4 Discuss product line pricing

5 Describe the role of pricing during periods of inflation and recession

The personal-computer industry is indeed in the doghouse. Worldwide growth is slowing from its once-guaranteed run of 20 percent-plus a year to somewhere closer to 10 to 15 percent a year. And while the state of the economy is always mentioned as a contributor to dropping demand, analysts seem worried about something greater: saturation.

If this were not enough, Dell Computer, the investment community's perennial favorite, has launched an aggressive price war. Speaking to the *Wall Street Journal* about the current price battle, IBM's former CEO Lou Gerstner noted, "Price wars in a commodity business are really dumb." All of this raises the question: Is this a commodity business? Or has Michael Dell become smitten with a strategy that, in Gerstner's words, is less than smart?

If a commodity is a product for which no one can establish a competitive advantage, then it follows that a commodity business is one in which no participant can obtain a competitive business advantage. However, even in tough times, Dell's business model stands head and shoulders above its competitors'. Dell's competitive advantage comes not from building better boxes per se, but from building them smarter and faster, and consuming fewer resources in the process.

Much has been written about Dell's direct model, which removes the intermediaries, along with their margin, from the sales process. And others have noted that Dell's incredible five days of inventory allow it to pass on component price declines faster than anyone else in the industry. But perhaps the unique aspect of Dell's business advantage is its negative cash conversion cycle. Because it keeps only five days of inventories, manages receivables to thirty days, and pushes payables out to fifty-nine days, the Dell model will generate cash—even if the company were to report no profit whatsoever.

Dell is clearly the low-cost leader when it comes to looking solely at the income statement. The company has continued to generate a substantial profit margin even as other vendors have struggled. For instance, IBM's personal and printing systems division lost $58 million on revenues of $3.18 billion in the first quarter of 2001. However, Dell's balance-sheet advantage is the added kicker here. Even in an environment where a price war eliminates all profitability—including that of Dell—the company will remain cash-flow positive. No wonder then that Dell would be willing to start a price war, and no wonder that IBM would find it "dumb."

By pushing for market share gains through a price war, Dell has presented its competitors with a true lose–lose dilemma. On the one hand, you can try to maintain market share by pricing against Dell. The problem is that because of its business model advantage, Dell can stand in the deep end of the pool forever. A competitor wading down there will likely run out of oxygen before too long. Currently, Gateway is the only player that has followed this path, and understandably so. As the only other large player with a completely direct strategy, Gateway is best equipped to ride out the war.

The other possible response, and the one that has been chosen by IBM and Hewlett-Packard, is to declare the price war "irrational." The problem here is that along the way they will lose market share, while Dell continues the tear that led it to become the No. 1 maker of PCs in the world. Sitting out the war is as dangerous as entering it, which is precisely why Dell's decision to push the pedal during these tough times is so remarkably shrewd.[1]

What type of basic price strategy is Dell following? What are some ways to fine-tune that strategy? What kinds of discounts can Dell offer?

How to Set a Price on a Product

1

Describe the procedure for setting the right price

Setting the right price on a product is a four-step process (see Exhibit 18.1):

1. Establish pricing goals.

2. Estimate demand, costs, and profits.

3. Choose a price strategy to help determine a base price.

4. Fine-tune the base price with pricing tactics.

The first three steps are discussed next; the fourth step is discussed later in the chapter.

Establish Pricing Goals

The first step in setting the right price is to establish pricing goals. Recall from Chapter 17 that pricing objectives fall into three categories: profit oriented, sales oriented, and status quo. These goals are derived from the firm's overall objectives.

A good understanding of the marketplace and of the consumer can sometimes tell a manager very quickly whether a goal is realistic. For example, if firm A's objective of a 20 percent target return on investment (ROI), and its product development and implementation costs are $5 million, the market must be rather large or must support the price required to earn a 20 percent ROI. Assume that company B has a pricing objective that all new products must reach at least 15 percent market share within three years after their introduction. A thorough study of the environment may convince the marketing manager that the competition is too strong and the market share goal can't be met.

All pricing objectives have trade-offs that managers must weigh. A profit maximization objective may require a bigger initial investment than the firm can com-

Exhibit 18.1

Steps in Setting the Right Price on a Product

mit or wants to commit. Reaching the desired market share often means sacrificing short-term profit because without careful management, long-term profit goals may not be met. Meeting the competition is the easiest pricing goal to implement. But can managers really afford to ignore demand and costs, the life-cycle stage, and other considerations? When creating pricing objectives, managers must consider these trade-offs in light of the target customer and the environment.

Estimate Demand, Costs, and Profits

Chapter 17 explained that total revenue is a function of price and quantity demanded and that quantity demanded depends on elasticity. After establishing pricing goals, managers should estimate total revenue at a variety of prices. Next, they should determine corresponding costs for each price. They are then ready to estimate how much profit, if any, and how much market share can be earned at each possible price. These data become the heart of the developing price policy. Managers can study the options in light of revenues, costs, and profits. In turn, this information can help determine which price can best meet the firm's pricing goals.

Choose a Price Strategy

The basic, long-term pricing framework for a good or service should be a logical extension of the pricing objectives. The marketing manager's chosen **price strategy** defines the initial price and gives direction for price movements over the product life cycle.

The price strategy sets a competitive price in a specific market segment, based on a well-defined positioning strategy. Changing a price level from premium to superpremium may require a change in the product itself, the target customers served, the promotional strategy, or the distribution channels. Thus, changing a price strategy can require dramatic alterations in the marketing mix. A carmaker cannot successfully compete in the superpremium category if the car looks and drives like an economy car.

A company's freedom in pricing a new product and devising a price strategy depends on the market conditions and the other elements of the marketing mix. If a firm launches a new item resembling several others already on the market, its pricing freedom will be restricted. To succeed, the company will probably have to charge a price close to the average market price. In contrast, a firm that introduces a totally new product with no close substitutes will have considerable pricing freedom.

Most companies do not do a good job of doing research to create a price strategy. A recent study found that only about 8 percent of the companies surveyed could be classified as conducting serious pricing research to support the development of an effective pricing strategy. In fact, 88 percent of them did little or no serious pricing research. McKinsey & Company's Pricing Benchmark Survey estimated that only about 15 percent of companies do serious pricing research. A 1997 Coopers & Lybrand study found that 87 percent of the surveyed companies had changed prices in the previous year. Only 13 percent of the price changes, however, came after a scheduled review of pricing strategy.[2]

These numbers indicate that strategic pricing decisions tend to be made without an understanding of the likely buyer or the competitive response. Further, the research shows that managers often make tactical pricing decisions without reviewing how they may fit into the firm's overall pricing or marketing strategy. The

price strategy
A basic, long-term pricing framework, which establishes the initial price for a product and the intended direction for price movements over the product life cycle.

New products with no close substitutes are less restricted in the pricing strategies they can pursue. How do you think Ceiva will price this Internet-connected digital picture frame? Keep in mind that other factors besides novelty may affect the pricing strategy.

data suggest that many companies make pricing decisions and changes without an existing process for managing the pricing activity. As a result, many of them do not have a serious pricing strategy and do not conduct pricing research to develop their strategy.

Companies that do serious planning for creating a price strategy can select from three basic approaches: price skimming, penetration pricing, and status quo pricing. A discussion of each type follows.

Price Skimming

price skimming
A pricing policy whereby a firm charges a high introductory price, often coupled with heavy promotion.

Price skimming is sometimes called a "market-plus" approach to pricing because it denotes a high price relative to the prices of competing products. Radius Corporation produces unique oval-headed toothbrushes made of black neoprene that look like a scuba-diving accessory. Radius uses a skimming policy, pricing the toothbrushes at $9.95, compared to around $2.00 for a regular toothbrush.[3]

The term **price skimming** is derived from the phrase "skimming the cream off the top." Companies often use this strategy for new products when the product is perceived by the target market as having unique advantages. For example, Caterpillar sets premium prices on its construction equipment to support and capture its high perceived value. Genzyme Corporation introduced Ceredase as the first effective treatment for Gaucher's disease. The pill allows patients to avoid years of painful physical deterioration and lead normal lives. A year's supply for one patient can exceed $300,000.

As a product progresses through its life cycle, the firm may lower its price to successfully reach larger market segments. Economists have described this type of pricing as "sliding down the demand curve." Not all companies slide down the curve. Genentech's TPA, a drug that clears blood clots, was still priced at $2,200 a dose four years after its introduction, despite competition from a much lower priced competitor.

Price skimming works best when the market is willing to buy the product even though it carries an above-average price. If, for example, some purchasing agents feel that Caterpillar equipment is far superior to competitors' products, then Caterpillar can charge premium prices successfully. Firms can also effectively use price skimming when a product is well protected legally, when it represents a technological breakthrough, or when it has in some other way blocked the entry of competitors. Managers may follow a skimming strategy when production cannot be expanded rapidly because of technological difficulties, shortages, or constraints imposed by the skill and time required to produce a product. As long as demand is greater than supply, skimming is an attainable strategy.

A successful skimming strategy enables management to recover its product development or "educational" costs quickly. (Often consumers must be "taught" the advantages of a radically new item, such as high-definition TV.) Even if the market perceives an introductory price as too high, managers can easily correct the problem by lowering the price. Firms often feel it is better to test the market at a high price and then lower the price if sales are too slow. They are tacitly saying, "If there are any premium-price buyers in the market, let's reach them first and maximize our revenue per unit." Successful skimming strategies are not limited to products. Well-known athletes, entertainers, lawyers, and hairstylists are experts at price skimming.[4] Naturally, a skimming strategy will encourage competitors to enter the market.

Penetration Pricing

penetration pricing
A pricing policy whereby a firm charges a relatively low price for a product initially as a way to reach the mass market.

Penetration pricing is at the opposite end of the spectrum from skimming. **Penetration pricing** means charging a relatively low price for a product as a way to reach the mass market. The low price is designed to capture a large share of a substantial market, resulting in lower production costs. If a marketing manager has made obtaining a large market share the firm's pricing objective, penetration pricing is a logical choice.

Penetration pricing does mean lower profit per unit, however. Therefore, to reach the break-even point, it requires a higher volume of sales than would a skimming policy. If reaching a high volume of sales takes a long time, then the recovery of product development costs will also be slow. As you might expect, penetration pricing tends to discourage competition.

A penetration strategy tends to be effective in a price-sensitive market. Price should decline more rapidly when demand is elastic because the market can be expanded through a lower price. Also, price sensitivity and greater competitive pressure should lead to a lower initial price and a relatively slow decline in the price later. Southwest Airlines' success is based on penetration pricing. By flying only the Boeing 737, it realizes efficiencies in stocking parts and training pilots and mechanics. It also saves by avoiding a costly computer reservation system, such as Apollo or SABRE, and by not serving meals. Southwest has a cost per seat mile of 7.0¢—the lowest in the industry. Costs per seat mile for other major carriers are US Airways, 10.8¢; United, 9.6¢; Delta, 9.4¢; Northwest, 9.1¢; and American, 8.9¢.

If a firm has a fixed cost structure and each sale provides a large contribution to those fixed costs, penetration pricing can boost sales and provide large increases to profits—but only if the market size grows or if competitors choose not to respond. Low prices can draw additional buyers to enter the market. The increased sales can justify production expansion or the adoption of new technologies, both of which can reduce costs. And, if firms have excess capacity, even low-priced business can provide incremental dollars toward fixed costs.

Penetration pricing can also be effective if an experience curve will cause costs per unit to drop significantly. The experience curve proposes that per-unit costs will go down as a firm's production experience increases. On average, for each doubling of production, a firm can expect per-unit costs to decline by roughly 20 percent. Cost declines can be significant in the early stages of production. Manufacturers that fail to take advantage of these effects will find themselves at a competitive cost disadvantage relative to others that are further along the curve.

The big advantage of penetration pricing is that it typically discourages or blocks competition from entering a market. The disadvantage is that penetration means gearing up for mass production to sell a large volume at a low price. What if the volume fails to materialize? The company will face huge losses from building or converting a factory to produce the failed product. Skimming, in contrast, lets a firm "stick its toe in the water" and see if limited demand exists at the high price. If not, the firm can simply lower the price. Skimming lets a company start out with a small production facility and expand it gradually as price falls and demand increases.

Penetration pricing can also prove disastrous for a prestige brand that adopts the strategy in an effort to gain market share and fails. When Omega—once a more prestigious brand than Rolex—was trying to improve the market share of its watches, it adopted a penetration pricing strategy that succeeded in destroying the watches' brand image by flooding the market with lower priced products. Omega never gained sufficient share on its lower priced/lower image competitors to justify destroying its brand image and high-priced position with upscale buyers. The Cadillac Cimarron and Lacoste clothing experienced similar outcomes from a penetration pricing strategy.

Sometimes marketers in other countries see the success of American companies' price strategies and decide to emulate them. Such was the case of Ryanair as explained in the "Global Perspectives" box.

Status Quo Pricing

The third basic price strategy a firm may choose is status quo pricing, or meeting the competition. (See also Chapter 17.) It means charging a price identical to or

Irish Airline Flies High Just Like Southwest Airlines

Europe's grand old airlines have hit a rough patch of air these days, and Michael O'Leary is proud to be a big part of their problem.

The chief executive of Ryanair Holdings didn't set out to rattle the once cozy world of European aviation. Ten years ago, when he was financial adviser to Irish tycoon Tony Ryan, he was asked by Ryan for some thoughts on fixing the struggling family-owned carrier. O'Leary's advice: "Shut the bloody thing down."

Instead, Ryan persuaded O'Leary to visit Southwest Airlines in Dallas and learn how the pioneer of low-cost air travel makes a big profit. There, under the Texas sun, O'Leary found cut-price religion. He agreed to run Ryanair, in the process taking on some of the biggest names in aviation.

Today, Ryanair stands foremost among a handful of European budget airlines, rewriting the rules and battering venerable flag carriers. Passengers grumble that flying Ryanair is like riding a bus, but they are doing it by the bus-

load. Ryanair carries seven million passengers in eleven countries each year—Britain, France, and Italy, among them—ranking its traffic volume above that of Ireland's state-owned Aer Lingus. That makes Ryanair Europe's first start-up to surpass a national carrier.

Ryanair's rise from Irish puddle-jumper to continental contender is more than one airline's growth story. The Gaelic upstart and its followers such as London-based EasyJet are fundamentally shifting the economics of flying around Europe. Some promotional Ryanair fares are as cheap as £1 ($1.45) to fly from one European city to another; the majority of the carrier's tickets are in the same price range as old-line carriers' bargain fares. But while major airlines make most of their money from premium travelers and offer discounts mainly to fill unsold seats, Ryanair is able to turn a profit at discount-fare levels.

The carrier, which today bases most of its flights in London, can make money on bargain fares be-

cause it pares costs to the bone and then keeps cutting. Frequent flyer plan? Forget about it. Want a snack or drink on board? You buy it. And Ryanair won't serve peanuts, because prying them out from between the seat cushions takes too long (and hence, costs too much money). In its no-frills fervor, Ryanair even refuses to use those extendable boarding corridors at airports because it's quicker to park a plane at the gate, roll stairs up to the front and back doors, and let passengers hustle across the tarmac. The result: Ryanair can break even with its planes almost half empty—although its average flight is 75 percent full, better than most major European carriers.[5]

What type of pricing strategy is Ryanair following? What might Europe's traditional airlines, like British Airways and Lufthansa, do to counteract Ryanair's success? What other problems might Ryanair face in following this pricing strategy?

---

very close to the competition's price. JCPenney, for example, makes sure it is charging comparable prices by sending representatives to shop at Sears stores.

Although status quo pricing has the advantage of simplicity, its disadvantage is that the strategy may ignore demand or cost or both. If the firm is comparatively small, however, meeting the competition may be the safest route to long-term survival.

2

Identify the legal and ethical constraints on pricing decisions

The Legality and Ethics of Price Strategy

As we mentioned in Chapter 3, some pricing decisions are subject to government regulation. Before marketing managers establish any price strategy, they should know the laws that limit their decision making. Among the issues that fall into this category are unfair trade practices, price fixing, price discrimination, and predatory pricing.

Unfair Trade Practices

unfair trade practice acts
Laws that prohibit wholesalers and retailers from selling below cost.

In over half the states, **unfair trade practice acts** put a floor under wholesale and retail prices. Selling below cost in these states is illegal. Wholesalers and retailers must usually take a certain minimum percentage markup on their combined merchandise cost and transportation cost. The most common markup figures are 6 percent at the retail level and 2 percent at the wholesale level. If a specific wholesaler or retailer can provide "conclusive proof" that operating costs are lower than the minimum required figure, lower prices may be allowed.

The intent of unfair trade practice acts is to protect small local firms from giants like Wal-Mart and Target, which operate very efficiently on razor-thin profit margins. State enforcement of unfair trade practice laws has generally been lax, however, partly because low prices benefit local consumers.

Price Fixing

Price fixing is an agreement between two or more firms on the price they will charge for a product. Suppose two or more executives from competing firms meet to decide how much to charge for a product or to decide which of them will submit the lowest bid on a certain contract. Such practices are illegal under the Sherman Act and the Federal Trade Commission Act. Offenders have received fines and sometimes prison terms. Price fixing is one area where the law is quite clear, and the Justice Department's enforcement is vigorous.

In the past several years, the Justice Department has vigorously pursued price-fixing cases. For example, a jury found three Archer-Daniels-Midland Company executives guilty of fixing the price of lysine, a livestock feed additive. Two of the executives spent two years in prison, and the company paid $197 million in fines.[6]

In another case, Dutch, Belgian, and U.S. companies paid more than $65 million in criminal fines for rigging bids for marine services in the North Sea and Gulf of Mexico. Under one agreement for heavy-lift barges, the conspirators agreed to divide customers, pool revenues, and split profits—and they put it all in writing.

BayerAG, the huge German multinational corporation (makers of Bayer aspirin), agreed to pay $46 million to settle a price-fixing lawsuit accusing it of conspiring with Archer-Daniels-Midland to fix citric acid prices. ADM also pleaded guilty to one criminal charge of price fixing.[7]

Recently, the Justice Department investigated five global paint manufacturers, including DuPont, Sherwin-Williams, and PPG Industries in the United States, for price fixing in the automotive refinishing industry. Concurrently, the Justice Department had at least twenty-five other price-fixing investigations under way in several industries. Supposedly, the paint firms met in Europe to fix wholesale prices in the United States.[8]

And in late 2001, A. Alfred Taubman, chairman of Sotheby's Holdings, the global auction house giant, was found guilty of price fixing. The jury determined that Taubman had conspired with the former chairman of rival Christie's International to fix fees charged to art clients.[9] He was later sentenced to a year and a day in prison and a $7.5 million fine.

Price Discrimination

The Robinson-Patman Act of 1936 prohibits any firm from selling to two or more different buyers, within a reasonably short time, commodities (not services) of like grade and quality at different prices where the result would be to substantially lessen competition. The act also makes it illegal for a seller to offer two buyers different supplementary services and for buyers to use their purchasing power to force sellers into granting discriminatory prices or services.

Six elements are therefore needed for a violation of the Robinson-Patman Act to occur:

Price Fixing

To find out more about current price-fixing cases, type "price fixing" into the AltaVista or Yahoo! Internet search engine. Compare the information you find there with some of the companies' own Web pages. How do companies deal with this type of scandal on their Web sites? Does this surprise you?

http://www.altavista.com

http://www.yahoo.com

On Line

price fixing
An agreement between two or more firms on the price they will charge for a product.

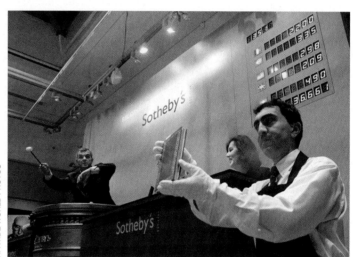

In a scandal that rocked the art world, Sotheby's and Christie's, two of the industry's most venerable auction houses, were caught in a price-fixing scheme. The CEOs of both companies received substantial fines and prison time.

- There must be price discrimination; that is, the seller must charge different prices to different customers for the same product.

- The transaction must occur in interstate commerce.

- The seller must discriminate by price among two or more purchasers; that is, the seller must make two or more actual sales within a reasonably short time.

- The products sold must be commodities or other tangible goods.

- The products sold must be of like grade and quality, not necessarily identical. If the goods are truly interchangeable and substitutable, then they are of like grade and quality.

- There must be significant competitive injury.

The Robinson-Patman Act provides three defenses for the seller charged with price discrimination (in each case the burden is on the defendant to prove the defense):

- *Cost:* A firm can charge different prices to different customers if the prices represent manufacturing or quantity discount savings.

- *Market conditions:* Price variations are justified if designed to meet fluid product or market conditions. Examples include the deterioration of perishable goods, the obsolescence of seasonal products, a distress sale under court order, and a legitimate going-out-of-business sale.

- *Competition:* A reduction in price may be necessary to stay even with the competition. Specifically, if a competitor undercuts the price quoted by a seller to a buyer, the law authorizes the seller to lower the price charged to the buyer for the product in question

Predatory Pricing

predatory pricing
The practice of charging a very low price for a product with the intent of driving competitors out of business or out of a market.

Predatory pricing is the practice of charging a very low price for a product with the intent of driving competitors out of business or out of a market. Once competitors have been driven out, the firm raises its prices. This practice is illegal under the Sherman Act and the Federal Trade Commission Act. Proving the use of the practice is difficult and expensive, however. The Justice Department must show that the predator, the destructive company, explicitly tried to ruin a competitor and that the predatory price was below the predator's average variable cost.

Prosecutions for predatory pricing suffered a major setback recently when a federal judge threw out a predatory pricing suit filed by the Justice Department against American Airlines. Instead of using the traditional predatory pricing definition of pricing below average variable cost, the Justice Department had argued that the definition should be updated and that the test should be whether there was any business justification, other than driving away competitors, for American's aggressive pricing. Under that definition, the Justice Department attorneys thought they had a great case. Whenever a fledgling airline tried to get a toehold in the Dallas market, American would meet its fares and add flights. As soon as the rival retreated, American would jack its fares back up.

Under the average variable cost definition, however, the case would be almost impossible to win. The reason is that like the high-tech industry, the airline industry has high fixed costs and low marginal costs. An airline's biggest expense is buying equipment—its airplanes. Once a flight is scheduled, the marginal cost of providing a seat for an additional passenger is almost zero. Thus, it is very difficult to prove that an airline is pricing below its average variable cost. The judge was not impressed by the Justice Department's argument, however, and stuck to the average variable cost definition of predatory pricing. The ruling likely marks the end of predatory pricing lawsuits for the foreseeable future, and it may well open the door for dominant companies to use predatory pricing to destroy smaller competitors, at least in industries with cost structures similar to the airline industry's.[10]

State Efforts to Drive Down Drug Prices

A recent development in the legality and ethicality of pricing strategies is occurring throughout the United States at the state-government level. Efforts by state governments to cut prescription-drug prices are sweeping across the nation, posing a serious challenge to the U.S. pharmaceutical industry. In mid-2001, Florida became the first state since federal Medicaid laws were overhauled in 1990 to extract additional price concessions from drugmakers. Under federal law, pharmaceutical companies that sell to state Medicaid programs must offer them the same prices they give their most-favored customers. Florida took this a step further, generally requiring companies to offer rebates averaging around 6 percent on top of the already-discounted prices.

Michigan's experiment is potentially even more far-reaching because it extends well beyond Medicaid-funded drugs and takes aim at drug companies' freedom to set prices. Instead of using the prices offered to companies' most-favored customers as a starting point, Michigan is trying to drive all prices down to a low common denominator. A similar movement in Europe, known as "reference pricing," has severely hurt drug company profits there.[11]

In Michigan, a committee of eleven doctors and pharmacists chose the best-in-class drugs in forty categories. These drugs are guaranteed a large portion of the $1.1 billion the state spends each year on prescription medicines for both Medicaid and a state-funded program for the elderly.[12] Doctors can prescribe drugs that aren't on the list but only after justifying their decision in a call to a phone bank of pharmacy technicians—a requirement that is expected to discourage use of unlisted drugs. Thus, all companies wanting to sell drugs under these programs risk losing market share unless they agree to slash prices to win a spot on the preferred list.

As expected, the pharmaceutical companies are filing lawsuits against the states. The companies claim that federal law allows states to limit access to Medicaid-funded drugs only if they offer no clinical benefit, not if the manufacturer doesn't offer a large enough price cut. The cases were still pending at the publication of this text.

State government interference in the pharmaceutical industry is threatening free markets in many states. State governments are beginning to require drugmakers to deeply discount their medications so that the states can save money on government-funded health initiatives and reimbursement programs.

Tactics for Fine-Tuning the Base Price

Explain how discounts, geographic pricing, and other special pricing tactics can be used to fine-tune the base price

base price
The general price level at which the company expects to sell the good or service.

After managers understand both the legal and the marketing consequences of price strategies, they should set a **base price**, the general price level at which the company expects to sell the good or service. The general price level is correlated with the pricing policy: above the market (price skimming), at the market (status quo pricing), or below the market (penetration pricing). The final step, then, is to fine-tune the base price.

Fine-tuning techniques are short-run approaches that do not change the general price level. They do, however, result in changes within a general price level. These pricing tactics allow the firm to adjust for competition in certain markets, meet ever-changing government regulations, take advantage of unique demand situations, and meet promotional and positioning goals. Fine-tuning pricing tactics include various sorts of discounts, geographic pricing, and special pricing tactics.

Discounts, Allowances, Rebates, and Value-Based Pricing

A base price can be lowered through the use of discounts and the related tactics of allowances, rebates, low or zero percent financing, and value-based pricing. Managers use the various forms of discounts to encourage customers to do what they

Edmunds

Which automakers are currently offering rebates? Go to Edmunds' advice page and check out the national and regional incentives, rebates, and leases to find out. What effect do you think rebates and incentives have on overall operating costs and company financial performance?

http://www.edmunds.com/advice/incentives/

 On Line

quantity discount
A price reduction offered to buyers buying in multiple units or above a specified dollar amount.

cumulative quantity discount
A deduction from list price that applies to the buyer's total purchases made during a specific period.

noncumulative quantity discount
A deduction from list price that applies to a single order rather than to the total volume of orders placed during a certain period.

cash discount
A price reduction offered to a consumer, an industrial user, or a marketing intermediary in return for prompt payment of a bill.

functional discount (trade discount)
A discount to wholesalers and retailers for performing channel functions.

seasonal discount
A price reduction for buying merchandise out of season.

promotional allowance (trade allowance)
A payment to a dealer for promoting the manufacturer's products.

rebate
A cash refund given for the purchase of a product during a specific period.

value-based pricing
Setting the price at a level that seems to the customer to be a good price compared to the prices of other options.

would not ordinarily do, such as paying cash rather than using credit, taking delivery out of season, or performing certain functions within a distribution channel. The following are of the most common tactics:

- *Quantity discounts:* When buyers get a lower price for buying in multiple units or above a specified dollar amount, they are receiving a **quantity discount**. A **cumulative quantity discount** is a deduction from list price that applies to the buyer's total purchases made during a specific period; it is intended to encourage customer loyalty. In contrast, a **noncumulative quantity discount** is a deduction from list price that applies to a single order rather than to the total volume of orders placed during a certain period. It is intended to encourage orders in large quantities.

- *Cash discounts:* A **cash discount** is a price reduction offered to a consumer, an industrial user, or a marketing intermediary in return for prompt payment of a bill. Prompt payment saves the seller carrying charges and billing expenses and allows the seller to avoid bad debt.

- *Functional discounts:* When distribution channel intermediaries, such as wholesalers or retailers, perform a service or function for the manufacturer, they must be compensated. This compensation, typically a percentage discount from the base price, is called a **functional discount** (or **trade discount**). Functional discounts vary greatly from channel to channel, depending on the tasks performed by the intermediary.

- *Seasonal discounts:* A **seasonal discount** is a price reduction for buying merchandise out of season. It shifts the storage function to the purchaser. Seasonal discounts also enable manufacturers to maintain a steady production schedule year-round.

- *Promotional allowances:* A **promotional allowance** (also known as a **trade allowance**) is a payment to a dealer for promoting the manufacturer's products. It is both a pricing tool and a promotional device. As a pricing tool, a promotional allowance is like a functional discount. If, for example, a retailer runs an ad for a manufacturer's product, the manufacturer may pay half the cost. If a retailer sets up a special display, the manufacturer may include a certain quantity of free goods in the retailer's next order.

- *Rebates:* A **rebate** is a cash refund given for the purchase of a product during a specific period. The advantage of a rebate over a simple price reduction for stimulating demand is that a rebate is a temporary inducement that can be taken away without altering the basic price structure. A manufacturer that uses a simple price reduction for a short time may meet resistance when trying to restore the price to its original, higher level.

- *Zero percent financing:* After the terrorist attacks on September 11, 2001, new-car sales plummeted. To get people back into the automobile showrooms, manufacturers offered zero percent financing, which enabled purchasers to borrow money to pay for new cars with no interest charge. The tactic created a huge increase in sales but not without cost to the manufacturers. A five-year interest-free car loan represented a cost of over $3,000 on a typical vehicle sold during the zero percent promotion. And several automakers were still offering such incentives over a year later!

Value-Based Pricing

Value-based pricing (also called *value pricing*) is a pricing strategy that has grown out of the quality movement. Instead of figuring prices based on costs or competitors' prices, it starts with the customer, considers the competition, and then determines the appropriate price. The basic assumption is that the firm is customer driven, seeking to understand the attributes customers want in the goods and services they buy and the value of that bundle of attributes to customers. Because very few firms operate in a pure monopoly, however, a marketer using value-based pricing must also determine the value of competitive offerings to customers. Customers determine the value of a product (not just its price) relative to the value of alternatives. In value-based pricing, therefore, the price of the product is set at a level that seems to the customer to be a good price compared with the prices of other options.

Procter & Gamble instituted a form of value pricing in 1992. In an effort to reduce operating costs and strengthen brand loyalty, it coupled value prices with increased advertising but a reduction in coupons, product displays, and other forms of sales promotion (see Chapter 16). The introduction of value pricing meant that average P&G prices fell across twenty-four product categories. Yet, as costs rose during the 1990s, there was a corresponding increase in the prices of P&G's products. P&G's change in pricing tactics, sales promotion, and advertising strategies resulted in an average 18 percent loss in market share across the twenty-four categories during the 1990s. Researchers, using sophisticated analytical models, found that most of the loss in market share was due to the severe cuts in coupons and sales promotion deals.[13] Because competitors' prices also rose during the decade, P&G's price increases played a lesser role in the loss of market share. P&G had hoped that increased advertising would strengthen brand loyalty and therefore increase sales, but it did not. As P&G's experience demonstrates, value pricing alone does not guarantee increased market share or profitability.

You read in Chapter 17 how the Internet is affecting pricing strategies, and that extends to the world of coupons and rebates. Many sites, like ebates.com, catalog rebate opportunities and pass information along to consumers who are willing to sign up.

Pricing Products Too Low

Sometimes managers price their products too low, thereby reducing company profits.[14] This seems to happen for two reasons. First, managers attempt to buy market share through aggressive pricing. Usually, however, these price cuts are quickly met by competitors. Thus, any gain in market share is short-lived, and overall industry profits end up falling. Second, managers have a natural tendency to want to make decisions that can be justified objectively. The problem is that companies often lack hard data on the complex determinants of profitability, such as the relationship between price changes and sales volumes, the link between demand levels and costs, and the likely responses of competitors to price changes. In contrast, companies usually have rich, unambiguous information on costs, sales, market share, and competitors' prices. As a result, managers tend to make pricing decisions based on current costs, projected short-term share gains, or current competitor prices rather than on long-term profitability.

The problem of "underpricing" can be solved by linking information about price, cost, and demand within the same decision support system. The demand data can be developed via marketing research. This will enable managers to get the hard data they need to calculate the effects of pricing decisions on profitability.

Occasionally, underpricing occurs by mistake. When this happens, what are the company's obligations to its customers? The "Ethics in Marketing" box explores this issue.

Geographic Pricing

Because many sellers ship their wares to a nationwide or even a worldwide market, the cost of freight can greatly affect the total cost of a product. Sellers may use several different geographic pricing tactics to moderate the impact of freight costs on distant customers. The following methods of geographic pricing are the most common:

- *FOB origin pricing:* **FOB origin pricing**, also called FOB factory or FOB shipping point, is a price tactic that requires the buyer to absorb the freight costs from the shipping point ("free on board"). The farther buyers are from sellers, the

FOB origin pricing
A price tactic that requires the buyer to absorb the freight costs from the shipping point ("free on board").

Less Than $30 to Paris? United Airlines Says "Oops"

Eric Bescher almost flew to Paris for less than $30. An elite-level United Airlines frequent flyer from Los Angeles, Bescher visited United's Web site to search for a low fare to Europe. The deal he found was a lot better than he'd bargained for—passage to France for less than the price of a bottle of good burgundy. A technical glitch at the site listed the round-trip fare from San Jose to Paris as just $27.98. "I snapped it up right away," he says.

Bescher wasn't alone in his good fortune. United Airlines says it inadvertently sold 143 tickets to destinations such as Hong Kong at *really* rock bottom prices via its Web site, ual.com, during a fifty-five-minute period.

United says a computer bug "zeroed out" the fare on a number of international flights so that the amounts shown reflected only a portion of the taxes and miscellaneous fees. In fact, fares were in a free-for-all: One minute a round-trip fare from San Francisco to Paris was $85.42; seconds later that same ticket sold for $24.98.

United spokesman Chris Brathwaite says the airline won't honor any tickets sold at those prices. "Anyone who thought they could fly from L.A. to Paris for $27 should have known better," Brathwaite says. He likens the situation to a bank error when the teller inadvertently hands the customer a $1,000 bill instead of $100. "It's clearly a mistake: Everyone knows you don't fly first class to Paris for $29," he says. "You don't get something for nothing."

United is in the process of contacting customers to let them know what the "correct" fare is. As a consolation, United says it will waive any cancellation fees should passengers not wish to pay the difference.

Some travelers are fuming nonetheless. One United flyer from Orange County, California, says United even sent an e-mail confirmation of his purchase of two tickets between San Jose and Paris for $85 each and now refuses to honor that price. As someone who spent more than $130,000 on United last year, the flyer, who asked that his name not be used, says he believes the airline has a responsibility to honor the tickets because its own Web site was responsible for the error.

Moments after purchasing his ticket to Paris, Bescher also received an e-mail confirmation of the $27.98 fare. But days later, United charged his credit card $573—what he assumes is the price he would have been quoted for the ticket had ual.com been working correctly.

Bescher immediately contacted United's customer service office about what he viewed as an unauthorized charge, and is still awaiting a response. "If they don't come through with a goodwill gesture," he says, "I'm going to dispute it."

In the meantime, prices returned to earth at ual.com. Two weeks after the glitch-driven fare sale, the lowest price for a round-trip ticket for travel between San Jose and Paris was $510.[15]

Should United honor the very low fares? Wouldn't United receive great publicity if it honors the fares? It could write off the cost as a promotional expense. Or were the mistakes like bank errors and customers should not expect United to honor the fares?

---

more they pay, because transportation costs generally increase with the distance merchandise is shipped.

- *Uniform delivered pricing:* If the marketing manager wants total costs, including freight, to be equal for all purchasers of identical products, the firm will adopt uniform delivered pricing, or "postage stamp" pricing. With **uniform delivered pricing**, the seller pays the actual freight charges and bills every purchaser an identical, flat freight charge.

- *Zone pricing:* A marketing manager who wants to equalize total costs among buyers within large geographic areas—but not necessarily all of the seller's market area—may modify the base price with a zone-pricing tactic. **Zone pricing** is a modification of uniform delivered pricing. Rather than placing the entire United States (or its total market) under a uniform freight rate, the firm divides it into segments or zones and charges a flat freight rate to all customers in a given zone. The U.S. Postal Service's parcel post rate structure is probably the best-known zone-pricing system in the country.

- *Freight absorption pricing:* In **freight absorption pricing**, the seller pays all or part of the actual freight charges and does not pass them on to the buyer. The manager may use this tactic in intensely competitive areas or as a way to break into new market areas.

uniform delivered pricing
A price tactic in which the seller pays the actual freight charges and bills every purchaser an identical, flat freight charge.

zone pricing
A modification of uniform delivered pricing that divides the United States (or the total market) into segments or zones and charges a flat freight rate to all customers in a given zone.

freight absorption pricing
A price tactic in which the seller pays all or part of the actual freight charges and does not pass them on to the buyer.

- *Basing-point pricing:* With **basing-point pricing**, the seller designates a location as a basing point and charges all buyers the freight cost from that point, regardless of the city from which the goods are shipped. Thanks to several adverse court rulings, basing-point pricing has waned in popularity. Freight fees charged when none were actually incurred, called *phantom freight*, have been declared illegal.

Special Pricing Tactics

Unlike geographic pricing, special pricing tactics are unique and defy neat categorization. Managers use these tactics for various reasons—for example, to stimulate demand for specific products, to increase store patronage, and to offer a wider variety of merchandise at a specific price point. Special pricing tactics include a single-price tactic, flexible pricing, professional services pricing, price lining, leader pricing, bait pricing, odd–even pricing, price bundling, and two-part pricing. A brief overview of each of these tactics follows, along with a manager's reasons for using that tactic or a combination of tactics to change the base price.

Single-Price Tactic

A merchant using a **single-price tactic** offers all goods and services at the same price (or perhaps two or three prices). Retailers using this tactic include One Price Clothing Stores, Dre\$\$ to the Nine\$, Your \$10 Store, and Fashions \$9.99. One Price Clothing Stores, for example, tend to be small, about three thousand square feet. Their goal is to offer merchandise that would sell for at least \$15 to \$18 in other stores. The stores carry pants, shirts, blouses, sweaters, and shorts for juniors, misses, and large-sized women. The stores do not feature any seconds or irregular items, and everything is sold for \$6.

Single-price selling removes price comparisons from the buyer's decision-making process. The consumer just looks for suitability and the highest perceived quality. The retailer enjoys the benefits of a simplified pricing system and minimal clerical errors. However, continually rising costs are a headache for retailers following this strategy. In times of inflation, they must frequently raise the selling price.

Flexible Pricing

Flexible pricing (or **variable pricing**) means that different customers pay different prices for essentially the same merchandise bought in equal quantities. This tactic is often found in the sale of shopping goods, specialty merchandise, and most industrial goods except supply items. Car dealers, many appliance retailers, and manufacturers of industrial installations, accessories, and component parts commonly follow the practice. It allows the seller to adjust for competition by meeting another seller's price. Thus, a marketing manager with a status quo pricing objective might readily adopt the tactic. Flexible pricing also enables the seller to close a sale with price-conscious consumers. If buyers show promise of becoming large-volume shoppers, flexible pricing can be used to lure their business.

The obvious disadvantages of flexible pricing are the lack of consistent profit margins, the potential ill will of high-paying purchasers, the tendency for salespeople to automatically lower the price to make a sale, and the possibility of a price war among sellers. The disadvantages of flexible pricing have led the automobile industry to experiment with one price for all buyers. General Motors uses a one-price tactic for some of its models, including the Saturn and the Buick Regal.

Professional Services Pricing

Professional services pricing is used by people with lengthy experience, training, and often certification by a licensing board—for example, lawyers, physicians, and family counselors. Professionals sometimes charge customers at an hourly rate, but sometimes fees are based on the solution of a problem or performance of an act

basing-point pricing
A price tactic that charges freight from a given (basing) point, regardless of the city from which the goods are shipped.

single-price tactic
A price tactic that offers all goods and services at the same price (or perhaps two or three prices).

flexible pricing (variable pricing)
A price tactic in which different customers pay different prices for essentially the same merchandise bought in equal quantities.

(such as an eye examination) rather than on the actual time involved. A surgeon may perform a heart operation and charge a flat fee of $5,000. The operation itself may require only four hours, resulting in a hefty $1,250 hourly rate. The physician justifies the fee because of the lengthy education and internship required to learn the complex procedures of a heart operation. Lawyers also sometimes use flat-rate pricing, such as $500 for completing a divorce and $50 for handling a traffic ticket.

Those who use professional pricing have an ethical responsibility not to overcharge a customer. Because demand is sometimes highly inelastic, such as when a person requires heart surgery or a daily insulin shot to survive, there may be a temptation to charge "all the traffic will bear."

Price Lining

price lining
The practice of offering a product line with several items at specific price points.

When a seller establishes a series of prices for a type of merchandise, it creates a price line. **Price lining** is the practice of offering a product line with several items at specific price points. For example, Hon, an office furniture manufacturer, may offer its four-drawer file cabinets at $125, $250, and $400. The Limited may offer women's dresses at $40, $70, and $100, with no merchandise marked at prices between those figures. Instead of a normal demand curve running from $40 to $100, The Limited has three demand points (prices). Theoretically, the "curve" exists only because people would buy goods at the in-between prices if it were possible to do so. For example, a number of dresses could be sold at $60, but no sales will occur at that price because $60 is not part of the price line.

Price lining reduces confusion for both the salesperson and the consumer. The buyer may be offered a wider variety of merchandise at each established price. Price lines may also enable a seller to reach several market segments. For buyers, the question of price may be quite simple: All they have to do is find a suitable product at the predetermined price. Moreover, price lining is a valuable tactic for the marketing manager, because the firm may be able to carry a smaller total inventory than it could without price lines. The results may include fewer markdowns, simplified purchasing, and lower inventory carrying charges.

Price lines also present drawbacks, especially if costs are continually rising. Sellers can offset rising costs in three ways. First, they can begin stocking lower quality merchandise at each price point. Second, sellers can change the prices, although frequent price line changes confuse buyers. Third, sellers can accept lower profit margins and hold quality and prices constant. This third alternative has short-run benefits, but its long-run handicaps may drive sellers out of business.

Leader Pricing

leader pricing (loss-leader pricing)
A price tactic in which a product is sold near or even below cost in the hope that shoppers will buy other items once they are in the store.

Leader pricing (or **loss-leader pricing**) is an attempt by the marketing manager to attract customers by selling a product near or even below cost in the hope that shoppers will buy other items once they are in the store. This type of pricing appears weekly in the newspaper advertising of supermarkets, specialty stores, and department stores. Leader pricing is normally used on well-known items that consumers can easily recognize as bargains at the special price. The goal is not necessarily to sell large quantities of leader items, but to try to appeal to customers who might shop elsewhere.

Leader pricing is not limited to products. Health clubs offer a one-month free trial as a loss leader. Lawyers give a free initial consultation. And restaurants distribute two-for-one coupons and "welcome to the neighborhood" free meal coupons.

Bait Pricing

bait pricing
A price tactic that tries to get consumers into a store through false or misleading price advertising and then uses high-pressure selling to persuade consumers to buy more expensive merchandise.

In contrast to leader pricing, which is a genuine attempt to give the consumer a reduced price, bait pricing is deceptive. **Bait pricing** tries to get the consumer into a store through false or misleading price advertising and then uses high-pressure selling to persuade the consumer to buy more expensive merchandise. You may have seen this ad or a similar one:

> REPOSSESSED . . . Singer slant-needle sewing machine . . . take over 8 payments of $5.10 per month . . . ABC Sewing Center.

This is bait. When a customer goes in to see the machine, a salesperson says that it has just been sold or else shows the prospective buyer a piece of junk no one would buy. Then the salesperson says, "But I've got a really good deal on this fine new model." This is the switch that may cause a susceptible consumer to walk out with a $400 machine. The Federal Trade Commission considers bait pricing a deceptive act and has banned its use in interstate commerce. Most states also ban bait pricing, but sometimes enforcement is lax.

Odd–Even Pricing

Odd–even pricing (or **psychological pricing**) means pricing at odd-numbered prices to connote a bargain and pricing at even-numbered prices to imply quality. For years, many retailers have priced their products in odd numbers—for example, $99.95 or $49.95—to make consumers feel they are paying a lower price for the product.

Some retailers favor odd-numbered prices because they believe that $9.99 sounds much less imposing to customers than $10.00. Other retailers believe that an odd-numbered price signals to consumers that the price is at the lowest level possible, thereby encouraging them to buy more units. Neither theory has ever been conclusively proved, although one study found that consumers perceive odd-priced products as being on sale.[16] The most recent research shows that consumers do purchase more at odd prices.[17]

Even-numbered pricing is sometimes used to denote quality. Examples include a fine perfume at $100 a bottle, a good watch at $500, or a mink coat at $3,000. The demand curve for such items would also be sawtoothed, except that the outside edges would represent even-numbered prices and, therefore, elastic demand.

Price Bundling

Price bundling is marketing two or more products in a single package for a special price. Examples include the sale of maintenance contracts with computer hardware and other office equipment, packages of stereo equipment, packages of options on cars, weekend hotel packages that include a room and several meals, and airline vacation packages. Microsoft offers "suites" of software that bundle spreadsheets, word processing, graphics, electronic mail, Internet access, and groupware for networks of microcomputers. Price bundling can stimulate demand for the bundled items if the target market perceives the price as a good value.[18]

Services like hotels and airlines sell a perishable commodity (hotel rooms and airline seats) with relatively constant fixed costs. Bundling can be an important income stream for these businesses because the variable cost tends to be low—for instance, the cost of cleaning a hotel room or putting one more passenger on an airplane. Therefore, most of the revenue can help cover fixed costs and generate profits.[19]

odd–even pricing (psychological pricing)
A price tactic that uses odd-numbered prices to connote bargains and even-numbered prices to imply quality.

price bundling
Marketing two or more products in a single package for a special price.

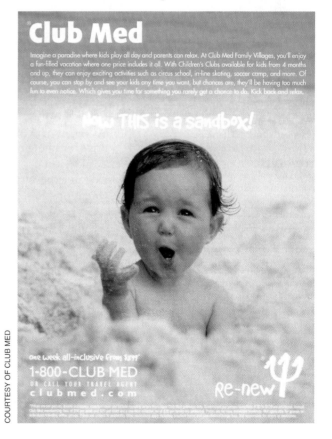

COURTESY OF CLUB MED

Club Med advertises an all-inclusive vacation for one from $899 in this humorous ad. Included in the price are the room, airfare, meals, sports, and children's clubs. However, several contingencies are placed on this bundled vacation—listed in the ad's fine print.

The automobile industry has a different motive for bundling. People buy cars only every three to five years. Thus, selling options is a somewhat rare opportunity for the car dealer. Price bundling can help the dealer sell a maximum number of options.

Bundling has also been used in the telecommunications industry. Companies offer local service, long distance, DSL Internet service, wireless, and even cable TV in various menus of bundling. Such bundling is not necessarily consumer focused. Telecom companies use bundling as a way to protect their market share and fight off competition by locking customers into a group of services. For consumers, comparison shopping may be difficult since they may not be able to determine how much they are really paying for each component of the bundle.[20]

A related price tactic is **unbundling**, or reducing the bundle of services that comes with the basic product. Rather than raise the price of hotel rooms, some hotel chains have started charging registered guests for parking. To help hold the line on costs, some stores require customers to pay for gift wrapping.

Some of the latest research has focused on how people consume certain bundled services. When people buy season tickets to a concert series, sporting event, or other activity, studies show that the sunk costs (price of the bundle) and the pending benefit (going to see an event) become decoupled. This reduces the likelihood of consumption of the event over time. For example, researchers found that theatergoers who purchased tickets to four plays were only 84 percent likely to use their first-play tickets and only 78 percent likely to use any given ticket across the four plays.[21]

In contrast, theatergoers who purchased tickets to a single play were almost certain to use those tickets. This is consistent with the idea that in a one-to-one transaction (i.e., one payment, one benefit), the costs and benefits of that transaction are tightly coupled, resulting in strong sunk cost pressure to consume the pending benefit. In other words, "I bought this ticket, now I've got to use it."

In practice, these findings mean that a theater manager might expect a no-show rate of 20 percent when the percentage of season ticket holders is high, but a no-show rate of only 5 percent when the percentage of season ticket holders is low. With a high number of season ticket holders, a manager could oversell performances and maximize the revenue for the theater. Airlines routinely overbook in anticipation of a predictable percentage of no-shows.

Price bundling of services can result in a lower rate of total consumption of that service. The same is not necessarily true, however, for products. Consider the purchase of an expensive bottle of wine, which can be inventoried until needed. When the wine is purchased as a single unit, its cost and eventual benefit are tightly coupled. As a result, the cost of the wine will be quite important, and a person will likely reserve that wine for a special occasion. When purchased as part of a bundle (e.g., as part of a case of wine), however, the cost and benefit of that individual bottle of wine will likely become decoupled, reducing the impact of the cost on eventual consumption. As a result, a person will likely find the wine appropriate for many more (not-so-special) occasions. Thus, in contrast to the price bundling of services, the price bundling of physical goods could lead to an increase in product consumption.

unbundling
Reducing the bundle of services that comes with the basic product.

AP/WIDE WORLD PHOTOS

In order to maximize revenue, managers could oversell tickets to an event for which season ticket subscriptions are high. This is because people who buy season tickets for an event, like these students from the University of Mississippi, holding their just-purchased season basketball tickets, are less likely to use all the tickets they purchase.

Two-Part Pricing

two-part pricing
A price tactic that charges two separate amounts to consume a single good or service.

Two-part pricing means establishing two separate charges to consume a single good or service. Tennis clubs and health clubs charge a membership fee and a flat fee each time a person uses certain equipment or facilities. In other cases they charge a base rate for a certain level of usage, such as ten racquetball games per month, and a surcharge for anything over that amount.[22]

Consumers sometimes prefer two-part pricing because they are uncertain about the number and the types of activities they might use at places like an amusement park. Also, the people who use a service most often pay a higher total price. Two-part pricing can increase a seller's revenue by attracting consumers who would not pay a high fee even for unlimited use. For example, a health club might be able to sell only 100 memberships at $700 annually with unlimited use of facilities, for total revenue of $70,000. However, perhaps it could sell 900 memberships at $200 with a guarantee of using the racquetball courts ten times a month. Every use over ten would require the member to pay a $5 fee. Thus, membership revenue would provide a base of $180,000, with some additional usage fees coming in throughout the year.

Consumer Penalties

More and more businesses are adopting **consumer penalties**—extra fees paid by consumers for violating the terms of a purchase agreement (see Exhibit 18.2 on the next page).

Businesses impose consumer penalties for two reasons: They will allegedly (1) suffer an irrevocable revenue loss and/or (2) incur significant additional transaction costs should customers be unable or unwilling to complete their purchase obligations. For the company, these customer payments are part of doing business in a highly competitive marketplace. With profit margins in many companies increasingly coming under pressure, organizations are looking to stem losses resulting from customers not meeting their obligations. However, the perceived unfairness of a penalty may affect some consumers' willingness to patronize a business in the future.

One study found that most consumers (53 percent) had paid a price penalty in the past year. A "fair" penalty exists when consumers believe that they are reimbursing the seller for actual lost revenue and not simply enabling the seller to make extra profit.[23]

consumer penalty
An extra fee paid by the consumer for violating the terms of the purchase agreement.

Product Line Pricing

Product line pricing is setting prices for an entire line of products. Compared to setting the right price on a single product, product line pricing encompasses broader concerns. In product line pricing, the marketing manager tries to achieve maximum profits or other goals for the entire line rather than for a single component of the line.

Discuss product line pricing

product line pricing
Setting prices for an entire line of products.

Relationships among Products

The manager must first determine the type of relationship that exists among the various products in the line:

- If items are *complementary,* an increase in the sale of one good causes an increase in demand for the complementary product, and vice versa. For example, the sale of ski poles depends on the demand for skis, making these two items complementary.

The demand curve is influenced by the relationship between products. For example, the demand for bindings depends on the demand for skis. This kind of relationship is described as complementary.

© INDEX STOCK IMAGERY/TOM STILLO

Exhibit 18.2

Common Consumer Penalties

1. Airlines

- Most airlines charge a penalty of $75 for changing reservations on discount tickets.
- A lost ticket can result in the traveler paying full price for a new ticket, with a possible refund later, but usually with an administration penalty fee added.
- Some travel agents charge an additional $10 to $20 penalty for canceled tickets with values under $200.

2. Automobiles

- Penalties are imposed for early terminations of car leases. In some cases, deposits on canceled leases can be subject to penalties.
- Car owners in England pay penalties, administration fees, and commissions if they cancel an insurance policy early.

3. Banks

- Penalties are often associated with early withdrawal of certificates of deposit.
- Some banks charge penalties for too many withdrawals in a month.
- Some have monthly penalties of $5 to $10 if a client's balance falls below a minimum level.
- Banks can charge late fees, in addition to interest, for tardy payments.
- The Senate Banking Committee is examining legislation to prohibit banks with ATMs from charging penalty fees to users who are customers of another bank.

4. Car Rentals

- Rental companies often have $25 to $100 penalties for no-shows for specialty vehicles. Budget, National, and Dollar/Thrifty are experimenting with no-show fees on all rentals.

5. Child Day Care

- Many day-care centers charge a penalty of up to $5 a minute when parents are late in picking up their children.

6. Cellular Phones

- Companies have cancellation penalties, often in the small print on the back of a contract, that can run as high as $525.

7. Credit and Debit Cards

- Some vendors now charge late fees (beyond normal interest). Lenders collect about $2 billion in late charges each year.
- GE Rewards MasterCard charges $25 a year for those who pay their bill each month, in full, on time. Advanta credit card company may charge $25 for six-month inactivity on an account and $25 to close an account.

8. Cruises

- If a cruise is sailing, even though there are hurricane warnings, some cruise lines will assess penalties if a passenger cancels.
- Even trip cancellation insurance will not ensure a refund if the traveler has embarked on the trip.
- Britain is trying to crack down on executive cancellation penalties on package holidays.
- The *Carnival Paradise* will disembark passengers found smoking.

9. Hotels

- Some hotels require 72 hours' cancellation notice, or the client must pay a penalty of one day's room cost.
- Most hotels have high charges for using in-room long-distance service.
- Hilton, Hyatt, and Westin have early departure fees ranging from $25 to $50.

10. Restaurants

- Some now charge up to $50 per person for no-show parties.

11. Retail Stores

- Circuit City and Best Buy are leading others in charging a 15 percent restocking fee on some items. A restocking fee is for putting a returned item back in inventory.

12. Trains

- Amtrak has a $20 penalty for a returned ticket and charges the same fee for changing a ticket.

13. Universities

- Universities will give only a partial tuition refund if a student becomes ill after a course begins.

SOURCE: Eugene Fram and Michael McCarthy, "The True Price of Penalties," *Marketing Management*, Fall 1999, 51.

- Two products in a line can also be *substitutes* for each other. If buyers buy one item in the line, they are less likely to buy a second item in the line. For example, if someone goes to an automotive supply store and buys paste Turtle Wax for a car, it is very unlikely that he or she will buy liquid Turtle Wax in the near future.

- A *neutral* relationship can also exist between two products. In other words, demand for one of the products is unrelated to demand for the other. For instance, Ralston Purina sells chicken feed and Wheat Chex, but the sale of one of these products has no known impact on demand for the other.

Joint Costs

Joint costs are costs that are shared in the manufacturing and marketing of several products in a product line. These costs pose a unique problem in product pricing. In oil refining, for example, fuel oil, gasoline, kerosene, naphtha, paraffin, and lubricating oils are all derived from a common production process. Another example is the production of compact discs that combine photos and music.

Any assignment of joint costs must be somewhat subjective because costs are actually shared. Suppose a company produces two products, X and Y, in a common production process, with joint costs allocated on a weight basis. Product X weighs 1,000 pounds, and product Y weighs 500 pounds. Thus, costs are allocated on the basis of $2 for X for every $1 for Y. Gross margins (sales less the cost of goods sold) might then be as follows:

	Product X	Product Y	Total
Sales	$20,000	$6,000	$26,000
Less: cost of goods sold	15,000	7,500	22,500
Gross margin	$ 5,000	($1,500)	$ 3,500

This statement reveals a loss of $1,500 on product Y. Is that important? Yes, any loss is important. However, the firm must realize that overall it earned a $3,500 profit on the two items in the line. Also, weight may not be the right way to allocate the joint costs. Instead, the firm might use other bases, including market value or quantity sold.

Beauty.com

Does Beauty.com use a product line pricing strategy? Choose a brand and view the product list and pricing sheet. What evidence do you see of product line pricing? Of other pricing strategies?

http://www.beauty.com

On Line

joint costs
Costs that are shared in the manufacturing and marketing of several products in a product line.

Pricing during Difficult Economic Times

Pricing is always an important aspect of marketing, but it is especially crucial in times of inflation and recession. The firm that does not adjust to economic trends may lose ground that it can never make up.

Describe the role of pricing during periods of inflation and recession

Inflation

When the economy is characterized by high inflation, special pricing tactics are often necessary. They can be subdivided into cost-oriented and demand-oriented tactics.

Cost-Oriented Tactics

One popular cost-oriented tactic is *culling products with a low profit margin* from the product line. However, this tactic may backfire for three reasons:

- A high volume of sales on an item with a low profit margin may still make the item highly profitable.

- Eliminating a product from a product line may reduce economies of scale, thereby lowering the margins on other items.

- Eliminating the product may affect the price–quality image of the entire line.

Another popular cost-oriented tactic is **delayed-quotation pricing**, which is used for industrial installations and many accessory items. Price is not set on the product until the item is either finished or delivered. Long production lead times force many firms to adopt this policy during periods of inflation. Builders of nuclear power plants, ships, airports, and office towers sometimes use delayed-quotation tactics.

Escalator pricing is similar to delayed-quotation pricing in that the final selling price reflects cost increases incurred between the time an order is placed and the time delivery is made. An escalator clause allows for price increases (usually across

delayed-quotation pricing
A price tactic used for industrial installations and many accessory items, in which a firm price is not set until the item is either finished or delivered.

escalator pricing
A price tactic in which the final selling price reflects cost increases incurred between the time the order is placed and the time delivery is made.

the board) based on the cost-of-living index or some other formula. As with any price increase, management's ability to implement such a policy is based on inelastic demand for the product. About a third of all industrial product manufacturers now use escalator clauses. Many companies do not apply the clause in every sale, however. Often it is used only for extremely complex products that take a long time to produce or with new customers.

Any cost-oriented pricing policy that tries to maintain a fixed gross margin under all conditions can lead to a vicious circle. For example, a price increase will result in decreased demand, which in turn increases production costs (because of lost economies of scale). Increased production costs require a further price increase, leading to further diminished demand, and so on.

Demand-Oriented Tactics

Demand-oriented pricing tactics use price to reflect changing patterns of demand caused by inflation or high interest rates. Cost changes are considered, of course, but mostly in the context of how increased prices will affect demand.

Price shading is the use of discounts by salespeople to increase demand for one or more products in a line. Often shading becomes habitual and is done routinely without much forethought.[24] Ducommun, a metals producer, is among the major companies that have succeeded in eliminating the practice. Ducommun has told its salespeople, "We want no deviation from book price" unless authorized by management.

To make the demand for a good or service more inelastic and to create buyer dependency, a company can use several strategies:

- *Cultivate selected demand:* Marketing managers can target prosperous customers who will pay extra for convenience or service. Neiman Marcus, for example, stresses quality. As a result, the luxury retailer is more lenient with suppliers and their price increases than is Alexander's Stores, a discounter. In cultivating close relationships with affluent organizational customers, marketing managers should avoid putting themselves at the mercy of a dominant firm. They can more easily raise prices when an account is readily replaceable. Finally, in companies where engineers exert more influence than purchasing departments do, performance is favored over price. Often a preferred vendor's pricing range expands if other suppliers prove technically unsatisfactory.

- *Create unique offerings:* Marketing managers should study buyers' needs. If the seller can design distinctive goods or services uniquely fitting buyers' activities, equipment, and procedures, a mutually beneficial relationship will evolve. Buyers would incur high changeover costs in switching to another supplier. By satisfying targeted buyers in a superior way, marketing managers can make them dependent. Cereal manufacturers have skirted around passing on costs by marketing unique value-added or multi-ingredient cereals, increasing the perceived quality of cereals and allowing companies to raise prices. These cereals include General Mills' Basic 4, Clusters, and Oatmeal Crisp; Post's Banana Nut Crunch and Blueberry Morning; and Kellogg's Mueslix, Nutri-Grain, and Temptations.

- *Change the package design:* Another way companies pass on higher costs is to shrink product sizes but keep prices the same. Scott Paper Company reduced the number of sheets in the smallest roll of Scott Clean paper towels from ninety-six to sixty and actually lowered the price by 10¢ a roll. The increases in costs for paper towels were tied to a 50 to 60 percent increase in the cost of pulp paper. The company also changed the names of the sizes to deemphasize the magnitude of the rolls. "We used to have three sizes: big, extra large, and megaroll," said Pete Judice, spokesperson for Scott. "We changed the names to single, double, and triple because they're easier [for the consumers] to relate to."[25]

- *Heighten buyer dependence:* Owens-Corning Fiberglas supplies an integrated insulation service (from feasibility studies to installation) that includes commercial and scientific training for distributors and seminars for end users. This practice freezes out competition and supports higher prices.

Recession

Kroger

How does Kroger's Web site promote its store brands? Is the site designed more to promote the store or its brands?

http://www.kroger.com

On Line

A recession is a period of reduced economic activity. Reduced demand for goods and services, along with higher rates of unemployment, is a common trait of a recession. Yet astute marketers can often find opportunity during recessions. A recession is an excellent time to build market share because competitors are struggling to make ends meet.

Two effective pricing tactics to hold or build market share during a recession are value-based pricing and bundling. *Value-based pricing*, discussed earlier in the chapter, stresses to customers that they are getting a good value for their money. Charles of the Ritz, usually known for its pricey products, introduced the Express Bar during a recession. A collection of affordable cosmetics and skin treatment products, the Express Bar sold alongside regular Ritz products in department stores. Although lower priced products offer lower profit margins, Ritz found that increases in volume can offset slimmer margins. For example, the company found that consumers will buy two to three Express Bar lipsticks at a time. "The consumer is very conscious of how she spends her income and is looking for value and quality that she can find elsewhere in department stores," said Holly Mercer, vice president of marketing for Ritz.[26]

Bundling or *unbundling* can also stimulate demand during a recession. If features are added to a bundle, consumers may perceive the offering as having greater value. For example, suppose that Hyatt offers a "great escape" weekend for $119. The package includes two nights' lodging and a continental breakfast. Hyatt could add a massage and a dinner for two to create more value for this price. Conversely, companies can unbundle offerings and lower base prices to stimulate demand. A furniture store, for example, could start charging separately for design consultation, delivery, credit, setup, and hauling away old furniture.

Recessions are a good time for marketing managers to study the demand for individual items in a product line and the revenue they produce. Pruning unprofitable items can save resources to be better used elsewhere. Borden's, for example, found that it made about 3,200 sizes, brands, types, and flavors of snacks—but got 95 percent of its revenues from just half of them.

Retailers also use recessions to drop or reduce shelf space for manufacturers' brands and introduce more store brands. Consumers increase their consumption of store brands during recessions because these products are typically less expensive. During the recession of the early 2000s, one out of every five items purchased at U.S. supermarkets, drugstores, and mass merchandisers such as Wal-Mart was a store brand.[27]

Kroger Company, the second largest U.S. supermarket operator, reported that house brands contributed to a tripling of net income in 2001. The Cincinnati company added hundreds of private-label products during the year, for a total of five thousand Kroger-branded products. Today, store brands generate over $50 billion in sales in the United States each year.[28]

Prices often fall during a recession as competitors try desperately to maintain demand for their wares. Even if demand remains constant, falling prices mean lower profits or no profits. Falling prices, therefore, are a natural incentive to lower costs. During the last recession, companies implemented new technology to improve efficiency and then slashed payrolls. They also discovered that suppliers were an excellent source of cost savings; the cost of purchased materials accounts for slightly more than half of most U.S. manufacturers' expenses. General Electric's appliance division told three hundred key suppliers that they had to reduce prices 10 percent or risk losing GE's business. Honeywell, Dow Chemical, United Airlines, General Motors, and DuPont made similar demands of their suppliers. Specific strategies that companies use with suppliers include the following:

- *Renegotiating contracts:* Sending suppliers letters demanding price cuts of 5 percent or more; putting out for rebid the contracts of those that refuse to cut costs.

- *Offering help:* Dispatching teams of experts to suppliers' plants to help reorganize and suggest other productivity-boosting changes; working with suppliers to make parts simpler and cheaper to produce.

- *Keeping the pressure on:* To make sure that improvements continue, setting annual, across-the-board cost-reduction targets, often of 5 percent or more a year.

- *Paring down suppliers:* To improve economies of scale, slashing the overall number of suppliers, sometimes by up to 80 percent, and boosting purchases from those that remain.

Tough tactics like these help keep companies afloat during economic downturns.

CONNECT IT

Dell Computer, as described at the beginning of the chapter, is using a penetration pricing strategy. The company can fine-tune the base price with discounts, FOB pricing or other geographic pricing tactics, price bundling, rebates, and leader pricing. Dell can offer a number of discounts. These include cash, cumulative quantity, noncumulative quantity, and seasonal discounts.

USE IT

 Auctions accounted for 29 percent of all e-commerce, or $129 billion, in 2002.[29] Why not join the crowd? You must, however, avoid the "winner's curse"—that is, overestimating the value of an item and bidding too much. The best way to avoid this is to be informed. On eBay (http://www.ebay.com), bidders can study past auctions of similar items and also read feedback about sellers.

To try something different, go to http://www. klik-klok.com, which is a Dutch auction. Modeled on Holland's famous flower markets, Dutch auctions are essentially the reverse of Yankee auctions: A set quantity of a certain item is available for a limited amount of time. On Klik-klok, for example, each auction lasts just two minutes, and there's an auction every three minutes. When the clock starts ticking, the item is available at its starting price. Then the price starts dropping—and keeps dropping by a few dollars every twenty seconds or so. Bidders try to hold out for the lowest price on the product that they want until just before all the items are bought by those willing to pay slightly more. The advantages of this format are obvious: The longer you play, the more prices go down instead of up—and you know immediately if your bid has "won."[30]

You can also save some money by using coupons. Whether you're shopping on-line or heading to the mall, make a pit stop at Ultimate-Coupons.com. The site features coupons from more than a hundred major retailers (mostly on the Web) in categories such as groceries and electronics. It also searches through offers on other coupon Web sites, so you'll get the best deals. One recent bargain: Save $10 when you spend $75 or more at Amazon.com. Printable coupons are available for brick-and-mortar stores; discount codes are provided for orders at e-tailers.

Compare prices before you buy. Rely on price comparison services like My Simon (http://www. mysimon.com) or Price Scan (http://www. pricescan.com).

(1) **Describe the procedure for setting the right price.** The process of setting the right price on a product involves four major steps: (1) establishing pricing goals; (2) estimating demand, costs, and profits; (3) choosing a price policy to help determine a base price; and (4) fine-tuning the base price with pricing tactics.

A price strategy establishes a long-term pricing framework for a good or service. The three main types of price policies are price skimming, penetration pricing, and status quo pricing. A price-skimming policy charges a high introductory price, often followed by a gradual reduction. Penetration pricing offers a low introductory price to capture a large market share and attain economies of scale. Finally, status quo pricing strives to match competitors' price.

1.1 A manufacturer of office furniture decides to produce antique-style rolltop desks reconfigured to accommodate personal computers. The desks will have built-in surge protectors, a platform for raising or lowering the monitor, and a number of other features. The quality, solid-oak desks will be priced far below comparable products. The marketing manager says, "We'll charge a low price and plan on a high volume to reduce our risks." Comment.

1.2 Janet Oliver, owner of a mid-priced dress shop, notes, "My pricing objectives are simple: I just charge what my competitors charge. I'm happy because I'm making money." React to Janet's statement.

1.3 What is the difference between a price policy and a price tactic? Give an example.

1.4 **TEAM** Divide into teams of four persons. Each team should choose one of the following topics: skimming, penetration pricing, status quo pricing, price fixing, geographic pricing, adopting a single-price tactic, flexible pricing, or professional services pricing. Each team should then pick a retailer that it feels most closely follows the team's chosen pricing strategy. Go to the store and write down examples of the strategy. Interview the store manager and get his or her views on the advantages and disadvantages of the strategy. Each team should then make an oral report in class.

(2) **Identify the legal and ethical constraints on pricing decisions.** Government regulation helps monitor four major areas of pricing: unfair trade practices, price fixing, predatory pricing, and price discrimination. Many states have enacted unfair trade practice acts that protect small businesses from large firms that operate efficiently on extremely thin profit margins; the acts prohibit charging below-cost prices. The Sherman Act and the Federal Trade Commission Act prohibit both price fixing, which is an agreement between two or more firms on a particular price, and predatory pricing, in which a firm undercuts its competitors with extremely low prices to drive them out of business. Finally, the Robinson-Patman Act makes it illegal for firms to discriminate between two or more buyers in terms of price.

2.1 **INFOTRAC® COLLEGE EDITION** What kind of factors can push a respectable firm to enter a price-fixing arrangement with a competitor? Using InfoTrac (**http://www. infotrac-college.com**), read about the price-fixing scandals that rocked the art auction industry or the Hollywood movie studios and Blockbuster Video during 2001 and 2002. If there are more current scandals, read a selection of articles on a particular industry. Then compile a list of business practices and pricing issues that are present in the reports of each scandal. Is each scandal unique, or are there overlapping characteristics? What conclusion can you draw about price fixing from the articles you read? How does the federal government deal with price fixing?

(3) **Explain how discounts, geographic pricing, and other special pricing tactics can be used to fine-tune the base price.** Several techniques enable marketing managers to adjust prices within a general range in response to changes in competition, government regulation, consumer demand, and promotional and positioning goals. Techniques for fine-tuning a price can be divided into three main categories: discounts, allowances, rebates, and value-based pricing; geographic pricing; and special pricing tactics.

The first type of tactic gives lower prices to those that pay promptly, order a large quantity, or perform some function for the manufacturer. Value-based pricing starts with the customer, considers the competition and costs, and then determines a price. Other tactics in this category include seasonal discounts, promotion allowances, and rebates (cash refunds).

Geographic pricing tactics—such as FOB origin pricing, uniform delivered pricing, zone pricing, freight absorption pricing, and basing-point pricing—are ways of moderating the impact of shipping costs on distant customers.

A variety of special pricing tactics stimulate demand for certain products, increase store patronage, and offer more merchandise at specific prices.

More and more customers are paying price penalties, which are extra fees for violating the terms of a purchase contract. The perceived fairness or unfairness of a penalty may affect some consumers' willingness to patronize a business in the future.

3.1 **WRITING** You are contemplating a price change for an established product sold by your firm. Write a memo analyzing the factors you need to consider in your decision.

3.2 Columnist Dave Barry jokes that federal law requires this message under the sticker price of new cars: "Warning to stupid people: Do not pay this amount." Discuss why the sticker price is generally higher than the actual selling price of a car. Tell how you think car dealers set the actual prices of the cars they sell.

3.3 Explain the difference between freight absorption pricing and uniform delivered pricing. When would it be appropriate to use each?

3.4 The U.S. Postal Service regularly raises the price of a first-class stamp but continues to operate in the red year after year. Is uniform delivered pricing the best choice for first-class mail? Explain your reasoning?

3.5 How is the "information age" changing the nature of pricing?

3.6 Have you ever paid a price penalty? How did it affect your attitude toward that company?

(4) **Discuss product line pricing.** Product line pricing maximizes profits for an entire product line. When setting product line prices, marketing managers determine what type of relationship exists among the products in the line: complementary, substitute, or neutral. Managers also consider joint (shared) costs among products in the same line.

4.1 Develop a price line strategy for each of these firms:

   a. a college bookstore

   b. a restaurant

   c. a video-rental firm

(5) **Describe the role of pricing during periods of inflation and recession.** Marketing managers employ cost-oriented and demand-oriented tactics during periods of economic inflation. Cost-oriented tactics include dropping products with a low profit margin, delayed-quotation pricing, and escalator pricing. Demand-oriented pricing methods include price shading and increasing demand through cultivating selected customers, creating unique offerings, changing the package size, and heightening buyer dependence.

To stimulate demand during a recession, marketers use value-based pricing, bundling, and unbundling. Recessions are also a good time to prune unprofitable items from product lines. Managers strive to cut costs during recessions in order to maintain profits as revenues decline. Implementing new technology, cutting payrolls, and pressuring suppliers for reduced prices are common techniques used to cut costs.

5.1 During a recession, what pricing strategies would you consider using to gain or maintain market share? Explain your answer.

5.2 **ON LINE** After a decade of astounding growth and prosperity, Americans were challenged by the economic downturn of 2000 and 2001. As a result, pricing became an issue for many consumers looking to pinch pennies. This was also true in areas where penny-pinching isn't a common occurrence, like high-end retailers. Search the *Wall Street Journal* on-line archives (**http://www.wsj.com**) to find an article by Teri Agins and Sarah Collins titled, "A Haggler's Christmas." Make a list of pricing concepts and tactics that are illustrated in the article.

5.3 Search for the following articles in the *Wall Street Journal*'s on-line archives (**http://www.wsj.com**):

Pamela Druckerman, "Argentina's Middle Class Makes Do: In a Crisis, Barter Clubs and Discount Hunting," May 1, 2002.
Michelle Wallin, "Argentines Hone Art of Shopping in a Crisis," May 28, 2002.

Read both articles and list the topics from the chapter that appear in each. How are Argentine consumers coping with serious economic difficulties? How are Argentine businesses changing their pricing to stay afloat? Write a brief summary of what you discover.

DEFINE IT

bait pricing 614
base price 609
basing-point pricing 613
cash discount 610
consumer penalty 617
cumulative quantity discount 610
delayed-quotation pricing 619
escalator pricing 619
flexible pricing (variable pricing) 613
FOB origin pricing 611
freight absorption pricing 612

functional discount (trade discount) 610
joint costs 619
leader pricing (loss-leader pricing) 614
noncumulative quantity discount 610
odd–even pricing (psychological pricing) 615
penetration pricing 604
predatory pricing 608
price bundling 615
price fixing 607
price lining 614
price shading 620

price skimming 604
price strategy 603
product line pricing 617
promotional allowance (trade allowance) 610
quantity discount 610
rebate 610
seasonal discount 610
single-price tactic 613
two-part pricing 616
unbundling 616
unfair trade practice acts 606
uniform delivered pricing 612
value-based pricing 610
zone pricing 612

APPLY IT

Application for Entrepreneurs

RoseAnn decided that time is, indeed, money. So she opened a Chinese buffet in Arlington, Texas. The new twist is that you pay by the minute. The restaurant, known as Rose's Chinese Buffet, is all-you-can-eat-by-the-minute.* The buffet table is piled with delectable seafood and steaming stir-fried dishes. Diners rush to their tables and wolf down spring rolls, fried noodles, fried rice, and other goodies. RoseAnn allows only the first thirty customers at lunch and dinner to pay by the minute. The rest must order from a traditional menu or pay the normal buffet price. By-the-minute lunch customers pay 30¢ a minute.

*Such restaurants do exist in Japan.

Questions

1. RoseAnn concedes that she only breaks even on her by-the-minute customers. Should she drop the concept?

2. What pricing tactics is she using?

3. Would such a restaurant be successful in your community?

Ethics Exercise

People feel better when they think that they are getting a great bargain when they shop. Knowing this, some retailers mark up items above the traditional retail price and then offer a 60 percent discount. If they had simply discounted the normal retail price by 20 percent the resulting "sale price" would have been the same. One retailer says that he is just making shoppers happy that they got a great deal when he inflates the retail price before discounting.

Questions

1. What do you think?

2. Does the AMA Code of Ethics address this issue? Go to **http://www.marketingpower. com** and review the code. Then, write a brief paragraph summarizing what the AMA Code of Ethics contains that relates to retail pricing.

TRY IT

Entrepreneurship Case

Setting the Right Price for a Special ISP

With only twenty-two thousand residents, Mercer Island is small enough to avoid recognition as a major market for anything. The affluent community, however, is situated on a small strip of land in the middle of Lake Washington on Seattle's western border. That means the community has major market needs and the means to fulfill them, but a group of ambitious entrepreneurs from the island's high school hopes to outdo Seattle when it comes to providing the island's Internet service.

At Mercer Island High School, information-technology teacher John Davis heads a team of students seeking to become the island's sole Internet service provider. He and his band of students call their nonprofit company IslanderISP, and together they hope that the profits from the business can be dedicated to funding the Mercer Island School District's technology needs.

The group hopes that it can prove to the world that it isn't necessary to have hundreds of thousands or millions of dollars in seed money from a venture capitalist to start a successful technology company. Having worked for the Navy, IBM, and Hewlett-Packard, Davis has the experience to lead his youthful partners. He sees the start-up as a means to developing more mature, experienced, and job-ready students in an increasingly competitive world. He plans to bolster his time-strapped staff by recruiting college students and retired teachers to work for them.

After incorporating as a nonprofit, staff members approached school officials about locating headquarters on high school property. They also contacted Qwest, which will provide them with connectivity to the Internet and advice on modem quantities and server locations. Qwest will also house IslanderISP's e-mail and Web servers, an arrangement that will give IslanderISP an advantage over most dial-up services by greatly reducing the time it will take for its customers to dial in to the information superhighway.

On campus, the young entrepreneurs are generating buzz through word of mouth and by handing out brochures at school sporting events. David Booth, a senior and public relations officer for the company, is pushing the school radio station and the local newspapers for exposure, as he hopes to benefit from the close-knit community and progressive atmosphere on the island. Between residences and businesses, the would-be ISP identifies ten thousand potential customers it hopes to sign to service subscriptions.

A subscription costs $22.50 per month. Customers who pay in full and up-front for the year receive one month free and pay only $247.50 for twelve months of service. Those who sign for a three-year subscription pay just $675, a discount equaling six months of free service at the introductory price. If it achieves 100 percent market penetration, IslanderISP projects a $2 million annual profit above the $400,000 to $500,000 incurred in maintenance, salary, rent, and Qwest service expenses.

With a dozen residents already signed, the students need to close eighty-eight more sales before activating the service. If the business fails to reach a hundred customers, the service agreements of the charter customers provide that the money they paid will be donated to Mercer Island School Foundation, a school system fund-raising entity.

Questions

1. Did IslanderISP thoroughly follow the procedure for setting the right price? Explain and critique.

2. What type of pricing strategy do you think would work best for IslanderISP?

3. Explain the special pricing tactics IslanderISP used in fine-tuning its base price.

4. If the company incurs $500,000 in expenses, how many one-year subscriptions (at $247.50) will it need to sell to break even? Do you think that is realistic? Explain.

 WATCH IT

Short

The *Marketing* PowerPoint CD-ROM contains two video ad clips embedded in the Chapter 18 slide presentation. How do Chrysler and Saturn advertise the ways that they fine-tune the base price of their cars? Are any special pricing strategies highlighted by the ads?

Medium **VIDEO**

Luxury products are typically insulated from the impact of an economic downturn. Watch a CNN report on the boom in yacht sales during the economic uncertainties of the past few years. Could yacht manufacturers use any pricing strategies to increase their sales even more without compromising the luxury of their products?

Long SmallBusinessSchool
the Series on PBS stations and the Web

For Chapter 18, Small Business School returns to Nicole Miler Fashion House in New York City. When you see the video this time, focus on how Nicole Miller used price to create her niche and how she establishes a price-quality relationship. Watch the segment and think about the kind of pricing strategy Nicole Miller uses for her products and her distribution channels.

 FLIP IT

 Flip to Chapter 18 in your *Grademaker Study Guide* for more review opportunities, including the pretest, vocabulary review, Internet activities, study test questions, and an application exercise based on pricing concepts. How do marketers set the right price? What government regulations constrain pricing decisions? Can you shut your book and list the ways that marketers can fine-tune the base price of their product or service? If not, then open your *Grademaker* and review.

CLICK IT

The *Marketing* Web site links you to all the Internet-based activities in this chapter, like the "Use It," "Review It" questions 2.1, 5.2, and 5.3 "Think About It," and the On-Line exercises in the chapter margins. As a review, do the

Still Shaky? Here's a Tip.

Chapter 18 is a good place to revisit study tips from Chapters 5, 7, and 12 (pages 183, 241, and 413). Try to find additional examples for each pricing technique described in the chapter. Associate a pricing strategy with each of your personal belongings (furniture, clothing, toiletries, electronics, bike, books, car, etc.).

Chapter 18 quiz and crossword puzzle. And don't forget the Career Exersite that shows you resources for exploring marketing career opportunities in pricing. Review the main concepts in the PowerPoint presentation for Chapter 18, too. Go to **http://lamb.swlearning. com**, read the material, and follow the links right from the site.

SPIN IT

 Spin your Xtra! CD-ROM to test your understanding of the pricing concepts in the chapter by completing the worksheet for exhibits 18.1 and 18.2. If your instructor has assigned a marketing plan project, templates on Xtra! can help you organize your work. In addition to the quiz on the Web site, there's another quiz on the Xtra! CD-ROM, plus video of the authors answering frequently asked questions about pricing topics, such as "What can managers do to get back some pricing control?" and "What is the importance of setting a base price?"

MARKETING MISCUES

Apple's Futuristic Cube Is Already a Thing of the Past

Based in Cupertino, California, Apple has been at the forefront in innovative computer design. The company ignited the computer revolution in the 1970s with the Apple II and then reenergized the personal computer market in the 1980s with the Macintosh. In an attempt to bring the PC market into the twenty-first century, Apple introduced its Cube in July 2000. Although Cube owners loved their Cubes, not enough customers were willing to pay the price for the futuristic box.

Price appears to have been a major factor in the Cube's market failure. At $1,799, it was one of the higher priced PCs in the marketplace. For this higher price, consumers got a PC that took up very little desk space. The Cube's features included the following:

- 64 MB of RAM
- 20 GB hard drive
- Mac OS 9.0.4
- DVD-ROM drive
- A silvery cube, eight inches on each side, inside a clear plastic column, ten inches high
- A power-on/off light indicator (requiring merely tapping to power up or down)
- Two baseball-shaped Harmon Kardon speakers
- A fan-free liquid cooling system (resulting in quieter running)
- A ball-free, buttonless optical mouse
- Reduced cable clutter

Although these features, particularly the product's futuristic design, were lauded by those closest to the system (Apple employees), the Cube failed to meet computer users' expectations on various fronts:
- A monitor was not included.
- The Cube lacked removable storage devices (e.g., Zip drive).
- The on/off switch was in a sensitive area on the case top, resulting in accidental touches.
- There was no floppy drive.
- There were no expansion slots.

Apple's share of the U.S. PC market was around 7 percent in the first half of 2000. Its worldwide market share was almost 4 percent. Apple aspired to increase its market share one to two percentage points per year, with each point worth around $1.3 billion in revenue. With average industry growth of 15 percent, Apple expected to grow at a rate of 34 percent. The Cube was to play a key role in meeting the company's growth targets. Sales forecasts for this cool-looking Cube were around 800,000 units in year one.

Unfortunately, the Cube failed to lead Apple in the right direction. The computer's liabilities apparently outweighed its assets. Several industry experts complained that the Cube's price was high in relation to the value it gave the user. Although it offered a new design, some questioned why anyone would pay the price for a computer so lacking in new, innovative technology. While the computer had been touted as a work of art, its pricey aesthetics failed to compensate for its unimpressive internal mechanics.

While competitors courted the multibillion-dollar corporate computer market, Apple's brand of individualism had led the company to target niche markets. Consumers in many of these niche markets have generally sought fun, easy-to-use computer systems. Unfortunately for Apple, consumers in its niche markets were not cool enough to pay the desired price for the Cube, and production was suspended only a year after it was introduced. In hindsight, the price was too high for the market, and the product had a low price–quality relationship.

Questions

1. Were Apple's pricing objectives profit oriented, sales oriented, or status quo oriented?

2. How could Apple have done a better job of setting the right price for the Cube?

CRITICAL THINKING CASE

Nokia's $20,000 Cellular Phone

Nokia's luxury-edition cellphone has it all—platinum or 18-karat gold housing, crystal screen, soft leather casings, upgradable internal components—all for only $21,240 (24,000 euros)! Why such a high-priced cellphone? Will anyone buy it?

The Mobile Phone Industry

The mobile phone industry has burgeoned in the past few years. By 2003, cellular penetration is expected to be as high as 80 percent in many European countries and slightly greater than 30 percent in the United States. Product innovation and pricing appear to be the drivers for this level of market penetration. Price-sensitive consumers are expected to purchase the low-end cellphones, while price-insensitive consumers will demand the latest and greatest in cellular technology.

By 2000, the mobile phone industry was thought to be the world's largest consumer electronics industry in terms of unit sales. Although overall market penetration has been phenomenal, such growth levels are not expected to continue. Rather, experts predict only modest growth in the mid- and late 2000s. Since first-time users accounted for over half of mobile phone purchases at the start of 2000, replacement sales are expected to comprise around 75 percent of sales in later years.

The mobile phone industry is dominated by major competitors including Ericsson (Sony), Motorola, Nokia, Qualcomm, Samsung, and Sanyo. Each of these companies offers cellular phones with numerous product options and various price ranges. Consumers' wants vary, but prevailing wisdom suggests that important phone features include size (the smaller the better), ease of use, and technological advances. Interestingly, cellphones may have a sexual connotation as well. One study suggests that men use their cellphones to attract women.

Nokia Corporation

With its American headquarters in Irving, Texas, Nokia Corporation (**http://www.nokia.com**) operates with estimated annual worldwide sales of $28 billion. A world leader in mobile communications, Nokia comprises two business groups: Nokia Networks and Nokia Mobile Phones.

With around 40 percent of the worldwide market for cellular phones, Nokia is the global leader in the development, manufacturing, and sales of mobile phones. In 2000, Nokia introduced twenty-two new cellphones. The company has been called the fifth most valuable brand in the world.

Attempting to differentiate its product offerings while building on its branding efforts, Nokia has founded the world's first luxury mobile phone company. This new, independent subsidiary, Vertu, Ltd., started operations in early 2002 and will cater to very wealthy consumers. A senior vice president in Nokia's Asia-Pacific division, Nigel Litchfield, will serve as president of London-based Vertu, Ltd.

Historically, Nokia has been known for marketing well-designed, user-friendly phones that are popular with the everyday phone user. The new Vertu phones, however, focus on the phone as a status symbol of the very wealthy and take Nokia into a niche market. Selling under the Vertu brand, the company's most expensive product carries a hefty price tag of $21,240. For this premium price, the rich and discerning customer gets a cellular phone that makes a fashion statement. In addition to its platinum handset and crystal display screen, this limited-edition luxury phone features evolutionary technology that will allow the phone's internal mechanisms to be upgraded while keeping the outside casing intact. The lower end of this elite product will feature similar internal technology inside a stainless steel casing. The low-end price is expected to be around $5,300. These luxury phones will be available by private showing only in the most distinguished shopping areas of Paris, London, Los Angeles, New York, and Hong Kong.

Nokia is not the only company offering limited-edition, high-end cellular phones. For many years, Ericsson has made gold-plated phones, and Motorola has an 18-karat gold, diamond-studded phone. Priced in the tens of thousands of dollars, both companies' phones have been particularly popular with oil sheiks in the Middle East. De Grisogono, a London-based jeweler, also provides diamond casings for mobile phone units. Reportedly, one celebrity paid $90 million for a diamond-studded phone. Although Nokia will be competing with these companies for the high-end market, the Vertu phone has the internal sophistication to allow it to stand alone in the marketplace—whatever and wherever that marketplace may be.

Questions

1. What are the determinants of Vertu's pricing strategy?

2. What pricing strategy is being followed?

3. Does Vertu's pricing strategy fit within Nokia's broader product line pricing strategy?

4. Why might Nokia have entered what appears to be a relatively small niche market?

MARKETING PLANNING ACTIVITIES

To complete all eight activities, use the Part 6 Marketing Planning Worksheets on your Xtra! CD-ROM. If you need a company for the basis of your work, follow the "Marketing Plan Project" link on the *Marketing* Web site (**http://lamb.swcollege.com**).

Pricing Decisions

For continued general assistance on business plans and marketing plans, visit **http://www.bplans.com** or **http://www.businessplans.org**. For electronic sources of information, search on the Electric Library at **http://www.elibrary.com** or the Internet Public Library at **http://www.ipl.org**. Another excellent source of information is the Sales and Marketing Executives Marketing Library at **http://www.sell.org**. You should also refer to Exhibit 2.7 for additional marketing plan checklist items (Part IV.B.4: Marketing Mix—Price).

You began your strategic marketing plan by stating your business mission and objectives and performing a detailed SWOT analysis. In the second part of the plan, you identified and described target market segments and identified sources of competitive intelligence and the need for further marketing research. Next, you began the process of defining the marketing mix, starting with the components of product, distribution, and promotion.

The next stage of the strategic planning process—pricing—completes the elements of the marketing mix. Pricing is a special challenge to the e-marketer because prices can be quickly and easily compared on the Internet. In any case, your goal should be to make pricing competitive and value driven, as well as to have it cover costs. Other features and benefits of your offering are likely to be more important than price.

Use the following exercises to guide you through the pricing part of your strategic marketing plan:

1. List possible pricing objectives for your chosen firm. How might adopting different pricing objectives change the behavior of the firm and its marketing plans?

2. Gather information on the tactics you selected for the first parts of your marketing plan. What costs are associated with those decisions? Will you incur more or fewer costs by selling on-line? Will your marketing costs increase or decrease? Why? Calculate the break-even point for selling your offering. Can you sell enough to cover your costs? Use the Internet to find a break-even analysis tool to help with your calculations.

3. Pricing is an integral component of marketing strategy. Discuss how your firm's pricing can affect or be affected by competition, the economic environment, government regulations, product features, extra customer service, changes in distribution, or changes in promotion.

4. Is demand elastic or inelastic for your company's product or service? Why? What is the demand elasticity for your offering in an off-line world? Whatever the level, it is likely to be *more* elastic on-line. What tactics can you use to soften or reduce this on-line price sensitivity?

5. What price policy should your firm use? Are there any legal implications of this choice? Will there be differences in on-line versus off-line pricing policies? Are these differences related to your cost structure in the on-line environment? Why? Are these differences legal?

6. Note how easy it is to compare prices on the Internet. Check out price comparison sites such as **http://www.pricescan.com**, **http://www.mysimon.com**, and **http://www.bizrate.com**. Given how products and prices are displayed, how can your offering show a competitive advantage if there is a price difference? As prices reach parity on the Internet, how else will you differentiate your products or services?

7. What kinds of price discounts can your company offer? Should on-line buyers be offered discounted prices that off-line buyers do not receive? Why might you charge your on-line customers less than your off-line customers?

8. As you work on the Internet component of your marketing plan, you must decide how to set geographic pricing policies. Will you appear as a nongeographic specific Internet provider and offer the same shipping costs to all, or will you have to charge more for longer distances? Will you market your product or services locally, regionally, or nationally? Just because you are on the Internet, does that mean you have to try to serve all markets? To check out how distances and even global transportation can affect your price, go to the United Parcel Rate Calculator at **http://www.ups.com/using/services/rave/rate.html** or **http://www.ltlrates.com**.

CROSS-FUNCTIONAL CONNECTIONS SOLUTIONS

Pricing to Satisfy Both Internal and External Demands

Questions

1. Should marketing play the lead role in coordinating the pricing decision? Explain why or why not.

   The marketing department is expected to be closest to the customer in terms of understanding consumer price elasticity. Additionally, marketing generally has the most current information on competitors' prices. The other business functions, however, focus on the cost component of pricing. Therefore, it is necessary to make the pricing process interactive in order to set the price at a level that ultimately will appeal to customers and make appropriate margins for the company.

2. How is activity-based costing more market oriented than traditional accounting methods?

   Traditional accounting methods do not make it easy to track marketing costs. Thus, the floor on price is determined by manufacturing's variable costs. Activity-based costing focuses on *all* costs related to bringing a product to market, which will allow marketers to more accurately utilize cost as the floor in the pricing process for individual customers. For example, ABC would include travel time to visit a customer as a customer-related cost, which would be reflected in the pricing process for that particular customer.

3. What kinds of internal problems are caused by price promotions?

   The major impact of a price promotion is felt in the manufacturing department. The manufacturing group has to increase its level of production just prior to the price promotion in order to have enough product on hand for delivery to the customer (unless, of course, the price promotion is a means of reducing inventory) during the promotional period. The manufacturing department may have to schedule overtime workers in order to meet demand. Even if the actual price promotion period does not cause much disruption in the manufacturing process, the promotion may have longer-term ramifications. If a retailer purchases more of the product than can be sold during the promotional period, normal shipments to the retailer will be reduced until the retailer's inventory is back to normal levels. The manufacturing group often finds itself struggling to maintain stability in its production processes.

Suggested Readings

Michael Gering, "Activity Based Costing and the Customer," *Management Accounting*, April 1999, 26–27.

Helen L. Richardson, "The New Shape of ABC," *Transportation & Distribution*, May 2000, 111–116.

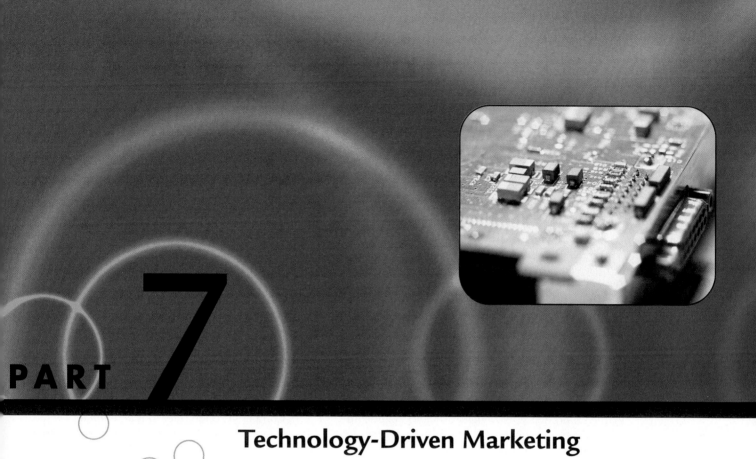

PART 7

Technology-Driven Marketing

TECHNOLOGY'S ROLE IN FACILITATING INTERACTIONS BETWEEN THE COMPANY AND ITS CUSTOMERS AND AMONG INTERNAL FUNCTIONS

Businesses in the twenty-first century are expected to respond quickly to customer demands. Companies such as Charles Schwab Corporation, Priceline.com, Bank One Corporation, and Amazon.com have been able to meet consumers' demand for immediate service and need fulfillment and, in doing so, have transformed their industries. Through their Web sites—**http://www.schwab.com**, **http://www.priceline.com**, **http://www.bankone.com**, and **http://www.amazon.com**—these companies have the ability to interact personally with their customers in a virtual environment. In the financial world, schwab.com made the corporation a full-service brokerage firm, and wingspan.com (Bank One) brought full-service banking to consumers. Priceline.com has changed the way consumers think about purchasing a wide variety of products, essentially bringing the pricing process into the consumer's home. Amazon.com was one of the first full-service retailers not associated with a bricks-and-mortar location. Through information technology, companies such as these have been able to attract consumers. However, the successful interaction of all business functions is what has kept customers returning to these companies as loyal and repeat users.

Understanding the marketplace and responding to its demands require technological linkages that were unheard of only a few decades ago. Advances in computer technology have already started to link marketing and its functional counterparts—all functions now have access to the same valuable market information. Although the benefits of networking functional departments, customers, and suppliers are vast, the process of bringing all of these groups together has not been without problems.

Internet marketing is leading to vast changes in the way all functional areas do business. Nevertheless, the necessary interaction between marketing and the information-technology group can contribute to a major point of contention within an organization. Information technologists generally have backgrounds in computer science, mathematics, or engineering—areas not known for their interaction with the customer. Now, however, these same information

technologists may be charged with developing the company's Web site.

Traditionally, the marketing group was in charge of developing the marketing communications program that reached the potential customer. Now the Web has dramatically changed the nature of a firm's marketing communications. In today's computer age, a company's Web site may be the customer's first and only contact with the company. Information that would once have been in a brochure or print ad is now on the consumer's computer screen instead. Often the responsibility for the actual development and functional capabilities of a company's Web site—a major element of the firm's marketing communications program—is in the hands of information-technology experts.

Companies often refer to marketers as the site/content *strategists* and information technologists as the site/content *implementators*. Unfortunately, the separation into strategy and implementation has tended to exacerbate the conflict between marketing and information technology. The information technologists do not like "taking orders" from marketers about something that has always come within their purview (computers). Likewise, marketers fear that letting information technologists build the Web site will result in something that emphasizes technology at the expense of customer appeal.

Not only must technologists and marketers work together in developing a company's Web page, but the legal department also has to become intimately involved in the process. Legal assistance is of utmost importance for issues such as domain registration (similar to trademarks and trade names), intellectual property rights, hidden language (called metatext), taxation, and privacy policies. The marketing and information-technology departments have to develop appropriate material—material that is both interesting and easy to navigate. Having a lawyer who specializes in cyberlaw working in tandem with both marketing and information technology is extremely important.

Once a company's Web site is up and running—that is, marketing and information technology have gotten past their functional biases and the lawyers have determined that the Web site is legally appropriate—marketing on the Internet begins to highlight necessary interactions between marketing and other business functions. Although the benefits of e-commerce can be substantial, doing business on-line entails considerable initial costs. In addition to the start-up costs for developing Web pages, the firm's security expenses increase when it engages in Internet marketing. As with many marketing initiatives, technology is treated by many companies as a cost center rather than an investment. This tends to create tension between marketing/technologists and accountants.

Cisco Systems has been one of the front runners in linking marketing and technology. The California-based company is a global leader in electronic commerce. With a clear understanding of the importance of cross-functional interactions, Cisco understands the importance of its human resources. In addition to their technological capabilities, Cisco personnel are well versed in customer service and in achieving customer satisfaction.

Not surprisingly, the Internet has worked wonders for customer service. Electronically fulfilling customer requests for technical support can dramatically improve customer satisfaction. Technicians can respond much more quickly to requests—bringing positive results to marketing in that customer satisfaction is increased—and to engineering in that fewer engineers are needed for product support. Consequently, the engineers can devote more time to new-product development.

Marketing directly to the consumer pays off from manufacturing's viewpoint, too. By using network capabilities and/or personal digital assistants, the company needs to keep little or no inventory on hand. Basically, when the consumer places an order, the firm's suppliers receive electronic messages indicating the raw materials that will be needed to satisfy the order. The raw materials are then shipped immediately to the manufacturing facility. The manufacturing facility will have received the order transmission at the same time as the suppliers so it will be ready to begin production as soon as the materials arrive. Technology also enables a manufacturer and a customer to collaborate on scheduling production processes that will be optimal for both companies.

Internet marketing also allows customers to receive their orders more quickly. No longer does a customer's order have to work its way through various steps before finally reaching the production people. Now electronic order taking can transmit the order directly to the company's order fulfillment center—drawing into focus the need for close relations with the logistics and transportation people.

Marketing via the Internet also calls for necessary interaction between marketing and research and development—particularly as it relates to what engineers can do and what customers desire. An example of an area where R&D exceeded consumers' wants and needs was television via the Internet. Known as video datacasting, the technology transmitted Internet data via the television airwaves and also allowed consumers to watch television on their personal computers. Unfortunately, the development engineers failed to recognize that consumers were unwilling to pay for having the television data-receiving cards installed in their computer systems. Compaq Computer manufactured such a card, but the consumer response was mediocre at best.

Technology is changing the way we market our products. It will also have long-term implications for a company's organizational structure and management processes. Changes in the way consumers interact with companies will no doubt lead to even greater challenges regarding cross-functional coordination.

Questions

1. How has today's technology altered the role of marketing both internally and externally?

2. What are some of the benefits of networking functional departments, customers, and suppliers?

3. Which functional areas are actively involved in making e-commerce a success? How?

CHAPTER **NINETEEN**
INTERNET MARKETING

Learning Objectives

1 *Describe the impact of the Internet on business practices*

2 *Describe the current Internet marketing environment*

3 *Discuss on-line business strategies*

4 *Discuss Internet marketing objectives and strategies*

19

GLOBAL PERSPECTIVES Internet Access and E-Commerce around the World

ETHICS IN MARKETING The Opt-In or Opt-Out Debate

Find the whole chapter on-line at
http://lamb.swlearning.com!

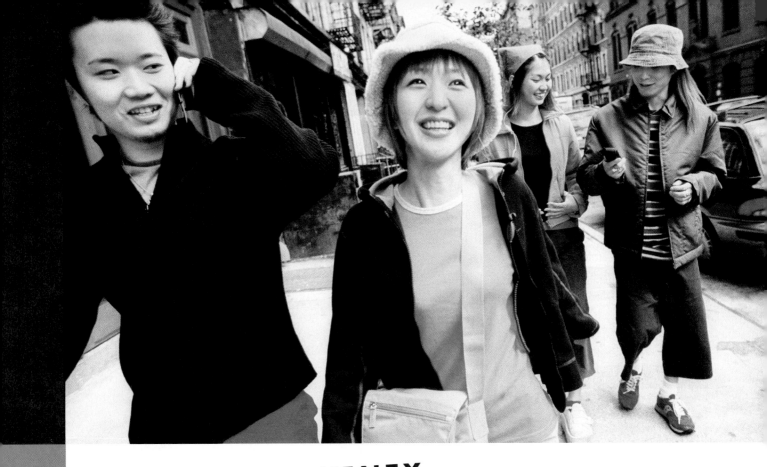

CHAPTER **TWENTY**

CUSTOMER RELATIONSHIP MANAGEMENT

Learning Objectives

1 *Define customer relationship management*

2 *Explain how to establish customer relationships within the organization*

3 *Explain how to establish and manage interactions with the current customer base*

4 *Outline the process of acquiring and capturing customer data*

5 *Describe the use of technology to store and integrate customer data*

6 *Describe how to analyze data for profitable and unprofitable segments*

7 *Explain the process of leveraging and disseminating customer information throughout the organization*

Even though it knows its customers, Student Advantage faces the challenge of pinning down a target market that moves on a regular basis. The typical customer for this Boston-based company is the college student looking for discounts on everything from bikes and backpacks to textbooks and airline tickets. Students have both a home and a university mailing address, though their school address often changes every year or two. Thus, students' actual physical location can be very tough to determine because of their mobility. Fortunately for Student Advantage, students are heavy e-mailers who frequently respond to on-line offers and targeted e-mail campaigns.

Student Advantage began as a local company in 1992, using discount cards to increase foot traffic among local businesses listed in the corresponding discount book. In 1997, Student Advantage became a national company when it secured American Express and AT&T as listings in its discount book. In 2001, Student Advantage launched its first Web site, which began as nothing more than an electronic billboard. By 2002, the company had expanded into a large, lucrative network of interactive, student discount and community sites.

Student Advantage earns its revenues from two sources: annual fees and advertising income. Members pay an annual fee, and business partners pay to advertise their services on the Web site and for e-mail campaigns. Student Advantage's services include its flagship discount book program; student and alumni communities, CollegeClub.com and FANSonly.com; a student loan resource center, eStudentloans.com; and a free newswire for college media called Uwire.com. Currently, Student Advantage has over fifteen thousand business partners (both brick and mortar and electronic) ranging from Amtrak and US Airways to Tower Records.

Recently, the company has begun using e-marketing and warehouse analysis tools in a focused customer relationship management (CRM) effort. The goal is to better understand how the company's products are being used and to maximize its clients' return on investment. Early in the CRM process, Student Advantage realized it was being overwhelmed with information about its customers. To be effective in its CRM efforts, it had to focus only on the types of demographic, geographic, and purchasing data it could use to better segment and analyze its various markets. As is typically the case, the volume of data collected quickly became large and unmanageable, and the storage and performance costs associated with maintaining this level of information became excessive. Rethinking its tracking strategy, Student Advantage trimmed the data fields it tracked to match what its business partners were looking for. Managers chose not to rely on telephone numbers (because they change frequently among college students) in favor of using mostly e-mail and Web sites. Student Advantage is now dicing its database of two million registered users into very small, granular-level segments. For example, AT&T wanted to target only students in Florida, and Dollar Rent a Car was seeking those students who were twenty-one years of age or older.

Another Student Advantage goal is to use CRM to simplify customer service from phone to e-mail and from e-mail to Web page FAQs. Updated FAQs keep the volume of e-mail questions down to a manageable level. Prompted e-mail responses likewise keep down calls to the customer service call center. As the emphasis has swung from phone to e-mail, Student Advantage claims to be handling twice as many questions in half the time, with fewer personnel. The level of customer service has increased without putting a drain on the company's resources.

In 2002, Student Advantage developed a membership renewal campaign to reach out to students instead of waiting for them to renew on their own. Students pay $20 to renew per year. Doing this via a direct-mail campaign would be cost-prohibitive because mailing addresses for students are notoriously incorrect. Student Advantage was able to re-sign thousands of students in just the first few weeks of its e-mail campaign, quickly generating over $70,000 in revenues.

To gather all this information, Student Advantage had to help students understand how they benefited from giving precise personal data. Many students don't see the value in filling out application forms correctly, so the company showed them what kinds of offers (like last-minute airfares, discounted concert tickets, and low-price hotel rooms) they could receive if the company could dependably and reliably contact them.

The next CRM initiative planned by Student Advantage involves a type of on-campus cash card that parents can add money to from any location. Students can then use the card to buy books, meals, and other college necessities. Information about purchases will feed back to the Student Advantage warehouse and provide even more granular and precise data about students' purchase patterns and behaviors. According to Student Advantage, the opportunities are boundless. Its managers believe that by unleashing the power of CRM on its various products and services, Student Advantage will be able to transform itself into the company it wants to be.[1]

Is Student Advantage creating strong customer relations with the college market? Is it offering college students exactly what they desire? How does a company go about setting up a CRM program? And once such a program is in place, how does the company use the information it collects to its advantage? We will answer these questions and more in this chapter.

What Is Customer Relationship Management?

Define customer relationship management

customer relationship management (CRM)
A company-wide business strategy designed to optimize profitability, revenue, and customer satisfaction by focusing on highly defined and precise customer groups.

Customer relationship management (CRM) is a company-wide business strategy designed to optimize profitability, revenue, and customer satisfaction by focusing on highly defined and precise customer groups. This is accomplished by organizing the company around customer segments, encouraging and tracking customer interaction with the company, fostering customer-satisfying behaviors, and linking all processes of the company from its customers through its suppliers. As described in the opening vignette, Student Advantage is a prime example of how CRM operates. Student Advantage is linking its suppliers (AT&T, American Express, etc.) directly with its customers (college students), building an interaction with those suppliers and customers, and using data obtained by the interaction to design customized product and service offerings that are extremely attractive to its market. With the introduction of its new cash card, Student Advantage is also poised to track the spending patterns and behaviors of college students so as to gain a better understanding of exactly what the college customer is seeking. All of this is accomplished by maintaining information about students, then using this information to increase customer service and satisfaction.

The Customer Relationship Management Cycle

On the surface, CRM may appear to be a rather simplistic customer service strategy. But while customer service is part of the CRM process, it is only a small part of a totally integrated, holistic approach to building customer relationships. CRM is often described as a closed-looped system that builds relationships with customers. Exhibit 20.1 illustrates this closed-looped system, one that is continuous and circular with no predefined starting or end point.[2]

To initiate the CRM cycle, a company must first *establish customer relationships within the organization.* This may simply entail learning who the customers are or where they are located, or it may require more complex information on the products and services they are using. For example, a bank may find it very beneficial to determine all the services a customer is using, such as loans, savings accounts, investment instruments, and so forth. Once the company identifies its customers and its popular products and services, it then *determines the level of interaction each customer has with the company.* The bank, for example, would determine how frequently each customer interacts with the bank and the channel used for the interaction (branch location, telephone call center, Web, etc.). Based on its knowledge of the customer and his or her interaction with the company, the company can then *acquire and capture all relevant information about the customer,* including measures of satisfaction, response to targeted promotions, changes in account activity, and even movement of assets. One industry that has acquired and captured relevant data about its customers is the digital cable industry. Through ongoing telephone surveys of more than 24,500 households conducted semiannually, industry monitors have discovered that digital cable subscribers, compared with direct broadcast satellite (DBS) subscribers,

If only you **knew** the **REAL me...**

CRM is a strategy designed to optimize business performance by focusing on highly defined customer groups. This Surado ad for SCM SQL is a perfect example of what CRM systems seek to know: The real customer.

Exhibit 20.1

SOURCE: Joseph Hair, Robert Bush, and David Ortinau, *Marketing Research: Within a Changing Information Environment,* 2nd ed. (Burr Ridge, Ill.: McGraw-Hill/Irwin, 2002).

are less likely to own their own home and are more likely to be single. They are as a group younger and better educated than DBS subscribers. They also are more likely to be black or Hispanic and live in a center city area.[3]

Technology plays a major role in any CRM system. It is used not only to enhance the collection of customer data, as will be discussed later in this chapter, but also to store and integrate customer data throughout the company. Customer data are the actual firsthand responses that are obtained from customers through investigation or asking direct questions. These initial data, which might include individual responses on questionnaires, responses on warranty cards, or lists of purchases recorded by electronic cash registers, have not yet been analyzed or interpreted. A critical component of a CRM system is the *use of the appropriate technology to store and integrate customer data.* The value of customer data depends on the system that stores the data and the consistency and accuracy of the data captured. Companies like General Motors, GEICO Insurance, Borders, and Amazon.com have taken great strides to improve their data-collection processes by using "data cleansing" and accuracy software such as "Validity Integrity Software."[4] Data cleansing software checks for inconsistencies and extracts them. It then organizes and streamlines the data. Obtaining high-quality, actionable data from various but complementary sources is a key element in a CRM system.

Every customer wants to be a company's main priority, yet not all customers are equally important in the eyes of a business. Some customers occupy segments that are simply more profitable for the company than others. Consequently, the company conducts data mining to *determine its profitable and unprofitable customer segments.* Data mining is an analytical process that compiles personal, pertinent, actionable data about the purchase habits of a firm's current and potential customers. (We will discuss data mining in greater detail later in the chapter.) Essentially, data mining transforms customer data into customer information, which consists of data that have been interpreted and to which narrative meaning has been attached. The data are subjected to a pattern-building procedure that profiles customers on variables such as profitability and risk. Customers may be categorized as highly profitable, unprofitable, high risk, or low risk, and these categories may depend on the customer's affiliation with the business. For example, the bank might categorize its customers as long-time customers, commercial clients, customers with little money in the bank, or customers with several accounts. Once the customer data are analyzed, they are assigned interpretative meaning (transformed into information) and *disseminated throughout the entire organization.* A primary objective of the CRM system is to spread customer information across all functional areas of the business. This is because the customer does not interact with only one function of the business (e.g., sales or marketing), but rather with all functions (e.g., operations, production, accounting, etc.). A company using a CRM system must view its customers comprehensively, understanding that they interact, either directly or indirectly, with all components of the internal business system from suppliers and manufacturers to wholesalers and retailers.

Although many would consider the retail industry to be at the forefront of CRM (think of Amazon.com and your supermarket shopper card), a Blue Martini Software survey conducted in 2002 revealed that the majority of retailers are not using CRM. The company conducted an e-mail poll of registered attendees at the 2002 National Retail Federation show in New York City. The survey's questions focused on retailers' ability to identify customers at the point of sale, access data about those customers in real-time, and "act on that information" to increase sales—all key steps in a CRM system. Results of the survey showed that only 45 percent of survey participants have technology to collect, aggregate, and analyze transaction data in a data warehouse. Additionally, only 41 percent of retailers surveyed can identify their "most profitable" customers and use that information for personalized promotions. And a paltry 10 percent of retailers are using individual customer data to drive promotional activities.[5]

Implementing a Customer Relationship Management System

Our discussion of the CRM system has assumed two key points. First, the customers, as represented by the information about them, take center stage in any organization. Focusing a company's energy in this way results in better customer understanding, increased customer access, and more efficient customer interactions. Second, the business must focus on the day-to-day management of the customer relationship across all points of customer contact throughout the entire organization. This factor is critical to the success of any CRM initiative and is the foundation of shared information throughout the organization. Charles Schwab understands these two points completely. Vice chairman and CIO Dawn Lepore says, "Our mission is to delight our most demanding customer in the busiest hour of the busiest day. The most demanding customers are great for our business. They're like our toughest competitors. They push us to do things we haven't thought about before."[6]

Keeping these two points in mind, let's now look at how a CRM system is implemented. We will follow the progression depicted in Exhibit 20.1 as we explain each step in greater detail.

Explain how to establish customer relationships within the organization

customer-centric
Under this philosophy, the company customizes its product and service offering based on data generated through interactions between the customer and the company.

Establishing Customer Relationships within the Organization

Companies that implement a CRM system adhere to a **customer-centric** focus or model. Customer-centric is an internal management philosophy similar to the marketing concept discussed in Chapter 1. Under this philosophy, the company customizes its product and service offering based on data generated through interactions between the customer and the company. This philosophy transcends all functional areas of the business (production, operations, accounting, etc.) producing an internal system where all decisions and actions of the company are a direct

The new iMac.

15" LCD flat screen. 800-MHz G4. CD/DVD-burning SuperDrive. Like nothing before. From $1,299.

result of customer information. A customer-centric company builds its system on what satisfies and retains valuable customers, while learning those factors that build long-lasting relationships with those customers. For example, before launching its PT Cruiser, DaimlerChrysler amassed a database of 450,000 interested customers. In addition to potential customer contact information, the database contained information on those features, options, and styling characteristics consumers wanted built into the vehicle.[7] Not only was this *information* important for the success of the PT Cruiser, but the *direct interaction* between customers and company engineers was equally important in shaping the product. The PT Cruiser development team was customer-centric.

Customer-centric organizations establish relationships with customers similar to those of the artisans of bygone years. Artisans sought to understand their customers' needs and expectations and negotiated with them a mutually satisfying commitment for product and service delivery. Artisans knew they could make flexible commitments to customers because they alone, not tens or hundreds of delegated representatives, were accountable for fulfilling their end of the bargain. This, in turn, allowed artisans to develop lasting relationships with customers, learn more about them, and generate repeat business. Similar to the artisans' approach, though expanded in scope, CRM is a company-wide process that focuses on learning, managing customer knowledge, and empowerment. It differs from one-to-one marketing, which we will discuss in Chapter 21, in a very important way: One-to-one marketing is an individualized marketing method that utilizes customer information to build a long-term, personalized and profitable relationship with each customer. CRM is broad and systemic, whereas one-to-one marketing is focused and individualized.

Learning

A customer-centric company and its representatives continually learn from customers about ways to enhance its product and service offerings. **Learning** in a CRM environment is normally an informal process of collecting customer information through customer comments and feedback on product or service performance. Dell Computer, for example, learned from its customers that they were experiencing difficulties unpacking its computers. The packaging was so strong that the customers were damaging the computers while removing them from the box. Dell responded with a simpler, more efficient packaging design that allowed customers to disassemble the packaging material in one easy procedure.[8] Likewise, Apple Computer learned from its customers that assembling the computer hardware devices was difficult. Apple's response was to produce a computer that required no assembly whatsoever.[9]

learning
An informal process of collecting customer data through customer comments and feedback on product or service performance.

Knowledge Management

Each functional unit of a business usually has its own way of recording what it learns and perhaps even its own customer information system. The disparate interests of departments make it difficult to pull together learned customer information into one place using a common format . To overcome this disparity,

knowledge management
The process by which learned information from customers is centralized and shared in order to enhance the relationship between customers and the organization.

companies operating in a CRM mode use knowledge management. **Knowledge management** is a process by which learned information from customers is centralized and shared in order to enhance the relationship between customers and the organization. The information collected includes experiential observations, comments, learned lessons, conclusions, and qualitative facts about the customer. All of these are formatted so that the information can be disseminated and shared throughout the entire organization.

A good example of knowledge management comes from General Electric's Appliance Division, where the GE Answer Center has provided service to GE appliance customers (and frequently to customers of other GE divisions) since the early 1980s. In the late 1980s, the GE Answer Center also became the GE Appliance Customer Knowledge Center, although it was never given that formal name. Each service representative records customer comments about appliances, dealers, or other relevant issues in a central system. This information is then reviewed by marketing, dealer relations, customer service, and, perhaps most important, manufacturing and new-product development managers. The service-based customer knowledge is also used to rapidly identify appliance problems in the field, such as an improper installation approach, that can be addressed with product or documentation changes, saving vast amounts in field dispatch costs.[10]

Empowerment

empowerment
Delegation of authority to solve customers' problems quickly—usually by the first person that the customer notifies regarding the problem.

interaction
The point at which a customer and a company representative exchange information and develop learning relationships.

As Chapter 1 explained, empowerment involves delegating authority to solve customers' problems. In other words, **empowerment** refers to the latitude organizations bestow on their representatives to negotiate mutually satisfying commitments with customers. Organizational representatives make commitments during interactions with customers (via phone, fax, e-mail, or Web communication, or face-to-face). An **interaction** is a point at which a customer and a company representative exchange information and develop learning relationships. In a CRM system, where the organization adheres to a customer-centric focus, the customer, not the organization, defines the terms of the interaction. The organizational response is to design products and services around the customer's desired experience.

Customers define the terms at the time of the interaction. For example, customer A may want a Whirlpool washing machine just as it is. Customer B may want a Whirlpool washing machine in a special color. Customer C may want a Whirlpool washing machine in a special color and delivered the next day. Customer D may want a price discount from the company because he or she is purchasing a Whirlpool washing machine, dryer, dishwasher, and refrigerator.

With a CRM system, the organization's representative becomes a knowledge worker and has the latitude to make on-the-spot decisions that affect the outcomes of the interaction. In the above example, the representative may determine that customers A, B, and D can be accommodated, but that customer C cannot be helped because the special-color washing machine is out of stock and cannot be delivered tomorrow. Thus, during the interaction, the organizational representative focuses on each individual customer and his or her requests; the representative is also concerned with achieving negotiations that will result in a mutually satisfying commitment and with learning from each interaction to create profitable, lasting relationships.

The success of CRM—building lasting and profitable relationships—can be directly measured by the effectiveness of the interaction between the customer and the organization. In fact, what further differentiates CRM from other strategic initiatives, such as one-to-one marketing and market development, is the organization's ability to establish and manage interactions with its current customer base. The more latitude (empowerment) a company gives its representatives, the more likely the interaction will conclude in a way that satisfies the customer.

Establishing and Managing Interactions with the Current Customer Base

The interaction between the customer and the organization is the foundation on which a CRM system is built. Only through effective interactions can organizations learn about the expectations of their customers, generate and manage knowledge about them, negotiate mutually satisfying commitments, and build long-term relationships.

Exhibit 20.2 illustrates the customer-centric approach for managing customer interactions. Following a consumer-centric approach, an interaction can occur through a formal communication channel, such as a phone, PC, or salesperson; through a previous relationship a customer has had with the organization, such as a past purchase or a response to a marketing research request; or through some current transaction by the customer, such as an actual product purchase, a request for repair service, or a response to a coupon offer. In short, any activity a customer has with an organization, either directly or indirectly, constitutes an interaction.

Companies that effectively manage customer interactions recognize that customers provide data to the organization that affect a wide variety of internal and external company touch points. In a CRM system, **touch points** are those areas of a business where customer data are gathered and used to guide and direct the decision making within that business unit. Touch points can be both internal and external to the company. External touch points might include a customer registering for some particular service, a customer communicating with customer service for product information, a customer completing and returning the warranty information card for a product, or a customer talking with salespeople, delivery personnel, and product installers. Data gathered at these external touch points, once interpreted, provide information that affects internal touch points. For example, when a customer purchases a new Sony TV from Sears, the point-of-sale interaction is an external touch point for Sony. If the customer purchases an extended warranty, the customer data obtained from that warranty application (an

Explain how to establish and manage interactions with the current customer base

touch point
All possible areas of a business where customers communicate with that business.

Exhibit 20.2

Customer-Centric Approach for Managing Customer Interactions

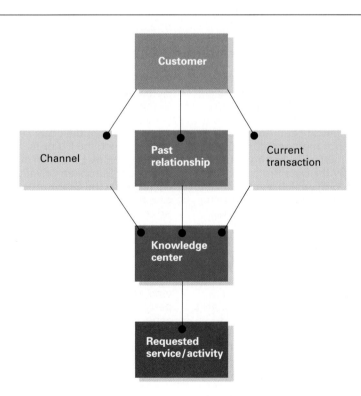

additional interaction) are then directed to an internal touch point, the repair and service department. Even though the repair and service department did not directly interact with the customer, it has an indirect interaction based on the information obtained from the warranty application. This information can be used to schedule routine and problematic repairs. In addition, customer information of this type can be directed to multiple internal touch points—marketing research, for developing profiles of extended warranty purchasers; production, for analyzing recurring problem and repair components; and accounting, for establishing cost-control models for repair service calls. This simple example illustrates one of the most compelling aspects of CRM: A single external customer interaction can generate multiple indirect interactions across multiple internal touch points within any given company.

An extremely common and almost standard touch point is the knowledge center. A **knowledge center** (call center) is an organization's internal operational component that manages and fulfills customer requests. It is the logistical system that reacts to, monitors, and controls the interaction between the customer and the organization. As seen in the earlier General Electric example, the knowledge center is responsible for obtaining customer information, evaluating the information, and directing the information to the appropriate department (touch point) within the company.

A knowledge center is a passive means of managing customer interactions because the customer must call to initiate the interaction. Companies themselves must also generate customer interactions, but doing so is becoming increasingly difficult. Consumers are often bombarded with unsolicited mailers and surveys that are sometimes viewed as intrusive. In these cases, consumers are more likely to refuse an opportunity for interaction than to accept. As the "Ethics in Marketing" box illustrates, rising privacy concerns are forcing companies to rethink their approaches to generating customer interactions. In a CRM system, the objective is to obtain this information in a nonintrusive manner and to allow customers to

knowledge center
An organization's internal operational component that manages and fulfills customer requests; the logistical system that reacts to, monitors, and controls the interaction between the customer and the organization.

ETHICS IN MARKETING

Collecting Customers' Data While Maintaining Their Privacy

Customer relationship management is one of the hottest concepts in business today. However, a key component of CRM is often overlooked: privacy. To remain competitive, businesses must consider adding privacy relationship management to their business practices.

The capture of personal data for marketing purposes is a long-standing practice in American business. Today, however, policies and laws that govern what businesses can do with customer information are changing. At the Direct Marketing Association/Internet Alliance 2001 Government Affairs Conference, it was reported that 465 privacy-related bills were introduced in forty-six states in 2001.

In other parts of the world, policies and laws regarding the use of customer data for marketing purposes are becoming increasingly restrictive. Argentina now has the strictest information protection law in Latin America. In Europe, each member of the European Union (EU) has agreed to abide by the Data Protection Directive of 1998, which is a formal set of privacy practices much stricter than those of the United States. With the implementation of this directive, the amounts and types of data flowing from the EU to the United States were severely restricted. In response, the U.S. Department of Commerce and the European Commission negotiated the "Safe Harbor," which was approved in July 2000. The Safe Harbor allows U.S. companies to voluntarily self-certify to the Department of Commerce that they

will adhere to certain privacy principles as stated by the European Commission. In this way, U.S. companies can avoid experiencing interruptions in their business dealings with the EU or facing prosecution by European authorities under European privacy laws. Adhering to the Safe Harbor will assure that U.S. businesses will provide adequate privacy protection as defined by the directive.[11]

How can a company create a privacy management program that will make customers and prospects feel comfortable when they provide personal data? Would a company with international markets, especially in Europe, be better off adhering to the Safe Harbor, negotiating separate contractual arrangements, or doing nothing at all regarding privacy?

---

freely relay information when they want to communicate it, not when the company wants it. Customer-centric organizations are implementing new and unique interactions specifically for this purpose, such as Web-based interactions, point-of-sale interactions, and transaction-based interactions.

Kroger

Does any part of Kroger's Web site constitute a point-of-sale interaction? Which part? In general, what elements of the CRM process are evident on Kroger.com?

http://www.kroger.com

On Line

Web-Based Interactions

E-mail addresses and Web sites are allowing customers to communicate with companies on their own terms. Instead of wasting time with phone numbers and mail surveys, companies are beginning to publicize their Web sites as the first touch point for customer interactions. Web users can purchase products, make reservations, input preferential data, and comment on the organization's services. The data from these **Web-based interactions** are then captured at the knowledge center, compiled, and used to segment customers, refine marketing efforts, develop new products, and deliver a degree of individual customization to improve customer relationships.

web-based interaction
Communications between customers and organizations using Web vehicles.

When users log on to Borders Books and Music Web site, for example, as either members or guests, their queries are recorded and tracked. From that initial touch point, every time users enter the site, their preferences are shown first. If they purchased any books or music in the past, the site will inform them of any new books or CDs from that author or artist. Similarly, if a customer requests a book by a particular author without making a purchase, the customer will still be informed on a subsequent visit of the new material that author has for sale.[12]

Point-of-Sale Interactions

Another method of generating customer interactions is through **point-of-sale interaction** in stores or at informational kiosks. Many point-of-sale software packages now allow customers to willingly reveal information about themselves without feeling violated. The information is then used in two ways: for marketing and merchandising activities, and for accurately identifying the store's best customers and the types of inventory they buy. The data collected at point-of-sale interactions are also used to increase customer satisfaction through the development of in-store services and customer recognition promotions.

point-of-sale interactions
Communications between customers and organizations that occur at the point of sale, normally in a store.

At selected Kroger locations, shoppers find informational kiosks throughout the stores. The purpose of these kiosks is to allow customers to interact directly and voluntarily with Kroger regarding services and product offerings. For example, one kiosk is located in the fresh seafood department. Customers purchasing seafood items can access information via the kiosk regarding cooking tips, recipes, complementary side dishes, and product safety information. Kroger, in turn, receives information from the customer regarding the type of seafood purchased, when it was purchased, by whom, and even the occasion at which it was served.[13]

Kroger also offers customers the option of becoming VIP "Plus" shoppers. Kroger can monitor the spending habits of its "Plus" card users and offer them special discounts and services.[14] The

At the University Village Starbucks in Seattle, Washington, customers can listen to the latest music on CDs at kiosks installed at the store. This kind of innovative point-of-sale interaction will help the company further tailor its product lines to match the lifestyles of customers who want to relax.

AP/WIDE WORLD PHOTOS

store also offers products tailored for different demographic segments. At a time when competition among grocery stores is extremely high and loyalty is difficult to establish, Kroger is appealing to customers by offering them added incentives to shop at its stores.

Transaction-Based Interactions

transaction-based interactions
The exchange of information that occurs between the customer and the company at the point of the actual transaction.

Transaction-based interactions differ from other interactions in that they focus on the exchange of information at the point of the actual transaction. Through the use of optical scanning technology and product bar codes, in conjunction with the payment method used by the customer (credit card or check), retailers can create parallel streams of information on each individual customer.

Once a credit card is swiped (or a check is processed for bank approval), two major streams of information are produced. First, optical scanning and bar coding allow retailers to capture information about which products the customer purchased and in what quantity. Second, by swiping a credit card or processing a bank check, the retailer can obtain all information contained in the customer's credit card file or checking account file. Thus, the retailer obtains information on both the customer's purchases and the customer's profile. These two streams of information can then be merged at the point of transaction and used in the retailer's knowledge center. To boost their data-collection capabilities, many retailers, including Kroger, are offering customers a Visa credit card positioned as a source of convenience for the customer. The stores also benefit, however. For example, the Kroger Visa generates additional income for the store while it is capturing customer-specific data at the point of transaction.

Acquiring and Capturing Customer Data

4

Outline the process of acquiring and capturing customer data

Vast amounts of data can be obtained from the interactions between an organization and its customers. Therefore, in a CRM system, the issue is not how much data can be obtained, but rather what types of data should be acquired and how they can effectively be used for relationship enhancement. Thus, before discussing the types of data to collect, we must understand how the data will be used in the CRM system. The guidelines for a CRM system include several ground rules regarding customer data:

1. The customer, as represented by the information obtained via the interaction, takes center stage in the organization.

2. Customer information must be centralized so that a single definitive source is established, typically within the knowledge center.

3. Information is retained beyond the initial contact with the customer and accumulated over the customer's entire life span with the organization.

4. Information must define the product and services the customer desires, and the customer's preferences for future products and services, as well as contact methods for future interaction.

These CRM guidelines suggest that specific data about customers be collected via interactions and then, once collected, be used in a capacity that will foster future relationships throughout the entire organization. Exhibit 20.3 illustrates how these guidelines operate regarding the collection of customer data. The channel, the transaction, and the product or service purchased all constitute external touch points between a customer and an organization that provide the opportunity for acquiring data from the customer.

 Once customer data is collected, the question of who owns that data collected becomes extremely salient. In its privacy statement, Toysmart.com declared that it would never sell information registered

Exhibit 20.3

Customer	Channel ──────►	Transaction ──────►	Product/Service
	Information Required	**Information Required**	**Information Required**
	Store	Contact	Brands and type
	Salesperson	Relationship	Volume
	Personal computer	Product usage	Prices
	Phone	Balances	Transaction method
	Wireless	Channel use	Reporting
		Transaction pattern	Performance
		Preferences profile	
		Lifestyle	
		Culture	
		Life stage	
		Profitability	
		Risk profile	
		Desirability	
		Loyalty profile	

at the site, including children's names and birth dates, to a third party. When the company filed for bankruptcy protection, it proclaimed that the information collected constituted a company asset that needed to be sold off to pay creditors.[15]

Despite the very vocal customer outrage at this announcement, many dot com companies closing their doors found that they had little in the way of assets and followed Toysmart's lead. The attorney general of Delaware filed suit against myseasons.com, a garden products seller, for selling its customer list despite promises to keep that information confidential.[16] The issue has become so alarming that North Dakota voters overwhelmingly rejected a state law that had allowed banks to sell customer information without written permission from the customers. Opponents of the law declared that customer information belongs to the customer, not the company.[17]

Channel

The traditional approach for acquiring data from customers is through channels. A **channel** is a medium of communication through which the customer interacts with a business at an external touch point. Channels include store visits, conversations with salespeople, interactions via the Web, traditional phone conversations, and wireless communications, such as cellphone conversations and satellite communications. What is important is the method of communication used by the customer, and not the data that can be collected from the channel. For example, a particular customer may develop a pattern of calling his or her bank every other Friday at 10 A.M. to check on account balances. This channel contact is an interaction, and, indirectly, customer information is exchanged. From this contact, the bank may realize that this particular customer calls every other Friday at 10 A.M. it can then use this pattern to communicate back to the customer. To create a nonintrusive interaction with this customer, the bank might call the customer at or around 10 A.M. on Fridays to communicate new services or introduce special promotions. Likewise, if Sears realizes that a certain group of customers visits a particular Sears location every Saturday afternoon, Sears can use this information to establish in-store promotions on Saturday afternoons appealing specifically to this customer group. In a CRM system, channel interactions are viewed as prime information sources based on the channel selected to initiate the interaction, rather than on the data acquired.

channel
A medium of communication through which the customer interacts with a business at an external touch point; the traditional approach for acquiring information from customers.

Transaction

A **transaction,** when viewed as an interaction between the company and the customer, presents the opportunity to collect vast amounts of data about the customer. The company can obtain not only simple contact information (name,

transaction
An interaction between a company and a customer involving an exchange of information as well as an exchange of products or services.

address, phone number), but also data pertaining to the customer's current relationship with the organization—past purchase history, quantity and frequency of purchases, average amount spent on purchases, sensitivity to promotional activities, and so forth.

From the transaction, product usage information can be obtained, along with the customer's preferred channel of contact with the company and preferred transaction pattern—payment by check, cash, credit card, or debit card. Many companies utilizing a CRM system also view the transaction as an opportunity to collect behavioral data on customers. GEICO Insurance Company, for example, at the time of policy renewal for its auto insurance customers, requests information pertaining to lifestyles (activities, interests, opinions, etc.), cultural factors (ethnicity, religion, etc.), and customer life stage (family composition, number and age of children, children living at home, etc.) for the purposes of pricing and customizing insurance packages for its customers. These data are also used for planning new-product offerings such as vehicle maintenance insurance and gap insurance for lease customers, along with cross-selling other GEICO services such as life insurance, home insurance, and marine insurance.[18]

By examining patterns or historical data relating to a customer's transaction, the company can also obtain information about the customer's profitability, risk, desirability, and loyalty. Profitability is the actual dollar amount a particular customer spends on a company's product over a specific time period. Risk refers to the amount of investment required to retain a customer. The higher the investment required to retain a customer, the higher the risk. For example, customers who buy General Motors cars only if GM is offering cash incentives would be considered high risk. Without cash incentives, the probability of these customers purchasing GM cars is reduced. These customers are high risk for GM because the company must offer incentives (higher investment) to win their business. In contrast, low-risk customers will periodically buy a GM vehicle regardless of the incentive.[19] Customers who, based on a pattern of current and past transactions, exhibit low risk and high profitability to the organization are highly desirable, as are customers who demonstrate high levels of loyalty by purchasing the same brand consistently over time. The company will seek to retain these customers but may choose not to make an effort to retain less desirable customers who exhibit high risk and low profitability.

Product and Service

The physical, as well as the psychological, consumption of the firm's product or service constitutes an additional external touch point for customer interaction. As an interaction point, it also represents an opportunity to acquire and capture customer data related to the consumption experience. The unique dimension of the product or service interaction is that it allows for the collection of customer data during the actual use of the product. As Exhibit 20.3 indicates, key customer data that can be captured at this interaction include the various brands and product types (package variations, sizes, colors, etc.) the customer consumes. The average length of time it takes to consume the product along with the volume consumed, the price paid, and the preferred transaction method can also be obtained.

Even more important are data related to the performance of the product and the method customers use to report performance-related issues. Because the interaction is typically initiated by the customer, these data are extremely valuable for the organization. Customers may call in to a company's knowledge center requesting information on product warranties, optional features, repair services, or installation requirements. Once these data are gathered and stored by the knowledge center, they can be translated into critical information and disseminated across all areas of the company, as we saw in the earlier General Electric example.

It should be obvious at this point that a voluminous amount of information can be captured from one individual customer across several external touch points. Multiply this by the thousands of customers across all of the touch points (both internal and external) within the organization, and the volume of data can rapidly become unmanageable for company personnel. The large volumes of data resulting from a CRM initiative can be managed effectively only through the use of technology.

Use of Technology to Store and Integrate Customer Data

As previously mentioned, customer data are only as valuable as the system in which the data are stored and the consistency and accuracy of the data captured. Customer data gathering is further complicated by the fact that the data needed by one unit of the organization, such as sales and marketing, often are generated by another area of the business or even a third-party supplier, such as independent marketing research firm. Lack of a standard structure and interface forces organizations to rely on technology to capture, store, and integrate strategically important customer information. This process of centralizing data in a CRM system is referred to as data warehousing.

A **data warehouse** (or *informational warehouse*) is a central repository of customer data collected by an organization. The data warehouse contains data from various functional areas of the organization that are stored and inventoried on a centralized computer system so that the resulting information can be shared across all functional departments of the business. The end result of the data warehouse is to provide the company with a system driven toward shared information. In a CRM environment, all customer data collected through customer interactions are stored in the data warehouse. Data pertaining to the channel, the transaction, and the product or service consumed by the customer are structured and categorized in the warehouse and made available to all internal touch points in the organization. To accomplish this task, the data warehouse contains three operational components: an information-access component, a system-management component, and a customer-initiated component.

The information-access component provides for the classification of customer data and enables any department of the business to access the data for any specific purpose. The system-management component defines and interprets the data in a longitudinal manner, allowing for the storage and structure of all data beginning with the initial contact made by the customer. The customer-initiated component stores and categorizes data initiated by the customer through various channel contacts.

American Airlines provides an excellent example of how data warehousing is being used in the airline industry. American Airlines extracts customer information from multiple customer touch points, including sources of data on competition. Its data warehouse maintains a complete historical information base about its customers,

Describe the use of technology to store and integrate customer data

data warehouse
A central repository for data from various functional areas of the organization that are stored and inventoried on a centralized computer system so that the information can be shared across all functional departments of the business.

American Airlines uses data warehousing to propel its customer-centric focus. Information collected at multiple touch points is stored and redistributed throughout the organization. Here, gate agent Debbie Bernard uses a Palm device to help a passenger find his seating assignment.

AP/WIDE WORLD PHOTOS

including information on demographics, flight usage and destination points, where customers live and work, and complete history of billing information.[20] The data warehouse enabled American Airlines to move from a traditional service-based carrier to a customer-centric, relationship management carrier. It allows the airline to examine its offerings on a customer-by-customer basis. For example, the individual flight packages offered by American Airlines are based on the customer's life stage, past ticket purchases, and past destination information.

The key to American Airlines' data warehouse system is its ability to respond to customer-initiated interactions. When a customer calls or accesses American Airlines' Web site, the airline will provide a customized offering—flight and hotel discounts, vacation packages, car rentals, tour packages—all based on information previously gathered about that particular customer. No matter what channel the customer uses to communicate with American Airlines (phone, e-mail, or Web), the customer will receive the same offer.[21] Any additional information obtained through the interaction is automatically stored in the data warehouse, and, if relevant, the offer presented to the customer will change to reflect the new information.

Data warehouses such as the one developed by American Airlines enable companies to better customize their products and services according to their customers' needs and wants. Such attention to customer preferences helps forge long-term relationships that benefit both customer and company. By combining the wealth of data collected through customer interactions, companies like American Airlines can target highly specific customer groups and offer them finely-tuned products or services. More importantly, organizations can use their data warehouses to monitor important financial aspects of the relationship, such as the current and potential value the customer represents to the organization. Through various predictive modeling techniques, data warehouses can generate customer profiles that categorize customers as either profitable or unprofitable to the business. The organization can then use this information to determine the amount of time and dollars required to build relationships with certain customers and to assess whether this investment will produce profitable relationships for the company.

Analyzing Data for Profitable and Unprofitable Segments

Describe how to analyze data for profitable and unprofitable segments

As a process strategy, CRM attempts to manage the interactions between a company and its customers. To be successful, organizations must identify customers who yield high profits or potential profits. To accomplish this task, significant amounts of data must be gathered from customers, stored and integrated in the data warehouse, and then analyzed and interpreted for commonalities that can produce distinct homogeneous segments that are different from other customer segments. Because all customers are not the same, organizations need to develop interactions that target *individual* customer needs and wants. Likewise, all customers do not contribute the same or generate the same revenue for the company. For example, Esure car insurance only offers its services to safe drivers, enabling the company to discount premiums by as much as 30 percent. Esure has, therefore, identified customers it does not want to service (unsafe drivers), because the resulting profit level would be unacceptable.[22] Recall from Chapter 7 that 80 percent of a company's revenue is generated by 20 percent of its customers (the 80/20 principle). Therefore, the question becomes, How do we identify the 20 percent of our customer base that contributes 80 percent to our revenue? In a CRM framework, the answer is data mining.

Data Mining

Data mining is the process of finding hidden patterns and relationships in the customer data stored in the data warehouse. It is a data analysis procedure that identifies significant patterns of variables and characteristics that pertain to particular customers or customer groups. Although businesses have been conducting such analyses for many years, the procedures were normally performed on small data sets containing as few as five hundred to a thousand customer respondent records. Today, with the development of sophisticated data warehouses, thousands and even hundreds of thousands of respondent records can be analyzed. Special data-mining tools have been developed for the specific purpose of analyzing customer patterns and characteristic relationships found in these extremely large data sets.

Citigroup has implemented Xchange, a software program designed to help the company to deliver the same level of service across all channels and to tailor promotional messages to customers according to their value to the company. Xchange helps Citigroup increase the profitability of each customer by identifying appropriate new products based on a life event, such as a marriage or retirement. Citigroup plans to use the software to develop targeted product pricing and discounts for its most profitable customers.[23]

Data-mining tools analyze significant relationships simultaneously among several customer dimensions within vast data warehouses. This procedure is conducted when the decision maker has limited knowledge of a particular subject. For example, the management of a casino may wish to identify the attributes of the gaming customers who had the largest gambling budget in the casino in the last year. Data-mining techniques would search the data warehouse, capture the relevant data, categorize the significant attributes, and form a profile of the high-budget gambler.

Two major capabilities associated with data mining are the automated prediction of trends and behaviors and the automated discovery of previously unknown patterns. Data mining automates the process of finding predictive customer information in large data warehouses. Questions that traditionally required extensive hands-on analysis can now be answered directly from the data. A typical example of a predictive problem is targeting certain customer groups. Data mining uses information on past customer behaviors to identify those customers most likely to maximize the return on investment from future marketing campaigns. Data-mining tools also sweep through data warehouses to identify previously hidden patterns of behavior that normally would not be recognized. For example, through the analysis of retail sales data, a store might identify a pattern of seemingly unrelated products that are often purchased together. Using these techniques, one supermarket learned that young fathers often purchase beer and disposable diapers on the same shopping trip. The store then strategically placed the beer display next to the diapers.

Many businesses operating in a CRM environment are turning to data-mining techniques to build and enhance relationships with highly profitable customer groups. For example, Carrier Corporation is using data mining to profile on-line customers and offer them customized packages on air conditioners and related products. Carrier began selling air conditioners, air purifiers, and related products to customers via its Web site (**http://www.buy.carrier.com**) in 1999, but initially its sales were low largely because it did not know exactly who its customers were and what they wanted. Carrier therefore initiated a program to raise awareness of its Web store and convert Internet traffic to sales. Using a combination of on-line sales data, data obtained from customer registrations for a sweepstakes, and demographic data provided by a third-party research firm, Carrier initiated a data-mining program to identify customers who were also high users of on-line shopping. The procedure matches customer profiles to zip codes, so when customers visit the Carrier Web site and type in their zip code, it is matched to their profile. Automatically, a pop-up window is displayed, offering customized products to specific customer groups, such as multiroom air conditioners to suburbanites and

data mining
A data analysis procedure that identifies significant patterns of variables and characteristics that pertain to particular customers or customer groups.

compact models to apartment dwellers.[24] These techniques have enabled Carrier to turn more Web visitors into buyers, increasing per-visit revenues from $1.47 to $37.42.[25] Data mining also revealed that Carrier's use of radio advertising to promote its Web store was not very effective. Profiles showed that Carrier's customers used public transportation, suggesting subway advertising would be more effective.

The Data-Mining Process

modeling
The act of building a model in a situation where the answer is known and then applying the model to another situation where the answer is unknown.

Data mining works through a process known as modeling. **Modeling** is simply the act of building a model in a situation where the answer is known and then applying the model to another situation where the answer is unknown. If the necessary information exists in the data warehouse, the data-mining process can model virtually any customer activity. The key is to find relevant patterns. Typical unknown situations data mining could address for a business include the following: "Which customers are most likely to suspend their cellphone service?" "What is the probability a customer will purchase $100 of merchandise from a particular store location?" and "Which potential customers are most likely to respond to a particular coupon?" Data mining builds models to answer such questions by using existing information from a data warehouse to predict future customer behavior. This behavior might be attrition at the end of a magazine subscription, purchasing of complementary products, willingness to use a debit card over a check, and so forth. The data-mining model assigns each prediction a score. The **score**, a numerical value that is assigned to each record in the data warehouse, indicates the likelihood that the customer whose record has been scored will exhibit the behavior in question. For example, if a model predicts customer attrition, a high score indicates that a customer is likely to leave, whereas a low score indicates the opposite. After a set of customers is scored, the numerical values are used to selectively target individual customers for a new marketing campaign.

score
A numerical value assigned to each record in a data warehouse that indicates the likelihood that the customer whose record has been scored will exhibit the behavior in question.

A wide range of companies have deployed data-mining applications successfully. Wal-Mart uses data mining to answer a number of questions, such as what commonly purchased items should be placed together on shelves and what soft drinks sell best in different parts of the country. After using data-mining techniques, Camelot Music discovered that a large number of senior citizens were purchasing rap and alternative music. When managers investigated further, they discovered seniors were buying the music as gifts for their grandchildren.[26] Data-mining technology can be applicable to most companies looking to leverage a large data warehouse to better manage their customer relationships. The two critical factors for success with data mining are (1) a large, well-integrated data warehouse and (2) a well-defined understanding of how the end result of the mining activities will be used and leveraged throughout the organization.

Leveraging and Disseminating Customer Information throughout the Organization

Explain the process of leveraging and disseminating customer information throughout the organization

Data mining identifies the most important (profitable) customers and prospects. Managers can then design tailored marketing strategies to best penetrate the identified segments. In CRM this is commonly referred to as leveraging and disseminating customer information throughout the organization to facilitate development of enhanced relationships among customers.

For example, Bayer Pharmaceutical Company analyzed its recent sales force activities to improve its targeting of high-value physicians and to determine which marketing activities would be most effective. Data in this analysis included competitor market activity and information about community health-care systems. Results of the analysis were distributed to the sales force via a wide area network that enabled the sales representatives to learn the key attributes used by physicians in selecting pharmaceutical vendors.[27] Ongoing analysis of the data warehouse enabled the best practices from throughout the organization to be applied in specific sales situations.

Another good example of leveraging customer information comes from American Express. American Express leveraged its vast warehouse of customer transaction data to identify customers most likely to be interested in a new credit card rewards program. Using a small test mailing, the company identified attributes of customers with an affinity for the new product. When the full campaign was rolled out, American Express had such a high response rate that the costs associated with the highly targeted mailing campaign decreased by twentyfold.[28]

In an attempt to increase the activity of its direct sales force, Federal Express applied data-mining techniques to identify the best prospects for its new ground delivery service. Using data mining to analyze its current customer base, FedEx discovered a unique segment of high-value business prospects. Information associated with this segment was then applied to a business database provided by Dun & Bradstreet, yielding a prioritized list of business customers across several regions in the United States.[29]

Lever Brothers, a large consumer packaged-goods company, applied data mining to improve the efficiency of its sales process to key retailers such as Wal-Mart, Target, and Kmart. Using data from consumer panels, order shipment invoices, and information on competitor activities, Lever Brothers developed a model identifying the reasons for brand and store switching behavior among consumers. From this analysis, Lever managers developed several unique promotional strategies to most effectively reach several distinct targeted segments.

These examples have a clear common denominator. In each case, the organization applied various data-mining techniques to leverage knowledge about its customers contained in a data warehouse. The information was then disseminated throughout the appropriate channels of the organizational structure. Indeed, one of the benefits of a CRM system is this capacity to share information throughout the organization.

Through campaign management, all functional areas of an organization participate in the development of programs targeted to its customers. **Campaign management** involves concentrating on outbound communications to customers designed to sell a company's product or service. The design of the campaign is based directly on data obtained from customers through various interactions. Campaign management includes monitoring the success of the communications based on customer reactions through sales, orders, call-backs to the company, and the like. If a campaign appears unsuccessful, it must be evaluated and possibly changed in order to achieve the company's desired objective. Consider Hilton Hotels, for example. Hilton has developed three ongoing campaigns targeted to the highly defined segment of business travelers. Focusing on the past experiences, expectations, and requirements as expressed by business travelers through key touch points, Hilton has designed the three campaigns, which are running simultaneously. One campaign offers room rates of $75, free breakfast, and complimentary airport shuttle service. This campaign is promoted only in airline in-flight magazines. The second campaign emphasizes a free night's stay, free tickets to a local opera, and complementary beverages. Campaign two is communicated only through travel agencies. The third campaign offers room upgrades, use of a rental car for one day, and bonus points added to the customers' frequent flyer program. Campaign three is promoted on national television. Each campaign is being monitored and evaluated relative to its success at penetrating the business traveler

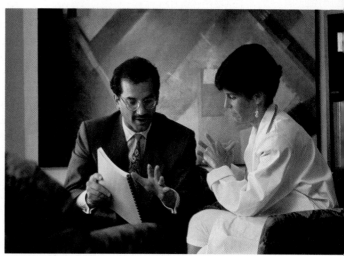

© JEFF ZARUBA/GETTY IMAGES/STONE

Collecting information is a wasted effort unless the company disseminates it throughout the organization. Bayer Pharmaceutical Company does just that. As a result, the company's sales force can increase efficiency by targeting high-value physicians.

campaign management
Developing product or service offerings customized for the appropriate customer segment and then pricing and communicating these offerings for the purpose of enhancing customer relationships

group. The campaign that is most successful will be continued, while the other campaigns will be modified to achieve more positive results. The key to success is how well the campaign conforms to the expectations of the individual customer while enhancing the opportunity for future relationships between the company and the customer. In a CRM context, this is known as personalization. Personalization is an attempt to develop and manage campaigns that meet the individual needs of a company's most profitable customer group.

Campaign management attempts to achieve personalization by developing customized product and service offerings for the appropriate customer segment, pricing these offerings attractively, and communicating these offerings in a manner that enhances customer relationships. Customizing product and service offerings requires managing multiple interactions with customers, as well as giving priority to those products and services that are viewed as most desirable for a specifically designated customer. Even within a highly defined market segment, individual customer differences will emerge. Therefore, interactions among customers must focus on individual experiences, expectations, and desires. Pricing, distributing, and communicating must be done on a continuous basis and modified according to the most recent information obtained from customer interactions.

Product and Service Customization

Using information stored in the data warehouse, highly customized, even personalized, products and services can be developed for customers. For example, e-Diets personalizes diet plans for its subscribers. Approximately forty thousand customers sign up for e-Diets' newsletter at a cost of $45 for a three-month subscription. The subscription entitles members to weekly fitness and meal plans personalized according to their eating habits, dietary preferences, medical condition, and emotional and weight-loss needs.[30] E-Diets relies on both customer and meal plan databases connected via software. The software extracts information from both databases to produce a customized diet plan for each individual member.

Similar to e-Diets, Reflect.com developed technology to customize skin-care, hair-care, and cosmetic products for women. When a customer visits Reflect.com and interacts with the company, she is prompted to fill out a questionnaire that will help Reflect.com create a product specifically for her. The customer might indicate, for example, that she gets dark circles or puffiness under her eyes, that she would like the skin under her eyes to be smoother, that she has laugh lines she wants reduced, or that her eyes are sensitive. The information is then transmitted to the product development center, which determines which ingredients should be included in the product, given the customer's information.[31] Once the product is developed, the information from the customer is stored for use in future interactions.

Pricing

Shared information from customer interactions can also be used to develop an individualized pricing plan for each customer. PSS World Medical supplies health-care organizations with more than fifty-six thousand products ranging from bandages and syringes to test tubes and petri dishes to diagnostic imaging equipment and X-ray technology. After physicians register with PSS

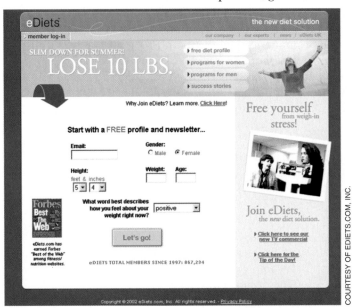

One of the major benefits of CRM is the ability to customize product and service offerings for each customer. E-Diets uses the information it collects from each of its customers to create a customized diet and/or fitness plan based on their individed needs.

World Medical, they can choose to see only products that are relevant to their practice. Once they begin placing orders, PSS maintains a real-time listing of all the products each physician ordered during the previous eighteen months, ranked in descending order by quantity and frequency of purchase.[32] Items purchased most frequently by physicians are given a priority pricing policy, allowing deep price discounts if the physician continues to purchase the item frequently.

Communication

Communication means interacting in a manner that is most effective and non-intrusive for the customer. For example, e-Diets', survival is based on customers returning to its Web site on a weekly basis and renewing their subscription every three months. To encourage this behavior, e-Diets uses the same technology it uses to personalize diets. For instance, if the system finds that a member hasn't logged on to the Web site for several weeks, it will automatically send that individual an e-mail encouraging him or her to stay on the plan. Unfortunately, this method of communication is not very effective when it comes to weight loss. With on-line weigh-ins, people have less motivation to stay on the program than they do with a face-to-face encounter as at Weight Watchers. To combat this problem, e-Diets supports chat rooms and bulletin boards, as well as toll-free phone numbers that members can call for help or support.[33] If a member calls and reports problems maintaining the diet because of being hungry all the time, e-Diets can access that member's information in its database, review the meal plan the customer is currently using, and adjust it as needed.

KidsDadsMoms (KDM) is another company that customizes products for its members. The company's mission is to help children learn and develop by enabling parents to identify the individual learning preferences of their children. Parents can build a profile about their child's strengths, weaknesses, and inclinations. KDM then suggests tools and toys that complement the child's unique learning style and preferences. KDM not only recommends appropriate items for each child; the company's Web site also enables parents to modify their children's profiles as they grow.[34] In a similar market, **SchoolKidz.com** allows parents to order customized boxes of school supplies developed for each grade. Customers can also send in their child's list of specific school supplies and receive a free quote. Teachers can also build a list of requirements for their students on **SchoolKidz.com.** Students in the class can then visit the site and purchase a school supplies kit tailor made for their particular class by their individual teacher.[35]

European companies have been somewhat slow to adapt campaign management and other CRM techniques. Nevertheless, as the "Global Perspectives" box describes, one European company is successfully implementing CRM.

KidsDadsMoms

Would you be comfortable building a profile about your child at **KidsDadsMoms.com?** Why or why not? What are the advantages of giving complete information? Are there any disadvantages? Can you use their highly customized site without building a learning profile for a child?

http://www.kidsdadsmoms.com

On Line

GLOBAL PERSPECTIVES

CRM in Europe

Americans ordering a meal at a restaurant in many southern European cities may wonder whether customer relationship management is a foreign concept in Europe. Compared to the United States, waiters frequently are less responsive to their customers. Certainly, European companies have been slow to adopt CRM. One reason for this reluctance has been the cultural differences between countries. In Spain, for example, sales cycles are longer than in many other European countries because Spanish customers are less inclined to move quickly on purchases. This means that a company has to take time nurturing its customers to develop relationships with them.

The adoption of CRM has also been slowed by political and geographic differences. While American companies can sell primarily to Americans, European companies must often sell in multiple countries, each with its own language and political structure. Such

continued

differences make CRM initiatives more complicated. Customer information has to be shared across borders, and transactions must be converted into different currencies. (Not all European Union countries have embraced the euro.) Inconsistencies of information make modeling and data mining more difficult.

Europe's widespread wireless infrastructure presents another complication. Many European companies already allow customers to access and change account information using wireless applications. Similarly, many European service organizations use wireless technology to handle field sales calls. Differences in wireless technology not only lead to disparities in the information obtained, but also make it more difficult to build data warehouses for capturing critical customer information.

Nevertheless, despite these difficulties, some European companies are adopting CRM as they look for ways to better understand and serve their customers. For example, Heineken Ireland recently implemented a CRM approach driven by a clear need to track its customers. In its traditional channel, the brewer sells beer directly to pubs or hotels through the pub owner. The company had little information about these customers and was not even tracking how much a pub purchased or when an order was due for replenishment. This lack of information meant that Heineken treated all customers the same with no attempt to distinguish between the top customers and less profitable ones.

A knowledge center and sales force automation became the foundations of Heineken's CRM initiative. The company restructured its sales organization and customer interaction processes so that it could track each customer's buying patterns and the marketing resources devoted to that customer. In addition, the knowledge center collected and managed this information, which was then shared throughout the marketing and sales divisions. Heineken now has visibility into its customer data, and its managers are able to predict customers' reactions and respond appropriately to them. The system allows Heineken to classify all customers in terms of importance to the company. High-value customers get weekly calls and visits from a dedicated salesperson, while lower value customers are contacted by direct methods through the knowledge center. As it developed its CRM program, Heineken had to keep Irish culture in mind; it therefore emphasized face-to-face contact and building friendships with its customers.[36]

CONNECT IT

The opening vignette described how Student Advantage started as a business that targeted products and services to college students. As the business grew, it developed more sophisticated marketing approaches to maximize profitability. One approach was the implementation of CRM. By creating interactions with students, Student Advantage was able to convince them of the value of the information it supplied, allowing for highly customized product and service offerings. This information also became part of the data warehouse maintained by Student Advantage for the purpose of applying data-mining techniques. Data mining allowed Student Advantage to develop new product offerings targeted toward the highly profitable student customer. Using campaign management, Student Advantage developed nonintrusive methods of communicating with students, measured the effectiveness of these communications, and delivered satisfying experiences to the market. The company has grown from a regional, single-service provider to a national organization with multiple service offerings and a high level of customer retention and profitability.

USE IT

Stay up-to-date on the latest developments in the CRM world. Because CRM is technology driven, the ways companies interact, collect customer information, and analyze that information are constantly changing. New and unique methods are being introduced along with new approaches in campaign management. To keep current with such changes and to understand how companies are using CRM, visit the Web site for the *Direct Marketing Review,* **http://www.dmreview. com.**This site provides access to the latest developments in CRM, case histories of companies using CRM, and trends that are shaping the industry.

① **Define customer relationship management.** Customer relationship management (CRM) is a company-wide business strategy designed to optimize revenue, profitability, and customer satisfaction by focusing on highly defined and precise customer groups. This is accomplished by organizing the company around customer segments, encouraging and tracking customer interaction with the company, fostering customer-satisfying behaviors, and linking all processes of a company from customers through suppliers.

1.1 Identify the six components of the CRMprocess.

1.2 Form a team and identify several local businesses that would benefit from a CRM strategy. Select one business and outline a plan for implementing a CRM strategy for that business. You may want to visit the company and interview managers about their current initiatives. When you have completed your CRM plan, share it with the class—and the company.

1.3 General Motors recently began installing the "On-Star" system in many of its vehicles. On-Star is a location, information, and communication system available to drivers who wish to subscribe to the service. Go to the On-Star Web site, **http://www.onstar.com**, and read about some of the services that are offered to consumers. Based on your discovery, write a short report describing the various ways that On-Star can be used as a CRM tool, specifically in the context of creating interactions, gathering customer data, and customizing service offerings to customers.

② **Explain how to establish customer relationships within the organization.** Companies that implement a CRM system adhere to a customer-centric focus or model. A customer-centric company builds its system on what satisfies and retains valuable customers, while learning the factors that build long-lasting relationships with those customers. Building relationships through CRM is a strategic process that focuses on learning, managing customer knowledge, and empowerment.

2.1 Briefly explain the concept of a customer-centric focus. Why is this so important in a CRM process?

2.2 What is meant by knowledge management? Why is it so important in a CRM system?

③ **Explain how to establish and manage interactions with the current customer base.** The interaction between the customer and the organization is the foundation on which a CRM system is built. Only through effective interactions can organizations learn about the expectations of their customers, generate and manage knowledge about them, negotiate mutually satisfying commitments, and build long-term relationships. Effective management of customer interactions recognizes that customers provide information to organizations across a wide variety of touch points. Customer-centric organizations are implementing new and unique approaches for establishing interactions specifically for this purpose. They include Web-based interactions, point-of-sale interactions, and transaction-based interactions.

3.1 Develop a plan for establishing and managing interactions with a business's customers. In this plan, identify the key touch points for customers, explain how the knowledge center would be designed, and indicate the main interaction methods that would be promoted to the customer.

④ **Outline the process of acquiring and capturing customer data.** Based on the interaction between the organization and its customers, vast amounts of information can be obtained. In a CRM system, the issue is not how much data can be obtained, but rather the type of data acquired and how the data can effectively be used for relationship enhancement. The channel, the transaction, and the product or service consumed all constitute touch points between a customer and the organization. These touch points represent possible areas within a business where customer interactions can take place and, hence, present opportunities for acquiring data from the customer.

4.1　Assume you are the manager for a Hard Rock Cafe. Your boss has asked you to evaluate how the company is using its Web site to gather customer data. Go to the Web site for the Hard Rock (**http://www.hardrock.com**) and provide a detailed critique on how the site is used for capturing customer data. Comment on the types of customer data the Web site is designed to capture, and explain how those data would benefit your local Hard Rock operation.

5 **Describe the use of technology to store and integrate customer data.** Customer data gathering is complicated because information needed by one unit of the organization (e.g., sales and marketing) is often generated by another area of the business or even a third-party supplier (e.g., an independent marketing research firm). Because of the lack of a standard structure and interface, organizations are relying on technology to capture, store, and integrate strategically important customer information. The process of centralizing data in a CRM system is referred to as data warehousing. A data warehouse is a central repository of customer information collected by an organization.

5.1　Briefly explain the concept of a data warehouse. In the context of a CRM framework, why is a data warehouse such an important tool?

5.2　INFOTRAC COLLEGE EDITION　What is being written about customer data in today's periodicals? Search the InfoTrac database of articles at **http://www.infotrac-college.com** using keywords like "customer data" and "data warehousing." Are certain industries better represented in the citation list generated by your search? Are certain issues more prevalent? Read a selection of at least three to four articles, and write a brief analysis of what is being discussed in the press regarding these CRM topics.

6 **Describe how to analyze data for profitable and unprofitable segments.** Customer relationship management, as a process strategy, attempts to manage the interactions between a company and its customers. To be successful, organizations must identify customers who yield high profits or potential profits. To accomplish this task, significant amounts of information must be gathered from customers, stored and integrated in the data warehouse, and then analyzed for commonalities that can produce segments that are highly similar, yet different from other customer segments. Data-mining tools identify significant relationships among several customer dimensions within vast data warehouses.

6.1　Explain the concept of data mining. Provide five examples of companies that are currently using data mining, and explain why each is using it.

7 **Explain the process of leveraging and disseminating customer information throughout the organization.** One of the benefits of a CRM system is the capacity to share information throughout the organization. This allows all functional areas of the organization to interact and develop programs targeted for their customers. This process is commonly referred to as campaign management. Campaign management involves developing customized product or service offerings for the appropriate customer segment and then pricing and communicating these offerings for the purpose of enhancing customer relationships.

7.1　Campaign management is a benefit derived by an organization's ability to leverage and disseminate information throughout the company. Briefly define campaign management and explain how a business may apply it to its daily operations. In your answer, select a particular business as an example of effective campaign management.

APPLY IT

Application for Entrepreneurs

Huey's Bar and Grill, a downtown Chicago restaurant, was established in the early 1990s. Since then, the establishment has flourished as one of the most popular attractions in the downtown area catering to the local business crowd and tourists. Huey's is particularly noteworthy for its famous Chicago-style Bar-B-Q and sear-sizzled steaks. In an attempt to grow the business, Huey opened a new location in the nearby northern suburb of Evanston. This community is a highly affluent, upwardly mobile market, consisting mainly of businesspeople and professionals. It also contains the campus of Northwestern University, so it is in some respects a college town.

To date, the Evanston restaurant has not experienced the same success as the downtown Huey's. As a result, Huey has begun to develop a CRM approach to increase traffic at the Evanston location. Huey is attempting to establish interactions with patrons in the area and to use the information gathered through these interactions to adjust his current business practices.

Questions

1. Conceptually design a CRM approach Huey can implement at his Evanston location. Specifically, design a program that will foster interactions between Huey and the community. Identify the customer information requirements that are critical in developing these relationships, and explain what channels of interaction would be best suited for this market.

2. What type(s) of customer data should Huey consider gathering from this process? Identify the key data requirements, and explain how they would assist Huey in designing future offerings (menu items, store atmosphere, prices, hours of operation, etc.) for this market.

3. Based on your answers to questions 1 and 2, design a campaign management approach that Huey can implement at the Evanston location. Be sure to explore the demographic makeup of the Evanston market before developing your campaign.

THINK ABOUT IT

Ethics Exercise

By combining several of its databases about parental purchasing behavior and the results of its market research, Maxwell Inc. believes it has the tools to launch one-to-one marketing messages for the six- to nine-year-old fans of its JoyMax educational toy products without violating the law. In spite of potential parental backlash, the company believes the approach will help to customize new children's products and increase the company's share of these profitable young customers.

Questions

1. What do you think? Should Maxwell use one-to-one marketing tools to communicate with children?

2. Does the AMA Code of Ethics address marketing to children in its Code of Ethics? Go to **http://www.marketingpower.com** and review the code. Then, write a brief paragraph on how the AMA Code of Ethics relates to Maxwell's dilemma.

Entrepreneurship Case

United Way of Greater Toronto

Nonprofit organizations do not typically come to mind when one thinks of entrepreneurs, but, in reality, most are entrepreneurs—even the well-known and firmly established United Way. Each city's branch of the United Way functions, in part, as its own entrepreneurial venture and is responsible for raising funds from local public and private donors. Those donors are, in effect, United Way's customers.

Philip King, vice president of e-business for the United Way of Greater Toronto (UWGT), realized that United Way could probably increase donations at his branch by implementing the type of CRM solutions commonly used by big businesses to establish more personal relationships with their customers. Because UWGT could not afford one of those systems on its own merit, United Way raised $2.3 million from major local businesses to fund the project.

Before its CRM program, UWGT, like most other philanthropic organizations, was able to reach its many diverse customers only by mass-mailing generic solicitations. Now the branch has the ability to draw from its previously built customer database to target solicitation messages to specific individuals or businesses. Dubbed UnitedWay@work, the system's primary focus is to increase contact with corporate donors by reaching employees who chair United Way giving campaigns within businesses.

UWGT piloted UnitedWay@work by sending 8,600 customized and personalized e-mails to sixteen different Canadian companies with regular histories of donating to United Way campaigns. Sent to companies based on identity and past donation levels, those e-mails gave employees HTML links to a personalized Web page with information on an individual's personal contributions and related United Way campaigns.

The Web page shows real-time updates on the amount of money raised by particular charitable campaigns, specific details on how those funds are being used in the community, and comparisons of the donation levels across departments within that employee's company. Individual contributors can also make donations on-line with credit cards or through payroll deductions, calculate tax implications, and elect to receive e-mail updates detailing exactly how their gifts are being applied throughout the year.

The personalization strategy is working. Almost 40 percent of those solicited returned $1.5 million in gifts—a $300,000 increase over the previous year—and 85 percent of those targeted by the new e-mail system pledged on-line. Combined with an estimated $200,000 savings in paper, data entry, administrative, and mailing costs, the new CRM program contributed $500,000 the UWGT's charitable causes in its first year.

Important to note, too, is how the system affected the behavior of individual contributors. First-time donors who gave on-line offered, on average, $100 more than first-time off-line givers, and returning givers who made donations on-line parted with 5 percent more than returning givers who paid off-line. UWGT combines what it learns from individuals acting on e-mail and Web site links with information in its existing database; then, together with the CRM system, it analyzes that information for use in developing future customer communications.

King points out that the change in customer behavior is incremental but still noteworthy. The eventual impact on the individual lives of those the United Way helps could be huge— and that, of course, is the ultimate goal. Following its successful pilot, UWGT plans to make UnitedWay@work available to sixty more companies in and around Toronto. It also plans to share the system with its partners in the United States. Six city branches are slated to pilot the system immediately, with the hope that all United Way branches will adopt it eventually.

Questions

1. Identify the six components of the CRM process, and explain which one the United-Way@work system employs.

2. Explain how the UnitedWay@work program establishes and manages interactions with its customers.

3. Describe how UWGT collects and integrates customer data. How has the use of these data affected it business?

WATCH IT

Short

Knowing and acting on what customers really want and need is the purpose of customer relationship management. The *Marketing* PowerPoint CD-ROM has one video ad clip, on M&M's, embedded in the Chapter 20 slide presentation related to CRM.

Medium **CNN VIDEO**

How much database technology do companies need? Apparently not as much as they purchased between 2000 and 2002. This CNN clip exposes the fact that many companies overspent on technology assets that they never installed! What are the implications of these findings for database marketers?

Long   **SmallBusinessSchool** ▪
the Series on PBS stations and the Web   For Chapter 20, Small Business School takes you to a Miami company that fills more prescriptions in Florida than CVS, Walgreen, Rite Aid, Eckerd, and every other pharmacy on the block. José and Louis Navarro will tell you how they built their successful chain of Navarro Pharmacy drugstores through building relationships with their customers.

FLIP IT

 Flip to Chapter 20 in your *Grademaker Study Guide* for more review opportunities, including the pretest, vocabulary review, Internet activities, study test questions, and an application exercise based on CRM concepts. What is the process for acquiring and capturing customer data? What do companies need to do to leverage the customer data they collect? If you don't know, then flip open your *Grademaker* and review.

CLICK IT

The *Marketing* Web site links you to all the Internet-based activities in this chapter, like the "Use It," "Review It" questions 1.3, 4.1, and 5.2, "Think About It," and the On-Line exercises in the chapter margins. As a review, do the Chapter 20 quiz and crossword puzzle. And don't forget the Career Exersite that shows you resources for exploring marketing career opportunities in customer relationship management. Review the main concepts in the PowerPoint presentation for Chapter 20, too. Go to **http://lamb.swlearning.com**, read the material, and follow the links right from the site.

SPIN IT

 Spin your Xtra! CD-ROM to test your understanding of CRM concepts in the chapter by completing the worksheets for exhibits 20.1, 20.2, and 20.3. If your instructor has assigned a marketing plan project, templates on Xtra! can help you organize your work. In addition to the quiz on the Web site, there's another quiz on the Xtra! CD-ROM, plus video of the authors answering frequently asked questions about CRM topics, such as "What does data mining have to do with marketing?"

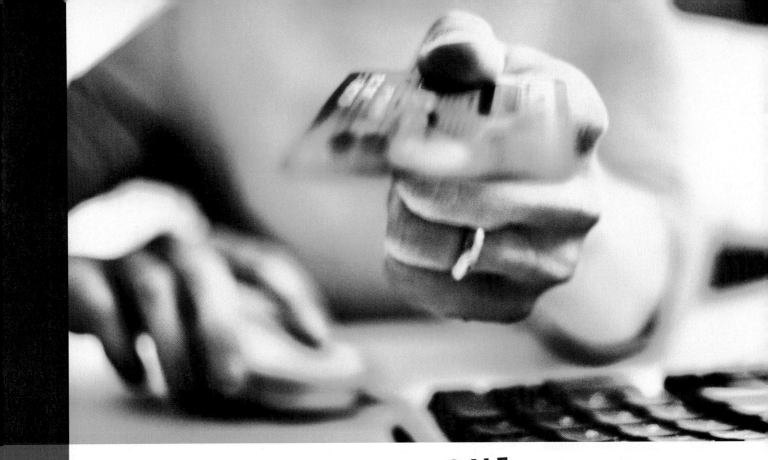

CHAPTER **TWENTY ONE**

ONE-TO-ONE MARKETING

Learning Objectives

1 *Define one-to-one marketing and discuss its dependence on database technology*

2 *Discuss the forces that have influenced the emergence of one-to-one marketing*

3 *Compare the one-to-one marketing communications process with the traditional mass-marketing communications process*

4 *List eight common one-to-one marketing applications*

5 *Discuss the basics of one-to-one marketing database technology*

6 *Describe one-to-one marketing using the Internet*

7 *Discuss privacy issues related to one-to-one marketing*

Amazon.com sells books, CDs, videos, electronic equipment, and more to over 38 million customers in 220 countries around the world. Its customers say they enjoy shopping at Amazon.com because of the product selection, convenience, and customer service. Company president Jeff Bezos says Amazon's success is due to the company's relentless commitment to its customers.

When Bezos started the company in 1995, his mission was to use the Internet to transform book buying into the fastest, easiest, and most enjoyable shopping experience possible. Since then, the company has grown to offer Earth's Biggest Selection, where customers can find anything they might want to buy on-line.

Everything Amazon does is based on exceeding customers' expectations. For instance, the Web site is designed to be easy to navigate, product selection is comprehensive, and fulfillment centers are spread around the globe to ensure prompt order delivery. All of these things contribute to the company's success. A large part of Amazon's $3.12 billion in sales, however, is due to the company's one-to-one marketing expertise.

The first time customers visit Amazon, they are encouraged to register. From that point on, anytime they log on from their own computer, they can expect to be greeted by name. When customers make a purchase, they immediately receive an order confirmation with a purchase tracking number via e-mail. When their order is shipped, they are again notified by e-mail.

Additionally, from the time a customer registers with Amazon, the company tracks the customer's browsing and purchasing behavior in order to learn about the customer's preferences. The company then uses that information to make product recommendations based on the customer's interest. For example, if a customer purchased *The One-to-One Future: Building Relationships One Customer at a Time* by Don Peppers and Martha Wang, the next time that customer visits Amazon, he or she may receive a recommendation for *Strategic Database Marketing* by Rob Jackson and Paul Wang. To improve the value of its recommendations, Amazon encourages customers to provide additional information about their likes and dislikes by rating the recommended items. Eventually, clients who shop and communicate with Amazon regularly find that Amazon makes valuable recommendations based on their individual preferences. As a result, customers find themselves looking forward to the recommendations and making more purchases.[1]

So how does Amazon communicate individually with 38 million customers? By developing, maintaining, and implementing a successful database system of one-to-one marketing. In this chapter, you will learn more about the advantages of one-to-one marketing and the technology that makes it possible.

What Is "One-to-One Marketing"?

1

Define one-to-one marketing and discuss its dependence on database technology

one-to-one marketing
An individualized marketing method that utilizes customer information to build long-term, personalized, and profitable relationships with each customer.

One-to-one marketing is the ultimate goal of a new trend in marketing that focuses on understanding customers as individuals instead of as part of a group. To do so, contemporary marketers are making their communications more customer-specific, like the personalized marketing efforts being initiated by Amazon.com.

Most businesses today use a mass-marketing approach designed to increase their *market share* by selling their products to the greatest number of people. For many businesses, however, it is more efficient and profitable to use one-to-one marketing to increase *share of customer*—in other words, to sell more products to each customer. **One-to-one marketing** is an individualized marketing method that utilizes customer information to build long-term, personalized, and profitable relationships with each customer. The goal is to reduce costs through customer retention and increase revenue through customer loyalty.[2] Customer relationship management (CRM), which you read about in Chapter 20, is a related marketing strategy that takes a broader approach.

The difference between one-to-one marketing and the traditional mass-marketing approach can be compared to shooting a rifle and a shotgun. If you have good aim, a rifle is the most efficient weapon to use. A shotgun, on the other hand, increases your odds of hitting the target when it is more difficult to focus. Instead of scattering messages far and wide across the spectrum of mass media (the shotgun approach), one-to-one marketers are now homing in on ways to communicate with each individual customer (the rifle approach).

The Evolution of One-to-One Marketing

It may surprise many readers—especially those who grew up to the sound of advertising jingles on television and the sight of billboards dotting the landscape—that one-to-one marketing is not at all new. In fact, before the Industrial Revolution introduced mass advertising, businesses understood that their success depended on their ability to build relationships with their customers. Merchants built their business by tracking customer purchases and making recommendations based on past purchases and the customer's interests. Moreover, products often were custom produced or modified to fit the customer's needs.

The Industrial Revolution brought about mass production and led to volume buying and mass advertising. Companies grew and prospered by manufacturing large quantities of the same product, advertising it through mass media, and profiting from sales volume.

As a result, marketers developed a different view of the customer. No longer viewed as unique, all customers were perceived as having the same needs and being reachable through the same channels with the same message. As Henry Ford said it, "We'll give you any color you want, as long as it's black."

Today, however, customers demand more choices; they seek to buy precisely what meets their needs and wants and expect individualized attention. Technology now makes it possible for companies to interact with these customers in new ways, by allowing companies to create databases that pull data from, and feed information to, those interactions. Companies are using technology that makes it possible to tailor products, service, and communications to meet those expectations.

© REUTERS NEWMEDIA INC./CORBIS

How serious are companies about giving customers individualized attention? Levi Strauss has a shrink tub in its San Francisco megastore so that customers can shrink their jeans to fit. After the shrink tub, they pass through the human dryer before leaving the store.

As a result of one-to-one marketing and the benefits of technology, companies are increasingly shifting from a product-driven orientation to a customer-driven emphasis. Early visionaries of this change were Stan Rapp and Tom Collins, who cowrote the 1987 book *Maxi-Marketing*, which summarized the new direction emerging at the time:[3]

> Every established norm in advertising and promotion is being transformed. . . . We are living through a shift from selling virtually everyone the same thing a generation ago to fulfilling the individual needs and tastes of better-educated consumers by supplying them with customized products and services. The shift [is] from a "get a sale now at any cost" to building and managing customer databases to track the lifetime value of your relationship with each customer. As the cost of accumulating and accessing data drops, the ability to talk directly with prospects and customers, building one-to-one relationships with them, will grow.

As one-to-one marketing takes hold, it is no longer enough to understand customers and prospects by aggregate profiles. The one-to-one future requires that marketers understand their customers and collaborate with them, rather than use them as targets. In fact, many early one-to-one marketing efforts failed because marketers bombarded customers with irrelevant, one-to-one communications before making an effort to understand the customers. The fundamental challenge of one-to-one marketing today is to combine the customer information gleaned from database technology with compelling marketing communications.[4]

The one-to-one future is still a goal, not a reality, for most companies. But progress toward one-to-one marketing is evident in the increase in personalized communications and product customization. The battle for customers will be won by marketers who understand why and how their customers buy their products and who will win them over one customer at a time.

New technology allows businesses to personalize messages to their customers. For example, a user of MyYahoo.com is greeted by name and presented with information in which the user has expressed interest. Similarly, RedEnvelope.com helps customers keep track of special occasions and offers personalized gift recommendations. The best-known example of one-to-one product customization is Dell Computer.

More and more companies are making it possible for customers to customize their purchases. For example, Reflect.com creates customized skin-care products for more than 400,000 customers monthly. Most automobile manufacturers offer limited customization of cars and trucks. Consumers can even create their own General Mills cereal at mycereal.com.[5]

Why One-to-One Marketing Needs Database Technology

How can marketers really communicate with their customers one at a time? How can huge corporations like FedEx and Williams-Sonoma communicate with each and every one of their thousands or millions of customers on a personal level?

The answer lies in *database technology*. Fundamentally, one-to-one marketing is no more than the relationship cultivated by a salesperson with the customer. A successful salesperson builds a relationship over time, constantly thinks about what the customer needs and wants, and is mindful of the trends and patterns in the customer's purchase history. A good salesperson often knows what the customer needs even before the customer knows. The salesperson may also inform, educate, and instruct the customer about new products, technology, or applications in anticipation of the customer's future needs or requirements.

This kind of thoughtful attention is the basis of one-to-one marketing. Database technology provides the tools marketers need to "get to know" their customers on a personal basis. Moreover, today's databases are capable of storing information about a company's customers, their purchasing history, and their preferences and then presenting it in a meaningful format that marketers can use to assess, analyze, and anticipate customer needs.

Reflect.com
Custom Chocolate

Create your own customized products at the Web sites of Reflect.com and Custom Chocolate. How did your experiences compare? Do you think that one type of product is more conducive to customization and on-line distribution than the other? Why?

http://www.reflect.com

http://www.custom-chocolate.com

On Line

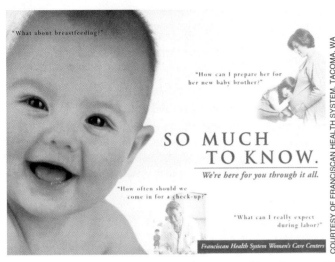

"What about breastfeeding?"

"How can I prepare her for her new baby brother?"

SO MUCH
TO KNOW.

We're here for you through it all.

"How often should we come in for a check-up?"

"What can I really expect during labor?"

Franciscan Health System Women's Care Centers

COURTESY OF FRANCISCAN HEALTH SYSTEM, TACOMA, WA

Being able to target ad mailings is a tremendous advantage for marketers. This brochure, designed specifically for pregnant women and new mothers, was sent out by Franciscan Health Systems as part of its Family Education Programs.

With the help of database technology, one-to-one marketers can track their customers as individuals, even if they number in the millions. Database technology enables marketers to sift through the millions of pieces of data to target the right customers, to develop the right communication based on these customers' needs, and to monitor the ongoing relationship, making adjustments in message strategy as needed.

The number of consumer names in many databases is astounding: American Express, 19 million names of prospective credit card holders; Mead Johnson, maker of Enfamil baby formula, 5 million names of expectant or new mothers; and hotel operator Marriott International, 12 million names of frequent travelers.[6] The data some companies collect can take up huge amounts of computer memory. Wal-Mart's database, considered second in size only to the Pentagon's, contains over two hundred terabytes (trillions of characters) of past customer transaction data. Wal-Mart uses its massive database to help each of its stores adapt its merchandising mix to local neighborhood preferences.[7]

Amazingly, many companies fail to use the information in their databases. Instead, they treat returning customers like first-time customers and continue to ask for the same information over and over again, thereby missing the opportunity to build a relationship. For instance, some hotel chains fail to track customers' room preferences, and many catalog companies require customers to provide their address and credit card information every time they place an order.[8]

Although developing databases for one-to-one marketing efforts can be expensive, the return on investment can be huge. KeyCorp, one of the largest financial services companies in the United States, realized a 364 percent return on investment from its one-to-one marketing efforts. KeyCorp collects data on its Web site where customers create a private profile, identifying their goals and interests. By knowing this information, KeyCorp was able to better respond to their financial needs, cross-selling additional products through direct mail, tellers, and the Internet.[9] Washington-based Franciscan Health Systems replaced its generic newsletters and mass mailings to its 37,000 female patients with a more targeted approach to get them to use its women's health services. The health provider segmented its database according to life stages, such as recently having a baby or being over sixty-five, and sent information that matched corresponding needs. The initiative brought in more female patients for its services and generated $783 for every dollar spent, versus only $263 for earlier marketing efforts.[10]

Forces Influencing One-to-One Marketing

2

Discuss the forces that have influenced the emergence of one-to-one marketing

Several forces have helped shape this new one-to-one focus on customers. They include a more diverse society, more demanding and time-poor consumers, a decline in brand loyalty, the explosion of new media alternatives, and demand for marketing accountability.[11]

Increasing Diversity

In the 1950s and 1960s, Americans strove for the *Leave It to Beaver* and *Dick and Jane* ideal of the perfect lifestyle. The ideal family was Caucasian and lived in a comfortable suburban house, the father worked to support the family, and mom stayed home to keep a tidy house and raise the children. Life was simple. Dad came home from work at five o'clock, the family ate dinner together, and later they gathered around the one television set to watch *Milton Berle*. Although not everyone of that era lived this lifestyle, nearly everybody agreed that it was the ideal.

Today, less than 7 percent of households fit this profile. Modern families are split into many smaller segments, such as unmarried couples living together, fathers or mothers heading households alone, married couples without children, homosexual couples, singles living alone or with roommates, older "empty nesters," and many other permutations. Even more important than the diversity of today's household, however, is society's acceptance of that diversity. Today, people acknowledge and accept diversity, and our definition of what is acceptable has changed as the family has changed.

More Demanding, Time-Poor Consumers

Consumers today are more strapped for time than any previous generation. Although the continuing rise in the number of women in the workforce, the increase in working mothers, and the rise in single-parent households mostly headed by women are not new trends, women now constitute the majority of American workers for the first time. As a result, consumers have less and less time to spend on anything but the most pressing details of their lives. This is having a profound impact on consumers' buying behavior. Consumers are becoming more demanding, more impatient, and much less likely to spend time agonizing over small purchases or driving across town to the mall. This is evident in the statistics showing that over 128 million Americans—more than two-thirds of the population—order goods or services by phone, mail, or on-line each year. The growth of Internet commerce also attests to Americans' lack of time. In 1999, one in five Americans purchased something over the Internet, up from virtually no one just four years earlier.[12]

Decreasing Brand Loyalty

In a 1975 survey of male and female heads of households, over three-quarters agreed with the statement "I try to stick to well-known brand names." Ten years later, only a little over half agreed with the same statement. This trend has continued through the 1990s and into the new century. Consumers are now more likely to experiment with generics or switch back and forth between major brands in a category. They are also more likely to shop for discounts and, if presented with two comparable brands, will likely choose based on price.

The decline in brand loyalty can be attributed in part to the excessive couponing, trade deals, and deep price promotions by manufacturers and retailers that have accustomed consumers to look for the best deal. Brand loyalty has also wavered due to the proliferation of brands available, with thousands more being introduced annually. With so many product choices, consumers often become confused about product differentiation or lack the time to learn about each new brand. As a result, consumers often resort to basing their purchases on price.

The decrease in brand loyalty can also be attributed to the increasing power of many retailers today. Retailers are increasingly taking control of their relationships with brand marketers, dictating level and type of in-store promotions, placement of product, and price. These retailers are also more sophisticated at developing their own customer communications programs, including multicoupon direct-mail and relationship-oriented marketing programs. As a result, consumers are building more of a relationship with a particular retailer than with a brand. For example, consumers may drive thirty or more miles to a Wal-Mart store to shop even though they can get the same brands at relatively the same prices in their own neighborhood.

Emergence of New Media Alternatives

Three decades ago, most Americans spent their evenings in front of their television set, watching network programming on NBC, CBS, or ABC. They were also more likely to read the newspaper and subscribe to a general news magazine such as *Life* or *Time*. Marketers reached consumers by blanketing mass media with image advertising.

Today's busy consumers are not at all likely to be found spending their evenings watching the latest sitcom on network television. Instead, they are probably surfing the hundreds of channels available through their direct satellite system, watching a rented movie, or visiting their favorite game or news site on the Internet. Newspapers and general-interest magazines have given way to an abundance of specialty publications that cater to a wide range of interests.

With the emergence of new and varied media alternatives, mass-media advertising will never be the same. Marketers must increasingly divvy up their marketing dollars among the various media available, concentrating on those that will bring them the most bang for the buck. Although mass-media advertising on network television or through general-interest magazines will continue to play an important role in communicating brand messages, it will never again be the dominant force it once was.

Demand for Accountability

The impact of mass-media advertising on sales has always been difficult to measure. Generations of marketers have quoted the comment of John Wanamaker, a late-nineteenth-century American merchant: "I know half of my advertising is wasted. I just don't know which half." Historically, the results of a newspaper or television advertising expenditure could be measured only through future sales of the advertised offering, its increase in market share, or the increase in store traffic. Even sales promotional tactics, which provide more measurability than mass-media efforts, have come under attack. For instance, coupons distributed through the free-standing inserts found in the Sunday paper are just as much a form of mass-media advertising as a full-page image ad in the same paper and, therefore, largely unaccountable. Manufacturers today are under pressure to maintain growth and profits for stockholders. It is no longer acceptable to say that sales increased after an advertising campaign. Management now wants proof that monies spent on advertising and marketing will deliver results.

How Have These Trends Influenced One-to-One Marketing?

What are these forces telling marketers? How are they pushing forward the customer-focused philosophy of one-to-one marketing?

For starters, a more diverse society has ruled that the one-size-fits-all marketing of yesteryear no longer fits. Consumers do not want to be treated like the masses. Instead, they want to be treated as the individuals they are, with their own unique sets of needs and wants. By its personalized nature, one-to-one marketing can fulfill this desire.

Second, more direct and personal marketing efforts will continue to grow to meet the needs of consumers who no longer have the time to spend shopping and making purchase decisions. With the personal and targeted nature of one-to-one marketing, consumers can spend less time making purchase decisions and more time doing the things that are important.

Third, consumers will be loyal only to those companies and brands that have earned their loyalty and reinforced it at every purchase occasion. One-to-one marketing techniques focus on finding a firm's best customers, rewarding them for their loyalty, and thanking them for their business.

Fourth, mass-media approaches will decline in importance as advances in market research and database technology allow marketers to collect detailed information on their customers, not just the approximation offered by demographics but the specific names and addresses. One-to-one marketing will increase in importance and offer marketers a more cost-effective avenue to reach customers. Finally, the demand for accountability will drive the growth of one-to-one marketing and justify its continued existence.

One-to-one marketing is a huge commitment and often requires a 180-degree turnaround for marketers who spent the last half of the twentieth century thick in mass-marketing efforts. Although mass marketing will probably always be part of the promotional mix, especially to create brand awareness or to remind consumers of a product, the advantages of one-to-one marketing cannot be ignored. Today, the new commandment of marketing's future rings loudly in every marketer's ears: "Know thy customer and communicate with him or her based on what you know."[13]

A Revised Marketing Communications Process

The traditional mass-marketing communications process, introduced in Chapter 14, in which everyone receives the same message through the same channel, no longer holds true in a one-to-one marketing environment. Recall that the mass-marketing communications process presented in Exhibit 14.3 depicts an advertiser or marketer sending a promotional message through some type of mass-marketing channel, such as a television ad or an outdoor billboard, to the target audience. Noise from competing advertisements affects the encoding and decoding of the message. Feedback on the effectiveness of the communication comes through market research and changes in sales levels or market share.

Now, compare this process with Exhibit 21.1, which depicts marketing communications using one-to-one marketing and database technology. The revised **one-to-one marketing communications process** flows as follows: (1) the one-to-one marketer, the *sender*, encodes individualized messages for customers and prospects identified from the database; (2) the message is then sent through a direct communications channel, such as direct mail, a salesperson, a telemarketer, or directly over the Internet; (3) the customer or prospect, the *receiver*, interprets the personalized message; (4) the customer or prospect responds to the communication through a response, a purchase, or other communication; (5) the one-to-one marketer captures this response, feeding it back into the marketing database where it will help shape the next marketing communication.

Although the flow of the communications process is still basically the same, from marketer to customer, there are a few significant differences. First, the encoded message is *personalized* to the individual. Rather than a mass communication

Compare the one-to-one marketing communications process with the traditional mass-marketing communications process

one-to-one marketing communications process
A revised marketing communications process that depicts the individualized communication between the one-to-one marketer and the customer; characterized by the use of personalized communication, the lack of interfering noise, and the ability to capture the response of the customer.

Exhibit 21.1

One-to-One Marketing
Communications Process

in which the same message is sent to a large group of potential respondents who may or may not be interested, a personalized, one-to-one communication is sent to relatively few individuals who are known to be interested. Novartis Seeds, Inc., a Minneapolis-based agriculture business, produces individually customized, full-color brochures for seven thousand farmers. Each piece features products selected by Novartis dealers specifically for the farmer based on information collected about the farm operation and the types of crops grown. Instead of the thirty-page catalog Novartis traditionally sent, these customers get a one-page brochure with only the five or six products they need, plus other complementary products dealers feel they should consider.[14]

Second, the channel used to send the message is a *direct* channel rather than a mass-media channel. With mass-media channels such as television or newspapers, marketers do not personally know the people with whom they are trying to communicate. With a direct one-to-one channel, the marketer has some information about each individual customer. Further, with mass-media channels, the company is unable to respond immediately to customers' reactions to its message. Instead, it must wait to see whether people are reacting positively or negatively by conducting research or by monitoring sales and market share. With a direct one-to-one channel, marketers can capture individual customer responses and use this information to shape future communications.

Third, notice that *noise*, or interference from competing advertisements, news articles, or other competing store displays, is not present in the one-to-one marketing communications process. This is because the communication occurs directly from the marketer to the customer or prospect, with minimal interference from competing messages. Although no communications environment is completely free of interfering noise—the dog may be barking, the children interrupting, or the telephone ringing—the one-to-one communications process comes as close as possible to being noise-free. With less interference, the receiver of the one-to-one marketing message is more likely to receive and interpret the communication correctly.

Last, in the one-to-one communications process the response of the individual can be captured, allowing the marketer to use the response to update the customer record, tailor the next marketing effort, and provide accountability for marketing dollars spent. Chris Zane, president of Zane's Cycles in Branford, Connecticut, uses past responses from customers to tailor future marketing communications. Every March, Zane searches his database for customers who bought baby seats three years earlier. Knowing that they may wish to buy a child's bike soon, Zane sends these customers a postcard showcasing his inventory of children's bikes and offering a small discount on the purchase. About 60 percent of those who receive the postcard return to buy a bike.[15]

One-to-One Marketing Applications

4

List eight common one-to-one marketing applications

As mentioned earlier, a marketing database is not an end in and of itself but rather a *tool* that helps marketers reach customers and prospects with one-to-one marketing communications. The information contained in marketing databases helps

Exhibit 21.2

Eight Common One-to-One
Marketing Applications

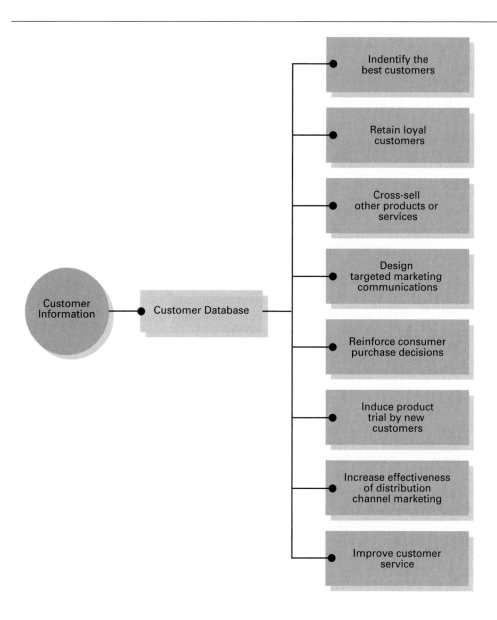

marketers know and understand their customers on an individual level. By analyzing and manipulating the information, marketers can identify sales opportunities and drive the communications process to address these opportunities. Several one-to-one applications for marketing databases are presented in Exhibit 21.2 and discussed in the text that follows.

Identifying the Best Customers

Smart marketers have found that not all customers are created equal; that is, a majority of sales will come from a minority of customers. When companies examine closely where their sales are coming from, most find that the 80/20 principle applies: 20 percent of the customer base accounts for 80 percent of sales. If a company could identify these customers and develop a relationship with them, chances are the company would enjoy enormous profitability. Thus, one of the most important values of a one-to-one marketing database is to track the 10 or 20 percent of customers who account for the majority of the sales. Casino operator Harrah's Entertainment, for instance, discovered that gamblers who spent between $100 and $499 a trip accounted for about 30 percent of its customer base but 80 percent of its revenue and nearly 100 percent of its profits. As a result, the company refocused its marketing efforts on this group it calls "avid players."[16] Conversely, discount brokerage firm Charles Schwab determined who its most costly customers were and revised the minimum balances required to qualify for free personal service. Now, those customers who are only comfortable talking to a company representative in a branch office may have to carry a certain balance or pay for the service.[17] Similarly, FedEx imposed double-digit rate increases on some major shippers that it identified as generating lots of expensive residential shipments, in essence telling several they could take their business elsewhere.[18]

Retaining Loyal Customers

It follows, then, that if a company knows who its best customers are, it should make every effort to maintain and increase their loyalty to retain their business. One study concluded that if a company retains an additional 5 percent of its customers each year, profits will increase by at least 25 percent. What's more, improving customer retention by a mere 2 percent can decrease costs by as much as 10 percent.[19]

Loyalty programs reward loyal consumers for making multiple purchases with the objective of building long-term, mutually beneficial relationships between a company and its key customers. Loyalty programs take advantage of database technology built around the identification of a firm's best customers. Marriott Hotels, for instance, rewards its best customers with special perks not available to customers who stay less frequently. Travelers who spend more than seventy-five nights a year in any of Marriott's brand hotels—Marriott, Renaissance, Fairfield, Courtyard, Residence Inn, SpringHill Suites, or TownePlace Suites—receive reservation guarantees, welcome gifts like fruit baskets or mineral water in their rooms, room upgrades, free phone service, and access to concierge lounges.[20] SportsLine USA rewards its loyal customers just for visiting its Web site. Members of its loyalty program receive points for viewing pages that can be redeemed for sports merchandise, event tickets, or private e-mail messages from sports celebrities. The Internet site uses the information collected to understand the unique behavior and tendencies of the sports fans who visit its site.[21]

In addition to rewarding good customers, loyalty programs provide businesses with a wealth of information about their customers and shopping trends that can be used to make future business decisions. For example, the 1.1 million members of Chico's Passport Club receive a 5 percent discount whenever they spend more than $500. These customers account for 80 percent of company sales. Every month, the company sends its members and another 1.3 million potential customers a catalog and a discount coupon, which allows the company to track the response down to each individual. Company officials then use the customer response to calculate future promotions and locations for future stores.[22]

Cross-Selling Other Products or Services

One-to-one marketing provides tremendous opportunities for cross-selling related products. A database allows marketers to match product profiles and consumer profiles to cross-sell customers other products that match their demographic, lifestyle, or behavioral characteristics. American Collegiate Marketing, a magazine subscription service targeted to students and educators, uses past customer purchase information gleaned from its database of millions of magazine subscribers to feature new magazines the customer may be interested in. Past purchase behavior may show that subscribers of *Sports Illustrated*, for instance, may also be interested in general news magazines such as *Time* or *Newsweek*. Similarly, the Internet music retailer CDNow develops profiles of music buyers who have purchased similar selections. When a buyer searches or purchases music titles that match a profile, he or she is then presented with titles that other buyers in the profile have bought.

Internet companies use product and customer profiling to reveal cross-sell opportunities while a customer is surfing their site. Past purchases, where a surfer goes on a site, and what site the surfer came from give on-line marketers clues about the surfer's interests and what items to cross-sell. Cyberian Outpost (outpost.com), a computer-goods e-tailer, adjusts the pages visitors see depending on what they click on at the site or what they purchased in the past. For instance, if a surfer always goes to computer game pages or has purchased simulation games in the past, Outpost will automatically put offers for other game titles on part of the screen. Depending on what a shopper puts in a shopping cart, Outpost will flash promotions for related materials—a leather case for someone who is buying a Palm Pilot, for example.[23]

Many banks are using one-to-one marketing techniques to encourage customers to visit a branch and to cross-sell new products such as life insurance and mutual funds. Washington Mutual recently redesigned its lobbies to create a more customer-friendly environment where customers enjoy doing business. Each lobby now features a concierge to welcome customers, a children's play area with cartoons and video games, and a shop with colorful calendars, piggy banks, and books on investing. Instead of sitting behind counters, bank tellers wearing khakis walk around the lobby offering to help customers with traditional services such as deposits and withdrawals or to explain the bank's new insurance and mutual fund products. Transactions are completed at kiosks where customers can view their accounts along with the teller. As a result of these efforts to reach out to customers, the banks are opening twice as many checking accounts and increasing insurance and financial-service sales.[24]

Designing Targeted Marketing Communications

Using transaction and purchase data, a database allows marketers to track customers' relationships to the company's products and services and modify the marketing message accordingly. For instance, a company may segment its customers as infrequent users, moderate users, and heavy users. It may then devise a segmented communications strategy based on which group the customer falls in. Marketing communications to infrequent users might encourage or stimulate a repeat purchase through a direct incentive such as a limited-time price discount for ordering again. Communications to moderate users may use fewer incentives and more reinforcement of past purchase decisions. Targeted communications to heavy users would be designed around loyalty and reinforcement of the purchase rather than price promotions.

Rite Aid Corporation's pharmacy division uses its database to create direct-to-patient targeted information in the form of informational pamphlets that also carry targeted advertising. A consumer filling a prescription for a diabetes medication, for example, will receive a pamphlet with different editorial content and advertising than a consumer filling a prescription for a hypertension drug.[25] Dick's Supermarkets, an eight-store chain in Wisconsin, uses transaction data from its loyalty card program to personalize shopping lists it mails every two weeks to its nearly thirty thousand members. The shopping lists contain timed offers based on past purchases. A consumer who bought Tide several weeks ago, for instance, may be offered a cents-off coupon to restock.[26]

Knowing other personal or demographic information besides past transaction data also allows marketers to tailor a message. For example, due to legal restrictions on mass advertising, R.J. Reynolds' Doral Tobacco brand relies on one-to-one marketing to maintain customer loyalty. In return for registration, Doral customers receive a personalized birthday card, a quarterly newsletter filled with recipes and coupons, and an invitation to annual customer appreciation events featuring free cigarettes, food, card games, and country music. Doral also uses its database to learn about customers' lifestyles and preferences. For instance, Doral found that a large percentage of its customers were veterans or had family members in the military. So the company recently hosted a "Red, White, and Blue Salute" weekend for veterans and their families. Similarly, since half of its customers enjoy collecting, the company created its own limited-edition cigarette cards.[27]

Reinforcing Consumer Purchase Decisions

As you learned in Chapter 5, *cognitive dissonance* is the feeling consumers get when they recognize an inconsistency between their values and opinions and their behavior. In other words, they begin to doubt the soundness of their purchase decision. A database offers marketers an excellent opportunity to reach out to customers to reinforce the purchase decision. By thanking customers for their purchase and letting them know that they are important to the business, marketers can help cement a long-term and profitable relationship. Guests staying at the quaint Village Country Inn nestled in the Green Mountains of Vermont receive a handwritten thank-you note from the inn's proprietors within a week of their stay. The note thanks the guests for visiting and encourages them to return in the future. Updating customers periodically about the status of their order also reinforces purchase decisions. Minutes after customers order merchandise from Amazon.com's Web site, for example, they receive an e-mail acknowledging their order. Every few days thereafter, customers receive updates that allow them to track the shipment of the order, from ship date to receipt. Postsale e-mails also afford the chance to provide more customer service or cross-sell another product or service. When customers purchase digital storage equipment from Iomega Direct, the site automatically sends a confirmation e-mail. Then, once a week, Iomega sends everyone who purchased in the previous week a message that provides links back to Iomega Direct's site, to a customer support site, and to a site where they can download Iomega software.[28]

Inducing Product Trial by New Customers

Although a significant portion of one-to-one marketing effort is expended on encouraging repeat purchases by a firm's best customers or market segments, a marketing database can also be used to identify new customers. Because a firm using a marketing database already has a profile of its best customers, it can easily find new customers who fit that profile.

One-to-one marketers generally use demographic and behavioral data overlaid on existing customer data to develop a detailed customer profile that is a powerful tool for evaluating lists of prospects. For instance, if a firm's best customers are thirty-five to fifty years of age, live in suburban areas, own luxury cars, like to eat at Thai restaurants, and enjoy mountain climbing, then the company can find prospects already in its database or customers who currently are identified as using a competitor's product who match this profile. Procter & Gamble uses its Web site to test customer interest in new products. Customers who visit the Web site are encouraged to sign up for free trial samples and then to provide feedback. The company uses the demographic data and customer feedback to make product and promotion decisions. In response to information gathered during a test for Crest Whitestrips, P&G decided to change language on the packaging and to focus promotions on women between the ages of thirty-five and fifty-four.[29]

One-to-one marketing has helped Boise Cascade know exactly who its customers are, who within the company takes care of which customers, and what the customers really want. The company can now compete more effectively against big box office supply stores, like Office Depot and Staples.

Increase the Effectiveness of Distribution Channel Marketing

In Chapter 12 you learned that a *marketing channel* is a business structure consisting of interdependent organizations, such as wholesalers and retailers, that move a product from producer to ultimate consumers. Most marketers rely on heavily layered, indirect channels to move their products to the end user. Thus, marketers often lose touch with the customer as an individual since the relationship is really between the retailer and the consumer. Marketers in this predicament tend to view their customers as aggregate statistics because specific customer information is hard to gather.

With one-to-one marketing databases, manufacturers now have a tool to gain insight into who is buying their products. Instead of simply unloading product into the distribution channel and leaving marketing and relationship-building to dealers, auto manufacturers today are taking a more active role in learning about their customers. Car makers now keep in touch with owners and prospects, learning their life stages and hobbies, understanding their vehicle needs, and developing relationships in the hopes that these consumers will reward them with brand loyalty in the future. Car manufacturers then pass on the information they collect to their dealers, so they can better understand their customers and tailor their dealerships to better meet customers' needs. Mercedes-Benz USA, for instance, has developed a database of some 1.5 million consumers who have expressed an interest in the brand. The car manufacturer offers owners individual Web sites to communicate directly with Mercedes-Benz. Similarly, DaimlerChrysler sends new buyers a thank-you mailing with a free oil change and an invitation to communicate with the company by phone, mail, or the Web.[30]

Improving Customer Service

One-to-one marketing techniques are increasingly being used to improve the customer service experience for customers. Boise Cascade Office Products is using one-to-one marketing techniques to compete against competitors like Office Depot. The company recently changed its whole culture to become more customer-centric. Sales reps were sent out to meet one-on-one with their customers. And now when a customer calls to place an order, a caller identification system automatically routes the call to a salesperson whose screen shows the customer's name and recent transaction history.[31] Capital One Financial Corporation, one of the top ten issuers of credit cards, made similar changes after it discovered that customers who called the company were waiting on hold for long periods of time or were routed to someone who was not trained to answer their questions. Using sophisticated data analysis and redesigned processes, Capital One can now predict the nature of the call even before the phone is answered. By sifting through customer contact data, the company developed a system that correctly categorizes and routes up to 70 percent of calls automatically, resulting in less waiting for the customer and faster information. The company is also able to capitalize on cross-sell opportunities. By decreasing call time by a third, the firm freed up customer service representatives to spend more time selling. Now Capital One cross-sells other services when customers call in and are more receptive to marketing.[32]

Procter & Gamble
What kind of product testing is currently going on at the Procter & Gamble Web site? Sign up to participate and find out how the company implements its one-to-one marketing plan through its Web site.

http://www.pg.com

On Line

The Basics of Marketing Database Technology

In almost all cases, one-to-one marketing is characterized by the creation of a large computerized file of customers' and potential customers' profiles and purchase patterns that are then used to direct marketing communications. One-to-one marketing using technology is commonly referred to as

5

Discuss the basics of one-to-one marketing database technology

data-driven marketing
The process of gathering, maintaining, and analyzing information about customers and prospects to implement more efficient and effective marketing communications. Another term for one-to-one marketing.

database
A collection of data, especially one that can be accessed and manipulated by computer software.

marketing database
The compilation of names, addresses, and other pieces of pertinent information about individual customers and prospects that affects what and how marketers sell to them.

data-driven marketing. That is, by gathering, enhancing, and analyzing information about customers and prospects, marketers will be able to implement more efficient and effective marketing communications and perform precise marketing. With data, technology, and statistical techniques, one-to-one marketers communicate to individuals, not to mass-market segments.

At the very core of one-to-one marketing is, of course, a database. As defined by *Random House Webster's Dictionary*, a **database** is "a collection of data, especially one that can be accessed and manipulated by computer software." More specifically, a **marketing database** is the compilation of names, addresses, and other pieces of pertinent information about individual customers and prospects that affects what and how marketers sell to them.

A database can store almost any kind of information about consumers. In its most basic form, database marketing relies on transactional processing systems that record the details of individual purchase transactions. For example, when a consumer makes a purchase using a credit card, a database records the store name, the store location, the date of the purchase, and the purchase price, among other things. Over time this produces a transaction history for every customer. This basic transactional system provides critical information about purchasing patterns and preferences that are valuable in creating new products or sales offers. Transaction data can be further enhanced with additional information about individual customers such as age and income level, interests, or something that reflects their lifestyle or attitudes. Exhibit 21.3 shows several different types of basic information that marketers could collect on their customers and prospects, divided by whether they are consumers or business-to-business customers.

Last quarter you had 1000 customers. This quarter you have 1000 customers. How many customers *did you lose?*

Where did they go? Why? Are the customers you gained as profitable as the ones you lost? Don't know the answers? Then you should know Business Objects. Our customer intelligence software mines the customer data that's scattered across your various systems – sales, marketing, customer support and finance – to give you an integrated 360° view of each and every customer. Then you, like the Global 1000 companies who use our software every day, will have the intelligence you need to grow your customer relationships. Instead of losing them. Call **1-800-527-0580** ext. 33 or visit **businessobjects.com/customer** and register for our free online "Customer Intelligence" seminar.

BUSINESS INTELLIGENCE. IF YOU HAVE IT, YOU KNOW.

BUSINESS OBJECTS

The Business Objects logo is a registered trademark of Business Objects S.A. ©2001 Business Objects S.A. All rights reserved.

COURTESY OF BUSINESS OBJECTS

In many cases, a database gives marketing decision makers access to the vast amounts of customer information traditionally stored in separate computer systems throughout a company. Data kept for other purposes, such as financial data kept by the billing department or customer service problems kept by the service area, are merged together into a data warehouse to provide a complete picture of the customer. Instead of the days, weeks, or months it traditionally took to create reports from data stored in different computer systems, a data warehouse allows today's managers to answer questions in seconds. Marketing decision makers can now ask a "what if" question such as "What if we sent the last offer only to the top 20 percent of our customers instead of the top 50 percent?" When decision makers can go from one question to the next in seconds rather than days or weeks, they ask not only more questions but better, and hopefully, the right questions.[33]

Marketers should remember, though, that having a marketing database is not a process in and of itself. Instead, the database is the *tool* used to achieve the full potential of one-to-one data-driven marketing. Any marketer can have a database of customer information, but if the right data are not collected and effectively manipulated to provide answers and insights, or if the data are not properly maintained to ensure their integrity, then the marketer has not fully achieved one-to-one marketing.

Marketing databases are critical for companies operating in fiercely competitive industries. This ad for Business Objects boils the issue down to the important truth of knowing who your customers are and if they are planning on defecting (if they haven't already).

Building a Marketing Database

As database marketing experts Rob Jackson and Paul Wang state in their book *Strategic Database Marketing*, "A database is only as powerful as the information it houses."[34] Data form the cornerstone of data-driven, one-to-one marketing. A company can have the most elaborate and expensive database system available and a staff of statistical professionals and marketing experts, but if the right data are not collected, then the other building blocks will never be used to their potential.

Many firms make it a point to gather customer information at the time of purchase at the same time transaction data are gathered. Toys "R" Us cashiers routinely

Exhibit 21.3

Basic Consumer and
Business-to-Business Data

Consumer Data	Business-to-Business Data
• Name, address, telephone number, e-mail address • Demographic data: age, income, gender, ethnicity, household size, etc. • Lifestyle and leisure interests • Financial characteristics such as credit history and rating • Recency, frequency, and monetary transaction history by date, dollar amount of purchase, and products purchased • Source of order, inquiry, or referral • Promotional response data	• Name, genderization (e.g., Mr./Mrs./Ms.), title of buyer, direct telephone number, e-mail address • Company name, address, and telephone number • Company demographics: NAICS code, number of employees, sales volume, number of branches, key contacts • Recency, frequency, and monetary transaction history by date, dollar amount of purchase, and products purchased • Financial characteristics such as credit history and rating • Predictive complementary product information (purchase behavior that indicates a propensity to purchase a complementary product) • Industry surveys • Assigned salesperson

ask for a phone number when the customer checks out. Walt Disney includes a postage-paid postcard in every video asking for customer information. Black & Decker includes product registration cards that can be returned with the purchase of every appliance. Marketers often provide an incentive in exchange for customer information. To gather customer demographic data and product feedback about Finditquick.com, a cross-promotion between books and Web sites, Golden Books gave away free book samples. As a result, the company learned that the books were appealing to an older audience than the company was targeting. It also learned that customers were more likely to purchase the books from a mass retailer or grocery store than a bookstore.[35]

 Data gathering can be overt or covert. Members of frequent shopper clubs generally understand that the retailer is collecting information about their purchases in exchange for discounts or gifts. For instance, Virgin Entertainment offers free Internet appliances to customers who are willing to part with their personal information. The Internet devices allow users to surf the Internet and send e-mail in exchange for answering questions about shopping preferences, music, and entertainment interests, where and how customers generally get on-line, and how they spend their time once they get on the Web. In accepting the Internet appliances, customers give Virgin the right to track their movements on the Web and also agree to receive targeted advertising and e-mails from Virgin and other marketers.[36] The Ritz Carlton's data gathering, on the other hand, is generally invisible to consumers but can create a special relationship over time. The hotel keeps track of guests' predilections and provides them with individualized service, right down to soft or firm pillows, whichever they prefer. The data gathering is very subtle—most guests don't even know their preferences are recorded in a database.[37]

Often the beginning of a marketing database is right under the marketer's nose in the form of a response list. A **response list** includes the names and addresses of individuals at home or in the workplace who have responded to an offer of some kind either by mail, telephone, direct-response television, product rebates, contests or sweepstakes, or billing inserts, to name a few.[38] Response lists tend to be especially actionable because past behavior is a strong predictor of future behavior. For instance, food products manufacturers often have the names of many people who responded to past offers of recipes using their products. Not only are these people a good place to start a database, but they have also shown significant interest in the product and are therefore more prone to purchase.

response list
A customer list that includes the names and addresses of individuals who have responded to an offer of some kind, such as by mail, telephone, direct-response television, product rebates, contests or sweepstakes, or billing inserts.

Other firms can get a jump-start on building a customer database by purchasing a compiled list. A **compiled list** generally includes names and addresses gleaned from telephone directories or membership rosters. A great many compilations are available, ranging from those owned by the large list companies such as American Business Lists, Database America, and Dun & Bradstreet for business-to-business data and Donnelley, Metromail, and R. L. Polk for consumer lists, to small groups or associations that are willing to sell their membership lists. Data compiled by large data-gathering companies are very accurate. American Business Lists, for instance, uses thousands of public sources, Securities and Exchange Commission records, 10-K reports, annual reports, trade journals, government publications, and newspapers to compile data on the nation's 11 million businesses. The company also utilizes a staff of hundreds of telemarketers to make over 16 million phone calls a year to verify and compile additional information on every U.S. business.

Multinational companies building worldwide databases often face difficult problems when pulling together internal data about their customers. Differences in language, computer systems, and data-collection methods can be huge obstacles that must be overcome. In spite of the challenges, many global companies are committed to building databases. Unilever has begun using the Internet not only to educate consumers about the brand but also to develop relationships with its customers by providing helpful information. Visitors to the Persil UK Web site can get information about removing stubborn stains. Customers also receive a discount on their next purchase in exchange for completing an on-line questionnaire. To date, the company has collected information on more than 30 million loyal customers.[39]

Enhancing Customer Data

A customer database becomes even more useful to one-to-one marketers when it is *enhanced* to include more than simply a customer's or prospect's name, address, telephone number, and transaction history. **Database enhancement** is the overlay of information to customer or prospect records for the purpose of better describing or better determining the responsiveness of customers or prospects. Types of enhancement data typically include demographic, lifestyle, or behavioral information about a customer.

There are three primary reasons to enhance a database with outside sources of information. First, marketers use database enhancement to learn more about customers or prospects. By overlaying demographic, lifestyle, and behavioral data onto customer records, marketers can gain a fuller picture of customers and their relative value to the company. For instance, a marketer of athletic equipment would find it valuable to know which of its customers were considered its best customers based on past transaction data. However, if that same marketer also knew that these customers have incomes over $50,000, enjoy outdoor recreation activities, especially biking and mountain climbing, and are also recent purchasers of mountain bikes, then the company would have a better understanding of who the customers really are.

Customer profiles allow marketers to distinguish different customer groupings by more than product purchases. For instances, direct marketer Spiegel's database contains the names of more than three million catalog shoppers who have purchased within the last eighteen months, each appended with credit data, demographic information, and dozens of other data points. Analysis of its data identified customer subgroups that Spiegel could better target through smaller specialty catalogs. Its On/View catalog, for example, is mailed to Spiegel's young career customers who prefer flowery, feminine clothing. Meanwhile, a subgroup of younger "post-feminist" shoppers culled from the On/View list now receives Spiegel Life, a catalog featuring relaxed natural fibers apparel.[40]

Second, database enhancement can increase the effectiveness of customer marketing programs. By learning more about the best and most profitable customers, marketers can understand how to maximize marketing communications and cross-selling opportunities. The same athletic equipment company, for example, now armed with a profile of its best customers, can tailor communications to these customers that showcase its line of mountain bike gear, such as helmets, protective pads, and clothing.

Finally, by understanding the profiles of their best customers, marketers can find prospects who match the profile and thereby can increase the success rate of future marketing communications and business expansions. For example, H-E-B Grocery Company uses database enhancement and customer profiling to identify and learn as much as possible about potential customers before opening a new store. Each store is then designed to be unique and to offer the products those customers want. When the company opened one of its upscale Central Market stores in Fort Worth, customer profiling indicated that Fort Worth residents have a strong sense of Western heritage. The Fort Worth location, therefore, is the only Central Market to offer customers chipotle-smoked barbecue ribs, game birds, and briskets. The store has also adjusted the way it cuts and sells beef to meet local preferences. In addition, H-E-B knows its best customers will fall into one of four groups: Hispanics, "Adventurous Diners" who like to try new things, "We've raised the kids and now it's our turn" customers who are interested in cooking for themselves, and "Soccer Moms" who don't have time to cook but want to give their family healthy meals. The store carries an expanded selection of peppers and fresh tortillas for its Hispanic customers. And it offers a large selection of healthy and gourmet prepared foods for those customers without the inclination or the time to cook for themselves. Once open, the stores continue to use databases to collect information about customer preferences to tweak product offerings and to encourage new-product trials.[41]

Compiled lists, mentioned earlier, are often enhanced with information gathered from public records, such as Census Bureau data, auto registrations, birth announce-ments, business start-ups, or bankruptcies. Thus, compiled data can indicate several key attributes about consumers that may suggest their financial status, demographics, buying preferences, lifestyle, or attitude patterns. Cox Direct, the cooperative mailer of both Carol Wright and Val-Pak coupons, launched its "See Them Grow" program targeted at parents of five- to eighteen-month-olds. "See Them Grow" is sent quarterly to a list of some 750,000 families with toddlers compiled from birth records. The mailing includes offers from Sears Portrait Studios, America Online, Gerber Life Insurance, and Grolier's Dr. Seuss & His Friends books.[42]

Another form of enhancement data is modeled data. **Modeled data** include information that has already been sorted into distinct groups or clusters of consumers or businesses based on census, household, or business-level data. Several organizations specialize in collecting these types of data to develop models of consumer purchase behavior based on the theory of *geographic behavioral patterns*—that is, people who live near each other will have similar characteristics and will behave similarly. These systems have the added advantage of being able to work within geographic areas that are significantly smaller than a zip code, most often down to the zip+4 level. These companies have conducted a great amount of research analyzing demographics, psychographics, and sometimes response patterns to determine these geographic "pockets" of similar decision makers.

The best known of these special database firms is Claritas, which created PRIZM (Potential Rating Index by zip Market). PRIZM is founded on the notion that "birds of a feather flock together." PRIZM breaks down the U.S. Census Bureau data by zip+4 codes and analyzes each code for social rank, mobility, ethnicity, family life cycle, and housing. Census data are blended with information from other municipal and regional government agencies, consumer surveys, and proprietary data from business partners like Equifax, Ford Motor Company, and Procter & Gamble. Zip+4 codes contain an average of six households.[43]

PRIZM defines every micro-neighborhood in the United States in terms of sixty-two demographically and behaviorally distinct types, or "clusters." Claritas can analyze a company's customer database and then tell the firm into which PRIZM clusters its customers fall. To get a better idea of how Claritas' PRIZM clusters work, do the "On-Line" activity at the top of the next page.

modeled data
Enhancement information that has already been sorted into distinct groups or clusters of consumers or businesses based on census, household, or business-level data.

custom data

Enhancement information acquired by the marketer, including customer surveys, customer participation programs, product registration, warranty cards, or loyalty marketing programs.

Marketers often have specific data enhancement elements on their wish list that cannot be collected via internal or external sources. Acquiring this information may require the marketers to use a little creativity to develop their own custom, primary source of enhancement data. Sources of **custom data** could include such things as customer surveys, customer participation programs, product registration, warranty cards, or loyalty marketing programs. Looking to capture more information about its customers' buying behavior, Ashford.com offers freebies such as a chance to win a trip to Ireland to customers who complete a questionnaire about themselves. Data from the questionnaire are then merged with the customer's purchasing history to help the company segment the customer into one of twelve categories. The company uses information about each segment to tailor marketing communications for that segment. For example, the high-end e-tailer will focus more marketing communications on members of the "jet set wannabes" than on the "bargain hunters." By using information collected from the customer surveys to create a more complete picture of its customers, Ashford.com improved the click-through rate of its communications from 2.5 percent to 20 percent overall, and 25 percent among its best customers.[44]

Finding Answers by Analyzing Customer Data

One of the most important aspects of one-to-one marketing is not the names and addresses stored but the ability to go beyond creating mere mailing lists to manipulating the data to profile the best customers or segments of customers, analyze their lifetime value, and, ultimately, predict their purchasing behavior through statistical modeling. Database marketing expert James R. Rosenfield's comments on database marketing sum it up: "Marketers confuse a marketing database, which can simply be stored information about customers, with database marketing, which is a dynamic approach to managing customers. You can't do database marketing without modeling and profiling—that's what it's all about."[45]

The real value of one-to-one marketing, therefore, is not in the data. Actually, large quantities of data can remove value from one-to-one marketing by making the exercise confusing and complex. That is not to say that data are not necessary, only that to be valuable, data must be turned into marketing information in the form of customer profiles, scores, and predictions. The data must be transformed from operational bits and bytes into the information that marketers need for successful marketing communication.

Common data analysis techniques for marketing databases include (1) customer segmentation, (2) recency-frequency-monetary analysis (RFM), (3) lifetime value analysis, (4) predictive modeling, and (5) data mining. Although other statistical and modeling techniques are available and widely used, these five types of data analysis are used quite often by one-to-one marketers. Most companies with customer databases should be able to conduct the first three data analysis techniques easily, if transaction data and enhancement data have been collected. Predictive modeling and data mining are more sophisticated techniques and generally require more data and expertise in statistical analysis. Predictive modeling provides an excellent means for marketers to ask "what if" questions, whereas data mining uses a variety of tools to uncover subtle patterns in consumer purchasing behavior.

Customer Segmentation

Customer segmentation is the process of breaking large groups of customers into smaller, more homogenous groups. One-to-one marketers use this analysis to paint a picture of what customers look like, in particular the best customers. By identifying a segment of customers in the database by any means, such as by survey, purchase data, response, or word of mouth, a firm then can find a way to compare the identified customer segment with the rest of its customers. These segmentations can be based on such characteristics as demographics, geographic location, previous purchase behavior, or psychographic variables. Some examples of these are shown in Exhibit 21.4. For instance, Fidelity Investments segments its customers into groups based on revenue, profitability, third-party data, and customer interaction. Fidelity uses these data to develop products and marketing programs for each group. As a result, the company increased customer loyalty, and improved the effectiveness of its marketing program while reducing the costs, and increased its share of financial-service customers.[46] Refer back to Chapter 7 for more information about segmentation.

Recency–Frequency–Monetary Analysis (RFM)

Research has shown that customers who purchase most recently and more often and who spend more money are more likely to purchase again. **Recency–frequency–monetary analysis (RFM)** identifies those customers most likely to purchase again because they have bought most recently, bought most frequently, or spent a specified amount of money with the firm. With these data a firm can build a simple equation to identify the "best customers" by assigning a score to customer records in the database based on how often, how recently, and how much they have spent. These customers are then ranked to determine which customers rise to the top of the list and which ones fall to the bottom. This ranking provides the basis for maximizing profits because it enables the firm to use the information in its customer database to select those persons who have proved to be good sources of revenue. As an example of RFM analysis, refer to Exhibit 21.5, which depicts the breakdown of customers in categories that describe their value at a hypothetical company.

Many marketers take RFM analysis one step further by introducing *profitability* into the equation. For instance, based on the monetary value of purchases, a customer may float to the top of the RFM list. If this customer only buys items on sale, however, then he or she is less profitable for the firm than a customer who buys the same dollar amount in nonsale items. Wachovia (formerly First Union) National Bank groups its customers into ten segments based on profitability. Top-ranking customers are routinely called by Wachovia relationship managers who

recency–frequency–monetary analysis (RFM)
A data manipulation technique that determines the firm's best customers by identifying those customers who have purchased most recently, most frequently, and who have spent the most money.

Exhibit 21.4

Four Major Groups of Segmentation Variables

Geographic	Demographic	Behavioral	Psychographic
• Country	• Age	• Purchase occasion	• Attitudes
• Region	• Gender	• Recent purchases	• Interests
• State	• Height/weight	• Benefits sought	• Opinions
• County	• Marital status	• User status (e.g., active or inactive)	• Activities
• Metropolitan type (urban, suburban, rural, etc.)	• Family size	• Usage rate	• Lifestyle
• Metropolitan statistical area	• Family life cycle	• Loyalty status (e.g., loyal users, frequent users, switchers, price buyers)	• Social class
• Census tract	• Ages of children		• Personality type
• Retail trading area	• Race	• Readiness stage (i.e., is the customer ready to purchase now, in 12 months, in 24 months?)	• Conspicuous consumption (e.g., mean current auto value, home value)
• Zip code	• Ethnicity		
• Telephone area code	• Nationality	• Attitude toward the product	
• Climate	• Country of birth	• Charities contributed to	
• Seasons	• First language	• Political affiliation	
	• Religion		
	• Education		
	• Occupation		
	• Industry		
	• Income		
	• Mobility		
	• Dwelling type		
	• Dwelling size		
	• Autos registered		

Exhibit 21.5   RFM Analysis: All Customers Are Not Created Equal

Best Customers N = 1,200 (10%)	Next-Best Customers N = 2,400 (20%)	Average Customers N = 3,600 (30%)	Poor Customers N = 4,800 (40%)
• High profit • Spent > $1,000 • Multiple purchases • Purchased in last six months • LTV: High • Total annual sales = $1,200,000	• Good profit • Spent approx. $500 • Multiple purchases • Purchased in last twelve months • LTV: Good • Total annual sales = $1,200,000	• Average profit • Spent $250 • One purchase • Purchased in last eighteen months • LTV: Average • Total annual sales = $900,000	• Low profit • Spent < $100 • One purchase • Purchased in last twenty-four months • LTV: Low • Total annual sales = $504,000

LTV = Lifetime value
N = Number of customers in category
Total annual sales = $3,804,000

Total number of customers: 12,000
Total number of orders per year: 20,000
Average order value: $190.20

SOURCE: Reprinted from *Desktop Database Marketing* by Jack Schmid and Alan Weber. © 1998. Used with permission of NTC/Contemporary Publishing Group, Inc.

may educate them about a new product or just thank them for their business. Lower-ranking unprofitable customers, on the other hand, are encouraged to use lower-cost services like automated teller machines.[47]

Lifetime Value Analysis (LTV)

lifetime value analysis (LTV)
A data manipulation technique that projects the future value of the customer over a period of years using the assumption that marketing to repeat customers is more profitable than marketing to first-time buyers.

Recency, frequency, and monetary data can also be used to create a lifetime value model on customers in the database. Whereas RFM looks at how valuable a customer is currently to a company, **lifetime value analysis (LTV)** projects the future value of the customer over a period of years. One of the basic assumptions in any lifetime value calculation is that marketing to repeat customers is more profitable than marketing to first-time buyers. It costs more to find a new customer in terms of promotion and gaining trust than to sell more to a customer who is already loyal.

Customer lifetime value has a number of uses: (1) It shows marketers how much they can spend to *acquire* a new customer, (2) it provides a level of profitable spending to *retain* a customer, and (3) it provides a basis for targeting new customers who look like a company's most profitable customers.[48] Lifetime value analysis allows a marketer to identify its most valuable customers and profit from them over the long term by building relationships. Cadillac has calculated the lifetime value of its top customers at $332,000. Similarly, Pizza Hut figures its customers are worth $8,000 in bottom-line lifetime value.[49]

Predictive Modeling

predictive modeling
A data manipulation technique in which marketers try to determine, based on some past set of occurrences, what the odds are that some other occurrence, such as a response or purchase, will take place in the future.

The ability to reasonably predict future customer behavior gives marketers a significant competitive advantage. Through **predictive modeling**, marketers try to determine, based on some past set of occurrences, what the odds are that some other occurrence, such as a response or purchase, will take place in the future. The occurrence a marketer is trying to predict through predictive modeling is described by the *dependent variable*, typically the likelihood of a response, making a sale, the amount of the sale, or all three. The *independent variables*, or predictor variables, are the things that affect the dependent variable. Past buying behavior, age, income, family size, or the neighborhood one lives in could all be independent variables that affect purchase behavior, the dependent variable. Colorado-based Abacus Direct, for example, compiles data on consumers who have purchased merchandise from over a thousand catalogs circulated in the United States. The third-party data provider's database now contains over 2.9 billion consumer catalog transactions that can be manipulated to predict future purchasing behavior. Catalogers, like Williams-Sonoma, J. Peterman, and Bloomingdale's, use the data collected by Abacus to augment their own customer databases, predicting future purchases of current customers, as well as finding new prospects who are most likely to purchase from their catalogs.[50]

The sharp rise in paper costs and postal rates a few years ago forced many catalog companies to turn to predictive modeling techniques in an effort to better target catalog mailings. Catalog retailer Fingerhut Corporation, based in Minnetonka, Minnesota, uses more than three hundred predictive models to scour its six-terabyte database. One model predicts the likelihood of someone responding to a targeted electronics catalog, while another scores the chances of a customer returning merchandise. Predictive modeling allows Fingerhut to reduce the number of catalogs sent while increasing sales and profits. As a result, response rates to catalogs have increased while the company saves more than $3.5 million a year in decreased mailing costs.[51]

Horchow

Does Horchow's Web site aid in the company's efforts at predictive modeling? If so, how? If not, what changes would you recommend to make the site a more effective one-to-one marketing tool?

http://www.horchow.com

On Line

Data Mining

As Chapter 20 described, data mining is a relatively new and sophisticated modeling technique. **Data mining** is the automated discovery of "interesting," nonobvious patterns hidden in a database that have a high potential for contributing to the bottom line. The discovery process often involves sifting through massive quantities of data such as electronic point-of-sale transactions, inventory records, and on-line customer orders matched with demographics.[52] Data-mining software accesses the data in the database and offers analysis tools such as decision trees, cluster analysis, neural networks, and regression analysis. Data mining can create customer profiles; help determine the reason for customer loyalty; analyze the potential return for pricing, promotion, and direct-mail strategies; and even help forecast sales.[53]

data mining
The process of using statistical analysis to detect relevant purchasing behavior patterns in a database.

One-to-One Marketing and the Internet

 Undoubtably, one of the most important trends in the field of one-to-one marketing is the emergence of one-to-one marketing over the Internet. While marketers have overwhelmingly adopted the Internet and World Wide Web as a new channel for promotions and commerce, many marketers are capitalizing on the Web's full set of interactive marketing capabilities. Internet companies are learning more about their customers and using this information to fine-tune their marketing efforts and build relationships with each customer on a more individual level. One-to-one marketers are always looking for better ways to communicate directly with their customers. To learn more about what the next one-to-one marketing channel may be, read "Mobile Marketing" in the "Global Perspectives" box.

6

Describe one-to-one marketing using the Internet

One advantage of on-line one-to-one marketing is the ability to deliver personalized promotional messages to each customer visiting a company's Web site. Past customer transaction history, clickstream data, and survey responses are used to identify buying patterns and interests. Based on information known about the customer visiting its site, such as color and brand preferences, geographic location, and past customer transaction data, the marketer can develop a targeted and personalized on-line promotion or custom catalog. For example, Amazon.com creates a personalized experience each time the same customer visits its Web site. Customers are greeted by name and instantly provided with a customized Web page offering book, music, and video suggestions based on their past purchasing and viewing behavior. Similarly, American Airlines' Web site has the ability to build custom pages, creating the potential for each of the airline's 32 million frequent flyers to have a unique experience when visiting the site. After logging in on the site's home page, members of its frequent flyer program,

Mobile Marketing

As the chapter pointed out, the Internet is currently the most popular medium for one-to-one marketing campaigns because new technology allows marketers to track their customers' on-line activities and continuously update their customer profiles. The technology even allows marketers to know when customers are on-line and what they have been viewing so that targeted messages can be sent at the right time. So what's the next frontier for one-to-one marketing?

The mobile communications industry is hoping the next one-to-one marketing medium will be mobile phones and personal data assistants (PDAs). In fact, the use of mobile data technology is already popular in Asia and is on the rise in Europe. To date, with the exception of Generation Y users, the U.S. market has been the slowest to embrace mobile technology. (Approximately 85 percent of mobile users reside outside the United States.)

The most common form of mobile data in use today is short message service (SMS), commonly referred to as text messaging. In some areas of Asia and the Middle East, technology has been upgraded to include general packet radio service (GPRS), which gives customers limited access to e-mail, personalized stock quotes, mobile banking, and location-based services such as assistance finding the nearest ATM. But according to industry leaders, the future of mobile data usage is Third Generation (3G) technology, which combines voice, text, image, and video capabilities. With 3G technology, users can use their mobile phones to watch their favorite television show while commuting or to participate in a videoconference. The first 3G networks have been launched in Japan, and companies like Nokia and Motorola are working with operators around the world to build more.

To fund the new 3G technology, mobile operators are looking for ways to increase mobile data service revenue. Many operators believe advertising revenue is the best option. Therefore, information-technology research firms are working to improve mobile marketing technology. In the future, mobile marketing will be able to target messages based on both individual customer profiles and customer location. For instance, when a customer arrives at the grocery store, a message could be sent to remind him or her to purchase laundry detergent or to pick up a copy of a newly released DVD at the video store next door.

Of course, mobile marketing is not this sophisticated yet. But marketers do know that the advantages of mobile marketing will include interactivity, personalization, location awareness, and always being with the user. In addition, mobile marketing will need to be personalized and permission based to be effective. According to a survey of mobile users in six countries, 80 percent of respondents are willing to accept promotional messages on their mobile devices if the messages are tailored to their personal interests, but 90 percent want control over the type and timing of those messages. Finally, as with one-to-one marketing on the Internet, privacy concerns are an issue for more than 50 percent of users.[54]

So what do you think? Will 3G technology increase the adoption rate of mobile data in the United States? Is it an appropriate medium for targeted advertising? How would you feel about receiving a personalized message from McDonald's when you are sitting in traffic across the street?

AAdvantage, can create profiles based on home airport, preferred destination and destination types, such as family, beach or golf, hub airports, hotel and rental car choices, preferred class of services, and seating preferences. Each time customers visit the site, they are greeted by name and the total number of accumulated frequent flyer miles. Based on their profile as well as past ticket purchase information, they are then shown relevant news, information, special offers, and travel packages as they page through the site.[55]

ON LINE When used in conjunction with on-line ad-serving technology, one-to-one marketing has the power to make the Internet an effective and cost-efficient advertising vehicle. On-line database marketing helps advertisers improve their return on investment by directing their banner ads to the consumers most likely to have an interest in their products or services. It also benefits consumers since they don't have to view ads that are of no interest to them.[56] Internet ad server

As technology develops, marketers are finding new media to convey their messages. 3G technology may become a powerful, mobile vehicle for targeted marketing messages. A Japanese woman, pictured here, tests a new 3G mobile phone relaying a live color image of her smiling face.

specialists like DoubleClick, RealMedia, and MatchLogic are building huge databases filled with anonymous profiles about consumers' activities on the Web with the goal of delivering ads that will home in on a Web surfer's interests. By profiling Web visitors, marketers can send banner ads and messages to just those who are likely to be interested instead of wasting money on sending advertisements to those who are not. The technology can also be used to capture the attention of target groups. DoubleClick recently worked with IBM to improve the effectiveness of entry-level recruitment ads on the IBM. com Web site. One-to-one technology enabled college students who visited the site using school computers to receive college-specific banner ads. For example, students at Boston University received ads that read "Boston University students, please click here." The targeted ads produced a 25 percent click-through rate compared to the average 1 percent click-through rate of typical banner ads.[57]

 Increasingly, more and more companies are realizing that e-mail is the ideal one-to-one medium, capable of establishing and building enduring customer relationships with highly targeted lists of prospects. This technique works much the same way as off-line one-to-one marketing campaigns: Companies build databases of e-mail addresses by enticing customers to register on a site in exchange for information or access to a special offer.[58] One-to-one e-mail campaigns are proving more effective than banner advertising on the Internet. Click-through rates for e-mail campaigns average 10 to 15 percent, compared to banner ad click rates that average around 1 percent, and traditional direct mail that averages between 0.5 and 2 percent.[59] For instance, RedEnvelope recently canceled its mass-communications advertising in favor of an ongoing e-mail campaign to communicate with its customers. The campaign, which is focused on 500,000 of RedEnvelope's customers, has a 50 percent click-through rate. As a result, RedEnvelope's sales have increased 75 percent, and the company's customer acquisition costs have dropped from $70 to $30.[60]

One-to-one e-mail marketing should be strictly permission based. That is, consumers should "opt-in" or give their permission to receive e-mail messages from a marketer. Amazon.com and other on-line booksellers ask customers to provide them with additional information about their likes and dislikes so that they can receive future book recommendations. But customers can indicate that they do not wish to receive recommendations. Similarly, Palm Computing, the maker of the Palm Pilot, sends messages to some 400,000 customers who have opted-in through Palm's Web site or registration cards to receive e-mail. The personalized messages include the recipient's name and contain information relevant to the product and model the person owns and tips on using it better.[61]

Privacy Concerns with One-to-One Marketing

 Before rushing out to invest in computer hardware and software to build a database, marketers should heed consumer reaction to the growing use of databases. One-to-one marketing concerns many Americans because of the potential for invasion of privacy, specifically the sheer volume of information that is aggregated in databases and the vulnerability of this information to unauthorized access and use. A fundamental aspect of one-to-one marketing is providing valuable services to customers based on knowledge of what customers really value. However, it is critical that marketers remember that these relationships should be built on trust. While database technology allows marketers to compile ever-richer information about their customers to build and manage relationships, if these customers feel their privacy is being violated, then the relationship becomes a liability.[62]

7
Discuss privacy issues related to one-to-one marketing

On Line

The popularity of the Internet for direct marketing, for consumer data collection, and as a repository of sensitive consumer data has alarmed privacy-minded consumers. On-line users have complained of being "spammed," the Internet's equivalent of junk mail. Web surfers, including children who are using the Internet, are routinely asked to divulge personal information in order to access certain screens or purchase goods or services on-line. Internet users who once felt fairly anonymous when using the Web are now disturbed by the amount of information marketers collect on them as they visit various sites in cyberspace. America Online, for instance, keeps records on more than 21 million subscribers, including names, addresses, and credit card numbers. The on-line service also tracks the movements of subscribers within its proprietary service where users spend over 80 percent of their time, including chat rooms, e-mail, news services, and other content. AOL sells names and addresses of subscribers to direct mailers and also buys information about its members, such as the type of computer owned, from outside data suppliers. It then uses this information to target advertising when a subscriber comes on-line.[63]

Most consumers are unaware of how personal information is collected, used, and distributed, and they are unaware of how technology helps in collecting personal data. The government actively sells huge amounts of personal information to list compilers. State motor vehicle bureaus sell names and addresses of individuals who get driver's licenses. Hospitals sell the names of women who just gave birth on their premises. Consumer credit databases, developed and maintained by large providers such as Equifax Marketing Services and TransUnion, are often used by credit card marketers to prescreen the targets for solicitations.

Further, there is widespread misunderstanding among consumers about existing privacy laws and regulations. Frustrated by their lack of control, consumers want more opportunities to determine how their personal information will be used. According to a recent poll by Forrester Research, Inc., 70 percent of Americans would like Congress to pass legislation protecting privacy on the Internet. Currently, only financial institutions, doctors, and insurance companies are prohibited from revealing certain information such as credit card numbers and medical records to third-party organizations. Therefore, privacy advocates are lobbying Congress to enact more federal regulations.[64]

While regulators have been debating future Internet privacy protection legislation, federal law to date is limited to the Children's Online Privacy Protection Act of 1998 (COPPA), which went into effect in 2000 and bars sites from collecting personal information from children under thirteen without parental consent.[65] The act does not, however, prohibit the anonymous collection of data about children's Internet activity, a fact that alarmed privacy advocates when N2H2 proposed the sale of data collected from school computers using its Web filter system.[66] Read more about the COPPA in the "Ethics in Marketing" box.

On-line privacy concerns were heightened recently when on-line advertising firm DoubleClick announced plans to combine its anonymous clickstream data—information captured by placing small computer files called "cookies" on surfers' hard drives that track their travels through cyberspace—with off-line consumer databases that would provide names and addresses. By matching cookie data with information in traditional direct marketing databases, DoubleClick hoped to create a powerful repository of consumer information that could be used to precisely target individuals for marketing purposes. Consumers and privacy advocates, however, became anxious that DoubleClick's pioneering techniques could create enormous privacy breaches. Their concerns triggered an investigation by the Federal Trade Commission.[67]

As a result of the FTC's interest in Web privacy, many Internet companies have now adopted privacy policies, and many are now giving Web users the ability to opt

Protecting Children On-line

Children's privacy on the Internet became a hot issue recently when it was discovered that nine out of ten Web sites aimed at children collected personal data about them, but only about 20 percent of those sites asked children to seek parental consent before supplying the information. In another study, researchers found that children and teens, when enticed with a free gift on-line, were willing to provide details about the family's buying habits, such as names of favorite stores and what kind of car the family drives. The same study found that younger children were more willing to offer more sensitive details, such as financial information or whether their parents missed work often or drank alcohol.

In a highly publicized case, the Federal Trade Commission charged Boston money manager Liberty Financial with failing to protect the anonymity of children on its Young Investor Web site, where young Web surfers were persuaded to fill out a survey by offering them a chance to win prizes and a free newsletter. Liberty maintained that the personal information would be maintained anonymously. According to the complaint, however, the young investor site asked survey questions that were deemed too personal, such as weekly allowances, spending habits, part-time work history, plans for college, and family finances, including ownership of any mutual funds. Further, the FTC

discovered that Liberty retained the names, addresses, and e-mails of those who participated in the Internet survey, even though the company stated that all personal information would be maintained anonymously.

As a result of this and other examples, legislators passed the Children's Online Privacy Protection Act, in an effort to protect children from unscrupulous data-collection techniques by Internet businesses. The act, which went into effect in 2000, requires Web sites targeting children under thirteen to prominently disclose what personal information they collect from children, how it is used, and whether it is shared with third parties. The Web site must also obtain "verifiable parental consent" before collecting any personal data from children. Consent from parents can take the form of a physically signed note, a credit card number, or an e-mail with a password.

While obtaining parental consent can be difficult in cyberspace, many Internet companies are developing their own methods of dealing with the law. Kid site Surf-Monkey.com, for instance, set up an 800 number so that parents can confirm that their children have permission to log on to the Web site's chat rooms and bulletin boards. Alloy.com banned all children under thirteen from its chat rooms and other interactive areas. America Online deleted on-line profiles of members who identified

Protecting children on the Internet is of prime concern to parents and children's sites. Many ISPs are now marketing their ability to filter out inappropriate sites before children happen upon them.

themselves as under age thirteen. Lycos.com now requires children and their parents to establish a family account with a credit card before they can even log on.[68]

Enforcing laws in cyberspace will prove to be a challenge for the federal government. Children will undoubtably forge parental consent, lie about their age, and discover ways to get around the law to be able to visit their favorite chat room or Web site. As a parent, how would you encourage your children to abide by the law?

---

out of data collection in an effort to avert federal legislation.[69] The Direct Marketing Association has also published new guidelines for its member companies to help assure consumers that their privacy is being respected (see Exhibit 21.6). But while an FTC study revealed that 90 percent of Web sites had posted privacy policies, only 20 percent met all the agency's proposed standards for privacy disclosure.[70]

GLOBAL While privacy policies for companies in the United States are largely voluntary and regulations on how personal data are collected and used are practically nonexistent, collecting data about consumers outside the United States is a different matter. For database marketers venturing in new data territories, success requires careful navigation of foreign privacy laws. Recall from Chapter 20 that under the European Union's *European Data Protection Directive*, for instance, any business that trades with a European organization must comply with

The Direct Marketing
Association Privacy Promise

In October 1997, The Direct Marketing Association made a Privacy Promise to American consumers as a public assurance that by July 1, 1999, all members of the DMA will follow certain specific practices to protect consumer privacy. These practices were designed to have a major impact on those consumers who wish to receive fewer advertising solicitations. Specifically, members of the DMA must abide by the following four privacy protection practices.

1. Notify customers that their names may be rented, sold, or exchanged for marketing purposes so that they are aware of their ability to opt out of these information exchanges.
2. Honor customer opt-out requests not to have their contact information transferred to others for marketing purposes.
3. Accept and maintain consumer requests to be on an in-house suppress file to stop receiving solicitations.
4. Use the DMA Preference Service suppression files, which allows consumers who do not wish to receive unsolicited marketing offers by mail or telephone (and soon e-mail) to make a single request for name removal.

SOURCE: The Direct Marketing Association, **http://www.the-dma.org**.

the EU's rules for handling information about individuals, or risk prosecution. This directive prohibits the export of personal data to countries not doing enough to protect privacy, in particular the United States.[71]

More than fifty nations have, or are developing, privacy legislation. Europe has the strictest legislation regarding the collection and use of consumer data, and other countries look to that legislation when formulating their policies. Australia, for instance, recently introduced legislation that would require private companies to follow a set of guidelines regarding the collection, storage, use, and transfer of personal information about individuals. Common privacy rules include obtaining data fairly and lawfully, using the information only for the original purpose specified, making sure it is accurate and up-to-date, and destroying data after the purpose for collection is completed. The EU requires that consumers be presented with an opt-out provision at the point of data collection.

CONNECT IT

As you recall from the opening story, Amazon.com, like many other marketers today, has embraced one-to-one marketing as an alternative to mass-media marketing. Knowing customers on an individual basis with the help of database technology provides marketers with an efficient and effective means of providing customers with the individualized attention that they demand. Amazon.com uses its database of past customer transaction data to develop personalized service and promotional offers and to cross-sell other merchandise.

USE IT

Protect Your Privacy On-line
Many Internet surfers don't realize that on-line companies can track their movements on the Web through the use of "cookie" files. To help maintain your anonymity on the Web, refrain from answering on-line questionnaires, entering sweepstakes, or divulging information to Web sites that do not post a privacy policy. Also, check out each site's privacy policy to learn about what it does or might do with your personal information.

It's also a good idea to periodically purge or clean out your cookie file on your hard drive. Keep only those cookie files for the sites you want to recognize you the next time you visit. To learn more about protecting your personal information as you surf, visit **http://www.junkbusters.com**. Become informed about your rights as a consumer by visiting the Direct Marketing Association at **http://www.the-dma.org**.

REVIEW IT

1 **Define one-to-one marketing and discuss its dependence on database technology.** One-to-one marketing is an individualized marketing method that utilizes customer information to build long-term, personalized, and profitable relationships with each customer. Database technology makes it possible for companies to interact with customers on a personal, one-to-one basis. A database stores pertinent information about a company's customers and contacts and makes it readily available to the sales and marketing staff for assessing, analyzing, and anticipating customers' needs. Database technology allows marketers to sift through the millions of pieces of data to target the right customers, to develop the right communication based on these customer needs, and to monitor the ongoing relationship, making adjustments in message strategy as needed.

1.1 Explain why one-to-one marketing today would not be possible without database technology.

2 **Discuss the forces that have influenced the emergence of one-to-one marketing.** Forces that have helped shape one-to-one marketing include a more diverse society, more demanding and time-poor consumers, a decline in brand loyalty, the explosion of new media alternatives, changing channels of distribution, and demand for marketing accountability. Consumers no longer want to be treated like the masses. One-to-one marketing allows consumers to be treated as individuals with their own unique sets of needs and wants. Consumers today also have less time to spend shopping for the products they need. Through its targeted nature, one-to-one marketing can decrease the time consumers need to make purchase decisions. Further, consumers are less brand loyal than they once were. One-to-one marketing techniques increase brand loyalty by focusing on finding a firm's best customers, rewarding them for their loyalty, and thanking them for their business. As mass-media approaches become less important, one-to-one marketing will increase in importance and offer marketers a more cost-effective avenue for reaching customers. Finally, the demand for marketing accountability will drive the growth of one-to-one marketing and justify its continued existence.

2.1 List several local businesses that you feel would benefit from one-to-one marketing. Choose one business and develop a one-to-one marketing plan, outlining the one-to-one applications that could be utilized, identifying what data should be collected about customers, and recommending data analysis methods. Also identify how the company could perform some of its one-to-one marketing using the Internet. Present your findings to the class.

③ Compare the one-to-one marketing communications process with the traditional mass-marketing communications process. The marketing communications process follows the flow of a marketing message from the marketer to the consumer. In the more traditional, mass-media version, an advertiser or marketer sends a promotional message through a mass-marketing channel to its target audience. Noise from competing advertisements affects the encoding and decoding of the message. Feedback on the effectiveness of the communication comes through market research and changes in sales levels or market share. In the one-to-one marketing communications process, the flow is similar; however, the message encoded by the marketer is personalized, there is relatively little noise to affect encoding and decoding, and the marketer has the ability to capture the response from the consumer and feed this information back into the marketing database for future use.

3.1 Explain the differences between traditional mass-media marketing communications and targeted one-to-one marketing communications. Why are these differences important to the success of one-to-one marketing?

④ List eight common one-to-one marketing applications. Common marketing applications of customer databases include (1) identifying the best customers, (2) retaining loyal customers, (3) cross-selling other products or services, (4) designing targeted marketing communications, (5) reinforcing consumer purchase decisions, (6) inducing product trial by new customers, (7) increasing the effectiveness of distribution channel marketing, and (8) improving customer service.

4.1 Assume that you are the manager of a local dry-cleaning business. What types of information do you currently collect about your customers that you could use to develop one-to-one relationships with your customers? What factors would determine your best customers?

4.2 As the marketing manager of a local retailing chain, you have just analyzed your database of customers and determined that your best customers constitute 12 percent of your customer database and provide nearly 80 percent of your sales. Additionally, you have discovered that about 50 percent of the customers in your database have not purchased in over two years. What can you do with this knowledge?

4.3 As marketing director for a regional chain of restaurants with a country gift shop theme, you have been assigned the task of developing a loyalty marketing program. Use the Internet to find a company that can help you. Once you select a provider, write a brief memo describing what the provider can do for your company. Identify in your memo which of the eight common one-to-one marketing applications your chosen provider can help you implement and how (see Exhibit 21.2). Also identify what tools your chosen provider has to help you with your segmentation, RFM anaylsis, LTV analysis, and predictive modeling.

⑤ Discuss the basics of one-to-one marketing database technology. One-to-one marketing is characterized by the creation of a large computerized database of customers' and potential customers' profiles and purchase patterns that are used to direct marketing communications. A marketing database is the compilation of names, addresses, and other pieces of pertinent information about individual customers and prospects that affects what and how marketers sell to them. In its most basic form, database marketing relies on transactional processing systems that record the details of individual purchase transactions. These data can then be enhanced using external sources of modeled **data or custom data. Marketers can analyze customer data using segmentation, recency–frequency–monetary analysis, lifetime value analysis, predictive modeling, or data-mining techniques.**

5.1 Explain the statement "A database is only as powerful as the information it houses."

5.2 Define the two different types of database enhancement and give examples of each.

5.3 Explain the concept of lifetime value. Why is this type of data manipulation so important to one-to-one marketers?

5.4 **ON LINE** The Data Warehousing Institute writes case studies of marketers who have provided their customers with data warehousing solutions using enterprise-wide data. Go to the site's case study page, found under the "What Works?" link on **http://www.dw-institute.com**. Read three to five case studies and make a list of all of the one-to-one marketing issues discussed in the chapter that also appear in the articles. Are there any "hot" issues that recur in each article? What conclusions can you draw from your list?

6 **Describe one-to-one marketing using the Internet.** Marketers have recently capitalized on the Internet's interactive capabilities as a one-to-one marketing tool. By collecting past customer transaction data and studying a user's movements on the Web, the on-line one-to-one marketer has the ability to create a personalized experience for each customer who visits its site. Additionally, banner advertising can be more efficiently targeted to just those Internet users who would be interested. An on-line marketer can also send personalized e-mail messages to those customers who give their permission.

6.1 **ON LINE** Visit the site developed by one-to-one marketing experts Don Peppers and Martha Rogers at **http://www.1to1.com** to read success stories of companies that have made one-to-one marketing strategies work for them. Select one of the articles at the "Publications" link (**http://www.1to1.com/publications/inside1to1**) and present a summary to the rest of the class.

7 **Discuss privacy issues related to one-to-one marketing.** One-to-one marketing concerns many Americans because of the potential for invasion of privacy, specifically the sheer volume of information that is aggregated in databases and the vulnerability of this information to unauthorized access and use. Most consumers are unaware of how personal information is collected, used, and distributed, and they are unaware of how technology helps in collecting personal data. Additionally, there is widespread misunderstanding among consumers about existing privacy laws and regulations. Frustrated by their lack of control, consumers want more opportunities to determine how their personal information will be used. The popularity of the Internet for direct marketing, for consumer data collection, and as a repository of sensitive consumer data has also alarmed privacy-minded consumers.

7.1 *INFOTRAC COLLEGE EDITION* Use InfoTrac (**http://www.infotrac-college.com**) to read how the Internet industry is taking privacy issues into its own hands. Request and read an article titled "Police Thyself" that appeared in *PC Week* magazine. Then conduct a keyword search to find out current conversations about consumer privacy in general and on-line privacy in particular.

DEFINE IT

compiled list 682
custom data 684
database 680
database enhancement 682
data-driven marketing 680
data mining 687
lifetime value analysis (LTV)
  686

marketing database 680
modeled data 683
one-to-one marketing 668
one-to-one marketing communications process
  673
predictive modeling 686

recency–frequency–monetary analysis (RFM) 685
response list 681

Application for Entrepreneurs

 Molly's Flowers is a small flower shop located in a medium-sized metropolitan area. The proprietor, Molly Edwards, has always measured the success of her business based on market share, which she estimates at roughly 10 percent. This is based on a report published by the local chamber of commerce that provides total flower sales from area flower shops in her city. This does not include flowers purchased at grocery stores.

Molly has used traditional mass-marketing approaches in an attempt to increase her market share, such as advertising heavily during holidays like Valentine's Day and Mother's Day and offering discounts during the low periods in between. These measures have increased sales, she believes, but she is not totally sure to what extent. Additionally, the ads cost money and the discounts eat into her profits. She knows that grocery stores cut into her business by offering lower prices on lower-quality flowers and arrangements, but she is not sure how to counter this because lowering her prices across the board would be devastating to her profits.

Molly knows that she has a number of customers who order from her time and again, but she has never thought much about how to take advantage of this loyal customer base. Shuffling through a stack of flower orders on her desk from the past year, she begins to look closely at the information that she actually does collect about her customers. Each order form contains the customer's name, address, telephone number, date of order, date flowers are to be delivered, type of flower arrangement requested, total price, to whom the flowers were sent, and what was to be printed on the card. Additionally, about nine out of ten orders were purchased over the phone with a credit card.

Questions

1. Suggest a one-to-one marketing plan in which Molly can use the customer information she collects to (1) identify her best customers, (2) increase sales from her best customers, and (3) reinforce their purchase decision.

2. Through credit card records, Molly can overlay data onto her customer database to provide more information about her customers. What additional enhancement data would you suggest she overlay?

3. What can Molly do to determine how much business her customers give to floral departments in grocery stores? With this information, what one-to-one marketing techniques could influence her customers to choose Molly's Flowers more often?

Ethics Exercise

Rani Pharmaceuticals is the maker of several popular drugs used to treat high blood pressure and arthritis. Over time, the company has developed a positive relationship with many of the patients who use its medications through a quarterly newsletter that offers all the latest information on new medical research findings and general health and fitness articles. The company has just been acquired by a group of investors who also own Soothing Waters Hot Tubs and Spas. The marketing director for Soothing Waters would like to use Rani's mailing list for a direct mail promotion.

Questions

1. What should Rani Pharmaceuticals do?

2. Does the AMA Code of Ethics address using customer information by multiple divisions of the same company in its Code of Ethics? Go to **http://www.marketingpower.com** and review the code. Then, write a brief paragraph on how the AMA Code of Ethics relates to Rani Pharmaceutical's dilemma.

Entrepreneurship Case

Green Hills Farms: Beating the Big Stores One Customer at a Time

© GETTY IMAGES/PHOTODISC

Managing to stay in business for sixty-eight years during the twentieth century was no small feat in any industry, let alone the hypercompetitive market for grocery sales. Everything from the supermarket to the megamarket to the hypermarket has been invented and built in the last fifty years, and most independently run stores have long since gone out of business. Independent grocer Gary Hawkins, however, has bucked the trend. In a neighborhood where the landscape is dominated by the megastores of large regional or national chains, Hawkins's family-run Green Hills Farms supermarket continues to thrive.

Grocery store shoppers are usually mercenaries, skipping from store to store to find the lowest prices on commodity-like goods. Hawkins's strategy has been to identify his customers, learn their shopping habits, and, no matter how much or how often they buy, entice them to return to the store. His program worked so successfully that his store was presented with a 1-to-1 Innovator Award from the prestigious Peppers and Rogers Group. To find the secret to Green Hills' success, one needs to look no farther than the one-to-one marketing tactics Hawkins uses to serve his most valuable customers.

Hawkins launched his frequent shopper rewards program in 1993, long before it was fashionable to collect shopper data. The store managed to sign 70 percent of its customers to the program within the first two years of its existence, and Hawkins then had the ability to identify more than 10,000 of his 15,000 customers by name. After giving cards to customers, Green Hills assigns them to one of five categories according to how much and how frequently they spend at the store.

Gem names—diamond, ruby, pearl, opal, and quartz—are used to describe the five spending segments, which signify a spending range from $100 per week at the diamond level to $10 per week at the quartz. Perks for customers who reach the diamond level include free Thanksgiving turkeys—fresh, not frozen—hand-selected Douglas fir trees at Christmas, $25 coupons for the garden shop in the spring, six coupons distributed throughout the year for 5 percent off a total purchase amount, and many postcard notifications of unadvertised specials.

That might seem rather costly, but Green Hills earns margins for diamond and ruby customers that are 10 percent above the average for the rest of the store's customers. In an industry where 1 percent margins are the norm for almost all stores and chains no matter their size, Hawkins hints that his are conservatively double that. Hawkins and his partners have been able to beat back *six* major competitors in the same neighborhood by making superior use of the data gained at the point of sale.

Lisa Piron, director of information services, applies database information toward promotion development. She targets known customers with customized offers on items in the area of the store that best meet their individual interests. Those promotions are far less costly to run than nontargeted mass-media advertising, and they yield much higher retention rates—96 percent of diamond-level customers, 80 percent of all customers—while satisfying the most valuable customers.

Green Hills has also reduced its weekly marketing costs by 50 percent by targeting its advertising to the zip codes where its most profitable customers live. That kind of commitment to identifying, collecting information, and targeting offers to the right customers in a timely fashion will probably keep Green Hills at the top of the hill for another sixty-eight years.

Questions

1. Explain how database technology makes possible the one-to-one marketing efforts at Green Hills Farms. Identify specific data that Green Hills is likely to collect and apply.

2. Describe how Green Hills' marketing communications are more effective than traditional methods.

3. Which of the eight common one-to-one marketing applications are made possible by the way Green Hills uses its marketing database?

Still Shaky? Here's a Tip.

Studying for comprehensive exams doesn't have to be a chore. Form a study group. Photocopy the *Marketing* 7e glossary and cut it into strips, one term per strip. Put all strips into a large bowl. Divide into teams and draw out one strip at a time. Quiz the opposing team and then read the correct answer. You can do the same with the summary sections at the end of each chapter. You can tabulate points, but you'll all win!

WATCH IT

Short

If knowing the customer is the foundation of database marketing, then protecting the customer's privacy when mining data is the mortar that holds it all together. The *Marketing* PowerPoint CD-ROM has one video ad clip, on Visa, embedded in the Chapter 21 slide presentation which illustrates both issues.

Medium

Is spam an invasion of privacy or a legitimate marketing tool? Watch people with opposing views on the subject defend their positions in the CNN clip for Chapter 21.

Long
the Series on PBS stations and the Web

For Chapter 21, Small Business School takes you to a company that uses a database of over 400,000 customers to mail three million catalogs a year and generate 50 cents to $1 profit per catalog mailed. Watch the video to see how International Wine Accessories has grown from a condo garage, where neighbors complained about forty-foot trailers rolling over their front lawns on delivery days, to a specialty catalog powerhouse, all through database marketing.

FLIP IT

Flip to Chapter 21 in your *Grademaker Study Guide* for more review opportunities, including the pretest, vocabulary review, Internet activities, study test questions, and an application exercise based on direct marketing concepts. What forces influence one-to-one marketing? Can you describe the basics of database technology? What about shutting your book and listing the eight one-to-one marketing applications? If not, then flip open your *Grademaker* and review.

CLICK IT

The *Marketing* Web site links you to all the Internet-based activities in this chapter, like the "Use It," "Review It" questions 4.3, 5.4, 6.1, and 7.1, "Think About It," and the On-Line exercises in the chapter margins. As a review, do the Chapter 21 quiz and crossword puzzle. And don't forget the Career Exersite that shows you resources for exploring marketing career opportunities in database marketing. Review the main concepts in the PowerPoint presentation for Chapter 21, too. Go to **http://lamb.swlearning.com**, read the material, and follow the links right from the site.

SPIN IT

Spin your Xtra! CD-ROM to test your understanding of the database marketing concepts in the chapter by completing the worksheets for exhibits 21.1, 21.2, 21.3, 21.4, and 21.5. If your instructor has assigned a marketing plan project, templates on Xtra! can help you organize your work. In addition to the quiz on the Web site, there's another quiz on the Xtra! CD-ROM, plus video of the authors answering frequently asked questions about database marketing topics, such as "Is one-to-one marketing realistic for most businesses?"

MARKETING MISCUES

Eli Lilly's Web Privacy Statement Fails to Protect Customers

Eli Lilly and Company develops and manufactures a wide variety of medicines. The company's mission is to help people live longer, healthier, and active lives. Medicines offered by Lilly include Evista (prevention and treatment of osteoporosis in postmenopausal women), Gemzar (pancreatic and non-small-cell lung cancer), Humatrope (growth hormone deficiency), Humulin (human insulin), Humalog (rapid-acting insulin), Humulin & Humalog Pens (prefilled insulin delivery service), Prozac (depression), Sarafem (premenstrual dysphoric disorder), Xigris (adult severe sepsis), and Zyprexa (schizophrenia and acute bipolar mania). The company also offers Actos (type 2 diabetes) and ReoPro (angioplasty/stenting) through its partners, Takeda Pharmaceuticals America, Inc., and Centocor B.V.

Through its research and development efforts, Lilly is able to successfully deliver one new drug out of about every hundred thousand drug development attempts. Since sales of a new drug are dependent upon both doctor and patient knowledge about the drug, Lilly provides a wealth of drug information to both target groups. The Web has become a critical outlet for getting information to the end user (the user of the prescription drug). Lilly provides current information about all of its medicines on its company Web site. Additionally, the company used its sophisticated on-line capabilities to provide services to its customers. Its Prozac Web service created a problem for the company, however, when Lilly inadvertently released confidential information about hundreds of Prozac users.

Millions of people suffer from depression. Though not fully understood, depression is believed to be caused by an imbalance in serotonin, a chemical that allows nerve cells in the brain to communicate with each other. In the late 1980s, drugs called selective serotonin reuptake inhibitors (SSRIs) were developed to help correct the serotonin imbalance. Prozac, initially approved in Belgium in 1986 to treat depression, was the first of this new class of drugs to be approved in the United States. Since 1987, more than 10 million people have taken Prozac for depression, with a success rate of 70 percent. SSRIs are also thought to be effective for sufferers of anxiety or panic disorders, post-traumatic stress, and eating disorders.

Although Lilly's competitors offer various other SSRI-related drugs including Zoloft, Paxil, Luvox, and Serzone, Prozac remains the most popular of all antidepressants. It is marketed in more than ninety countries and used by over 40 million people worldwide. Some experts claim that the other SSRIs do the same thing as Prozac, but since Prozac was the first on the market, it received considerable press. At the time of its market introduction, Prozac was featured on the covers of the *New Yorker* and *Newsweek*. Additionally, approximately 3,500 articles about the drug have been published in medical and scientific journals.

In its continual efforts to build customer relationships, Eli Lilly offered an on-line Medi-Messenger service to its Prozac customers. This messenger sent daily e-mail messages to its Prozac customers, reminding them to take their prescribed dose of Prozac. Close to seven hundred Prozac users signed up for this on-line reminder service. Lilly's privacy statement told these customers that the company had security measures in place to protect the confidentiality of any information about the on-line recipient.

On June 27, 2001, however, Lilly sent an e-mail to all of its 669 service subscribers announcing that the company would be discontinuing the Medi-Messenger service that was linked to its prozac.com Web site. Unfortunately, the e-mail displayed all 669 message recipients. Suddenly, a Prozac customer was no longer anonymous to at least 668 other Prozac users. Whether the incident resulted from a computer program glitch or human error, the company had violated the customers' right to privacy and confidentiality. The American Civil Liberties Union (ACLU) asked the Federal Trade Commission (FTC) to investigate the privacy breach as an unfair or deceptive trade practice. Additionally, the ACLU claimed that the identification of people suffering from various forms of depression could cause them to be discriminated against in the future.

Although no fine was imposed on Lilly, the FTC required the company to take steps to ensure the security of data by putting a four-stage information security program in place. Lilly apologized to its Prozac subscribers and promised to abide by the FTC guidelines.

Questions

1. If you were one of the 669 Prozac subscribers whose names were released in the e-mail, how would you feel?

2. How can Eli Lilly mend its potentially broken relationship with these Prozac customers?

CRITICAL THINKING CASE

Peapod and Royal Ahold Combine to Keep Serving the Internet Consumer

E-commerce has quickly become a "way of life" for both consumers and retailers. By 2000, grocery sales accounted for about $200 million of e-commerce activity. That $200 million is small, however, compared to future projections for this growing segment of e-commerce. By 2005, e-grocery sales are expected to reach $7.5 billion. Even at that figure, e-grocery sales will only be beginning to tap into the overall grocery market of $400 billion.

The Grocery Customer

Grocery trends in the United States reflect consumers' desire to eat at home without a lot of effort. A study conducted for the Food Marketing Institute, reported the following findings:

- 44 percent of weekday dinners are prepared in less than half an hour.
- 74 percent of consumers eat home-cooked meals at least three times a week.
- More than 40 percent of shoppers use cleaned, precut, and bagged vegetables at least once a week.
- The older the shoppers, the more likely they are to cook from scratch.
- One-third of shoppers under forty years of age cook from scratch less than once a week.
- 67 percent of shoppers eat main meals out at least once a week.
- Supermarket takeout accounts for 20 percent of all takeout foods.

Such findings support the on-line grocery shopping phenomenon.

The typical on-line grocery consumer can be described as follows:

- A dual-income family
- Household income of at least $75,000

- Children living at home in 50 percent of households
- Prefer to shop after 8 P.M.
- Average order size of $117
- Time-starved
- Pet owner
- Not interested in packaging (products can be delivered in plain boxes)

The on-line grocery consumer also likes to have flexibility in both ordering and delivery. Many prefer unattended deliveries. Convenience appears to be the initial driver in on-line grocery shopping.

Peapod

Headquartered in Chicago, Peapod (**http://www.peapod.com**) is credited with introducing on-line grocery shopping to the U.S. marketplace in 1989. Though the company faced many obstacles, it eventually became the largest and most successful U.S. e-grocer. Nevertheless, this pioneer in the area of Internet food delivery was not immune to the general e-commerce shakeout that took place in the late 1990s. As this industry liquidity crisis unfolded, however, Peapod was approaching profitability. Nonetheless, Peapod still required a large capital infusion from its largest shareholder, Royal Ahold, a Dutch supermarket operator. By the end of 2001, Ahold had purchased all outstanding shares of Peapod, which then became an Ahold subsidiary.

Royal Ahold

Royal Ahold (**http://www.ahold.com**) is a holding company for retail food providers and food-service companies. The company began in the Netherlands in 1887 as a small grocery store. By 2000, the company had annual sales of 65 billion euros (€) and was serving over 40 million customers in almost thirty countries throughout the world. As a public company still based in the Netherlands, Royal Ahold's shares are listed on the Amsterdam, Zurich, and New York stock exchanges.

Not including Peapod's sales, the company's U.S. operations posted sales revenue of around $35 billion in 2001, accounting for almost 60 percent of the company's total sales. Of this, $23 billion was a result of Royal Ahold's six retail operating companies: Stop & Shop, Giant-Landover, Giant-Carlisle, Bi-Lo, Tops, and Bruno's. The company's wholly owned food-service subsidiaries, U.S. Foodservice, Alliant Foodservice, PYA/Monarch, Parkway, and Mutual, had sales revenue of $12 billion in 2001.

Royal Ahold operates around seven thousand retail stores in Europe. In 2001, these stores had sales of €22 billion. The company is active in ten Latin American countries, with approximately 750 stores generating 2001 sales revenue of €5 billion. The company's hundred supermarkets in Asia produced sales revenue of €400 million in 2001.

Royal Ahold's mission states that the company must be the best in all of its operations. In striving to accomplish this mission, the company's strategy relies on organic growth, new acquisitions, and joint ventures. The company's multichannel strategy allows it to serve customers in various formats—supermarkets, superstores, specialty stores, hypermarkets, minihypers, convenience stores, gasoline stations, and e-commerce/home delivery.

Isn't E-Grocery Dead?
The early 2000s were a difficult period for many online grocery retailers. At the start of 2000, there were around ten Internet-only, home-delivery grocery retailers. By the beginning of 2002, this number had dropped dramatically. With the demise of several popular on-line grocers including Webvan, Home-Runs.com, and Kozmo, Peapod faced an awareness battle. These much-publicized Internet failures, caused many consumers to assume that all Internet-based, home-delivery grocery retailers had gone out of business. Of course, the failures were garnering much more media attention than the still-struggling Peapod.

Although partnering with Royal Ahold has provided Peapod with the financial stability it needed to stay out of bankruptcy, Peapod now must build brand awareness. With basically no competition in the on-line grocer marketplace, Peapod needs to use this time to build customer awareness and loyalty. Given the projected size of the e-grocery marketplace, company executives know that bricks and clicks (large supermarket chains) are likely to provide Internet services in the near future.

Questions

1. What marketing tactics can Peapod use to help convince consumers that it is still a thriving concern?

2. Can electronic customer relationship management systems help Peapod better understand its customer base?

MARKETING PLANNING ACTIVITIES

To complete all fifteen activities, use the Part 7 Marketing Planning Worksheets on your Xtra! CD-ROM. If you need a company for the basis of your work, follow the "Marketing Plan Project" link on the *Marketing* Web site (**http://lamb.swlearning.com**).

Technology-Driven Marketing
For continued general assistance on business plans and marketing plans, visit **http://www.bplans.com** or **http://www.businessplans.org**. For electronic sources of information, search on the Electric Library at **http://wwws.elibrary.com** or the Internet Public Library at **http://www.ipl.org**. Another excellent source of information is the Sales and Marketing Executives Marketing Library at **http://www.sell.org**. You should also refer to Exhibit 2.7 for additional marketing plan checklist items (Part V: Implementation, Evaluation, and Control).

You began your strategic marketing plan by stating your business mission and objectives and conducting a detailed SWOT analysis. In the second part of the plan you identified and described target market segments and identified sources of competitive intelligence and the need for further marketing research. Next, you defined aspects of the marketing mix, including product, distribution, promotion, and pricing tactics. Now you must clearly identify the ways in which your company will leverage the capabilities of database technology and the Internet in product, distribution, promotion, and pricing decisions. Also, refer to Exhibit 2.7 for additional marketing plan subjects.

Use the following exercises to guide you through the additional technology aspects of a strategic marketing plan:

1. Assume your company is or will be marketing its products and/or services over the Internet. How should your company enter this electronic marketplace? How will technology issues affect your firm?

2. How will marketing over the Internet modify your target market segment(s)? Redefine the demographics, psychographics, geographics, economic factors, size, growth rate, trends, and any other applicable qualities of the target segment(s) you intend to reach through the Internet. How do your potential on-line customers compare with off-line customers? For customer profiles visit **http://www.cc.gatech.edu/gvu/user_surveys**. Other information about on-line users is at **http://www.survey.net**.

3. One of the most important aspects of having an e-marketing offering is to select the right Internet service provider (ISP). Different ISPs offer different prices and services. Checking up on e-commerce capabilities for secure on-line transactions will be particularly important. To find and compare ISPs and Web hosts, go to **http://thelist.internet.com**. For a comprehensive list of Web design firms, go to **http://www.firmlist.com/main.shtml**.

4. Choosing a domain name that is easy to remember and spell, as well as one that uniquely identifies your firm, is an important challenge. Does your domain name have to be the same as your company name? To see if your desired domain name is already being used, go to **http://411direct.com/domainnamereg.htm**. Or check the "Who Is" area of **http://www.networksolutions.com**.

5. Web site development is a key tool to identify your offering, brand, and company. Development of a unique, secure, and user-friendly site will take time and money. Should you legally protect the contents of your site? Check out **http://www.benedict.com** to check on copyright issues for your Web site contents. Internet patent and trademark information is shown on **http://www.micropat.com**.

6. What kinds of consumer or business product or service is your firm planning to market over the Internet? Identify ways that marketing over the Internet will change the basic design of your core product or service. How will modification of the product or service affect your costs? Identify any modification to your return policies that will need to be made to address new Internet customers.

7. Discuss the implications of adding the Internet as a channel to your already developed distribution network. How will this affect channel relationships? The final price offered to Internet customers? Any promotional efforts launched over the Internet?

8. How can e-mail newsletters be a beneficial marketing tool? Should your company create and distribute one? If so, who will create the content, and what will the content be?

9. Should your company participate in, monitor, or sponsor a mailing or on-line discussion list? One of the hottest topics in Internet marketing is how to build a "sticky" on-line community at e-commerce sites—in other words, a community that keeps visitors at the site for a long time. Would your site benefit from having community resources? Why or why not? If so, what features would you add to build a community presence? How will you make it "sticky"? To search for lists in your company's area of interest, go to **http://www.liszt.com**.

10. Investigate the expansion of your marketing efforts to include a one-to-one database marketing program. How will you collect data? How will you use the data? What effect will the creation of the database have on your diverse marketing methods (mailings, catalogs, e-mailings, coupon distribution, product sample distribution, and so on)? Write your on-line privacy policy. Consult the AMA Code of Ethics for information on privacy (**http://www.marketingpower.com**).

Implementation

The last and concluding part of a strategic marketing plan deals with implementation, evaluation, and control. A strategic plan is effective only when it is acted upon, so implementation guidelines should list specific action plans and a recommended time frame. Evaluation is needed to see if actual marketing activities are resulting in expected objectives. If not, control measures will need to take place.

Use the following exercises to conclude your strategic marketing plan with implementation, evaluation, and control:

1. Project management tools are the best way to set up your implementation, evaluation, and control program. For a free timeline utility tool, visit **http://www.smartdraw.com**. Decide whether the marketing or operations department will manage the implementation and control of the plan.

2. Make sure performance standards are set for each area of the marketing plan. Because **performance** will be compared against objectives, the objectives must be stated in numerical terms. What will your objectives be in terms of traffic (hits), sales, page views, visits per customer, and length of average visit (in minutes)? Which measurement is most important? Why?

3. What is the financial impact on the plan if performance standards are met? How long can you last if they are not met? For on-line extensions of off-line businesses, how many resources should the

off-line business put behind its on-line counterpart? Use financial spreadsheet software to set up a calendar-based pro-forma statement outlining expected sales and costs over the course of the marketing cycle.

4. Using additional spreadsheets, compare actual versus expected performance. Where actuals exceed expectations, what are the sources of success that should be further capitalized on? When actuals fail to meet expectations, what are the sources of the problems, and how can they be corrected? Are the sources directly related to doing business on-line?

5. What other marketing research is needed to assist in the evaluation and modification of your strategic marketing plan? Looking back over your now complete marketing plan, do marketing costs appear to be more or less intensive in the on-line business environment than in the traditional one?

CROSS-FUNCTIONAL CONNECTIONS SOLUTIONS

Technology's Role in Facilitating Interactions between the Company and Its Customers and among Internal Functions

Questions

1. How has today's technology altered the role of marketing both internally and externally?

Advertising and promoting products on the Internet have caused the marketing department, which in the past has been responsible for creating and developing the entire communications program for products/services, to share its marketing communications responsibilities with other functional groups within the company. Marketing has been forced to relinquish sole ownership of the creative process, due to its inability to design a Web site that echoes its vision for the communications program. Marketing must now work closely with information technology, a group that translates the vision into a visual, interactive Web site. Traditionally, a product was marketed to a mass audience through brochures and/or print ads. Marketing departments created communications campaigns on a grand, informal scale to promote products. Due to the Internet, however, companies are marketing their products to consumers directly. Marketing must now develop, along with information technologists, Web sites (which may ultimately replace print ads and brochures) that clearly communicate the company, as well as the products, to the on-line user.

2. What are some of the benefits of networking functional departments, customers, and suppliers?

Very broadly, benefits include the following:

Facilitation of cross-functional communication: All functional groups have access to the same information, at the same time.

Speed of transaction: Customer orders can be sent electronically and simultaneously to all departments that will perform steps in processing the order, allowing all necessary groups to begin fulfilling tasks to get the order out the door (e.g., accounting can begin checking the firm's credit records, production can check stock for adequate levels, shipping can begin preparing to get the product to the customer).

Immediate delivery of component parts, materials, etc.: Suppliers become as aware of stock level as the customer, and they ship based on their reporting processes rather than waiting for the customer to place an order.

3. Which functional areas are actively involved in making e-commerce a success? How?

Marketing, information technology, legal, finance/accounting, and research and development are all functional areas that are involved in making e-commerce a success. Marketing and information technology partner to create a visual communication to the customer while lawyers, specialized in cyber law, analyze the site's legal logistics. Finance and accounting evaluate the costs of maintaining the site and determine its budget. Research and development continuously work on improving the product offering. Together, these departments work to create a successful cyber experience.

Suggested Readings

Parry Aftab, "Master of the Domain," *Working Woman*, April 2000, 58.

Jerry Luftman and Tom Brier, "Achieving and Sustaining Business-IT Alignment," *California Management Review*, Fall 1999, 109–122.

Appendix

CAREERS IN MARKETING

One of the most important decisions in your life is deciding on your career. Not only will a career choice affect your income and lifestyle, but it also will have a major impact on your happiness and self-fulfillment. Probably the most difficult part of job hunting is deciding exactly what type of work you would like. Many students have had no working experience other than summer jobs, so they are not sure what career to pursue. Too often, college students and their parents rush toward occupational fields that seem to offer the highest monetary payoff or are currently "hot," instead of looking at the long run over a forty- to fifty-year working life.

In order to help you as you begin thinking about career goals and job hunting, the *Marketing* Web site contains an appendix titled "Careers in Marketing." Not only can it inform you about career opportunities in the marketing field, it also provides a wealth of information to help you at each stage of your job search:

- A self-assessment tool
- Career listings with compensation ranges
- Features-advantages-benefits model to help you determine job fit
- Resources for job prospecting
- How to write your résumé
- How to write a professional cover letter
- Self-preparedness test to determine readiness to interview
- Pre-interview checklist
- Tips to keep in mind while preparing for an interview
- More than seventy frequently asked job interview questions
- Questions to ask an interviewer
- How to conduct yourself during an interview
- How to handle objections raised by an interviewer
- Tips on following up after an interview
- How to write a letter accepting a job offer
- How to write a letter declining a job offer

Visit **http://lamb.swlearning.com** to find out how to market yourself to the marketing industry.

GETTING STARTED

Getting started can be the toughest part of job hunting, especially if you are uncertain about what career you want to pursue. The careers appendix can help you in this initial stage with its self-assessment tool, career and compensation lists, features-advantages-benefits (FAB) matrix, and listing of resources for job prospecting.

A self-assessment tool can help you identify your personal needs, capabilities, characteristics, strengths, weaknesses, and desires. The on-line careers appendix includes a thirteen-question assessment tool that can help you begin to analyze what is important to you in choosing the kind of work you will do and the kind of employer for whom you will work. There is also a complete listing of careers available in the marketing industry, with compensation figures for each. This information can help you determine what marketing fields interest you and meet your income needs. Using the FAB matrix, you can plot your abilities and skills against the employer's job requirements. Once you complete the model, you will have a better idea of what you have to sell a potential employer. If you have identified a career that suits you but are having trouble finding an employer that offers that particular career opportunity, the on-line careers appendix can help. It provides a list of resources that can be useful when prospecting for an employer. Information on where to locate and how to use the various resources is also included.

ARE YOU READY TO INTERVIEW?

Once you have moved through the initial phase of your job search, the on-line careers appendix can still help you. It shows you how to write your résumé and cover letter so that you convey a positive and professional attitude. The information in the appendix can also help you determine how ready you are for a job interview. It provides you with a self-preparedness test, a pre-interview checklist, and a list of considerations to keep in mind when preparing for your interview.

Since interviewing can often be a source of nervousness and anxiety, the on-line careers appendix gives you tools you can use to feel calm and prepared during an interview. A list of over seventy frequently asked job interview questions is provided along with a list of questions for you to ask the interviewer. You can receive guidance on how to conduct yourself professionally during the interview and how to handle objections raised by the interviewer. You can also find tips on following up after the interview and on accepting or declining a job offer.

GO ON-LINE!

Many of the basic concepts of marketing introduced in this book can be used to help you get the career you want by marketing yourself. This complete on-line appendix, "Careers in Marketing," is designed to help you do just that, so visit **http://lamb.swlearning.com** to begin learning how to successfully market yourself to prospective employers!

More resources are available at South-Western's "Career Café" on **http://www.swcollege.com.** Link out to popular career sites, order resources on-line, and discover what kind of career advice experts like John Zweig of Apple Computer, Peter Bowen of General Electric, and Anne Gordon of Microsoft, have to offer.

Glossary

A

accessory equipment Goods, such as portable tools and office equipment, that are less expensive and shorter-lived than major equipment.

adopter A consumer who was happy enough with his or her trial experience with a product to use it again.

advertising Impersonal, one-way mass communication about a product or organization that is paid for by a marketer.

advertising appeal Reason for a person to buy a product.

advertising campaign Series of related advertisements focusing on a common theme, slogan, and set of advertising appeals.

advertising objective Specific communication task a campaign should accomplish for a specified target audience during a specified period.

advertising response function Phenomenon in which spending for advertising and sales promotion increases sales or market share up to a certain level but then produces diminishing returns.

advocacy advertising Form of advertising in which an organization expresses its views on controversial issues or responds to media attacks.

agents and brokers Wholesaling intermediaries who facilitate the sale of a product from producer to end user by representing retailers, wholesalers, or manufacturers and who do not take title to the product.

AIDA concept Model that outlines the process for achieving promotional goals in terms of stages of consumer involvement with the message; the acronym stands for Attention, Interest, Desire, and Action.

applied research Attempts to develop new or improved products.

Asia-Pacific Economic Cooperation (APEC) A trade agreement that includes most ASEAN countries plus eleven other nations.

Association of Southeast Asian Nations (ASEAN) A trade agreement among ten Asian nations.

aspirational reference group Group that someone would like to join.

assurance The knowledge and courtesy of employees and their ability to convey trust.

ATC. *See* **average total cost.**

atmosphere The overall impression conveyed by a store's physical layout, decor, and surroundings.

attitude Learned tendency to respond consistently toward a given object.

audience selectivity Ability of an advertising medium to reach a precisely defined market.

automatic vending The use of machines to offer goods for sale.

AVC. *See* **average variable cost.**

average total cost (ATC) Total costs divided by quantity of output.

average variable cost (AVC) Total variable cost divided by quantity of output.

B

baby boomers People born between 1946 and 1964.

bait pricing Price tactic that tries to get consumers into a store through false or misleading price advertising and then uses high-pressure selling to persuade consumers to buy more expensive merchandise.

base price The general price level at which the company expects to sell the good or service.

basic research Pure research that aims to confirm an existing theory or to learn more about a concept or phenomenon.

basing-point pricing Price tactic that charges freight from a given (basing) point, regardless of the city from which the goods are shipped.

BehaviorScan Scanner-based research program that tracks the purchases of three thousand households through store scanners.

belief Organized pattern of knowledge that an individual holds as true about his or her world.

benefit segmentation The process of grouping customers into market segments according to the benefits they seek from the product.

brainstorming Getting a group to think of unlimited ways to vary a product or solve a problem.

brand A name, term, symbol, design, or combination thereof that identifies a seller's products and differentiates them from competitors' products.

brand equity The value of company and brand names.

brand loyalty A consistent preference for one brand over all others.

brand mark The elements of a brand that cannot be spoken.

brand name That part of a brand that can be spoken, including letters, words, and numbers.

break-even analysis Method of determining what sales volume must be reached before total revenue equals total costs.

business analysis The second stage of the screening process, at which time preliminary figures for demand, cost, sales, and profitability are calculated.

business e-commerce Electronic transactions between companies.

business marketing The marketing of goods and services to individuals and organizations for purposes other than personal consumption.

business product (industrial product) Product used to manufacture other goods or services, to facilitate an organization's operations, or to re-sell to other customers.

business services Expense items that do not become part of a final product.

buyer Department head who selects the merchandise for his or her department and may also be responsible for promotion and personnel.

buyer for export Intermediary in the global market that assumes all ownership risks and sells globally for its own account.

buying center All those persons in an organization who become involved in the purchase decision.

C

campaign management Developing product or service offerings customized for the appropriate customer segment and then pricing and communicating these offerings for the purpose of enhancing customer relationships.

cannibalization Situation that occurs when sales of a new product cut into sales of a firm's existing products.

cash cow In the portfolio matrix, a business unit that usually generates more cash than it needs to maintain its market share.

cash discount A price reduction offered to a consumer, an industrial user, or a marketing intermediary in return for prompt payment of a bill.

category killers Term often used to describe specialty discount stores because they so heavily dominate their narrow merchandise segment.

central-location telephone (CLT) facility A specially designed phone room used to conduct telephone interviewing.

chain stores Stores owned and operated as a group by a single organization.

channel Medium of communication—such as a voice, radio, or newspaper—for transmitting a message.

channel (CRM) A medium of communication through which the customer interacts with a business at an external touch point; the traditional approach for acquiring information from customers.

channel conflict Clash of goals and methods between distribution channel members.

channel control Situation that occurs when one marketing channel member intentionally affects another member's behavior.

channel leader (channel captain) Member of a marketing channel that exercises authority and power over the activities of other channel members.

channel members All parties in the marketing channel that negotiate with one another, buy and sell products, and facilitate the change of ownership between buyer and seller in the course of moving the product from the manufacturer into the hands of the final consumer.

channel partnering (channel cooperation) The joint effort of all channel members to create a supply chain that serves customers and creates a competitive advantage.

channel power Capacity of a particular marketing channel member to control or influence the behavior of other channel members.

CLT. *See* **central-location telephone facility.**

closed-ended question An interview question that asks the respondent to make a selection from a limited list of responses.

cobranding Placing two or more brand names on a product or its package.

code of ethics A guideline to help marketing managers and other employees make better decisions.

cognitive dissonance Inner tension that a consumer experiences after recognizing an inconsistency between behavior and values or opinions.

cold calling Form of lead generation in which the salesperson approaches potential buyers without prior knowledge of the prospects' needs or financial status.

commercialization The decision to market a product.

communication Process by which we exchange or share meanings through a common set of symbols.

comparative advertising Form of advertising that compares two or more specifically named or shown competing brands on one or more specific attributes.

competitive advantage The set of unique features of a company and its products that are perceived by the target market as significant and superior to the competition.

competitive advertising Form of advertising designed to influence demand for a specific brand.

competitive intelligence An intelligence system that helps managers assess their competition and their vendors in order to become more efficient and effective competitors.

compiled list A customer list that was developed by gathering names and addresses from telephone directories and membership rosters, usually enhanced with information from public records, such as census data, auto registrations, birth announcements, business start-ups, or bankruptcies.

component lifestyles Practice of choosing goods and services that meet one's diverse needs and interests rather than conforming to a single, traditional lifestyle.

component parts Either finished items ready for assembly or products that need very little processing before becoming part of some other product.

computer-assisted personal interviewing Interviewing method in which the interviewer reads the questions from a computer screen and enters the respondent's data directly into the computer.

computer-assisted self-interviewing Interviewing method in which a mall interviewer intercepts and directs willing respondents to a nearby computer where the respondent reads questions off the computer screen and directly keys his or her answers into the computer.

concentrated targeting strategy A strategy used to select one segment of a market or targeting marketing efforts.

concept test Test to evaluate a new product idea, usually before any prototype has been created.

consumer behavior Processes a consumer uses to make purchase decisions as well as to use and dispose of purchased goods or services; also includes factors that influence purchase decisions and the use of products.

consumer decision-making process A five step process used by consumers when buying goods or services.

consumer penalty An extra fee paid by the consumer for violating the terms of the purchase agreement.

consumer product Product bought to satisfy an individual's personal wants.

Consumer Product Safety Commission (CPSC) A federal agency established to protect the health and safety of consumers in and around their homes.

consumer sales promotion Sales promotion activities targeting the ultimate consumer.

continuous media schedule Media scheduling strategy, used for products in the latter stages of the product life cycle, in which advertising is run steadily throughout the advertising period.

contract manufacturing Private label manufacturing by a foreign company.

control The mechanisms for evaluating marketing results in light of the plan's goals and for correcting actions that do not help the organization reach those goals within budget guidelines.

convenience product A relatively inexpensive item that merits little shopping effort.

convenience sample A form of nonprobability sample using respondents who are convenient or readily accessible to the researcher, for example, employees, friends, or relatives.

convenience store A miniature supermarket, carrying only a limited line of high-turnover convenience goods.

cooperative advertising Arrangement in which the manufacturer and the retailer split the costs of advertising the manufacturer's brand.

core service The most basic benefit the consumer is buying.

corporate social responsibility Business's concern for society's welfare.

cost competitive advantage Being the low-cost competitor in an industry while maintaining satisfactory profit margins.

cost per contact The cost of reaching one member of the target market.

countertrade A form of trade in which all or part of the payment for goods or services is in the form of other goods or services.

coupon Certificate that entitles consumers to an immediate price reduction when they buy the product.

credence quality A characteristic that consumers may have difficulty assessing even after purchase because they do not have the necessary knowledge or experience.

crisis management Coordinated effort to handle the effects of unfavorable publicity or of another unexpected, unfavorable event.

cross-tabulation A method of analyzing data that lets the analyst look at the responses to one question in relation to the responses to one or more other questions.

culture Set of values, norms, attitudes, and other meaningful symbols that shape human behavior and the artifacts, or products, of that behavior as they are transmitted from one generation to the next.

cumulative quantity discount A deduction from list price that applies to the buyer's total purchases made during a specific period.

custom data Enhancement information acquired by the marketer, including customer surveys, customer participation programs, product registration, warranty cards, or loyalty marketing programs.

customer-centric Under this a philosophy, the company customizes its product and service offering based on data generated through interactions between the customer and the company.

customer relationship management (CRM) A company wide business strategy used to optimize profitability, revenue, and customer satisfaction by focusing on highly defined and precise customer groups.

customer satisfaction The feeling that a product has met or exceeded the customer's expectations.

customer value The ratio of benefits to the sacrifice necessary to obtain those benefits.

D

database A collection of data, especially one that can be accessed and manipulated by computer software.

database enhancement The overlay of information to customer or prospect records for the purpose of better describing or better determining the responsiveness of customers or prospects.

database marketing The creation of a large computerized file of customers' and potential customers' profiles and purchase patterns.

data-driven marketing The process of gathering, maintaining, and analyzing information about customers and prospects to implement more efficient and effective marketing communications; another term for one-to-one marketing.

data mining The process of using statistical analysis to detect relevant purchasing behavior patterns in a database.

data warehouse A very large, corporate-wide database in which the data are culled from a number of legacy systems, such as billing/accounting, order fulfillment, distribution, customer service, and marketing and sales, that are already in place within the organization.

decision support system (DSS) An interactive, flexible computerized information system that enables managers to obtain and manipulate information as they are making decisions.

decline stage A long-run drop in sales.

decoding Interpretation of the language and symbols sent by the source through a channel.

delayed-quotation pricing Price tactic used for industrial installations and many accessory items, in which a firm price is not set until the item is either finished or delivered.

demand The quantity of a product that will be sold in the market at various prices for a specified period.

demographic segmentation Segmenting markets by age, gender, income, ethnic background, and family life cycle.

demography The study of people's vital statistics, such as their age, race and ethnicity, and location.

department store A store housing several departments under one roof.

derived demand The demand for business products.

development Stage in the product development process in which a prototype is developed and a marketing strategy is outlined.

differential advantage One or more unique aspects of an organization that cause target consumers to patronize that firm rather than competitors.

differential competitive advantage Advantage achieved when a firm provides something that is unique and valuable to buyers beyond simply offering a lower price than the competition offers.

diffusion The process by which the adoption of an innovation spreads.

direct channel Distribution channel in which producers sell directly to consumers.

direct foreign investment Active ownership of a foreign company or of overseas manufacturing or marketing facilities.

direct marketing (direct-response marketing) Techniques used to get consumers to make a purchase from their home, office, or other non-retail setting.

direct retailing The selling of products door-to-door, office-to-office, or at home parties by representatives.

discount store A retailer that competes on the basis of low prices, high turnover, and high volume.

discrepancy of assortment Lack of all the items a customer needs to receive full satisfaction from a product or products.

discrepancy of quantity Difference between the amount of product produced and the amount a customer wants to buy.

distribution resource planning (DRP) Inventory control system that manages the replenishment of goods from the manufacturer to the final consumer.

diversification A strategy of increasing sales by introducing new products into new markets.

dog In the portfolio matrix, a business unit that has low growth potential and a small market share.

DRP. *See* **distribution resource planning.**

drugstore A retail store that stocks pharmacy-related products and services as its main draw.

DSS. *See* **decision support system.**

dual distribution (multiple distribution) Use of two or more channels to distribute the same product to target markets.

dumping The sale of an exported product at a price lower than that charged for the same or a like product in the "home" market of the exporter.

E

EDI. *See* **electronic data interchange.**

EDLP. *See* **everyday low prices.**

80/20 principle Principle that holds that 20 percent of all customers generate 80 percent of the demand.

elastic demand Situation in which consumer demand is sensitive to changes in price.

elasticity of demand Consumers' responsiveness or sensitivity to changes in price.

electronic data interchange (EDI) Information technology that replaces the paper documents that usually accompany business transactions, such as purchase orders and invoices, with electronic transmission of the needed information to reduce inventory levels, improve cash flow, streamline operations, and increase the speed and accuracy of information transmission.

electronic distribution Distribution technique that includes any kind of product or service that can be distributed electronically, whether over traditional forms such as fiber-optic cable or through satellite transmission of electronic signals.

empathy Caring, individualized attention to customers.

empowerment Delegation of authority to solve customers' problems quickly—usually by the first person that the customer notifies regarding a problem.

encoding Conversion of the sender's ideas and thoughts into a message, usually in the form of words or signs.

environmental management When a company implements strategies that attempt to shape the external environment within which it operates.

environmental scanning Collection and interpretation of information about forces, events, and relationships in the external environment that may affect the future of the organization or the implementation of the marketing plan.

escalator pricing Price tactic in which the final selling price reflects cost increases incurred between the time the order is placed and when delivery is made.

ethics The moral principles or values that generally govern the conduct of an individual.

evaluation Gauging the extent to which the marketing objectives have been achieved during the specified time period.

evoked set (consideration set) Group of brands, resulting from an information search, from which a buyer can choose.

exchange The idea that people give up something to receive something they would rather have.

exclusive distribution Form of distribution that establishes one or a few dealers within a given area.

executive interviews A type of survey that involves interviewing businesspeople at their offices concerning industrial products or services.

experience curves Curves that show costs declining at a predictable rate as experience with a product increases.

experience quality A characteristic that can be assessed only after use.

experiment Method a researcher uses to gather primary data.

expert Someone with in-depth knowledge of a subject or activity.

export agent Intermediary who acts like a manufacturer's agent for the exporter. The export agent lives in the foreign market.

export broker Intermediary who plays the traditional broker's role by bringing buyer and seller together.

exporting Selling domestically produced products to buyers in another country.

express warranty A written guarantee.

extensive decision making Most complex type of consumer decision making, used when buying an unfamiliar, expensive product or an infrequently bought item; requires use of several criteria for evaluating options and much time for seeking information.

external information search Process of seeking information in the outside environment.

extranet A private network that uses Internet technology and a browser interface, also a network that links a company with its suppliers and customers.

F

factory outlet An off-price retailer that is owned and operated by a manufacturer.

family brand The marketing of several different products under the same brand name.

family life cycle (FLC) A series of stages determined by a combination of age, marital status, and the presence or absence of children.

Federal Trade Commission (FTC) A federal agency empowered to prevent persons or corporations from using unfair methods of competition in commerce.

feedback Receiver's response to a message.

field service firm A firm that specializes in interviewing respondents on a subcontracted basis.

fixed cost Cost that does not change as output is increased or decreased.

FLC. *See* **family life cycle.**

flexible pricing (variable pricing) Price tactic in which different customers pay different prices for essentially the same merchandise bought in equal quantities.

flighted media schedule Media scheduling strategy in which ads are run heavily every other month or every two weeks, to achieve a greater impact with an increased frequency and reach at those times.

FOB origin pricing Price tactic that requires the buyer to absorb the freight costs from the shipping point ("free on board").

focus group Seven to ten people who participate in a group discussion led by a moderator.

follow-up Final step of the selling process, in which the salesperson ensures that delivery schedules are met, that the goods or services perform as promised, and that the buyers' employees are properly trained to use the products.

Food and Drug Administration (FDA) A federal agency charged with enforcing regulations against selling and distributing adulterated, misbranded, or hazardous food and drug products.

four Ps Product, place, promotion, and price, which together make up the marketing mix.

frame error Error that occurs when a sample drawn from a population differs from the target population.

franchise The right to operate a business or to sell a product.

franchisee Individual or business that is granted the right to sell another party's product.

franchiser Originator of a trade name, product, methods of operation, and so on, that grants operating rights to another party to sell its product.

Free Trade Agreement of the Americas (FTAA) A regional trade agreement that, when signed, will create a regional trading zone encompassing 36 countries in North and South America.

freight absorption pricing Price tactic in which the seller pays all or part of the actual freight charges and does not pass them on to the buyer.

frequency Number of times an individual is exposed to a given message during a specific period.

frequent buyer program A loyalty program in which loyal consumers are rewarded for making multiple purchases of a particular good or service.

full-line discount store A retailer that offers consumers very limited service and carries a broad assortment of well-known, nationally branded "hard goods."

fully industrialized society The fifth stage of economic development, a society that is an exporter of manufactured products, many of which are based on advanced technology.

functional discount (trade discount) Discount to wholesalers and retailers for performing channel functions.

G

gap model A model identifying five gaps that can cause problems in service delivery and influence customer evaluations of service quality.

General Agreement on Tariffs and Trade (GATT) Agreement that provided loopholes that enabled countries to avoid trade-barrier reduction agreements.

Generation X People born between the years 1965 and 1978.

Generation Y People born between the years 1979 and 1994.

generic product A no-frills, no-brand-name, low-cost product that is simply identified by its product category.

generic product name Name that identifies a product by class or type and that cannot be trademarked.

geodemographic segmentation Segmenting potential customers into neighborhood lifestyle categories.

geographic segmentation Segmenting markets by region of the country or world, market size, market density, or climate.

global brand A brand where at least 20 percent of the product is sold outside its home country or region.

global marketing Marketing to target markets throughout the world.

global marketing standardization Production of uniform products that can be sold the same way all over the world.

global vision Recognizing and reacting to international marketing opportunities, being aware of threats from foreign competitors in all markets, and effectively using international distribution networks.

gross margin Amount of money the retailer makes as a percentage of sales after the cost of goods sold is subtracted.

group dynamics Interaction essential to the success of focus group research.

growth stage The second stage of the product life cycle when sales typically grow at an increasing rate, many competitors enter the market, large companies may start acquiring small pioneering firms, and profits are healthy.

H

horizontal conflict Channel conflict that occurs among channel members on the same level.

hypermarket Retail store that combines a supermarket and full-line discount store in a space ranging from 200,000 to 300,000 square feet.

I

ideal self-image The way an individual would like to be.

IMC. *See* **integrated marketing communications.**

implementation The process that turns marketing plans into action assignments and ensures that these assignments are executed in a way that accomplishes the plans' objectives.

implied warranty An unwritten guarantee that the good or service is fit for the purpose for which it was sold.

independent retailers Retailers owned by a single person or partnership and not operated as part of a larger retail institution.

individual branding Using different brand names for different products.

industrializing society The fourth stage of economic development when technology spreads from sectors of the economy that powered the takeoff to the rest of the nation.

inelastic demand Situation in which an increase or a decrease in price will not significantly affect demand for the product.

inflation A general rise in prices without a corresponding increase in wages, which results in decreased purchasing power.

infomercial Thirty-minute or longer advertisement that looks more like a TV talk show than a sales pitch.

informational labeling Labeling designed to help consumers make proper product selections and lower their cognitive dissonance after the purchase.

InfoScan A scanner-based sales-tracking service for the consumer packaged-goods industry.

innovation A product perceived as new by a potential adopter.

institutional advertising Form of advertising designed to enhance a company's image rather than promote a particular product.

intangibility Characteristic of services that cannot be touched, seen, tasted, heard, or felt in the same manner in which goods can be sensed.

integrated marketing communications (IMC) The careful coordination of all promotional messages for a product of service to assure the consistency of messages at every contact point where a company meets the customer.

intensive distribution Form of distribution aimed at having a product available in every outlet at which target customers might want to buy it.

interaction The point at which a customer and a company representative exchange information and develop learning relationships.

internal information search Process of recalling past information stored in the memory.

internal marketing Treating employees as customers and developing systems and benefits that satisfy their needs.

interpersonal communication Direct, fact-to-face communication between two or more people.

introductory stage The full-scale launch of a new product into the marketplace.

inventory control system Method of developing and maintaining an adequate assortment of products to meet customer demand.

involvement Amount of time and effort a buyer invests in the search, evaluation, and decision processes of consumer behavior.

J

JIT. *See* **just-in-time production.**

joint costs Costs that are shared in the manufacturing and marketing of several products in a product line.

joint demand The demand for two or more items used together in a final product.

joint venture A venture in which a domestic firm buys part of a foreign company or joins with a foreign company to create a new entity.

just-in-time production (JIT) Redefining and simplifying manufacturing by reducing inventory levels and delivering raw materials just when they are needed on the production line.

K

keiretsu A network of interlocking corporate affiliates.

keystoning Practice of marking up prices by 100 percent, or doubling the cost.

knowledge center An organization's internal operational component that manages and fulfills customer requests; the logistical system that reacts to, monitors, and controls the interaction between the customer and the organization.

knowledge management The process by which learned information from customers is centralized and shared in order to enhance the relationship between customers and the organization.

L

lead generation (prospecting) Identification of those firms and people most likely to buy the seller's offerings.

lead qualification Determination of a sales prospect's (1) recognized need, (2) buying power, and (3) receptivity and accessibility.

leader pricing (loss-leader pricing) A price tactic in which a product is sold near or even below cost in the hope that shoppers will buy other items once they are in the store.

learning Process that creates changes in behavior, immediate or expected, through experience and practice.

learning (CRM) An informal process of collecting customer data through customer comments and feedback on product or service performance.

licensing The legal process whereby a licensor agrees to let another firm use its manufacturing process, trademarks, patents, trade secrets, or other proprietary knowledge.

lifestyle Mode of living as identified by a person's activities, interests, and opinions.

lifetime value analysis (LTV) A data manipulation technique that projects the future value of the customer over a period of years using the assumption that marketing to repeat customers is more profitable than marketing to first-time buyers.

limited decision making Type of decision making that requires a moderate amount of time for gathering information and deliberating about an unfamiliar brand in a familiar product category.

logistics The process of strategically managing the efficient flow and storage of raw materials, in-process inventory, and finished goods from point of origin to point of consumption.

logistics information system Information technology that integrates and links all of the logistics functions of the supply chain.

loyalty marketing programs Promotional program designed to build long-term, mutually beneficial relationships between a company and its key customers.

LTV. *See* **lifetime value analysis.**

M

Maastricht Treaty Agreement among twelve countries of the European Community to pursue economic, monetary, and political union.

major equipment (installations) Capital goods such as large or expensive machines, mainframe computers, blast furnaces, generators, airplanes, and buildings.

mall intercept interview Survey research method that involves interviewing people in the common areas of shopping malls.

management decision problem Broad-based problem that requires marketing research in order for managers to take proper actions.

manufacturers' brand The brand name of a manufacturer.

marginal cost (MC) Change in total costs associated with a one-unit change in output.

marginal revenue (MR) The extra revenue associated with selling an extra unit of output or the change in total revenue with a one-unit change in output.

market People or organizations with needs or wants and the ability and willingness to buy.

market development Attracting new customers to existing products.

market opportunity analysis The description and estimation of the size and sales potential of market segments that are of interest to the firm and the assessment of key competitors in these market segments.

market orientation Philosophy that assumes that a sale does not depend on an aggressive sales force but rather on a customer's decision to purchase a product.

market penetration A marketing strategy that tries to increase market share among existing customers.

market segment A subgroup of people or organizations sharing one or more characteristics that cause them to have similar product needs.

market segmentation The process of dividing a market into meaningful, relatively similar, and identifiable segments or groups.

market share A company's product sales as a percentage of total sales for that industry.

marketing The process of planning and executing the conception, pricing, promotion, and distribution of ideas, goods, and services to create exchanges that satisfy individual and organizational goals.

marketing audit A thorough, systematic, periodic evaluation of the goals, strategies, structure, and performance of the marketing organization.

marketing channel (channel of distribution) Set of interdependent organizations that ease the transfer of ownership as products move from producer to business user or consumer.

marketing concept The idea that the social and economic justification for an organization's existence is the satisfaction of customer wants and needs while meeting organizational objectives.

marketing-controlled information source Product information source that originates with marketers promoting the product.

marketing database The compilation of names, addresses, and other pieces of pertinent information about individual customers and prospects that affects what and how marketers sell to them.

marketing information Everyday information about developments in the marketing environment that managers use to prepare and adjust marketing plans.

marketing mix A unique blend of product, distribution, promotion, and pricing strategies designed to produce mutually satisfying exchanges with a target market.

marketing myopia Business defined in terms of goods and services rather than in terms of the benefits that customers seek.

marketing objective A statement of what is to be accomplished through marketing activities.

marketing plan A written document that acts as a guidebook of marketing activities for the marketing manager.

marketing planning Designing activities relating to marketing objectives and the changing marketing environment.

marketing research The process of planning, collecting, and analyzing data relevant to a marketing decision.

marketing research objective Specific information needed to solve a market research problem; the objective should provide insightful, decision-making information.

marketing research problem Determining what information is needed and how that information can be obtained efficiently and effectively.

marketing strategy The activity of selecting and describing one or more target markets and developing and maintaining a marketing mix that will produce mutually satisfying exchanges with target markets.

markup pricing Cost of buying the product from the producer plus amounts for profit and for expenses not otherwise accounted for.

Maslow's hierarchy of needs Method of classifying human needs and motivations into five categories in ascending order of importance: physiological, safety, social, esteem, and self-actualization.

mass communication Communication of a concept or message to a large audience.

mass customization (build-to-order) Production method whereby products are not made until an order is placed by the customer; also a strategy that uses technology to deliver customized services on a mass basis, with products being made according to customer specifications.

mass merchandising Retailing strategy using moderate to low prices on large quantities of merchandise and lower service to stimulate high turnover of products.

materials-handling system Method of moving inventory into, within, and out of the warehouse.

materials requirement planning (MRP) Inventory control system that manages the replenishment of raw materials, supplies, and components from the supplier to the manufacturer.

maturity stage A period during which sales increase at a decreasing rate.

MC. *See* **marginal cost.**

measurement error Error that occurs when there is a difference between the information desired by the researcher and the information provided by the measurement process.

media mix Combination of media to be used for a promotional campaign.

media planning The series of decisions advertisers make regarding the selection and use of media, allowing the marketer to optimally and cost-effectively communicate the message to the target audience.

media schedule Designation of the media, the specific publications or programs, and the insertion dates of advertising.

medium Channel used to convey a message to a target market.

merchant wholesaler Institution that buys goods from manufacturers and resells them to businesses, government agencies, and other wholesalers or retailers and that receives and takes title to goods, stores them in its own warehouses, and later ships them.

Mercosur The largest new trade agreement, which includes Brazil, Argentina, Uruguay, and Paraguay.

mission statement The firm's long-term vision based on a careful analysis of benefits sought by present and potential customers and analysis of existing and anticipated environmental conditions.

modeled data Enhancement information that has already been sorted into distinct groups or clusters of consumers or businesses based on census, household, or business-level data.

modeling The act of building a model in a situation where the answer is known and then applying the model to another situation where the answer is unknown.

modified rebuy Situation in which the purchaser wants some change in the original good or service.

morals The rules people develop as a result of cultural values and norms.

motive Driving force that causes a person to take action to satisfy specific needs.

MR. *See* **marginal revenue.**

MRP. *See* **materials requirement plan.**

multiculturalism A situation in which all major ethnic groups in an area-such as a city, county, or census tract-are roughly equally represented.

multinational corporation A company that is heavily engaged in international trade, beyond exporting and importing.

multiplier effect (accelerator principle) Phenomenon in which a small increase or decrease in consumer demand can produce a much larger change in demand for the facilities and equipment needed to make the consumer product.

multisegment targeting strategy A strategy that chooses two or more well-defined market segments and develops a distinct marketing mix for each.

mystery shoppers Researchers posing as customers who gather observational data about a store.

N

NAICS. *See* **North American Industry Classification System.**

need recognition Result of an imbalance between actual and desired states.

needs assessment Determination of the customer's specific needs and wants and the range of options a customer has for satisfying them.

negotiation Process of both the salesperson and the prospect offering special concessions in an attempt to arrive at a sales agreement.

networking Process of finding out about potential clients from friends, business contacts, coworkers, acquaintances, and fellow members in professional and civic organizations.

new buy A situation requiring the purchase of a product for the first time.

new product Product new to the world, the market, the producer, the seller, or some combination of these.

new-product strategy Linking the new-product development process with the objectives of the marketing department, the business unit, and the corporation.

newsgroups Function like bulletin boards on the Internet. They are established to focus on a particular topic.

niche One segment of a market.

niche competitive advantage Advantage achieved when a firm seeks to target and effectively serve a small segment of the market.

noise Anything that interferes with, distorts, or slows down the transmission of information.

nonaspirational reference group Group with which an individual does not want to associate.

noncumulative quantity discount A deduction from list price that applies to a single order rather than to the total volume of orders placed during a certain period.

nonmarketing-controlled information source Product information source that is not associated with advertising or promotion.

nonprobability sample Any sample in which little or no attempt is made to get a representative cross section of the population.

nonprofit organization An organization that exists to achieve some goal other than the usual business goals of profit, market share, or return on investment.

nonprofit organization marketing The effort by nonprofit organizations to bring about mutually satisfying exchanges with target markets.

nonstore retailing Shopping without visiting a store.

norm Value or attitude deemed acceptable by a group.

North American Free Trade Agreement (NAFTA) An agreement between Canada, the United States, and Mexico that created the world's largest free-trade zone.

North American Industry Classification System (NAICS) A detailed numbering system developed by the United States, Canada, and Mexico to classify North American business establishments by their main production processes.

O

observation research Research method that relies on three types of observation: people watching people, people watching activity, and machines watching people.

odd–even pricing (psychological pricing) Price tactic that uses odd-numbered prices to connote bargains and even-numbered prices to imply quality.

OEM The acronym OEM stands for original equipment manufacturer. OEM's buy business goods that they incorporate into the products that they produce for eventual sale to other producers or to consumers.

off-price retailer Retailer that sells at prices 25 percent or more below traditional department store prices because it pays cash for its stock and usually doesn't ask for return privileges.

on-line retailing A type of shopping available to consumers with personal computers and access to the Internet.

one-to-one marketing An individual marketing method that utilizes customer information to build long-term, personalized, and profitable relationships with each customer.

one-to-one marketing communications process A revised marketing communications process that depicts the individualized communication between the one-to-one marketer and the customer. The process is characterized by the use of personalized communication, the lack of interfering noise, and the ability to capture the response of the customer.

open-ended question An interview question that encourages an answer phrased in the respondent's own words.

opinion leader Individual who influences the opinions of others.

optimizer Type of business customer that considers numerous suppliers, both familiar and unfamiliar, solicits bids, and studies all proposals carefully before selecting one.

order processing system System whereby orders are entered into the supply chain and filled.

outsourcing (contract logistics) Manufacturer's or supplier's use of an independent third party to manage an entire function of the logistics system, such as transportation, warehousing, or order processing.

P

penetration pricing Pricing policy whereby a firm charges a relatively low price for a product initially as a way to reach the mass market.

perception Process by which people select, organize, and interpret stimuli into a meaningful and coherent picture.

perceptual mapping A means of displaying or graphing, in two or more dimensions, the location of products, brands, or groups of products in customers' minds.

personality Way of organizing and grouping the consistencies of an individual's reactions to situations.

personalized economy Delivering goods and services at a good value on demand.

personal selling A purchase situation in which two people communicate in an attempt to influence each other.

persuasive labeling Labeling that focuses on a promotional theme or logo with consumer information being secondary.

pioneering advertising Form of advertising designed to stimulate primary demand for a new product or product category.

planned obsolescence The practice of modifying products so those that have already been sold become obsolete before they actually need replacement.

planning The process of anticipating future events and determining strategies to achieve organizational objectives in the future.

PLC *See* **product life cycle.**

point-of-purchase display Promotional display set up at the retailer's location to build traffic, advertise the product, or induce impulse buying.

point-of-sale interactions Communications between customers and organizations that occur at the point of sale, normally in a store.

portfolio matrix Tool for allocating resources among products or strategic business units on the basis of relative market share and market growth rate.

position The place a product, brand, or group of products occupies in consumers' minds relative to competing offerings.

positioning Developing a specific marketing mix to influence potential customers' overall perception of a brand, product line, or organization in general.

poverty of time Lack of time to do anything but work, commute to work, handle family situations, do housework, shop, sleep, and eat.

preapproach A process that describes the "homework" that must be done by the salesperson before he or she contacts the prospect.

predatory pricing The practice of charging a very low price for a product with the intent of driving competitors out of business or out of a market.

predictive modeling A data manipulation technique in which marketers try to determine, based on some past set of occurrences, what the odds are that some other occurrence, such as a response or purchase, will take place in the future.

preindustrial society A society in the second stage of economic development, involving economic and social change and the emergence of a middle class with an entrepreneurial spirit.

premium Extra item offered to the consumer, usually in exchange for some proof of purchase of the promoted product.

prestige pricing Charging a high price to help promote a high-quality image.

price That which is given up in an exchange to acquire a good or service.

price bundling Marketing two or more products in a single package for a special price.

price equilibrium Price at which demand and supply are equal.

price fixing An agreement between two or more firms on the price they will charge for a product.

price lining Practice of offering a product line with several items at specific price points.

price shading Use of discounts by salespeople to increase demand for one or more products in a line.

price skimming Pricing policy whereby a firm charges a high introductory price, often coupled with heavy promotion.

price strategy Basic, long-term pricing framework, which establishes the initial price for a product and the intended direction for price movements over the product life cycle.

primary data Information collected for the first time; can be used for solving the particular problem under investigation.

primary membership group Reference group with which people interact regularly in an informal, face-to-face manner, such as family, friends, or fellow employees.

private brand A brand name owned by a wholesaler or a retailer.

probability sample A sample in which every element in the population has a known statistical likelihood of being selected.

problem child (question mark) In the portfolio matrix, a business unit that shows rapid growth but poor profit margins.

processed materials Products used directly in manufacturing other products.

product Everything, both favorable and unfavorable, that a person receives in an exchange.

product advertising Form of advertising that touts the benefits of a specific good or service.

product category All brands that satisfy a particular type of need.

product development Marketing strategy that entails the creation of new products for present markets; process of converting applications for new technologies into marketable products.

product differentiation A positioning strategy that some firms use to distinguish their products from those of competitors.

product item A specific version of a product that can be designated as a distinct offering among an organization's products.

product life cycle (PLC) A concept that provides a way to trace the stages of a product's acceptance, from its introduction (birth) to its decline (death).

product line A group of closely related product items.

product line depth The number of product items in a product line.

product line extension Adding additional products to an existing product line in order to compete more broadly in the industry.

product line pricing Setting prices for an entire line of products.

product mix All products an organization sells.

product mix width The number of product lines an organization offers.

product modification Changing one or more of a product's characteristics.

product offering The mix of products offered to the consumer by the retailer, also called the product assortment or merchandise mix.

production orientation A philosophy that focuses on the internal capabilities of the firm rather than on the desires and needs of the marketplace.

product/service differentiation The provision of something that is unique and valuable to buyers beyond simply offering a lower price than the competition's.

profit Revenue minus expenses.

profit maximization A method of setting prices that occurs when marginal revenue equals marginal cost.

promotion Communication by marketers that informs, persuades, and reminds potential buyers of a product in order to influence an opinion or elicit a response.

promotional allowance (trade allowance) Payment to a dealer for promoting the manufacturer's products.

promotional mix Combination of promotion tools—including advertising, public relations, personal selling, and sales promotion—used to reach the target market and fulfill the organization's overall goals.

promotional strategy Plan for the optimal use of the elements of promotion: advertising, public relations, personal selling, and sales promotion.

PSA. *See* **public service advertisement.**

psychographic segmentation Market segmentation on the basis of personality, motives, lifestyles, and geodemographics.

publicity Public information about a company, good, or service appearing in the mass media as a news item.

public relations Marketing function that evaluates public attitudes, identifies areas within the organization that the public may be interested in, and executes a program of action to earn public understanding and acceptance.

public service advertisement (PSA) Announcement that promotes a program of a federal, state, or local government or of a nonprofit organization.

pull strategy Marketing strategy that stimulates consumer demand to obtain product distribution.

pulsing media schedule Media scheduling strategy that uses continuous scheduling throughout the year coupled with a flighted schedule during the best sales periods.

push money Money offered to channel intermediaries to encourage them to "push" products—that is, to encourage other members of the channel to sell the products.

push strategy Marketing strategy that uses aggressive personal selling and trade advertising to convince a wholesaler or a retailer to carry and sell particular merchandise.

pyramid of corporate social responsibility A model that suggests corporate social responsibility is composed of economic, legal, ethical, and philanthropic responsibilities and that firm's economic performance supports the entire structure.

Q

quantity discount Price reduction offered to buyers buying in multiple units or above a specified dollar amount.

quota Statement of the individual salesperson's sales objectives, usually based on sales volume alone but sometimes including key accounts (those with greatest potential), new accounts, and specific products.

R

random error Error that occurs because the selected sample is an imperfect representation of the overall population.

random sample A sample arranged in such a way that every element of the population has an equal chance of being selected as part of the sample.

raw materials Unprocessed extractive or agricultural products, such as mineral ore, lumber, wheat, corn, fruits, vegetables, and fish.

reach Number of target consumers exposed to a commercial at least once during a specific period, usually four weeks.

real self-image The way an individual actually perceives himself or herself.

rebate Cash refund given for the purchase of a product during a specific period.

receiver Person who decodes a message.

recency–frequency–monetary analysis (RFM) A data manipulation technique that determines the firm's best customers by identifying those customers who have purchased most recently and most frequently and who have spent the most money.

recession A period of economic activity when income, production, and employment tend to fall—all of which reduce demand for goods and services.

reciprocity A practice in which business purchasers choose to buy from their own customers.

recruited Internet sample Sample in which respondents are prerecruited and, after qualifying to participate, are sent a questionnaire by e-mail or directed to a secure Web site to fill out a questionnaire.

reference group Group in society that influences an individual's purchasing behavior.

referral Recommendation to a salesperson from a customer or business associate.

relationship marketing A strategy that entails forging long-term partnerships with customers.

relationship selling (consultative selling) Sales practice of building, maintaining, and enhancing interactions with customers in order to develop long-term satisfaction through mutually beneficial partnerships.

reliability The ability to perform a service dependably, accurately, and consistently.

repositioning Changing consumers' perceptions of a brand in relation to competing brands.

research design One that specifies which research questions must be answered, how and when the data will be gathered, and how the data will be analyzed.

response list A customer list that includes the names and addresses of individuals who have responded to an offer of some kind, such as by mail, telephone, direct response television, product rebates, contests or sweepstakes, or billing inserts.

responsiveness The ability to provide prompt service.

retailer Channel intermediary that sells mainly to consumers.

retailing All the activities directly related to the sale of goods and services to the ultimate consumer for personal, nonbusiness use.

retailing mix Combination of the six Ps—product, place, promotion, price, personnel, and presentation—to sell goods and services to the ultimate consumer.

return on investment (ROI) Net profit after taxes divided by total assets.

revenue The price charged to customers multiplied by the number of units sold.

RFM. *See* **recency–frequency–monetary analysis.**

ROI. *See* **return on investment.**

routine response behavior Type of decision making exhibited by consumers buying frequently purchased, low-cost goods and services; requires little search and decision time.

S

sales orientation The idea that people will buy more goods and services if aggressive sales techniques are used and that high sales result in high profits.

sales presentation Face-to-face explanation of the sales proposal to a prospective buyer.

sales process (sales cycle) The set of steps a salesperson goes through in a particular organization to sell a particular product or service.

sales promotion Marketing activities—other than personal selling, advertising, and public relations—that stimulate consumer buying and dealer effectiveness.

sales proposal A formal written document or professional presentation that outlines how the salesperson's product or service will meet or exceed the prospect's needs.

sample A subset of a population.

sampling Promotional program that allows the consumer the opportunity to try the product or service for free.

sampling error Error that occurs when a sample somehow does not represent the target population.

satisficer Type of business customer that places an order with the first familiar supplier to satisfy product and delivery requirements.

scaled-response question A closed-ended question designed to measure the intensity of a respondent's answer.

scanner-based research A system for gathering information from a single group of respondents by continuously monitoring the advertising, promotion, and pricing they are exposed to and the things they buy.

score A numerical value assigned to each record in a data warehouse that indicates the likelihood that the customer whose record has been scored will exhibit the behavior in question.

scrambled merchandising The tendency to offer a wide variety of nontraditional goods and services under one roof.

screened Internet sample Internet sample with quotas based on desired sample characteristics.

screening The first filter in the product development process that eliminates ideas that are inconsistent with the organization's new-product strategy or are obviously inappropriate for some other reason.

search quality A characteristic that can be easily assessed before purchase.

seasonal discount A price reduction for buying merchandise out of season.

seasonal media schedule Media scheduling strategy that runs advertising only during times of the year when the product is most likely to be used.

secondary data Data previously collected for any purpose other than the one at hand.

secondary membership group Reference group with which people associate less consistently and more formally than a primary membership group, such as a club, professional group, or religious group.

segmentation bases (variables) Characteristics of individuals, groups, or organizations.

selective distortion Process whereby a consumer changes or distorts information that conflicts with his or her feelings or beliefs.

selective distribution Form of distribution achieved by screening dealers to eliminate all but a few in any single area.

selective exposure Process whereby a consumer notices certain stimuli and ignores other stimuli.

selective retention Process whereby a consumer remembers only that information that supports his or her personal beliefs.

self-concept How a consumer perceives himself or herself in terms of attitudes, perceptions, beliefs, and self-evaluations.

selling against the brand Stocking well-known branded items at high prices in order to sell store brands at discounted prices.

sender Originator of the message in the communication process.

service The result of applying human or mechanical efforts to people or objects.

service mark Trademark for a service.

shopping product Product that requires comparison shopping, because it is usually more expensive than a convenience product and found in fewer stores.

simulated (laboratory) market testing Presentation of advertising and other promotion materials for several products, including a test product, to members of the product's target market.

simultaneous product development A team-oriented approach to new-product development.

single-price tactic Policy of offering all goods and services at the same price.

social class Group of people in a society who are considered nearly equal in status or community esteem, who regularly socialize among themselves both formally and informally, and who share behavioral norms.

socialization process Process by which cultural values and norms are passed down to children.

societal marketing orientation The idea that an organization exists not only to satisfy customer wants and needs and to meet organizational objectives but also to preserve or enhance individuals' and society's long-term best interests.

spatial discrepancy Difference between the location of the producer and the location of widely scattered markets.

specialty discount store Retail store that offers a nearly complete selection of single-line merchandise and uses self-service, discount prices, high volume, and high turnover.

specialty product A particular item that consumers search extensively for and are very reluctant to accept substitutes for.

specialty store Retail store specializing in a given type of merchandise.

star In the portfolio matrix, a business unit that is a fast-growing market leader.

status quo pricing Pricing objective that maintains existing prices or meets the competition's prices.

stimulus Any unit of input affecting one or more of the five senses: sight, smell, taste, touch, hearing.

stimulus discrimination Learned ability to differentiate among similar products.

stimulus generalization Form of learning that occurs when one response is extended to a second stimulus similar to the first.

straight commission Method of compensation in which the salesperson is paid some percentage when a sale is made.

straight rebuy Buying situation in which the purchaser reorders the same goods or services without looking for new information or investigating other suppliers.

straight salary Method of compensation in which the salesperson receives a salary regardless of sales productivity.

strategic alliance (strategic partnership) A cooperative agreement between business firms.

strategic business unit (SBU) A subgroup of a single business or collection of related businesses within the larger organization.

strategic channel alliance Cooperative agreement between business firms to use the other's already established distribution channel.

strategic planning The managerial process of creating and maintaining a fit between the organization's objectives and resources and evolving market opportunities.

subculture Homogeneous group of people who share elements of the overall culture as well as unique elements of their own group.

supercenter Retail store that combines groceries and general merchandise goods with a wide range of services.

supermarket A large, departmentalized, self-service retailer that specializes in food and non-food items.

supplementary services A group of services that support or enhance the core service.

supplies Consumable items that do not become part of the final product.

supply The quantity of a product that will be offered to the market by a supplier at various prices for a specified period.

supply chain The connected chain of all of the business entities, both internal and external to the company, that perform or support the logistics function.

supply chain management Management system that coordinates and integrates all of the activities performed by supply chain members into a seamless process, from source to the point of consumption that results in enhanced customer and economic value.

supply chain team Entire group of individuals who orchestrate the movement of goods, services, and information from the source to the consumer.

survey research the most popular technique for gathering primary data in which a researcher interacts with people to obtain facts, opinions, and attitudes.

sustainable competitive advantage A differential advantage that cannot be copied by the competition.

SWOT analysis One that identifies internal strengths (S) and weaknesses (W) and also examines external opportunities (O) and threats (T).

T

takeoff economy The third stage of economic development that involves a period of transition from a developing to a developed nation.

tangibles The physical evidence of a service, including the physical facilities, tools, and equipment used to provide the service.

target market A group of people or organizations for which an organization designs, implements, and maintains a marketing mix intended to meet the needs of that group, resulting in mutually satisfying exchanges.

teamwork Collaborative efforts of people to accomplish common objectives.

telemarketing The use of the telephone to sell directly to consumers.

temporal discrepancy A situation that occurs when a product is produced but a customer is not ready to buy it.

test marketing The limited introduction of a product and a marketing program to determine the reactions of potential customers in a market situation.

touch point All possible areas of a business where customers communicate with that business.

trade allowance Price reduction offered by manufacturers to intermediaries, such as wholesalers and retailers.

trademark The exclusive right to use a brand or part of a brand.

trade sales promotion Sales promotion activities targeted to a channel member, such as a wholesaler or retailer.

traditional society A society in the earliest stages of economic development, largely agricultural, with a social structure and value system that provide little opportunity for upward mobility.

transaction Any interaction between a company and a customer involving an exchange of information as well as an exchange of products or services.

transaction-based interactions The exchange of information that occurs between the customer and the company at the point of the actual transaction.

two-part pricing Price tactic that charges two separate amounts to consume a single good or service.

U

UCC. *See* **Uniform Commercial Code filings.**

unbundling Reducing the bundle of services that comes with the basic product.

undifferentiated targeting strategy Marketing approach that views the market as one big market with no individual segments and thus requires a single marketing mix.

unfair trade practice acts Laws that prohibit wholesalers and retailers from selling below cost.

uniform delivered pricing Price tactic in which the seller pays the actual freight charges and bills every purchaser an identical, flat freight charge.

unique selling proposition Desirable, exclusive, and believable advertising appeal selected as the theme for a campaign.

unitary elasticity Situation in which total revenue remains the same when prices change.

universal product codes (UPCs) Series of thick and thin vertical lines (bar codes), readable by computerized optical scanners, that represent numbers used to track products.

universe The population from which a sample will be drawn.

unrestricted Internet sample One in which anyone with a computer and modem can fill out the questionnaire.

unsought product A product unknown to the potential buyer or a known product that the buyer does not actively seek.

UPCs. *See* **universal product codes.**

Uruguay Round An agreement to dramatically lower trade barriers worldwide.

usage-rate segmentation Dividing a market by the amount of product bought or consumed.

V

value Enduring belief that a specific mode of conduct is personally or socially preferable to another mode of conduct.

value-based pricing The price set at a level that seems to the customer to be a good price compared to the prices of other options.

variable costs Costs that vary with changes in the level of output.

venture team A market-oriented group staffed by a small number of representatives from different disciplines.

vertical conflict Channel conflict that occurs between different levels in a marketing channel, most typically between the manufacturer and wholesaler or between the manufacturer and retailer.

W

want Recognition of an unfulfilled need and a product that will satisfy it.

warehouse membership clubs Limited-service merchant wholesalers that sell a limited selection of brand-name appliances, household items, and groceries on a cash-and-carry basis to members, usually small businesses and groups.

warranty Confirmation of the quality or performance of a good or service.

web-based interactions Communications between customers and organizations using Web vehicles.

World Trade Organization (WTO) A new trade organization that replaces the old General Agreement on Trade and Tariffs (GATT).

World Wide Web (Web) Component of the Internet designed to simplify text and images.

WTO. *See* **World Trade Organization.**

Y

yield management systems (YMS) A technique for adjusting prices that uses complex mathematical software to profitably fill unused capacity by discounting early purchases, limiting early sales at these discounted prices, and overbooking capacity.

Z

zone pricing Modification of uniform delivered pricing that divides the United States (or the total market) into segments or zones and charges a flat freight rate to all customers in a given zone.

CHAPTER 1

1. D. M. Osborne, "Taking On Procter & Gamble," *Inc.*, October 2000, 67–73. Used with permission.
2. "About Us," American Marketing Association (on-line). Available at http://www.marketingpower.com/index. January 14, 2002.
3. Philip Kotler, *Marketing Management*, millennium ed. (Upper Saddle River, N.J.: Prentice-Hall, 2000), 12.
4. Nora Isaacs, "Crash & Burn," www.upsidetoday.com, March 2001, 186–192.
5. Ibid.
6. Rekha Balu, "Listen Up," *Fast Company*, May 2000, 304–316.
7. Lucy McCauley, "Unit of One," *Fast Company*, March 2000, 94.
8. Ibid.
9. David W. Cravens, Charles W. Lamb, Jr., and Victoria L. Crittenden, *Strategic Marketing Management Cases*, 7th ed. (New York: McGraw-Hill Irwin, 2002), 2.
10. Balu, 312.
11. Cravens, Lamb, and Crittenden, 3.
12. Isaacs, 190.
13. Joann Muller, "It Doesn't Get Any Bigger Than This," *Business Week*, September 4, 2000, 84.
14. Sandra Dolbow, "Kmart May Be Down, But Don't Count It Out," *Brandweek*, January 28, 2002, 5.
15. Ibid.
16. Jerry Wind and Arvind Rangaswamy, "Customerization: The Next Revolution in Mass Customization," *Journal of Interactive Marketing* 15 (no. 1), 2001, 18.
17. Christopher J. Zane, "Creating Lifetime Customers," *The Retailing Issues Letter*, September 2000, 2.
18. "Top 10 Things That Irked Holiday Shoppers," *Business Week*, February 7, 2000, EB12.
19. Tony Pachi, "Sublime Service," *Customer Relationship Management*, October 2001, 25–26.
20. "Return to Sender," *Marketing News*, June 18, 2001, 3.
21. Scott Thurm, "How to Drive an Express Train," *Wall Street Journal*, June 1, 2000, B1.
22. Ibid.
23. Robert Bibb and Eric Gehm, "The 360-Degree View," *Customer Relationship Management*, June 2001, 23–24.
24. "Ask Yourself, What the Hell Really Works Here?" *Fast Company*, May 2001, 82.
25. Dana Jones, "Respondez-Vous, B-to-B," *Marketing News*, May 22, 2000, 1, 9, 10.
26. Robert Levering and Milton Moskowitz, "The 100 Best Companies to Work For," *Fortune*, January 10, 2000, 81–110.
27. John Yokoyama and Jim Bergquist, "The World Famous Pike Place Fish Story," *The Retailing Issues Letter*, November 2001, 5. Center for Retailing Studies, Texas A & M University.
28. Alessandra Galloni, "Coke to Launch Powerade Drink across Europe," *Wall Street Journal*, October 16, 2001, B11E. Used with permission.
29. Geoffrey A. Fowler, "Green Sales Pitch Isn't Moving Many Products," *Wall Street Journal*, March 6, 2002, B1, B4. Reprinted with permission of the *Wall Street Journal* ©2002 Dow Jones & Co., Inc. All rights reserved worldwide.
30. Kotler, 22.
31. Gina Imperato, "Get Your Career in Sight," *Fast Company*, March 2000, 326.

CHAPTER 2

1. Erin White, "How Stodgy Turned Stylish," *Wall Street Journal*, May 3, 2002, B1, B3. Used with permission.
2. Chris Reidy, "Lands' End to Join Sears Family for $1.9 Billion," *Knight Ridder Tribune Business News*, May 14, 2002, 1.
3. Monica Roman, "Pepsi Blue or Vanilla Coke?" *Business Week*, May 20, 2002, 50.
4. Jennifer Dixon, "Shoppers Abandon Kmart Stores; Wal-Mart, Target Pick Up Business," *Knight Ridder Tribune Business News*, March 30, 2002, 1.
5. Christine Bittar, "S. C. Johnson Flushes Line with New Wipes" *Brandweek*, January 28, 2002, 4.
6. http://www.aspca.org/site/PageServer?pagename=apcc_centoverview.
7. "Technology Brief—Hewlett-Packard Co.: Officials Don't Get Bonuses Because of Failed Objectives," *Wall Street Journal*, January 30, 2002, B5.
8. Andrew Park and Peter Burrows, "Dell, The Conqueror," *Business Week*, September 24, 2001, 92–102.
9. Ann Zimmerman and David Armstrong, "How Drug Makers Use Pharmacies to Push Pricey Pills," *Wall Street Journal*, May 1, 2002, A1, A12. Used with permission.
10. Khanh T. L. Tran, "Nike Puts Its Swoosh on MP3 Players, Walkie-Talkies, Heart Monitors," *Wall Street Journal*, May 10, 2000, B1, B4.
11. "Designing Products around Customer Needs," *Fortune*, Special Advertising Section, July 23, 2001, S18.
12. Jim Wilson, "Airbag Shield Foils Terrorists," *Popular Mechanics*, June 2000, 17.
13. Sandra I. Irwin, "Smart Armor Shield Deploys Like Air Bag to Stop Bullets," *National Defense*, May 2000, 23. Reprinted from National Defense with permission.
14. Ibid.

CHAPTER 3

1. Sarah Ellison, "Levi Strauss, Losing Ground to Rivals, Is Set to Iron Wrinkles Out of Jeans Sales," *Wall Street Journal*, February 12, 2001, A23B. Used with permission.
2. The "coming of age" material is adapted from Charles Schewe, Geoffrey Meredith, and Stephanie Noble, "Defining Moments: Segmenting by Cohorts," *Marketing Management*, Fall 2000, 47–53.
3. "No Place Like Home," *Wall Street Journal*, June 16, 1997, R4.
4. David Wolfe, "The Psychological Center of Gravity," *American Demographics*, April 1998, 16–19.
5. James Steinberg, "The Millennial Mind Set," *American Demographics*, January 1999, 60–64.
6. "Leisure Squeeze," *Roper Reports*, January 1999, 1.
7. Ibid.
8. "For Harried Workers in the Twenty-first Century, Six Trends to Watch," *Wall Street Journal*, December 29, 1999, B1. Used with permission.
9. "Latest Backlash against Dual Earners Ignores Some Realities," *Wall Street Journal*, May 14, 1997, B1.
10. "Sorry, Boys—Donna Reed Is Still Dead," *American Demographics*, September 1995, 13–14.
11. "Women-Owned Businesses Booming, But So Are Obstacles," *Associated Press Newswires*, April 11, 2000.
12. Gerry Myers, "Selling to Women," *American Demographics*, April 1996, 36–42.
13. Ibid.
14. Christy Harvey, "A Guide to Who Holds the Purse Strings," *Wall Street Journal*, June 22, 2000, A14. Used with permission.
15. Ibid.
16. Shelly Branch, "Irradiated Food by Any Other Name Might Just Win Over

Consumers," *Wall Street Journal,* August 14, 2001, B1, B4. Used with permission.

17. Pamela Paul, "Getting Inside Gen Y," *American Demographics*, September 2001, 43–49.

18. Rebecca Gardyn, "Swap Meet," *American Demographics*, July 2001, 51–55.

19. "Hotels Target Generation X; Young Travelers Demand High-Tech Services, Amenities," *USA Today*, February 10, 2000, 1B.

20. "Harley-Davidson's New 'Buell Blast' Roars into 18–34 Year-Old Novice Market," *PR Newswire*, March 16, 2000.

21. "Survey Sheds Light on Typical Boomer," *Marketing News*, January 31, 1994, 2.

22. Cheryl Russell, "The Master Trend," *American Demographics*, October 1993, 28–37.

23. "Booming Business," *American Demographics*, December 1999, 32–35.

24. "Boomer Havens and Young Adult Magnets," *American Demographics*, September 2001, 22–24.

25. Howard Willens and Leslie Harris, "The Mature Market . . . Is It for Real?" *Quirk's Marketing Research Review*, May 2001, 40–43. Reprinted with permission.

26. Ibid.

27. Ibid.

28. "Marketers Tweak Strategies as Age Groups Realign," *Wall Street Journal*, May 15, 2001, B1, B4. Used with permission.

29. "Work Slowdown," *American Demographics*, March 1996, 4–7.

30. William Frey, "Micro Melting Pots," *American Demographics*, June 2001, 20–23.

31. Ibid.

32. "An Almost-Invisible $1 Trillion Market," *Business Week*, June 11, 2001, 151.

33. Steve Rabin, "How to Sell across Cultures," *American Demographics*, March 1994, 56–58.

34. "P&G Reaches Out to Hispanics," *Wall Street Journal*, October 13, 2000, B1, B4. Used with permission.

35. "Diversity in the Main Stream," *Marketing News*, May 21, 2001, 1, 13.

36. "The Web Goes Multicultural," *Advertising Age*, November 29, 1999, 51, 54.

37. Ibid.

38. "Creating the Digital Dividend," *Business2.com*, March 6, 2001, 60.

39. Ibid.

40. Ibid.

41. Hassan Fattah, "The Rising Tide," *American Demographics*, April 2001, 48–53.

42. http://www.census.gov, October 12, 2001.

43. U.S. Department of Commerce: Bureau of Economic Analysis (http://www.bea.gov), October 12, 2001.

44. "How Prosperity Is Reshaping the American Economy," *Business Week*, February 14, 2000, 101–110.

45. "Masters of Innovation," *Business Week 50*, Spring 2001, 162.

46. Stacy Perman, "Automate or Die," http://www.ecompany.com, July 2001, 60–67.

47. Peter Landers, "Electronics E-Commerce in Japan Held Back by Retail Traditions," *Wall Street Journal,* March 30, 2000, A22. Used with permission.

48. The Tide story is from Katrina Brooker, "A Game of Inches," *Fortune*, February 5, 2001, 98–100.

49. Based on Edward Stevens, *Business Ethics* (New York: Paulist Press, 1979). Reprinted with permission. Used with permission of Paulist Press.

50. Anusorn Singhapakdi, Skott Vitell, and Kenneth Kraft, "Moral Intensity and Ethical Decisionmaking of Marketing Professionals," *Journal of Business Research* 36, March 1996, 245–255; Ishmael Akaah and Edward Riordan, "Judgments of Marketing Professionals about Ethical Issues in Marketing Research: A Replication and Extension," *Journal of Marketing Research*, February 1989, 112–120. See also Shelby Hung, Lawrence Chonko, and James Wilcox, "Ethical Problems of Marketing Researchers," *Journal of Marketing Research*, August 1984, 309–324; Kenneth Andrews, "Ethics in Practice," *Harvard Business Review*, September–October 1989, 99–104; Thomas Dunfee, Craig Smith, and William T. Ross, Jr., "Social Contracts and Marketing Ethics," *Journal of Marketing*, July 1999, 14–32; and Jay Handleman and Stephen Arnold, "The Role of Marketing Actions with a Social Dimension: Appeals to the Institutional Environment," *Journal of Marketing*, July 1999, 33–48.

51. O. C. Ferrell, Debbie Thorne, and Linda Ferrell, "Legal Pressure for Ethical Compliance in Marketing," *Proceedings of the American Marketing Association*, Summer 1995, 412–413.

52. "Ethics Programs Aren't Stemming Employee Misconduct," *Wall Street Journal*, May 11, 2000, A1. Used with permission.

53. This section is adapted from Archie B. Carroll, "The Pyramid of Corporate Social Responsibility: Toward the Moral Management of Organizational Stakeholders," *Business Horizons*, July–August 1991, 39–48; see also Kirk Davidson, "Marketers Must Accept Greater Responsibilities," *Marketing News*, February 2, 1998, 6.

54. "Business Ethics: Three Companies Show How Business Might Evolve Ethically in the Next Century," *PR Newswires*, November 16, 1999.

55. "The Best Corporate Reputations in America," *Wall Street Journal*, September 23, 1999, B1, B20.

56. "The Promise of the New Economy Is at Risk," *Fast Company*, March 2000, 166–167.

57. Amy Borrus, "Commerce Reweaves the Social Fabric," *Business Week*, August 28, 2000, 187–189.

58. Ibid.

59. "Survey Rates Companies' Reputations, And Many Are Found Wanting," *Wall Street Journal*, February 7, 2001, B1, B6.

60. Sankar Sen and C. B. Bhattacharya, "Does Doing Good Always Lead to Doing Better? Consumer Reactions to Corporate Responsibility," *Journal of Marketing Research*, May 2001, 225–243.

CHAPTER 4

1. Bill Spindle, "Cowboys and Samurai: The Japanizing of Universal," *Wall Street Journal*, March 22, 2001, B1, B6. Used with permission.

2. "The Big Myth about U.S. Manufacturing," *Fortune,* October 2, 2002, 44.

3. Statistics obtained from http://www.usatradeonline.gov, October 18, 2001.

4. Ibid.

5. Ibid.

6. Ibid.

7. See http://www.bxa.fedworld.gov/faq.html. This is the Web site of the Bureau of Export Administration.

8. "Anti-Trade/Pro-Poverty," *Fortune*, January 10, 2000, 40.

9. Sara Terry, "Free Trade Isn't Fair," *Fast Company,* September 2000, 254–256.

10. "Anti-Trade/Pro-Poverty," 40.

11. "The Pros and Cons of Globalization," *Business Week*, April 24, 2000, 41.

12. "Globalization: What Americans Are Worried About," *Business Week*, April 24, 2000, 44.

13. "Toy Story," *Fortune,* June 26, 2000, 270.

14. "Hurting in Lockstep," *Business Week,* October 22, 2001, 30.

15. "Up the Ladder," *Business Week,* November 6, 2000, 78–85.

16. Ibid.

17. "What's at Stake," *Business Week,* October 22, 2001, 34–37.

18. Neil Jacoby, "The Multinational Corporation," *Center Magazine*, May 1970, 37.

19. "The Stateless Corporation," *Business Week*, May 14, 1990, 98–105. See also Bruce Kogut, "What Makes a Company Global?" *Harvard Business Review*, January–February 1999, 165–170; and Neil Bruce Holbert, "Worldwide Marketing Must Not Assume Imperialistic Air," *Marketing News*, February 14, 2000, 20.

20. "See the World, Erase Its Border," *Business Week,* August 28, 2000, 113–114.

21. Theodore Levitt, "The Globalization of Markets," *Harvard Business Review*, May–June 1983, 92–102.

22. Saeed Samiee and Kendall Roth, "The Influence of Global Marketing Standardization on Performance," *Journal of Marketing*, April 1992, 1–17. See also Aviv Shoham, "Global Marketing Standardization," *Journal of Global Marketing*, September 1995, 91–119.

23. "For Peruvians, Fizzy Yellow Drink Is the Real Thing," *International Herald Tribune*, December 27, 1995, 3.

24. Sherrie Zhan, "Marketing across Cultures," *World Trade*, February 1999, 80–82.

25. "Research Meaning When Giving International Gifts," *Cincinnati Business Courier*, July 28, 2000, 36.

26. "Selling Overseas Complex Endeavor," *Marketing News,* July 30, 2001, 4.

27. For an excellent article on culture and marketing, see Cheryl Nakata and K. Sivakauar, "Instituting the Marketing Concept in a Multinational Setting: The Role of National Culture," *Journal of the Academy of Marketing Science,* Summer 2001, 255–275.

28. "Portrait of the World," *Marketing News*, August 28, 1995, 20–21.

29. "Who's Free, Who's Not," *Wall Street Journal,* November 1, 2000, A26.

30. Robert Frank, "Thai Food for the World," *Wall Street Journal,* February 6, 2001, B1, B4.

31. http://www.wto.org, October 19, 2001.

32. "Beijing's Phony War on Fakes," *Fortune*, October 30, 2000, 190–199.

33. "Motorcycle Makers from Japan Discover Piracy Made in China," *Wall Street Journal*, July 25, 2001, A1, A4.

34. "NAFTA's Scorecard: So Far, So Good," *Business Week,* July 9, 2001, 54–56.

35. Material for the sections on FTAA, ASEAN, and APEC is reprinted from C. Williams, *Management,* 2nd ed. (Cincinnati, Ohio: South-Western, 2003) 274–275. Original sources for the material are provided in notes. G. Smith, E. Malkin, J. Wheatley, P. Magnusson, and M. Arndt, "Betting on Free Trade: George Bush Wants to Turn North and South America into the World's Biggest Single Market. Is It for Real or Just a Dream?" *Business Week*, April 23, 2001, 32.

36. Declaration of Principles, Summit of the Americas, "Free Trade Area of the Americas." [On-line] Available http://www.ftaa-alca.org/EnglishVersion/miami_e.htm, January 27, 1999.

37. G. Smith, E. Malkin, J. Wheatley, P. Magnusson, and M. Arndt, 32.

38. "ASEAN Free Trade Area (AFTA): An Update," Association of South East Nations. [On-line] Available http://www.aseansec.org/view.asp?file=/general/publication/afta-upd.htm, September 10, 2001.

39. "Member Economies' Web sites," Asia-Pacific Economic Cooperation. [On-line] Available http://www.apecsec.org.sg/member/memb_websites.html, September 10, 2001.

40. "Trustbusting's Top Cop," *Business Week,* April 30, 2001, 88–90.

41. Tony Horwitz, "Europe's Borders Fade, And People and Goods Can Move More Freely," *Wall Street Journal,* May 18, 1993, A1, A10. Used with permission.

42. http://www.franchise.org, October 22, 2001.

43. Polly Larson, "Opening Doors to Emerging Economies," http://www.franchise.org, October 22, 2001.

44. For an excellent article on joint ventures, see Mark Houston and Shane Johnson, "Buyer-Supplier Contracts versus Joint Ventures: Determinants and Consequences of Transaction Structure," *Journal of Marketing Research,* February 2000, 1–15.

45. "Mondavi Likes the Taste of Global Joint Ventures," *The Plain Dealer,* December 15, 1999, 3F.

46. "How the Chevy Name Landed on an SUV Using Russian Technology," *Wall Street Journal,* February 20, 2001, A1, A8.

47. "Making Global Alliances Work," *Fortune,* December 17, 1990, 121–123.

48. "P&G Squabbles with Vietnamese Partner," *Wall Street Journal,* February 27, 1998, A10.

49. "How Well Does Wal-Mart Travel?" *Business Week,* September 3, 2001, 82–84.

50. "Wal-Mart's European Beachhead," *International Herald Tribune,* March 13, 2001, 11.

51. "Could Your Job Go to China?" CNN.com, September 7, 2001.

52. "TI Teams Up in Asia," *Dallas Morning News,* February 4, 1996, H1.

53. "Herbal Remedies Aimed at East and West," *Wall Street Journal,* January 31, 2000, A26.

54. "Can TV Save the Planet?" *American Demographics,* May 1996, 43–47.

55. "Indian Company Thrives with Simple Marketing," *Wall Street Journal,* December 1, 2000, B19A.

56. "Kiddi Just Fine in the U.K., But Here It's Binky," *Marketing News*, August 28, 1995, 8.

57. Adam Sage, "McDonald's Rebrands Itself as 100 Percent Pure French," http://www.thetimes.co.uk, March 31, 2001.

58. Phred Dvorak, "Japanese Dairy Pours on the Apologies," *Wall Street Journal,* July 12, 2000, A21. Used with permission.

59. "Exxon Centralizes New Global Campaign," *Wall Street Journal,* July 11, 2001, B6.

60. Vijay Mahajan, Marcos V. Pratini de Moraes, and Jerry Wind, "The Invisible Global Market," *Marketing Management,* Winter 2000, 31–35.

61. Ilan Greenberg, "UPS Targets Logistics Business in Asia," *Wall Street Journal,* April 26, 2001, A12.

62. "Payment System Lets Customers Choose Currency," *Information Week,* April 2, 2001, 33.

63. "In Japan, The Hub of E-Commerce Is a 7-Eleven," *Wall Street Journal,* November 1, 1999, B1, B4.

64. "In Europe, Surfing a Web of Red Tape," *Wall Street Journal,* October 29, 1999, B1, B4.

65. "E-Commerce Discovers Europe," *International Herald Tribune,* December 24, 1999, 15.

66. "Europe Defines Itself against U.S. on the Internet," *Wall Street Journal,* April 2, 2001, B9E.

67. Roger Collis, "Savvy Trekkers Map Out Routes to Career Success," *International Herald Tribune,* August 17, 2001, 7.

CHAPTER 5

1. Paul Glader, "One Industry Is Booming in the Aftermath of Attacks," *Wall Street Journal*, November 7, 2001, B1; Brian Caulfield, Matthew Maier, Ryan Tate, and Owen Thomas, "The Tipping Point," *Business 2.0*, November 2001, 42; Allison Fass, "Agencies Tread Carefully in Messages to Consumers," *New York Times*, October 18, 2001; Rick Lyman, "This Season Fewer Soldiers March Onscreen," *New York Times*, October 16, 2001; Eryn Brown, "Just Another Product Launch," *Fortune*, November 12, 2001, 102; Joseph Pereira, "Toyland Sounds a Call to Arms," *Wall Street Journal*, November 7, 2001, B1; Timothy Aeppel, "Now Is the Time to Sell 'U.S.-Made,'" *Wall Street Journal*, October 22, 2001, B1; Patricia Callahan and Amy Merrick, "Greeting-Card Firms Hasten to Serve Nation's New Mood," *Wall Street Journal*, October 4, 2001, B4; David Handelman, "In Pensive Times, Comfort Magazines Find an Audience," *New York Times*, October 29, 2001; Shelly Branch, "Campbell's Soup Shipments Rise as Buyers Stock Pantries," *Wall Street Journal*, November 15, 2001, B4.

2. Michael Totty, "Information, Please," *Wall Street Journal*, October 29, 2001, R6.

3. Emily Nelson, "P&G Checks Out Real Life," *Wall Street Journal*, May 17, 2001, B1.

4. Nancy Ann Jeffrey and Sarah Collins, "The Grandparent Industry," *Wall Street Journal*, November 2, 2001, W1.

5. "A Leg Up," *Continental*, November 2001, 22.

6. Lee Gomes, "Download, Downshift and Go: MP3 Takes to the Road," *Wall Street Journal*, February 27, 2001, B1.

7. Suzanne Bidlake, "P&G to Roll Laundry Tablet in Europe," *Advertising Age,* March 1, 1999, 18.

8. Nancy Shepherdson, "New Kids on the Lot," *American Demographics,* January 2000.

9. Ronald Alsop, "Survey Rates Companies' Reputations, And Many Are Found Wanting," *Wall Street Journal*, February 7, 2001, B1. See also Gordon Fairclough, "Philip Morris Seeks to Mold Its Image into an Altria State," *Wall Street Journal*, November 16, 2001, A3.

10. Thomas E. Weber, "To Get Expert Advice about Digital Cameras, Check Out These Sites," *Wall Street Journal*, November 5, 2001, B1.

11. Ernest Beck, "Boosting Diageo's Sprits," *Wall Street Journal*, February 23, 2001, B1.

12. David P. Hamilton, "Not an Easy Sell: TiVo, ReplayTV and Other 'PVRs' Don't Take Off," *Wall Street Journal*, February 7, 2001, B1.

13. Emily Nelson, "Too Many Choices," *Wall Street Journal*, April 20, 2001, B1.

14. Ronald Alsop, "The Best Corporate Reputations in America: Johnson & Johnson (Think Babies!) Turns Up Tops," *Wall Street Journal*, September 23, 1999, B1. See also Alsop, "Survey Rates Companies' Reputations, And Many Are Found Wanting."

15. Princeton Research Survey Associates, "Consumer Behavior, Experiences and Attitudes: A Comparison by Age Groups," *AARP*, March 1999.

16. Frederic M. Biddle, "After Years of Disdain, Korean Cars Rev Up Sales," *Wall Street Journal*, August 18, 1999, B1, B4.

17. Michael Totty, "Making the Sale," *Wall Street Journal*, September 24, 2001, R6.

18. Stephanie Thompson, "Marketers Embrace Latest Health Claims," *Advertising Age,* February 28, 2000, 20–22.

19. Ibid. See also John Urquhart, "A Health Food Hits Big Time," *Wall Street Journal*, August 3, 1999, B1, B4.

20. Dean Bonham, "Hispanic Fans Make It to Big Leagues," *Rocky Mountain News*, June 23, 2001, 5C; Rodney Ho, "Radio One Deploys an Urban Beat to Make Revenue Jump," *Wall Street Journal*, November 16, 2001, B6; Jeffrey Ball, "Chrysler's Latest Ads for Minivans Stress Multicultural over Motherly," *Wall Street Journal*, December 18, 2001, B9.

21. Cathleen Egan, "Kellogg, General Mills Battle over Bars," *Wall Street Journal*, March 26, 2001, B10.

22. Bill Stoneman, "Beyond Rocking the Ages: An Interview with J. Walker Smith," *American Demographics*, May 1998, 44–49.

23. Pamela Paul, "Getting Inside Gen Y," *American Demographics*, September 2001, 42–49. See also Pooja Bhatia, "Look Who's Reading," *Wall Street Journal*, November 9, 2001, W1.

24. Miriam Jordan, "Global Craze for Diet Drugs," *Wall Street Journal*, August 24, 2001, B1. See also Leslie Chang, "Bring Science to Weight Loss in China," *Wall Street Journal*, August 24, 2001, B1.

25. Bill Spindle, "Cowboys and Samurai: The Japanizing of Universal," *Wall Street Journal*, March 22, 2001, B1.

26. Erla Zwingle, "A World Together," *National Geographic,* August 1999, 10–33; Hillary Mayell, "Death of the Mother Tongue," nationalgeographic.com/NEWS, February 25, 1999; Oliver Burkeman and Emma Brockes, "Trouble Brewing," *The Guardian,* December 3, 1999; "'Americanization' Fears Seem Misplaced," *Canberra Times,* October 24, 1999, 19; Swaminathan S. Ankleesaria Aiyar, "Does Globalisation Threaten Indian Culture?" *The Economic Times,* December 22, 1999; Naomi Klein, "The Tyranny of Brands," *Australian Financial Review,* February 11, 2000, 1; Sally Beatty and Carol Hymowitz, "How MTV Stays Tuned In to Teens," *Wall Street Journal,* March 21, 2000, B1, B4.

27. Joshua Harris Prager, "People with Disabilities Are Next Consumer Niche," *Wall Street Journal*, December 15, 1999, B1, B6.

28. Devon Spurgeon, "Hold the Oatmeal! Restaurants Now Court the Breakfast Burger Eater," *Wall Street Journal*, September 4, 2001, B1.

29. Eduardo Porter, "For Hispanic Marketers, Census Says It All," *Wall Street Journal*, April 24, 2001, B8. See also Bonham, "Hispanic Fans Make It to Big Leagues."

30. Heidi J. Shrager, "Closed-Circle Commerce," *Wall Street Journal*, November 19, 2001, B1.

31. Rebecca Piirto Heath, "Life on Easy Street," *American Demographics*, April 1997.

32. Elia Kacapyr, "Are You Middle Class?" *American Demographics*, October 1996.

33. Rebecca Piirto Heath, "The New Working Class," *American Demographics*, January 1998, 51–55.

34. Suein L. Hwang, "Dot-Coms Head Down-Market for Dollars," *Wall Street Journal*, July 16, 2001, B1.

35. Michael J. Weiss, "A Tale of Two Cheeses," *American Demographics*, February 1998, 16–17.

36. Bhatia, "Look Who's Reading."

37. Barbara Cooke, "Radar Fine-Tuned to 'Cool' Sets Some Teens Apart," *Chicago Tribune,* March 5, 2000, 1.

38. Erin White, "Abercrombie Seeks to Send Teeny-Boppers Packing," *Wall Street Journal*, August 30, 2001, B1.

39. Norihiko Shirouzu, "Japan's High-School Girls Excel in Art of Setting Trends," *Wall Street Journal*, April 24, 1998, B1, B6.

40. Matt Haig, "Teenage Clicks," *The Guardian*, October 25, 2001, 46.

41. Kortney Stringer, "Young and Restless," *Wall Street Journal*, September 24, 2001, R8; Nina Munk, "Peddling Cool: How Teens Buy," *Fortune*, April 13, 1998, 28–30.

42. Greg Winter, "States Try to Limit Sales of Junk Food in School Buildings," *New York Times,* September 9, 2001, 1; Betsy McKay, "Coke Finds Its Exclusive School Contracts Aren't So Easily Given Up," *Wall Street Journal,* June 26, 2001, B1; Randy Southerland, "Schools' Soda Deals Losing Fizz? Challenges Mount over Issues of Nutrition, Commercialization," *Atlanta Journal-Constitution,* September 26, 2001, JA1.

43. John Gaffney, "The Kids Are Doing It. Should You?" *Business 2.0*, November 2001, 141.

44. Jonathan Eig, "Edible Entertainment," *Wall Street Journal*, October 24, 2001, B1.

45. Janice Rosenberg, "Tweens Mesh Latest Fads, Moms & Dads," *Advertising Age*, February 14, 2000, 40.

46. Nancy Shepherdson, "New Kids on the Lot," *American Demographics*, January 2000.

47. Matthew Klein, "He Shops, She Shops," *American Demographics*, March 1998, 34–35.

48. Khanh T. L. Tran, "Women Assert Computer Games Aren't Male Preserve," *Wall Street Journal*, February 26, 2001, B1. See also Meeyoung Song, "Credit-Card Companies Cater to Korean Women," *Wall Street Journal*, June 6, 2001, B4.

49. Emily Nelson, "Forget Supermodels—Revlon's New Face Gets Lipstick on Her Teeth," *Wall Street Journal*, March 30, 2001, B1.

50. Wendy Bounds and Rebecca Quick, "Men Who Shop: Retailers Target Male Shoppers as Santa's New Helpers; Gift-Wrapping Tips for Guys," *Wall Street Journal*, November 12, 1999, W1, W4.

51. Diane Crispell, "Fruit of the Boom," *Marketing Tools*, April 1998.

52. Vanessa O'Connell and Jon E. Hilsenrath, "Advertisers Are Cautious as Household Makeup Shifts," *Wall Street Journal*, May 15, 2001, B1.

53. Anita Lienert, "A More Visible Altima," *Detroit News*, September 26, 2001, 01.

54. Lisa Vickery, Kelly Greene, Shelly Branch, and Emily Nelson, "Marketers Tweak Strategies as Age Groups Realign," *Wall Street Journal,* May 15, 2001, B1.

55. Nora J. Rifon and Molly Catherine Ziske, "Using Weight Loss Products: The Roles of Involvement, Self-Efficacy and Body Image," in *1995 AMA Educators' Proceedings,* ed. Barbara B. Stern and George M. Zinkhan (Chicago: American Marketing Association, 1995), 90–98.

56. Amy Merrick, "Counting on the Census," *Wall Street Journal,* February 14, 2001, B1.

57. Sarah Hall, "What Color Is Your Cart?" *Self,* September 1999, 150.

58. Jane L. Levere, "New Campaign for Ivory Soap," *New York Times* on-line, October 25, 2001.

59. Joshua Rosenbaum, "Guitar Maker Looks for a New Key," *Wall Street Journal,* February 11, 1998, B1, B5.

60. Elizabeth J. Wilson, "Using the Dollarmetric Scale to Establish the Just Meaningful Difference in Price," in *1987 AMA Educators' Proceedings,* ed. Susan Douglas et al. (Chicago: American Marketing Association, 1987), 107.

61. Sunil Gupta and Lee G. Cooper, "The Discounting of Discounts and Promotion Thresholds," *Journal of Consumer Research,* December 1992, pp. 401–411.

62. Mark Stiving and Russell S. Winer, "An Empirical Analysis of Price Endings with Scanner Data," *Journal of Consumer Research,* June 1997, 57–67. See also Robert M. Schindler and Patrick N. Kirby, "Patterns of Rightmost Digits Used in Advertised Price: Implications for Nine-Ending Effects," *Journal of Consumer Research,* September 1997, 192–201.

63. Sheila Muto, "What's in an Address? Sometimes, A Better Image," *Wall Street Journal,* September 5, 2001, B14.

64. Rhonda L. Rundle, "In Stores Now: Full Body Scans," *Wall Street Journal,* July 24, 2001, B1.

65. Stuart Elliot, "Growing Number of Airlines Resume Image Advertising," *New York Times* on-line, November 6, 2001.

66. Kevin Helliker, "How Hardy Are Upscale Gyms?" *Wall Street Journal,* February 9, 2001, B1.

67. Deborah Ball, "Despite Downturn, Japanese Are Still Having Fits for Luxury Goods," *Wall Street Journal,* April 24, 2001, B1.

68. Eryn Brown, "Just Another Product Launch," *Fortune,* November 12, 2001, 102.

69. Gene Del Vecchio, "Keeping It Timeless, Trendy: From Barbie to Pez, 'Ever-Cool' Kids Brands Meet Both Needs," *Advertising Age,* March 23, 1998, 24.

70. Chris Gaither, "Microsoft Explores a New Territory: Fun," *New York Times* on-line, November 4, 2001.

71. Steven Lipin, Brian Coleman, and Jeremy Mark, "Pick a Card: Visa, American Express, And MasterCard Vie in Overseas Strategies," *Wall Street Journal,* February 15, 1994, A1, A5.

72. Evan Ramstad, "Digital-Camera Makers Focus Their Attention on Printing," *Wall Street Journal,* February 8, 2001, B6.

73. Leila Jason, "Simple PCs Can Help Speed Elderly onto Net," *Wall Street Journal,* July 16, 2001, B5.

74. Jim Carlton, "Recycling Redefined," *Wall Street Journal,* March 6, 2001, B1.

75. Chang, "Bring Science to Weight Loss in China."

76. Jack Neff, "James River Puts Muscle Behind Dixie Paper Brand," *Advertising Age,* June 16, 1997, 22.

77. Miriam Jordan, "Debut of Rival Diet Colas in India Leaves a Bitter Taste," *Wall Street Journal,* July 21, 1999, B1, B4.

CHAPTER 6

1. Gregory L. White, "In Asia, GM Pins Its Hopes on Delicate Web of Alliances," *Wall Street Journal Interactive Edition,* October 23, 2001, on-line. Used with permission.

2. For a more thorough discussion of marketing on the Internet, see Chapter 19.

3. Ward Hanson, *Internet Marketing* (Cincinnati, OH: South-Western, 2000), 6.

4. "E-Procurement Could Save Trillions," *eMarketer,* December 18, 2001, on-line.

5. "Saluting Solutions," *eMarketer,* December 19, 2001, on-line.

6. Paul C. Judge, "How I Saved $100 Million on the Web," *Fast Company,* February 2001, 174–181.

7. Ibid.

8. Ibid.

9. Alex Frangos, "Just One Word: Plastics," *Wall Street Journal,* May 21, 2001, R20.

10. Ibid.

11. David Sims, "Bringing Online Help to the B2B World," *Customer Relationship Management,* August 2001, 32–36.

12. Fara Warner and Rick Brooks, "Ford Is Hiring UPS to Track Vehicles in Transit from Factories to Dealers," *Wall Street Journal Interactive Edition,* February 2, 2001, on-line.

13. Karen L. Lundegaard, "Online Exchange of Auto's Big Three Clears Final Hurdle," *Wall Street Journal,* September 27, 2000, B10.

14. Jocelyn Parker, "As Covisint Auto Market Materializes, Concerns Arise over Smaller Suppliers," *Wall Street Journal,* September 18, 2000, B18H.

15. Karby Leggett, "In Rural China, GM Sees a Frugal but Huge Market," *Wall Street Journal,* January 16, 2001, A1. Used with permission.

16. U.S. Census Bureau, "North American Industry Classification System (NAICS)—United States," http://www.census.gov/epcd/www/naics.html.

17. Mark Tatge, "Caterpillar's Truck Engine Sales May Skid amid High Inventories," *Wall Street Journal Interactive Edition,* March 13, 2000, on-line.

18. "Lockheed Wins JSF Contract," *Fort Worth Star-Telegram,* December 30, 2001, 6F.

19. http://www.lockheedmartin.com/about/ethics/code-of-ethics.html.

20. James W. Taylor, *The Marketing Strategy & Planning Workbook,* (South Nyack, NY: Wellington Press, 2000), 9.

CHAPTER 7

1. Thea Singer, "Little Clippers," *Inc.,* July 2001, 25–28. Used with permission.

2. Pamela Sebastian Ridge, "Chico's Scores with Its Nonjudgmental Sizes," *Wall Street Journal,* March 8, 2001, B1, B4.

3. Leslie Chang, "Bringing Science to Weight Loss in China," *Wall Street Journal,* August 21, 2001, B1, B7. Used with permission.

4. Nichole L. Torres, "It's Child's Play," *Entrepreneur,* December 2001, 24–26.

5. Kristina Feliciano, "The Kids Are Alright," *Consumer Magazines,* March 6, 2000, M8.

6. Anne D'Innocenzio, "Stores Are Catering to Tastes of Tweens," *Fort Worth Star Telegram,* September 5, 2000, 1C, 5C.

7. Torres, "It's Child's Play."

8. "Graying Boomers, Booming Teens," *Inc.,* May 15, 2001, 86–87.

9. Meg Jones, "Milking It," *Fort Worth Star Telegram,* October 29, 2001, 1F, 6F.

10. Lisa Vickery, Kelly Greene, Shelly Branch, and Emily Nelson, "Marketers Tweak Strategies as Age Groups Realign," *Wall Street Journal,* May 15, 2001, B1.

11. Ibid.

12. Dave Carpenter, "Fountain of Youth," *Fort Worth Star Telegram,* January 23, 2001, 1C, 10C.

13. Vickery, Greene, Branch, and Nelson, "Marketers Tweek Strategies."

14. "Mature Audience," *Business 2.0,* April 17, 2001, 59.

15. Kevin J. Clancy, "Getting Serious about Building Profitable Online Retail

Brands," *Arthur Andersen Retailing Issues Newsletter*, Center for Retailing Studies, Texas A&M University, 12:6, November 2000, 3.

16. Khanh T. L. Tran, "Women Assert Computer Games Aren't Male Preserve," *Wall Street Journal*, February 26, 2001, B1, B8.

17. Emily Nelson, "Beauty Makers Now Go Where the Boys Are," *Wall Street Journal*, August 10, 2000, B1, B4.

18. Erin White, "Teen Mags for Guys, Not Dolls," *Wall Street Journal*, August 10, 2000, B1, B4.

19. Ann Zimmerman, "Taking Aim at Costco, Sam's Club Marshals Diamonds and Pearls," *Wall Street Journal*, August 9, 2001, A1, A4.

20. Chuck Paustian, "Anybody Can Do It," *Marketing News*, March 26, 2001, 23.

21. Chris Rooney, "Ethnic Marketing: It's the Aspiration, Stupid," *Brandweek*, September 11, 2000, 44.

22. Paustian, "Anybody Can Do It."

23. Roger O. Crockett, "Attention Must Be Paid: The African American Web Community Is Swelling and Underserved," *Business Week*, February 7, 2000, EB16.

24. Eduardo Porter, "Why the Latino Market Is So Hard to Count," *Wall Street Journal*, October 13, 2000, B1, B4.

25. Dana James, "Lingua Franca: Human Touch Translates into Better Research of Hispanic Market," *Marketing News*, January 3, 2000, 17.

26. Sonia Reyes, "Hormel Takes Herdez North of Border w/$4M," *Brandweek*, February 12, 2001, 5.

27. Joel Millman, "U.S. Marketers Adopt Cinco de Mayo As National Fiesta," *Wall Street Journal*, May 1, 2001, B1, B4.

28. Eduardo Porter, "It's Not Easy to Bottle the Coolness and Heat of J. Lo's Decolletage," *Wall Street Journal*, August 9, 2001, A1, A6.

29. Vanessa O'Connell and Jon E. Hilsenrath, "Advertisers Are Cautious as Household Makeup Shifts," *Wall Street Journal*, May 15, 2001, B1, B4.

30. Ibid.

31. Alex Taylor III, "Porsche Slices Up Its Buyers," *Fortune*, January 16, 1995, 24.

32. Karen Benezra, "The Fragging of the American Mind," *Superbrands*, June 15, 1998, S12–19.

33. Beverly Bundy, "Central Market Says It Knows What You Want to Eat, Even If You Don't," *Fort Worth Star Telegram*, October 10, 2001, 1F, 2F.

34. Amy Merrick, "The 2000 Count: Counting on the Census—New Data Will Let Starbucks Plan Store Openings, Help Blockbuster Stock Its Videos," *Wall Street Journal*, February 14, 2001, B1.

35. "Downsizing Megamarkets: A Return to Mom-and-Pops?" *Firstlight*, March 2000, 22.

36. Jennifer Ordonez, "Cash Cows: Hamburger Joints Call Them 'Heavy Users'—But Not to Their Faces," *Wall Street Journal*, January 12, 2000, A1, A10.

37. David Armstrong, "Here's to the Net," *Wall Street Journal*, April 23, 2001, R30. Used with permission.

38. Ginger Cooper, "Centricity," *Customer Relationship Management*, December 2001, 35–40.

39. Dennis J. Chapman, "Clients, Customers and Buyers," *Customer Relationship Management*, March 2001, 65–71.

40. Anick Jesdanun, "AOL Gambit Works A-OK," *Fort Worth Star Telegram*, January 3, 2001, 1C, 3C.

41. Tricia Bisoux, "Niche Marketing Makes Its Mark," *Biz Ed*, November/December 2001, 45–47.

42. Lisa Bannon, "Let's Play Makeover Barbie," *Wall Street Journal*, February 17, 2000, B1, B4.

43. "Can Levi's Be Cool Again?" *Business Week*, March 13, 2000, 144, 148.

44. Kim T. Gordon, "Different Strokes," *Entrepreneur*, January 2002, 99.

45. Abbey Klaassen, "St. Joseph: From Babies to Boomers," *Advertising Age*, July 9, 2001, 1, 38.

46. Ian Johnson, "Herbal Remedies Aimed at East and West," *Wall Street Journal*, January 31, 2000, A26.

CHAPTER 8

1. Joseph Rydholm, "Preserving the Preservationists," *Quirk's Marketing Research Review,* March 2000, 18–19, 74–75. Reprinted by permission.

2. "Fantastic Voyage," *Fast Company,* March 2000, 178–200.

3. "Keebler Learns to Pay Attention to Research Right from the Start," *Marketing News*, March 11, 1996, 10.

4. "Why Some Customers Are More Equal Than Others," *Fortune*, September 19, 1994, 215–224.

5. Kendra Parker, "Got Questions? All You Have to Do Is Ask," *American Demographics*, November 1999, 36–39.

6. www.casro.org, October 29, 2001.

7. Eileen Moran, "Managing the Minefields of Global Product Development," *Quirk's Marketing Research Review,* November 2000, 24–28. Used with permission.

8. Molly Williams, "Monkey See," *Wall Street Journal*, April 23, 2001, R32. Used with permission.

9. Dana James, "The Future of Online Research," *Marketing News*, January 3, 2000, 1, 11.

10. Chris Yalonis, "The Revolution in E-research," *CASRO Journal*, 1999, 131–134.

11. Ibid.

12. Dana James, "Precision Decision," *Marketing News*, September 27, 1999, 23–24.

13. This section was adapted from James Watt, "Using the Internet for Quantitative Survey Research," *Quirk's Marketing Research Review*, June/July 1997, 67–71.

14. Carl McDaniel and Roger Gates, *Contemporary Marketing Research*, 5th ed. (Cincinnati: International Thomson Publishing, 2002).

15. Phone conversation between Kevin Bender, Information Resources, Inc., and Carl McDaniel on April 17, 2000.

16. Sheena Sharp, "New Techniques for Corporate Foresight," *Research Conference Report*, May 1998, 7–8.

CHAPTER 9

1. Stephanie Clifford, "The Grill of Their Dreams," *Business 2.0*, February 2002, 96. © 2002 Time Inc. All rights reserved.

2. "Oral-B Unveils Age-Pegged Toothbrushes for Kids," *BusinessWeek Online*, October 4, 2001. http://www.businessweek.com/reuters market/8/REUT-8KW.HTM.

3. "GM Isn't Giving Up on the Pontiac Aztec Yet," *WSJ.com*, November 27, 2001, http://interactive.wsj.com.

4. Teri Agins, "Hilfiger Returns to Preppy Roots, But Sales Slump," *Wall Street Journal*, February 2, 2001, B1, B6.

5. Christine Bittar, "Shiseido Rolls Color, Light and $7M in Major Cosmetic Repositioning," *Brandweek*, October 16, 2000, 6.

6. Sonia Reyes, "Minute Maid Juices Up Calcium Fortified Line," *Brandweek*, March 13, 2000, 323.

7. Mike Beirne, "Hershey Chews on Gum, Mint Plans; Jolly Rancher Eyes Preemptive Strike," *Brandweek*, February 26, 2001, 9.

8. Katrina Brooker, "A Game of Inches," *Fortune*, February 5, 2001, 98–100.

9. Betsy McKay, "Drinks for Developing Countries," *Wall Street Journal*, November 27, 2001, B1, B6. Used with permission.

10. Steve Jarvis, "Lesson Plans," *Marketing News*, June 18, 2001, 1, 9, 10.

11. Gerry Khermouch, Stanley Holmes, and Moon Ihlwan, "The Best Global Brands," *Business Week*, August 6, 2001, 50–57.

12. Brian O'Keefe, "Global Brands," *Fortune*, November 26, 2001, 102–110.

13. Fara Warner, "C'Mon, Get Closer," *Fast Company*, August 2001, 129–139.

14. Lauren Gold and Michael Gold, "Change the Rules of Private-Label Packaging," *Marketing News*, November 22, 1999, 20–21.

15. Peter Galuszka and Wendy Zellner, "Soap Opera at Wal-Mart," *Business Week*, August 16, 1999, 44.

16. Mike Beirne, "Hey, Partner: Ramada Joins AmEx, Continental in Big Co-Brand Push," *Brandweek*, November 13, 2000, 18.

17. Frederic M. Biddle, "American Express, Lexus in Co-Brand Pact," *Wall Street Journal,* February 9, 2000, B12.

18. Stephanie Thompson, "The Mouse in the Food Aisle," *Advertising Age*, September 10, 2001, 73.

19. James Heckman, "Trademarks Protected through New Cyber Act," *Marketing News*, January 3, 2000, 6.

20. Sonia Reyes, "Sunsweet Updates Look, Tells Families: 'Be Good,' " *Brandweek*, February 7, 2000, 10.

21. Jonathan Eig, "Food Companies Grab Kids' Attention by Packaging Products As Toys, Games," *WSJ.com*, October 26, 2001, http://interactive.wsj.com.

22. Kenneth Hein, "Miracle-Gro Seeds TV, Radio, Print; $20M Push Targets Spring Planters," *Brandweek*, February 12, 2001, 4.

23. Gerry Khermouch, "Guinness Pours It On in Chicago," *Brandweek*, February 28, 2000, 18.

24. Herbert M. Meyers, "The Internet's Threat to Branding," *Brandweek*, December 4, 2000, 30.

CHAPTER 10

1. William J. Holstein, "Daimler-Chrysler's Net Designs," *Business 2.0*, April 17, 2001, 26–28. © 2001 Time Inc. All rights reserved.

2. William J. Holstein, "Dump the Cookware," *Business 2.0*, May 1, 2001, 69–72.

3. Gary Strauss, "Squeezing New from Old," *USA Today*, January 4, 2000, B1, B2.

4. Sonia Reyes, "Groove Tube," *Brandweek*, October 16, 2000, M111.

5. David Koenig, "Product Adds Softer Touch to Tissue Issue," *Fort Worth Star-Telegram*, January 17, 2001, C1.

6. Strauss, "Squeezing New from Old," B1.

7. Gerry Khermouch, "Beefeater Gin Sets New Bottle, First Radio Ads on Renewal Drive," *Brandweek*, December 4, 2000, 17.

8. Strauss, "Squeezing New from Old," B2.

9. Gordon Fairclough, "A Potentially Less Toxic Cigarette Gets National Push," *Wall Street Journal*, November 5, 2001, B1, B4. Used with permission.

10. "Acquire a Taste for Lower Cholesterol," *Fort Worth Star-Telegram*, June 25, 2001, 3D.

11. Anna Muoio, "GM Has a New Model for Change," *Fortune*, December 2000, 62–64.

12. Alex Taylor III, "Kellogg Cranks Up Its Idea Machine," *Fortune*, July 5, 1999, 181–182.

13. Reyes, "Groove Tube," M114.

14. "Phytol Products Take Market Test," *Food Ingredients News*, August 2001, on-line.

15. Philip Brasher, "Teens Sample Milk from Vending Machines," *Fort Worth Star-Telegram*, April 5, 2001, 10A.

16. John Gaffney, "How Do You Feel about a $44 Tooth-Bleaching Kit?" *Business 2.0*, October 2001, 125–127.

17. Ibid.

18. Roy Attaway, "Man with the Plan," *Sea Ray Living*, Summer 2001, 46–52.

19. David W. Cravens, *Strategic Marketing*, 6e. (New York: Irwin McGraw-Hill, 2000) 235.

20. Gregory L. White, "How the Chevy Name Landed on SUV Using Russian Technology," *Wall Street Journal*, February 20, 2001, A1, A8.

21. Karby Leggett, "GM Confirms Plans to Produce Less Costly Buick for the Chinese," *Wall Street Journal*, October 24, 2000, A21.

22. Michael Flagg, "Coca-Cola Is Adopting Strategy in Asia of Inventing Drinks Tied to Local Tastes," *Wall Street Journal*, July 30, 2001, B9C.

23. Ibid.

24. Alessandra Galloni, "Coke to Launch Powerade Drink across Europe," *Wall Street Journal*, October 16, 2001, B11E.

25. James Daly, "Restart, Redo, Recharge," *Business 2.0*, May 1, 2001, 11.

26. Holstein, "DaimlerChrysler's Net Designs," 28.

CHAPTER 11

1. Chuck Salter, "On the Road Again," *Fast Company*, January 2002, 50–58. Used with permission.

2. Valarie A. Zeithaml and Mary Jo Bitner, *Services Marketing* (New York: McGraw-Hill, 2000).

3. Joel Milliman, "Services May Lead U.S. to Trade Surplus," *Wall Street Journal*, December 14, 2000, A1. Used with permission.

4. Christina Binkley, "From Orange Shag to Pin Stripes: Sheraton Gets a Makeover," *Wall Street Journal*, April 19, 2000, B1, B10.

5. Zeithaml and Bitner, *Services Marketing*.

6. Susan Greco, "Fanatics!" *Inc.*, April 2001, 35–48.

7. Luey McCauley, ed., "Unit of One," *Fast Company*, March 6, 2000, 104.

8. Zeithaml and Bitner, *Services Marketing*.

9. "Exceeding Customer Expectations," *Fortune*, March 6, 2000, S3.

10. Stacey L. Bell, "Puttin' on the Ritz," *Customer Relationship Management*, May 2001, 35–40.

11. Much of the material in this section is based on Christopher H. Lovelock, *Services Marketing* (Upper Saddle River, NJ: Prentice-Hall, 2001), 39–41.

12. Wendy Perrin, "Bells and Whistles," special business supplement 2000 to *Conde Nast Traveler*, 21–22.

13. Ibid.

14. Susan Kuchinskas, "Organic San Francisco," *IQnews*, February 14, 2000, 36.

15. Calmetta Coleman, "Banks Cozy Up to Customers," *Wall Street Journal*, April 26, 2001, B1, B4.

16. Lovelock, *Services Marketing*, 262–265.

17. Lovelock, *Services Marketing*, 149–150.

18. Much of the material in this section is based on Leonard L. Berry and A. Parasuraman, *Marketing Services*, (New York: Free Press, 1991), 132–150.

19. Sue Shellenberger, "To Win the Loyalty of Your Employees, Try a Softer Touch," *Wall Street Journal*, January 26, 2000, B1.

20. Berry and Parasuraman, *Marketing Services,* 151–152.

21. Kirsten Downey Grimsley, "At Your Service," *Fort Worth Star-Telegram*, March 1, 2000, C1.

22. Ellen Graham, "Marriott's Bid to Patch the Child-Care Gap Gets a Reality Check," *Wall Street Journal*, February 2, 2000, B1.

23. Joel Milliman, "Exporting Management Savvy," *Wall Street Journal*, October 24, 2000, B1, B18.

24. Ann Zimmerman, "Promotional Ties to Charitable Causes Help Stores Lure Customers," *Wall Street Journal*, December 4, 2000, B1, B4.

25. Joanne R. Halperin, "All for the Cause," *Business 2.0* On-line, October 24, 2000. © 2000 Time Inc. All rights reserved.

CHAPTER 12

1. Jeffery A. Tannenbaum, "Beverage Marketers See Refreshing Distribution Possibilities," *Wall Street Journal*, May 29, 2001, B2. Used with permission.

2. "Dell Seizes No. 1 Market Position in U.S. Corporate Desktop PC Sales," September 10, 1997, Dell Computer Corporation press release, http://www.dell.com.

3. Nicole Harris, " 'Private Exchanges' May Allow B-to-B Commerce to Thrive After All," *Wall Street Journal*, March 16, 2001, B1; Michael Totty, "The Next Phase," *Wall Street Journal*, May 21, 2001, R8.

4. Amy Merrick and Emily Nelson, "Sears Says Stores Won't Sell Makeup,

A Setback for Avon's New Line," *Wall Street Journal*, July 11, 2001, B1.

5. Gary McWilliams and Kortney Stringer, "Dell Tries Selling in Kiosks, On TV as PC Sales Drop," *Wall Street Journal*, December 20, 2001, B1.

6. Wade Lambert, "Publisher Puts Story Machines in London Tube," *Wall Street Journal*, February 22, 2001, B1.

7. Nick Wingfield, "Amazon Links with Circuit City to Boost Its Electronic Business," *Wall Street Journal*, August 21, 2001, B4; Wingfield and Amy Merrick, "Amazon Sets Citibank Deal, Expands Target Pact," *Wall Street Journal*, November 6, 2001, B8.

8. Matthew Schifrin, "Partner or Perish," *Forbes Best of the Web*, May 21, 2001, 26; Jonathan Eig, "H.J. Heinz, Japan's Kagome Agree to Investments as Part of Alliance," *Wall Street Journal*, July 26, 2001, B11.

9. Jonathan Welsh, "Auto Makers Now 'Slam' Cars Right in the Factory," *Wall Street Journal*, October 30, 2001, B1.

10. David Frederick Ross, *Competing Through Supply Chain Management: Creating Market-Winning Strategies Through Supply Chain Partnerships* (New York: Chapman & Hall, 1998), 9–12.

11. Matthew Boyle, "Supply Chains Get Sexy," *Fortune*, December 12, 2001, 272.

12. Owen Keates, "Flow Control," *Management*, March 2001, 28.

13. Rob Wherry, "Ice Cream Wars: Dreyer's Conquered Supermarket Freezers. Now It's Going After the Corner Store," *Forbes*, May 28, 2001, 160.

14. Karen Lundegaard, "Bumpy Ride," *Wall Street Journal*, May 21, 2001, R21.

15. Leigh Muzslay, "Shoes That Morph from Sneakers to Skates Are Flying Out of Stores," *Wall Street Journal*, July 26, 2001, B1.

16. Shelly Branch, "P&G Buys Iams: Will Pet-Food Fight Follow?" *Wall Street Journal*, August 12, 1999, B1, B4.

17. Evan Ramstad, "Inside Radio Shack's Surprising Turnaround," *Wall Street Journal*, June 8, 1999, B1, B16.

18. Daniel Machalba, "High-speed Grain Terminals Bode Change for Rural U.S.," *Wall Street Journal*, December 26, 2001, B2.

19. G. Bruce Knecht, "Independent Bookstores Are Suing Borders Group and Barnes & Noble," *Wall Street Journal*, March 19, 1998, B10.

20. Leslie Kaufman, "Luxury's Old Guard, Battered by New Realities," *New York Times* on-line, December 16, 2001.

21. Ellen Neuborne, "Big Brands (Small Companies)," *Business Week*, August 13, 2001, 12.

22. Laura M. Holson, "Military Contractors Set to Begin Rare Experiment in Cooperation," *New York Times* on-line, December 17, 2001.

23. Faith Keenan, "The Marines Learn New Tactics—From Wal-Mart," *Business Week*, December 24, 2001, 74.

24. Norihiko Shirouzu, "Fickle Consumers Force Auto Makers to Be More Flexible," *Wall Street Journal*, September 10, 2001, B8.

25. Carlita Vitzthum, "Just-in-Time Fashion," *Wall Street Journal*, May 18, 2001, B1; Julie Creswell, "Confessions of a Fashion Victim," *Fortune*, December 10, 2001, 48.

26. Thomas A. Foster, "3PL's Serve Up Supply Chain Innovation," *Logistics Management & Distribution Report*, November 1999.

27. Nick Wingfield, "In the Beginning . . . ," *Wall Street Journal*, May 21, 2001, R18.

28. Stephanie Strom, "A Brighter Holiday (If the Goods Hold Out)," *New York Times* on-line, December 9, 2001.

29. Ross, *Competing Through Supply Chain Management*, 232.

30. Russ Dixon, "Tomorrow's Warehouse," *Snack Food & Wholesale Bakery*, May 2000, TD10.

31. Anna Wilde Mathews, "Cargo in Ships Offers Clues to What Will Go under Tree," *Wall Street Journal*, August 6, 1997, B1.

32. Greg Ip, "As Security Worries Intensify, Companies See Efficiencies Erode," *Wall Street Journal*, October 24, 2001, A1.

33. James Aaron Cooke, "Clicks and Mortar," *Logistics Management & Distribution Report*, January 31, 2000.

34. James Aaron Cooke, "Making the Global Connection," *Logistics Management & Distribution Report*, June 1999.

35. Caitlin Kelly, "Rolling Onward," *Supply Chain Management* on-line, September 30, 2001.

36. Renee Boucher Ferguson, "Outsourcing Supply Chains," *eWeek*, April 2, 2001, 17.

37. "Ford Hands Off Vehicle Delivery to Third Party," *Logistics Management & Distribution Report*, March 2000.

38. Michael Selz, "Outsourcing Firms Venture Beyond Primary Functions," *Wall Street Journal*, June 26, 2001, B2.

39. Don Clark, "Canceled Programs: Software Is Becoming an Online Service, Shaking Up an Industry," *Wall Street Journal*, July 21, 1999, A1, A6.

40. George Anders, "Ebay, E-Stamp in Tie-Up to Market Online Postage," *Wall Street Journal*, January 12, 2000, B6.

41. Rhonda L. Rundle, "New Battlefield for E-Tickets: Home Printers," *Wall Street Journal*, February 17, 2000, B1, B4; Bruce Orwall, "Six Theater Chains Will Join in Venture to Sell Movie Tickets via Web, Phone," *Wall Street Journal*, March 3, 2000, B4.

42. Martin Peers, "Video on Demand Arrives—Sort Of," *Wall Street Journal*, January 29, 2001, B1.

43. Nick Wingfield, "Digital Video Recorders Stir Up a New Battle," *Wall Street Journal*, December 17, 2001, B4; Jon Healy, "Studios Spur Measures to Thwart Digital Piracy," *Los Angeles Times*, January 18, 2002, C1; Amy Harmon, "A Wave of Video Piracy," *San Diego Union-Tribune*, February 11, 2002; Scott Wooley, "Steal This Movie," *Forbes*, February 18, 2001, 66.

44. Ken Bensinger, "Can You Spot the Fake?" *Wall Street Journal*, February 16, 2001, W1; Todd Zaun and Karby Leggett, "Motorcycle Makers from Japan Discover Piracy Made in China," *Wall Street Journal*, July 25, 2001, A1.

45. Alejandro Reyes, "Against a World of Giants," *AsiaWeek* wire report, February 2, 2001; Todd Zaun and Karby Leggett, "Motorcycle Makers from Japan Discover Piracy Made in China," *Wall Street Journal*, July 25, 2001, A1; "Meeting of the Minds," *Supply Chain Management Review* on-line, September 30, 2001; Andrew Tanzer, "Chinese Walls," *Forbes*, November 12, 2001, 74.

46. Louis Uchitelle, "Globalization Marches On, As U.S. Eases Up on the Reins," *New York Times* on-line, December 17, 2001.

47. Jon E. Hilsenrath, "Globalization Persists in Precarious New Age," *Wall Street Journal*, December 31, 2001, A1.

48. Kevin Hogan, "Borderline Savings," *Business 2.0*, May 17, 2001, 34. © 2001 Time Inc. All rights reserved.

49. Richard Gibson, "Merchants Mull the Long and the Short of Lines," *Wall Street Journal*, September 3, 1998, B1, B4.

50. Neal Templin, "Electronic Kiosks Check In Guests at More Hotels," *Wall Street Journal*, February 16, 1999, B1, B4.

51. Martha Brannigan, "Cruise Lines Go Online—To Tout Travel Agents," *Wall Street Journal*, August 23, 2001, B1.

52. Deborah Lohse, "Allstate Plans Direct Insurance Sales by Phone, Internet," *Wall Street Journal*, November 11, 1999, B12

53. Patrick Barta, "Home Rules," *Wall Street Journal*, October 29, 2001, R12.

54. Chuck Martin, "Oprah Fans Scoop Up Graeter's," *Cincinnati Enquirer*, June 4, 2002, on-line.

CHAPTER 13

1. Vivian Chu, "Hip Goods, Enticing Stores: How Target Beat Kmart," *Reuters* on-line, February 4, 2002; Lee Clifford, "Getting Malled," *Fortune*, December 10, 2001, 114; Alice Z. Cuneo,

"On Target," *Advertising Age*, December 11, 2000; http://www.target.com.

2. Karen J. Sack, "Massive Retail Industry Propels U.S. Economy," *Standard & Poor's Industry Surveys*, November 25, 1999, 5.

3. U.S. Census Bureau, Monthly Retail Trade Report, 2001.

4. David Schulz, "The Nation's Biggest Retail Companies," *Stores* on-line, July 1, 2001.

5. Ibid.

6. David Schultz, "The Definitive Ranking of the Nation's Biggest Specialty Chains," *Stores* on-line, August 2001.

7. Pamela Sebastian Ridge, "Chico's Scores Big with Its 'Nonjudgmental' Sizes," *Wall Street Journal*, March 8, 2001, B1.

8. Leigh Gallagher, "Rebound," *Forbes*, May 3, 1999, 60.

9. Maureen C. Carini, "Retailing: Supermarkets and Drugstores," *Standard & Poor's Industry Surveys*, vol. 166, no. 14, sec. 1, April 2, 1998, 12–13.

10. Joel A. Baglole, "Loblaw Supermarkets Add Fitness Clubs to Offerings," *Wall Street Journal*, December 27, 1999, B4.

11. Alexei Barrionuevo and Ann Zimmerman, "Lastest Supermarket Special —Gasoline," *Wall Street Journal*, April 30, 2001, B1.

12. Carini, "Retailing," 13.

13. Matt Nannery, "Pigging Out," *Chain Store Age*, July 1999, 77.

14. Carini, "Retailing," 12.

15. Wal-Mart Web site, http://www.walmart.com.

16. Emily Nelson, "Overhauling Its Web Site, Wal-Mart Will Push Toys and Electronics," *Wall Street Journal*, October 1, 1999, B1, B4.

17. Schulz, "The Nation's Biggest Retail Companies."

18. Tony Lisanti, "Extreme Segment, Extreme Growth," *Discount Store News*, July 26, 1999, 13.

19. Company News Release, "Toys "R" Us Reports Fourth Quarter and 2000 Fiscal Year Results," March 7, 2001.

20. Ann Zimmerman, "Taking Aim at Costco, Sam's Club Marshals Diamonds and Pearls," *Wall Street Journal*, August 9, 2001, A1.

21. Ray A. Smith, "Outlet Centers Go Upmarket with Amenities," *Wall Street Journal*, June 6, 2001, B12.

22. National Restaurant Association, "Industry at a Glance," January 24, 2002.

23. Eatzi's Market and Bakery Web site at http://www.eatzis.com.

24. Rodney Ho, "Vending Machines Make Change," *Wall Street Journal*, July 7, 1999, B1, B4.

25. Cathleen Egan, "Vending-Machine Technology Matures, Offering Branded Foods, Convenience," *Wall Street Journal*, December 13, 2001, B13.

26. Ibid.; Dow Jones Newswire, "Pepsi Plans to Launch New Vending Machines That Take Credit Cards," December 13, 2001.

27. Nigel Powell, "PC Salesmen Go Door to Door," *The Times* (London), July 16, 1997, 6; "Reaching Out to Small-Town USA: Move Over Amway, PC Sales Firm Hand Technologies Adds Hi-Tech Touch," *South China Morning Post*, May 12, 1998, 8; Barbara Carton, "PCs Replace Lettuce Tubs at Sales Parties," *Wall Street Journal*, March 26, 1997, B1; "Hand Technologies: Background Information," *M2 Presswire*, May 2, 1997; Chad Kaydo, "Are PCs Like Tupperware? *Sales & Marketing Management*, June 1998, 20.

28. Elizabeth Lee, "Parties That Sell," *Atlanta Journal-Constitution*, September 6, 2001, BE12.

29. Dennis Berman, "Is the Bell Tolling for Door-to-Door Selling? *Business Week*, November 1, 1999. 58–60; Rachel Beck, "Amway Puts Direct Selling Model Online," *Marketing News*, March 29, 1999, 12.

30. Amy Lo, "Selling Dreams the Mary Kay Way," *AsiaWeek*, June 29, 2001.

31. Dell Computer Web site, http://www.dell.com/us/en/gen/corporate.

32. QVC Web site, http://www.qvc.com.

33. The Online Group of the National Retail Federation's Web site, http://www.shop.org/learn/stats.

34. Ibid.

35. CDNow Web site, http://www.CDNow.com.

36. Amazon.com Web site, http://www.Amazon.com.

37. The Online Group of the National Retail Federation Web site, http://www.shop.org; Ernst & Young press release, "Despite Dot.com Woes, On-line Retailing Growth in 2000 Confirmed by New Ernst & Young Global Study," *Business Wire*, January 15, 2002; "Amazon.com: The First Global Cyber-Brand," *Ernst & Young Global Online Retail Report* at Stores on-line, January 2000, 24; Amazon.com press release, "Amazon.com Announces 4th Quarter Profit," www.Amazon.com, January 22, 2002.

38. Timothy Henderson, "Multi-Channel Retailers Increasingly Rely on Internet-Based Kiosk to Bridge Gap Between Channels," *Stores* on-line, October 1, 2001.

39. Alexandra Peers and Nick Wingfield, "Sotheby's, eBay Team Up to Sell Fine Art Online," *Wall Street Journal*, January 31, 2002, B8.

40. McDonald's Corporation, Inside the U.S. Franchising Fact Sheet, http://www.mcdonalds.com/corporate/franchise/inside/factsheet/factsheet.html.

41. International Franchise Association Web site, http://www.franchise.org.

42. Domino's Pizza Web site, http://www.dominos.com/Franchise.

43. Brian O'Keefe, "Global Brands," *Fortune*, November 26, 2001, 104.

44. Louise Lee, "Gap: Missing That Ol' Mickey Magic," *Business Week*, October 29, 2001, 86–88.

45. Michael Totty, "Making the Sale," *Wall Street Journal*, September 24, 2001, R6.

46. Rebecca Quick, "Ann Taylor Gets Its Groove Back," *Wall Street Journal*, February 16, 1999, B1, B4.

47. Patrick McGuire, "The Analytics Divide," *Stores* on-line, October 2001.

48. Eleena De Lisser, "Online Retailers Slice and Dice Niches Thinner Than Julienne Fries," *Wall Street Journal*, November 29, 1999, B1, B6.

49. "An Exclusive Club," *Chain Store Age*, October 1998.

50. Jack Neff, "Wal-Mart Stores Go Private (Label)," *Advertising Age*, November 29, 1999, 1, 34–38; Emily Nelson, "For Wal-Mart, A Soap War Looms against Mighty P&G," *Wall Street Journal*, August 6, 1999, B1, B3.

51. Alice Z. Cuneo, "On Target," *Advertising Age*, December 11, 2000, 1.

52. Dean Starkman, "Mall Developers Envision Shopping Paradise, And It's Called Las Vegas," *Wall Street Journal*, July 11, 2001, B1.

53. Dean Starkman, "The Mall, Without the Haul," *Wall Street Journal*, July 25, 2001, B1.

54. Calmetta Y. Coleman, "Making Malls (Gasp!) Convenient," *Wall Street Journal*, February 8, 2000, B1, B4.

55. Anne Faircloth, "Value Retailers Go Dollar for Dollar," *Fortune*, July 6, 1998, 164–166.

56. Calmetta Cloeman, "Kohl's Retail Racetrack," *Wall Street Journal*, March 13, 2001, B1.

57. Emily Nelson, "Why Wal-Mart Sings, 'Yes, We Have Bananas!'" *Wall Street Journal*, October 6, 1998, B1, B4.

58. James Lardner, "Branching Out," *Business 2.0*, November 2001, 137.

59. Kate Murphy, "A Sales Pitch Right Under Your Nose," *New York Times*, September 13, 1998, 8.

60. "Playful Touches Dress Up the Box," *Chain Store Age*, June 1998, 110–111.

61. Chad Terhune, "Home Depot's Home Improvement," *Wall Street Journal*, March 8, 2001, B1.

62. Totty, "Making the Sale," *Wall Street Journal*, November 24, 2001, R6.

63. Timothy P. Henderson, "Perception That Some Merchants Practice Racial Profiling Generates Debate," *Stores* on-line, June 2001; Tanya Eiserer, "A Question of Security," *Fort Worth Star-Telegram*, October 28, 2001, 1;

Associated Press Newswires, "Protesters Rally outside Store Where Accused Shoplifter Died," *Associated Press*, online, February 18, 2001.

64. John C. Koopman, "Successful Global Retailers: A Rare Breed," *Canadian Manager*, Spring 2000, 22.

65. Teri Agins, "Brooks Brothers Wines, Dines Potential New Customers," *Wall Street Journal*, September 7, 2001, B4; Agins, "Trunk Show Chic," *Wall Street Journal*, February 5, 2001, B1.

66. "More Consumers Shopping at Super Centers," *Chain Store Age* online, February 4, 2002.

67. Susan Reda, "On-line Retail Grows Up," *Stores on-line*, February 2002.

68. Jack Neff, "Dawn of the Online Icebox," *Advertising Age*, March 15, 1999, 7.

CHAPTER 14

1. Dale Buss, "The British Are Coming!" *Sales & Marketing Management*, August 2001, 32–40; Verne Gray, "Newsstand Seductress," *Brandweek*, October 23, 2000, M80; Jill Feiwell and Bill Higgins, "Maxim Maxed," *Daily Variety*, August 14, 2000, 20; http://www.maximonline.com.

2. Jack Neff, "Male Mystique Rises a Degree," *Advertising Age*, December 31, 2001, 3.

3. Frank Witsil, "Spam I Am," *Tampa Tribune*, February 9, 2002, 1; Frances Katz, "Putting the Lid on SPAM: Almost Everybody Hates the Kudzu of E-mail, But There's No Magic Formula," *Atlanta Journal and Constitution*, August 5, 2001, Q1; "Privacy Action," *Advertising Age*, October 15, 2001, 14; Donna Gillin, "Privacy Issues Take Center Stage in 2001," *Marketing Research*, Spring 2001, 36; William M. Savino and Stephen J. Smirti, Jr., "Privacy Please!" *Marketing Management*, Winter 2000, 46.

4. Sally Beatty, "HBO Marches into Battle," *Wall Street Journal*, July 18, 2001, B1, B4; "Brothers Roll Out," *Broadcasting & Cable*, September 17, 2001, 24.

5. Stephanie Thompson, "Marketers Embrace Latest Health Claims," *Advertising Age*, February 28, 2000, 20–22.

6. Ibid.

7. "Promo Shorts," *Marketing Magazine*, September 3, 2001, P4.

8. "Showering in the Streets," *Marketing Magazine*, May 21, 2001, 1.

9. Frank G. Bingham, Jr., Charles J. Quigley, Jr., and Elaine M. Notarantonio, "The Use of Communication Style in a Buyer–Seller Dyad: Improving Buyer–Seller Relationships," Proceedings: Association of Marketing Theory and Practice, 1996 Annual Meeting,

Hilton Head, South Carolina, March 1996, 188–195.

10. Michael Beverland, "Relationship Selling and the Selling Dyad," *Journal of Personal Selling & Sales Management*, Summer 2001, 207.

11. Karen Raugust, "Marketing 1000: Nestlé Crunch," *Advertising Age*, October 8, 2001, S10–S30.

12. Philip J. Kitchen, "Marketing Communications Renaissance," *Internal Journal of Advertising*, 12 (1993), 367–386.

13. Amy Shipley, "Extreme Winter Games: Olympics Targeting a Younger Audience," *Washington Post*, November 25, 2001, A01.

14. Ibid.

15. Kitchen, "Marketing Communications Renaissance," 372.

16. Kellie Searle, "The Brown Trucks Are Coming! The Brown Trucks Are Coming! UPS Joins the Global Revolution," *Sales, Advertising & Marketing*, November 1, 2001, http://www.sammag.com; Allyson L. Stewart-Allen, "Sense of Identity Crucial for Fast Food Worldwide," *Marketing News*, November 19, 2001, 12; Thomas T. Semon, "Cutting Corners in Language Risky Business," *Marketing News*, 9; Thomas J. Madden, Kelly H. Hewett, and Martin S. Roth, "Managing Images in Different Cultures: A Cross-National Study of Color Meanings and Preferences," *Journal of International MKT*, vol. 8, no. 4, 2000; Yumiko Ono, "U.S. Superstores Find Japanese Are a Hard Sell," *Wall Street Journal*, February 14, 2000, B1, B4.

17. The AIDA concept is based on the classic research of E. K. Strong, Jr., as theorized in *The Psychology of Selling and Advertising* (New York: McGraw-Hill, 1925) and "Theories of Selling," *Journal of Applied Psychology*, 9 (1925), 75–86.

18. Thomas E. Barry and Daniel J. Howard, "A Review and Critique of the Hierarchy of Effects in Advertising," *International Journal of Advertising* 9 (1990), 121–135.

19. Kim Cleland, "Marketing 1000: Poo-Chi," *Advertising Age*, October 8, 2001, S10–S30.

20. "New Loyalty Program Earns 'Grocery Miles,' " *MMR*, May 8, 2000, 58.

21. Sandra Dolbow, "BriteSmile Sinks Its Teeth into $20M Push," *Brandweek*, December 17, 2001, 6.

22. Hilary Chura "Marketing 1000: Smirnoff Ice," *Advertising Age*, October 8, 2001, S10–S30.

23. Bill Adams, "Talking about Integrated Communications," *Public Relations Tactics*, February 2001, 26.

24. Brad Zeller, "Lord of the Rings Redux," *Publishers Weekly*, September 10, 2001, 23, used with permission;

J. D. Andrews, "The Lord of the Onion Rings: Burger King Is Offering Magical Premiums to Hungry Fellowship Fans," *Point of Purchase*, December 2001, 6.

25. Lynne Eagle, Philip Kitchen, Ken Hyde, Wina Fourie, and Mani Padisetti, "Perceptions of Integrated Marketing Communications among Marketers and Ad Agency Executives in New Zealand," *International Journal of Advertising*, February 1999, 79–94.

CHAPTER 15

1. Kenneth Hein, "A Bull's Market," *Brandweek*, May 28, 2001, 21; Hein, "Red Bull Charges Ahead," *Brandweek*, October 15, 2001, M38; Rebecca Flass and Jack Feuer, "Red Bull Hands Media to Lunch, Its Creative Shop," *Adweek Western Edition*, September 10, 2001, 5; "Turn Up the Juice," *Drug Store News*, July 23, 2001, 37; Hillary Chura, "Grabbing Bull by Tail," *Advertising Age*, June 11, 2001, 4; David Noonan and Kevin Peraino, "Red Bull's Good Buzz," *Newsweek*, May 14, 2001, 39.

2. "Domestic Advertising Spending by Medium," *Advertising Age*, September 24, 2001, s12.

3. U.S. Department of Commerce. Bureau of the Census, *Statistical Abstract of the United States* (Washington DC: Government Printing Office, December 2000), 420.

4. "2000 Advertising-to-Sales Ratios for the 200 Largest Ad Spending Industries," *Advertising Age*, July 24, 2000, 44.

5. Tom Reichert, "Sexy Ads Target Young Adults," *USA Today Magazine*, May 2001, 50.

6. Amitava Chattaopadhyay and Kunal Basu, "Humor in Advertising: The Moderating Role of Prior Brand Evaluation," *Journal of Marketing Research*, November 1990, 466–476.

7. Rajiv Grover and V. Srinivasan, "Evaluating the Multiple Effects of Retail Promotions on Brand Loyalty and Brand Switching Segments," *Journal of Marketing Research*, February 1992, 76–89; see also S. P. Raj, "The Effects of Advertising on High and Low Loyalty Consumer Segments," *Journal of Consumer Research*, June 1982, 77–89.

8. David Goetzl, "Boeing Ads Focus on Space-Based Image," *Advertising Age*, May 1, 2000, 76.

9. Trevor Jensen and Scott Bryan, "Boeing Looks to Tomorrow," *Adweek Eastern Edition*, July 23, 2001, 2.

10. "Philip Morris Says It's Sorry for Death Report," *Wall Street Journal*, July 26, 2001, B1, B6.

11. Tobi Elkin, "Microsoft to Focus on Experience," *Advertising Age*, February 26, 2001, 26.

12. Tobi Elkin, "Window XP's $200 Million Launch Kicks Off," *AdAge.com*, October 11, 2001.

13. Louise Kramer, "As Sales Flatten, Top Pizza Chains Turn Up the Heat," *Advertising Age*, February 23, 1998, 4.

14. Louise Kramer, "Papa John's New Salvo Intensifies Pizza Battle," *Advertising Age*, September 27, 1999, 3.

15. Amy Merrick, "Target and Kmart Both Claim Victory in Spat over Ads," *Wall Street Journal,* September 4, 2001, B6.

16. Maryann Napoli, *Health Facts*, October 2001, 2.

17. Sebastian Rupley, "No False Ads," *PC Magazine*, July 3, 2001, 64.

18. www.adageglobal.com, "Absolut Vodka Must Pull Campaign in Italy," February 2, 2001.

19. www.adageglobal.com, "Yahoo! Korea Complains about Comparative Ads," September 21, 2001.

20. Fahad S. Al-Olyan and Kiran Karade, *Journal of Advertising*, Fall 2000, 69.

21. "Rainmakers," *Advertising Age's Creativity*, October 2001, 14.

22. Reprinted with permission from "The Best Awards," *Advertising Age*, May 28, 2001, s2. Copyright Crain Communications, Inc., 2001.

23. Betsy McKay, "Sports Drinks Refresh Rivalry for Coke, Pepsi," *Wall Street Journal*, May 8, 2001, B1, B4.

24. Barbara Lippert, "Power Trips," *Adweek Eastern Edition*, September 3, 2001, 18.

25. Laura Q. Hughes and Wendy Davis, "Revival of the Fittest," *Advertising Age*, March 12, 2001, 18–19.

26. Marc G. Weinberger, Harlan Spotts, Leland Campbell, and Amy L. Parsons, "The Use and Effect of Advertising Media," *Journal of Advertising Research*, May/June, 1995, 44–56.

27. Mike Beirne, "Can Your Beer Do This?" *Brandweek*, October 15, 2001, M50.

28. Suzanne Vranica, "Focus Groups Favor Nostalgic Messages," *Wall Street Journal*, October 10, 2001, B6.

29. Roger Thurow, "Shtick Ball: In Global Drive, Nike Finds Its Brash Ways Don't Always Pay Off," *Wall Street Journal*, May 5, 1997, A1, A10.

30. Johnny K. Johansson, "The Sense of 'Nonsense': Japanese TV Advertising," *Journal of Advertising*, March 1994, 17–26.

31. Russell Abratt and Deanna Cowan, "Client Agency Perspectives of Information Needs for Media Planning," *Journal of Advertising Research*, November 1999, 37.

32. "Domestic Advertising Spending by Medium," *Advertising Age*, September 25, 2000, s12.

33. "Domestic Advertising Spending by Media," *Advertising Age,* September 25, 2000, s4.

34. "Radio: No Longer an Advertising Afterthought," *Standard & Poor's Industry Surveys*, July 20, 1995, M36; Rebecca Piirto, "Why Radio Thrives," *American Demographics*, May 1994, 40–46.

35. Edmund O. Lawler, "B-to-B Skewed Cable Now Mainstream Buy," *Advertising Age*, May 7, 2001, 32.

36. Wayne Friedman, "TV Networks' New Reality," *Advertising Age*, September 24, 2001, 1, 70.

37. Wayne Friedman, "Second Down," *Advertising Age*, September 3, 2001, 3.

38. Jim Edwards, "The Art of the Infomercial," *Brandweek*, September 3, 2001, 14.

39. Barbara Martinez, "City Sight: Giant Ads Spring from Holes in the Ground," *Wall Street Journal*, August 18, 1999, B1, B10.

40. "Top 10 Advertising Categories in 2000," Outdoor Advertising Association of America.

41. Kate Fitzgerald, "Out of Home," *Advertising Age*, July 9, 2001, s1, s4.

42. *Absolut Collectors Society Newsletter* issue 237, July 31, 2000.

43. "Internet Advertising Revenue Holds Steady As All Ad Sectors Decline," http://www.iab.com, December 4, 2001.

44. Jennifer Rewick, "Brand Awareness Fuels Strategies for Online Advertisers Next Year," *Wall Street Journal*, December 28, 2000, B2.

45. Ibid.

46. Vanessa O'Connell, "Looking Beyond Banners to Revive Web Advertising," *Wall Street Journal*, February 26, 2001, B1, B12.

47. Jack Neff, "Floors in Stores Start Moving," *Advertising Age,* August 20, 2001, 15.

48. Cara Beardi, "Video Venue Joins the Line for Gas-Pump Advertising," *Advertising Age*, April 23, 2001, 8.

49. Suzanne Vranica, "Think Graffiti Is All That's Hanging in Subway Tunnels? Look Again," *Wall Street Journal*, April 4, 2001, B1, B4.

50. Suzy Bashford, "Sorry Ladies, This Bit of Scots Beef Is Already Taken," *Marketing*, November 1, 2001, 56; Maryann Lorusso, "Sex and Sensibility," *Footwear News*, June 11, 2001, 6; Barbara Lippert, "Kinky R Us," *Adweek*, April 2, 2001, 20; David Hakala, "Mind Your Manners, Ad Writers," *Sm@rt Partner*, March 19, 2001; Michael Miller, "The Ploy of Sex," *Pittsburgh Business Times*, April 28, 2001, 22; Tom Reichert, "Sexy Ads Target Young Adults," *USA Today Magazine*, May 2001, 50; Lauren Booth, "I Have Become Lynda Lee-Potter, Reactionary and Scared of a Little Innuendo," *New Statesman*, July 16, 2001, 63; Alessandra Galloni, "Clampdown on 'Porno-Chic' Ads Is Pushed by French Authorities," *Wall Street Journal*, October 25, 2001, B4; Hillary Chura, "Spirited Sex," *Advertising Age*, July 9, 2001, 1.

51. Sara Teasdale, "Study Challenges Three-Plus Viewing Rule," *Business Marketing*, December 1995, 5; Hugh M. Cannon and Edward A. Riordan, "Effective Reach and Frequency: Does It Really Make Sense?" *Journal of Advertising Research*, March 1994, 19.

52. Cannon and Riordan, "Effective Reach and Frequency," 19; Erwin Ephron, "A New Media-Mix Strategy: As Advertisers Eye Obvious Decline of TV, Agencies Expand Options," *Advertising Age*, February 28, 2000, s10.

53. Kate Lynch and Horst Stripp, "Examination of Qualitative Viewing Factors for Optimal Advertising Strategies," *Journal of Advertising Research*, May 1999, 7.

54. Sally Beatty, "Ogilvy's TV-Ad Study Stresses 'Holding Power' Instead of Ratings," *Wall Street Journal*, June 4, 1999, B2.

55. Chuck Ross, "Study Finds Continuity vs. Flights," *Advertising Age*, April 19, 1999, B2.

56. Erwin Ephron, "Recency Planning: A New Media Approach," *Advertising Age*, July 1, 1999, 21.

57. Nicholas Maiesse, " 'Blair Witch' Casts Its Spell," *Advertising Age*, March 20, 2000, s8; Nancy Coltun Webster "The Marketing 100: 'The Blair Witch Project' Amorette, Jones," *Advertising Age*, June 26, 2000, s22.

58. Jean Sherman Chatzky, "Whose Name Here? It Seems No Event Is Too Personal to Have a Corporate Sponsor," *Money*, October 1, 2001, 196.

59. James R. Hagerty, "Krispy Kreme at a Krossroads," *Wall Street Journal*, February 24, 2000, B1, B4.

60. Melanie Wells, "Who Really Needs Madison Avenue?" *Forbes*, October 29, 2001, 131.

61. "The Bulgari Connection," *Natural Life*, November/December 2001, 22.

62. Teri Agins, "Armani Touts Urban Chic with 'Shaft,' " *Wall Street Journal*, June 19, 2000, 16.

63. Kate Fitzgerald, "It's the Wheel Thing," *Advertising Age*, November 15, 1999, 30.

64. Laura Petrecca, "Defying Gravity: NBC, Petersen Connect with Cynical Teens via Sports Fest," *Advertising Age*, October 11, 1999, 36–40.

65. Peter Wonacott, "Chinese TV Discovers Product Placement," *Wall Street Journal*, January 26, 2000, B12, used with permission; Normandy Madden, "Sponsors Follow Twists of Chinese Soap Operas," *Advertising Age International*, January 1, 2000, 9.

66. Kate Fitzgerald, "Maui Comes To the Mall," *Advertising Age*, February 7, 2000, 30–32.

67. "Modernista! Adds Avon, to Unveil Holiday Gap Ads" *Adweek*, November 12, 2001, 32.

68. Michael Jay Polonsky, "Reevaluating Green Marketing: A Strategic Approach," *Business Horizons*, September/October 2001, 21.

69. Kathleen Cholewka, "The 5 Best E-Marketing Campaigns," *Sales & Marketing Management,* January 2001, 53.

70. Ibid.

71. Maxine Lans Retsky, "More Steps to Avoid McDonald's Situation,*" Marketing News*, November 19, 2001, 11.

72. Bruce Orwall and Nancy Keates, "Disney Ship's Maiden Voyage Delayed Again," *Wall Street Journal*, February 19, 1998, B1, B12.

73. George Anders, "eBay to Refund Millions after Outrage," *Wall Street Journal*, June 14, 1999, B8; George Anders, "eBay Scrambles to Repair Image after Big Crash," *Wall Street Journal*, June 14, 1999, B1, B4.

CHAPTER 16

1. Andy Cohen, "Is This Guy for Real?" *Sales & Marketing Management*, May 2001, 36–45; John Helyar, "A Team of Their Own," *Fortune*, May 14, 2001, 190; Devin Gordon, "A True Maverick," *Newsweek*, April 23, 2001, 52; Richard Hoffer, "Pro Basketball: Dallas Maverick Iconoclastic Dotcom Billionaire Mark Cuban Thought It Might Be a Lot of Fun to Own an NBA Franchise," *Sports Illustrated*, November 6, 2000, 80.

2. "2001 Annual Report: Industry Report 2001," *PROMO Magazine*.

3. "Merger and Acquisition Activity Impacts Coupon Promotion Volume, Study Finds," *The Food Institute Report*, March 5, 2001, 4.

4. "2001 Annual Report: Industry Report 2001."

5. Shelly Branch, "Crooner May Find New Audience in Barter Deal with Earth's Best," *Wall Street Journal*, January 25, 2001, B9.

6. Anne Kandra, "Bait and Rebate," *PC World*, September 2001, 45.

7. "Right Up Their Alley; McDonald's, Toys 'R' Us Share a Holiday Happy Meal," *PROMO Magazine*, December 1, 2001, 11.

8. Mark Lacek, "Loyalty Marketing No Ad Budget Threat," *Advertising Age*, October 23, 1995, 20.

9. Ginger Conlon, "True Romance," *Sales & Marketing Management*, May 1996, 85–90.

10. Liz Mullen, "NBA Teams Reward Fans with Loyalty Programs," *Washington Business Journal*, December 10, 1999, 22.

11. Amanda Beeler, "Heady Rewards for Loyalty: Cars, Trips and Hot Tickets Expand Offerings Beyond Store Merchandise for Retailers in Touch with Rich," *Advertising Age*, August 14, 2000, S8.

12. Vincent Alonzo, "Money Isn't Everything," *Sales & Marketing Management*, April 2000, 47–48.

13. "HGTV, Sears, Join Forces for House Giveaways," *Advertising Age*, February 7, 2000, 30.

14. "2001 Annual Report: Industry Report 2001."

15. Lafayette Jones, "Ethnic Product Sampling: The Hidden Opportunity," *Retail Merchandiser*, August 2001, 45.

16. Stephanie Fagnani, "A Taste of Success: The Practice of Product Sampling Combines Favorable Location, Product Innovation, Thorough Promotion and Timely Execution," *Supermarket News*, August 27, 2001, 33.

17. Stephanie Thompson, "Ben & Jerry's Goes Alternative with New Effort: Marketer Sticks to Its Grassroots Via Print, Radio," *Advertising Age*, May 8, 2000, 111.

18. Andy Cohen, "A Marketing Touchdown," *Sales & Marketing Management*, October 2001, 16.

19. Geoffrey A. Fowler, "When Free Samples Become Saviors," *Wall Street Journal*, August 14, 2001, B1, B4.

20. "Point-of-Purchase: $17 Billion," *PROMO Magazine,* October 29, 2001, 3.

21. Erin Strout, "Doctoring Sales," *Sales & Marketing Management*, May 2001, 53–60; Joseph P. Shapiro and Stacey Schultz, "Prescriptions: How Your Doctor Makes the Choice," *U.S. News & World Report*, February 19, 2001, 58; Bill Brubaker, "Drug Firms Still Lavish Pricey Gifts on Doctors; Ethics Debated as Freebies Flow," *Washington Post*, January 19, 2002, E01; Ed Susman, "U.S. Doctors Touchy on Topic of Pharmaceutical Gifts," *Medical Post,* July 17, 2001.

22. "MasterCard Unwraps Priceless Holiday Prizes," *PROMO Xtra,* November 5, 2001, 22.

23. Dean Takahashi, "Sega Will Give Away Dreamcast Players to Lure Subscribers to the Web," *Wall Street Journal*, April 4, 2000, B1, B4.

24. Roger O. Crocket, "Penny-Pinchers' Paradise," *Business Week*, January 22, 2001, EB12.

25. Deborah Cohen, "Burger King First to Serve Up Hamburger Miles," *Reuters Business Report*, January 13, 2002, 1.

26. Libby Estell, "Economic Incentives," *Sales & Marketing Management*, October 2001, S2–S4.

27. Ben Chapman, "The Trade Show Must Go On," *Sales & Marketing Management*, June 2001, 22.

28. Elana Harris, "Standing Tall," *Sales & Marketing Management*, December 2000, 84.

29. Michael Beverland, "Contextual Influences and the Adoption and Practice of Relationship Selling in a Business-to-Business Setting: An Exploratory Study," *Journal of Personal Selling & Sales Management*, Summer 2001, 207.

30. Richard Morrison, *"*The Business Process of Customer Retention and Loyalty," C*ustomer Interaction Solutions*, October 2001, 4.

31. "The Right Questions and Attitudes Can Beef Up Your Sales, Improve Customer Retention," *Selling*, June 2001, 3.

32. Andy Cohen, "Copy Cats," *Sales & Marketing Management*, August 2000, 50–58.

33. Erika Rasmusson, "How to Manage Long Term Leads," *Sales & Marketing Management*, January 1998, 77.

34. Roger Brooksbank, "The New Model of Personal Selling: Micro-Marketing," *Journal of Personal Selling & Sales Management*, Spring 1995, 61–66; Donald W. Jackson, Jr., "Relationship Selling: The Personalization of Relationship Marketing," *Asia-Australia Marketing Journal*, August 1994, 45–54.

35. Jean Halliday, "Ford Finds E-Leads Productive," *Advertising Age*, January 22, 2001, 28.

36. Sarah Lorge, "The Best Way to Prospect," *Sales & Marketing Management*, January 1988, 80; Tricia Campbell, "What's a Referral Worth to You?" *Sales & Marketing Management*, September 1997, 103.

37. Alf Nucifora, "Need Leads? Try a Networking Group," *Business News New Jersey*, November 14, 2000, 22.

38. Mike Grebb, "The Customer Connection: Living Up to Your Sales Pitch," http://www.sammag.com, March 1, 2001.

39. "Leads Are a Terrible Thing to Waste," *Sales & Marketing Management,* August 1997, 108; Center for Strategic Communication.

40. Marvin A. Jolson and Thomas R. Wortruba, "Selling and Sales Management in Action: Prospecting: A New Look at This Old Challenge," *Journal of Personal Selling & Sales Management*, Fall 1992, 59–66.

41. Janelle Rice, "Show and Sell: Filling the Sales Manager's Shoes," *Sales,* http://www.sammag.com, July 2001.

42. Robyn Griggs, "Qualifying Leads Online," *Sales & Marketing Management*, July 1997, 68.

43. Marvin A. Jolson, "Broadening the Scope of Relationship Selling," *Journal of Personal Selling and Sales Management,* Fall 1997, 75.

44. Adapted from Bob Kimball, *Successful Selling* (Chicago: American Marketing Association, 1994).

45. "Five Steps to Wrapping Up a Sales Call," *Sales & Marketing Management,* January 1998, 75.
46. Jolson, "Broadening the Scope of Relationship Selling."
47. Gina DeLapa, "Something to Write Home About," *Sales & Marketing Management,* December 2000, 33–34.
48. Scott Cressman, "Eight Tips for Highly Effective Presentations," *Sales,* http://www.sammag.com, May 1, 2001.
49. Colleen Cooper, "Overcoming Last Minute Objections," *Sales & Marketing Management,* March 1997, 32; Sarah Lorge, "How to Close a Deal," *Sales & Marketing Management,* April 1998, 84.
50. Cooper, "Overcoming Last Minute Objections."
51. Michelle Marchetti, "Hey Buddy, Can You Spare $113.25?" *Sales & Marketing Management,* August 1997, 69–77.
52. Cliff Ennico, "Cynical? Insecure? Ruthless? You're Hired. Essential Characteristics for Sales Success," http://www.sammag.com, May 1, 2001.
53. "Can Your Reps Sell Overseas?" *Sales & Marketing Management,* February 1998, 110.
54. David Garfinkel, "The E-Vangelist: Autoresponse Marketing," *Sales & Marketing Management,* May 2001, 27.
55. Andy Cohen, "Global Dos and Don'ts," *Sales & Marketing Management,* June 1996, 72; Esmond D. Smith, Jr., and Cuong Pham, "Doing Business in Vietnam: A Cultural Guide," *Business Horizons,* May/June 1996, 47–51; "Five Tips for International Handshaking," *Sales & Marketing Management,* July 1997, 90, from Dorothea Johnson, director of The Protocol School of Washington; Tricia Campbell, "What to Give Overseas," *Sales & Marketing Management,* September 1997, 85; "Negotiating: Getting to Yes, Chinese-Style," *Sales & Marketing Management,* July 1996, 44–45; Michelle Marchetti, "Selling in China? Go Slowly," *Sales & Marketing Management,* January 1997, 35–36; Sergey Frank, "Global Negotiating: Vive Les Différences!" *Sales & Marketing Management,* May 1992, 64–69.
56. Andy Cohen, "The Traits of Great Sales Forces," *Sales & Marketing Management,* October 2000, 67–72.
57. "Reorganizing a Sales Force: How DoubleClick Aligns Its Salespeople with Its Customers," *Sales & Marketing Management,* March 2000, 90.
58. Erika Rasmusson, "The 10 Traits of Top Salespeople," *Sales & Marketing Management,* August 1999, 34–37.
59. "America's 25 Best Sales Forces: Best at Sales Training," *Sales & Marketing Management,* July 2000, 68.
60. Gabriel Landriault, "In Class, Online," *Computing Canada,* March 1, 2001, 11.

61. Arun Sharma, Customer Satisfaction–Based Incentive Systems: Some Managerial and Salesperson Considerations," *Journal of Personal Selling & Sales Management,* April 1997, 61.
62. Cohen, "The Traits of Great Sales Forces."
63. Cliff Ennico, "Ideas@work: Thanks for Your Service, Now Go Away," http://www.sammag.com, May 1, 2001.
64. Libby Estelle, "Rewarding and Improving Performance Motivate Employees and Customers to Grab the Brass Ring," *Sales & Marketing Management,* October 2001, S1–S4.
65. James Champy, "Waiting for Change," *Sales & Marketing Management,* August 2001, 30.
66. Kathleen Cholewka, "E-Market Stats," *Sales & Marketing Management,* September 2001, 21.
67. Brent Keltner, "Just Another Channel?" *Sales & Marketing Management,* January 2000, 23–34.
68. Ginger Conlon, "No Turning Back," *Sales & Marketing Management,* December 1999, 50–55.
69. Keltner, 23–34; Brent Keltner, "Harnessing the Internet's Potential," *Sales & Marketing Management,* February 2000, 29.

CHAPTER 17

1. Christopher T. Heun, "Log Me On to the Ball Game—For a Price," *Informationweek.com,* April 2, 2001, 33. Used with permission.
2. "Cost-Conscious Shoppers Seek Secondhand," *USA Today,* March 14, 1996, B1.
3. "Retailers Are Giving Profits Away," *American Demographics,* June 1994, 14.
4. "DaimlerChrysler's Freightliner Puts New Chief at the Wheel," *Wall Street Journal,* May 29, 2001, B4.
5. "India's Mobile Users Hit 4.5 Million," *CNN.com,* September 19, 2001.
6. "Financing Deals for New Cars Shake Up Market for Used Cars," *Wall Street Journal,* November 16, 2001, B1, B4.
7. Ramarao Desuaju and Steven Shugan, "Strategic Service Pricing and Yield Management," *Journal of Marketing,* January 1999, 44–56.
8. Michael Mendano, "Priced to Perfection," *Business2.com,* March 6, 2001, 40–41.
9. "Your Room Costs $250 . . . No! $200 . . . No," *Wall Street Journal,* May 5, 1999, B1, B16.
10. Gordon Fairclough, "Governments Can Be Addicted to Cigarettes," *Wall Street Journal,* October 2, 2000, A1. Used with permission.
11. "The Common Good," *The Economist,* December 2, 2001. © 2001 The Economist Newspaper Ltd. All rights reserved. Reprinted with permission.

Further reproduction prohibited. www.economist.com
12. David Henderson, "What Are Price Wars Good For? Absolutely Nothing," *Fortune,* May 12, 1997, 156.
13. See Joseph Cannon and Christian Homburg, "Buyer-Supplier Relationships and Customer Firm Costs," *Journal of Marketing,* January 2001, 29–43.
14. Most of this section is taken from: David Hamilton, "The Price Isn't Right," *Wall Street Journal,* February 12, 2001, R8, R10. Used with permission.
15. Ibid.
16. Ibid.
17. Ibid.
18. Gary Hamel, "Edison's Curse," *Fortune,* March 5, 2001, 175–178. See also Florian Zettlemeyer, "Expanding to the Internet: Pricing and Communications Strategies When Firms Compete on Multiple Channels," *Journal of Marketing Research,* August 2000, 292–308; and Subir Bandyopadhyay, Guang Bo Lin, and Yan Zhong, "Under the Gavel," *Marketing Management,* November/December 2001, 25–28.
19. "Price Buster," *Wall Street Journal,* July 17, 2000, R12.
20. "Value Driven," *Fortune,* May 1, 2000, 74.
21. Cindy Waxer, "When Price Takes a Back Seat," *Business2.com,* June 26, 2001, 37.
22. "Stores' Demands Squeeze Apparel Companies," *Wall Street Journal,* July 15, 1997, B1, B12; Timothy Matanovich, Gary Lilien, and Arvind Rangaswamy, "Engineering the Price-Value Relationship," *Marketing Management,* Spring 1999, 48–53.
23. Praveen Kopalle and Donald Lehmann, "The Effects of Advertised and Observed Quality on Expectations about New Product Quality," *Journal of Marketing Research,* August 1995, 280–290; Akshay Rao and Kent Monroe, "The Effect of Price, Brand Name, and Store Name on Buyers' Perceptions of Product Quality: An Integrative Review," *Journal of Marketing Research,* August 1989, 351–357; Gerard Tellis and Gary Gaeth, "Best Value, Price-Seeking, and Price Aversion: The Impact of Information and Learning on Consumer Choices," *Journal of Marketing,* April 1990, 34–35; Dawar Niraj and Phillip Parker, "Marketing Universals: Consumers' Use of Brand Name, Price, Physical Appearance, and Retailer Reputation as Signals of Product Quality," *Journal of Marketing,* April 1994, 81–95; and R. Chandrashekaran, "The Implications of Individual Differences in Reference to Price Utilization for Designing Effective Price Communications," *Journal of Business Research,* August 2001, 85–92.

24. William Dodds, Kent Monroe, and Dhruv Grewal, "Effects of Price, Brand, and Store Information on Buyers' Product Evaluations," *Journal of Marketing Research*, August 1991, 307–319. See also Akshay Rao and Wanda Sieben, "The Effect of Prior Knowledge on Price Acceptability and the Type of Information Examined," *Journal of Consumer Research*, September 1992, 256–270; Ajay Kalra and Ronald Goldman, "The Impact of Advertising Positioning Strategies on Consumer Price Sensitivity," *Journal of Marketing Research*, May 1998, 210–224.

25. Phillip Parker, "Sweet Lemons: Illusory Quality, Self-Deceivers, Advertising, and Price," *Journal of Marketing Research*, August 1995, 291–307; Michael Etgar and Naresh Malhotra, "Determinants of Price Dependency: Personal and Perceptual Factors," *Journal of Consumer Research*, September 1981, 217–222; Jeen-Su Lim and Richard Olshavsky, "Impacts of Consumers' Familiarity and Product Class on Price-Quality Inference and Product Evaluations," *Quarterly Journal of Business and Economics,* Summer 1988, 130–141.

26. Donald Lichtenstein and Scott Burton, "The Relationship between Perceived and Objective Price—Quality," *Journal of Marketing Research*, November 1989, 429–443.

27. "Store-Brand Pricing Has to Be Just Right," *Wall Street Journal*, February 14, 1992, B1. See also George Cressman, Jr., "Snatching Defeat from the Jaws of Victory," *Marketing Management*, Summer 1997, 9–19.

28. Merrie Brucks, Valarie Zeithaml, and Gillian Naylor, "Price and Brand Name as Indicators of Quality Dimensions for Consumer Durables," *Journal of the Academy of Marketing Science*, Summer 2000, 359–374.

CHAPTER 18

1. J. William Gurley, "Above the Crowd: Why Dell's War Isn't Dumb," *Fortune*, July 9, 2001, 134–136. © 2001 Time Inc. All rights reserved.
2. Kent Monroe and Jennifer Cox, "Pricing Practices That Endanger Profits," *Marketing Management*, September/October 2001, 42–46.
3. "Building a Better Mousetrap Is No Claptrap," *Business Week*, February 1, 1999, 47.
4. "Take Me Out to the Ballgame, James," *Business Week*, March 13, 2000, 142.
5. Daniel Michaels, "No-Frills Irish Airline Flies High," *Wall Street Journal*, September 6, 2000, B1, B4. Used with permission.

6. "Jury Convicts Ex-Executives in ADM Case," *Wall Street Journal*, September 18, 1998, A3, A4.
7. "Justice's Cartel Crackdown," *Business Week*, July 27, 1998, 30–32.
8. "Five Paint Firms Are Scrutinized for Price Fixing," *Wall Street Journal*, June 4, 2001, A4.
9. "Sotheby's Chief Is Convicted of Price-Fixing," *Wall Street Journal*, December 6, 2001, B1, B4.
10. Dan Carney, "Predatory Pricing: Cleared for Takeoff," *Business Week*, May 14, 2001, 50.
11. "States Square Off against Drug Firms in Crusade on Prices," *Wall Street Journal*, December 7, 2001, A1, A13.
12. Ibid.
13. Kusum L. Ailawadi, Donald Lehmann, and Scott Neslin, "Market Response to a Major Policy Change in the Marketing Mix: Learning from Procter & Gamble's Value Price Strategy," *Journal of Marketing*, January 2001, 44–61. See also Kusum L. Ailawadi, Scott Neslin, and Karen Gedenk, "Pursuing the Value-Conscious Consumer: Store Brands versus National Brand Promotions," *Journal of Marketing*, January 2001, 71–89; Kissan Joseph, "On the Optimality of Delegating Pricing Authority to the Sales Force," *Journal of Marketing*, January 2001, 62–70.
14. Joel Urbany, "Are Your Prices Too Low?" *Harvard Business Review,* October 2001, 26–27.
15. Jane Costello, "$27.98 Airfare to Paris, China? United: 'Oops,'" *Wall Street Journal*, February 15, 2001, B1, B14. Used with permission.
16. Charles Quigley and Elaine Notarantonio, "An Exploratory Investigation of Perceptions of Odd and Even Pricing," in *Developments in Marketing Science*, ed. Victoria Crittenden (Miami: Academy of Marketing Science, 1992), 306–309.
17. "Nine Cents of Separation," *American Demographics*, May 1998, 41.
18. "Three-for-$3 and Other Numerical Pitches Work Magic in Stores," *Wall Street Journal*, March 12, 1998, A1. See also Herman Simon and Robert Dolan, "Price Customization," *Marketing Management*, Fall 1998, 11–17; and Margaret Campbell, "Perceptions of Price Unfairness: Antecedents and Consequences," *Journal of Marketing Research*, May 1999, 187–199.
19. Francis Mulhern and Robert Leone, "Implicit Price Bundling of Retail Products: A Multiproduct Approach to Maximizing Store Profitability," *Journal of Marketing*, October 1991, 63–76; Dorothy Paun, "Product Bundling: A Normative Model Based on an Orientation Perspective," in *Developments in Marketing Science*, ed. Victoria Crittenden (Miami: Academy of

Marketing Science, 1992), 301–305; Manjit Yadav and Kent Monroe, "How Buyers Perceive Savings in a Bundle Price: An Examination of a Bundle's Transaction Value," *Journal of Marketing Research*, August 1993, 350–358; R. Venkatesh and Vijay Mahajan, "A Probabilistic Approach to Pricing a Bundle of Services," *Journal of Marketing Research*, November 1993, 509–521; Asim Ansari, S. Siddarth, and Charles Weinberg, "Pricing a Bundle of Products or Services: The Case of Nonprofits," *Journal of Marketing Research*, February 1996, 86–93; Francis Mulhern, Jerome Williams, and Robert Leone, "Those with More Buy Less," *American Demographics*, April 1999, 18–20.
20. "Why Bundling Its Consumer Services Hasn't Benefited AT&T," *Wall Street Journal*, October 24, 2000, B1, B4.
21. Dilip Soman and John Gourville, "Transaction Decoupling: How Price Bundling Affects the Decision to Consume," *Journal of Marketing Research*, February 2001, 30–44.
22. Vicki Morwitz, Eric Greenleaf, and Eric Johnson, "Divide and Prosper: Consumers' Reactions to Partitioned Prices," *Journal of Marketing Research*, November 1998, 453–463.
23. This material on price penalties is from Eugene Fram and Michael McCarthy, "The True Price of Penalties," *Marketing Management*, Fall 1999, 49–54.
24. "Ask and It Shall Be Discounted," *Business Week*, October 6, 1997, 116–118.
25. "Marketers Try to Ease Sting of Price Increases," *Marketing News*, October 9, 1995, 5.
26. "Value Strategy to Battle Recession," *Advertising Age*, January 7, 1991, 1, 44.
27. "Brand X No Longer Plan B for Shoppers," *Dallas Morning News*, July 14, 2001, 3F.
28. Ibid.
29. "Going, Going, Gone," *Business Week*, April 12, 1999, 30.
30. "What a Deal," *Fast Company*, November 1998, 298.

CHAPTER 20

1. Student Advantage, Inc. Annual Report (SEC Form 10-k), April 2, 2001; Student Advantage Corporate Profile, http://www.ir.studentadvantage.com; Seth Fienberg, "An Interview with Ray Sozzi, CEO, Student Advantage," January 13, 2000, http://www.channelseven.com; Student Advantage, Inc. Annual Report (SEC Form 10-k), April 2, 2002; Mary Hildebrand, "Student Advantage Adds Five New Retail Partners," *E- Commerce Times*, September 9, 1999, 45.

2. Joseph Hair, Robert Bush, and David Ortinau, *Marketing Research: Within a Changing Information Environment,* 2nd ed. (Burr Ridge, IL: McGraw-Hill/Irwin, 2002) 128.

3. Louis Chunovic, "Digital Cable, Satellite Studies Target Churn," *Electronic Media,* February 18, 2002, 4.

4. Thomas Hicks, "Establishing and Maintaining Customer Relationships," *SGB,* August 23, 2000, 9.

5. Sara Fraser, "Many Retailers Cannot Identify Most Valuable Customers," *Customer Interface,* March 2002, 17. See also "Blue Martini Software Demonstrates Integration with Point of Sale Devices at National Retail Federation Show," *PR Newswire,* January 14, 2002.

6. Clinton Wilder, "Squeaky Wheel Drives Innovation," *InformationWeek,* December 11, 2000.

7. "Chrysler to Unveil New PT Cruiser," *Associated Press,* On-line, March 27, 2002, http://www.ptcruiserforum.com/pressrelease/press-03-27-2002.

8. Kenneth Cramer and Jason Dedrick, "Dell Computers: Organization of a Global Production Network," *Center for Research on Information Technology and Organizations*, 2001, http://www.crito.uci.edu/git/publications/pdf/dell.pdf.

9. Scott Rosenburg, "Brilliant Careers: Steve Jobs," *Salon,* January 5, 1999, http://www.salon.com/bc/1999/01/cov-05bc.html.

10. Robert Slater, *Jack Welch and the GE Way,* (New York: McGraw-Hill, 1998); Slater, *Get Better or Get Beaten* (New York: McGraw-Hill, 2001).

11. An interesting interpretation of the Safe Harbor can be found at http://www.atw%cv.the-dma.org/library/privacy/safeharbor5.shtml. Additional information on privacy can be found at http://www.privacy.org and http://www.privacyexchange.org.

12. "Heading to the Border: Borders Books and Music Celebrates Three Decades of Prosperity Thanks to Its Successful Retailing Recipe," *Shopping Center World*, December 1, 2001, http://www.scwonline.com.

13. "Ralph's Supermarkets to Offer Club Card Members Webmiles Rewards through Southern California," March 20, 2001, http://www.webmiles.com.

14. Ibid.

15. Sean Doherty, "Keeping Data Private," *Network Computing,* June 25, 2001, 83.

16. "Attorney General Files Motion to Prevent Bankrupt Company from Selling Customer Information," *M2 Presswire,* December 17, 2001.

17. "North Dakota Voters Reject Referendum to Allow Banks to Sell Customer Information without Written Permission," *Mondaq Business Briefing,* June 27, 2002.

18. "Group 1 and iWay Software Partner to Enhance Enterprise Wide Data Quality and Customer Data Integration," Press release: iWay Software, January 15, 2002.

19. Larry Stevens, "CRM by the Slice: Running Analytics Is Expensive, So Companies Are Focusing on Areas with Customers," *Internetweek,* April 3, 2001, http://www.internetweek.com/indepth01/indepth040301.

20. "American Airlines Web Site Features Atg Online CRM Offering" Press release from American Airlines. http://industry.java.sun.com/javanews/stories/story2. May 15, 2002; "Strategic Directions: Staying Ahead of the Curve, Closing the CRM Loop" CIO White Paper Library, November 15, 2000, http://www.cio.com/sponsors/1100crm; "American Airlines Redesigns Its Web Site." May 16, 2002, http://www.m-travel.com/20516.shtm; Brett Bush, "American Airlines: Flying High with Advantages." February 2, 1998, http://www.digitrends.net/marketing/13641_8661.htm.

21. Ibid.

22. Ross Sleight, "Being Aware of Your Customer's True Value," *New Media Age,* March 7, 2002, 20.

23. *Jennifer Maselli,* "Citigroup Follows the Money—Financial-Services Company Adopts Xchange CRM to Target Its Most-Profitable Customers," *InformationWeek,* November 12, 2001, 87.

24. "Carrier Relies on Ascential Data Integration Software to Enhance Product Quality," *Businesswire,* February 4, 2002.

25. Ibid.

26. Carol Krol, "Data Warehouse Generates Surprise Leads for Camelot," *Advertising Age,* January 4, 1999, 20; Todd Wasserman, Gerry Khermouch, and Jeff Green, "Minding Everyone's Business," *Brandweek,* February 28, 2000, 32.

27. "AvantGo Introduces Mobile Application Built Specifically for Pharmaceutical Sales," *Business Wire,* March 4, 2002.

28. "Card Members to Receive Double Membership Rewards for Charges in Metro Atlanta Restaurants," June 4, 1996, http://www.cardtrack.com; "American Express to Run Rewards Program," *Digitrend,* January 31, 2000, http://www.digitrend.com.

29. Curt Hall, "The Move to Real-Time Data Warehousing and Business Intelligence," May 22, 2001, http://www.cutter.com/consortium/research; "D+B and Netegrity Forge Strategic Alliance to Minimize Risk in E-Business Transactions," Press release: Netegrity, Inc., March 18, 2002.

30. http://www.Ediets.com/programs.

31. http://www.Reflect.com.

32. PSS World Medical, Inc. Quarterly Report (SEC Form 10q), February 11, 2002

33. http://www.Ediets.com/programs.

34. http://www.kidsdadsmoms.com

35. http://www.schoolkidz.com

36. Jeff Sweat, "CRM Migration," *InformationWeek,* May 21, 2001, 57–64. Used with permission.

CHAPTER 21

1. Stewart Alsop, "I'm Betting on Amazon.com," *Fortune* online, April 20, 2001; Alex Frangos, "Here's My Advice. . . ," *Wall Street Journal*, January 14, 2002, R15; Company press release, "Amazon.com Announces 4th Quarter Profit," Amazon.com, January 22, 2002; company Web site, Amazon.com/About Amazon.com.

2. Susan Fournier, Susan Dobscha and David Glen Mick, "Preventing the Premature Death of Relationship Marketing," *Harvard Business Review,* January/February 1998, 2–8.

3. Gerri Knilans, "Database Marketing: Fad, Fantasy or Reality?" *Direct Marketing,* May 1997, 48.

4. J. Walker Smith, "Marketing with Attitude," *Marketing Management*, January/February 2002, 48.

5. Evantheia Schibsted, "Say Goodbye to Mass Selling: Designer Products: Personalized Product Marketing the Net's New Frontier," *National Post*, April 2, 2001, E2.

6. Carol Krol, "Cayman Visits AmEx," *Advertising Age*, February 15, 1999, 18; Krol, "Case Study: Mead Johnson Finds Winning Formula for Reaching Moms," *Advertising Age*, April 26, 1999, 25; Christina Binkley, "Marriott to Give Additional Perks to Frequent Guests," *Wall Street Journal*, April 25, 2000, B15; Jennifer Lach, "Data Mining Digs In," *American Demographics*, July 1999.

7. Todd Wasserman, Gerry Khermouch, Jeff Green, "Minding Everyone's Business," *Brandweek,* February 28, 2000, 32.

8. Fournier, Doscha, and Mick.

9. Don Peppers, "Banking on Strong Customer Relationships," *Inside 1to1,* March 16, 2000, http://www,.1to1.com/publications.

10. Ann Diver, "A Healthy Dose of ROI," *Inside 1to1,* April 27, 2000, http://www.1to1.com/publications.

11. This section based on Rob Jackson and Paul Wang, *Strategic Database Marketing* (Lincolnwood, IL: NTC Business Books, 1997), 4–11; and Frederick Newell, *The New Rules of Marketing: How to Use One-to-One Relationship Marketing to Be the Leader in Your Industry* (New York: McGraw-Hill, 1997), 10–32.

12. Direct Marketing Association, http://www.the-dma.org.

13. Jackson and Wang, *Strategic Database Marketing,* 11.

14. Chad Kaydo, "Planting the Seeds of Marketing Success," *Sales & Marketing Management,* August 1998, 73.

15. Ibid.

16. Christina Binkley, "Lucky Numbers: A Casino Chain Finds a Lucrative Niche: The Small Spenders," *Wall Street Journal,* May 4, 2000, A1, A10.

17. Julie Pitta, "Garbage In, Gold Out." *Forbes,* April 5, 1999, 125–126.

18. David Bank, "Know Your Customer," *Wall Street Journal,* June 21, 1999, R18.

19. Ginger Conlon, "True Romance," *Sales & Marketing Management,* May 1996, 85–90.

20. Binkley, "Marriott to Give Additional Perks to Frequent Guests."

21. Debra Aho Williamson, "Program Rewards Frequent Visitors," *Advertising Age,* May 17, 1999, 50.

22. Alice Z. Cuneo, "Chico's: Jim Frain," *Advertising Age,* October 8, 2001, S19.

23. William M. Bulkeley, "We're Watching You," *Wall Street Journal,* November 22, 1999, R32, R46.

24. Calmetta Coleman, "Banks Cozy Up to Customers," *Wall Street Journal,* April 26, 2001, B1.

25. Carol Krol, "Database Marketing Proves Rx Value," *Advertising Age,* March 15, 1999, s18.

26. Jennifer Lach, "Can We Talk?" *American Demographics,* March 1999.

27. Kenneth Hein and Mike Beirne, "A Singular Sensation," *Brandweek,* February 26, 2001, 32.

28. Chad Kaydo, "As Good As It Gets," *Sales & Marketing Management,* March 2000, 55–60.

29. Michael Totty, "Information, Please," *Wall Street Journal,* October 29, 2001, R6.

30. Jean Halliday, "Carmakers Learn to Mine Databases," *Advertising Age,* April 17, 2000, s6; Michele Marchetti, "Shifting Gears," *Sales & Marketing Management,* December 1999, 38–48.

31. Eric Schurenberg, "Boise Cascade Gets That Old Data Religion," *Business 2.0,* November 2001, 68; Jim Kirk, "Boise Taking Its Business Personally," *Chicago Tribune,* January 6, 2002, C1.

32. "Customer Relationship Management: A Senior Management Guide to Technology for Creating a Customer-Centric Business-Executive Summary," *PriceWaterhouseCoopers and the Direct Marketing Association,* http://www.the-dma.org; Meryl Davids, "How to Avoid the 10 Biggest Mistakes in CRM," *Journal of Business Strategy,* November 1999, 22.

33. Jack Schmid and Alan Weber, *Desktop Database Marketing* (Lincolnwood, IL: NTC Business Books, 1998), 33–34.

34. Jackson and Wang, 83.

35. Hein and Beirne.

36. Julia Angwin, "Virgin to Trade Web Use for Personal Data," *Wall Street Journal,* April 10, 2000, B16.

37. Rebecca Piirto Heath, "Loyalty for Sale: Everybody's Doing Frequency Marketing—But Only a Few Companies Are Doing It Well," *Marketing Tools,* July 1997, 40.

38. Denny Hatch, "The Business of Business Lists: A Look at This Incredibly, Unbelievably Complex World," *Target Marketing,* January 1997, 65.

39. Andrew Fisher, "How IT Underpins Groups Global Business Strategy," *Financial Times* online, August 8, 2001.

40. Diane Cyr, "Spiegel's Power Play," *Catalog Age,* April 30, 2000.

41. Beverly Bundy, "Central Market Says It Knows What You Want to Eat, Even If You Don't," *Fort Worth Star-Telegram,* October 10, 2001, Life and Arts, 1.

42. Carol Krol, "Targeting Toddlers," *Advertising Age,* April 20, 1998, 29.

43. Greg Johnson, "Census Breakdowns Help Marketers 'Follow the Money' Consumers," *Los Angeles Times,* May 12, 2001, A15.

44. Paul Kaihla, "Want to Slim Down Customer Costs?" *eCompany Now* online, March 13, 2001.

45. James R. Rosenfield, "The Myth of Database Marketing," *Direct Marketing,* February 1998, 28.

46. Larry Seldon and Geoffrey Colvin, "A Measure of Success," *Business 2.0,* November 2001, 62.

47. Michele Marchetti, "In Search of Profitable Revenues," *Sales & Marketing Management,* August 1998, 74.

48. Newell, *The New Rules of Marketing,* 82.

49. Heath, "Loyalty for Sale," 40.

50. "Alliance of Catalogers Creates Immense Database," *Direct Marketing,* March 1999, 41.

51. Lach, "Data Mining Digs In"; Amanda Beeler, "Fingerhut Uses Optimization to Reduce Cascade of Catalogs," *Advertising Age,* June 5, 2000, 35.

52. Peter R. Peacock, "Data Mining in Marketing: Part 1: The Revolution Is upon Us, So Choose Your Weapons Carefully," *Marketing Management,* Winter 1998, 9–18.

53. Skip Press, "Fool's Gold?" *Sales & Marketing Management,* June 1998, 58–62.

54. Nokia Web site, http://www.Nokia.com; Business Wire, "Motorola and ETISALAT Bring First High Speed Mobile Data to Middle East,"

TheFeature.com, October 23, 2001; Steve Wallage, "Advertising to Save Mobile Operators?" *TheFeature.com,* September 3, 2001; Ray Hegarty, "Asia Leads the Wireless Way," *TheFeature.com,* September 17, 2001; Peggy Salz, "Look Who's Watching," *TheFeature.com,* October 29, 2001; Wallage, "Mobile Marketing—Use Your Imagination!" *TheFeature.com,* January 28, 2002.

55. Amanda Beeler, "Customer Service Gets Boost from New Tech," *Advertising Age,* March 27, 2000, 44.

56. Don Peppers and Martha Rogers, "Opening the Door to Customers," *Sales & Marketing Management,* October 1998, 22–29.

57. Stephanie Miles, "Selling Strategies—People Like Us," *Wall Street Journal,* April 23, 2001, B2.

58. Ira Teinowitz, "Consumers to Be Notified about Profiling," *Advertising Age,* November 15, 1999, 52.

59. Sarah Lorge, "Banner Ads vs. E-Mail Marketing," *Sales & Marketing Management,* August 1999, 15.

60. Jennifer Gilbert, "A Dotcom That's Doing Things Right," *Business 2.0,* August/September 2001, 168.

61. Kaydo, "As Good As It Gets," 56–57.

62. Jim Costelli, "How to Handle Personal Information," *American Demographics,* March 1996, 50–58.

63. Nick Wingfield and Glenn R. Simpson, "With So Much Subscriber Data, AOL Walks a Cautious Line on Privacy," *Wall Street Journal,* March 15, 2000, B1, B4.

64. Johanna Bennett, "It's My Life," *Wall Street Journal,* October 29, 2001, R9.

65. Julia Angwin, Nick Wingfield, and Khanh T. L. Tran, "New Children's Privacy Rules Pose Obstacles for Some Sites," *Wall Street Journal,* April 24, 2000, B8.

66. Jason Anders, "Web Filter Data from Schools Put Up for Sale," *Wall Street Journal,* January 26, 2001, B1.

67. Andrea Petersen, "A Privacy Firestorm at DoubleClick," *Wall Street Journal,* February 23, 2000, B1, B4; Andrea Petersen and Jon G. Auerbach, "Online Ad Titans Bet Big in Race to Trace Consumers' Web Tracks," *Wall Street Journal,* November 8, 1999, B1, B4.

68. Aaron Lucchetti, "FTC Shows Line Drawn for Internet Ads," *Wall Street Journal,* May 7, 1999, B2; John Simons, "New FTC Rules Aim to Protect Kid Web Privacy," *Wall Street Journal,* April 21, 1999, B1, B4; Jennifer Gilbert and Ira Teinowitz, "Compliance Deadline Looms for Kids' Sites," *Advertising Age,* April 17, 2000, 54; Julia Angwin and Nick Wingfield, "New Children's Privacy Rules Pose Obstacles for Some Sites," *Wall Street Journal*, April 24, 2000, B8; Ted Bridis, "Teens Will Likely Disclose Family Data over the Internet for a Free Gift Online," *Wall Street Journal*, May 17, 2000, B2.

69. Richard B. Schmitt, "Online Privacy: Alleged Abuses Shape New Law," *Wall Street Journal*, February 29, 2000, B1, B4.

70. Ira Teinowitz, "FTC Policy Draft Provokes Debate about Web Privacy," *Advertising Age*, May 15, 2000, 3, 84.

71. Erika Rasmusson, "The Perils of International Direct Mail," *Sales & Marketing Management*, April 2000, 107; "E-Commerce III: Nations Fall Slowly in Line on Privacy-Protection Laws," *The Globe and Mail*, November 30, 1999, E25; Mark Ward, "Connected: EU Deal with U.S. over Privacy," *The Daily Telegraph*, March 23, 2000, 3; Beverley Head, "No Privacy, But at Least Some Control," *Business Review Weekly*, April 20, 2000, 44; Wasserman, Khermouch, and Green, "Minding Everyone's Business"; "U.S., EU Make Safe Harbor Agreement, No Shelter for Financial Institutions," *Retail Delivery News*, March 2000.

CHAPTER 1

Try It

Jan Jaben Eilon, "Small Business Entices Marketers." *Bank Technology News,* June 2002, 1, with permission of Bank Technology News, a division of The Thomson Corporation.

CHAPTER 2

Try It

Joyceann Cooney-Curran, "All About 'Me': Noodé Provides a Fun Yet Effective Skin-Care Line to the 'Generation Me' Demographic," *Global Cosmetic Industry,* November 2000, 62.
Andrea Grossman, "It's a Noodé for Skin Care," *WWD,* January 5, 2001, 13.
———, "Noodé Aims to Shield Sun's Rays," *WWD,* January 4, 2002, 10.
———, "Small Firms Win with Samples, Moxie," *WWD,* January 11, 2002, 10. "Noodé for the Me Generation," *Soap & Cosmetics*, November 2000, 72.

CHAPTER 3

Try It

"Joseph J. Atick," *Business Week,* 14 January 2002, 75; "Why Visionics Is Flying Higher," *Business Week,* 14 January 2002, 42; "Mobile Recognition Device to Be Utilised by Winter Olympics Police," *Telecomworldwire,* 12 February 2002, no page available; C. A. Mangis, "It's Written All Over Your Face," *PC Magazine,* 15 January 2002, 25; M. Edmunds, "Biometrics Still in Its Infancy." *Financial Times,* 13 March 2002, 11; www.visionics.com.

CHAPTER 4

Try It

David Greenfield. "Israeli Entrepreneurs Go Optical: The Market Downturn Hasn't Stopped Several Israeli Start-ups from Chasing the Optical Dream." *Lightwave* 19, issue 2, February 2002, 103–104. Portions reprinted with permission from *Lightwave,* February 2002, © 2002 IEEE.

Marketing Miscues

www.bluelight.com
Scott Carlson. "Expert Says Wal-Mart, Target Likely to Benefit from Kmart Bankruptcy." *Knight Ridder Tribune Business News,* January 23, 2002, 1.
Sudeep Reddy and Steve Quinn. "Kmart Faces Short-Term, Long-Term Challenges." *Knight Ridder Tribune Business News,* January 23, 2002, 1.

Critical Thinking Case

www.hp.com
"Hewlett-Packard Laboratories Tests Total Web Environment." *Philadelphia Inquirer,* August 3, 2000, on-line, Gale Group, March 20, 2002.
Brian Milner. "Fiorina Claims Victory in Fight of Her Life." *The Globe and Mail Metro,* March 20, 2002, A1.
Sam Omatseye. "HP Serves Up Initiatives for Increasingly Mobile World." *RCR Wireless News,* October 15, 2001, 10.s
Neil Orman. "Hewlett-Packard Seeks Livelier Image through 'Net Tech.'" *Sacramento Business Journal,* July 13, 2001, 24.

CHAPTER 5

Try It

Kevin Coupe, "A Theme Retailing Failure and Some Views on Restaurant and Pub Trends," *Store Equipment & Design*, January 2001, 24. Danielle Furfaro, "Entrepreneur Opens Family-Centered Restaurant in Albany, N.Y.," *Knight-Ridder Tribune Business News,* February 18, 2002. "McDonald's Launches World's First 'Town Center' Restaurant: New Restaurant Is Second Largest in U.S., Features Family 'Edu-Tainment,'" PR *Newswire,* April 30, 2002. "New Amex Seminars Focus on Consumer Dining Trends," *Nation's Restaurant News,* May 20, 2002, 200.
Richard L. Papiernik, "Industry Sales for 2002 Projected to Hit \$407 B," *Nation's Restaurant News,* January 7, 2002, 1.

CHAPTER 6

Try It

Alicia Neumann. "How It Works—A Better Mousetrap Catalog" *Business 2.0,* February 2000, 117–118.
Aaron Baar. "Grainger Targets Purchasers." *Adweek,* May 31, 1999, 6.
Peter Girard. "The Spin-off Payoff." *Catalog Age New Canaan,* March 15, 2000, 1, 18–21.
Melanie Warner, Daniel Roth, Erick Schonfeld, and Marc Gunther. "Ten Companies That Get It." *Fortune,* Novembr 8, 1999, 115–117.

CHAPTER 7

Try It

Kipp Cheng. "eBay Best Viral Marketing." *Adweek,* June 28, 1999, IQ42.
eBay Web site: http://www.ebay.com/community/aboutebay/overview/index.html
Claire Tristram. "Takin' It to the Street." *MC Technology Marketing Intelligence,* February 1999, 22–28.

CHAPTER 8

Try It

C. Pappas, "Pop Culture—Where It's At: Cool and How to Find It," *Advertising Age,* May 10, 2002, 16.
R. A. Jones, "L.A. Duo Serves Fresh Trends Fast," *WWD,* December, 14, 2000, 11.
T. Coffey, "Researchers Review Youth Buying Trends," *San Diego Business Journal,* November 13, 2000, 55.

Marketing Miscues

"A Review of the Ricochet Wireless Internet Service," 2002. On-line: http://www.wherry.com/gadgets/ricochet/.
Peter Benesh, "Did Marketing Miscues Doom Metricom's Ricochet?" *Investor's Business Daily,* August 10, 2001, A6.
Corey Grice, "Metricom Feels the Need for Wireless Speed," *CNET News.com* on-line, December 20, 1999.
Margo McCall, "Wireless Pioneer Files Bankruptcy," *Wireless Week,* July 9, 2001, 1.
Dan Meyer, "Metricom Seeks Financing As Rising Star Crashes," *RCR Wireless News,* February 12, 2001, 3.

Critical Thinking Case

——— "Golf Company Shifts Focus to Women Players," *Marketing to Women: Addressing Women and Women's Sensibilities,* May 2001, 5.
Liz Consavage, "Square Two Gains with Women's Lines," *Golf World,* May 18, 2001, S6.
www.womensgolfunlimited.com
E. Michael Johnson, "The Total Package," *Golf World Business,* August 2000, 30.
——— "Women's Business Square Two's Focus," *Golf World,* July 14, 2000, S6.

E. Michael Johnson, "Women Wanted," *Golf World,* August 10, 2001, S2.

CHAPTER 9

Try It

Stephanie Stoughton, "Path to Success," *Boston Globe*, June 17, 2000, C1–C2.

"Topozone Launches Interactive Topographic Map Size, Revolutionizes Topographic Map Industry," *PR Newswire,* November 30, 1999, on-line. http://www.topozone.com

CHAPTER 10

Try It

Risa Brim, "Lexington, Ky.-Based Motor Oil Producer Steps Out of Mold," *Lexington Herald-Leader*, November 5, 2001, available on-line at http://www.wsj.com.

Lucy May, "Ashland Launches Spirit 3-D Foam," *Business Courier Serving Cincinnati-Northern Kentucky*, October 12, 2001, 13.

CHAPTER 11

Try It

"Chicago-Based 'Dot-Org' i.c.stars Adapts Web Approaches to Not-for-Profit Initiative," *PR Newswire,* May 23, 2000, on-line.

"i.c.stars Addresses Digital Divide and Creates a New Business Model for Not-for-Profits," *PR Newswire,* May 16, 2000, on-line.

Darcy Evon, "Crossing Electronic Lines," *Chicago Software News,* March 2000. On-line.

Howard Wolinsky, "Tech Leaders Push to Close Digital Divide," *Chicago Sun-Times,* April 18, 2000, on-line. http://www.iccapital.com http://www.icstars.org

Marketing Miscues

http://www.moxi.com

"Moxi's Fortunes Rely on Middleware," *CED,* February 2002, 10.

Richard Cole, "Perlman to Unveil Home-Networking Set-Top," *Cable World,* January 7, 2002, 2.

Ben Elgin, Linda Himelstein, and Cliff Edwards, "Jazzy Product, Sizzling Start, Lots of Trouble," *Business Week,* March 4, 2002, 92–94.

Chris Marlowe, "Perlman's Moxi Shows Off Digital Entertainment Hub," *Hollywood Reporter,* January 8, 2002, 2.

Critical Thinking Case

http://www.dekaresearch.com http://www.segway.com

"Mystery Project Revealed," *Design Engineering,* January 2002, 7.

Gareth Cook, and Nicholas Thompson, "Ginger's Rough Ride," *Boston Globe,* February 5, 2002, C1–C3.

" 'Ginger' Revealed to be Electric Scooter," *Electric Vehicle Online Today,* December 4, 2001, on-line.

Karl Greenberg, "The 'IT' Girl," *Brandweek,* November 12, 2001, 37.

John Heileman, "Here 'IT' Is: The Inside Story of the Secret Invention That So Many Are Buzzing About," *Time,* December 10, 2001, 76.

CHAPTER 12

Try It

CarsDirect.com Web site at http://www.carsdirect.com.

Robert Elder, Jr., and Jonathan Weil, "To Sell Cars in Texas, Online Firms Are Forced to Enter the Real World," *Wall Street Journal,* January 26, 2000, T1, T4.

Maynard M. Gordon, "Battle Lines Forming in the Wild World of the Automotive Web Sites," *Ward's Dealer Business,* June 1, 2000, 12.

Chris Knap, "Online Car Sales Will Rise, Analysts Say," *KRTBN Knight-Ridder Tribune Business News: The Orange County Register—California,* September 19, 1999.

Jennifer Montgomery, "Texas State Law Bars Residents from Buying Cars Online," *KRTBN Knight-Ridder Tribune Business News: Houston Chronicle—Texas,* March 19, 2000.

Fara Warner, "Racing for Slice of a $350 Billion Pie, Online Auto-Sales Sites Retool," *Wall Street Journal,* January 24, 2000, B1, B6.

———, "New Tactics Shake Up Online Auto Retailing," *Wall Street Journal,* October 18, 1999, B1.

———, "CarsDirect.com Bets on One-Stop, Desktop Showroom," *Wall Street Journal,* May 17, 1999, B4.

Scott Woolley, "A Car Dealer by Any Other Name," *Forbes,* November 29, 1999, 113–116.

CHAPTER 13

Try It

Soozhana Choi, "Funky Fashions for Teen-Age Girls," *Gannett News Service,* March 16, 1999.

Becky Ebenkamp, "Stephen Kahn," *Brandweek,* November 8, 1999, 32.

Laura Keating, "The In Crowd: Retail Rushes to Keep Pace with Generation Y," *Shopping Center World,* May 30, 2000.

Melanie Kletter, "Catalogs Lose Teen Appeal," *WWD,* March 2, 2000, 11.

Paul Miller, "Apparel: Trends Analysis," *Catalog Age,* March 15, 2000, 65–69.

David S. Murphy, "Delia's Next Big Step," *Fortune,* February 15, 1999, 192[C]–192[H].

Vicki M. Young, "Playing the Junior Game," *WWD,* October 27, 1999, 20.

———, "Teen Shopping Heats Up On-line," *WWD,* February 3, 2000, 26B.

Marketing Miscues

"Kraus Gains Super Bowl Airtime via Mail Boxes Promo," *Brandweek,* January 8, 1999, 8.

"Jeremy's MicroBatch Ice Creams," *Frozen Food Age,* January 2000, 42.

"Dip Shops Part of New Management's Plans at Jeremy's," *Ice Cream Reporter,* September 20, 2000, 1.

"Obits," *Inc.,* February 1, 2001, 33.

Critical Thinking Case

http://www.oreillynet.com http://www.streamcastnetworks.com

Dawn Chmielewski, "Movie, Film Groups Sue File-Swapping Services, Alleging Online Piracy," *San Jose Mercury News,* October 4, 2001. On-line.

Lisa Rein and David Sims, "O'Reilly P2P Directory," *The O'Reilly Network,* October 20, 2000, On-line.

Erick Schonfield, "Goodbye Napster, Hello Morpheus," *ZDNet,* March 18, 2002. On-line.

Clay Shirky, "What Is P2P . . . and What Isn't," *The O'Reilly Network,* November 24, 2000, On-line.

Scott Woolley, "Steal This Movie," *Forbes,* February 18, 2002, 66.

CHAPTER 14

Try It

Katrina Burger, "A Drink with an Attitude," *Forbes,* February 10, 1997.

Joel Kurtzman, "Advertising for All the Little Guys," *Fortune,* April 12, 2000, 162.

Greg Masters, "All Juiced Up," *Discount Merchandiser,* July 1999, 107.

Gwen Moran, "Go, Granny, Go," *Entrepreneur Magazine,* March 2000.

Nantucket Nectars Web site at http://www.juiceguys.com.

"Nantucket Nectars Will Tie Up in Denver," *Denver Rocky Mountain News,* February 14, 1999.

Nancy Coltun Webster, "Squeezed Nectars: Chris Testa," *Advertising Age,* June 26, 2000, s4.

"What Have You Become?" *Entrepreneur Magazine,* May 2000.

CHAPTER 15

Try It

Bill Carter, "Will This Machine Change Television?" The *New York Times,* 5 July 1999, p. 1.

Jim Cooper, "Inside the Box," *Brandweek*, 8 May 2000, p. C32.
Marla Matzer Rose, "TV Advertisers Worry About Growth of New PVRs," *Chicago Tribune*, 14 April 2000, p. 4.
Erin Strout, "The End of TV Advertising?" *Sales & Marketing Management*, January 2000, p. 15.
TiVo Web site at http://www.tivo.com
"TiVo Signs Showtime," *Advertising Age*, 16 May 2000.

CHAPTER 16

Try It

VarsityBooks.com Web site at http://www.varsitybooks.com.
Jeff Gottlieb, "Internet Vendors Test College Textbook Market," *Los Angeles Times*, June 25, 2000, B-1.
Ann M. Mack, "Textbook Case," *Brandweek*, August 7, 2000, IQ30.
Karen Solomon, "College Bound," *Business 2.0*, April 1999.
Jeffrey A. Tannenbaum, "Marketers on Campus: A New Bag of Tricks," *Wall Street Journal*, January 31, 2000, B1, B8.
"Varsity Nears Breakeven on Lower Revenues," *Publishers Weekly*, April 8, 2002, 14.
"Varsity Year Ends with New Business Model," *Educational Marketer*, April 15, 2002, page not available.
Steven M. Zeitchik, "Capitalism on Campus," *Business 2.0*, May 2000.
http://www.publishers.org

Marketing Miscues

http://www.gillette.com
"The Gillette Co.," *Drug Store News-Newsfirst,* February 13, 2002, 1.
Ann Davin, "Duracell Launches New Advertising for America's Favorite Battery," Company press release, November 19, 2001, 1.
Daniel Golden and Suzanne Vranica, "Advertising: Duracell's Duck Ad Will Carry Disclaimer," *Wall Street Journal,* February 7, 2002, B7.
Jack Neff, "Energizing Their Bases: Duracell and Energizer Focus Ads on Flagships," *Advertising Age,* June 4, 2001, 4.

Critical Thinking Case

http://www.philipmorris.com
Philip B. Clark, "Marketing Execs like Sound of 'Altria,'" *B to B*, December 10, 2001, 3.
David Grainger, "Identity," *Fortune*, December 10, 2001, 36.

Julie Hood, "Altria vs. Altria Is David vs. Goliath," *PR Week*, December 10, 2001, 3.
Tom McGhee, "Denver-Based Venture Capital Firm Challenges Philip Morris over New Name," *Denver Post,* December 6, 2001, On-line.
Michael Stetz, "Philip Morris Name Change Viewed with Suspicion," *San Diego Union-Tribune.* December 31, 2001, B1.

CHAPTER 17

Try It

Interview with Mark James, CEO of A Taste of Class, December 12, 2001.

CHAPTER 18

Try It

Angela Lo, "Young Entrepreneurs' Dream Is to Become Mercer Island's Sole Internet Provider," *Seattle Times,* February 13, 2002.
http://www.mercerislandchamber.org

Marketing Miscues

http://www.apple.com
"Apple," *Business Week,* July 31, 2000, 102.
Jerry Langton, "Cube on Centre Stage," *Computer Dealer News,* August 11, 2000, 30.
Harry McCracken, "Coolness Cubed: Apple's Radical New Mac," *PC World,* November 2000, 106.
Josh Quittner, "Apple's New Core," *Time*, January 14, 2002, 46–52.

Critical Thinking Case

http://www.nokia.com
"Could Diamonds Be Nokia's Best Friend?" *Reuters*, January 14, 2002, On-line: http://www.asia.cnet.com.
Elisa Batista, "The Jewel of Cell Phones," *Wired News*, January 31, 2001, On-line: http://www.wired.com.
Aloysius Choong, "Nokia Asia Exec Takes Helm at Vertu," *CNETAsia*, January 25, 2002, On-line.
Jonathan Liew, Sipho Majola, Sohil Parekh, and Peter Weed, "Wireless Voice Data: The Impact on the Consumer," On-line: http://www.ksg.harvard.edu/project6.
Hillary Smith, "For the Person with Everything, Nokia Offers Jeweled Handset," *RCR Wireless News,* January 28, 2002, On-line.

CHAPTER 20

Try It

Marion Agnew, "CRM Becomes a Charitable Application," *InformationWeek,* October 16, 2000, 176.
Patricia Odell, "The Web Way," *Direct*, May 15, 2001, 63.
Susan Stellin, "A Non-Profit Uses Customer-Relationship Management Software to Net $1.5 Million," *ECompany.com*, July 2001.

CHAPTER 21

Try It

"One to One," *Progressive Grocer,* February 15, 2002, 8.
S. Mulholland, "Mining for Diamonds: An Upstate New York Independent Is Reaping Rewards through a Multi-Pricing System That Recognizes Its Best Shoppers," *Supermarket News,* February 11, 2002, 17.
S. Greco, "Inc. Case Study—Green Hills Farms 67-Year-Old Grocery Store," *Inc.,* June 2001, 54.

Marketing Miscues

http://www.lilly.com
"All about Prozac," *Making the Prozac Decision: A Guide to Antidepressants* (RGA Publishing Group, 1997), On-line: http://www.my.webmd.com.
"FTC to Settle Eli Lilly Privacy Probe," *Reuters,* January 11, 2002, On-line: http://www.cnet.com.
Patrick Thibodeau, "FTC, Eli Lilly Settle Privacy Case," *Computerworld,* January 18, 2002, On-line: http://www.computerworld.com.

Critical Thinking Case

http://www.peapod.com
http://www.ahold.com
"An Emerging Power in the U.S.," *MMR,* January 14, 2002, 18.
Research International USA, "Trends in the United States: Consumer Attitudes and the Supermarket, 2001," A report prepared for the Food Marketing Institute, 2001, On-line.
Ameet Sachdev, "Despite Doubts, On-line Grocer Still Delivering," *Chicago Tribune* January 31, 2002, 1.
John Schultz, "Groceries Via the Net," *MMR,* December 19, 2000, 25.
Jenny Summerour, "Click by Brick," *Progressive Grocer,* October 2001, 28.

Index

Internet Index